Accounting Information Systems

INTERNATIONAL ADAPTATION

Accounting Information Systems
Connecting Careers, Systems, and Analytics

INTERNATIONAL ADAPTATION

Arline Savage, PHD, CA
The University of Alabama at Birmingham
Birmingham, Alabama, USA

Danielle Brannock, CPA, CSPO
Intuitive
Atlanta, Georgia, USA

Alicja Foksinska, CISA, CFE
Protective Life Corporation
The University of Alabama at Birmingham
Birmingham, Alabama, USA

Accounting Information Systems
Connecting Careers, Systems, and Analytics

INTERNATIONAL ADAPTATION

John Wiley & Sons, Inc., Hoboken, New Jersey

Cover image: © Adobe Stock

Contributor details: Dr K Lubza Nihar, Associate Professor, GITAM School of Business, India

Founded in 1807, John Wiley & Sons, Inc. has been a valued source of knowledge and understanding for more than 200 years, helping people around the world meet their needs and fulfill their aspirations. Our company is built on a foundation of principles that include responsibility to the communities we serve and where we live and work. In 2008, we launched a Corporate Citizenship Initiative, a global effort to address the environmental, social, economic, and ethical challenges we face in our business. Among the issues we are addressing are carbon impact, paper specifications and procurement, ethical conduct within our business and among our vendors, and community and charitable support. For more information, please visit our website: www.wiley.com/go/citizenship.

ISBN: 978-1-119-88938-0

ISBN: 978-1-119-88939-7 (ePub)

ISBN: 978-1-119-88940-3 (ePdf)

Printed and bound by CPI Group (UK) Ltd, Croydon, CR0 4YY

C9781119889380_040324

To Archer, Mirabel, and Lillianna, my most special small people, for their tolerance and patience when I couldn't spend time with them. To Paul and Karen, who kept me going. To Kay and Frank, for everything. To Vyxsin, for food.

Arline Savage

Dylan, who brings me water. Kaetlan, who always understands. Alicia, who keeps me sane. Brant, who makes the best meals. My mom, who reminds me why. Eddie, who believes. Modem, who waits.

Danielle Brannock

To my parents, Renata and Mirosław, my sisters, Aleksandra and Julia, my brother, Jan, and my fiancé, Adam, for their love, patience, and encouragement to help my literary dreams come true. To my manager, Rusty, and colleagues Baron and Grant for teaching me how to be a successful IT auditor.

Alicja Foksinska

From the Authors

Many students may find it difficult to understand how an accounting information systems (AIS) course is relevant to their idea of what an accounting professional does. It's not until they enter their careers that they see the value of concepts learned in an AIS course. Our goal is to present you with a view of AIS that strongly aligns the concepts in this course with your other accounting coursework while practically preparing you for your future accounting career. This course is designed by current accounting professionals for future accounting professionals—and that means you!

Remember, regardless of which accounting career path you pursue, you'll encounter the concepts covered in this course. To help you develop the skills you need to be successful in the workplace, we have embedded our professional experience and the experiences of our colleagues throughout this course. We help you become job-ready by including:

- Thoughts from our **extensive network of accounting professionals across all accounting areas,** who provide current and compelling examples of how this AIS course is relevant to their domains.
- A **storybook approach to data visualization cases** that will help you succeed as a trusted advisor in your career, regardless of what software your company uses.
- A focus on the **relevance of data analytics to all parts of a business** and its operations through integration of data analytics and dashboards in most chapters.
- Early career and data analytics **assignments based on our on-the-job experiences** that explore the critical thinking and practical skills increasingly expected of accounting graduates.

To emphasize how AIS is at the center of every business, we use a continuing story that takes you through a company's journey from a small startup to a national corporation—and all the related risks and controls along the way. This approach clearly connects how data analytics, internal controls, risk management, and business processes all work together to create a company's business operations.

To be successful in this course, we recommend that you:

- Pay close attention to what you're learning in the first eight chapters. This content lays a foundation of concepts that are applied throughout business scenarios in the rest of the course.
- Focus on gaining an education—not a training—in data analytics. This course is designed to expose you to and teach you the principles of data analytics. It's not meant to be an in-depth training for specific software. You'll get that training from your employer. Focus on learning the concepts and how they apply to a company.
- Think holistically about what you are learning. It's easy for accounting professionals to focus only on the details. This AIS course is the "big picture" of how accounting integrates into a company's operations. From purchasing raw materials to issuing financial statements, accounting is present. We look at the AIS from a business-first perspective by focusing on how each chapter fits into the overall organization of a company.

We are excited to be a part of your accounting journey. Remember, this class is the keystone that ties all your other accounting courses together!

Arline Savage, PhD, CA
Danielle Brannock, CPA, CSPO
Alicja Foksinska, CISA, CFE

About the Authors

The University of Alabama at Birmingham

Eric Bern Studio

Photo Courtesy of Tyler Furgerson

ARLINE SAVAGE, PHD, CA is Professor and Sallie W. Dean Faculty Fellow in Accounting in the Collat School of Business at The University of Alabama at Birmingham (UAB). She has taught a wide variety of courses across multiple countries, including her birthplace of South Africa, Canada, and the United States. She is the recipient of numerous teaching awards, most recently the 2021 UAB President's Award for Excellence in Teaching for exceptional accomplishments in teaching. Arline received her bachelor's, master's, and doctoral degrees in accounting from Nelson Mandela Metropolitan University in South Africa. She began teaching at UAB in 2012 and has served as chair of the Accounting and Finance department. She currently serves on the board of directors of the Federation of Schools of Accountancy.

Arline's research in accounting education has received international recognition; based on BYU accounting research rankings, she ranks 12th for the world over the last 12 years and 26th for all time. Arline has published more than 40 academic and professional publications as well as two scholarly books and two other textbooks. She is a past President of the Accounting Information Systems Educator Association and founding Editor-in-Chief of the *AIS Educator Journal*. Arline serves on the editorial boards of two highly ranked accounting education journals, *Issues in Accounting Education* and *Journal of Accounting Education*.

As a Chartered Accountant (CA), Arline has worked as an auditor and accountant for one of the biggest CPA firms and at General Motors. She has also consulted or served as an accounting advisor on various accounting and finance projects in the wholesale food, apparel, engineering, health care, and manufacturing industries. She brings these experiences to her classroom to provide real-world context to her students to prepare them for success in the accounting profession.

DANIELLE BRANNOCK, CPA, CSPO is an Internal Audit Data Analyst at Intuitive, a robotics firm that provides surgeons assistance in performing minimally invasive procedures by using robots, such as the da Vinci Surgical System.

Danielle is a licensed CPA in the state of Georgia, a certified Core Alteryx Designer, and a Certified Scrum Product Owner (CSPO), which is a project management certification for Agile and scrum software development frameworks. Prior to starting at Intuitive, Danielle performed internal audit data analytics at WestRock and Invesco after a career in external audit data analytics at both PwC and EY.

Danielle was named the 2020 Young Accounting Alum of the Year and 2015 Outstanding Accounting Undergraduate Student at The University of Alabama at Birmingham (UAB) and was the recipient of the 2015 Alabama Society of CPA's Accounting Achievement Award.

With a passion for public speaking, and educating both accounting professionals and academics, Danielle has presented at more than 10 conferences and in many classrooms since 2016. Danielle is a past board member of the Beta Alpha Psi international organization and served as an officer of the Delta Chi chapter during her undergraduate program.

Danielle has a BS in accountancy and an AAS in paralegal research. Currently, Danielle is pursuing an MIS in computer science at Boston University's part-time online program, while working full-time, writing books, and managing a household of humans, dogs, and cats. There are over 200 board games on the shelf in Danielle's home office.

ALICJA FOKSINSKA, CISA, CFE has been Lead IT Auditor at Protective Life Corporation since 2015. At Protective, Alicja spearheaded the creation of data analytics, visualization, and storytelling efforts in the (world's greatest) Internal Audit department, becoming the data specialist of the team. She is currently managing and maturing the newly created Data Analytics shop. Alicja is also an instructor at The University of Alabama at Birmingham (UAB), where she teaches classes in accounting information systems and data visualization for business.

Alicja earned BS degrees in information systems and in management (business administration) from UAB. She also earned an MS in business analytics from Indiana University. In addition to being a Certified Information Systems Auditor (CISA) and Certified Fraud Examiner (CFE), Alicja is a certified Tableau Desktop Specialist.

She serves on the board of directors of a local chapter of ISACA (Birmingham, Alabama) as the current President, where she leads more than 300 IT audit, risk, compliance, and governance professionals.

Alicja is a recipient of the UAB Rising Star Award and a graduate of Momentum Upward Leadership Program, which is Alabama's premier women's leadership program. She is a past Senior Data Fellow for the Magic City Data Collective program, which is a community partnership that creates a pipeline of students who are uniquely qualified for jobs in the data industry.

Outside of the profession, Alicja serves on The Bell Center for Early Intervention Programs' Junior Board and is one of the Co-Chairs of the Collat Young Alumni Council.

Alicja is an immigrant from Poland who enjoys celebrating her Polish culture. She loves spending time with her wonderful family, raising awareness and advocating for individuals with Down syndrome, and immersing herself in different cultures through travel.

Our Approach

Career Focus

This International Adaptation of *Accounting Information Systems* prepares students for a changing workplace, emerging technologies, and increased expectations for accounting professionals.

Featured Professional Text Interviews

Each chapter ends with an interview spotlighting a real accounting professional. These *Featured Professional* boxes discuss individuals' career paths, how these professionals apply course concepts students are learning in their day-to-day lives, and the professional skills they developed to get to where they are.

Sample Job Postings

Each chapter begins with a sample job posting. These postings, which are based on actual LinkedIn job postings, demonstrate the importance of the skills individuals in the field would require for various positions. These sample postings provide an engaging way for students to connect with course material and help them understand how job opportunities connect to the skills they're developing. These postings also help students visualize the different career paths related to AIS.

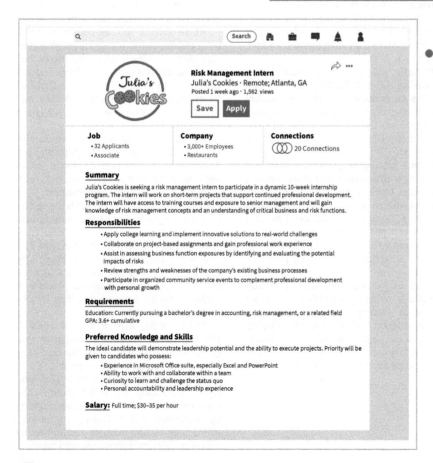

Why Does It Matter to Your Career?

Throughout each chapter, *Why Does It Matter to Your Career?* feature boxes help students process the information they have learned and provide some professional insights into how that information is relevant to their current and future career paths.

Why Does It Matter to Your Career?

Thoughts from a Tax Senior, Public Accounting

- One of the most valued skillsets for accounting professionals is an analytic mindset. This is a buzzword with employers because this mindset is valuable in a new hire. You don't have to know how to code or even do advanced Excel analysis. It's the curiosity about data, interest in learning, and ability to ask a question and find out what data can answer it that makes an accounting professional stand out as having next-generation skills.

- Using data analysis may require working alongside trained IT professionals who may not understand the business side of accounting. Entering your role with a basic understanding of both the business and technology sides can make you a valuable translator between your team and the IT professionals in your company.

In the Real World LEGO

The LEGO company was founded in 1932 by Ole Kirk Christiansen, a carpenter whose primary business of producing household goods had suffered due to the Great Depression. Initially producing wooden toys, the company later developed a system of interlocking bricks.

LEGO decided to go for an Agile transformation to address several challenges they were facing. In a pre-Agile environment, there was considerable confusion, inefficiencies, and lack of customer collaboration, leading to an ineffective and wasteful work environment. To achieve the vision, LEGO felt that they needed dynamism, high levels of responsiveness, and full adjustment to constantly moving targets. To succeed, LEGO realized their employees had to innovate, test, and learn in a world that is in constant flux. The LEGO Digital Solutions team consisted of 20 teams, so there was significant change and realignment required. According to Henrik Kniberg and Thyrsted Brands-gård, the coaches who led the Agile transformation for LEGO Digital Solutions (DS), the following problems were identified:

- Cross-team alignment
- Client collaboration
- Release planning
- Platform development

It decided to move toward Scaled Agile Framework (SAFe) in 2014. The Agile transformation at th LEGO Group was launched in early 2018 and included the introduction of a new digital operating model. One year into the transformation, the impact of the new model began to show as a significant reduction in the time required to respond to change—from months to weeks—in the company's core functions. The new way of working improved motivation and satisfaction among employees in the two departments that kicked off the Agile transformation—contributing to a significant positive increase in the yearly employee motivation and satisfaction survey score.

Have you heard of Agile before this course? What kind of environment would you rather work in: one featuring Agile or Waterfall? What if you were an end user? Would you prefer receiving updates at the end of project completion (Waterfall) or being involved in the development of your system (Agile)?

In the Real World

Drawing connections to real businesses and business practices helps students understand the relevance and application of what they are learning. The *In the Real World* feature box in each chapter provides examples of how the concepts in the chapter apply to a real-world company or business. Each box ends with a few thought-provoking questions to help students think more critically.

Data Analytics

Students will develop a future-ready skillset with an integrated approach to data analytics. *Accounting Information Systems* includes the following foundational content:

- **Chapters 5 and 6** help students understand the foundations of data and databases, while **Chapters 17 and 18** introduce data analytics and data visualization techniques and how they are applied in the business world.

- Each of the **business process chapters—Chapters 9 through 13**—has a learning objective that applies chapter concepts to data analytics.

- **Data analytics topics** are integrated across multiple chapters and across many end-of-chapter questions.

Tableau Case: Julia's Cookies' IT Help Desk

What You Need

Download Tableau to your computer. You can access www.tableau.com/academic/students to download your free Tableau license for the year, or you can download it from your university's software offerings.

Download the following file from the book's product page on www.wiley.com:

Chapter 5 Raw Data.xlsx

Case Background

Big Picture:

Examine IT issues and requests.

Details:

Why is this data important, and what questions or problems need to be addressed?

- Every company has an IT help desk that employees can call to report a system outage or login issues, among many others. It is important for the company to monitor this help desk information to see if there is a larger underlying problem that it might need to address. It is also important to track these tickets to ensure that they are being addressed in an appropriate time frame so as not to severely disrupt the business.
- To examine the issue and request patterns that Julia's Cookies employees are communicating with the IT help desk, we should consider the following questions: Which issue category has the most tickets requested? How long does it take, on average, to close a severe ticket? Which ticket group has the most unsatisfied requestors?

Plan:

What data is needed, and how should it be analyzed?

- The data needed to answer the objective is pulled from the central ticketing management system.
- The data should be filtered to an appropriate time frame that would allow IT to identify patterns.
- This data looks at eight months: March through October.

Now it's your turn to evaluate, analyze, and communicate the results!

Gradable Continuing Case: Tableau or Excel

The Tableau continuing case assessment question is an extension of the Julia's Cookies continuing case. Students are given a specific business scenario with questions and must answer the questions using Tableau. In addition, an Excel version is available online. The data sets for this case follow the data structure used with popular software. The data sets range in size; one data set is around a quarter of a million rows in size, ensuring that students get hands-on experience with realistically large data sets.

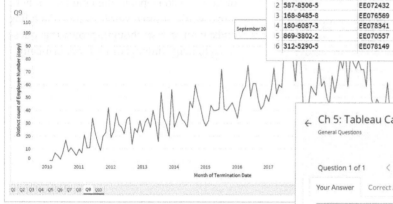

	A	B	C	D	E
1	Ticket Number	Requestor ID	Requestor Name	Ticket Group	Issue Categ
2	411-8513-9	EE077805	Alexander, Nick	Architecture	Systems
3	523-2507-2	EE075449	Alley, Timothy	Security and Governance	Access/Logi
4	979-2433-9	EE071209	Attaway, Lesmore	Hardware	Hardware
5	579-9227-1	EE076604	Banks, Megan	Hardware	Systems
6	184-6074-4	EE079642	Barajas, Leisha	Hardware	Systems
7	691-6969-7	EE071470	Bell, Norah	Architecture	Systems
8	723-9106-4	EE079094	Berquist, Frances	Hardware	Hardware
9	609-8836-7	EE080061	Bhusari, Calvin	Networking	Hardware
10	860-7573-7	EE075583	Black, Christian	Architecture	Systems
11	836-9414-9	EE074774	Blubaugh, Stephen	Security and Governance	Access/Logi
12	587-8506-5	EE072432	Boozer, Timothy	Hardware	Systems
13	168-8485-8	EE076569	Campbell, Wade	Security and Governance	Access/Logi
14	180-6087-3	EE078341	Casey, Teresa	Architecture	Hardware
15	869-3802-2	EE070557	Childress, Taylor	Hardware	Hardware
16	312-5290-5	EE078149	Fallin, Jessica	Security and Governance	Access/Logi

Ch 5: Tableau Case: Julia's Cookies' IT Help Desk

General Questions

Interactive view ON + ADD

Question 1 of 1 < >

Your Answer | Correct Answer (Used)

✔ Your answer is correct.

Which month has the highest number of tickets submitted?

July 2022

Solution

Unique Pedagogical Approach

Accounting Information Systems takes a unique pedagogical approach to help students master content and prepare them for a successful career in accounting. Practice is integrated in the text at the point of learning with the Julia's Cookies continuing case.

Chapter Roadmap ········•

The Chapter Roadmap lists the learning objectives and topics students will learn about in the chapter. It also provides an overview of the applied learning opportunities provided with the Julia's Cookies continuing case.

Chapter Roadmap

LEARNING OBJECTIVES	TOPICS	JULIA'S COOKIES APPLIED LEARNING
5.1 Differentiate between data elements and data types.	• Data Elements • Data Types • Data That Changes	Unstructured Data: Call Center
5.2 Explain how data is stored.	• Introduction to Databases • Types of Data Storage	Data Acquisition: Budget Data
5.3 Summarize the five characteristics of big data.	• Volume • Velocity • Variety • Veracity • Value	Big Data: Mobile App Limitations

ABOUT US Julia's Cookies was founded after midnight on a cold October morning in 2010. Five accounting majors working on a group project for their international financial accounting class had a sudden craving for something sweet, but all of the local bakeries were closed due to the late hour. It was then that a business idea was born: Wouldn't it be great to have fresh-baked cookies at any time—even the middle of the night?

MISSION Our mission is simple: to satisfy late-night cravings by delivering delicious cookies from our kitchens to your doors.

VISION Innovate our approach in baking to ensure low prices without sacrificing quality.

VALUES

Simplicity: Cut down barriers and make the process as simple as possible.

Selflessness: Care for the success and well-being of the team.

Social Responsibility: Care for our customers and our c[...]

Sustainability: Care for our planet.

•········ Illustrations and Icons

The accounting and business professions often use icon-style art in presentations and when communicating important information. To help students become familiar with this type of visual representation, carefully curated icons are used throughout the course.

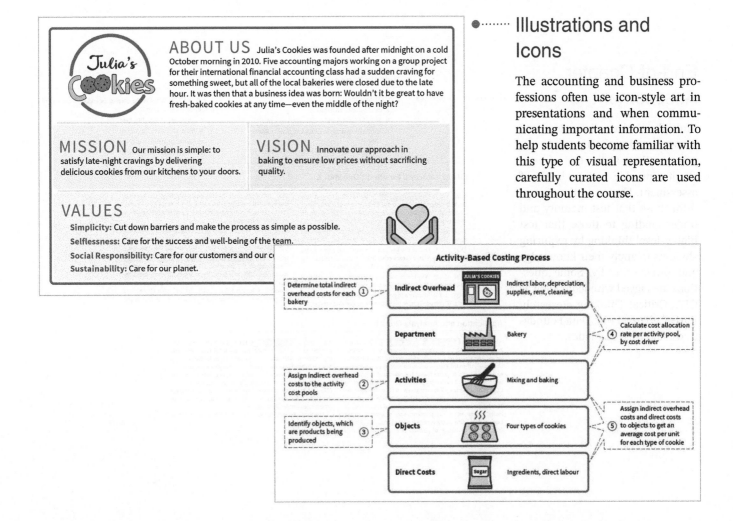

Career-centric Assessments

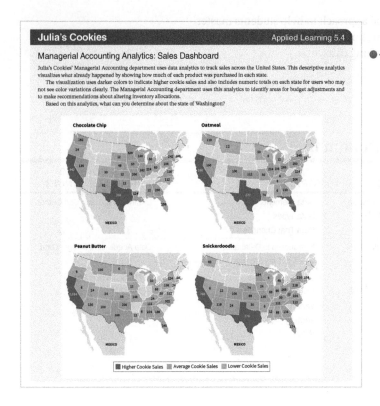

Julia's Cookies Continuing Case

The Julia's Cookies continuing case allows students to apply AIS topics to realistic company scenarios. In each learning objective, students come across Julia's Cookies case references and questions that help them see how topics come to life in various business scenarios. The continuing case gives students practice using various accounting applications and functions as Julia's Cookies continues to grow and expand.

End-of-Chapter Assessment

Multiple choice, discussion and research, and application and analysis questions at the end of each chapter provide various levels of assessment. These questions range from those that test memory and understanding to those that test higher-level thinking by requiring students to apply their knowledge and think critically. Some questions are tagged with icons such as CPA, Critical Thinking, Research, Early Career, Fraud, Data Foundations, and Data Analytics.

Multiple Choice Questions

1. (LO 1) Structured data
   a. can be displayed in tables.
   b. includes images and social media content.
   c. is difficult to analyze using traditional software tools.
   d. represents about 80% of a company's data.

2. (LO 1) **CPA** What is the correct ascending hierarchy of data elements in a system?
   a. Character, record, file, field
   b. Field, character, file, record
   c. Character, field, record, file
   d. Field, record, file, character

Discussion and Research Questions

DQ1. (LO 1) **Critical Thinking** Why should accountants be knowledgeable about the difference between structured and unstructured data? What opportunities and challenges do these types of data present to accounting professionals?

DQ2. (LO 1) Compare and contrast structured and unstructured data.

DQ3. (LO 1) Define the key data elements and demonstrate how they are related to each other in a hierarchy by explaining how data elements compose other data elements.

DQ4. (LO 2) Why is it important for accounting professionals to understand the structure of a relational database?

DQ5. (LO 3) Identify and define the 5Vs that characterize big data. Which one is most important for accounting profession-

DQ7. (LO 4) Describe the four primary types of data analytics and explain the question that each type is best suited to answer. Provide an example of how accounting professionals could use each type of analysis.

DQ8. (LO 4) Explain, using an example, how a corporate tax accountant might use data analytics. Also, identify the primary type of analytics the accountant would use for your example.

DQ9. (LO 4) **Research** **Data Analytics** **Critical Thinking** Choose *one* of the following areas of accounting: financial accounting, audit and compliance (including fraud examination), managerial accounting, or taxation. Using the examples provided in Section 5.4 as a guide, research your chosen area and provide your own examples of each type of data analy-

Application and Analysis Questions

A1. (LO 1–5) **Early Career** **Critical Thinking** Alicia's Accessories is a global manufacturer of jewelry and hair accessories. The company currently relies on the COSO Internal Control—Integrated Framework to manage its corporate governance and risk response plans. The new chief information security officer (CISO) has proposed that leadership adopt the COBIT 2019 framework to strengthen its IT governance process. The CISO wants to use COBIT 2019 to help identify key IT internal controls that can mitigate some of Alicia's Accessories' biggest technology problems, such as users accessing inappropriate data, inappropriate system changes resulting in failures, loss or damage of physical IT equipment where its

A2. (LO 2) **Critical Thinking** TLL Motors is an online motorcycle equipment store that sells motorcycle helmets, boots, jackets, and more. With no brick-and-mortar stores, it relies on many systems to provide an excellent customer buying experience.

You are the accounting director at TLL Motors and are overseeing the implementation of a new general ledger system called GL Solutions. As part of the final steps of implementing the system, you need to assign users to the appropriate user access roles within GL Solutions.

Users can be assigned to only one of four roles or can be denied access:
   A. Administrator

New to the International Adaptation

The following are some of the changes made in this edition:

- New international cases in "In the Real World" feature, including those on Volkswagen, Cantey Technology, MillerCoors, LEGO, and Java Golf Club
- Expanded coverage, with new sections on
  - Components of an AIS
  - Database Forms and Reports
  - Software Tools for Graphical Documentation
  - Directive 2014/56/EU of the European Parliament
  - Financial Modeling for Decision Making
  - Recent Cybersecurity Attacks on Optus and National Health Service (NHS)
- Each of the sections are followed by Concept Review questions focused on key points students need to remember

Engaging Online Resources

The following resources are available for instructors in the book's product page on www.wiley.com.

- Test Bank
- PowerPoint Lecture Slides
- Instructor Manual
- Solutions Manual
- Solutions to Julia's Cookies problems (answers in both Excel and Tableau)

Acknowledgments

Accounting Information Systems was significantly improved through the participation of our featured professionals network, meetings with our advisory board members, input from students who piloted this course in class, feedback from instructors who class-tested the material, comments from chapter reviewers, and the work of our editorial team. We very much appreciate the recommendations and comments from everyone who supported us throughout the writing of this material, and we thank the instructors who participated in development and authoring activities for this edition.

Featured Professionals

Miriam Bolus
Donny Shimamoto
Cindy Wyatt
Laniesha Williams
Eliza Sheu
Dominic Sylvester
Kevin Wang
Catalina Ballesteros
Jonathan Cullen
Holly Giang
Yanek Michel
Bharti Sukhani
Hafiz Chandiwala
Mark Thomas
John Aubrey Pickens
Rob Valdez
Joshua Giles
Alana Baumann
Latei Rudolph

Advisory Board Members

Deniz Appelbaum, *Montclair State University*
Vipin Arora, *Oregon State University*
Alisa DiSalvo, *Saint Mary's University of Minnesota*
Jessie George, *University of Houston, Downtown*
Matthew Holt, *University of Dayton*
Venkataraman Iyer, *University of North Carolina, Greensboro*
Gregory Kogan, *Long Island University, Brooklyn*
Britton McKay, *Georgia Southern University*
Matthew Sargent, *University of Texas, Arlington*
Richard Savich, *University of California, Riverside*
George Schmelzle, *Missouri State University*
Julie Staples, *Jacksonville State University*

Reviewers

Jane Adams, *Henderson State University*
Kevin Agnew, *Elon University*
Mark Allan, *Metropolitan State University, St. Paul*
Rihab Alzubaidi, *Westfield State University*
Sara Amstutz, *Saint Mary-of-the-Woods College*
Benjamin Anderson, *San Jose State University*
Deniz Appelbaum, *Montclair State University*
Barbara Arel, *University of Vermont*
Vipin Arora, *Oregon State University*
Benjamin Bae, *California State University, Bakersfield*
Karen Baker, *Loyalist College*
Ryan Baxter, *Boise State University*

Martin Blaine, *Columbus State Community College*
Jane Bloodgood, *Kansas State University*
Stacey Bolin, *East Central University*
Sunday Boniface, *Western Michigan University*
Michael Borbacs, *Georgetown University*
Faye Borthick, *Georgia State University*
Felix Buabeng, *College of the Albermarle*
Stacey Callaway, *Rowan College of South Jersey*
Jack Cathey, *University of North Carolina, Charlotte*
Luis Cedeno, *University of Houston, Downtown*
Sandra Cereola, *James Madison University*
Siew Chan, *University of North Georgia*
C. Catherine Chiang, *Elon University*
Gerald Childs, *Waukesha County Technical College*
Lawrence Chui, *University of St. Thomas*
Susan Clark, *Asnuntuck Community College*
Eve-Lynn Clarke, *University of St. Francis, Fort Wayne*
Susan Cockrell, *Austin Peay State University*
Ciril Cohen, *Fairleigh Dickinson University*
Scott Collins, *Penn State University, University Park*
John Covone, *Cairn University*
Joshua Coyne, *University of Memphis*
Susann Cuperus, *University of Mary*
Kathleen Davisson, *University of Denver*
Julie Dawson, *Carthage College*
Laurence DeGaetano, *Montclair State University*
Sebahattin Demirkan, *Manhattan College*
Sandra Devona, *Northern Illinois University*
Brandon Di Paolo Harrison, *Austin Peay State University*
Alisa DiSalvo, *Saint Mary's University of Minnesota*
Dawna Drum, *Western Washington University*
Lisa Dunbar, *University of Southern Maine, Portland*
Steven Ernest, *Baton Rouge Community College*
Richard Evans, *University of Virginia*
Samantha Falgout, *Nicholls State University*
Kurt Fanning, *Grand Valley State University*
Julie Flaiz-Windham, *University of California, Irvine*
Thomas Francl, *National University*
Donna Free, *Oakland University*
Sonia Gantman, *Bentley University*
Jessie George, *University of Houston, Downtown*
Tatiana Gershberg, *California State University, Los Angeles*
Peter Gillett, *Rutgers State University, New Brunswick*
Sunita Goel, *Siena College*
Mary Beth Goodrich, *University of Texas, Dallas*
Richard Green, *Texas A & M University, San Antonio*
Kristie Gregar-Skillman, *Colorado State University*
Michael Griffin, *University of Massachusetts, Dartmouth*
Deborah Habel, *Wayne State University*
John Hagan, *University of Texas, Dallas*

Md Hasan, *Old Dominion University*
Holly Hawk, *University of Georgia*
Betsy Haywood-Sullivan, *Rider University*
Megan Hiner, *Florida Atlantic University*
David Hinrichs, *Lehigh University*
Kristen Hockman, *University of Missouri, Columbia*
Jamie Hoelscher, *Southern Illinois University, Edwardsville*
Matthew Holt, *University of Dayton*
J. Michael Hoppe, *Wake Technical Community College*
Amy Igou, *University of Northern Iowa*
Venkataraman Iyer, *University of North Carolina, Greensboro*
Derek Jackson, *Saint Mary's University of Minnesota*
Diane Janvrin, *Iowa State University*
Ron Jastrzebski, *University of Illinois, Chicago*
Yonghua Ji, *University of Alberta*
Jennifer Johnson, *University of Texas, Dallas*
Patricia Johnson, *Southern New Hampshire University*
Kevin Jones, *University of California, Santa Cruz*
Scot Justice, *Appalachian State University*
Stani Kantcheva, *Cincinnati State University*
Andrea Kelton, *Middle Tennessee State University*
Debra Kiss, *Davenport University*
Bonnie Klamm, *North Dakota State University*
Gregory Kogan, *Long Island University, Brooklyn*
Mark Koscinski, *Moravian College*
Juliana Kralik, *University of South Florida*
Bradley Lail, *Baylor University*
Michael Lawson, *Brigham Young University*
Yvette Lazdowski, *University of New Hampshire*
Chih-Chen Lee, *Lehigh University*
Lorraine Lee, *University of North Carolina, Wilmington*
Miriam Lefkowitz, *City University of New York, Brooklyn*
Jacob Lennard, *University of Central Florida*
Robert Lin, *California State University, East Bay*
Qi Liu, *University of Rhode Island*
Tina Loraas, *Auburn University*
Valissa Lowery, *Robeson Community College*
Sakthi Mahenthiran, *Butler University*
Lois Mahoney, *Eastern Michigan University*
Bushra Malik
Robert Markley
David Marks, *The University of Texas, Tyler*
Karen Mattison, *Presbyterian College*
Donna McGovern, *Golden West College*
Britton McKay, *Georgia Southern University*
Suzann Medicus, *University of Maryland, Baltimore County*
Karen Miller, *Union University*
Susan Minke, *Purdue University, Fort Wayne*
Ashley Minnich, *Park University*
Preston Mitchell, *New Mexico State University, Las Cruces*
Robert Monaghan, *University of North Carolina, Charlotte*
Bonnie Morris, *Duquesne University*
Christine Naaman, *Murray State University*
Ramesh Narasimhan, *Montclair State University*
Ikechukwu Ndu, *University of Southern Maine*
Pam Neely, *State University of New York, Brockport*
Renee Olvera, *Texas Christian University*
Alyssa Ong, *Pepperdine University*
Diaeldin Osman, *Alabama State University*
Vincent Owhoso, *Northern Kentucky University*
Tillie Parmar, *Trinity Western University*
Veronica Paz, *Colorado State University*

Joanne Pencak, *University of Vermont*
Matthew Pickard, *Northern Illinois University*
Jeffrey Pickerd, *University of Mississippi*
Elizabeth Pierce, *Saginaw Valley State University*
Ronald Premuroso, *Colorado State University*
Jeffrey Pullen, *University of Maryland, Global Campus*
Nirmalee Raddatz, *University of Memphis*
Joseph Ragan, *Saint Joseph's University*
Dan Ramey, *University of Houston*
David Repp, *Strayer University*
Sherilyn Reynolds, *San Jacinto College*
Marie Rice, *West Virginia University*
Allison Richardson, *College of the Holy Cross*
Laura Rickett, *Cleveland State University*
Jennifer Riley, *University of Nebraska, Omaha*
Doug Roberts, *Appalachian State University*
Constance Rodriguez, *State University of New York, Empire State College*
Paulette Rodriguez, *University of Texas, El Paso*
Jorge Romero, *Towson University*
Silvia Romero-Andrade, *Montclair State University*
Rebecca Rosner, *Long Island University, Post Campus*
Karen Saboe, *College of Charleston*
Matthew Sargent, *University of Texas, Arlington*
Richard Savich, *University of California, Riverside*
Brenden Schaaf, *Metropolitan St University, St. Paul*
George Schmelzle, *Missouri State University*
Karen Schuele, *John Carroll University*
Joann Segovia, *Winona State University*
Angela Seidel, *Saint Francis University*
Vincent Shea, *Saint John's University*
Milton Shen, *University of Alabama, Huntsville*
Alice Sineath, *Forsyth Technical Community College*
Ankita Singhvi, *Texas A&M University, Central Texas*
Roger So, *St. John's University*
Qian Song, *Rochester Institute of Technology*
Gregory Springate, *MacEwan University*
Julie Staples, *Jacksonville State University*
Ashley Stewart, *Delta State University*
John Strong, *Santa Ana College*
Li Sun, *University of Tulsa*
Pavani Tallapally, *Slippery Rock University*
Calvin Tan, *Kapiolani Community College*
Michael Tang, *Florida International University*
Haimeng Teng, *The Pennsylvania State University, Harrisburg*
Houda Trabelsi, *Athabasca University*
Jill Trucke, *University of Nebraska, Lincoln*
Alli Vainshtein, *Saint Paul College*
James Vogt, *San Diego State University*
Richard Walstra, *Dominican University*
Kun Wang, *Texas Southern University*
Lin Wang, *Midwestern State University*
TJ Wang, *Governors State University*
Cassandra Weitzenkamp, *Peru State College*
Veronda Willis, *University of Texas, Tyler*
Jon Winchenbach, *Framingham State University*
Bradley Winton, *University of Southern Mississippi*
Suzanne Wright, *The Pennsylvania State University*
John Wronkovich, *Kent State University*
Yan Xiong, *California State University, Sacramento*
Xiaoli Yuan, *Elizabeth City State University*
Chuancai Zhang, *Cal Poly, San Luis Obispo*

We also want to thank the talented people who helped us move this product from concept to publication. We appreciate the support and guidance of Veronica Schram, who has gone above and beyond as our lead editor, and the rest of our amazing team at Wiley, including Natalie Munoz, Ed Brislin, Wendy Ashenberg, Christina Koop Minarik, Maureen Shelburn, Emily Marcoux, Shelley Lea, Lisa Holloway, and Kali Ridley. We couldn't have created this unique product without the input of our talented developmental editors, Jessica Carlisle and Kitty Wilson, our copyeditor, Sarah Perkins, or our art lead, Jodie Bernard. Thank you to all involved for believing that we can disrupt the way AIS is taught.

We believe that feedback is as important to this course as it is to career development, and we appreciate suggestions and comments about this course from instructors and students. You can send them to us at AIS.Savage.Wiley@gmail.com.

Contents

FROM THE AUTHORS   vi
ABOUT THE AUTHORS   vii
OUR APPROACH   viii
ACKNOWLEDGMENTS   xiv

Part I: Foundations of AIS

1 Accounting as Information

1.1 **Why Is Accounting Information Important?**   **1-2**
Good Information Leads to Good Decisions   **1-2**
Transforming Data into Information   **1-3**
Components of an AIS   **1-4**
Meet Julia's Cookies   **1-6**
Julia's Cookies Applied Learning 1.1   **1-7**
Understanding Business Operations   **1-8**
1.2 **How Have Accounting Information Systems Evolved?**   **1-13**
Acquisitions and Payments Processes   **1-14**
Julia's Cookies Applied Learning 1.2   **1-15**
Conversion Processes   **1-16**
In the Real World: McDonald's Regrets Changing Its Conversion Process   **1-17**
Marketing, Sales, and Collections Processes   **1-17**
1.3 **How Does Management Use Information?**   **1-19**
Management's Responsibility for Business Processes   **1-20**
Data-Driven Decision Making   **1-21**
Julia's Cookies Applied Learning 1.3   **1-24**
1.4 **What Is the Relationship Between Accounting and Data Analytics?**   **1-25**
Reporting Versus Analytics   **1-26**
Data Analytics in Accounting   **1-27**
Julia's Cookies Applied Learning 1.4   **1-27**
Data Analytics Skills   **1-28**
Featured Professional: Accounting Support Services   **1-29**
Tableau Case: Cookies Cares Charitable Foundation   **1-38**

2 Risks and Risk Assessments

2.1 **How Do We Understand Risk?**   **2-2**
Importance of Risk   **2-2**
Applying Risks to a Business   **2-3**

Enterprise Risk Management   **2-5**
Identifying Risks   **2-6**
Julia's Cookies Applied Learning 2.1   **2-7**
2.2 **What Are the Types of Risks?**   **2-8**
Internal Risks   **2-8**
External Risks   **2-10**
In the Real World: Volkswagen Emissions Scandal   **2-11**
Risk Inventory   **2-12**
Julia's Cookies Applied Learning 2.2   **2-13**
2.3 **How Do We Prioritize Risk?**   **2-14**
Evaluating Risk Severity   **2-14**
Julia's Cookies Applied Learning 2.3   **2-15**
Using Risk Formulas   **2-16**
Creating Risk Matrices   **2-18**
2.4 **How Do We Respond to Risk?**   **2-19**
Assess the Risk   **2-20**
Respond to the Risk   **2-21**
Julia's Cookies Applied Learning 2.4   **2-23**
Featured Professional: Nontraditional CPA Firm   **2-24**
Tableau Case: Julia's Cookies' Risk Profile   **2-34**

3 Risk Management and Internal Controls

3.1 **How Do Internal Controls Mitigate Risk?**   **3-2**
Preventive Controls   **3-3**
Detective Controls   **3-5**
Corrective Controls   **3-5**
Julia's Cookies Applied Learning 3.1   **3-7**
3.2 **How Are Controls Classified?**   **3-8**
General Controls   **3-9**
Application Controls   **3-10**
In the Real World: Cantey Technology's Contingency Response   **3-10**
Implementing Controls   **3-11**
Continuous Monitoring   **3-14**
Julia's Cookies Applied Learning 3.2   **3-15**
3.3 **How Do We Assess Internal Controls?**   **3-17**
Management: First and Second Lines of Defense   **3-18**
Julia's Cookies Applied Learning 3.3   **3-20**
Internal Audit: Third Line of Defense   **3-21**
3.4 **Why Are Internal Control Frameworks Important?**   **3-23**
Sarbanes-Oxley Act of 2002 (SOX)   **3-23**
Directive 2014/56/EU of the European Parliament   **3-25**

COSO Internal Control—Integrated
Framework   **3-25**
COSO Enterprise Risk Management
Framework   **3-28**
Julia's Cookies Applied Learning 3.4   **3-29**
Featured Professional: Managing Partner,
Risk Management Firm   **3-30**
Tableau Case: Control Mapping at Julia's Cookies   **3-40**

4   Software and Systems

**4.1   How Do Systems Capture and Process
Data?   4-2**
Information Systems   **4-2**
Transaction Processing   **4-3**
Software   **4-5**
Cloud Computing   **4-7**
Julia's Cookies Applied Learning 4.1   **4-9**
**4.2   How Do Startups and Small Businesses Use
Technology?   4-11**
Technology for Startups   **4-11**
Managing Risks   **4-14**
Julia's Cookies Applied Learning 4.2   **4-15**
**4.3   What Are the Characteristics of
Information Systems for Growing
Companies?   4-16**
Acquisition-Based Growth   **4-16**
Systems Integration   **4-17**
Systems Configurations   **4-18**
Julia's Cookies Applied Learning 4.3   **4-21**
**4.4   Why Are Enterprise Resource Planning (ERP)
Systems Considered Ideal?   4-22**
A Solution for Systems Integration   **4-22**
Julia's Cookies Applied Learning 4.4   **4-25**
Implementing an ERP System   **4-25**
In the Real World: MillerCoors: An ERP Disaster
Story   **4-27**
Featured Professional: Senior Accountant at a Local
Startup   **4-29**
Tableau Case: Julia's Cookies' System
Conversion   **4-35**

5   Data Storage and Analysis

5.1   What Is Data?   5-2
Data Elements   **5-2**
Data Types   **5-3**
Data That Changes   **5-6**
Julia's Cookies Applied Learning 5.1   **5-7**
5.2   How Is Data Stored?   5-9
Introduction to Databases   **5-9**
Types of Data Storage   **5-10**
Julia's Cookies Applied Learning 5.2   **5-12**

5.3   What Makes Data "Big Data"?   5-13
Volume   **5-14**
Velocity   **5-14**
Variety   **5-15**
Veracity   **5-15**
In the Real World: Uber's Data Platform   **5-16**
Value   **5-16**
Julia's Cookies Applied Learning 5.3   **5-17**
**5.4   How Do Accounting Professionals Use
Data?   5-18**
Audit and Compliance   **5-20**
Financial Accounting   **5-21**
Managerial Accounting   **5-22**
Julia's Cookies Applied Learning 5.4   **5-23**
Tax Accounting   **5-24**
Featured Professional: MBA Business Analytics
and Management Information Systems
Candidate   **5-26**
Tableau Case: Julia's Cookies' IT Help Desk   **5-33**

6   Designing Systems and Databases

6.1   How Are Systems Developed?   6-2
Pre-Implementation   **6-3**
System Build   **6-6**
Go-Live and Beyond   **6-6**
Julia's Cookies Applied Learning 6.1   **6-8**
**6.2   Which Methodology Should Be
Used?   6-9**
Waterfall Methodology   **6-9**
Agile Methodology   **6-10**
In the Real World: LEGO   **6-13**
Selecting a Methodology   **6-13**
Julia's Cookies Applied Learning 6.2   **6-15**
**6.3   What Type of Database Should
Be Used?   6-16**
Relational Databases   **6-16**
Julia's Cookies Applied Learning 6.3   **6-18**
Object-Oriented Databases   **6-19**
NoSQL Databases   **6-20**
**6.4   How Are Relational Databases
Designed?   6-21**
The Conceptual ERD: Identifying Tables and
Relationships   **6-22**
The Logical ERD: Adding Details   **6-23**
The Physical ERD: Creating the Technical
Design   **6-24**
Julia's Cookies Applied Learning 6.4   **6-25**
**6.5   How Do We Interact with Data in a
Database?   6-30**
The Basic SELECT Statement   **6-31**
The WHERE Clause   **6-34**

The JOIN Operator **6-35**
Putting It Together **6-38**
Julia's Cookies Applied Learning 6.5 **6-39**
6.6 How Can We Create Database Forms and Reports? 6-40
Forms **6-40**
Reports **6-42**
Featured Professional: Finance Digital Transformation Analyst **6-43**
Tableau Case: Julia's Cookies' IT Help Desk Employee Insights **6-53**

7 Emerging and Disruptive Technologies

7.1 How Do Companies Approach Emerging and Disruptive Technologies? 7-2
Differentiating Emerging and Disruptive Technologies **7-3**
Risk and Risk Mitigation **7-3**
Julia's Cookies Applied Learning 7.1 **7-6**
7.2 How Do Disruptive Technologies Provide Business Opportunities? 7-7
Internet of Things (IoT) **7-7**
Extended Reality (XR) **7-9**
Gamification **7-10**
Autonomous Things (AuT) **7-11**
Julia's Cookies Applied Learning 7.2 **7-12**
7.3 How Does Robotic Process Automation (RPA) Benefit Accounting Professionals? 7-13
Types of Automation **7-14**
Logic Behind RPA **7-14**
Accounting Use Cases **7-17**
Julia's Cookies Applied Learning 7.3 **7-21**
Creating Efficiencies and Opportunities **7-22**
In the Real World: Automation at Airbus: Saving Millions on Finance Tasks **7-23**
7.4 What Is Blockchain? 7-24
The Basics of Blockchain **7-25**
Cryptology **7-26**
Blockchain Ledgers **7-26**
Fundamental Principles of Blockchain Technology **7-29**
Types of Blockchain Systems **7-30**
Julia's Cookies Applied Learning 7.4 **7-31**
7.5 Why Should Accountants Care About Blockchain? 7-32
Evolving Career Opportunities **7-33**
Improving Data Quality **7-35**
Julia's Cookies Applied Learning 7.5 **7-36**
Featured Professional: Director of Innovation, Public Accounting Firm **7-37**
Tableau Case: Julia's Cookies' Smart Freezers **7-43**

8 Documenting Systems and Processes

8.1 Why Do We Document Systems and Processes? 8-2
Systems Documentation **8-2**
Program Documentation **8-3**
Operator Documentation **8-4**
User Documentation **8-4**
Julia's Cookies Applied Learning 8.1 **8-5**
8.2 How Do We Know Which Type of Documentation to Use? 8-6
Documenting the Overall Business **8-7**
Documenting Processes and Systems **8-8**
Documenting Data **8-10**
Julia's Cookies Applied Learning 8.2 **8-12**
8.3 How Do Flowcharts Illustrate Systems or Business Processes? 8-13
Flowchart Shapes **8-14**
Julia's Cookies Applied Learning 8.3 **8-16**
Flowchart Swim Lanes **8-18**
In the Real World: A Picture Is Worth a Thousand Words **8-18**
8.4 How Do Data Flow Diagrams Show Information Flow? 8-20
DFD Shapes **8-20**
DFD Levels **8-21**
Julia's Cookies Applied Learning 8.4 **8-24**
8.5 What Software Tools Can Be Used for Graphical Documentation? 8-26
Featured Professional: Big Four External Auditor **8-28**
Tableau Case: Julia's Cookies' System Migration **8-35**

Part II: Business Processes

9 Human Resources and Payroll Processes

9.1 How Are Human Resources and Payroll Related? 9-2
Human Resources: Employee Operations **9-2**
Payroll: Employee Compensation **9-4**
Integrating HR and Payroll **9-5**
Julia's Cookies Applied Learning 9.1 **9-6**
9.2 How Are New Employees Hired? 9-6
Employee Onboarding Process **9-7**
Risks and Control Activities **9-8**
Julia's Cookies Applied Learning 9.2 **9-12**

9.3 What Happens When an Employee Is Terminated? 9-14
Employee Termination Process **9-15**
Risks and Control Activities **9-15**
Julia's Cookies Applied Learning 9.3 **9-19**
9.4 How Do We Compensate Employees for Their Work? 9-20
Payroll Journal Entries **9-21**
Payroll Process **9-23**
Risks and Control Activities **9-24**
In the Real World: Java Golf Club **9-26**
Julia's Cookies Applied Learning 9.4 **9-28**
9.5 How Can Human Resources and Payroll Data Be Used to Identify Risks? 9-29
Database Design **9-30**
Reporting and Insights **9-31**
Julia's Cookies Applied Learning 9.5 **9-36**
Featured Professional: Director of SOX Compliance **9-37**
Tableau Case: Julia's Cookies' People Analytics **9-46**

10 Purchasing and Payments Processes

10.1 What Is the Relationship Between Purchasing, Inventory Management, and Supply Chain Management? 10-2
Inventory Purchasing and Payments Processes **10-3**
In the Real World: Purchasing Gone Wrong **10-4**
Inventory Management **10-6**
Supply Chain Management **10-7**
Julia's Cookies Applied Learning 10.1 **10-8**
10.2 How Are Inventory and Other Goods and Services Purchased? 10-9
Purchasing Process **10-10**
Internal Control over Purchasing **10-10**
Julia's Cookies Applied Learning 10.2 **10-14**
10.3 What Makes Fixed Assets Unique to Purchasing and Payments? 10-17
Fixed Asset Acquisitions Process **10-18**
Internal Control over Fixed Asset Acquisitions **10-21**
Julia's Cookies Applied Learning 10.3 **10-22**
10.4 How Do We Evaluate the Credit Payments Process? 10-24
Credit Payments Process **10-25**
Internal Control over Payments to Vendors **10-27**
Julia's Cookies Applied Learning 10.4 **10-28**
10.5 How Does the AIS Capture Purchasing and Payments Data? 10-29
Database Design **10-29**
Julia's Cookies Applied Learning 10.5 **10-30**

Reporting and Insights **10-32**
Featured Professional: External Auditor for Private Companies **10-38**
Tableau Case: Accounts Payable Red Flags at Julia's Cookies **10-45**

11 Conversion Processes

11.1 What Is the Relationship Between Conversion Processes, Inventory, and Supply Chain Management? 11-2
Conversion Processes **11-3**
Julia's Cookies Applied Learning 11.1 **11-9**
Managing Inventory and Product Life Cycle **11-11**
11.2 Why Is Cost Accounting Important to the Accounting Information System? 11-14
Traditional Cost Accounting **11-14**
Activity-Based Cost Accounting **11-18**
Julia's Cookies Applied Learning 11.2 **11-19**
Product Costing Internal Controls **11-20**
11.3 What Is Digital Manufacturing? 11-22
Digital Manufacturing Environment **11-22**
In the Real World: Inside the Siemens Digital Factory **11-23**
Opportunities and Challenges **11-23**
Digital Manufacturing Use Cases **11-24**
Julia's Cookies Applied Learning 11.3 **11-25**
11.4 How Is Data Collected and Used? 11-26
Database Design **11-27**
Julia's Cookies Applied Learning 11.4 **11-28**
Reporting and Insights **11-29**
Featured Professional: Program Manager, Electric Vehicle Manufacturer **11-31**
Tableau Case: Julia's Cookies' Raw Ingredient Costs **11-40**

12 Marketing, Sales, and Collections Processes

12.1 How Do Marketing, Sales, and Collections Complete the Business Model? 12-2
Business-to-Consumer Sales **12-3**
Managing Inventory and Product Flow **12-9**
Julia's Cookies Applied Learning 12.1 **12-10**
12.2 Why Are Business Credit Sales More Complex Than Consumer Cash Sales? 12-11
Marketing **12-12**
Pricing and Contracts **12-13**
Julia's Cookies Applied Learning 12.2 **12-15**
Sales Orders **12-16**
Shipping **12-17**

Billing and Collections   **12-20**
Credit Sales Process Flowchart   **12-22**
12.3   How Do We Ensure That Revenue Is Correctly Recognized?   12-23
Revenue Recognition Model   **12-24**
In the Real World: Wirecard and the Missing $2 Billion of Revenue and Cash   **12-25**
Controlling for Mistakes and Fraud   **12-25**
Julia's Cookies Applied Learning 12.3   **12-28**
12.4   How Are Customer Payments Collected?   12-29
Receiving Payments   **12-29**
Bank Deposits   **12-30**
Recording Cash Receipts   **12-32**
Collections Process Flowchart   **12-33**
Julia's Cookies Applied Learning 12.4   **12-34**
12.5   Which Reports and Analytics Give Insights into These Processes?   12-36
Database Design   **12-36**
Reporting and Insights   **12-38**
Julia's Cookies Applied Learning 12.5   **12-41**
Featured Professional: Finance Transformation Manager   **12-45**
Tableau Case: Julia's Cookies' Accounts Receivable Analysis   **12-55**

13 Financial Reporting Processes

13.1   How Is an AIS Involved in Financial Reporting?   13-2
Meeting Financial Reporting Objectives   **13-2**
Julia's Cookies Applied Learning 13.1   **13-4**
Consolidated Reporting Requirements   **13-4**
13.2   How Are Financial Statements Generated by an AIS?   13-6
Chart of Accounts   **13-6**
The Financial Reporting Process   **13-7**
Julia's Cookies Applied Learning 13.2   **13-11**
Financial Reporting Internal Controls   **13-13**
13.3   How Does XBRL Create Efficient Financial Reporting?   13-16
Tagging Financial Data   **13-16**
Standardized Financial Reporting   **13-17**
XBRL in Action   **13-18**
Julia's Cookies Applied Learning 13.3   **13-19**
13.4   Are There Other Important Financial Accounting Reports?   13-20
Cost Accounting   **13-20**
Responsibility Accounting   **13-21**
Balanced Scorecard   **13-22**
Julia's Cookies Applied Learning 13.4   **13-24**
13.5   How Is Financial Reporting Data Used for Insights and Decision Making?   13-25

In the Real World: A New Financial Reporting and Management Accounting System   **13-26**
Database Design   **13-27**
Julia's Cookies Applied Learning 13.5   **13-28**
Financial Modeling for Decision Making   **13-29**
Reporting and Insights   **13-30**
Featured Professional: Chief Financial Officer   **13-33**
Tableau Case: Julia's Cookies' General Ledger Journal Entries   **13-43**
Appendix A: Expanding the Accounting Equation: From Balance Sheet to Statement of Cash Flows   **13-45**

Part III: Risk Assurance

14 Information Systems and Controls

14.1   What Framework Can We Use to Mitigate Risk Around Our Systems?   14-2
Introducing COBIT   **14-2**
Julia's Cookies Applied Learning 14.1   **14-3**
The Five Domains of COBIT   **14-3**
14.2   How Do We Decide Who Can Access Systems?   14-6
Assigning and Authenticating Users   **14-7**
Julia's Cookies Applied Learning 14.2   **14-8**
Adding and Removing Users   **14-9**
Reviewing Existing Users   **14-11**
User Access Internal Controls   **14-12**
14.3   How Do We Physically Protect Our Systems?   14-13
Data Center Components and Security   **14-14**
In the Real World: Google and Amazon Data Centers   **14-15**
Julia's Cookies Applied Learning 14.3   **14-17**
Physical Access Internal Controls   **14-17**
14.4   How Do We Keep Our Systems Running?   14-19
Business Continuity Planning   **14-19**
Julia's Cookies Applied Learning 14.4   **14-20**
Backup Sites   **14-21**
Backup Strategies   **14-22**
Backup Cycles   **14-25**
Data Storage Internal Controls   **14-26**
14.5   How Do We Make Changes to Systems?   14-28
The Change Management Process   **14-29**
Julia's Cookies Applied Learning 14.5   **14-33**
Differentiating Between Normal and Emergency Changes   **14-33**
Change Management Internal Controls   **14-34**

Featured Professional: IT Governance Thought
        Leader   **14-35**
Tableau Case: Change Management at
        Julia's Cookies   **14-44**

15   Fraud

15.1   What Is Fraud?   **15-2**
        Fraud Is a Risk   **15-2**
        External Fraud   **15-4**
        Occupational Fraud   **15-4**
In the Real World: A Fraud with Deadly
        Consequences   **15-6**
        Behavioral Red Flags   **15-6**
Julia's Cookies Applied Learning 15.1   **15-7**
15.2   How Do We Manage Fraud Risk?   **15-8**
        The Fraud Triangle   **15-9**
Julia's Cookies Applied Learning 15.2   **15-11**
        Preventing Fraud   **15-11**
        Detecting Fraud   **15-13**
**15.3   How Does Asset Misappropriation Result
        in Fraud?**   **15-14**
        Skimming   **15-15**
        Larceny   **15-17**
        Fraudulent Disbursements   **15-18**
Julia's Cookies Applied Learning 15.3   **15-19**
**15.4   What Are the Characteristics of Financial
        Statement Fraud?**   **15-23**
        Overstating Financial Performance   **15-24**
Julia's Cookies Applied Learning 15.4   **15-28**
        Understating Financial Performance   **15-30**
        Management's Involvement in Financial
        Statement Fraud   **15-32**
Featured Professional: Fraud Analytics Specialist   **15-34**
Tableau Case: Employee Reimbursement
        Expenses at Julia's Cookies   **15-42**

16   Cybersecurity

**16.1   How Is Cybersecurity Relevant to the
        Accounting Profession?**   **16-2**
        Recent Cybersecurity Threats   **16-3**
        Relevance to Accounting Professionals   **16-4**
        Governance and Policies   **16-6**
Julia's Cookies Applied Learning 16.1   **16-8**
16.2   How Do Cybercriminals Plan Attacks?   **16-8**
        Physical Reconnaissance Attacks   **16-9**
Julia's Cookies Applied Learning 16.2   **16-11**
        Logical Reconnaissance Attacks   **16-13**
**16.3   How Do Hackers Gain Unauthorized
        Access?**   **16-15**
        Physical Access Attacks   **16-15**

Julia's Cookies Applied Learning 16.3   **16-16**
        Logical Access Attacks   **16-17**
**16.4   How Do Attackers Shut Down
        a System?**   **16-20**
        Denial-of-Service Attacks   **16-21**
        Malware Attacks   **16-23**
In the Real World: Hostage Systems   **16-26**
Julia's Cookies Applied Learning 16.4   **16-27**
Featured Professional: Public Accounting
        Cybersecurity Director   **16-28**
Tableau Case: Network Logins at Julia's
        Cookies   **16-35**

Part IV: Technology and Analytics

17   Data Analytics

**17.1   How Is Data Analytics Changing the
        Accounting Profession?**   **17-2**
        Types of Analysts   **17-2**
In the Real World: Employment Opportunities in
        Accounting Data Analytics   **17-3**
Julia's Cookies Applied Learning 17.1   **17-4**
        Types of Analytics   **17-4**
        Machine Learning (ML)   **17-5**
**17.2   How Do We Explore a Data
        Set?**   **17-7**
        Anomaly Detection   **17-8**
        Data Summarization   **17-8**
        Clustering and Classification   **17-10**
Julia's Cookies Applied Learning 17.2   **17-13**
**17.3   How Do We Investigate Interesting
        Occurrences in a Data Set?**   **17-14**
        Linear Regression   **17-15**
Julia's Cookies Applied Learning 17.3   **17-16**
        Forecasting   **17-16**
        Monte Carlo Simulation   **17-17**
**17.4   Which Analytics Techniques Are
        Gaining Popularity in the Accounting
        Profession?**   **17-19**
        Process Mining   **17-19**
Julia's Cookies Applied Learning 17.4   **17-21**
        Network Analysis   **17-21**
        Geospatial Analytics   **17-23**
        Natural Language Processing
        (NLP)   **17-24**
Featured Professional: Audit Data Analytics
        Manager   **17-26**
Tableau Case: Julia's Cookies' Call Center
        Performance   **17-34**

18 Data Visualization

18.1 How Does Visualization Tell a Story with Data?   18-2
In the Real World: Charles Schwab's Tableau Center of Excellence   **18-3**
Turning Data into a Story   **18-3**
Designing for a User   **18-5**
Setting the Tone   **18-5**
Julia's Cookies Applied Learning 18.1   **18-6**
18.2 What Are the Fundamentals of Design?   18-7
Color   **18-7**
White Space   **18-10**
Typography and Iconography   **18-11**
Julia's Cookies Applied Learning 18.2   **18-12**
18.3 How Do Visualizations Help Us Explore Data?   18-13
Composition and Comparison   **18-15**
Distribution   **18-19**
Relationships   **18-21**
Geospatial Maps   **18-24**
Julia's Cookies Applied Learning 18.3   **18-25**
18.4 When Should Explanatory Visualizations Be Used for Storytelling?   18-26
Infographics   **18-27**
Dashboards   **18-27**
Storyboards   **18-30**
Julia's Cookies Applied Learning 18.4   **18-33**
Featured Professional: Health Insurance Business Analyst   **18-34**
Tableau Case: Julia's Cookies' Sales Dashboard   **18-48**

GLOSSARY   G-1
INDEX   I-1

Online Chapter

19 Audit Assurance

19.1 What Is the Difference Between Internal Audit and External Audit?   19-2
Audit Specializations   **19-2**
External Auditors   **19-3**
In the Real World: Arthur Andersen and Enron   **19-5**
Julia's Cookies Applied Learning 19.1   **19-7**
19.2 How Are Internal Audits Performed?   19-8
The Internal Audit Process   **19-8**
Planning an Audit   **19-10**
Julia's Cookies Applied Learning 19.2   **19-12**
19.3 How Is Testing Performed?   19-13
Information Gathering   **19-14**
Tests of Controls   **19-15**
Substantive Procedures   **19-16**
Julia's Cookies Applied Learning 19.3   **19-20**
19.4 What Happens After an Audit?   19-21
Wrap-up   **19-21**
Julia's Cookies Applied Learning 19.4   **19-23**
Reporting   **19-23**
Follow-up   **19-24**
Featured Professional: External Auditor, Big Four Firm   **19-25**
Tableau Case: Julia's Cookies' Internal Audit Analytics   **19-34**

CHAPTER 1

Accounting as Information

Accounting Intern—Finance Leadership Rotational Program

Julia's Cookies · Remote, Chicago, Atlanta, San Francisco

Posted 1 week ago · 1,189 views

Save | **Apply**

Job	**Company**	**Connections**
• 25 Applicants	• 3,000+ Employees	⬭ 20 Connections
• Associate	• Restaurants	

Summary

Julia's Cookies is seeking participants in a two-year rotational program designed to develop high-potential accounting talent into future finance leaders. Participants in the Finance Leadership Rotational Program (FLRP) spend time in the following departments:

- Corporate Accounting and Finance
- Internal Audit
- Tax
- Financial Planning and Analysis
- Risk Management

You will be challenged to:

- Demonstrate adaptability and agility by working in varied rotations throughout the organization
- Gain well-rounded professional experience and exposure to key business processes and departments
- Engage in leadership and development activities
- Ensure compliance with regulatory standards around data privacy and security

This program provides support for CPA certification, including study materials. Upon completion of the FLRP, graduates have transitioned into roles such as staff accountant, internal auditor, tax analyst, or financial analyst.

Requirements

Education: Currently pursuing a bachelor's degree in accounting or related field

GPA: 3.2+ cumulative

Preferred Knowledge and Skills

Preference will be given to candidates who have related internship or business experience in finance or accounting and who have demonstrated leadership via school clubs, volunteer work, or other organizations.

Salary: Part time; $25–35 per hour, depending on region

CHAPTER PREVIEW   The public often imagines accountants as wearing pocket protectors and sitting in cubicles, like stereotypical bookkeepers and IRS auditors. In reality, accounting is at the center of every business. Accounting professionals use critical thinking to make decisions like how to report, record, and categorize accounting activities. As technology continues influencing how companies operate, accounting professionals are becoming more strategic in their focus—moving away from "crunching numbers" and following checklists and toward becoming valuable advisors helping businesses meet their strategic objectives.

In order to provide strategic value, accounting professionals make decisions by using economic and business information. In this chapter, you will learn about where this information comes from and why information systems are an integral part of operations, including:

- How an information system supports business operations
- How accounting information systems have evolved
- How management uses information
- The relationship between data analytics and accounting

This chapter also introduces a company, Julia's Cookies, that you will encounter throughout the course. Focusing on a single company will help you understand the big picture of how the key concepts in this course integrate and influence business operations. Although Julia's Cookies is fictitious, it is modeled after real-world businesses, and the scenarios in the course are based on the real-life experiences of accounting professionals. The Julia's Cookies' job postings that appear throughout the book, like the Finance Leadership Rotational Program intern posting at the beginning of the chapter, are based on real job openings posted on online career websites such as LinkedIn. Companies post jobs just like this, and they are looking for accounting professionals just like you.   ■

Chapter Roadmap

LEARNING OBJECTIVES	TOPICS	JULIA'S COOKIES APPLIED LEARNING
1.1 Explain how accounting affects both the demand for and supply of information.	• Good Information Leads to Good Decisions • Transforming Data into Information • Components of an AIS • Meet Julia's Cookies • Understanding Business Operations	Accounting Skills: Rotational Internship Candidates
1.2 Compare traditional transaction-based accounting systems with process-based information systems.	• Acquisitions and Payments Processes • Conversion Processes • Marketing, Sales, and Collections Processes	Acquisitions and Payments Processes: Ordering Flour
1.3 Explain management's relationship to information and information systems.	• Management's Responsibility for Business Processes • Data-Driven Decision Making	Useful Information: Selecting Relevant Data Points
1.4 Describe the relationship between accounting and data analytics.	• Reporting Versus Analytics • Data Analytics in Accounting • Data Analytics Skills	Accounting Analytics: Capturing Data from Business Events

CPA   You will find the CPA tag throughout the chapter to call out any important topics you may see on the CPA exam.

1.1 Why Is Accounting Information Important?

Learning Objective ❶
Explain how accounting affects both the demand for and supply of information.

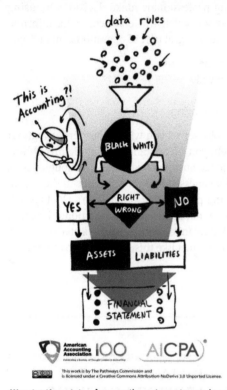

Illustration 1.1 Accounting stereotypes lead to misconceptions about the kind of work accounting professionals perform.

Source: The Pathways Commission, sponsored by the American Accounting Association and the American Institute of CPA. CC BY-ND 3.0.

Do you remember your introductory accounting course and your first perception of accounting? Have you seen movies that portray accountants as boring or nerdy? What about the public perception of IRS auditors? **Illustration 1.1** shows some common accounting misperceptions[1]:

- Accountants are boring bean counters who "crunch numbers."
- Accounting is a mechanical process with rigid black-and-white rules and yes-or-no answers.
- Accountants focus on debits and credits and are removed from business events and activities.

These misperceptions could not be further from the truth. Auditors are not the police, ready to write you up for failing to perform your job. That misconception still exists in many companies today, and internal and external auditors alike are fighting to prove they are here to help and innovate—even using phrases like "trusted advisor" to rebrand themselves.

Good Information Leads to Good Decisions

We call accounting the "language of business" because it measures and communicates the financial outcomes of a company's business strategy for three crucial categories of business activities: operating, investing, and financing. The results of these measurements can exceed, meet, or fail to meet expectations. Management uses these outcomes to make plans and execute them accordingly.

The reality of accounting is that it:

- Requires knowledge of economic contexts to fuel accounting judgments
- Consists of a mix of rigid black-and-white rules and many shades of gray
- Provides a source of useful information for decision making
- Helps support a prosperous society
- Serves the public interest
- Demands strong critical-thinking skills

Illustration 1.2 emphasizes the importance of critical-thinking skills for accounting professionals, which include (from the bottom up in the illustration):

- Using economic contexts to make accounting judgment calls for financial reporting. Generally accepted accounting principles (GAAP) allow for discretion in making accounting choices where there are shades of gray.
- Assessing the usefulness of reported accounting information resulting from these judgment calls.
- Making good business decisions based on this useful information.

Illustration 1.2 also shows both the demand for and supply of information, which often occur in real time due to advances in technology. The arrows indicate a flow of cause and effect. The supply of information flows from the information preparers at the bottom to the information users and decision makers at the top. During this process, accounting professionals

---

[1]We use, acknowledge, and appreciate the guidance provided by the American Accounting Association (AAA) and the AICPA's Pathways Commission in their Pathways Vision Model and accompanying explanatory materials.

should make judgment calls on what most appropriately reflects the business reality of economic activity. For example, an accounting professional must understand and interpret whether to use FIFO, LIFO, or a weighted average method for inventory valuation (covered in financial accounting courses). These judgments affect the usefulness of information, which then affects the users' decisions. Good business decisions lead to a prosperous society, which is how accounting professionals serve the public interest.

We can also look at the arrows in reverse by emphasizing the demand for information, which starts at the top of the model with users, or decision makers, who are seeking information about economic activity to help make decisions. Accounting has consequences. These decisions based on accounting information result in more economic activity, which starts the process over again.

It is important to note that the term "information system" can include all the people and processes involved in this supply of information. For the purposes of this accounting information systems course, however, we use "information system" and "accounting information system" to reference computer systems, whose definitions follow.

Transforming Data into Information

CPA An **information system** consists of interrelated components including physical hardware like monitors and laptops, the software that users interact with, databases used for storage, and networks that send data and information throughout the system. An information system also includes the people who use and maintain it. **Illustration 1.3** shows how an information system:

- Captures raw and unorganized data, which is the **input**
- Processes and stores that data (action)
- Reports information in formats that are useful to users, which is the **output**

You will learn about data later in the course, but for now, you just need to know that **data** consists of facts or statistics about a person or an object, like a transaction, that are collected for reference or analysis. Data is useless to a business until it is transformed into information.

An **accounting information system (AIS)** performs the same data collection, transformation, and reporting as all other information systems, but it is specific to accounting and financial data:

- The informational output of an AIS consists of accounting reports used by investors, tax authorities, creditors, and other stakeholders.
- The AIS involves a subset of all business data, which makes it one part of a firm's overall information system. It captures accounting data created by business events (or activities) that involve an exchange of economic resources.

The term **business event** refers to a single business activity in a business process. Business events are definable activities that take place during the normal operation of a business. Examples of business events include "Sell goods to customer" and "Purchase equipment." These events give rise to accounting transactions because they involve an exchange of economic resources that impacts the accounting equation. An example of a business event that does not give rise to an accounting transaction is "Take customer order." Even though it is essential for the business to collect data about customer orders in its information system, this event's data does not flow through to the AIS. It is filtered out and stored in other parts of the company's information system (**Illustration 1.4**).

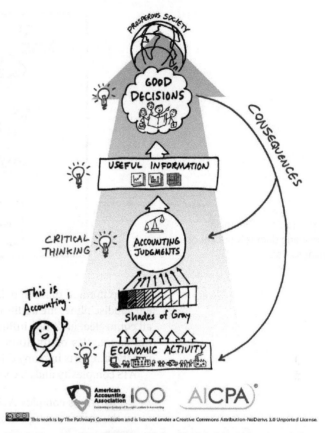

Illustration 1.2 The Pathways Vision Model shows how accounting professionals are involved in using judgments to make good decisions.

Source: The Pathways Commission, sponsored by the American Accounting Association and the American Institute of CPA. CC BY-ND 3.0.

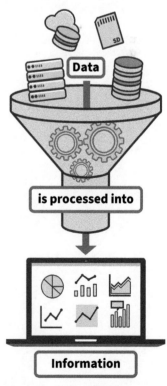

Illustration 1.3 Data (input) is captured by an information system and then processed into useful information (output).

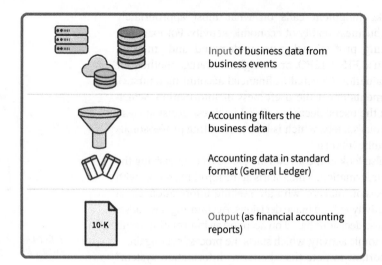

	Input of business data from business events
	Accounting filters the business data
	Accounting data in standard format (General Ledger)
10-K	Output (as financial accounting reports)

Illustration 1.4 Financial accounting data is a subset of business data.

Keep in mind that financial accounting is one subdiscipline of accounting. Other important subdisciplines are auditing and assurance, taxation, and managerial accounting. They are all connected, and they influence the AIS of a company. These connected disciplines extend the boundaries of traditional accounting information outputs from the AIS to provide a variety of reports in many different formats.

AIS complexity and size vary based on a company's needs:

- **CPA** A less complex AIS is a stand-alone system used by small businesses that focuses on the accounting equation and financial implications of the underlying business events.
- **CPA** An AIS with higher complexity can fully integrate with the company's enterprise-wide information system.

As companies grow, their information systems grow in complexity. An integrated AIS enables accounting reports far broader than simply tracking assets, liabilities, and owner's equity. Thanks to technological advances, data that used to be captured during a business event and later input into multiple systems—often manually—is now captured once when the business event occurs, often in real time. Now data automatically flows throughout the integrated information system to the various functional areas that need it. Benefits include quick access to that data, robust and real-time reporting, and the ability to make decisions faster. For example, a mobile-app-based company generates large amounts of data in real time that are instantly captured in the company's AIS as business events take place. We use a fictional company called Julia's Cookies to apply the concepts of AIS to a modern digital business model.

Components of an AIS

Traditionally, the users of accounting information retrieved the relevant information from an accounting system, maintained manually in paper-based forms. With the advent of technology and its increased adoption by businesses, records are maintained using computer systems. Today, AIS is a set of processes, procedures, and systems that captures, processes, summarizes, and reports accounting data that arise from a series of business events related to various business processes using technology (see **Illustration 1.5**).

The advancement of technology with the integration of business processes, cutting across functional domains, enables users to get quick access to real-time data. It supports the decision makers with robust information and real-time reporting for decision making.

The components of an AIS include:

Data

The AIS stores and retrieves data about the business's assets, liabilities, and equity. It also includes data on revenues, expenses, taxes, and other nonfinancial information captured during business events. The data supports the decision makers to create or generate meaningful

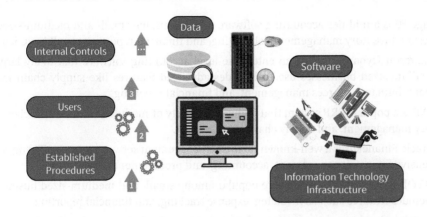

Illustration 1.5 Components of an accounting information system.

reports. Some examples of data are sales orders, customer billing statements, sales analysis reports, purchase requisitions, vendor invoices, general ledger, inventory data, and payroll information. The type of data captured and stored in an AIS varies across business processes, the nature of business, and the type of industry.

Established Procedures

The consistency of the AIS can be ensured by following predetermined and established procedures. Procedures provide clarity on steps to be followed while using the AIS. The procedures can be in terms of recording accounting records, source documents, and using a system for coding the business's financial transactions and financial reports. As the AIS is software-based, it is prone to threats of loss or destruction of data. There should be procedures for backup and recovery of data too.

Internal Controls

The internal control systems in place play an essential role in maintaining the reliability and efficiency of the AIS. The **internal controls** may be preventive, detective, or corrective measures. We may take the example of ordering inventory. An internal control mechanism must be in place to verify the quantity received with the purchase order, verify receiving report and purchase order to approve invoices, and update the accounts payable records. The restrictions or conditions of who will authorize transactions and activities, the fund limits the different managerial positions are authorized to sanction, and access to information are necessary to be built in the AIS as an internal check mechanism.

Information Technology (IT) Infrastructure

The AIS uses hardware for its operation. The hardware comprising computers, servers, routers, barcode scanners, printers, surge protectors, backup power supplies, and other components are referred to as IT infrastructure. An optimized IT infrastructure requires compatibility with the software selected for the AIS.

Software

AIS software is a tool that companies use to automate their accounting function and design real-time reports. The **software** simplifies accounting and finance control functions and can be customized. The AIS software makes the database management systems work. There are accounting software designed for specific operations like billing and invoice systems and payroll management systems. There is also integrated software connected to all functions in the business, such as enterprise resource planning (ERP) system. Some of the popular AIS software are:

- QuickBooks is a well-known accounting software for small businesses. It includes functions like invoicing, expense tracking, and financial reporting.

- Sage 50 is a mid-tier accounting software popular among small- and medium-sized businesses. Inventory management, job costing, and financial reporting are all included in it.
- Microsoft Dynamics GP is an enterprise-level accounting software that many large- and medium-sized businesses use. It includes advanced features like supply chain management, human resources management, and financial reporting.
- SAP is a popular ERP system that includes a variety of modules, such as financials, inventory management, and supply chain management.
- Oracle Financials is a well-known financial management software system offering comprehensive financial management, accounting, and procurement capabilities.
- MYOB is an accounting software popular among small- and medium-sized businesses. It includes features such as invoicing, expense tracking, and financial reporting.
- Xero is a cloud-based accounting software that includes features such as invoicing, expense management, and bank reconciliation.
- Wave is a free cloud-based accounting software for small businesses with invoicing, expense management, and financial reporting features.

Users

Users of accounting information can be divided into two broad groups: internal users and external users. The reports and statements generated by the AIS are consumed by external users like investors, creditors, government agencies, trading partners, regulatory agencies, journalists, and the general public. This information and reports may be used to evaluate the business's performance, risk, and compliance. The internal users of the AIS are owners, managers, and employees. They use AIS-generated information for decision making, analysis, target setting, budgeting, pricing, and forecasts.

Meet Julia's Cookies

Julia's Cookies is a national bakery offering fresh-baked cookies for pickup or delivery, with a limited selection of cookies available for walk-in customers. Every cookie is placed in the oven at the time it is ordered, so customers are served fresh, delicious cookies all day. The company was founded by a group of college students who wanted to satisfy the late-night cravings of finals week (**Illustration 1.6**).

As they discussed opening a late-night bakery together, the group realized that students aren't the only ones who crave late-night treats. Nurses, doctors, firefighters, restaurant workers, and many other professionals also keep late hours and might appreciate having cookies

ABOUT US Julia's Cookies was founded after midnight on a cold October morning in 2010. Five accounting majors working on a group project for their international financial accounting class had a sudden craving for something sweet, but all of the local bakeries were closed due to the late hour. It was then that a business idea was born: Wouldn't it be great to have fresh-baked cookies at any time—even the middle of the night?

MISSION Our mission is simple: to satisfy late-night cravings by delivering delicious cookies from our kitchens to your doors.

VISION Innovate our approach in baking to ensure low prices without sacrificing quality.

VALUES

Simplicity: Cut down barriers and make the process as simple as possible.

Selflessness: Care for the success and well-being of the team.

Social Responsibility: Care for our customers and our community.

Sustainability: Care for our planet.

Illustration 1.6 Julia's Cookies' business model includes achieving its mission, vision, and values.

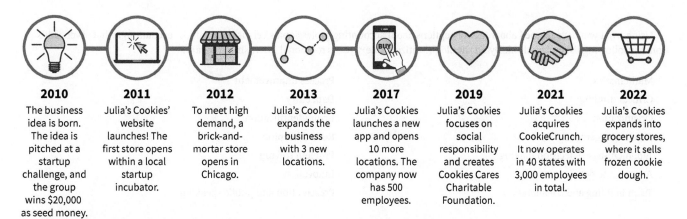

Illustration 1.7   Julia's Cookies began as a startup idea and is now found in grocery stores throughout the United States.

available any time. By targeting late-night hours and the convenience of ordering freshly baked cookies delivered directly to the customer, the group could meet a niche market need that nobody else in town was fulfilling. If they could obtain funding for the startup, the competitive advantage of their unique business model just might be successful. The group entered a startup challenge at their university and won seed money to fund the initial business.

Over the next decade, Julia's Cookies expanded its operations through both organic growth and acquisitions. Today, Julia's Cookies has more than 3,000 employees and operates in 40 states (**Illustration 1.7**).

Throughout your AIS course, you will use Julia's Cookies to learn skills employers look for in accounting graduates:

- Each chapter begins with a job posting for Julia's Cookies that demonstrates technical skills and concepts needed for an accounting position related to that chapter's topics. These job postings are based on real jobs for companies like Home Depot, Uber, and TikTok.
- Each learning objective includes an Applied Learning exercise for Julia's Cookies. You will have an opportunity to help employees at Julia's Cookies make important business decisions, solve problems, and perform data analytics.

Julia's Cookies uses a smart phone app to connect customers to its local stores, where cookies are baked fresh when ordered before they are delivered right to each customer's location. This app-based business model is how real businesses like Tiff's Treats, Insomnia Cookies, and many other companies in the food service industry stay relevant. In today's world, third-party companies like Uber Eats, DoorDash, and Grubhub can connect customers to a restaurant from their phones while charging fees to both the customer and the restaurant for the service. Offering a proprietary app for direct ordering can save the restaurant money, which subsequently increases the restaurant's profitability. You will learn more about profitability and business models next, but first take a moment to explore the Internal Audit department at Julia's Cookies and help the vice president prioritize skills for next year's Internal Audit internship program in Applied Learning 1.1.

Julia's Cookies   Applied Learning 1.1

Accounting Skills: Rotational Internship Candidates

Dylan is the vice president of Internal Audit at Julia's Cookies. He's meeting next week with a campus recruiter, Lauren, from the Human Resources department to discuss what skills his team is looking for as a department participating in the company's Finance Leadership Rotational Program. Lauren's team will attend career fairs at local colleges and meet with student candidates for the program this fall. She needs to understand what skills and personality traits Dylan's team needs so she can screen candidates for interview slots.

Lauren sends Dylan a list of skills the Internal Audit, Accounting, and Finance departments have historically looked for in candidates for this program.

Using what you have learned about misconceptions about accounting professionals versus the reality of accounting, what seven skills from the following list do you think Dylan should prioritize for next year's rotational internship program?

Mathematics	Process improvement
Critical thinking	Data entry
Organization	Error identification
Time management	Record keeping
Judgment-based decision making	Problem solving
Attention to details	Innovation
Team building and collaboration	Presentation and public speaking

SOLUTION

Dylan should focus on relationship building and collaboration skills first. As trusted advisors to their companies, Internal Audit team members need these and other soft skills that enable them to interact effectively and harmoniously with others:

Critical thinking	Process improvement
Judgment-based decision making	Innovation
Problem solving	Presentation and public speaking
Team building and collaboration	

Candidates need these skills in addition to fundamental accounting knowledge gained in an accounting program. This is not to say the other skills are unnecessary, but Dylan's team will have an easier time training an intern in areas like data entry and record keeping. Soft skills improve over time and can be difficult for an employer to teach.

Understanding Business Operations

The **purpose of a business** is to make a profit and generate enough cash flow to continue operating. Without the profit motive, it would not be a business (at least not for very long). There are two reasons for the profit motive:

- Stockholders will not invest in a company if they do not expect to earn a competitive return, which is determined by the company's profits. These profits can increase stock value or be paid to stockholders in the form of dividends.

- Profit is reinvested into the company to expand operations and fund activities. Do you remember Retained Earnings? Profits not declared or paid back to the investor are closed out to Retained Earnings for future reinvestment in the business.

To earn these profits, a business engages in activities called business operations. Learning about AIS requires a strong foundation in business operations, so we will review some key business terms that will be used throughout this course.

Business Models

CPA A **business model** is a company's plan for operations. It includes identifying the customer base, products, operation plans, and sources of revenue and financing. Companies make strategic plans that consider profitability, investor input, risk, and social responsibility to create a business model. Social responsibility is part of a business model that helps a company be socially accountable to its internal and external stakeholders, its community, and the public. The business world has seen a drastic shift in how companies prioritize social responsibility. Initiatives such as sponsoring employees to volunteer on company time, matching employee donations, and eliminating paper products in office buildings have become more popular. An example is Julia's Cookies' social responsibility campaign, Cookies Cares (**Illustration 1.8**). Companies use their profits to sponsor these initiatives, so it is important for a company to achieve its primary purpose of profitability to be able to cover these additional expenses.

Illustration 1.8 Julia's Cookies' social responsibility campaign is called Cookies Cares.

There are many types of business models, including:

- The **franchise business model** allows individuals to purchase and run a franchise of a popular fast food chain (for example, McDonald's).
- The **subscription business model** involves charging a monthly subscription fee for unlimited access to a service or product (for example, Netflix).
- The **freemium business model** involves offering free services but charging a fee to access upgraded features (for example, Dropbox).
- The **peer-to-peer business model** connects individuals with one another (for example, Airbnb).
- The **direct-to-consumers business model** involves selling directly to customers. For example, Julia's Cookies uses a mobile app to sell cookies directly to customers instead of using a third-party delivery vendor like DoorDash.

While Julia's Cookies' primary business model is direct-to-consumers cookie delivery via mobile app sales, the company recently began selling frozen cookie dough to local grocery stores. This product line uses a traditional **retailer business model**. Large corporations may have multiple business models designed specifically for their different product lines. Successful businesses integrate different types of business models to create customized approaches to their operations.

Business Processes

Business models are achieved through well-designed business processes. **CPA** A **business process** is a group of related business events designed to accomplish the strategic objectives of the business. Recall that a business event is an activity that takes place during company operations.

At a high level, business processes take inputs of resources to create products and services as outputs. These outputs must have value to customers, or they will not sell. In its simplest form, a **basic business model** consists of three primary types of business processes (**Illustration 1.9**).

You will learn more about these three types of business processes and how they are recorded in the AIS later in this chapter. For now, remember that the three key steps of an information system are collecting data, processing and storing data, and reporting information. **Illustration 1.10** compares each type of business process to each of the three key steps of an information system.

When viewed this way, it is clear that a business itself is a system. It has inputs (acquisitions), processing and storage (conversion), and outputs (products and/or services). These components are linked in a continuous value chain between suppliers of resources, the firm's operations, and customers. To achieve this business model, a company needs well-designed and interrelated business processes.

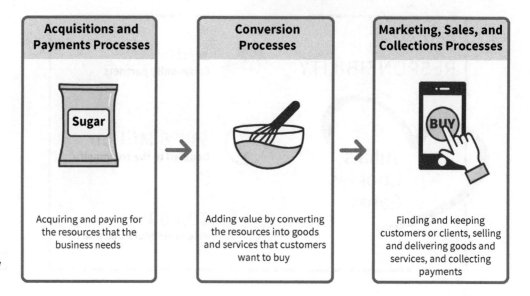

Illustration 1.9 A basic business model has three primary types of business processes.

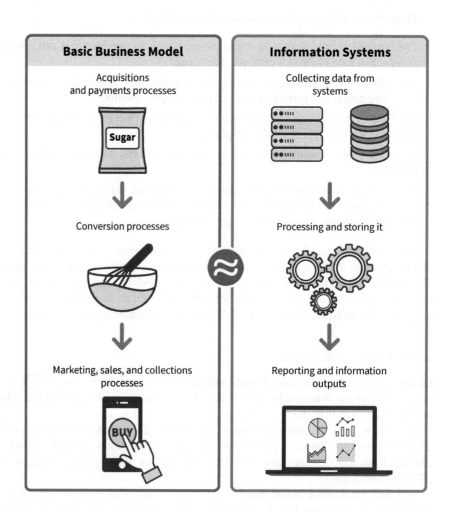

Illustration 1.10 The basic business model is comparable to an information system.

The business events in business processes generate data, which is input into the AIS. Accounting filters and records that data appropriately and transforms it into usable information. Accounting's role in turning business data into usable information is so important that accounting was among the few disciplines chosen for the earliest purposes of computers.

Every business process comprises one or more interrelated business events. For example, one of the marketing, sales, and collections business processes is "Sell cookies to online customers." This business process is made up of multiple business events, which we discuss next.

Business Events

You have learned that an AIS captures data generated from business events that result in economic activities, like transactions. Now let's look more closely at what a business event, also called a **business activity**, really is.

A business event always includes a verb and a noun that is the object of the verb. For example:

- Sell (verb) goods (noun) to customer.
- Purchase (verb) equipment (noun).

There are four types of business events or activities:

- **CPA** **Operating events:** Occur during the normal operations of a company's business and directly relate to the company's creating and providing a good or service to its customers. Examples include:
  - Collect customer payment
  - Hire employee
  - Pay employee
  - Deliver goods
- **CPA** **Financing events:** Help the company operate by acquiring incoming cash flows to fund operating events. Examples include:
  - Issue stocks
  - Declare dividends
  - Apply for a loan
  - Pay loan installment
- **CPA** **Investing events:** Provide long-term value to the company by purchasing long-term assets that will deliver value in the future. Examples include:
  - Buy/sell property, plant, and equipment
  - Buy/sell marketable securities
  - Buy/sell other businesses

CPA These three types of business events should seem familiar. They are the three types of activities on the cash flow statement: operating activities, financing activities, and investing activities. The fourth business event is unique in that it does not result in an exchange of economic resources:

- **Information events:** Involve an exchange of information and never involve an exchange of economic resources. Examples include:
  - Take customer order
  - Create purchase order
  - Interview candidate
  - Print report

These different types of business events combine to create a business process. Remember the Julia's Cookies business process "Sell cookies to online customers"? Three interrelated business events create this business process (**Illustration 1.11**):

- **Take customer order:** Customers order cookies on the mobile app.
- **Collect customer payment:** Customers pay via the mobile app.
- **Deliver goods to customer:** Local delivery drivers deliver directly to the customer's location.

In this example, how many of the three business events result in the exchange of economic resources? The answer is only two: "Collect customer payment" and "Deliver goods to customer." These two events generate accounting transactions captured in the AIS.

Does this mean that "Take customer order" is not important? Of course not. Without taking a customer's order, there would be no sale, revenue, or cash. Information events are crucial

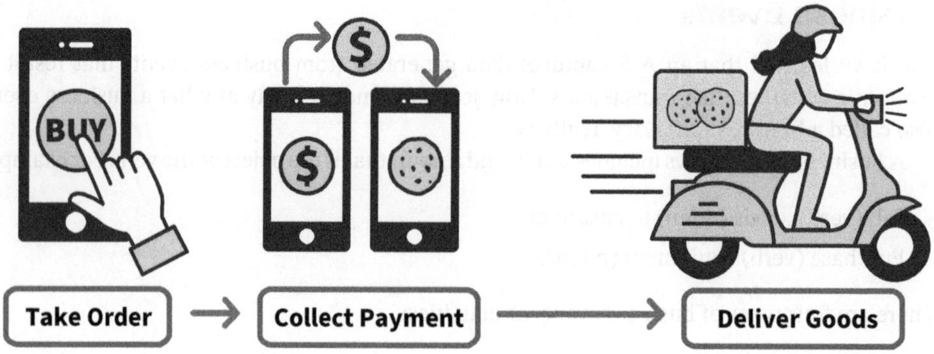

Illustration 1.11 Julia's Cookies' business process for online ordering has three major business events.

business events that often combine with the other three types of events to create business processes.

The company's information system captures the data *of interest* about these business events. The information system does not have to capture all the data about a specific business event—only the data that the company needs. For a customer paying cash at a grocery store, there may be no need to capture the data for customer name and customer address. For credit sales, that data is essential. The information system transforms the captured data into usable information. You will learn how management uses this information later in the chapter.

Why Does It Matter to Your Career?

Thoughts from an Internal Audit Intern, Manufacturing

- There is high demand for accounting professionals who embrace technological agility and their role as information professionals. Changing the widely held public misperception of accounting and accounting information systems is a slow process, so companies want to hire individuals who already embrace this reality.

- Once you join a team, you may find that some team members are resistant to change. As a member of the newest generation of accounting professionals, you will be in a position to influence your teams. An important skill is driving change while respecting the opinions of others.

- Familiarity with business processes and how the information system captures data about those processes gives accounting professionals a holistic view of the business—a valuable perspective that will help you provide meaningful solutions and ideas for your team.

CONCEPT REVIEW QUESTIONS

1. **CPA** What is an information system?
   Ans. An information system consists of interrelated components, including physical hardware like monitors and laptops, software that users interact with, databases used for storage, and networks that send data and information throughout the system.

2. What is an accounting information system (AIS)?
   Ans. An AIS is a set of processes, procedures, and systems that captures, processes, summarizes, and reports accounting data that arise from a series of business events related to various business processes using technology.

3. **CPA** What is a business model?
   Ans. A business model is a company's plan for operations. It includes identifying the customer base, products, operation plans, and revenue and financing sources.

4. Identify the differences between franchise and subscription business models.
   Ans. The franchise business model allows individuals to purchase and run a franchise of a popular fast food chain (for example, McDonald's). The subscription business model charges a monthly subscription fee for unlimited access to a service or product (for example, Netflix).

5. **CPA** What is a business process?

   Ans. A business process is a group of related business events designed to accomplish the business's strategic objectives.

6. Define business events or business activity in a business.

   Ans. A business event is also called a business activity or transaction resulting in an exchange of value between two or more parties involved in the transaction. When the event has an economic impact on the business, it is considered an accounting event. The business events in business processes generate data, which is input into the AIS.

7. **CPA** What are operating events?

   Ans. Operating events occur during the normal operations of a company's business and directly relate to the company creating and providing goods or services to its customers.

8. **CPA** What are financing events?

   Ans. Financing events help the company operate by acquiring incoming cash flow to fund operating events.

9. **CPA** What are investing events?

   Ans. Investing events provide long-term value to the company by purchasing long-term assets that will deliver value in the future.

10. What are information events?

    Ans. Information events involve an exchange of information and never involve an exchange of economic resources.

1.2 How Have Accounting Information Systems Evolved?

Learning Objective ❷
Compare traditional transaction-based accounting systems with process-based information systems.

Before the advent of the sophisticated, integrated, **process-based information systems** we use today, firms used **transaction-based AIS** to record only accounting transactions. These systems were limited in that they ignored nonfinancial data and the relationships between business events and business processes. They still exist today, especially in small businesses, and you may encounter them in your career.

Regardless of the type of information system used, accounting professionals must understand financial accounting transactions, which are the business events that result in economic exchanges of resources. Recall that business events combine to create a business process, but not all business events result in economic exchanges of resources. Many business processes include informational events, which (as you have learned) involve the exchange or creation of information.

Let's summarize what you have learned so far:

- Business processes are made up of business events.
- Business events create data.
- Data of interest is stored and processed by an information system.
- Information is generated for decision-making purposes.

The basic business model, composed of three main types of business processes, reappears in more detail in **Illustration 1.12**.

While operating, financing, and investing events take place in a business, there are also information events, such as a marketing employee retrieving customer lists or the company accountant printing out a set of financial statements at month end. These reports might be slide presentations, spreadsheets, or charts and graphs. They provide the basis for management's and other users' decision-making activities or events. Simply put, an information event can involve printing or generating reports.

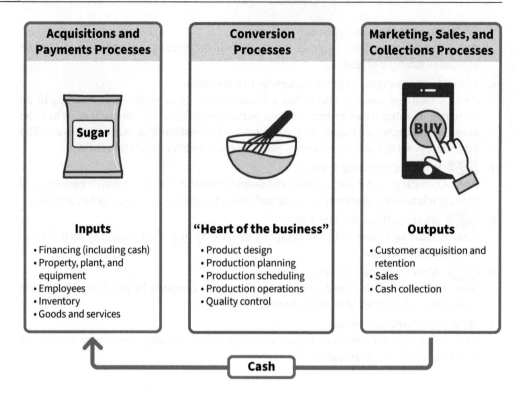

Illustration 1.12 The basic business model includes all of the acquisitions and payments, conversion, and marketing, sales, and collections processes that make up a company's operations.

Let's look at an acquisitions and payments process that includes three business events:

- Order raw materials from vendor
- Receive raw materials from vendor
- Pay vendor

What data should the business collect for "Order raw materials from vendor"? The data could include date of order, vendor name, product ID, order quantity, price, and promised delivery date.

Recall that a transaction-based AIS captures only accounting business events, while a process-based information system captures all the data of interest generated in a business process, including informational events. Let's next compare the transaction-based AIS to the process-based information system for the three types of business processes:

- Acquisitions and payments processes
- Conversion processes
- Marketing, sales, and collections processes

Acquisitions and Payments Processes

CPA Management's first task before the business can actually *do* business is to buy and pay for the resources the company needs. These processes become an ongoing commitment throughout the life of the business. The types of resources vary across companies and industries. Common resources include:

- Financing (cash is central to a business)
- Property, plant, and equipment
- Employees (yes, employees are a resource a company acquires)
- Inventory
- Other goods and services

Acquiring the resources that a business needs is an *input* to the business. A manufacturing company must hire employees to work on the manufacturing line and purchase the

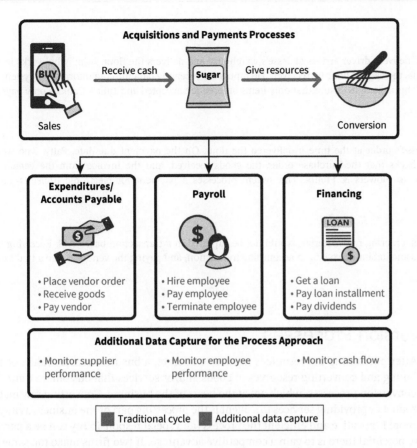

Illustration 1.13 A process-based system for acquisitions and payments processes captures additional useful information.

equipment needed to manufacture its products. It must also purchase raw materials to transform into its final product. These are all inputs to the company's operations. However, hiring employees is not an exchange of economic resources. In fact, hiring and paying employees are two separate business events—and only paying them is a traditional accounting transaction. With a transaction-based AIS, hiring employees would not be captured as part of the AIS data.

Illustration 1.13 compares the traditional accounting transactions to the business processes captured in a process-based information system. The blue terms indicate examples of data captured in traditional accounting cycles. A business-process approach includes this data but also captures the other data about the business events, shown in green. This process-based approach is more inclusive, capturing both financial and nonfinancial data, and nonfinancial information can be just as useful for decision making as financial information.

For example, employee terminations may not result in accounting transactions, but accounting professionals can use this data to calculate monthly employee turnover—the percentage of employees leaving the company each month—to analyze the risks in each of the company's plants. High turnover can create opportunities for fraud, reduce a plant's productivity, and result in high costs related to hiring and training new employees, which can cost thousands of dollars and take weeks—all factors of interest to accounting professionals.

Help Jesse decide which business events are captured in a transaction-based AIS in Applied Learning 1.2.

Julia's Cookies   Applied Learning 1.2

Acquisitions and Payments Processes: Ordering Flour

Jesse orders ingredients for all the Julia's Cookies shops in the greater Chicagoland area.

As part of the acquisitions and payments processes, Jesse orders flour and creates the following three associated business events. Which of these are operating events that would be captured by a transaction-based AIS?

1. *Order raw materials from vendor*

   On Monday morning, Jesse sends an order for flour to Flowers & Flours, a local artisanal flour company. Jesse frequently partners with local suppliers to support Chicago area businesses and to provide high-quality, locally sourced ingredients to Julia's Cookies' customers.

2. *Receive raw materials from vendor*

Wednesday afternoon, Flowers & Flours' delivery driver arrives at Jesse's warehouse and delivers the flour. John, who works in the warehouse, accepts the delivery and counts the bags of flour he received. He inputs the receiving data into the information system for matching to the order prior to payment. This is done to ensure that only items ordered are accepted and Julia's Cookies only pays for items that are ordered and received.

3. *Pay vendor*

Flowers & Flours sent an invoice for Jesse's order at the time it delivered the flour. On the payment due date, Patty, who works in the Accounts Payable department, checks that the purchase order, the goods received, and the invoice from the vendor all match. She then approves the payment to Flowers & Flours. The system processes a payment for electronic transmission to Flowers & Flours.

SOLUTION

While all three of these are operating events, ordering raw materials would not be captured in a transaction-based AIS. Receiving raw materials increases physical inventory counts and liabilities, so it is an accounting transaction, and paying the vendor is also a traditional accounting transaction.

Conversion Processes

CPA After purchasing the resources needed to operate, a business creates value, or profit, by combining and converting resources to goods and/or services that customers want. These are the conversion processes, which are at the heart of the business. Converting raw materials into a product or providing services to a client is the *processing* part of the business as a system.

The more innovative and efficient the process (and social responsibility can be a part of it), the more potential there is to gain a competitive advantage. If two firms make the same product or perform a service in the same way, they will have difficulty differentiating themselves in the market. Remember how products are an essential part of a business model? A unique product with no competition could command a higher price from customers.

Illustration 1.14 compares data captured in a transaction-based AIS to the more robust data captured in a process-based information system:

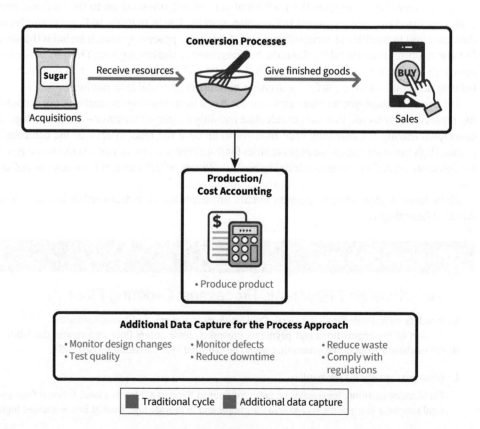

Illustration 1.14 Conversion processes also generate additional useful information that is not captured in a traditional transaction-based system.

In addition to those in the illustration, nonfinancial business events include the following:

- Design product
- Test product
- Plan production
- Schedule production
- Assemble product
- Package product

As we discussed earlier, social responsibility and sustainability have become more important to companies. The conversion processes can also capture sustainability data, which is used to measure a company's environmental footprint and societal and economic impacts. For example, an organization may collect data on:

- Supply chain miles
- Water usage
- Carbon footprint
- Product recycling rate
- Energy consumption
- Waste reduction rate

In the Real World McDonald's Regrets Changing Its Conversion Process[2]

McDonald's started out as a hot dog stand in California in the late 1930s. Today, McDonald's is one of the most widely recognized name brands in the world. It climbed to international success because of its strategy of efficient and reliable food delivery, with a streamlined conversion process (converting raw materials into fast food) to provide a product that is fast, cheap, and consistent in quality. However, the road has not always been smooth for this highly successful company. Management has made costly mistakes along the way. One of the most notable mistakes occurred when the leadership team shifted focus with a change in business strategy, which it implemented by changing the production process.

The Change	Management changed the production process to introduce a concept called "Made for You." Orders were prepared to suit individual customer preferences, which required expensive equipment upgrades in addition to the process change. These changes resulted in enhanced food quality, but it took more time to make those upscale burgers.
The Outcome	Management failed to balance innovation and a shift to a different product with production process efficiency. The old, efficiently produced products were familiar to customers. People knew what to expect when they came to McDonald's—food that was fast, cheap, and always tasted the same. They did not want a nicer-tasting burger that was more expensive and took more time to prepare. Customers were suddenly waiting much longer for their food, and the new options were more expensive. This was not what McDonald's customers wanted. "Made for You" eventually failed—an expensive mistake with advertising costing over $200 million. As a result, the company lost value on the stock market when its stock price declined because of this fiasco.
The Lesson	Don't make changes to business strategy and production processes to support the strategy if the changes do not align with customer wants and needs. CFOs and other accounting professionals who are part of a management team can learn a lesson from the mistake that McDonald's made.

What could McDonald's have done differently before implementing the changes described here to ensure that the changes aligned with customer wants and needs? Do you think this situation put the success of McDonald's at any kind of risk?

Marketing, Sales, and Collections Processes

CPA After converting resources into products and/or services, a business needs to generate revenue by marketing and selling them and collecting the cash from the sales. The cash flows back to resources and replenishes the cash balance so the firm can pay its commitments.

Selling and collecting cash from sales are the *outputs* of the business. **Illustration 1.15** compares data captured by a traditional transaction-based AIS to data captured by a modern process-based information system.

Remember, if a company loses its customers, it loses its source of revenue. With profitability as the primary goal of a business, capturing data related to customers and sales—beyond accounting transactions—is essential to monitor operations and identify areas for improvement.

---

[2]www.business2community.com/business-innovation/3-companies-failed-adapt-went-wrong-01895678

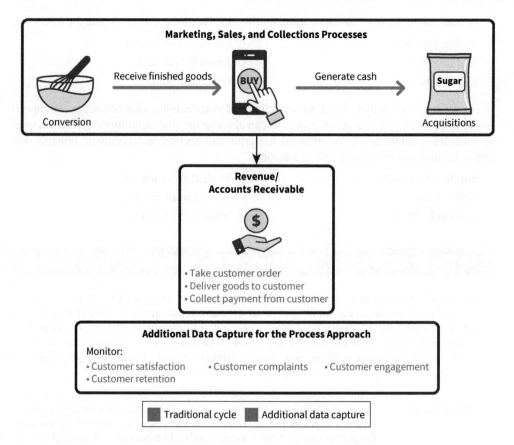

Illustration 1.15 Turning finished goods into cash generates useful information not captured by traditional transaction-based systems.

What additional data do you think a company may want to capture about customers in a process-based information system? It is critically important to focus on customer satisfaction, and other nonfinancial information that could be invaluable includes:

- Conversion rate from first contact with potential customers to their becoming customers
- Online search engine rankings
- Online click-through rate
- Online engagement level
- Social media posts

As you continue your AIS course, you will continue learning about business processes. Subsequent chapters explore the risks, controls, and reporting related to business processes. Now that you have been introduced to companies, their information systems, and their key business processes, in the following chapters, you will apply these foundational principles to identifying and managing risks related to companies' information systems and business processes.

Why Does It Matter to Your Career?

Thoughts from an Accounting Data Analytics Intern, Public Accounting

- Data from older, nonintegrated systems may not be current or accurate. It may be inconsistent with the data in other separate systems in the same company, even though the data is supposed to be identical. These older systems and systems integration issues present significant concerns when leveraging data.

- Accounting decision making and problem solving require an understanding of business processes. Your ability to solve problems improves through understanding different levels of sophistication in systems.

- Maintaining a competitive advantage for your clients or your company requires capturing better data. You can help by recommending how your clients or company can capture robust data from its business processes. Data analytics can transform this data into useful insights—something all businesses are increasingly doing.

CONCEPT REVIEW QUESTIONS

1. What is an AIS software?

   Ans. An AIS software is a tool that companies use to automate their accounting function and design real-time reports. The software simplifies the accounting and finance control functions and can be customized.

2. What is an integrated process-based information system?

   Ans. Business events combine to create a business process. This may lead to the generation of economic exchange of resources and the exchange or creation of information. The integrated process-based information system records the financial and nonfinancial information.

3. What do you understand by the term "information event"?

   Ans. Many business processes lead to the exchange or creation of information, termed as information event. For example, hiring and paying employees are two different business events. Hiring may be considered as an information event, while payment is a business event involving economic exchange.

4. What is transaction-based AIS?

   Ans. Transaction-based AIS records only accounting transactions. These systems were limited as they ignored nonfinancial data and the relationships between business events and business processes.

5. **CPA** What are acquisitions and payments processes?

   Ans. Companies need to acquire resources and pay for them according to their business needs. These processes of acquisitions and payments become an ongoing commitment throughout the business's life cycle. The needs of various resources differ for different companies and vary across industries. The common resources acquired and paid are finances, inventory, property, plant, and equipment.

6. **CPA** Write a short note on conversion processes.

   Ans. After purchasing the resources needed to operate, a business creates value, or profit, by combining and converting resources to goods and/or services that customers want. Converting raw materials into a product or providing services to a client is the conversion processing part of the business as a system.

7. **CPA** What are marketing, sales, and collections processes?

   Ans. After converting resources into products and/or services, a business needs to generate revenue by marketing, selling, and collecting cash from the sales. The cash flows back to resources and replenishes the cash balance so the firm can pay its commitments.

1.3 How Does Management Use Information?

Learning Objective ❸
Explain management's relationship to information and information systems.

"Management," "end users," "users," "stakeholders," and "decision makers" are interchangeable terms for people who use the information created by an information system.

Management uses information for decision making. A significant part of the management function in any company is making decisions about business processes. These business processes must produce outcomes that align with the company's strategic plan. Business processes and related information systems change because of management decisions. Management oversees business processes through planning, implementing, monitoring, and changing and improving processes.

Management's Responsibility for Business Processes

An AIS provides financial and other metrics that determine how well management is implementing and controlling business processes. Management's responsibilities for overseeing business processes include:

Planning

- Developing a strategic plan to create a sustainable competitive advantage
- Designing business processes focused on achieving strategic goals
- Identifying key performance indicators and benchmarks
- Identifying opportunities and assessing their risks
- Forecasting future performance

Implementing

- Implementing, or putting into place, a strategic plan
- Dividing high-level business objectives into smaller processes and events
- Assigning employees to perform activities
- Motivating employees to maximize their performance
- Embedding internal controls in processes and systems to prevent and detect errors and fraud

Monitoring

- Evaluating the operating results and financial position
- Assessing whether strategic objectives are being attained by:
  - Analyzing financial statements (which you learn about in financial accounting classes)
  - Using data to monitor risks in real time (which you learn about in this course)
  - Monitoring key performance indicators and comparing them to benchmarks (which you learn about in management accounting classes)
  - Auditing processes, systems, controls, and transactions (which you learn about in external and internal auditing classes)
  - Comparing actual performance and metrics to forecasts and budgets (which you learn about in management accounting classes)

Changing and improving processes

- Changing designs of business processes or events so that actual results meet expectations
- Improving the design and correcting identified issues
- Prosecuting occupational fraudsters to the full extent of the law and sending a message of zero tolerance for fraud to management and other employees
- Improving internal controls to decrease opportunities for errors and fraud

One of the many responsibilities of management is identifying ways to assess and monitor the performance of the company and its business processes. A popular method is to implement **key performance indicators (KPIs)**, which are quantifiable metrics used to measure and evaluate the success of a company based on its objectives. Most businesses use KPIs, which means that benchmarks—points of reference for a company's industry—are often readily available. Julia's Cookies can use benchmarks for the bakery or food service industry to compare its performance against its competitors. Many KPIs are accounting ratios you learn about in financial or managerial accounting classes, like net profit margin, return on assets, or earnings before interest, taxes, depreciation, and amortization (EBITDA).

The relationship between business processes, the information system, and management is iterative (**Illustration 1.16**) because the responsibilities of management (planning, implementing, monitoring, and changing and improving) relate to the business processes. Management decisions affect business processes, which affect the data the information system captures, which affects the information management receives, which again affects decision making that may result in changes to business processes.

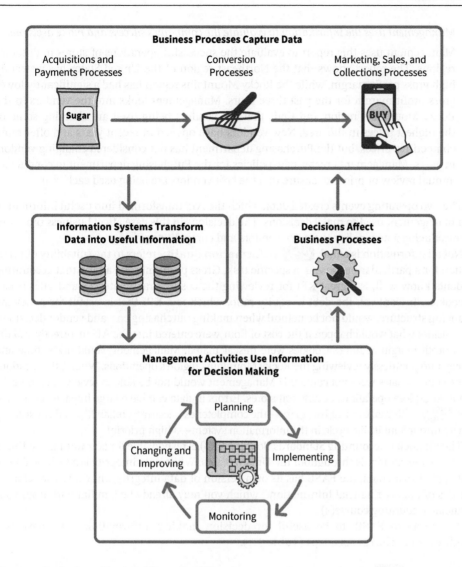

Illustration 1.16 There is an iterative relationship between management, information system, and business processes.

Data-Driven Decision Making

Because the data in an information system is used to generate information for decision making, it is important for management to be able to rely on its accuracy. Decision-making data, including the data to perform calculations for KPIs, comes from the business's information systems—often the accounting information system.

Management combines the principles of *quality of information* and *decision context* to identify the information needed from an AIS for decision-making activities.

Quality of Information

At Julia's Cookies, the following steps create the iterative relationship between management and the AIS:

1. *Business events create data.*

   Business operating event: Employees at the local factory purchase raw ingredients from local vendors, which are then used to make cookies. This event creates data—the cost of the ingredient (cost), the vendor it is purchased from (vendor), the location where the purchase was made (region), and the date of the purchase (year).

   Business operating event: A customer buying cookies creates data—the location where the sale took place (region), the amount of the sale (revenue), and the date of the sale (year).

2. *The AIS transforms raw data into useful information.*

   The AIS stores the purchasing and sales data. It is used to create a report that includes the KPI gross profit margin. Gross profit margin is calculated as (Revenue − Cost of goods sold)/Revenue. The purchasing and sales data (inputs) create this KPI (output).

3. *Management uses the information to evaluate the company's success and make decisions.*

Management uses this report to evaluate the successful operations of stores in different regions. The report shows that the Northeast region of the United States has a steadily high gross profit margin, while the Rocky Mountains region has had a significantly lower gross profit margin for the past three years. Management looks into the vendors in the Rocky Mountains region and finds that the vendors being used are charging some of the highest prices in the area. New vendors have opened in recent years and offer more competitive prices, but the Purchasing department has not considered changing vendors in years. Management creates new policies for the Purchasing department to conduct an annual review of prices to ensure that the best vendors are being used each year.

The two operating events created data, which the AIS transformed into useful information that management used to make decisions. The decisions in this case affect business processes by introducing a new policy to review vendors and competitive pricing.

Not all information is equal. **CPA** **Information quality** refers to the suitability of information for a particular purpose in a specific task. Gross profit margin, a ratio that accounting students know well, is a great KPI for reviewing the costs of raw materials and sales prices of cookies. In contrast, the debt-to-equity ratio, which is a KPI that is useful for reviewing financing structure, would not be helpful when making purchasing cost and vendor decisions.

Consider what would happen if the cost of flour were entered into the AIS incorrectly and the gross profit margin at Julia's Cookies were miscalculated. Management would invest time and money into pointlessly reviewing the Rocky Mountains region's operations. What if the locations of the cookies' sales were not captured? Management would not be able to review operations by region to explore operations at different stores. Errors in data can have large impacts on companies. **CPA** This makes **data integrity**—the completeness, accuracy, reliability, and consistency of data throughout its life cycle in the information system—a high priority.

The Financial Accounting Standards Board (FASB) is responsible for accounting and financial reporting standards throughout the United States. While data integrity is a technical term that applies to all data, the FASB has its own version of data integrity, known as the "characteristics of quality financial information," which you may already be familiar with from your financial accounting course(s).

According to FASB, to be useful for decision making, information must have two **fundamental characteristics (Table 1.1)**.

TABLE 1.1 **CPA** Fundamental Characteristics of Useful Information

Relevance	Information must be capable of influencing a decision. Relevant information has: • Predictive value: Applicable to future events • Confirmatory value: Ability to either confirm or change previous decisions • Materiality: Significant impact on the decision (not including it would influence the decision)
Faithful representation	Information must be unbiased and accurate. Faithfully represented information is: • Complete: With all information necessary included • Neutral: Not favoring a particular outcome • Error free: Accurate

The usefulness of information increases in the presence of four **enhancing characteristics**, which are optional (**Table 1.2**).

These characteristics are discussed in FASB's Statement of Financial Accounting Concepts No. 8. The FASB's fundamental characteristics and enhancing characteristics are shown in **Illustration 1.17**.

CPA Regardless of how many of these characteristics are present, an overall constraint on the usefulness of information is its cost-effectiveness. If the benefit of using useful information exceeds the costs of providing it, then the decision to provide the information is cost-effective. A cost-benefit analysis is necessary to ensure that information is worth the resources needed

TABLE 1.2 CPA Enhancing Characteristics of Useful Information

Verifiability	Information results in the same conclusions by independent and knowledgeable individuals.
Timeliness	Information is recent and available in time to influence relevant decisions.
Understandability	Information is easy to understand because it is properly classified and presented clearly.
Comparability	Information presents similar items in the same manner to make it easy to identify similarities and differences when necessary.

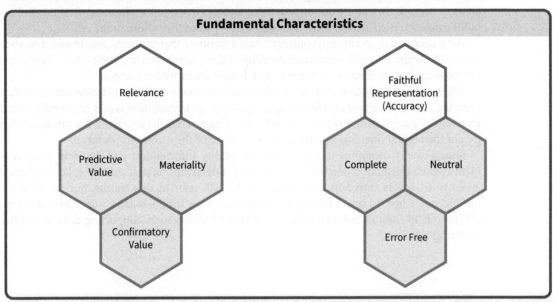

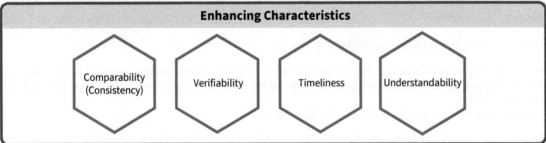

Illustration 1.17   The two fundamental characteristics—relevance and faithful representation—work with the enhancing characteristics to create useful information.

to access it. The cost of using information can be simple, as at Julia's Cookies, where the AIS can easily generate a report on the gross profit margin. It can also be complex, as in a company where data is stored in different information systems, files, and formats throughout the business; with this type of complexity, an analyst may spend significant time compiling the sales and purchasing data needed to create a simple KPI.

Why Does It Matter to Your Career?

Thoughts from an Internal Audit Data Analytics Manager, Financial Services

- As an accounting professional, in order to work with data, you need to understand where the data originates and where it is stored.

- As a new accounting graduate, you can leverage your knowledge of business processes and information systems in the job market. Employers value people who ask questions about how the job they are applying for fits into the company's overall business processes and information systems. "Big picture" thinking is an essential skill for accounting professionals, and thinking about the big picture in terms of technology is even better.

Decision Context

Ideally, quality information includes all of the fundamental and enhancing characteristics; however, the cost-benefit constraint means that there are often trade-offs in the real world. For example, it may be difficult to get data that is both understandable and timely. If an analyst has to spend significant time working on sales and purchasing data, it may be difficult to obtain the gross sales margin in a timely manner. The choice may be between meeting a deadline and producing highly accurate information. Such decisions are made using the decision context.

The **decision context** is the preferences, constraints, and other factors that affect how a decision is made. In other words, the decision context helps you understand the intended use of information: Who are the users, and why do they need the information?

For a perspective on context, consider Uber, a business that connects people with transportation. Uber needs context—an understanding of drivers, vehicles and their whereabouts, and the customer's preferences—in order to match up a driver with a customer.

When choosing whether accuracy or timeliness is more important, management considers what the information is being used to accomplish. If the information is part of a weekly status meeting for a sales team, timeliness may be more important. In contrast, if the information is part of the annual financial reports, accuracy will be of the utmost importance.

Management combines the principles of quality information and decision context to identify the information needed from the AIS for decision-making activities. You will learn about how data is stored in a database for the AIS later in this course, but for now you need to know how to select the right data for making a simple business decision. Test your ability to help Julia's Cookies connect a business decision to its supporting data in Applied Learning 1.3.

Julia's Cookies   Applied Learning 1.3

Useful Information: Selecting Relevant Data Points

Rodriguez works in the Purchasing department of Julia's Cookies in the Baltimore area. One of the local stores received a large corporate catering order for next week. Rodriguez needs to check inventory to determine if the regional factory can prepare the large order or if he needs to order additional inventory.

Which of these data sources does Rodriguez need in order to make his decision?

- On-hand raw ingredients (flour, butter, sugar, etc.)
- Equipment (bowls, mixers, baking pans, etc.)
- On-hand packaging (cookie boxes, paper liners, etc.)
- Catering orders (cookie types, quantities, etc.)
- Pricing (costs of flour, butter, sugar, etc.)
- Store information (store name, phone number, general manager, etc.)
- Recipes (ingredient types, ingredient quantities, etc.)

SOLUTION

While there is useful information in all these categories, Rodriguez's business decision is about inventory. In order to decide if he has enough inventory on hand, Rodriguez needs to answer the following questions with data from the sources listed:

How many cookies and what types are being ordered? Data source: catering orders

What ingredients are needed for these cookies? Data source: recipes

What ingredients are available to make these cookies? Data source: on-hand raw ingredients

What packaging is available to send these cookies? Data source: on-hand packaging

Although the factory needs equipment to bake the cookies, equipment is not purchased regularly. The factory is already fully operational with needed equipment.

CONCEPT REVIEW QUESTIONS

1. Who is the management in a business?

   Ans. There are three levels of management in an organization—top, middle, and operational. The persons at these levels manage resources and make decisions about business processes. The objective is to align the business outcomes with the strategic plan. The group of individuals involved in the management function is the company's management, who use AIS to make decisions. The management oversees business processes through planning, implementing, monitoring, and changing and improving processes.

2. Who are the end users of information in an AIS?

   Ans. The end users of information in an AIS may include accountants, consultants, business analysts, managers, and chief financial officers.

3. What are key performance metrics (KPIs) in a business?

   Ans. KPIs are quantifiable metrics used to measure and evaluate a company's success based on its objectives. These are benchmarks or points of reference for a company and its industry that are readily available.

4. **CPA** What is information quality?

   Ans. Information quality refers to the suitability of information for a particular purpose in a specific task. Gross profit margin is a great KPI for reviewing the costs of raw materials and sales prices of products and services.

5. **CPA** What is meant by data integrity?

   Ans. Errors in data can have significant impacts on companies. Data integrity ensures that data is complete, accurate, reliable, and consistent throughout its life cycle in the information system.

6. **CPA** Write a short note on the cost-benefit analysis of information.

   Ans. An overall constraint on the usefulness of information is its cost-effectiveness. Suppose the benefit of using useful information exceeds the costs of providing it, then the decision to provide the information is cost-effective.

7. What is meant by decision context of information?

   Ans. The decision context involves defining what decision is being made and why, as well as its relationship to other decisions previously made or anticipated. The decision context helps to understand the intended use of information—who are the users, and why do they need it? For example, the choice may be between meeting a deadline and producing highly accurate information. Selecting a particular alternative may depend on the decision context.

1.4 What Is the Relationship Between Accounting and Data Analytics?

Learning Objective ❹

Describe the relationship between accounting and data analytics.

Accounting is an information-centric profession, and accounting professionals have been performing financial analysis since before computers existed. How companies perform financial analysis and the types of analysis they prioritize have evolved with the digitalization of business. Business events capture data digitally even in small companies, which enables financial analysis to be performed using technology.

This section introduces the role of reporting and data analytics in the accounting profession. In the Data Storage and Analysis chapter, we explore data analytics in depth, including real-world applications of analytics in the various accounting specialties: tax, audit, managerial accounting, and financial accounting. Additional chapters teach hands-on data management and analytics skills, including the various categories of data analytics. For now, we focus on the role of data analytics in accounting.

Why Does It Matter to Your Career?

Thoughts from an External Audit Manager, Public Accounting

- One of the most important skills employers want in an accounting new hire is the ability to identify use cases for data analytics. Turning business questions into data analytics scenarios and identifying the data needed to answer the questions are essential skills.

- Even if you are not specializing as a data analyst, you will likely work alongside them. Understanding and speaking their language will make you a valuable addition to any team you join.

Reporting Versus Analytics

You have learned that management makes decisions with the help of useful information, but how do those users get that information? By using data that is generated during business events, companies use two processes, reporting and data analytics:

- **CPA** **Reporting** is the process of aggregating data into information on the activities and performance in a company.

- **CPA** **Data analytics** is the process of using technology to transform raw data, or facts, into useful information.

Reporting provides a strictly descriptive view of what happened and does not seek insights into the context or reasons. Many information systems have integrated reporting capabilities. Such reports are usually static but can offer customization for users to choose filters, aggregation levels, and more. An AIS can generate reports on KPIs such as gross profit margin.

In contrast, data analytics answers strategic questions beyond historical reporting by transforming data into insights. Sounds a lot like the definition of an information system, right? The difference is nuanced: an information system captures and processes data, and data analytics uses the data from the information system. Data analytics is performed by a trained professional who creates custom test parameters, which specify precisely what the analytic is going to produce—usually through software outside the information system.

Data analytics goes beyond tracking historical figures that reporting provides. **CPA** In fact, data analytics can use either raw data from an information system or reports generated by the information system.

Management uses historical performance information tracked in reporting with data analytics insights to understand what's happened and make decisions on how to improve business processes. Reporting and data analytics are dependent on one another, and both are useless without a robust information system capturing the business process data (**Illustration 1.18**).

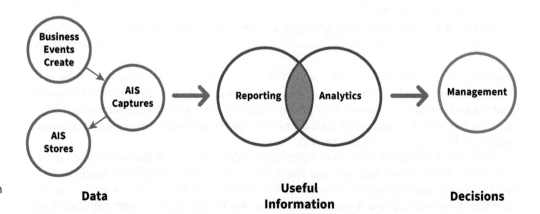

Illustration 1.18 The relationship between data, useful information, and decisions is supported by both reporting and analytics.

Data Analytics in Accounting

Accounting is information focused, so it is not surprising that the accounting profession has transitioned from viewing data analytics as cutting edge to considering it a mandatory process in many industries. Businesses that are not using data analytics to understand their accounting data are behind their peers.

Accounting data analytics does not have to be complex, but it can be. Think about comparing the KPIs that are accounting ratios. **CPA** Accounting professionals use accounting ratios to compare a company's performance across time, compare one company to another, or compare a company to industry standards. Financial analysis like analyzing KPIs has been part of accounting for a long time, but doing such analysis with technology is considered data analytics. Similarly, horizontal and vertical analysis of financial statements used to be a manual pen-and-paper process, but now it is done using data from an AIS and is considered data analytics. You probably learned about these types of analysis in your introduction to financial accounting courses.

For processes accountants have been doing manually for decades, we can now use technology to achieve faster and more comprehensive results. Consider these data analytics examples for Julia's Cookies:

- **Comparing total flour purchased each month to the amount of flour used:** This will identify excess ordering and inventory waste.
- **Checking whether a vendor sent multiple invoices for the same order:** This will identify if Julia's Cookies has paid the same invoice twice, which is a financial loss.
- **Calculating the number of days it took to pay invoices from a vendor:** This will check whether Julia's Cookies is meeting payment terms that qualify it for payment discounts. It is important because discounts reduce the cost of goods sold and increase profits, as seen in the gross profit margin.
- **Performing a three-way match between the purchase order, the goods received, and the invoice from the vendor:** This is usually performed manually but can be done with data analytics to increase efficiency.

There is nothing innovative about these examples; accounting professionals have been doing these activities for years. But because tasks like these use data that is stored in an AIS, data analytics allows them to be performed faster and more efficiently.

As accounting tasks continue to become digital and data driven, the skills accounting professionals need are also evolving. Discover how much data is created and stored in less than an hour at Julia's Cookies in Applied Learning 1.4.

Julia's Cookies | Applied Learning 1.4

Accounting Analytics: Capturing Data from Business Events

Martin is a new customer at Julia's Cookies and signs up for an account on the Julia's Cookies mobile app. He creates a profile and orders a half dozen chocolate chip cookies for immediate delivery to his home address. Forty-five minutes after he initially downloads the mobile app, his first cookie order arrives on his doorstep.

What business events just took place? What data do you think Julia's Cookies' AIS captured in these 45 minutes?

SOLUTION

Multiple business events took place during these 45 minutes:

1. New profile created
2. Cookies ordered
3. Payment collected
4. Cookies baked
5. Cookies delivered

The data captured from these business events includes:

1. Customer profile data: Name, home address, payment method
2. Order data: Cookie type, quantity, price
3. Payment transaction: Payment method, price, taxes, fees, driver tip
4. Inventory: Cookie inventory depleted
5. Cookies delivered: Delivery time, delivery driver

Data Analytics Skills

 Have you ever tracked your grades for a semester in a spreadsheet? What about using that information to calculate the grade you need on a final exam to pass or to earn an A in a class? If you have completed tasks like these in a spreadsheet using formulas to calculate the weights of your grades, then you have performed data analytics.

Data analytics can range from small data transformation in software like Excel to advanced predictive modeling using artificial intelligence. Anyone can perform data analytics, and many people already do so on a regular basis without even realizing it. However, advanced analytics requires specialized skills in technology—and sometimes even in statistics, depending on the question you want to answer.

Most employers understand that accounting majors are already learning a lot in their college programs. Graduating with an accounting degree, especially if you pursue eligibility for the CPA exam, is no small feat. If you find the technical aspects of data you learn throughout this course exciting, consider taking some classes—or even double majoring—in information systems or computer science.

That path is not for everyone, though, and not every accounting professional needs to code advanced predictive analytics algorithms in data analytics programming languages. **CPA** Employers look for candidates who are data minded. Awareness, curiosity, excitement, and creative thinking are just some of the soft skills that show employers you are data minded. Most employers expect that accounting graduates will need to be trained in data analytics.

In the first years of your career, you will need to develop some fundamental data analytics skills to stay relevant. It is not necessary to be an expert in all of the skills in **Table 1.3** the day you graduate, but you will likely be expected to learn them quickly, so start preparing yourself now. The table includes key data analytics skills for new accounting professionals and indicates where these skills are covered in this course.

To build a solid foundation for your career, focus on applying these skills to your accounting coursework whenever possible.

TABLE 1.3 Essential Data Analytics Skills Course Roadmap

Identify what data can be used to answer a business question	Embedded throughout the course
	End-of-chapter questions labeled "Data Foundations"
	End-of-chapter questions labeled "Data Analytics"
	Julia's Cookies Tableau/Excel Cases accompanying each chapter
Recognize data quality issues	FASB characteristics of useful information in Section 1.3
Know the fundamentals of how data is stored so you can retrieve it	Data Storage and Analysis chapter
	Database design sections of the Designing Systems and Databases chapter
	End-of-chapter questions labeled "Data Foundations"
Display data analytics skills that can be applied to any software	End-of-chapter questions labeled "Data Foundations"
	End-of-chapter questions labeled "Data Analytics"
Perform data analytics using common software like Excel	Julia's Cookies Excel Case accompanying each chapter
Collect, clean, and prepare data	Database design sections of the Designing Systems and Databases chapter
	Julia's Cookies Tableau/Excel Cases accompanying each chapter
Recognize when advanced data analytics tools are needed	Data Analytics chapter
	Financial Reporting Processes chapter
	Data Visualization chapter
Perform data visualization and report the results of an analysis	Financial Reporting Processes chapter
	Data Visualization chapter
	Julia's Cookies Tableau Case accompanying each chapter

CONCEPT REVIEW QUESTIONS

1. `CPA` What is reporting?

Ans. Reporting is the process of aggregating data into information on the activities and performance of a company. Reporting provides a strictly descriptive view of what has happened and does not seek insights into the context or reasons.

2. `CPA` What is meant by the term "data analytics"?

Ans. Data analytics is the process that includes collection, transformation, and organization of data to make predictions, and drive informed decision making using technology.

3. `CPA` What do you understand by "being data-minded"?

Ans. Employers look for candidates who are data-minded. Awareness, curiosity, excitement, and creative thinking are some soft skills that show employers that the person is data-minded.

FEATURED PROFESSIONAL | Accounting Support Services

Photo courtesy of
Miriam Semaan Bolus

Miriam Bolus, CPA

Miriam spent the first three years of her career as an external auditor at a Big Four firm. She then transitioned to her current role as a market accountant in the health care industry, where she provides accounting support services to various ambulatory surgery centers throughout the Southeast market. Miriam has bachelor's and master's degrees in accounting. In addition to her role as an accounting professional, Miriam is active in her local community and participates in various networking and mentorship organizations, including co-chairing the Young Alumni Council of her alma mater.

How do you use data analytics in your current accounting role?

Everyone in accounting performs data analytics to some extent. In my work, I use a report that compares this quarter's financial metrics to the prior quarter. This report comes from the AIS. However, data analytics showcases which of these metrics are standing out above the threshold, which allows me to focus my time and effort on the critical thinking and judgment aspect by digging into why this metric increased or decreased. Data analytics like this help me provide more value to my team by allowing me to focus more on critical thinking and decision making.

How do you use the characteristics of useful information in your daily work?

Comparability is something we use regularly in data analytics. Our AIS creates reports that show me monthly, yearly, and quarterly analysis, which allows me to compare prior activities to recent activities. This helps me focus on how we're progressing or regressing on specific financial statement line-item areas and what adjustments to make moving forward.

Do you have any tips for current accounting students who are starting internships or their first full-time position?

A positive attitude can go a long way. Remember that you are new to the company, and that will bring challenges. Being a team player, bringing a fresh outlook and positive energy to your team, and seeking out opportunities will help you be successful in your new role. If you face technical challenges, try to do the work yourself first by taking an "initial stab" at things before you turn to your colleagues for help. When you present the problem to your leaders, be ready with a potential solution to showcase you attempted to solve it on your own. Combining a positive attitude with this kind of hard work won't go unnoticed.

Review and Practice

Key Terms Review

accounting information system (AIS)	business event	data
basic business model	business model	data analytics
business activity	business process	data integrity

decision context	information quality	peer-to-peer business model
direct-to-consumers business model	information system	process-based information system
enhancing characteristics	input	purpose of a business
financing event	internal controls	reporting
franchise business model	investing event	retailer business model
freemium business model	key performance indicator (KPI)	software
fundamental characteristics	operating event	subscription business model
information event	output	transaction-based AIS

Learning Objectives Review

❶ Explain how accounting affects both the demand for and supply of information.

- Good Information Leads to Good Decisions
- Transforming Data into Information
- Components of an AIS
- Meet Julia's Cookies
- Understanding Business Operations

The demand for accounting information comes from decision makers, who need information about economic activity to help make decisions. The supply of accounting information flows from the information preparers to the decision makers.

Accounting professionals make judgment calls about what most accurately reflects the business reality of economic activity.

An accounting information system (AIS):

- Captures data about business events that give rise to accounting transactions (data input)
- Processes and stores that data (action)
- Reports information in formats that are useful to users (information output)

The components of an AIS are:

- Data
- Established procedures
- Internal controls
- Information technology (IT) infrastructure
- Software
- Users

A business event or activity (such as "Accept customer order") is a definable activity that takes place during the normal operation of a business.

An example of the output from an AIS is a set of financial statements.

To earn profits and generate sufficient cash flow from operations, a business engages in activities called business operations. To succeed, a business needs to use a hierarchical structure:

- Business model(s)
- Business processes
- Business events

Business models are achieved through well-designed business processes. A business process is a group of related business events designed to accomplish the strategic objectives of the business.

A basic business model consists of the three primary types of business processes:

- Acquisitions and payments processes: For acquiring resources
- Conversion processes: For converting resources into a product or service
- Marketing, sales, and collections processes: For selling goods and services and collecting cash

There are four types of business events:

- Operating
- Financing
- Investing
- Information

❷ Compare traditional transaction-based accounting systems with process-based information systems.

Traditional transaction-based accounting information systems record only accounting transactions.

Today, many companies use sophisticated, integrated, process-based information systems, which collect and process all data of interest to the business and connect all the processes. An AIS is a module of an integrated system and not a stand-alone system.

Common resources acquired during the acquisitions and payments processes include:

- Financing
- Property, plant, and equipment
- Employees
- Inventory
- Other goods and services

Conversion processes are at the heart of any business. They convert resources into products or provide services to clients or customers.

The marketing, sales, and collections processes involve marketing and selling products or services and collecting the cash from the sales. The cash flows back to resources and replenishes the cash balance so that the firm can pay its commitments.

❸ Explain management's relationship to information and information systems.

Management needs information to make decisions about business processes. Much of this information comes from the output of a company's information system(s). Management uses this information to determine whether the business is meeting its strategic objectives. The information generated by the information system(s) helps monitor business process outcomes and results in changes and improvements to the processes, which in turn should improve the chances of meeting objectives.

Management is responsible for:

- Planning processes
- Implementing processes
- Monitoring processes
- Changing and improving processes

Business events making up the business processes create the data stored in a company's database(s).

Management combines the principles of information quality and decision context to identify information needs for decision-making activities.

Information quality refers to the suitability of information for a particular purpose in a specific task.

To be useful for decision making, quality information must have two fundamental characteristics:

- Relevance
- Faithful representation

The usefulness of information increases in the presence of four enhancing characteristics:

- Verifiability
- Timeliness
- Understandability
- Comparability

An overall constraint on the usefulness of information is cost-effectiveness.

Decision context refers to the preferences, constraints, and other factors that affect how a decision is made, such as who is going to use the information, and why.

❹ Describe the relationship between accounting and data analytics.

By using data that is generated by business events, companies use two processes:

- Reporting is the process of aggregating data into information on the activities and performance in a company.
- Data analytics is the process of using technology to transform raw data, or facts, into useful information.

Management combines the historical performance information provided by reporting with data analytics insights to understand what happened and to make decisions on how to improve business processes.

Data analytics skills that new accounting professionals need:

- Identify what data can be used to answer a business question
- Recognize data quality issues
- Know the fundamentals of how data is stored so that you can retrieve it
- Display data analytics skills that can be applied to any software
- Perform data analytics using common software like Excel
- Collect, clean, and prepare data
- Recognize when advanced data analytics tools are needed
- Perform data visualization and report the results of an analysis

CPA questions, as well as multiple choice, discussion, analysis and application, and Tableau questions and other resources, are available online.

Multiple Choice Questions

1. **(LO 1)** Accounting communicates to stakeholders
   a. minimally required public financial data.
   b. the financial outcomes of operating, investing, and financing activities.
   c. the sales strategy for the operating, marketing, and sales activities.
   d. black and white details about the economics of operating activities.

2. **(LO 1)** Accounting information systems differ from larger business information systems in that they
   a. consist of a subset of the data stored in the entire information system.
   b. focus on data from business events involving exchanges of economic resources.
   c. collect, process, store, and analyze data and report information.
   d. All of the above

3. **(LO 1)** Input to an information system consists of
   a. raw and unorganized data.
   b. hardware and software.
   c. reported information.
   d. processed data.

4. **(LO 1)** Which of the following is *not* a business event?
   a. Hire a new employee
   b. Order raw materials
   c. Deliver goods to customer
   d. Accounts receivable

5. **(LO 2)** In which of the three types of business processes in the basic business model does a business deliver products to its customers?
   a. Sales and collections
   b. Acquisitions and payments
   c. Conversion
   d. Delivery contracts

6. **(LO 2)** Which of the following accounting data components is an acquisitions and payments process?
   a. Expenditures
   b. Payroll
   c. Financing
   d. All of the above

7. **(LO 2)** In which of the three types of business processes in the basic business model does a business transform resources into a product or service that customers want?
   a. Sales and collections
   b. Acquisitions and payments
   c. Conversion
   d. Accounts receivable

8. **(LO 2)** Which of these business events does *not* result in an accounting transaction?
   a. Declare a dividend
   b. Pay a dividend
   c. Order supplies from vendor
   d. Deliver product to customer

9. **(LO 2)** Which statement about the conversion process is false?
   a. Businesses create value by combining and converting resources to goods and/or services.
   b. The conversion process includes the acquisition of resources.
   c. The conversion process includes regulatory compliance.
   d. Businesses create value by being innovative and efficient in their processing.

10. **(LO 2)** McDonald's could have avoided massive financial losses from changing its conversion processes if it had
   a. used data to analyze market trends and customer desires.
   b. used robots to create the made-to-order meals.
   c. spent more money on marketing.
   d. changed them sooner.

11. **(LO 3)** Which characteristic refers to the suitability of the information for a particular purpose in a specific task?
   a. Information integrity
   b. Information quality
   c. Data integrity
   d. Data quality

12. **(LO 3)** In the iterative relationship of data-driven decision making, what occurs after business events create data?
   a. Management decision making
   b. Business process updates
   c. Transformation of raw data into useful information
   d. Control activities through monitoring

13. **(LO 3)** The information quality characteristic that refers to knowledgeable and independent people reaching agreement about whether information is representative of a real-world fact or occurrence is
   a. relevance.
   b. faithful representation.
   c. verifiability.
   d. reliability.

14. **(LO 3)** Which characteristic refers to the completeness, accuracy, reliability, and consistency of data?
   a. Information integrity
   b. Information quality
   c. Data integrity
   d. Data quality

15. **(LO 3)** **CPA** Within the context of qualitative characteristics of accounting information, which of the following is a fundamental qualitative characteristic?
   a. Relevance
   b. Timeliness
   c. Comparability
   d. Confirmatory value

16. **(LO 3)** **CPA** A tire company is evaluating the following measures: customer lifetime value (the value the company realizes from each customer), customer acquisition cost (cost of acquiring each customer), customer satisfaction and retention, and number of new and existing customers. Which of the following best describes this initiative?

a. Data analytics

b. KPIs

c. Audit data analytics

d. Decision making

17. **(LO 3)** `CPA` Which of the following KPIs (ratios) would be used to evaluate a company's profitability?

a. Current ratio

b. Inventory turnover ratio

c. Debt to total assets ratio

d. Gross margin ratio

18. **(LO 3)** Quantifiable metrics used to measure and evaluate the success of an organization based on its objectives are known as

a. data integration metrics.

b. business event indicators.

c. key performance indicators.

d. data quality points.

19. **(LO 3)** Relevant information must

a. be applicable to future events.

b. have confirmatory value.

c. have a significant impact on the decision.

d. All of the above

20. **(LO 4)** Which of the following is an example of data analytics?

a. A student uses Excel to calculate weights of grades and determine the grade needed on the finals.

b. A student uses Excel to record their time spent studying for each class and perform statistical analysis on the time spent versus grade earned.

c. An accountant uses software to horizontally and vertically analyze financial statements to compare with prior quarters.

d. An accountant uses software to generate reports that contain ratios of historical financial data.

21. **(LO 4)** `CPA` Roles for accountants in data include all of the following *except*

a. assessing the quality and integrity of data.

b. integrating data into evaluations of internal controls.

c. building big data systems.

d. data analytics.

22. **(LO 4)** The two types of outputs that are generated with data created during a business event are reports and

a. timesheets.

b. invoices.

c. analytics.

d. decisions.

23. **(LO 4)** Which of the following is an important skill related to data analytics that new accounting professionals need to learn?

a. How to code programming languages

b. How to use statistical algorithms

c. Web design

d. How to recognize data quality issues

Discussion and Research Questions

DQ1. (LO 1) Find or create two memes: (1) one that demonstrates common misconceptions about accounting professionals and what they do and (2) one that shows the reality of the work that accounting professionals do. The second meme can also show the reason you chose to be an accounting major.

DQ2. (LO 1) Explain to your supervisor how accounting (1) meets the demand for information while at the same time it (2) affects the supply of information. Use the Pathways Vision Model as a reference.

DQ3. (LO 1) `Critical Thinking` You have successfully taught yourself how to program apps by using online resources like Datacamp, Coursera, and Codeacademy. You have an idea for a new app that will inform students whether their backpacks are missing important items on a particular day, like textbooks, Scantron forms for exams, laptops, or financial calculators. You develop a business plan and win the $50,000 first prize in a competition run by Innovation Depot, the epicenter for technology startups in Birmingham, Alabama. You are about to graduate, and you want to launch your own startup with the prize money. At a high level, explain (1) the primary purpose of business and how it relates to your business, (2) your business model in terms of inputs of resources and outputs of goods and services (refer to Illustration 1.12 for guidance), and

(3) the cash flow implications of your business model, including how you are going to generate cash.

DQ4. (LO 1) Explain the relationship between business events and business processes.

DQ5. (LO 1) Explain how accounting information differs from other information in an information system.

DQ6. (LO 2) Using an example, explain how the context in which a decision is made can have a significant impact on the prioritization of the characteristics of quality information.

DQ7. (LO 2) `Critical Thinking` You have launched a successful business that is starting to grow. You are considering the acquisition and implementation of a process-based information system. Explain to your business partner, who is a traditional accountant, the relationship between business processes and the information system and how a traditional accounting system differs from a process-based system.

DQ8. (LO 2) For acquisitions and payments processes, identify four examples of socially responsible business activities for which data can be collected. This data could be financial or nonfinancial. Identify the related resource—for example, raw materials, supplies, human resources, and fixed assets.

DQ9. (LO 2) For a firm that manufactures off-road vehicles, identify four examples of socially responsible business activities for which nonfinancial data related to the conversion process can be collected.

DQ10. (LO 2) At a conceptual level, discuss whether business processes determine the information system or whether the information system determines the business processes.

DQ11. (LO 3) Describe each of the following management functions: (1) planning, (2) implementing, (3) monitoring, and (4) changing and improving. Explain the relationship between these functions and a firm's information system.

DQ12. (LO 3) What is quality information? Choose one fundamental characteristic and one enhancing characteristic of quality information. Compare and contrast what makes each of your choices a fundamental versus an enhancing characteristic. Provide an example that demonstrates why information quality would be compromised if the chosen fundamental characteristic did not have the enhancing characteristic.

DQ13. (LO 4) `Early Career` `Data Foundations` Use the internet to research skills related to data analytics that accounting professionals need. You can look at websites from global and regional accounting firms to see the types of services they offer or look at LinkedIn for job postings in your area or a major metro area near you. List at least five technical, data-related skills and identify where you found each of them.

Application and Analysis Questions

A1. (LO 1) `Critical Thinking` If you walk into a local coffee shop and order a fresh-baked scone from the cashier, a variety of business events will take place. Identify at least four business events, in order, and label each of them as an operating event or an information event.

A2. (LO 2) For each of the business events listed in the following table, (1) identify the business process for the event in a process-based approach and (2) identify the traditional accounting cycle(s) for the event. For nonaccounting events, write "not applicable."

Business Event	Business Process Approach	Traditional Accounting Cycle(s)
1. Ship goods to credit customer	Sales and collection	Revenue/accounts receivable
2. Pay hourly employees for the week		
3. Sell goods for cash		
4. Order a new factory machine		
5. Receive raw materials from vendor		
6. Receive payment from credit customer		
7. Take out a loan to pay for new factory machine		
8. Pay a dividend to shareholders		
9. Manufacture a product		
10. Write off an uncollectible account		
11. Issue new common stock		

ID	Date	Item	Customer First Name	Customer Last Name	Amount
000238	4/8/2020	Chocolate chip cookies	Johnny	Ramirez	$9.56
239	4/9/2020	Oatmeal raisin cookies	Johnny	Ramirez	$8.51
000240	4/31/2020	Snickerdoodle cookies	Julia	Rodriguez	$4.20
000241	4/10/2020	PBC	Annette	Álvarez	$6.51
000242	4/11/2020	Chocolate chip cookies	Brian		$11.23

A3. (LO 3) `Data Foundations` `Critical Thinking` You have a table full of data and have started finding some quality issues in it. Go through the table above and identify the data quality issues that you notice, the field in which each issue occurs, and how you would fix it. Choose from the following data quality characteristics: comparability (consistency), understandability, error free, completeness, confirmatory value.

A4. (LO 3) `Critical Thinking` For each of the information situations listed below, match the following information quality characteristic that either most accurately applies to the situation or would be the best characteristic to improve the information. Where more than one characteristic could apply, choose the most appropriate one.

Information quality characteristics:

A. Completeness

B. Relevance

C. Predictive value

D. Understandability

E. Timeliness

F. Faithful representation

G. Confirmatory value

H. Comparability

Information Situation	Characteristic
1. At the beginning of the COVID-19 pandemic, the United States was behind many other countries in testing people for the coronavirus. News reports said that people with symptoms struggled for access to tests, often in vain. The lack of testing availability resulted in reports of COVID cases that bore no resemblance to the reality of how much the virus had really spread. Consequently, there was fear and uncertainty.	
2. This characteristic strongly factors into the reason for reporting land and buildings at historical cost in a company's Balance Sheet, even though this value may bear no resemblance to the fair market value of the asset.	
3. In the income statement of a company, sales transactions included in the revenue amount are only those that reflect revenue earned during the reporting period—no more and no less.	
4. In the management decision to replace a long-haul transportation truck used for the past 10 years, inclusion of information about the original cost of the truck in a report has no _____ (fill in the characteristic).	
5. Disney World provides guests with Magic Bands, which are wristbands that collect data on who the guests are, where they are, what rides they go on, and what they buy. Disney characters greet children wearing the bands by name. Magic Bands provide Disney with an incredible amount of data about guest profiles and preferences. Information like this can help Disney improve decision making for optimal management of its resorts.	
6. Alicia's Accessories is developing a proprietary big data system called Just-in-Time. The intention of the system is to continuously monitor and improve operations, products, marketing, sales, and employee training and to improve competitive advantage. The data comes from the company's point-of-sale systems, inventory systems, promotions, customer feedback and surveys, and loyalty programs. Just-in-Time provides information every 30 minutes at headquarters for immediate decision making. Operational glitches get immediate attention.	
7. According to the magazine *Fast Company*, not making the content of business websites available to people with disabilities means potentially losing around $500 million in spending power. This amount does not include losses from lawsuits. *Fast Company* provides examples of businesses that have been sued for failing to offer ADA-compliant websites, including Domino's and Beyoncé's Parkwood Entertainment.	
8. Oil and gas companies consistently apply the same industry-specific accounting standards to their financial statements, and so there should be a high level of _____ (fill in the characteristic) within that industry.	
9. A company with information about a probable and material lawsuit must report it in the notes to its financial statements. An attempt to withhold this information indicates bias and *not* _____ (fill in characteristic).	
10. Financial statements include information on cash flows so that financial analysts and investors can evaluate the accuracy of their past predictions.	
11. Financial analysts and investors use past financial statements as a basis to chart performance trends and make predictions about future performance, including profitability and cash flow, for business valuation purposes.	

Business Event/Activity	O, F, or I?	Related Information Event	Related Decision Activity
1. Ship goods to a credit customer	O	Retrieve a report that compares shipment date to delivery date and shows time taken for successful delivery	Monitor efficiency and effectiveness of couriers
2. Pay hourly employees for the week			
3. Return a defective product to the supplier			
4. Order a new factory machine			
5. Receive raw materials from a vendor			
6. Pay an invoice received from a vendor			
7. Take out a loan to pay for a new factory machine			
8. Pay a dividend to shareholders			
9. Manufacture a product			
10. Write off an uncollectible account			
11. Issue new common stock			

A5. (LO 1–4) For each of the business events listed above, (1) identify it as an operating, financing, or investing event or activity; (2) identify a related information event; and (3) identify a related decision activity.

A6. (LO 1–4) **Early Career** **Critical Thinking** Clever Cabinets is a small but growing company specializing in the manufacture and installation of a variety of cabinets and fixtures. The company has approximately 55 employees. It does commercial subcontracting work for general contractors like construction firms. The company's work results from a competitive bidding process, and the final price is fixed. The company bears the risk of a loss if the bid is too low.

Management is concerned about the lack of integration between the company's traditional accounting and other management information systems. Inputs of the same data take place multiple times because of disconnected information systems and lack of a single database for the company. Recently, an audit revealed that the same data item had different values in different systems, resulting in a lack of data integrity and a lack of trust in the information delivered by these disparate systems. Clever Cabinets retains the CPA firm where you are an intern to propose an integrated, process-based information system to help the business grow with a more value-added emphasis and with access to better information.

Your manager sends you on a site visit to Clever Cabinets. You take the following notes about the current system for the acquisition and payment of raw materials, plus some additional information for later use:

Generic purchasing, which is the purchase of raw materials common to all jobs (such as plywood, glue, and nails) is on an as-needed basis, depending on how low inventory levels are or on the deal the company can get from a supplier at a particular time. When a supplier offers a good deal to the company, it often results in bulk purchases. The purchasing manager generates a purchase order (PO) for the supplier

without a purchase requisition (PR). The main difference between a PO and a PR is that firms use a PR to authorize a purchase. This authorization happens before the issuance of a purchase order to the vendor. A PR often starts the purchasing process.

The request to buy raw materials for a successfully bid job comes from the job cost estimator. If a bid is successful, the estimator issues a PR unique to a particular bid job. The PR contains product descriptions, quantity, bid purchase price, and (often) vendor name. The purchasing manager reviews the PR to determine which raw materials are already in inventory (the result of generic purchasing). If the materials are not in stock, they prepare a PO based on the information shown on the PR and send it to the supplier.

An employee in the Receiving department accepts delivery of an order and signs the vendor-generated delivery report as proof of receipt. A copy of the proof of receipt goes to accounts payable, and the delivered goods go into the raw materials store. The various manufacturing supervisors remove raw materials from the store as required. There is no perpetual inventory system.

Once the accounts payable clerk receives the PR (optional), PO, and vendor-generated receiving record, they update the accounts payable records. Upon receipt of the vendor invoice, they match all these documents. They prepare a check on the due date for signing by an authorized signatory. The check signatory cancels the supporting documentation at this point. The accounts payable clerk mails the check to the vendor and updates the accounts payable records.

In discussions with management, you find out that the company wants to incorporate the following into a business-process approach for the acquisition of raw materials:

- Cost Accounting and Inventory Management want to adopt a perpetual inventory system using the weighted average inventory valuation method.

- When materials requisitions for raw materials are sent to the materials store, store employees will check inventory on hand and decide what to order. Store employees will issue a purchase requisition for inventory that is not on hand, and they will immediately issue items that are on hand to production. The new rule is that a materials requisition must support removal of raw materials from the storeroom. A store person should be the only person with physical access to the raw materials.

- The Purchasing department receives all purchase requisitions. It aggregates purchase requisitions to get bulk discounts and issues purchase orders to individual vendors. For generic (bulk) inventory items, the Purchasing department sets a minimum order quantity, and the perpetual inventory system triggers a purchase requisition to purchasing when it reaches a minimum level for an inventory item. This happens once a day, with all reorder items for that day listed on one request.

- The store person checks receipts of new shipments and signs the delivery documents accompanying the order as evidence of receipt of all goods in good order. The stores person also generates a receiving report detailing the quantity and description of accepted items. Rejected shipments go back to the vendor.

- The receiving report then goes to accounts payable for payment of the correct amount to the vendor on the due date.

You are back at the office, and you are getting ready for a meeting with your manager to discuss your findings. To prepare for this meeting, you must perform the following tasks:

1. List the business events that lead to accounting transactions in the traditional expenditures and accounts payable accounting system, based on the existing system.

2. List, in sequential order, the business events that apply to the proposed process-based acquisitions and payments system for raw materials. Identify those events that give rise to accounting transactions, and compare this answer to your answer to question 1. What do you notice?

3. Identify three other possible monitoring activities in the new process-based system that a traditional accounting system would not record.

Pop-up Stall Scenario

Answer questions A7 and A8 using this scenario:

You are opening a limited-time pop-up coffee stall in your campus's business building. Your pop-up will use the space of an existing sandwich shop that is only open from 11:00 a.m. to 2:00 p.m. Monday through Friday. Your coffee stall will be open from 3:00 p.m. through 9:00 a.m. the three weeks leading up to and during midterms and finals weeks. The sandwich shop already has a lot of things you need, like refrigerator space and display counters, but it doesn't have any coffee equipment.

A7. (LO 1–4) `Critical Thinking` Match the following business events related to setting up and operating your pop-up

to one of the three types of business processes discussed in Learning Objective 1.1:

A. Acquisitions and payments processes

B. Conversion processes

C. Marketing, sales, and collections processes

Business Event	Business Process
1. Buy an espresso machine	
2. Transfer the receipts from today from your mobile payment app to your pop-up's bank account	
3. Sell your first latte	
4. Pay your friends who work as baristas at the end of the week	
5. Pay for pour-over coffee filters	
6. Pay a fair-trade coffee provider for beans delivered last week	
7. Prepare batches of cold brew to steep overnight the night before it is sold	
8. Order a custom chalkboard sign from an Etsy shop for your daily menus	
9. Make a macchiato for a customer	
10. Order milk from a local dairy farm's stall at a farmer's market that will be delivered next Tuesday	
11. Bake scones to sell the next day	
12. Send your customer an e-receipt via text message	

A8. (LO 1–4) `Data Foundations` `Critical Thinking` Your university approved your pop-up for this semester, but those in charge want to see if you are successful before they approve your opening again in future semesters. Choose three of the following pieces of information that you collected while operating your pop-up, state which of the three business processes generated each piece of information, and explain how you would use those three pieces of information together to show the university which parts of your pop-up were successful or failed.

1. Total number of coffees sold (including all types)	3,600
2. Total amount earned (before depreciation)	$ 18,000.00
3. Cost of all ingredients and supplies purchased	$ 3,026.00
4. Cost of fixed asset purchases (like espresso machine)	$ 1,598.00
5. Cost of paying baristas	$ 8,640.00
6. Average wait time (length of line)	15 minutes
7. Total number of students who had finals during this time	6,523
8. Total number of customers	242

A9. (LO 1–4) **Data Foundations** **Critical Thinking** You are running four successful popsicle stores in Los Angeles and are about to prepare a purchase order for raw materials for each store but need to know how much to purchase. Your stores are in four different areas of the city, but you don't want to drive around to physically count the inventory. Furthermore, you have learned that, for each of the stores, sales differ drastically by customer preferences for different popsicle flavors. You decide to utilize your database to perform some analytics prior to placing the order. What type of information should you gather to make an inventory decision without physically seeing the inventory? Identify three sources of information. How would you use the information to calculate your inventory needs?

A10. (LO 1–4) In the following table, match each of the items from List A with the appropriate items from List B. Every item in List A matches *one or more* items in List B. Each item in List B has *zero or one* matches in List A. (Item 14 is an exception since it can have more than one match.)

List A	List B	Answer
A. The practice of accounting	1. Input into an information system	
B. Sales and collections processes	2. No connection with business events	
C. Conversion processes	3. Profits not declared or paid as dividends	
D. Data	4. Order raw materials from vendor	
E. Acquisitions and payments processes	5. Inputs of resources into a business	
F. Output	6. Information or product	
G. Cost versus benefit	7. Timeliness and verifiability	
H. Misperception(s) about accounting	8. Acquire and retain customers	
I. Both enhancing characteristics of information quality	9. Business event	
J. Information quality	10. Serves the public interest and promotes prosperity	
K. Take customer order	11. Combine resources to add value	
L. Retained earnings	12. Rigid black-or-white rules; no flexibility in accounting choices	
	13. Accessibility	
	14. There is no match for this item.	

Tableau Case: Cookies Cares Charitable Foundation

What You Need

Download Tableau to your computer. You can access www.tableau.com/academic/students to download your free Tableau license for the year, or you can download it from your university's software offerings.

Download the following file from the book's product page on www.wiley.com:

Chapter 1 Raw Data.xlsx

Case Background

Big Picture:
Analyze the corporate social responsibility of the Cookies Cares Charitable Foundation.

Details:
Why is this data important, and what questions or problems need to be addressed?

- It is important to analyze the Cookies Cares Charitable Foundation's charitable giving efforts to ensure that Julia's Cookies is fulfilling its corporate social responsibility promise to grow its charitable efforts from year to year.

- To analyze the financial gifts that the Cookies Cares Charitable Foundation has given over the years, consider the following questions: How much was given? To whom were the charitable gifts allocated? Where are the charities located?

Plan:

What data is needed, and how should it be analyzed?

- The data needed is captured by the Accounts Payable department and extracted from the database that supports the Financial module of the ERP system. Accounts Payable manages the charitable giving process because charitable donations are business expenses that are subject to specific internal controls.
- To isolate the charitable giving expenses for the Cookies Cares Charitable Foundation, the data is filtered on the Cost Center field to only show cost center 12542. Cost centers identify the departments where expenses are allocated. The data includes charitable donation expenses from 1/1/2019 through 12/31/2022.

Now it's your turn to evaluate, analyze, and communicate the results!

Questions

1. How many banks did Julia's Cookies use for charitable giving?
2. How many transactions were processed through Wells Fargo? (Hint: Each line item is a transaction.)
3. Which bank processed the fewest total transactions?
4. What was the total dollar amount of charitable giving expenses in 2021?
5. Which bank processed the smallest total dollar amount of transactions in 2021? How much was it?
6. Which bank processed the highest total dollar amount of transactions overall? How much was it?
7. What three charities received the largest dollar amounts of donations?
8. Which state received the largest dollar amount of donations?

Take it to the next level!

9. In what month and year was the largest dollar amount of charitable giving donated?
10. Which charity received the largest donation during that month and year?

CHAPTER 2
Risks and Risk Assessments

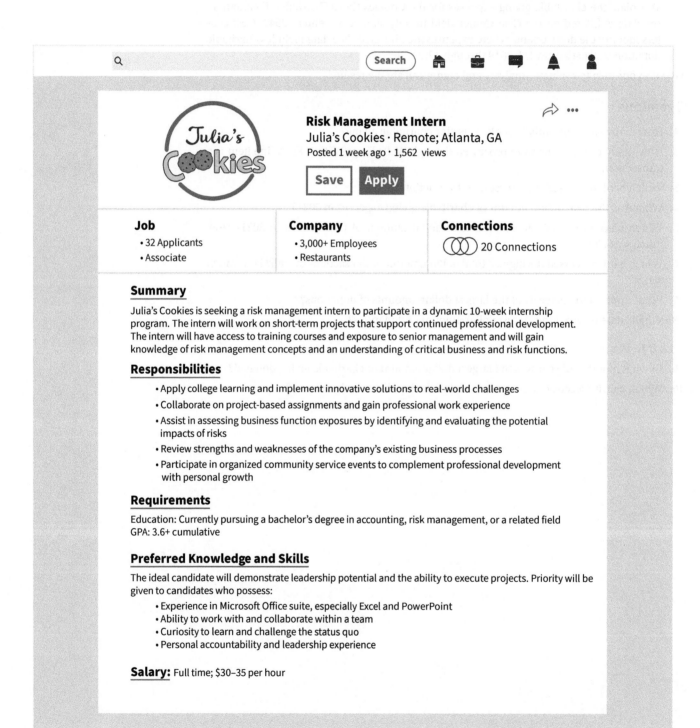

Risk Management Intern

Julia's Cookies · Remote; Atlanta, GA

Posted 1 week ago · 1,562 views

Save Apply

Job
- 32 Applicants
- Associate

Company
- 3,000+ Employees
- Restaurants

Connections
20 Connections

Summary

Julia's Cookies is seeking a risk management intern to participate in a dynamic 10-week internship program. The intern will work on short-term projects that support continued professional development. The intern will have access to training courses and exposure to senior management and will gain knowledge of risk management concepts and an understanding of critical business and risk functions.

Responsibilities

- Apply college learning and implement innovative solutions to real-world challenges
- Collaborate on project-based assignments and gain professional work experience
- Assist in assessing business function exposures by identifying and evaluating the potential impacts of risks
- Review strengths and weaknesses of the company's existing business processes
- Participate in organized community service events to complement professional development with personal growth

Requirements

Education: Currently pursuing a bachelor's degree in accounting, risk management, or a related field
GPA: 3.6+ cumulative

Preferred Knowledge and Skills

The ideal candidate will demonstrate leadership potential and the ability to execute projects. Priority will be given to candidates who possess:

- Experience in Microsoft Office suite, especially Excel and PowerPoint
- Ability to work with and collaborate within a team
- Curiosity to learn and challenge the status quo
- Personal accountability and leadership experience

Salary: Full time; $30–35 per hour

CHAPTER PREVIEW   You have learned that accounting information systems produce information for decision making that serves a broader public interest purpose and that accountants don't spend their days "crunching numbers." In fact, accounting professionals are some of the most important employees in a company. Every industry needs professionals who can evaluate economic activities, make accounting judgments about poorly defined business situations, and turn insights into useful information.

An important area where judgment transforms gray areas into useful information is risk. You will recognize a pattern about risk in this chapter: there are not always clear solutions.

This chapter explores concepts related to risk and risk assessment that will guide you throughout your AIS course:

- The nature of risk
- Categorizing risk
- Prioritizing risk
- Responding to risk

If you think risk management is boring, think again. Risk management is an area where accounting professionals are free to use their imaginations, critical-thinking skills, educational knowledge, and personal perceptions to bring unique value to companies. Accounting professionals are often sought for unique job opportunities like the risk management internship at Julia's Cookies, which is based on a real job posting for a risk management internship at a well-known financial services company. The first step to risk management is understanding the fundamentals of risks and how they impact a company. ■

Chapter Roadmap

LEARNING OBJECTIVES	TOPICS	JULIA'S COOKIES APPLIED LEARNING
2.1 Describe the nature of risk.	• Importance of Risk • Applying Risks to a Business • Enterprise Risk Management • Identifying Risks	Risk Identification: Boise Store
2.2 Classify risks into different risk categories.	• Internal Risks • External Risks • Risk Inventory	Categorizing Risks: Boise Store
2.3 Determine the quantitative value of risk.	• Evaluating Risk Severity • Using Risk Formulas • Creating Risk Matrices	Prioritizing Risks: Boise Store
2.4 Explain how businesses respond to risk.	• Assess the Risk • Respond to the Risk	Selecting a Risk Response: Oven Fires

CPA   You will find the CPA tag throughout the chapter to call out any important topics you may see on the CPA exam.

2.1 How Do We Understand Risk?

Learning Objective ❶
Describe the nature of risk.

It is essential for accounting professionals to understand risk, including emerging trends in risk management. Technology is propelling massive and fast-paced changes in how a business functions. It also poses a unique challenge: technology provides new ways to *manage* risk while also *creating* risks related to its use. Employers rely on accounting professionals who understand these two competing realities. Careers in risk-focused areas are growing as companies build specialized teams to address areas where the business might suffer losses.

Identifying and managing risk are essential functions of a business. Every business takes risks, and it is important for businesses to decide how to deal with the negative outcomes of those risks. Regardless of specialization, accounting professionals assess and address risk constantly, both formally and informally:

- Internal audit departments perform formal risk assessments when creating audit plans.
- External auditors assess a client's audit risk when creating audit plans.
- Cost accountants examine risk from financial and operational perspectives.
- Financial accountants implement controls—that is, specific procedures—to address risk.
- Tax accountants comply with regulations designed to protect their companies and clients from risk.

Importance of Risk

Anything that can *possibly* hinder a business in achieving its goals or cause a loss is an unfavorable event, and **risk** is the likelihood of an unfavorable event occurring. Risks differ by business type, size, industry, and location. The local coffee shop near you doesn't face the same risks as a global technology behemoth like Amazon.

Some examples of risks at Julia's Cookies, a bakery specializing in delivering fresh-baked cookies to your door via a mobile app order, are:

- Employees burning themselves on ovens
- Running out of raw materials
- Delivering the wrong order to a customer
- Public opinion focusing on healthy snacks and discouraging customers from buying cookies
- Employees stealing cash from the cash register
- Fires burning down stores
- Delivery drivers getting into car accidents while delivering cookies
- Cyber attackers stealing customer data

Risk often drives innovation. A company that takes on significant risk may have a competitive advantage over a company that avoids that risk. Think of modern-day innovators like Elon Musk (SpaceX), Mark Zuckerberg (Facebook), Steve Jobs (Apple), Jack Ma (Alibaba), and Jeff Bezos (Amazon). Without taking significant risks, their companies would not have become the success stories that have made them household names.

CPA If a company wants to be at the forefront of its industry, it must be willing to accept calculated risk. Different companies may view the same risk as negative or as an opportunity. A brick-and-mortar store may find online shopping a negative risk, while another retail store may see it as an opportunity to increase its market share and revenues. **Illustration 2.1** shows how companies can find the "sweet spot"—the optimal level of risk-taking that yields enough value to make taking the risk worthwhile.

A risk-aware culture lets businesses proactively identify and manage risk. **CPA** A risk-aware culture at a business is characterized by leadership that sets a risk-awareness tone at the top, management that encourages employees to discuss risks openly and honestly, and an alignment of risk across all corporate initiatives, including salaries and incentive programs. One of the most important proactive risk-awareness techniques that companies use is formally assessing risk. Formal **risk assessments** identify, categorize, and prioritize individual risks so companies can leverage their understanding of risk in strategic planning. After assessing risk, management decides how to manage it.

Applying Risks to a Business

The number and magnitude of risks in a particular company—and in each business process—vary. Risk identification takes place at many levels in an organization, all the way down to an individual project. For the purposes of this course, we narrow our scope to risks at the business-process level.

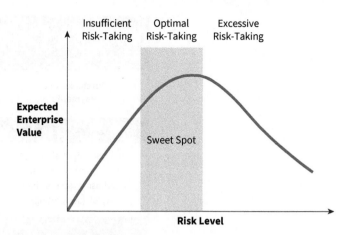

Illustration 2.1   There is a sweet spot for risk.

Recall that a business process is a group of related business events intended to accomplish the strategic objectives of a business. **Illustration 2.2** shows the three primary types of business processes that make up a basic business model for Julia's Cookies.

When considering risk, companies need to know where the risk exists within their organizational structures. It is not enough to know that the risk for a business process applies to the "marketing, sales, and collections" area since that is a very broad categorization and doesn't specify the location of the risk. To address this, companies consider risk at a business function level. A **business function** is a high-level business area or department that performs business processes to achieve company goals. More than one business function may be necessary to complete a single business process.

There is no specific guidance for how a company identifies a business function. A company could classify it broadly, like "accounting," or narrowly by separating accounting into multiple business functions, like "payroll" and "purchasing." The broader the definition of the business function, the less specific the business can be in identifying its risks. This is why we use a narrower, granular approach. Even with granularity, some business functions cross many areas—especially business functions that are involved in technology, like information technology (IT) security, design, and services.

Illustration 2.3 is not a comprehensive depiction of Julia's Cookies, but it shows examples of business functions and how they relate to some of the business processes we have been discussing. It moves from the highest level (company) down to a granular level (risks for each business process).

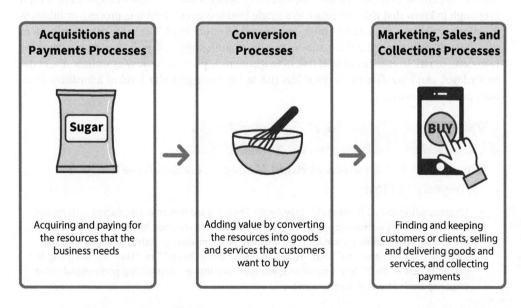

Illustration 2.2   Recall that the basic business model is made up of three categories, or business processes.

Company		
Types of Business Processes		
Purchases and Payments	**Conversion**	**Marketing, Sales, and Collections**
Business Functions		
Supply chain Vendor management Purchasing (accounting) Payroll (accounting)	Production Quality Research and development Distribution	Sales Customer relations Store operations Deliveries Mobile app
Individual Business Processes		
Purchasing raw inventory Receiving raw inventory Onboarding a new employee	Manufacturing raw cookie dough Delivering raw cookie dough to a store Developing a new cookie recipe	Face-to-face sales Online sales Mobile app sales with delivery
Risks		
Duplicate payments to vendors Unauthorized access to employee data Payroll fraud	Excess inventory Unauthorized access to research data Inventory fraud	Customer dissatisfaction Unauthorized access to customer data Revenue fraud

Illustration 2.3 Some risks at Julia's Cookies are related to individual business processes.

It is easiest to learn these concepts by applying them to separate business functions and processes, but in the real world, a single business process is rarely isolated, or siloed. Companies are moving toward integrated operations, which means that a business process is usually implemented by multiple business functions. We can use Julia's Cookies as an example:

- The purchasing business function must work with the warehouse and production teams to understand what inventory they need to have and what is already available in inventory.
- The business process "purchasing raw inventory" will have many business events executed across these business functions.

You will learn more about how business processes are cross-functionally executed when you learn to document processes in the Documenting Systems and Processes chapter. For now, it is enough to know that risk can relate to a single business event, business process, or business function, or risk can relate to an entire company at an entity level. The more granular its identification, the more specific the business can be in addressing it. **CPA** Businesses combine two views of risk to ensure optimal risk management. A **portfolio view** examines risk at the entity level, and a **profile view** considers risk at the more granular level of a business function, process, or event.

Why Does It Matter to Your Career?

Thoughts from an Internal Audit Manager, Global Asset Management Firm

- Understanding and addressing risk may sound like it is a tedious, micromanaging activity, but it really is not. It's a strategic opportunity for a company to enhance its operations by making the most of its available resources. It is a creative problem-solving activity. The objective isn't "What are we doing wrong?" but "How can we do things better?" or "How are we going to make the best of this?" It is a creative space that may interest accounting professionals who want to pursue a more strategic career.

- Many companies don't yet have robust risk programs. Some are getting started, while others are just reaching maturity. In other words, companies are hiring for these roles. If you are interested in a career in risk, starting as an auditor (external or internal) is one of many ways you can get experience that will help you learn the skills needed to transition into an enterprise risk management role.

Enterprise Risk Management

Just as risk can exist at different levels, from single business events to entity-wide corporate risks, risk identification can be performed at different levels of the company. An individual team can do a risk assessment to identify risks to its projects or budgets. Alternatively, risk can be viewed at the entity level, which means it is looked at across the entire organization. **CPA** When a company looks at entity-level risk, it can leverage its understanding of the identified risks to:

- Create the organization's strategic plan
- Plan which audits the internal audit department will perform this year
- Report risk to the audit committee and board of directors
- Select which projects different departments should prioritize
- Design information systems and data analytics solutions
- Assess and design internal controls, which are discussed in the next chapter
- Meet regulatory requirements
- Investigate areas for potential fraud
- Create policies and procedures
- Design physical security and infrastructure plans

This holistic view of risk at an entity level is becoming more popular in all industries. **CPA** **Enterprise risk management (ERM)** is the comprehensive process of identifying, categorizing, prioritizing, and responding to a company's risks. The first three of these ERM processes combine to create a formal risk assessment, and the final process is the act of addressing the risk (**Illustration 2.4**).

You will learn the first step of ERM, identifying risks, next. The remaining sections of this chapter explore categorization, prioritization, and response.

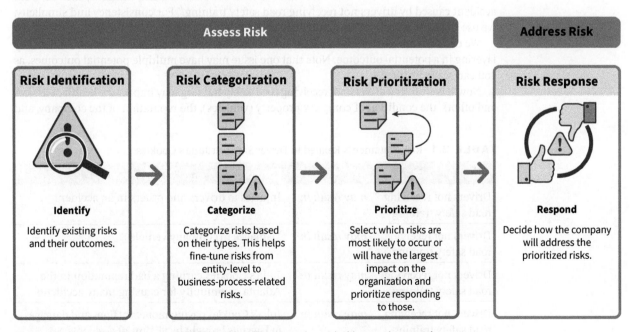

Illustration 2.4   The four steps of ERM are identify, categorize, prioritize, and respond.

Identifying Risks

Identify

Identifying a risk is not as simple as looking at a list of potential risks and figuring out which ones apply to your business. Accountants use critical thinking to analyze all possible outcomes. Identifying risks is a "worst-case scenario" exercise. It uses a Murphy's Law approach: anything that *can* happen *will* happen. While this negative outlook is rarely true, identifying risks requires assuming the worst. **CPA** There are a number of ways to identify risks, such as by conducting brainstorming exercises, using data to investigate historic events to predict future occurrences, diagramming business processes to look for weaknesses, and developing assumptions about operations and risks. Regardless of the method, it is essential to craft a well-formed risk statement.

As an example of finding risks, let's consider Julia's Cookies' delivery drivers in the Atlanta, Georgia, area:

- Julia's Cookies hires delivery drivers of any age as long as they have state-issued driver's licenses. Newly hired drivers receive one day of training on how to provide the best customer experience. That training does not cover driving safety. Delivery drivers use company vehicles.

- In the state of Georgia, individuals are eligible for a driver's license at age 16 after completing a 30-hour driver's education course. However, a driver's education course is not required for individuals over 16 years of age. Instead, candidates for a state-issued driver's license receive a discount on most insurance policies if they have taken a voluntary driver's education course.

We can easily identify the following issues:

- Drivers don't receive safety training from Julia's Cookies.
- Drivers may never have received road safety training if they didn't take a driver's education course.

At this stage, we have identified *issues*. These are not yet clearly defined risk statements. **CPA** A **risk statement** contains two parts: the issue and the possible outcome. Companies care about more than just what the risk *is*; they also care about what the risk *does*. A possible outcome gives business leaders a "why this is important" perspective. The outcome of an individual risk can vary greatly, from preventing the success of an entire company all the way down to delaying the launch of a single information system.

Risk statements come in many forms. Some common keywords are "because," "caused," and "possible." Sometimes the issue is worded to include what caused the issue, such as "a car accident caused by drivers not receiving road safety training." For consistency and simplicity, we use the basic wording "This issue *may result in* this outcome."

We can turn our identified issues for Julia's Cookies into clearly defined risk statements by layering in a potential outcome. Note that one issue may have multiple potential outcomes, as you can see in **Table 2.1**.

Now it is clear that drivers not receiving road safety training may impact the health of drivers and others, the condition of company property (vehicles), the reputation of the company, and

TABLE 2.1 Risk Statements Related to Driver Safety at Julia's Cookies

Issue		Outcome
Drivers not receiving road safety training	*may result in*	Injuries to drivers and others in an accident
Drivers not receiving road safety training	*may result in*	Damages to company vehicles
Drivers not receiving road safety training	*may result in*	Julia's Cookies earning a bad reputation in the Atlanta community for causing many accidents
Drivers not receiving road safety training	*may result in*	Julia's Cookies paying monetary fines and damages in lawsuits brought by victims of accidents

the finances of the company. Julia's Cookies will address each of these individual risk statements separately. You can work through another risk scenario for Julia's Cookies in Applied Learning 2.1.

Julia's Cookies   Applied Learning 2.1

Risk Identification: Boise Store

Julia's Cookies' products are made at factories throughout the United States. Raw ingredients are turned into dough, and the dough is packaged and sent in refrigerated trucks to local brick-and-mortar stores. Once there, dough has a limited shelf life before it is discarded.

Store employees have multiple job duties, including working the cash register for face-to-face sales, baking cookies in the kitchen, preparing delivery orders for drivers, and receiving deliveries of raw packaged cookie dough. Store staffs are small to keep overhead costs down.

At the Boise, Idaho, location, Julia's Cookies' staff consists of two employees on weekdays from 7:00 a.m. to 11:00 a.m., as this is the store's slowest time of day for business. The kitchen has one large oven, which can handle the store's demands. Deliveries arrive daily at 9:00 a.m., and one employee accepts the delivery while the other runs the kitchen and cash register. Business can be slow at this location, and sometimes raw cookie dough is thrown away due to a lack of customers.

What issues do you see with the Boise location? Find at least three separate issues and turn them into risk statements by adding a "*may result in*" outcome to the end of the statement.

SOLUTION

With risk identification, there are no wrong and right answers. Every person will see a situation in a different light. Risk specialists often work as a team to gain different perspectives. Here are three examples of risk statements for the Boise location:

1. An employee calling in sick for the 7:00 a.m. shift *may result in* lack of store coverage during the 9:00 a.m. delivery.

2. A malfunction in the only oven onsite *may result in* store operations closing for the day.

3. A slow week of sales *may result in* increased expenses and reduced profits because large amounts of expired products must be discarded.

CONCEPT REVIEW QUESTIONS

1. **CPA** Briefly discuss the importance of risk.
   Ans. Anything that can hinder a business's success in achieving its goals or cause a loss is an unfavorable event, and risk is the likelihood of an unfavorable event occurring.

2. How would you define a business function?
   Ans. Business function is a group of inter-related activities that are grouped as an area of department that performs business processes to achieve company goals. They can be classified, for instance, broadly as accounting or with a narrow scope like payroll and purchasing.

3. **CPA** What is the difference between portfolio and profile view in the context of examining risk?
   Ans. There are two views for optimal risk management in businesses. A portfolio view examines risk at the entity level, whereas a profile view considers risk at a more granular level of a business function, process, or event.

4. **CPA** What is enterprise risk management (ERM)?
   Ans. Enterprise risk management (ERM) is a term used in business to describe risk management methods. It is a comprehensive process of identifying, categorizing, prioritizing, and responding to a company's risks. The first three ERM processes combine to create a formal risk assessment, and the final process addresses the risk.

5. **CPA** What is a risk statement?
   Ans. A risk statement specifically describes risks that everyone can easily understand so that they can prioritize and mitigate the risks accordingly.

2.2 What Are the Types of Risks?

Learning Objective ❷
Classify risks into different risk categories.

Categorize

The second step of ERM is categorizing identified risks based on their type. Because risks can be found at the entity level and across every business process in a company, it is important to know how to classify them. Often, different risks in the same categories can be addressed with the same risk responses, which you will learn about later.

The first step in categorizing a risk is to determine where it comes from:

- **Internal risks** occur throughout a company's operations and arise during normal operations. Most internal risks are preventable through careful risk identification and management. It's important to note that an internal risk may relate to an external party, such as the company's reputation with customers. The key is to remember that internal risk arises from normal operations. For example, if an external party like Forbes ranks a business poorly, it still ties to the company's operations and performance, which makes this reputational risk an internal risk.

- Risks that are not related to business operations and come from outside the company are called **external risks**. While external risks are often unpredictable, companies still prepare for them to the best of their abilities. External risks are distinguished from internal risks because they are not related to business operations. For example, a stock market crash during a pandemic and a hurricane destroying corporate warehouses are not related to the company's operations or performance. They are outside events that the business has no control or influence over.

The determination of whether a risk is external or internal is done to identify the source of the risk. It is a company's responsibility to be accountable for all its risks—even the ones that are beyond its control. An identified risk is most useful when it is mapped to one source category. If a risk feels like it can be classified as both internal and external, the company fine-tunes its risk statement to make it more granular until it maps clearly to one source. Consider this risk statement at Julia's Cookies:

> "Customer dissatisfaction may result in loss of customers and sales revenue."

"Customer dissatisfaction" is a high-level term. It could be an internal risk that comes from issues with products—such as a new cookie recipe that was not properly researched before being offered to customers—or an external risk that comes from customers preferring a competitor's prices or products. Before the ERM team at Julia's Cookies can address this risk, it needs to be fine-tuned into granular risk statements that clearly identify a singular source:

> "Customers preferring a competitor's products may result in loss of customers and sales revenue." This is an external risk related to market competition and strategy.

> "Poorly researching a new cookie recipe may result in poor reception by customers and a loss of sales revenue." This is an internal risk related to operations.

Internal and external risks can each be classified into three different, commonly encountered risk categories. **Table 2.2** summarizes the six types of risk.

Internal Risks

Internal risk is categorized as operational, financial, or reputational risk.

Operational Risk

The most important type of risk for AIS is **operational risk**, which occurs during day-to-day business operations and causes breakdowns in business activities. These risks are a priority for AIS because they result from inadequate or failed procedures within the company. The computer system

TABLE 2.2 Six Types of Risk and Examples

Source	Type	Example
Internal risks	Operational	Technology interruption
	Financial	Failed investments
	Reputational	Data breach making the news
External risks	Compliance	Regulatory fines
	Strategic	Beaten by competitor
	Physical	Natural disasters

could fail, employees could commit fraud, or procedures could fail to outline the proper steps in a business process. Throughout this course, we take an in-depth look at many different operational risks.

The previous example of delivery drivers for Julia's Cookies is an operational risk; it stems from daily business operations within the company. Other operational risks related to delivery drivers include a driver failing to arrive at work on time, delivery vehicles failing to start due to mechanical issues, and GPS system failures causing drivers to get lost during deliveries.

A specific subset of operational risk that is of interest to AIS is technology risk. **Technology risk** exists when technology failures have the potential to disrupt business. Technology failures include threats, vulnerabilities, and exposures of information.

Have you ever waited until the last minute to submit an assignment to an online course portal like Blackboard or Canvas? If it is 11:55 p.m. and your assignment is due at 11:59 p.m., you face the risk that a slow internet connection or computer crash will prevent your submission from being uploaded in time. A business considers similar technology risks. For example, power outages or poor connections can result in interruption of company operations. Other serious technology concerns include fraud, cybercrime (like data breaches), security issues, and the condition of physical equipment.

For Julia's Cookies' delivery drivers, a GPS system failure is a technology risk. A more serious technology risk Julia's Cookies faces is the increased traffic on its mobile app during peak times of the day. More customers placing orders at once may cause the mobile app to crash. This is an internal, operational technology risk!

Cyber risk is a unique type of technology risk that occurs when an external party accesses the company's technology assets and performs unauthorized actions that are malicious. Cyberattacks can cause data breaches, lock down a company's systems and hold them for ransom, or even be meant simply to prove that the attacker has the skill needed to perform the attack successfully. You will explore technology risk throughout this course as it relates to specific business processes, and you will also look at stand-alone risks specific to a company's technological infrastructure.

Financial Risks

While most risks can result in financial loss, **financial risk** specifically refers to money going into and out of a company and the potential loss of a substantial sum. This type of risk is associated with financial transactions of various types, including investments, sales, purchases, and loans. We will not go into detail about the different types of financial risk, but it is important to understand that financial transactions create a unique type of risk.

Julia's Cookies began as a startup by accepting money from venture capital investors—specialized investors who take on the high risk of investing in a startup because they understand that the return if the company is successful can be quite large. To supplement the remaining money it needed to launch, Julia's Cookies took out some large loans. Large amounts of debt increase financial risk because changes to interest rates can cause large additional costs, and the inability to pay back debt can cause significant financial losses—and even bankruptcy.

Reputational Risks

Reputational risk occurs when the reputation—or good name—of a company is damaged. With reputational risk comes financial loss through a loss of customers and revenue. Reputational risk can be both internal and external in nature. We classify it as internal because a company can reduce reputational risk by implementing appropriate policies, safety procedures, and customer relations initiatives. The exact financial loss tied to a reputational risk is hard to quantify, but reputation is so important to a company that in accounting we consider it an intangible asset.

Reputational risk has grown in importance as more people use and access social media. Once on the internet, posts and reviews can't be reversed. Companies must monitor these sources of complaints to prevent public relations nightmares. Not all customer posts are negative. Many very happy customers post about a business or its products; however, it is that one negative post that will be remembered. **Illustration 2.5** shows Julia's Cookies tagged in a tweet by a dissatisfied customer.

Illustration 2.5 Social media poses a major reputational risk to businesses.

Keep in mind that reputational risk doesn't only stem from customer dissatisfaction. Remember the risk statement concerning a Julia's Cookies' delivery driver getting in a car accident? There is a reputational risk that the community will not want to order from Julia's Cookies if the company's drivers cause multiple car accidents and injuries due to lack of safety training. Volkswagen faced reputation risk when its sales dropped as more and more countries started penalizing the company for noncompliance of emission norms (see In the Real World).

External Risks

External risks are less predictable and harder to control than internal risks. The three external risks we discuss are compliance, strategic, and physical risks.

Compliance Risk

Compliance risk occurs when a company fails to follow regulation and legislation and is subjected to legal penalties, including fines. Between changing laws and business growth, it can be hard to keep up with applicable regulations:

- Julia's Cookies started in San Francisco as a local bakery and was subject to health codes.
- When its mobile app expanded its online presence, the company had to follow online commerce regulations.

In the Real World   Volkswagen Emissions Scandal[1]

Warren Buffet said it best: "It takes 20 years to build a reputation and five minutes to ruin it."

Volkswagen, founded in 1937, is the world's largest automaker in car production. It has a long history of serving customers worldwide. Volkswagen climbed to success by building trust with its customers. Its reputation took a major hit when in early 2017, the automaker pleaded guilty to three criminal felony charges related to defrauding the U.S. government.

Let's look at what happened.

The Fraud	The U.S. Environmental Protection Agency (EPA) found that Volkswagen cheated the emissions tests using software attached to the car's engine so that they can sell those cars in the United States.
The Method	It was found that 482,000 Volkswagen cars sold in the United States had a "defeat device"—or software—in diesel engines that could detect that they were being tested, and alter their performances accordingly to lower emissions. However, when on road, the engines emitted nitrogen oxide pollutants up to 40 times above what is allowed in the United States.
The Motivation	Volkswagen has had a major push to sell diesel cars in the United States, backed by a huge marketing campaign focusing on cars' low emissions.
The Discovery	A nonprofit public policy think tank, the International Council on Clean Transportation (ICCT) performed independent—and crucial on-road—emissions tests on the Volkswagen cars that were detected with the unusual difference in the performance of on-road and stationary tests and referred the case to the EPA.
The "Income"	Volkswagen admitted that about 11 million cars sold worldwide, including 8 million in Europe, were fitted with the so-called defeat device.
The Costs	The investigations started in the United States and were initiated across the United Kingdom, Italy, France, South Korea, Canada, and Germany. This led to Volkswagen recalling 8.5 million cars in Europe, including 2.4 million in Germany and 1.2 million in the United Kingdom, and 500,000 in the United States. With Volkswagen recalling millions of cars worldwide, it set aside €6.7 billion to cover costs. The cost to the company was €31.3 billion in fines and settlements as in 2020.

Volkswagen's sales dropped significantly and its reputation took a beating as more and more countries started penalizing the company for noncompliance of emission norms. The company rebuilt itself in terms of leadership, by restructuring the organization, redeveloping strategy, and rebranding the products to move away from the scandal.[2]

Did you know about this fraud? What are your impressions about Volkswagen after knowing about this fraud? How is Volkswagen doing now?

- Launching its first gluten-free cookie option required compliance with Food and Drug Administration (FDA) regulations for labeling.
- As the company began shipping raw cookie dough out of state to website customers, interstate shipping regulations became a concern.
- When Julia's Cookies decided to become a publicly traded company, it had to comply with new financial regulations.
- Now, as Julia's Cookies prepares to open its first international store, extensive research must be done into the regulatory requirements in a new country.

Failing to comply with regulations can lead to substantial legal penalties, financial losses, and even reputational loss. Would you want to purchase a car if you knew the manufacturer had recently been fined for violating safety regulations when installing seatbelts? Probably not.

Strategic Risk

Remember when we said not all risk is bad? **Strategic risk** is the inevitable risk that results when a strategy becomes less effective. Companies constantly update their strategies—and change their risks—to stay ahead of the competition. Adopting new technology, overhauling a product design, and changing vendors to avoid high costs of materials are all examples of companies taking proactive measures to avoid strategic risk.

[1]https://www.bbc.com/news/business-34324772
[2]https://www.emerald.com/insight/content/doi/10.1108/JBS-04-2018-0068/full/html

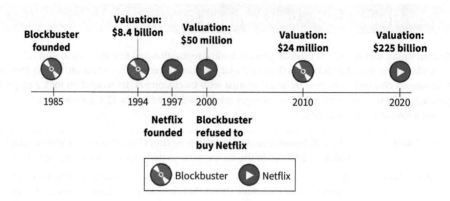

Illustration 2.6 Blockbuster passed on the opportunity to buy Netflix in 2000.

When companies face strategic risk, they either adapt or fail. Consider Blockbuster. In September 2000, the CEO of Blockbuster was given the option to purchase Netflix for $50 million. Netflix had been requesting meetings with Blockbuster for months, in hopes of striking a deal. At the time, Netflix was losing money steadily and worried about bankruptcy. Netflix was desperate for Blockbuster's investment. The Blockbuster CEO turned down the opportunity—refusing to even counteroffer Netflix's $50 million asking price. Both companies were faced with strategic risk. Blockbuster's strategy was to deny the internet boom as a potential success and pursue other avenues. The movie-rental-store giant partnered with Enron and turned its back on the first major development of wide-scale movie streaming because the company was too focused on its then-lucrative brick-and-mortar stores. In the end, Blockbuster failed and filed for bankruptcy with $1 billion of debt (**Illustration 2.6**).

After being rejected by Blockbuster, Netflix faced potential bankruptcy. Instead of accepting this strategic risk, the company adapted, innovated, and moved on. Netflix's founders looked at their business from the customer's perspective and focused on a 5- to 10-year plan that was continuously updated. In 2021, the streaming giant was valued at $260 billion.

Physical Risk

Threats such as adverse weather, crimes, and physical damage are **physical risks**. Physical risk is the easiest type of risk to understand, and it is one of the most important types of risk to identify because the impact is usually high. The losses from physical risks range from financial loss to legal actions and reputational loss due to mismanagement of assets. Physical risks in the form of disasters are a key priority for businesses. Entire career fields are devoted to recovering a business from disrupted operations. We talk about how businesses respond to the potential of disruptions throughout this course.

Risk Inventory

CPA Once a company has identified and categorized risks, the risks are compiled into a **risk inventory**, which is a listing of all the business's known risks. Using an entity-wide risk inventory allows the ERM team to map risks to business objectives, business processes, and one another. This is an essential part of approaching risk at the entity level and creating a portfolio view.

Why Does It Matter to Your Career?

Thoughts from a Lead IT Auditor, Health Care

Risk categorization is deceptive. It seems like an easy concept, but in application it is complex. As with most things surrounding risk, there are not often clear answers. Risk is a gray area that requires critical-thinking skills and willingness to step outside the box. For categorization, you must be willing to take your original idea and rework it until it fits into categories.

See if you can identify internal and external risks for Julia's Cookies in Applied Learning 2.2.

| Julia's Cookies | Applied Learning 2.2 |

Categorizing Risks: Boise Store

Recall the three risk statements identified for the Julia's Cookies store in Boise (Applied Learning 2.1):

1. An employee calling in sick for the 7:00 a.m. shift *may result in* lack of store coverage during the 9:00 a.m. delivery.

2. A malfunction in the only oven onsite *may result in* store operations closing for the day.

3. A slow week of sales *may result in* increased expenses and reduced profits because large amounts of expired products must be discarded.

Is each of these risks internal or external?

SOLUTION

All three of these risks are internal risks. Specifically, they are all operational risks; each is the result of Julia's Cookies' operations. These risks are preventable: Julia's Cookies can change the way it operates to address each of these risks.

CONCEPT REVIEW QUESTIONS

1. What are internal risks?

   Ans. Internal risks occur throughout a company's operations and arise during the normal course of business operations. These risks may relate to an external party, such as the company's reputation with customers. Most internal risks are preventable through careful risk identification and management.

2. What do you understand by external risks?

   Ans. Risks that are unrelated to business operations and whose source is from outside the company are called external risks. These are difficult to control as compared to internal risks. While external risks are often unpredictable, companies still prepare for them to the best of their abilities.

3. What are operational risks?

   Ans. Operational risks are internal risks and these affect the AIS too. These risks are a priority for AIS because they result from inadequate or failed procedures within the company and affect normal business activities. For instance, the computer system could fail, employees could commit fraud, or procedures could fail to outline the proper steps in the business process.

4. What is common between technology risk and operational risk?

   Ans. Technology risk is a subset of operational risk. It is caused during business operations. Technology risk exists when technology failures have the potential to disrupt business activities. Technology failures include threats, vulnerabilities, and exposures of information.

5. What is cyber risk?

   Ans. Cyber risk is a unique technology risk that occurs when an external party accesses the company's technology assets and performs malicious and unauthorized actions. Cyberattacks can cause data breaches, lock down a company's systems, and hold them to ransom.

6. What do you understand by the term "financial risk"?

   Ans. Financial risk refers to the risks and chances of losses associated with an investment. The risk is classified as an internal risk. This type of risk is associated with financial transactions of various types, including investments, sales, purchases, and loans.

7. What is meant by reputational risk?
   Ans. Reputational risk occurs when the reputation of a company is damaged. It can be both internal and external. Reputational risk has now become important as more people use and access social media.

8. What is strategic risk?
   Ans. Strategic risk is the inevitable risk that results when a strategy becomes less effective. Companies constantly update their strategies—and change their risks—to stay ahead of the competition.

9. **CPA** What is a risk inventory?
   Ans. Risk inventory is a listing of all the business's known risks. Using an entity-wide risk inventory allows the ERM team to map risks to business objectives, business processes, and one another. This is an essential part of approaching risk at the entity level and creating a portfolio view.

2.3 How Do We Prioritize Risk?

Learning Objective ❸
Determine the quantitative value of risk.

Prioritize

How can you determine how serious a risk is? The answer will vary depending on the industry the business is in. In the software industry, the biggest risks are typically technology risks, since these companies use software to support their operations and sell software products to customers. In farming, physical risk may be of the highest concern. Adverse weather could destroy an entire crop and put a farm out of business.

Prioritizing risk is a crucial step for businesses. Because companies have limited resources—equipment, space, people, and budgets—they must determine which risks those resources should be used to address. While many methods can be used to prioritize risk, the most common is prioritizing by severity. This may seem like a subjective exercise, but when calculating risk, fact-based, measurable criteria are used as much as possible. A good risk identification and prioritization looks at monetary values, historical data, and external benchmarks.

Evaluating Risk Severity

CPA **Risk severity** is the *likelihood* of risks occurring and their potential *impact* on the company:

- **Likelihood** is the estimated probability of risk occurrence. Companies use different methods to calculate likelihood, but likelihood is always ranked on a spectrum. Data-driven risk analysis applies statistical values, while judgment-based risk analysis makes estimates that rely on the experience of company leaders. In different industries, likelihood can be described as "frequency" or "probability"; these terms are synonymous. We use the term "likelihood" in this course, based on experience in our companies.

- **Impact** is the estimation of damage that could be caused if a risk occurs. Earlier in this chapter, we started with an issue and defined a possible outcome to form a risk statement. The outcome is the impact (**Table 2.3**).

TABLE 2.3 The Outcome of a Risk Statement Is the Impact

Risk Statement		
Issue		**Impact**
Drivers not receiving road safety training	*may result in*	Julia's Cookies paying monetary fines and damages in lawsuits from victims of accidents

Other terms used for impact include "magnitude" and "consequence." Impact is measured on a scale, just like likelihood. Impact consists of different types of damage that can occur. Financial, customer, and reputational loss are some of the many factors that companies consider to determine overall impact.

CPA Likelihood and impact are measured on a scale from low to high. Some companies use these words, and others apply numeric values. We'll explore how numeric values can be helpful later. For now, **Illustration 2.7** shows the scale of terms used to rank both likelihood and impact. Risks are prioritized using *both* factors—never just one. For example, the likelihood for Julia's Cookies' risk of a delivery driver getting into a car accident is medium low (ML); that is, it is somewhat unlikely. The impact of vehicle damage, reputational damage, legal fines, and even loss of life are high (H); these outcomes are extreme and highly undesirable.

As a student, you prioritize risk without realizing it. For example, you prioritize risk when you organize your study schedule. If you have two finals coming up on the same day, you may calculate what grade you need to earn on each test to achieve your desired overall grade. Time is your limited resource, and you need to allocate it appropriately. The factors you need to consider are the class where you need a higher exam grade and the exam you most need to study for to do well. By combining the outcomes of these two considerations—and identifying for which course the impact and likelihood of a lower final exam grade are higher—you can prioritize the exam to study for.

Now that you have learned about risk levels, help Julia's Cookies' Boise location prioritize the risks it faces in Applied Learning 2.3.

Risk Level	Abbreviation
High	H
Medium High	MH
Medium	M
Medium Low	ML
Low	L

Illustration 2.7 Risk levels range from low to high.

Julia's Cookies   Applied Learning 2.3

Prioritizing Risks: Boise Store

Julia's Cookies' Boise location has already identified (Applied Learning 2.1) and categorized (Applied Learning 2.2) its risk statements, and it's now time to prioritize them.

Rate the likelihood and impact of each risk statement as high, medium high, medium, medium low, or low.

Risk	Likelihood	Impact
1. An employee calling in sick for the 7:00 a.m. shift *may result in* lack of store coverage during the 9:00 a.m. delivery.		
2. A malfunction in the only oven onsite *may result in* store operations closing for the day.		
3. A slow week of sales *may result in* increased expenses and reduced profits because large amounts of expired products must be discarded.		

SOLUTION

While there are no official right or wrong answers here, you might give the risk statements the following ratings:

Risk	Likelihood	Impact
1. An employee calling in sick for the 7:00 a.m. shift *may result in* lack of store coverage during the 9:00 a.m. delivery.	High	Medium
2. A malfunction in the only oven onsite *may result in* store operations closing for the day.	Medium low	High
3. A slow week of sales *may result in* increased expenses and reduced profits because large amounts of expired products must be discarded.	Medium low	Medium

Notice that so far you have not been given a lot of explanation about what "high" and "low" mean. Keep reading to find out how risk formulas bring more clarity to these rankings.

Using Risk Formulas

What happens if you only use the qualitative words for risk prioritization? How do you know that your interpretation of "high" is the same as your boss's interpretation of "high"? When a company uses only qualitative assessments, multiple risks may have the same rankings. To address this, the qualitative approach is first used to assign likelihood and impact, and then a quantitative method is used to score each risk. A point value of 1–5 is applied to the likelihood and impact rankings, with 1 being the lowest and 5 being the highest value. You can then calculate a final risk score by multiplying the two numbers together.

Note that each company will have its own criteria for what each point value means. For Julia's Cookies, **Illustrations 2.8** and **2.9** show criteria used to rank likelihood and impact, respectively. Julia's Cookies considers $25 million to $50 million to be a medium high financial impact, but another company, like a small local business, might consider a medium high risk to be a smaller amount, such as $1 million. Applying formal criteria ensures that everyone in the company has the same understanding of the risk.

Risk Level	Likelihood Score	Category	Annual Occurrence Percentage
High	5	Imminent	> 15%
Medium High	4	Probable	10–15%
Medium	3	Reasonably Possible	5–10%
Medium Low	2	Unlikely	2.5–5%
Low	1	Rare	< 2.5%

Illustration 2.8 Likelihood is scaled from 1 to 5, based on the probability of an outcome occurring.

Risk Level	Impact Score	Category	Financial Impact	Customer Impact	Reputational Impact
High	5	Detrimental	> $50 million	> 10,000	International long-term
Medium High	4	Serious	$25–$50 million	1,000–10,000	National long-term
Medium	3	Moderate	$10–$25 million	100–1,000	National short-term
Medium Low	2	Minor	$1–$10 million	50–100	Local short-term negative
Low	1	Insignificant	< $1 million	< 50	Limited local media

Illustration 2.9 Impact is scaled from 1 to 5, based on the impact the outcome could have on the business.

A risk such as a tsunami might have a low likelihood (scored 1) but a high impact (scored 5), which would result in a risk score of 5. Alternatively, a risk such as an employee forgetting the login password to a company system might have a high likelihood (scored 5) but a low impact (scored 1), which would also result in a risk score of 5. **CPA** Risks with similar risk scores may be treated differently, based on judgmental decision making. Risk scores are often complex, using decimal points, products, averages, and more to eliminate unnecessary information. Every company's approach to risk calculations is different. In other words, there's no universally accepted best practice for how these numbers are generated. For the purposes of this course, the simplified risk calculation of multiplying the two rankings to create a risk score is sufficient to give you an understanding of the purpose of a risk score in prioritizing risks—and this is the most important takeaway from this section.

Julia's Cookies came up with the risk rankings shown in **Table 2.4** for some of its risk statements.

TABLE 2.4 Risk Score Calculations at Julia's Cookies

Risk Statement	Likelihood Score		Impact Score		Risk Score
A. An employee baking cookies in the oven *may result in* a burn.	4	×	2	=	8
Management reasoning: Management evaluated this criterion as "daily accidental burns." People accidentally touch hot surfaces all the time, so a medium high likelihood is appropriate. A quick touch of a hot surface should not send anyone to a hospital, but an employee might have to leave for the day or seek medical attention, which would be a medium low impact.					
B. An employee stealing from a cash register *may result in* loss of cash.	3	×	2	=	6
Management reasoning: While it is tempting to steal cash, the likelihood is only reasonably probable. Furthermore, since most people order and pay through the app, there is very little cash at any single store, so the impact on the company would be insignificant.					

TABLE 2.4 (*Continued*)

Risk Statement	Likelihood Score		Impact Score		Risk Score
C. An oven fire *may result in* destruction of a store.	1	×	5	=	5
Management reasoning: While it would be detrimental if a store burned down (high impact), the likelihood of that happening is low, as there aren't very many fires daily, and most fires are contained before destroying an entire store.					
D. A delivery driver getting into a car accident while delivering cookies *may result in* injuries to drivers and others in the accident.	2	×	5	=	10
Management reasoning: Management evaluated this criterion as a worst-case scenario. The likelihood is low, but if someone is injured, the impact could be significant.					
E. A cybersecurity attack *may result in* theft of customer data.	3	×	5	=	15
Management reasoning: A cookie company isn't a prime target for a cybersecurity attack, which is why the ranking is medium. However, if an attack happened, all of the credit card numbers of customers would be compromised, which would be a high impact.					
F. A store employee getting sick *may result in* the employee backing out of a shift at the last minute.	5	×	1	=	5
Management's reasoning: It's unavoidable that employees will get sick. Shifts are scheduled in such a way that the impact of a sick employee is minimal.					

Once each of the risks has a rank for likelihood and impact, management multiplies the values to create the final risk score. The highest-scored items are the highest priority for a company to address. **Table 2.5** shows how Julia's Cookies prioritizes these risks.

TABLE 2.5 Prioritization of Risks at Julia's Cookies

Risk Score	Risk
15	(E) A cybersecurity attack *may result in* theft of customer data.
10	(D) A delivery driver getting into a car accident while delivering cookies *may result in* injuries to drivers and others in the accident.
8	(A) Employees baking cookies in the oven *may result in* a burn.
6	(B) An employee stealing from a cash register *may result in* loss of cash.
5	(C) An oven fire *may result in* destruction of a store.
5	(F) A store employee getting sick *may result in* the employee backing out of a shift at the last minute.

Note specifically where risks (C) and (F) fall in this prioritization. Both have the same risk score of 5. Risk ranks for impact and likelihood might use decimals to further prioritize items. We have simplified this example for learning purposes by using only whole numbers. Ties still occur, and many times, when there is a tie between risks, management will prioritize the risks that have the highest impact.

Why Does It Matter to Your Career?

Thoughts from a Risk and Advisory Specialist, Telecommunications

The ability to identify the likelihood and impact of risks is a key part of the job for many accounting professionals—especially those who work in public accounting, internal audit, or advisory services. For example, a risk and advisory consultant will perform a risk assessment and meet with the company's leadership to help make decisions on where to invest company resources.

Creating Risk Matrices

CPA A **risk matrix** helps paint a clearer picture of risk than just a number. Recall that Table 2.4 includes likelihood and impact spanning from low to high for different risks. Some of the risks in that table have the same final risk score, and it is impossible to tell at a glance which of them is more serious. A risk matrix like the one shown in **Illustration 2.10** helps users visualize variations in risk scores. Using a risk matrix allows management to plot risk and move prioritization around; this is especially helpful for the risks that are scored the same numerically. Each of the boxes in Illustration 2.10 represents a likelihood and impact combination. The letter or letters before the dash indicate the impact, and the letter or letters after the dash indicate the likelihood. For example, the risk of a delivery driver getting into a car accident is ranked "H–ML" because it has an H impact and an ML likelihood.

	H–L	H–ML	H–M	H–MH	H–H
	MH–L	MH–ML	MH–M	MH–MH	MH–H
Impact	M–L	M–ML	M–M	M–MH	M–H
	ML–L	ML–ML	ML–M	ML–MH	ML–H
	L–L	L–ML	L–M	L–MH	L–H

Likelihood

Illustration 2.10 Risk rankings appear on a colored heat map.

CPA A **heat map** is a type of risk matrix that uses different colors to represent values of data in a map or diagram format. The different colors in the risk matrix heat map in Illustration 2.10 represent the priority of a risk based on the risk score; green is lower priority, and red is higher priority. Note that some of the squares on the heat map are the same color despite having different scores for likelihood and impact. This is because some risks may have different locations on the risk map but are considered equal in prioritization. For example, the MH–L, M–ML, ML–M, and L–MH squares are all the same shade of yellow. These four squares on the heat map have risk score values near one another.

A heat map provides a holistic, big-picture view of risk. Risk analysts can use a heat map to easily explain to management which areas are the highest risk for the company. However, it is important to remember that a heat map is only as good as the risk identification, categorization, and prioritization steps taken to calculate the risk scores.

Illustration 2.11 shows Julia's Cookies' risks plotted in a heat map. Even though two of the risks, (C) and (F), have a risk score of 5, they are in different areas of the risk matrix. This is because they have inverse values for impact and likelihood rankings.

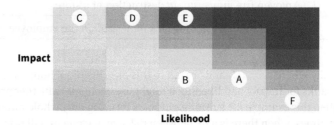

Impact

Likelihood

Illustration 2.11 Julia's Cookies' risks plotted on the likelihood versus impact matrix.

CONCEPT REVIEW QUESTIONS

1. **CPA** Define likelihood and impact in the context of risk severity and assessment.

    Ans. Likelihood is the estimated probability of risk occurrence. Companies use different methods to calculate likelihood, but likelihood is always ranked on a spectrum. In different industries, likelihood can be described as "frequency" or "probability."

    Impact is the estimation of damage that could be caused if a risk occurs. The outcome is the impact. Other terms used for impact include "magnitude" and "consequence." Impact is measured on a scale, just like likelihood. Impact consists of different types of damage that can occur. Financial, customer, and reputational loss are some of the many factors that companies consider to determine overall impact.

2. **CPA** What is meant by risk severity?
   Ans. Risk severity is the likelihood of risks occurring and their potential impact on the company.

3. **CPA** What are risk scores?
   Ans. Risk scores are often complex, using decimal points, products, averages, and more to eliminate unnecessary information. Every company's approach to risk calculations is different. In other words, there's no universally accepted best practice to generate these numbers.

4. What is the difference between data-driven and judgment-based risk analysis?
   Ans. Data-driven risk analysis applies statistical values, while judgment-based risk analysis makes estimations that rely on the experience of company leaders.

5. **CPA** What is a risk matrix?
   Ans. A risk matrix is a risk analysis tool that presents a clearer picture of risk than just a number. Using a risk matrix allows management to plot risk and move prioritization around, specifically when the risks are scored the same numerically. For example, the risk of a delivery driver getting into a car accident is ranked "H–ML" because it has a high (H) impact and medium low (ML) likelihood.

6. **CPA** What is a heat map?
   Ans. A heat map is a type of risk matrix that uses different colors to represent values of data in a map or diagram format. The risk priority is based on the risk score interpreted as green being a lower priority and red being a higher priority. A heat map provides a holistic, big-picture view of a risk. Risk analysts can use a heat map to easily explain to management which areas are the highest risk for the company.

2.4 How Do We Respond to Risk?

Learning Objective ❹
Explain how businesses respond to risk.

Risk management is a complex part of a business. It requires critical-thinking and decision-making skills to understand the entire situation and come up with the appropriate combination of risk responses. Companies are becoming more risk aware and seeking individuals who specialize in this area, so careers in risk management are growing. The U.S. Bureau of Labor and Statistics anticipates a 17% growth rate from 2020 to 2030 in jobs for financial managers, especially those with a focus on risk management.[3] Accounting professionals are uniquely qualified for work in this area due to their training in business processes, risk identification, and holistic business operations.

Regardless of the size of a business, risk is always present, and companies are constantly managing risk. You have learned that risk assessment involves identifying, categorizing, and prioritizing risks. Now it is time to learn the last step of ERM: responding to the risk.

Respond

In smaller companies, it is the responsibility of the leadership team and executives to manage risk. If a company is large enough, then risk management is also part of the board of directors' responsibilities. To decide the optimal risk response, risk management professionals must calculate a risk's likelihood and its potential impact on the success of the business. From there, risks are prioritized, and a risk response is chosen for each risk. **CPA** Illustration 2.12 shows the four traditional risk responses from which to choose. You'll learn more about each of these risk responses in the next section, but for now it's

[3]www.bls.gov/ooh/management/financial-managers.htm#tab-6

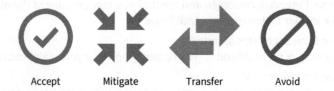

Illustration 2.12 The four traditional risk responses are accept, mitigate, transfer, and avoid.

Accept   Mitigate   Transfer   Avoid

important to know that companies implement different types of responses based on each risk they face.

When selecting one of these risk responses, a company must also consider its risk appetite. **Risk appetite** is the amount of risk a company is willing to take on at a particular time. Risk appetite is part of a company's culture. When considering it at the entity level, the risk appetite for the entire business is taken into consideration. For example, if a company has already taken on a lot of risk by adopting new communications software for its sales department, it may not want to take on the risk of migrating its email system at the same time. To ensure that the new email client migration fits its risk appetite, a company could choose a risk response that minimizes the risks the new project brings.

Why Does It Matter to Your Career?

Thoughts from an Internal Audit Analytics Manager, Financial Services

You can apply these same principles at a project level for your job. You will encounter risks daily! Knowing how your team can react to them will help you make appropriate decisions. Should you try new data analytics software in the middle of busy season? Probably not. Trying it during the down season may be less risky.

Assess the Risk

Risk is either inherent or residual. This classification is different from classification into a specific type, such as operational risk. Inherent and residual refer to the nature of the risk. It helps to think of them as the "before" and "after" of risk response.

Inherent Risk

Before a business takes any action to address a risk, that risk is considered an inherent risk. **CPA** **Inherent risk** is the natural level of risk in a business process or activity if there are no risk responses in place. It is the risk *before* implementing a risk response. Inherent risk consists of two parts—likelihood and impact—which you learned to calculate while prioritizing risks.

Consider the risk of damaging your smart phone to the point that it can't be repaired. If you are clumsy and have dropped your phone in the past, if you carry your phone in your pocket with your keys, or if you work on a construction site and use your phone while you work, then the likelihood of damaging your phone is higher than if you carry it in a dedicated pocket in your bag and have never dropped it. Assume in this instance that the likelihood of damaging your phone is a 3.

Next, the impact must be identified. For your smart phone, the impact of replacing it will depend on the model. Damaging the latest iPhone purchased through your mobile service provider will have a higher impact than damaging a budget phone due to the cost of replacement. Assume in this instance that the impact of replacing the phone is a 4.

Recall that the likelihood and impact are multiplied, and the product is the risk score. In this case, you face an inherent risk of 12 ($4 \times 3 = 12$). **Illustration 2.13** shows what this inherent risk score of 12 looks like on a heat map.

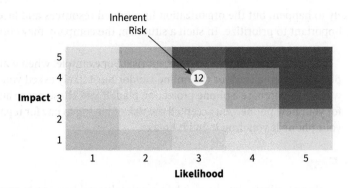

Illustration 2.13 The inherent risk of damaging a cell phone is plotted on a heat map.

Residual Risk

After conducting a risk assessment, an organization chooses a risk response to decide how to deal with each risk, which you'll learn more about in the next section. **CPA** **Residual risk** is the remaining risk posed by a process or an activity once a plan to respond to the risk is in place. It is the risk *after* implementing a risk response. Companies establish a **target residual risk**, which is the goal after implementing a risk response, and they also measure the **actual residual risk**, which is what really happens after the risk is addressed.

The inherent risk of damaging a smart phone beyond repair may be very high for a construction worker who carries the latest iPhone. Using a heavy-duty case for the phone is a type of risk response. That is, the phone case decreases the likelihood of damaging the phone beyond repair. So, the inherent risk minus the safety provided by the case results in the residual risk.

Let's assume that using a heavy-duty phone case decreases the risk of damaging your phone beyond repair by 50%. The phone case makes it less likely that you will damage your phone if you drop it, and it also lessens the impact. **Illustration 2.14** shows how the inherent risk score of 12 decreases by 50% to create a residual risk score of 6. Here, risk response is a percentage translated into a numeric value to place the risk on the heat map.

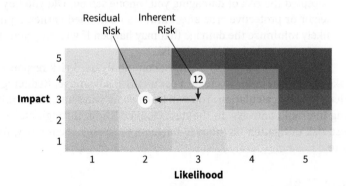

Illustration 2.14 The residual risk of damaging a cell phone moves the risk score lower on a heat map.

The residual risk is compared to the company's risk appetite to determine if the risk response is adequate. If a company is not comfortable with the residual risk, it changes its risk response until the residual risk is acceptable. In the case of your cell phone, if you were uncomfortable with a risk score of 6, you would seek out additional or different risk responses to bring the residual risk score down further.

Respond to the Risk

Now that you have learned how companies determine if a risk response is adequate by calculating residual risk, let's examine the four types of risk response a company can use. These responses can be used individually or in combination with one another to address risk.

Accept the Risk

CPA **Risk acceptance** occurs when an inherent risk is present but the organization chooses not to act. Sometimes a risk is small or unlikely to happen. Other times a risk may be large or likely to happen, but the organization has limited resources and faces other risks that are more important to prioritize. In such a situation, the company may choose to accept the risk.

 We all sometimes choose to accept risk. For example, when you bought your phone, the store clerk or the online vendor most likely asked you whether you wanted to purchase a phone protection plan. If you chose not to buy that option for your new phone, you accepted the risk of having to pay for repairs or replace your phone if you drop it and it breaks.

Avoid the Risk

CPA **Risk avoidance** eliminates the risk by completely avoiding the events causing the risk. Rather than accept or reduce risk, companies avoid risk when it is both significant and highly likely to occur. For example, a company may eliminate the source of a risk, such as eliminating a product line or closing stores in a particularly high-risk geographic location.

 You may not be able to reasonably avoid risk entirely. In the smart phone example, the only way to avoid the risk to your smart phone is to not purchase it. But many of us use our phones throughout the day, for work and otherwise. Not having a phone is not a realistic option for many people! Similarly, a company is often unable to completely avoid risk and will choose to partially avoid the risk while using an additional risk response for what it can't avoid.

Mitigate the Risk

CPA When a company decides to accept the risk but to minimize its impact in the event that it occurs, the firm mitigates the risk internally by implementing methods or procedures that affect business processes and activities or using other mitigation tools to reduce the risk.

We know that if you chose not to purchase the phone protection plan, you accepted the risk of damaging your phone screen. Did you buy a screen protector or protective case afterward? As mentioned earlier, a phone case will likely minimize the damage that may happen if you drop your phone. When you use one, you mitigate the risk.

Risk mitigation is the most commonly used risk response. It enables a company to take on risks in order to create a competitive advantage. Reducing risk requires careful consideration and calculation. You will learn about ways businesses mitigate risks—including using internal controls—in the next chapter. Then, throughout this course, you will apply those risk mitigation methods to business processes, technology, fraud opportunities, and more.

Transfer the Risk

CPA **Risk transfer** involves shifting a risk to a third party. In other words, a third party assumes the liabilities for the risk. Most often, this is done through a contract. For example, an insurance policy transfers risk from an individual to an insurance company. Transferring the risk in this way comes with associated costs, like insurance policy premiums.

 Returning to our phone example, if you know that you tend to often drop your phone, the likelihood of damage is high. The insurance policy you were offered may cost significantly less than a new phone or repairs. If you accept the phone protection plan offer, you transfer the risk to a third party, and you can rest assured that the costs of damage to the phone are covered by the insurance company.

A company's choice of risk response is not as simple as picking one of the four responses just discussed. Companies can minimize residual risk through a combination of risk responses. **CPA** However, there will always be residual risk, regardless of the combination of responses. In this sense, some level of risk acceptance is inevitable. Risk management requires deciding how much residual risk is acceptable and what combination of risk responses will be most effective in getting there. Cost-benefit analysis and feasibility play a huge role in the selection of responses. For example, Julia's Cookies can't completely avoid the inherent risks of using equipment like ovens without changing its entire business model, so it chooses the best combination of responses to achieve an acceptable level of residual risk. Test your ability to select an appropriate risk response combination in Applied Learning 2.4.

Now that you have learned the four parts of ERM, you are ready to learn more about risk mitigation and its importance to the accounting profession in the next chapter.

Julia's Cookies | Applied Learning 2.4

Selecting a Risk Response: Oven Fires

Julia's Cookies' mission statement includes "satisfy late-night cravings by delivering delicious cookies from our kitchens to your doors." This means that Julia's Cookies acknowledges in its mission statement that its stores use ovens on their premises. While using ovens seems like an everyday activity, ovens involve inherent risks. One of the biggest risks is that an oven could start a fire and burn down a Julia's Cookies store. Julia's Cookies believes there is a moderate likelihood that this could happen and that the impact would be a significant financial loss to the company.

Using the four traditional types of risk response, what combination of the following do you recommend to Julia's Cookies?

1. *Risk acceptance*

   Julia's Cookies can accept the risk that a store might burn down. If this happens, Julia's Cookies will be financially responsible for the losses.

2. *Risk avoidance*

   Julia's Cookies can avoid the risk of using ovens by only selling prepared cookie dough for customers to bake at home.

3. *Risk mitigation*

   Julia's Cookies can mitigate the risk by installing smoke detectors, buying state-of-the-art fire extinguishers, training employees for emergency response, following the fire code, and periodically undergoing inspections.

4. *Risk transference*

   Julia's Cookies can transfer the risk of losses to a third party by purchasing a fire insurance policy.

SOLUTION

1. This risk response is not recommended for Julia's Cookies. The likelihood and impact of a fire are too high to accept.
2. This risk response changes the entire business model of Julia's Cookies. It is not recommended unless the company wants to change its business model for other reasons.
3. This risk response is a good approach. These mitigations lessen the impact of a fire spreading so far that it burns down an entire building. They also reduce the likelihood of such fires by including preventive measures such as following fire codes and conducting inspections.
4. This risk response is a good approach as well. Transferring the risk to an insurance company will reduce the impact of the financial losses in the event of the risk happening. This response does not address the likelihood of a fire occurring, though.

The best choice for Julia's Cookies is a combination of risk mitigation (3) and risk transference (4). Together, these options provide more protection to lessen both the impact of a fire and the likelihood that it will happen.

CONCEPT REVIEW QUESTIONS

1. What is meant by risk appetite?

   Ans. Risk appetite is the amount of risk a company is willing to take on at a particular time. It is part of a company's culture.

2. **CPA** What is an inherent risk?

   Ans. Inherent risk is the natural level of risk in a business process or activity if there are no risk responses in place. It is the risk before implementing a risk response. Inherent risk consists of two parts—likelihood and impact.

3. Distinguish between target and actual residual risks?

   Ans. Residual risk is the remaining risk posed by a process or an activity once a plan to respond to the risk is in place. It is the risk after implementing a risk response. Companies establish a target residual risk, which is the goal after implementing a risk response, and they also measure the actual residual risk, which is what really happens after the risk is addressed.

4. **CPA** What is the meaning of risk acceptance?

   Ans. Risk acceptance occurs when an inherent risk is present, but the organization chooses not to act. Sometimes a risk is small or unlikely to happen. Other times a risk may be large or likely to happen. However, the organization has limited resources and faces other more important risks to prioritize. In such a situation, the company may choose to accept the risk.

5. **CPA** What is meant by risk avoidance?

   Ans. Risk avoidance eliminates the risk by completely avoiding the events causing the risk. Rather than accept or reduce risk, companies avoid risk when it is significant and highly likely to occur.

6. **CPA** What is risk mitigation?

   Ans. Risk mitigation is the most commonly used risk response. It enables a company to take on risks in order to create a competitive advantage. Reducing risk requires careful consideration and calculation.

7. **CPA** What is risk transfer, and how is it done?

   Ans. Risk transfer involves shifting risk to a third party. In other words, a third party assumes the liabilities for the risk. Most often, this is done through a contract. For example, an insurance policy transfers risk from an individual to an insurance company.

FEATURED PROFESSIONAL | Nontraditional CPA Firm

Photo courtesy of Donny Shimamoto

Donny Shimamoto, CPA, CITP, CGMA

Donny started his career in a Big Four firm and later founded his own consulting and management team, which he considers a "nontraditional CPA firm." It specializes in organizational development and business process improvements. Donny uses his expertise and experience from Big Four clients to leverage cost-effective enterprise technology to enable small and mid-sized organizations to gain a competitive advantage. His firm strategically applies the right technology to solve problems and improve the quality of information available to management to enable better, fact-based decision making.

Why is it important for accounting students to learn about risk assessment? How will understanding risk assessment and risk responses be relevant in their first two years on the job?

As more of the transactional work in accounting becomes automated, the role of accountants will shift to focus on either information insights (e.g., data analysis) or risk assessment. As an entry-level auditor (internal or external), you need to be able to assess an entity's risks and control environment so that you can properly focus your audit procedures. If you are going into finance, you also need to be able to identify where there may be risk so that you can help reduce your organization's risks. Being able to do this well in either case demonstrates strong critical-thinking skills and will help you to stand out from your peers and advance your career.

In what ways have you seen your clients struggle with risk management?

Risk assessment is an art, not a science—and the effectiveness of a company's risk management process is only as good as the professional judgment of those involved in doing risk assessment and designing mitigation strategies. Part of what makes me strong at assessing risk is that I have worked with many organizations in different industries, so I have seen a lot of different approaches to mitigating the same types of risks. I have also seen what works and what doesn't work—and when something didn't work, how a client changed things to make it more effective. Conversely, clients who have only worked in or seen a few organizations may only know one or two ways to address a particular risk—so their ability to envision other approaches to mitigating the risk may be more limited.

Do you think it is better to look at risk at a business-process level only or to approach it from an enterprise-wide risk management perspective?

You actually need to do both. Just like when we look at financial statements, we look at individual accounts and also the financial statements as a whole; you must do the same with risk. Materiality concepts have parallel, too. A large number of immaterial exceptions at the account level may become material at the financial statement level, and a lot of low-risk situations in individual business processes may turn into moderate or high risks when aggregated to the enterprise level.

Review and Practice

Key Terms Review

actual residual risk	likelihood	risk avoidance
business function	operational risk	risk inventory
compliance risk	physical risk	risk matrix
cyber risk	portfolio view	risk mitigation
enterprise risk management (ERM)	profile view	risk severity
external risk	reputational risk	risk statement
financial risk	residual risk	risk transfer
heat map	risk	strategic risk
impact	risk acceptance	target residual risk
inherent risk	risk appetite	technology risk
internal risk	risk assessment	

Learning Objectives Review

① Describe the nature of risk.

Anything that can possibly hinder a business in achieving its goals or cause a loss is an unfavorable event. Risk is the likelihood of an unfavorable event occurring. Companies accept higher risk in exchange for higher rewards.

Risks may be present in business functions, projects, or the entire enterprise. The portfolio view of risk examines the entity-level risks, while the profile view of risk examines the business function or process level. Combining both views optimizes a company's risk assessment and management program.

The four steps of enterprise risk management (ERM) are:

- Identifying
- Categorizing
- Prioritizing
- Responding

Identifying risks requires crafting risk statements that include the issue and possible outcome.

② Classify risks into different risk categories.

Categorizing risks involves determining whether a risk is:

- Internal: Occurring from a company's operations
- External: Coming from outside the company

There are three major internal risk categories:

- Operational risk
- Financial risk
- Reputational risk

There are three major external risk categories:

- Compliance risk
- Strategic risk
- Physical risk

A company can create a risk inventory listing all the business's known risks and map them to business objectives, processes, and each another to look at risk from the entity level and portfolio view.

3 Determine the quantitative value of risk.

Risk severity is determined based on the likelihood and impact of risk. Likelihood and impact are measured from low to high in a risk matrix that includes five levels:

5. High

4. Medium high

3. Medium

2. Medium low

1. Low

After determining the likelihood and impact scores for a risk, an organization can multiply those two numbers to come up with a risk score. For example, at Julia's Cookies, if "An employee baking cookies in an oven may result in a burn" has a likelihood of 4 and an impact of 2, the risk score is 8 ($2 \times 4 = 8$).

Companies use risk matrices to visualize the risk scores of a risk inventory, usually as a heat map:

- Horizontal axis: Likelihood rating
- Vertical axis: Impact rating

4 Explain how businesses respond to risk.

Companies first determine their risk appetites to identify how much risk they are willing to take on at a particular time. This is part of the company's culture.

Before a risk response is implemented, the risk has an inherent risk—the natural level of the risk. After a risk response is implemented, the residual, or remaining, risk is measured. The target residual risk identifies the residual risk the company wishes to achieve, and the actual residual risk measures the risk actually achieved by the risk response.

There are four risk responses:

1. Accept: Participate in the activity without doing anything
2. Mitigate: Use a method or methods to lessen the risk
3. Transfer: Move the risk to a third party
4. Avoid: Don't participate in the activity at all

CPA questions, as well as multiple choice, discussion, analysis and application, and Tableau questions and other resources, are available online.

Multiple Choice Questions

1. (LO 1) _____ is propelling massive and fast-paced changes in how businesses function.

    a. Technology

    b. Accounting

    c. Sales

    d. Service

2. (LO 1) **CPA** Demanding higher performance usually requires accepting more

    a. tolerance.

    b. vision.

    c. risk.

    d. performance severity.

3. (LO 1) A risk statement is composed of an

    a. issue and a categorization.

    b. impact and a possible outcome.

    c. issue and a possible outcome.

    d. issue and a risk score.

4. (LO 1) **Fraud** Which of the following is *not* an example of a risk statement?

    a. Delivery drivers not receiving road safety training may result in reputational damage due to accidents in the community.

    b. Unauthorized access to the data center may result in physical theft of computer equipment.

    c. A single employee authorizing and paying invoices may result in fraudulent payments being disbursed to fake vendors.

    d. Adopting new technology may result in gaining competitive advantage and market share.

5. (LO 1) Which of the following best explains risk identification?

    a. Deciding how the company will address the prioritized risks

    b. Selecting which risks are most likely to occur or will have the largest impact

    c. Categorizing risks based on their types

    d. Identifying existing risks and their outcomes

6. (LO 1) **CPA** While both views highlight risk severity, the _____ view of risk is from the entity-wide level, while the _____ view of risk is from the perspective of units or levels with the entity.

    a. incident; root cause

    b. root cause; incident

    c. portfolio; profile

    d. profile; portfolio

7. (LO 1) **CPA** Which of the following is *not* a strategic risk for a car rental company?

    a. Customer accident and damage incidents may be higher than expected.

    b. Customers may choose only low-margin cars and options.

    c. Investing in the stock market may result in financial losses.

    d. Cars may be stolen.

8. (LO 1) The business function that aligns with the purchases and payments processes is

    a. production.

    b. customer relations.

    c. marketing.

    d. supply chain management.

9. (LO 2) Blockbuster went out of business because its top management was unable to properly manage the company's

    a. operational risk.

    b. compliance risk.

    c. strategic risk.

    d. financial risk.

10. (LO 2) Which of the following risk categories relate to external risk rather than internal risk?

    a. Physical, compliance, and strategic risk

    b. Physical, compliance, and reputational risk

    c. Operational, strategic, and financial risk

    d. Compliance, physical, and reputational risk

11. (LO 2) Volkswagen suffered significant damage as a result of

    a. reputational risk.

    b. compliance risk.

    c. strategic risk.

    d. physical risk.

12. (LO 2) U.S. health care reform legislation is a high-risk area for the pharmaceutical industry. This risk belongs to which risk category?

    a. Internal risk, strategic

    b. External risk, compliance

    c. External risk, strategic

    d. Internal risk, compliance

13. (LO 2) Pride College is an online university that grants various business degrees at a steep cost. These degrees are not yet competitive in the market. This is a risky situation for Pride College. In which risk category does this risk belong?

    a. Internal risk, reputational

    b. External risk, reputational

    c. Internal risk, operational

    d. External risk, strategic

14. (LO 2) Which of the following is a major internal risk category?

    a. Compliance risk

    b. Strategic risk

    c. Operational risk

    d. Physical risk

15. (LO 3) Risk severity can be evaluated by

    a. estimating the harm that could potentially result if a risk becomes a reality.

    b. estimating the probability of the risk occurring.

    c. prioritizing risks by ranking their likelihood of occurring and their potential impact to the organization.

    d. calculating "frequency" or "probability of the risk inherent in a scenario."

16. (LO 3) The risk score formula is

    a. Likelihood – Impact

    b. Likelihood × Impact

    c. Likelihood/Outcome

    d. Likelihood/Average impact

17. (LO 3) **CPA** Each of the following is considered by management to be part of a risk assessment, *except*

    a. inherent risk.

    b. unknown risk.

    c. actual residual risk.

    d. target residual risk.

18. (LO 3) **CPA** A heat map used as a part of assessing risks plots the _____ on the vertical axis and the _____ on the horizontal axis.

    a. impact rating; likelihood rating

    b. inherent risk; risk appetite

    c. target residual risk; actual residual risk

    d. internal control; inherent risk

19. (LO 3) An organization has the following likelihood risk scale and impact risk scale:

Likelihood Risk Scale		Impact Risk Scale	
Risk Level	Likelihood Score	Risk Level	Impact Score
High	5	High	5
Medium High	4	Medium High	4
Medium	3	Medium	3
Medium Low	2	Medium Low	2
Low	1	Low	1

What is the final risk score for a defined risk with a high likelihood and a medium low impact?

    a. 3   **c.** 5

    b. 2.5   **d.** 10

20. **(LO 4)** The amount of risk a company is willing to take on at a particular time is called
    a. residual risk.
    b. risk appetite.
    c. risk tolerance.
    d. inherent risk.

21. **(LO 4)** Which of the following statements about residual risk is true?
    a. It is gross risk.
    b. It is the level of risk after considering controls and other mitigating factors.
    c. It is the natural level of risk inherent in a business process or activity.
    d. When an inherent risk is present and management chooses not to act, it has chosen to accept the risk.

22. **(LO 4)** Traditional risk responses available to management are
    a. defeat, amplify, purchase, and accept.
    b. accept, mitigate, cancel, and amplify.
    c. accept, mitigate, transfer, and avoid.
    d. accept, implement internal controls, and ignore.

23. **(LO 4)** Using smoke detectors and fire extinguishers is an example of _____ risk.
    a. accepting
    b. transferring
    c. mitigating
    d. avoiding

24. **(LO 4)** If a company closes stores in a particularly high-risk geographical location, how are they responding to the risk?
    a. Accepting the risk
    b. Avoiding the risk
    c. Mitigating the risk
    d. Transferring the risk

25. **(LO 4)** **CPA** A manufacturer actively monitors a foreign country's political events whenever a supply chain disruption occurs within the country that exceeds 90 days. The manufacturer is following which of the following risk-response strategies?
    a. Share
    b. Avoid
    c. Accept
    d. Reduce

26. **(LO 4)** **CPA** Match each statement below with the appropriate term that best describes it:
    i. After considering implemented controls, the desired level of the risk of a major cyberattack is low.
    ii. Before considering controls, the level of risk of a major cyberattack is high.
    iii. After considering implementing controls, the level of the risk of a major cyberattack is medium.
    a. (i) Internal control; (ii) inherent risk; (iii) target residual risk
    b. (i) Target residual risk; (ii) internal control; (iii) inherent risk
    c. (i) Target residual risk; (ii) actual residual risk; (iii) assessed risk
    d. (i) Target residual risk; (ii) inherent risk; (iii) actual residual risk

27. **(LO 4)** Which of the following best describes a technology risk?
    a. When technology failures have the potential of improving business
    b. When technology failures have the potential of disrupting business
    c. When technology is deployed to solve business problems
    d. When technology is removed from business operations

28. **(LO 4)** Which of the following provides best definition of impact?
    a. Impact prioritizes risks by ranking their likelihood of occurring and the potential impact on the company.
    b. It is the estimated probability of a risk occurrence.
    c. It is the estimation of damage that could be caused if the risk occurs.
    d. It is an estimation of the loss of goodwill.

29. **(LO 4)** A company identifies the following risks with a risk score as given below:

Risk	Risk Score
An oven fire may result in the destruction of a store.	5
A cybersecurity attack may result in the theft of customer data.	15
A store employee getting sick may result in them backing out of their shift last minute.	4
An employee stealing from a cash register may result in loss of cash.	6

Which risk has the lowest priority?
    a. An oven fire may result in the destruction of a store.
    b. A cybersecurity attack may result in the theft of customer data.
    c. A store employee getting sick may result in them backing out of their shift last minute.
    d. An employee stealing from a cash register may result in loss of cash.

30. **(LO 4)** What is the first step of ERM?
    a. Risk identification
    b. Risk categorization
    c. Risk prioritization
    d. Risk response

Discussion and Research Questions

DQ1. (LO 1) Explain what IT risk is and why it is an important consideration in risk management.

DQ2. (LO 1) `Critical Thinking` Is taking on significant business risk always negative? How could a business benefit from taking on significant business risk? Explain and provide examples.

DQ3. (LO 1) Explain what it means to consider enterprise risk management at an entity level.

DQ4. (LO 2) `Critical Thinking` Boeing grounded its best-selling plane, the 737 MAX, in March 2019 after two fatal crashes killed 346 people. These crashes, and the subsequent grounding of planes, significantly damaged Boeing's reputation. Investigators linked faults with the plane's software design to both crashes. Boeing halted production in January 2020 and has a large inventory of undelivered 737 MAX planes in storage. Was this calamity a result of (1) an identifiable internal risk or (2) the threat of an external risk? Explain why and prepare a risk statement for this crisis, mapping it to a single internal or external risk category.

DQ5. (LO 2) Use an internet search engine to find a credible definition of "compliance risk" and to identify an example of compliance risk. Cite your source(s).

DQ6. (LO 2) `Critical Thinking` Pacific Gas and Electric (PG&E) in California sought bankruptcy protection when it faced an estimated $30 billion in wildfire liabilities resulting from devastating wildfires, death, and destruction caused by its old and deteriorating transmission lines. PG&E has been linked to several wildfires in California, including the Camp Fire, which caused 86 deaths and destroyed 14,000 homes, more than 500 businesses, and 4,300 other buildings. Victims claimed that the company did not follow state regulations for proper maintenance to keep the transmission lines safe. Was this situation a result of (1) an identifiable internal risk or (2) the threat of an external risk? Explain why and prepare a risk statement that maps to a single internal or external risk category.

DQ7. (LO 3) Is risk 100% controllable by management? Explain.

DQ8. (LO 3) `Early Career` `Critical Thinking` You land a lucrative and highly competitive internship at a company whose vision statement describes it as a "platform business" from a technology perspective. The company leverages personal computers, the internet, mobile communications, and related technologies. You research the term "platform business," as you do not know what it means. You find out that big names like Amazon, Google, Facebook, and Apple are dominant in the platform economy and that some see the business

world as divided into two parts: the conventional economy and the platform economy. Platform companies create value far beyond that of conventional companies because they use digital innovation to their advantage so that businesses and people can interact in innovative ways that are not possible in the traditional economy. Explain how being a technology-enabled platform business may impact risk for your company. Keep your discussion at a high level and base it on chapter content.

DQ9. (LO 3) `Data Analytics` Refer to the following heat map and risk matrix. There are five risks in different areas of the risk matrix. Rank these risks from the highest risk to the lowest and explain your ranking. Use the colors in your explanation, as well the risk levels provided to you. In other words, explain how to read this heat map.

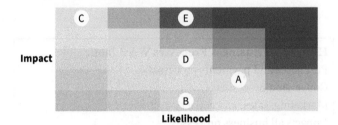

Risk Level	Abbreviation
High	H
Medium High	MH
Medium	M
Medium Low	ML
Low	L

DQ10. (LO 3) `Critical Thinking` Say that the majority (96%) of a company's customers pay online via credit card, PayPal, or similar payment method. One risk at this company is that an employee may manipulate the accounts receivable balance. Identify the likelihood and impact of this risk, using the risk levels high, medium high, medium, medium low, and low. Assume that this area of the business has strong controls in place that make it more difficult for an employee to commit fraud.

DQ11. (LO 4) Risk is always present in a business. Who is responsible for addressing business risk, and how would that be done?

DQ12. (LO 4) Distinguish between inherent risk and residual risk.

DQ13. (LO 4) Identify and briefly describe each of the four traditional or common types of risk responses. Provide an example of each that differs from examples provided in the chapter.

Application and Analysis Questions

A1. (LO 1) `Early Career` `Critical Thinking` You work for a new electric car company, Ion, which gives tours of its car plant to visitors every Friday. This week, you join the tour to learn more about your company. While on the tour, you notice some issues that might have an impact on your company. You

decide to record these issues in a table after the tour so you can present your concerns to your manager. Finish the following table with your analysis of the potential outcome each issue could have on the company.

Issue	Outcome/Potential Impact
The door to one of the machines is propped open, even though it has a sign "keep closed"	*may result in*
Some employees are not wearing hard hats in hard-hat zones	*may result in*
Some employees are taking shortcuts around the machines and not following the clearly marked lines on the ground, showing where it is safe to walk	*may result in*
An employee was eating a bag of chips while changing the machine settings	*may result in*
A piece of duct tape is used to hold one of the machine pieces together	*may result in*

A2. (LO 1) For the 10 risk statements in the following table, identify the high-level business process to which it relates and potential business functions (that is, where in the company the risks take place). Choose from the word banks provided. You will not use all the options in the word banks.

Business Functions Word Bank

Production operations

Human resources

Sales

Marketing research

Board of directors and executives

Treasury management

Purchasing

Internal audit

Information technology

Payroll

Customer service

All functional areas

High-Level Business Processes Word Bank

Purchases and payments processes

Conversion processes

Marketing, sales, and collections processes

Impacts all business processes

Risk Statement	Business Process	Business Function(s)
1. Because wiring from suppliers does not meet specifications, it will be necessary to return the wiring to the suppliers for a refund.		
2. Because working conditions for employees in the factory are not safe, there may be legal consequences like compensation for lost wages, medical bills, and production delays in the event of accidents.		
3. Because of sales staff members lacking knowledge about the features and benefits of a new service the company is selling, prospective customers are confused and don't subscribe to the service, resulting in decreased sales revenues.		
4. Because of poor strategic planning, the business may not meet its earnings forecasts and may therefore suffer financial losses, reputational loss, and a decrease in its stock price.		
5. If product reliability test failures exceed 5%, the resulting schedule delay to fix failures would exceed two weeks, causing increased cost and customer dissatisfaction.		
6. Poor short-term financial forecasts may result in cash flow issues, negatively impacting the company's credit rating and its ability to borrow at a reasonable cost.		
7. Customer data theft caused by defective system changes could result in significant financial fraud losses due to fines, loss of customers, and regulatory sanctions.		
8. Returns by customers in a superstore are at risk of being diverted, with the returned goods never reaching the warehouse, resulting in inventory shrinkage.		

Risk Statement	Business Process	Business Function(s)
9. Because of inadequate background checks, an employee with a criminal background may be hired, with the potential for losses from fraud or theft in the workplace.		
10. Because of inadequate timekeeping, employees could be paid for time not worked, resulting in fictitious costs and reduced profits.		

Risk Scenario	Risk Category
1. Employees are required to work from home, remotely, if there is no need for a physical presence in the workplace. Because managers cannot supervise employees in person, the employees may not be as productive as when they are on the premises, resulting in much lower productivity for the same cost to the organization.	
2. Because of COVID-19, walk-in customers, the main revenue source for the business, can no longer come to the store due to the shutdown. The CFO arranges to borrow money from a bank at a higher-than-usual rate of interest in an attempt to bridge the gap in the revenue stream. She is concerned about the company's ability to repay the loan principal by the due date specified in the debt agreement.	
3. At a university, in an effort to ensure that the football program starts the season, the board of trustees mandates a restart of face-to-face classes before the rate of infection from the virus has decreased in that state. The board proposes mandatory monitoring of the health of faculty and students through the use of an app, testing, distancing in class and on campus, and mask wearing. The university faces a risk of lawsuits by faculty and students who are infected by the virus on campus, regardless of the precautions, resulting in a financial loss due to settlements and legal fees.	
4. A commercial diving school continues to run its certification program during the COVID-19 pandemic. It uses an app for instructors and students to mandatorily report on their health conditions every three days. Administration discloses to colleagues, without permission, that an instructor has reported an underlying condition of concern. The instructor rightly claims that the school has breached the law (HIPAA) by disclosing his medical condition to colleagues.	
5. A member of the executive team at a major corporation has joked on social media about the coronavirus and mocked people infected with the virus. He also used a racial slur against an Asian man who responded to one of his posts. The public relations department is trying to manage the public outrage resulting from the executive's posts.	

A3. (LO 2) Critical Thinking Organizations around the globe have faced challenges with risk management during the COVID-19 pandemic. While COVID-19 is an external threat, and organizations can't control it, they can control how they respond to the risks. In this sense, risks related to COVID-19 can be either internal or external.

The table above lists various COVID-19 scenarios. Label each scenario with the risk category to which it belongs. The risk categories are compliance, strategic, financial, reputational, physical, and operational risk. Each risk category is only used once, and not all risk categories will be used.

A4. (LO 3) Early Career Critical Thinking You own an online shop on a website like Etsy, where you sell laptop stickers you have designed. You have identified five risks you would like to address. When you perform a risk prioritization, you find that all five risks have similar risk scores.

You meet your best friend at a local coffee shop to brainstorm about your risks and get your friend's input. While there, you write your reasoning for each risk on a separate note card—one for each risk—and place the cards in order of the priority that you and your friend have agreed on. On the walk back to your apartment, you drop the note cards, and they are now out of order. You need to re-create your prioritization from the coffee shop.

Match each note card reasoning for priority with its appropriate risk and then rank the risks from 1 to 5, with 1 being the *highest* priority and 5 being the *lowest* priority.

Your note card choices are as follows:

A. This store is a source of income for you. You need to protect yourself by making sure you do not send merchandise to a customer until the customer's credit card clears the system and the payment is in your account.

B. Turning on notifications on your shop's social media accounts and other sites where a customer may write a review will ensure that you are monitoring commentary and engagement with your brand—whether positive or negative. Your brand's image is essential, and one bad review can ruin your customer base.

C. A lawsuit could be awful. You should publish a list of materials used in your products—adhesive, printer ink, etc. People are allergic to many things, and this disclosure will prevent a potential lawsuit by providing disclosure to buyers.

D. Damaged goods are probably unavoidable, so you will keep a budget to cover these losses. To keep your

customer happy, you need to refund the purchase price. A solid refund policy will protect you from excessive refunds.

E. If a customer receives a wrong item, you can simply apologize, send the correct item, and possibly include a bonus sticker as a small gift of apology. Keeping customers happy is essential to avoid bad reviews.

Risk	Note Card Letter	Priority
A customer receiving the wrong order may result in an upset customer.		
A customer posting a negative review on the social media page may result in reputational damage.		
A customer returning a used/damaged laptop sticker and demanding a full refund may result in a loss of revenue.		
A customer suffering an allergic reaction to the glue on the sticker may result in an upset customer and a possible lawsuit.		
A customer providing a fake credit card number may result in loss of revenue.		

Risk	Likelihood	Impact	Risk Score	Manager Reasoning	Priority
Important influencers with contracts to publish content only on this platform leaving the site may result in significant revenue loss due to lower customer traffic.					
An influencer making offensive remarks during a live stream may result in reputational damage to the site.					
A lack of proper security processes may result in a hacker stealing customer information such as names and credit card numbers.					

A5. (LO 3) Critical Thinking You are an enterprise risk manager at a new video streaming platform. In today's risk meeting, your team has identified three emerging risks. As the manager, your job is to use the risk table above to rate the likelihood, rate the impact, calculate the risk score, and prioritize these three risks. You must also include the reasoning behind your rankings.

Remember: Likelihood and impact are rated on a scale of 1–5, with 1 being the *lowest* and 5 being the *highest*. Priority is ranked as 1, 2, or 3, with 1 being the *most important*.

A6. (LO 4) Early Career Critical Thinking You have plans to go out for dinner with friends tonight. When you text one of them that you are on your way, she mentions the exam you both have in financial accounting tomorrow morning. You completely forgot about this exam, and you have not studied for it! You will lower your letter grade for the class if you don't get at least an 82% on this exam. For the last few exams, you

have studied and felt prepared, and your grades have been between 80% and 90%. You think it is highly likely you will not get an 82% on this test if you don't do something about it. Listed below are the actions you could take. Match each action with one of the following risk responses: acceptance, avoidance, mitigation, or transfer. An action may fit more than one risk response type, so choose the ones you think match best.

1. You cancel your plans and stay up all night cramming. You risk being tired during the test, but you think you can cram enough to just maybe pull this off.

2. You cancel your plans and study for two hours before your normal bedtime and get a good night's rest. Maybe that is going to be enough.

3. You go to dinner but come home right after to study the rest of the night. You think you can manage both.

4. You go to dinner and stay out with your friends afterward. It is going to be what it is going to be, and it is too late for whatever studying you can do to make any difference anyway.

5. You tell your friends you are sick and tell your professor you are too sick to attend class the next day. You schedule a makeup exam for next week and spend adequate time studying for it.

6. You pay someone else to take the exam for you. (Note: It happens, although this is a terrible idea. Never do this! It is unethical, and the consequences may be severe.)

A7. (LO 1-4) `Critical Thinking` As a risk management consultant, you have been hired to help DataBots Inc. improve its new server room. The project parameters follow.

DataBots Project Parameters

Project Name: Server Room Enhancements

Project Timeline: 4 months

Project Requirements:

i. Server room must provide access to appropriate personnel only.

ii. Server room enhancements are the company's highest-priority project currently; cost is not a concern.

iii. Physical changes to the room are limited to adding security measures and equipment. Walls, layout, and location of the server room cannot be changed.

Review the project and its risks. Select *one* of the key risks for DataBots Inc. and provide your solution. Your solution should have two parts: (1) Explain what you would do to address the risk. (2) Identify which of the four risk response types you have used in your solution.

Key risks to address:

1. The server room houses extra IT equipment like network cables and chargers. Door access is granted via badges. Employees have been caught handing their badges to unauthorized employees to grant them access to the room when they need a piece of equipment. This results in a risk of unauthorized access to the servers, which contain sensitive data.

2. There are desks and chairs in one corner, where IT employees gather to socialize. This has led to food and drinks being open near sensitive equipment. Additionally, there are often too many employees in the server room at one time. There is a risk of spilling food or drinks on the equipment and losing important data and equipment.

3. The outlets in the server room are outdated. The most recent fire inspection revealed a risk of short circuiting the breakers due to the amount of equipment connected. This creates a high risk of fire in the building.

Bamboozled Doggos Scenario

Use the following scenario to complete questions A8 through A10:

Bamboozled Doggos is a dog treat company that claims its products taste so good that dogs don't know that they are good for them. Located in Lincoln, Nebraska, Bamboozled Doggos makes all its products onsite at its local bakery.

Its signature product, the "Heckin' Bamboozled," has a hollow center, where dog owners insert medication in pill or tablet form. The treat is soft and melts in the dog's mouth, masking the taste and smell of the medication.

Bamboozled Doggos only uses local, natural ingredients in its products. Bamboozled Doggos offers its product line in grain-free, vegan, and dairy-free versions by request. Its most popular products use locally sourced Floral Flours wheat flour that is made from wheat grown at a local farm called Serenity Acres. Bamboozled Doggos prides itself on sourcing flour from this single provider. By keeping the supply chain small, Bamboozled Doggos believes it can provide quality products to its customers.

Meteorologists are predicting a warm winter this year, which could be detrimental to Nebraska's wheat fields, as it creates an environment that increases the risk of wheat virus diseases such as High Plains virus and wheat streak mosaic virus. These viruses can be avoided using proper planting techniques. Bamboozled Doggos is not involved with or aware of Serenity Acres' planting practices.

Perform a risk assessment by identifying, categorizing, and prioritizing the risks around Bamboozled Doggos and its wheat supply chain.

A8. (LO 1-4) `Early Career` `Critical Thinking` **Identify**

1. Find three issues in Bamboozled Doggos' supply chain. Try to find at least one that can be mapped to an internal risk and one that can be mapped to an external risk.

2. Identify a risk statement with a "may result in" outcome for each issue.

A9. (LO 1-4) `Early Career` `Critical Thinking` **Categorize**

1. Map each risk statement to a risk category.

2. Label each risk statement and its category as either internal or external risk.

A10. (LO 1-4) `Early Career` `Critical Thinking` **Prioritize**

1. Rank the likelihood of each risk statement from 1 (lowest) to 5 (highest) likelihood.

2. Rank the impact of each risk statement from 1 (lowest) to 5 (highest) impact.

3. Calculate the risk score.

4. Order the risks in priority from highest priority to lowest priority.

Tableau Case: Julia's Cookies' Risk Profile

What You Need

Download Tableau to your computer. You can access www.tableau.com/academic/students to download your free Tableau license for the year, or you can download it from your university's software offerings.

Download the following file from the book's product page on www.wiley.com:
   Chapter 2 Raw Data.xlsx

Case Background

Big Picture:
Determine which areas of the business should be subject to frequent internal audits due to being high risk.

Details:
Why is this data important, and what questions or problems need to be addressed?

- Internal auditors analyze company risk on an ongoing basis to ensure that they are targeting high-risk areas for audits. Of course, all areas of the company need to be audited; however, higher-risk areas need to be audited more often, as they have a higher likelihood of occurring and/or impact to the company.
- When determining which areas of a company to audit, the Internal Audit department divides the company into "auditable entities." An auditable entity represents a group of business processes that are closely related. Auditable entities are often based on existing business functions of an organization, such as those shown in Illustration 2.3.
- To illustrate the risk of some areas of the company, consider the following questions: Which risk has the highest inherent risk score? How many risks have a high inherent impact?

Plan:
What data is needed, and how should it be analyzed?

- The data needed is pulled from the internal audit GRC (governance, risk, and compliance) software, which houses the Internal Audit department's assessment and ratings of corporate risks.
- The data was filtered to include only the auditable entities that were subject to internal audit last year.

Now it's your turn to evaluate, analyze, and communicate the results!

Questions

1. How many business processes does the auditable entity "Business Continuity and Disaster Recovery Management" have?
2. Which two auditable entities have the highest total number of risks? (Hint: Each row is a unique risk.)
3. Which risk owner is responsible for the smallest total number of risks?
4. How many risks belong to the risk category "internal fraud"?
5. How many risks have an inherent impact rating of "high"?
6. How many risks have an inherent likelihood rating of "low"?
7. Which risk has the highest risk score? (Hint: Use MAX.)
8. Which business process belongs to two risk owners?

Take it to the next level!

9. How many risks have an inherent likelihood rating of "medium" and inherent impact rating of "medium"?
10. Which risk owner is responsible for five risks that have an inherent likelihood rating of "medium" and inherent impact rating of "medium"?

CHAPTER 3
Risk Management and Internal Controls

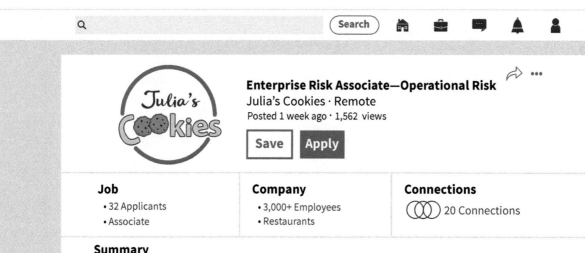

Enterprise Risk Associate—Operational Risk
Julia's Cookies · Remote
Posted 1 week ago · 1,562 views

Save   **Apply**

Job	Company	Connections
• 32 Applicants	• 3,000+ Employees	20 Connections
• Associate	• Restaurants	

Summary

Julia's Cookies is seeking a recent college graduate who is passionate about using creative thinking to help the company address risk. The enterprise risk associate is responsible for identifying, categorizing, prioritizing, and recommending responses to risks on an ongoing basis to support our corporate business functions. The role is vital to ensure that we achieve our goals and comply with local and global legal and compliance requirements. Join a team that partners across the organization to shape the future of our evolving risk program.

The role can work remotely and travel to the Chicago, Atlanta, or San Francisco corporate office for in-person trainings.

Responsibilities

- Develop enterprise risk management tools, practices, and policies for analysis and reporting
- Help establish the enterprise risk management strategy for the company
- Understand business processes, regulations, and controls to develop meaningful tests to assess whether controls are operating effectively
- Collaborate with other departments to ensure that the company appropriately prioritizes, manages, and monitors risk

Requirements

Preferred Education: Bachelor's degree or higher in accounting, finance, management information systems, economics, engineering, or related subject
Preferred Certifications: CPA eligibility, COSO Enterprise Risk Management–Integrated Framework or other risk framework certification

Preferred Knowledge and Skills

The ideal candidate will demonstrate a basic understanding of audit processes and information technology—particularly how systems integrate with business processes and operations. Preference will be given to candidates who demonstrate:

- Ability to work independently and to effectively execute multiple complex projects on time
- Critical thinking, sound judgment, and analytical skills
- Resourcefulness and ability to seek out information sources without supervision

Salary: $55,000–60,000

CHAPTER PREVIEW Many risk factors exist that might make it hard for a company to reach its business objectives. Risk identification includes outlining the details of risks, how likely they are to occur, their potential financial impact, and their possible impact on business operations.

Risk mitigation is the most popular type of risk response, and this chapter explains why. Management mitigates risk through a variety of procedures and methods, but this chapter focuses on risk mitigation through internal controls. A company's internal control environment consists of policies and procedures implemented by management to mitigate risks by providing reasonable assurance that:

- Financial statements are fairly presented.
- Operations are efficient and effective.
- Laws and regulations are followed.

Why is this topic so important to accounting information system (AIS)? First, technology is a significant risk area in companies of any size. Second, the AIS of a company is high risk not only from a technology standpoint but also from a regulatory perspective. Companies must comply with a multitude of laws and regulations, and accounting information systems are a repository for a significant amount of confidential and regulated information. One of the major goals of risk mitigation is to prevent material misstatements in the financial statements, which means the information produced by the AIS must meet the regulatory standards of quality. It also requires a financial risk assessment to comply with Section 404 of the Sarbanes-Oxley Act of 2002 (SOX 404). Under SOX 404, a public company's annual report must include an attestation of its own assessment of internal control over financial reporting, as well as an external auditor's attestation.

In this chapter, you will learn:

- How risk is mitigated through internal controls
- Classifications of internal controls
- Methods to assess whether internal controls are working
- Regulatory importance of the internal control environment

Risk management is an aspect of business that most accounting professionals are involved with in one way or another. Whether your career takes you to audit, tax, managerial accounting, or a specialized risk position like the enterprise risk associate role at Julia's Cookies, you will be a part of your employer's internal control environment. ∎

Chapter Roadmap

LEARNING OBJECTIVES	TOPICS	JULIA'S COOKIES APPLIED LEARNING
3.1 Distinguish among the three functions of internal controls.	• Preventive Controls • Detective Controls • Corrective Controls	Internal Control Functions: Controlling a Risk
3.2 Characterize a control by its location and implementation method.	• General Controls • Application Controls • Implementing Controls • Continuous Monitoring	Internal Control Classification: Policies and Procedures
3.3 Explain the three lines of defense to ensure effectiveness of internal controls.	• Management: First and Second Lines of Defense • Internal Audit: Third Line of Defense	Assessing Internal Controls: Business Process Maturity Model
3.4 Describe the importance of frameworks in an internal control environment.	• Sarbanes-Oxley Act of 2002 (SOX) • Directive 2014/56/EU of the European Parliament • COSO Internal Control–Integrated Framework • COSO Enterprise Risk Management Framework	Risk Management: Selecting a Framework

CPA You will find the CPA tag throughout the chapter to call out any important topics you may see on the CPA exam.

3.1 How Do Internal Controls Mitigate Risk?

Companies address risk by either accepting, mitigating, transferring, or avoiding it. Of the four risk responses, the most commonly used response in business is risk mitigation. By mitigating risk, which involves applying internal controls to business processes to reduce its exposure, a company can take on risks and create a competitive advantage for its business while still carefully considering, calculating, and reducing those risks.

At the center of business processes and management responsibilities are internal controls. In other words, a crucial management responsibility for the AIS of a company is to provide an adequate internal control process.

 CPA **Internal control** is a process that specifically mitigates risks to the company's financial information. An adequate process creates assurance that (1) accounting information is reliable, complete, and valid; (2) operations are effective and efficient; and (3) the business is complying with laws and regulations. The first consideration, reliable accounting information, includes ensuring the security, privacy, and integrity of the AIS. Internal control, as it relates to accounting information, focuses on providing quality information to internal decision makers and external stakeholders.

Management mitigates the risk of poor-quality information by implementing internal controls over business processes, including directly in the AIS. **CPA** Proper internal controls can:

- Create quality information
- Lessen the risk of financial statement misstatements
- Prevent fraud
- Identify financial issues
- Safeguard assets from theft and waste
- Increase operating efficiency
- Measure business objectives and goals
- Ensure compliance with applicable laws and regulations
- Provide investors with reassurance

Regulators mandate internal controls for specific types of organizations, such as public companies, or controls may be adopted voluntarily by other organizations that want the benefits the controls provide. Internal controls provide *reasonable assurance*, which means not absolute mitigation but enough mitigation to give the company confidence that risk is at an acceptable level.

An internal control process implements individual control activities. **Controls**, or control activities, are the mechanisms, like rules, policies, and procedures, that make up the process. In order to understand internal controls, consider the enterprise risk management (ERM) processes you have learned so far, which include performing risk assessments and selecting risk responses. After applying controls, companies compare actual residual risk to their target residual risk to determine if further risk mitigation is necessary to meet the business's risk appetite, which you may recall is how much risk the business is willing to take on.

about complying with regulations; it is also about using best practices to add value to your company.

- Accounting professionals must adhere to a variety of regulations that specify required internal controls. Understanding the types of controls and how they relate to corporate risk will help you connect potentially tedious regulatory requirements to their business applications. This can help you understand the "why" instead of just the "what."

- Internal controls can often seem like regulatory red tape. This isn't true, but it contributes to the public misconception of accountants being "bean counters" or auditors being "the police." Internal controls are actually crucial to a company's risk response plan.

The number of controls a company implements can be large. No universal document exists to provide companies with predefined controls they must use. Instead, businesses design controls in response to their risk assessments, and so controls are customized to a company's unique risks and risk appetite.

Controls differ in function, location in business processes, and style of implementation. These differences characterize a control. You will learn more about classifying controls in the next section, but first you need to know that different controls serve different functions. The function of a control is to do one of the following:

- Prevent
- Detect
- Correct

Preventive Controls

People take preventive measures with their vehicles by taking them for scheduled maintenance checks. Car manufacturers usually recommend a regular maintenance schedule of 30,000, 60,000, and 90,000 miles.

 Taking a car in for a check at those intervals, even if it has not broken down, is a control. This control allows the mechanic to check various parts of the car to prevent breakdowns and prolong its life.

CPA **Preventive controls** prevent problems from happening. An example is a firewall to prevent unauthorized access to an organization's computer network. One of the most common preventive controls is policy and procedure documentation. By specifying how employees should execute procedures and clarifying company policies, an organization lowers its risk of error and misconduct.

One particular kind of preventive control has a special name because it is so important for error and fraud prevention. The American Institute of Certified Public Accountants (AICPA) describes it as a basic building block of internal control. **CPA** **Segregation of duties**, also called separation of duties, is a type of preventive control that lessens the risk of error and fraud by ensuring that different employees are responsible for the separate parts of a business activity: authorizing, recording, and custody. The work of one employee acts as a check on the work of another employee. Management should structure work assignments to separate these three specific activities when it is cost-effective to do so (**Illustration 3.1**).

Segregation of duties can be enforced via policies, or it can be programmed directly into the AIS. Management implements an embedded segregation of duties control by assigning different capabilities, known as "roles," to each user in the system. You may have encountered roles in your life if you've ever had read-only access to a file or added someone to a Google Drive document as "Viewer." Much as read-only access prohibits a user from editing a file, system roles dictate what activities users can perform. Let's look at some of the responsibilities and system roles of the AIS users involved in purchasing and paying for inventory at Julia's Cookies (**Table 3.1**).

Authorizing

business transactions
and decisions

*Signing checks, authorizing
requests for checks, approving
vendor payments, approving
purchase orders, approving
compensation adjustments*

Recording

data about
business activities

*Preparing source documents,
inputting data into the
information system, recording
journal entries, and maintaining
accounting records, files, and
databases*

Custody

of business assets

*Overseeing and distributing
cash, inventory, fixed assets,
computer equipment, tools,
and supplies*

Illustration 3.1 Segregation of duties ensures that different employees perform each of these three key activities.

TABLE 3.1 User Responsibilities and System Roles

Ordering Ingredients from Vendor				
Business Title	**Responsibilities**	**Duty**	**System Role**	**System Restrictions**
Purchasing employee	Ordering ingredients and other raw materials for production of cookies	Recording	Purchaser	*Allowed:* Input data into system *Prohibited:* Approve purchase orders
Purchasing manager	Approving purchase orders	Authorizing	Approver	*Allowed:* Approve purchase orders *Prohibited:* Input data into system
Receiving employee	Checking shipments received from suppliers and accepting or rejecting goods	Custody	Receiver	*Allowed:* Scan acceptable goods received into system *Prohibited:* Alter inventory records
Paying for Ingredients Received from Vendor				
Business Title	**Responsibilities**	**Duty**	**System Role**	**System Restrictions**
Accounts Payable analyst	Processing invoices received from vendors	Recording	Processer	*Allowed:* Input data into system *Prohibited:* Approve invoice payments
Accounts Payable manager	Approving invoice payments	Authorizing	Approver	*Allowed:* Approve invoice payments *Prohibited:* Input data into system
Accounts Payable clerk or automated system process	Paying invoices from vendors	Custody	Payer	Payments are either made by writing a physical check (Accounts Payable clerk) or automatically processed through the system once approved
Recording Journal Entry for Purchase and Payment				
Business Title	**Responsibilities**	**Duty**	**System Role**	**System Restrictions**
Financial accountant or bookkeeper	Recording journal entries in the general ledger	Recording	Accountant	*Allowed:* Create and post journal entries *Prohibited:* Approve journal entries
Chief financial officer (CFO) or controller	Approving journal entries	Authorizing	Approver	*Allowed:* Approve journal entries *Prohibited:* Create and post journal entries

Detective Controls

While scheduled maintenance is a preventive control for vehicles, indicator lights in vehicles are detective controls. The icons on the car dashboard light up when an issue is detected.

CPA **Detective controls** alert management to an issue once it has occurred. These controls monitor business processes to identify problems like fraud risk, quality control, or legal compliance.

At Julia's Cookies, the store managers count the cash drawer nightly and then reconcile the cash with the total sales recorded in the sales log for that day (**Illustration 3.2**). This detective control protects the cash assets of the company. It also discourages employees from stealing cash from the cash register because they know about the nightly reconciliation procedure.

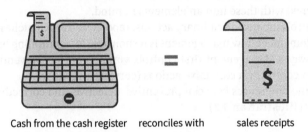

Cash from the cash register   reconciles with   sales receipts

Illustration 3.2 Cash in the register must reconcile with sales receipts.

Another detective control you will encounter if you pursue a career in audit is performing a physical inventory count. This control requires a person to count the quantity of each type of inventory currently on hand and compare it to the totals in the inventory system. It is designed to detect irregularities from errors or fraud. Errors may be the result of an employee improperly inputting a transaction into the system, whereas fraud could occur if an employee is stealing inventory from a warehouse. Most auditors—whether internal or external—find themselves performing inventory counts in the first few years of their careers.

Corrective Controls

What if a driver ignores the preventive control of scheduled maintenance and the detective control of a check engine light on a vehicle? The vehicle may break down. At this point, the only thing that can be done is to correct the situation. Ordering a tow truck to take the vehicle to the repair shop and having a mechanic fix the issue are corrective actions.

CPA **Corrective controls** change undesirable outcomes and occur after the potential outcome of a risk has become a reality. While it may seem counterintuitive to have corrective controls, sometimes it is not cost-effective to implement preventive or detective controls to mitigate a specific risk. For such risks, corrective controls are used instead. Corrective controls are also used as a backup plan in the event of a failure of preventive or detective controls.

While we always hope that controls will work as intended, we can never have absolute confidence that they will. Controls are not infallible. They can, and regularly do, fail. Regardless of the policies and procedures a business implements, companies can only provide reasonable assurance on the effectiveness of internal controls. This is because human judgment is often an element of internal controls.

Control Weaknesses

CPA **Management override** occurs when internal control activities don't work because management is not following policy or procedure—such as by telling an employee who reports directly to them to ignore a specific control. For example, a control may require additional approvals for journal entries over a certain dollar amount. If an accounting manager insists that a member of their team input a journal entry above this threshold without proper approval, management has ignored the existing control. This is called management override. The AICPA describes management override as the Achilles heel of fraud prevention.[1]

A control will also not work if two or more people collude to override the control. What if a control requires one employee to input invoices into the accounts payable system and a different employee to approve payments for the invoices? If these two employees work together, they can commit fraud by inputting a fictitious invoice and authorizing the payment to go to a bank account they control. This is **collusion**. CPA When two employees collude, they work together to circumvent controls. This is teamwork at its worst.

Management override and collusion are major concerns when it comes to management's responsibilities for business processes and internal control. Good business processes and controls are designed with these human elements in mind.

Corrective controls include disciplinary actions, reports, software patches, and even policy updates. CPA Remember how management is responsible for controlling business processes in two different ways? Management first controls via monitoring (preventive and detective controls) and then controls via corrective actions (corrective controls).

To remember the differences between preventive, detective, and corrective controls, think of a bank robbery (**Illustration 3.3**).

Preventive	**Detective**	**Corrective**	**All**
Prohibits or deters a risk outcome from occurring	Identifies a risk during or after outcome occurrence	Remedies the outcome after a risk outcome occurrence	Functions as all three simultaneously
Security: physical security of the vault and bank, locked doors, and walls designed to be difficult to penetrate prohibit culprits from accessing or deter culprits due to the effort of bypassing them.	*Monitoring: security cameras, trip sensors, and motion sensors create alerts if an activity, like a culprit trying to enter the vault, is detected. Camera videos can also be used to identify culprits after a theft.*	*Reaction and recovery: police being called to the scene of a crime, chasing the culprits, and recovering the stolen assets.*	*Combination: security guards deter a culprit (preventive), can catch a thief in the act (detective), and can respond to a theft by chasing culprits and recovering the stolen assets (corrective).*

Illustration 3.3   Controls have three functions: preventing, detecting, and correcting the occurrence of a risk outcome.

Time-Based Model of Controls

Companies use controls with preventive, detective, and corrective functionality to create an effective control environment. Consider information security risks specifically. If an intruder breaks into a company's systems, the impact can be detrimental. CPA The **time-based model of controls** measures the residual risk for technology attacks by comparing the relationship of the three control functions (**Illustration 3.4**). If $P > (D + C)$, then the controls are effective. Otherwise, the security measures are inadequate to protect the company's systems from intruders.

This is just one example of how the three different controls can be combined to create a robust system of internal control over business processes. In fact, a single business event may have all three of these controls if the risk score is high enough to merit it. Help Julia's Cookies categorize its technology risks in Applied Learning 3.1.

---

[1]www.aicpa.org/ForThePublic/AuditCommitteeEffectiveness/DownloadableDocuments/achilles_heel.pdf

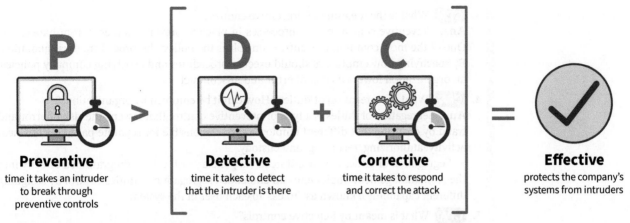

Illustration 3.4 The time-based model of controls is specific to the time it takes for a technology attack to bypass preventive controls compared to the company's detective and corrective control reaction times.

Julia's Cookies   Applied Learning 3.1

Internal Control Functions: Controlling a Risk

Julia's Cookies' business model is connecting customers to freshly baked cookies via a mobile app. This means technology risks are a big concern. The ERM team is presenting the internal control process to the chief technology officer (CTO) and has assembled the following list of new controls that management has designed and implemented this year.

These controls must be categorized before the presentation to the CTO. Can you categorize each one as preventive, detective, or corrective?

1. A system scans the network to identify unexpected network activity that might indicate hackers.
2. Antivirus software scans everything downloaded to a company computer and blocks items with red flags that indicate virus infection.
3. Viruses detected in the systems are immediately quarantined via specially programmed software.
4. Locks are installed at the entrance to the room where computer equipment is stored.
5. Access to new users of a system is authorized by a manager and added to the system by a different employee in the IT department.

SOLUTION

Preventive controls include the antivirus software (2) that blocks items before they are downloaded to the company computers, locks (4) that prevent unauthorized access to company computer equipment, and the separation of duties (5) that has one employee authorize users and a different employee add the users to the system. All three of these occur before a potential risk outcome occurs to prevent it from ever taking place.

A detective control is the network scanning software that looks for potential hacker activity (1). This control detects possible threats after they have accessed the system.

A corrective control is quarantining viruses (3). The virus is already in the system, so this control occurs after the fact and mitigates risk by reacting to the event.

CONCEPT REVIEW QUESTIONS

1. What is assurance in the context of internal controls?
   Ans. An adequate process creates assurance that (1) accounting information is reliable, complete, and valid; (2) operations are effective and efficient; and (3) the business is complying with laws and regulations.

2. What is meant by reasonable assurance?
   Ans. Reasonable assurance means not absolute mitigation but enough mitigation to give the company the confidence that risk is at an acceptable level.

3. **CPA** What is the meaning of preventive control?

   Ans. Preventive control means processes in place to prevent problems from happening. One of the most common preventive controls is the policy and procedure documentation. By specifying how employees should execute procedures and clarifying company policies, an organization lowers its risk of error and misconduct.

4. **CPA** What is segregation of duties? How can it be enforced by organizations?

   Ans. Segregation of duties is a type of preventive control that lessens the risk of error and fraud by ensuring that different employees are responsible for separate parts of a business activity: authorizing, recording, and custody.

   Segregation of duties can be enforced via policies, or it can be programmed directly into the AIS. Management implements an embedded segregation of duties control by assigning different capabilities, known as "roles," to each user in the system.

5. **CPA** What is meant by detective controls?

   Ans. Detective controls alert the management to an issue once it has occurred. These controls monitor business processes to identify problems like fraud risk, quality control, or legal compliance.

6. **CPA** Write a brief note on corrective controls.

   Ans. Corrective controls change undesirable outcomes and occur after the potential outcome of a risk has become a reality. While it may seem counterintuitive to have corrective controls, sometimes it is not cost-effective to implement preventive or detective controls to mitigate a specific risk. For such risks, corrective controls are used instead. Corrective controls are also used as a backup plan in the event of a failure of preventive or detective controls.

7. **CPA** What is meant by collusion?

   Ans. When two or more employees join hands together and work to circumvent controls, it is known as collusion.

8. **CPA** What is the meaning of time-based model of controls?

   Ans. The time-based model of controls measures the residual risk for technology attacks by comparing the relationship of the three control functions, namely, preventive, detective, and corrective controls.

3.2 How Are Controls Classified?

Learning Objective ❷
Characterize a control by its location and implementation method.

In addition to classifying a control by its function to either prevent, detect, or correct risk, we can also characterize a control based on where in a business process it exists. The first step in determining where a control exists involves a question: Is the control in a computer environment or not? The answer indicates whether the control is a physical control or an information technology (IT) control. There are three locations for controls (**Illustration 3.5**):

- Physical controls
- IT general controls (ITGCs)
- IT application controls

A physical control is the most straightforward type of internal control, as it is tangible and governs individuals and their activities. For this reason, we focus on the two types of IT controls in the remainder of this section.

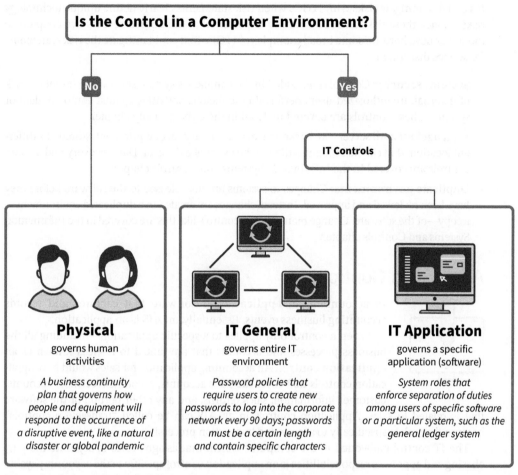

Illustration 3.5 Each type of control governs one of these three locations.

General Controls

CPA **ITGCs** apply to the entire operation of the full system and its environment. All corporate applications, like email, web browsers, time-keeping software, benefits management systems, and more, are subject to ITGCs. Julia's Cookies' preventive antivirus controls, detective network activity monitoring program, and corrective virus quarantine controls in Applied Learning 3.1 are all ITGCs. They relate to all the technology throughout Julia's Cookies.

The technological infrastructure of a company is essential to maintaining operations. Imagine if Netflix's servers went down for a significant time. The servers that support the streaming platform are part of the company's technology environment. Netflix uses extensive ITGCs to prevent this from happening.

Don't let the name "general" controls trick you. These controls, like all other controls, target specific risk statements. Simply saying "the risk of servers crashing may result in a disruption of service" is not specific enough for a company like Netflix to implement proper controls. Instead, detailed risk statements, like these, can create a clear roadmap to designing adequate ITGCs:

- An unauthorized user accessing the system and hijacking servers may result in a disruption of service.

- A natural disaster destroying the data center housing servers may result in a disruption of service.

- Updates to streaming software that contain errors may result in a disruption of service.

It's easier to mitigate risks with ITGCs when risk statements clearly define unique technology risks. In fact, these risks and ITGCs are so important that this course devotes two chapters to them. For now, here are some broad examples of ITGCs that could mitigate the risk statements for service disruption:

- **Systems security:** Controls embedded in the company's system specifically target the risk of external, unauthorized users performing malicious activities against company data or systems. These controls are covered in detail in the Cybersecurity chapter.
- **Data backups:** All servers are backed up to a secondary set of equipment, stored at a different location, that can be brought online in the event of a disaster. Data recovery and backup controls are covered in the Information Systems and Controls chapter.
- **Duplicate environments:** Changes to systems are not released to the software before they have been reviewed and approved. Instead, changes are created in a duplicated environment—a copy—of the software. Change management controls like this are covered in the Information Systems and Controls chapter.

Application Controls

In accounting, an **application** is software that captures and records accounting business events. Essentially, an AIS is an application.

When a control only applies to a specific application—including all the business processes and accounts that are linked to it—it is known as an **application control**. An accounting application for sales would have application controls that cover the sales accounts, accounts receivable accounts, customer information, sales returns, and any other portion of the software that is related to sales. Application controls in an AIS can be called "transaction controls" because they relate specifically to accounting transaction processing.

The IT control embedded in the computer system that assigns roles to separate the purchasing and approvals responsibilities is an application control specific to the accounts payable software. Another example of an application control is a validity check that verifies entered data is formatted correctly. For example, when creating a profile for a website account, a user must input their date of birth in MM/DD/YYYY format. If a user inputs 1/24/94, the system sends an error message.

In the Real World   Cantey Technology's Contingency Response

Cantey Technology, founded and led by Willis Cantey, is a South-Carolina-based IT firm that specializes in providing top-notch IT solutions and consulting services in Charleston, the Southeast, and beyond. Established in 2007, the company offers a range of services, including managed IT, cloud and storage solutions, network and server management, and cyber security. With multiple offices across South Carolina in cities like Charleston, Columbia, Greenville, Spartanburg, and Summerville, Cantey Technology is well positioned to serve its clients effectively.

The company has established strong partnerships with renowned technology firms, reinforcing its capabilities and service offerings. These partnerships include being a Microsoft Solutions Partner and Cisco/Meraki Select Partner, utilizing Amazon Web Services, being a VMWare Cloud Service Provider, and collaborating with Dell Technologies.

In 2013, Cantey Technology faced a significant challenge when their office building in Mount Pleasant, South Carolina, experienced a major fire due to a lightning strike. The fire destroyed their network infrastructure and computer hardware, which seriously threatened their ability to provide services, especially since they hosted servers for over 200 clients. However, due to a well-thought-out business continuity plan devised by Willis Cantey, the company was able to avert a disaster.

Anticipating potential risks and disasters, Cantey had already moved its client servers to a remote data center as part of their business continuity plan. This strategic decision ensured that continual backups were in place, preventing substantial data loss and enabling a quick recovery. When the fire occurred, the company swiftly shifted its operations to the off-site data center, ensuring no disruption in services provided to their clients. Employees temporarily relocated to this site, showcasing the effectiveness of their comprehensive business continuity plan in maintaining service continuity even during unforeseen and challenging circumstances.

Do you think Cantey Technology's Comprehensive Business Continuity Plan helped? Is there any other way employees' temporary dislocation could have been avoided?

Implementing Controls

As you have seen, controls can be characterized by function—whether they prevent, detect, or correct a risk. You have also seen that we can characterize controls by the location they govern—whether that is physical activities, the general IT environment, or a specific application.

We can also characterize controls by how they are implemented. There are two methods of implementing a control: manual and automated (**Illustration 3.6**).

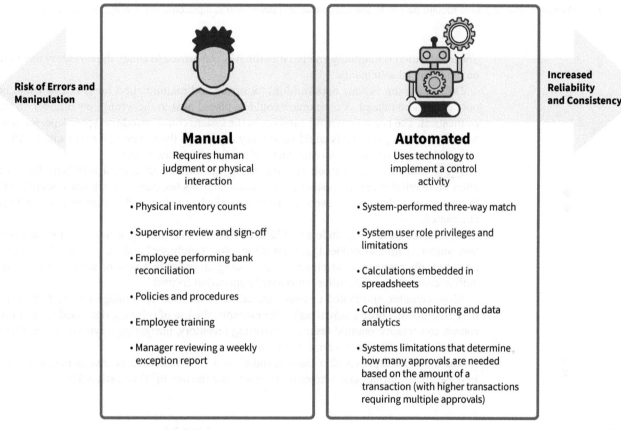

Risk of Errors and Manipulation ← → **Increased Reliability and Consistency**

Manual
Requires human judgment or physical interaction

- Physical inventory counts
- Supervisor review and sign-off
- Employee performing bank reconciliation
- Policies and procedures
- Employee training
- Manager reviewing a weekly exception report

Automated
Uses technology to implement a control activity

- System-performed three-way match
- System user role privileges and limitations
- Calculations embedded in spreadsheets
- Continuous monitoring and data analytics
- Systems limitations that determine how many approvals are needed based on the amount of a transaction (with higher transactions requiring multiple approvals)

Illustration 3.6 A control's implementation is either manual or automated.

Manual controls might sound antiquated, but they play a significant role because they are used when human judgment or physical interaction is required. Note that there is a difference between the terms "manual control" and "physical control." Manual controls are executed by people or physical interaction, while physical controls mitigate risks related to people and their actions. **CPA** Manual controls are subject to human error or intentional manipulation and override, which means there is an increased risk that a manual control might fail. For this reason, auditors—both internal and external—frequently focus on manual controls during their assessments, as described in more detail at the end of this chapter.

Manual controls are often unavoidable when it comes to physical inventory and document review. For example, Julia's Cookies is proud to sell individual serving-sized bottles of local milk at all its brick-and-mortar stores. For Baltimore, that means working with a small dairy farm in northwestern Maryland called North Green Farms. Dairy cows are part of North Green Farms' inventory and are counted regularly (**Illustration 3.7**). Employees manually tag the cows with asset tags—like a barcoded label or a number. On a regular basis, employees must physically count the cows to ensure that all are accounted for in the pastures. This manual process involves walking through fields or feedlots with a clipboard and pen.

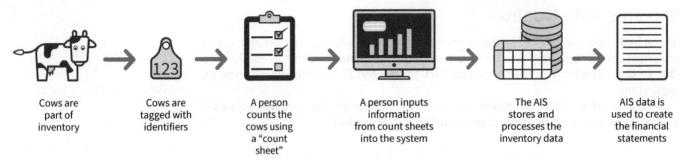

| Cows are part of inventory | Cows are tagged with identifiers | A person counts the cows using a "count sheet" | A person inputs information from count sheets into the system | The AIS stores and processes the inventory data | AIS data is used to create the financial statements |

Illustration 3.7 Manual inventory counts require people to use clipboards and paper and to input data into the system by hand.

The information is manually entered into the AIS and is used to create the inventory line item on the financial statements.

Do you see the various opportunities for errors and manipulation here? A cow could be out of sight and missed. A checkmark could be placed next to the wrong cow number on the count sheet. The person entering numbers in the system could introduce typos. A person who is tired of walking the fields could lie and say a cow was there when he never saw it. All of these risks could result in a misstatement of the financial statements.

CPA **Automated controls** use technology to implement control activities. They are often more reliable and consistent than manual controls because they are not susceptible to human error, judgment, or override. To be classified as automated, a control must be fully automated.

Automated controls include embedded IT controls like the separation of duties application control at Julia's Cookies that assigns the roles "purchaser" and "approver." This control automatically prevents a purchaser from sending an order to a vendor without the proper authorization. It is a preventive, automated application control.

More complex automated controls use other automation technologies to perform what have traditionally been manual tasks. For example, the use of robotics, discussed later in this course, can remove manual tasks like counting inventory, navigating a system, or creating a file. Let's use North Green Farms as an example.

Third-party companies offer "feedlot audit" services to automate the inventory of livestock. In these audits, drones take photos of the cows, like the one in **Illustration 3.8**.

DJI_0332   Count: 289

Count Completed By: John Gibson   August 07, 2018

Illustration 3.8 Photograph of cattle in a feedlot taken by a drone during an automated feedlot audit.

These photos are automatically fed into artificial intelligence (AI) software programmed to recognize each cow, and the software assigns a count to the picture. The AI connects directly to an information system and inputs the total count. This fully automated control alleviates any risk of human miscount, laziness, typos, or fraud (**Illustration 3.9**).

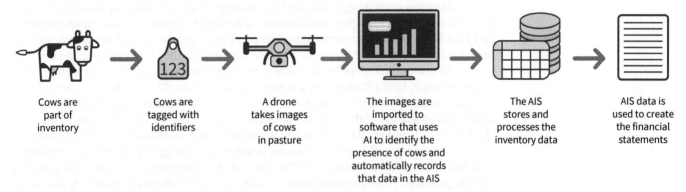

| Cows are part of inventory | Cows are tagged with identifiers | A drone takes images of cows in pasture | The images are imported to software that uses AI to identify the presence of cows and automatically records that data in the AIS | The AIS stores and processes the inventory data | AIS data is used to create the financial statements |

Illustration 3.9 Automating inventory counts can involve using drones to scan large geographic areas and import data to the system directly.

Is it feasible for all dairy farms to implement this level of automation? Not really. North Green Farms is a small dairy farm that only provides products to local restaurants and small businesses. Given the size of their herd, overhead, and budget for technology, it is unlikely that they would implement this fully automated control. North Green Farms would also have to consider what controls there should be around the technology in use. Would appropriate security be in place when they connected the third-party AI to their system? How would they provide assurance that the third-party AI was reliable? Are they equipped with technology personnel who are experienced enough to own this process and provide adequate oversight?

For a relatively small operation like North Green Farms, a good solution may be to use drones for photos, then have a human review the pictures to count the cows and input that number into the system. This approach combines automated and manual controls in a budget-friendly way.

Many controls consist of a mixture of manual and automated components. A company may need to determine which is more effective: human or computer. To adequately address risk, a business needs a combination of both manual (human) and automated (computer) controls. While automated solutions may seem like the answer to keeping manual controls up to date, even the most sophisticated and powerful programs are limited when it comes to insights and nuances. Artificial intelligence cannot completely replace human judgment, and its cost can also be a limiting factor for many companies, like North Green Farms. Ultimately, by combining human expertise and insights from powerful automated systems, businesses can optimize their risk response programs.

Why Does It Matter to Your Career?

Thoughts from a Risk and Advisory Specialist, Global Private Company

- Accounting professionals are often in charge of sensitive or regulated information. Understanding the types of risk mitigation your company implements to protect its data will help you know where your job function fits into the company's strategy.

- You are going to hear about internal controls, regardless of which area of accounting you choose to pursue. Accounting professionals often are involved with implementing (financial accounting, tax accounting) or assessing (external audit, internal audit, advisory) controls.

Continuous Monitoring

Internal auditors, who are data analysts, use **continuous monitoring** technology to create detective controls that use rules-based programming to monitor a business's data for red flags of risks.

Continuous monitoring is often programmed to keep tabs on key performance indicators (KPIs), like gross profit margin, or to look for red flags, like fraud risk indicators. The business uses this monitoring to confirm that a process is working properly or to notify management in real time when risk events occur. Automating risk management procedures allows management to identify and eliminate potential problems as soon as the red flags appear and not afterward, which is the difference between a proactive approach and a reactive approach to risk.

For example, Julia's Cookies has a service level agreement (SLA)—which is a formal commitment between two parties—with a call center. The SLA requires that operators answer a call within 90 seconds of the customer placing the call. Julia's Cookies continuously monitors the KPI for call answer rate to confirm that the call center answers calls in a timely manner.

In this instance, call center continuous monitoring is mitigating the risk of reputational loss, as the company is making sure that the call center employees answer calls according to a set guideline. This enhances customer satisfaction and reduces the possibility that Julia's Cookies' reputation will be damaged. **Illustration 3.10** shows an example of how data analytics can be used to create a continuous monitoring call center dashboard.

Continuous monitoring is an internal control that merits special attention, as it deals with multiple aspects of the AIS:

- Continuous monitoring uses data stored in the AIS for analysis. The data must be accurate.
- The continuous monitoring program is often a separate information system that creates its own technology risks.

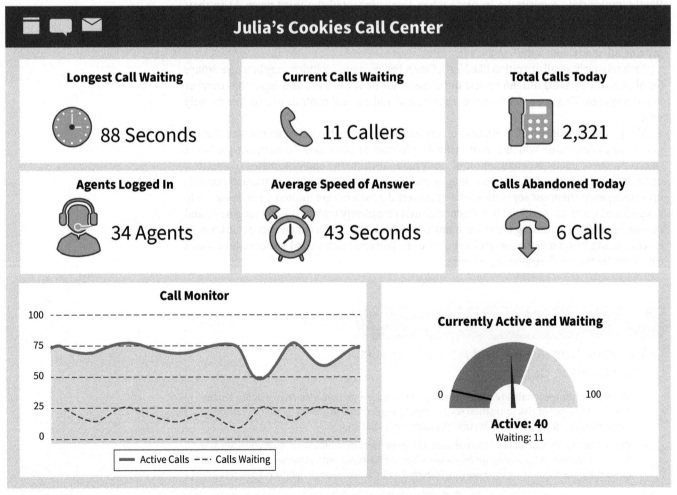

Illustration 3.10 This continuous monitoring dashboard presents visuals of KPIs at Julia's Cookies.

Even though continuous monitoring is a type of internal control, additional internal controls are often applied to the source data *and* the continuous monitoring program itself.

To summarize, remember that a control is characterized by its function (preventive, detective, or corrective), plus its location in the business processes (physical, IT general, or IT application), plus how it is implemented (manual or automated) (**Illustration 3.11**). Help the ERM team at Julia's Cookies classify controls in Applied Learning 3.2.

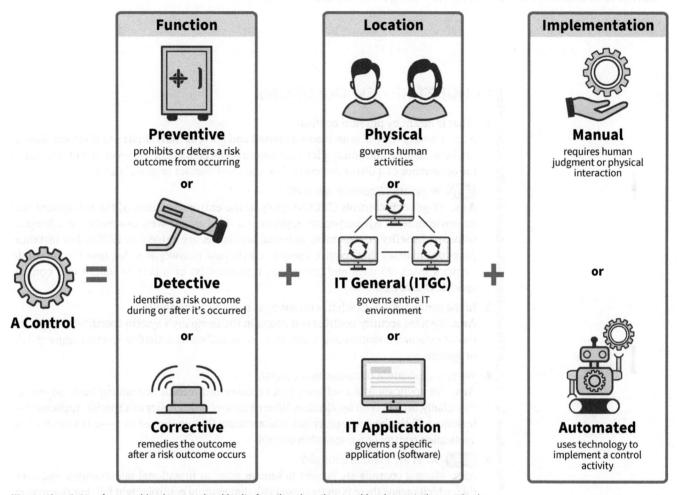

Illustration 3.11   A control is characterized by its function, location, and implementation method.

Julia's Cookies   Applied Learning 3.2

Internal Control Classification: Policies and Procedures

As Julia's Cookies began expanding and hiring more employees, it became clear to leadership that many employees were unsure of whether they could use their laptops for personal things like ordering groceries.

The ERM team developed written policies and procedures for employees to follow regarding use of company-provided devices. New employees also receive training during their first day.

Can you characterize these two controls based on their function (preventive, detective, or corrective), location (physical, IT general, or IT application), and implementation (manual or automated)?

SOLUTION

Function:

These are preventive controls. By providing up-front guidance on what employees are permitted to do with company-provided devices, Julia's Cookies reduces the likelihood that employees will use their devices inappropriately.

Location:

These are physical controls. While they relate to computer equipment, they are governing the people who use the equipment and are not embedded in the computer systems.

Implementation:

These are manual controls. Someone must oversee employees reading, and hopefully signing, a document acknowledging that they have read and understood the policies and procedures. Training is also facilitated manually.

CONCEPT REVIEW QUESTIONS

1. What is meant by physical control?

   Ans. Physical control is an internal control and governs individuals and their activities. It can be a business continuity plan that governs how people and equipment will respond to the occurrence of a disruptive event, like a natural disaster or global pandemic.

2. **CPA** What are IT general controls?

   Ans. IT general controls (ITGCs) apply to the entire operation of the full system and its environment. All corporate applications, like email, web browsers, time-keeping software, benefits management systems, and more, are subject to ITGCs. For instance, password policies that require users to create new passwords to log into the corporate network every 90 days and passwords that must be of a certain length and contain specific characters.

3. In the context of ITGC, what is meant by systems security control?

   Ans. Systems security controls embedded in the company's system specifically target the risk of external, unauthorized users performing malicious activities against company data or systems.

4. What is application or transaction control?

   Ans. An application is a software that captures and records accounting business events. Essentially, an AIS is an application. When a control only applies to a specific application—including all the business processes and accounts that are linked to it—it is known as an application control or a transaction control.

5. **CPA** What are manual controls?

   Ans. Manual controls are subject to human error or intentional manipulation and override, which means there is an increased risk that manual control might fail. For this reason, auditors—both internal and external—frequently focus on manual controls during their assessments.

6. **CPA** What is meant by automated controls?

   Ans. Automated controls use technology to implement control activities. They are often more reliable and consistent than manual controls because they are not susceptible to human error, judgment, or override. To be classified as automated, a control must be fully automated. For instance, this control automatically prevents a purchaser from sending an order to a vendor without a proper authorization. It is a preventive, automated application control.

7. What do you understand by the term "continuous monitoring"?

   Ans. Continuous monitoring is an internal control that merits special attention, as it deals with multiple aspects of the AIS. Continuous monitoring uses data stored in the AIS for analysis. The continuous monitoring program is often a separate information system that creates its own technology risks.

3.3 How Do We Assess Internal Controls?

> ## Learning Objective ❸
> Explain the three lines of defense to ensure effectiveness of internal controls.

You have learned about different risks and business processes that exist in a company. We have discussed how a company identifies risks during its risk assessment and mitigates risks by implementing internal controls. Now let's look at who makes sure those internal controls are doing their jobs. Remember that we can never have absolute confidence that a control will work as intended. Manual controls are subject to human error or manipulation, like management override or collusion, and even automated controls can have technological malfunctions.

CPA Companies must continuously assess both the overall internal control environment and individual controls to determine if they are functioning properly and addressing risk appropriately. Assessments can be performed either internally or externally by management, internal auditors, or external auditors. These business functions can be divided into three lines of defense, based on their involvement in combating risk to protect the company:

- **Management**—Management provides both the first and second lines of defense:
  - **First line of defense:** Business operations. **CPA** Management has the ownership and the responsibility of enforcing mitigating measures to prevent identified risk from occurring. As you have learned, management is responsible for developing, implementing, and controlling business processes. This is where financial accountants, tax accountants, system analysts, and other accounting professionals who are not auditors or compliance officers work.
  - **Second line of defense:** Risk management and compliance. In many companies, ERM and compliance operations are combined, while in others they might be separate departments. Recall that the ERM team is responsible for identifying and assessing organizational risks. This line of defense aids the first line of defense in ensuring that controls are designed to adequately address risk, then monitors the controls to ensure that the first line of defense is complying with internal control requirements. Accounting professionals who specialize in compliance—such as designing and monitoring internal controls, performing risk assessments and responses, or assisting the legal team—work here.
- **CPA** **Internal audit:** The **third line of defense**, internal audit, is an independent function of the company that has a unique reporting relationship in an organization. Internal audit directly reports both to executive management and to the board of directors, while the other two lines of defense report only to executive management. The primary objective of internal audit is to test internal controls to provide assurance of their effectiveness to executive management and the board of directors.

Illustration 3.12 shows the Institute of Internal Auditors' model for three lines of defense and the reporting structure adopted by most companies. In 2020, the Institute of Internal Auditors released this updated three lines of defense model, which stresses the importance of communication among the three lines, indicated by the arrows connecting them all. In this model, the first line and second line combine to create "management." Management aligns, communicates, and collaborates with the internal audit department. Both management and internal audit are accountable to and report to the governing body (board of directors).

CPA Note that external auditors are not part of the three lines of defense of a company. Instead, they are outside parties who are categorized as external assurance providers. External audit plays an important role in the overall structure, as it provides additional assurance to the company's shareholders and management regarding the effectiveness of risk mitigation. You will learn about external audit and how it compares to internal audit in the Audit Assurance chapter.

The IIA's Three Lines Model

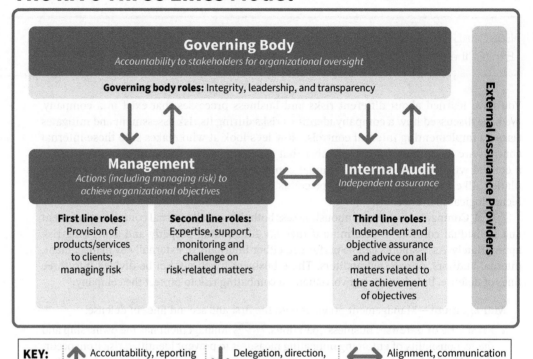

Illustration 3.12   Business functions are divided into three lines of defense that protect an organization against risk.

Source: *IIA Issues Important Update to Three Lines Model*, LAKE MARY, Fla. (July 20, 2020). Copyright © 2020 The Institute of Internal Auditors, Inc. All rights reserved.

Why Does It Matter to Your Career?

Thoughts from a Manager—External Audit, Big Four Public Accounting Firm

You are going to be part of the three lines of defense model. You could be a financial accountant in the first line, risk specialist in the second line, internal auditor in the third line, external auditor in the external assurance providers, or one day a member of the audit committee or CFO in the governing body. Every role in a company has a place in this model. Consider where yours is once you begin your career.

Management: First and Second Lines of Defense

Management includes both the first line of defense, business operations, and the second line of defense, compliance and ERM teams. Management controls business processes and mitigates risk through preventive, detective, and corrective actions. Internal auditors are not part of designing or implementing controls; in other words, they are not control owners. **CPA** The responsibility for processes and controls rests solely with management, and internal audit provides a complementary, objective assessment. Management performs self-assessments to determine the effectiveness of its own controls.

Companies constantly work to achieve the optimal state of business processes and controls. While there are many ways management can assess business processes' levels of maturity and internal controls, a single approach is used throughout this course for consistency. It is a model used in the real world by management, compliance, ERM teams, and third-party consultants to assess the performance of business processes and their related controls by comparing the current state to an ideal operating state.

A **maturity model** shows how far along a company is on its journey to reach the ideal state by comparing the current state to a predetermined set of best practices. Companies use maturity models to judge their current performance and create a roadmap, or plan, for continuous improvement. Maturity models can be custom-designed tools, but there are many resources available for companies to leverage as they design their models. For example, the Institute of Internal Auditors provides guidance in its publication *Selecting, Using, and Creating Maturity Models: A Tool for Assurance and Consulting Engagements*, which sets out guidelines for designing a maturity model. By using best practices to design or select a maturity model, companies gain:

- A guide for envisioning the future—both the desired state and the development needed to get there
- Benchmarks for the organization to use in comparing processes internally or externally
- Insights into the improvement path from an immature model to a mature model
- Disciplined methods that are easy for management to understand and implement

A given company's maturity model can differ greatly from a competitor's, as each is designed using KPIs and benchmarks specific to that company's business model and risks. To assess the maturity of business processes and their related controls, Julia's Cookies uses the maturity model in **Illustration 3.13**. This model has four phases that correlate with the size and sophistication of the company. For Julia's Cookies, a nationally recognized food service company with more than 3,000 employees, the goal is to achieve Phase 4—Optimized. Smaller companies may lack the resources to realistically reach this phase or may determine through a cost-benefit analysis that a lesser phase is their ideal state. The maturity model Julia's Cookies uses is generic in that it is designed to be applied to all business processes and related controls across the company. Spend a while reviewing the following explanations of the phases. As you progress through this AIS course, you will use this business process maturity model to assess the current state of operations in Julia's Cookies' business processes.

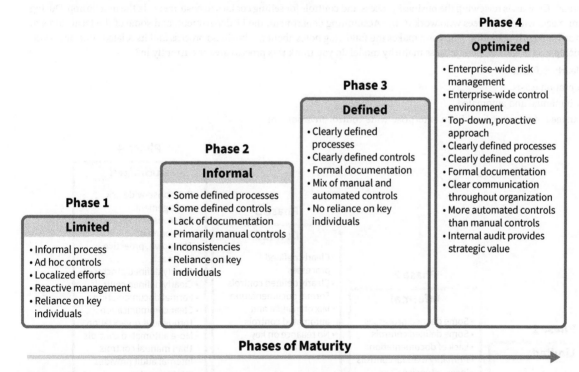

Illustration 3.13   The four phases on Julia's Cookies' business process maturity model are (1) limited, (2) informal, (3) defined, and (4) optimized.

Phase 1—Limited: In Phase 1, a company's business processes are poorly defined, and employees may use multiple ways to achieve the same outcome. Supervisors and managers make their own decisions on which controls to implement, and there's not an enterprise-wide risk assessment or control environment. This is a reactive environment, and management only addresses issues after something has gone wrong. The team relies on key individuals who have strong knowledge of the team's responsibilities. If a key employee quits or is out of office, the business processes suffer due to lack of documentation for others to follow.

Phase 2—Informal: Some processes and controls are defined, but documentation, inconsistencies, and reliance on key individuals still exist. Overall, everything is more defined, but informal maturity business processes lack enterprise-wide oversight and implementation.

Phase 3—Defined: Policies, procedures, and controls are formally documented, which creates a consistent environment where key employees are no longer relied on. Automated controls provide more protection against errors and manipulation. Many companies may never achieve a higher phase of maturity than Phase 3 due to resource limitations.

Phase 4—Optimized: As the ideal state, Phase 4 is considered the gold standard in business process maturity. Risk management and controls are managed at an enterprise-wide level, with leadership taking a top-down, proactive approach to risk. Because the processes are running so well, internal audit can shift its focus away from control reviews and toward more innovative projects that provide strategic support for decision makers. Every company should strive for the best practices of Phase 4, even if resource limitations prevent them from implementing all of them.

Make sure you thoroughly understand these four phases, as you will apply them to Julia's Cookies throughout this course when business processes are reviewed. To get started, assist the ERM team in assessing the maturity of the sales processes in Applied Learning 3.3.

Julia's Cookies　　　　　　　　　　　　　　　　　　　　　　Applied Learning 3.3

Assessing Internal Controls: Business Process Maturity Model

The ERM team at Julia's Cookies is reviewing the business process and controls for selling cookies to customers via the mobile app. During the review, the team meets with employees who work in the Accounting department, the IT department, and some of the local stores to discuss how things are currently operating. The team makes the following notes about the business process and its related controls. Based on these notes, which phase of the business process maturity model do you think this process area is currently in?

- Processes are clearly defined.
- Formal documentation exists.
- Controls are both manual and automated.
- Controls are managed at an entity level in an enterprise-wide control environment.

Phase 4

Optimized
- Enterprise-wide risk management
- Enterprise-wide control environment
- Top-down, proactive approach
- Clearly defined processes
- Clearly defined controls
- Formal documentation
- Clear communication throughout organization
- More automated controls than manual controls
- Internal audit provides strategic value

Phase 3

Defined
- Clearly defined processes
- Clearly defined controls
- Formal documentation
- Mix of manual and automated controls
- No reliance on key individuals

Phase 2

Informal
- Some defined processes
- Some defined controls
- Lack of documentation
- Primarily manual controls
- Inconsistencies
- Reliance on key individuals

Phase 1

Limited
- Informal process
- Ad hoc controls
- Localized efforts
- Reactive management
- Reliance on key individuals

Phases of Maturity

- Business process would not function as intended if key personnel were absent.
- Risk management at Julia's Cookies is enterprise-wide.
- Internal audit recently performed an advisory project to provide strategic advice that included this model.

SOLUTION

The first step of this solution is to identify in which phase each of these items belongs:

- Phase 3/4: Processes are clearly defined.
- Phase 3/4: Formal documentation exists.
- Phase 3: Controls are both manual and automated.
- Phase 4: Controls are managed at an entity level in an enterprise-wide control environment.
- Phase 2: Business process would not operate if key personnel were absent.
- Phase 4: Risk management at Julia's Cookies is enterprise-wide.
- Phase 4: Internal audit recently performed an advisory project to provide strategic advice that included this process.

While it looks at first as if this process is operating at Phase 4, there are still some Phase 2 and Phase 3 areas to improve. For that reason, the ERM team will use its judgment to make the decision between assessing this area as Phase 3 or Phase 4. In assessments like this, there are not often clear answers. Usually, professionals use facts like the ones provided in the notes, combined with professional skepticism and critical thinking, to make a judgment call.

In this instance, the ERM team classifies this process area as Phase 3—Defined. There is still room for improvement.

Internal Audit: Third Line of Defense

Internal audit adds value to a business by providing assurance, insight, and objectivity to the company (**Illustration 3.14**).

Assurance	Ensures that the organization is operating in accordance with management's plan
Insight	Discovers improvements for policies, procedures, controls, and risk management
Objectivity	Assesses the company from an independent consulting point of view

Illustration 3.14 Internal audit provides assurance, insight, and objectivity to a company.

Some businesses outsource their internal audit departments by hiring contractors to perform internal audit work, while other companies hire as many as 400 internal auditors as employees. There are also many companies that have only a handful of internal auditors.

Internal auditors are employees of their organizations; however, they must remain independent of all business functions that they audit. **CPA** **Independence** means an auditor is removed from the business process and has no stake in or influence over the outcome of the business processes that they are auditing. It is important to remain independent in order to audit the business objectively.

Internal auditors provide insights into company policies, procedures, processes, controls, and even culture. They present the results of their audit engagements to both company leadership and the **audit committee**, which is a committee of the company's board of directors that includes outside committee members with special qualifications in finance or accounting. The audit committee provides objective oversight of a company, and the company's internal audit department has a direct line of communication to this committee.

Imagine that the Internal Audit department at Julia's Cookies discovers that Darlene, the CFO, has been committing fraud. Rather than tell the chief executive officer, who could be colluding with Darlene, the Internal Audit department can report these suspicions directly to the audit committee.

While some companies are required to have an internal audit department, including publicly traded companies listed on different stock exchanges, companies that are exempt from this regulation may still choose to establish an internal audit department because of the value this team brings by:

- Assessing whether controls are well designed
- Determining if controls are functioning as designed
- Providing objective insight because of its independence
- Ensuring that the company is complying with regulations
- Identifying opportunities for strategic improvements

CONCEPT REVIEW QUESTIONS

1. **CPA** In the three lines of defense model, which business function is considered as the first line of defense?

   Ans. Management has the ownership and the responsibility of enforcing mitigating measures to prevent identified risk from occurring. Management is responsible for developing, implementing, and controlling business processes. This is where financial accountants, tax accountants, system analysts, and other accounting professionals who are not auditors or compliance officers work. They are the doers involved in business operations and act as the first line of defense.

2. Which is the second line of defense?

   Ans. In many companies, risk management and compliance team is the second line of defense. The ERM team is responsible for identifying and assessing organizational risks. This line of defense aids the first line of defense to ensure that controls are designed to address risk adequately. It then monitors the controls to ensure that the first line of defense complies with internal control requirements. Accounting professionals specializing in compliance—designing and monitoring internal controls, performing risk assessments and responses, or assisting the legal team—work here.

3. **CPA** Which is the third line of defense?

   Ans. Internal audit is an independent function of the company that has a unique reporting relationship in an organization. Internal audit directly reports to the executive management and the board of directors, while the other two lines of defense report only to the executive management. The primary objective of internal audit is to test internal controls to provide assurance of their effectiveness to executive management and the board of directors.

4. Write a note on maturity model.

   Ans. A maturity model shows how far a company is on its journey to reach the ideal state by comparing the current state to a predetermined set of best practices. Companies use maturity models to judge their current performance and create a roadmap or plan for continuous improvement.

5. **CPA** What do you mean by auditor independence in risk management?

   Ans. Independence means an auditor is removed from the business process and has no stake in or influence over the outcome of the business processes that they are auditing. It is important to remain independent in order to audit the business objectively. Internal auditors provide insights into company policies, procedures, processes, controls, and even culture. They present the results of their audit engagements to both company leadership and the audit committee.

6. What is an audit committee?

   Ans. The audit committee with the company's board of directors includes outside committee members with special qualifications in finance or accounting. The audit committee provides objective oversight of a company, and the company's internal audit department has a direct line of communication to this committee.

3.4 Why Are Internal Control Frameworks Important?

> ## Learning Objective ❹
> Describe the importance of frameworks in an internal control environment.

Risk assessments, risk management, and internal control are complex parts of a business. Entire departments and large budgets are often dedicated to these areas. Risk management is so important that there are regulations focused on ensuring that companies have appropriate internal controls and risk management plans in place. How do businesses know how to comply with these requirements? This is where companies turn to frameworks.

CPA A **framework** is a published set of specifications and criteria that defines a strategy to achieve certain objectives. Frameworks come in many types and are not exclusive to the accounting industry. For example, accounting frameworks are specific to the information appearing in a company's financial statements, and risk management frameworks focus on how a company defines its strategy for eliminating or minimizing the impact of risks.

A framework provides a set of instructions for businesses to follow. Frameworks are often referred to as roadmaps as they provide a path to follow but don't specify what mode of transportation to use. In other words, they are not prescriptive. They give an outline for companies to follow regarding how to approach a topic. In some ways, your class syllabus is like a framework. It provides an outline for your class, including course objectives, expectations, rules, timelines, and things you can do to be successful in achieving your goal of earning a good grade. If you don't follow your syllabus, there's a chance you may put in a lot of work for the class that doesn't meet your professor's expectations. This is a high-risk approach that most students choose not to take. Why risk failing a course when your professor provided you with a framework for success at the beginning of the term? Your syllabus is not prescriptive either. It doesn't tell you exactly what every assignment should look like. Instead, it gives you an outline of what types of assignments are coming.

Companies use frameworks to guide them in implementing internal controls and meeting regulatory requirements. To better understand how regulations and internal controls affect companies, we can look at how the Sarbanes-Oxley Act became a reality.

Sarbanes-Oxley Act of 2002 (SOX)

Many of the largest accounting scandals in U.S. history took place between 1995 and 2005. Scandals involving companies like Enron, Tyco, and WorldCom cost corporations and their investors billions of dollars. These financial statement frauds shook the financial markets and the trust of investors, resulting in a large-scale move by the U.S. government to enact a bill that would restore the trust of the public and increase the liability of corporate leaders for their companies' actions.

CPA The goal of the **Sarbanes-Oxley Act of 2002 (SOX)** is to protect investors from fraud and other risks by improving the reliability and accuracy of financial statements. Does that seem familiar? It is very similar to the definition of internal controls. This is because SOX primarily focuses on the internal control structure of a company. While internal controls and reporting requirements had been around for decades, SOX changed the way companies operate by mandating audit trails and shifting the responsibility for financial reporting misstatements. Responsibility for control failures moved directly to management, and violation of internal control requirements now comes with serious criminal penalties—with fines up to $5 million and/or imprisonment for up to 20 years.

CPA SOX compliance is required for:

- Publicly traded companies in the United States and their subsidiaries
- Foreign companies that are publicly traded and do business in the United States
- Private companies planning their initial public offerings (IPOs) to become publicly traded companies
- Accounting firms performing audits of the above SOX-regulated companies

While private companies, nonprofits, and charities are generally not required to fully comply with SOX regulations, they cannot intentionally destroy or falsify relevant information and are subject to SOX penalties if they do. Many also find that complying with SOX provides enhanced efficiencies and security for their businesses and choose to do so voluntarily.

CPA SOX has many requirements—far too many to cover here. Some of the most significant SOX requirements are:

CPA Chief executive officers (CEOs) and CFOs are responsible for:

- The accuracy and documentation of financial statements
- Ensuring that financial statements are reviewed by management
- Overall internal control structure reports provided to the Securities and Exchange Commission (SEC)
- Informing external auditors about any significant internal control issues or fraud concerns

CPA An internal control report that:

- Is included in the company's annual financial statements
- States that management is responsible for implementing and maintaining an adequate system of internal control
- Contains an assessment of the effectiveness of the system of internal control

CPA An external audit that:

- Evaluates management's assessment of the effectiveness of the system of internal control and provides an audit opinion on management's report
- Includes disclosure of significant internal control deficiencies, which are controls that are not operating correctly
- Includes disclosure of instances where the internal control environment is not in compliance with SOX

CPA Formal data security policies that:

- Are communicated and enforced throughout the company
- Ensure protection of all financial data in storage and in use

These are only some of the regulatory requirements for companies subject to SOX compliance.

The U.S. SEC is the government agency that oversees trading and securities transactions and has the legal authority to issue rules under federal securities laws. The SEC first required publicly traded companies to file financial reports in 1934. After SOX became law in 2002, the SEC required publicly traded companies to select and use a formal internal control framework for implementing and annually reporting on the effectiveness of internal controls. The framework selected by a company must (1) be free from bias, (2) provide consistent measurements of internal controls, (3) be complete enough to include any relevant factor that could alter the opinion about a company's effectiveness of internal controls, and (4) have relevance to an evaluation of internal controls as they relate to financial reporting.

Why Does It Matter to Your Career?

Thoughts from an Internal Audit Manager—Analytics, Financial Services

- While some frameworks can feel overwhelming, there are good resources that summarize them. Infographics and charts are good sources of on-the-job references.
- Using a framework can give you leverage when speaking to leadership. When going into a meeting to update leaders on the results of a project, saying that the team "used COSO" or did something "in accordance with SOX" will get their attention. Because the control environment is so important to leadership—who are responsible for all of this under SOX rules—they often pay closer attention when specific frameworks and regulations are mentioned. This kind of knowledge will add credibility to your work.

Directive 2014/56/EU of the European Parliament

The European Union (EU) equivalent of the Sarbanes-Oxley Act (SOX) for internal controls is the EU Audit Regulation and Directive (**Directive 2014/56/EU**) which was adopted in 2014. This directive was an amendment to Directive 2006/43/EC.[2] The goal of the directive is to set out the framework for all statutory audits, strengthen public oversight of the audit profession, and improve cooperation between competent authorities in the EU.

Some of the main changes introduced by this directive include the following:

1. The directive enables statutory auditors and audit firms to develop their statutory audit service activities within the Union by allowing them to provide such services in a Member State other than that in which they were approved.

2. The aim is to eliminate barriers to developing statutory audit services between Member States and facilitate the integration of the Union audit market.

3. The competent authorities shall establish procedures for the approval of statutory auditors who have been approved in other Member States.

4. Statutory auditors and audit firms should be bound by strict rules on confidentiality and professional secrecy, which should not, however, block the proper enforcement of this Directive and of Regulation (EU) No 537/2014 or cooperation with the group auditor during the performance of the audit of consolidated financial statements when the parent undertaking is in a third country.

5. The power to adopt supervisory measures by, and the sanctioning powers of, competent authorities should be enhanced.

Directive 2014/56/EU[3] has introduced stricter requirements on the statutory audits of public-interest entities, such as listed companies, credit institutions, and insurance undertakings. It aims to improve statutory audits in the EU by reinforcing auditors' independence and professional suspicion toward the management of the audited company. The directive also enables statutory auditors and audit firms to develop their statutory audit service activities within the Union by enabling them to provide such services in a Member State other than that in which they were approved. This would contribute to the integration of the Union audit market. Additionally, the power to adopt supervisory measures and the sanctioning powers of competent authorities have been enhanced. Overall, this directive strengthens public oversight of the audit profession and improves cooperation between competent authorities in the EU.

COSO Internal Control–Integrated Framework

To comply with SOX and the SEC requirement of using an internal control framework, most publicly traded companies turn to an organization called the **Committee of Sponsoring Organizations of the Treadway Commission (COSO)**. This organization, which is committed to fighting corporate fraud, is composed of five private organizations that focus on providing guidance to executives and government entities on fraud prevention and response. CPA The respected private sector groups that comprise COSO are:

- The American Accounting Association (AAA)
- The American Institute of Certified Public Accountants (AICPA)
- The Institute of Internal Auditors (IIA)
- The Institute of Management Accountants (IMA)
- The Financial Executives Institute (FEI)

---

[2]https://finance.ec.europa.eu/capital-markets-union-and-financial-markets/company-reporting-and-auditing/auditing-companies-financial-statements_en?prefLang=pllegislation

[3]https://eur-lex.europa.eu/legal-content/EN/TXT/?uri=CELEX:32014L0056

COSO's guidance for SOX compliance comes in the form of a framework. The **Internal Control–Integrated Framework** is a control-based approach to risk management that is widely accepted as the authoritative guidance on internal controls and SOX compliance. It defines internal control and gives the criteria for developing, implementing, and monitoring an effective internal control system. Many companies that are not required to follow SOX still choose to leverage the Internal Control–Integrated Framework, as it provides a solid foundation to help companies enhance the following areas:

- Cybersecurity protection against fraud and threats
- Handling the advanced complexities of a business
- Meeting high expectations of oversight from leadership
- Operating in global markets
- Performing robust and detailed risk assessments
- Adhering to complex requirements of regulations, laws, and standards
- Improving efficiencies in operations
- Providing increased reliability of financial reporting
- Adapting and reacting to evolving technologies
- Providing cost savings
- Improving the effectiveness of internal controls

The Internal Control–Integrated Framework consists of two key parts and a visualized model:

- Control objectives
- Components and related principles
- COSO Cube

Control Objectives

CPA The Internal Control–Integrated Framework focuses on achieving results in three areas, called **control objectives**:

- *Operations objectives* relate to the effectiveness and efficiency of the company's daily functions, allocation of resources, operation and financial performance, and prevention of losses.
- *Reporting objectives* relate to the reporting of financial information internally and externally and the reporting of nonfinancial information. These objectives relate to the characteristics of useful information, including relevance, representational faithfulness, timeliness, and reliability.
- *Compliance objectives* relate to internal control goals for adhering to applicable laws and regulations.

Control Components

The five key steps involved in implementing an effective system of internal controls are the **control components**. They flow from the top to the bottom of a business, starting with the control environment and ending with monitoring. **CPA** Control components and their related principles help framework users understand what an effective control is and how to judge whether a control is effectively designed and implemented (**Table 3.2**).

Throughout this course, you have been using some of the components of the COSO Internal Control–Integrated Framework without even knowing it. Do you see how relevant this framework is and why so many businesses choose to adopt it even when regulations don't specifically require it?

COSO Cube

CPA COSO shows how the parts of an effective control system are related in the COSO Cube (**Illustration 3.15**). The three control objectives are at the top—they make up the columns of the cube. The rows reflect the five interrelated control components. The third dimension—on

TABLE 3.2 CPA COSO Internal Control–Integrated Framework Control Components and Related Principles

Control Component	Related Principles	Key Course Concept
1. **Control environment:** This is the foundation for other components and includes the attitude of management concerning integrity and ethical behavior. It is the most important component because it sets the overall tone for the organization. When the tone at the top leadership is poor, the control environment suffers. Recall that companies should adopt a risk-aware culture, which starts with leadership setting an example, and conduct entity-level risk activities. A lax control environment presents a higher risk for management override of internal controls, which can have a significant impact on an organization's internal control efforts. To ensure that the control environment is regularly assessed, SOX compliance requires a routine test of how internal controls are monitored and an annual control review by external auditors.	1. Demonstrates commitment to integrity and ethical values 2. Exercises oversight responsibility 3. Establishes structure, authority, and responsibility 4. Demonstrates commitment to competence 5. Enforces accountability	• Risk appetite • Enterprise-wide risk management • Business process maturity model • Management override • SOX regulations
2. **Risk assessment:** This component requires management to continuously identify, categorize, and prioritize risk by looking at both internal and external risks to the company. This is done by performing a risk assessment. The risk assessment also identifies the potential for fraud and any changes that could impact the functionality of the internal controls.	6. Specifies suitable control objectives 7. Identifies and analyzes risk 8. Assesses fraud risk 9. Identifies and analyzes significant change	• Risk appetite • Risk identification • Risk categorization • Risk scores • Risk prioritization • Heat maps
3. **Control activities:** This component consists of the policies and procedures that address risk and support achievement of the company's objectives. You have learned how risks are mitigated through internal control. This entire chapter is about controls, which are an essential part of the COSO Internal Control–Integrated Framework.	10. Selects and develops control activities 11. Selects and develops general controls over technology (ITGCs) 12. Deploys through policies and procedures	• Risk responses • Internal controls
4. **Information and communication:** This component consists of internal and external communications, including financial reports, policies, and procedures. Remember the policy Julia's Cookies created to inform its employees of when they are allowed to use a company computer? That falls under information and communication. Don't forget that the characteristics of quality information are an important part of a company's information and communication.	13. Uses relevant information 14. Communicates internally 15. Communicates externally	• Quality information • Reporting • Data analytics • Internal audit • Management • Audit committee • Financial statements
5. **Monitoring:** This component is about assessing internal controls and determining whether changes should be made. Management monitors business processes with detective controls and ensures that the controls are working appropriately. You learned about assessing internal controls in an earlier section of this chapter.	16. Conducts ongoing and/or separate evaluations 17. Evaluates and communicates deficiencies	• Management assessments • Internal audits • Audit committee reporting

the right of the image—relates to a company's organizational structure. The organizational structure includes different levels of business, starting with the entity as a whole and drilling all the way down to an individual job function. Recall that you looked at the drill-down of Julia's Cookies from entity level through business function to business processes and risks in the previous chapter. COSO uses different terminology for this, but it is the same principle as what you have already learned. The sides of the cube work three dimensionally to show how everything is connected.

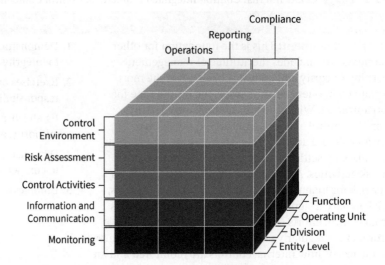

Illustration 3.15 The COSO Cube depicts how all parts of the Internal Control–Integrated Framework are related.

Source: www.coso.org/Documents/ COSO-ICIF-11x17-Cube-Graphic.pdf

COSO Enterprise Risk Management Framework

COSO has developed another widely used framework specifically for risk management. In 2004, COSO published its Enterprise Risk Management–Integrated Framework to provide organizations with a roadmap to managing risk. The framework included four objectives and eight components displayed in a COSO Cube like the Internal Control–Integrated Framework. In 2017, COSO recognized that the complexity of risk was changing and set out to address new risks that had emerged for businesses. Its updated framework reflects the importance of risk management in strategic planning and encourages companies to incorporate risk management throughout their departments and functions. The eight components were changed to five components, and the objectives and cube presentation are gone (COSO still uses a cube presentation for its Internal Control–Integrated Framework). **CPA** The new publication, called Enterprise Risk Management–Integrating with Strategy and Performance (**ERM Framework**), is a set of five interrelated components that highlight the importance of risk in creating strategies and driving a company's performance (**Table 3.3**).

The components and principles of the COSO ERM Framework are aligned with the steps and concepts you have learned so far in this course. You have been using the COSO ERM Framework without realizing it.

CPA The ERM Framework aims to improve the risk management process by addressing more than internal control:

- It embeds risk management throughout the organization as a prime responsibility of management and the board of directors.

- It is more comprehensive than the COSO Internal Control–Integrated Framework because it focuses on *all* types of risks. It uses a risk-based approach, where the risk is at the forefront of thought. The COSO Internal Control–Integrated Framework is a controls-based approach, with internal control efficiency at the forefront.

- Its principles apply to all functions across all levels of an organization, just like the components of the COSO Internal Control–Integrated Framework (the third dimension of the COSO Cube). Enterprise risk management is present throughout the strategy formation—from a company's mission, vision, and core values all the way through the strategy's implementation and performance.

While there are many types of frameworks, all of them have this in common: they provide companies with ways to address risk. Even if you do not work for a company that is required to be SOX compliant, you are likely to encounter frameworks in your career. Companies of all sizes and subject to different types of regulations choose to voluntarily invest in human resources and processes needed to implement the SOX and COSO frameworks because of the logical and detailed guidance they provide to manage risk. Help Julia's Cookies determine which framework to use in Applied Learning 3.4.

TABLE 3.3 CPA COSO ERM Framework Components and Principles Tied to Course Concepts

Component	Related Principles	Key Course Concept
1. Governance and culture: This component is about setting the company's tone and establishing oversight responsibilities for ERM.	1. Exercises board risk oversight 2. Establishes operating structures 3. Defines desired culture 4. Demonstrates commitment to core values 5. Attracts, develops, and retains capable individuals	• Business model • Values and mission • Business objectives • Sustainability • Culture
2. Strategy and objective setting: This component is about the strategic planning process, which combines ERM, strategy, and objective setting to determine the risk appetite and align it with the business objectives.	6. Analyzes business context 7. Defines risk appetite 8. Evaluates alternative strategies 9. Formulates business objectives	• Decision-making context • Risk appetite • Business objectives
3. Performance: This component is about assessing and identifying risks and responding to risks at a portfolio-view level. It is also about reporting results to key stakeholders.	10. Identifies risk 11. Assesses severity of risk 12. Prioritizes risks 13. Implements risk responses 14. Develops portfolio view	• Risk identification • Risk categorization • Risk scores • Risk prioritization • Heat maps • Risk responses • Internal controls • Portfolio-level risks
4. Review and revision: This component is about reviewing performance to consider how well ERM is functioning and identify necessary revisions.	15. Assesses substantial change 16. Reviews risk and performance 17. Pursues improvement in ERM	• Internal audits • Management assessments • Business process maturity model
5. Information, communication, and reporting: This component is about continually obtaining and sharing necessary information, from both internal and external sources, flowing up, down, and across the company.	18. Leverages information and technology 19. Communicates risk information 20. Reports on risk, culture, and performance	• Quality information • Reporting • Data analytics • Management assessments • Internal audits • Audit committee reporting

Julia's Cookies   Applied Learning 3.4

Risk Management: Selecting a Framework

Management wants to improve the corporate structure of the business by implementing a framework to help align its business objectives to its risk management approach, including identifying risks, selecting responses, and continuously assessing whether the risk approach is appropriately managed. Which framework would you suggest that Julia's Cookies use, and why?

SOLUTION

Julia's Cookies should use the COSO ERM Framework. This framework specifically addresses the risk management approach and alignment with strategic objectives. It includes components dedicated to assessing the risk management process and revising how the company is managing risks. The COSO Internal Control–Integrated Framework focuses on reviewing and communicating control activities, not the risk management process.

CONCEPT REVIEW QUESTIONS

1. What is the importance of frameworks in an internal control environment?

   Ans. A framework is a published set of specifications and criteria that defines a strategy to achieve certain objectives. It provides a set of instructions for businesses to follow. Frameworks are often referred to as roadmaps as they provide a path to follow but don't specify what mode of transportation to use. In other words, they are not prescriptive.

2. What is the goal of the Sarbanes-Oxley Act of 2002 (SOX)?

   Ans. The Sarbanes-Oxley Act of 2002 (SOX) was enacted to protect investors from fraud and other risks by improving the reliability and accuracy of financial statements.

3. **CPA** What is an internal control report?

   Ans. An internal control report is a report that states that the management is responsible for implementing and maintaining an adequate system of internal control and contains an assessment of the effectiveness of the system of internal control.

4. **CPA** What is an external audit?

   Ans. An external audit evaluates the management's assessment of the internal control system's effectiveness. It provides an audit opinion on the management's report. It includes disclosure of significant internal control deficiencies, which are controls that are not operating correctly. It also includes disclosure of instances where the internal control environment is not in compliance with SOX.

5. What is the Internal Control–Integrated Framework?

   Ans. The Internal Control–Integrated Framework is a control-based risk management approach, widely accepted as the authoritative guidance on internal controls and SOX compliance. It defines the internal controls and gives the criteria for developing, implementing, and monitoring an effective internal control system.

6. **CPA** Write a short note on control objectives.

   Ans. The Internal Control–Integrated Framework focuses on achieving results in three areas called control objectives. The three areas are operations objectives, reporting objectives, and compliance objectives.

7. **CPA** What are control components?

   Ans. The key steps involved in implementing an effective system of internal controls are the control components. They flow from the top to the bottom of a business, starting with the control environment and ending with monitoring. Control components and their related principles help framework users understand what effective control is and how to judge whether a control is effectively designed and implemented.

8. What is the goal of Directive 2014/56/EU?

   Ans. The goal of Directive 2014/56/EU is to set out the framework for all statutory audits, strengthen public oversight of the audit profession, and improve cooperation between competent authorities in the European Union (EU).

FEATURED PROFESSIONAL | Managing Partner, Risk Management Firm

Photo courtesy of Cindy Wyatt

Cindy Wyatt, CPA, CITP, CFF, CFE

Cindy is the managing partner of a firm that specializes in risk management, internal control, and business processes. She is passionate about helping clients manage risk, implement best practice internal controls, and improve their operational performance. Cindy is an avid learner who loves new opportunities. She has a bachelor of science degree in accounting with a minor concentration in information systems. In her personal time, Cindy enjoys traveling, and her goal is to visit all 50 states and every continent.

What are your top interview tips for candidates?

- Be prepared—thoroughly research the company, the position, and the interviewer, if possible.

- Dress professionally and make sure you have a firm handshake.

- Bring a notebook and be prepared to ask questions.
- Make sure you know where you are going and allow yourself plenty of time to get there.
- Be able to confidently provide an overview of yourself.
- Research common interview questions and practice, practice, practice!

What is your favorite thing about your job?

I love working with internal controls as I get to see every aspect of a company and understand how it operates.

How does your company address its own internal risk?

We have a unique risk perspective since we get to work with many different companies and see a broad spectrum of the types of risks that businesses face. We use a twofold approach to addressing risk within our firm. We address certain emerging risks, such as new security risks, in real time to minimize any potential impacts. In addition, we have periodic internal meetings where we perform internal risk assessments.

What is your best career advice for professionals?

People often think technical skills are the most important but often forget that professional and people skills are equally important. My best professional advice is:

- Always show up early with a positive attitude.
- View work as an opportunity, not a burden.
- Get out of your comfort zone and be willing to accept new challenges.
- Seek out every opportunity you can to make or strengthen relationships.
- Always keep your commitments and take responsibility for your mistakes.
- Work fervently on listening, presentation, and relationship skills, which are critical to success.

Review and Practice

Key Terms Review

application
application control
audit committee
automated control
collusion
Committee of Sponsoring
   Organizations of the Treadway
   Commission (COSO)
continuous monitoring
control
control component

control environment
control objective
corrective control
detective control
Directive 2014/56/EU
ERM Framework
first line of defense
framework
independence
internal audit
internal control

Internal Control–Integrated Framework
IT general control (ITGC)
management override
manual control
maturity model
preventive control
Sarbanes-Oxley Act of 2002 (SOX)
second line of defense
segregation of duties
third line of defense
time-based model of controls

Learning Objectives Review

❶ Distinguish among the three functions of internal controls.

The most commonly used risk response is risk mitigation. Internal control is a process specifically designed to mitigate risks to the company's financial information.

Internal control creates assurance that:

- Accounting information is reliable, complete, and valid.
- Operations are effective and efficient.
- The company is complying with laws and regulations.

An internal control, or control activity, is a mechanism a company implements to create the internal control process.

Controls have three functions, and a single control can be a combination of two or more of these functions:

- Prevent: Prohibit or deter a risk from occurring
- Detect: Identify a risk outcome during or after it occurs
- Correct: Remedy the risk outcome after it occurs

Separation of duties is a special type of preventive control that lessens the risk of fraud by ensuring that different employees are responsible for each of these three key activities:

- Authorizing business transactions and decisions
- Recording data about business activities
- Having custody of business assets

We can never have absolute confidence that controls will work correctly. They can, and regularly do, fail.

There are two important considerations when designing controls to prevent fraud:

- Management override occurs when a well-designed internal control fails because management is not following policy or procedure.
- Collusion occurs when two or more employees work together to circumvent controls.

❷ Characterize a control by its location and implementation method.

Controls are characterized by the three locations they can govern:

- Physical controls: Govern human activities
- IT general controls (ITGCs): Govern the entire IT environment
- IT application controls: Govern a specific application (software)

Controls are implemented in one of two ways:

- Manual: Requires human judgment or physical interaction
- Automated: Uses technology to implement a control activity

Manual controls have a higher risk of error or manipulation than automated controls, which are more reliable and consistent.

Many controls have both manual and automated components.

Continuous monitoring uses data analytics to create automated controls that detect risk parameters, called red flags. Monitoring is often used to keep an eye on KPIs and fraud risks.

A control is defined as:

(Function) Preventive *or* Detective *or* Corrective
+
(Location) Physical *or* ITGC *or* IT application
+
(Implementation) Manual *or* Automated

❸ Explain the three lines of defense to ensure effectiveness of internal controls.

Business functions can be decomposed into the three lines of defense model:

- Management, which includes:
  - Business operations: First line
  - Risk management and compliance: Second line
- Internal audit: Third line

Management performs self-assessments and is responsible for controlling business processes and mitigating risk through monitoring and corrective action.

A business process maturity model is used to assess how a business process and its controls compare to benchmarks defined as phases.

Internal audit remains independent by staying unbiased and separate from the business process that is subject to audit. Internal audit also reports directly to the audit committee, a committee of the board of directors that includes outside board members who have expertise in accounting and finance.

Internal audits bring value to a business by:

- Assessing control design
- Determining control functionality
- Providing objective insights
- Ensuring regulatory compliance
- Identifying strategic opportunities

❹ Describe the importance of frameworks in an internal control environment.

A framework is a published set of specifications and criteria that assists companies in achieving objectives. It is not prescriptive, rather, it is a guide.

The Sarbanes-Oxley Act of 2002 (SOX) requires certain companies to implement an internal control framework. The EU equivalent of the Sarbanes-Oxley Act (SOX) for internal controls is the EU Audit Regulation and Directive—Directive 2014/56/EU.

Most companies use the COSO Internal Control–Integrated Framework to meet SOX requirements. This framework consists of the following three control objectives:

- Operations objectives
- Reporting objectives
- Compliance objectives

This framework has five interrelated control components:
- Control environment
- Risk assessment
- Control activities
- Information and communication
- Monitoring

COSO's ERM Framework is used to guide companies' enterprise risk management processes. While it includes designing controls as part of the risk mitigation response, it focuses less on the controls and more on the process of managing risk. It consists of five components:

- Governance and culture
- Strategy and objective setting
- Performance
- Review and revision
- Information, communication, and reporting

CPA questions, as well as multiple choice, discussion, analysis and application, and Tableau questions and other resources, are available online.

Multiple Choice Questions

1. (LO 1) **CPA** Controls are classified according to the categories—preventive, detective, and corrective. Which of the following is a preventive control?

a. Contingency planning

b. Quality information

c. Reconciliations

d. Access control software

2. (LO 1) In what ways do companies address risk?

a. Mitigating it

b. Transferring it

c. Avoiding it

d. All of the above

3. (LO 1) Which of the following is an example of proper segregation of duties for an invoice payment?

a. Sarah authorizes the payment; Johanna inputs the data into the system and makes the payment.

b. Sarah and Luke both authorize the payment; Sarah inputs the data into the system; Johanna makes the payment.

c. Sarah authorizes the payment; Johanna and Luke both input data into the system; Luke makes the payment.

d. Sarah authorizes the payment; Johanna inputs the data into the system; Luke makes the payment.

4. (LO 1) A company's process of implementing internal controls provides reasonable assurance that

a. financial statements are fairly presented.

b. operations are efficient and effective.

c. laws and regulations are being followed.

d. All of the above

5. (LO 1) When a person in charge decides not to follow an internal control, it is called

a. inadequate monitoring.

b. collusion.

c. lack of skilled employees.

d. management override.

6. (LO 1) Reconciling the cash from a cash register with sales transaction receipts at the end of a shift is an example of a

a. preventive control.

b. detective control.

c. hybrid control.

d. corrective control.

7. (LO 1) The time-based model of controls equation is

a. $P < (D + C)$.

b. $(P + D) > C$.

c. $P > D > C$.

d. $P > (D + C)$.

8. (LO 2) ITGCs apply to

a. communication software, including email and messaging systems.

b. accounting payment systems.

c. all corporate applications.

d. cybersecurity programs.

9. (LO 2) Which type of control has a higher risk of failure?

a. Manual

b. Automated

c. IT general

d. IT application

10. (LO 2) A business monitors the call answer rate every day to confirm that its call center answers calls in a timely manner. This is an example of

a. a risk assessment.

b. internal control.

c. an external audit.

d. continuous monitoring.

11. (LO 2) **CPA** Which of the following statements presents an example of a general control for a computerized system?

a. Limiting entry of sales transactions to only valid credit customers

b. Turning data into quality information using AIS reporting

c. Restricting entry of accounts payable transactions to only authorized users

d. Restricting access to the computer center by use of biometric devices

12. (LO 2) Rural Enterprises raise sheep and cattle for meat production. As a technologically advanced ranching operation, Rural Enterprises have experimented with using drones to capture images of herds grazing to assist employees in obtaining physical inventory counts. Employees then count the animals in the images and record the data in the information system. What type of control classification best characterizes their inventory system?

   a. Manual control

   b. Automated control

   c. Combination of manual and automated controls

   d. Continuous monitoring

13. **(LO 3)** Internal audit is an independent function of the company that is part of the

   a. first line of defense.

   b. second line of defense.

   c. third line of defense.

   d. external parties.

14. **(LO 3)** Which of the phases in the business process maturity model includes a lack of documentation, inconsistencies, and some defined processes?

   a. Phase 1—Limited

   b. Phase 2—Informal

   c. Phase 3—Defined

   d. Phase 4—Optimized

15. **(LO 3)** In the 2020 update of the three lines of defense model, which two lines of defense were combined to create "Management"?

   a. First and second

   b. Second and third

   c. First and external parties

   d. Second and governing bodies

16. **(LO 3)** Enterprise risk management (ERM) provides which line of defense in combating risk?

   a. First

   b. Second

   c. Third

   d. All of the above

17. **(LO 3)** The primary focus of internal audit includes

   a. internal control evaluation, process and procedure reviews, and risk management.

   b. material misstatement identification, ethics, and internal control environment.

   c. legal and regulatory compliance, testing procedures, and significant management estimates.

   d. internal control evaluation, ethics, and risk of material misstatement evaluation.

18. **(LO 3)** **CPA** Covington Financial, a large financial services corporation, has a unit responsible for conducting regular, recurring reviews to prevent and detect fraud. This unit should be part of the _____ function at Covington.

   a. IT

   b. HR

   c. Legal

   d. Internal Audit

19. **(LO 4)** According to SOX, which group is responsible for implementing effective systems of internal control in public companies?

   a. External auditors

   b. Internal auditors

   c. Data security leadership

   d. Management

20. **(LO 4)** Which of the following is *not* one of the interrelated components of COSO's Internal Control–Integrated Framework?

   a. Monitoring

   b. Control environment

   c. Control activities

   d. Planning

21. **(LO 4)** **CPA** According to COSO, which of the following components addresses the need to respond in an organized manner to significant changes resulting from international exposure, acquisitions, or executive transitions?

   a. Control activities

   b. Risk assessments

   c. Monitoring activities

   d. Information and communication

22. **(LO 4)** The goal of the Sarbanes-Oxley Act of 2002 is to protect

   a. the U.S. government from fraudulent acts committed by U.S. companies.

   b. investors from fraud and other risks by improving the reliability and accuracy of financial statements.

   c. companies from the U.S. government interfering in how they present financial statements.

   d. investors from the risk of increased taxes impacting the financial statements of companies in which they are invested.

23. **(LO 4)** **CPA** In the COSO Cube model, all of the following are components of internal control *except*

   a. monitoring.

   b. control activities.

   c. operations control.

   d. risk assessment.

24. **(LO 4)** _____ is a set of criteria that defines a strategy to achieve certain objectives without being prescriptive; it provides a path but doesn't specify exactly how to get there.

   a. An internal control report

   b. A control objective

   c. A framework

   d. An assurance activity

25. (LO 4) Internal controls are

a. defined based on industry specifications.

b. customized to fit a company's unique risks and risk appetite.

c. predefined for public companies.

d. All of the above

26. (LO 4) Which of the following statements is true about the Directive 2014/56/EU?

a. It restricts public oversight of the audit profession.

b. It's a framework for all statutory audits to improve cooperation between competent authorities in the EU.

c. It disintegrates the Union's audit market.

d. The statutory auditors and audit firms are restricted from developing their statutory audit service activities.

Discussion and Research Questions

DQ1. (LO 1) Critical Thinking Your colleague, Adam, complains to you at work about the corporate policy that doesn't allow him to directly order and receive supplies that he needs. He thinks that it is inefficient for someone in purchasing to order the supplies and then for someone in receiving at the warehouse to verify receipt of the shipments. Only then does Adam have access to the supplies. Why can't he just order and receive them himself? Explain to Adam the concept and importance of segregation of duties.

DQ2. (LO 1) Distinguish between preventive, detective, and corrective controls. Provide an example of each that differs from examples provided in the chapter.

DQ3. (LO 1) Why is management override such a threat to an effective internal control environment? Provide an example that differs from the examples in the chapter.

DQ4. (LO 2) Discuss the importance of continuous monitoring to management and provide an example that differs from examples provided in the chapter.

DQ5. (LO 2) Distinguish between manual and automated controls. Provide examples of manual and automated controls that differ from the examples provided in the chapter. Which type of control is more reliable?

DQ6. (LO 3) Fraud Critical Thinking In the notorious Arthur Andersen and Enron fraud case, the external auditor, Arthur Andersen, surrendered its licenses to practice

accounting in every U.S. state. As a result, more than 85,000 Arthur Andersen employees lost their jobs. Three years later, the U.S. Supreme Court unanimously overturned the conviction, and Arthur Andersen was once again allowed to practice. Due to its reputational loss, the firm was unable to regain its footing as one of the Big Five public accounting firms. Do you believe the revocation of Andersen's right to practice was an appropriate response to the Enron scandal and Arthur Andersen's act of destroying audit documents to cover up their shortcomings? Given that the U.S. Supreme Court overturned Andersen's conviction, do you think the loss of more than 85,000 jobs could have been avoided? Discuss the balance of protecting the public from fraud and protecting the victims employed at Arthur Andersen who were not involved in the scandal.

DQ7. (LO 3) Research The Institute of Internal Auditors (IIA) recently changed its three lines of defense model to combine the first line and second line of defense into a single entity called "Management." Use the internet to research why the IIA made this change. Explain at least one reason why the IIA decided to update its model. Do you think this change will make it easier or more complicated for businesses to recognize who is responsible for overseeing the internal control environment?

DQ8. (LO 4) Which of the five interrelated components of the COSO Internal Control–Integrated Framework is the most important, and why?

Application and Analysis Questions

A1. (LO 1) Fraud Early Career Critical Thinking Josephine is the accounting supervisor in a medium-sized, family-owned company, Cape Renovations. Josephine has a bachelor's degree with a major in accounting. She has worked for Cape Renovations for 11 years. The company performs renovation work on damaged properties in Florida.

Josephine manages and maintains the general ledger for Cape Renovations. She is also responsible for the day-to-day, routine operations in the Accounting department. She reports to the chief accountant, Jerome Gonzales.

On Fridays, Josephine collects all the invoices scheduled for payment the following week. She collects and prepares the documentation to support check preparation. Libby, an Accounts Payable accountant, processes the payments to the vendors, arranges for the printing of the checks, which are signed electronically, and prepares the cash payments listing.

Libby collects the signed checks and sends them to the mailing clerk for timely mailing. She then gives a printout of the cash payments listing to Jerome, who performs the monthly bank reconciliation, and she files the invoices and supporting documentation. Libby is also responsible for reconciling the accounts payable subsidiary ledger to the control account in the general ledger each month.

You are interning at a local CPA firm for the semester, and the owners of Cape Renovations have engaged your firm to help improve its system of internal control. The company's financial statement ratios over time are showing some disturbing trends, with no logical explanation. Your assignment is to review the controls, specifically separation of duties, over Accounts Payable. Identify segregation of duties deficiencies in the accounts payable function at Cape Renovations. If you find deficiencies, explain what the consequences could be and how to mitigate that risk.

A2. (LO 1–2) `Early Career` `Critical Thinking` Southeastern Paper is a paper manufacturing company located in the southeastern United States. At its mills, Southeastern Paper turns trees into pulp and manufactures cardboard boxes, rolls of industrial paper, and more. This spring, a hurricane hit the town of Southeastern Paper's largest mill on the Georgia coastline. The mill has been closed for five months, and Southeastern Paper has been making efforts to clean, rebuild, and reopen operations.

A variety of risks have been identified in relation to the shutdown. As part of its risk response efforts, Southeastern Paper has implemented internal controls. Match each risk in Column A below with the appropriate internal control in Column B.

(A) Risk	(B) Internal Control
1. Southeastern Paper hired new vendors for cleanup work. The new vendors are no longer needed, but the billing system was overloaded during the shutdown, and because of the resulting confusion, Southeastern Paper thinks some cleanup vendors may still be receiving payments when they are no longer doing work.	A. Southeastern Paper hires temporary security guards to monitor inventory and ensure that only authorized personnel have access to the warehouse.
2. Southeastern Paper is afraid there will be theft of inventory while the paper rolls are being stored in a temporary warehouse located at a distance from the mill property. This warehouse lacks the security that the mill had.	B. Southeastern Paper creates a remote work plan that includes testing the equipment of all corporate personnel and ensuring that they have appropriate network access from home.
3. Southeastern Paper lost data stored on local hard drives at the mill due to water damage from the hurricane. If a hurricane hits one of its other mills, the company may face additional data loss.	C. Southeastern Paper's data analysts create a vendor payment dashboard. It shows payments made to vendors by category, including the category Temporary Vendors. Southeastern Paper's management can look at this dashboard to see if any payments are made to temporary vendors after the mill has reopened. The dashboard also sends an email to management if any temporary vendors receive payments over a certain amount so management can review the payments for appropriateness.
4. Southeastern Paper's Accounting department was located at a corporate office down the road from where the hurricane hit. While the Accounting department was not affected, Southeastern Paper realizes it would have been unprepared if it had been.	D. Southeastern Paper sends out the Internal Audit team to assist its warehouse personnel in valuing the lost inventory. The group does a physical inventory count and ties the data to the most recent inventory count or to the perpetual inventory records before the hurricane. This is standard procedure for Southeastern Paper, but it moved up the inventory count to immediately after the hurricane to ensure an accurate assessment of damage.
5. Southeastern Paper lost a lot of physical inventory in the hurricane. With the year-end audit coming up, Southeastern Paper is worried that there will not be sufficient documentation of the lost inventory and its value.	E. Southeastern Paper creates a server backup location at a network operations center facility in Ohio, where there is less chance of a natural disaster. This facility backs up all the data stored at all Southeastern Paper's mills.

A3. (LO 3) Map the following numbered terms to their locations in the three lines of defense model shown below. A letter in the model may be used for more than one numbered term.

1. Second line of defense
2. Board of directors
3. Managing risk
4. External audit
5. Regulators
6. Support on risk-related matters
7. Third line of defense
8. Internal audit
9. Risk management and compliance
10. First line of defense
11. Management
12. Independent advice

The IIA's Three Lines Model

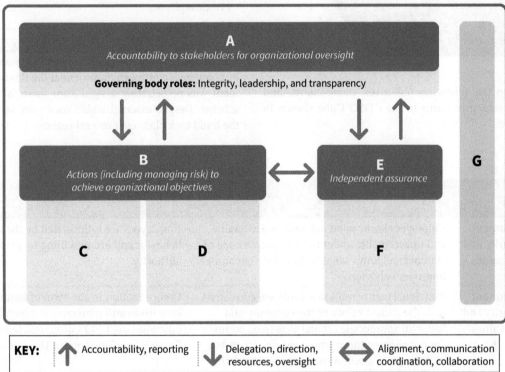

A4. (LO 4) Label each of the following facts with the related governing body or framework in the word bank. Word bank terms may be used more than once.

1. Control environment, risk assessment, control activities, information and communication, monitoring.
2. Public companies must select and use a formal internal control framework for implementing and reporting annually on the effectiveness of internal controls.
3. Created in response to the accounting scandals from 1995 to 2005, specifically, those involving Enron, Tyco, and WorldCom.
4. Consists of 3 objectives, 5 components, and 17 principles.
5. The CEO and CFO must certify that the company's financial statements fairly present financial reality, are not misleading, and were reviewed by management.

Word Bank

SOX

COSO Internal Control–Integrated Framework

SEC

A5. (LO 4) Critical Thinking Portia's Ports, a seller of fine wine and spirits, is considering going public, which means the company will offer common stock to be purchased by the public. This will make Portia's Ports a publicly traded company. In preparation for its initial public offering (IPO), management, led by the ERM team, is reviewing regulatory requirements for publicly traded companies and considering the current internal control environment. The ERM team has identified the following risk statement related to going public: The highly regulated environment of a publicly traded company creates regulatory risk that may result in fines or reputational damage.

Portia's Ports already has an entity-level control environment, a risk management approach, an Internal Audit department that assesses control activities, and continuous monitoring for both KPIs and fraud risk. Do you think Portia's Ports is well prepared to go public? What framework could the ERM team use to assess the company's readiness?

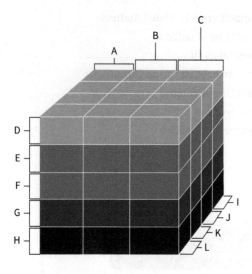

1. Control environment   _____
2. Reporting   _____
3. Entity level   _____
4. Operating unit   _____
5. Control activities   _____
6. Operations   _____
7. Monitoring activities   _____
8. Information and communication   _____
9. Division   _____
10. Risk assessment   _____
11. Compliance   _____
12. Function   _____

A6. (LO 4) Map the following objectives, components, and organizational structure terms to the COSO Cube shown in the figure above.

A7. (LO 1–4) `Fraud` `Early Career` `Critical Thinking`
The following audit program provides an assessment of a public company's control environment at the time that top management was perpetrating a significant financial statement fraud scheme. Despite external audits each year, as required by law, the fraud took place over several years.

#	COSO Principle	Control Objective	Audit Observations
1	Commitment to integrity and ethical values	Employees know what behavior is acceptable and unacceptable under the company's code of conduct and know what to do if they encounter improper behavior.	Employees are intimidated by the CEO's harsh behavior and are unwilling to question his authority.
2	Commitment to integrity and ethical values	Individual compensation awards are consistent with the ethical values of the company and foster an appropriate ethical tone (e.g., bonuses are not given to those who meet objectives but in the process circumvent established policies, procedures, or controls).	Compensation in the form of bonuses for executives and managers is dependent on following the CEO's directives to improve the financial performance of the company.
3	Commitment to integrity and ethical values	There is regular identification, measurement, and reporting of losses arising from violations of laws and regulations.	Medicare has filed a lawsuit against the company for falsifying records. Management ignored these violations until details of the lawsuit became public. There was no identification or mention of potential losses in prior management and audit reports.
4	Management's competence	Company personnel have the competence and training necessary for their assigned duties.	Top management employees are competent to perform their roles due to prior experience and professional qualifications. There is no reason to suspect that management is incompetent.
5	Proper oversight by board of directors and audit committee	Board committees exist. The board is an independent governing body that provides oversight for management's activities.	There is little evidence that the board of directors provides oversight over top management. Board members do not question the financial statements provided by management. The CEO handpicked the board and exerts control over them.
6	Proper oversight by board of directors and audit committee	The audit committee meets privately with the chief accounting officer, internal auditors, and external auditors to discuss the reasonableness of the financial reporting process and system of internal control.	There is no evidence of the board questioning the reasonableness of the financial statements. Consequently, the audit committee did not raise issues about the financial reporting process or the system of internal control.

(Continued)

#	COSO Principle	Control Objective	Audit Observations
7	Management's philosophy and operating style	There is a monitoring process for turnover of management and supervisory personnel. There is an assessment of the reasons for significant turnover.	There has been significant turnover in the chief financial officer position, with five different CFOs over the past eight years. There is no evidence of a monitoring process for turnover and no record of the reason for this phenomenon.
8	Management's philosophy and operating style	Management exemplifies attitudes and actions reflecting a sound control environment and commitment to ethical values, including for financial reporting as it relates to appropriate resolution of disputes over application of accounting treatments.	There is evidence that the CEO has tried to circumvent generally accepted accounting practices by coercing his employees to "fix" the financial statements.
9	Organizational structure	Executives understand their responsibility for and authority over business activities. They understand how they relate to the business as a whole.	It seems, based on an interview with the CEO, that he does not hold himself responsible for the actions of his employees. He said he is not an accountant and that he did not understand "why I am expected to know what the accountants do."
10	Assignment of authority and responsibility	Employees are empowered, when appropriate, to correct problems or implement improvements.	The control environment is very autocratic. Employees do not feel empowered. They are afraid of the CEO.
11	Assignment of authority and responsibility	The board of directors and/or audit committee adequately considers their understanding of how management identifies, monitors, and controls business risks.	There is no evidence that the board of directors has an understanding of management's process for assessing and monitoring risk.
12	Human resources policies and procedures	Disciplinary actions send a message of intolerance for violations of expectations regarding behavior.	There is evidence that top management violated behavioral expectations. For instance, executives often used the company jet and helicopter for personal reasons, without any disciplinary action against them.

First, identify whether each of the 12 controls in the audit program exist in the company. Then, based on the observations recorded in the program, explain how you would assess the control environment of this company. Are there red flags leading you to be suspicious of fraud occurring in this firm? Explain.

A8. (LO 1–4) Internal controls are often categorized using the COSO Internal Control–Integrated Framework. In the following table, Column 1 shows the COSO internal control objectives and components, and Column 2 lists examples of internal controls.

Perform the following tasks:

1. For the items listed in Column 1, identify each as a control objective or as one of the interrelated components of the internal control framework. Then, for the interrelated components, list them in the correct sequential order.

2. Match each control in Column 2 with:
   a. One or more internal control objectives from Column 1.
   b. The single most appropriate internal control component from Column 1.

COSO IC Objectives or IC Components	Controls Implemented for Firm ABC
A. Operations	1. The executive team meets quarterly to review all business risks (including the potential for fraud), implements risk responses, and manages risk, including making changes to the system of internal control.
B. Risk assessment	2. The executive team meets each month to review the monthly financial statements and accounting ratios provided by the controller and approved by the CFO. The main objective of this review is to see whether the firm has met operational and financial performance goals.
C. Monitoring	3. The employee who performs bank reconciliations is someone other than the employees who handle cash and generate payments from the firm.

(Continued)

COSO IC Objectives or IC Components	Controls Implemented for Firm ABC
D. Information and communication	**4.** Management implemented a code of ethics, which includes policies on conflicts of interest. All employees, including executives, electronically sign an acknowledgment that they have read, understand, and agree to abide by the code.
E. Compliance	**5.** Management implemented continuous monitoring over the call center to confirm that the call center answers the calls in a timely manner.
F. Control activities	**6.** Strong controls are in place to ensure proper accounting for and timely payment of statutory payroll deductions, like (1) federal, state, and local income taxes and (2) Social Security and Medicare deductions and firm contributions, to the respective governmental agencies.
G. Control environment	**7.** The human resources department has processes in place to ensure that employees at all levels have the qualifications, experience, and training to efficiently and effectively perform their work.
H. Reporting	**8.** There are controls in place to ensure that the audit committee receives reports in a timely manner on internal control deficiencies identified by the internal audit department.

Tableau Case: Control Mapping at Julia's Cookies

What You Need

Download Tableau to your computer. You can access www.tableau.com/academic/students to download your free Tableau license for the year, or you can download it from your university's software offerings.

Download the following file from the book's product page on www.wiley.com:

Chapter 3 Raw Data.xlsx

Case Background

Big Picture:
Determine whether internal controls are effectively mitigating risks.

Details:
Why is this data important, and what questions or problems need to be addressed?

- Besides analyzing company risk, internal auditors test internal controls to ensure that risks are being mitigated. When auditors test internal controls, they test to ensure that a control is designed appropriately and that it functions as intended. Some risks might have one mitigating internal control, while other risks might require multiple internal controls to reach a desired level of residual risk. After an internal control is tested, it is rated as effective, ineffective, or marginal.

- To illustrate how well a control is mitigating the risk, we should consider the following questions: How many risks have a residual risk score that is less than its inherent risk score, which would be the result of an internal control mitigating the risk? How many controls were rated as ineffective?

Plan:
What data is needed, and how should it be analyzed?

- The data needed to answer the objective is pulled from the internal audit GRC (governance, risk, and compliance) software that houses the Internal Audit department's assessment and ratings of corporate risks, including internal controls and their determined effectiveness.

- The data was filtered to only include the auditable entities that were subject to an internal audit last year.

Now it is your turn to evaluate, analyze, and communicate the results!

Hint: This data includes auditable entities, business processes, risks, and internal controls, as illustrated on the next page. One auditable entity can include one or more business processes. One business process can be subject to one or more risks. One risk can be mitigated by one or more internal controls.

Auditable Entity

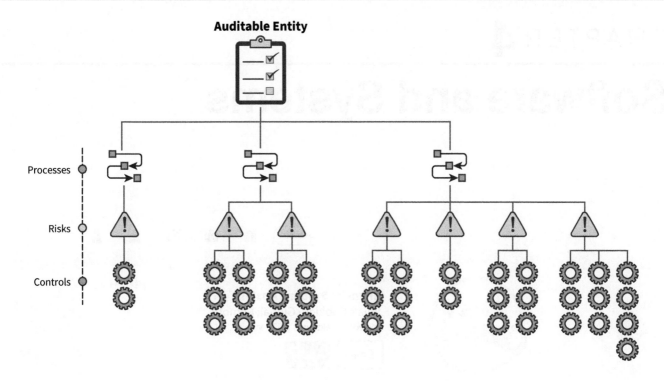

When calculating risks in Tableau, use the Risk ID field to perform distinct counts. When calculating internal controls in Tableau, use the Control ID field to perform distinct counts. To do this, you must convert the Risk ID and Control ID fields from dimensions to measures.

Questions

1. Which auditable entity is responsible for the largest number of internal controls?

2. Which business process includes the largest number of internal controls?

3. Which risk is mitigated by the largest number of internal controls?

4. How many risks started with the inherent likelihood score "medium high" but now have a residual likelihood score of "medium," due to the implementation of internal controls?

5. How many risks started with the inherent likelihood score "medium low" but now have a residual likelihood score of "low," due to the implementation of internal controls?

6. How many risks started with the inherent impact score "high" but now have a residual likelihood score of "medium," due to the implementation of internal controls?

7. How many risks started with the inherent impact score "medium high" but now have a residual likelihood score of "medium low," due to the implementation of internal controls?

8. How many internal controls did the Internal Audit department identify as "ineffective"? (Hint: Use Test Result.)

Take it to the next level!

9. A risk owner is the employee responsible for the portion of the business process that relates to a specific risk. The risk owner usually reports to the business process owner. Which risk owner is responsible for risks that have, on average, the highest inherent risk score? Which risk owner has the highest *average inherent risk*? (Hint: Risk = Impact × Likelihood.)

10. A business process owner is the employee responsible for the entire business process. The business process owner usually has other employees, such as the risk owners, who report to them. Which business process owner is responsible for risks that have, on average, the lowest residual risk score? (Hint: Risk = Impact × Likelihood.)

CHAPTER 4

Software and Systems

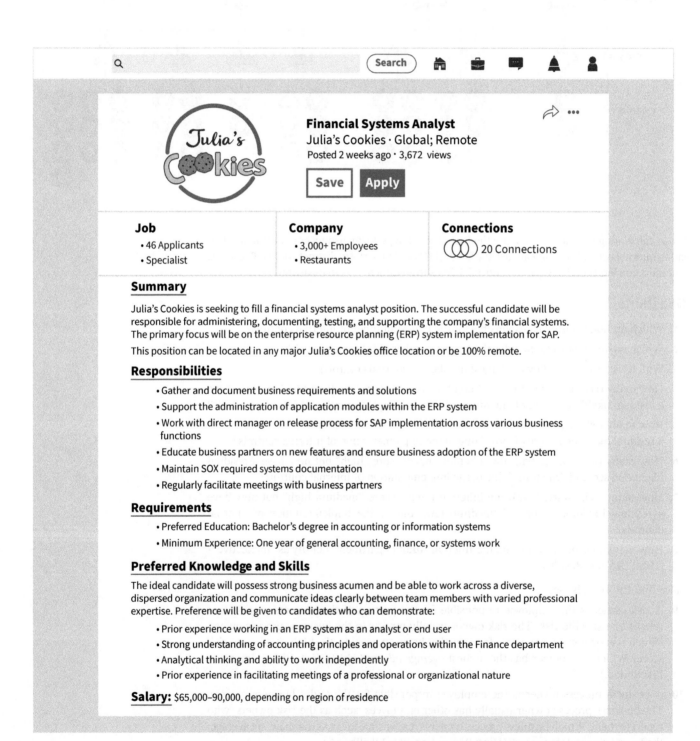

Q | Search | 🏠 💼 💬 🔔 👤

Financial Systems Analyst
Julia's Cookies · Global; Remote
Posted 2 weeks ago · 3,672 views

[Save] [Apply]

Job	**Company**	**Connections**
• 46 Applicants	• 3,000+ Employees	〇〇〇 20 Connections
• Specialist	• Restaurants	

Summary

Julia's Cookies is seeking to fill a financial systems analyst position. The successful candidate will be responsible for administering, documenting, testing, and supporting the company's financial systems. The primary focus will be on the enterprise resource planning (ERP) system implementation for SAP.

This position can be located in any major Julia's Cookies office location or be 100% remote.

Responsibilities

- Gather and document business requirements and solutions
- Support the administration of application modules within the ERP system
- Work with direct manager on release process for SAP implementation across various business functions
- Educate business partners on new features and ensure business adoption of the ERP system
- Maintain SOX required systems documentation
- Regularly facilitate meetings with business partners

Requirements

- Preferred Education: Bachelor's degree in accounting or information systems
- Minimum Experience: One year of general accounting, finance, or systems work

Preferred Knowledge and Skills

The ideal candidate will possess strong business acumen and be able to work across a diverse, dispersed organization and communicate ideas clearly between team members with varied professional expertise. Preference will be given to candidates who can demonstrate:

- Prior experience working in an ERP system as an analyst or end user
- Strong understanding of accounting principles and operations within the Finance department
- Analytical thinking and ability to work independently
- Prior experience in facilitating meetings of a professional or organizational nature

Salary: $65,000–90,000, depending on region of residence

CHAPTER PREVIEW   Einstein taught us that all things are relative. This is certainly true when it comes to accounting information systems. An AIS can be a stand-alone system or integrated with a pre-existing system, custom-built system, or sophisticated enterprise-wide system. They all perform essentially the same tasks: recording data, retrieving information, and generating reports. Often, different accounting information systems look similar because their purposes and subject matter are the same.

This chapter focuses on introducing you to software and information systems that are important to your career, including:

- Data processing in an information system
- Information systems for startup businesses
- Information systems for expansion and growth
- How companies strive for an ideal state in information systems

Companies need accounting professionals with an interest in information systems to perform specialized roles like the financial systems analyst at Julia's Cookies. This is a great example of a job opportunity where an information systems major could qualify, but the company may prefer to hire an accounting professional that they can train to manage the technical systems side of the job. Accounting is, after all, an information system. ■

Chapter Roadmap

LEARNING OBJECTIVES	TOPICS	JULIA'S COOKIES APPLIED LEARNING
4.1 Summarize the characteristics and components of information systems.	• Information Systems • Transaction Processing • Software • Cloud Computing	Cloud Computing: Mitigating SaaS Risks
4.2 Identify technologies used by startups and small businesses.	• Technology for Startups • Managing Risks	Small Business: Software Selection
4.3 Explain how growing businesses enhance their systems.	• Acquisition-Based Growth • Systems Integration • Systems Configurations	Systems Configuration: New Regional Office
4.4 Describe the features of and implementation considerations for an enterprise resource planning (ERP) system.	• A Solution for Systems Integration • Implementing an ERP System	ERP Modules: Locating the Data

CPA You will find the CPA tag throughout the chapter to call out any important topics you may see on the CPA exam.

4.1 How Do Systems Capture and Process Data?

To be successful in a competitive environment, companies must adapt. Whether as a result of changes in the industry, tools available, or company size, businesses adapt by adopting appropriate information technology (IT) that supports their data processing and information system needs. These IT tools and systems equip employees and business leaders to complete their responsibilities efficiently and effectively. Adoption of these technologies is driven by the need to create efficient and effective processes to create more value for the business. The right technology choices can help companies of all sizes achieve their strategic objectives.

You have learned that an information system captures raw data and processes it into useful information for decision makers. In this section, we take a closer look at the types of information systems and software available, including the accounting information system (AIS). Remember, an AIS is a type of information system that focuses specifically on executing and capturing data generated by accounting business events.

Information Systems

When information systems are fully online and performing real-time activities, they are considered one of two types of online processing systems:

- An **online transaction processing (OLTP)** system supports core business functions by handling sales, accounting, purchasing, and more.
- In contrast, **online analytical processing (OLAP)** systems focus on leveraging the data for information.

OLTP and OLAP systems work together to capture and transform data into useful information. **Table 4.1** summarizes the differences between OLTP and OLAP systems.

TABLE 4.1 Comparing OLTP and OLAP Systems

	Online Transaction Processing (OLTP)	Online Analytical Processing (OLAP)
What	Processes transactions	Processes reports and analytics
How	Modifies the database by adding and changing transaction data	Queries the database to answer questions
When	Real time	Real time
Example	A Julia's Cookies customer orders six peanut butter cookies on the mobile sales app. The OLTP system immediately records the sales data to the relevant sales database tables.	A Julia's Cookies manager wants to know how many peanut butter cookies were ordered from the St. Louis store last month. The OLAP system queries the sales database tables to identify all peanut butter cookie sales records for the St. Louis store.

CPA There are different levels of information systems, each providing information for users at different levels of the company:

- **Executive support systems (ESS)** support strategic decision making and are a subset of decision support systems.

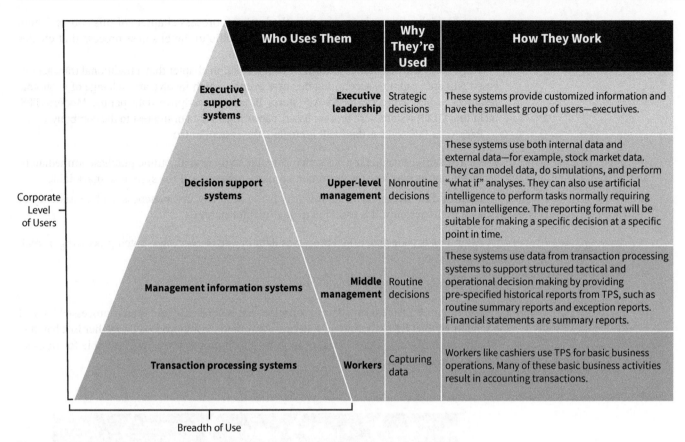

	Who Uses Them	Why They're Used	How They Work
Executive support systems	**Executive leadership**	Strategic decisions	These systems provide customized information and have the smallest group of users—executives.
Decision support systems	**Upper-level management**	Nonroutine decisions	These systems use both internal data and external data—for example, stock market data. They can model data, do simulations, and perform "what if" analyses. They can also use artificial intelligence to perform tasks normally requiring human intelligence. The reporting format will be suitable for making a specific decision at a specific point in time.
Management information systems	**Middle management**	Routine decisions	These systems use data from transaction processing systems to support structured tactical and operational decision making by providing pre-specified historical reports from TPS, such as routine summary reports and exception reports. Financial statements are summary reports.
Transaction processing systems	**Workers**	Capturing data	Workers like cashiers use TPS for basic business operations. Many of these basic business activities result in accounting transactions.

Corporate Level of Users

Breadth of Use

Illustration 4.1 The four levels of information systems serve unique purposes for a business.

- **Decision support systems (DSS)** assist in solving nonroutine problems and unstructured decision making.
- **Management information systems (MIS)** assist in routine management activities.
- **Transaction processing systems (TPS)** process day-to-day business activities, provide a foundation for other systems, and capture data that is fed through the higher-level systems.

Illustration 4.1 describes these systems.

The AIS is primarily a TPS. Understanding where an AIS fits within the levels of different information systems highlights the importance of quality information and controls. Because an AIS is a TPS that captures data that is fed upward through other information systems levels, a poor control environment can negatively impact decisions made using MIS, DSS, and ESS.

Why Does It Matter to Your Career?

Thoughts from an Accounting Manager, Financial Services

Every aspect of a business uses a system. Whether to store, retrieve, or process data, you will use systems and software in your career. Many of the terms and concepts here are things you are going to hear in business meetings.

Transaction Processing

A modern-day TPS collects data continuously, in real time, for day-to-day business activities. Data collection should be efficient and should preserve the integrity of the data. The TPS generates business-process documents, such as pay slips, customer orders, invoices, and receipts, which you can learn about in the business process chapters of this course. These documents are each a type of internal control specific to the business process that creates them.

You already learned in the Accounting as Information chapter that a traditional transaction-based AIS only captures accounting business events, which involve an exchange of economic resources, while a process-based AIS stores broader, descriptive data points. Modern TPS, including OLTP systems, are process based, capturing all data of interest to the company.

Because a TPS collects data as it is created, the system must:

- **Be available:** Imagine if a customer is unable to process an online purchase immediately. The business may lose the customer, or many customers, if the system is unavailable.

- **Ensure data integrity:** Data integrity is the accuracy, completeness, and consistency of data in the systems. It is essential to quality information.

After data is collected, a TPS processes data in one of two ways: batch processing or real-time processing.

Batch Processing

CPA In **batch processing**, data is collected as it is generated and then is processed later, at a scheduled time (**Illustration 4.2**). Because transactions are processed together in a batch—whether at the end of a day, week, or month—batch processing is most suitable for transactions that are not time sensitive.

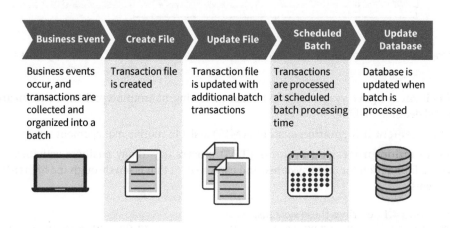

Business Event	Create File	Update File	Scheduled Batch	Update Database
Business events occur, and transactions are collected and organized into a batch	Transaction file is created	Transaction file is updated with additional batch transactions	Transactions are processed at scheduled batch processing time	Database is updated when batch is processed

Illustration 4.2 Batch processing creates and stores a file of transactions that is processed at a scheduled time.

A good example of batch processing is payroll. Businesses have scheduled payroll cycles, such as each week, every other week, or on the last day of the month. The hours worked may be recorded in real time and data collected as it's generated, but the payroll transactions aren't processed until the end of the payroll cycle, when the entire pay-period batch is processed.

Journal entries are also often entered into the general ledger system in batches to eliminate the need for accounting employees to enter journal entries as each transaction arises. The general ledger system records the "batch number," which uniquely identifies which journal entries were input in a particular batch. This is useful as an audit trail for error correction, analysis, and auditing.

Batch processing has three main benefits:

- **Efficiency:** There are economies of scale due to optimizing the use of employees and processing many like transactions through a system at the same time.

- **Simplicity:** Once the batch processing schedules are established, it is easy to maintain the scheduled stream of processing. The processes and systems are less complex, and there is an established audit trail.

- **Quality of data:** Since the data flows through the same pre-established steps and schedule, there are fewer errors.

Real-Time Processing

CPA In **real-time processing**, a transaction is processed as it occurs (**Illustration 4.3**). This requires the company to have high processing capabilities readily available.

Think of sending money to a friend for the pizza they bought you for dinner. You might use a mobile app like Venmo or Zelle to quickly transfer the funds. Those apps use real-time processing systems, so your friend is paid back immediately. The benefit of real-time processing is that the accounting records are always current. However, the system is more complex than a batch processing system.

An example of batch versus real-time processing is how different retailers process their customers' credit card payments:

- **Batch processing:** The retailer collects credit card payments throughout the day. When purchases are made, an approval request is sent to the customer's bank to ensure that funds are available for the payment. However, transactions are not processed and sent to the customer's bank until the end of the day, which is why the customer will not see the transaction posted to the account until a later time or date.

- **Real-time processing:** When purchases are made, the retailer immediately sends the approval request and transaction to the customer's bank. The transaction immediately posts to the customer's account.

Now that we have explored the types of processing that TPS use, let's take a closer look at an important part of an information system that you likely use regularly.

Illustration 4.3 Real-time processing eliminates the batch steps and updates the database at the time a transaction occurs.

Software

Recall that an information system consists of interrelated components—hardware, software, databases, and networks. **CPA** **Software** is the interface between the components and the users. It governs how the other components work with one another and provides users with the means of interacting with the system. You likely use software every day, like mobile apps and internet browsers.

Software is created using **programming languages**, which are written sets of coded instructions that the system understands. These instructions can be as simple as opening a file or as complex as performing calculations for a rocket to land on the moon. While computer science majors are most often associated with coders who "speak" these complex programming languages, accounting professionals can use programming skills, too. For example, a financial accountant may use Structured Query Language (SQL) for extracting data from a database (**Illustration 4.4**). The Data Storage and Analysis chapter introduces you to databases and SQL. Then, you will learn how to write the SQL code in the Designing Systems and Databases chapter!

```
SELECT * FROM Customers AS Customers
FULL OUTER JOIN Orders AS Orders
ON Orders.Customer_ID = Customers.Customer_ID
LEFT JOIN Products AS Products
ON Orders.Product_ID = Products.Product_ID
```

Illustration 4.4 SQL code can be used to model and extract data.

Popular software programming languages include:

- JavaScript
- Java
- HTML
- Python
- C# (pronounced "C sharp")
- C++ (pronounced "C plus plus")
- Go
- Scala

Let's look at some popular types of software and their associated risks.

Systems Software

A system is a set of interrelated components, and there must be a way for these components to communicate. **Systems software** is specialized software that runs a computer's hardware and other software. It's a platform for other software that coordinates all the activities throughout the system.

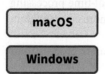

When you turn on your computer, do you know how the hardware inside knows what to do? It receives instructions from the **operating system (OS)**, which supports a computer's basic functions, such as task management, executing applications, and even starting up and shutting down. Two widely used operating systems are Microsoft Windows and Apple macOS.

Other types of systems software coordinate specific activities throughout a system (**Table 4.2**).

TABLE 4.2 Systems Software Examples

Systems Software	Description	Examples
Database management system (DBMS)	Software used to define, manipulate, retrieve, and manage data in a database	MySQL, SQL Server, Oracle, Microsoft Access
Data communication software	Software used to provide remote access to exchange data between computers and users	Messaging and email software, File Transfer Protocol (FTP) client
Utility programs	Software used for analyzing, configuring, optimizing, and maintaining a computer	Network Manager, antivirus software, backup software, disk cleaners, file compression software (zip)

You will learn more about how a DBMS allows users to interact with stored data in the Data Storage and Analysis chapter. For now, let's look at a type of software that may be even more familiar: software that helps users accomplish tasks.

Application Software

Illustration 4.5   Microsoft Office is a popular suite of application software.

Application software, also known as an app, is an end-user program that performs specific functions. For example, the Microsoft Office suite includes Word, Outlook, Excel, PowerPoint, and more (**Illustration 4.5**). This application software is designed for general use and can be purchased readily through digital downloads. Other application software may be custom developed for a specific function. For example, your favorite store may have a custom-built mobile app for shopping.

You will learn about specific accounting application software later in this chapter.

Software Sourcing

Whether they need systems software or application software, companies must decide where to acquire it:

• Software can be purchased from a third-party vendor, as when a company buys a license to use Microsoft Office application software.

• Alternatively, companies can develop software from scratch, called **in-house development**. Here, the software is programmed by the company's own software developers.

Both methods of software sourcing involve risks. With software purchased from third-party vendors, businesses can face disruptions, breaches, and even copyright issues that are beyond their own control (**Table 4.3**).

TABLE 4.3 Risks Related to Purchasing Third-Party Software

Area	Risk
Copyright infringement	If the business isn't adhering to the software licensing policies of the software vendor, the business could face legal allegations and reputational loss.
Data breaches	Since the business isn't the one creating the code, the business is trusting that the third-party software vendor created the software properly. If the third-party software is not properly secure, the company is vulnerable to hackers and malicious programs.
Disruptions	If the third-party vendor closes, the business could be disrupted, as the vendor no longer supports the software. The business should ensure that the third-party vendor provides a source code escrow agreement, which would give the business access to the software's source code under certain circumstances, such as vendor closure.
Updates	The vendor may require unnecessary updates, giving the vendor an excuse to bill additional hours to its customers that cannot be refused.

Alternatively, in-house-developed software is subject to project management risks, like budgeting risk, scheduling risk, and fraud risk (**Table 4.4**).

TABLE 4.4 Risks Related to In-House-Developed Software

Area	Risk
Budgeting	The company must employ the talent to write necessary code and maintain the system, which can be expensive.
Scheduling	Software may take longer to create than expected.
Technical specifications	Software may not be properly developed.
External market	By the time the software is developed and implemented, there might be industry and market changes that cause the software to require extensive updates.
Fraud	Software programmers cannot write the code and implement that code within the production environment. By doing so, they could program the software to circumvent fraud controls like allowing unauthorized access or granting unapproved permissions to users.

The build-versus-buy decision isn't the only infrastructure choice that businesses face. They also must choose whether or not to use the cloud.

Cloud Computing

Traditionally, when software was purchased from a third-party vendor, it was installed locally on the target computer, with enough memory and storage space to support the software's use. These days, businesses and individuals can rent these resources from providers and use them on demand instead of buying and owning them.

Do you use Google Drive or Dropbox? These are two of many cloud-based storage options designed for personal use. These subscription-based business models provide free storage for basic members and charge increasing prices for upgrades in storage sizes. If you upload a photo to Google Drive, the file is stored in one of Google's databases, which is running on one of Google's servers, so you save money by not having to purchase, install, or maintain expanded storage of your own. Your file is now in the "cloud," which is a network of servers accessed via the internet.

Cloud computing provides access to shared resources over the internet, such as computer processing, software applications, data storage, and other services. In the business context, cloud computing allows companies to minimize computer resources kept on hand, which can be expensive to both purchase and securely store. The costs are absorbed by the cloud provider, which maintains the physical equipment at its facility and provides access to customers via the cloud network.

Cloud Deployment

Cloud solutions can be deployed through three different deployment models, which we summarize in **Table 4.5**.

TABLE 4.5 Three Cloud Deployment Models

Model	Definition	Advantages
Private cloud	Exclusive for one business and always maintained on a private network. Hardware and software are dedicated solely to that one business.	• Customizable • High security
Public cloud	Available to the public through a provider. If an organization uses a public cloud, it will still be secured; however, the user accesses these services through a web browser.	• Readily available • Lower costs
Hybrid cloud	Mixture between private and public cloud with a divider between the two. In this environment, the data and applications can move between the two environments.	• Increased flexibility • Moderate costs • Moderate security

Service Models

We gave an example of Google Drive for general cloud computing, but the cloud isn't just for accessing software. In fact, Google Drive is an example of only one of the three types of cloud service models, each of which gives customers remote access to specific cloud solutions based on the end-user requirements (**Table 4.6**).

TABLE 4.6 Cloud Computing Service Models

Cloud Computing Service Model	Provides Access To	Examples
Software as a service (SaaS)	Utilizes the internet to provide customers with applications that are managed by the third-party provider. The software leverages the provider's data storage and IT infrastructure.	Google Drive, Salesforce, Slack, Microsoft Office 365, Tableau Server
Platform as a service (PaaS)	Provides customers a platform for software development that is delivered remotely. Developers have access to maintained operating systems, servers, storage, and networks and focus on design and building of application software.	Google App Engine, OpenShift, Apache Stratos
Infrastructure as a service (IaaS)	Provides customers with fully self-service computers, networking, storage, and operating systems through virtualized environments. Customers are responsible for managing all of their own operating systems, data, and applications.	Amazon Web Services (AWS), Microsoft Azure, Rackspace

Some cloud solutions are combinations of these models. For example, Azure SQL Database is a database hosted in the cloud that is both SaaS and PaaS. The underlying data storage is a platform, while the database management system is software.

For the purposes of this course, our focus is on SaaS because of its particular usefulness for accounting. In SaaS solutions, the cloud provider manages both the software and the underlying infrastructure, including storing the customer's data.

Advantages of SaaS include:

- Users have access to information from anywhere, at any time, and on any device.
- It doesn't require the maintenance costs and time of owning the hardware and software.
- It reduces the need for capital expenditures and software costs.
- It offers more flexibility and scalability to meet changing conditions.

Cloud Risks

The risks you have reviewed related to purchasing third-party software also apply to cloud-based solutions. Because cloud solutions are accessed via internet networks, they also carry some unique risks. Companies must rely fully on the third-party provider, and impacts to the systems may be beyond customers' control (**Table 4.7**).

TABLE 4.7 Risks of Using SaaS Cloud Providers

Area	Risks
Reliability	• If the customer loses internet connectivity, then it cannot use the system to access or maintain data because the system cannot be used offline. • If the provider is unreliable in providing the software, monitoring and managing the software, and delivering a secure environment, then the system may fail.
Privacy	• If the provider does not take steps to make data privacy a priority and deliver a secure environment, then it puts the customer's business at risk of litigation and loss of reputation in the event of a breach of the data privacy requirements of state and federal law.
Security	• If the provider does not take steps to make data security a priority, then the customer's system and data may be accessed and used maliciously, resulting in the potential for significant financial loss.

Now that you have reviewed the types of cloud service models and related risks, determine which route Julia's Cookies should pursue for its new general ledger in Applied Learning 4.1.

Julia's Cookies — Applied Learning 4.1

Cloud Computing: Mitigating SaaS Risks

The current AIS is a third-party-provided system purchased from a vendor that has since gone out of business. It's time for a change!

Lyn, a financial systems analyst, is researching and identifying risks related to using a software as a service (SaaS) solution for the replacement AIS. The information they gather will be presented to executive leadership to assist in decision-making activities.

Lyn needs to consider:

1. The size and structure of the company and the complexity of its operations
2. The company's controls over its internal data and user access to the SaaS application
3. The SaaS vendor that the company selects
4. The corporate culture (innovative or resistant to change) and system user buy-in

What are the risks of implementing a cloud-based SaaS system? What can Lyn recommend for mitigating each of these risks?

SOLUTION

Lyn presents the following risks and recommendations to executive leadership:

Risk 1: Cloud computing services may be disrupted by natural disasters or denial-of-service attacks that exploit software vulnerabilities via the internet.

Mitigation: Using an established and reputable third-party provider rather than a startup provider

Risk 2: Cloud computing is done over the internet, with its related connectivity and security risks.

Mitigation: Using IT general controls (ITGCs) like securing the network or using encryption

Risk 3: Employees of the third-party providers have access to sensitive and proprietary data and information.

Mitigation: Engaging in continuous auditing of the systems, software, networks, and services provided by the SaaS vendor

Risk 4: Company employees may access SaaS data on devices that have software vulnerabilities or other vulnerabilities, risking malicious attacks on the system.

Mitigation: Requiring company data to be stored on company networks and not personal devices

CONCEPT REVIEW QUESTIONS

1. What is an online transaction processing (OLTP)?
   Ans. An online transaction processing (OLTP) system supports core business functions by handling sales, accounting, purchasing, and more. It modifies the database by adding and changing transaction data in real time.

2. What is an online analytical processing (OLAP)?
   Ans. In contrast to OLTP, online analytical processing (OLAP) systems focus on leveraging the data for information. It processes reports and analytics by precalculating queries in the database to answer questions.

3. **CPA** What are the different levels of information systems?
   Ans. There are different levels of information systems that provide information to users at different levels of the company. Executive support systems (ESS) support strategic decision making and are a subset of decision support systems (DSS). DSS assist in solving nonroutine problems and unstructured decision making. Management information systems (MIS) assist in routine management activities. Transaction processing systems (TPS) process day-to-day business activities, provide a foundation for other systems, and capture data that is fed through the higher-level systems.

4. **CPA** What is batch processing?
   Ans. Business events and transactions are collected and organized into a batch. The transaction file is created and updated with additional batch transactions. Transactions are processed at the scheduled batch processing time. An example of batch processing is payroll.

5. **CPA** What is real-time processing?
   Ans. In real-time processing, transactions are processed in real time and the database is updated immediately. An example of real-time processing is customers' credit card payment.

6. **CPA** What is software?
   Ans. Software is the interface between components and users. It governs how the other components work with one another, and it provides users with the means of interacting with the system.

7. What is the difference between systems software and application software?
   Ans. Systems software is a specialized software that runs a computer's hardware and other software. It's a platform for other software that coordinates all the activities throughout

the system (e.g., database management systems). Application software, or an app, is an end-user program that performs specific functions. For example, the Microsoft Office suite.

8. What is meant by cloud computing?

Ans. Cloud computing provides access to shared resources over the internet, such as computer processing, software applications, data storage, and other services.

4.2 How Do Startups and Small Businesses Use Technology?

Learning Objective ❷
Identify technologies used by startups and small businesses.

Ideas for startups happen every day. Many college students go on to open businesses of their own, like microbreweries, accounting and tax firms, and graphic design and event planning services. Household names like Google, Microsoft, Square, Tesla, and Dell started in garages or dorm rooms. These businesses did not grow overnight, which is why it is important to understand how systems and technology evolve to meet a company's current needs and strategy.

Throughout this section, we explore popular systems and technology for startups and small businesses. You may recognize the names of some popular options throughout, but they are only a small selection of the many technology solutions available. We use Julia's Cookies to explore how the various software and systems are used.

Technology for Startups

Many startups have little more than laptops and basic application software for their employees in the beginning. The lack of capital and the business need to purchase more complex systems make startups the perfect candidates for purchasing third-party vendor software or for using SaaS.

Let's look at the software Julia's Cookies used when it started out. Remember, these examples are only a glimpse of the software that small businesses use.

Payment Processing with Square

Square One of the most important business processes a company needs technology to support is receiving payments from customers. Julia's Cookies used Square, a payment processing software that supports customer payments via magstripes, chip cards, NFC phone tap payments, and more:

- Square provides a device that attaches to the business owner's phone or tablet to receive payments.
- The setup for Square is simple, and businesses pay a flat rate for each payment that is processed.
- Square also offers a point-of-sale system, which is software that businesses use to complete retail transactions.

Square is one of the most popular payment processing software programs available, especially for startups, individual proprietors, and small businesses. Alternatives to Square include GoPayment, SumUp, and Clover.

Because Square uses the SaaS model, it stores business customers' data on its own servers, saving the customers the various expenses required to maintain their own data.

Data Processing with Excel

Companies also need to store information, perform data analytics and calculations, and manage other finance-related functions. Excel is a spreadsheet application program that supports these functions (**Illustration 4.6**):

- It's often used for budgeting, analyzing sales data, tracking information, and performing data visualization.
- Excel is part of the Microsoft Office suite and can be purchased as locally installed software or through a SaaS subscription with Microsoft Office 365. Excel's competitors include Google Sheets and Numbers for Mac.

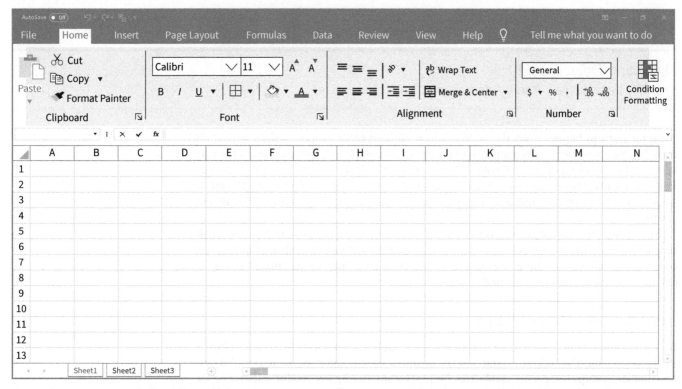

Illustration 4.6 In a single Excel file, multiple sheets can contain different types of data that can be linked with Excel functions.

Julia's Cookies initially used Excel to track performance and analyze the sales data it downloaded from Square's servers. It also used Excel to manage employees, inventory, and other resources. For example, one Excel file at Julia's Cookies contained information about inventory, including inventory types, on-hand quantities, and related costs.

Companies of all sizes use Excel, even international corporations like Coca-Cola and Netflix. As an accounting professional, you are likely to work with Excel files daily. Pro tip: Before graduating, get comfortable using Excel by learning shortcuts and important formulas and functions (**Table 4.8**).

TABLE 4.8 Important Excel Formulas and Functions

Excel Function	Purpose	Format
SUM	Calculates the sum total of a range of cells or input numbers.	=SUM([cell name]:[cell namer])
AVERAGE	Calculates a simple average of selected cells or input numbers.	=AVERAGE([number 1],[number 2],...)
MIN	Finds the minimum value in the range of selected cells or input numbers.	=MIN([number 1],[number 2],...)

TABLE 4.8 *(Continued)*

Excel Function	Purpose	Format
MAX	Finds the maximum value in the range of selected cells or input numbers.	=MAX([number 1],[number 2],...)
TRIM	Removes leading and trailing spaces in the selected cell, which are unnecessary characters.	=TRIM([Cell Name])
IF	Applies conditional logic to select cells to determine a true or false outcome.	=IF(Conditional Logic,[value if true],[value if false])
VLOOKUP	Locates values in Table A that are related to values in Table B by connecting and looking up identical values in the two tables.	=VLOOKUP([Identical Value 1],[Location of Identical Value 2],[Value to Locate],[Should Value 1 and Value 2 be exactly identical or approximately identical])
CONCAT	Concatenates, or combines two or more columns into one new column.	=CONCAT([Cell Name 1],[Cell Name 2],...)

Data Storage in Access

 While data can be stored in Excel files, many small businesses soon grow to need a more manageable approach to local data storage. At Julia's Cookies, it didn't take long—only a few months—for the business to reach a point where a database solution was required.

Microsoft Access is a database system used to store, query, and report data. You will learn more about databases in the Data Storage and Analysis chapter. For now, it's important to understand that Access is a database system that best supports smaller businesses that need smaller-sized databases. Larger companies will implement more sophisticated databases, which you will learn about in the Designing Systems and Databases chapter.

Access differs from Excel because it can store millions of lines in one table. Like Excel, Access can be purchased as software locally installed on a computer or through the SaaS delivery model. Major competitors include Zoho and Knack.

Internet of Things (IoT)

The Internet of Things (IoT) connects everyday devices via the internet to send and receive data. Physical objects like sensors and machines are networked together to collect data that is leveraged in decision making.

Even when Julia's Cookies was still a young startup company, it invested in some IoT technologies, like the following:

- **Google Assistant:** An intelligent voice assistant embedded in mobile devices can connect calendars, notes, and task management systems to create efficiencies.
- **Smart locks:** Locks on the business premises that can be controlled remotely by mobile devices and web apps allow managers to monitor access to the business after hours and manage and record entry activities at the building.
- **Cloud-supported security cameras:** Cameras that capture footage that is stored in the cloud and viewable on mobile devices and web apps mitigate the risks of theft or damage.
- **Philips Hue light bulbs:** Smart light bulbs controlled by mobile devices and web apps generate significant energy savings by automatically adjusting lighting based on sensors in the room.
- **Nest thermostat:** Sensor-driven, cloud-based thermostats control temperatures based on schedules controlled on a mobile device or web app, resulting in energy savings.

Accounting with QuickBooks

 Companies need more accounting support than just what's required to capture sales data. Businesses need reliable software that provides core accounting functionality and user-friendly reporting capabilities. The ideal accounting software will also easily scale, or grow, with a company as it expands its operations.

Because many startups and small businesses don't have the resources to support a dedicated IT professional, it's important that this type of software is easy to configure and use.

There are a number of great accounting software products companies can choose from, including one of the most popular options on the market, QuickBooks. QuickBooks is used to manage:

- Financial reporting
- Time tracking
- Payroll
- General Ledger
- Paying bills

QuickBooks makes it easy for businesses like Julia's Cookies to track their financial health, analyze sales, and leverage financial data for decision making. It offers both local software and SaaS services. If you work for a small business, you will likely encounter QuickBooks or one of its competitors, like Xero, Sage Intacct, NetSuite, or FreshBooks.

Why Does It Matter to Your Career?

Thoughts from an External Staff Auditor, Public Accounting

External audit clients vary in industry and size, and auditors encounter data extracted from many different systems. They need to understand what information is needed and where it's located in that system. Even as an auditor for a Big Four firm, you may encounter client data from Access or QuickBooks. You will be exposed to all kinds of systems early in your career if you pursue the external audit career path.

Managing Risks

All companies face risks. For startups and small businesses, some of these risks are different from those faced by their large, corporate counterparts. For example, a startup may be less likely than a global corporation to experience financial statement fraud, where management manipulates the financial statements to misrepresent the company's current state. In contrast, a startup has fewer resources to mitigate its risks than a large corporation. Small business owners must carefully consider risk management, prioritizing risks to make the best use of scarce resources. **Compensating controls** can also be used to reduce the risk when more expensive or more complex controls are missing.

Table 4.9 examines three common internal controls and the ways small businesses can adapt these controls for limited resources.

TABLE 4.9 Control Activity Considerations for Small Businesses

Control Activity	Use in Small Businesses
Segregation of duties	It can be expensive for small businesses with few employees to enforce proper segregation of duties, and incompatible functions are often combined. A small business should focus on segregating duties where it makes financial sense and implementing compensating controls such as manager supervision.
Physical access	Physical access controls prevent unauthorized individuals from accessing physical resources like buildings, computers, hard drives, inventory, and more. Because many employees in small businesses use personal devices for work, enforcing controls can be difficult. Companies should focus on bring-your-own-device policies and procedures that are both flexible for the work environment and address these unique risks. Any company data should be saved on the company's secure network and not on personal device hard drives.
Logical access	Logical access controls prevent unauthorized users from accessing systems on a network, workstation, database, or application. These controls can also assign different access privileges to different persons, depending on their roles, and authenticate users' identities. Because small companies often cannot afford to implement complex, sophisticated security measures, small businesses can practice safety by requiring employees to use strong usernames and passwords that are tied to the functions they are allowed to access.

Based on what you've learned in this section about common software solutions that startups and small businesses use to support various business processes, consider whether Julia's Cookies should choose stand-alone accounting software or the SaaS delivery model in Applied Learning 4.2.

Julia's Cookies	**Applied Learning 4.2**

Small Business: Software Selection

Julia's Cookies decided to use QuickBooks for its AIS and must decide which type of QuickBooks product to purchase:

- QuickBooks Desktop (QBD): A desktop system with the software installed locally and data storage residing in-house
- QuickBooks Online (QBO): A cloud-based accounting solution (SaaS) with the software residing on the web and data storage provided by the vendor

Should the AIS move to the cloud with QBO? Help executive leadership decide by identifying the benefits of adopting cloud-based computing for Julia's Cookies.

SOLUTION

Benefits of QBO include the following:

- SaaS applications are ready to be used immediately once the subscription is activated, with no initial costs.
- Users with access to the QBO system are offered more mobility and freedom, as they can log in at the same time and can log in at any time, from anywhere, and from any device (desktop, laptop, smart phone, tablet), as long as they have an internet connection.
- QBO provides real-time access to financial information, enabling more timely decision making and problem solving.
- QBO performs automatic updates as soon as they become available at no additional cost.
- Automatic backups ensure uninterrupted access to data in the event of a disaster.
- For a small business without a sophisticated IT system, a cloud service improves IT security, and data stored in the cloud is encrypted.
- The company does not have to maintain its own computing infrastructure with its own employees. Instead, it pays for the service as it is used, lowering the costs related to systems management, backups, updates, upgrades, and data security.
- QBO does not require up-front investment in a system. With a monthly subscription, the costs are expensed each month.
- QBO offers more scalability for higher data volume and therefore more flexibility for businesses that grow.
- Less time and fewer resources are needed to manage the technology, and more time is available to manage business operations.
- Cloud customers benefit from the most recent technological innovations, as they are integrated into the product by the vendor, which needs to remain on top of developments to remain competitive.
- SaaS helps equalize advances in IT systems for businesses in various stages of growth by making IT more accessible to small businesses. Cost flexibility allows small businesses to afford IT tools and computing power that would normally be out of their reach.

Based on these benefits, the executive leadership team chooses the cloud-based accounting option.

CONCEPT REVIEW QUESTIONS

1. What is meant by compensating controls in managing risk?
   Ans. It can be expensive for small businesses with few employees to enforce proper segregation of duties, and incompatible functions are often combined. A small business should focus on segregating duties where it makes financial sense and implementing compensating controls such as manager supervision. Compensating controls can also be used to reduce the risk when more expensive or more complex controls are missing.

2. What is logical access control?
   Ans. Logical access controls prevent unauthorized users from accessing systems on a network, workstation, database, or application. These controls can also assign different access privileges to different persons, depending on their roles, and authenticate users' identities.

3. What activities can be managed by accounting software products such as QuickBooks?
   Ans. QuickBooks can be used to manage business processes such as financial reporting, time tracking, payroll, general ledger, and paying bills. This helps the business to track its financial health, analyze sales, and leverage financial data for decision making.

4.3 What Are the Characteristics of Information Systems for Growing Companies?

During the startup years, companies often use technology that is low cost, stable, and simple. As companies grow, they explore other options to fit their needs. Growth often means companies expand locations where they operate. For example, Lyft, a rideshare company, was launched in 2012 and offered ride services in California for years before expanding to New York City in 2014 and Canada in 2017. In 2019, Lyft's initial public offering (IPO) was the first in rideshare company history and valued the business at $24.3 billion. Lyft's successful growth over the years has come with risks and changes in technology requirements.

Throughout this section, you will learn about the information system complexities that growing companies face.

Acquisition-Based Growth

CPA Companies can grow in two ways:

- **Organic growth** occurs when a company uses its own resources and business processes to increase sales, customers, and market share.
- **Acquisition-based growth** occurs as a company purchases and integrates other companies into its infrastructure.

Many companies grow through a combination of these methods. Companies often pursue acquisition-based growth because it allows them to increase their capabilities more quickly. An acquired company often comes with resources that make acquisition more cost beneficial than pursuing that level of growth organically. There are two terms you should know when it comes to this type of growth (**Illustration 4.7**):

- A **merger** is the combination of two separate companies into a new legal entity. A pure merger is unusual, as one of the companies generally maintains its leadership and operating environment. For the purposes of this section, we discuss information systems for acquisitions, but mergers may experience the same complications around systems integration.
- An **acquisition** happens when one company purchases all or the majority of another company's shares to gain control over that company.

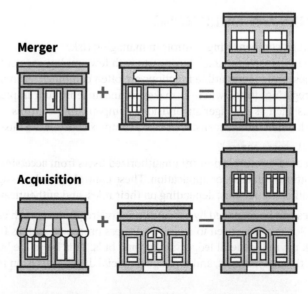

Illustration 4.7 A merger results in a new company that combines the two merged businesses, while an acquisition results in one company taking control of the other.

In 2008, Disney held 10% of the market share in its industry. In 2019, after a combination of organic growth and acquisitions like those of Marvel, Lucasfilm (*Star Wars*), and 21st Century Fox, it represented just under 40% of the film market in the United States. This is a staggering increase!

And what about Lyft? It's also experienced growth through acquisitions. In fact, in 2018, Lyft entered the bicycle-sharing market by acquiring an existing company.

So why does understanding organic and acquisition-based growth matter in an AIS course? Often, systems are taught as existing in a clearly designed, optimal state. In reality, systems can be complex, poorly integrated, and even messy. When you start your career, the odds are low that you will encounter a perfectly integrated system that functions the way textbooks describe. Companies do their best to manage their information systems with the resources available to them.

Julia's Cookies gained ownership of existing factories, stores, employees, and systems when it acquired a competitor, Cookie Crunch. The integration of Cookie Crunch's existing processes with Julia's Cookies required training employees, reviewing business processes for overlaps and risks, refining the employee base to remove redundant or underperforming roles via layoffs, and integrating all of Cookie Crunch's existing data and systems into Julia's Cookies' IT environment.

Systems Integration

Systems integration is the process of joining different systems or subsystems into one larger system and ensuring that they function as one system. Consider the AIS:

- If a company uses System A and acquires a company that uses System B, how will that business combine the data and systems to create quality information?

In its worst state, a business may run both systems in parallel and aggregate the information after it's been generated by the two different systems. This can be a complicated and inefficient endeavor. Data is stored differently in individual systems, and combining the data after the fact is often a tedious task that creates the risk of redundancies, errors, and inaccuracies. None of these characteristics support the creation of quality information.

Companies may have hundreds of applications and databases that must be integrated and must decide if they will integrate these systems gradually or immediately.

Lift and Shift, Then Integrate

One of the easiest and lowest-cost ways to integrate systems is a lift and shift. In a **lift and shift**, the acquiring company moves the acquired systems, physically placing the systems' servers in the data center and maintaining the existing systems as they are. Users have access to all the systems simultaneously. Consider this example at Julia's Cookies, which is based on a real situation at a global manufacturing firm:

- At the time of acquisition, Cookie Crunch used the accounting software Tallie to manage employees' corporate expenses and reimbursements. Julia's Cookies used SAP Concur.

- After acquiring Cookie Crunch, Julia's Cookies assumed control of Tallie and kept it operational. The legacy employees—those who worked at Cookie Crunch at the time of acquisition—continued to submit expenses in Tallie, while Julia's Cookies employees used Concur.

- The IT department and accounting team managed both systems simultaneously and aggregated data from the systems to create financial reports. This didn't continue indefinitely, however. Once Julia's Cookies finished integrating systems that were a higher priority, it migrated legacy employees to Concur and shut down the Tallie system.

You may find yourself working for or auditing an acquisition-driven company. If so, you will be working with legacy systems that have been lifted and shifted during acquisitions. While burdensome to corporate employees who must manage and aggregate data from these systems, lift and shift is often an efficient way to complete an acquisition's terms within legal deadlines. After the acquisition is complete, systems are reviewed, and the company determines if and when full integration is necessary.

Immediate Integration

As an alternative to lift and shift, a company can immediately integrate systems, often focusing on priority systems. Integrating multiple systems requires converting existing data in the systems to be retired and migrating it into the new system. The original systems are then eliminated. While it may seem like a simple copy-and-paste exercise, it's a complex problem, as data in the different systems will not likely be in the same format:

- At Julia's Cookies, the customer account numbers are 10 characters long, and the vendor management system is programmed not to accept entry of an account number that is longer or shorter than 10 characters.
- Cookie Crunch, however, used a 12-character account number. It's impossible to simply import that vendor data into Julia's Cookies' system as is.
- The account numbers from Cookie Crunch must be updated to 10 characters, or the controls in Julia's Cookies' vendor management system must change to allow 12-character account numbers.

During an acquisition, it's often not reasonable to integrate the acquired systems within the time limits legally given for the acquisition. Therefore the "lift and shift, then integrate" method is more commonly used.

Systems Configurations

You have learned that businesses have many systems—some internally developed, some purchased, and some acquired. Businesses want these disparate information systems to "talk" to one another and provide users with easier access to data. Let's use an example at Julia's Cookies to understand how this works:

- Management in Chicago may need to access sales order data generated at a Julia's Cookies' store in Atlanta, and where that data is stored impacts how easily the data can be accessed across multiple locations.
- There isn't a "right answer" when it comes to choosing a systems approach. A business must weigh the advantages and disadvantages of each approach to choose the appropriate method of addressing systems as they grow.

There are three systems configurations that consolidate and coordinate data across multiple locations. Cloud computing makes it easier to incrementally grow or scale any of these systems. Let's compare each option as a solution for Julia's Cookies' Chicago and Atlanta offices.

Centralized Systems

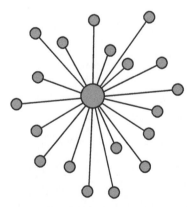

Illustration 4.8 A centralized network has one central location to which all systems connect.

CPA A **centralized system** connects all users to one central location built around a server or cluster of servers that all authorized users can access. All the network's main business processing occurs at, and business information is stored in, that one place (**Illustration 4.8**).

If Julia's Cookies used a centralized system, the sales transaction in Atlanta would be sent over a network and stored on a centralized server in Chicago, where all orders would be stored. This single system in Chicago would be the only point of access users needed to obtain data. Like all other systems configurations, this setup has both favorable and unfavorable characteristics (**Table 4.10**).

TABLE 4.10　Advantages and Disadvantages of Centralized Systems

Advantages	Disadvantages
It is the easiest to set up.	The risk of business disruption is greater because any disruption impacts the entire system.
There is better security of the central location as there is only one point of access to protect.	A single system may experience transaction bottlenecks if processing traffic is high because only one system is performing all the processing.
Data is easy to access for authorized users.	Users in other locations may experience lag time for data access because of network and remote complications.
There is consistency in processing.	
Cost is lower, as there is only one central location to maintain.	

Decentralized Systems

CPA Rather than having a single location, a **decentralized system** utilizes multiple locations that each maintain a copy of the data needed for its connected systems. In a decentralized network, there are multiple access points for users, but not all users are connected to all access points (**Illustration 4.9**). Decentralized systems may be used when there are regional offices that process data, then summarize it and communicate the data back to headquarters.

If Julia's Cookies' Southeast regional office in Atlanta stores all the sales transaction data for its region, including Atlanta, and only reports aggregated numbers for financial reporting purposes to the corporate office in Chicago, then that is a decentralized system. If someone in Chicago needs to see the detailed transactions, that person would access the regional system in Atlanta. This means the system uses less power and storage but also that risks are higher since raw data is stored disparately and requires aggregation at headquarters (**Table 4.11**).

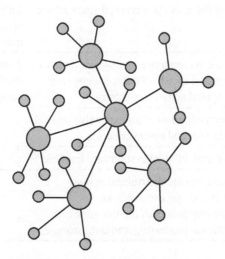

Illustration 4.9　A decentralized network has multiple access points to which aggregated data is sent.

TABLE 4.11 Advantages and Disadvantages of Decentralized Systems

Advantages	Disadvantages
With an increase in locations processing and storing their own transactional data, the processing power and data storage needed at the central site is reduced.	Since each location has its own system, there is an increase in security risk, as more systems must be protected and monitored.
There is higher responsiveness from the decentralized systems at remote locations, as each location has its own system to process and retrieve its data.	The cost of installing and maintaining multiple systems across different locations is higher.
Processing bottlenecks are reduced because employees aren't competing for processing power.	
If one system fails, the other systems can still process transactions.	

Distributed Systems

Illustration 4.10 A distributed system has no central location, and all data is communicated to all interconnected nodes.

CPA A **distributed system** is like a decentralized system; however, it goes a step further, as all the users and systems are directly connected to one another across the network (**Illustration 4.10**). In a distributed system, the processing and databases are distributed among several business locations. All users have access to all data, depending on their user access privileges, and all users are connected throughout the business.

In contrast to the decentralized system, where Atlanta reported aggregated sales data to be stored in Chicago, all the transactional-level sales data is stored in the distributed network. In other words, there are servers and databases everywhere that communicate over the network:

- When a sales transaction is completed in Atlanta, it's immediately available to Chicago users who have access to the network.
- In fact, a store manager in Atlanta will also have access to the transactions of a store in Chicago (if they have that level of authorization within the system).

Many industries benefit from this level of communication—for example, Netflix and Uber, which have remote workers, global operations, and vast volumes of data generated and processed on an hourly basis. Of course, these benefits come with a higher price tag (**Table 4.12**).

TABLE 4.12 Advantages and Disadvantages of Distributed Systems

Advantages	Disadvantages
Communication among the users is increased since all are connected.	This is the most expensive option, as it involves higher maintenance costs.
Real-time transaction details are more readily available to users. Access and processing speed are faster because the processing workload is spread across the system.	This option can be difficult to implement as it is the most complex of the three methods.
Reduction or complete elimination of an expensive central processing site results in reduced hardware costs.	
Incremental growth and scalability of systems are possible.	
With processing and data storage distributed across the system, the failure of a single site is not as damaging because other computers in the network can accommodate the additional processing and data storage.	

When Julia's Cookies opened its second corporate office in Atlanta, management had to decide which of these three systems configurations to implement. Determine whether they made a good decision in Applied Learning 4.3.

| Julia's Cookies | Applied Learning 4.3 |

Systems Configuration: New Regional Office

Organic growth has led Julia's Cookies to open a regional corporate office in Atlanta to support increasing sales in the Southeast region. This new office will allow Julia's Cookies to create a diverse corporate team closely connected to its southeastern U.S. operations.

As part of the office opening, Julia's Cookies needs to decide which systems configuration will grow with the business, reliably support business processes, and have reasonable maintenance costs.

Ahmad, the chief technology officer at Julia's Cookies, suggests rating the three types of systems configurations as high, medium, or low, based on these characteristics:

- Probability of business disruption
- Maintenance costs
- Scalability
- Security vulnerability

Rank the systems based on these criteria and recommend which one Ahmad should propose to the executive team.

System Configuration	Probability of Business Disruption	Maintenance Costs	Scalability (Growth) of Network	Security Vulnerability
Centralized				
Decentralized				
Distributed				

SOLUTION

The systems approaches can be ranked as follows:

System Type	Probability of Business Disruption	Maintenance Costs	Scalability (Growth) of Network	Security Vulnerability
Centralized	High	Low	Low	Low
Decentralized	Medium	Medium	Medium	Medium
Distributed	Low	High	High	High

Julia's Cookies needs a configuration that can grow with the business but that is still budget-friendly:

- The transactions occurring in Atlanta have no effect on a store in Chicago, so a distributed system isn't necessary.
- A centralized system may not be ideal due to the number of transactions Julia's Cookies anticipates in each region and for future expansion. The processing power needed from a single server could be difficult to achieve while growing and staying within budget.

Ahmad should propose a decentralized system. It provides a moderate solution that suits the operating model of regional stores and will assist continued growth.

CONCEPT REVIEW QUESTIONS

1. **CPA** Differentiate between organic and acquisition-based growth.
   Ans. Organic growth occurs when a company uses its own resources and business processes to increase sales, customers, and market share. Acquisition-based growth occurs as a company purchases and integrates other companies into its infrastructure.

2. What is the difference between merger and acquisition?
   Ans. A merger results in a new company that combines the two merged businesses, while an acquisition results in one company taking control of the other. Both are acquisition-based growth.

3. What is meant by systems integration?
   Ans. Systems integration is the process of joining different systems or subsystems into one larger system and ensuring that they function as one system.

4. What is a lift and shift way to integrate systems?
   Ans. One of the easiest and low-cost ways to integrate systems is a lift and shift. In a lift and shift way, the acquiring company moves the acquired systems, physically placing the

systems' servers in the data center and maintaining the existing systems as they are. Users have access to all the systems simultaneously.

5. **CPA** What is a centralized system?

Ans. A centralized system connects all the users to one central location built around a server or cluster of servers that all authorized users can access. The network's main business processing occurs at, and business information is stored in, that one place.

6. **CPA** What is a decentralized system?

Ans. Rather than having a single location, a decentralized system utilizes multiple locations that maintain a copy of the data needed for its connected systems. In a decentralized network, there are multiple access points for users, but not all users are connected to all access points. Decentralized systems may be used when there are regional offices that process data, then summarize it, and communicate the data back to headquarters.

7. **CPA** What is a distributed system?

Ans. A distributed system has no central location, and all the data is communicated to all interconnected nodes. In a distributed system, the processing and databases are distributed among several business locations. All the users have access to all data, depending on their user access privileges, and all the users are connected throughout the business.

4.4 Why Are Enterprise Resource Planning (ERP) Systems Considered Ideal?

Learning Objective ❹
Describe the features of and implementation considerations for an enterprise resource planning (ERP) system.

Remember how complicated it is for users to aggregate data from different information systems? It's not easy to reformat 12-character account numbers to integrate with a system designed for 10-character account number entry. This creates challenges across the entire company, from the IT personnel who maintain the systems to the end users who need to generate reports from the system's data.

While you learned about this example in the context of an acquisition, the problem isn't exclusive to acquisition-based integrations:

- A company may use System A for its sales department and System B for its inventory management department. To calculate gross profit, end users require the total sales revenue from System A and the cost of goods sold from System B. If System A formats a product name as, say, A-1234 and System B formats it as A1234, data will need to be transformed to either remove the dash from System A data or add a dash to the data from System B.

- A company may use PeopleSoft for human resources management and Concur for employee expense reimbursement management. During a fraud investigation, the internal audit department must combine data from PeopleSoft—employee names, addresses, bank account numbers, and more—with Concur data to compare employees' information with their expense reports. If employee IDs are formatted differently in the two systems, data transformation will be required.

Startups and small businesses often adopt different systems to serve individual functions because it's cost-effective. The issue of having disparate systems becomes apparent as businesses grow, departments become larger, and data expands.

A Solution for Systems Integration

To address the issue of disparate systems that cannot easily communicate with one another, businesses turn to a solution that offers a single system with aggregated parts that meet the needs of each business function. **CPA** Known as an **enterprise resource planning (ERP)** system, this solution integrates multiple systems into a single, cohesive communication system. ERP systems are often described as the "ideal state" of a system:

- They offer integrated, enterprise-wide systems with a unified interface so businesses can improve operating and financial performance.
- They provide TPS, MIS, and DSS system functions in a single system.
- They support multiple business functions, like human resources and accounting.
- Their location is flexible. They can exist onsite or as cloud-based solutions.
- They connect to customer and vendor systems to manage supply chain communication.
- Risk is mitigated since internal controls like application controls and ITGCs are embedded in the software.

Benefits of an ERP System

An ERP system is a complex and expensive technology. The integration of all systems into a unified ERP system has several goals:

- **Improved data transparency and quality:** All the business data resides in a single system, making it accessible to authorized users who need it to perform their tasks. This improves data quality because the data is only stored once in a central location. It also breaks down departmental silos by enabling automated communications among employees. Having insight into all data also helps with compliance, as auditors and risk management employees have insights into the company's overall "snapshot" from a single database, which allows them to pinpoint risk more easily.
- **Future cost savings:** While the initial implementation cost and any customization of an ERP system is expensive, the long-term costs may be less as a result of owning one system, as opposed to multiple systems.
- **Increased business efficiency:** With the availability of real-time data all in one place, an ERP system simplifies the collection, analysis, and reporting of business data and improves business decisions.
- **Quality improvement:** With continuous collection, analysis, and reporting of business data, management can better benchmark the business against its competitors. Furthermore, with all of the information in one system, responses to inquiries are faster. For example, customers who call a customer representative can receive their answers far more quickly, leading to an increase in customer satisfaction, trust, and retention.
- **Automation of routine business processes:** By embedding best practices within the software infrastructure for accounting, payroll, inventory management, and purchasing, for example, the company can save money and increase efficiency. However, processes that are unique to a company and provide it with competitive advantage are not suitable for standardization. For example, by switching to common processes for manufacturing and doing the same thing as everybody else, a company may lose its competitive advantage.

Modules and Features

CPA Successful ERP systems support the core business processes in a company's operations, including the accounting function. Every function within an ERP system is called an **ERP module**. ERP modules can be purchased as a full, all-inclusive package or individually to create custom combinations that meet the business's needs.

Within each ERP system module, various business processes may have their own **ERP features**, which are specific capabilities. For example, the Financial module is likely to include features such as Financial Reporting, Accounts Receivable, General Ledger, Accounts Payable, and more. Each of these features is specifically designed to support the unique requirements of those business processes.

ERP modules vary with the system provider and range from six to more than ten categories. For this course, we focus on six common ERP modules:

- **Financial module:** The most important ERP module, which captures accounting data and generates financial documents, including financial statements, tax forms, and receipts. Accounting data from all other modules flows to the financial module for reporting.

- **Supply Chain Management (SCM) module:** Coordinates the entire supply chain, from purchasing of raw materials and supplies to inventory management and warehousing. It also has the ability to manage supplier relationships.
- **Production module:** Manages production activities, including machine operations and scheduling. The Production module should communicate seamlessly with the Supply Chain Management module.
- **Customer Relationship Management (CRM) module:** Captures and stores all customer information. It captures communication with customers like emails and phone calls and can generate leads of prospective customers for sales team members to contact.
- **Sales Management module:** Tracks orders from the time they are received from customers through shipment of products. It is important for the Sales Management module to communicate with the Supply Chain Management and Production modules because sales requirements drive what production will prioritize and when.
- **Human Resources Management (HRM) module:** Manages detailed employee records, training and development, and even time tracking. The HRM module must communicate with the Financial module because employee data and timekeeping are in the HRM module, while payroll processing is in the Financial module.

Illustration 4.11 shows these six major ERP modules and their key features. You will find variations of this illustration throughout each of the business process chapters, highlighting which part of the ERP system is involved in that chapter's processes.

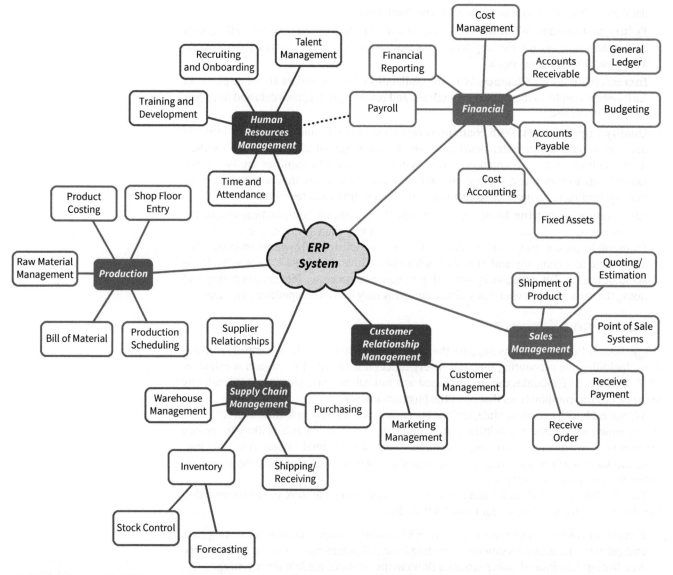

Illustration 4.11 This ERP system contains six modules, each with several features dedicated to support unique business processes.

Because Julia's Cookies is a manufacturing company, it needs all six modules to manage employees, customers, production, and supply chain logistics. Not all companies require every module. For example, an insurance company would not need the Production module because it doesn't produce physical goods. Companies must know how many modules and features they need when selecting which ERP solution to implement.

It's important for accounting professionals to be familiar with the structure of an ERP system and its modules. Understanding where in the system data is generated and stored will make it easier to locate data in the business that is needed to complete your work. Help Brant, an internal auditor, identify the location of the data he needs in Applied Learning 4.4.

Julia's Cookies	Applied Learning 4.4

ERP Modules: Locating the Data

As an internal auditor, Brant performs a lot of data analytics. Currently, he needs to create data analytics that answer the following questions. But first, Brant must identify where in the business the data he needs is located.

In which of the six ERP modules Julia's Cookies uses can Brant find the data he needs for each of the following business questions?

1. How many chocolate chip cookies were sold in Denver last year?
2. What ingredients are currently available to make cookies in the San Francisco factory?
3. Which journal entries were posted to the inventory account in December of last year?
4. How many cookies are forecasted to be sold next quarter?
5. Did any new hires join the company last month?
6. What marketing promotions are planned for next quarter?

SOLUTION

The data needed to answer each question is captured and stored in these ERP modules:

1. Sales
2. Production
3. Financial
4. Supply Chain Management
5. Human Resources Management
6. Customer Relationship Management

Implementing an ERP System

Implementing an ERP system is a complex process. A business must select a vendor, assess expected costs—including the cost of the system itself and implementation-related expenses—and convert relevant existing systems to the new ERP system. Due to the complex, expensive nature of this type of system implementation, businesses considering adopting a new ERP system should:

- Ensure that leadership is willing to intervene when issues impact the implementation project and to champion adoption of the system across the company
- Choose an ERP solution vendor that has a solid reputation in the industry
- Choose an ERP solution that meets company needs with as little customization as possible
- Allocate sufficient time and resources for post-implementation training of employees on using the new system
- Embed internal controls in the ERP system during implementation to create a cohesive control environment

Successfully implementing an ERP system is an extensive process that can span many years, and failed ERP system implementations are common horror stories in the business world. Success is possible, though. In fact, in 2020, Refratechnik Group, a German-based production company involved in the industrial minerals industry, performed a successful migration to SAP fully remotely during the COVID-19 pandemic. Careful planning and risk assessment of the ERP system and its implementation can mitigate the risks of a failed ERP system implementation. You can learn more about specific system implementation methods and risks in the Designing Systems and Databases chapter.

Vendor Selection

 One of the largest decisions businesses make when implementing an ERP system is selecting which solution to adopt. Many vendors provide ERP solutions. In this course, we focus on SAP (pronounced "S-A-P"), as it is widely used in large businesses; however, as you enter the workforce, you may also see ERP solutions from vendors like Oracle, Microsoft, Sage, Workday, and many more.

Using an ERP solution can be compared to driving a car. If you learn to drive using a Honda, you can translate that knowledge to drive another car, like a Subaru. Once you have learned to navigate one ERP system, it's easier to use ERP systems from other vendors. The difference between education and training is straightforward:

- Education is learning about generalities so you can later learn specifics of software when you encounter them.
- Training is learning the specific keystrokes required to operate the software.

For this AIS course, your goal is to gain an education. Your company will provide system-specific training on the solution of its choice.

All ERP solutions include the option of a Financial module that businesses can use as their AIS. The most fundamental feature of the Financial module is the General Ledger, which supports the function of posting journal entries by allowing the entry of debits and credits. The General Ledger feature must also capture beginning balances, debits, credits, ending balances, and appropriate audit trail documentation for posted transactions. You may have to do some exploring to find this feature in a given ERP system. For example, the General Ledger feature is called the Activity Report in one ERP system and Miscellaneous Report in another system.

Why do common accounting reports have different names in these systems? Software is generally developed by computer programmers, not by accountants. Communication between the two during development is often suboptimal. As an ERP software user, you need to recognize what you are searching for by its content and not just by the common name that you have learned in your accounting classes.

Why Does It Matter to Your Career?

Thoughts from a Senior Auditor, Public Accounting

If you pursue a career in external audit, ERP will be a commonly used term in your vocabulary. You will learn how to audit an ERP system, and it won't matter which system you learn first. Your clients will all have different systems and configurations. It can get difficult when clients customize their ERPs, as that creates more areas your team needs to audit.

Solution Types

Most vendors offer different types of solutions for companies to choose from when selecting an ERP system. There are three common types:

- **Out-of-the-box ERP system:** This system is preconfigured to work one way and will work that way immediately when implemented. Customers are expected to adapt their business processes to match the system's existing configuration. This is like purchasing a base model of a Honda Civic currently available at your local car dealership.

- **Configurable ERP system:** This system has some add-ins and features that can be customized for customers' needs. This is like purchasing a Honda Civic but upgrading the stereo and getting a special paint color, both of which are offered by Honda for additional fees. You will pay more for these improvements and may wait longer for the dealership to order this version of the car to be delivered.

- **Customizable ERP system:** This system's features are fully customized for an individual customer's needs. This is like purchasing a Honda Civic and taking it to a local auto shop to have a customized paint job applied, personalized white leather seats made, and a one-of-a-kind spoiler installed. None of these features are offered by Honda in a ready-to-purchase vehicle, so it will take a lot of money and time to have these customizations made. While it seems cool to design your own vehicle, the expense may not be worth it. You will also likely pay more for future maintenance if the car doesn't use standard parts.

Sometimes companies think they need a particular type of ERP solution and then make subsequent changes. For example, Seagate, a leader in the data storage solutions industry, recently replaced its highly customized ERP system with an industry-standard solution from SAP. SAP's flexible platform allows for configuration but is standardized enough to address issues Seagate faced with its previous system.

If a company chooses the wrong type of ERP system, it may find itself among other businesses that abandon ERP system implementation projects after investing millions of dollars. Many ERP system implementations fail due to incompatibility with existing IT infrastructure, lack of top management support, and insufficient planning.

In the Real World   MillerCoors: An ERP Disaster Story

Without proper planning, ERP system implementation can go horribly wrong. One such case is the MillerCoors' ERP disaster.[1]

MillerCoors was a beer brewing company in the United States. It was formed in 2008 as a joint venture between SABMiller and Molson Coors to combine their brewing, marketing, and sales operations in the United States.[2]

MillerCoors wanted to upgrade its IT system in 2013, so it hired HCL to deploy the enterprise software SAP. MillerCoors and HCL Technologies entered into a series of contracts under which HCL agreed to review and document MillerCoors' existing business-process blueprints and then plan, build, and test a customized version of SAP eWM in MillerCoors' warehouses. The goal was to drive efficiencies, innovation, and growth across MillerCoors' various breweries by implementing a standard set of best practices and business processes in a new enterprise SAP software solution. HCL's expertise would best fit their IT initiative because the project involved customizing various SAP modules.

The engagement was complex, multi-year, and required significant staffing contributions from both parties. The contract was approximately $53 million, with an additional $9.6 million added to the initial contract price to account for time constraints. However, the implementation was subject to delays and cost overruns. The relationship between the parties deteriorated to the point that MillerCoors refused to accept and pay three invoices and ultimately terminated the work order related to the implementation.

MillerCoors then terminated the contract in 2016 and filed a $100 million lawsuit against HCL Technologies, India's fourth-largest technology services firm, and its U.S. arm for breach of contract in a project to implement business software SAP.[3] The lawsuit claims that HCL failed to meet the deadline for the enterprise software implementation project and staff the project. The lawsuit also claimed that the software contained flaws.

MillerCoors in 2018 released a statement that all claims between the firms "have been amicably resolved," and the lawsuit "has been dismissed without any finding or determination by the court of any issue either for or against any of the parties."

It was acquired by Molson Coors in 2016, folded into Molson Coors North America in 2020, and is defunct now.[4]

Molson Coors, in its 2013 annual filings on risks specific to the U.S. Segment and MillerCoors, states that:

> We may incur unexpected costs or face other business issues from MillerCoors due to challenges associated with integrating operations, technologies and other aspects of the operations. The MillerCoors management team continues to focus on fully

[1]https://www.cms-connected.com/News-Archive/March-2017/ERP-SAP-Implementation-Failure-MillerCoors-Sues-HCL-for-$100M
[2]https://www.disputesoft.com/cases/millercoors-v-hcl-technologies-limited/
[3]https://economictimes.indiatimes.com/tech/ites/breach-of-contract-millercoors-sues-hcl-tech-for-100-million/articleshow/57819765.cms
[4]https://d18rn0p25nwr6d.cloudfront.net/CIK-0000024545/fe288027-0447-4074-8ccb-898debc56974.pdf

integrating ours and SABMiller's U.S. operations, technologies and services, as well as the distribution networks, including resolving disputes arising from the consolidation of distributors arising from the MillerCoors joint venture. The failure of MillerCoors to successfully integrate the two operations could adversely affect our financial results or prospects.

What problems are to be considered when executing large IT initiatives?

- Budget and deadline overruns
- A lack of transparency about the process involved
- Staff struggles to adapt to the new processes
- Choosing the right ERP solutions

Do you think this is an unusual case or something that happens in most companies?

Implementation Costs

Implementing an ERP system is a costly endeavor that includes multiple types of expenditures:

- **Licensing fees:** In addition to the base licensing cost of the ERP system, additional modules or features can add more costs.
- **Customization:** Costs to customize the ERP system to business-specific processes can add up very quickly.
- **Hardware:** Using a cloud-based solution can minimize hardware costs.
- **Consultants:** Third-party contractors can dedicate time and specialized skills to the implementation that the business's employees may not have.
- **Training:** Without proper training on how to use the ERP system, the implementation will fail, as employees will be reluctant to adopt its use.

In addition to these financial costs, ERP system implementation takes time. Low-end solutions may only take a few weeks or months to implement, while a sophisticated, customized ERP system can take multiple years to be fully functional.

Overall, companies can anticipate total ERP system implementation costs between $75,000 and $10 million. Implementation can take between three months and three years to complete, depending on the company size and the selected solution.

CONCEPT REVIEW QUESTIONS

1. **CPA** What is an enterprise resource planning (ERP) system?
   Ans. Enterprise resource planning (ERP) system integrates multiple systems into a single, cohesive communication system. ERP systems are often described as the "ideal state" of a system as they offer integrated, enterprise-wide systems with a unified interface so businesses can improve operating and financial performance. They support multiple business functions, like human resources and accounting. They can exist onsite or as cloud-based solutions.

2. **CPA** What is meant by an ERP module?
   Ans. Every function within an ERP system is called an ERP module. ERP modules can be purchased either as a full, all-inclusive package or individually to create custom combinations that meet the business's needs.

3. What are the types of ERP solutions?
   Ans. There are three types of ERP solutions offered by most vendors: (1) Out-of-the-box ERP system: this system is preconfigured to work one way and will work that way immediately when implemented. Customers are expected to adapt their business processes to match the system's existing configuration. (2) Configurable ERP system: this system has some add-ins and features that can be customized for customers' needs. (3) Customizable ERP system: this system's features are fully customized for an individual customer's needs.

FEATURED PROFESSIONAL | Senior Accountant at a Local Startup

Photo courtesy of Laniesha Williams

Laniesha Williams

Laniesha's career began with college internships, which provided firsthand experience with accounting operations, various-sized teams, and the kinds of technology being used by corporations. After graduating with a bachelor's degree in accounting, Laniesha worked as an internal auditor at a Fortune 500 company before moving into a staff accountant position at a local startup company. Currently, Laniesha is a senior accountant who manages a team of four. While working at this startup, Laniesha has created new processes and policies, helped create the documentation required to receive capital funding, and assisted in the implementation of an ERP system. When not at work, Laniesha enjoys hiking, local events, and gardening.

What role did you and your accounting team play during your company's ERP system implementation?

During the ERP system implementation, our accounting team members wore "many hats," and many of the functions we performed were tasks that an entire team would be dedicated to at a larger corporation. Because we are a startup, and our team is small, we found it difficult to prioritize the important features we needed from the system. We were creative and a bit futuristic with our policies, processes, and controls. Many of us were the assigned leaders for specific features and modules. We each had to learn the system quickly and accept the new process of how the system input the data that flows to our financial reports. We redesigned business processes so they would work with the ERP system and focused on risk mitigation whenever possible.

What advice do you have for accounting students about using technology in the workplace?

Don't be afraid to be creative. I truly believe there's more than one way to reach the same result. While you may hear about the "ideal" route to perform a task, use the flexibility that technology provides to your advantage.

Review and Practice

Key Terms Review

acquisition
acquisition-based growth
application software
batch processing
centralized system
cloud computing
compensating control
configurable ERP system
Customer Relationship Management (CRM) module
customizable ERP system
decentralized system
decision support system (DSS)
distributed system

enterprise resource planning (ERP)
ERP feature
ERP module
executive support system (ESS)
Financial module
Human Resources Management (HRM) module
in-house development
lift and shift
management information system (MIS)
merger
online analytical processing (OLAP)
online transaction processing (OLTP)
operating system (OS)

organic growth
out-of-the-box ERP system
Production module
programming language
real-time processing
Sales Management module
software
Supply Chain Management (SCM) module
systems integration
systems software
transaction processing system (TPS)

Learning Objectives Review

① Summarize the characteristics and components of information systems.

There are different levels of information systems, each serving a unique function for users at different levels of the company:

- Transaction processing systems (TPS) provide the foundational system used by workers to process day-to-day business activities and capture data. The AIS is a TPS.

- Management information systems (MIS) generate prespecified reports such as routine summary and exception reports for middle managers to make routine management decisions.

- Decision support systems (DSS) provide information to upper-level managers to assist in solving nonroutine problems and in unstructured decision making. Using internal data and external data, they can model data, do simulations, perform "what if" analyses, and use artificial intelligence to perform tasks.

- Executive support systems (ESS) are a subset of decision support systems. They provide customized reports for top executives to help with strategic decision making.

These systems are classified as either:

- Online transaction processing (OLTP) systems, which process data transactions

- Online analytical processing (OLAP) systems, which query a database for analysis

After data is collected, a TPS processes it in one of two ways:

- Batch processing, where data is collected over a period of time and processed later, at a scheduled time. It is suitable for transactions that are not time sensitive. The data is processed together in a batch at the end of specific time period (day, week, month, etc.).

- Real-time processing, where transactions are processed immediately as they occur. This requires the company to have high processing capabilities that are readily available.

Software is created using programming languages, which are written sets of instructions in code. There are two categories of software:

- Systems software, which is a program that runs the computer's hardware and applications. An example of systems software is an operating system (OS) to manage the other programs in the system. It manages communication between the computer hardware and the software, and it is the interface between the user and the hardware.

- Application software, which is an end-user program that performs specific functions, such as Microsoft Word and Excel.

Cloud computing is deployed using one of three models:

- Private cloud

- Public cloud

- Hybrid cloud

The three types of cloud computing service models differ based on the level of involvement and resources the customer requires:

- Software as a service (SaaS)

- Platform as a service (PaaS)

- Infrastructure as a service (IaaS)

Software as a service (SaaS) provides software applications that a business can rent and use on demand from cloud computing providers, normally on a subscription basis, instead of buying and owning them. SaaS for accounting has become increasingly popular.

Important cloud risks include:

- Reliability

- Privacy

- Security

❷ Identify technologies used by startups and small businesses.

Technology for startups is usually simple and includes the following examples of technologies:

- Payment processing software (e.g., Square)

- Data processing software (e.g., Excel)

- Data storage (e.g., Access)

- The Internet of Things (IoT)

- Accounting package (e.g., QuickBooks)

The IoT uses the internet to network physical objects and devices like sensors and machines to systems for collecting data and leveraging it for decision-making purposes.

A company's software and systems can be in-house desktop systems or cloud-based systems. A cloud-based system has many advantages over an in-house system.

Internal control activities that are important to consider:

- Segregation of duties

- Physical access controls

- Logical access

❸ Explain how growing businesses enhance their systems.

Companies can grow in two ways:

- Organic growth

- Acquisition-based growth

An acquisition happens when one company purchases all or most of another company's shares to gain control over that company, while a merger is the combination of two separate companies into a new legal entity. In either case, the companies must integrate their information systems. Systems integration is the process of joining different systems or subsystems into one larger system and ensuring that they function as one system. Timing is important. Management can integrate systems in different ways:

- Lift and shift, then integrate: This process involves physically moving the acquired servers to the data center and maintaining the existing systems as they are. Integration may happen later. Integrating the two systems means converting the data and eliminating one system by incorporating it into the primary system.

- Integrate immediately, which is often not feasible, as it requires time and effort.

There are three systems configurations to consolidate and coordinate data across multiple locations:

- A centralized system connects all users to one central location built around a server or cluster of servers that all authorized users can access. All the network's main business processing occurs at, and business information is stored in, that one place.

- A decentralized system utilizes multiple locations that each maintain a copy of the data needed for its connected systems. In a decentralized network, there are multiple access points for users, but not all users are connected to all access points.

- A distributed system distributes the processing and databases among several business locations. All users have access to all data, depending on their user access privileges, and all users are connected throughout the business.

4 Describe the features of and implementation considerations for an enterprise resource planning (ERP) system.

An enterprise resource planning (ERP) system is an integrated set of programs providing support for core business processes. It has several benefits:

- It provides transaction processing, management, and decision-making support in a single, integrated, organization-wide system with a unified interface.

- The system can be an onsite or cloud-based system and enables real-time reporting.

- A well-functioning ERP system is considered an ideal system because it embeds "best practices" in business processes in the software infrastructure, including internal controls.

An ERP package is made up of ERP modules. Companies can pick and choose which modules to buy. Modules include Supply Chain Management, Financial, Human Resources Management, Customer Relationship Management, Sales Management, and Production.

Implementing an ERP system involves selecting a vendor and a solution type and considering the costs involved.

There are three different solution types for ERP systems:

- Out of the box: The software works immediately when implemented. The expectation is that the business will adapt its business processes to match the software's pre-existing configuration.

- Configurable: The software has some custom add-ins that the vendor provides for the customer to implement.

- Customizable: The software functionality and workflows are custom made for the business, which can add significantly to the expense and complexity of a new implementation.

CPA questions, as well as multiple choice, discussion, analysis and application, and Tableau questions and other resources, are available online.

Multiple Choice Questions

1. (LO 1) An online information system that supports core business functions like handling sales, accounting purchasing, and more is considered what type of a(n) system?

    a. An online transaction processing system (OLTP)

    b. An online analytics processing system (OLAP)

    c. A batch transaction processing system (BTP)

    d. A batch analytics processing system (BAP)

2. (LO 1) There are four different levels of information systems that provide information to users at different levels of the company. Match the systems with who uses the system.

A. Executive support system	I. Executive leadership
B. Decision support system	II. Upper level management
C. Management information system	III. Middle management
D. Transaction processing system	IV. Workers

    a. A and I, B and II, C and III, D and IV

    b. A and II, B and I, C and II, D and IV

    c. A and III, B and II, C and I, D and IV

    d. None of the above

3. (LO 1) The level of information system that provides the foundation for the other levels is the

    a. management information system.

    b. executive support system.

    c. decision support system.

    d. transaction processing system.

4. (LO 1) Jellyfish has a unique manufacturing process that is not suitable for one-size-fits-all, preconfigured systems software. The company maintains its competitive advantage because of the uniqueness of its process. You are a consultant advising Jellyfish on the implementation of a new system. What type of manufacturing process software would be *most* suitable for Jellyfish?

    a. General-purpose systems software

    b. Custom-built systems software

    c. Hybrid application software

    d. A custom-built database

5. (LO 1) Which of the following is *not* a cloud computing service model?

    a. Application as a service

    b. Software as a service

c. Infrastructure as a service

d. Platform as a service

6. (LO 2) Companies need to store information, perform data analytics and calculations, and manage other financial-related functions. What tool did Julia's Cookies use for these data analytics functions?

a. Square

b. Microsoft Excel

c. QuickBooks

d. Google Sheets

7. (LO 2) Logical access controls prevent access to

a. inventory storage areas.

b. computer systems.

c. databases only.

d. computer hardware.

8. (LO 2) Why might businesses use Access instead of Excel?

a. Easier to use

b. Advanced interface

c. Stores larger amounts of data

d. Creates better shortcuts and formulas

9. (LO 2) The chapter discussed three control activity considerations for small businesses. In a smaller business, incompatible business functions are often combined. A small business may prevent unauthorized individuals from accessing resources like buildings, computers, hard drives, and inventory. This is an example of what control activity?

a. Segregation of duties

b. Physical access

c. Logical access

d. Environmental access

10. (LO 2) What type of accounting system provides a subscription-based model with no up-front investment?

a. A desktop system with software installed locally and data storage residing in-house

b. An ERP system installed locally and data storage residing in-house

c. A cloud-based accounting solution with the software residing on the web and data storage provided by the vendor

d. A batch-processing system with cloud storage

11. (LO 3) Increasing sales, customers, and market share by using the company's own resources and business processes is called

a. organic growth.

b. merger.

c. expansion of locations.

d. acquisition.

12. (LO 3) What is a purpose of an acquisition?

a. Replace organic growth

b. Increase the stock price

c. Achieve corporate growth

d. Decrease complexities

13. (LO 3) RAM Manufacturing LLC is a rapidly growing manufacturer of parts for the automotive industry. RAM Manufacturing maintains a lot of inventory and uses NetSuite to manage its inventory. RAM Manufacturing recently acquired Top Automotive LLC. Top Automotive uses Sellbrite to manage its inventory. If RAM Manufacturing decides to allow the Top Automotive operations to continue to run Sellbrite at Top Automotive's facility, which systems integration approach has RAM Manufacturing taken?

a. Shut down both systems

b. Run both systems in parallel

c. Lift and shift, then integrate

d. Immediate integration

14. (LO 3) What is *not* an element of a distributed system?

a. All users can have access to the data.

b. All users are connected throughout the system.

c. Processing workload is spread across the system.

d. It has a central location for data processing and storage.

15. (LO 4) The three ways of implementing a preconfigured ERP system like SAP do *not* include its being

a. customizable.

b. internally developed.

c. configurable.

d. out of the box.

16. (LO 4) Which two systems work together to support transaction and business decisions?

a. TCP and ODP

b. ISP and ISDN

c. OLTP and OLAP

d. ERP and AIS

17. (LO 4) Successful ERP systems support the core business processes in a company's operations. Every function within the ERP is called a module. What is the best definition of the Production module?

a. The most important ERP module that captures accounting data and generates financial documents, including financial statements, tax forms, and receipts.

b. Coordinates the entire supply chain, from purchasing of raw materials and supplies to inventory management and warehousing.

c. Manages production activities including machine operations and scheduling.

d. Captures and stores all customer information.

18. (LO 4) Which of the following statements about ERP systems is *not* true?

a. ERP systems are modular.

b. ERP systems have multiple databases.

c. ERP systems use best practices to automate standard business processes.

d. An ERP system is a single, integrated, organization-wide system with a unified interface.

Discussion and Research Questions

DQ1. (LO 1) You are an intern at a small CPA firm in your hometown. The owner/managing member, Gaurav, knows that you recently earned an A in your AIS course. Later today, he has a meeting with a potential client, who specifically wants an explanation of the main types of information systems and their functions. He asks you to give him a refresher before he goes to the meeting. Briefly explain to him the four main types of information systems and their functions.

DQ2. (LO 1) Accounting systems are what type of processing system, and how does this type of system handle data?

DQ3. (LO 1) How does batch processing differ from real-time processing, and what are the benefits of batch processing?

DQ4. (LO 2) Accounting software packages such as Quick-Books are immensely popular with small businesses. List the major advantages of this type of software.

DQ5. (LO 2) You are evaluating the controls in a small business. Which controls are often lacking in small businesses, and why should you keep them in mind?

DQ6. (LO 3) What are the three main system approaches to consolidating and coordinating data across multiple locations?

DQ7. (LO 3) Two providers of sports programming, SSN (Super Sports Network) and TSP (Total Sports Programming), are considering the possibility of joining forces in an acquisition to better compete with the main provider of sports programming, WOAS (We Own All Sports). You are a partner in a local accounting firm and have been friends with the CFO of SSN for many years. The CFO has informed you that the CIO has questions about how the ongoing business would function from a systems perspective. The CFO has not had time to talk with the CIO, but they want to be better prepared for the discussion. They have asked you to help them understand the main system approaches. What information would the CFO need to have a productive discussion with the CIO?

DQ8. (LO 3) Research Research merger and acquisition information systems integration failures, choose one case, and then explain why the implementation failed and how management could have prevented that failure.

DQ9. (LO 4) Why is important to correctly size an ERP system to the organizational needs?

DQ10. (LO 4) You are a new hire at Dovleena Enterprises, having spent the last four years at a Big Four CPA firm. You are on a team tasked with advising top management on a potential ERP implementation. The company currently uses a number of disparate systems, each with its own database. In your first meeting with the team, discuss the three different ways to implement an ERP system and align the system and the business processes.

DQ11. (LO 4) ERP system implementations can be a high-risk endeavor, and the risk is not always understood by company executives in the planning stages. While disparate information systems impede an organization's long-term growth, there may be unrealistic expectations regarding what ERP systems can provide and how they are the right choice for a specific organization. If you were speaking with a group of executives, how would you explain the purpose of the ERP system and help set the correct expectations?

DQ12. (LO 4) Research The decision to implement an ERP system is a high-risk/high-reward project that corporate executives sometimes embark on without considering the risk and enormity of the project. There are often unrealistic expectations about what ERP systems can provide and how they are the right choice for a specific organization. The evidence to support this statement is out there! Research ERP failures, choose one case, and then explain how the implementation failed and how management could have prevented that failure.

Application and Analysis Questions

A1. (LO 1) Critical Thinking As an accounting systems analyst at Joy's Accessories, it's important for you to understand the different types of system processing approaches to understand how the systems you use daily are functioning. For each of the following situations, identify whether the activity would take place in an OLTP or OLAP system.

1. Fulfilling an order for 300 necklaces for a Joy's Accessories store in Denver
2. Forecasting the sales of an earring style for the Louisville regional stores
3. Comparing website sales with in-person retail sales
4. Processing a refund for a customer who is returning a bracelet
5. Looking up a customer to determine what product that customer most recently purchased and at which location

A2. (LO 1) You are a new associate in the Accounting department at KiCo, which engages in consulting services for a variety of industries. Sheryl Cohen, who is an intern in the IT department, heard you mention that you had taken accounting information system classes. Sheryl asks for your help in determining the best processing method for various types of business activities. The choices are batch processing and real-time processing. Choose the best alignment for the following business activities by labeling each with the processing option that captures that data.

1. Parts sold daily at a small local auto parts store
2. Filling prescriptions at a drugstore
3. Daily ATM deposits
4. Weekly customer address updates
5. Daily credit card transactions

6. Monthly bill generation

7. Twice-per-day payment method updates

8. Purchasing tickets for a concert

9. Point-of-sale transactions

10. Biweekly payroll

A3. (LO 2) You are the director of IT audit for a small but growing fintech organization. The new VP of operations is concerned that risks are not being managed appropriately within the department. He provides you with the current alignment between activities and risks and asks you to review them and ensure that items are aligned correctly. Label each of the following control activities with the type of risk it mitigates.

Risks:

- Inadequate segregation of duties
- Unauthorized physical access
- Unauthorized logical access

Control activities:

1. Only the warehouse manager can unlock the main door.

2. Software programmers cannot write the code and implement that code within the production environment.

3. All guests must check in with security personnel at the front deck.

4. Tiered access is based on job function.

5. Only employees with Level 4 badges may enter the data center.

6. The same personnel should not prepare bank deposits and verify cash receipts.

7. Accounts payable clerks may not process payments for receivables.

8. Users must authenticate to join the wireless network.

9. All passwords must have at least 10 characters and must be changed every 60 days.

A4. (LO 2) When Crunchie Cookies was a startup, software was chosen that best fit the needs of the task at the time. The software chosen was Excel, Access, and QuickBooks. Align each task with the software that best meets the need of the task. Also identify gaps that cannot be filled by the software listed and mark this unmet need as GAP.

1. Show differences between sales by cookie type

2. Generate income statements

3. Create a pivot table to summarize data

4. Run a query on the average sales per month

5. Create job-based access criteria for the accounting system

6. Update the rate of pay for employees

7. Create a graph showing which products are the most profitable

8. Create a new process for counting cash in cash registers

9. Add new vendor information for making a payment

A5. (LO 3) Lillianna's Crafts is a fast-growing company based in Swindon that sells innovative craft supplies to retailers, with an existing regional office in Bristol. Due to organic growth, management decides to open another regional corporate office in Exeter to support the very high volume of increasing sales. This regional office will allow Lillianna's to hire talent in another part of the country to create a diverse corporate team closely connected to its Swindon and Bristol operations.

A task force, in which you represent the accounting function, must recommend to the leadership team a systems configuration—centralized, decentralized, or distributed—that will best meet the needs of the business by reliably supporting business processes, having reasonable maintenance costs, and having the ability to grow with the business.

As a first step, for each of the following criteria, indicate which of the three configurations would be most suitable, which would be least suitable, and which would be in the middle. Describe why you make each selection.

1. Lowest probability of business disruption

2. Lowest maintenance costs

3. Most scalable (in terms of growth of system)

4. Most efficiency in processing large volume of transactions

A6. (LO 4) Research You are the software procurement specialist for a mid-sized benefits services organization. At the beginning of the fiscal year, the finance manager asks to meet with you to discuss opportunities to upgrade the system that is currently being used. The finance manager tells you that she knows little about the different types of software or how they can be adapted and asks for your help. Using the information below, research the software and the preferred ways to adapt the software and align each software option with the correct method of adoption.

Method of adoption:

A. Out of the box

B. Configurable

C. Customizable

Software:

1. SAP

2. Quicken

3. SAGE300

4. Excel

5. Salesforce

6. Apache

7. Oracle PeopleSoft for Benefits Admin

8. SAS Viya

9. Microsoft Windows

A7. (LO 1 and 4) Software can be internally developed by members of the organization, or it can be purchased through a third party responsible for the development. Both types of software can present risks to the organization. Using the information below, label each risk with the appropriate risk area and identify the type of implementation the risk involves.

Risk areas:

- Budget overrun
- Technical risk
- Copyright infringement
- Data breach

- External risk
- Business disruption

Implementation type:

- In-house development
- Third-party purchase
- Both

Business risks:

1. The company must employ developers to write necessary code and maintain the system, which can be expensive.
2. If the business isn't adhering to the software's licensing policies, the business could face legal issues and reputational loss.
3. If the software is not properly secured, the company is vulnerable to hackers and malicious programs.
4. Software may not be properly developed.
5. There might be industry and market changes that cause the software to require extensive updates.
6. Source code cannot be obtained for review.

A8. (LO 2–4) You landed an internship at a local consulting firm. Your first assignment is to team up with your mentor to guide the owners of a small auto-repair business in their selection of an appropriate accounting information system. Using the lists below, help your client make a decision by aligning the type of accounting system with the appropriate criterion. A criterion may have more than one matching system. Which system would you suggest for the client?

Systems:

A. Stand-alone desktop
B. SaaS
C. Onsite ERP system

Client Criteria
1. Centralized system
2. Low initial up-front cost
3. Low maintenance costs
4. Minimal updating of the system
5. Ability to monitor financial performance
6. Ease of implementation
7. Minimal technical expertise requirements
8. Data security
9. Access from anywhere, at any time, and from any device
10. Most flexibility and scalability

Tableau Case: Julia's Cookies' System Conversion

What You Need

Download Tableau to your computer. You can access www.tableau.com/academic/students to download your free Tableau license for the year, or you can download it from your university's software offerings.

Download the following file from the book's product page on www.wiley.com:

Chapter 4 Raw Data.xlsx

Case Overview

Big Picture:

Monitor system conversions.

Details:

Why is this data important, and what questions or problems need to be addressed?

- Many businesses grow through acquisitions. When one business acquires another one, their systems are rarely compatible. This situation challenges the IT department to make decisions regarding the system housing the newly acquired data. The IT department can either run the newly acquired system in unison with the main system or convert the newly acquired system into the main IT solution. It is important to monitor where the data resides, as data must be converted from one system to another.
- To monitor the systems conversions, consider the following questions: Which system has the most orders? Which system is being decommissioned and when? How many systems are being supported?

Plan:

What data is needed, and how should it be analyzed?

- The data needed for this analysis is pulled from systems that Julia's Cookies supports. Due to the size of the data, and for the purposes of this assignment, you have received only 20% of the original data. Julia's Cookies has millions of orders each year, but we help you with loading and uploading the data by giving you a subset of that data.

Now it's your turn to evaluate, analyze, and communicate the results!

Questions

1. How many systems does Julia's Cookies support as of 2022?
2. Julia's Cookies decommissioned one system and successfully transferred this system's data to another system. Which system was decommissioned? (Hint: "Decommissioned" means that the system received no more orders after a certain date.)
3. For the decommissioned system identified in question 2, in what month and year did that system last have data inputs?
4. For the decommissioned system identified in question 2, into what system was all the data transferred? (Hint: Look to see which system had a positive spike, or an uptick, in payment counts.)
5. Which customer spends, on average, the most money? In which system are this customer's orders placed?
6. What was the dollar amount of the most expensive order?
7. Which state had the highest number of orders processed in 2023?
8. Which bank processed the largest total dollar amount of deposits in 2021? What was the total dollar amount for this bank's deposits in 2021?

Take it to the next level!

9. For all systems in the data set, what was the average number of days between when a customer made a payment and when the received customer payment was recorded in the system?
10. Which system had the shortest average number of days between when the customer made a payment and when the received customer payment was recorded in the system? How many days was it?

CHAPTER 5
Data Storage and Analysis

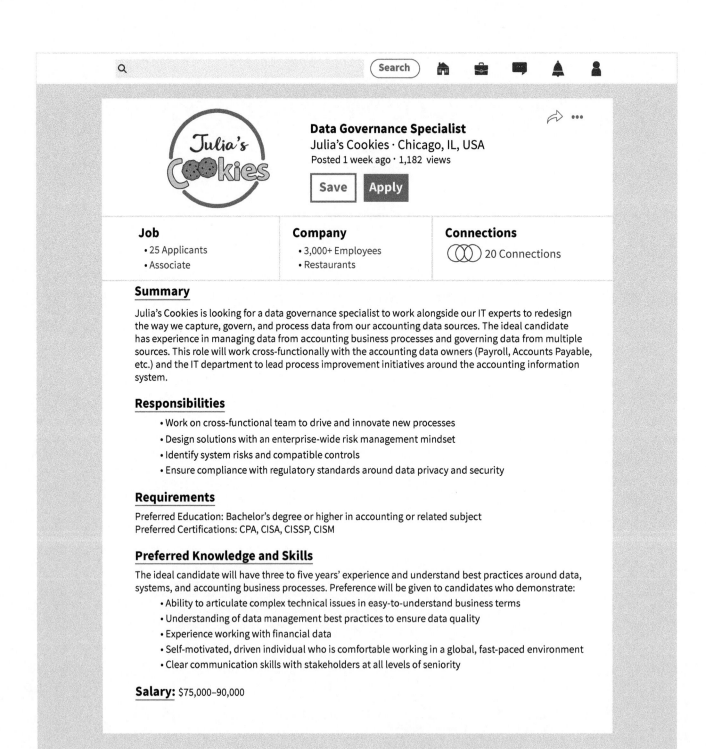

Summary

Julia's Cookies is looking for a data governance specialist to work alongside our IT experts to redesign the way we capture, govern, and process data from our accounting data sources. The ideal candidate has experience in managing data from accounting business processes and governing data from multiple sources. This role will work cross-functionally with the accounting data owners (Payroll, Accounts Payable, etc.) and the IT department to lead process improvement initiatives around the accounting information system.

Responsibilities

- Work on cross-functional team to drive and innovate new processes
- Design solutions with an enterprise-wide risk management mindset
- Identify system risks and compatible controls
- Ensure compliance with regulatory standards around data privacy and security

Requirements

Preferred Education: Bachelor's degree or higher in accounting or related subject
Preferred Certifications: CPA, CISA, CISSP, CISM

Preferred Knowledge and Skills

The ideal candidate will have three to five years' experience and understand best practices around data, systems, and accounting business processes. Preference will be given to candidates who demonstrate:

- Ability to articulate complex technical issues in easy-to-understand business terms
- Understanding of data management best practices to ensure data quality
- Experience working with financial data
- Self-motivated, driven individual who is comfortable working in a global, fast-paced environment
- Clear communication skills with stakeholders at all levels of seniority

Salary: $75,000–90,000

CHAPTER PREVIEW   Regardless of where your career takes you, data will be there. Without data, accounting can't be done. This chapter focuses on data and its importance to your career, including:

- Types of data
- How we store data
- Characteristics of data
- How we use data

From human resources to payroll to tax schedules, the spreadsheets, websites, emails, and internal documents we use are all forms of data. While a small company's data may be stored in a collection of Excel workbooks, a larger company is likely to have database storage solutions.

Because data is everywhere, accounting professionals are being expected to enter the workforce with more technical skills and data familiarity than ever before. Unique careers are available to accounting professionals with an interest in understanding data. From accounting analysts, to cybersecurity specialists, to financial crime investigators, the job market is full of opportunities if technology and data become your passion.

Accounting professionals can be a valued resource for data-centric positions in a company. Because of their understanding of processes, security, and controls, accounting professionals with interest and experience in technology are often sought after to fill positions like the data governance specialist position at Julia's Cookies. By working with the IT team, the person in this role will make decisions on best practices that consider the company's risks, controls, and technical capabilities. Even though the person won't be building the database or programming the system, they will be in a position to advise others on what critical items the company must consider when implementing these projects.   ■

Chapter Roadmap

LEARNING OBJECTIVES	TOPICS	JULIA'S COOKIES APPLIED LEARNING
5.1 Differentiate between data elements and data types.	• Data Elements • Data Types • Data That Changes	Unstructured Data: Call Center
5.2 Explain how data is stored.	• Introduction to Databases • Types of Data Storage	Data Acquisition: Budget Data
5.3 Summarize the five characteristics of big data.	• Volume • Velocity • Variety • Veracity • Value	Big Data: Mobile App Limitations
5.4 Apply data analytics to accounting problems.	• Audit and Compliance • Financial Accounting • Managerial Accounting • Tax Accounting	Managerial Accounting Analytics: Sales Dashboard

CPA You will find the CPA tag throughout the chapter to call out any important topics you may see on the CPA exam.

5.1 What Is Data?

You have learned that there are many different types of information systems companies can choose. Regardless of whether it is a network of Excel files, simple software like QuickBooks, or an integrated enterprise resource planning (ERP) system, an information system has a universal purpose: to turn raw data into useful information. This leads to a major question: What exactly is data?

The concept of data has been around for a long time; in fact, its definition has nothing to do with computers. **Data** consists of facts and statistics (about a person or an object, for instance) that are collected for reference or analysis. Data can include numbers, words, measurements, observations, or even just descriptions. For example, your personal data includes your first and last names, birthdate, address, and more. This information doesn't have to be stored on a computer to be considered data.

 A computer information system stores and uses data with a two-symbol system. All information and instructions (recall that software is a set of instructions that tells the system what to do) are executed on a computer in **binary code**, which uses the digits 1 and 0 to represent a letter, digit, or other character. **CPA** You may be wondering why this is important to an accounting information systems student, but this is on the CPA exam, so don't let your attention wander just yet.

Let's review two key topics that accounting professionals need to understand about data:

- Data elements
- Data types

Data Elements

CPA For accounting purposes, there are six data elements that together comprise a computer system:

Bit: A binary digit, which is an individual 1 or 0 in binary code.

Byte: A group of bits, usually in clusters of eight, that represents an alphabetic or numeric character or a symbol.

Field: A group of bytes (characters) that identifies a characteristic of an entity. Each field is defined as a specific data type, such as date, text, or number.

Record: A group of related fields that describes an individual instance of an entity.

File: A group of records for one specific entity.

Database: A set of logically related files.

To illustrate these six data elements, **Table 5.1** presents personal data stored in a table format.

The binary digits—bits—combine into binary code to create a byte. This byte generates the alphabetic character "D." This byte combines with other bytes to create the entire field, or cell in the table, which contains the word "Delilah" and is a text data type. A field consists of a group of bytes. It contains a unit of data about some entity that consists of specific **data types**, such as text, number, or date, whether the data is in a spreadsheet like Excel or a sophisticated database.

TABLE 5.1 Personal Data Stored in a Table

First Name	Last Name	Birthdate	Address	City	State
Delilah	Zhang	August 5	2168 Peachtree Rd.	Atlanta	GA
Jeremy	Brown	June 12	100 6th St. NE	Atlanta	GA

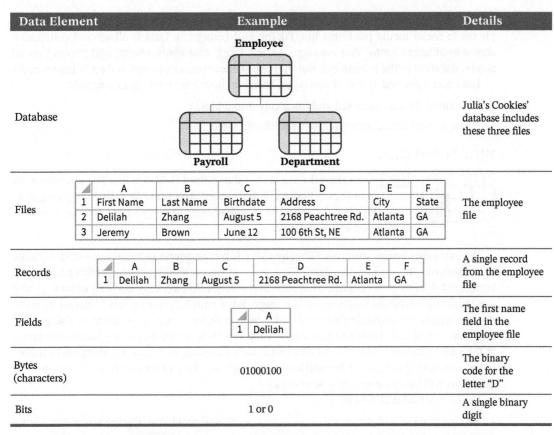

Data Element	Example	Details
Database	Employee / Payroll / Department	Julia's Cookies' database includes these three files
Files	(spreadsheet: First Name, Last Name, Birthdate, Address, City, State; Delilah Zhang August 5 2168 Peachtree Rd. Atlanta GA; Jeremy Brown June 12 100 6th St, NE Atlanta GA)	The employee file
Records	(single record: Delilah Zhang August 5 2168 Peachtree Rd. Atlanta GA)	A single record from the employee file
Fields	(field: Delilah)	The first name field in the employee file
Bytes (characters)	01000100	The binary code for the letter "D"
Bits	1 or 0	A single binary digit

Illustration 5.1   The hierarchy of data elements is demonstrated using the Julia's Cookies employee file.

TABLE 5.2 **CPA** Hierarchy of Data Elements

Data Element	
Databases	are composed of files
Files	are composed of records
Records	are composed of fields
Fields	are composed of bytes
Bytes (characters)	are composed of bits
Bits	are the smallest elements in a computer system

This field combines with all the other fields in this row to create a record about Delilah that includes fields for her last name, birthdate, address, city, and state. This record combines with the other record—the row for Jeremy—to create the file. (Hint: *File* is another word for *table*.) Assume Delilah and Jeremy work for Julia's Cookies. The file shown in Table 5.1 combines with other files about the company's employees to create a database. The database may have files with data about employees' pay, hire dates, departments they work for, and which company provided their health insurance plans. **Illustration 5.1** presents this example visually. An easy way to remember the names of these data elements is to memorize them in order of their hierarchy, from largest to smallest. **CPA** Table 5.2 is a quick reference study guide that shows how you might see this topic on the CPA exam.

Data Types

Consider the data you generate in your daily life. Your class assignments may be saved as Excel, Word, or PowerPoint files and stored on your computer or in the cloud. If you own a phone, the log of phone calls you make is stored by the phone company. The last meal you ordered from Uber Eats or DoorDash created a sales order for both the delivery app company and the restaurant that made your food. You probably send text messages and post videos and photos to social media platforms like TikTok and Instagram. Data is all around you, and it comes in different forms. Text messages, videos, bank statements, tweets, and photos may all appear different to the human eye, but they are all electronically stored as data in binary code.

Data is categorized as one of two types, based on how it is stored in a computer:

- Structured data is organized and fits nicely into tables.
- Unstructured data doesn't fit into a traditional table.

Structured Data

 CPA **Structured data** is stored in a fixed field of a file. The data elements example in Illustration 5.1 demonstrated structured data, including employee data. Whether it's stored in a spreadsheet or a database, data in a table is considered structured data.

We can easily access structured data by using filters or querying languages—code specific to a database—to analyze the data. Most accounting professionals are proficient in using structured data to gain insights, as accounting information systems are well organized and use traditional database tables for data storage. For example, you may have learned in introductory financial accounting courses that when analyzing an asset account in the general ledger, we must add the debits and subtract the credits from the beginning balance to arrive at the ending balance. Most of the databases, data analytics, and data reporting encountered in the accounting industry today will leverage structured data. On the CPA exam, data-related questions will likely cover this type of data.

In short, structured data is:

- Easily stored in tables
- Made up of specific data types like date, numeric, and text
- Stored using less storage space and allows for easy scalability
- Easier to manage than unstructured data

Unstructured Data

 CPA **Unstructured data** is any data that is *not* stored in a fixed field of a record or a file. Photographs, emails, and PDFs are just some examples of unstructured data accounting professionals encounter daily. Text may seem like it is a structured data type, but often text is stored in formats that are unstructured data, like PDFs, .txt files, or even large text fields of forms where users type open answers. To remember the difference, focus on whether the data is already or easily can be stored in a table. Remember that PDFs and .txt files are not structured data.

CPA Documents may contain data that can be **scraped**, which is the act of pulling and cleaning textual data from an unstructured format and placing it into a structured table. Even audio files can be converted to analyzable data by using voice-to-text transcription software to convert audio to a text file script of the content. While this script isn't structured—it wouldn't fit into a table—advanced data analytics tools can analyze large chunks of unstructured text data to look for the recurrence of words. The results can be used to generate a word cloud—a visualization of the most popular or commonly used words in the unstructured text data.

Other unstructured data items, such as photographs, can never be transformed into structured data. A human who is not visually impaired can easily interpret an image of a green turtle swimming. A computer doesn't "see" that, which means this type of data cannot be easily analyzed. Searching a database for the word "green" won't return a photo of a green turtle swimming. To work around this, computer systems use meta tags to identify unstructured data. **Meta tags** are keywords that help describe content. For example, a human can categorize the image of the green turtle swimming with meta tags such as "turtle," "green," "swimming," "animal," and "happy." These meta tags convert the image into data that is searchable. This is how search engines work! If you type the keywords "happy green turtle" into a Google Image search, Google takes those keywords and searches all the meta tags on all the photos in its database to match the terms you searched.

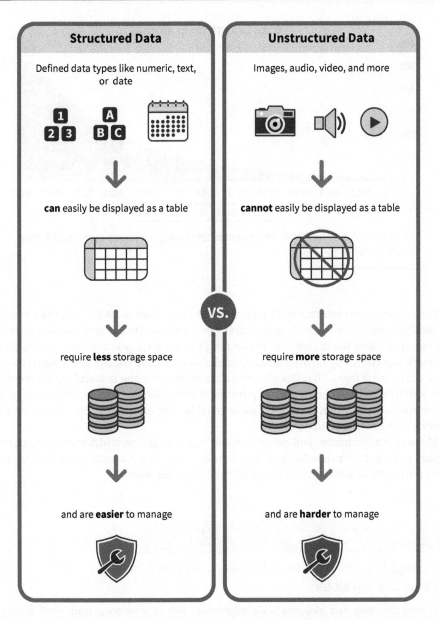

Illustration 5.2 The key differences between structured and unstructured data relate to format and storage.

Many accounting professionals struggle to use unstructured data. Ideas like analyzing tweets when making product pricing and inventory management decisions don't come naturally to everyone. Understanding the basic concepts of unstructured data and knowing how to use it to add value to your company can make you more valuable in the accounting industry. **Illustration 5.2** summarizes the key differences between structured and unstructured data.

Web 2.0

Did you know that 80% of business data is unstructured? Companies primarily use structured data to make their decisions, which means most business decisions are based on only 20% of the company's available data.

The amount of unstructured data has increased for several reasons—the most notable of which is the birth of Web 2.0. **Web 2.0** refers to user-generated content and user participation on the internet. The internet was once a "read-only" environment where users mainly consumed published content. Web 2.0 is rich in interactive applications and socialization—truly a "read and write" environment.

The Web 2.0 revolution resulted in the creation of enormous amounts of unstructured data (**Illustration 5.3**). People can easily post photos, videos, and voice recordings—all of which are hard for a business to analyze. Social media sites like TikTok, X (formerly Twitter), Instagram, and Facebook, podcasts, user-created wikis, and video-sharing sites like YouTube are all examples of Web 2.0.

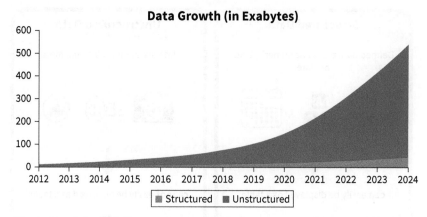

Illustration 5.3 Over time, unstructured data has grown much more quickly than structured data.

Source: www.arborsys.com

For example, you interact with unstructured data when a CAPTCHA asks you to verify that you are not a robot. It may present you with an image and ask you to select all squares containing street signs. By performing this exercise, you are helping Google refine its search algorithms by turning unstructured data (the image of the street signs) into structured data—meta tags—that Google can utilize when someone is searching for street signs. This activity also has an even greater purpose: it helps Google train its artificial intelligence algorithms to be smarter, faster, and more reliable. You are helping transform the way we interact with unstructured data!

Memory is now cheaper and easier to obtain than ever before, which means companies can capture more data. The challenge of how to utilize this data prevents many companies from using unstructured data to make meaningful business decisions.

Why Does It Matter to Your Career?

Thoughts from an Internal Audit Analytics Manager, Financial Services

- Understanding data elements is essential in any line of accounting work—and employers want to hire students who already understand these basics. You'll encounter structured data in tables throughout your career and need to know how to communicate about these tables to others.

- Many of the new members of the workforce have never experienced Web 1.0. They've only known Web 2.0—full of unstructured data and interaction. Companies are struggling to catch up with this generation's expectations and the impact unstructured data has on their operations. Fresh talent that understands what unstructured data is and has ideas about how to use it—even if they won't code it themselves—is critical for companies seeking to stay relevant.

Data That Changes

Another important characteristic of data is whether it is static or dynamic. **Static data** doesn't change once it's created. Think of static data like a book: once it's printed, its pages do not change. In contrast, **dynamic data** may change after it is recorded and must be updated. Dynamic data is like a website: users can update the content at any point in time, causing the data to change when they do so. If you have a social media profile and have ever changed your name, the city you live in, or your relationship status, you have updated dynamic data that the website stores for your profile.

Companies must consider the impact of dynamic data when planning their data strategy. As an internal auditor at Julia's Cookies, Kae uses data to create reports for company leaders. If the data she uses is dynamic, Kae must make sure she's using the most recent version of the data to provide relevant information in her reports. This is one of many considerations she needs to address when using data. Find out how Kae uses unstructured data to analyze what's happening at Julia's Cookies' call center in Applied Learning 5.1.

Julia's Cookies　　　　　　　　　　　　　　　　　　Applied Learning 5.1

Unstructured Data: Call Center

Julia's Cookies' customer service calls are all directed to the company's corporate call center. Calls are recorded as audio files and saved to the call center's computer system.

Kae wants to know the most common customer complaint that the call center employees receive. However, calls are hard to analyze since each one is stored as an unstructured data type—an audio file.

To analyze the calls, Kae would have to listen to many hours of calls to determine how to categorize each one or come up with a better idea. How can Kae utilize this unstructured data?

SOLUTION

Kae recommends using the following process to utilize the unstructured data:

1. Use software to convert unstructured calls into scripts.
2. Save the scripts as text files.
3. Analyze call scripts using a word cloud tool.
4. Scan the words to create a word bank (or word cloud).

Here is the result of Kae's analysis:

From the word cloud created using data from the calls, Kae concludes that most people who called to complain had problems with:

- Late deliveries
- Poor customer service
- Orders

This data analytics tool created a high-level word bank that allows the Internal Audit team to investigate the call scripts more deeply and choose a targeted sample for testing. When Kae selects one of the words, like "delivery," the word cloud directs her to a listing of all the calls that include the word "delivery" for her team review. By drilling down into the word "late," Kae discovers that customers have been unhappy about deliveries taking longer than expected. She recommends the auditors look into the specific locations with "late" included in the transcript to investigate the problem by location.

CONCEPT REVIEW QUESTIONS

1. What is a binary code?

   Ans. A computer information system stores and uses data with a two-symbol system. All information and instructions are executed on a computer in binary code, which uses the digits 1 and 0 to represent a letter, digit, or other character.

2. Identify field, record, and file from the given employee details table extract.

A	B	C	D
First Name	**Last Name**	**Address**	**Country**
John	Wales	123, 7th Street	Australia
Mary	Jose	102, Cherry Blossoms	Japan

   Ans.

A
John

   It is the first name field from the employee details file.

A	B	C	D
Mary	Jose	102, Cherry Blossoms	Japan

   It is a single record from the employee details file.

A	B	C	D
First Name	**Last Name**	**Address**	**Country**
John	Wales	123, 7th Street	Australia
Mary	Jose	102, Cherry Blossoms	Japan

   It is an employee details file.

3. What is the basic difference between structured and unstructured data?

   Ans. Data is categorized as one of two types based on how it is stored in a computer:

   - Structured data is organized and fits nicely into tables.
   - Unstructured data does not fit into a traditional table.

4. **CPA** What is structured data?

   Ans. Structured data is stored in a fixed field of a file. We can easily access structured data by using filters or querying languages—codes specific to a database—to analyze the data. Most accounting professionals are proficient in using structured data to gain insights, as accounting information systems are well organized and use traditional database tables for data storage.

5. **CPA** What is unstructured data?

   Ans. Unstructured data is any data that is not stored in a fixed field of a record or a file. Photographs, emails, and PDFs are some examples of unstructured data.

6. What is meant by data scrapping?

   Ans. Pulling and cleaning textual data from an unstructured format and placing it into a structured table is data scrapping. For example, audio files can be converted to analyzable data using voice-to-text transcription software to convert audio to a text file script of the content.

7. What do you know about Web 2.0?

   Ans. Web 2.0 refers to user-generated content and user participation on the internet. The Web 2.0 revolution resulted in the creation of enormous amounts of unstructured data.

8. What is the difference between static and dynamic data?

   Ans. Static data doesn't change once it's created. Think of static data like a book: its pages do not change once it's printed. In contrast, dynamic data may change after it is recorded and must be updated. Dynamic data is like a website: users can update the content at any point in time, causing the data to change when they do so.

5.2 How Is Data Stored?

Learning Objective ❷
Explain how data is stored.

Imagine you are in the entrance of a large library. In front of you, thousands of books are spread out on shelves and organized by topic. One section may have fiction, while another section houses autobiographies. The books are organized using a classification system like the Dewey Decimal Classification you may have learned in elementary school. Books relating to the same topic—like social sciences, technology, or literature—may all be stored on shelves near one another, in alphabetical order by author.

If you are looking for books on a specific topic, you can use the library's catalog to look up books by topic. Classic library catalogs, which were popular before digital options became available, consist of drawers with cards inside. Each card in the catalog includes information about one book and tells you where in the library that book is stored. Once you find the card for a book you want, you can go to the shelf and personally take the book down to read.

A library full of books that allows visitors to search for specific content and retrieve a book from a shelf is a lot like a database.

Introduction to Databases

A **database** is a set of logically related tables (files) containing an organized collection of data that is accessible for fast searching and retrieval. Like books in a library, data related to the same topic is stored in a table or group of tables.

There are different types of databases, which are characterized by the relationships between the tables they hold. The most common type of database you'll encounter as an accounting professional is a relational database. **CPA** **Relational databases** organize structured data in interrelated tables connected by similarities between tables. The data elements field, record, and file (table) are fundamental parts of a relational database, as data within relational databases is stored in tables that share commonalities—relationships—with one another (**Illustration 5.4**).

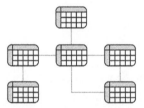

Illustration 5.4 Tables with commonalities are connected to one another in a relational database.

You'll learn more about the complexities of how tables in a relational database are connected in the Designing Systems and Databases chapter. **CPA** For now, there are key terms that will help you understand the basics of databases:

- **Database management systems (DBMS):** The systems that manage a database and retrieve data for a user are called database management systems (DBMS). These systems include the user interface, which is a screen where a user logs in and interacts with the computer system and where users can write code and queries. You learned about DBMS in the Software and Systems chapter, including popular systems like Oracle, MySQL, SQL Server, and Microsoft Access.

- **Queries:** Queries are requests for data that is stored within a database. A query results in the requested data being displayed on the screen or sent to a new location like a new table or report that the user specifies. Querying is much like looking up a book by topic in a library catalog.

- **Querying languages:** Queries are written in a querying language that is unique to the database management system. An example of a commonly used querying language is Structured Query Language (SQL). Variations of SQL are used in different database management systems for relational databases. Accounting professionals with a basic knowledge of how to write SQL queries are highly sought after by employers because most companies have databases that rely on SQL for querying.

- **Schema:** When a company implements a database, it customizes the layout of data tables within it. A database schema is a logical diagram of a database's structure and organization. It depicts relationships between tables and acts as both a blueprint for database administrators when setting up a new database and a guide for users who access an established database.

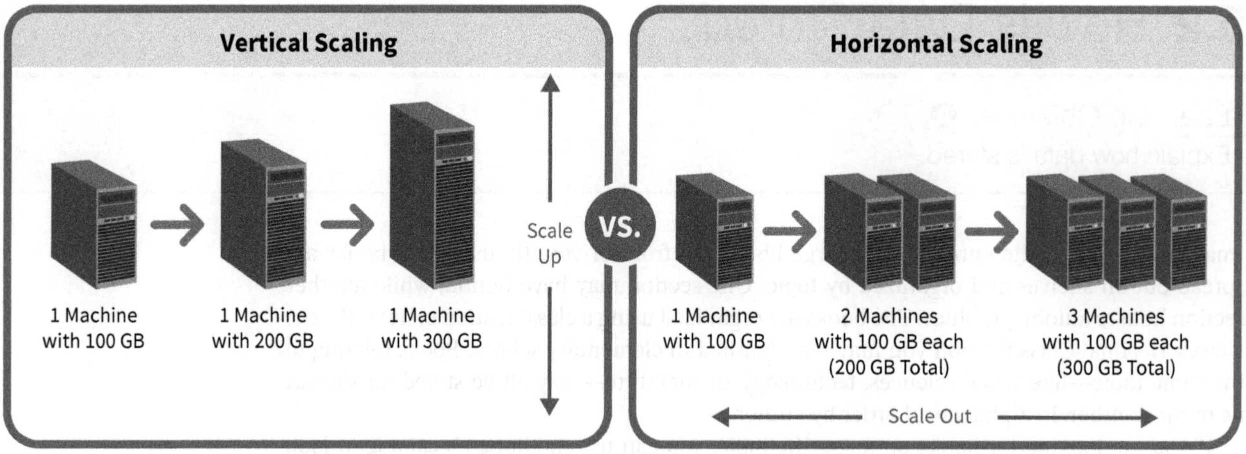

Illustration 5.5 Vertical scaling increases the size of the machine, while horizontal scaling increases the number of machines.

- **Database scalability:** Much like system scalability, database scalability is the capability of a database to manage increasing demands. A database can be scaled vertically by adding more capacity to the existing machine or horizontally by spreading the database across multiple machines that all work together to manage the database. Think of this as scaling up versus scaling out (**Illustration 5.5**).

- **Production database:** A database that is connected to an information system that is used for transactions in a business process is a production database. This database is "live"—the data is created and stored in real time as a result of a transaction being processed. For example, a production database is used for processing orders on Julia's Cookies' mobile app. At an investment firm, a production database supports orders that traders place on the stock market by recording the order data in real time. Production databases are the backbone of a company's operations.

Types of Data Storage

While data is created in a production database, that's often not where users access it. Production databases support operations. This means that if a large task, such as a user performing a complex query, slows down the database, the information system and business process it supports are also impacted. For this reason, alternative data storage is used to save copies of data where users can access it to query and perform activities that support decision making. Retrieving data from these data stores allows a company to meet its data objectives without placing strain on the production database.

Two types of data stores you'll likely encounter in your career are data lakes and data warehouses.

Data Lakes

Data in its raw format—before it's cleaned, aggregated, or filtered—is stored in a data lake. A **data lake** is a vast pool of data. It is designed to contain all of a company's data and acts as a central repository for data that is stored even though its purpose may not yet be known. One of the key benefits of a data lake is that it is cost-effective. Large companies implement data lakes to store all their data, regardless of whether it is structured or unstructured. Bulk data like social media feeds and websites is stored effectively in data lakes because a data lake doesn't have a predefined schema. Instead, a data lake uses an agile structure that adapts to new types of data as they are ingested into the data lake.

Data lake implementation is an enterprise-wide initiative. Companies often set up dedicated teams for data lake implementation, and a project like this can take years to roll out completely. Users who access data in a data lake need to know what they are looking for and

> ## Why Does It Matter to Your Career?
>
> ### Thoughts from a Recruiter, Public Accounting
>
> - Data storage is a growing issue for companies in all industries. Whatever type of company you join, you are going to be exposed to initiatives like data lakes and data warehouses. Many companies are just rolling out these programs—and they can take many years to complete.
>
> - Technical skills are no longer "bonuses" for accounting professionals—they're requirements for new hires. In an interview, ask questions about what technology a team uses. It may help you stand out to interviewers, even if you don't have technical experience. Companies are looking for students who are passionate about innovation and excited to learn what the business is doing.

how to transform it into a usable format for their analysis. For this reason, data lakes require someone with deep technical knowledge of data—like a data scientist—to transform the data into useful information.

Data Warehouses

CPA In contrast to a data lake, a **data warehouse** is designed specifically for reporting and data analysis and contains relevant data that has already been transformed for reporting use. Data warehouses are relational databases; they store historical data that's structured into related tables. Since a data warehouse is designed to be used for reporting, it has a predefined schema, and data ingested into the warehouse must fit that format. **CPA** A **data mart** is a subset of a data warehouse that is designed for a specific business function. A department uses a data mart for its individual reporting needs. Companies often have multiple data marts throughout their various business areas.

Data warehouses, like data lakes, are implemented enterprise-wide. If you are looking for data to perform an analysis, a data warehouse is the first place you should look. Since the data has already been transformed into an analytics-friendly format, data analysts and business users can use this data easily. Keep in mind that a data warehouse is updated on a scheduled basis and does not contain real-time data, as would a production database or data lake. Users need to understand how frequently a data warehouse is updated to ensure their reports are relevant. **Table 5.3** summarizes the differences between a data lake and a data warehouse for your review.

In a company that has both a data lake and data warehouse, the data lake is the first stop for newly generated data. From there, applicable data is cleansed and aggregated before it flows into the data warehouse, where analysts can access it (**Illustration 5.6**).

While data lakes and data warehouses are different in many ways, both are designed to manage large quantities of data across a business—known as "big data." We explore the characteristics of big data in the next section. In the meantime, see if you can identify where Julia's Cookies' budgeting and forecast data might be stored in Applied Learning 5.2.

TABLE 5.3 The Differences Between a Data Lake and a Data Warehouse

	Data Lake	Data Warehouse
Type of data	Unstructured and structured data from across the company (raw data)	Historical data in a structured format designed for a relational database (processed data)
Purpose	Cost-effective storage of big data	Aggregated big data for analytics and business decisions
Users	Data scientists	Data analysts
Activities	Storing big data	Supporting business analysis
	Big data analytics (data science)	Read-only queries for aggregating or extracting data
Scope of data	All data in a company	Only data relevant to reporting and analytics

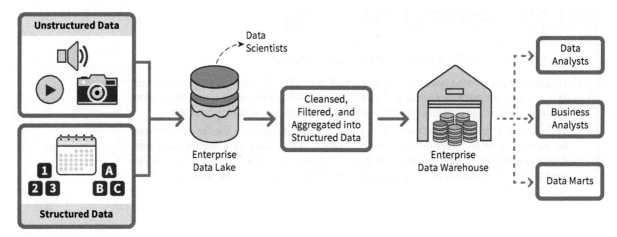

Illustration 5.6 Data flows through an enterprise data lake to an enterprise data warehouse.

Julia's Cookies
Applied Learning 5.2

Data Acquisition: Budget Data

Annika, who was hired for their accounting background, is on a development team that works on department-wide budgeting and forecasts at Julia's Cookies. The team has never done this before, so none of the data is readily available.

Annika is looking for historical budget data that is captured by the Accounting department. While meeting with one of the accounting analysts, they learn that the budget data is stored in a production database. Additionally, Julia's Cookies is currently in the middle of implementing an enterprise data lake, and the data that's in the lake already feeds to an accounting data warehouse. The accounting analyst isn't sure if this data has been ingested into the data lake or data warehouse yet and suggests Annika ask someone from the IT department who works on either of those projects.

Would you recommend that Annika meet with the project owners of the enterprise data lake or the project owners or the data warehouse first?

SOLUTION

Annika's first stop would be the data warehouse owners. If Julia's Cookies already has an accounting data warehouse established, that's where Annika could access the budgeting data. If that data isn't already in the warehouse, the data warehouse owners will know if there is a plan to eventually include that data—and if there isn't, they can work with Annika to develop a plan to do so for the development team's purposes.

CONCEPT REVIEW QUESTIONS

1. **CPA** What are database management systems (DBMS)?
   Ans. The systems that manage a database and retrieve data for a user are called database management systems (DBMS). These systems include the user interface, which is a screen where a user logs in and interacts with the computer system and where users can write code and queries. Popular DBMS are Oracle, MySQL, SQL Server, and Microsoft Access.

2. **CPA** What are querying languages?
   Ans. Queries are written in a querying language that is unique to the database management system. An example of a commonly used querying language is Structured Query Language (SQL). Variations of SQL are used in different database management systems for relational databases.

3. **CPA** What is a schema?
   Ans. When a company implements a database, it customizes the layout of data tables within it. A database schema is a logical diagram of a database's structure and organization. It depicts the relationships between tables and acts as both a blueprint for database administrators when setting up a new database and a guide for users who access an established database.

4. **CPA** What is the difference between vertical and horizontal database scalability?

Ans. Much like system scalability, database scalability is the capability of a database to manage increasing demands. A database can be scaled vertically by adding more capacity to the existing machine or horizontally by spreading the database across multiple machines that all work together to manage the database.

5. **CPA** What is a production database?

Ans. A database that is connected to an information system that is used for transactions in a business process is a production database. This database is "live"—the data is created and stored in real time as a result of a transaction being processed. At an investment firm, a production database supports orders that traders place on the stock market by recording the order data in real time. Production databases are the backbone of a company's operations.

5.3 What Makes Data "Big Data"?

Learning Objective ❸
Summarize the five characteristics of big data.

Information systems and databases have limitations that impact the type and amount of data they can process or store. The greater the capabilities of a system or database, the more expensive it is to purchase, implement, and maintain. For this reason, companies perform cost-benefit analyses to determine the systems and databases that can best achieve company goals and handle data processing and storage needs without raising costs unnecessarily.

When making these decisions, one of the largest factors is how much big data a company generates and wishes to analyze. **CPA** **Big data** refers to extremely large and complex data sets that can be analyzed to reveal patterns and associations. In our internet-driven world, vast amounts of new data are created every minute, at a very fast rate. Big data often is so large, generated so fast, and so unstructured that it surpasses the limitations of traditional systems and databases.

Big data has five characteristics, called the 5Vs (**Illustration 5.7**).

Illustration 5.7 Big data is characterized by five attributes call the 5Vs.

Volume

 CPA One of the first attributes used to define big data is **volume**, which is the quantity and scale of data generated every second. In other words, it's not big data if it isn't big.

As people and processes become more connected, the amount of data is growing exponentially:

- The size of the entire internet in 1997 was 88 terabytes (TB)—a value we'll examine more closely shortly.

- The internet now is so large that scientists cannot agree on a number.

Accountants are expected to use a large volume of data in financial decision making, and standard software like Excel and Access are not equipped to handle large sets of data. The financial decision-making tools you use will depend on your company's size, data volume, and available resources.

To measure the size of data, recall that a byte is composed of 8 bits (binary digits). Because the next smallest data element is a single binary digit, a byte is the smallest unit of memory—which is storage—that a computer has. All larger measures of memory size are based on bytes. For example, a kilobyte (KB) is approximately 1,000 bytes, a megabyte (MB) is approximately 1 million bytes, and a gigabyte (GB) is approximately 1 billion bytes. This means that a smart phone with 64 GB of storage has around 64 billion bytes of memory.

To keep up with rapid growth in data volume, the terms used to describe data sizes have also grown. **CPA** Table 5.4 gives examples of data for each of the terms commonly used to describe the size of data.

TABLE 5.4 **CPA** Data Measurements and Examples[1-3]

Bit	A bit, or binary digit, is either 1 or 0.
Byte	A letter on a keyboard, such as "p," is 1 byte.
Kilobyte (KB)	A typical text message is less than 1 KB.
Megabyte (MB)	Most emails allow up to 25 MB of attached files.
Gigabyte (GB)	The average-size USB flash drive that a college student uses is 2–8 GB.
Terabyte (TB)	Streaming 4K movies for over 100 hours would use around 1 TB of data.
Petabyte (PB)	The human brain can store memories equal to about 2.5 PB of data.
Exabyte (EB)	Around 32 million Blu-ray discs could be stored in 1 EB.
Zettabyte (ZB)	It is estimated the world created around more than 59 ZB of data in 2019.
Yottabyte (YB)	There is no practical use for yottabytes, as all the world's data can still be measured in zettabytes.

Velocity

 Where does all this data come from? The simple answer is *everywhere*. In addition to the internet, every digital interaction with the world—from paying for a cup of coffee with a debit card or smart phone app to checking the time on a phone's screen—is recorded. Businesses use their collected data for insights and decision making by processing it through their information systems.

[1]www.scientificamerican.com/article/what-is-the-memory-capacity/
[2]www.seagate.com/files/www-content/our-story/trends/files/idc-seagate-dataage-whitepaper.pdf
[3]www.idc.com/getdoc.jsp?containerId=prUS46286020

Velocity is the speed at which data is generated. When data is generated, it must be processed and stored somewhere in real time. Companies can find it overwhelming to deal with the speed of data creation and the arrival of data in their systems. System limitations are a key factor in managing data velocity; an information system must have the processing power to handle the large amounts of data being created at fast speeds.

Variety

Data variety is a challenging aspect of managing big data for a business. **Variety** is the diversity of data created or collected. Data variety can refer to the difference between unstructured and structured big data or the different types of unstructured data. As you already learned, unstructured data is challenging, and the challenge grows exponentially when you add more file types to the mix.

Companies generate unstructured data like photographs, PDFs, employee chat conversations, and emails each day. Externally, customers generate social media posts, customer service requests, customer chat bot conversations, and more. Many companies are not equipped to handle the types of unstructured data they have and use manual processes for accessing and reviewing files instead of leveraging advanced technology to organize, manage, and query unstructured data.

Why Does It Matter to Your Career?

Thoughts from a Manager of Tax Data and Insights, Manufacturing

- If your company doesn't have advanced tools, you may be expected to manually review files like PDFs and emails. Ask your interviewers what types of tools and processes their team uses to work with data. They may be impressed you have an interest, and you may find out the job description is more manual than you hoped. If the team is working on implementing new technology, it's an opportunity for you to join the team and have an impact in shaping the team's future.

- Accounting professionals of all types work with data regularly and handle large amounts of data at a time. Most accounting professionals use Excel, but Excel isn't equipped for large data sets. Work on your technology skills, like basic database querying languages (like SQL), and you will be able to start a job equipped with a set of skills that will instantly add value to the team.

Veracity

Veracity is the accuracy and truthfulness of data—the extent to which the data can be trusted for insights. Unstructured data is inherently prone to many imprecisions and inaccuracies due to high velocity and variety. Data must be accurate, objective, and relevant to be useful and have value.

When we ask advice only from people who share our own worldview, we risk hearing only what we want to hear. This is called **confirmation bias.** By using inherently biased data for an analytics task, we risk decision making that omits relevant facts about the big picture. Data preparation and cleansing are important steps before performing data analytics because these tasks improve veracity.

The core accounting principles—accuracy and completeness—are not just management assertions for financial accounting. These principles apply to all aspects of accounting practice and are a cornerstone of sound decision making. Ensuring that we can trust the data—that it is free from biases—ties directly to data veracity and is critical for accountants.

In the Real World   Uber's Data Platform

Uber Technologies is a multi-billion-dollar company that owns popular services for ride sharing, package and food delivery, and even electric bicycle and motorized scooter rentals. As a mobile app–based company, Uber generates a lot of data every day.

The company originally stored limited amounts of data in several traditional production SQL databases. These databases weren't integrated, meaning they didn't communicate with one another, so users had to access each database individually and combine the data themselves. Because Uber is a global company, this decentralized approach led to issues in achieving an enterprise-wide understanding of the business. As the velocity and volume of incoming data continued to increase, Uber needed to move to a scalable, centralized data platform.

The data platform's first generation focused on migrating data to a single repository. An online SQL querying service allowed users to easily interact with data from a single access point without needing to understand the underlying querying language. For the first time, Uber had a global view of its data. As more data continued to be ingested into the warehouse, Uber realized the warehouse was becoming more of a data lake—where raw data is not usable to analysts.

For the second generation of its data platform, Uber focused on horizontal scalability with a more structured schema in the data warehouse that improved storage efficiency and costs. A separate data lake was introduced to hold raw data from external sources that didn't require transformation during ingestion. This freed up the data warehouse for its purpose: housing transformed, analytics-ready data.

Uber faced new challenges as tens of petabytes of data were added to its data platform. Latency—the time between the creation of data in a system and when that data is available to users—was too great for real-time decision making, and the number of queries executed was putting too much pressure on the system.

The third generation of the data platform focused on faster, incremental data ingestion. With a data library, users can incrementally extract only the data that changed since their last access. This update reduced data latency from 24 hours to 1 hour between the time the data is created and when it's available to users. The company's future goal is to reduce latency to only 5–10 minutes.

Uber's data analytics infrastructure is an advanced, cross-functional collaboration. Uber makes this offer: "If working on big data challenges that boggle the limits of scale interests you, consider applying for a role in our San Francisco and Palo Alto–based teams."[4]

How do you think a project like Uber's data platform affects a company's accounting professionals? Does it seem relevant to your future career to understand these types of IT projects?

Value

CPA **Value** is arguably the most important of the 5Vs because data isn't useful to a business unless it can be converted into valuable information. Given the significant resources allocated to collecting, storing, and analyzing data, it is essential to identify data value. While companies may capture large quantities of big data, they may lack the capabilities to interpret how to turn that data into useful information. We can identify the value of data by determining the costs and benefits. We ask questions like:

- Is this the right data to answer my question?
- Is collecting this data worth the effort?
- Is this data of a high quality?
- Is this enough data?
- Is this data reliable?
- Has this data already been collected and stored somewhere else in the company?
- Is storing this data cost beneficial?
- Is the time spent preparing and analyzing this data worthwhile?

Now that you have learned all five of the characteristics of big data, try to troubleshoot Julia's Cookies' mobile app limitations in Applied Learning 5.3.

---

[4]eng.uber.com/uber-big-data-platform/

Julia's Cookies	Applied Learning 5.3

Big Data: Mobile App Limitations

Julia's Cookies' customers place orders on a mobile app that routes the orders to the customers' local stores. Orders are baked fresh and delivered to a customer's front door in less than 40 minutes. The app provides real-time tracking to allow customers to see the status of their order—including a map that tracks the location of the delivery driver.

Julia's Cookies' IT department believes that system and database limitations may make it impossible to keep up with the demands this process places on the IT infrastructure. The IT department recommends that Julia's Cookies invest in upgrading related systems and databases.

Do you think any of the 5Vs—volume, velocity, variety, veracity, and value—may be impacting Julia's Cookies' systems and databases?

SOLUTION

Volume: As Julia's Cookies' business keeps expanding, so does its customer base. The increased number of customers and orders may be putting a strain on Julia's Cookies' database storage capabilities due to increased volume.

Velocity: Due to the real-time nature of Julia's Cookies' order and delivery process, the underlying systems may be struggling to keep up with high processing speeds that result from the speed at which data is being created.

CONCEPT REVIEW QUESTIONS

1. **CPA** What is meant by big data?
   Ans. Big data refers to extremely large and complex data sets that can be analyzed to reveal patterns and associations. In our internet-driven world, vast amounts of new data are created every minute, at a very fast rate. Big data is often so large, generated so fast, and so unstructured that it surpasses the limitations of traditional systems and databases.

2. Describe the "value" characteristic of big data with respect to limited resources in a company.
   Ans. Value is the worth of the data from the decision-making perspective. Value is arguably the most important of the 5Vs because data isn't useful to a business unless it can be converted into valuable information. If a company has limited resources, it should consider if the data is reliable, of high quality, and enough before investing time and money in its collection, storage, and analysis.

3. **CPA** Fill in the right answer in the following sentences:
   a. A bit, or binary digit, is either _____ or _____.
   b. A letter on a _____, such as "p," is 1 byte.
   c. A typical text message is less than 1 _____.
   d. Most emails allow up to _____ of attached files.
   e. The average-sized USB flash drive is 2–8 _____.
   f. Streaming 4K movies for over 100 hours would use around 1 _____ of data.
   g. The human brain can store memories equal to about 2.5 _____ of data.
   h. EB is _____.
   i. The full form of ZB is _____.
   j. The full form of YB is _____.
   Ans. a. 1 or 0; **b.** keyboard; **c.** Kilobyte (KB); **d.** 25 Megabyte (MB); **e.** Gigabyte (GB); **f.** Terabyte (TB); **g.** Petabyte (PB); **h.** Exabyte (EB); **i.** Zettabyte (ZB); **j.** Yottabyte (YB)

4. What do you understand by data variety?
   Ans. Data variety can refer to the difference between unstructured and structured big data or the different types of unstructured data. Companies generate unstructured data such as photographs, PDFs, employee chat conversations, and emails each day. Externally,

customers generate social media posts, customer service requests, customer chatbot conversations, and more.

5. Define veracity in the context of big data.

Ans. Veracity means the accuracy and truthfulness of data—the extent to which the data can be trusted for insights. Unstructured data is inherently prone to many imprecision and inaccuracies due to high velocity and variety. Data must be accurate, objective, and relevant to be useful and have value.

5.4 How Do Accounting Professionals Use Data?

Learning Objective ❹
Apply data analytics to accounting problems.

Just as companies use different types and sizes of information systems based on individual needs, they also use different approaches to using data. Some companies may not use data at all and have no plans to do so in the near future. One company may only use data to look at historical information, while another company might use data to drive predictions and decisions about the future. Data-focused companies integrate data analysis goals into their organizational strategies. Viewing data as a strategy—rather than as a technology issue to be addressed—changes the way a company approaches data analytics.

 Recall that data analytics is the process of using technology to transform raw data, or facts, into useful information. Accounting professionals use their financial analysis and critical-thinking skills to apply data analytics to problems using technology.

CPA There are four widely accepted categories within data analytics, and each one answers a question:

- **Descriptive analytics:** *What has* happened?
- **Diagnostic analytics:** *Why* did it happen?
- **Predictive analytics:** *What is likely* to happen?
- **Prescriptive analytics:** *How* should we act?

We apply these four categories of analytics to specific accounting uses, often with the help of dashboards. **Dashboards** are interactive, real-time reports that are presented as **visualizations**—graphical representations of information and data (**Illustration 5.8**).

While not all accounting professionals will learn how to code these analytics in advanced programming languages like SQL or Python, employers still look for technical skills that can help their departments pursue innovative solutions and increase their data analytics capabilities. **CPA** Some of the most valued data analytics–focused skillsets employers look for in accounting professionals are:

- An "analytic mindset," including the ability to apply critical-thinking skills to data—for example, asking a question, transforming data to answer the question, and communicating the answer to leadership
- Understanding of basic data elements and structures
- Knowledge of data visualization and analytics software
- Ability to use traditional tools such as Excel and Access to help migrate processes to newer analytics tools

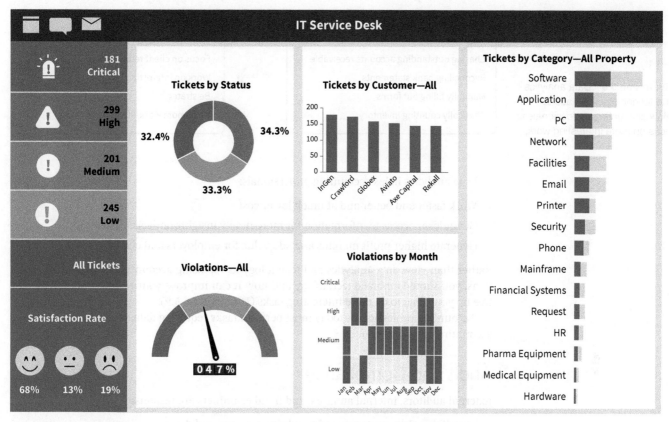

Illustration 5.8 Dashboards with visualizations are graphical representations of information and data.

Why Does It Matter to Your Career?

Thoughts from a Tax Senior, Public Accounting

- One of the most valued skillsets for accounting professionals is an analytic mindset. This is a buzzword with employers because this mindset is valuable in a new hire. You don't have to know how to code or even do advanced Excel analysis. It's the curiosity about data, interest in learning, and ability to ask a question and find out what data can answer it that makes an accounting professional stand out as having next-generation skills.

- Using data analysis may require working alongside trained IT professionals who may not understand the business side of accounting. Entering your role with a basic understanding of both the business and technology sides can make you a valuable translator between your team and the IT professionals in your company.

Data analytics has transformed the accounting profession. A few years ago, proficiency in data analytics was a cutting-edge skill for accounting professionals, but now management and audit committees expect it. Data analytics requires investments in technology, but the technology is useless without the human element. Employers are often willing to make the technological investment but struggle to find accounting professionals who have the necessary technical skills.

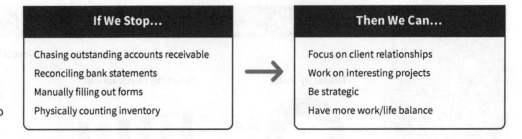

Illustration 5.9 Data analytics and technology innovations allow accounting professionals to focus on more interesting work.

Data analytics helps accounting professionals:

- Work faster and better and at much lower cost
- Get quicker access to information for more timely insights or decision making
- Generate higher profit margins and add value for employers and clients

Rather than view data analytics and technology as replacing accounting professionals' positions, you should embrace technology and how it can improve your team's productivity and free up your time to do more interesting tasks (**Illustration 5.9**).

Accounting professionals today must perform tasks requiring data analytics in all areas of accounting specialization.

Audit and Compliance

External auditors, internal auditors, and fraud examiners are responsible for:

- Identifying risks, patterns, and trends in processes and data
- Advising business leaders on best practices and regulatory requirements
- Performing audit tests to gain assurance over populations of data

Historically, audit testing relied on population sampling. The population is the entire group you want to draw a conclusion about—in this case, the data. With manual testing, auditors were unable to test entire populations. They instead randomly selected samples—a minimum number of records from the data—and relied on them to indicate the state of the entire population. Audit teams are now using data analytics to test 100% of the population and provide higher levels of assurance while using fewer resources.

The Big Four public accounting firms all use audit data analytics. For example, EY's Helix includes a series of visual ledgers that allow auditors to follow the flow of transactions through all stages of the reporting process. The software flags suspicious transactions. Its dashboards are fully interactive. By clicking on the graphics, an auditor can drill down to the underlying data.

Table 5.5 shows examples of audit data analytics for each of the four types of data analytics.

TABLE 5.5 Auditing and Data Analytics

Descriptive: What has happened?	
Data Analytics	**Explanation**
Three-way match for purchasing	For the whole population of inventory purchases for the period, match the firm's purchase order with the firm's receiving documentation and the vendor's invoice. Agree the quantity per the invoice to the quantity received and to the quantity ordered. Agree the price per the invoice to the price on the purchase order. Then examine discrepancies and determine internal control deficiencies.

TABLE 5.5 (*Continued*)

Diagnostic: Why did it happen?	
Data Analytics	**Explanation**
Three-way match for purchasing	Descriptive analysis results revealed that 0.9% of the transactions were not subject to the three-way match. Drilling down to the data and investigating revealed that only one vendor and one accounts payable supervisor were involved in these transactions. The supervisor manually approved the invoices for payment without matching purchase orders and receiving documentation. This led to the discovery of a purchasing fraud scheme. The brother of the supervisor had received payment for nonexistent purchases.
Predictive: What is likely to happen?	
Data Analytics	**Explanation**
Allowance for doubtful accounts	Build a model to predict the amount of the allowance for doubtful accounts by using inputs such as payment history, debt types, and industry norms. Compare this prediction to the balance in the ledger.
Prescriptive: How should we act?	
Data Analytics	**Explanation**
Intelligent audit planning	Run historical audit findings and observations data through an artificial intelligence algorithm to analyze risks and activities. Predict which audits should be performed next, based on past risk indicators.

Financial Accounting

Financial accountants are responsible for:

- Preparing and analyzing financial statements
- Managing financial accounting information systems
- Ensuring compliance with regulatory requirements

Financial accountants have always analyzed financial statements to assess the performance of a firm. The difference today is that newer technologies like interactive data visualization, machine learning, and artificial intelligence have revolutionized and significantly expanded the insights gained from data analysis (**Table 5.6**).

TABLE 5.6 Financial Accounting and Data Analytics

Descriptive: What has happened?	
Data Analytics	**Explanation**
Perform financial statement analysis	Use ratio analysis, horizontal analysis, and vertical analysis to analyze a company's financial statements and display the results on an interactive dashboard. Knowledge of these ratios is essential for accounting certifications like the CPA, CMA, and CFE. Ratios include profitability, liquidity, solvency, and activity ratios.

(Continued)

TABLE 5.6 (*Continued*)

Diagnostic: Why did it happen?	
Data Analytics	**Explanation**
Compare accounting ratios and vertical analyses to competitors and the industry using XBRL[5] data	Benchmark a company's ratios by comparing them to the firm's own past performance, competitors' ratios, and industry ratios. For example, if there is a return on equity (ROE) ratio of 15% this year and 12% for the prior year, this indicates that managers are employing the funds entrusted to them by the shareholders to generate improved returns. If the company's main competitor has an ROE of 18%, the company is being outperformed. If the industry ratio is 13%, then the company outperformed the industry this year but not last year. You can also drill down into ROE on an interactive dashboard to decompose it into the numerous underlying ratios that help pinpoint areas for improvement. Decomposing ROE is like peeling back the layers of an onion to get to the underlying explanations for changes.
Predictive: What is likely to happen?	
Data Analytics	**Explanation**
Predict future financial performance	Produce forecasts of the income statement, statement of cash flows, and balance sheet for each of the next five years. Horizontal analysis over the past several years should identify trends. There are key drivers for this task—normally the sales forecast and profit margin. If a company is sensitive to the economic cycle, it is necessary to consider macroeconomic conditions in the forecasts.
Prescriptive: How should we act?	
Data Analytics	**Explanation**
Classify leases as finance or operating	Use machine learning based on previous lease classifications to evaluate new leases and assign a classification to each for compliance with U.S. GAAP, continuously using historical data to further train the program.

Managerial Accounting

Managerial, or management, accountants focus on three areas:

- Cost management and reporting
- Performance measurement and analysis
- Supporting management's planning and decision-making efforts

Management accountants are responsible for a diverse range of tasks and responsibilities. They may be tasked with special projects aimed at determining the costs and benefits of a course of action or be asked to develop a budget and control system for a business unit. The explosion of big data allows management accountants to expand their traditional boundaries. For example, the availability of **geotags**, which digitally assign a geographic location to a piece of data like a photo, and other locational data allows management accountants to provide analyses that are more extensive and substantive. Explore the managerial accounting analytics examples in **Table 5.7**, then see how a dashboard is used at Julia's Cookies for managerial accounting reporting in Applied Learning 5.4.

---

[5]XBRL (eXtensible Business Reporting Language) is a language used for the consistent exchange of business information, particularly financial reporting information for public companies. XBRL makes data easy to analyze across companies and platforms. The Financial Reporting Processes chapter covers this topic.

TABLE 5.7 Managerial Accounting and Data Analytics

Descriptive: What has happened?	
Data Analytics	**Explanation**
Develop key performance metrics	Display key performance metrics for a firm on a digital dashboard to monitor performance, including gross profit margin, operating profit margin, EBITDA (earnings before interest, taxes, depreciation, and amortization), customer retention rate, market share, market growth rate, time to market, employee churn rate, recycling rate, waste reduction rate, carbon footprint, and water footprint.
Diagnostic: Why did it happen?	
Data Analytics	**Explanation**
Perform variance analysis by comparing actual performance to benchmark performance and identifying causes for significant variances	A firm's days sales outstanding has significantly increased. This means that the firm is taking longer to collect accounts receivable. Use diagnostic analysis to provide insights into why this has happened.
Predictive: What is likely to happen?	
Data Analytics	**Explanation**
Reduce employee turnover costs	Identifying employees at risk of resigning and reducing the resignation rate through early intervention could lead to significant savings. In performing the analysis, the input data could include employee reviews, pay data, peer reviews, time at the firm, time since last promotion, and LinkedIn data. Remember that big data may know when you'll resign before you do!
	Assume that a firm has 2,000 employees, average salary is $50,000, cost to replace employees is an average of 120% of the employee's annual salary, and voluntary resignations average 10% per year (or 200 employees). A quick calculation reveals that the annual cost of employee turnover averages $12 million!
Prescriptive: How should we act?	
Data Analytics	**Explanation**
Determine the best crops to plant	A multinational agricultural corporation identifies the optimal mix of crops to plant in different geographic locations by utilizing artificial intelligence and inputs such as real-time weather patterns and climate change indicators.

Julia's Cookies
Applied Learning 5.4

Managerial Accounting Analytics: Sales Dashboard

Julia's Cookies' Managerial Accounting department uses data analytics to track sales across the United States. This descriptive analytics visualizes *what* already happened by showing how much of each product was purchased in each state.

The visualization uses darker colors to indicate higher cookie sales and also includes numeric totals on each state for users who may not see color variations clearly. The Managerial Accounting department uses this analytics to identify areas for budget adjustments and to make recommendations about altering inventory allocations.

Based on this analytics, what can you determine about the state of Washington?

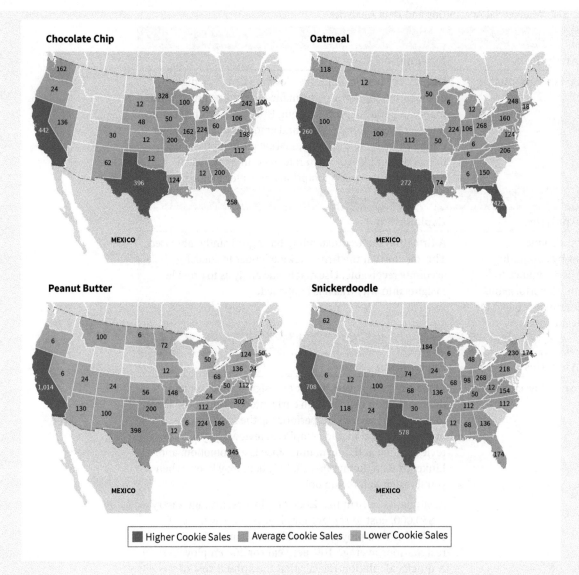

SOLUTION

It's clear that Washington cookie sales are going well—chocolate chip and oatmeal had steady sales. The lack of a single peanut butter cookie sale is unusual. It could mean that peanut butter cookies just are not very popular in Washington; however, it could also mean that there's something wrong with the peanut butter cookies in that region—maybe a supplier's ingredients are low quality or there's something wrong with the way the stores in Washington are baking the cookies. The Managerial Accounting department can use diagnostic analytics to further investigate *why* there are no peanut butter cookie sales in Washington.

Tax Accounting

Tax accountants' responsibilities include:

- Ensuring compliance with a multitude of income tax codes (federal, state, and local)
- Collecting and paying sales taxes
- Advising management on tax strategy, implications, and consequences
- Attending to tax audit issues

Recent legislation concerning online sales by companies like Amazon have complicated the collection of sales taxes, as these companies must now collect sales taxes for sales in different states, all with their own sales tax rates. Most of the data to support calculations associated with these tax determinations are in separate systems and data sources throughout the business and externally, and much of this data will not be in a standard format.

One example of a technology that is helping solve this problem is the **tax data hub**, which is a specialized database designed to provide a centralized store for tax-related data. It automatically extracts data from source systems and loads it in a standard format optimized for the tax department. In addition to increasing efficiency, tax data hubs reduce errors and enable data analytics. **Table 5.8** offers more examples.

TABLE 5.8 Tax Accounting and Data Analysis

Descriptive: What has happened?	
Data Analytics	**Explanation**
Develop key performance metrics on tax costs	Display key performance metrics on tax costs for a corporation on a digital dashboard over a five-year period, including income before tax, effective tax rate, taxes paid, deferred taxes, and impact of losses carried forward.
Diagnostic: Why did it happen?	
Data Analytics	**Explanation**
Create a trend analysis for sales taxes paid in different states to identify and investigate anomalies	An online company sells goods in all 50 states. Sales tax penalties for underpayment can be severe.
Predictive: What is likely to happen?	
Data Analytics	**Explanation**
Advise a wealthy couple on the tax consequences of residing part time in certain countries	Prince Harry and Meghan Markle consult a tax partner to provide scenarios of future tax liabilities in the United States and Canada before deciding where to live.
Prescriptive: How should we act?	
Data Analytics	**Explanation**
Develop an online Q&A for tax clients	Accountants use artificial intelligence to answer online tax questions from clients.

CONCEPT REVIEW QUESTIONS

1. **CPA** List the four widely accepted categories within data analytics.
   Ans. There are four widely accepted categories within data analytics, and each one answers a question:
   - **Descriptive analytics:** *What has* happened?
   - **Diagnostic analytics:** *Why* did it happen?
   - **Predictive analytics:** *What is likely* to happen?
   - **Prescriptive analytics:** *How* should we act?

2. What are dashboards?
   Ans. Dashboards allow us to use and see interactive, real-time reports presented as visualizations—graphical representations of information and data.

3. What do you understand by the term "tax data hub"?
   Ans. A tax data hub is a specialized database designed to provide a centralized store for tax-related data. It automatically extracts data from source systems and loads it in a standard format optimized for the tax department. In addition to increasing efficiency, tax data hubs reduce errors and enable data analytics.

FEATURED PROFESSIONAL | MBA Business Analytics and Management Information Systems Candidate

Photo courtesy of Yih-Shan Sheu

Eliza Sheu, CPA

Eliza earned a master's degree in accounting and then began working in a Big Four firm, serving clients in diverse industries. Later, Eliza transitioned to a financial analyst position. After a couple years of industry experience and realizing the importance of having a data analytics skillset, Eliza pursued an MBA degree with a specialization in business analytics while simultaneously completing a management information systems dual major. Outside work, Eliza enjoys aerobic exercise and yoga.

Why are accounting information systems important?

Accounting is the language of business, and accounting information systems provide a mechanism to record detailed transactions and produce accounting reports needed for decision making. Also, knowledge about integrated systems and how data can be extracted from these systems to provide useful information provides students with a jumpstart to their careers. You can think of accounting and financial reporting as the body and the information system and data streams as the arteries.

Why did you decide to go back to school to pursue a master's in information systems and business analytics?

Before I went back to school for analytics, I had experience in systems implementation projects. I wanted to know the full pipeline of data and how it's collected in systems automatically, how it's extracted and transformed into valuable information, and how a user interacts with systems throughout this process.

What's the most important thing you think accounting professionals should know about data?

Big data technologies have significantly impacted various industries and business functions; the accounting profession is no exception. It is important for accounting professionals to have the skillset to bridge gaps in the business, technology, and finance domains to provide information that is useful for making efficient and effective decisions.

Review and Practice

Key Terms Review

big data	descriptive analytics	structured data
binary code	diagnostic analytics	tax data hub
confirmation bias	dynamic data	unstructured data
dashboard	geotag	value
data	meta tag	variety
data lake	predictive analytics	velocity
data mart	prescriptive analytics	veracity
data type	relational database	visualization
data warehouse	scraped	volume
database	static data	Web 2.0

Learning Objectives Review

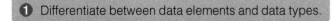

1 Differentiate between data elements and data types.

Data consists of facts and statistics that are collected for reference or analysis.

There are six data elements:

- Bit: A binary digit
- Byte: A group of bits, usually in clusters of eight
- Field: A group of bytes that identify a characteristic of an entity

- Record: A group of related fields that describe an individual instance of an entity
- File: A group of records for one specific entity
- Database: A set of logically related files (tables)

How data is stored determines whether it is structured or unstructured. Structured data is easily stored in a table; includes specific data types, such as date, numeric, and text fields; uses less storage space; and is easier to manage. Unstructured data includes photographs, emails, and more. It requires more storage space and is harder to manage. Meta tags are often used to label unstructured data with keywords that can be searched in a database. A person must assign these keywords. Web 2.0 creates user-generated content that contributes to the large amounts of unstructured data businesses own. Data can be static or dynamic. Static data doesn't change after creation, while dynamic data is changed and updated after creation.

❷ Explain how data is stored.

A database organizes data by grouping like items together in tables and using queries to retrieve data that a user needs. Queries are written using a querying language such as SQL.

A database management system (DBMS) includes a user interface where users log in and interact with the system.

A database schema is a logical diagram of the structure and organization of a database. Databases can be structured in a variety of ways. In a relational database, structured data is connected by similarities between the tables.

Companies like Uber consider a database's scalability to ensure that the database can grow with the business's needs. Projects like data lakes and data warehouses enable businesses to store data that users need to analyze without granting access to production databases.

The key differences between a data lake and data warehouse are:

- Data lakes store unstructured and structured data from across the company that has not been transformed. They store all data the company generates.
- Data warehouses store historical data that has been transformed into a consistent, structured format. They are relational databases that aggregate data for users to analyze for business decisions.

❸ Summarize the five characteristics of big data.

The five characteristics of big data are:

- Volume: The quantity and scale of data generated every second

- Velocity: The speed at which data is generated
- Variety: The diversity of data collected—whether it includes tables, photos, videos, emails, etc.
- Veracity: The accuracy of data and the extent to which it can be trusted for insights
- Value: The usefulness of data to a business through its conversion into information

Value is considered the most important because companies must turn data into useful information to justify the cost benefit of storage and analysis. Questions that can help determine data's value include:

- Is this the right data to answer my questions?
- Is collecting this data worth the effort?
- Will it cost too much to make it usable?
- Is storing this data cost beneficial?
- Is analyzing this data worthwhile?

❹ Apply data analytics to accounting problems.

Data analytics can be categorized into one of four types:

- **Descriptive analytics:** *What* is happening?
- **Diagnostic analytics:** *Why* did it happen?
- **Predictive analytics:** *What is likely* to happen?
- **Prescriptive analytics:** *How* should we act?

Data analytics transforms raw data into useful information that can be presented by compiling visualizations into interactive, real-time reports called dashboards.

Employers seek accounting professionals who have an analytic mindset and can use critical-thinking skills to ask questions that data can answer.

Data analytics helps accounting professionals work faster, get answers more quickly, and add value for employers and clients. Accounting professionals use data analytics for audit and compliance, financial accounting, managerial accounting, tax accounting, and more.

CPA questions, as well as multiple choice, discussion, analysis and application, and Tableau questions and other resources, are available online.

Multiple Choice Questions

1. (LO 1) Structured data

   a. can be displayed in tables.

   b. includes images and social media content.

   c. is difficult to analyze using traditional software tools.

   d. represents about 80% of a company's data.

2. (LO 1) **CPA** What is the correct ascending hierarchy of data elements in a system?

   a. Character, record, file, field

   b. Field, character, file, record

   c. Character, field, record, file

   d. Field, record, file, character

3. **(LO 1)** An example of unstructured data is a
   a. sales order.
   b. cash payment.
   c. digital image.
   d. loan amount from a bank.

4. **(LO 1)** How are meta tags used to identify unstructured data?
   a. Meta tags are used as the primary key.
   b. Meta tags are key words that help describe the content.
   c. Meta tags are used as foreign keys.
   d. Meta tags represent tables in the database.

5. **(LO 1)** **CPA** The following customer data is stored in the sales processing system of a regional produce distributor:
   CustomerNumber, CustomerName, CustomerPhone, CustomerContact, CustomerCreditLimit
   Which of the following is true?
   a. CustomerNumber is an example of a field.
   b. CustomerNumber is an example of a data value.
   c. CustomerNumber is an example of a record.
   d. CustomerNumber is an example of a file.

6. **(LO 2)** **CPA** SQL is *most* directly related to
   a. string question language processing.
   b. the "grandfather, father, son" method of record retention.
   c. electronic commerce.
   d. relational databases.

7. **(LO 2)** How can a database be scaled vertically?
   a. A database can be scaled vertically by removing capacity from the existing machine.
   b. A database can be scaled vertically by consolidating the database onto a single machine.
   c. A database can be scaled vertically by adding more capacity to the existing machine.
   d. A database can be scaled vertically by spreading the database across multiple machines that work together to manage the database.

8. **(LO 2)** Which of the following best describes a database?
   a. A database is several interconnected computers, machines, or operations.
   b. A database is a software that acts as a bridge to applications.
   c. A database is a set of logically related files containing an organized collection of data that is accessible for fast searching and retrieval.
   d. A database is a program or group of programs designed for end users.

9. **(LO 2)** **CPA** A specialized version of a data warehouse that contains data that is preconfigured to meet the needs of specific departments is known as
   a. a functional warehouse.
   b. a data mart.
   c. a data store.
   d. an object-oriented database.

10. **(LO 3)** Which of the following is one of the five characteristics of big data?
    a. Vastness
    b. Vital
    c. Vanity
    d. Value

11. **(LO 3)** Which of the following best describes extremely large and complex data sets that can be analyzed using recent technological innovations to reveal patterns and associations?
    a. Production databases
    b. Test databases
    c. Big data
    d. Data lakes

12. **(LO 3)** What is confirmation bias?
    a. The inclination to interpret new information as validation of existing beliefs
    b. Confirmation of an accounts receivable balance that is incorrect
    c. A bias toward always seeing the positive side of an issue
    d. Sending a bank confirmation request to the wrong bank

13. **(LO 3)** System limitations are a key factor in managing data
    a. value.   c. veracity.
    b. velocity.   d. volume.

14. **(LO 3)** According to the In the Real World: Uber's Data Platform case, Uber's first-generation data platform was a
    a. data mart.   c. data warehouse.
    b. data lake.   d. production database.

15. **(LO 4)** Which of the following is the area in which financial accountants focus?
    a. Performance measurement and analysis
    b. Collecting and paying sales taxes
    c. Ensuring compliance with regulatory requirements
    d. Auditing transactions

16. **(LO 4)** Which of the following is *not* an example of audit data analytics?
    a. Auditing the entire population rather than a sample
    b. Forecasting sales and other metrics
    c. Identifying and analyzing patterns, trends, and anomalies
    d. Identifying purchase transactions not subjected to a three-way match

17. **(LO 4)** Which of the following types of data analysis can tell a company which of its products will have the highest sales next year?
    a. Descriptive   c. Prescriptive
    b. Predictive   d. Diagnostic

18. **(LO 4)** Investigating anomalies in sales taxes paid by state to avoid sales tax payments is a type of
    a. predictive analytics.
    b. diagnostic analytics.
    c. descriptive analytics.
    d. prescriptive analytics.

Discussion and Research Questions

DQ1. (LO 1) `Critical Thinking` Why should accountants be knowledgeable about the difference between structured and unstructured data? What opportunities and challenges do these types of data present to accounting professionals?

DQ2. (LO 1) Compare and contrast structured and unstructured data.

DQ3. (LO 1) Define the key data elements and demonstrate how they are related to each other in a hierarchy by explaining how data elements compose other data elements.

DQ4. (LO 2) Why is it important for accounting professionals to understand the structure of a relational database?

DQ5. (LO 3) Identify and define the 5Vs that characterize big data. Which one is most important for accounting professionals, and why?

DQ6. (LO 3) For each of the 5Vs of big data, identify one challenge faced by businesses.

DQ7. (LO 4) Describe the four primary types of data analytics and explain the question that each type is best suited to answer. Provide an example of how accounting professionals could use each type of analysis.

DQ8. (LO 4) Explain, using an example, how a corporate tax accountant might use data analytics. Also, identify the primary type of analytics the accountant would use for your example.

DQ9. (LO 4) `Research` `Data Analytics` `Critical Thinking` Choose *one* of the following areas of accounting: financial accounting, audit and compliance (including fraud examination), managerial accounting, or taxation. Using the examples provided in Section 5.4 as a guide, research your chosen area and provide your own examples of each type of data analysis: descriptive, diagnostic, predictive, and prescriptive. Using Tables 5.5 through 5.8 as a guide, create your own table of examples and explanations.

Application and Analysis Questions

A1. (LO 1) `Data Foundations` Regardless of industry or size, every company or business uses unstructured data. Unstructured data enriches the structured data stored in information systems by associating an item of unstructured data with a structured data record in a database. The following chart shows a list of unstructured data items. You need to decide which table of a business's database would be the best fit for each of these items. Using the options below, fill in the correct letter to match up each database table with the appropriate data item. The same database table can match more than one unstructured data item.

A. Patients   F. Employees

B. Property   G. Inventory

C. Banks   H. Vehicles

D. Customers   I. Vendors

E. Product List   J. Purchase Orders

Unstructured Data Item	Database Table(s)
A photo of an inventory item that the firm sells	1. _____
A bar code that is assigned to an item in the company's warehouse	2. _____
Results of X-rays and MRIs in a doctor's office	3. _____
Satellite and topographical imagery of land and buildings that a business owns	4. _____
Scripts of calls from the customer call center	5. _____
Scanned copy of a paper notification that the company's overdraft limit has been increased	6. _____

Unstructured Data Item	Database Table(s)
Facebook posts of customer complaints about poor service	7. _____
Text messages about products the firm ordered	8. _____
Survey data about a new product that the firm sells	9. _____
Patient symptoms during a doctor's visit	10. _____

A2. (LO 1) `Data Foundations` As a payroll analyst at DXL Contractors, you are responsible for ensuring that new employee data is properly stored in the company's database. The following chart shows data elements related to the payroll data you oversee. Using the options below, fill in the correct letter to match up each data element with the appropriate example.

Employee ID	Start Date	Pay Rate Code	Salary	Exempt/Non Exempt
02365	08/02/202X	5—Executive	$168,000	Exempt
03685	03/16/201X	3—Individual Contributor	$58,000	Exempt

A.

B. $58,000

Employee ID	Start Date	Pay Rate Code	Salary	Exempt/Non Exempt
03685	03/16/201X	3—Individual Contributor	$58,000	Exempt

C.

D. 00000101

Data Element	Example	Details
Database	**Employee**  **Payroll Department**	The database includes these three files
Files	1. _____	The payroll file
Records	2. _____	A single record from the payroll file
Fields	3. _____	The salary field in the payroll file
Bytes (characters)	4. _____	The binary code for the number 5
Bits	1 or 0	A single binary digit

A3. (LO 2) `Early Career` `Data Analytics` `Critical Thinking`

Kim's Auto Dealership sells late-model used cars with lower mileage and in good condition. The following three illustrations show partial tables from the firm's database.

Answer the following questions based only on the data provided in the Customers, Customer Orders, and Vehicles tables:

1. Which vehicles have not been sold?
2. The dealership enters prospective customers into the system when they visit the dealership and are willing to receive marketing materials. Which customers visited the dealership but did not buy a vehicle?
3. Did any customers receive sales discounts? Identify the customer(s), the vehicle(s), and any discount amounts.
4. Have all vehicles ordered by customers been delivered?
5. Explain the relationships between the tables by identifying columns that are in at least two tables (relationships).

	A	B	C	D	E	F	G
1	**Customer ID**	**Last Name**	**First Name**	**City**	**State**	**Phone**	**Email**
2	601	Spencer	Jon	Madison	AL	256-826-9983	jhm56@yahoo.com
3	602	Xu	Chen	Bessemer	AL	205-673-5834	xuchen@gmail.com
4	603	James	Susan	Hoover	AL	205-782-9276	susanj22@gmail.com
5	604	Zebo LLC		Birmingham	AL	205-729-8826	zebocabs@zebos.com
6	605	Haku	Julian	Nashville	TN	615-689-8992	hakujul@sbc.net
7	606	Fiala	Lillianna	Harvest	AL	256-780-3887	lillijoy@gmail.com

Customers

	A	B	C	D	E	F	G
1	**Orders**						
2	**Order ID (PK)**	**Customer ID (FK)**	**Order Date**	**Promise Date**	**Delivery Date**	**Stock ID (PK)**	**Selling Price**
3	10045	604	01/12/20XX	02/12/20XX	02/12/20XX	6116	$ 22,998
4	10045	604	01/12/20XX	02/12/20XX	03/12/20XX	6121	$ 21,000
5	10046	601	01/12/20XX	02/12/20XX	02/12/20XX	6118	$ 25,998
6	10047	606	01/12/20XX	03/12/20XX		6120	$ 34,998
7	10048	604	02/12/20XX	02/12/20XX	03/12/20XX	6115	$ 32,998

Orders

Note: Two attributes together, Order ID and Stock ID, uniquely identify a row for CUSTOMER ORDERS

	A	B	C	D	E	F	G
1	**Stock ID (PK, FK)**	**Make**	**Model**	**Year**	**Color**	**List Price**	**VIN Number**
2	6115	Toyota	Sienna LE	2020	White	$ 34,998	5TDKK3DC4GS759511
3	6116	Ford	Edge SEL	2019	White	$ 23,998	2FMPK4J97KBB57437
4	6117	Ford	F150 XLT	2019	Blue	$ 30,998	1FTEW1E50KFA67177
5	6118	GMC	Arcadia	2018	Yellow	$ 25,998	1GKKNNLS8HZ200186
6	6119	Honda	Accord EX	2018	Red	$ 22,998	1HGCV1F43KA033006
7	6120	Cadillac	CT16 Platinum	2017	Beige	$ 34,998	1GYS3HKJ1GR228514
8	6121	Ford	Fusion Hybrid	2019	White	$ 22,998	3FA6P0RU3KR184886

Vehicles

A4. (LO 2) `Early Career` `Critical Thinking` As a newly hired accounting analyst, you are attending your first team meeting. The meeting is led by your manager, who is the business owner of an accounting information system and its related database. During the meeting, your manager says the following:

> "I think our team should consider connecting our database to a new data storage solution. Every time Internal Audit or the Financial Reporting department wants to access data from our (1) _____, we have to plan the SQL (2) _____ that accesses the data to run after hours so we don't disrupt ongoing operations. Since all our data is (3) _____ that fits into tables nicely and many different groups want to access our data, I think a (4) _____ would be an ideal solution."

Fill in the blanks in your manager's quote, using terms from the following word bank so that what your manager says makes sense.

Word Bank:

production database	scalable	DBMS
data warehouse	data lake	structured data
unstructured data	query	data mart

A5. (LO 3) `Data Foundations` `Critical Thinking` Pizza Palace, a global pizza company, has a mobile app that allows customers to create profiles, place orders, earn rewards points, write reviews, and more. For each of the following scenarios for the Pizza Palace mobile app, specify which characteristic of big data (5Vs) best relates to it and explain why you made that choice.

1. The Pizza Palace mobile app allows users to review their pizzas. Pizza review data is stored on the Pizza Palace systems in a database. Pizza Palace uses review information for a variety of data analysis projects. Pizza reviews include user profile information from the app, a ranking of 1 to 5 stars, large text fields for writing reviews, and photo uploads.

2. Pizza Palace has thousands of mobile app users in the United States. For every app user, Pizza Palace stores a large number of different data points, such as name, contact information, payment information, order history, preferences, and marketing demographics. For every mobile app order, Pizza Palace stores a large number of data points, such as order date, number and types of pizzas ordered, delivery addresses, estimated delivery time, actual delivery time, delivery driver name, and delivery driver's car.

3. About 60% of the mobile app pizza reviews Pizza Palace received this year do not include a text entry. Users selected a star ranking and did not provide comment feedback. If Pizza Palace uses an advanced data analytics tool to analyze keywords in text entry reviews, it will spend significant time preparing the pizza review data for the word cloud tool, and it will be looking at only 40% of the pizza reviews received this year. After a cost-benefit analysis, Pizza Palace decides to build the analytics.

4. Pizza Palace stores directly receive local pizza orders from the mobile app and bake them fresh to order. The app provides real-time tracking of your pizza status, including a map that tracks the location of your delivery driver. For every order, Pizza Palace goes from order to door in less than 40 minutes.

5. Pizza Palace wants to use pizza reviews to plan improvements for its recipes and make decisions about marketing. It has a word cloud tool that can analyze the text reviews and identify when a review has common words or phrases such as "good," "bad," "loved it," and "didn't like." The mobile app provides an open text field for users to write reviews. There is no spellcheck, and users can make typos, use slang, and include hashtags. A review may not be identified by the tool, for example, if a user types "lovedit" instead of "loved it."

A6. (LO 1–4) `Data Analytics` `Critical Thinking` You are a management accountant at Mirabel Enterprises, which provides maintenance services. Your CEO, Karen Norman, has asked you to do two things. First, Karen wants you to determine why the number of maintenance contract renewals has decreased from year to year. Second, Karen wants you to recommend ways to increase the retention and expansion of maintenance contract customers. Karen knows that you recently completed an accounting degree with a concentration in data analytics and is excited to see what you come up with.

You know that Mirabel's systems are well integrated and that getting the data to answer questions won't be difficult. This data is stored in an easy-to-access data warehouse and is already structured and stored in tables. The challenge will be knowing what questions to ask, what procedures to perform, and how to interpret the data.

You decide that you need to answer the following two questions before you can proceed with the task:

- When did the firm begin to see a decline in maintenance contract renewals?

- Are there any indicators that point to why the decline in maintenance contract renewals was occurring?

Based on these insights, you can begin to formulate a plan for what actions you will recommend to management to address Karen's second request. Would you perform descriptive, diagnostic, predictive, or prescriptive analytics? You may perform more than one type of analytics. Explain your choice.

A7. (LO 1–4) `Early Career` `Data Analytics` `Critical Thinking` You are an internal audit data analytics consultant at a Big Four firm and have been hired by The Royal Cooks, a cookware supplier to commercial kitchens, to consult on an accounts receivable project. As part of the accounts receivable project, your team is looking at collection communications—specifically, emails sent to customers who owe balances. The Royal Cooks' communications team can view whenever a customer opens an email, including collections and marketing messages. This data is stored in a structured table in a relational database that can easily be analyzed by your team.

The Accounts Receivable team has noticed an increase in unopened emails recently, and they are concerned that customers may not be opening their collections emails due to having too many marketing emails in their inboxes.

Maeva Han is the senior director of Marketing at The Royal Cooks. When you meet with her, Maeva tells you that The Royal Cooks sends email marketing communications seasonally. The Royal Cooks is currently in a peak season, with a variety of marketing campaigns running, including an increase in email marketing communications. Maeva provides you with the times of year in which her team engages in "peak marketing."

To determine if the Accounts Receivable team's concerns are valid, you acquire data from the Communications team for all emails sent for collections and marketing within the last two years. You filter this data by opened and unopened communications and then separate it into the peak and non-peak marketing seasons.

Placing this data into a percentage column chart, you see that the percentage of collections emails opened during peak marketing season is significantly lower than the percentage of collections emails opened during the non-peak marketing times.

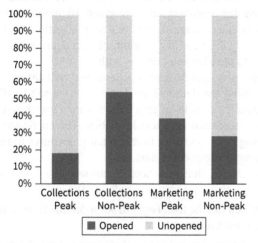

Based on this chart and the project specifications, did you use descriptive, diagnostic, predictive, or prescriptive analytics? What analytic question did your analysis answer?

A8. (LO 1–4) `Early Career` `Data Analytics` `Critical Thinking`
As an internal audit data analyst at a global investment firm, you have received the following request from the internal audit team you are assisting on an engagement:

> Most securities are priced using external sources for valuation. Securities that cannot be priced using an external source are called "Hard to Price Securities." The pricing team reviews Hard to Price Securities every month and

assigns them a level of complexity from 1 to 3. The level of complexity indicates how difficult it is to find a price for that security in the given month. The expectation is that securities will be reviewed and given a complexity level each month and that the complexity level will stay consistent from month to month. The attached data is for Q1 202X. Perform preliminary analytics on this data and provide us an explanation of the analysis performed and related results.

You perform the analytics and provide the audit team with a response. Use the following descriptions and the sample of data provided in the spreadsheet excerpt to categorize each analytic you performed as descriptive, diagnostic, predictive, or prescriptive.

1. Identified securities that are missing a complexity level for a month. The data includes January, February, and March pricing dates. One security was missing a month of data:

   Security ID 20022L, February 202X

2. Identified securities with inconsistent complexity levels from month to month. The following securities had more than one complexity level:

   Security ID 00012A   Security ID 20022L

3. Investigated securities with high complexity scores to see if a specific security type is the reason for the complexity level by finding the average complexity level for each security type. Preferred stock securities have consistently higher complexity scores. This suggests that the high complexity scores are caused by preferred stock securities that are harder to price.

	A	B	C	D
1	**Security ID**	**Pricing Date**	**Complexity**	**Security Type**
2	00012A	1/13/20XX	1	Common stock
3	00012A	2/15/20XX	1	Common stock
4	00012A	3/16/20XX	2	Common stock
5	2235B	1/13/20XX	3	Preferred stock
6	2235B	2/15/20XX	3	Preferred stock
7	2235B	3/16/20XX	3	Preferred stock
8	20022L	1/13/20XX	1	Common stock
9	20022L	3/16/20XX	3	Common stock
10	6248X	1/13/20XX	3	Preferred stock
11	6248X	2/15/20XX	3	Preferred stock
12	6248X	3/16/20XX	3	Preferred stock
13	MN0031	1/13/20XX	2	Preferred stock
14	MN0031	2/15/20XX	2	Preferred stock
15	MN0031	3/16/20XX	2	Preferred stock

Tableau Case: Julia's Cookies' IT Help Desk

What You Need

Download Tableau to your computer. You can access www.tableau.com/academic/students to download your free Tableau license for the year, or you can download it from your university's software offerings.

Download the following file from the book's product page on www.wiley.com:

Chapter 5 Raw Data.xlsx

Case Background

Big Picture:

Examine IT issues and requests.

Details:

Why is this data important, and what questions or problems need to be addressed?

- Every company has an IT help desk that employees can call to report a system outage or login issues, among many others. It is important for the company to monitor this help desk information to see if there is a larger underlying problem that it might need to address. It is also important to track these tickets to ensure that they are being addressed in an appropriate time frame so as not to severely disrupt the business.

- To examine the issue and request patterns that Julia's Cookies employees are communicating with the IT help desk, we should consider the following questions: Which issue category has the most tickets requested? How long does it take, on average, to close a severe ticket? Which ticket group has the most unsatisfied requestors?

Plan:

What data is needed, and how should it be analyzed?

- The data needed to answer the objective is pulled from the central ticketing management system.

- The data should be filtered to an appropriate time frame that would allow IT to identify patterns.

- This data looks at eight months: March through October.

Now it's your turn to evaluate, analyze, and communicate the results!

Questions

1. Which month had the highest number of tickets submitted?
2. On July 6, 2022, there was a peak number of tickets submitted. What issue category did the most tickets belong to?
3. Which requestor submitted the most tickets?
4. Which ticket group had the most tickets submitted on April 18, 2022?
5. What issue category had the largest number of open tickets? (Hint: Consider ticket status.)
6. Which issue category had the highest *average* of open days?
7. Which severity level had an *average* days open of 4.686?
8. Which ticket group had the most unsatisfied requestors in May 2022?

Take it to the next level!

9. What month did Joni Kelly have the most *3-high severity* tickets submitted?
10. How many *3-highly satisfied* tickets did the issue category *Hardware* have in August 2022?

Designing Systems and Databases

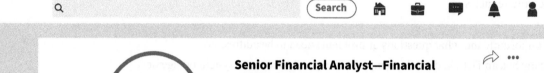

Senior Financial Analyst—Financial Reporting

Julia's Cookies · Chicago, IL; Atlanta, GA; Remote

Posted 1 week ago · 1,182 views

Save | **Apply**

Job	**Company**	**Connections**
• 10 Applicants	• 3,000+ Employees	20 Connections
• Associate	• Restaurants	

Summary

Julia's Cookies is looking for a senior financial analyst to assist in preparation of financial and operational reporting and analysis and to provide insight into key performance indicators through recurring reports and ad hoc analysis. This role will collaborate with stakeholders, business analysts, database administrators, and core development teams to deliver high-quality analytics solutions in an Agile software development and project management environment.

This role can work remotely and travel to the Chicago or Atlanta corporate office for in-person trainings.

Responsibilities

- Work with large data sets, leveraging SQL to generate reports and analytics
- Conduct special financial projects and coordinate with other departments
- Compile and prepare reports, graphs, and charts of data developed
- Yield value-generating, action-oriented insights to key business partners
- Recommend changes in financial analysis methods and procedures
- Assist and supervise financial analysts in the daily preparation and conduct of their work

Requirements

Preferred Education: Bachelor's degree or higher in accounting, finance, or related field

Preferred Knowledge and Skills

The ideal candidate will have two or three years' experience working with data using a variety of database applications and analytics tools, such as SQL. Preference will be given to candidates who demonstrate:

- Ability to extract and analyze big data from relational database environments
- Understanding of accounting processes and data
- Experience using analytics to answer business questions and provide insights
- Ability to work with end users and core development team on analytics development projects
- Experience working on Agile teams and collaborating with end users throughout a project's life cycle

Salary: $75,000–95,000

CHAPTER PREVIEW   Implementing a new information system and a database to support it involves many people. In the IT department, systems analysts, application programmers, database designers, and other technical specialists play key roles in designing and building the technical aspects. Developing a new system or database also requires involvement from non-IT areas of the business. The people who will use the new system must explain why it is necessary, describe what it needs to do, and eventually test the system to ensure that it functions correctly. The same users are also involved in database creation. They must describe the business events that create the data so database designers can properly structure how the data is stored in the new database.

In this chapter, we explore:

- Systems development
- Development methodologies
- Types of databases
- Relational database design
- Queries to access data
- Usefulness of database forms and reports

While you may not pursue a career in the IT department creating systems and databases, you are likely to be a user of a system, a user of data in a database—like the person who fills the senior financial analyst job opening at Julia's Cookies—or an auditor who reviews how an IT project was executed and whether proper controls are in place. The topics covered in this chapter will prepare you to interact with systems and databases during your accounting career. ∎

Chapter Roadmap

LEARNING OBJECTIVES	TOPICS	JULIA'S COOKIES APPLIED LEARNING
6.1 Outline the systems development life cycle (SDLC) stages.	• Pre-Implementation • System Build • Go-Live and Beyond	Systems Development: Pre-Implementation Audit
6.2 Compare and contrast the Waterfall and Agile systems development methodologies.	• Waterfall Methodology • Agile Methodology • Selecting a Methodology	Selecting a Methodology: Agile Pilot
6.3 Distinguish among different types of modern databases.	• Relational Databases • Object-Oriented Databases • NoSQL Databases	Relational Database: Brainstorming Field Names
6.4 Design relational database tables by using an entity relationship diagram (ERD).	• The Conceptual ERD: Identifying Tables and Relationships • The Logical ERD: Adding Details • The Physical ERD: Creating the Technical Design	Primary and Foreign Keys: Designing Relationships
6.5 Construct queries to retrieve data and answer business questions.	• The Basic SELECT Statement • The WHERE Clause • The JOIN Operator • Putting It Together	SQL Statements: Querying for Answers
6.6 Explain how database forms and reports are useful for businesses.	• Forms • Reports	

CPA   You will find the CPA tag throughout the chapter to call out any important topics you may see on the CPA exam.

6.1 How Are Systems Developed?

Learning Objective ❶
Outline the systems development life cycle (SDLC) stages.

When a company needs a system, such as a new accounting information system (AIS), it faces the dilemma of whether to build or buy:

- **Buy:** Purchasing may be quicker, but the system won't be customized. And costs of systems can quickly add up over time.
- **Build:** Developing an in-house system allows for customization but requires specific talent and comes with its own costs, including time.

Companies with adequate resources often elect to build their own systems, especially if the system is going to be implemented enterprise-wide for critical functions and will benefit from customization. These technology projects are expensive and long-term endeavors that can take months, or even years, to complete.

CPA A systems development project involves several risks:

- Lack of management support may result in constraints on financial, time, and other necessary resources.
- Evolving emerging technologies may result in incompatibility between the system being developed and the existing IT infrastructure. In other words, a company may want to move forward with a new technology but may be restrained by limitations on its own capabilities.
- Resistance of key stakeholders may result in failure to prioritize the development project or unwillingness to adopt the new system once it's ready for deployment.
- Inadequate design and testing may result in a final product that is rushed, doesn't meet the needs of end users, or functions poorly.
- Inadequate end-user training may result in poor adoption of the system. Without users, the system is a failure.

Companies address these risks by using frameworks to guide their systems development projects to completion. **CPA** The **systems development life cycle (SDLC)** is a project management framework with clearly defined stages for creating and deploying new systems. This framework includes seven stages (**Illustration 6.1**).

Like other frameworks, the SDLC provides a standardized process that companies customize for their individual risks and operations. Regardless of how the SDLC is implemented, the basic model creates a structured approach to systems development that focuses on identifying key roles and responsibilities, requirements, and project milestones.

We explore the seven SDLC stages using a Julia's Cookies example. Until now, Julia's Cookies has offered mobile cookie purchases to customers only through third-party mobile applications (apps) like DoorDash and Uber Eats. Now, the company is launching an app that will allow customers to order directly from Julia's Cookies. Having a customized customer ordering system will build a stronger brand with users and cut costs by eliminating the delivery fees that third-party apps charge. The team has decided to develop this new app in-house.

This mobile app is a transaction processing system (TPS) and captures data from accounting transactions and information business events. The data will be stored in the Sales Management module of the enterprise resource planning (ERP) system. The accounting transaction data will flow from the Sales Management module to the Financial module, where it will be processed for reporting. This makes the new mobile app part of Julia's Cookies' AIS.

As you work through this section, you will find that the SDLC stages can be very technical. To help make this content easier to understand, we divide the seven stages into three sections: what happens before (pre-implementation), during (system build), and after (go-live and beyond) the system is developed.

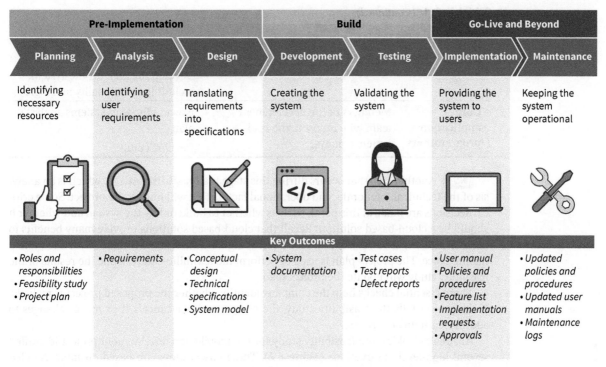

Illustration 6.1   The seven stages of the SDLC are planning, analysis, design, development, testing, implementation, and maintenance.

Pre-Implementation

Before programmers can begin developing a system, the project must be planned and the system analyzed and designed.

Planning

The first stage of every SDLC project is the **planning stage**, which includes defining the scope of the project, identifying necessary resources, and determining if the project will likely be successful. These three steps can be performed in any order and often occur in tandem.

To start, a **project plan** is created that identifies the system scope and project goals. **CPA** Project plans cover three elements:

- Critical factors that must be met for the project to be successful
- A defined project scope, including an overview of goals and limitations
- Milestones and responsibilities that break down project goals into timelines and identifying individuals responsible for each goal

During planning, necessary resources are also identified. Part of identifying necessary resources is considering the people who will be involved, including determining necessary roles, responsibilities, and technical skills. **CPA** While team composition varies depending on the scope of the project, some roles are consistent across projects of all sizes (**Table 6.1**).

TABLE 6.1   Roles and Responsibilities During the SDLC

Role	Description	Responsibilities
IT steering committee	Representatives from business areas throughout the company, including the IT department	• Approve and prioritize proposed projects for systems development
End users	Individuals who will use the system in their daily job functions	• Identify business need • Propose system to address need • Use final product in daily job duties

(Continued)

TABLE 6.1 *(Continued)*

Role	Description	Responsibilities
Lead systems analyst	Manager of the development team that programs the project	• Work with end users directly • Develop the plan for the system, including functionality and logic
Core application programmers	Members of the development team who report to the lead systems analyst	• Execute the lead systems analyst's plan • Develop code

CPA Another step that occurs during this stage is a **feasibility study**, which is an analysis of the technical, economic, and operational factors that will impact the project. Some critical decisions are made at this point, such as whether to build or buy the system and whether it should be a cloud-based solution. Recall that cloud-based solutions provide many benefits to businesses, such as lower expenses for purchasing hardware, storing equipment, and system maintenance. The project plan is used to perform the feasibility study, while the results of the feasibility study will update the project plan.

These essential checks help the company identify whether the proposed project is realistic. If the project fails the feasibility study, the company either cancels it or makes changes to address feasibility concerns.

At Julia's Cookies, the feasibility study for the mobile app development project identified several high-level observations (**Table 6.2**). These observations are based on more detailed information, such as cost estimates and sales forecasts.

TABLE 6.2 Feasibility Study Questions

Feasibility	Questions Asked	Observations
Technical feasibility	• Do we have the talent necessary to build it, or do we need to hire a contractor? • Should we buy the system instead of building it?	• Development team lacks necessary experience. • System needs to be highly customized and requires in-house development. • Company needs to hire talent with mobile app development experience to deliver systems development project.
Economic feasibility	• Do we need the system? • Do the system benefits outweigh the costs of development? • Should we support the system locally or choose a cloud-based delivery method?	• System is essential, as it supports the core business process of customer sales. • Forecasted increase in customers and sales are benefits that outweigh cost of project. • System will be supported on existing cloud-based Amazon Web Services (AWS) platform.
Operational feasibility	• How well will the system integrate into the company's current systems and environments?	• Minimal changes will be required in existing IT infrastructure. • Proposed system can be designed to integrate with existing systems.

Based on these observations, Julia's Cookies determines that the systems development project passes the feasibility study.

Analysis

The second stage of the SDLC is the **analysis stage**. Systems analysts meet with end users to understand business requirements of the project, which is a critical step in a systems development project. The information captured here is the roadmap for programmers. The **requirements definition** formally documents the final project goal, identifies the steps needed to achieve it, and outlines the overall system plan.

At Julia's Cookies, the project's lead systems analyst meets with end users in the Sales and Accounting departments to discuss system requirements. In the Sales department, employees share details about how the sales business processes work, including how customers will interact with the mobile app, the types of products that will be sold, and the way some of the seasonal promotions will work. In the Accounting department, employees walk the lead systems analyst through examples of accounting processes for creating journal entries, posting to the general ledger, and financial reporting. Knowing how the data will be used in the Accounting department helps the lead systems analyst ensure that the system is designed properly for all end users, including data users outside the Sales department.

Examples of some of the requirements for the mobile app include:

- A new customer creating a profile with a login
- Customers placing orders for both pickup and delivery
- Customers making payments for orders
- Customers tracking status of their deliveries, including a live map of their delivery drivers' progress
- Customers reviewing products and rating orders

Design

CPA The **design stage** translates the requirements definition into technical specifications:

1. The lead system analyst creates a **conceptual design** summarizing the system's purpose, resource requirements, and planned flow of data through the system.

2. The lead systems analyst creates **technical architecture specifications** that identify software, hardware, and network technologies the system will need.

3. The lead systems analyst creates graphical models, such as flowcharts and data flow diagrams (DFDs), to create a **systems model** that describes in technical detail how the system will interact with users, other technologies, and systems processes and components. You can learn about systems flowcharts and DFDs in the Documenting Systems and Processes chapter.

4. Finally, the lead systems analyst and core programmers create a mockup of the **graphical user interface (GUI)** that shows the screen that will allow users to interact with the system. It includes colors, layout, and style decisions.

The lead systems analyst and core programmers at Julia's Cookies create a mockup of the mobile app's GUI (**Illustration 6.2**). Once the design and GUI are approved by project stakeholders, the systems analysts begin writing the code to build the system.

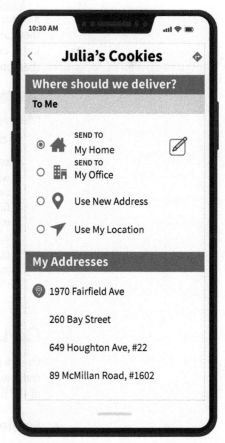

Illustration 6.2   The Julia's Cookies mobile app GUI includes a screen to order cookies and a screen to input the delivery address.

System Build

To develop the new system, programmers write code that is then tested multiple times, both by the programmers and by independent testers.

Development

During the **development stage,** programmers create the system based on technical specifications identified in the design stage. It's critical that programmers write code that is:

- Based on requirements and design specifications
- Compatible with other systems throughout the company
- Error free

CPA Since correcting code after the development stage is expensive, programmers test their own code as they are writing it to ensure that it's as error free as possible.

Testing

After the system is developed, it goes to another team for independent testing. During the **testing stage**, the system is evaluated against the design specifications and requirements definition to ensure that it meets expectations. Testers evaluate systems to answer a number of questions:

- Does each piece of the system work correctly?
- Does the system work together as a whole?
- Does the system work with existing systems it must connect to?
- Does the system accomplish its primary purpose?

CPA The last question is answered through **user acceptance testing (UAT),** in which a select group of end users get access to the system before it is officially available to users so they can use the system and verify that it meets their expectations. They are provided scenarios to execute, such as ordering a cookie on the Julia's Cookies' mobile app, and then record their observations and any errors encountered.

Why Does It Matter to Your Career?

Thoughts from a Manager of Accounting, Banking

- While you may think you don't need to understand technical IT content, you may be surprised where your career takes you. Many accounting professionals are the end users of systems such as payroll and accounts receivable systems. If your company migrates these systems, you could find yourself on the end-user side of an SDLC project. The CPA exam is evolving to reflect the increased expectation that accounting professionals understand technology.
- People at the director level or higher see the business from all sides and work with people like the chief information security officer (CISO), chief technology officer (CTO), and more. Understanding how these functions work together will prepare you for your future role—whatever that may be.

Go-Live and Beyond

Once a system is developed and tested, it's ready for **system go-live,** which is when it is officially available to users. This critical event in the SDLC is followed by ongoing maintenance of the live system.

Implementation

The **implementation stage** begins when the system is moved into production and goes live for use in the company. This stage is the culmination of the work put into the systems development project. Because implementing a new system can be a complex process, companies use one of four implementation methods (**Table 6.3**). Note that these methods can be used whether a system is developed in-house or purchased from a third-party vendor.

The direct cutover implementation method can go horribly wrong if the new system fails or users are ill prepared to use it. Companies should only use this method for small, low-priority systems because it is so high risk.

A pilot implementation can be based on company departments, customer types, or even geographic regions. Julia's Cookies chooses a geographic pilot implementation for its new system, and the mobile app is rolled out to customers in the Chicago area for pilot testing. Feedback from this pilot is used to update the system before it's implemented nationally.

It's also important that the implementation stage and system go-live include adequate employee training for the end users of the new system. Remember how ERP implementations can fail because users are not confident in using the new system? The same risk applies to all new systems implementations, whether developed in-house or purchased.

TABLE 6.3 System Implementation Methods

Implementation Method	Explanation	Example
Direct cutover	• Like flipping a switch, this method turns the old system off and new system on, with no overlap. • There is no backup plan for dealing with failure of the new system. • This method involves low cost and high risk.	Old System → New System
Parallel implementation	• The new system begins to be used before old system is turned off. • Systems run concurrently until there is confidence that new system works properly. • The cost of maintaining both systems simultaneously is high, but the risk is low.	Old System / New System
Phased implementation	• Both systems are divided into modules, and one module is implemented at a time. • For example, an ERP system might be implemented starting with a financial module while the rest of the company remains on the old systems. • This method involves moderate cost and moderate risk.	Old System → New System
Pilot implementation	• Both systems are divided into groups based on users. • A few users pilot the new system before it goes live for the rest of the company. • Feedback is collected from the pilot users and integrated into future implementations. • This method involves moderate cost and moderate risk.	Old System → New System

Maintenance

After the system goes live, the final SDLC stage continues throughout the system's life. During this **maintenance stage**, the system is monitored, updated, and changed. Changes to the system go through the company's formal change management process, which is part of the information technology controls environment. You can learn more about change management in the Information Systems and Controls chapter.

For now, help Julia's Cookies' internal auditor, Kae, understand what to expect during the SDLC stages in Applied Learning 6.1.

Julia's Cookies

Systems Development: Pre-Implementation Audit

Kae is working on a pre-implementation audit of the new accounts payable system. This means Kae is involved in the project before and during its implementation and can provide valuable feedback to the systems development team and end users as the project is being built. During which stage of the SDLC will Kae experience the following scenarios?

1. The accounts payable analysts are given access to a test version of the system and asked to record their feedback on whether it is functioning correctly.
2. The system owner receives a change request for a new segregation of duties control that prevents certain user IDs from approving payments.
3. An assessment of whether Julia's Cookies has the right talent on its development team to program the system is performed.
4. Programmers write code to build the system and perform ad hoc tests to check its functionality.
5. The direct cutover method is used to launch the new system.
6. The accounts receivable team provides a wish list of features for the new system.
7. Functional requirements for the users to access the system are turned into a GUI mockup.

SOLUTION

Kae can expect these scenarios to occur during the following SDLC stages:

1. Testing
2. Maintenance
3. Planning
4. Development
5. Implementation
6. Analysis
7. Design

CONCEPT REVIEW QUESTIONS

1. **CPA** What is the systems development life cycle (SDLC)?
   Ans. SDLC is a project management framework with clearly defined stages for creating and deploying new systems. Like other frameworks, the SDLC provides a standardized process that companies customize for their individual risks and operations.

2. What is the first stage of the SDLC?
   Ans. The first stage of every SDLC project is the planning stage, which includes defining the scope of the project, identifying necessary resources, and determining if the project will likely be successful.

3. What is the analysis stage in the SDLC?
   Ans. The second stage of the SDLC is the analysis stage. System analysts meet with end users to understand business requirements of the project, which is a critical step in a systems development project. The information captured here is the roadmap for programmers. The requirements definition formally documents the final project goal, identifies the steps needed to achieve it, and outlines the overall system plan.

4. **CPA** What does the design stage of the SDLC accomplish?
   Ans. The design stage translates the requirements definition into technical specifications. The lead system analyst creates a conceptual design, technical architecture specifications, systems model, and finally lead systems analyst and core programmers create a mock-up of the graphical user interface (GUI) that shows the screen that will allow users to interact with the system.

5. What is the significance of the development stage?
   Ans. During the development stage, programmers create the system based on technical specifications identified in the design stage.

6. What is the testing stage in the SDLC model?

Ans. During the testing stage, the system is evaluated against the design specifications and requirements definition to ensure that it meets expectations. Testers evaluate systems to answer a number of questions:

- Does each piece of the system work correctly?
- Does the system work together as a whole?
- Does the system work with existing systems it must connect to?
- Does the system accomplish its primary purpose?

7. **CPA** What do you understand by the term "user acceptance testing (UAT)"?

Ans. In UAT, a select group of end users get access to the system before it is officially available to users so they can use the system and verify that it meets their expectations. They are provided scenarios to execute and then record their observations and any errors encountered.

8. What is the implementation stage? List the four system implementation methods.

Ans. The implementation stage begins when the system is moved into production and goes live for use in the company. This stage is the culmination of the work put into the systems development project.

The four system implementation methods are direct cutover, parallel implementation, phased implementation, and pilot implementation.

9. What is the maintenance stage?

Ans. After the system goes live, the final SDLC stage continues throughout the system's life. During this maintenance stage, the system is monitored, updated, and changed. Changes to the system go through the company's formal change management process, which is part of the information technology controls environment.

6.2 Which Methodology Should Be Used?

Learning Objective ❷

Compare and contrast the Waterfall and Agile systems development methodologies.

Frameworks like the SDLC offer companies guidance for achieving an objective but are not prescriptive. How a framework is executed is up to company discretion. The SDLC outlines best practices for the stages of systems development, and companies can use formal SDLC methodologies or ad hoc, custom approaches to execute these stages.

All frameworks involve risk. Individual risks, costs and benefits, and available resources influence a business's methodology choice. For example, one methodology may work best for decentralized teams that are spread across time zones, while another works best for a team located in the same office building and meeting face-to-face regularly. In our world of remote work, this is a critical consideration when companies select an approach to the SDLC.

Let's explore two popular methodologies for implementing the SDLC framework: Waterfall and Agile.

Waterfall Methodology

CPA The **Waterfall methodology** breaks the SDLC into formal stages, which must be executed in a linear fashion (**Illustration 6.3**):

- Much like its namesake, each stage flows downstream to the next sequential stage.
- There is no overlap; every stage is performed in its entirety before the next begins.
- Waterfall usually uses the seven stages of the SDLC framework, but companies can customize this approach by adding, removing, or renaming stages.

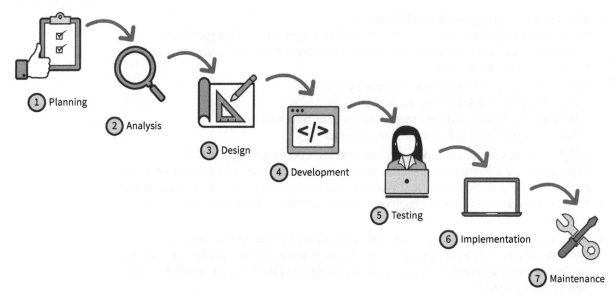

Illustration 6.3 The seven stages of the SDLC are performed in a sequential, cascading order when using the Waterfall methodology.

Waterfall is an effective and traditional method that companies still use today, but other methodologies have gained favor over the years because Waterfall's linear nature can make it difficult to respond to real-time risks and changes.

To understand these risks, imagine that a college course requires you to submit ten essays at the end of the term. You won't receive any feedback between essays, and you won't know if your work meets your professor's expectations. You can't improve throughout the term or correct issues that began with the first essay. To avoid this, most professors use a modular approach, dividing course-work into modules with incremental deadlines. This approach allows your professor to provide feedback in real time so you have an opportunity to address it in your next submission.

Waterfall presents similar risks. Completing systems development projects takes signifi-cant resources and time. The time from the planning stage to the implementation stage can span months. Waterfall creates risks when developers don't receive feedback until the project's completion. Between the analysis stage, where user requirements are gathered, and the imple-mentation stage, there may be:

- Changes in end users' expectations
- Changes in business processes that will use the system
- Turnover in leadership that causes a change in requirements or makes the project obsolete
- Disconnect between developers and end users that prevents end users from being excited about the system once it's implemented

In reality, most SDLC projects that use Waterfall don't use a pure Waterfall approach, so these risks are an extreme example of what may happen if the process is followed academi-cally. Instead, companies adapt the Waterfall methodology to meet their unique project needs.

Agile Methodology

A direct contrast to the linear approach of Waterfall is **Agile methodology,** a group of SDLC meth-odologies that focus on iterative development, collaboration, and self-organized, cross-functional teams. Characterized by multiple short cycles of work that simultaneously include multiple SDLC stages, Agile involves end users in real-time decision making as the project progresses.

Agile was created in response to the risks of traditional methodologies like Waterfall where the final product is not revealed until the end of the SDLC stages. To address the risks, Agile breaks the project into smaller pieces and involves end users throughout the development project. By the end of a project, end users know exactly what they are receiving because they have been part of the design, feedback, and testing processes. Agile methodology focuses on:

- Ensuring customer satisfaction
- Supporting, trusting, and motivating people

- Encouraging collaboration between business stakeholders and programmers
- Regularly reflecting on ways to improve
- Adjusting to change mid-development
- Creating self-organized teams of equals without structured leadership

Agile can be implemented using different project management styles, and in reality, businesses use combinations of different project management styles to customize Agile to meet their needs.

Why Does It Matter to Your Career?

Lead Internal Auditor, Financial Corporation

Agile is not limited to systems development. Many accounting and audit departments have successfully implemented it in their processes. Performing an audit, for example, can translate easily to an Agile project management approach, where there is constant communication among the audit team and the auditee, especially if the auditor identifies a finding. If you are considering a career in audit, ask your interviewers if their team is implementing any Agile practices.

Scrum Roles and Responsibilities

One of the most popular project management styles for implementing Agile methodology is **scrum**. Scrum is a set of project management practices focused on daily communication and flexible planning. This flexible planning allows mid-project changes that do not impact budgets or timelines. Scrum breaks a systems development project into short cycles of work. After each cycle, the team reflects on successes and failures, and appropriate adjustments are made before continuing to the next cycle. A scrum systems development project involves four parties: the end user and the three roles on the scrum team. If you compare the roles of scrum to the traditional SDLC roles and responsibilities, as in **Table 6.4**, the Agile principles of being customer oriented—where the end user is the customer—and having self-organized teams of equals become evident.

TABLE 6.4 Scrum Roles and Responsibilities and SDLC Counterparts

Role	Description	Responsibilities	SDLC Counterpart
Business stakeholders	Individuals who will use the system in their daily job functions	• Communicate regularly with product owner • Provide real-time feedback after each project iteration	End users
Product owner	Champion of the system	• Understand end-user requirements • Communicate end-user requirements and feedback to core development team	Lead systems analyst
Scrum master	Champion of the core development team—often called a "servant leader"	• Motivate core development team • Ensure core development team focuses on Agile principles • Clear obstacles from core team's path • Facilitate core team's dialogue	None
Core development team	Self-organized team of programmers without formal leadership	• Conduct project execution and testing • Self-manage timelines • Self-manage responsibilities • Be open to scrum master's motivations and guidance • Commit to transparency and accountability within the team	Core application programmers

Teams of all types use scrum methodologies and roles to manage their projects. Even internal audit departments have begun adopting Agile auditing, where auditors take on scrum roles to complete audit projects, treating the audit as the "system" and the area of business they are auditing as the "stakeholders."

Scrum Timeboxing

To efficiently integrate feedback and respond to changes in real time, scrum projects use careful time management:

- **Sprints** are single iterations of the systems project that include multiple SDLC stages. Sprints can be monthly or weekly increments, with two weeks being the most common. After each sprint, the core team regroups to discuss what went well and how to improve work during the next sprint.

- **Timeboxing** allocates a fixed length of time to each activity to both define the activity and limit the amount of time dedicated to it.

- Timeboxing prevents **scope creep**—which occurs when a project evolves during development beyond its original specifications and becomes too large to meet its deadlines. This is often the result of end users asking "Can it also do this?" and adding more features. Scrum addresses this risk by ordering the suggestions of the end users by priority.

Everything is subject to change during Agile systems development except the timeboxing. New features can be added, technology can be changed mid-project, and core members can transition in and out of teams, but the final deadline of the systems development project never extends. If all features are not finished, they are added to a future update.

Scrum Artifacts

In order to ensure transparency and clear communication of project information to all parties involved, scrum uses three artifacts: the product backlog, sprint backlog, and product increment.

The **product backlog** is a list of all the desired features for the system being developed. Each feature is its own item on the backlog. As the team works through the project, it builds all the features through to completion, in order of priority:

- Features are divided into categories based on whether they are crucial, or fundamental, or are additional features that would be nice to have. If there's time in the planned project once the fundamental features are complete, the core team will develop the additional features. The product owner has final authority in prioritization decisions but considers feedback from business stakeholders and the development team.

- If changes arise and the core team needs to spend more time on the fundamental features, that is as far as the project will go.

- The remaining features become future updates instead of being part of the initial implementation.

Recall the requirements definition for the Julia's Cookies' mobile application. Let's assume that the IT department is using scrum to manage this project. The product owner works with the business stakeholders to prioritize these features into fundamental features and additional features (**Table 6.5**).

The features in the product backlog are then allocated to the sprint backlog. As each sprint is a short iteration of work, the **sprint backlog** contains what the core team will

TABLE 6.5 Julia's Cookies Mobile Features

Fundamental Features	Additional Features
• New customer creating a profile with a login	• Customers reviewing products and rating orders
• Customers placing orders for both pickup and delivery	• Customers tracking status of their deliveries, including a live map of their delivery drivers' progress

develop during the current sprint. Features on the product backlog are broken into smaller parts and worked on simultaneously by the core team. Rather than one developer working on the ordering feature and another working on customer profiles for Julia's Cookies' mobile application, the full core team is dedicated to building the highest-priority item first—the customer profile.

At the end of the sprint, the product owner presents the **product increment**, the current version of the system, to the business stakeholders for feedback. Feedback is returned to the core team, which prioritizes the feedback, adjusts the product backlog accordingly, and creates a sprint backlog for the next sprint.

In the Real World LEGO[1]

The LEGO company was founded in 1932 by Ole Kirk Christiansen, a carpenter whose primary business of producing household goods had suffered due to the Great Depression. Initially producing wooden toys, the company later developed a system of interlocking bricks.

LEGO decided to go for an Agile transformation to address several challenges they were facing. In a pre-Agile environment, there was considerable confusion, inefficiencies, and lack of customer collaboration, leading to an ineffective and wasteful work environment. To achieve the vision, LEGO felt that they needed dynamism, high levels of responsiveness, and full adjustment to constantly moving targets. To succeed, LEGO realized their employees had to innovate, test, and learn in a world that is in constant flux. The LEGO Digital Solutions team consisted of 20 teams, so there was significant change and realignment required. According to Henrik Kniberg and Thyrsted Brandsgård, the coaches who led the Agile transformation for LEGO Digital Solutions (DS), the following problems were identified:

- Cross-team alignment
- Client collaboration
- Release planning
- Platform development

It decided to move toward Scaled Agile Framework (SAFe) in 2014. The Agile transformation at the LEGO Group was launched in early 2018 and included the introduction of a new digital operating model. One year into the transformation, the impact of the new model began to show as a significant reduction in the time required to respond to change—from months to weeks—in the company's core functions. The new way of working improved motivation and satisfaction among employees in the two departments that kicked off the Agile transformation—contributing to a significant positive increase in the yearly employee motivation and satisfaction survey score.

Have you heard of Agile before this course? What kind of environment would you rather work in: one featuring Agile or Waterfall? What if you were an end user? Would you prefer receiving updates at the end of project completion (Waterfall) or being involved in the development of your system (Agile)?

Selecting a Methodology

You have learned that Waterfall is a structured, sequential process that creates risks by not presenting the product to end users until the end of the project. In contrast, Agile involves end users, or business stakeholders, throughout the entire journey by providing product increments for feedback after every sprint. As a result, risks are managed in real time (**Illustration 6.4**).

Even so, deciding whether to use Waterfall or Agile is a complicated process. Best practice is to have the entire IT department operating on the same methodology and to make these decisions at an enterprise level to create consistency in processes, reporting, and risk management activities. In reality, many IT decisions are made in business units, making project scopes small, so that it is difficult to respond to changing business needs. For example, if the web development team decides to use Agile while database developers use Waterfall, the teams may have difficulty coordinating projects where they need to collaborate.

There are times and places for both Waterfall and Agile in systems development projects. In fact, while Agile is growing in popularity, the shift to remote work in 2020 due to the COVID-19 pandemic impacted many Agile teams because Agile is not as conducive to decentralized, virtual work—especially where there are large time zone differences between team members. Rather, Agile excels in situations where teams can meet in person daily. **Table 6.6** summarizes various factors companies consider when deciding whether to use Waterfall or Agile.

---

[1]https://bootcamp.uxdesign.cc/agile-success-story-lego-and-their-agile-transformation-2ac474d07ad7; https://www.lego.com/en-in/themes

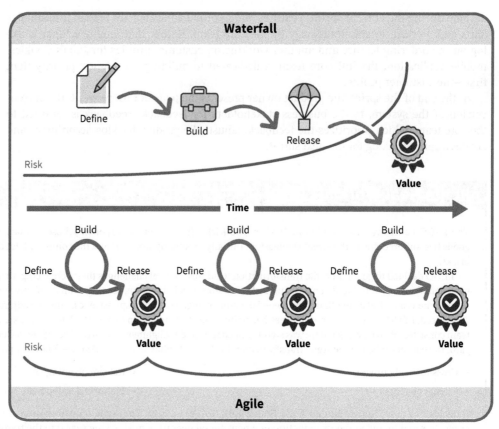

Illustration 6.4 Risks build up over time in Waterfall but are mitigated at the end of each sprint during an Agile project.

TABLE 6.6 Guide for Selecting the SDLC Methodology

	Waterfall	Agile
Requirements and regulations	Many initial requirements and regulations with little room to make changes during development	Fewer initial requirements and regulations, allowing developers to use creativity and make improvements along the way
Leadership involvement	Project manager with low level of involvement who only wants periodic updates	Hands-on product owner who wants to be heavily involved in real-time decision making
New versus updates	Updating an existing project with clear definitions of change management needs	Creating a new system from scratch
Budget	Firm budget that requires a predictable outcome	Flexible budget that allows for expenses needed to prioritize features and increase speed of completion
Current IT infrastructure	Formal procedures already operating under traditional SDLC stages with a corporate culture that supports traditional methods	Less formal procedures, enabling teams to be flexible in their approach to projects, and a corporate culture of accepting failure and trying new things
Team composition	Minimal communication requirements; appropriate for both in-person teams and decentralized or remote teams	Daily communication that works best among teams that can meet in person and sit in the same office

At Julia's Cookies, the IT department is considering migrating to an Agile SDLC methodology. Evaluate whether Ginny's HR and payroll project is a good candidate to pilot an Agile approach in Applied Learning 6.2.

Julia's Cookies   Applied Learning 6.2

Selecting a Methodology: Agile Pilot

Ginny, the new director of Human Resources at Julia's Cookies, requests a migration of Julia's Cookies' HR processes from its current stand-alone system to an integrated Human Resources Management (HRM) module in the ERP system. When the request is approved by the IT steering committee, Ginny meets with the systems development project leader, Jorge, who tells her that they are piloting test projects using an Agile methodology called scrum. The IT team can deploy the new HRM module in the ERP system using the Agile approach, but Jorge is willing to use the traditional Waterfall approach if she prefers.

While this is a migration from an existing process to a new system, Ginny knows she has a lot of changes. She may as well be building the features from the ground up. She is excited to work with Jorge's team to develop features and application controls that will meet the needs of her team. She has a firm budget, but she is willing to request more funding if the benefits justify the costs.

Do you think Ginny should let her systems development project be part of the Agile pilot?

SOLUTION

Ginny seems like a hands-on director who is excited for change. She may benefit from an Agile approach by being involved in the design and development process through recurring sprints and product increments. Since she is willing to incorporate the expertise of Jorge's team in this project, she will likely enjoy the collaborative, team-focused approach of Agile. She has a firm budget, however, and she will need to keep that in mind as they prioritize features and feedback throughout the systems development project.

We have covered best practices and methodologies for developing a new system. But what about storing data that the system captures? Companies must also select, design, and develop databases to support their information systems. In the next section, we cover the types of databases companies can implement.

CONCEPT REVIEW QUESTIONS

1. What is Waterfall methodology?

   Ans. The seven stages of the SDLC are performed in a sequential, cascading order when using the Waterfall methodology. Waterfall is an effective and traditional method that companies still use today, but other methodologies have gained favor over the years because Waterfall's linear nature can make it difficult to respond to real-time risks and changes.

2. What is Agile methodology?

   Ans. Agile methodology is a group of SDLC methodologies that focus on iterative development, collaboration, and self-organized, cross-functional teams. Characterized by multiple short cycles of work that simultaneously include multiple SDLC stages, Agile involves end users in real-time decision making as the project progresses.

3. What do you understand by the term "scrum"?

   Ans. The most popular project management style for implementing Agile methodology is scrum. Scrum is a set of project management practices focused on daily communication and flexible planning. This flexible planning allows mid-project changes that do not impact budgets or timelines. Scrum breaks a systems development project into short cycles of work.

4. What are the three scrum artifacts to ensure transparency and clear communication of project information?

Ans. In order to ensure transparency and clear communication of project information to all parties involved, scrum uses three artifacts: the product backlog, sprint backlog, and product increment.

6.3 What Type of Database Should Be Used?

Learning Objective ❸
Distinguish among different types of modern databases.

At this point in the course, you have been introduced to the fundamentals of systems, software, and databases, and now you have seen how a system is developed and implemented through the SDLC. What about the database that stores the data generated by a new system?

Companies use an enterprise-wide risk management approach to selecting databases. This ensures that all technology solutions in the business align with the enterprise vision, direction, and strategy. It also guarantees that the new database fits into the existing control environment. Making this decision at a business unit level, instead of the company-wide level, increases risk. If the Accounting department at Julia's Cookies establishes its own database without consulting the IT department, the database may not have the appropriate controls and security, the IT department may not have the correct skills and resources to support it, and the IT department may have been able to recommend potentially better options.

There are several considerations when selecting a database to implement (**Table 6.7**).

TABLE 6.7 Database Selection Considerations

Consideration	Questions Asked
Data variety	• Will the database be capturing structured data, unstructured data, or both?
Data volume	• What amount of data is expected to be captured daily? • What about long term?
Scalability	• What are the current performance requirements, and how will they be improved over time as demands increase?
Purpose	• Is this a data warehouse, data lake, or other type of data store?

Databases can be characterized by how stored data is formatted. While understanding the nuances of every database type isn't necessary for an accounting professional, we discuss three popular database types you are likely to encounter during your career.

Relational Databases

You have learned that most accounting information systems use relational databases. Let's look at some key terms you learned in the Data Storage and Analysis chapter and their relational database counterparts (**Table 6.8**). We use relational database terms throughout the remainder of this chapter.

CPA Recall that the six data elements, from smallest to largest, are bit, byte, field, record, file, and database.

TABLE 6.8 Comparing Data Storage Terminology

Data Element	Definition	Relational Database Terminology
Field	Group of bytes (characters) that identify a characteristic of an entity	Field or attribute
Record	Group of related fields that describe an individual instance of an entity	Record
File	Group of records for one specific entity	Table
Database	Set of logically related files	Database

Now that we have reviewed database versions of the terms that you are familiar with, let's add two new terms that relational databases use:

- **Column:** A collection of data fields aligned vertically in a table that are all of the same data type, such as text, dates, or numbers.
- **Field name:** Descriptive label, or name, given to a column that identifies the contents of that column. Also known as a header.

In **Illustration 6.5**, we use these terms to expand on the example of the human resources (HR) database and Employee table from the Data Storage and Analysis chapter.

Database Term	Example	Details
Database	**Employee** / **Payroll** **Department**	Julia's Cookies' HR database includes these three tables
Table	A: First_Name, Last_Name, Birthdate, Address, City, State (row 1); Delilah, Zhang, August 5, 2168 Peachtree Rd., Atlanta, GA (row 2); Jeremy, Brown, June 12, 100 6th St, NE, Atlanta, GA (row 3)	The Employee table
Column	A: First_Name (1), Delilah (2), Jeremy (3)	A single column from the Employee table
Field name	A: First_Name (1)	The field name for the second column in the table

Illustration 6.5   Julia's Cookies' Employee table is used to demonstrate database columns and field names.

Illustration 6.6 applies everything you have learned so far to the HR database and Employee table at Julia's Cookies.

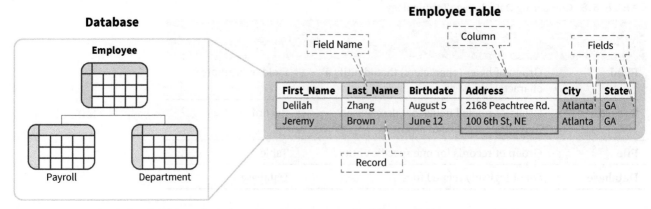

Illustration 6.6   A relational database includes tables that have records, columns, field names, and fields.

Because most accounting-related data is structured data, and relational databases store structured data in two-dimensional tables of rows and columns, this is one of the most widely used database types you will encounter during your accounting career. Consider a customer purchase with Julia's Cookies' newly developed mobile application. The transactional data generated by this business event is shown in **Illustration 6.7**.

Customer_Name	Customer_Phone	Product_1	Product_2	Product_3	Price_1	Price_2	Price_3	Total_Price	Payment_Method
Humphrey Rotham	616-921-0026	Chocolate Chip Cookie	Peanut Butter Cookie	Chocolate Chip Cookie	1.05	1.25	1.05	3.35	Venmo

Illustration 6.7   Customer and order data is generated by a customer order business event.

This data is broken into multiple tables of related fields that are connected to one another. To start, the fields related to the customer's profile are placed in one table (**Illustration 6.8**), and the fields related to the order details are placed in a separate table (**Illustration 6.9**).

Customer_Name	Customer_Phone	Payment_Method
Humphrey Rotham	616-921-0026	Venmo

Illustration 6.8   Customer profile data is placed in one table.

Product_1	Product_2	Product_3	Price_1	Price_2	Price_3	Total_Price
Chocolate Chip Cookie	Peanut Butter Cookie	Chocolate Chip Cookie	1.05	1.25	1.05	3.35

Illustration 6.9   Order detail data is placed in a second table.

These two tables are part of the relational database that stores data generated by and used during the sales business process. Now help Julia's Cookies' systems development core team begin designing a database for the sales order data in Applied Learning 6.3.

Julia's Cookies   Applied Learning 6.3

Relational Database: Brainstorming Field Names

Chris is a product owner working on the mobile app systems development project. He meets with the system's end users in the Accounting department to discuss how the data captured by the system should be stored. The Accounting department provides multiple scenarios of ways the application would be used by customers and explains the key data points the system needs to collect for the department.

Chris decides to categorize the data into the following tables:

- Customers
- Orders
- Stores
- Products

Help Chris categorize each of the following field names into one of above four tables.

Field Name	Description
1. Delivery_Address	Address with house/apartment number and street name
2. Region	Geographic region of delivery store
3. Unit_Price	Price of the product
4. General_Manager	Employee ID of the general manager at that location
5. Rewards_Number	Number associated with the points earned for purchases made
6. Quantity	Amount of product that was purchased
7. In_Stock	Indicator of whether something is available to purchase

SOLUTION

The field names are categorized as follows:

1. Customers
2. Stores
3. Products
4. Stores
5. Customers
6. Orders
7. Products

Object-Oriented Databases

Because relational databases can only store structured text and numeric data, they are not suitable for unstructured data like audio, video, graphics, social media posts, texts, PDFs, and emails. The need to store this complex data led to the development of object-oriented databases.

An **object-oriented database** is a hybrid database because it has a relational database framework with the data presented and stored in a form other than tables. It can store both structured numbers and text and complex unstructured data. Companies tend to use either relational databases or object-oriented databases, not both.

In object-oriented databases, database designers determine the data that needs to be connected and the similarities of various objects within the data (**Illustration 6.10**):

- Instead of using tables and relationships, a **class** connects similar objects together.
- An **object** is an item contained within a class. It is like a record in a relational database.

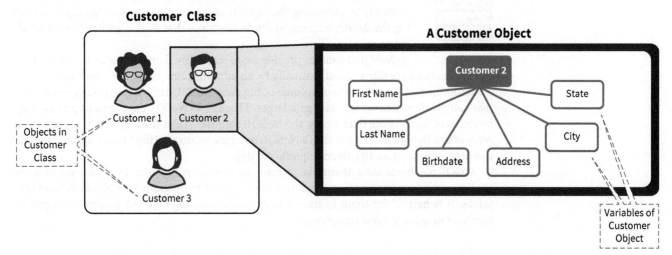

Illustration 6.10 Object-oriented databases assign variables to objects that are associated with one another in a class.

- **Variables** are the names assigned to similar characteristics of objects in a class, much like fields in a relational database.

When a user queries a class, all objects contained in that class are returned. Users do not directly query records, as they do in a relational database.

Classes can be compared to car engines. An engine is composed of multiple parts, including the cylinder block and pistons. Each of these is a stand-alone item. Once the parts are assembled and bolted together, they are together referred to as an engine. Much like engines, classes are composed of multiple objects, or stand-alone items. Objects can be groupings of structured data, or they can be unstructured data referenced with meta tags. A class is referenced as a collective unit so that the database does not have to go into each object separately.

NoSQL Databases

To respond to the increasing velocity of big data and the need for faster processing of unstructured data, NoSQL databases were introduced. A **NoSQL database** stores each item individually, rather than in rows and columns, and retrieves them by using key values. There is no structured schema, resulting in a flexible storage solution for unstructured data.

These databases support both structured and unstructured data and are often referred to as "Not Only SQL." They use more than just the SQL language; programming languages like Java, C#, and Python can be used to access the data. This makes NoSQL databases compatible with websites and other applications, like YouTube and Facebook. NoSQL databases are an ideal solution for storing user-generated content.

While NoSQL databases can store both structured and unstructured data, they are not considered ideal for structured data because they are not designed to support transaction processing systems. In other words, they don't make good production databases. A company chooses a NoSQL database under certain circumstances:

- The company wants to store and retrieve vast volumes of data.
- The data is unstructured.
- The data changes continuously.
- Data volume is growing, requiring the database to be regularly scaled.

While NoSQL databases have gained popularity in recent years, many organizations have yet to adopt them, as relational and object-oriented databases continue to meet their needs. Because NoSQL databases must run on machines with high specifications, they are often implemented by companies as cloud-based solutions. A cloud-based solution is housed on the service provider's machines and accessed by the users via the internet.

 Do you remember what scalability is? It's the ability of a database to grow as the requirements of data and performance increase. Databases can scale vertically by increasing the capacity of one machine or horizontally by spreading the database across multiple machines that work together to support the database.

NoSQL databases provide more scalability than relational databases. Relational databases are often scaled manually by an administrator when space becomes limited. To accommodate the velocity and volume of big data, NoSQL databases are designed to automatically scale whenever the data gets larger. This allows NoSQL databases to process huge amounts of data. As the data grows, the NoSQL database scales itself to maximize efficiency. AWS offers DynamoDB as Amazon's NoSQL database solution. These cloud-based databases can process more than 10 trillion requests per day.

NoSQL databases are a disruptive technology that many organizations have yet to adopt. While most accounting professionals are not expected to program NoSQL databases themselves, it is helpful for them to have a basic understanding of these databases to provide business insights to their companies.

CONCEPT REVIEW QUESTIONS

1. What is meant by an object-oriented database?

   Ans. An object-oriented database is a hybrid database with a relational database framework and the data presented and stored in a form other than tables. It can store both structured numbers and text and complex unstructured data.

2. What is NoSQL database?

   Ans. NoSQL database stores each item individually, rather than in rows and columns, and retrieves them by using key values. There is no structured schema, resulting in a flexible storage solution for unstructured data.

6.4 How Are Relational Databases Designed?

Learning Objective ❹
Design relational database tables by using an entity relationship diagram (ERD).

Tables in a relational database are connected in a specific order, like puzzle pieces. As more tables are added, more data is available to create the final picture. This data is transformed via reporting and analytics to help us understand a business and its operations. But before data in a database can be used to create information for decision makers, the database must be designed. In this section, you will learn how relational databases are designed to create meaningful connections between tables that can be leveraged for information.

Designing a relational database requires understanding and planning for the data it will store. **Data modeling** allows us to document data that will be stored in a database and identify its specifications. These specifications include the fields that will be stored, the associations between fields and tables, and the rules that govern the associations.

Database design can be approached in many ways. For the purpose of this course, we are using the customer order data collected by the new Julia's Cookies mobile application as our real-world example. We will highlight the most important steps for an accounting professional and design the database for the second requirement of the system: customers placing orders for both pickup and delivery.

The Conceptual ERD: Identifying Tables and Relationships

The first step in designing a relational database is to identify the entities, or tables, the database will need to capture. Recall that an order on the Julia's Cookies mobile app generated data that was easily categorized into two tables: Customers and Orders. Upon further brainstorming, the core systems development team and the Accounting department have identified additional entities (**Illustration 6.11**).

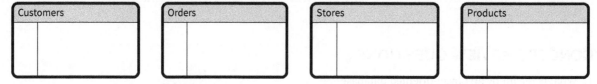

Illustration 6.11 Data generated by the customer purchasing a product business event is categorized into four tables: Customers, Orders, Stores, and Products.

Do you remember what an entity relationship diagram (ERD) is? In the Data Storage and Analysis chapter, you learned that ERDs model relationships among tables in a relational database. The type of ERD used is determined by its intended purpose:

- **CPA** Conceptual ERDs and logical ERDs are used by business analysts to model the plans for the database.
- Physical ERDs are elaborate blueprints for the database designer who implements the structure by creating the database.

To identify the connections between a pair of tables, we turn them into statements of relationships based on the business events that will happen:

- A customer places an order.
- An order is placed for a product.
- An order is placed at a store.
- A store sells products.

A conceptual ERD is created based on these statements. The ERD in **Illustration 6.12** shows an overview of the relationships between entities by adding connecting lines between them.

Illustration 6.12 Lines connecting the four tables demonstrate how tables are related to one another in a conceptual ERD.

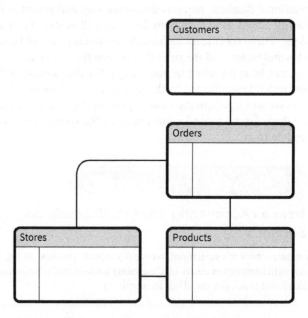

Notice that the Customers table is only connected to the Orders table. Meanwhile, the Orders, Products, and Stores tables are all connected to one another. This is because a customer's only way of interacting with a store or product on the mobile application is by placing an order.

The Logical ERD: Adding Details

CPA Next, the conceptual ERD is enhanced by adding field names for each table. All fields in a table must describe the appropriate records. For example, if there is a Phone_Number field, the phone number for each record must belong to the individual named in that record. **Illustration 6.13** shows a logical ERD used by the Julia's Cookies Accounting department to finalize its portion of the data modeling. Consider what fields from other entities would be stored in a table. For example, the Orders table needs to include the customer who placed the order. For the logical ERD at Julia's Cookies, Customer_Name is added as a field name to the Orders table. Also note that the Products table contains Selling_Price, while the Orders table also contains Price. These repetitions will be turned into a relationship by the core development team when the physical ERD is created.

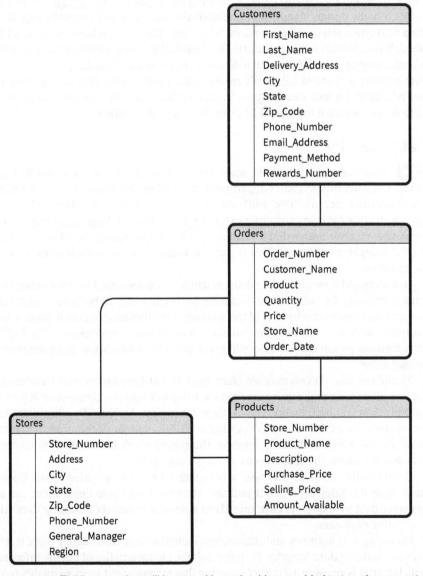

Illustration 6.13 Field names that will be stored in each table are added to turn the conceptual ERD into a logical ERD.

Currently, the field names are conversational terms. As the database design project progresses, they will be replaced with system field names. For example, Purchase_Price in the Products table may be called Price_1, and Selling_Price in the same table may be called Price_2.

A **data dictionary** provides a detailed description of and data type (text, numeric, date, etc.) for the fields located in each table. It provides descriptions that end users can reference when they need data from the database. If you are not sure if you need a field name, always check with the system owner. Using the wrong field for your work can have disastrous results, and any assumptions you make should always be validated with someone who knows the system. Public accounting auditors often receive data from their clients with system field names. Assuming a date field ambiguously labeled "Date" is the actual journal entry date without confirming with your client may result in your performing journal entry tests over inaccurate data. Imagine explaining that to your manager after they have been embarrassed in front of the client for presenting something incorrect. It's always best to validate.

The Physical ERD: Creating the Technical Design

The final ERD level in database design is creating the physical ERD. **CPA** Recall that the physical ERD is the design blueprint of a relational database. It enhances the logical model by adding field types, sizes, and constraints, which are rules about what can and can't be put into a field. It is important for an accounting professional to understand that the physical ERD adds the relationships and the items that define them to the database design.

Before creating a physical ERD, let's review some risks around data storage that a well-designed relational database can mitigate. To explain these concepts, we focus on the Customers and Orders tables from the logical ERD for the rest of this section.

Data Integrity

CPA **Data redundancy** exists when the same piece of data is stored in multiple places. Consider this: the Sales department stores all the information for every customer who places an order in a table, while the Accounts Receivable department also stores all the information for every customer in its own table. When billing a customer, Accounts Receivable receives notice that a customer's contact information has changed. How will the Sales department know? This is just one example of the complexities data redundancy brings.

To understand how tables in a relational database are connected to one another, first you must understand the basics of data redundancy. The first step in building a relationship is to ensure that every table has a field that uniquely identifies every record it holds. Using the Customers table as an example, the first name of a customer is not unique to that individual. More than one person may live at an address or use a phone number, so those identifiers can't be used either.

To address this, ID columns are often used. If you have an account number at your doctor's office or a unique user name you use to log in when you shop online at your favorite store, then you have unique IDs for those businesses. Unique IDs allow a database to retrieve only the record related to a particular ID. For example, if there are two customers at Julia's Cookies named James Johnson, the system won't know which to retrieve if it uses only the name. Instead, it needs to use the unique ID.

For the Julia's Cookies database, a customer ID column is added to the Customers table. Both the Sales department and the Accounts Receivable department can access customer data by using the customer ID to reference necessary customer data without duplicating its storage.

Managing data accuracy and consistency, including data redundancy risks, is referred to as maintaining *data integrity*. Do you recall the characteristics of quality information? Data integrity is an essential part of ensuring that management receives quality information for decision making.

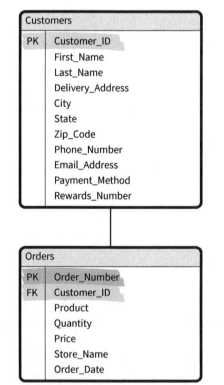

Illustration 6.14 The Customer_ID field is a key that relates the Customers and Orders tables to one another.

Primary and Foreign Keys

Relational databases use unique IDs and relationships to eliminate data redundancy by referencing data a table needs that is already stored in a different table. The information about the customer will only be stored in the Customers table, and the Orders table will reference it by having a customer ID column that identifies which customer placed the order (**Illustration 6.14**).

CPA The unique IDs that identify the records in the database are called **keys,** and they are the center of the database's relationships:

- **CPA** If the key is the unique ID of a table, such as the customer ID in the Customers table, it's called a **primary key (PK).**
- **CPA** When the key is referenced by another table, such as the customer ID in the Orders table, it's called a **foreign key (FK).**
- The connection between a PK in one table and an FK in another table is the relationship.
- **Referential integrity** states that an FK can't be entered into a table unless it exists as a PK in the base table. For example, you cannot enter the customer ID into the Orders table if the customer ID does not exist in the Customers table.
- The primary key cannot be **null,** which means empty. This is called **entity integrity.**

Defining keys is one of the most essential steps in database design. For Julia's Cookies, the core development team asks the end users in the Accounting department to review their plans to ensure that the plans meet the expectations of the users' business rules. Decide if any changes are needed in Applied Learning 6.4.

Julia's Cookies   Applied Learning 6.4

Primary and Foreign Keys: Designing Relationships

The Accounting department at Julia's Cookies must confirm that the primary and foreign keys in the Orders and Stores tables meet the expectations for the new relational database. Jennifer, a financial reporting analyst who works with the accounting systems regularly, is given the following ERD to review. Do you think Jennifer should suggest any changes to the selected keys?

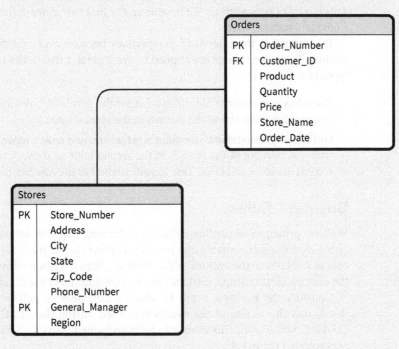

SOLUTION

Jennifer needs to suggest the following two changes:

1. **The Stores table:** The General_Manager column is not the primary key (PK) of the Stores table. It is likely a foreign key (FK) that references employee information stored in the Employees table of the database. Jennifer should ask the core development team about this potential relationship.

2. **The Orders table:** The Store Name column should be replaced by the primary key (PK) of the Stores table—Store_Number—and labeled as a foreign key (FK) in the Orders table.

Cardinality

Once it's been established that two tables are related to one another, the relationship must be characterized by identifying its cardinality. **Cardinality** is the numeric relationship between data in one table and data in another table. To understand cardinality, you must first understand perspective. In a relationship between two tables, there are two perspectives:

- The way that the first table relates to the second table.
- The way the second table relates to the first table.

For example, for the four tables at Julia's Cookies—Orders, Customers, Products, and Stores—the perspectives are the ways in which:

- Orders relate to Customers
- Customers relate to Orders
- Orders relate to Products
- Products relate to Orders
- Orders relate to Stores
- Stores relate to Orders
- Products relate to Stores
- Stores relate to Products

This is a lot of perspectives! We'll focus on the first two as we define the cardinality for Julia's Cookies' database.

It's important to understand perspectives because every relationship is subject to constraints. These constraints are applied to every perspective in the relationship. There are two types of constraints:

- **Plurality constraint:** Identifies whether the first table's records are associated with only one or more than one of the records in the second table.

- **Optionality constraint:** Identifies whether the first table's records must have a relationship with one or more of the records in the second table or if they can be related to none of the records in the second table. This identifies whether the relationship is mandatory or optional.

Business Rules

With the principles of cardinality in mind, the next step is to define business rules. **Business rules** are written statements that precisely capture the business event occurring during a process as it relates to the entities in the database. When written correctly, business rules define the entities, relationships, cardinalities, and constraints of the database.

Consider the business event in which a customer of Julia's Cookies places an order. Recall that this is one of the events identified during the SDLC analysis stage for Julia's Cookies' mobile app. This event can be transformed into two business rules, one from each perspective (**Table 6.9**).

TABLE 6.9 Writing Business Rules

Business Event	Business Rules	Plurality	Optionality
A customer places an order.	One customer may place many orders.	One to many (1:M)	Optional
	One order is placed by one customer.	One to one (1:1)	Mandatory

The optionality of these two business rules determines whether a record must exist in the second table if one exists in the first table. For example, it's possible a customer may make a profile on the mobile app and never place an order, so there can be a record in the Customers table that is not related to any Orders table records. On the contrary, orders must be placed by a customer, so a record in the Orders table must be related to a record in the Customers table.

Crow's Foot Notation

Now that the cardinality and constraints between the Orders and Customers tables are identified, the physical ERD is enhanced by adding shapes to the end of each line between entities using a formal diagramming notation called **crow's foot notation**. Each side of the relationship line has two symbols: one for the plurality constraint and one for the optionality constraint (**Table 6.10**).

TABLE 6.10 Crow's Foot Notation for Plurality and Optionality Constraints

Plurality Crow's Foot Notation	
Plurality Constraint	**Crow's Foot Notation Symbol**
One	—————┼
Many	—————<
Optionality Crow's Foot Notation	
Optionality Constraint	**Crow's Foot Notation Symbol**
Optional	—————○—
Mandatory	—————┼

The plurality notation is added closest to the table, with the optionality notation attached to its other side, and combined they create the four types of cardinalities shown in **Table 6.11**.

TABLE 6.11 Crow's Foot Cardinality Notations

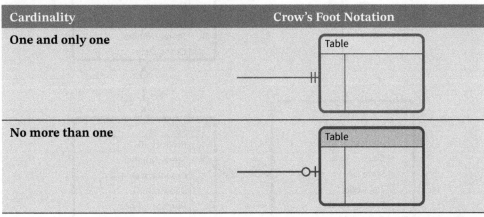

Cardinality	Crow's Foot Notation
One and only one	
No more than one	

(Continued)

TABLE 6.11 (*Continued*)

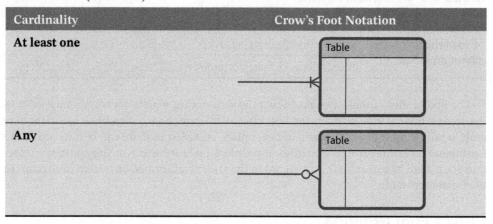

Cardinality	Crow's Foot Notation
At least one	
Any	

Putting It Together

Putting these concepts together, Julia's Cookies' physical ERD for the Customers, Orders, Products, and Stores tables can be created (**Illustration 6.15**). The database designers will

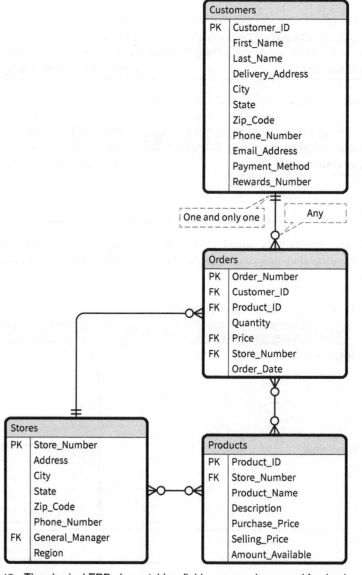

Illustration 6.15   The physical ERD shows tables, field names, primary and foreign keys, and relationship cardinality.

use it as their blueprint for the creation of the relational database. It's important to note that there are further considerations the database designers will implement before building this relational database. The topic of database design is a complex area of study that is beyond the scope of this AIS course. While the physical ERD will undergo further changes before it's fully ready to be implemented, the understanding you have gained to this point will adequately prepare you for your future accounting courses, the CPA exam, and your first role as an accounting professional.

We have covered a lot of specifics in this section. To summarize, here are some of the key rules for designing a relational database:

- Every column contains a single data type, like numbers, dates, or text.
- The primary key cannot be empty, or null. This rule, called "entity integrity," is one of the most important rules of database design.
- A foreign key cannot be used in a table unless it corresponds to an existing primary key in the base table. This rule, called "referential integrity," ensures that logical dependencies exist between primary and foreign keys.
- All fields in a record describe the object identified by the primary key.
- Relationships are defined by cardinality and optionality.

CONCEPT REVIEW QUESTIONS

1. What do you understand by data modeling?
   Ans. Data modeling is the process of documenting data that will be stored in a database and identifying its specifications. These specifications include the fields that will be stored, the associations between fields and tables, and the rules that govern the associations.

2. What is an entity relationship diagram (ERD)? What are the different types of ERDs?
   Ans. An entity relationship diagram, also known as ERD, ER diagram, or ER model, is a type of structural diagram used in database design.
   Conceptual and logical ERDs are used by business analysts to model the plans for the database. Physical ERDs are elaborate blueprints for the database designer who implements the structure by creating the database.

3. What is meant by a data dictionary?
   Ans. A data dictionary provides a detailed description of and data type (text, numeric, date, etc.) for the fields located in each table. It provides descriptions that end users can reference when they need data from the database.

4. **CPA** What are keys in database management systems?
   Ans. The unique IDs that identify the records in the database are called keys, and they are the center of the database's relationships.

5. **CPA** What is a primary key?
   Ans. In database terminology, a primary key is a unique identifier. Each record in a table is assigned a primary key. If the key is the unique ID of a table, such as the customer ID in the Customers table, it is called a primary key (PK).

6. **CPA** What is a foreign key?
   Ans. When the key is referenced by another table, such as the customer ID in the Orders table, it is called a foreign key (FK).

7. What do you understand by the term "referential integrity"?
   Ans. Referential integrity states that an FK can't be entered into a table unless it exists as a PK in the base table. For example, you cannot enter the customer ID into the Orders table if the customer ID does not exist in the Customers table.

8. What are business rules?
   Ans. Business rules are written statements that precisely capture the business event occurring during a process as it relates to the entities in the database. When written correctly, business rules define the entities, relationships, cardinalities, and constraints of the database.

9. What is a crow foot notation?

Ans. The physical ERD is enhanced by adding shapes to the end of each line between entities using a formal diagramming notation called crow's foot notation.

6.5 How Do We Interact with Data in a Database?

Learning Objective ❺
Construct queries to retrieve data and answer business questions.

Now that you have explored how relationships connect data between different tables in a relational database, it's time to interact with that data. A key characteristic of relational databases is that they can be used to create ad hoc reports from the data they store by using a querying language. You have learned that a querying language is used to retrieve data from the database, but that is not the only use of a database language.

CPA Do you remember what SQL stands for? It stands for Structured Query Language, and different variations of SQL are available for different database management systems.

SQL uses **commands** to send instructions to a database to perform tasks like creating items and querying existing data. These commands are classified into *languages* based on their purpose. Before we start exploring how to write SQL, let's review the five subsets of SQL and some important SQL commands in **Table 6.12**.

TABLE 6.12 Overview of SQL Languages and Commands

SQL Language	SQL Commands	Purpose
CPA A **data definition language (DDL)** changes the structure of a database by adding or changing tables and relationships.	CREATE	Adds a new empty table to the database
	ALTER	Changes a characteristic of an existing table, such as adding a new column
	DROP	Deletes an existing table and all records it contains
	TRUNCATE	Deletes all the records contained in an existing table but does not delete the table
CPA A **data manipulation language (DML)** modifies the data within a database.	INSERT	Adds a new record of data to a table
	UPDATE	Changes the value of an existing field
	DELETE	Removes one or more records from a table
A **data control language (DCL)** grants access to or removes access from a database user.	GRANT	Gives access permissions to a user
	REVOKE	Removes access permissions from a user
Transaction control language (TCL) interacts with DML commands when transactions are processed in the database.	COMMIT	Saves all pending transactions to the database
	ROLLBACK	Undoes pending transactions that have not yet been saved by undoing entire transactions
CPA **Data query language (DQL)** retrieves data from a database based on user requests.	SELECT	The only DQL command; the beginning of all queries written to retrieve data for viewing, copying, or updating

For the purposes of an accounting course, we are focusing on the DQL SELECT command and its many uses for retrieving data. It's good to be familiar with commands for the remaining languages, but unless you specialize as a database administrator, it's unlikely that you will be required to write those queries as an accounting professional. On the other hand, DQL is used to extract data for analysis and is something you will likely encounter on the job.

The Basic SELECT Statement

SQL commands are communicated to a database through written syntax called **SQL statements**. Within a database management system (DBMS), which includes the interface that allows a user to interact with the database, SQL commands are written into SQL statements and executed.

Illustration 6.16 shows the query window and results window for a DBMS called Microsoft SQL Server Management Studio. **CPA** Other examples of relational DBMSs include Oracle Database, Oracle MySQL, and Teradata. The remainder of this chapter uses Microsoft SQL Server Management Studio, but it's good to know the other names if you take the CPA exam.

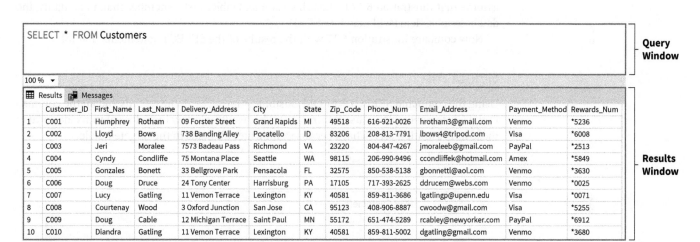

Illustration 6.16   Microsoft SQL Server Management Studio has a query window to write SQL commands and a results window to review the data the query retrieves.

Illustration 6.16 shows a simple SELECT statement that starts with the **SELECT command**, which is entered in the query window. This DQL command retrieves data from the database, and its basic form is:

SELECT [field name] FROM [table name]

The result of a simple SELECT statement is a list of data from the specified table in the database, which is displayed in the results window. In place of the name of a field, the SELECT statement can use * to retrieve all the columns in the specified table, as shown in Illustration 6.16.

To further understand how SELECT statements work, first review the database sample of Julia's Cookies' Customers table in **Illustration 6.17**. We'll assume for the sake of this example that it represents a complete list of customers. Note that the field names in Illustration 6.16 match the comprehensive list of field names in the ERD in the last section. However,

	Customer_ID	First_Name	Last_Name	City	State	Payment_Method
1	C001	Humphrey	Rotham	Grand Rapids	MI	Venmo
2	C002	Lloyd	Bows	Pocatello	ID	Visa
3	C003	Jeri	Moralee	Richmond	VA	PayPal
4	C004	Cyndy	Condliffe	Seattle	WA	Amex
5	C005	Gonzales	Bonett	Pensacola	FL	Venmo
6	C006	Doug	Druce	Harrisburg	PA	Venmo
7	C007	Lucy	Gatling	Lexington	KY	Visa
8	C008	Courtenay	Wood	San Jose	CA	Visa
9	C009	Doug	Cable	Saint Paul	MN	PayPal
10	C010	Diandra	Gatling	Lexington	KY	Venmo

Illustration 6.17 Julia's Cookies' Customers table includes relevant information about its customers, including addresses, contact information, and payment methods.

Illustration 6.17 is missing some of those fields. This is because we are removing some field names for the rest of our discussion to ensure that the tables are clear and easy to follow. We'll assume that Illustration 6.17 is the full Customers table. Just remember that, in actuality, the database table fields will match the ERD.

Now compare Illustration 6.17 with the results of the SELECT statements that follow.

Select All

Using the command SELECT * FROM Customers retrieves all the records and all the columns in the Customers table (**Illustration 6.18**). The results window includes columns identical to those in Illustration 6.17. That's because * indicates all fields in the targeted table.

SELECT * FROM Customers

100 % ▾

	Customer_ID	First_Name	Last_Name	City	State	Payment_Method
1	C001	Humphrey	Rotham	Grand Rapids	MI	Venmo
2	C002	Lloyd	Bows	Pocatello	ID	Visa
3	C003	Jeri	Moralee	Richmond	VA	PayPal
4	C004	Cyndy	Condliffe	Seattle	WA	Amex
5	C005	Gonzales	Bonett	Pensacola	FL	Venmo
6	C006	Doug	Druce	Harrisburg	PA	Venmo
7	C007	Lucy	Gatling	Lexington	KY	Visa
8	C008	Courtenay	Wood	San Jose	CA	Visa
9	C009	Doug	Cable	Saint Paul	MN	PayPal
10	C010	Diandra	Gatling	Lexington	KY	Venmo

Illustration 6.18 Executing SELECT * FROM Customers in the query window generates the full Customers table in the results window.

Select One Column

The command SELECT Customer_ID FROM Customers retrieves only the Customer_ID column values from all the records (**Illustration 6.19**).

Illustration 6.19 Executing SELECT Customer_ID FROM Customers in the query window generates only the Customer_ID column from the Customers table in the results window.

Select Multiple Columns

SELECT Customer_ID, First_Name, Last_Name FROM Customers retrieves all the records for the three specified columns in the Customers table (**Illustration 6.20**).

Illustration 6.20 Executing SELECT Customer_ID, First_Name, Last_Name FROM Customers in the query window generates the Customer_ID, First_Name, Last_Name columns from the Customers table in the results window.

The SELECT statement is the foundation for all data querying. It always begins with the SELECT command but can be modified with additional functions to achieve more complex results, which we explore next.

Why Does It Matter to Your Career?

Thoughts from an Internal Audit Manager, Asset Management

The ability to form requests for data in logical ways will impress your clients. Database administrators are used to answering requests from traditional accounting professionals. They don't expect you to know what you want from their systems. If you are able to articulate and understand basic principles of databases and querying, you can form data requests that are clear and considerate. Building those relationships as an auditor will put you in a position to become a trusted advisor to your clients or your company.

The WHERE Clause

The SELECT command and subsequent field names control which columns you retrieve from the database, but what if you want to control which records you retrieve?

The **WHERE clause** is added to a SELECT statement to filter which records the query returns by adding values such as mathematical comparisons (=, <, <=, >, >=, <>) or special operators (BETWEEN, LIKE, IN, etc.). There are many criteria that a WHERE clause can specify. Let's learn how to use the WHERE clause for mathematical comparisons. Note that we can use two of these mathematical comparisons on text fields: is equal to (=) and is not equal to (<>), which we will do next.

The basic form of a SELECT statement with a WHERE clause is:

SELECT [field name] FROM [table name] WHERE [expression]

We'll use the WHERE clause to answer three questions.

Question 1: Which Customers Use the Venmo Payment Method?

The first step to answering this question is to isolate customer records that contain Venmo in the Payment_Method field. This query retrieves the name and customer ID for each customer who uses the Venmo payment method:

SELECT Customer_ID, First_Name, Last_Name, Payment_Method FROM Customers WHERE Payment_Method = 'Venmo'

This query shows that C001, C005, C006, and C010 all use Venmo payments (**Illustration 6.21**).

SELECT Customer_ID, First_Name, Last_Name, Payment_Method FROM Customers WHERE Payment_Method = 'Venmo'				
100 % ▾				
▦ Results 📄 Messages				
	Customer_ID	First_Name	Last_Name	Payment_Method
1	C001	Humphrey	Rotham	Venmo
2	C005	Gonzales	Bonett	Venmo
3	C006	Doug	Druce	Venmo
4	C010	Diandra	Gatling	Venmo

Illustration 6.21   Adding a WHERE clause for Payment_Method that equals Venmo returns four records.

When referring to a value in a text field in a WHERE clause, the referenced text is placed within single quotation marks. This is why Payment_Method = 'Venmo' is used in the previous example. Numeric fields do not require quotation marks in the SELECT statement.

Question 2: How Many Customers Live in Kentucky?

This time, the SELECT statement targets the State field name and looks for the field value KY, the abbreviation for Kentucky. The following query retrieves two records:

SELECT Customer_ID FROM Customers WHERE State = 'KY'

There are two customers who live in Kentucky (**Illustration 6.22**).

Note that the WHERE clause uses 'KY' instead of 'Kentucky'. The query only recognizes what is typed into the statement.

- Query writers must know how the data is formatted within the database in order to create accurate SELECT statements. If the query uses 'Kentucky' and not 'KY', then the results will be inaccurate.

- The details of how the states are formatted is found in the data dictionary.

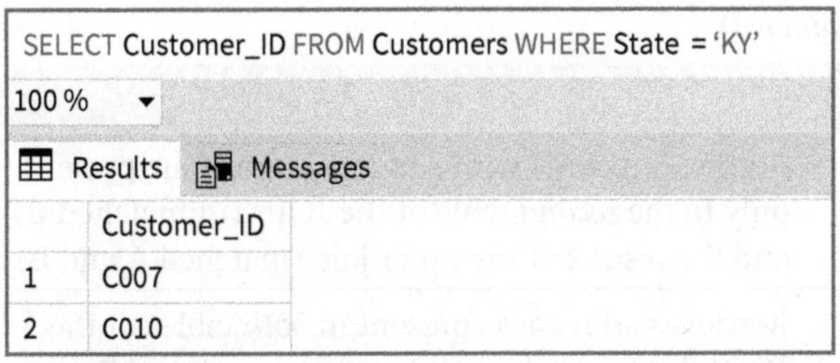

SELECT Customer_ID FROM Customers WHERE State = 'KY'

100 %   ▾

⊞ Results   📄 Messages

	Customer_ID
1	C007
2	C010

Illustration 6.22   Adding a WHERE clause for State = 'KY' returns two records.

Question 3: Are There Customers with the First Name Doug Who Are Not Doug Druce?

Finally, we isolate First_Name fields that contain Doug while ignoring Last_Name fields that contain Druce by using the syntax for "does not equal," which is <>. The following query retrieves all records where the First_Name field contains Doug and the Last_Name field does not contain Druce:

SELECT Customer_ID, First_Name, Last_Name FROM Customers WHERE First_Name = 'Doug' AND Last_Name <> 'Druce'

There is one other Doug in the database (**Illustration 6.23**).

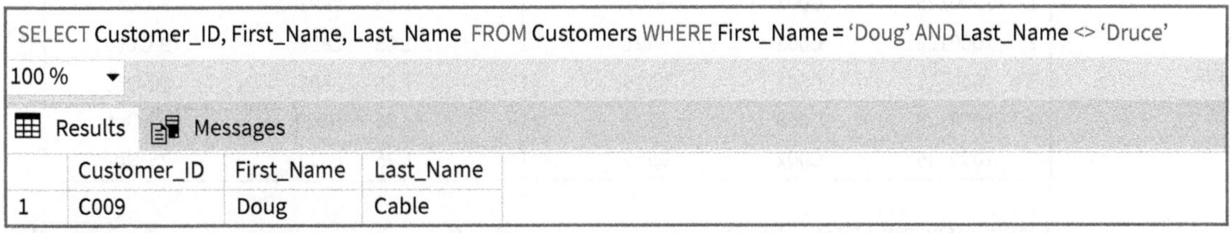

SELECT Customer_ID, First_Name, Last_Name FROM Customers WHERE First_Name = 'Doug' AND Last_Name <> 'Druce'

100 %   ▾

⊞ Results   📄 Messages

	Customer_ID	First_Name	Last_Name
1	C009	Doug	Cable

Illustration 6.23   Adding a WHERE clause for First_Name that equals Doug and Last_Name that does not equal Druce returns one record.

The JOIN Operator

Since the primary purpose of a relational database is to store data in separate tables connected by relationships, knowing how to retrieve data from multiple tables at once is crucial. The **JOIN operator** retrieves interconnected data from related tables by declaring a primary key and foreign key relationship as the join column. For example, when joining the Customers and Orders tables, the Customer_ID column is the join column: it's the primary key in the Customers table and a foreign key in the Orders table.

JOIN operations are classified by the desired results of the SQL statements. In other words, which records does the user want to see? A join can be either inner or outer. Outer joins are further classified into three types, depending on which sets of records are desired (**Table 6.13**). All three outer joins return values that are *not* present in both tables.

TABLE 6.13 Four Types of JOIN Operations

Join	Definition	Example
Inner join	Retrieves a record only if its join column value is present in *both* tables (matched)	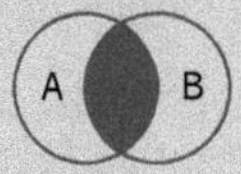
Left outer join	Retrieves records with a join column value present only in the *first* table of the JOIN (unmatched A) and the results of the inner join (matched A and B)	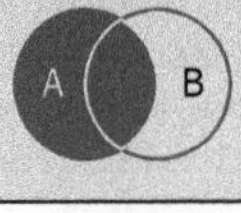

(Continued)

TABLE 6.13 (*Continued*)

Join	Definition	Example
Right outer join	Retrieves records with a join column value present only in the *second* table of the JOIN (unmatched B) and the results of the inner join (matched A and B)	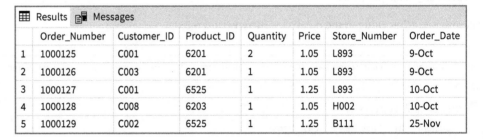
Full outer join	Retrieves all records present in *both* tables of the JOIN (both matched and unmatched A and B)	

JOIN operators are complex SQL statements. While it's not necessary to know how to write these statements, it's essential to understand the four types of joins you have just learned. The most commonly used join is the left outer join. We next provide SQL statement examples comparing a left outer join to a full outer join to help you understand the types of results these operations retrieve.

Left Outer Join Example

In addition to the Customers table, Julia's Cookies' database also houses an Orders table. **Illustration 6.24** shows a sample.

Illustration 6.24 Julia's Cookies' database includes an Orders table that captures important information from customer orders.

	Order_Number	Customer_ID	Product_ID	Quantity	Price	Store_Number	Order_Date
1	1000125	C001	6201	2	1.05	L893	9-Oct
2	1000126	C003	6201	1	1.05	L893	9-Oct
3	1000127	C001	6525	1	1.25	L893	10-Oct
4	1000128	C008	6203	1	1.05	H002	10-Oct
5	1000129	C002	6525	1	1.25	B111	25-Nov

LEFT OUTER JOIN with Customers used as the first table retrieves every record in the Customers table (A) and the records from the Orders table that have customer IDs from the Customers table (B) (**Illustration 6.25**). Note that the syntax includes AS Cus and AS Ord.

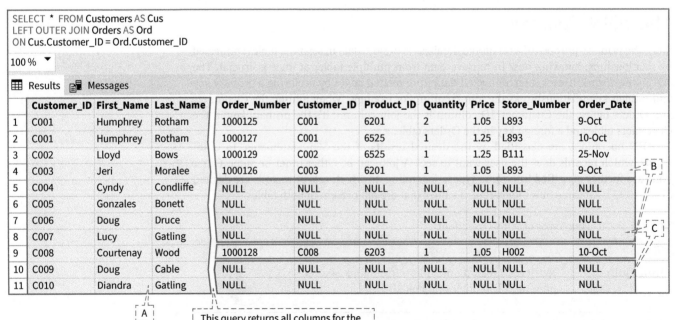

```
SELECT * FROM Customers AS Cus
LEFT OUTER JOIN Orders AS Ord
ON Cus.Customer_ID = Ord.Customer_ID
```

	Customer_ID	First_Name	Last_Name	Order_Number	Customer_ID	Product_ID	Quantity	Price	Store_Number	Order_Date
1	C001	Humphrey	Rotham	1000125	C001	6201	2	1.05	L893	9-Oct
2	C001	Humphrey	Rotham	1000127	C001	6525	1	1.25	L893	10-Oct
3	C002	Lloyd	Bows	1000129	C002	6525	1	1.25	B111	25-Nov
4	C003	Jeri	Moralee	1000126	C003	6201	1	1.05	L893	9-Oct
5	C004	Cyndy	Condliffe	NULL	NULL	NULL	NULL	NULL	NULL	NULL
6	C005	Gonzales	Bonett	NULL	NULL	NULL	NULL	NULL	NULL	NULL
7	C006	Doug	Druce	NULL	NULL	NULL	NULL	NULL	NULL	NULL
8	C007	Lucy	Gatling	NULL	NULL	NULL	NULL	NULL	NULL	NULL
9	C008	Courtenay	Wood	1000128	C008	6203	1	1.05	H002	10-Oct
10	C009	Doug	Cable	NULL	NULL	NULL	NULL	NULL	NULL	NULL
11	C010	Diandra	Gatling	NULL	NULL	NULL	NULL	NULL	NULL	NULL

This query returns all columns for the Customers table. Only Customer_ID, First_Name, and Last_Name are shown in this illustration for simplicity.

Illustration 6.25 LEFT OUTER JOIN returns all records in the Customers table and matched records from the Orders table.

AS assigns an alias to the tables being selected immediately before the AS. The alias is then used in the ON clause to indicate the JOIN is connecting tables using Customer_ID from the Customers table (Cus.Customer_ID) and Customer_ID from the Orders table (Ord.Customer_ID). An alias can be any word or label and makes it easy to reference the same item throughout a query.

No orders are excluded from the results in this case. You learned earlier that the business rules state that every order *must* have one customer associated with it. In contrast, there are customers who have no orders (C). This is because the business rules contain an optionality constraint stating that customers *may* have one or more orders. Also note that Customer_ID C001 appears in two rows. This is because customer C001 has two orders in the Orders table, so the data is duplicated in the Customers table with this join.

Full Outer Join Example

JOIN operators can be combined to join multiple tables. For example, in addition to the Customers and Orders tables, Julia's Cookies uses a Products table, which contains the data shown in **Illustration 6.26**.

	Product_ID	Product_Name
1	6201	Chocolate Chip Cookie
2	6525	Peanut Butter Cookie
3	6203	Sugar Cookie
4	6205	Snickerdoodle

Illustration 6.26 The contents of the Products table relate to the Orders tables.

Using FULL OUTER JOIN with these three tables retrieves all records in Customers (A), Orders (B), and Products (C) (**Illustration 6.27**).

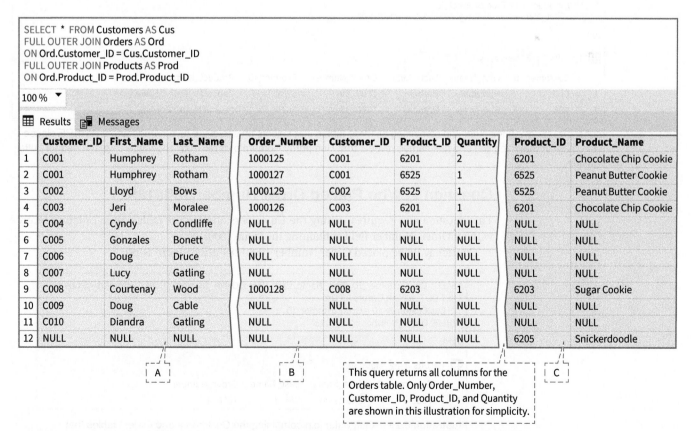

```
SELECT * FROM Customers AS Cus
FULL OUTER JOIN Orders AS Ord
ON Ord.Customer_ID = Cus.Customer_ID
FULL OUTER JOIN Products AS Prod
ON Ord.Product_ID = Prod.Product_ID
```

100 % ▼

Results   Messages

	Customer_ID	First_Name	Last_Name	Order_Number	Customer_ID	Product_ID	Quantity	Product_ID	Product_Name
1	C001	Humphrey	Rotham	1000125	C001	6201	2	6201	Chocolate Chip Cookie
2	C001	Humphrey	Rotham	1000127	C001	6525	1	6525	Peanut Butter Cookie
3	C002	Lloyd	Bows	1000129	C002	6525	1	6525	Peanut Butter Cookie
4	C003	Jeri	Moralee	1000126	C003	6201	1	6201	Chocolate Chip Cookie
5	C004	Cyndy	Condliffe	NULL	NULL	NULL	NULL	NULL	NULL
6	C005	Gonzales	Bonett	NULL	NULL	NULL	NULL	NULL	NULL
7	C006	Doug	Druce	NULL	NULL	NULL	NULL	NULL	NULL
8	C007	Lucy	Gatling	NULL	NULL	NULL	NULL	NULL	NULL
9	C008	Courtenay	Wood	1000128	C008	6203	1	6203	Sugar Cookie
10	C009	Doug	Cable	NULL	NULL	NULL	NULL	NULL	NULL
11	C010	Diandra	Gatling	NULL	NULL	NULL	NULL	NULL	NULL
12	NULL	NULL	NULL	NULL	NULL	NULL	NULL	6205	Snickerdoodle

A   B   This query returns all columns for the Orders table. Only Order_Number, Customer_ID, Product_ID, and Quantity are shown in this illustration for simplicity.   C

Illustration 6.27 FULL OUTER JOIN used with the Customers, Orders, and Products tables returns all records, whether they are matched or not.

Product ID 6205, which is the Snickerdoodle, is included in these results even though no customers have ordered it. The FULL OUTER JOIN operator returns all records in the specified tables.

Putting It Together

Now that we have covered the basic SELECT statement and some of the expanded functions often used to query a database, let's put it all together and examine some data querying use cases.

The SQL statements that follow use SELECT statements with JOIN operators and WHERE clauses to retrieve the answers to three questions. As you work through them, focus on understanding the results of these examples and how the JOIN operators and WHERE clauses work together to query the database tables for answers.

Question 1: What Types of Cookies Did Humphrey Rotham Order?

To answer this question, we need to combine the Customers table, Orders table, and Products table, then use the WHERE clause to isolate orders from a customer with the first name Humphrey and last name Rotham.

Humphrey Rotham ordered both chocolate chip and peanut butter cookies (**Illustration 6.28**). Note in this query that we include the alias for the Customer_ID and Product_ID fields in the initial SELECT statement. This is because the fields are duplicated as a PK and an FK in related tables, so we specify which to return to avoid seeing the same column twice.

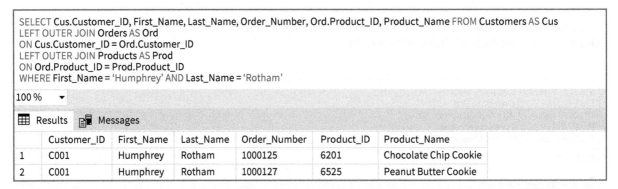

Illustration 6.28   A left outer join combining all three tables that selects only relevant field names and a WHERE clause searching for matching first and last names reveals that Humphrey Rotham ordered both chocolate chip and peanut butter cookies.

Question 2: Who Placed Order Number 1000128?

This question also requires joining the Customers and Orders tables, then isolating records with an Order_Number field containing the value 1000128.

Courtenay Wood placed Order Number 1000128 (**Illustration 6.29**).

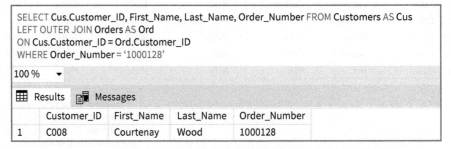

Illustration 6.29   A left outer join combining the Customers and Orders tables that selects only relevant field names and a WHERE clause searching for a specific order number reveals that Courtenay Wood placed order number 1000128.

Question 3: Who Ordered Peanut Butter Cookies?

This last question combines three tables and searches for a Product_Name field containing peanut butter cookies.

Humphrey Rotham and Lloyd Bows ordered peanut butter cookies (**Illustration 6.30**).

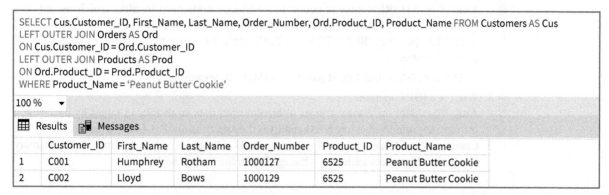

```
SELECT Cus.Customer_ID, First_Name, Last_Name, Order_Number, Ord.Product_ID, Product_Name FROM Customers AS Cus
LEFT OUTER JOIN Orders AS Ord
ON Cus.Customer_ID = Ord.Customer_ID
LEFT OUTER JOIN Products AS Prod
ON Ord.Product_ID = Prod.Product_ID
WHERE Product_Name = 'Peanut Butter Cookie'
```

100 %   ▼

⊞ Results   📄 Messages

	Customer_ID	First_Name	Last_Name	Order_Number	Product_ID	Product_Name
1	C001	Humphrey	Rotham	1000127	6525	Peanut Butter Cookie
2	C002	Lloyd	Bows	1000129	6525	Peanut Butter Cookie

Illustration 6.30   A left outer join combining all three tables that selects only relevant field names and a WHERE clause searching for a specific product name reveals that Humphrey Rotham and Lloyd Bows purchased peanut butter cookies.

Querying languages are an important tool in data analytics because they connect the user to the data in the database. If a data analyst needs data but can't access the relational database, then the data can be extracted by either saving it to a file outside the database or directly importing it via database queries to an analysis tool like Python or Alteryx.

You may be surprised to discover how valuable knowledge of SQL querying will be in your accounting career. You can practice your new query writing skills in Applied Learning 6.5.

Julia's Cookies   Applied Learning 6.5

SQL Statements: Querying for Answers

Joshi is an accounting analyst at Julia's Cookies. His manager has asked for a list of all inactive vendors in the vendor main table to provide the internal audit team, which is conducting a fraud review.

The vendor main table is named VendorMain and contains the following column field names:

Vendor_ID

Vendor_Name

Vendor_Address

Vendor_BankAccount

Vendor_ActiveDate

Vendor_Status

Which SQL statement do you think Joshi should use to retrieve the information his manager wants to see?

1. SELECT Vendor_Name, Vendor_Address, Vendor_BankAccount, Vendor_Status FROM VendorMain WHERE Vendor_Status = 'Inactive'
2. SELECT VendorMain WITH Vendor_Name IF Vendor_Status = 'Inactive'
3. SELECT Vendor_Name FROM VendorMain WHERE Vendor_Status = 'Inactive'
4. SELECT Vendor_Name FROM VendorMain WHEN Vendor_Status <> 'Active'

SOLUTION

Statement #3 is a correctly formatted SQL statement. #1 is also a correctly formatted SQL SELECT statement, but the only column Joshi's manager asked to see is the Vendor_Name field, so he should use #3.

CONCEPT REVIEW QUESTIONS

1. What does the SELECT command do?

   Ans. The Select command retrieves data from the database, and its basic form is:

   SELECT [field name] FROM [table name]

2. How do you use the WHERE clause?

   Ans. The WHERE clause is added to a SELECT statement to filter which records the query returns by adding values such as mathematical comparisons (=, <, <=, >, >=, <>) or special operators (BETWEEN, LIKE, IN, etc.). There are many criteria that a WHERE clause can specify.

   SELECT [field name] FROM [table name] WHERE [expression].

3. What is a JOIN operator?

   Ans. The JOIN operator retrieves interconnected data from related tables by declaring a primary key and foreign key relationship as the join column. For example, when joining the Customers and Orders tables, the Customer_ID column is the join column: it's the primary key in the Customers table and a foreign key in the Orders table.

6.6 How Can We Create Database Forms and Reports?

Learning Objective ❻

Explain how database forms and reports are useful for businesses.

Most business users interact with a relational database primarily through forms and reports—forms for entering data and reports for displaying data.

Forms

A **form** is a user interface that allows users to enter data into the database. It is designed to gather information for one record of the database at a time. For example, if you have a database of customers, you might have a form that allows you to enter information about one customer at a time.

A database form is a user interface that can be used to enter, edit, or display data from a data source such as a table or query. It can be used to control access to data, such as which fields or rows of data are displayed. For example, certain users might need to see only several fields in a table with many fields. Providing those users with a form that contains only those fields makes it easier for them to use the database. You can also add command buttons and other features to a form to automate frequently performed actions. Forms can be used by businesses to gather information via web browsers. Modern database form builders allow the users to customize the forms by adding colors, their brand logo, backgrounds, a variety of fields such as bar codes. We can also include conditional statements in these database forms and handle dynamic behavior. Different types of database forms are used by businesses these days, including contact forms, lead generation forms, survey forms, order forms, booking forms, applicant tracker forms, and user feedback forms.

Relational database systems include the ability to create and customize database forms. A good database form creator can collect information via the web and mobile browsers, customize the look and feel of the form, and handle dynamic if-then behavior. Many forms can be created depending on the organization's needs.

For example, an organization's procurement department developed a purchase order form to streamline purchase requests. This form collects all relevant information about a purchase request and forwards it to the approving manager for further processing.

Illustration 6.31 shows a database form—a custom-designed screen for adding new records to a database table. This form is divided into three major sections:

1. A heading section at the top of the form, that is, a New Order Form
2. A detail section, which usually takes up most of the space on the form and displays the record information
3. Form submission, which always appears at the bottom of the form

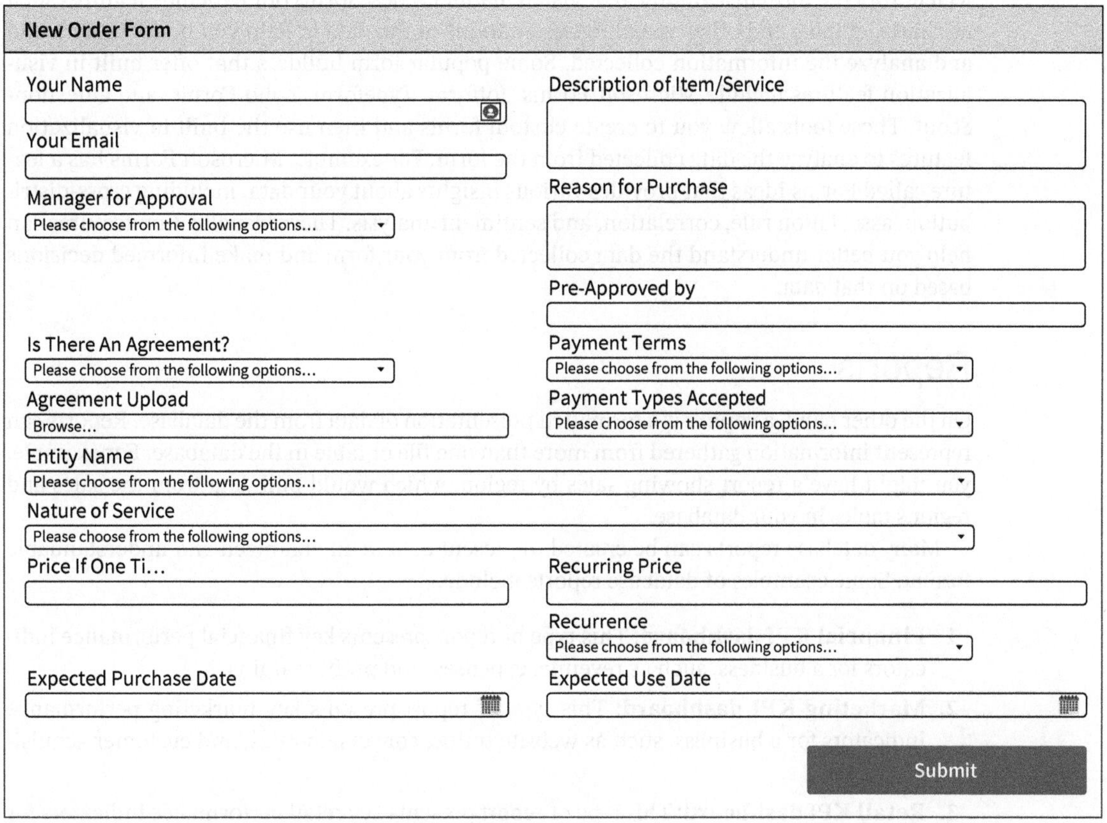

New Order Form

Your Name

Your Email

Manager for Approval
Please choose from the following options...

Is There An Agreement?
Please choose from the following options...
Agreement Upload
Browse...
Entity Name
Please choose from the following options...
Nature of Service
Please choose from the following options...
Price If One Ti...

Description of Item/Service

Reason for Purchase

Pre-Approved by

Payment Terms
Please choose from the following options...
Payment Types Accepted
Please choose from the following options...

Recurring Price

Recurrence
Please choose from the following options...
Expected Use Date

Expected Purchase Date

Submit

Illustration 6.31   Database form—a custom-designed screen for adding new records to a database table.

There are several ways to create a database form and report.

Creating a Form in Microsoft Access

1. **From an existing table or query in Access:** To create a form from a table or query using the database, in the Navigation Pane, click the table or query that contains the data for the form that is required, and on the Create tab, click Form.
2. **Blank form:** On the Create tab, click Blank Form. Access opens a blank form in Layout view and displays the Field List pane. In the Field List pane, click the plus sign (+) next to the table or tables that contain the fields that you want to see on the form.
3. **Split form:** A split form gives two views of the data at the same time—a Form view and a Datasheet view. The datasheet portion of the form can be used to quickly locate a record, and use the form portion to view or edit the record. The two views are connected to the same data source and are synchronized at all times. A new split form can be created using the Split Form tool; in the Navigation Pane, click the table or query that contains the data, and then on the Create tab, click More Forms, and then click Split Form.

4. **Create a form that displays multiple records:** A multiple item form, also known as a continuous form, is useful if the requirement is to display multiple records. This is more customizable than a datasheet. In the Navigation Pane, click the table or query containing the data you want to see on the form.

Another way to create a database form is using an online builder like WorkMap.ai (formerly HyperBase). With WorkMap.ai, you can create custom forms that can be accessed via web and mobile browsers. You can also customize the look and feel of the form and handle dynamic if-then behavior.

Forms with built-in visualization are available that allow you to visualize the data collected from the form in a graphical or visual manner. These forms often include features such as charts, graphs, and other visual representations of the data to help you better understand and analyze the information collected. Some popular form builders that offer built-in visualization features include Microsoft Forms, Jotform, Typeform, Zoho Forms, and Question-Scout. These tools allow you to create custom forms and then use the built-in visualization features to analyze the data collected from the form. For example, Microsoft Forms has a feature called Forms Ideas that provides various insights about your data, including cross-distribution, association rule, correlation, and sentiment analysis. These visualization features can help you better understand the data collected from your form and make informed decisions based on that data.

Reports

On the other hand, a **report** is a formatted presentation of data from the database. Reports can represent information gathered from more than one file or table in the database. For example, you might have a report showing sales by region, which would pull data from the sales and regions tables in your database.

Many database reports can be created to present data in an organized and understandable format. Some examples of database reports include:

1. **Financial KPI dashboard:** This type of report presents key financial performance indicators for a business, such as revenue, expenses, and profit margins.

2. **Marketing KPI dashboard:** This type of report presents key marketing performance indicators for a business, such as website traffic, conversion rates, and customer acquisition costs.

3. **Retail KPI dashboard:** This type of report presents key retail performance indicators for a business, such as sales, inventory levels, and customer satisfaction.

4. **Customer support dashboard:** This type of report presents key customer support performance indicators for a business, such as response times, resolution rates, and customer satisfaction.

These are just a few examples of the many different types of database reports that can be created to present data in an organized and understandable format. The specific type of report you choose to create will depend on the data you want to present and the audience you are presenting it to.

There are many tools available for creating database reports. Some popular tools include:

1. **Microsoft Excel:** This tool is widely used for creating reports and charts from data stored in spreadsheets.

2. **SQL Server Reporting Services (SSRS):** This server-based report-generating software system from Microsoft allows you to create, deploy, and manage reports.

3. **Crystal Reports:** This business intelligence application is used to design and generate reports from a wide range of data sources.

4. **Tableau:** This data visualization tool allows you to create interactive dashboards and reports.

5. **QlikView:** This business intelligence tool allows you to create interactive dashboards and reports.

A variety of different reports can be created using Access. The starting point is to identify the report's record source. Understand whether the report is a simple listing of records or a grouped summary of sales by region. First, determine which fields contain the data you want to see in your report, and in which tables or queries they are found.

After choosing the record source, creating the report using the Report Wizard will usually be easy. The Report Wizard is a feature in Access that guides you through a series of questions and generates a report based on your answers.

Creating a Report using Wizard in Microsoft Access

1. On the Create tab, in the Reports group, click Report Wizard.
2. Follow the directions on the Report Wizard pages. On the last page, click Finish.

CONCEPT REVIEW QUESTIONS

1. What is a database form?

   Ans. A database form is a user interface that allows users to enter data into the database. It is designed to gather information for one record of the database at a time. For example, if we have a database of customers, we have a form that allows us to enter information about one customer at a time.

2. What is a database report?

   Ans. A database report is a formatted presentation of data from the database. Reports can represent information gathered from multiple files or tables in the database. For example, we can have a report showing sales by region, which would pull data from the sales and regions tables in our database.

FEATURED PROFESSIONAL | Finance Digital Transformation Analyst

Photo courtesy of Dominic Sylvester

Dominic Sylvester, CPA

Dominic is a process improvement specialist who began his career as an audit associate at a Big Four firm. He quickly moved into a specialized role as a digital accelerator, where he focused on developing new systems and processes for automation, process improvement, and analytics solutions. He continues to utilize his skills in process automation and analytics to increase productivity within the finance function for a large technology company. Using his dual major of accounting and information systems, Dominic has carved a unique role for himself in the accounting industry. He has a master of science degree in finance with a concentration in digital innovation, a degree combination that focuses on leveraging software development skills and financial theory to build financial applications for areas like corporate finance, risk management, and investments. As a subject matter expert, Dominic has trained hundreds of accounting professionals in analytics solutions including Alteryx and Tableau. He enjoys coding in his spare time.

Why do you think it's important for accounting professionals in traditional roles like audit and tax to understand the systems development process?

During the development phase, being able to translate the business needs into systems requirements can ensure quality in the development process. From a user's perspective, understanding how systems are developed and the information stored within them can greatly influence the interactions the traditional roles have with other departments along with enhancement requests for IT.

What technical skills do you think accounting majors should obtain before entering the workforce?

The first is understanding SQL for accessing data within databases. Most, if not all, company data is stored in various databases, and having the ability to access and understand where to find the information is a great tool to have. The second is the ability to identify processes for automation. As a great number of companies begin to accelerate their adoption of process improvement initiatives and digital transformation efforts, understanding when you should automate a manual process is going to be a great tool for accounting professionals.

How would you recommend students gain exposure to systems and databases before starting their careers?

For training, there are a great many resources on YouTube that can help you learn about various technologies and how to use them. For process automation, students can enroll for free in the UiPath Academy, a learning management system that provides instructions on how to build automation solutions with UiPath. Alteryx offers similar free training. Codecademy is another great resource for learning about coding languages, specifically Python and SQL. It even has a quiz to assess where you should begin your training.

Review and Practice

Key Terms Review

Agile methodology
analysis stage
business rule
cardinality
class
commands
conceptual design
crow's foot notation
dashboard
data control language (DCL)
data definition language (DDL)
data dictionary
data manipulation language (DML)
data modeling
data query language (DQL)
data redundancy
design stage
development stage
entity integrity

feasibility study
foreign key (FK)
form
graphical user interface (GUI)
implementation stage
JOIN operator
key
maintenance stage
NoSQL database
null
object
object-oriented database
planning stage
primary key (PK)
product backlog
product increment
project plan
referential integrity
report

requirements definition
scope creep
scrum
SELECT command
sprint
sprint backlog
SQL statement
system go-live
systems development life cycle (SDLC)
systems model
technical architecture specifications
testing stage
timeboxing
transaction control language (TCL)
user acceptance testing (UAT)
variable
Waterfall methodology
WHERE clause

Learning Objectives Review

❶ Outline the systems development life cycle (SDLC) stages.

The systems development life cycle (SDLC) enables users to transform a systems project idea into an operational one. The seven stages of the SDLC are:

1. Planning
2. Analysis
3. Design
4. Development
5. Testing
6. Implementation
7. Maintenance

During the planning stage, roles and responsibilities are identified. The project also undergoes a feasibility study, and the project plan is created.

The analysis stage focuses on acquiring user requirements for the system's purpose and functions.

Requirements are translated into technical specifications during the design stage.

Programmers write the code that creates the system during the development stage and send the system's code for validation during the testing stage. User acceptance testing provides selected end users an opportunity to use and provide feedback about the system.

System implementation is a complex stage where the system goes live and is available to users. Systems can be implemented through:

- Direct cutover
- Parallel implementation
- Phased implementation
- Pilot implementation

After a system goes live, the maintenance stage ensures that it stays operational and updated.

② Compare and contrast the Waterfall and Agile systems development methodologies.

The SDLC is a framework that can be implemented using Waterfall or Agile methodologies.

Waterfall methodology progresses through the stages of the SDLC in sequential order and provides end users a product only after the full project is completed.

Agile methodology uses short iterations of work, called sprints, and engages end users throughout the development process to address risks and changes in real time.

Key roles in scrum project management are:

- Business stakeholders
- Product owner
- Scrum master
- Core development team

Scrum is a type of Agile project management that uses timeboxing and sprints to prevent scope creep.

Three important scrum artifacts are:

- Product backlogs
- Sprint backlogs
- Product increments

Waterfall is suitable for projects that require little change throughout development and require predictable outcomes. Agile is better suited for projects that have few initial requirements and require mid-development decisions, changes, and prioritization.

③ Distinguish among different types of modern databases.

When selecting a database type, companies consider:

- Data variety
- Data volume
- Scalability
- Purpose

Relational databases are made up of:

- Tables
- Records
- Columns
- Field names
- Fields

Relational databases are suited for storing structured data and are commonly used for accounting purposes.

Object-oriented databases are made up of:

- Classes
- Objects
- Variables

Object-oriented databases can store structured and unstructured data.

NoSQL databases can store both structured and unstructured data and use SQL language along with other programming languages like Java and Python to access the data. NoSQL databases are easy to scale and are a disruptive technology companies are currently adopting.

④ Design relational database tables by using an entity relationship diagram (ERD).

There are three types of entity relationship diagrams (ERDs):

- Conceptual: Used for basic design planning
- Logical: Include more details for developers
- Physical: Capture all relationships, rules, and primary and foreign keys and used for database development

Relational databases mitigate the risk of data redundancy.

Primary keys are unique identifiers in tables. Foreign keys are references to primary keys in other tables. These keys create the relationship between two tables in a relational database.

Cardinality is a numeric relationship between two tables and consists of two constraints:

- Plurality: One or many
- Optionality: Optional or mandatory

Together, these two constraints combine to make four cardinalities for a relational database:

- One and only one
- No more than one
- At least one
- Any

Business rules define cardinality constraints and the relationships between tables.

⑤ Construct queries to retrieve data and answer business questions.

There are five types of SQL languages, each utilizing specific commands:

- Data definition language (DDL): Changes a database by adding or altering tables
- Data manipulation language (DML): Modifies data within a database
- Data control language (DCL): Grants and removes user access rights
- Transaction control language (TCL): Processes transactions
- Data query language (DQL): Retrieves data from the database

The basic SQL SELECT statement is:

SELECT [field name] FROM [table name]

This SELECT statement is used to select all field names from a table:

SELECT * FROM [table name]

The WHERE clause filters which records the SELECT statement returns:

SELECT [field name] FROM [table name] WHERE [expression]

JOIN operators are used to combine two or more tables in a relational database. There are four types of joins:

- Inner join, which returns all matching records in Table A and Table B
- Left outer join, which returns all records in Table A and matching records in Table B
- Right outer join, which returns matching records in Table A and all records in Table B
- Full outer join, which retrieves all records present in both Tables A and B

> **6** Explain how database forms and reports are useful for businesses.

Most business users interact with a relational database primarily through:

- Forms for entering data
- Reports for displaying data

Some popular form builders that offer built-in visualization features include:

- Microsoft Forms
- Jotform
- Typeform
- Zoho Forms
- QuestionScout

Some popular tools for creating reports are:

- Microsoft Excel
- SQL Server Reporting Services (SSRS)
- Crystal reports
- Tableau
- QlikView

CPA questions, as well as multiple choice, discussion, analysis and application, and Tableau questions and other resources, are available online.

Multiple Choice Questions

1. (LO 1) **CPA** The systems development life cycle (SDLC) is the traditional methodology for developing information systems. In which phase of the SDLC would the activity of identifying the problem(s) to be solved is most likely to occur?

a. Analysis

b. Implementation

c. Planning

d. Development

2. (LO 1) **CPA** Mr. Shankley's Medical Services Corp. operates in all states and territories of the United States. It is developing a new patient relationship management system that is approaching completion and is behind schedule. Which implementation method would be potentially fastest but also involves the most risk?

a. Pilot testing

b. Direct cutover

c. Phased implementation

d. Parallel implementation

3. (LO 1) A new system moves to production and goes live for company use in the

a. development stage.

b. implementation stage.

c. design stage.

d. maintenance stage.

4. (LO 1) **CPA** Which of the following is responsible for overall program logic and functionality?

a. IT steering committee

b. Lead systems analyst

c. Application programmers

d. End users

5. (LO 2) Agile methodology focuses on all the following *except*

a. ensuring customer satisfaction.

b. reflecting on improvement opportunities.

c. adjusting to change in real time.

d. working in cascading sequential phases.

6. (LO 2) Which role is responsible for understanding end-user requirements?

a. Scrum master

b. Business stakeholder

c. Product owner

d. Development team

7. (LO 2) Which of the following statements about the Waterfall systems development methodology is true?

a. The Waterfall method must be executed in a linear fashion with each step overlapping the next.

b. The Waterfall method uses the seven stages of the SDLC framework and is not customizable.

c. Each stage in the Waterfall method is completed before continuing to the next stage.

d. The first stage in the Waterfall method is planning; the final stage is implementation.

8. **(LO 3)** Determining current performance requirements for a database design project relates to

a. data variety.

b. purpose.

c. data volume.

d. scalability.

9. **(LO 3)** In the table below, the shaded row represents a

First Name	Middle Initial	Last Name	Birthdate	Phone Number
Willie	H	Nelson	April 29, 1933	123-456-7890
Waylon	A	Jennings	June 15, 1937	987-654-3210

a. field.

b. record.

c. column.

d. file.

10. **(LO 3)** The element of an object-oriented database that is most like a relational database record is the

a. class.

b. variable.

c. object.

d. query.

11. **(LO 4)** "One employee is hired by one manager" is a business rule with _____ plurality.

a. 1:M

b. 1:1

c. M:M

d. M:1

12. **(LO 4)** Monica is designing the physical ERD for a new database. What element must Monica include?

a. Tables

b. Relationships

c. Keys

d. All of the above

13. **(LO 4)** **CPA** Which term describes the unique identifier that identifies a specific record in a table?

a. A foreign key

b. A primary key

c. A secondary key

d. A schema

14. **(LO 5)** Which type of SQL language grants or removes access from a database user?

a. Data definition language

b. Data manipulation language

c. Data control language

d. Data querying language

15. **(LO 5)** Which SELECT statement returns all fields and records in the Customers table?

a. SELECT all FROM Customers

b. SELECT * FROM Customers

c. SELECT Customers FROM Table

d. SELECT All Names FROM Customers Table

16. **(LO 5)** In the Employee table, the field EmployeeStatus indicates whether employees are active, retired, or terminated. Which of the following SELECT statements returns all fields and records of employees who have *not* been terminated in the Employee table?

a. SELECT * FROM Employee WHERE EmployeeStatus = 'Active'

b. SELECT All FROM Employee WHERE EmployeeStatus <> 'Terminated'

c. SELECT * FROM Employee WHERE EmployeeStatus <> 'Terminated'

d. SELECT * FROM Employee WHERE EmployeeStatus = 'Terminated'

17. **(LO 6)** Which view in Microsoft Access is used to create and modify a form?

a. Query design view

b. Form design view

c. Relationship design view

d. Table design view

18. **(LO 6)** The formatted way used to retrieve data from one or more tables of the database and represent it in the way it is required is a

a. table.

b. relationship.

c. form.

d. report.

Discussion and Research Questions

DQ1. (LO 1) **Critical Thinking** Aabid's Accessories is implementing a new ERP system and must choose a system implementation method. The project has a large budget, and the company has a low to moderate risk appetite. Leadership would like the implementation to be cost-effective. Choose the system implementation method Aabid's Accessories should use and explain how it works. Explain why you chose it and describe its associated costs and risks.

DQ2. (LO 1) **Critical Thinking** WanderLust LLC is a fast-growing manufacturer of adventure and outdoor gear. The company wants to replace its semiautomated batch production line system with an automated mass production line system, using the same floor space in the factories. Which implementation methodology would you recommend, and why?

DQ3. (LO 1–2) You are a senior financial analyst for an innovative and growing technology company, experienced at working as a team member on applications and systems development projects. The VP for finance asks you whether the Waterfall systems development life cycle approach is still relevant, given the popularity of the Agile approach. How would you respond?

DQ4. (LO 2) Critical Thinking Gellin's Gelatins, a dessert manufacturer, is developing a new payment portal for customers to review and pay invoices. The existing system is third-party software, and developing in-house software is a new project. The development team works together, in person, at the corporate office and is known for creative problem solving and design. The system has many predefined requirements due to the sensitivity of processing payments and capturing sensitive customer data, including some regulatory specifications.

Should Gellin's Gelatins use the Waterfall or Agile SDLC management methodology? Explain your selection, including why your methodology is a suitable choice for the described project.

DQ5. (LO 3) Explain the relationship between a defined class and the objects in the class in an object-oriented database.

DQ6. (LO 3) Compare and contrast how a relational database and a NoSQL database handle scalability.

DQ7. (LO 4) After a meeting with users about the development of a new analytics system for accounts receivable, your manager at a CPA firm asks you to explain the distinction between conceptual, logical, and physical ERDs because the manager was confused during the meeting. How would you respond?

DQ8. (LO 4) What are primary and foreign keys in a relational database? What function do they serve, and why are they so important?

DQ9. (LO 5) You are an audit partner conducting a training session for new hires at a large CPA firm. Explain to these new hires why a working knowledge of SQL is important for employees at your firm.

DQ10. (LO 5) You are an audit partner conducting a training session for new hires at a large CPA firm. Provide at least four examples for these new hires of how SQL can be used on the job.

Application and Analysis Questions

A1. (LO 1) Critical Thinking You are an IT auditor for a public accounting firm, and your team is performing a pre-implementation audit of your client's planned employee expense reimbursement system. Your team just received descriptions of system requirements and specifications from the client. Label each of the following descriptions with the appropriate document type from the word bank. One document type may be used for more than one description.

Word Bank:	
conceptual design	systems model
technical architecture	requirements definition
specifications	
graphical user interface (GUI)	

Descriptions:

1. Managers approve employees' submitted expenses in the system.

2. A data flow diagram shows technical details about how the credit card data will enter the system from the credit card provider's system.

3. The login button will be orange.

4. Employees will import credit card charges to their expense reports.

5. The system-generated data will flow into the HR database, but technical details aren't available yet.

6. The system will operate on the same cloud server as the previous system.

A2. (LO 1) Critical Thinking Chrystelle is a luxury clothing brand whose products are sold in high-end department stores

throughout Europe. You are a member of Chrystelle's finance transformation team, whose objective is to identify opportunities throughout the Finance and Accounting departments to leverage technology to improve processes and drive efficiencies. Currently, your team is working with the IT department to develop a website that will be a single-stop portal for all things related to accounting analytics. Employees will log into the website to request data analytics to be performed by the analyst team, access existing dashboards, and post comments and discussions related to analytics ideas throughout the department.

Perform a feasibility study by reviewing the following facts about the project and labeling each with the type of feasibility it addresses. Then determine whether the project passes the feasibility study.

Types of feasibility:

- **A.** Technical feasibility
- **B.** Economic feasibility
- **C.** Operational feasibility

Project facts:

1. The website will streamline communication about analytics throughout the department and allow teams to leverage one another's ideas and programming easily.

2. The website will be developed by existing web developers who regularly build and support internal websites such as this.

3. The website will use existing web page templates and be accessible through the existing corporate home page.

4. The website will be housed on existing company web servers and cost a minimal amount to build and maintain.

A3. (LO 1) You are a senior financial analyst for a growing technology company. The VP of finance, Charlena, is concerned that a new analytics development project is not following the stages of the systems development life cycle (SDLC). Charlena knows that you are experienced at working with end users and the core development team on development projects. She asks you to provide her with the alignment between the stages of the SDLC and the ten key outcomes that she is particularly interested in for follow-up. Label each of the ten key outcomes that follow with the applicable SDLC stage from the word bank.

Word Bank:

planning	testing
analysis	implementation
design	maintenance
development	

Ten key outcomes:

1. Translating the design specifications into computer code
2. Preparing a blueprint of technical system specifications
3. Assessing whether the computer coding will produce the expected results
4. Making the system available to users
5. Specifying the business problem that needs a solution
6. Gathering information to determine the specific requirements that the new system must satisfy
7. Detecting errors or bugs in the computer code
8. Determining whether the project is financially feasible
9. Specifying system inputs, outputs, and user interfaces
10. Updating the system for changes in business conditions

A4. (LO 2) Critical Thinking You are a newly hired member of an internal audit department that uses Agile methodology to manage audit engagements. During each audit engagement, team members are assigned a specific role and responsibilities. Match each individual with their appropriate Agile scrum role.

Agile roles:

A. Business stakeholder
B. Product owner
C. Scrum master
D. Core team member

Individuals:

1. Champion of the audit who ensures that the audit project is completed and communication with business stakeholders is facilitated
2. Manager in the business who oversees the part of the company currently being audited
3. Motivational leader who ensures that the audit team is focused on Agile principles
4. Staff auditor who executes audit tasks and manages his or her own timelines and responsibilities

A5. (LO 2) Critical Thinking You are a core development team member on a mobile payment application development project at Reliant, Inc. You are currently on a video call with Rachael, another developer from your team, discussing the next steps for the project. Rachael is concerned that the client isn't happy with the current state of the project. Fill in the following conversation with the appropriate Agile terms from the word bank.

Word Bank:

sprint	product increment
timebox	product backlog
product owner	Agile principles
scope creep	

Rachael: Did you hear that the client wants us to change the layout on the login page? We finished that weeks ago. They should have said something when they saw that _____.

You: That is true. But John, our _____, is meeting with them tomorrow. He knows we need to continue to _____ our work and focus on the essential parts of the app.

Rachael: Yeah, changing layouts isn't essential. John should add that to the _____. We can work on that during the next _____ if we have time.

You: Exactly. Otherwise, we are going to miss our deadlines due to _____. John wouldn't let that happen. That is not part of our _____.

A6. (LO 2) You are a financial analyst working for a dynamic young company. One of the founders asks you for your opinion on using an Agile versus Waterfall project management approach for systems development and asks you to contrast the two for each of the following project attributes. Label each of the following descriptions with the correct project attribute from the word bank. Identify whether each description applies to Agile or Waterfall.

Word Bank:

stages	metrics for progress
goal	metrics for success
scope	availability of working product or system
schedule and budget	

1. Set, based on predefined scope of project
2. Create a bare-bones application or system that performs at a minimal level and then iterate to improve it
3. Measured against the project plan and well documented
4. Measured by whether the project delivery is on time, within budget, and to scope
5. Well defined prior to starting development
6. More flexible in that it can be set or based on feedback from each iteration
7. Typically not available until at least the testing stage
8. Linear and inflexible, with each stage of the project completed before the next stage begins

9. Normally available in early phases of the project

10. Measured by whether the project meets end-user requirements

11. Create a completed application or system

12. Iterative and flexible, with the ability to move forward and backward across stages if necessary

13. Measured against a minimal level of performance with minimal documentation

14. Undefined prior to starting with development

A7. (LO 3) Research Choose one of the following popular database management systems: Oracle, SQL Server, MongoDB, or Amazon DynamoDB. Use the internet to research and answer the following questions:

1. What type of database(s) does the DBMS support?

2. Does it support structured data, unstructured data, or both?

3. Does the DBMS primarily use SQL or a different querying or programming language?

4. For the DBMS you chose, are there clear answers to these questions, or are the answers difficult to find?

5. How do you think the answer to question 4 affects a business's decision to adopt a DBMS?

Traditional General Journal Entries					
			Account	Dr.	Cr.
1.	7/1/202X	Cash	1001	5,000	
		Accounts Receivable	1004	70,000	
		Sales	4001		75,000
		Credit sale with down payment			
2.	7/1/202X	Cost of goods sold	5001	40,000	
		Inventory	1030		40,000
		Cost of goods sold			
3.	7/2/202X	Accounts Payable	2001	8,000	
		Cash	1001		8,000
		Payment of invoice			

A8. (LO 3–4) Jerilee's team is working on a sales systems development project using the Waterfall approach and is currently at the systems analysis stage. The team meets with the system's end users in the accounting department to discuss how the data captured by the system should be stored. The accounting team provides multiple scenarios of ways the system will be used and explains the key data points the system needs to collect for their department.

Jerilee decides to categorize the data into the following tables:

Customer_Order   Pizza

Order_Details   Customer

Help Jerilee place each of the following field names in one of these four tables and identify the primary and foreign keys for each table.

Customer_ID	Customer_Name
Order_No	Order_Date
Pizza_Name	Total_Price
Customer_Phone	Unit_Price
Pizza_Code	Pizza_Code
Ordered_Qty	Customer_Address

A9. (LO 4) Data Foundations Critical Thinking You are a new accounting graduate, and this is your first week as a new hire at a large CPA firm in Atlanta. This week is dedicated to orientation and training for new employees. Your next training session is about the fundamentals of systems design and databases. The senior partner conducting this session is Ms. Lupita Schmidt. She walks into the room, and introductions follow. She explains that every one of you will be dealing with databases throughout your careers at the firm, regardless of area of specialization.

The new hires in this session, all accounting graduates except one from information systems, have a wide range of exposure to databases, from hardly any to advanced database courses. Ms. Schmidt wants to get a baseline of each employee's knowledge before proceeding, and she also wants to present a challenge to the new hires to test their critical-thinking skills. She provides everyone with a simple general journal with three entries. She says: "This is not a team project, so each of you must come up with your own input for the class discussion after the break. I will give you hints on how to proceed by providing you with the business rules—a topic we just discussed."

Ms. Schmidt provides you with the following business rules for this stage of the analysis:

- The journal entry number will reset to 1 at the beginning of the next fiscal year.

- For each journal entry resulting from an accounting transaction, the total of the debits must equal the total of the credits.

- The account number from the chart of accounts can't be used more than once for a single journal entry.

1. Transform the general journal given on previous page into a single, two-dimensional, flat-file table with no empty cells and only one value in each cell. Abbreviate the explanations so that they fit neatly in each cell in the explanation column. Call this flat file of similar records Table 1.

2. Identify the combination of columns that together uniquely identify a row in Table 1, assuming that Table 1 is expanded to include all transactions over two fiscal years. Explain your choice.

3. Break down the data into logical, smaller, more manageable units to simplify the organization of data for relational database purposes. Do this by dividing your Table 1 into three tables (Tables A, B, and C), assuming the following additional business rules:

- No attribute in a column must be dependent on only a portion of the unique identifier for a row. Each attribute must be dependent on the entire identifier in your new tables.
- The value of an attribute cannot be deduced from the value of another attribute. Hint: Collapse two columns into one to resolve this issue.

Invoice Number	Date	Customer ID	Customer Name	Inventory ID	Inventory Name	Qty	Unit Price
345	6/3/20XX	567	A Corp	567835CT	Micro Chip Axl	1000	125
345	6/3/20XX	567	A Corp	489352AZ	Circuit Board 221-L	200	48
345	6/3/20XX	567	A Corp	156783MI	Circuit Board 224-M	500	64
346	6/12/20XX	467	Z Inc	567835CT	Micro Chip Axl	1200	125
347	6 13/20XX	239	M Corp	913784ME	Graphics Card VXG2	600	20
347	6/13/20XX	239	M Corp	489352AZ	Circuit Board 221-L	120	48

A10. (LO 4) `Data Foundations` `Critical Thinking` As an intern at a CPA firm, you are assisting the database design team in the creation of a new relational database to house sales data for a new client. A customer orders products. Upon delivery and acceptance of the products by the customer, revenue recognition takes place. The customer is immediately billed, and an invoice is generated and sent to the customer. Each invoice includes the customer's ID and key information related to the sale.

You have been provided the table shown above, which contains data related to the sales but is not in the correct database form. Complete the following steps to transform this table into relational database format.

Limit your answer to the attributes given in the table above. In a real-life situation, there will be other attributes of interest (customer address, inventory unit cost, quantity on hand, etc.), but disregard these for purposes of this assignment.

1. Write the business rules related to one of the following business events: "Deliver goods to customer" or "Sell goods to customer."

2. Divide the table into multiple tables, each containing data related to only one part of the business event. (The nouns in your business rules are a good source for table names.)

3. Transform your tables into a physical ERD, including relationships and cardinalities, and label the primary and foreign keys.

A11. (LO 4) Archer Solutions needs to store the following data about customers and sales in a relational database:

Product ID	Customer name
Order date	Customer phone
Customer ID	Selling price (per unit)
Customer address	Quantity sold

Purchase order number	Salesperson name
Product description	Salesperson commission
Salesperson ID	rate

You are an intern at a local CPA firm. You have been asked by your supervisor to draw a physical ERD for Archer Solutions to illustrate relationships and field names for these tables in a relational database. You must also identify the primary keys and foreign keys that relate the tables. You may add additional field names, as necessary. For example, salesperson would have a first name and a last name.

A12. (LO 5) `Early Career` `Critical Thinking` You are a first-year external auditor at a Big Four public accounting firm. You have just received data from your client, and the systems administrator included a screenshot of the SQL code she wrote to extract the data you requested. Review the provided SQL statements and determine whether each of the following requests was executed correctly.

1. All fields where an employee is currently active and was hired after 2021:

    SELECT * FROM Employee WHERE Status = 'Active' AND HiredYear > '2021'

2. All fields where an employee is a salaried employee and not an hourly employee or a contractor:

    SELECT * FROM Employee WHERE EmploymentType <> 'Salary'

3. All fields where employees scored a 1 or 2 on their performance review:

    SELECT FirstName, LastName FROM Employee WHERE PerformanceScore < '3'

A13. (LO 5) `Fraud` `Early Career` `Critical Thinking`
You are an external auditor performing a fraud analytics test analyzing expenses employees have submitted for the company to reimburse. You are currently joining the expense report table (Table A) with the employee table (Table B) to identify the job titles of employees and compare that to the type of purchases they submitted in their expense reports.

What type of join combines Table A with Table B and gives Table C as the result?

TABLE A Expense Report Data

Employee ID	Expense Report Date	Expense Report Name
E0013925	9/20/202X	Software Subscriptions
E0013925	10/21/202X	Software Subscriptions
E0058291	9/28/202X	College Recruiting Event
E0513950	10/15/202X	Inventory Trip
E0285011	10/06/202X	Warehouse Parts

TABLE B Employee Data

Employee ID	First Name	Last Name	Hire Date	Job Title
E0013925	James	Addison	6/1/202X	Sr. Analyst
E0250682	Renee	Emerald	9/14/202X	Warehouse Manager
E0058291	Sawyer	Green	2/25/202X	Director of Human Resources
E0513950	Richard	Longhorn	5/12/202X	Staff Internal Auditor

TABLE C Joined Data

Employee ID	Expense Report Date	Expense Report Name	First Name	Last Name	Hire Date	Job Title
E0013925	9/20/202X	Software Subscriptions	James	Addison	6/1/202X	Sr. Analyst
E0013925	10/21/202X	Software Subscriptions	James	Addison	6/1/202X	Sr. Analyst
E0058291	9/28/202X	College Recruiting Event	Sawyer	Green	2/25/202X	Director of Human Resources
E0513950	10/15/202X	Inventory Trip	Richard	Longhorn	5/12/202X	Staff Internal Auditor
E0285011	10/06/202X	Warehouse Parts				

A14. (LO 5) `Critical Thinking` Using the data in the spreadsheet below, fill in the blanks in the following SQL statements to address each request.

Requests:

1. The first and last names of all executive employees:

   _____ First_Name, Last_Name _____
   Employee _____ Department _____
   'Executive'

2. The first name, last name, and annual salary of all employees who work for Kelly Arnold:

   _____ First_Name, Last_Name, _____
   FROM Employee _____ Manager _____
   '_____'

3. The first name, last name, and job title of all employees who make more than $100,000 per year:

   _____ _____, _____, Job_Title
   _____ Employee _____ _____ >
   _____

	A	B	C	D	E	F	G
1	First_Name	Last_Name	Job_Title	Manager	Department	Monthly_Salary	Annual_Salary
2	Harold	Austin	Chief Financial Officer	Lawrence Cheville	Executive	23,333	280,000
3	Lyra	Chen	Administrative Vice President	Lawrence Cheville	Executive	17,000	204,000
4	Bernard	Lorentz	Programmer	Justine Levvy	IT	6,000	72,000
5	Austin	Greenberg	Programmer	Justine Levvy	IT	8,750	105,000
6	Sarah	Kochran	Programmer	Justine Levvy	IT	7,167	86,000
7	Kelly	Arnold	Finance Manager	Nina Kelly	Finance	12,000	144,000
8	Prya	Argentine	Accountant	Kelly Arnold	Finance	9,000	108,000
9	Zach	Moonfield	Accountant	Kelly Arnold	Finance	7,833	94,000

Tableau Case: Julia's Cookies' IT Help Desk Employee Insights

What You Need

Download Tableau to your computer. You can access www.tableau.com/academic/students to download your free Tableau license for the year, or you can download it from your university's software offerings.

Download the following file from the book's product page on www.wiley.com:

Chapter 6 Raw Data.xlsx

Case Background

Big Picture:

Identify help desk employee patterns.

Detail:

Why is this data important, and what questions or problems need to be addressed?

- IT help desk information helps the company monitor underlying problems that need to be addressed within systems. This information is useful to the ERM team, Internal Audit department, and management, as recurring technology issues can indicate failing internal controls or unmitigated risks.
- The data generated by the IT help desk offers more insight when it is combined with another data source, such as the human resources file. Enriching the help desk data set through a join of the human resources data will allow management to monitor which departments' employees are submitting a larger number of tickets than employees in other departments, which may indicate a need for retraining.
- To identify help desk employee patterns, we should consider the following questions: Which office location had the most help desk tickets? Which department had the highest help tickets per employee ratio? Which department had the lowest requestor overall satisfaction score?

Plan:

What data is needed, and how should it be analyzed?

- The necessary data is extracted from the central ticketing management system, which for Julia's Cookies is ServiceNow.
- To ensure an appropriate amount of data is available to identify patterns, we use data covering a period of eight months: 3/1/202X through 10/31/202X.
- The second data set is a human resource set of all active employees.

Now it's your turn to evaluate, analyze, and communicate the results!

Hint: Connect the data using a left join as follows:

Questions

1. What percentage of tickets submitted belonged to the "Main Campus—Chicago" location?
2. Which employee type submitted a total percentage of 0.08% of all tickets during this time period?
3. Which department had the lowest number of tickets submitted related to login issues? (Hint: Issue category "Access/Login.")
4. How many tickets were submitted by employees with less than two years' tenure?
5. What percentage of employees in the Finance department are dissatisfied with the help desk?
6. How many "medium severity" tickets were submitted by employees in the Investments department?
7. On what date did employees in the Marketing department submit the most help desk tickets?
8. How many of the currently open tickets were submitted by employees in the Accounting department?

Take it to the next level!

9. Which department has the lowest help tickets per employee ratio?
10. Which department has a 3.0 ratio of help tickets per employee?

CHAPTER 7

Emerging and Disruptive Technologies

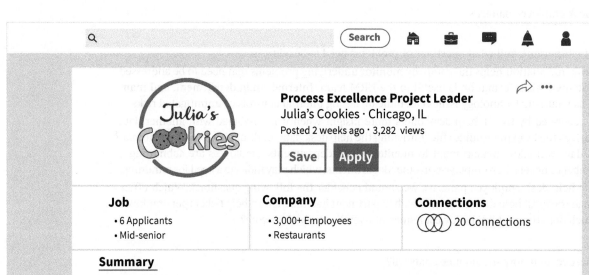

Process Excellence Project Leader
Julia's Cookies · Chicago, IL
Posted 2 weeks ago · 3,282 views

[Save] [Apply]

Job	Company	Connections
• 6 Applicants	• 3,000+ Employees	◯◯ 20 Connections
• Mid-senior	• Restaurants	

Summary

Julia's Cookies is looking for a process excellence project leader to work on the Finance Innovation and Transformation team, which helps finance leaders move away from traditional, mostly manual transactional processes to a predictive and proactive mindset. This team reports to the corporate controller and is composed of integrated competency centers that drive value realization, including Business Process Optimization, Data Analytics, and the Automation Center of Excellence. These centers form a digital hub and work cross-functionally with business partners.

This role is responsible for leading projects that capture existing business processes, identifying opportunities for improvement, proposing improvements, and aligning projects with leadership objectives.

Responsibilities

- Perform process analysis to evaluate enhancement and automation opportunities
- Use knowledge of current and emerging technologies to eliminate waste and variability in business processes
- Capture customer business requirements
- Translate requirements into functional specifications for programmers
- Build trust and maintain cross-functional relationships by being well informed about business initiatives, system implementations, and organizational changes

Requirements

- Preferred Education: Master's degree in accounting, finance, or information systems
- Minimum Experience: Minimum of five years in accounting and/or business analysis

Preferred Knowledge and Skills

The ideal candidate will demonstrate experience in:

- Business process reengineering and continuous improvement
- Implementation of financial processes and systems

Salary: $130,000–145,000

CHAPTER PREVIEW   Companies rely on historical and external information to perform risk assessments. Research, combined with the expertise and personal experience of company team members, helps enterprise risk management professionals make reliable decisions about various technologies and their associated risks.

The problem is that historical information, experience, and data don't exist for new technology. Companies that adopt a technology before their competitors are often the test subjects for everything that could go wrong. But new technologies can bring great opportunities. Being the first to implement a new technology can put a company at the forefront of its industry and ahead of its more cautious competitors. Since new technology often focuses on helping employees work smarter and be more productive, it can enable employees like accounting professionals to dedicate more time to strategic, innovative new projects.

New technologies that become successful can disrupt the way businesses operate. While it's impossible to predict which new technologies will be successful, companies should be aware of emerging technology trends that have potential to impact their industries.

This chapter introduces you to new technologies that are currently entering the market or that are disrupting the old way of doing things:

- What is the difference between emerging and disruptive technology?
- Which technology innovations are currently disrupting businesses?
- How can robotic process automation increase efficiency in business processes?
- What are the fundamentals of blockchain?
- How is blockchain influencing the accounting profession?

Businesses address the unknown impacts of these technologies by hiring specialists like the process excellence project leader at Julia's Cookies. This role is based on a real position at a global home improvement chain's corporate office. ■

Chapter Roadmap

LEARNING OBJECTIVES	TOPICS	JULIA'S COOKIES APPLIED LEARNING
7.1 Explain how businesses identify risks and opportunities associated with emerging and disruptive technologies.	• Differentiating Emerging and Disruptive Technologies • Risk and Risk Mitigation	New Technology Risks: Case for Hiring Specialists
7.2 Identify business opportunities provided by disruptive technologies.	• Internet of Things (IoT) • Extended Reality (XR) • Gamification • Autonomous Things (AuT)	Disruptive Technology: Prioritizing New Technology Projects
7.3 Apply the principles of robotic process automation (RPA) to accounting use cases.	• Types of Automation • Logic Behind RPA • Accounting Use Cases • Creating Efficiencies and Opportunities	RPA Use Cases: Accounting Feasibility Analysis
7.4 Identify the fundamental principles and technologies of blockchain.	• The Basics of Blockchain • Cryptology • Blockchain Ledgers • Fundamental Principles of Blockchain Technology • Types of Blockchain Systems	Blockchain: Business Feasibility
7.5 Explain blockchain's relevance to accounting professionals.	• Evolving Career Opportunities • Improving Data Quality	Blockchain: Contaminated Raw Materials

CPA You will find the CPA tag throughout the chapter to call out any important topics you may see on the CPA exam.

7.1 How Do Companies Approach Emerging and Disruptive Technologies?

Learning Objective ❶
Explain how businesses identify risks and opportunities associated with emerging and disruptive technologies.

Technology changes the world all the time, and innovations and new capabilities are invented regularly. With information widely available on the internet, including free classes, we have access to knowledge that once required hours in a library to discover. Technology has significantly disrupted education in recent years. Online classes make education possible for those who work full time or don't live near institutions of higher learning. You may be reading this material in a digital textbook or an online course—two options that are changing how professors teach and making education accessible to more people. Businesses, like professors, must consider technological advances in relation to:

- Disruption of business activities and operations versus the potential for increased efficiencies and competitive advantage
- Identification of risks associated with the technology and integrating it into the existing control environment

Companies rely on accounting professionals to be trusted advisors when making decisions about implementing new technologies and identifying the associated risks and internal controls. A key consideration for a company adopting a new technology is where that technology is in its life cycle. **Illustration 7.1** shows the **Rogers Adoption Curve**, which explains the five stages of technology adoption.[1]

As you continue through this chapter, consider examples of real companies as innovators, early adopters, early majority, late majority, or laggards.

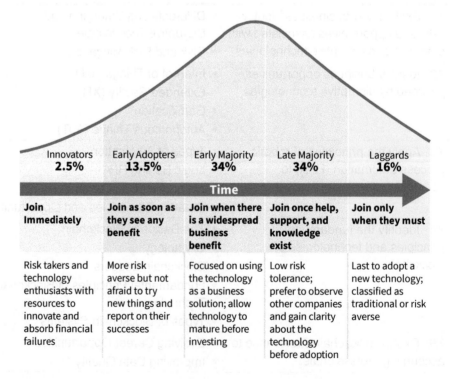

Innovators 2.5%	Early Adopters 13.5%	Early Majority 34%	Late Majority 34%	Laggards 16%
Join Immediately	**Join as soon as they see any benefit**	**Join when there is a widespread business benefit**	**Join once help, support, and knowledge exist**	**Join only when they must**
Risk takers and technology enthusiasts with resources to innovate and absorb financial failures	More risk averse but not afraid to try new things and report on their successes	Focused on using the technology as a business solution; allow technology to mature before investing	Low risk tolerance; prefer to observe other companies and gain clarity about the technology before adoption	Last to adopt a new technology; classified as traditional or risk averse

Illustration 7.1 The Rogers Adoption Curve shows the percentage of businesses that fall in each technology adoption category.

[1]Rogers, E. M. 2003. *Diffusion of innovations*, 5th ed. New York: Free Press of Glencoe.

Differentiating Emerging and Disruptive Technologies

New technology can be described as either emerging or disruptive:

- **CPA** When a new technology enters the market but is not yet regularly used by companies, it is called an **emerging technology.**

- As emerging technologies continue through their life cycles, they will either fail—and not be widely adopted—or become widely used. **CPA** As more companies adopt an innovation, it becomes a **disruptive technology,** which changes the way businesses function. Disruptive technologies force companies to adapt their operations to stay competitive.

Over time, successful technology goes from emerging to disruptive and then to widely used (**Illustration 7.2**).

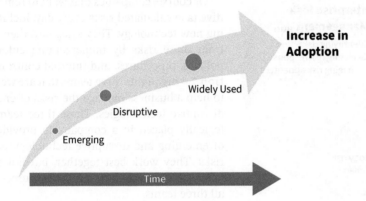

Increase in Adoption

Widely Used

Disruptive

Emerging

Time

Illustration 7.2   Successful new technologies start as emerging, move to disruptive, and then become widely used.

Not every emerging technology becomes disruptive, as not all technologies are successful. Google Glass, a hands-free device released in 2014, is a pair of smart glasses that brings smartphone contents to your eyes and allows you to interact with it via voice commands. Google expected it to disrupt the consumer smart device industry. After a few years of privacy concerns (such as concerns about the device's cameras capturing people around the user without consent) and customer pushback, Google stopped supporting updates for the consumer version of the device in 2019. In 2020, Amazon released its Echo Frames to the general public. These smart glasses connect to your Amazon Alexa but don't project your phone's contents to the glasses. The initial reception has been mixed, and only time will tell if Amazon can succeed where Google did not.

Netflix provides an example of an innovation that gained market share and went on to be widely adopted. Netflix was originally a DVD rental company that sent movies to customers through the mail. Already successful at disrupting the DVD rental operating model, Netflix next began investing in an emerging technology: video streaming. Over time, customers stopped going to brick-and-mortar rental stores like Blockbuster to rent movies, ordering physical DVDs from Netflix, or even owning a DVD player. Did you know Blockbuster had the opportunity to *purchase* Netflix early on? The risk-averse decision not to invest in Netflix has left Blockbuster a relic in the memory of its previous clientele.

As Netflix's popularity grew, other businesses had to adopt streaming technology to ensure that they weren't left behind. Currently, streaming is widely adopted and has evolved from an emerging technology to a disruptive technology. Even Netflix's own operations were disrupted, and it retired its DVD rental service and migrated to a fully online streaming platform.

Risk and Risk Mitigation

While emerging and disruptive technologies can increase efficiency and make tasks easier, they also bring unpredictable risk to the business. The earlier the stage of adoption, the higher the risk because unknown variables and a lack of history mean that companies can't rely on past experiences to perform risk assessments.

Illustration 7.3 Risks related to new technologies include business disruptions, financial loss, security vulnerabilities, and regulatory risks.

Business disruptions
due to integration issues with existing systems

Financial losses
from investments if the technology fails

Security vulnerabilities
due to unknown variables in the technology

Regulatory risks
due to new or unrefined regulatory requirements

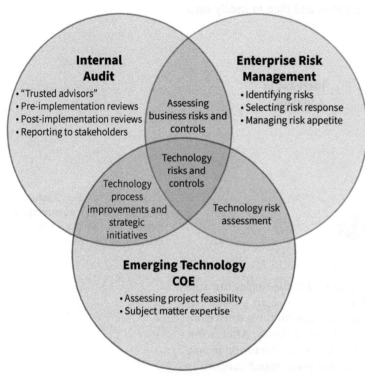

Illustration 7.4 Internal audit, enterprise risk management, and an emerging technology COE support one another in the oversight of technology risks and controls.

There are several risks related to emerging and disruptive technology (**Illustration 7.3**).

Of course, companies that want to remain competitive take calculated risks every day, including adopting new technology. They safeguard their businesses from these risks by implementing enterprise-wide policies, procedures, and internal controls. **Illustration 7.4** highlights three teams that are well equipped to help a business manage the risks of emerging and disruptive technologies. These three teams are strategically placed in a company to provide oversight of emerging and disruptive technology projects and risks. They work best together, but not every company is large enough or has the resources to support all three teams.

Internal Audit

While not every company will have a dedicated enterprise risk management (ERM) or emerging technology team, many have an internal audit department. Since internal auditors have unique insight into all areas of the business, they can brainstorm to identify risks from the implementation of emerging technologies and their integration with existing systems.

When auditing emerging technologies, internal auditors should:

- Understand which emerging and disruptive technologies are being used
- Identify how these technologies can disrupt current processes
- Remain professionally skeptical about management's risk assessments
- Assess how these technologies will impact current controls
- Identify control gaps and recommend new controls management can implement

Internal audit can be involved in a pre-implementation review before a new technology is adopted, in a post-implementation review after a technology is adopted, or even throughout an entire project, from planning through the system going live. It's best practice for the internal audit team to be involved as early as possible because it's easier to address control gaps during implementation, which is when system settings and processes are put into place, than to add new controls after the technology is already operational.

Why Does It Matter to Your Career?

Thoughts from an Accounting Manager, Financial Services

- Emerging technologies aren't just hype. They are changing how accountants perform their jobs. Understanding these technologies is important—especially when it comes to how they relate to data creation in your company. For example, if your company uses chatbots for conversing with customers, that is a new area of data your company can leverage for analysis and a new area of data your company needs to protect.

- Technology will only continue to move forward, so you must embrace it, understand it, and become a key partner in decision making for emerging technology implementation.

Enterprise Risk Management Team

The ERM team formally defines the company's risk appetite and assesses the risk of emerging technology using the company's risk strategy. This team is in a strategic position to focus on emerging and disruptive technology risks because of its members' expertise in risk assessment and management.

Recall that formal risk assessments identify, categorize, and prioritize risks to provide input into the company's strategic planning, while enterprise risk management is the comprehensive process of planning, organizing, and managing these risks.

The ERM team works with the information technology (IT) department to strategize and approve emerging technologies the company wants to implement.

To understand how an ERM team is involved with emerging and disruptive technologies, let's look at Julia's Cookies. The IT department wants to implement facial recognition software that detects employees coming into the office building to replace the current practice of using a physical badge for access. Access will be granted to employees when their faces are "recognized," or invisibly scanned, at the entrance.

During the risk assessment of this software, the ERM team performs a risk analysis of facial recognition software to determine if the value it brings is worth the risk. The team communicates its list of benefits and risks to the Internal Audit team at Julia's Cookies. Internal Audit agrees with the benefits and risks identified by ERM and adds one additional risk (**Table 7.1**).

TABLE 7.1 Risk Analysis for Biometric Authentication

	Benefits	Risks
ERM team	• Simplified process for employees • Increased security of facilities • Reduced workload on facilities for badge creation and replacement	• Employees may be resistant to change. • The cost of installing facial recognition scanners may be high.
Internal Audit	*Agrees with ERM team's assessments*	• Biometric data from facial scans is subject to regulatory privacy requirements that the company is not currently implementing.

After considering Internal Audit's feedback on regulatory requirements, the ERM team members go into action:

- They review the regulatory requirements for storing this data and determine the cost of implementing this new technology while complying with regulatory standards.
- They meet with key stakeholders in the IT department, and together they determine that facial recognition software is worth adopting because the benefits outweigh the costs.

Next, the ERM team and Internal Audit work closely with the team responsible for implementing this new technology to ensure the proper design and integration of controls into the new system.

Emerging Technology Center of Excellence

A **center of excellence (COE)** is a specialized team in a company that is dedicated to providing unique support, usually technological, to the entire business. The primary objective of an **emerging technology COE** is to evaluate emerging and disruptive technologies to see how they may fit into current operations. Even if a company isn't an innovator or early adopter, it should monitor technology trends and competitors that are taking these risks.

Emerging technology COEs identify the most impactful technologies for their companies and provide resources and strategies to adopt particular technologies. In addition, they report on the risks and the trade-offs of adopting a new technology.

Emerging technology COEs also review existing technology in a company to determine what new technologies may already be in use outside of the internal control environment. For example, a team may have an employee who is skilled in coding advanced technologies that have automated processes without ERM team or IT department knowledge. Stand-alone innovations like this may appear attractive and provide value to the business, but it is essential that technology adoption be under the umbrella of the IT department's internal control structure.

Emerging technology COEs meet with business leadership and stakeholders to understand existing technology and oversee implementation of emerging and disruptive technology projects. Emerging technology COEs provide an interesting career path for accounting professionals with an interest in innovative technologies.

Some companies may not have emerging technology COEs because their size, risk appetite, or technology use doesn't merit a dedicated team. At Julia's Cookies, Internal Audit and the ERM team work together to oversee technology risk. Help the company decide if it should take the step of forming a dedicated emerging technology COE in Applied Learning 7.1.

Julia's Cookies	Applied Learning 7.1

New Technology Risks: Case for Hiring Specialists

Recently, multiple departments at Julia's Cookies have tried to simplify their business processes. As a result, new technology has been appearing throughout the company regularly. While the new systems and tools are improving efficiencies, there are some risks involved:

- There is no oversight or corporate governance that prescribes how these systems are built and what technology is used.
- The company does not have a formal review process to ensure that these tools have been designed accurately and meet company security standards.

Julia's Cookies' ERM team knew that using new technology to simplify processes was trending in the industry, but it didn't consider the risks that would occur should the practice be adopted within the company.

What should Julia's Cookies do to prevent this kind of widespread risk in the future?

SOLUTION

Due to the recurring technology advances at Julia's Cookies, the ERM team should consider whether it is worth the investment required to create a dedicated Emerging Technology COE. Its Emerging Technology COE could research and plan for these kinds of technology risks before they impact the business and provide valuable insight on technology risks, both existing and potential, during the enterprise risk assessment.

CONCEPT REVIEW QUESTIONS

1. What are the stages in the Rogers Adoption Curve?

   Ans. The five stages are Innovators, Early Adopters, Early Majority, Late Majority, and Laggards.

2. **CPA** What is an emerging technology?

   Ans. When a new technology enters the market but is not yet regularly used by companies, it is called an emerging technology. As emerging technologies continue through their life cycles, they will either fail and not be widely adopted or become widely used.

3. **CPA** What is a disruptive technology?
   Ans. As more companies adopt an innovation, it becomes a disruptive technology that changes how businesses function. Disruptive technologies force companies to adapt their operations to stay competitive. For example, Netflix's adoption of streaming technology.

4. List the three teams that mitigate risks of emerging and disruptive technologies in a company.
   Ans. The internal audit team, the enterprise risk management team, and the emerging technology center of excellence (COE) support one another in the oversight of technology risks and controls.

5. What are the objectives of a center of excellence (COE)?
   Ans. COE is a specialized team in a company that is dedicated to providing unique support, usually technological, to the entire business. The primary objective of an emerging technology COE is to evaluate emerging and disruptive technologies to see how they may fit into current operations. Even if a company is not an innovator or early adopter, it should monitor technology trends and competitors that are taking these risks.

7.2 How Do Disruptive Technologies Provide Business Opportunities?

Learning Objective ❷
Identify business opportunities provided by disruptive technologies.

Awareness of emerging and disruptive technologies, even at a conceptual level, is important because these technologies directly impact the way businesses—and the accounting profession—operate, which in turn impacts business processes and the controls over those processes. This chapter covers six disruptive technologies that every accounting professional should be aware of. We cover four of them at a high level in this section. The rest of the chapter is dedicated to a closer look at the final two.

As you explore each of these technologies, consider where you have seen them in your own life. Have you encountered a smart fridge or earned a LinkedIn badge? Have you played Pokémon GO? For consumers, such technologies seem exciting and new, but for companies, new technologies cause disruptions to business processes and create an ever-evolving risk environment.

Internet of Things (IoT)

CPA The **Internet of Things (IoT)** is a collection of electronic devices (the "things") connected to the internet through sensors, software, and other technologies. The IoT is designed to monitor and control devices while extracting the data each device generates. Most physical items can be transformed into IoT devices. For example, smart light bulbs like the Philips Hue connect to the internet and are controllable via an app on your phone. These light bulbs can be programmed with automated decision statements that create a smart home environment.

The IoT has two distinct business impacts, which are business opportunities provided by:

- IoT products that are consumer facing
- IoT products used in business operations

Many companies sell IoT products and services to their customers. For example, the home appliance industry offers smart refrigerators, dishwashers, washers and dryers, and more. Having a sensor in a smart refrigerator adds value to homeowners in several ways:

- Immediately alerting the consumer if the refrigerator stops working
- Sending push notifications if the door is ajar
- Allowing consumers to adjust internal temperature from their phones
- Creating an inventory of items updated in real time to generate shopping lists

CPA The data generated by these activities creates business opportunities in both customer-facing products and products used during the course of business operations. Explore more examples of IoT uses and the business opportunities these products create in **Table 7.2**.

TABLE 7.2 Internet of Things Products and Business Opportunities

Consumer-Facing IoT Products	Business Opportunities
Appliances Examples: Refrigerators, washers and dryers, light bulbs	Manufacturers leveraging big data collected from consumer IoT products to: • Design new products • Create marketing opportunities
Vehicles Examples: Sensors monitoring activities in personal vehicles	Insurance industry monitoring driver activity to: • Determine safe driver discounts • Reward safe driving behaviors
IoT wearables Examples: Fitbit, Apple Watch	Life insurance companies using big data collected from wearables to: • Monitor heart rate, calorie burn, sleep quality, and more • Estimate an individual's longevity to calculate a premium for that individual's lifestyle
Business Operations IoT Products	Business Opportunities
Appliances Examples: Manufacturing machinery, safety equipment	Using sensors and big data to: • Predict machinery downtime • Monitor production efficiencies and capacity • Send alerts when storage tanks are full or when safety equipment needs maintenance
Vehicles Examples: Sensors monitoring activities in delivery trucks	Using sensors and big data on corporate vehicles to: • Optimize delivery routes and provide GPS tracking • Reduce errors • Alert when vehicles need maintenance • Fully monitor the supply chain, including delivery
IoT wearables Examples: Smart glasses, health trackers	Upgrading items employees already wear such as: • Manufacturing safety glasses that include sensors or extended reality • Using health trackers to monitor air quality and employee health metrics in high-risk jobs like mining

New technology, even when it is useful, always comes with risks and often creates public controversy. IoT is no exception. These devices create big data, which companies must store securely. Recall that the 5Vs of big data create unique risks (**Illustration 7.5**). From scalability to privacy, companies that use IoT must manage their big data appropriately.

CPA There has been some public pushback against consumer-facing IoT products, specifically due to privacy concerns. While it is fun for runners using wearable devices like a Fitbit to see if their pace is improving on their daily jogs, the collected data stores the GPS locations of users. An unauthorized individual could use this data to analyze the wearers' habits and identify opportunities for breaking into their homes while the runners are out exercising.

CPA It is important for you, as an accounting professional, to understand IoT devices, even if you don't plan on owning any of your own:

• Auditors need to know what data is available to perform analytic testing on data collected by an IoT device.

• Cybersecurity specialists must understand privacy regulations and risks around the sensitive data these devices collect.

Illustration 7.5 When using IoT products, companies must manage risks related to the 5Vs of big data.

- Managerial accountants may work with data from IoT devices in company operations like manufacturing machinery and should understand how that data is collected and used.

Despite mixed reactions from the public, IoT is gaining momentum and seeing adoption in both consumer-facing and business operations use cases.

Extended Reality (XR)

Experiencing extended, digitally crafted realities is not a new concept. However, recently this technology has found its way into affordable, accessible consumer devices, and companies are also finding creative ways to implement these technologies to enhance business operations. **CPA** **Extended reality (XR)** technology takes three forms, which progress from completely real to completely virtual (**Illustration 7.6**).

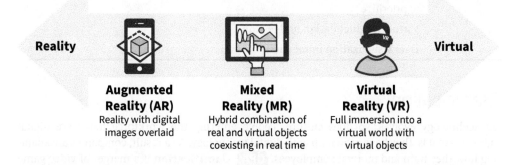

Illustration 7.6 Extended reality (XR) progresses from reality to AR, MR, and VR.

Mixed reality (MR), which is a hybrid, is newer on the market, and we focus on augmented reality (AR) and virtual reality (VR) in the following discussion. It is important to understand the differences between AR and VR (**Illustration 7.7**) before exploring the use cases and opportunities.

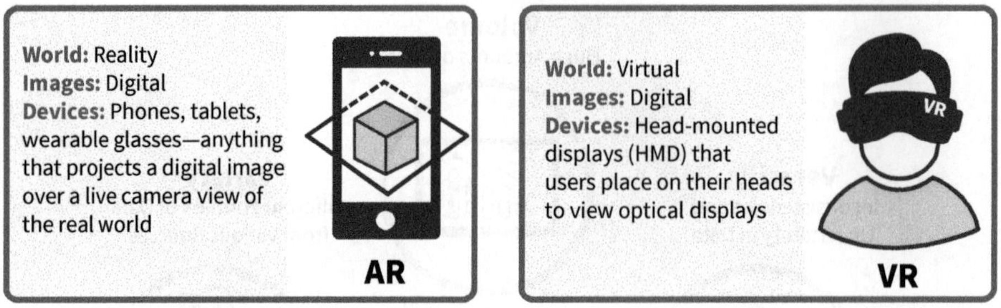

World: Reality
Images: Digital
Devices: Phones, tablets, wearable glasses—anything that projects a digital image over a live camera view of the real world

AR

World: Virtual
Images: Digital
Devices: Head-mounted displays (HMD) that users place on their heads to view optical displays

VR

Illustration 7.7 AR and VR differ in world, images, and devices.

From consumer-facing AR products like devices that project a digital image of a furniture store product into the user's home to business operations using VR to simulate on-the-job training, companies are implementing XR technologies for a variety of uses (**Table 7.3**).

TABLE 7.3 Extended Reality Technologies and Business Opportunities

XR Technology	Business Opportunities
Augmented reality (consumer facing) Examples: Pokémon GO, shopping AR environments that project a product into consumers' homes, Snapchat filters	Pokémon GO collects personal data, including: • Calories likely burned during a play session • Distance traveled • Promotions engaged in • Location data, such as place of work or restaurants visited All of this data can be used for marketing, future product design, and other consumer-metric-driven analysis.
Augmented reality (business operations)	Businesses may provide employees with wearable glasses, phones, or tablets that can: • Create training environments that partially immerse the employee in a scenario • Project information onto an existing product or machine in manufacturing • Support product design by displaying prototypes in reality
Virtual reality (consumer facing)	VR users can sail down the canals of Venice or physically fight the Joker while defending Gotham City, and while they do, the HMD manufacturers and video game companies collect their usage data.
Virtual reality (business operations)	Business are using VR for: • Training employees—one of the most popular business uses of VR to date—to respond to cyberattacks, security threats, and other situations that are hard to replicate in reality • Tracking customers' gazes in retail stores to determine areas of retail displays to prioritize • Virtual product design and testing • Data visualization immersion

Gamification

As technology evolves, so does culture. People entering the workforce today are digital natives—that is, they have grown up with digital technology. As a result, companies are adapting how they train and motivate employees. **CPA** **Gamification** is a merger of video game principles and real-world simulations in which users earn badges and points while they learn new skills they might need on the job. Gamification can be a low-key badge-earning system, as when a public accounting firm awards employees badges and points for engaging in health and wellness activities. Gamification can also be complex, as when gamification principles are combined with VR and HMDs to create job simulations (**Table 7.4**).

TABLE 7.4 Gamification Techniques and Business Opportunities

Gamification Technique	Business Opportunities
Badge achievements Example: LinkedIn badges	Promoting positive activities in the workplace by rewarding employees for: • Completing trainings • Engaging in health and wellness activities • Meeting milestones
Video game environments Example: VR training	Creating scenarios (virtual or real) for employees to engage in: • Executing daily tasks • Responding to high-stress scenarios • Earning points for completion

Why Does It Matter to Your Career?

Thoughts from an Audit Manager, Public Accounting

- All the examples in this section exist right now. The popularity of these technologies is only going to increase.
- The field of auditing is evolving. Auditors must learn ways to audit emerging and disruptive technologies that don't fit the traditional control environment that companies historically used. Auditors must be curious and flexible about learning and applying new auditing techniques. Companies are looking to new hires to lead these initiatives and to instill a culture of innovation and change in their teams.

Autonomous Things (AuT)

CPA **Autonomous things (AuT)** are physical devices controlled by computers using complex algorithms. Human interaction is required to establish the programming, but from there, these devices are self-regulating. The devices come in the form of drones and robots. As AuT becomes more widely adopted, you may encounter instances of AuT being either fully autonomous or semi-autonomous (**Table 7.5**).

TABLE 7.5 Autonomous Things Examples and Business Opportunities

Autonomous Things	Business Opportunities
Drones	Using autonomous or semi-autonomous robots to: • Monitor crops for weed contamination or nutrient deficiencies • Perform physical inventory counts or land measurements for an audit • Review safety regulation compliance at a construction site • Handle package delivery, such as Amazon's Prime Air
Robots	Using autonomous robots to: • Conduct security checks in a parking deck • Carry out manufacturing processes • Deliver medication in hospitals and room service to guests in hotels • Collaborate with humans to complete tasks (PwC calls these "cobots") • Handle warehouse fulfillment tasks such as fetching, monitoring inventory, packing, and inspecting

Performing a site survey for safety regulation can take an audit team two to three weeks using traditional methods, but drone imaging can decrease that time to only a few hours. PwC uses drone technology to audit coal reserves; the drones measure piles of coal to identify volume. These measurements have resulted in 99% accuracy.

Amazon provides several examples of robots in daily life. Not only is Amazon Prime Air taking to the sky, but Amazon Scout is now roaming the streets (**Illustration 7.8**). This friendly-looking miniature tank, which is actually a cooler, began roaming the streets of Snohomish County in Washington State during 2019. The fully autonomous robot delivers packages by moving along sidewalks at human walking speed. It navigates with a camera and many sensors and plans its route and navigation in real time using artificial intelligence. Amazon Scout is being piloted in multiple cities across the United States, and it is only a matter of time before Amazon rolls it out on a larger scale.

Top management at Julia's Cookies has made it a priority to consider new technologies that have potential for adding value at the company. Consider the scenario in Applied Learning 7.2.

Illustration 7.8 Amazon Scout is a small tank that drives on sidewalks at walking speed to make deliveries.

Julia's Cookies   Applied Learning 7.2

Disruptive Technology: Prioritizing New Technology Projects

Marianna, the director of IT Audit, is tasked with reviewing the emerging technologies list that she received from the Audit Committee. The Audit Committee wants her to name a potential business application for each of the emerging technologies and prioritize them so that Julia's Cookies knows which ones it should focus on adopting first and which ones it should monitor for potential future adoption.

Marianna added the following examples to each of the emerging technologies she was given. How do you think she should prioritize these items?

- Virtual reality: Creating virtual reality training for employees to help them learn what types of customers and situations they might encounter while working in the bakery
- Internet of Things: Connecting kitchen equipment and monitoring its condition based on sensors
- Autonomous things: Adding drones to the fleet of delivery vehicles so that a drone could deliver cookies in a shorter range and eliminate the need for a delivery driver in some cases

SOLUTION

There is no right or wrong answer here. Each of these three items could be prioritized for any of the following reasons. Many business decisions have no right or wrong answer, and companies can only make the decisions they feel are the *best* for them. Marianna and the Audit Committee will need to prioritize by considering the company's strategic goals and the costs of implementing each of the options.

Virtual reality: Many companies might benefit from creating helpful training simulations. This might have a smaller impact on a business than the other options, as it would typically affect only newly hired employees.

Internet of Things: Julia's Cookies is updating its kitchen equipment, and most equipment comes with smart technology already built in. This would be an expensive choice; however, it is doable, as the technology is now standard. Monitoring the kitchen equipment and other equipment in the store might result in efficiency gains or even mitigation of safety risks, such as alerting employees that something is wrong with an oven or that refrigerator doors were left open by accident, possibly leading to food spoilage.

Autonomous things: This is the most expensive of these emerging technologies, and it would require an expensive trial. It would cause the largest disruption for the company, as delivery drivers wouldn't be utilized as much, which would decrease the risk of drivers being in car accidents.

CONCEPT REVIEW QUESTIONS

1. **CPA** What is Internet of Things (IoT)? How does IoT create business opportunities?

Ans. IoT is a collection of electronic devices (the "things") connected to the internet through sensors, software, and other technologies. IoT is designed to monitor and control devices while extracting data that each device generates. The data generated by these activities creates business opportunities in both customer-facing products and products used during the course of business operations.

2. **CPA** Why should accounting professionals know about IoT devices?

Ans. Auditors need to know what data is available to perform analytic testing on data collected by an IoT device. Managerial accountants may work with data from IoT devices in company operations like manufacturing machinery and should understand how that data is collected and used.

3. **CPA** What are the three forms of extended reality (XR)?

Ans. Extended reality (XR) technology takes three forms: augmented reality, virtual reality, and mixed reality. Augmented reality uses digital images and uses phones, tablets, and wearable glasses to create business opportunities that may be consumer-facing or related to business operations. Virtual reality uses digital images and uses head-mounted displays (HMD) that users place on their heads to view optical displays to create business opportunities that may be consumer-facing or related to business operations. Mixed reality is a hybrid combination of real and virtual objects coexisting in real time.

4. **CPA** What is gamification?

Ans. Gamification is a merger of video game principles and real-world simulations in which users earn badges and points while they learn new skills they might need on the job. It can be a low-key badge-earning system, as when a public accounting firm awards employees badges and points for engaging in health and wellness activities. Gamification can also be complex, as when gamification principles are combined with VR and HMDs to create job simulations.

5. **CPA** Define autonomous things (AuT).

Ans. AuT are physical devices controlled by computers using complex algorithms. Human interaction is required to establish the programming, but from there, these devices are self-regulating. The devices come in the form of drones and robots.

7.3 How Does Robotic Process Automation (RPA) Benefit Accounting Professionals?

Learning Objective ❸
Apply the principles of robotic process automation (RPA) to accounting use cases.

For a century, computer science and engineering have looked to creating robots to perform human tasks. From a pair of robotic arms installing parts at an automobile manufacturing company, to robotic software downloading and analyzing journal entry data files, to artificial intelligence in a self-driving car, the capabilities of robotics are only limited by current technology and the risk appetite of consumers.

As an accounting professional, you may offer advice on improving the controls around robots or evaluating business processes performed more efficiently with robotics. If this area sparks your interest, consider that many accounting professionals have double-majored in computer science—or learned skills on the job—to help them pursue a more technical career path.

CPA Companies are implementing robotic process automation and artificial intelligence in **business process automation**, which is the process of managing information, data, costs, resources, and investments by increasing productivity through automating key business processes with computing technology.

Types of Automation

Accounting professionals, even in traditional accounting roles like tax, audit, and financial accounting, are likely to encounter two types of automation (**Table 7.6**):

- CPA **Robotic process automation (RPA)** involves software that can be programmed and managed easily, using a drag-and-drop interface that does not require coding knowledge. With RPA, you basically create a software robot that can launch and operate other software.
- CPA **Artificial intelligence (AI)** involves computer systems that are trained to perform tasks that typically require human intelligence. It uses complex algorithms to learn and solve problems without human intervention.

TABLE 7.6 Differences Between RPA and AI

Robotic Process Automation (RPA)	Artificial Intelligence (AI)
Follows pre-programmed "rules"	Simulates human decision making
Smart enough to follow "orders"	Self-selects appropriate responses
Ideal for repetitive tasks	Ideal for eliminating human efforts in complex analysis
Initially programmed tasks never change	Initially programmed tasks evolve through self-learning

Consider the evolution of the Roomba robot vacuum, which uses sensors to maneuver hands-free within a home. When they first entered the market, Roombas used simple pre-programmed decision making, and they frequently bumped into walls because their RPA didn't allow them to memorize the room layout. The AI of more recent Roomba models has dramatically evolved. The vacuum scans a room, records the size, marks obstacles on its internal map, and records and processes each possible route to determine the most efficient route path. If a Roomba encounters a new stool in the kitchen, it adds this to its memory and performs new calculations that account for the stool during its next run. While a Roomba's memory maps are only stored short term, it records its decisions after each map and reflects on the most recent decisions when calculating its next route. A Roomba can actually determine and remember if a sofa is flat on the ground so that it can't get through or lifted on legs so that it can vacuum underneath the sofa, as long as it avoids the legs.

The evolution of technologies in business has been similar to the evolution of Roombas. The original models were similar to RPA and used rules-based, predetermined automation. Newer models use AI to make decisions through advanced algorithms.

RPA and AI are different methods of business process automation. We will discuss AI in the Data Analytics chapter, but for now let's explore the technical workings of RPA.

Logic Behind RPA

RPA, which was an emerging technology in the early 2000s, is currently a disruptive technology being implemented at a rapid rate across companies of all sizes. At companies with RPA COEs, programmers are building automation software solutions for teams throughout the business. As shared service centers for the rest of the company, RPA COEs often have enormous project backlogs. Prioritizing projects requires analysis of feasibility, benefits, and risks enterprise-wide. To understand what makes a business process feasible for RPA, you must understand how RPA works.

RPA uses **conditional statements**, in the form of "IF THIS THEN THAT," to pre-program "rules," or decisions, into the software. Conditional statements are used in a variety of programming situations besides RPA, such as data analytics, systems and software development, and website development. You can even program a conditional statement in an Excel field.

In RPA, a conditional statement involves a trigger, which is a scenario, and a subsequent action, or decision (**Illustration 7.9**).

Illustration 7.9   In RPA, the "IF THIS THEN THAT" conditional statement involves a trigger and an action.

These decision statements help us understand the feasibility of RPA. First, let's look at an everyday example of an "IF THIS THEN THAT" statement to understand its functionality (**Illustration 7.10**). Note that the example of automated bill pay in Illustration 7.10 is *not* RPA but illustrates how conditional statements are used.

Illustration 7.10   Automatic bill pay in an online bank account is an example of a conditional statement.

An RPA conditional statement's biggest limitation is that it cannot deviate from its pre-programmed orders. To demonstrate this, consider a smart home that is programmed to turn on the front porch lights when the owner comes home (**Illustration 7.11**). Programmers must consider as many scenarios as possible, and the resulting statements can get quite complex. Programmers can increase the complexity of a scenario by adding conditional statements, including "AND" (**Illustration 7.12**) and "OR" (**Illustration 7.13**).

Illustration 7.11   A smart home turns on the lights when the owner returns home.

Illustration 7.12 Adding an "AND" conditional statement allows programmers to specify a more complex scenario.

Illustration 7.13 Adding an "OR" conditional statement allows programmers to specify multiple scenarios.

Notice the brackets in the "OR" example (Illustration 7.13). The brackets act like mathematical parentheses, indicating how the software reads the decision statement. In this instance, the brackets encase the "OR" statement. When the owner returns home and either of the following two scenarios takes place—either it is after 6:00 p.m. *or* the weather is cloudy— then the lights are turned on. Regardless of which "OR" scenario takes place, the owner *must* return home as well in order to trigger the action.

Programmers also consider what happens if the scenario is not true by adding "ELSE" to capture all scenarios not specified (**Illustration 7.14**).

If an owner comes home and it is not dark—which in this example means that it's either after 6:00 p.m. or the weather is cloudy—the smart home doesn't need to turn on the light. It only unlocks the door. This is a pre-programmed decision, and the automation cannot deviate from it.

Illustration 7.14 The final "ELSE" captures what the automation should do in the event that none of the specified scenarios occur.

To address multiple scenarios, programmers use "IF" in a conditional statement in the form of "ELSE IF." Programmers use these complex decision statements to design RPA that considers all possible scenarios. You will see examples of "ELSE IF" in the following accounting use cases.

Why Does It Matter to Your Career?

Thoughts from a Financial Center of Innovation Team Member, Manufacturing

- There are many opportunities for accounting professionals who are passionate about innovating through automation. It is easier for employers to train accounting professionals on the technical aspects of this type of work than it is to train computer science majors about accounting principles.

- If you aren't interested in a technical career, then focus on use cases. The biggest skill gap employers are seeing in candidates is that accounting majors often struggle to apply technology concepts like automation and data analytics to use cases. You don't have to code it—you just have to know when to use it.

Accounting Use Cases

How does a conditional statement affect the feasibility of a use case for RPA? To be feasible, a proposed RPA use case must fit into the rigid structure of the rules-based programming RPA uses. Ideal projects are processes that are:

- Routine
- Consistent
- Digital

- Time-consuming
- Performed frequently

The following two use cases demonstrate how RPA uses decision statements to automate accounting business processes from the current state to an automated, efficient RPA state.

Accounts Payable Invoice Process

The following is a feasibility analysis for automating a portion of the accounts payable process with RPA.

Current state   When a vendor sends an invoice, the accounts payable clerk opens the email, reviews the attachment, and saves it to that vendor's folder on the shared network drive. The accounts payable clerk then opens the accounts payable information system and inputs the details of the invoice—vendor, amount, due date—into the system.

Feasibility analysis   This process is highly compatible with RPA because:

- There is no decision making that requires judgment.
- This activity is performed frequently.
- The same steps occur each time.

RPA state   The RPA software receives an alert when an email is received and automatically saves the invoice file to the shared network drive. The RPA opens the file, identifies the key data in the file, opens the accounts payable information system, and copies that data from the file into the system.

Often in RPA, "IF THIS THEN THAT" statements specify actions that are steps in a process the program will take. The sequential steps of this use case are indicated in **Illustration 7.15** as numbered steps.

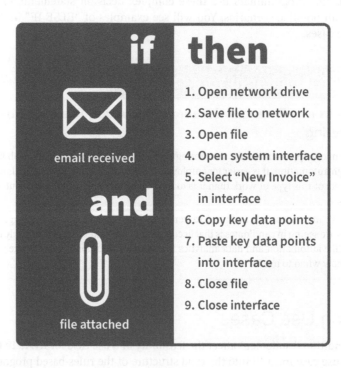

if email received **and** file attached

then
1. Open network drive
2. Save file to network
3. Open file
4. Open system interface
5. Select "New Invoice" in interface
6. Copy key data points
7. Paste key data points into interface
8. Close file
9. Close interface

Illustration 7.15   A sample conditional statement for accounts payable processing RPA includes multiple actions in sequential order.

What happens if an email is received without an attachment? The decision statement adds an "ELSE IF" statement to handle this situation (**Illustration 7.16**).

Illustration 7.16 An "ELSE IF" is an additional scenario that may occur in a conditional statement.

Internal Audit User Access Testing

Another area prime for RPA automation is in repetitive audits, such as the SOX test of user access, which is an annual test of controls mandated by U.S. federal law.

Current state The internal audit team:

- Sends an email to the IT department, requesting a list of all users who have requested new access to a database in the past year
- Randomly selects 10 names
- Asks the IT department for copies of these individuals' request tickets in the IT system

The IT department:

- Exports the request tickets into PDF files
- Emails them back to the internal audit team

The internal audit team:

- Sends an email to the human resources department, requesting an updated extract of the employee main table

Human resources:

- Exports the file to an Excel document
- Emails it to the internal audit team

The internal audit team:

- Opens each PDF file
- Reviews every file manually to make sure there is a name in the "Approver" section of the ticket
- Searches the employee main table data to find the job title of the person who approved the request

- Compares the job title in the employee main table data to a list of appropriate job titles (as only job titles on this list are expected to be approving requests for access to system)
- Adds to a file requests where job titles aren't included in the appropriate job title list
- Sends email to the IT department, asking for further information

This is only part of the audit, which can take three to four weeks and is performed every year as part of SOX testing.

Feasibility analysis   This process is highly compatible with RPA because:

- It is repeated annually.
- The process is rules based. (The same tasks are performed every year.)
- There is a lot of digital information.

RPA state   The RPA software is directly connected to data sources, which eliminates the need for the internal audit team, IT department, and human resources department to be involved in data acquisition every year.

The RPA software connects to the IT department's request ticket database and:

- Downloads the table that lists all requests this year
- Downloads the data tables that are used to create the request tickets, which include the approver data

The RPA software connects to the human resources department's database and:

- Downloads an extract of the employee main table

The RPA software then:

- Saves these files to a predetermined location
- Executes an automated data analytics workflow

RPA often performs tasks at the beginning or end of a data analytics workflow to create end-to-end automation. In this example, the RPA is programmed to acquire and save the data sources that the data analytics flow will now analyze.

The data analytics workflow:

- Combines the files into a single table that includes all needed data related to the test: name of requestor, date requested, name of approver, date approved, and job title of approver
- Uses the primary list of appropriate job titles that the internal audit department programmed when building this workflow to compare the job titles of the approvers to the job titles that have been determined to be appropriate

If a record includes inappropriate jobs, the data analytics workflow saves those names in a file in a folder the RPA tool can access. If the file is in the folder, the RPA software opens that file and sends a pre-scripted email to the IT department, requesting information about these approvers and why they were allowed to approve the requests.

The audit team does not get involved until the IT department sends a response explaining the exceptions, and the entire population—every access request received throughout the year—is tested instead of a sample. If there are no exceptions, the internal audit team is notified by the RPA software.

This complex process uses many conditional statements. The sample conditional statement in **Illustration 7.17** is executed at the end of this process when emails are sent to the IT department.

The RPA program will email the IT department about follow-up only if there is a file with names stored in the folder, as indicated in the "IF" portion of this statement. If there is no file in the folder, this indicates to the RPA that there are no exceptions, and the RPA software instead emails the internal audit department with a notice of no exceptions, which is the "ELSE" portion of the conditional statement.

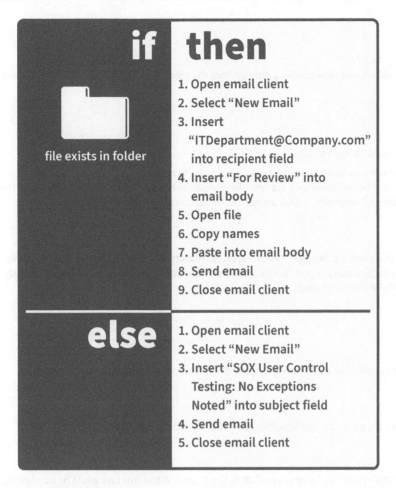

Illustration 7.17 A sample conditional statement for user access testing shows how multiple actions can be assigned to the "ELSE" portion of the statement.

Help the Automation COE at Julia's Cookies perform a feasibility analysis and prioritize use cases for RPA adoption in the Finance department in Applied Learning 7.3.

Julia's Cookies — Applied Learning 7.3

RPA Use Cases: Accounting Feasibility Analysis

Julia's Cookies' Automation COE is part of a team of competency centers that provide digital innovation to the company's Finance department. This Financial Innovation and Transformation team includes a group dedicated to identifying business process candidates for optimization via automation. The Process Optimization team has created a large backlog of initiatives suitable for RPA. Of the following proposed use cases, which are feasible projects for the Automation COE?

Use Case 1: Vendors

Department: Accounts Payable

Process: Onboarding new vendors

Description: New vendors submit a complete "New Vendor" form that is an Excel file. Accounts Payable opens this file and manually inputs the new vendor information into the vendor main table within the information system.

Time spent: Significant

Frequency: Often

Suggestion: Have an RPA solution copy new vendor information from the Excel file and paste it into the new vendor intake interface in the information system.

Use Case 2: Audit Documentation

Department: Internal Audit

Process: Creating audit documentation and workpapers

Description: Internal Audit records its findings and recommendations in an online system throughout an audit engagement. These descriptions are copied and pasted into a PowerPoint presentation for the business stakeholders at the conclusion of each audit.

Time spent: Moderate

Frequency: Very often

Suggestion: Have an RPA solution pull findings and recommendations directly from the Internal Audit system and copy the text into a PowerPoint presentation.

Use Case 3: Fraud Risk

Department: Employee Expenses

Process: Reviewing red flags that indicate the potential for fraud

Description: Finance employees log into the fraud monitoring system on an ad hoc basis to check for any existing red flags in the dashboard. They do not know when red flags are identified unless they log into the system. Then they must manually open the Time and Expense reporting system and filter on the identified employee to find the red flag transaction.

Time spent: Moderate

Frequency: Ad hoc

Suggestion: Have an RPA solution review the fraud red flag dashboard and send an email alert to the Finance employees whenever a new red flag is indicated. The RPA solution could also generate a report that includes the transaction data for each red flag in the body of the email to eliminate the need to log in and search for the transaction.

Use Case 4: Financial Statements

Department: Financial Reporting

Process: Creating the annual report

Description: Financial reporting employees copy and paste a disclaimer to a new document every year during annual reporting.

Time spent: Minimal

Frequency: Infrequent

Suggestion: Have an RPA solution copy and paste the prior year verbiage into the current year document.

SOLUTION

The only one of these use cases that seems infeasible for the Automation COE is Use Case 4. While this task could be automated, it currently requires minimal time and occurs only once a year. The amount of time needed to design an RPA solution is not worth the value it would add to the finance function.

The other three projects pass the feasibility test and should be prioritized based on the impact of the efficiencies to be gained and the risks addressed. For example, while Use Case 3 may not offer the most significant efficiency gain, it addresses the risk of fraud in the organization and provides an ongoing fraud-monitoring program, which may make it more important than the other two suggestions.

Creating Efficiencies and Opportunities

CPA Robotics and automation won't replace the need for accountants, but they are causing a shift in the way accountants work—and the skills needed for the job. Companies are hiring well-rounded accounting students with core accounting knowledge who also understand technology use cases and data fundamentals.

Business process automation in particular is opening up new opportunities for accounting professionals. The Pathways Vision Model discussed in the Accounting as Information chapter emphasizes the critical-thinking skills accounting professionals need in the technologically influenced workplace.

Recall that the Pathways Vision Model describes the misperception that accountants are number crunchers and the reality that accounting professionals are trusted advisors and decision makers who use accounting to make judgment-based decisions.

Thanks to RPA, instead of performing routine, manual tasks like reconciliations, collections of accounts receivable, and check writing, accounting professionals have time to advise leadership, analyze results, and engage in business processes when an accounting judgment-based decision is required.

For public accounting firms, the benefits of RPA are exponential. Memes about busy season are everywhere. "Welcome to public accounting, where busy season never ends, and the PTO isn't real" and "One does not simply 'have a good weekend' in the middle of busy season" are only two examples of jokes that ring true with those in the public accounting field. With RPA, the future of busy season can be changed.

CPA Accounting jobs will evolve around automation and AI to allow humans in these jobs to:

- Partner with robots to monitor and improve company performance and results
- Oversee robotic uses in accounting and auditing tasks and determine use cases for automation versus humans
- Develop new and refine existing robotic applications
- Execute human-centric tasks such as working on client relationships and innovation and even small tasks that are not feasible for automation

RPA is a disruptive technology—it is here, and it is staying—that won't replace accounting professionals. Instead, it is freeing accounting professionals to focus their time on strategic initiatives. It allows us to focus on more exciting things!

Throughout this course, consider how RPA can be applied to create efficiency in business processes or partner with data analytics concepts to create end-to-end automated workflows like those in the internal audit example described earlier. Employers are looking for idea generators. Understanding use cases for RPA will set you apart from your peers, even if you choose not to go on to be a person who programs RPA software.

In the Real World　Automation at Airbus: Saving Millions on Finance Tasks[2]

Airbus, which employs over 100,000 people globally, designs, manufactures, and sells military and commercial aerospace products, including commercial aircraft. Its revenues in 2019 were approximately $79 billion. Airbus is setting its sights on automating the processing of invoices and expense reports.

According to Richard Masci, the head of financial system services and compliance at Airbus Americas, in 2017 the company had four employees who reviewed 25,000 travel and expense reports filed annually by employees from across the United States. This process took an hour or more per expense report—and even more time if there were red flags like missing receipts that required follow-up.

In 2018, Masci oversaw a transition to an expense report review system that utilizes automation software:

- The system matches reports against a repository of accepted vendors, expense categories, and expense amounts to identify red flag outliers. It looks at the vendor's identity, the type of expense, and the amount to determine when things don't match.
- Today, an employee only needs to review the system's output of red flag, or noncompliant, expenses. For example, Airbus' expense policy prohibits expensing alcohol that isn't part of a meal on a business trip. The approval system flags employees who file dinner expenses from bars that the system knows don't serve food. This kind of information is something a human may not know or catch in a manual review.
- Since adding this automated reviewing system, the average time between an employee submitting an expense report and being approved has gone from multiple weeks to only a few days, and the reviewers' workload has been cut in half.

Within the first partial year of implementing this system in the Americas division, Airbus paid off the initial investment of $50,000 and saw an additional net savings of $50,000. The company anticipates growth to $200,000 per year of savings—just in the Americas division.

This process initially automated 53% of the expense report approval process, but Airbus isn't stopping there. Its goal is to reach 80% automation by refining the system's ability to recognize red flag transactions.

This isn't Airbus' first adventure into automation in its Finance department. A similar project uses scanning technology to automate invoice approvals and prevent employees from working overtime to locate information that is missing from invoices.

Masci expects these successful automation projects to pave the way for additional digitization efforts. This division's initiative to use RPA and AI to reduce costs in the finance function could save millions of dollars annually if rolled out to the global company.

Do you think this example describes a form of AI or RPA? If employees are currently manually reviewing the receipts for transactions that the system has red-flagged, how could Airbus use RPA to improve this automation process? What do you think would happen to the employees who have been reviewing the expense reports?

---

[2] www.wsj.com/articles/airbus-harnessing-ai-in-bid-to-save-millions-on-finance-tasks-11566207002

CONCEPT REVIEW QUESTIONS

1. **CPA** Write a note on business process automation.

   Ans. Business process automation is the process of managing information, data, costs, resources, and investments by increasing productivity through automating key business processes with computing technology.

2. **CPA** What is meant by robotic process automation (RPA)?

   Ans. RPA involves software that can be programmed and managed easily, using a drag-and-drop interface that does not require coding knowledge. With RPA, we basically create a software robot that can launch and operate other software.

3. **CPA** Write in brief your understanding of artificial intelligence (AI).

   Ans. AI involves computer systems that are trained to perform tasks that typically require human intelligence. It uses complex algorithms to learn and solve problems without human intervention.

4. What is the logic behind RPA?

   Ans. RPA uses conditional statements, in the form of "IF THIS THEN THAT," to pre-program "rules," or decisions, into the software.

7.4 What Is Blockchain?

Learning Objective ❹

Identify the fundamental principles and technologies of blockchain.

CPA A **blockchain** system enables the recording of digital transactions packaged in *blocks* that form a sequence, like a *chain*, in a peer-to-peer network. These blocks are distributed and visible to all participants in the network in a way that makes changing, cheating, or hacking the system almost impossible.

We can trace the origin of blockchain to a 2008 whitepaper titled *Bitcoin: A Peer-to-Peer Electronic Cash System*.[3] As "peer-to-peer" (P2P) implies, blockchain technology removes intermediaries or some central authority in a transaction between two parties. In a P2P network, the "peers" are computer systems connected to each other via the internet.

For example, in a P2P transaction, if you want to send a wire transfer to a family member from your bank account to the family member's bank account, banks would be the trusted intermediaries to validate the transaction. They do this in exchange for service fees. Blockchain does the same without the intermediary, and it does it much faster and at a much lower cost. The most successful and notable use case of blockchain is bitcoin, a cryptocurrency (or virtual currency) traded in a public blockchain. Anyone can join the bitcoin network and be a participant.

CPA Blockchain is a disruptive technology for the accounting profession, with significant potential for widespread use in business. Its recent inclusion as a topic on the CPA exam indicates its importance to the accounting profession.

Before getting into the technical aspects of blockchain, let's review what a blockchain transaction looks like (**Illustration 7.18**). Don't worry if these terms don't make sense right away; we'll use this illustration as a guide when we get into the details.

---

[3]bitcoin.org/bitcoin.pdf

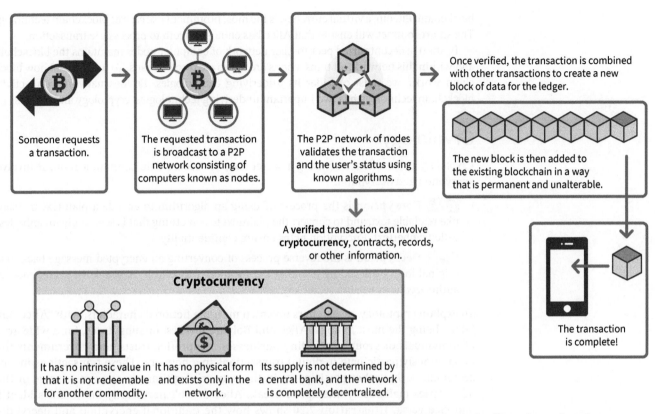

Illustration 7.18 A high-level overview of a blockchain transaction includes important technologies like nodes and cryptocurrency.

The Basics of Blockchain

CPA Blockchain is a type of distributed ledger with essential underlying technologies. It is a sequence of blocks containing unchangeable ledgers of transactions. Each block in the chain has a logical relationship with the preceding block. These blocks of data are stored on **nodes**, which are the computers, laptops, or servers of participants in the network who choose to be miners. **Miners** create the ledgers of transactions in chained blocks by using their computing power (nodes in the network) to solve the mathematical encryption puzzles that secure the transactions.

Miners, then, are people who participate in the process of verifying and adding transactions to the blockchain using their computing hardware. In other words, they own the computing power that does the "mining." Nodes connect to one another and continually exchange the latest blockchain ledgers so that all the nodes stay up-to-date all the time (**Illustration 7.19**). They store, distribute, and update the blockchain data.

Some network participants do not want to be nodes. They only want to use the blockchain network for peer-to-peer transactions. **CPA** These entities use **wallet applications** that allow them to broadcast and receive transactions with their wallets, using smart contracts. **Smart contracts** are computer programs that act as intermediaries to create, execute, and settle contracts automatically under certain conditions. An accounting example is the automatic payment of an invoice after the program checks that goods have been received, that they match the purchase order, and that sufficient funds are available in the buyer's bank account to pay the invoice. Think of Alice transferring bitcoin to Bob in a sales transaction on a

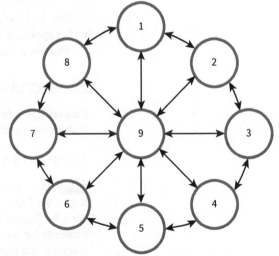

Illustration 7.19 Nodes in a blockchain network are connected computers, laptops, or servers of blockchain participants.

blockchain. Bitcoin, a virtual currency, is the most prominent use case of blockchain technology. The smart contract will ensure that Alice has enough bitcoin to process the transaction.

In short, a decentralized peer-to-peer network of computer nodes maintains the blockchain, and within this network, all transactions are approved by consensus. To understand how blockchain works, we must consider its underlying technologies. Besides network connectivity, blockchain technology has two important underlying technologies: cryptology and ledgers.

Cryptology

Cryptology is the science of using a secret code for secure data communication. It involves encryption and decryption:

- **CPA** **Encryption** is the process of using an algorithm to encode a plaintext message, like readable text, and to convert the plaintext to something that is seemingly meaningless, called ciphertext. Encryption helps ensure confidentiality.

- **CPA** **Decryption** is the reverse process of converting an encrypted message back to its original form by decoding it so that the recipient can read it. To break the secret code, an authorized user needs a secret key.

To explain cryptology, researchers invented multiple fictional characters, with "Alice" and "Bob" being the most famous. Alice and Bob are proxies, or substitutes, for a wide array of individuals or groups, including businesses, nonprofits, trusts, and governments that anonymously participate in digital transactions in a network. These transactions involve secret codes that other participants in the network legitimately attempt to solve or that adversaries maliciously attempt to break. Alice doesn't necessarily know Bob's identity and vice versa. **Illustration 7.20** shows how the traditional encryption and decryption process works on a network.

Illustration 7.20 The encryption and decryption process uses a secret key to transfer between the sender and recipient.

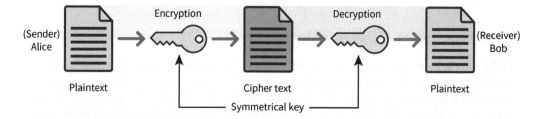

Now let's look at a transaction between Alice and Bob (**Illustration 7.21**). Note where the wallet applications, cryptology process, and miner nodes exist in this transaction.

We have covered the essentials, so it is time to get more technical.

Blockchain Ledgers

Ledgers have been used since ancient times to record transactions involving economic exchanges. There are three types of blockchain ledgers (**Illustration 7.22**).

Centralized Ledgers

CPA In a **centralized ledger** system, all participants have access to a central ledger. The ledger we know best is the traditional centralized ledger that businesses use as the backbone for financial accounting—the general ledger. The general ledger contains all the ledger accounts for recording transactions related to a company's assets, liabilities, owners' equity, revenue, and expenses.

- There is only *one* general ledger per company, making it the *central* repository for all accounting transactions, administered by the controller and CFO of the company and audited by an independent third-party intermediary, the external auditor.

- Like other traditional centralized ledger systems, a centralized general ledger requires trusted intermediaries (management) to verify transactions to ensure validity. After approval, transactions are recorded in the general ledger.

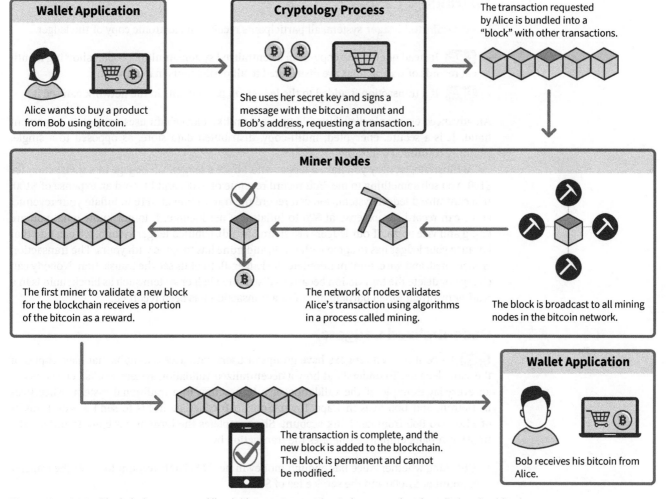

Illustration 7.21 Blockchain use case: Alice initiates a transaction to buy a product from Bob using bitcoin.

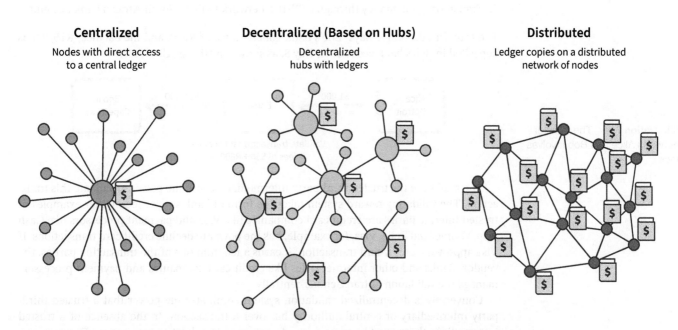

Illustration 7.22 The three types of blockchain ledgers are centralized, decentralized, and distributed.

Distributed Ledgers

In a **distributed ledger** system, all participants receive an electronic copy of the ledger.

- **CPA** Instead of only one copy, as in a centralized system, multiple copies showing identical records of transactions are distributed to all participants in a network.
- **CPA** If a transaction is added to the ledger, *all* participants in the network can see it.

An advanced electronic distributed ledger system like blockchain uses *encryption* to prevent fraud. It is a secure, encrypted, multi-copy, distributed data store, as opposed to a single, centrally controlled data store.

To illustrate, let's say you have a ledger, and I have a ledger. We engage in a transaction for $100. You sell something to me. You record revenue of $100, and I record an expense of $100. In a centralized ledger system, you can record the transaction at $110 to inflate your revenue, and I can record my expense at $90 to inflate my net income. I do not know what you are doing and vice versa. If our ledgers are shared in a distributed ledger system, we can't do that because your ledger has to agree with mine, and mine has to agree with yours. The transaction is encrypted, and we cannot manipulate the ledger. Both of us see the transaction. Nobody can change or delete the transaction because a distributed ledger system such as blockchain is in a *read-only* format for all participants after a transaction has been recorded.

Decentralized Ledgers

CPA **Decentralized ledgers** have groups of users with access to hubs that have copies of the same ledgers. To understand how a decentralized validation system works, let's consider an everyday example of the validation of a transaction in a traditional system. Alice lives in Detroit, and Bob lives in Cape Town, South Africa. Alice needs to send a wire transfer of $1,000 to Bob from her bank account. She completes the form at her bank to initiate the transfer. A bank employee validates the transaction by:

1. Checking whether Alice has enough money in her U.S. bank account to cover the transfer amount of $1,000 and the service fee of $50
2. Verifying the information for Bob's bank account in South Africa
3. Converting the $1,000 to its equivalent in South African rand: R16,000
4. Transferring the money through a SWIFT network to Bob's South African bank account

The transfer takes three days. Bob's bank collects a fee of R600, and the balance, R15,400, is deposited in Bob's bank account on Day 3, as shown in **Illustration 7.23**.

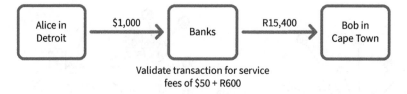

Illustration 7.23 The transfer between Alice and Bob involves fees.

The banks are the trusted third-party intermediaries with the power to validate this transaction. The validating reward system takes the form of bank service fees. Other examples of trusted intermediaries are credit card companies like Visa and payment processors like Cash App, Venmo, and Zelle. Visa, for example, has the power to decline credit card transactions. If Visa approves a credit card transaction, it earns a fee from one of the transacting parties, the vendor. Banks and other intermediaries like credit card companies and payment processors manage the validation of transactions centrally.

Conversely, a decentralized validation system eliminates the power that a trusted third-party intermediary or central authority has over a transaction. In the absence of a trusted intermediary, there must be some form of consensus to validate a transaction. Furthermore, this decentralized validation happens in an apolitical and unbiased manner.

A real-life example illustrates the power that intermediaries can exert in transactions between two parties. During the COVID-19 pandemic, a portrait studio in Tacoma, Washington, received an email from a payment processor, Square, which is the intermediary in transactions between the studio and its customers. The email notified the studio that Square would start holding back 30% of each of the studio's payments from customers for 120 days "to protect you and Square from unexpected loss events." The studio had never had a disputed transaction in three years with Square as the intermediary.[4] In this situation, there would have been no holdback of payments in a decentralized validation system, even in the midst of a pandemic.

CPA **Bitcoin**, the first cryptocurrency, has been the most successful use case of blockchain technology because of the decentralized and transparent validation of bitcoin transactions. Bitcoin provides a proven consensus protocol, called **proof of work**, to replace third-party intermediaries or a central authority. With bitcoin, no third-party intermediaries are necessary to approve and enter transactions in the system. This eliminates reliance on a central bank or other third-party entities. You may remember from economics that the central bank of the United States, the Federal Reserve System, controls the country's official currency; however, it does not control cryptocurrency like bitcoin.

Proof of work functions as follows:

- Blockchain participants use their own computer resources to form a node in the network. Remember that nodes form the computer infrastructure of a blockchain network. Many thousands of nodes can be online simultaneously. Anyone can run a node by downloading the transaction history of a blockchain.

- Miners use computing powers to solve encryption puzzles and create a ledger. Miners are essential participants in a blockchain. They provide the mining nodes, which may require much heavier processing power than other nodes.

- These miners, by consensus of the majority, create and validate new blocks to add to a blockchain and eliminate fraudulent blocks. They attempt to solve the mathematical puzzles in the encrypted transactions using their computing power.

- A miner who provides the most comprehensive proof of work found acceptable by the majority verifies a block of transactions and *by consensus* validates a new block to add to the chain.

In a bitcoin blockchain, miners compete against one another. The first to solve the equation and successfully add the next block to the chain receives a portion of the bitcoin traded in the transaction as reward. The portion of the bitcoin reward is a predetermined amount that has changed over time.

Why Does It Matter to Your Career?

Thoughts from Internal Audit Data Analytics Manager, Financial Services

Many accounting professionals don't understand how blockchain works. Given that blockchain runs on a ledger system for transactions, it seems natural that accounting professionals would be interested in and understand this technology. It is past time that blockchain is demystified for accountants.

Fundamental Principles of Blockchain Technology

Now that you know more about blockchain technology, let's summarize three interrelated fundamental principles of the technology that build on one another:

- Decentralization
- Transparency
- Immutability

---

[4]www.wsj.com/articles/hit-by-coronavirusand-a-30-holdback-by-the-payment-processor-11592040601

A distributed ledger doesn't have to be decentralized. **CPA** However, **decentralization** eliminates the need for an intermediary or a central authority to process, validate, or authenticate transactions. Decentralization of power leads to transparency, which in turn leads to immutability. **Immutability** gives blockchain users assurance that their assets and information are secure. Intermediaries like banks normally provide this assurance to us. Bitcoin's immutability relies on proof of work, which secures a blockchain through powerful computer computations.

CPA Every transaction in the distributed ledger is timestamped and given a unique cryptographic signature. All participants can view all of the transactions. The technology provides a verifiable and auditable history of all the data about all the transactions stored in the blockchain. Many ledgers form blocks in the chain, and these blocks are stored across many servers. These servers communicate to all network participants for **transparency**, thus ensuring *by consensus* maintenance of the most accurate and recent record of transactions (or ledgers) arranged in transaction blocks. The transactions are recorded in the ledger only after the network participants reach consensus.

CPA The biggest threat or risk to a blockchain system is the possibility that a single entity or malicious collusive parties will control more than 50% of the computing power on a network. By consensus, they would control the network and the process of recording new blocks. Thus, they would have a monopoly on creating new blocks. The bigger the network, the lower this risk (**Illustration 7.24**).

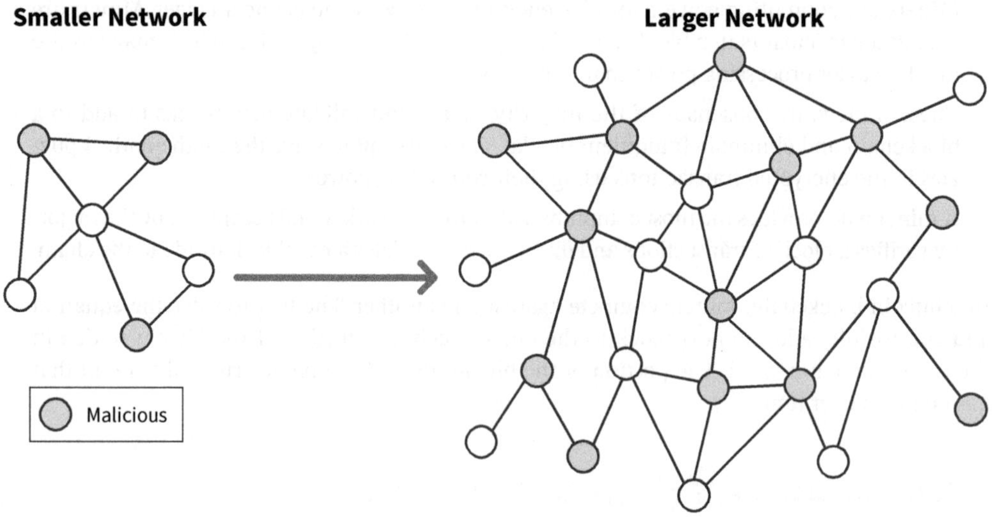

Smaller Network   **Larger Network**

Malicious

Illustration 7.24 It is harder for malicious parties to gain consensus in larger networks, where more malicious parties would need to be involved.

Types of Blockchain Systems

The blockchain technology that bitcoin uses is a public network that is open to all, with no restrictions on accessing or leaving the network. However, private and partially private consortium blockchains have since emerged to make the technology a better fit for traditional business use. We explore the three main types of blockchains next.

The **public blockchain** systems mentioned above have several benefits:

- All transactions are public, and users can choose to remain anonymous.
- They provide decentralization of power, with no one entity having control.
- There is full transparency of the ledger of transactions.
- They are fast, secure systems and are less expensive than traditional accounting systems.
- Any persons or other entities with internet access can participate in the verification of transactions and set themselves up as nodes because the systems are permissionless.

A **private blockchain** *does* have an intermediary. A single entity (the business) governs the network. A private blockchain system has the following characteristics:

- One entity has full control and predetermines the selection of a few nodes.
- Participants require permission to join, so there are no miners with economic incentive to validate transactions by performing complex proof of work computations, as in a

"permissionless" blockchain system; instead, users enter and, by consensus, validate the transactions, allowing for greater efficiency and speed than in other blockchain systems.

- Whereas public networks feature anonymity, with private blockchain, the identity of each validator is known.

A private blockchain network is suitable for a business that may want to replace its traditional accounting system with blockchain technology and still maintain privacy. There are different levels of access, and network participants need permission to read, add transactions, or audit the blockchain. Encryption may protect confidential information. There is privacy in a private network! Only the entities participating in a transaction have knowledge of it, and only entities with the appropriate permissions can access the transaction.

From a business perspective, a **consortium blockchain** allows a consortium of companies to collaborate and leverage information to improve workflows, accountability, and transparency. An example is a manufacturer working with logistics companies to form a blockchain supply chain. This type of blockchain allows for transaction privacy, with a selected group of participating members controlling the network and setting the rules. Its permissions structure is more complex than for a private blockchain, as individual companies still want to keep certain transactions private.

For many, blockchain systems can seem daunting. When broken down into transactions and technology, however, it is easier to get an understanding of what is taking place. There is more to learn in the next section, including blockchain's relevancy to accounting professionals and examples of real business use cases. Armed with what you already know, help Julia's Cookies determine the feasibility of using blockchain in Applied Learning 7.4.

Julia's Cookies   Applied Learning 7.4

Blockchain: Business Feasibility

Emilia, Julia's Cookies' CEO, has heard about businesses in the food service delivery industry adopting blockchain technology.

Given what you have learned so far, do you think Emilia should consider blockchain's feasibility for Julia's Cookies?

SOLUTION

Businesses of all sizes can benefit from blockchain by establishing a blockchain-backed payment solution that uses cryptocurrency, smart contracts that are self-executing and avoid third-party involvement, and even blockchain-backed supply chains. You will explore these applications in the next section.

CONCEPT REVIEW QUESTIONS

1. **CPA** What is a blockchain system?
   Ans. A blockchain system enables the recording of digital transactions packaged in blocks that form a sequence, like a chain, in a peer-to-peer network. These blocks are distributed and visible to all participants in the network in such a way that makes changing, cheating, or hacking the system almost impossible.

2. What is blockchain mining?
   Ans. Blockchain mining is the process of verifying and adding transactions to a blockchain block. Miners create the ledgers of transactions in chained blocks by using their computing power (nodes in the network) to solve the mathematical encryption puzzles that secure the transactions.

3. What are smart contracts?
   Ans. Smart contracts are computer programs that act as intermediaries to create, execute, and settle contracts automatically under certain conditions.

4. **CPA** Differentiate between encryption and decryption.
   Ans. Cryptology is the science of using a secret code for secure data communication. It involves encryption and decryption.

   Encryption is the process of using an algorithm to encode a plaintext message, like readable text, and to convert the plaintext to something that is seemingly meaningless, called ciphertext. Encryption helps ensure confidentiality.

Decryption is the reverse process of converting an encrypted message back to its original form by decoding it so that the recipient can read it. To break the secret code, an authorized user needs a secret key.

5. **CPA** What is a bitcoin?

   Ans. Bitcoin is the first cryptocurrency which has been the most successful use case of blockchain technology because of the decentralized and transparent validation of bitcoin transactions. It is a virtual currency designed to act as a form of payment outside the control of any authority, thus removing the need for third-party involvement in financial transactions.

6. What is the difference between a public and private blockchain?

   Ans. The blockchain technology that bitcoin uses is a public network that is open to all, with no restrictions on accessing or leaving the network. A private blockchain does have an intermediary. A single entity (the business) governs the network.

7.5 Why Should Accountants Care About Blockchain?

Learning Objective ❺
Explain blockchain's relevance to accounting professionals.

According to Deloitte, "Blockchain is a trustless, distributed ledger that is openly available and has negligible costs of use. The use of Blockchain for accounting use-cases is hugely promising. From simplifying the compliance with regulatory requirements to enhancing the prevalent double entry bookkeeping, anything is imaginable."[5]

Blockchain has the potential to significantly disrupt the accounting profession. A traditional accounting information system has numerous trusted third-party intermediaries, or watchdogs, including independent auditors, banks, and the government (for example, the IRS). Accounting processes could become more automated by leveraging blockchain technology for more transparency and immutability while still complying with regulatory requirements. Progress like this could potentially reduce the need for independent auditors.

The American Institute of Certified Public Accountants (AICPA) and the Wall Street Blockchain Alliance, a nonprofit trade association promoting blockchain technology for business use, are collaborating to promote the use of blockchain technology in the accounting profession. According to AICPA president and CEO Barry Melancon, "The accounting profession is built on confirmation and verification, and that's what blockchain is all about."[6]

Why Does It Matter to Your Career?

Thoughts from a Financial Center of Innovation Manager, Manufacturing

- Blockchain is one of those technologies that companies either work with or don't—there is not much middle ground. This means professionals are either educated on the content or not. If you understand the material in this section, you are going to be ahead of many accounting professionals who are still turning a blind eye to the fact that blockchain isn't going away.

- Blockchain technology has the potential to impact financial reporting processes. This includes the manner in which accounting transactions are initiated, authorized, processed, recorded, and reported.

[5]www.finyear.com/Blockchain-Technology-A-game-changer-in-accounting_a35816.html
[6]www2.deloitte.com/content/dam/Deloitte/de/Documents/Innovation/Blockchain_A%20game-changer%20in%20accounting.pdf

Evolving Career Opportunities

The accounting profession is evolving in response to the use of blockchain technology in business. Besides the expansion of consulting opportunities, this technology impacts accounting functions across the board. Let's explore a few ways you may encounter blockchain in your career as an accounting professional.

Audit Professionals

Let's explore a few examples of the impact of blockchain on the auditing profession. Internal and external auditors must understand how transactions are recorded in the blockchain and:

- Acquire sufficient evidence about the nature of blockchain transactions
- Audit the blockchain to ensure confidence in the system and data integrity
- Track and validate cryptocurrency transactions
- Verify ownership of transactions, which becomes difficult when anonymity is inherent in a public blockchain
- Drill down to the code level to ensure that a blockchain system is functioning correctly technologically

A transaction recorded in a blockchain may still be unauthorized, fraudulent, or illegal, executed between related parties and not disclosed as such, linked to a side agreement that is "off-chain," or incorrectly classified in the financial statements.

While auditors must overcome a number of technological challenges, blockchain could change the way audits are performed by automating many audit processes. If this happened, audit fees and compliance costs would plummet as less time would be spent on these engagements.

To understand how an audit team could use blockchain to conduct its review, let's consider the importance of verifying the accuracy of a record for auditors. Inherent immutability in a blockchain means that certain data integrity risks would not apply to the new system. Blockchain enables verification of the integrity of a record. **CPA** Each record has a **hash string**, which is created with an algorithm as part of the encryption process. This hash string ensures that third parties are unable to access the information. The hash string is embedded in the blockchain, and auditors search for the hash string within the blockchain. If the search is successful, the auditors know the record has remained unmodified (**Illustration 7.25**).[7]

CPA If an audit team can begin with a transaction record that is reliable and doesn't need to be audited because it is immutable, it can save time and client money in executing audits—and the team can focus on activities that provide more strategic value.

Other Accounting Functions

Companies involved in a specific transaction maintain separate traditional double-entry accounting systems. By implementing blockchain at a large scale, which would require buy-in and adoption globally, blockchain could replace the double-entry system and serve as a single transaction entry that captures both companies' accounting (**Illustration 7.26**).

CPA Imagine the cost savings for audit and compliance if companies used a single blockchain for their transactions. These cost savings are an important outcome of blockchain implementation. This business transformation through blockchain isn't likely to occur soon, but it will eventually. The possibility demonstrates the disruption that is possible if blockchain is widely adopted.

Businesses and consortiums are already creating immutable, real-time financial records that are easy to verify and difficult to change. This presents a challenge to the traditional double-entry accounting system, which remains labor intensive, and to accountants who

---

[7]www.finyear.com/Blockchain-Technology-A-game-changer-in-accounting_a35816.html

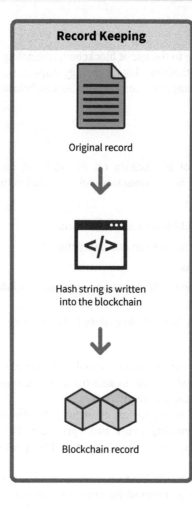

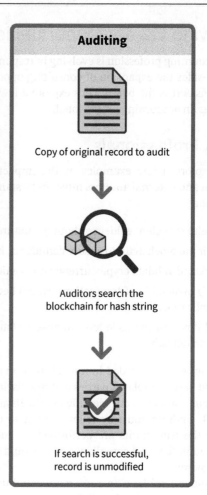

Illustration 7.25 Hash strings can enable auditors to identify whether a record has been modified through blockchain.

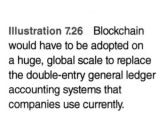

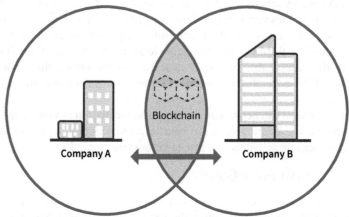

Illustration 7.26 Blockchain would have to be adopted on a huge, global scale to replace the double-entry general ledger accounting systems that companies use currently.

are unable to operate in a technologically advanced environment. This could be the first step toward blockchain replacing individual double-entry ledgers entirely.

Blockchain is already changing the way accounting professionals work. Current impacts on other accounting functions include the following:

- Financial accountants must record transactions related to buying and selling cryptocurrencies. The public ledger shows basic information, including a date and timestamp, but it doesn't include everything an accountant needs. An accountant must do additional work after pulling a participant's data from the blockchain.

- Tax accountants can use blockchain to simplify and automate tax compliance and transparency. Tax authorities can obtain access to blockchain data to calculate and enforce tax payments, reduce tax fraud opportunities, and reduce the need for labor-intensive tax services.

- Purchasing accountants are seeing changes in how supply chains are operating. Secured payments are often sent to suppliers as soon as materials are received—through real-time scanning and recording using tags. Data on receipts includes time received, quality indicators, and the item's location, based on GPS data. This information is shared through the blockchain distributed ledger to create a transparent supply chain.

Small Businesses

Accountants are often trusted advisors to small businesses, own their own small businesses, or work for smaller businesses. Blockchain systems offer advantages that small businesses could adopt. For example:

- Blockchain systems provide increased security through strong authentication processes.
- Distribution of all the data to different computers in different locations vastly mitigates any risk of data manipulation or deletion.
- **CPA** Blockchain technology includes programmed self-executing contracts, which are smart contracts that eliminate the need for intermediaries like lawyers, significantly lowering costs.
- **CPA** Blockchain-backed payment platforms provide alternatives to cash through the option to transfer funds directly, securely, and instantly and without intermediaries, lowering the costs of collections and payments in a secure environment that reduces the possibility of fraud.

Improving Data Quality

Compared to traditional ledgers, blockchain systems have many advantages related to accounting data characteristics (**Table 7.7**). These advantages alone explain the disruptive forces that blockchain presents for accounting professionals.

TABLE 7.7 Comparison of Blockchain Systems and Traditional Ledgers for Good Data Quality

Characteristic of Good Data	Blockchain Systems	Traditional Ledgers
Data integrity	Data is immutable once entered into a blockchain ledger and can't be changed or deleted.	The risk of subsequent manipulation is greater with traditional ledgers.
Data retention	Each node can potentially back up the entire blockchain ledger to provide multiple copies.	Backups are far more restricted.
Data validity	Miners verify validation of transactions by a majority consensus prior to entry.	Verification of transactions may be limited to a single person.
Data transparency	A blockchain is widely distributed.	A traditional ledger is not widely distributed.
Data security	A majority of participants must generally collude for fraud to happen.	A single fraudster can jeopardize a traditional system.

Now that you have learned about blockchain and how it can impact a company, consider whether Julia's Cookies should adopt a supply chain blockchain initiative in Applied Learning 7.5.

Julia's Cookies — Applied Learning 7.5

Blockchain: Contaminated Raw Materials

Emilia, Julia's Cookies' CEO, has an accounting background. She was reading the *Journal of Accountancy* one Sunday afternoon, and a report about a blockchain implementation by Walmart caught her attention.[8] She had already been considering blockchain as a solution for the company's supply chain. She knows that business transformation through blockchain is eventually likely to occur, once there is widespread adoption. She does not want Julia's Cookies to be in the laggard category for adoption.

A recent multistate outbreak of *Escherichia coli* was linked to romaine lettuce. This unfortunate event and subsequent recall of romaine lettuce significantly impacted Walmart because the source of the contamination was unknown and took a lot of time to pinpoint. This resulted in the removal of millions of bags and heads of romaine lettuce from stores, whether contaminated or not and regardless of origin. Walmart experienced a loss of consumer confidence as well as a negative financial impact, which extended to suppliers and farmers. Walmart decided to use blockchain to mitigate this risk.

Walmart implemented a private blockchain network called the *Walmart Food Traceability Initiative*, in which its suppliers and associated farmers of fresh produce participate. Suppliers and farmers use a web-based portal for data entry. The blockchain uses smart contracts to trace fresh produce from its source and throughout the supply chain. Walmart can now accurately pinpoint sources of contamination, so it can handle recalls much more quickly and with less waste. Walmart reported that it had reduced the amount of time it takes to track a food item from a Walmart store back to its source to seconds rather than the days or weeks required under a traditional system.

Do you think a similar initiative might help Julia's Cookies? Why or why not? What are factors to consider? Please help Emilia brainstorm.

SOLUTION

An important factor is whether Julia's Cookies' products could be contaminated to such an extent that a national recall of its products might become necessary. A Google search reveals numerous recalls of cookie dough—for example, because of *Listeria* contamination. An initiative similar to Walmart's, tailored to Julia's Cookies, warrants further consideration.

Other factors to consider:

- Julia's Cookies would most likely need to pilot the new technology in collaboration with numerous suppliers, customers, and a technology platform.
- Considering in-house expertise, Julia's Cookies may need to engage a consultant to help steer this initiative. Examples would be CPA firms specializing in blockchain.
- Do the benefits outweigh the costs?
- Is blockchain technology a good strategic fit for Julia's Cookies?
- Suppliers, transportation participants, and customers need to be convinced of the value add to them of engaging in this initiative.
- Combining blockchain with IoT technology by installing sensors in refrigerated trucks to monitor and record transportation conditions would keep these conditions transparent to all participants in the blockchain in real time. This would help fix responsibility for contamination prior to transferring ownership to customers and also help prevent contamination by sending real-time alerts if the temperature falls outside the pre-programmed range.

CONCEPT REVIEW QUESTIONS

1. **CPA** What is a hash string and how do auditors use it?

   Ans. Each record in a blockchain system has a hash string created with an algorithm as part of the encryption process. This hash string ensures that third parties are unable to access the information. The hash string is embedded in the blockchain, and auditors search for it within the blockchain. If the search is successful, the auditors know the record has remained unmodified.

2. Accountants are often trusted advisors to small businesses, own their own small businesses, or work for a smaller business. Blockchain systems offer advantages that small businesses could adopt. Discuss.

   Ans. Blockchain systems offer following advantages: (1) Increased security with a strong authentication process. (2) All data is distributed to different computers in different locations, vastly mitigating any risk of data manipulation or deletion. (3) Blockchain technology includes programmed self-executing contracts that avoid the need for intermediaries like lawyers, significantly lowering costs. (4) Blockchain-based payment platforms provide alternatives to cash through the option to transfer funds directly, securely, and instantly.

---

[8]www.journalofaccountancy.com/issues/2019/aug/blockchain-services-jagruti-solanki-cpa.html

FEATURED PROFESSIONAL | Director of Innovation, Public Accounting Firm

Photo courtesy of Kevin Wang

Kevin Wang, CPA, CITP, CGFM

Kevin works for a regional public accounting firm headquartered in the southeastern United States. His career began in external audit after he earned both a bachelor's and a master's in accounting. After a number of years as an external auditor, and upon being promoted to senior manager, Kevin shifted roles in his firm to become the first director of innovation. In this unique role, Kevin identifies and proposes areas where technology, organizational structure, and daily practices can be combined and refined to drive his firm toward its business goals. Kevin is a recognized leader in emerging technologies such as AI, blockchain, and automation.

What is your favorite part of your job?

I am fascinated with learning. In my current position, I am beyond grateful to have the freedom and flexibility to continue my pursuit to be a lifelong learner. Reading about how the latest in technology saved hundreds of processing hours or how a new web application created a unique customer experience is what drives me every day.

Which technology platforms and software are most critical to your career?

As fast as technology is moving, the most critical technology platform or software is constantly changing, so naming one is hard. If I had to name a certain technological aspect that's most important to learn, it would be the ins and outs of data. The power of data is extremely fascinating to me, and I think we've only hit the tip of the iceberg in terms of what can be done with data. If you think about it, all emerging technologies have something to do with data.

How do you keep current on the happenings/emerging subjects/technologies in your field? How do you balance technology needs?

I utilize Google Alerts to keep up to date on the latest in technologies pertinent to my areas of expertise. Every morning, I receive a daily digest of various articles, blog posts, and news stories about the topics I've chosen. This saves me from having to scour the internet for information or wait to get the latest from others.

What are some of the initiatives your team has worked on related to emerging technologies in your company?

We are constantly evaluating the relevancy and effectiveness of various technologies that can support us and our clients. To name one, we successfully developed a robotic process automation (RPA) bot that has the potential to replace hundreds of hours of mundane, repetitive data entry work. These saved hours can now be shifted to focusing on more critical areas of our clients' finances and processes.

As a student in accounting, did you think that technology would play such a big role in your job?

I can't honestly say that I saw this much technology coming in my career. I thought the extent of technology was spreadsheets such as Microsoft Excel and data analysis programs, such as ACL. I was severely mistaken!

Review and Practice

Key Terms Review

artificial intelligence (AI)
autonomous things (AuT)
bitcoin
blockchain
business process automation
centralized ledger
center of excellence (COE)
conditional statement
consortium blockchain
decentralization
decentralized ledger

decryption
disruptive technology
distributed ledger
encryption
emerging technology
emerging technology COE
extended reality (XR)
gamification
hash string
immutability
Internet of Things (IoT)

miner
node
private blockchain
proof of work
public blockchain
robotic process automation (RPA)
Rogers Adoption Curve
smart contract
transparency
wallet application

Learning Objectives Review

> **❶** Explain how businesses identify risks and opportunities associated with emerging and disruptive technologies.

Companies are defined as being in one of five stages of technology adoption, depending on when they adopt new technologies:

- Innovators: First adopters who are risk takers and technology enthusiasts
- Early adopters: More risk averse but not afraid to try new things
- Early majority: Wait for technology to mature before adopting
- Late majority: Need full clarity and understanding before adopting
- Laggards: Adopt only when they must

New technology that is successful goes through a life cycle of emerging, becoming disruptive, and eventually being widely used.

Four risks of emerging and disruptive technologies are:

- Business disruptions
- Financial loss
- Security vulnerabilities
- Regulatory risk

Three teams in a company are uniquely positioned to work together to manage new technologies:

- Internal audit team
- ERM team
- Emerging technology COE

> **❷** Identify business opportunities provided by disruptive technologies.

The six disruptive technologies every accounting professional should be aware of are:

- Internet of Things (IoT)
- Extended reality (XR)
- Gamification
- Autonomous things (AuT)
- Robotic process automation (RPA)
- Blockchain

> **❸** Apply the principles of robotic process automation (RPA) to accounting use cases.

Robotic process automation (RPA) is a type of business process automation specific to software that automates and manages digital workflows in place of a human.

There are important differences between RPA and artificial intelligence (AI):

- RPA: Rules based, follows orders, handles repetitive tasks, requires initial programming that never changes
- AI: Simulates human thinking, self-selects responses in real time, eliminates human efforts, has initial programming evolve through self-learning

RPA uses logic called a conditional statement to create triggers and subsequent actions in the automation software. RPA conditional statements are formatted as IF [trigger] THEN [action]. A complex RPA conditional statement adds additional clauses, such as IF [trigger] AND ([trigger] OR [trigger]) THEN [action] ELSE IF [second trigger] THEN [second action] ELSE [default action].

Ideal project candidates for RPA are:

- Routine
- Consistent
- Digital
- Time-consuming
- Performed frequently

Many areas in which accounting professionals work are opportunities for RPA projects:

- Accounts payable processing
- Internal audit annual testing

Accounting professionals will adapt to work with RPA and AI to:

- Partner with robots to achieve efficiencies
- Oversee robotic uses in accounting and auditing tasks
- Develop and define existing robotic application use cases
- Execute human-centric tasks such as building relationships and innovating

> **❹** Identify the fundamental principles and technologies of blockchain.

Blockchain is a disruptive technology with significant potential for widespread use in business. Blockchain fundamentals include:

- Nodes, which are computers, laptops, or servers of network participants
- Wallet applications used to broadcast and receive transactions via smart contracts
- Miners who create ledgers

Cryptology uses encryption and decryption to provide a secret code for secure data communication.

There are three types of blockchain ledgers:

- Centralized: Everyone has access to a central ledger.
- Decentralized: Groups of users have access to hubs, each of which has ledgers.

- Distributed: Everyone receives an electronic copy of the ledger.

The fundamental principles of blockchain are decentralization, transparency, and immutability. Decentralization of power leads to transparency, which ensures through consensus that the most accurate records of the ledgers are in the transaction blocks. Transparency leads to immutability, which is the ability of the blockchain to remain unchanged.

Blockchains are either:

- Public: Blockchain technology that was created for bitcoin is a public network that is open to everyone, with no restrictions.
- Private: Private blockchains and partially private (consortium) blockchains have emerged.
- Consortium: Consortium blockchains allow companies to collaborate and leverage information to improve workflows, accountability, and transparency.

Blockchain applications in various industries and sectors like supply chain management, health care, intellectual property rights, and government services are extensively implemented because of the advantages businesses get due to the fundamental principles of blockchain.

⑤ Explain blockchain's relevance to accounting professionals.

Accounting professionals can be involved in blockchain in many ways, including the following:

Auditors:

- Understanding blockchain to audit it
- Gathering sufficient evidence to audit blockchain

- Validating cryptocurrency transactions
- Verifying ownership of transactions in spite of encryption

Financial accountants:

- Blockchain can replace the double-entry ledger system by creating a single ledger linking both companies involved in a transaction.
- Public blockchain ledgers often don't have all the information financial accountants need, so accountants must be comfortable acquiring additional data.

Tax accountants:

- Tax authorities with access to blockchain data can calculate and enforce tax payments, reduce tax fraud risk, and lessen the labor-intensive work of tax professionals.

Small businesses can also benefit from blockchain:

- Increased security with strong authentication processes
- Mitigated risk of data manipulation or deletion
- Lower third-party costs due to self-executing contracts
- Blockchain payment platforms

Blockchain has advantages related to data quality:

- Data integrity: Data is immutable once in blockchain.
- Data retention: Each node can back up an entire blockchain.
- Data validity: Minders verify validation of transactions by majority consensus.
- Data transparency: Data is distributed.
- Data security: A majority, or consensus, of participants must collude for fraud to occur.

CPA questions, as well as multiple choice, discussion, analysis and application, and Tableau questions and other resources, are available online.

Multiple Choice Questions

1. (LO 1) Disruptive technologies
   a. force companies to adapt their operations to stay competitive.
   b. have entered the market but are not yet regularly used by companies.
   c. are difficult to analyze using traditional software tools.
   d. may eventually become emerging technologies.

2. (LO 1) When adopting new technologies, companies can safeguard their businesses from related risks by implementing policies and procedures and internal controls that identify, assess, and mitigate the risk. These include all of the following *except*

   a. establishing an emerging technology center of excellence as part of the organizational structure.
   b. auditing emerging technologies.
   c. waiting to be one of the last companies to adopt a technology.
   d. conducting enterprise-wide risk assessments.

3. (LO 1) Which of the following is the best descriptor for innovators in the Rogers Adoption Curve?
   a. Join immediately
   b. Join as soon as they see any benefit
   c. Join when there is widespread business benefit
   d. Join only when they must

4. (LO 2) Which of the following is the best definition of Internet of Things (IoT)?

    a. Internet of Things is the collection of electronic devices connected to the internet through sensors, software, and other technologies.

    b. Internet of Things takes three forms, which progress from completely real to completely virtual.

    c. Internet of Things is the merger of video game principles and real-world simulations where the user can achieve badges and earn points while they learn new skills.

    d. Internet of Things are physical devices controlled by computers using complex algorithms.

5. (LO 2) CPA Which of the following is *not* an example of gamification?

    a. Building graphics and video displays into simulations to teach workers about dangers at a factory

    b. A competition among salespeople to earn points

    c. Dressing up as a cow to promote a fast-food restaurant

    d. Creating a game to teach students about managerial accounting

6. (LO 2) CPA Cool-Refreshing Beverages sponsors a contest for its programmers, with prizes for the winning teams. This is an example of _____ that is intended to _____.

    a. online marketing; build social media data

    b. industrial espionage; build internal data

    c. gamification; build motivation and team rapport

    d. data mining; use big data

7. (LO 3) Which of the following statements about robotic process automation (RPA) is false?

    a. Follows pre-programmed rules

    b. Simulates human decision making

    c. Suitable for repetitive tasks

    d. Always performs programmed tasks in the same way

8. (LO 3) Which of the following is a feature of artificial intelligence?

    a. Follows pre-programmed "rules"

    b. Ideal for repetitive tasks

    c. Initially programmed tasks never change

    d. Self-selects appropriate responses in real time

9. (LO 3) Review the illustration below. Which word fits best for B?

    a. If

    b. This

    c. Then

    d. That

10. (LO 4) Which of the following is true?

    a. Bitcoin trading is an example of robotic process automation.

    b. Bitcoin trading uses gamification.

    c. Bitcoin trading uses extended reality.

    d. Bitcoin trading uses blockchain technology.

11. (LO 4) Which underlying technology does blockchain *not* depend on?

    a. Network connectivity

    b. Cryptology

    c. Centralized ledgers

    d. Distributed ledgers

12. (LO 4) A blockchain system enables the recording of digital transactions packaged in _____ that form a sequence, like a chain, in a peer-to-peer network.

    a. circles

    b. squares

    c. blocks

    d. wedges

13. (LO 4) Which statement about public blockchains is false?

    a. Participants need permission to join public blockchains.

    b. Public blockchains require proof of work.

    c. Public blockchains are transparent.

    d. Public blockchains are immutable.

14. (LO 5) Compared to traditional ledgers, blockchain systems have the following advantage from a data perspective:

    a. Data retention: Backups of blockchain data are more restrictive.

    b. Data security: A majority of participants in a blockchain must engage in fraud malfeasance for the fraud to be successful.

    c. Data verification: Blockchain transactions are approved by an accounting manager.

    d. Data integrity: A blockchain system relies on an object-oriented database for data storage.

15. (LO 5) The accounting profession is evolving in response to the use of blockchain technology in business. Which of the following best describes how accounting professionals would be impacted by the use of blockchain?

    a. Record transactions related to buying and selling cryptocurrencies

    b. Verify ownership of transactions

    c. Simplify and automate tax compliance and transparency

    d. Secured payments are sent to suppliers as soon as materials are received

16. (LO 5) Aroha wires money from her bank account to her brother Ari in New Zealand for a fee of NZD35. The role of her bank is that of a(n)

    a. intermediary.   **c.** blockchain participant.

    b. miner.   **d.** payee.

17. (LO 5) `CPA` Business transformation through blockchain is likely to occur _____ and requires _____ adoption.

  a. quickly; supplier

  b. eventually; widespread

  c. eventually; supplier

  d. quickly; widespread

18. (LO 5) `CPA` Which of the following is an important outcome of the use of blockchain?

  a. Closed-form accounting

  b. Reduced auditing and compliance costs

  c. Increased centralization of accounting systems

  d. Impenetrable authentication

19. (LO 5) `CPA` At Mega-Construction, secured payments are sent to suppliers as soon as materials are received and scanned. Many attributes of the received goods are also scanned and recorded immediately on receipt (for example, time received, quality indicators, item location through GPS functionality). This information is shared through a distributed ledger. Mega-Construction is likely using _____.

  a. blockchain

  b. TCP/IP

  c. bitcoin

  d. timestamp

Discussion and Research Questions

DQ1. (LO 1) Why should accountants be knowledgeable about new technologies that companies want to adopt? What opportunities and challenges do new technologies present to accounting professionals?

DQ2. (LO 1) Your supervisor asks you to explain the difference between emerging and disruptive technologies. Compare and contrast emerging and disruptive technologies.

DQ3. (LO 1) There are five stages of technology adoption, based on when a business adopts compared to the market. Innovators in the first stage are businesses that are risk takers and have the resources to innovate. Many of their innovations might fail, but they can absorb financial failures. According to *Forbes* magazine, it took 50 years for electricity to be adopted by 60% of the households in the United States and 10 years for cell phones to be adopted. Discuss the potential adoption of self-driving cars in the United States and the business opportunities that this initiative would provide.

DQ4. (LO 2, 5) `Research` Visit the website of one of the Big Four accounting firms (PwC, Deloitte, KPMG, EY). Research the top emerging and disruptive technologies identified recently by the firm you select, list them, and find an example of how that technology works in the real business world. (Specific company names are not required but welcomed.)

DQ5. (LO 3) `Research` `Critical Thinking` Do research to answer the following question: Given that RPA is relatively new, what controls might be most effective for monitoring and managing RPA in a business? Cite your source(s).

DQ6. (LO 3) `Critical Thinking` What knowledge, skills, and abilities do companies need in order to implement and manage RPA?

DQ7. (LO 4) `Critical Thinking` How can blockchain help make the food supply chain more reliable by providing the ability to trace the origins of contaminated food?

DQ8. (LO 5) Explain why knowledge of blockchain is important to external auditors and identify risks of material misstatement associated with blockchain transactions.

Application and Analysis Questions

A1. (LO 1–4) Match up each of the scenarios below with the most appropriate emerging or disruptive technology. The same technology can match more than one scenario.

Emerging and disruptive technologies:

  A. VR

  B. Internet of Things

  C. Drones

  D. Robots and cobots

  E. Blockchain

  F. RPA

Scenarios:

1. A parking deck is patrolled without the need for security personnel to leave their office.

2. A large manufacturer of food packaging products developed an algorithm to predict wear and tear on manufacturing machine parts by collecting historical data like temperature, pressure, and vibration to predict breakdowns and alert maintenance to replace parts and prevent unplanned downtime.

3. A large retailer uses head-mounted displays to train its employees to respond to Black Friday shopping scenarios.

4. A property management company uses technology to survey the condition of land and buildings that its clients own.

5. In a factory, this technology works alongside human workers, augmenting their performance. Their movements are programmed, enabling them to perform specific repetitive manufacturing tasks.

6. In the music industry, this technology is used for smart contracts. By entering into a decentralized, transparent contract, musicians agree to royalties and are paid in full and on time without the involvement of intermediaries.

7. In a call center, this technology does website scraping and collects customer data, does the required data manipulation, and gives the call center manager a single view with all the information about a customer.

8. An accounting firm uses this technology to count cattle in fields during the audits of its farming clients.

9. In a warehouse, this technology moves inventory past humans and other objects because it is programmed with advanced collision avoidance capabilities.

A2. (LO 3) `Research` A survey by consulting firm Protiviti[9] found that 74% of companies that are leaders in robotic process automation (RPA) involved finance and accounting. Research and identify reasons why the majority of leading companies in RPA adoption might include accounting tasks.

A3. (LO 3) `Early Career` `Critical Thinking` The Internal Audit department at Pluto-Cola assigns its team members to special working groups every year. Each group is assigned specific types of internal projects, like data analytics or training, to benefit the operations of the Internal Audit department. This year, you have been assigned to the Process Improvement working group. This working group focuses on identifying opportunities for improvements from formats of audit report templates to automating audit processes.

Pluto-Cola's RPA COE only has capacity to work on two projects for the Internal Audit department this year. As a kickoff this year, your working group is meeting to review suggestions for automation that were collected from the rest of the internal auditors last month. Your working group needs to prioritize the top three suggestions to present to the Internal Audit leadership team. From there, the leadership team will provide feedback on which two should be selected for this year's initiatives.

Choose three of the following automation suggestions and explain why you believe each of them is a top candidate for RPA transformation:

A. Quarterly board reporting requires collecting information from the past quarter's audit reports, which are saved in uniform audit report files on a shared drive. The Internal Audit strategy director must access every report to copy and paste audit issues and conclusions into the board-reporting PowerPoint deck.

B. Each year, the regional audit directors perform an annual audit risk assessment. One metric they use is the "prior year's audits," which indicates how many years it has been since a risk category has been audited. To achieve this, they open the prior year's audit plan and manually add the names of the areas that were audited last year.

C. Every year the audit department must perform a specific regulatory review. It takes three auditors two weeks to complete this engagement. One step is manually reviewing about 10 contracts to verify that the prices match with what is in the business's Excel file.

D. Before each audit engagement, the audit team sends an email announcement, informing the leadership of the department to be audited that an audit is forthcoming. This email includes specifics like the reason this area was selected for an audit this year, which is unique to each audit.

E. During an audit, the team records information in an audit template that captures things like findings, commentary, and recommendations. These items are eventually copied and pasted into the formal audit report template, which will later be sent out to the stakeholders. Every audit uses the same template for capturing information during the engagement and the same template for the formal audit report.

F. Every year, there are two or three audit engagements that are advisory in nature. This means they are special projects focused on providing feedback to the business on how to improve a specific process or provide subject matter expertise. Heavy amounts of ad hoc communication are involved, including emails, memos, and reports.

A4. (LO 3) `Fraud` `Data Fundamentals` `Critical Thinking`
In Applied Learning 7.3, Julia's Cookies' RPA COE was prioritizing potential RPA projects in the finance department. The following RPA project was considered a feasible use case.

Department: Employee Expenses

Process: Reviewing fraud red flags

Description: Finance employees log into the fraud monitoring system on an ad hoc basis to check for any existing red flags in the dashboard. They do not know when red flags are identified unless they log into the system. Then they must manually open the Time and Expense reporting system and filter on the identified employee to find the red flag transaction.

Time spent: Moderate

Frequency: Ad hoc

Suggestion: Have an RPA solution review the fraud red flag dashboard and send an email alert to the Finance employees whenever a new red flag is indicated. The RPA solution could also generate a report that includes the transaction data for each red flag in the body of the email to eliminate the need to log in and search for the transaction.

---

[9]www.protiviti.com/US-en/insights/rpa-survey

Identify an RPA conditional statement ("IF THIS THEN THAT") that includes at least one "AND" clause that you could use in this project.

Remember: Conditional statements must include the "ELSE" clause, which is the default action if the trigger (scenario) does not occur.

Hint: Your "THEN" can be either a summarized statement of the action or a step-by-step sequence of events.

A5. (LO 4–5) `Early Career` `Critical Thinking` In recent business news, China's state-run shipping container line, Cosco Shipping Holdings, entered into an agreement to collaborate with Alibaba Group Holding and the Ant Financial Group on a blockchain project to track cargo in the shipping supply chain. Ant operates the largest blockchain platform in China and processes payments for up to a billion users a day. This new initiative will connect the cargo owners, shipping operators, logistics companies, and ports on a blockchain platform.

You are majoring in accounting, and you secured an exciting summer internship at a company in Seattle. This company ships goods to China using Cosco. The CFO tells you that the company received an invitation to join the blockchain as a trusted participant. During your interview, you told the CFO that you learned all about emerging and disruptive technologies in your AIS class that semester, and you specifically mentioned blockchain. Well, you must have impressed her. The CFO asks you to please explain how participation in the blockchain might benefit the company. Outline how would you respond, beginning with the differences in types of blockchain.

A6. (LO 5) `Critical Thinking` Blockchain systems have a number of advantages over traditional ledgers from a data perspective. Match each of the advantages listed below with one of the following terms: data integrity, data validity, data transparency, data security, data retention.

1. Miners verify validation of transactions by a majority consensus prior to entry in a blockchain ledger.

2. Each node can potentially back up the entire blockchain ledger to provide multiple copies.

3. A transaction is immutable once entered into a blockchain ledger and cannot be changed or deleted.

4. A majority of participants in a blockchain must generally engage in fraud malfeasance for it to happen.

5. A blockchain is widely distributed, whereas a traditional ledger is not.

Tableau Case: Julia's Cookies' Smart Freezers

What You Need

Download Tableau to your computer. You can access www.tableau.com/academic/students to download your free Tableau license for the year, or you can download it from your university's software offerings.

Download the following file from the book's product page on www.wiley.com:

Chapter 7 Raw Data.xlsx

Case Background

Big Picture:
Identify opportunities to minimize food waste costs.

Details:
Why is this data important, and what questions or problems need to be addressed?

- By adopting emerging and disruptive technologies, companies create opportunities to gain advanced insights from the new data these technologies capture. Most recently, Julia's Cookies replaced all of its freezers with "smart" versions. The new freezers can monitor, record, and alert employees of internal temperature changes. Since all of Julia's Cookies' products must be stored frozen until they are ready to be baked, it is important that freezers are monitored. A technical issue with a freezer may result in dangerous bacteria in food products, product waste, and financial losses.

- To avoid food waste and the costs associated with it, the "smart" freezers monitor internal temperatures and inform company analysts if any of the freezers are malfunctioning. This allows technicians to be alerted immediately if a freezer needs maintenance.

- It is important to consider the following questions: What is the daily average temperature in each freezer? What is the average number of times a freezer door is being opened throughout the day? Was any freezer door left open for an unexpected length of time?

Plan:

What data is needed, and how should it be analyzed?

- The data needed to answer the objective is captured by a stand-alone system provided by the freezer manufacturer and stored in a SQL database owned by the Production department.
- The data was filtered to include data for only one Julia's Cookies' location, in Atlanta, Georgia, that has two freezers: F001 and F002. The data set contains data for Q3 and Q4, which include dates from July 1 through December 31.

Now it's your turn to evaluate, analyze, and communicate the results!

Questions

1. How many times, on average, were both Freezer F001 and F002 opened during the day? (Hint: One unique ActivityID = a door opening.)

2. On July 3, how many times, in total, was freezer F002 opened?

3. What was the highest average temperature recorded for freezer F001?

4. Which freezer has an average overall temperature of 0.83°F?

5. On what date did freezer F002 record the *lowest* temperature of −3.63°F? (Hint: Use MIN.)

6. What was the *highest* temperature that freezer F002 recorded? (Hint: Use MAX.)

7. For how many minutes, in total, was freezer F001 opened?

8. For how many minutes, in total, was freezer F001 opened on July 3?

Take it to the next level!

9. On how many days in Q3 and Q4 was freezer F001 opened for 100 minutes or more?

10. In which month did freezer F001 reach the temperature 20°F four different times?

CHAPTER 8

Documenting Systems and Processes

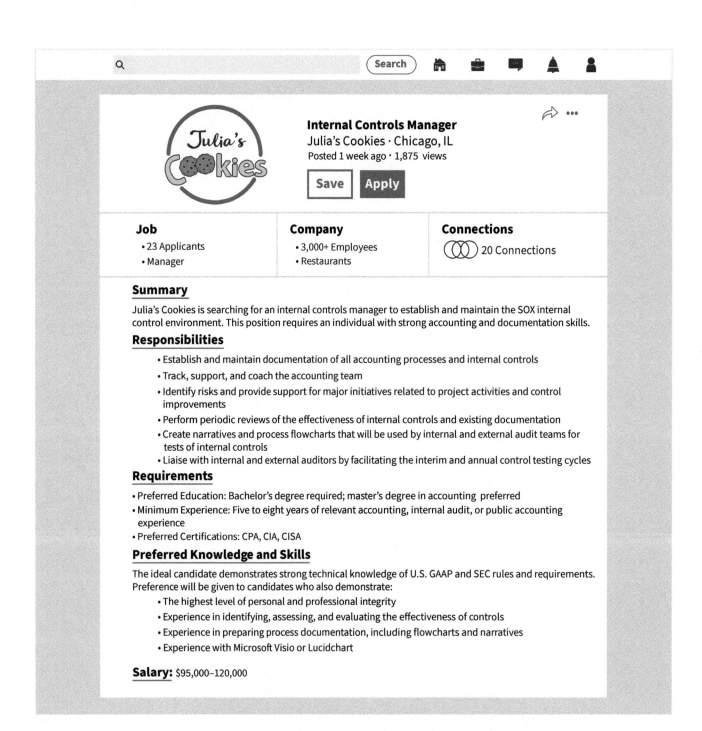

Internal Controls Manager
Julia's Cookies · Chicago, IL
Posted 1 week ago · 1,875 views

Save | Apply

Job	Company	Connections
• 23 Applicants • Manager	• 3,000+ Employees • Restaurants	20 Connections

Summary

Julia's Cookies is searching for an internal controls manager to establish and maintain the SOX internal control environment. This position requires an individual with strong accounting and documentation skills.

Responsibilities

- Establish and maintain documentation of all accounting processes and internal controls
- Track, support, and coach the accounting team
- Identify risks and provide support for major initiatives related to project activities and control improvements
- Perform periodic reviews of the effectiveness of internal controls and existing documentation
- Create narratives and process flowcharts that will be used by internal and external audit teams for tests of internal controls
- Liaise with internal and external auditors by facilitating the interim and annual control testing cycles

Requirements

- Preferred Education: Bachelor's degree required; master's degree in accounting preferred
- Minimum Experience: Five to eight years of relevant accounting, internal audit, or public accounting experience
- Preferred Certifications: CPA, CIA, CISA

Preferred Knowledge and Skills

The ideal candidate demonstrates strong technical knowledge of U.S. GAAP and SEC rules and requirements. Preference will be given to candidates who also demonstrate:

- The highest level of personal and professional integrity
- Experience in identifying, assessing, and evaluating the effectiveness of controls
- Experience in preparing process documentation, including flowcharts and narratives
- Experience with Microsoft Visio or Lucidchart

Salary: $95,000–120,000

CHAPTER PREVIEW   Companies are complex, evolving entities with lots of moving parts. Managing the risks hidden in those parts is crucial to their long-term success. Consistency in operations can mitigate those risks, and one way to accomplish consistency is to document a process so others can systematically repeat it.

Whether you create it or use it, documentation will be part of your accounting career. This chapter focuses on documentation and its relevance to accounting professionals, including:

- Why businesses document processes and systems
- Types of documentation techniques
- How to document business processes and information flows throughout a company
- How to document data movements in a company's systems

When a process is properly documented, it can be consistently repeated by anyone. Documentation also shows a business's stakeholders how a specific process is performed. For example, auditors review systems documentation to understand how a system is designed, and management uses it to ensure that business processes are executing the company's strategy.

First-year accounting professionals are often asked to create or use documentation, especially the narratives and flowcharts you will learn about in this chapter. It's one of the first skills you will learn as an intern or new hire. The job posting at Julia's Cookies for an internal controls manager is based on a real job posting on LinkedIn for a global credit card company. Even at this level of seniority, experience with documentation is an essential skill for candidates.   ∎

Chapter Roadmap

LEARNING OBJECTIVES	TOPICS	JULIA'S COOKIES APPLIED LEARNING
8.1 Explain the goals of documenting systems and processes.	• Systems Documentation • Program Documentation • Operator Documentation • User Documentation	Documentation Levels: Staying Up to Date
8.2 Differentiate among various documentation techniques.	• Documenting the Overall Business • Documenting Processes and Systems • Documenting Data	Documentation Forms: An External Audit Request
8.3 Show how a flowchart illustrates a system or business process.	• Flowchart Shapes • Flowchart Swim Lanes	Process Flowchart: Bank Reconciliation
8.4 Summarize how a data flow diagram (DFD) shows the flow of information in a system.	• DFD Shapes • DFD Levels	Level 1 Diagram: New Customer Accounts
8.5 Summarize the various software and their use for graphical documentation by accounting professionals.	• Graphical Documentation • Software for Graphical Documentation	

CPA You will find the CPA tag throughout the chapter to call out any important topics you may see on the CPA exam.

8.1 Why Do We Document Systems and Processes?

Learning Objective ❶
Explain the goals of documenting systems and processes.

If you have stopped at a typical fast food restaurant to stretch your legs and get something to eat during a long road trip, you may have noticed something about your burger, fries, or salad. No matter where you are in the United States, food from big restaurant chains like McDonald's and Burger King tastes the same. This is because most locations use identical ingredients and sequences to create each order, right down to the amount of ketchup on the burger. If your food ever tastes different, then it's probably because employees didn't follow the process correctly. Documentation of processes and procedures makes this kind of precision and consistency possible.

CPA **Documentation** is a formal record that describes a system or process. Documentation can serve as a future reference, such as a user guide for training, or as an official record, such as an audit trail. Companies use documentation for several reasons:

- Complying with laws and regulations
- Troubleshooting and maintenance
- Consistency across employees' work and how employees are trained
- Capturing usable information for process improvements
- Documenting and evaluating internal control activities

CPA Documentation of systems or processes ranges from organizational charts to complex diagrams that show the flow of information through a system. We will examine the different types of documentation in the following sections.

Section 404 of the Sarbanes-Oxley Act of 2002 (SOX) requires public companies to document their internal control procedures. Documentation is essential for identifying risks related to fraud and errors, as well as issues with business processes. It also helps internal and external auditors evaluate controls to comply with SOX.

Let's look at some nuances related to documenting computer systems. **CPA** Companies maintain four levels of documentation, with each level capturing different elements of the system. Together, they provide a holistic view of the system's operations. These levels start at the bottom with the most detailed description of the system's design and move up to the highest level of instructions for how a user should interact with the system (**Illustration 8.1**).

Why Does It Matter to Your Career?

Thoughts from an Associate, Public Accounting

- Documentation is the best gift a client could give you. When documentation is well organized and thorough, an audit is easier, and you have fewer questions for the client. If your company is undergoing an audit, then this piece of advice could make your life easier.
- Outside of audit, you may be involved with maintaining or reviewing documentation for your company. Accounting professionals are included in discussions related to process improvements, ensuring that appropriate documentation levels are maintained, and using documentation to support their interactions with a system.

Systems Documentation

The developers of a system need to have a clear understanding of the system's purpose and design. This helps them create successful new systems, maintain existing systems, and

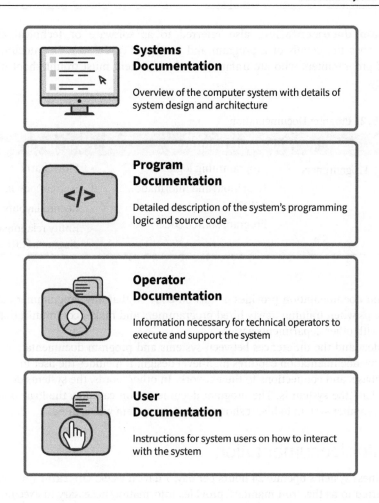

Systems Documentation

Overview of the computer system with details of system design and architecture

Program Documentation

Detailed description of the system's programming logic and source code

Operator Documentation

Information necessary for technical operators to execute and support the system

User Documentation

Instructions for system users on how to interact with the system

Illustration 8.1 Documentation levels form a hierarchy, starting with the technical system detail and moving to user tutorials.

troubleshoot problems. **Systems documentation** provides an overview of a computer system and gives the most granular type of documentation (**Table 8.1**). Systems developers need a clear understanding of the system's purpose and design and use systems documentation to help create new systems, maintain existing systems, and troubleshoot problems.

TABLE 8.1 Systems Documentation

Primary Users	Elements Captured	Forms of Documentation
• **CPA** Developers (most often) • Auditors (to understand the architecture and design of the system they are auditing)	• System architecture • Technical design • User interface design • Inputs and outputs • High-level processing logic • How the system interacts with other systems in the business	• Narrative descriptions • Flowcharts • Data flow diagrams • Entity relationship diagrams (ERDs)

Program Documentation

The programmer who designs a system will know the system code, logic, and layout, as well as the data that has to be input and the information for output. But what happens when that programmer isn't available? Employees take vacations, quit, or are simply unavailable when a system breaks down. Proper documentation mitigates the risks of excessive reliance on key personnel, like the original programmer.

Program documentation, also referred to as software or technical documentation, describes the details of a program and its logic (**Table 8.2**). This documentation is helpful if programmers who are unfamiliar with a system must troubleshoot it during an emergency.

TABLE 8.2 Program Documentation

Primary Users	Elements Captured	Forms of Documentation
• **CPA** Programmers	• Programming logic • Data input and information output • Program source code	• Flowcharts • Source code listings • Record layouts • Entity relationship diagrams (ERDs)

Program documentation provides details on code so that any programmer can interpret it. This helps when training newly hired programmers and makes communication about the program with other departments easier.

To understand the differences between systems and program documentation, remember that systems documentation captures high-level design. It includes the user interface, underlying database, and connections to the network. In other words, the systems documentation shows "what" the system is. The program documentation captures the logic and code that brings a computer system to life. It shows "how" the system was created.

Operator Documentation

Most business systems operate 24 hours per day, 7 days a week. **Operator documentation**, often referred to as the "run manual," provides information necessary to execute a program and make it work (**Table 8.3**).

TABLE 8.3 Operator Documentation

Primary Users	Elements Captured	Forms of Documentation
• **CPA** Exclusively computer operators	• Required equipment and supplies • Execution commands • Error messages • Verification procedures • Expected output • Troubleshooting guidelines • Protocols for backup and recovery of data	• Narrative descriptions • Flowcharts

Computer operators who work in the network operations center (NOC) are trained to keep systems working and troubleshoot any overnight problems before the systems programmers arrive at work the next day.

User Documentation

You have most likely encountered a user manual outlining how to use or assemble a new purchase, such as a laptop or a piece of furniture. This type of user manual typically includes a list of parts, necessary tools, assembly instructions, and troubleshooting tips. Businesses also prepare this type of documentation for their employees. **User documentation** is the content provided to system users to ensure that they are successful at using the system (**Table 8.4**).

TABLE 8.4 User Documentation

Primary Users	Elements Captured	Forms of Documentation
• **CPA** End users of the system • Auditors reviewing documentation to compare how the system should be used to how employees are actually using it	• How to use the system, such as tutorials • System functionalities and features • Tips, such as frequently asked questions • Common errors and how to resolve them • Instructions for inputting data into the system • Instructions to request reports from the system • Procedures for verifying data accuracy	• Narrative descriptions • Flowcharts

At Julia's Cookies, accounting systems documentation is maintained for all four levels of the system, but it has been some time since the documentation was updated. Help Vanessa decide which documentation levels should be updated first in Applied Learning 8.1.

Julia's Cookies   Applied Learning 8.1

Documentation Levels: Staying Up to Date

Vanessa, a staff accountant at Julia's Cookies, is reviewing the accounting systems documentation to ensure that each system is properly documented. They're performing this documentation analysis in preparation for an upcoming external audit.

Vanessa takes notes about the documentation levels missing for each system and rates the documentation from most to least important. They want to ensure that the system owners will focus on creating the most necessary documentation first.

The accounts payable system in particular has outdated documentation—it's more than three years old. Vanessa tells the system owner to update all of the documentation for this system.

Which of these documentation updates do you think should be prioritized, and why would that documentation update be more important than the others?

1. Systems documentation: The overview of the system design, used by system developers and auditors
2. Program documentation: The detailed code and program logic, used by programmers
3. Operator documentation: The technical instructions to operate the system, used by computer operators
4. User documentation: The instructions to use the system, used by end users

SOLUTION

Vanessa should ensure that all regulatory required documentation is created first, and this depends on what type of review is being performed and what is missing.

From there, the system's owner should prioritize the systems documentation. This documentation provides an overview of the system design and includes interactions with other systems in the business. Systems documentation is most often used by systems developers, but it's a helpful aid for auditors to understand the company and where data flows throughout the business. Since this update is being done to prepare for an external audit, Vanessa's team will want to provide this documentation to the external auditors to assist them in their review. Remember, systems documentation is useful for external parties who need to understand the system's design and functionality.

CONCEPT REVIEW QUESTIONS

1. **CPA** What do you understand by documentation?

   Ans. Documentation is a formal record that describes a system or process. It can serve as a future reference, such as a user guide for training or as an official record, such as an audit trail. Documentation of systems or processes ranges from organizational charts to complex diagrams that show the flow of information through a system.

2. **CPA** What are the different levels of documentation that companies maintain?

   Ans. Companies maintain four levels of documentation, with each level capturing different elements of the system: systems documentation, program documentation, operator documentation, and user documentation. Together they provide a holistic view of the system's operations. These levels start at the bottom with the most detailed description of the system's design and move up to the highest level of instructions for how a user should interact with the system.

8.2 How Do We Know Which Type of Documentation to Use?

Learning Objective ❷
Differentiate among various documentation techniques.

Documentation is used to create, capture, evaluate, and audit processes in an accounting information system (AIS). When an area of the business is well documented, a company benefits through:

- **Efficient knowledge transfer:** New employees can quickly familiarize themselves with the department's work and processes.
- **Standardized processes:** Similar processes throughout the company are performed consistently.
- **Process improvements:** Documentation empowers thorough reviews of a department and can point directly to areas where efficiency and effectiveness can be improved.
- **Effective audits:** Internal and external auditors need detailed information to understand an area of the business they are auditing.

In order for documentation to provide these benefits to your company, you must know which form of documentation to use. The appropriate form of documentation depends on the combination of what is being documented and how the documentation will be used:

- Documenting the overall business
- Documenting processes and systems
- Documenting data

In this section, we briefly examine organizational charts, questionnaires, narratives, and entity relationship diagrams (ERDs). Note that using an ERD is a complex method of documenting a database, which we covered in the Designing Systems and Databases chapter. Here, we look at the role an ERD plays in formal documentation. The remainder of this chapter is dedicated to an in-depth discussion of flowcharts and data flow diagrams.

Documenting the Overall Business

Documenting the business involves capturing the people who work there or the state of operations and internal controls. Organizational charts, checklists, and questionnaires are tools that can be helpful in documenting the business.

Organizational Charts

An **organizational chart**, often called an "org chart" for short, is a diagram that shows the employees in the company and their reporting relationships with one another. The chief executive officer (CEO) or the company president is usually at the top of the org chart, with everyone else cascading down from there.

Org charts have many uses, including the following:

- Visualizing an employee directory
- Showing employee responsibilities and how employees fit into the overall company structure
- Depicting reporting relationships
- Showing segregation of duties

Auditors (both internal and external) rely on organizational charts and include them in all their testing. This helps the auditors to test for segregation of duties, independence, turnover within reporting lines, and more. As an accounting professional, you will use your company's organizational chart to identify who to talk to when you need to collaborate or request information from other teams.

An organizational chart can be "tall" (vertical) or "flat" (horizontal) (**Illustration 8.2**). A company is tall when numerous levels of management report to the CEO at the top. As a first-year new hire in such an organization, you will have many people between you and the CEO, such as seniors, managers, senior managers, directors, and more.

Large and complex companies usually have a tall organizational structure to ensure that managers have greater oversight of their employees. Consequently, employees receive more guidance and direction from their immediate managers, which is an advantage. The disadvantage is that employees who are farther down in the structure are far removed from executive management and may feel disconnected.

An org chart is flat, or horizontal, when there are fewer levels of management reporting to the CEO at the top. Managers in this type of structure have more employees reporting to them. A flat organization allows for a greater sense of responsibility and autonomy for employees. Managers generally can't provide as much supervision because they manage so many employees. As a first-year new hire, you may have only a few leaders between you and the CEO, such as a manager, director, and vice president.

Think about which structure you would prefer. Organizational structure is a good topic to ask about during an interview!

Checklists and Questionnaires

CPA Sometimes people outside the business, like auditors, need to understand what is happening. They use a **questionnaire**, which is a list of questions to ask the business team in charge of the process, to gather information about specific procedures and internal controls. Auditors may refer to questionnaires as **checklists**. Audit checklists can consist of questions, items to review, or steps to perform during an audit engagement. Audit questionnaires and checklists are created using standardized templates and client-specific knowledge (external audit) or business process-specific knowledge (internal audit).

In a physical inventory observation, auditors travel to the physical site of the observation and meet with warehouse management. As part of the meeting, auditors go through a list of

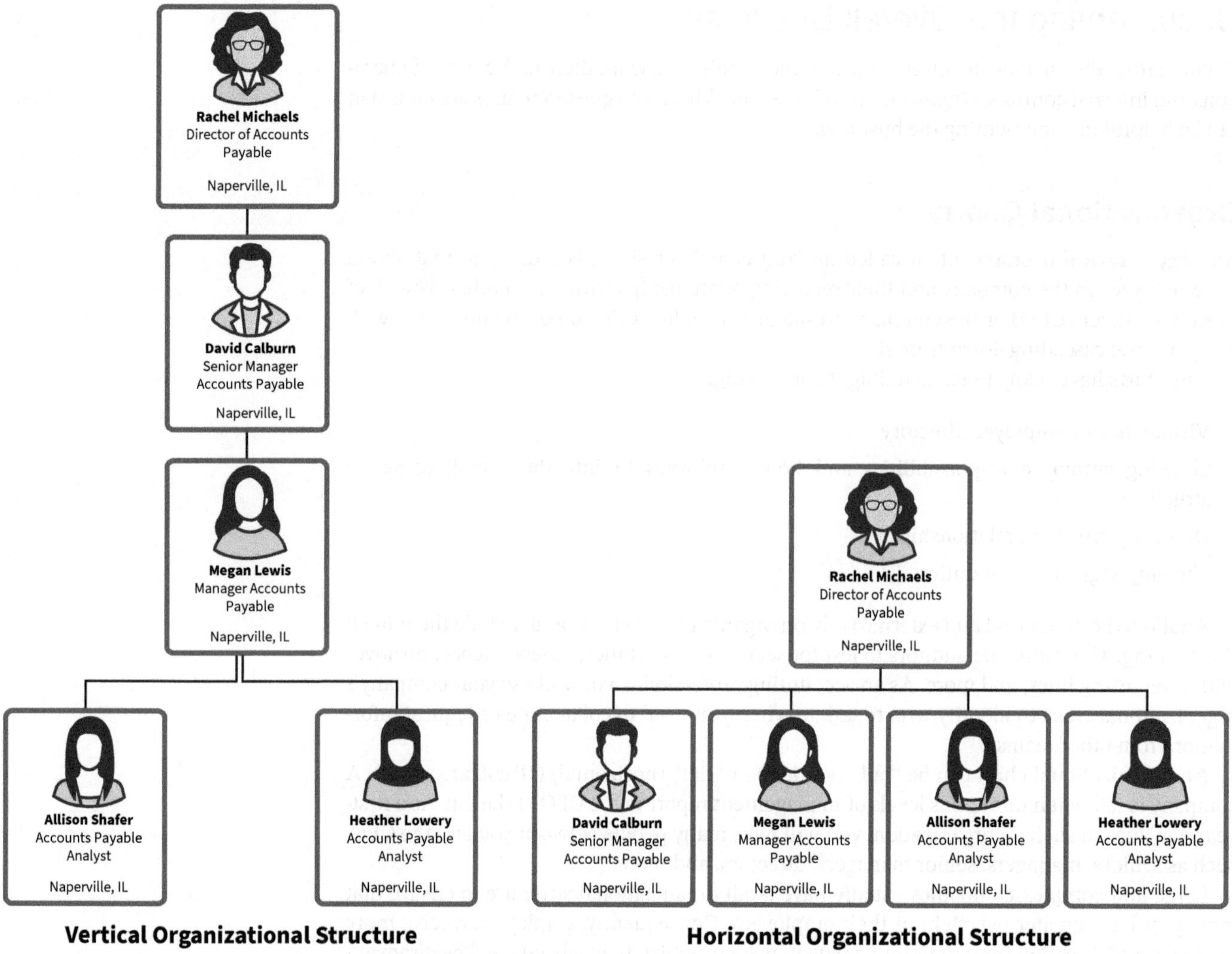

Vertical Organizational Structure

Horizontal Organizational Structure

Illustration 8.2 Tall (vertical) organizational structures have more layers of reporting between the lowest level and the highest level than flat (horizontal) organizational structures.

procedures and controls that the warehouse must follow in order to be compliant. Auditors ask several questions during the warehouse walkthrough, either orally or in writing, with checklists or preformatted questionnaires.

The warehouse management would answer questions such as:

- Has there been any theft during the audit period?
- Were counts checked or were inventory items recounted by persons other than those making original counts?
- Are the counts, as recorded, the final quantities to be used in the inventory listings?
- Was production suspended during the inventory count?
- Were shipping and receiving operations suspended during the inventory count?

Checklists and questionnaires provide further insight and answers to questions and ensure that audits are performed consistently. They are often a required part of many audit engagements, even in our world of audit automation and analytics. Using a checklist or questionnaire also means an auditor will be less likely to forget a step in the process, which might be detrimental to the audit.

Documenting Processes and Systems

Processes and systems can be documented with narrative descriptions or more complex flowcharts, which can be costly to build and maintain. Every time the process or system changes, the documentation becomes obsolete and must be updated. It's easier to update a narrative, so flowcharts may only be used for critical processes and systems, while less critical items have narratives.

Narratives

CPA Businesses use written descriptions of systems and processes as a form of documentation. These **narratives** describe responsibilities in detail, as well as the processes and controls that are in place. A narrative is often accompanied by a visual depiction, such as a flowchart, which you will learn about next. Many first-year accounting professionals are asked to translate an existing narrative into a flowchart, so these concepts are important to understand as you begin your professional accounting career.

An example of a narrative at Julia's Cookies explains the process of a customer ordering a cookie:

> If the customer buys the cookie in store, the customer pays for the cookie at the register and receives the cookie at the counter. If the customer orders the cookie through the mobile application, the customer pays for the cookie on the mobile app at the time of ordering. The cookie is then delivered to the customer's door by a delivery driver.

You will transform this narrative into a flowchart in the next section, but first you need to understand what a flowchart is.

Flowcharts

CPA A **flowchart** depicts the actions or movements of individuals or items in a system or process. Flowcharts present visuals of the management, operations, controls, outside vendors, and systems involved in a business process. A flowchart may be able to fit on a single page, or it might span multiple pages.

CPA Flowcharts are versatile charts that can depict computerized and manual processes, making them a popular choice in business and other professions. Anywhere there is a process or system, there can be a flowchart to help people:

- Understand a process from beginning to end
- Create a visual record of the process, which is used by auditors as formal audit documentation
- Find opportunities for process improvements
- Communicate intricate processes easily and clearly
- Plan a project and evaluate its feasibility
- Evaluate internal controls, since the chart can identify control failures like those involving segregation of duties

The type of flowchart used depends on the focus of the end user, as shown in **Table 8.5**.

Throughout this course, process flowcharts are used to depict business processes that generate data that is captured through an AIS. In the next section, you will learn how to read and create process flowcharts.

Business Process Model and Notation (BPMN)

Business Process Model and Notation (BPMN) is a documentation method that depicts the steps of a business process from start to finish. BPMN is a standardized methodology managed by the Object Management Group, which is an organization that offers certifications for process improvement specialists to become credentialed BPMN analysts.

Like process flowcharts, BPMN creates a visual that can be easier to understand than a narrative description. Process flowcharts and BPMN differ in the shapes and technical layouts they use, but they both serve the same purpose and can be used interchangeably, based on the preference of the creator or business stakeholders who will use the visual aid. This course uses process flowcharts rather than BPMN due to the prevalence of process flowcharts in the accounting profession today.

TABLE 8.5 Flowchart Types

Flowchart Type	Description	Example
Document flowchart	This type of flowchart shows the flow of documents, such as physical or digital purchase orders, through a process.	A document flowchart may show the movement of a purchase requisition and purchase order through the purchasing process. Eventually the purchase order is used by accounts payable in a three-way match with the vendor invoice and receiving documents. All of these documents and their movements to different departments can be depicted in the flowchart.
Systems flowchart	This type of flowchart illustrates the flow of information through a system, including how information is accessed and where data is stored.	In the purchasing process, a purchase order may be digital and part of the system. A systems flowchart shows the data captured when a purchase order is created and where it is stored in a database. It also shows how and when users log into the system during the process. It's the same purchasing process as in the document flowchart but from the perspective of the system.
Program flowchart	This type of flowchart shows the sequence of coded instructions in a computer program that enable it to perform specified logical and mathematical operations.	A purchasing system is built using programming languages. A program flowchart shows the underlying code and logic that supports each of the process steps in the purchasing system.
Process flowchart	This type of flowchart shows the flow of activity through the company, including the key parties and actions that they perform. Process flowcharts are also known as business-process diagrams.	The purchasing process can be visualized from the perspective of actions and people. Systems are included in process flowcharts, but databases and login points are not the focus. The focus is instead on the business process and related internal controls.

Why Does It Matter to Your Career?

Thoughts from an Internal Audit Data Analytics Manager, Financial Services

- Newly hired accounting professionals are expected to read and understand most types of documentation. The more you understand, the more valuable you are to the company.
- If you choose a career in audit, you will likely be asked to document a system or process within your first year. One of the most common tasks you will perform is translating a narrative to a flowchart.

Documenting Data

While systems flowcharts capture the flow of information through a system, sometimes more technical documentation is needed. In such cases, developers create documentation that captures data movement within a system and how data is stored in its database.

Data Flow Diagrams

CPA A **data flow diagram (DFD)** is a graphical representation of the flow of data in an information system. A DFD describes the processes involved in a system to manage the life cycle of the data, from generation (input) to storage (databases) to reporting (output). For most people, visuals are easier to comprehend than complicated text.

CPA A DFD is not the same as a flowchart. A flowchart details the flow of information, documents, or activities in a system or process. A DFD uses different shapes and rules to depict the flow of data through a system at a technical level. While flowcharts are often used to evaluate controls in a system, DFDs are used when developing new systems.

Advantages of a DFD include:

- Shows system functionality and limits
- Documents a business process from the perspective of its related data
- Easier to use than a text description
- Offers an easy-to-understand system diagram for users to comprehend the data flow
- Helps new employees understand a system
- Familiarizes auditors with the system they are auditing

You will learn how to read and create DFDs in the last section of this chapter.

Entity Relationship Diagrams (ERDs)

CPA You have learned that a relational database organizes structured data in interrelated tables that are connected based on similarities between the tables, known as relationships. In the Designing Systems and Databases chapter, we explained how an **entity relationship diagram (ERD)** is a graphical illustration of all the tables in a database and their relationships (**Illustration 8.3**).

Remember that an ERD is not the same as a database schema, which is a logical diagram of a database's structure and organization that depicts the relationships between tables and acts as a blueprint for database administrators. These two types of tools have different uses.

Database administrators use database schemas to build databases, and developers use them to understand and access the data in databases. In contrast, ERDs are designed for business end users who don't have the technical skills to read a database schema. ERDs help these users understand the layout and data within a relational database.

Recall that there are three types of ERDs, each with its own complexity, uses, and requirements (**Table 8.6**). ERDs are an important part of database design and are used by accounting professionals when performing data analytics to ensure that the correct data is being used.

Illustration 8.3 An entity relationship diagram shows the way tables in a relational database are connected by different types of relationships.

TABLE 8.6 Three Types of Entity Relationship Diagrams

	Conceptual ERD	Logical ERD	Physical ERD
Complexity	Simplest model	Introduces more detail	Most complex model
Use	Used by business end users and database designers to capture business needs and to understand the general plan for the database	Used by database designers to refine the business needs of the database and begin modeling data at a more technical level	Created by database designers and used by database administrators and developers (along with a database schema) to build and access the database
Minimum requirements	Table names and lines connecting related tables together	Table names, lines connecting related tables together, and lists of fields included in each table	Table names, lists of fields in each table, data types, restrictions to be programmed into the database, and technical details about how each table is connected to another

Now that you have reviewed the different forms of documentation, help Annamary select the best type of documentation for her external audit team in Applied Learning 8.2.

Julia's Cookies   Applied Learning 8.2

Documentation Forms: An External Audit Request

Annamary, an external auditor whose client is Julia's Cookies, is in the documentation request phase of her audit engagement. During this phase, the audit team sends requests for the documentation they need to review to gain an understanding of the company's control environment.

Annamary's manager provides her with a list of documentation requirements, but first Annamary needs to identify the type of documentation required for each. Annamary will choose from:

- Narrative
- Data flow diagram
- Organizational chart
- Flowchart

Which type of documentation do you think will best fill each of the following needs?

1. Reporting lines between CFO, the Accounting department, and Internal Audit
2. How information flows within the General Ledger system and the payroll process
3. A detailed description of guidelines followed prior to posting payroll for the pay period
4. A step-by-step outline of ordering raw materials

SOLUTION

1. Organizational chart: This visual shows the reporting lines between employees in the organization.
2. Data flow diagram or systems flowchart: Both of these methods present the movement of data or information through a system or process.
3. Narrative and/or process flowchart: A narrative gives a detailed description of a process and is often accompanied by a process flowchart, which provides a visual snapshot of the process.
4. Process or document flowchart: A process flowchart follows the people involved, and a document flowchart follows purchase orders and other documents; in either case, the flowchart explains the process.

CONCEPT REVIEW QUESTIONS

1. What is an organizational chart?

   Ans. An organizational chart, often called an "org chart", is a diagram that shows the employees in the company and their reporting relationships with one another. The chief executive officer (CEO) or the company president is usually at the top of the org chart, with everyone else cascading down from there.

2. What are the two types of organizational chart?

   Ans. The two types of organizational chart are "tall" (vertical) and "flat" (horizontal). A company is tall when numerous levels of management report to the CEO at the top. An org chart is flat, or horizontal, when there are fewer levels of management reporting to the CEO at the top.

3. **CPA** How do auditors use questionnaires and checklists for assessing internal control environment?

   Ans. Sometimes people outside the business, like auditors, need to understand what is happening. They use a questionnaire, which is a list of questions to ask the business team in charge of the process, to gather information about specific procedures and internal controls.

4. **CPA** What are flowcharts and what do they depict?

   Ans. A flowchart depicts the actions or movements of individuals or items in a system or process. Flowcharts present visuals of the management, operations, controls, outside vendors, and systems involved in a business process. Flowcharts are versatile charts that can depict computerized and manual processes, making them a popular choice in business and other professions.

5. Match the following:

Flowchart Type	Description
1. Document flowchart	**A.** This type of flowchart shows the sequence of coded instructions in a computer program that enables it to perform specified logical and mathematical operations.
2. Systems flowchart	**B.** This type of flowchart shows the flow of documents, such as physical or digital purchase orders, through a process.
3. Program flowchart	**C.** This type of flowchart shows the flow of activity through the company, including the key parties and actions that they perform.
4. Process flowchart	**D.** This type of flowchart illustrates the flow of information through a system, including how information is accessed and where data is stored.

Ans. 1-B, 2-D, 3-A, 4-C

6. What is Business Process Model and Notation (BPMN)?

Ans. BPMN is a documentation method that depicts the steps of a business process from start to finish. BPMN is a standardized methodology managed by the Object Management Group, which is an organization that offers certifications for process improvement specialists to become credentialed BPMN analysts.

7. **CPA** Compare flowcharts and data flow diagrams (DFDs).

Ans. A DFD is not the same as a flowchart. A flowchart details the flow of information, documents, or activities in a system or process. A DFD uses different shapes and rules to depict the flow of data through a system at a technical level. While flowcharts are often used to evaluate controls in a system, DFDs are used when developing new systems.

8.3 How Do Flowcharts Illustrate Systems or Business Processes?

Learning Objective ❸
Show how a flowchart illustrates a system or business process.

A typical day for most people consists of a series of actions and decisions. Even something as simple as ordering breakfast can be described as a series of completed steps and decisions. For example, if you order a breakfast sandwich at a local restaurant, you must decide whether you also want coffee. If you don't want coffee, then your breakfast order is complete. Ordering coffee adds an extra step to the sequence of events. We can capture this sequence of events and decisions in a flowchart like the one shown in **Illustration 8.4**.

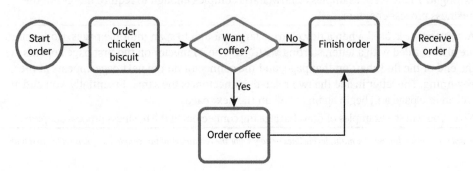

Illustration 8.4 The process of ordering breakfast can be depicted using a process flowchart.

While flowcharts can be hand drawn, software such as Lucidchart and Microsoft Visio are used extensively in the business world and in the accounting profession. Flowcharting capabilities are also available in basic Microsoft software including Word, Excel, and PowerPoint. Creating and interpreting flowcharts are essential skills for accounting professionals. The type of flowchart you use will depend on your task and focus. Recall that a process flowchart shows the flow of activity through a company. In this course, you will find process flowcharts depicting business activities and controls for key business processes that make up the basic business model. This section explains the most important elements of a flowchart.

Flowchart Shapes

A flowchart consists of various shapes, each with its own meaning. The type of flowchart determines which shapes are used. **Table 8.7** shows the six shapes used in a process flowchart, which is the simplest flowchart and requires the fewest shapes.

TABLE 8.7 Process Flowchart Shapes

Shape		Description
Terminator (circle or oval)	Start/End	The **terminator shape** marks the start or end of a process. It can be filled with either the word "Start" or "End" or a description of the beginning of a process. The flowcharts in this chapter use "Start," but you will encounter process flowcharts in other chapters with more specific beginning terminators, such as "Year-End Reporting Begins." Note: Every flowchart should start and end with a terminator.
Process (rectangle)	Process	The **process shape** represents an event, or step, within the flow. A flowchart could be as detailed as having a process shape for every step of baking cookies, such as "Add one egg" followed by "Stir ingredients together," or as general as "Bake cookies." Note: A process shape always has a single line entering it and can have multiple lines exiting it. This is because flowcharts can split into two paths if a process event results in two subsequent events, such as sending an email to two different departments.
Flowline (arrow)	→	The **flowline** connects shapes together. Each shape in a flowchart must have at least one incoming flowline and one outgoing flowline, unless it's a terminator. The arrow of the line points in the direction of the flowchart flow. Note: Flowlines cannot have arrows on both sides.
Decision (diamond)	Decision	The **decision shape** represents a yes/no or true/false question that must be answered for the process to continue on the correct flowline. When the flowchart reaches a decision, it splits into two branches—one for the answer "Yes" and one for the answer "No." For example, if a customer orders a cookie, there is a decision on whether the order is placed in a store or in the app. You'll see a decision for "Purchased in store?" in the process flowchart example that follows. Note: A decision shape must have a single flowline entering it and two flowlines exiting it.
Merge* (triangle)	Merge	The **merge shape** connects two or more paths of a flowchart into a single flowline. There is no limit on the number of paths that can merge through this shape. Note: A merge should always have multiple flowlines entering it and a single flowline exiting it. You will see examples of flowcharts complex enough to require merges in the business process chapters.
Connector* (circle)	A	A **connector** is used when a flowchart is large enough to span multiple pages. Connectors are always filled with a letter, starting with "A." The connector on the first page appears at the end of the flowchart on that page, and the connector on the next page appears at the beginning. The letter inside the two related connectors is the same. Essentially, you end at "A" on one page and begin again at "A" on the next page. Note: You will see examples of flowcharts using connectors in the business process chapters.

*Merge and connector shapes are used only for complex processes that require multiple flowlines or pages. For the remainder of this chapter, we focus on the first four shapes to build a foundation of the basics.

Since process flowcharts provide a high-level view of a process, they only utilize these first six shapes. But if more detail is necessary, such as depicting when something is done manually versus automatically in a system, then we can use more shapes. **Table 8.8** shows additional shapes that can be used in a systems or document flowchart.

TABLE 8.8 Additional Flowchart Shapes

Document (rectangle with wavy bottom)	Document	The document shape represents a physical or digital document, such as an email, a report, or an invoice.
Input/output (parallelogram)	Input/output	The input/output shape represents data or information coming into the process or leaving the process, such as an order coming in to the bakery.
Database (cylinder)	Database	The database shape represents data storage. Data is input into the database, and information is retrieved.
Manual input (trapezoid)	Manual input	The manual input shape depicts data that is manually input into a system, such as a user typing in a username and password to access the system.
Manual operation (trapezoid)	Manual operation	The manual operation shape is used when a user physically takes an action, such as placing a printout of a report on someone's desk or physically placing freshly baked cookies on a cooling rack. Note: Manual operation is different from manual input, as no new data is being input into the system during a manual operation.

Flowchart shapes combine to create a logical path of sequential steps, such as for a business process, which is what we focus on for the remainder of this section. A flowchart is either vertically or horizontally oriented, based on what looks best visually. For a PowerPoint slide, horizontal orientation may be ideal, whereas vertical orientation works best in the pages of a textbook.

Let's go back to Julia's Cookies and explore the business activity of converting resources into the cookies sold in stores. Consider the following narrative:

> After Julia's Cookies purchases ingredients from local vendors, the cookie dough is mixed at factories and then frozen. The frozen cookie dough is shipped to regional stores and baked when a customer orders a cookie. If the customer buys a cookie in store, the customer pays for the cookie at the register and receives the cookie at the counter. If the customer orders a cookie through the mobile application, the customer pays for the cookie on the mobile app, and the cookie is delivered to the customer's door by a delivery driver.

Why Does It Matter to Your Career?

Thoughts from a First-Year Risk Assurance Associate, Public Accounting

- In auditing, most walkthroughs require the creation of a flowchart. Internal auditors may create flowcharts from scratch, while external auditors rely on documentation created by the client. These flowcharts facilitate understanding of the business process to help the audit team to correctly evaluate the risk within the process.

- When you start at a company, ask for flowcharts that depict your department's processes. They will help you understand the business activities that make up the processes, responsibilities within your department, and how the department integrates with other functional areas.

By using the first four shapes—terminator, flowline, process, and decision—we can transform this narrative into a process flowchart (**Illustration 8.5**). Process flowcharts like these

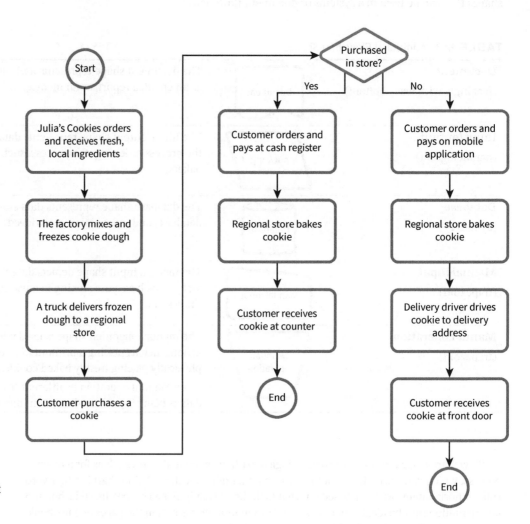

Illustration 8.5 This process flowchart depicts the high-level purchases-to-sales processes at Julia's Cookies.

are useful for documenting financial reporting processes. Help the Accounting department at Julia's Cookies create a process flowchart for posting journal entries in Applied Learning 8.3.

Julia's Cookies | Applied Learning 8.3

Process Flowchart: Bank Reconciliation

Jasmin works in the Accounting department at Julia's Cookies. They outline the process for recording accounting transactions in the General Ledger during the month with a narrative so that they can easily explain the process to the new hire that they're training:

Accounting transactions are identified as either routine or nonroutine. Routine transactions are recorded in special journals like sales, purchases, cash receipts, and cash payments journals. Then subsidiary ledgers like accounts payable, accounts receivable, and inventory ledgers are updated. Nonroutine transactions are recorded in the general journal. Special and general journal entries are all eventually posted to the General Ledger.

Jasmin has also created the flowchart below. What steps do you think are missing for the shapes numbered 1, 2, 3, and 4?

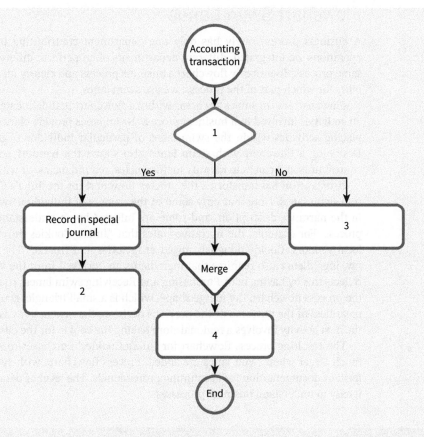

SOLUTION

Jasmin is missing:

1. This decision shape should depict which path to take for a routine versus a nonroutine transaction.

2. This process shape should depict the subsidiary ledgers. Routine transactions are recorded in special journals and then recorded in subsidiary ledgers.

3. This process shape should depict the general journal. Nonroutine transactions are recorded only in the general journal.

4. This process shape should depict the General Ledger. Both routine and nonroutine transactions are posted to the General Ledger, which requires the two paths to merge before the process shape.

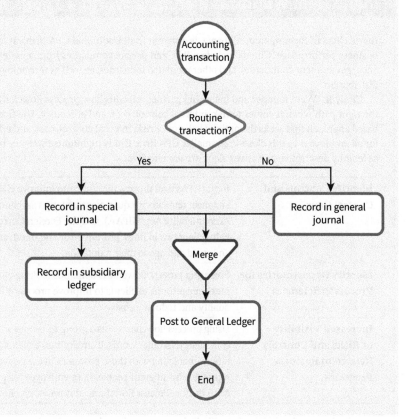

Flowchart Swim Lanes

A business process rarely has only one department contributing to it. Because company operations are integrated, different departments often perform different activities within the same process. To properly flowchart a business process and clearly identify who has responsibility for which part of the process, we use swim lanes.

Flowchart **swim lanes** are areas within a flowchart that delineate the responsibilities for all activities involved in a business process. Swim lanes provide clarity and accountability by placing activities within the swim lanes of particular individuals, groups, or departments. Designing a flowchart with swim lanes also shows the handoff points between different contributors and can help identify inefficiencies, redundancies, or waste in the process.

Illustration 8.6 transforms the process flowchart for the Julia's Cookies business model into swim lanes. Note that only some of the owners of individual swim lanes are identified in the narrative description, and some are inferred by an understanding of the accounting process. For example, the narrative states that "Julia's Cookies purchases ingredients from local vendors. Cookie dough is mixed at factories and frozen." The process of purchasing raw ingredients also requires that ingredients are received from the vendors. Illustration 8.6 reflects this by having both Purchasing and Receiving swim lanes. To reduce redundancies in the process flowchart, the merge shape, which is a small triangle, is used. This indicates that regardless of the outcome of the previous decision, the next activity is the same. In this case, the next activity involves a regional store baking the cookie for the customer.

The resulting process flowchart for Julia's Cookies' purchases-to-sales business model is much larger when swim lanes are added. Process flowcharts with swim lanes are a favorite form of documentation for accounting professionals. The level of detail and visual aid makes it easy to understand business processes.

In the Real World | A Picture Is Worth a Thousand Words

Insyte CPAs in Birmingham, Alabama, is different from traditional CPA firms. It focuses only on risk management, internal control, and business performance. Clients include public and private companies from a variety of industries, including health care, banking, insurance, government contractors, and other regulated industries, as well as technology, professional service companies, and manufacturing/distribution.

Cindy B. Wyatt, founder and managing partner, explains how process flowcharts provide a roadmap to assess whether the client is on the right path when it comes to risk, internal control, cost, and efficiency. The firm's internal control engagements all begin with a risk-based approach that seeks the optimal balance of risk, internal control, cost, and efficiency. This makes expertise in flowcharting essential for all employees in this close-knit, smaller CPA firm. Cindy highlights three key benefits of process mapping for her firm and its clients, as lengthy descriptive narratives alone are not effective.

Identify Controls and Control Gaps	Insyte CPAs uses process flowcharts to improve clients' internal controls so they can manage risk and meet regulatory requirements, such as Sarbanes-Oxley, the Health Insurance Portability and Accountability Act (HIPAA), and the Foreign Corrupt Practices Act (FCPA). In this context, the company helps clients avoid fines, prevent error and fraud, avoid discovery of deficiencies during external audits, and avoid damage to their reputation.
Identify Opportunities for Process Efficiencies	Preparing process flowcharts demands looking closely at each part of the process. This helps Insyte make suggestions to clients to improve process efficiency and effectiveness by improving process quality and reducing costs.
Increased Visibility of Risks and Controls Related to Business Processes	Using process flowcharts puts a group of people on a level playing field, eliminates silos, and promotes consistency. In other words, it streamlines collaboration between process and control owners and others interacting with those processes in the organization. With proper documentation, processes are repeatable by different people. If an employee resigns, then a new employee can use the flowcharts to learn the job. Process flowcharts also provide a checklist of existing controls.

A few last words of advice from Cindy: keep process flowcharts updated, as processes are a work in progress, with changes and updates occurring as a business grows and evolves.

Why do you think it is important to document business processes? Is this a skill you feel prepared to use when you graduate? If not, what can you do now to get ready?

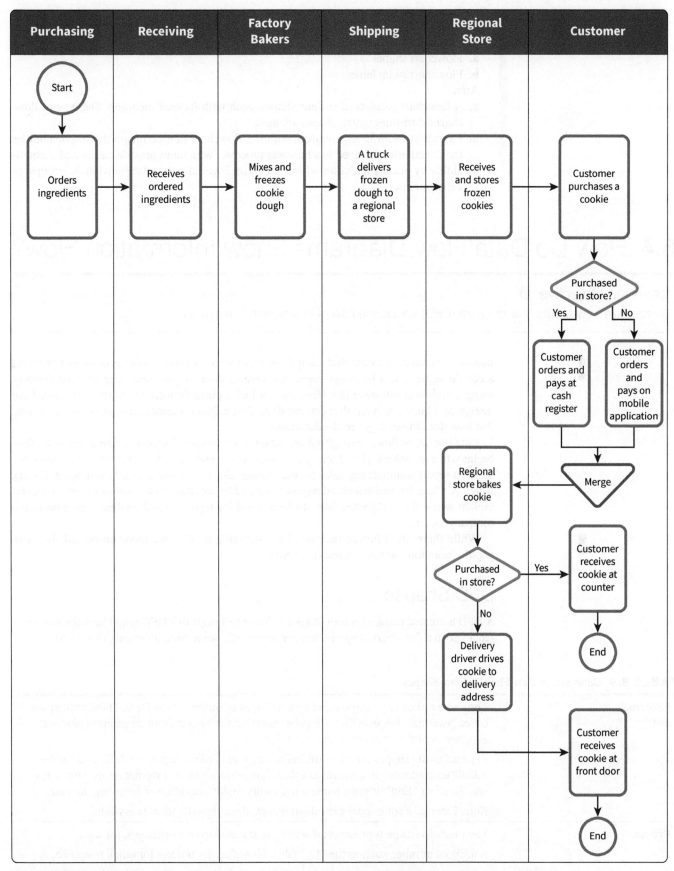

Illustration 8.6 Adding swim lanes to the process flowchart for Julia's Cookies presents a more detailed and granular view of the process.

> **CONCEPT REVIEW QUESTION**
>
> 1. Write a short note on:
>   a. Flowchart shapes
>   b. Flowchart swim lanes
>   **Ans.**
>   a. A flowchart consists of various shapes, each with its own meaning. The type of flow-chart determines which shapes are used.
>   b. Flowchart swim lanes are areas within a flowchart that delineate the responsibilities for all activities involved in a business process. Swim lanes provide clarity and account-ability by placing activities within the swim lanes of particular individuals, groups, or departments.

8.4 How Do Data Flow Diagrams Show Information Flow?

Learning Objective ❹

Summarize how a data flow diagram (DFD) shows the flow of information in a system.

Business events create data that companies must store. A Julia's Cookies customer ordering a cookie delivery is a business event that creates data. If you have ever ordered delivery using a mobile application like Uber Eats or had a pizza delivered to your home, you have instigated a business event that created data. When data is created, it's stored in a database. But how does the data get to the database?

Data travels, or flows, throughout an organization through its information systems. Its flow begins when an order is placed and goes onward to the end users, like the chief financial officer seeing a report summarizing sales for the quarter. Businesses use a data flow diagram (DFD), which you have learned is a visual representation of information flow within a system, to clearly explain where data originates, how it's being used for reporting and analysis, and who in the company sees it.

While there are different methods for visualizing a DFD, we focus on one of the most popular notation methodologies: Gane-Sarson.

DFD Shapes

A DFD is created using only four shapes. While a rectangle in a DFD might look the same as a rectangle in a flowchart, it symbolizes, or represents, something different (**Table 8.9**).

TABLE 8.9 Gane-Sarson Data Flow Diagram Shapes

External entity	External entity	The **external entity shape** represents an input or output of the DFD. These entities are called "external" because they are either entering the system from an external place or exported out of the system to an external place.
		External entity shapes are often the beginning and ending shapes of a DFD and can be called "terminators." In contrast to a flowchart terminator, an external entity cannot just say "Start" or "End"; it must name a real entity that is providing or receiving the data.
		Note: External entities only provide or receive data; they do not process data.
Process	1.0 Process	The **process shape** represents an activity that transforms, or changes, the data.
		A decimal number, such as the "1.0" label, identifies the process for quick reference.
		Processes are always expressed as a singular verb and a singular noun, such as "Verify order" or "Apply payment."
		Note: A process shape must be connected to at least one external entity.

TABLE 8.9 (*Continued*)

Data store	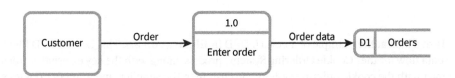	The **data store shape** represents a data repository such as a database or data warehouse. The data store retains data for later use.
		A data store can also be the beginning or ending of a data flow diagram.
		A "D" and numeric, such as the "D1" label, identifies the data store for quick reference.
		The name of a data store describes what the store is storing, such as "Inventory" or "Orders."
Data flow	⟶	The **data flow line** illustrates movement of data between external entities, processes, and data stores.
		The data flow line is labeled with the type of data being transmitted, such as "Purchase order" or "Order data."
		Note: Data flow lines can have arrows at both ends to depict a two-way flow of information, unlike flowlines in flowcharts, which must always move in one direction.

Illustration 8.7 provides a simple example of a DFD created by Julia's Cookies.

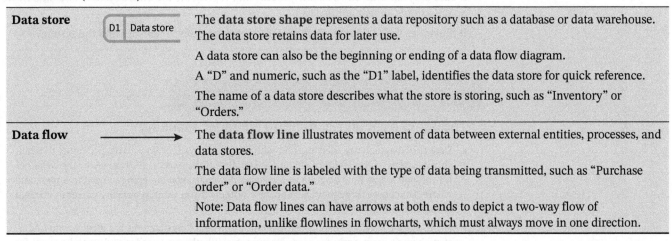

Illustration 8.7 Julia's Cookies' process depicted in a data flow diagram shows the movement of data from its generation to storage.

This DFD describes a simple process: a customer (*external entity*) enters an order (in a mobile app, for example—a *process*), and the order data is stored in an Orders database (*data store*) for future use by the system.

For a data flow to be valid, data must flow:

- Between a process and an external entity (either direction)
- Between a process and a data store (either direction)
- Between two processes that are guaranteed to be running at the same time

To keep things simple for the purposes of an AIS, we focus on the first two types of data flows. This means that a data flow diagram can begin and end with either an external entity or a data store.

DFD Levels

You might have noticed that Illustration 8.7 is a very short and simple diagram for a complicated process. To capture the detailed complexities of a process, there are three different levels to a DFD. Each new layer adds details and complexities on the data flow. To find the inefficiencies in the data flow, an IT professional might depend on the greatest level of detail that is offered in a diagram, while business end users may prefer a high-level overview of the DFD to understand the big picture of the flows.

Level 0 Diagrams

A **Level 0 diagram**, also referred to as a context diagram, is a summary that gives a high-level overview of data flows:

- It must fit on one page.
- It provides a snapshot of the data flow that is designed to be understood by all business audiences—from stakeholders to developers.

- It uses only external entities, one process that represents the entire system, and data flows; no data stores appear at this level.
- It illustrates the exchange of information between external entities and the system.

Why Does It Matter to Your Career?

Thoughts from an Accounting Manager, Banking

- Data flow diagrams are used together with narratives, systems flowcharts, and entity relationship diagrams to give auditors a full understanding of the systems they are reviewing. Whether it's through a data flow diagram or a systems flowchart, you are going to need to understand where data moves throughout a company's systems if you want to pursue a career in internal or external audit.

- For those not interested in a career in audit, using data flow diagrams is a great way to understand how a system works for your own purposes. Whether you need to understand systems for a certification exam like the CPA, CIA, or CISA or just want to become comfortable with your own work environment and the impact you have on your company's systems, using data flow diagrams is a helpful way to view a system.

Take a look at the example of a Level 0 DFD in **Illustration 8.8**. This Level 0 DFD illustrates the data flow for the "Cookie Ordering System" process, along with the key external entities that interact with the cookie ordering system: the customer, the supplier, and a Julia's Cookies store.

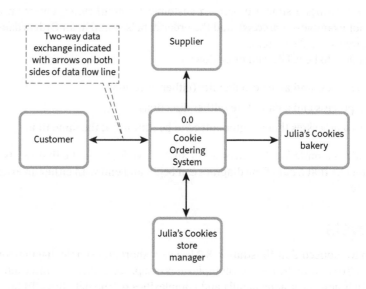

Illustration 8.8 A Level 0 DFD includes only one process and external entities.

Level 1 Diagrams

When more details are needed than are given in a Level 0 diagram, a Level 1 diagram is used. A **Level 1 diagram** highlights the main functions carried out by the system and drills down further into the DFD process by "decomposing" the system. It breaks down each process into further subprocesses.

Illustration 8.9 breaks down the single process "Cookie Ordering System" from our Level 0 example into multiple processes.

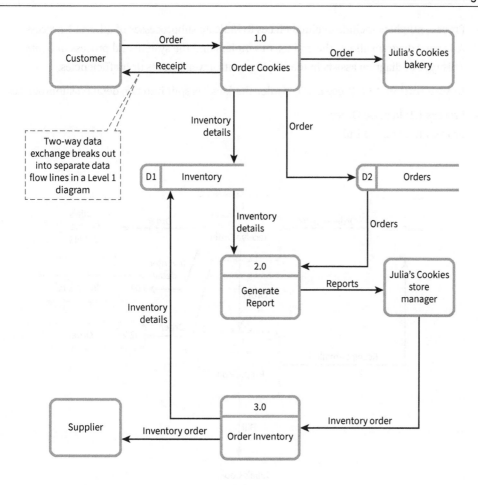

Illustration 8.9 A Level 1 DFD shows multiple processes, external entities, and data stores.

The Level 1 diagram decomposes the single original process into three processes:

Process 1.0: Order Cookies

- Customer places order and receives receipt (external entity)
- Process transforms customer order
- Process sends order to bakery (external entity)
- Process updates inventory details in inventory (D1 data store)
- Process updates order in orders (D2 data store)

Process 2.0: Generate Report

- Process accesses inventory details from inventory (D1 data store)
- Process accesses orders data from orders (D2 data store)
- Process generates a report
- Process sends report to store manager (external entity)

Process 3.0: Order Inventory

- Store manager (external entity) uses the report to create an inventory order
- Process places inventory order with supplier (external entity)
- Process updates inventory details in inventory (D1 data store)

Level 2 Diagrams

The Level 1 diagram shows multiple processes and external entities. However, each process is still high level. For example, "Order Cookies" (Process 1.0) is a multistep, complex process with its own data flow. To see the detailed data flow within the "Order Cookies" process, we create a Level 2 diagram.

A **Level 2 diagram** is usually the most detailed DFD:

- Process numbers include decimal places to indicate subprocesses of a Level 1 process.
- A Level 2 diagram allows the end user to understand the system and process in depth.
- This type of diagram assists in identifying control weaknesses or inefficiencies.

In **Illustration 8.10**, Process 1.0, "Order Cookies," is split into two detailed subprocesses:

- Process 1.1: Receive Order
- Process 1.2: Prepare Bill

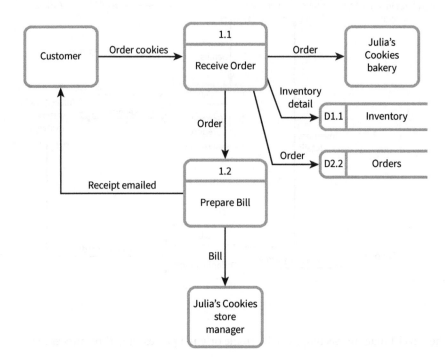

Illustration 8.10 A Level 2 DFD breaks processes from a Level 1 DFD into subprocesses labeled with decimal point reference numbers.

Julia's Cookies needs a Level 1 data flow diagram to capture the movement of data when customers create new accounts. Help decide which external entities, processes, and data stores need to be included in the DFD in Applied Learning 8.4.

Julia's Cookies   Applied Learning 8.4

Level 1 Diagram: New Customer Accounts

Mila Ivanov, an account specialist, is preparing a DFD of the customer account system. Her manager requested that she create a Level 1 DFD for an internal auditor, who is currently learning about the system. Mila wrote out the process in narrative form:

Every time a new customer makes an order through the mobile app or a website, they must create a new account. The system creates a new customer account by storing the new customer information in the customer database and then emails the customer confirmation that their account has been created.

Which external entities, processes, and data stores does Mila need to include in the Level 1 diagram?
Hint: Remember that a business event or activity includes a singular verb and a singular noun, and a data store is described by what data it contains.

SOLUTION

Mila's Level 1 diagram needs to include:

- External entity:
  New customer (both the beginning and the ending)
- Processes:
  1.0: Create Account
  2.0: Send Confirmation
- Data store:
  Customers

Mila's Level 1 diagram will look like this:

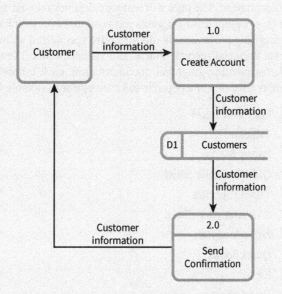

CONCEPT REVIEW QUESTIONS

1. What is a data flow diagram (DFD)?
   Ans. A DFD is a visual representation of information flow within a system to clearly explain where data originates, how it's being used for reporting and analysis, and who in the company sees it.

2. How many levels can there be to a DFD?
   Ans. There are three different levels to a DFD. Each new layer adds details and complexities on the data flow.

   Level 0, also referred to as a context diagram, is a summary that gives a high-level overview of data flow that fits in one page. It provides a snapshot of the data flow that is designed to be understood by all business audiences—from stakeholders to developers.

   When more details are needed than are given in a Level 0 diagram, a Level 1 diagram is used. A Level 1 diagram highlights the main functions carried out by the system and drills down further into the DFD process by "decomposing" the system. It breaks down each process into further subprocesses.

   To see the detailed data flow within a process, we create a Level 2 diagram. A Level 2 diagram is usually the most detailed DFD.

8.5 What Software Tools Can Be Used for Graphical Documentation?

Learning Objective ⑤
Summarize the various software and their use for graphical documentation by accounting professionals.

Graphical documentation refers to the use of visual elements, such as diagrams, charts, graphs, illustrations, and other graphical representations, to convey information, concepts, or instructions. It is a method of presenting information in a visual format, which can make complex ideas easier to comprehend. The choice of software depends on your specific needs and preferences, such as the type of graphics or diagrams you want to create, your level of expertise, and your budgets. Accounting professionals often require specialized software for graphical documentation to create financial reports, charts, and visualizations. There are numerous software tools available for creating graphical documentation, each tailored to specific needs and preferences. Here is a list of some popular software options available for accounting professionals:

a. Microsoft Excel

b. Tableau

c. Power BI

d. QlikView/Qlik Sense

e. TIBCO Spotfire

f. SAP Analytics Cloud

g. Zoho Analytics

h. QuickBooks

i. Xero

j. Google Sheets

k. Sage Intacct

These software are used for graphical visualizations of the accounting and financial information to enable effective decisions. These software support:

a. **Data integration:** Accounting professionals often deal with data from various sources, including financial systems, spreadsheets, and databases. Software tools can connect to these diverse data sources, helping accounting professionals consolidate and integrate financial data into a single platform.

b. **Data visualization:** Data visualization is a graphical representation of data using a wide range of visualization options, including bar charts, line graphs, scatter plots, heatmaps, and other visual aids. Accounting professionals can use these charts to represent financial data in a visually appealing and easy-to-understand format.

c. **Interactive dashboards:** An interactive dashboard is a graphical user interface (GUI) tool used to display and visualize data in a dynamic and user-friendly manner. It typically consists of various data visualizations, such as charts, graphs, tables, and widgets, presented on a single screen or a page. The key characteristic of an interactive dashboard is that users can actively engage with the displayed data, making it a valuable tool for data analysis, monitoring, and decision making.

　　Accounting professionals can create interactive dashboards, which allow users to explore financial data dynamically. These dashboards can include filters, drill-down capabilities, and tooltips to provide detailed insights into specific financial metrics or trends.

d. **Financial reports:** Software tools can be used to design and generate financial reports that include charts, graphs, and tables. These reports can be customized to meet specific reporting requirements, such as balance sheets, income statements, and cash flow statements.

e. **Budgeting and forecasting:** Accounting professionals can use these software for budgeting and forecasting by visualizing historical financial data and projecting future scenarios.

The tool's data modeling capabilities enable them to create predictive models for financial planning.

f. **Profitability and expense analysis:** The tools can help accounting professionals analyze the profitability of products, services, or business units by creating profit and loss (P&L) statements and visualizing key performance indicators (KPIs). Visualizations can highlight cost-saving opportunities and areas where expenses can be optimized.

g. **Compliance and audit:** Software tools can assist in compliance and audit processes by creating visual representations of financial data that make it easier to identify anomalies, track changes, and ensure regulatory compliances.

h. **Scenario analysis:** These software facilitate scenario analysis by visualizing the impact of different variables on financial outcomes. This is essential for risk assessment and decision making.

When choosing graphical documentation software for accounting, consider factors such as ease of use, integration with your existing accounting systems, collaboration features, and the specific types of financial visualizations and reports you need to create. Additionally, some organizations may have industry-specific accounting software that includes built-in visualization tools, so it's essential to explore the options available within your accounting ecosystem.

The software that are used frequently for specific functions are:

1. **Data visualization and charting**

   Tableau: Powerful data visualization software for creating interactive charts and dashboards

   Microsoft Excel: Widely used for creating charts and graphs from data

   Google Charts: A free web-based tool for creating various types of charts

   D3.js: A JavaScript library for creating custom data visualizations

2. **Mind mapping and flowcharts**

   MindMeister: Online mind mapping tool for brainstorming and organizing ideas

   XMind: A popular open-source mind-mapping and brainstorming software

   Lucidchart: Also suitable for creating flowcharts and diagrams

3. **Flowchart and process diagrams**

   Draw.io: A free, web-based tool for creating flowcharts, diagrams, and wireframes

   Microsoft PowerPoint: Often used for creating basic flowcharts and process diagrams

The choice of software depends on your specific needs and preferences, such as the type of graphics or diagrams you want to create, your level of expertise, and your budget. Many of these tools offer free trials or free versions with limited features, so you can explore and choose the one that best suits your requirements.

CONCEPT REVIEW QUESTIONS

1. What is meant by graphical documentation?

   Ans. Graphical documentation refers to the use of visual elements, such as diagrams, charts, graphs, illustrations, and other graphical representations, to convey information, concepts, or instructions.

2. List the software that can be used for data visualization and charting.

   Ans. The software that can be used for data visualization and charting are:

   Tableau: Powerful data visualization software for creating interactive charts and dashboards

   Microsoft Excel: Widely used for creating charts and graphs from data

   Google Charts: A free web-based tool for creating various types of charts

   D3.js: A JavaScript library for creating custom data visualizations

3. How can accounting professionals use interactive dashboards?

   Ans. Accounting professionals can create interactive dashboards, which allow users to explore financial data dynamically. These dashboards can include filters, drill-down capabilities, and tooltips to provide detailed insights into specific financial metrics or trends.

FEATURED PROFESSIONAL | Big Four External Auditor

Photo courtesy of Catalina Ballesteros

Catalina Ballesteros

Catalina started studying accounting as a nontraditional student when she returned to college as a single mother and part-time nanny. She currently works as an external auditor at a Big Four public accounting firm and recently completed—and passed!—the final section of the CPA exam. Catalina will be applying for her CPA license as soon as her work requirements are completed. Catalina fell in love with accounting when completing a course that was required for all business majors. She went on to receive a bachelor's and master's in accounting, with a focus on assurance.

What are the benefits of using a process flowchart?

Because a flowchart provides us with a visual representation of a business process, it can be easier to understand than documentation in narrative form. Flowcharts allow us to efficiently gain an understanding of a process and aid in identifying key elements within the flow of information. Gaining an adequate and clear understanding of business processes is vital during an audit.

Why is clear documentation important?

Clear documentation is key to the quality, efficiency, and success of an audit. Taking time to gain an understanding of a process through documentation reduces the number of questions that may arise when performing other audit procedures.

What is your favorite thing about your job?

My favorite thing about my job is the vast number of technical and professional skills that I get to learn and develop on a daily basis. I also love that I get to work in a collaborative environment that allows me to help my team and learn from others.

How do you use data analytics in your work?

The use of data analytics in auditing is rapidly increasing. Because data analytics helps us understand and evaluate data more efficiently and helps improve audit quality, it is important that I keep up with this technology. As I approach my second year at the firm, I will be learning how to use Power BI and Alteryx so that I can apply these technologies to automate audit procedures.

What characteristics are important for an aspiring external auditor?

• Good communication, both written and oral
• Organization
• Leadership
• Collaboration

These skills are strengthened through experience. However, the most important quality a good auditor has is the ability to act with integrity at all times, no matter the circumstances.

Review and Practice

Key Terms Review

Business Process Model and
 Notation (BPMN)
checklist
connector
data flow diagram (DFD)
data flow line
data store shape
data visualization
decision shape
document flowchart
documentation
entity relationship diagram (ERD)

external entity shape
flowchart
flowline
graphical documentation
interactive dashboards
Level 0 diagram
Level 1 diagram
Level 2 diagram
merge shape
narrative
operator documentation
organizational chart

process flowchart
process shape
program documentation
program flowchart
questionnaire
swim lane
systems documentation
systems flowchart
terminator shape
user documentation

Learning Objectives Review

① Explain the goals of documenting systems and processes.

Documentation is a formal record that describes a system or process. Companies use documentation for:

- Complying with regulations
- Troubleshooting and maintenance
- Consistency across employees' work and how employees are trained
- Capturing usable information for process improvements
- Documenting and evaluating control activities

SOX Section 404 requires public companies to document their internal control procedures. Documentation is essential for identifying the risks of fraud, error, and issues with business processes.

For a computer system, companies maintain four levels of documentation, with each level capturing different elements of the system:

- Systems documentation
- Program documentation
- Operator documentation
- User documentation

These levels start at the most detailed description of the system's design and move up to the highest level of instructions for how a user should interact with the system.

② Differentiate among various documentation techniques.

An organizational chart is a diagram that shows the employees in the company and their reporting relationships with one another. Organizational charts are used for:

- Visualizing an employee directory
- Showing employee responsibilities and how employees fit into the overall company structure
- Depicting reporting relationships
- Showing segregation of duties

An organizational chart can be "tall" (vertical) or "flat" (horizontal):

- A company is tall when numerous levels of management report to the CEO at the top. Large and complex organizations usually have tall organizational charts.
- An org chart is flat, or horizontal, when there are fewer levels of management. Managers have more employees reporting to them, with the CEO at the top. A flat organization allows for a greater sense of responsibility and autonomy for the employee.

Checklists and questionnaires are used to gather information about specific procedures and internal controls. Using a checklist or questionnaire means an auditor will be less likely to forget a step in the audit process.

Narratives are written descriptions of systems and processes that describe responsibilities and the processes and controls that are in place. A narrative is often associated with a visual depiction, such as a flowchart.

Flowcharts present visuals of the management, operations, controls, outside vendors, and systems involved in a business process. They help a company to:

- Understand a process from beginning to end
- Create a historical record of the process, which is useful for an audit
- Find opportunities for process improvements and efficiency gains
- Communicate intricate processes easily and clearly
- Plan a project and evaluate its feasibility
- Evaluate process controls, since they can identify control failures like those involving segregation of duties

Types of flowcharts used depend on the focus of the end user:

- Document flowcharts: Show the flow of documents through a process
- Systems flowcharts: Illustrate the flow of information through a system, including how information is accessed and where data is stored
- Program flowcharts: Provide the sequence of coded instructions in a computer program that enable it to perform specified logical and arithmetic operations
- Process flowcharts: Depict the flow of activity through the company and include key parties and the actions they perform

Business Process Model and Notation (BPMN) is used to visually document a business process, much like a process flowchart.

A data flow diagram (DFD) is a visual representation of an information flow within a system. Advantages of a DFD include:

- Shows system functionality and limits
- Easier to use than a text description
- Offers an easy-to-understand system diagram for users to comprehend the data flow
- Helps new employees understand a system
- Familiarizes auditors with the system they are auditing

An entity relationship diagram (ERD) is a graphical illustration of all the tables and their relationships in a database. An ERD helps end users understand the layout and data within a relational database. There are three kinds of ERDs: conceptual, logical, and physical.

❸ Show how a flowchart illustrates a system or business process.

Flowcharts use specific shapes to convey meaning. The six shapes used in a process flowchart are:

- Terminator (oval): Indicates the start or end of the process
- Process (rectangle): Indicates an event or a step in the flow
- Flowline (arrow): Indicates what comes next
- Decision (diamond): Poses a yes-or-no question that determines which direction the flow goes next
- Merge (triangle): Joins two or more paths in the flowchart back into a single flowline
- Connector (circle): Indicates where a flowchart is joined together when it is so large it spans multiple pages

Systems and document flowcharts use more shapes:

- Document: Indicates a physical or digital document
- Input/output: Indicates data or information coming into or leaving the process
- Database: Indicates data storage where data is stored or retrieved
- Manual input: Indicates data manually entered into a system
- Manual operation: Indicates that physical action takes place

Swim lanes are areas in a flowchart that delineate responsibilities. Swim lanes provide clarity and accountability by placing activities within the swim lanes of particular individuals, groups, or departments. They can be vertical or horizontal.

❹ Summarize how a data flow diagram (DFD) shows the flow of information in a system.

A data flow diagram (DFD) depicts the travel of data or information throughout a company's systems. One of the most popular notation methodologies is Gane-Sarson. DFDs use only four shapes:

- External entity: An input or output of the DFD
- Process: An activity that transforms the data

- Data store: A data repository such as a database or data warehouse
- Data flow: An arrow indicating the flow of data through the system

A DFD can be one of three levels:

- Level 0: This is a context diagram that gives a high-level overview of the data flow.
- Level 1: This diagram includes more details that highlight main functions carried out by the system.
- Level 2: This diagram provides the most detailed breakdown of the multistep, complex processes from the Level 1 DFD.

❺ Summarize the various software and their use for graphical documentation by accounting professionals.

Graphical documentation refers to the use of visual elements, such as diagrams, charts, graphs, illustrations, and other graphical representations, to convey information, concepts, or instructions.

Accounting professionals often require specialized software for graphical documentation to create financial reports, charts, and visualizations.

The software that are used frequently for specific functions are:

1. Data visualization and charting
   Tableau
   Microsoft Excel
   Google Charts
   D3.js
2. Mind mapping and flowcharts
   MindMeister
   XMind
   Lucidchart
3. Flowchart and process diagrams
   Draw.io
   Microsoft PowerPoint

CPA questions, as well as multiple choice, discussion, analysis and application, and Tableau questions and other resources, are available online.

Multiple Choice Questions

1. **(LO 1)** Which of the following is the best definition of user documentation?
   a. Overview of the computer system with details of system design and architecture

   b. Detailed description of the system's programming logic and source code
   c. Information necessary for technical operators to execute and support the system

d. Instructions for system users on how to interact with the system

2. (LO 1) How can documentation benefit employees?

a. By increasing the time necessary to perform a task

b. By helping them understand what to do when faced with uncertainties or problems

c. By creating the need for additional oversight from management

d. By providing minimal information on the systems used

3. (LO 1) What is the importance of a record retention plan?

a. Identifying documents to be maintained or destroyed

b. Providing insights into system operations

c. Creating roadmaps for process improvement

d. Keeping records with low importance to the organization

4. (LO 1) Which of the following is an element captured in systems documentation?

a. Programming logic

b. Error messages

c. Systems architecture

d. Instructions for inputting data into the system

5. (LO 1) **CPA** Sameer Khan wrote software for the Valencia Clown Revue. One fine day, however, having grown tired of computers and software, he became a juggler, fire eater, and fainting goat farmer. After his departure, the Valencia Clown Revue was unable to maintain and upgrade the systems that Sameer had written. The best control for preventing this failure would be

a. automated accruals and deferrals.

b. user documentation.

c. operator documentation.

d. program documentation.

6. (LO 1) **CPA** Mary & Jones, a regional public accounting firm, has recently accepted a contract to audit On-the-Spot, Inc., a mobile vending service that provides vending machines for large events. On-the-Spot uses a computerized accounting system, portions of which were developed internally to integrate with a standard financial reporting system that was purchased from a consultant. What type of documentation will be most useful to Mary & Jones in determining how the system as a whole is constructed?

a. Operator documentation

b. Program documentation

c. Systems documentation

d. User documentation

7. (LO 2) What is the purpose of an entity relationship diagram (ERD)?

a. Showing an outline of the organization

b. Providing a graphical representation of tables and relationships

c. Showing the flow of data through the system

d. Providing process documentation

8. (LO 2) Which of the following is a use of org charts?

a. Showing table relationships in a relational database

b. Visualizing computer connectivity

c. Demonstrating customer relationship management

d. Visualizing an employee directory

9. (LO 2) Auditors also refer to questionnaires as

a. org charts.

b. process question forms.

c. checklists.

d. vertical graphs.

10. (LO 3) Which of the following is *not* a type of flowchart?

a. Document   **c.** Process

b. System   **d.** Data

11. (LO 3) How can a flowchart help with the evaluation of controls?

a. Identify control weaknesses

b. Identify process improvements

c. Identify project plans

d. Identify decision points

12. (LO 3) Which of the following flowchart shapes represents a decision?

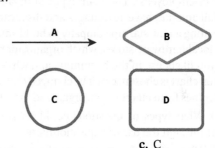

a. A   **c.** C

b. B   **d.** D

13. (LO 3) How is a connector represented in a flowchart?

a. As a line with an arrow

b. As a circle

c. As a triangle

d. As a square

14. (LO 3) Which of the following DFD shapes represents data?

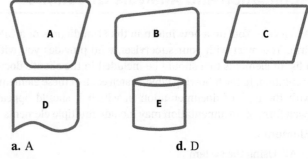

a. A   **d.** D

b. B   **e.** E

c. C

15. **(LO 4)** What does a DFD represent?

   a. Execution of computer code

   b. Management decision points

   c. Information flow within a process or system

   d. Roles and responsibilities within a process

16. **(LO 4)** Within a DFD, which level highlights the main system functions?

   a. Level 0

   b. Level 3

   c. Level 2

   d. Level 1

17. **(LO 4)** A data flow diagram helps a user understand

   a. the sources of data in a system and the destinations of that data.

   b. the flow of documents through an organization.

   c. the processing steps in an AIS

   d. the processing logic of application programs.

18. **(LO 5)** Data can be presented in a simpler way using

   a. bars and charts.

   b. heatmaps.

   c. treemaps.

   d. All of the above

19. **(LO 5)** Which of the following is not part of an interactive dashboard?

   a. Filters

   b. Drill-down capabilities

   c. Tooltips

   d. Data cleaning

Discussion and Research Questions

DQ1. (LO 1) Explain why a company must use documentation.

DQ2. (LO 1) What is the best documentation to use in outlining how to resolve system errors? Why is it better for this purpose than other types of documentation?

DQ3. (LO 2) [Critical Thinking] An organizational chart is a diagram used to show the employees within an organization and the reporting relationships between employees (and groups of employees). The main types of organizational structures, tall and flat, have advantages and disadvantages. If you were creating a new startup company to build small workbenches for local hardware stores, which organizational structure would you likely use in the beginning, and why? Once an organizational chart is chosen, can it be changed? What are the possible outcomes from changing an organizational structure?

DQ4. (LO 2) What types of questions could an auditor ask management through the use of a questionnaire?

DQ5. (LO 2) What is the primary purpose of narrative descriptions, and how often should they be updated?

DQ6. (LO 3) What are flowcharts, and how do they help organizations?

DQ7. (LO 3) Do all six common shapes have to be used in a flowchart? What is an example of a shape that is used in every flowchart?

DQ8. (LO 3) During a training session for process management employees, you are asked to demonstrate your familiarity with flowchart symbols. For each of the following shapes, describe what the symbol represents and give at least two examples of how the shape could be used: (A) database, (B) decision, (C) document, (D) manual operation.

DQ9. (LO 4) Which level of DFD is used to present the greatest level of detail? How does the detail differ from that supplied by other levels?

DQ10. (LO 3–4) [Early Career] [Critical Thinking] You are a senior internal auditor who works at Beeman Sports, a local sporting goods store. You have been assigned to mentor Anila, who is a first-year associate on your team. During your monthly peer meeting with Anila, she mentions she was recently asked to create a flowchart of a business process for an audit engagement, but the audit manager sent back review notes on her diagram, mentioning that it's more of a data flow diagram than a flowchart. Anila is confused about the difference between those two documentation methods.

Explain to Anila the difference between a data flow diagram and a flowchart, in what context each would be more appropriate to use, and other factors she should be aware of the next time she's creating documentation.

Application and Analysis Questions

A1. (LO 1) You are a new intern in the IT audit area of a CPA firm. You meet with your supervisor, who provides you with a list of elements that should be included in the client's documentation. In the following table, match each of these elements with the type of documentation in which it should appear. Each form of documentation may include multiple elements.

Elements:

   A. Using the system

   B. Error messages

   C. Error resolution

   D. Input data and information output

   E. Technical design

   F. Execution commands

   G. Source code

   H. Processing logic

   I. System features

   J. Troubleshooting guidelines

Documentation	Elements
Operator documentation	1. _____
Program documentation	2. _____
Systems documentation	3. _____
User documentation	4. _____

A2. (LO 1) Documentation is vital in helping employees understand different organizational components. Documentation serves various purposes and is used by different types of employees. In the following table, match the type of documentation to the employees who are most likely to use it. Each type of documentation may be used more than once.

Type of documentation:

- A. Operator documentation
- B. Program documentation
- C. Systems documentation
- D. User documentation

Employee	Type of Documentation
Call center employee	1. _____
Systems developer	2. _____
Accounting clerk	3. _____
IT auditor	4. _____
System administrator	5. _____
NOC associate	6. _____
CFO	7. _____
Programmer	8. _____

A3. (LO 2) `Fraud` `Data Analytics` `Critical Thinking`
Dylan Michaels is a senior manager of client services at an investment management firm. Recently, an anonymous tip was submitted to the employee whistleblower hotline, suggesting that Dylan may be submitting expenses that are not company related to the expense reimbursement system.

As an internal auditor, you are tasked with reviewing Dylan's expenses to identify any fraud red flags. The data in the table below includes some of Dylan's transactions from Q1 202X. Using the data and the organizational chart below:

1. Identify at least four suspicious transaction IDs
2. Explain why they are suspicious
3. Explain how the organizational chart helped you identify these transactions

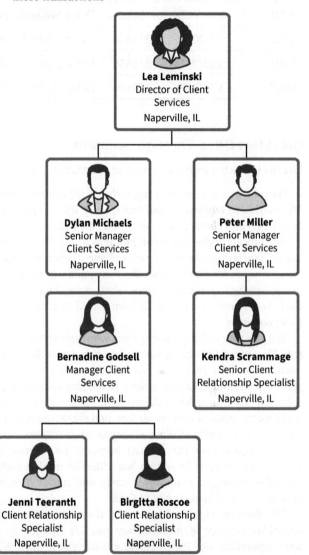

Transaction ID	Transaction Date	Amount	Employee	Merchant	Merchant Local	Expense Description	Approver
10012	1/18/202X	$88.24	Dylan Michaels	Verizon	Atlanta, GA	Company cell phone bill	Lea Leminski
10013	1/22/202X	$100.84	Dylan Michaels	The Hill House	Baltimore, MD	Dinner while traveling	Lea Leminski
10014	1/23/202X	$23.45	Dylan Michaels	Starbucks	Baltimore, MD	Breakfast while traveling	Lea Leminski
10015	2/23/202X	$268.94	Dylan Michaels	Hilton	Baltimore, MD	Hotel	Lea Leminski
10016	2/10/202X	$8.94	Dylan Michaels	Best Buy	Naperville, IL	Ethernet cable	Lea Leminski
10017	2/15/202X	$345.28	Dylan Michaels	Hilton	Naperville, IL	Hotel	Matthew Tildon

(Continued)

(*Continued*)

Transaction ID	Transaction Date	Amount	Employee	Merchant	Merchant Local	Expense Description	Approver
10018	2/15/202X	$22.85	Dylan Michaels	Chipotle	Naperville, IL	Lunch while traveling	Matthew Tildon
10019	2/16/202X	$12.34	Dylan Michaels	Starbucks	Naperville, IL	Breakfast while traveling	Matthew Tildon
10020	2/18/202X	$88.24	Dylan Michaels	Verizon	Atlanta, GA	Company cell phone bill	Lea Leminski
10021	2/19/202X	$11.94	Dylan Michaels	Starbucks	Naperville, IL	Breakfast while traveling	Matthew Tildon
10022	3/3/202X	$185.94	Dylan Michaels	Maggianos	Naperville, IL	Team lunch	Lea Leminski
10023	3/15/202X	$195.99	Dylan Michaels	Maggianos	Naperville, IL	Dinner while traveling	Matthew Tildon
10024	3/18/202X	$88.24	Dylan Michaels	Verizon	Atlanta, GA	Company cell phone bill	Lea Leminski

Breakfast Drive-Through Scenario

Use the following scenario to answer questions A4 and A5:

On your way to work, you regularly use the drive-through at McDonald's to buy your usual breakfast of black coffee and a bacon, egg, and cheese bagel, but without the bacon.

The process begins when you pull into one of the two lanes, where there is a speaker and a microphone. There are sensors in the ground under your vehicle, and they make a beeping sound in the headsets of the employees taking drive-through orders. Each lane's sensors make a different sound to identify which lane you are in.

You give your order to the employee, who inputs it into the system. The order and price appear on the screen next to the speaker/ microphone. Once your order has been taken, the employee tells you the price and asks you to drive to the first window to pay. After you pay with either cash or a card, the order goes through to the second window and the kitchen, and the employee will ask you to drive to the next window, where you can pick up your order.

The employee in the kitchen prepares your order and places your wrapped bagel in a bag while the employee at the second window gets your coffee ready and hands it to you, quickly followed by your bag of food.

The drive-through process is on a timer. Anything over a particular number of minutes (say four) is reported as too time-consuming, and the employee will ask you to park in the waiting bay. An employee will come out, confirm your order, and deliver your order to you out there. Then you drive off to work.

A4. (LO 2) For the breakfast drive-through scenario, prepare a narrative description of the user documentation for the employees taking the order, collecting payment at the first window, and delivering the meal at the second window.

A5. (LO 3) Prepare a process flowchart for the breakfast drive-through scenario. Your instructor will decide which tool you should use. (PowerPoint and Lucidchart are great options.)

A6. (LO 3) You can create a basic flowchart for a process by identifying business events or activities and decisions and separating them with arrows. For example, if you were preparing a monthly bank reconciliation for your company, you would write the following description:

Start process -> Clear last month's outstanding items against this month's bank statement -> List items that have not cleared the bank -> Investigate long-outstanding items for resolution -> Compare cash receipts journal entries with deposits on bank statement -> Compare cash payments journal entries to payments on bank statement -> Prepare adjusting journal entries for approval and processing by accounting department -> Prepare bank reconciliation that reconciles the General Ledger control account balance to the balance on the bank statement

For each of the following examples, create a description of a basic flowchart that shows the events or activities separated by arrows.

1. A computer is ordered by the purchasing department, received by the receiving department, and entered into inventory.

2. A customer enters a restaurant to order a take-out breakfast. During the ordering process, the customer makes choices about the types of eggs (scrambled or over-medium) and whether to have coffee or orange juice with the meal. The customer pays for the order. The order is prepared and given to the customer.

3. You order and pay for tickets for an upcoming concert via the order app on your phone.

A7. (LO 4) Critical Thinking In Applied Learning 8.4, Mila used the narrative form and a Level 1 flow diagram to describe the process of creating new customer accounts; their narrative and data flow diagram are repeated below. Review the process and identify at least three controls that could help mitigate the risk of error or fraud in the process and identify whether they are detective, preventive, or corrective controls.

Every time a new customer makes an order through the mobile app or a website, they must create a new account. The system creates a new customer account by storing the new customer information in the customer database and then emails the customer confirmation that their account has been created. The system also saves the new customer information into a customer database.

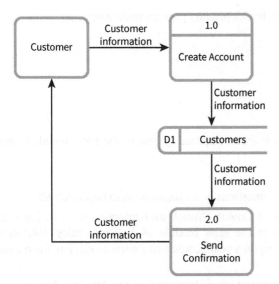

A8. (LO 4) Health Foods Corporation is a food distributor specializing in high-quality meat-substitute products in Auckland. The company recently adopted new purchasing software to support its purchasing and accounts payable business processes. You are an internal auditor at Health Foods Corporation, performing a post-implementation review of the new software. The system owner provided you a DFD of the system to help familiarize you with how it has been implemented.

Review the following DFD and identify whether it is a Level 0, Level 1, or Level 2 DFD.

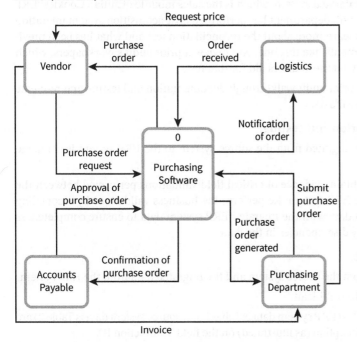

A9. (LO 3–4) You are the new IT auditor at a regional bank called Cobblestone, a London-based company. For your first assignment, you are tasked with writing a narrative description of the process for a bank customer withdrawing cash from a bank account using an ATM. You deliver the description below to your manager, Abigail, who knows the process well and approves your work. Abigail especially likes the way you decomposed the process into business activities in your description. You say it makes the process easier to understand.

For your second assignment, Abigail asks you to transform your narrative description into visual documentation. Decide whether the narrative description would best be presented as a process flowchart or a data flow diagram and create the documentation for Abigail to review. Your instructor will decide which tool you should use. (PowerPoint and Lucidchart are great options.)

Cobblestone Bank

Narrative Description of Process: Bank Customer Withdraws Cash from ATM

1. **Insert bank card:** The customer inserts their bank card into the ATM's card reader. The system allocates an ATM transaction identifier to track the transaction.
2. **Read bank card:** The system reads the bank card information.
3. **Authenticate customer:** The system authenticates the customer or rejects the card.
4. **Select bank account type:** The customer selects from the ATM display a checking or savings account from which to withdraw cash.
5. **Select type of transaction:** The customer selects from the ATM display the type of available service options. The customer selects "Withdraw cash."
6. **Select or input amount of transaction:** The system displays a list of standard withdrawal amounts or allows the customer to input a custom amount of their choice, but the amount must be a multiple of £20.
7. **Confirm withdrawal:** The system assesses available funds and confirms the withdrawal.
8. **Eject bank card:** The system ejects the customer's bank card, and the customer takes it back.
9. **Dispense cash to customer:** The system dispenses the cash to the customer and records a transaction for the withdrawal.

Tableau Case: Julia's Cookies' System Migration

What You Need

Download Tableau to your computer. You can access www.tableau.com/academic/students to download your free Tableau license for the year, or you can download it from your university's software offerings.

Download the following file from the book's product page on www.wiley.com:

Julia's Cookies ERP Data.xlsx

Cookie Crunch Source Data.xlsx

Case Background

Big Picture:

Validate the migration of sales data from an acquired system to the ERP module to ensure completeness and accuracy.

Details:

Why is this data important, and what questions or problems need to be addressed?

- Julia's Cookies recently acquired Cookie Crunch and migrated the existing data in Cookie Crunch's sales system to the sales module of Julia's Cookies' ERP system. As an IT auditor, you are working on a post-acquisition review to validate the migration of Cookie Crunch's data.

- When migrating data to a new system, there is a risk that the data transfer may not be complete. Records may be missing or inaccurate due to data formatting and other issues. Reconciling the source data with the imported data in the new system validates the completeness and accuracy of the data migration. Questions to consider when reconciling are: Which transactions are stored in one system but not in the other? Is there a difference in total dollar amounts between the two systems?

Plan:

What data is needed, and how should it be analyzed?

- The data needed is pulled from the original source system, which is Cookie Crunch's sales system, and the migrated system, which is the sales module of Julia's Cookies' ERP system. The Internal Audit department has performed post-acquisition system migration reviews in the past. To learn more about the reconciliation test and what has been previously done on engagements like this one, you review a prior audit's workpapers, which include details about what the auditors did for that test.

- Follow along with the prior audit walkthrough documentation and testing and re-create the testing using this year's data.

System Migration Validation and Testing:

- Test Name: Sales data migrated from the source system to the ERP system is complete and accurate.

- Testing Procedures: Obtain evidence of critical field validations performed between the source system and the ERP system. Re-perform the business validations by reconciling the raw source system data with the migrated ERP system data to ensure completeness and accuracy. Note any discrepancies in the data.

Prior Audit Testing Steps:

1. Obtain the raw data from the source system and the migrated data from the ERP system.

2. Pull the two data files into Tableau.

3. Ensure that the two tables (ERP system data is Table 1 and source system data is Table 2) are joined with an outer join option (as illustrated) on the field Transaction ID.

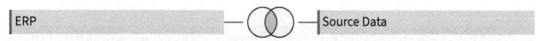

4. Open Sheet 1 (the two combined files in Tableau) and answer the following questions to reconcile the two files.

Now it's your turn to evaluate, analyze, and communicate the results!

Questions

1. What was the total dollar amount of sales recorded in the source system for the selected day?

2. What was the total dollar amount of sales recorded in the ERP system for the selected day?

3. How many transactions match in the source system and the ERP system from the data chosen for testing?

4. When comparing the source system and ERP system data, how many transactions were recorded in the source system but not in the ERP system? (Hint: Listed as "Null.")

5. For the transactions recorded in the source system but not in the ERP system, in which states were the missing transactions?

6. What was the total dollar amount of the transactions that were missing from the ERP system? (Hint: Round up.)

7. When analyzing the dollar amount in the ERP system, what was the largest order of the day for the southwest region? In which state was that order placed?

8. When analyzing the dollar amount in the ERP system, what was the lowest order of the day for the southwest region? In which state was that order placed?

Take it to the next level!

9. For the transactions that matched in the source system and the ERP system (not "null"), how many transactions differed in dollar amount? (Hint: Creating a set to assist with filtering might be helpful.)

10. For the transactions that matched in the source system and the ERP system (not "null") in the state of Texas (TX), how many transactions differed in dollar amount? (Hint: Creating a set to assist with filtering might be helpful.)

Human Resources and Payroll Processes

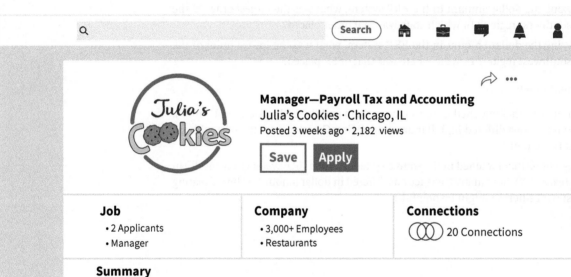

Manager—Payroll Tax and Accounting
Julia's Cookies · Chicago, IL
Posted 3 weeks ago · 2,182 views

Save   Apply

Job	Company	Connections
• 2 Applicants	• 3,000+ Employees	20 Connections
• Manager	• Restaurants	

Summary

Julia's Cookies is seeking a manager of payroll tax and accounting to be responsible for payroll-related accounting, reporting, and tax functions. The manager is responsible for all payroll-related systems and has primary responsibility for future system upgrades, enhancements, and data maintenance. This position works closely with the IT, HR, and Accounting departments.

Responsibilities

- Oversee payroll postings to the General Ledger and monthly accounting accruals
- Ensure timely General Ledger account reconciliations
- Ensure payroll tax filings are timely and accurately prepared by third-party providers
- Develop payroll reporting and analytics, including comparison of actual payroll expenses to budgets and forecasts
- Manage all payroll reporting to support analysis for other departments and audits
- Oversee review of compensation plans and agreements to ensure IRS compliance
- Ensure compliance with internal controls; document and develop new procedures when required
- Liaise with internal and external auditors, providing audit deliverables as needed

Requirements

Preferred Education: Master's degree or higher in accounting or related field

Preferred Certification: CPA

Preferred Knowledge and Skills

The ideal candidate has five to seven years' experience in payroll or accounting and an understanding of internal controls, payroll accounting, and reconciliations. Preference given to candidates who demonstrate:

- Current knowledge of federal, state, and local payroll/income tax law
- Ability to research payroll tax-related changes
- Experience in seeking and taking advantage of any payroll-related tax credits

Salary: $110,000–125,000

CHAPTER PREVIEW This chapter explores business processes that focus on a company's people. From hiring new employees to compensating active ones, we will follow the human resources and payroll business processes through the accounting information system. We also examine how to drive insights and change by utilizing the data created by these systems. In addition to learning about risks, control activities, and the impact on financial statements, you will discover:

- How human resources and payroll are both related and segregated
- Who should extend an offer letter to potential new hires and why
- Why so many departments are involved in the termination of employment
- What makes payroll a high-risk area for fraud and what can be done to mitigate the risk
- How data captured by the related systems is used for reporting and insights

Employees are the key to success for every company. People provide the innovation, strength, and brainpower companies need to create and achieve strategic goals. While technological advances like artificial intelligence and robotic process automation continue to eliminate daily job tasks in business processes, they don't eliminate the need for people. These process improvements instead provide employees with opportunities to devote more time to job duties that require creativity and critical thinking.

Besides involvement in human resources and payroll processes as an employee of an organization, there are various career paths that accounting professionals can follow in this area. The manager of payroll tax and accounting at Julia's Cookies is an example of an accounting position that combines financial accounting, information systems, and tax skills. This position is modeled after a real job posting in New York City at one of the largest airlines in North America. ■

Chapter Roadmap

LEARNING OBJECTIVES	TOPICS	JULIA'S COOKIES APPLIED LEARNING
9.1 Explain the relationship between human resources and payroll.	• Human Resources: Employee Operations • Payroll: Employee Compensation • Integrating HR and Payroll	Segregation of Duties: Payroll Audit
9.2 Evaluate the employee onboarding process.	• Employee Onboarding Process • Risks and Control Activities	Employee Onboarding Maturity: Starting Somewhere
9.3 Evaluate the employee termination process.	• Employee Termination Process • Risks and Control Activities	Employee Termination Maturity: Things Look Better
9.4 Assess the payroll processing process.	• Payroll Journal Entries • Payroll Process • Risks and Control Activities	Payroll Processing: Mitigating Risks
9.5 Connect the data in the underlying system and database to important reports and data analytics.	• Database Design • Reporting and Insights	Payroll Analytics: Identifying Data Requirements

CPA You will find the CPA tag throughout the chapter to call out any important topics you may see on the CPA exam.

9.1 How Are Human Resources and Payroll Related?

Learning Objective ❶
Explain the relationship between human resources and payroll.

If you have ever received a paycheck or applied for a job opening, then you have been involved in the human resources (HR) and payroll business processes of a company. These two sets of business processes work together and are essential to a company's operations; after all, a company with no employees would find it difficult to do business.

Recall that a business process is a group of related *business events or activities* intended to accomplish the strategic objectives of the business.

At a high level, a business process takes inputs of resources to create products or provide services as outputs. These outputs must have value to customers, or they will not sell. One of the most important inputs into a business is HR. In the basic business model, HR and payroll business processes are part of the acquisition and payment processes stage. In **HR processes**, we acquire and manage our employees, while in **payroll processes**, we pay for these employees' work (**Illustration 9.1**).

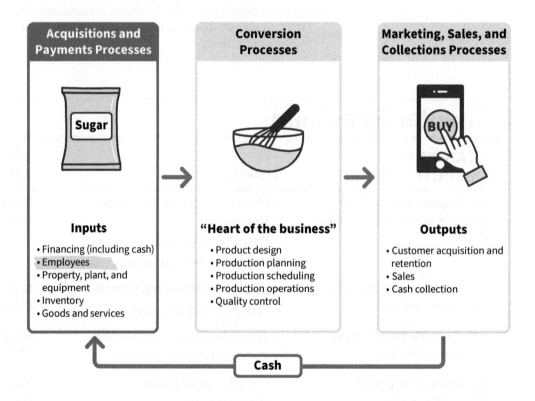

Acquisitions and Payments Processes	Conversion Processes	Marketing, Sales, and Collections Processes
Inputs	**"Heart of the business"**	**Outputs**
• Financing (including cash)	• Product design	• Customer acquisition and retention
• Employees	• Production planning	• Sales
• Property, plant, and equipment	• Production scheduling	• Cash collection
• Inventory	• Production operations	
• Goods and services	• Quality control	

Cash

Illustration 9.1 The basic business model shows employees as part of the acquisitions and payments business processes.

Now that we have learned where HR and payroll processes fit into a company's business model, let's examine them more closely.

Human Resources: Employee Operations

CPA The **human resources (HR)** business function is responsible for all employees and employee-related operations. An HR department is responsible for a number of major activities:

- Recruiting and hiring employees
- Training and developing employees

- Determining salaries and benefits
  - Compensation
  - **Employee benefits**, which include medical and life insurance, retirement, and more
  - Paid time off (PTO) and leaves
- Monitoring and evaluating employees
  - Performance evaluations
- Transitioning employees
  - Voluntary and involuntary termination
  - Retirement
  - Promotion
  - Changing roles within the company
- Updating and maintaining employee data in the main table

Companies may move certain HR activities to an **outsourced HR model**, where a third-party company is responsible for certain administrative tasks. Examples include companies that specialize in administration of benefits such as health insurance and search firms that find the best candidates for a key position. This outsourced model frees up the company's dedicated HR team to perform more value-driven tasks such as increasing the company's competencies in:

- Strategic hiring and workforce training
- Innovation, creativity, and flexibility
- Development and support of new approaches to the work model, such as remote work, career development planning, and rotational programs that allow employees to experience different parts of the business

Consider the employment life cycle of Alex, who was hired as the manager of Payroll Tax and Accounting at Julia's Cookies (**Illustration 9.2**).

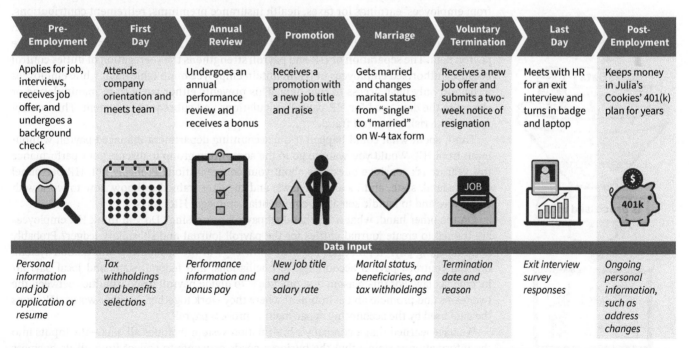

Pre-Employment	First Day	Annual Review	Promotion	Marriage	Voluntary Termination	Last Day	Post-Employment
Applies for job, interviews, receives job offer, and undergoes a background check	Attends company orientation and meets team	Undergoes an annual performance review and receives a bonus	Receives a promotion with a new job title and raise	Gets married and changes marital status from "single" to "married" on W-4 tax form	Receives a new job offer and submits a two-week notice of resignation	Meets with HR for an exit interview and turns in badge and laptop	Keeps money in Julia's Cookies' 401(k) plan for years
Data Input							
Personal information and job application or resume	*Tax withholdings and benefits selections*	*Performance information and bonus pay*	*New job title and salary rate*	*Marital status, beneficiaries, and tax withholdings*	*Termination date and reason*	*Exit interview survey responses*	*Ongoing personal information, such as address changes*

Illustration 9.2 A career at Julia's Cookies starts at the job interview, and the relationship with the company continues even after the last day.

Throughout Alex's career, HR has been involved in overseeing these key career events—all of which have resulted in data inputs to the HR information system.

Payroll: Employee Compensation

One of HR's business process objectives is to compensate employees. To achieve this objective, HR oversees and owns the data used in the payroll processes. **Payroll** calculates wages (hourly, salary, commission) and compensates employees with their entitled pay.

CPA HR should be separate from payroll because they are two distinct areas of a business. HR personnel are in the "people" business and primarily deal with employee relations and maintenance of employee main table data, while payroll handles the compensation of employees for their work. Each department has distinct functions, but they intersect at times—for example, when employees are hired or fired, when someone gets a raise, and when a worker wants some time off.

Payroll involves calculations for salaries and wages, commissions, bonuses, severance pay, overtime, employee reimbursements, and PTO. Payroll also involves making deductions from employees' earnings for taxes, health insurance premiums, retirement contributions, and so forth. As a best practice, the accounting department should process payroll, with input data coming from the HR team and the accounting information system housing the payroll data. The separation of HR and payroll strengthens the segregation of duties control because authorized employees in HR maintain employee main table data, while employees in payroll only have access to that data. This prevents either party from manipulating or changing the data used for HR payroll calculations and subsequent payment. This control reduces the risk of payroll fraud.

Think about what could happen if the accounting department managed payroll without input from HR. Would you want to go to the accounting group to discuss your performance this year or ask sensitive questions about your compensation? Probably not. HR personnel know federal, state, and local labor laws, and they are trained to know how to work with employees and to handle sensitive, confidential, and legal HR issues.

On the other hand, what if HR handled payroll processing? Do you think HR employees are trained to create journal entries for the payroll journal and subsidiary ledger? Probably not. Managing payroll processes requires knowledge of the accounting information system, internal controls, payroll accounting, reconciliations, and federal, state, and local payroll/income tax law. For this reason, best practice is to divide payroll responsibilities between the two teams and promote an environment where they work together. In other words, HR owns the data used by the accounting department to process payroll.

We have learned that a company's information system includes all data—the inputs into the information system—that the business needs or wants to collect from all its business processes. Recall that an accounting information system (**Illustration 9.3**):

- Captures data about business events that involve an exchange of economic resources
- Processes and stores that data
- Produces financial reports that are useful for decision making

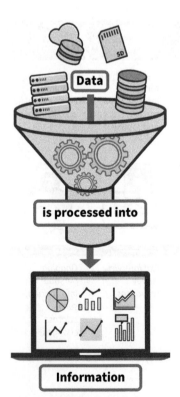

Data

is processed into

Information

Illustration 9.3 An information system turns data into useful information.

CPA Compensating employees is a business process that results in an exchange of economic resources. This process generates accounting transactions that require regulatory compliance with both generally accepted accounting principles and tax regulations. In the United States, companies must calculate and withhold deductions for federal and state taxes, Social Security, Medicare, and unemployment insurance. Payroll can also include deductions that employees elect to have withheld from their paychecks. Examples include health insurance and life insurance premiums, retirement contributions, and contributions to a pre-tax account that can be spent on specific expenses, such as child care, health care, or even commuting. We'll explore the details of these activities and their related journal entries later.

Integrating HR and Payroll

Business processes for HR and payroll can be categorized into groups based on the types of processes and associated outcomes. Companies have their own methods of categorization based on their organizational structures. Some of these processes are suitable for outsourcing—for example, payroll, health insurance, and retirement plan administration. Outsourcing changes the design of relationships between business processes.

Throughout the remainder of this chapter, we consider the HR and payroll processes at Julia's Cookies. As shown in **Illustration 9.4**, Julia's Cookies' HR and payroll business processes fall into six categories. Visualizing its business processes this way enables Julia's Cookies to see how the different business processes work together. While risks and controls vary for all these business processes, we're going to focus in this chapter on three essential areas in HR and payroll:

- Employee administration: employee onboarding
- Employee administration: terminations
- Payroll processing

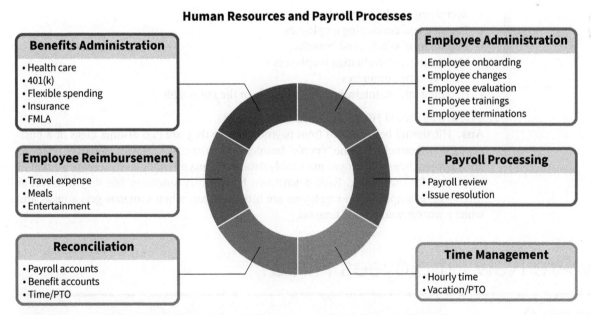

Human Resources and Payroll Processes

Benefits Administration
- Health care
- 401(k)
- Flexible spending
- Insurance
- FMLA

Employee Reimbursement
- Travel expense
- Meals
- Entertainment

Reconciliation
- Payroll accounts
- Benefit accounts
- Time/PTO

Employee Administration
- Employee onboarding
- Employee changes
- Employee evaluation
- Employee trainings
- Employee terminations

Payroll Processing
- Payroll review
- Issue resolution

Time Management
- Hourly time
- Vacation/PTO

Illustration 9.4   Julia's Cookies' HR and payroll business processes fall into six categories.

Now that you have learned how HR and payroll are both segregated and integrated, help Brant, an internal auditor, summarize his interview notes from an internal audit in Applied Learning 9.1.

Julia's Cookies	Applied Learning 9.1

Segregation of Duties: Payroll Audit

Brant, an internal auditor at Julia's Cookies, is currently working on an engagement reviewing the payroll processes. He is meeting with his audit manager tomorrow to share the outcome of an interview with the manager of payroll operations. Brant has the following notes from the interview:

Payroll is part of the Finance and Accounting department. Payroll employees report to the chief financial officer, not the chief people officer.

Payroll receives employee information from the HR department via files shared on a network drive and updates the payroll system manually by copying data from the files.

When employees have questions about their pay, they contact Payroll directly—not the HR department. Sometimes Payroll receives questions about benefit withholdings on paychecks. Payroll must direct employees to the HR department for these questions.

Based on these notes, what are some key points Brant should share with his manager tomorrow?

SOLUTION

Some key points Brant could share with manager are:

- There is segregation of duties between Payroll and HR employees.
- There is a risk of errors or manipulation in the manual entry of employee data into the payroll system. Recommend that the process of receiving data from the HR department be automated to minimize the risk of error and fraud.
- The company intranet should direct employees to HR first about benefit- or pay-related questions. Employees should contact their HR representative, who can contact Payroll on their behalf. Payroll employees are not trained for employee-relations management.
- Sensitive Payroll information such as employee salaries is available to a wide range of company personnel via the shared drive.

CONCEPT REVIEW QUESTIONS

1. **CPA** Define human resources (HR) business function.
   Ans. The HR business function is responsible for all employees and employee-related operations. The major activities undertaken by HR are:
   - Recruiting and hiring employees
   - Training and developing employees
   - Determining salaries and benefits
   - Monitoring and evaluating employees
   - Transitioning employees
   - Updating and maintaining employee data in the main table

2. **CPA** Why should HR be separated from payroll?
   Ans. HR should be separated from payroll because they are two distinct areas of a business. HR personnel are in the "people" business and primarily deal with employee relations and maintenance of employee main table data, while payroll handles the compensation of employees for their work. Each department has distinct functions, but they intersect at times—for example, when employees are hired or fired, when someone gets a raise, and when a worker wants some time off.

9.2 How Are New Employees Hired?

Learning Objective ❷
Evaluate the employee onboarding process.

HR contributes to many parts of a company, and all those parts have a common denominator: people. Imagine that you have accepted an internship at your dream accounting job—whether it is a public accounting role or an industry role. After being shown to your desk and receiving login credentials for your computer, you are left alone without instructions. You don't even know where the nearest break room or bathroom is. You sit awkwardly all day and wait, unsure of whether anyone around you is a part of your team. Does that sound like a great first-day experience? Of course not.

When it comes to first impressions, HR has only one chance to get it right, and it happens during onboarding of new employees.

Employee onboarding is the process of establishing new employees in the company's systems and helping them quickly adapt to their positions and the company:

- Onboarding starts when a job offer is made and continues through an employee's first day, weeks, or even months.
- While accounting professionals involved in employee onboarding typically focus on the administrative process of establishing a new employee in the company's systems, employee onboarding involves more than just administrative tasks.
- A best practice onboarding process includes socializing new employees with their teams and exposing them to the corporate culture.

 For example, at Julia's Cookies, each new hire receives a packet of information about volunteer opportunities to ensure that they are exposed to the company's culture of giving back to the community. At Big Four accounting firms, groups of new hires go through days or weeks of training together, and the relationships made there may last throughout their careers.

Some important aspects of HR onboarding that go beyond the traditional business processes and controls can benefit the company as well as new hires:

- Ensuring that new hires are comfortable, facilitating socialization, and providing them exposure to the company helps new hires buy into the company, thus increasing the likelihood of retention.
- **CPA** When new hires buy into the company, it mitigates many risks associated with high employee turnover, such as decreased productivity, expenses of training, and diminished company reputation. Retaining high-performing employees is critical to success for businesses of all types.

Companies today face new risks related to hiring in a virtual environment. With the corporate workforce shifting primarily to a work-from-home environment due to COVID-19, and with many companies planning to maintain this arrangement long term, businesses are navigating how to interview, hire, and onboard employees they have never met in person. Controls such as extensive background checks and robust training play an essential role in helping the HR department navigate this new virtual working arrangement.

Why Does It Matter to Your Career?

Thoughts from a Risk Advisory Consultant, Public Accounting

Employee onboarding is often an overlooked opportunity for process improvements. Simple changes such as providing comprehensive employee onboarding, following up with new hires after orientation to see how they are adjusting, and making sure employees have access to building floorplans and local restaurants can greatly improve employees' outlooks on their new company. These tiny details can reduce risks around turnover.

Employee Onboarding Process

In order to evaluate Julia's Cookies' employee onboarding process, you need to understand how it works and how responsibilities are distributed among employees. It is also important to know whether the process as it is documented is up to date with what is taking place in the business. A process flowchart makes it easy to review a business process for accuracy and currency. Talking to employees will reveal whether the process as it is documented truly reflects the current operations. Process flowcharts are also used to evaluate controls in a system or process.

Recall that a process flowchart is a graphical representation of a business process in a flowchart format. The steps of the process are represented by different shapes to create a step-by-step diagram of what takes place.

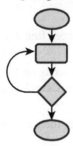

Julia's Cookies uses the process flowchart in **Illustration 9.5** to document its current business process of employee onboarding. Three areas are involved in this process: HR generalist, HR benefits team, and Payroll. Julia's Cookies outsources payroll to a third-party **payroll service administrator**. Automatic Data Processing, Inc. (ADP) is a provider of human resources management software and services, including payroll. ADP must set up a new hire in its system so it can manage payroll activities on behalf of Julia's Cookies. Julia's Cookies reviews ADP's system inputs to ensure that employee information is accurate.

The Julia's Cookies' process flowchart refers to some specific terminology and steps:

- **Offer letter:** The initial offer contains the position details and salary for the prospective employee and states that the employment offer is contingent on a background check.

- **Background check:** A third-party company verifies the prospective hire's historical residential addresses, prior employment, and criminal history.

- **New hire package:** This email contains the start date, summary of benefits offered, where to report on the first day, and a link to an online portal the employee will use to provide information before starting employment.

- **Expense tracking system:** This system, maintained by the Accounting department, allows employees to input their reimbursable business expenses with appropriate documentation (such as receipts). Such a system is often purchased from a third-party software company (Julia's Cookies uses SAP Concur) but directly administered by the company's Accounting department.

- **Employee personal information:** Before starting employment, the employee is given access to the online company portal to provide additional information such as emergency contacts, tax ID number, tax withholding details, and mailing address.

Risks and Control Activities

Companies mitigate the risks in employee onboarding by implementing and enforcing effective control activities. In the summary of controls provided in **Table 9.1**, we explore risk statements and identify the employee(s) typically responsible for each control activity to ensure proper segregation of duties.

Recall that a clearly defined risk statement is formed by identifying the issue and the potential outcome: [The issue] *may result in* [the outcome]. For example: "System records created for a nonexistent employee may result in payroll fraud."

In earlier chapters, you learned that companies consider inherent risk, likelihood, impact, cost-benefit, and residual risk when determining what controls to implement. As with everything else in business, the cost of a control activity should not exceed the benefit. While frameworks like COSO provide guidance to companies on how to create an effective control environment, business processes like HR and payroll do not have comprehensive lists of recommended controls. Companies are left to interpret guidance and design controls that meet the specific needs of their business. The sample control activities listed in Table 9.1 are just some of the many critical controls for employee onboarding. After you review this list of control activities, explore what control deficiencies a CPA firm found for employee onboarding at Julia's Cookies in Applied Learning 9.2.

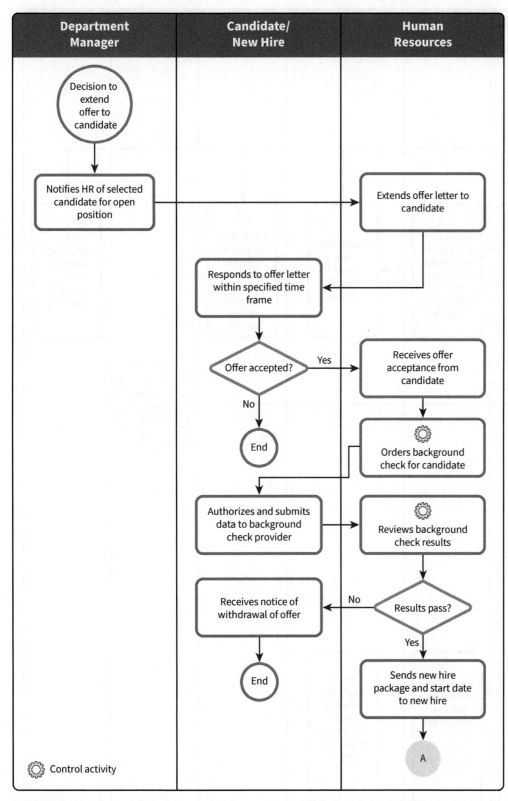

Illustration 9.5 A process flowchart makes it easy to see Julia's Cookies' onboarding process and related control activities. (*Continued*)

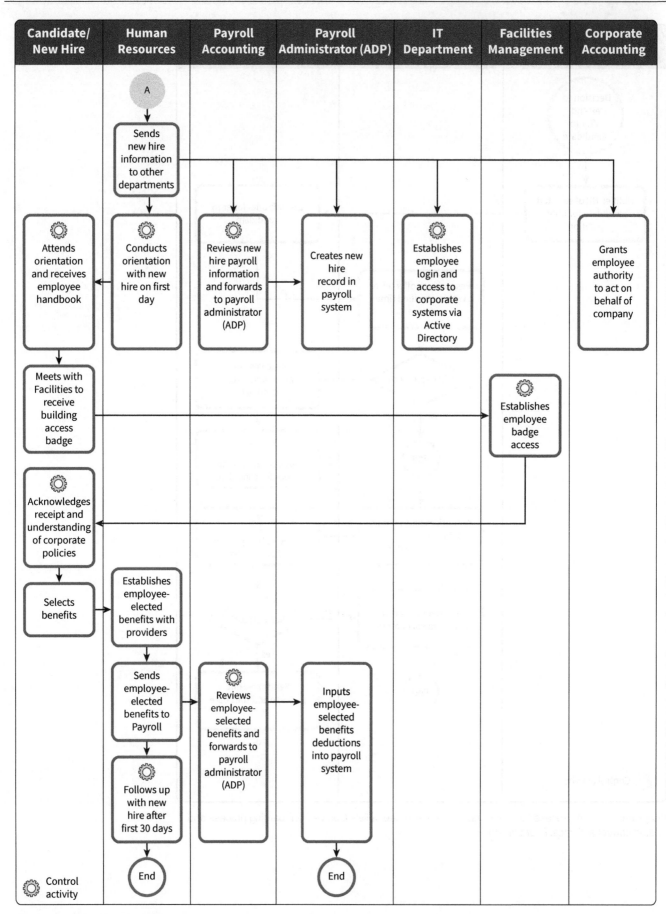

Illustration 9.5 (*Continued*)

TABLE 9.1 Summary of Risks and Controls in Employee Onboarding

Risk Statement: These control activities apply to all potential risks in this business process.

Sample Control Activity	Control Owner
Follow documented and authorized policies and procedures for hiring	HR manager
Complete a new hire checklist to ensure receipt of required documentation prior to employee record creation	HR manager

Risk Statement: CPA Hiring someone with a poor employment record or criminal history may result in an employee being unsuitable for the position and possibly future loss.

Sample Control Activity	Control Owner
Perform comprehensive background checks before finalizing offers of employment	HR manager

Risk Statement: CPA Employee records created for a nonexistent employee may result in fraudulent payments to a fictitious employee.

Sample Control Activity	Control Owner
Prior to employee record creation, have employees complete a new hire package that includes a method (manual or digital) of acquiring: • New employee profile form • W-4 form • Employment eligibility form • State tax form • Direct deposit form • Benefits enrollment form	HR manager
Review new hire documentation prior to employee record creation	Payroll manager
CPA Secure employee data so that additions or changes are documented and performed only by authorized individuals	HR manager
CPA Conduct an independent review of new hire data in the system to ensure validity and accuracy	Payroll manager/HR manager

Risk Statement: CPA Violation of employment laws for hiring may result in lawsuits, fines, legal penalties, or reputational damage.

Sample Control Activity	Control Owner
Ensure that only the HR department extends offer letters for employment	HR manager
Ensure that third-party background check providers have an independent internal control report in place to ensure confidentiality and security of personal information	HR manager/background check provider

Risk Statement: New hires failing to understand their duties, obligations, and company policies may result in misunderstandings and negative impacts on productivity.

Sample Control Activity	Control Owner
As part of the new hire package, have an employee sign an employment agreement that includes the job description and the employee's responsibilities to the company	HR manager
Have new hires attend an employee orientation before beginning their job duties	HR manager
Maintain a comprehensive employee handbook and provide it to all employees	HR manager
Ensure that new hires acknowledge receipt and understanding of these policies: • Professional conduct policy • Travel and expense policy • Harassment policy • Confidentiality and nondisclosure agreement • Employment agreement	HR manager

(Continued)

TABLE 9.1 *(Continued)*

Risk Statement: CPA New hires feeling disconnected from the company culture and their teams may result in high turnover, which leads to increased hiring and training costs and decreased team morale.

Sample Control Activity	Control Owner
Provide comprehensive onboarding for new employees including: • Opportunities to socialize • Robust orientation to the company and its culture • A personalized first-day experience • Ongoing training and engagement with employees after their onboarding	HR manager

Julia's Cookies   Applied Learning 9.2

Employee Onboarding Maturity: Starting Somewhere

Ginny, the new director of Human Resources at Julia's Cookies, hires a CPA firm to evaluate the onboarding process and its related controls. The firm assesses the maturity of this business process to provide Ginny with a starting point to identify and measure areas for improvement. Her goal is for Julia's Cookies' HR and payroll processes to meet those of a best-in-class company, which is Phase 4 of the maturity model.

The CPA firm identifies four control deficiencies and makes recommendations to Ginny for improvement. An assessment of the likelihood and impact of the risk for each control deficiency results in the assignment of a priority level of high, medium, or low.

Based on the following report from the CPA firm and the business process maturity model, which recommendation do you think Ginny should implement first? What is the maturity level of the employee onboarding process?

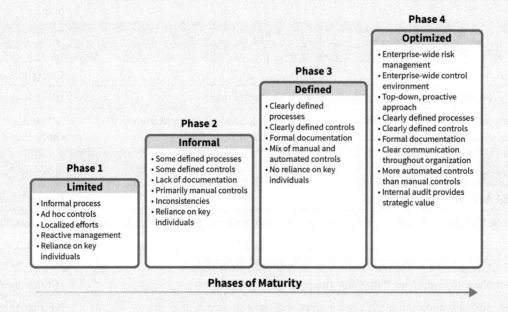

KEY OBSERVATIONS

Julia's Cookies does not enforce a consistent process for employee onboarding. The hiring manager sometimes issues offer letters before involving HR.

Most controls are manual.

CONTROL DEFICIENCIES

1. Deficiency: The hiring manager sometimes issues offer letters before notifying the HR department.

   Recommendation: Ensure that only HR extends offer letters to prevent premature hiring, employment law violations, and inconsistencies in hiring procedures

   Priority: High

2. Deficiency: The third-party background check provider does not have an independent internal control report in place.

   Recommendation: Require vendors with access to confidential information to have an internal control report issued by a CPA firm prior to engagement in order to prevent lawsuits

   Priority: Medium

3. Deficiency: The new hire package does not include a detailed job description.

   Recommendation: Streamline job descriptions and communicate them to employees upon hire

   Priority: Medium

4. Deficiency: There are multiple stand-alone policies instead of a single comprehensive employee handbook.

   Recommendation: Aggregate policies into a comprehensive employee handbook for clearer communication and process efficiency

   Priority: Medium

SOLUTION

Ginny uses a cost-benefit analysis and the priority ratings to determine which recommendations to implement first.

Because it is a high priority and an easily implemented recommendation, Ginny should first focus on Deficiency #1 by enforcing the formally documented employee onboarding process and requiring that HR draft and extend all offer letters directly to prospective employees.

Based on the CPA firm's report and the business process maturity model, Julia's Cookies' employee onboarding process is in Phase 2—Informal. Processes, while somewhat defined and documented, are not enforced, and controls are predominantly manual. For example, Julia's Cookies' process flowchart shows that all offer letters come from the HR department, but Deficiency #1 reveals that this control is not enforced, and hiring managers sometimes send letters directly. This means there is inconsistency in handling these business activities.

Ginny has a lot of work to do!

CONCEPT REVIEW QUESTIONS

1. What do you understand by employee onboarding process?

   Ans. Employee onboarding is the process of establishing new employees in the company's systems and helping them quickly adapt to their positions and the company. Onboarding starts when a job offer is made and continues through an employee's first day, weeks, or even months.

2. **CPA** Consider the risk statement: "Hiring someone with a poor employment record or criminal history may result in an employee being unsuitable for the position and possibly future loss." What control activity the process owner needs to execute to mitigate this risk?

   Ans. The HR manager should perform comprehensive background checks before finalizing offers of employment.

3. **CPA** For the risk statement, "Employee records created for a nonexistent employee may result in fraudulent payments to a fictitious employee," what could be a sample control activity?

   Ans. HR managers should secure employee data so that additions or changes are documented and performed only by authorized individuals. Payroll managers or HR managers should conduct an independent review of new hire data in the system to ensure validity and accuracy.

9.3 What Happens When an Employee Is Terminated?

Learning Objective ❸
Evaluate the employee termination process.

With all the work that goes into onboarding a new employee, it should come as no surprise that removing an employee also requires quite a bit of effort. From managing personalities and emotions to ensuring the safety of the company's data, HR has several responsibilities upon termination of employment.

The **employee termination** business process involves managing the removal of an employee from active employment status:

- A termination may be voluntary (resignation, retirement), involuntary (layoffs, firing), or medical (disability, death).
- HR guides conversations, answers questions from departing employees and their leadership, and minimizes potential damage during this process.
- The HR department implements controls to ensure that company policy and procedures are enforced during this often-stressful time.

While HR's involvement is driven by corporate culture, best practices require HR to be strategically involved in the entire termination process. In the case of resignation, HR is notified immediately after the employee's supervisor receives notice. For firings, HR is involved to ensure that the situation doesn't escalate and to mitigate the risk of a retaliatory ex-employee filing a lawsuit.

CPA In some situations, it is necessary for employees to gather their belongings and leave immediately. This is especially true at public accounting firms, where employees often have their exit interviews and are sent home on the same day they turn in their resignations. The goal of such a speedy exit is to protect company information and property. In the case of public accounting, requiring a newly terminated employee to leave immediately also prevents conflicts of interest that arise when the exiting employee has already accepted a job offer from a firm that is a direct competitor. With these types of fast-paced, often unexpected voluntary terminations, HR employees are trained to act efficiently with short notice.

Why Does It Matter to Your Career?

Thoughts from an Internal Audit Director, Private Company

One day you may be responsible for firing an employee. It is important to follow policy and procedures to protect your company—and yourself—from legal retaliation. Remain professional no matter what happens and work closely with your HR department throughout the process.

In addition to managing the human element of employee terminations, HR is also responsible for the administrative process, which includes these business activities:

- Receiving company assets from the departing employee
- Terminating employee access to systems
- Administering retirement or death benefits to the appropriate beneficiaries

While some of these activities are executed solely by HR, others require a partnership with other areas of the company.

Julia's Cookies' HR department is responsible for informing the IT department about terminated employees who should have their access to systems removed. The IT department performs the system access removal. Controls for this process require mitigating both the risks in the HR department and the risks in the IT department. Given that a company will have many cross-functional business processes like this, the further along the maturity model, the more coverage the company's controls will have. An enterprise-level risk management approach is required to see the big-picture impact of business processes and to ensure that controls exist to address the unique risks across teams.

Employee Termination Process

You have learned that a process flowchart is a type of formal documentation of a process and its related controls. Based on the business maturity model, formal documentation exists at Phase 3—Defined. This means that not all processes will have formal documentation, and a lack of documentation indicates a lack of maturity in the business process.

At Julia's Cookies, a process flowchart for employee terminations did not exist before Ginny joined the HR team. To create one, Ginny met with the responsible manager and their team members to discuss daily activities and all the scenarios that occur when an employee is terminated. Ginny discovered that an employee termination is initiated in four major ways: voluntary resignation, involuntary termination (firing or layoff), retirement, and death. Because retirement and death are less common, Ginny focused on creating a process flowchart for the more likely scenarios of voluntary resignation and involuntary termination (**Illustration 9.6**). Note that there are many departments in the swim lanes of this flowchart, and they indicate in which part of the business the process occurs. The termination process affects every area of the business where that employee had access—even the buildings.

These notes will help you understand the employee termination process flowchart:

- **Severance:** For an involuntary termination, such as a layoff, that is not the result of poor employee performance, exiting employees may be entitled to a severance pay package that includes a percentage of their salary.

- **Exit interview:** On the last day of employment, employees meet with HR to discuss why they are leaving, provide forwarding contact information, and learn about benefits post-termination. This is also when employees turn in their badges, equipment, and corporate credit cards. HR then escorts employees from the building.

Risks and Control Activities

Ending a professional relationship between an employee and a company can be a sensitive time for all parties involved. In addition to being subject to administrative risks, this business process carries a high risk for emotional reactions that can result in reputational loss, lawsuits, and even retaliatory action. The HR department needs to take a consistent and professional approach as it facilitates terminations.

Controls that mitigate the risks in employee terminations focus on both the personal side of the process and the administrative risks it brings. **Table 9.2** identifies sample controls and control owners for each of these common risks. Note that some of the sample control activities cover more than one risk. In an effective control environment, controls are designed to provide maximum risk coverage. This creates a higher value in the cost-benefit analysis of which controls to implement.

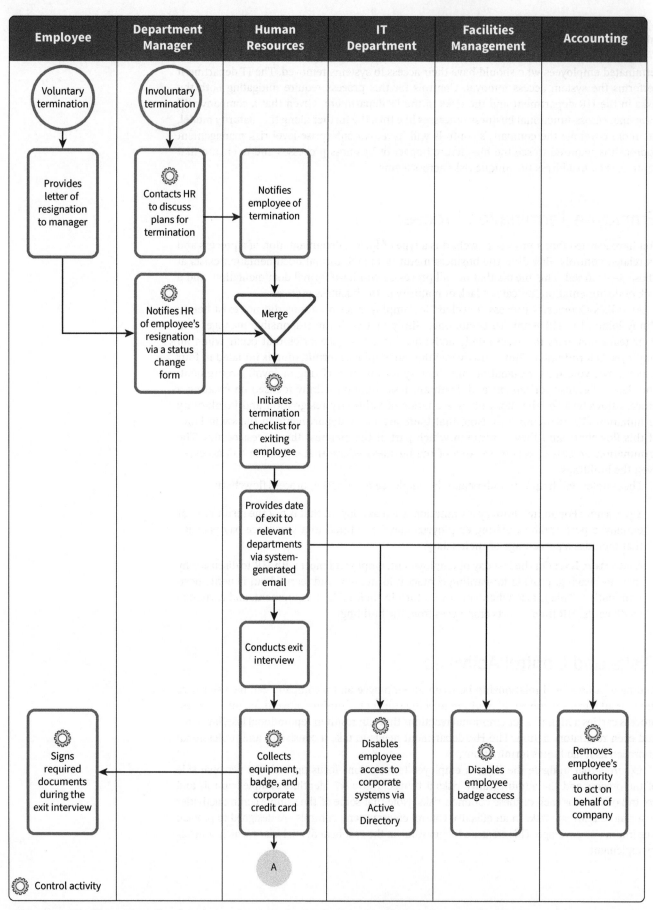

Illustration 9.6 The process flowchart for employee termination begins with either a voluntary or involuntary termination and ends with the employee's final payroll. (*Continued*)

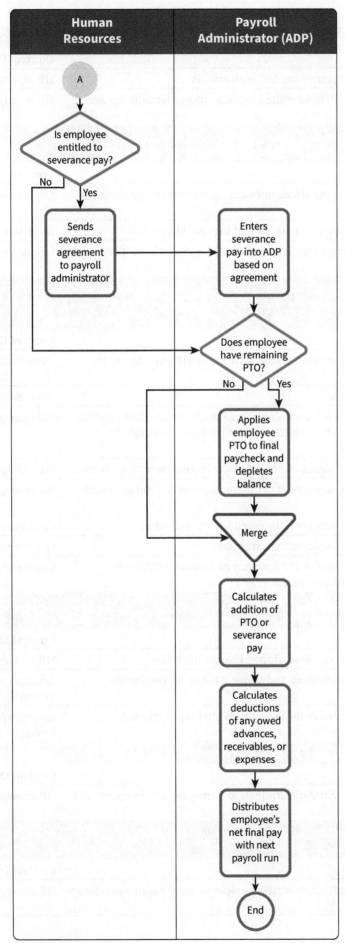

Illustration 9.6 *(Continued)*

TABLE 9.2 Summary of Risks and Controls in Employee Terminations

Risk Statement: These control activities apply to all potential risks in this business process.	
Sample Control Activity	**Control Owner**
Follow documented and authorized policies and procedures for terminations	HR manager
Complete a termination checklist to ensure that all tasks related to the employee termination are performed	HR manager
Risk Statement: CPA An involuntary termination that doesn't follow legal regulations may result in a wrongful termination lawsuit requiring costly litigation and reputational damage.	
Sample Control Activity	**Control Owner**
Provide notification of involuntary termination to the HR department via a status change form the day the employee is terminated	Department manager
Complete an HR-authorized employee termination checklist. Submit the checklist to HR	Department manager
Document involuntary terminations with a severance agreement executed by both the employee and the employee's direct manager	HR manager
Risk Statement: Terminated employees who continue to have access to company systems, resources, and physical locations have inappropriate access to confidential information, data, and business activities and may perform retaliatory or malicious actions against the company, which may result in breaches, data losses, financial losses, and reputational damage.	
Sample Control Activity	**Control Owner**
Provide notification of voluntary termination via a status change form to the HR department the same day that notice is received	Department manager
Remove employee system access in a timely manner	IT manager
During the exit interview, collect company property from the employee, such as computers, mobile phones, corporate credit cards, badges, keys, and employee ID, and return it to the responsible department	HR manager
Execute a return of company property agreement signed by the employee during the exit interview	HR manager
Provide a copy of the return of company property agreement to the employee at the end of the exit interview	HR manager
Disable electronic access to the facilities immediately upon the employee's termination	Facilities manager
Disable access to systems immediately upon the employee's termination	IT department
Remove the employee's authority to act on the behalf of the company and conduct company business (such as executing checks, contracts, and purchases)	Legal/accounting
Risk Statement: Terminated employees who continue to have access to a corporate credit card might charge unauthorized expenses to the company, which may result in financial liability for the company.	
Sample Control Activity	**Control Owner**
Collect corporate credit cards in possession of the employer during the exit interview	HR manager
Finalize expense reimbursement documentation for clearance and payment before the employee's termination date	Accounts payable manager
Pay and close corporate credit card account at the end of the billing cycle after the employee's termination date	Accounts payable manager
Risk Statement: CPA Employee turnover may result in the loss of valued, high-performing employees.	
Sample Control Activity	**Control Owner**
Capture and formally document the reasons for voluntary termination during the exit interview and investigate, if necessary	HR manager
Risk Statement: CPA Employee records remaining active in the payroll system for a terminated employee may result in fraudulent payments to the terminated employee.	
Sample Control Activity	**Control Owner**
HR conducts an independent review of the payroll administrator's employee record status to validate that it is no longer active	HR manager

TABLE 9.2 (*Continued*)

Risk Statement: Terminated employees owing outstanding advances and employee receivables may result in uncollected funds and financial losses.	
Sample Control Activity	**Control Owner**
Clear all advances and employee receivables prior to the employee's final paycheck	Accounts receivable

Risk Statement: **CPA** Terminated employees with knowledge of secret or sensitive information about operations, clients, customers, strategy, and more may result in market share loss, financial losses, and customer losses.	
Sample Control Activity	**Control Owner**
Have an employee sign a noncompete agreement during the exit interview	HR manager
Provide a copy of the signed noncompete agreement to the employee at the exit interview	HR manager

Employee terminations are a sensitive and risk-filled area of business. Evaluate the maturity of Julia's Cookies' processes in Applied Learning 9.3.

Julia's Cookies   Applied Learning 9.3

Employee Termination Maturity: Things Look Better

After its successful work on the onboarding process, Ginny extends the contract with the CPA firm to have the contractors assess the termination process and its related controls.

The CPA firm identifies only two control deficiencies for this business process. An assessment of the likelihood and impact of the risk for each control deficiency results in the assignment of a priority level of high, medium, or low.

Review the following report from the CPA firm and compare the deficiencies to the business process maturity model. Which recommendation should Ginny implement first? What is the maturity level of the employee termination business process?

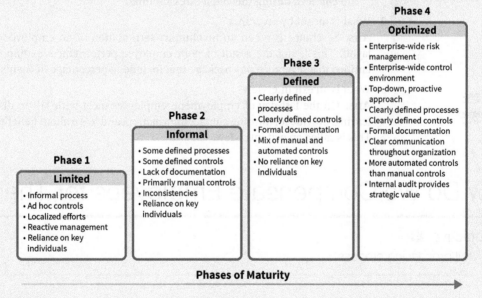

Phases of Maturity

KEY OBSERVATIONS

Julia's Cookies does not consistently enforce its process for involuntary employee terminations. Department managers sometimes terminate an employee without first working with HR and having HR issue the notice to the employee. In addition, exit interviews are conducted inconsistently.

Employee termination data is used in risk management activities. The enterprise risk assessment uses employee termination reports and a dedicated dashboard populated with exit interview data to assess risks at an enterprise level. Retention and turnover are not considered in the enterprise risk assessment.

CONTROL DEFICIENCIES

1. Deficiency: In some instances, the department manager terminates an employee without first providing notice to HR.

   Recommendation: Julia's Cookies should ensure that HR is notified and engaged in the termination process prior to communication to the employee. This will prevent premature termination and mitigate the risk of wrongful termination lawsuits.

   Priority: High

2. Deficiency: Exit interviews are conducted inconsistently. HR does not formally review the results.

Recommendation: Julia's Cookies should regularly review exit interview results and leverage exit interview comments from terminated employees along with turnover statistics to evaluate areas for improvement.

Priority: Medium

SOLUTION

While both recommendations should be implemented in Julia's Cookies' journey toward the Phase 4—Optimized maturity level, the most impactful and potentially damaging deficiency is Deficiency #1. HR has the knowledge base to determine whether a termination is warranted and also has the expertise to ensure that it is enacted in a legal manner.

It appears that Julia's Cookies' employee termination process is more mature than its hiring process. This process is somewhere between Phase 2—Informal and Phase 3—Defined. Processes and controls appear to be clearly defined, but Ginny had to create her own process flow diagram. There are inconsistencies in the enforcement of the controls as well, as indicated by the two deficiencies the CPA firm identified. It is likely the CPA firm would rate this business process as Phase 2—Informal and add commentary that it is already moving into Phase 3—Defined.

CONCEPT REVIEW QUESTIONS

1. What activities are involved in the employee termination business process?
   Ans. A termination may be voluntary (resignation and retirement), involuntary (layoffs and firing), or medical (disability and death). The employee termination business process involves managing the removal of an employee from active employment status:
   - HR guides conversations, answers questions from departing employees and their leadership, and minimizes potential damage during this process.
   - The HR department implements controls to ensure that company policy and procedures are enforced during this often-stressful time.

2. What is meant by severance?
   Ans. Severance is when an involuntary termination of an employee is done, such as a layoff. This is not the result of poor employee performance; exiting employees may be entitled to a severance pay package that includes a percentage of their salary.

3. What is an exit interview?
   Ans. On the last day of employment, employees meet with HR to discuss why they are leaving, provide forwarding contact information, and learn about benefits post-termination. This is called an exit interview.

9.4 How Do We Compensate Employees for Their Work?

Learning Objective ❹
Assess the payroll processing process.

The primary goal of a company is to maximize profits. The same can be said for its employees. Finding a job that you love and "never working a day in your life" may be your goal, or you may make trade-offs and sacrifice personal fulfillment in the name of financial gain. If you don't love your job, you will likely find yourself faced with what is known in economics as the **labor-leisure trade-off**. This trade-off is the balance between the amount of time you spend earning your salary and the satisfaction you receive during your leisure, or unpaid, time. The primary determinant of this balance is the amount of salary you are earning.

Recall that the *payroll* function in an organization calculates wages (hourly, salary, and commission) and compensates employees with their entitled pay. It therefore follows that employees and their time worked are at the heart of a company's payroll business process.

Companies take various approaches to HR and payroll systems, including subcontracting these activities out to a third-party payroll provider, as

Julia's Cookies does, or implementing HR and payroll modules and features in a fully integrated enterprise resource planning (ERP) system, which is a Phase 4—Optimized maturity-level approach. Many factors, including these, determine the degree of integration between a company's HR and payroll systems:

- Cost of an enterprise-wide system
- Size of the business
- Support from management
- Ability to generate user buy-in

You have learned that HR and payroll generate and use large amounts of employee-related data. From this perspective, there are advantages for a company to pursue a higher level of maturity and integrate the information systems for these processes:

- Creating a single source for HR and payroll data
- Reducing data redundancies
- Improving data quality
- Minimizing effort required for data collection (that is, entering data into only one system)
- Providing streamlined and quick access to data for business users

If a cost-benefit analysis indicates that integrated systems are not the best option for a business, it may choose to outsource payroll to a vendor instead. Julia's Cookies originally decided to outsource payroll to ADP when it wanted to reduce costs in its early years of operations. Even though Julia's Cookies' payroll administration is performed by a third-party vendor, the company still has a payroll manager on its corporate accounting team. The corporate Payroll department is responsible for managing ADP and acting as a control owner over various payroll control activities, which we'll explore later.

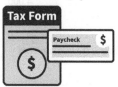

CPA Keep in mind that payroll is not as straightforward as simply distributing hourly rates or annual salaries to employees. Wages must be taxed based on federal, state, and local regulations, which results in several financial accounting journal entries. Before we examine the payroll business process and related control activities, let's review these journal entries to illustrate the impact of payroll on the financial statements, which are a critical output of the accounting information system.

Payroll Journal Entries

To examine the impact of payroll on the financial statements, let's assume that Julia's Cookies' Internal Audit department has 14 employees. These employees earned a total of $100,000 during the month of July and are paid monthly, on the first of the subsequent month. The following taxes, deductions, and benefits apply to these wages:

Federal taxes withheld from employees, to be paid to the IRS	$20,000
State taxes withheld from employees, to be paid to the state tax agency	$4,000
Social Security tax rate	6.2% each for employee and the employer
Medicare tax rate	1.45% each for employee and the employer
Federal unemployment tax, paid by employer	$4,500
State unemployment tax, paid by employer	$3,000
Employee portion of health insurance premiums, payable to Kaiser	Varies by employee; 20% paid by employee, 80% paid by employer
Employee retirement investment, payable to Schwab Retirement Services	5% of pay by employee and matched by employer
Life insurance premiums, 100% paid by the employer and payable to Protective Life	$500
Vacation and PTO accrual	$16,769

Illustration 9.7 shows the journal entries for the Internal Audit department's July payroll.

	Dr.	Cr.
Salaries and Wages Expense (gross pay)	100,000	
Federal Tax Withholdings Payable		20,000
State Tax Withholdings Payable		4,000
Social Security Taxes Payable (6.2%)		6,200
Medicare Taxes Payable (1.45%)		1,450
Employee Health Insurance Payable (20%)		4,000
Employee Retirement Investment Payable (5%)		5,000
Salaries and Wages Payable		59,350

Gross pay—an expense to the company—less employee payroll deductions, which are liabilities to the company until paid to third parties

	Dr.	Cr.
Payroll Tax Expense	15,150	
Social Security Tax Payable (employer's match)		6,200
Medicare Tax Payable (employer's match)		1,450
Federal Unemployment Tax Payable		4,500
State Unemployment Tax Payable		3,000

The company's share of payroll taxes—an expense to the company and liabilities until paid to third parties

	Dr.	Cr.
Employee Benefits Expense	21,500	
Employee Health Insurance Payable (employer's 80%)		16,000
Employee Retirement Investment Payable (employer's 5% match)		5,000
Employee Life Insurance Payable		500

The company's employee benefits expense owed to third parties are liabilities until paid

	Dr.	Cr.
Employee Vacation and PTO Expense	16,769	
Employee Vacation and PTO Liability		16,769

Accrual for future employee time off—liability is reduced as employees use this benefit

Illustration 9.7 Julia's Cookies' payroll journal entries for the Internal Audit department.

The total payroll expense (salaries plus benefits) for Julia's Cookies' Internal Audit department for the month of July is $153,419 ($100,000 + $15,150 + $21,500 + $16,769).

When the related liabilities are settled, the journal entry will be Dr. Liability and Cr. Cash to deplete the liability accounts in the first three journal entries in Illustration 9.7. This reduces liabilities and the cash balance, which is a current asset. Recall from the employee termination business process that when employees leave the company, any accrued vacation or PTO benefits will be paid in cash in the final paycheck. The Employee Vacation and PTO Liability is adjusted each month to reflect the liability outstanding at the end of that month. The other side of the journal entry for the adjustment goes to the Employee Vacation and PTO Expense account. Assuming that the Employee Vacation and PTO Liability balance should be $15,998 at the end of August, the adjusting journal entry at the end of August is as shown in **Illustration 9.8.**

		Dr.	Cr.
August 31, 202X	Employee Vacation and PTO Liability	771	
	Employee Vacation and PTO Expense		771

Illustration 9.8   Adjusting journal entries are posted every month to recognize the liability outstanding at month end.

You may recall from financial accounting that expenses appear on the Income Statement, and liabilities appear on the Balance Sheet. Let's look at how business activities that create inputs to the information system also affect the outputs. Journal entries for payroll (inputs) create the following financial statement effects (outputs):

- Paying expenses reduces Net Income, which reduces Stockholders' Equity on both the Balance Sheet and the Statement of Stockholders' Equity.
- Paying liabilities reduces Cash on the Balance Sheet and reduces Cash Flow from Operations on the Statement of Cash Flows.

There are two different kinds of journal entry processing:

- Online, real-time journal entry processing occurs upon input of the data (when employee hours are recorded in timekeeping) and the expense and liability are recorded immediately in the accounting information system.
- In contrast, **batch processing** accumulates transactions into groups and processes them at regular intervals. These intervals can be daily, weekly, biweekly, or monthly. If a reporting period ends before batch processing takes place, the company uses an adjusting journal entry to post and accrue unpaid salaries, wages, and benefits. Payroll is an ideal area for batch processing because employees receive their pay at periodic intervals.

Now that we have reviewed the effect of payroll processing on the financial statements, let's look at the business process itself.

Payroll Process

Payroll processing at Julia's Cookies is formally documented in a process flowchart (**Illustration 9.9**). When reviewing the process flowchart, remember that Julia's Cookies outsources payroll to ADP. In the employee onboarding and termination processes, ADP is responsible for creating and terminating access for employees. In the payroll process, ADP performs its core service for Julia's Cookies by calculating, creating, and distributing payroll.

ADP maintains its own set of independent internal controls over the payroll process. For purposes of Julia's Cookies' payroll process flowchart, ADP's services are summarized in the terminator "Calculates and distributes payroll." This flowchart focuses on the payroll preparation, review, and authorization steps that take place before the transactions are sent to ADP for distribution.

Here are some key terms that will help you understand the payroll process flowchart:

- **Payroll batch:** The batch consists of the accumulated transactions for batch processing.
- **Timekeeping system:** Because salaried employees do not typically record their work in a timekeeping system, only hourly paid employees perform this step.
- **Paid time off:** PTO includes paid vacation, personal, or sick time, which requires approval from the employee's manager.

- **Overtime:** Only hourly employees are generally entitled to overtime, which requires prior approval from the employee's manager.

Risks and Control Activities

CPA Important internal control activities over payroll provide reasonable assurance that:

- Payroll is appropriately authorized
- Payroll expenses and liabilities are calculated accurately

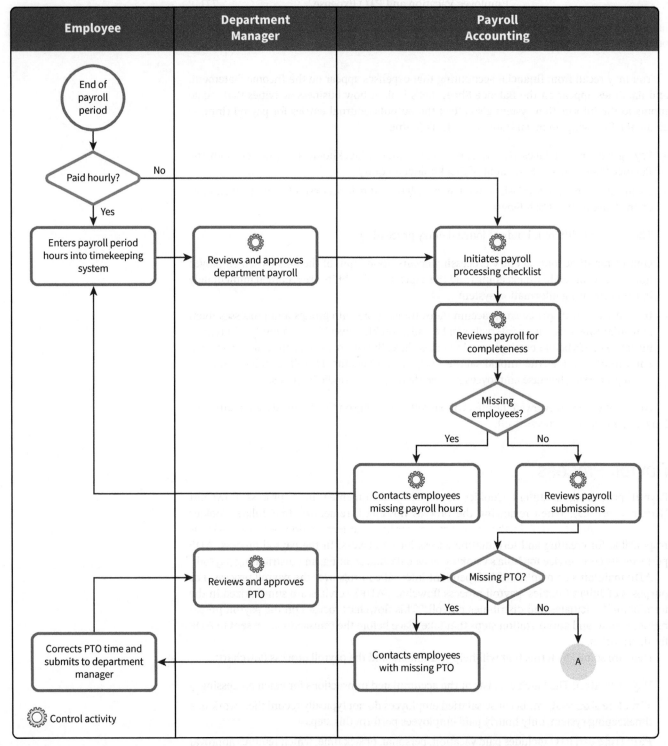

Illustration 9.9 Presenting the payroll process in a process flowchart makes it easy to see all the necessary control activities. (*Continued*)

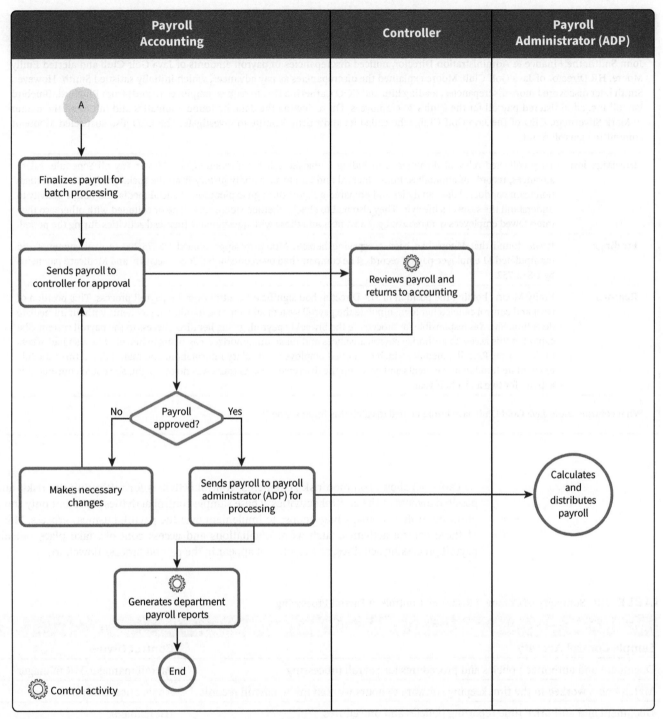

Illustration 9.9 (*Continued*)

- Payroll withholdings are remitted to appropriate agencies
- Sensitive personal information is protected

You have learned that the HR and payroll processes are part of the payments and acquisitions section of the basic business model. Payroll connects to the payments process, as payroll payments are cash disbursement transactions. For example, payroll payable, payroll taxes payable, and payroll withholdings payable are all cash disbursements for resources in the same way as disbursements made when the company purchases raw materials and incurs payable liabilities for those resources.

In the Real World   Java Golf Club[1]

John Smith, the Finance & Administration Director, noticed discrepancies in payroll amounts of Java Golf Club and alerted Emily Moore, HR Director of Java Golf Club. Moore explained the discrepancies as pay advances, which initially satisfied Smith. However, Smith later discovered more discrepancies, leading him and COO Catherine Doe to request employee records from Bluebird. Bluebird Payroll Inc. administered payroll for the Club's 20 employees. On reviewing the data, he found anomalies and informed the matter to Mark Silverman, CEO of the Java Golf Club, who called its audit firm Deloitte to investigate. The CEO also suspected Moore of committing payroll fraud.

Investigation	They collected relevant documents, including employee salary information, the Master Payroll Schedule, salary advances, records of anomalies, from Bluebird and employee activity history from the social media. The investigation team conducted data analytics and prepared a report through exploration of social media and online activity to understand the suspect's lifestyle. They also had to check whether Moore was alone or colluded with others, so they interviewed employees who received pay advances and those with questionable financial activities during the period.
Findings	It was found that Moore had been overpaying herself. Moore misappropriated US$75,200 in overpayments and manipulated 11 employee payroll records. The company had overcontributed Social Security and Medicare payments by US$5,752.
Reasons	Emily Moore, holding the position of HR Director, had significant control over the payroll process. This position of trust and control enabled her to manipulate the payroll system and approve fraudulent payments without immediate detection. She was responsible for processing the biweekly payroll, giving her direct access to the payroll system. She exploited this access to authorize payroll advances and make unauthorized payments to herself. She also had access to the Master Payroll Schedule, which contained employee and salary information. She manipulated this schedule to facilitate fraudulent payments and cover up the discrepancies. As there was no oversight, she could continue this activity for two and a half years.

What controls could Java Gold Club have implemented to catch this fraud sooner?

Table 9.3 shows common risk statements, control activities for mitigating the risks, and possible owners of the control activities. These sample control activities represent only some of the controls a company may choose to implement over the payroll business process. Many of these control activities, such as reconciliations and access controls, take place outside payroll processing activities, so they do not appear in the payroll process flowchart.

TABLE 9.3 Summary of Common Risks and Controls in Payroll Processing

Risk Statement: These control activities apply to all potential risks in this business process.	
Sample Control Activity	**Control Owner**
Document and authorize policies and procedures for payroll processing	Payroll manager/HR manager
Match hours worked in the timekeeping software to hours worked in the payroll records	Application control
Document and authorize time reporting policies and procedures	HR manager
Document and authorize changes to the employee main table data and payroll records	Payroll manager/HR manager
CPA Restrict access to employee main table data to a limited number of individuals, segregated from payroll processing	HR manager
CPA Segregate payroll preparation duties from payroll authorization, the HR department, check signing, and payroll distribution	Payroll manager/accounts payable manager/HR manager
Store payroll payments, payroll records, and employee records that have been validated by the system in the same database	Payroll manager/accounts payable manager

[1]https://www.at-mia.my/2018/03/01/java-golf-club-a-payroll-fraud-case-study/

TABLE 9.3 (*Continued*)

Risk Statement: Incorrect employee data may result in incorrect payments to employees.

Sample Control Activity	Control Owner
Reconcile data in the payroll records to the HR main table on a regular basis to confirm current pay rates, tax codes, deductions, and so on and ensure the use of current, valid, authorized data for payroll	Payroll manager/HR manager
Have the employee make changes directly to employee personal information via an online portal to eliminate the risk of error when entering data from a paper form into the system	Employee/HR manager

Risk Statement: Unauthorized access to the employee main table and payroll records may result in destruction and loss of data, disclosure of confidential information, the addition of fictitious and fraudulent records, or other unauthorized changes.

Sample Control Activity	Control Owner
Compare the list of employees receiving paychecks to other credible employee listings, such as Active Directory or active company telephone numbers, to validate the existence of each paid employee	Controller
Ensure that an independent review of the employee main table data is conducted to look for duplicate names, addresses, bank accounts, etc., to identify fraud risks	HR manager

Risk Statement: Processing of unauthorized payroll transactions may result in a misappropriation of assets.

Sample Control Activity	Control Owner
Review and approve the payroll journal prior to distribution of payments	Payroll manager/controller
CPA Ensure that the controller reviews and signs payroll checks	Controller

Risk Statement: Inaccurate payroll data and inappropriate payments to employees (whether hours are unpaid or extra hours are paid) may result in inaccurate data, records, reports, and financial statements.

Sample Control Activity	Control Owner
CPA Reconcile payroll and employee records	Payroll manager
Regularly review hours worked and payroll to identify unusual balances or variances between pay periods, job responsibilities, or departments	Department manager
Distribute payroll expense reports to the appropriate cost center or department. Ensure that department managers compare against forecasts and explain variances	Payroll manager/department manager

Risk Statement: Payroll processing that is incomplete or inaccurate may result in financial statement misrepresentation.

Sample Control Activity	Control Owner
Complete a payroll processing checklist for each pay period	Payroll manager
Provide a payroll calendar for each payroll type (hourly and salaried) to all employees and include payroll processing periods and cutoff dates	Payroll manager

Risk Statement: Noncompliance with statutory requirements may result in fines, interest payments, and other penalties.

Sample Control Activity	Control Owner
Mail an annual tax report to each employee for tax filing purposes	Payroll manager
Reconcile employee compensation and payments made to government agencies	Payroll manager
Remit payroll withholdings on a timely basis to government agencies	Accounts payable
CPA Reconcile both payroll withholdings and the General Ledger accounts	Accounting manager
Reconcile the list of employees receiving tax reports to the employee main table to verify that all employees are accounted for	Payroll manager

Now that you've reviewed the risks and control activities related to payroll processing, consider which control activities the Internal Audit department should recommend at Julia's Cookies in Applied Learning 9.4.

Julia's Cookies   Applied Learning 9.4

Payroll Processing: Mitigating Risks

Dylan, the head of Internal Audit, receives a list of risks from the corporate controller. These risks are in the Payroll department, and Dylan needs to provide recommendations for control activities to mitigate each of the risks.

Which control activities do you think will best mitigate each of the following risks?

1. An employee elects a certain amount for federal tax withholding, but inaccurate data is entered in the system. As a result, the employee owes thousands of dollars in federal income taxes at the end of the year.

2. A disgruntled terminated employee who resents her manager still has access to the department's database and sabotages the department by deleting three months' data.

3. A payroll clerk creates a fictitious employee and then deposits the paycheck of that employee into their personal bank account.

4. The IRS implements a penalty equal to a percentage of payroll taxes based on the number of days late the company is in paying them.

SOLUTION

A number of control activities could address each of these risks. The following table shows examples from Table 9.3 for each risk.

Risk	Sample Control Activities
1. An employee elects a certain amount for federal tax withholding, but inaccurate data is entered in the system. As a result, the employee owes thousands of dollars in federal income taxes at the end of the year.	Reconcile data in the payroll records to the HR main table on a regular basis to confirm current pay rates, tax codes, deductions, and so on and ensure the use of current, valid, authorized data for payroll
	Have the employee make changes directly to employee personal information via an online portal to eliminate the risk of error when entering data from a paper form into the system
2. A disgruntled terminated employee who resents her manager still has access to the department's database and sabotages the department by deleting three months' data.	Compare the list of employees receiving paychecks to other credible employee listings, such as Active Directory or active company telephone numbers, to validate the existence of each paid employee
	Ensure that an independent review of the employee main table data is conducted to look for duplicate names, addresses, bank accounts, etc., to identify fraud risks
3. A payroll clerk creates a fictitious employee and then deposits the paycheck of that employee into their personal bank account.	Review and approve the payroll journal prior to distribution of payments
	Ensure that the controller reviews and signs payroll checks
4. The IRS implements a penalty equal to a percentage of payroll taxes based on the number of days late the company is in paying them.	Mail an annual tax report (W-2) to each employee for tax filing purposes
	Reconcile employee compensation and payments made to government agencies
	Remit payroll withholdings on a timely basis to government agencies
	Reconcile both payroll withholdings and the General Ledger accounts
	Reconcile the list of employees receiving W-2s to the employee main table to verify that all employees are accounted for

CONCEPT REVIEW QUESTION

1. Discuss the advantages for a company to pursue a higher level of maturity and integrate the information systems for payroll processes.

   Ans. An integrated system includes a single source for HR and payroll data. The single source reduces redundancy and as a result improves data quality. Efforts are minimized for data collection and entry, and access to data is streamlined providing quick access to the HR department and to department managers and supervisors.

9.5 How Can Human Resources and Payroll Data Be Used to Identify Risks?

Learning Objective ❺
Connect the data in the underlying system and database to important reports and data analytics.

Human resources and payroll processes are essential to every business, regardless of size or industry. The systems that capture HR and payroll data enable the HR department to support the business and its employees and enable the finance department to capture and process payroll according to regulations. In an ERP environment, the Payroll feature speaks to, or connects to, the Human Resources Management module for clear communication across processes. This ensures a seamless process for managing the employee main table data, processing timecards, and processing payroll (**Illustration 9.10**).

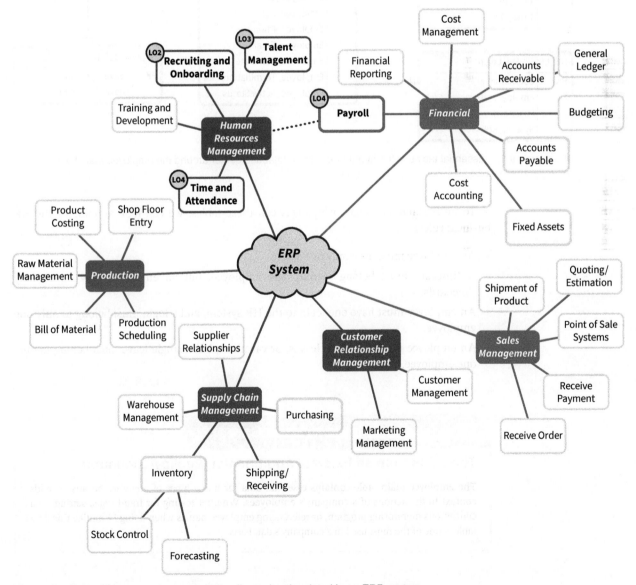

Illustration 9.10 Human resources and payroll are closely related in an ERP system.

Database Design

In the Human Resources Management module of an ERP system, data is centered around the employee main table. It is possible to retrieve data from this table about employees such as salaries, timecards, and vacation hours used. **Illustration 9.11** presents some of the key human resources tables in an entity relationship diagram (ERD).

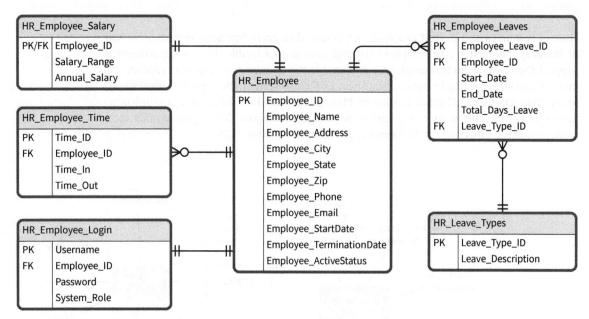

Illustration 9.11 Essential tables in the human resources database center around the employee main table.

To understand the relationships between these tables, we can look at some of the HR business rules:

- An employee must have only one salary.
- A timecard must belong to only one employee, but an employee may have many timecards.
- An employee must have one login to the HR system, and a login must belong to only one employee.
- An employee may take many leaves, or vacations, but a single leave must belong to only one employee.

Why Does It Matter to Your Career?

Thoughts from an External Audit Senior, Public Accounting

The employee main table contains essential data for many types of analytics because it adds context to the actions of a company's employees. Whether testing for fraud risks, setting up a continuous monitoring program, or referencing employee names when doing IT audits, this data table is one of the most used in a company's database.

Reporting and Insights

In this section, we explore important reports and analytics that utilize HR and payroll data. When internal fraud occurs, employees are the perpetrators. Therefore, HR data is a valuable resource for fraud detection. You'll see a variety of fraud tests and dashboards throughout this section.

Employee Onboarding

All business processes generate data that is stored in the information system and converted to useful information through reporting and analysis. The data created during the employee onboarding process includes new hire personal details, start dates, job descriptions, salaries, benefits selections, tax withholding statuses, system logins, bank account numbers, tax IDs, and more. This data is transformed into employee onboarding reports or analyzed using various data analyses. **Table 9.4** lists and describes a number of reports that can be used for employee onboarding.

 Recall that reporting involves aggregating raw data to provide a view of historical activities without context. It is used to inform management of past performance and to show what has happened. Analysis focuses on providing context for the historical data. It gives management meaningful insights to make decisions on how to improve a process. Analysis uses either the raw data or existing reports originating from that data.

TABLE 9.4 Employee Onboarding Reports

Report	Description
New hires	Number and types of new hires. Can be summarized by departments, hiring managers, or time periods.
Hiring violations	Number and types of hiring violations detected.
Hiring issues	Number and types of issues reported by new hires.
Compliance fines and penalties	Number and amounts of compliance fines and penalties. Can be summarized by departments or time periods.
Unfilled positions	Number and types of unfilled positions. Can be summarized by departments.
Internal control exceptions	Number and types of internal control exceptions noted by management or Internal Audit.
Employee main table	Centralized and comprehensive list of all employees, including the hire date and current employment status for each one. Often used alongside other data sources to perform fraud analytics.

Employee onboarding data can also be analyzed to detect risks. **Table 9.5** shows examples of analytics related to employee onboarding.

TABLE 9.5 Employee Onboarding Analytics Examples

Analytic	Example
Compensation variance	Comparison of new hire compensation packages to departmental budgets to identify variances. This analytic can help detect inappropriate hiring practices and financial risks.
Training gaps	Time analysis of the percentage of tenured employees versus newly hired employees, based on length of employment. This analytic can help identify departments that may benefit from increased training because they have many new hires.
Employee feedback	Analysis of post-onboarding surveys completed by new hires to identify whether there are trends in feedback about HR employees, onboarding steps, and so forth. This analytic can help detect risks in the onboarding process.

(Continued)

TABLE 9.5 *(Continued)*

Analytic	Example
Hiring manager feedback	Analysis of post-onboarding surveys completed by hiring managers to identify the skills new hires are expected to have upon completing onboarding, determine whether all access needed has been granted, and identify whether department managers could benefit from any additional changes in onboarding processes. This analytic can help detect risks in the onboarding processes, including skill gaps in newly hired employees.
Vendor–employee comparison	Comparison of vendor telephone numbers, addresses, emails, and bank accounts to the employee main table. This analytic can help look for red flags indicating fraud, such as an employee establishing a fictitious vendor to receive fraudulent payments.
Fictitious employees test	Analysis of employee data to identify employees with matching information, such as different names but the same bank accounts. This analytic provides a fraud test for fictitious employees.

At Julia's Cookies, the Internal Audit department maintains a new hire risk dashboard that uses data generated in the employee onboarding process to show key risk indicators across the company (**Illustration 9.12**). The department uses this dashboard to monitor the number of new hires in each area of the company. When there is a sudden increase in hiring, such as in the IT department between the third and fourth quarters, the department considers things like:

- Could new employees create increased risks due to lack of training and lack of company knowledge?
- Why are there suddenly job openings? Did people quit or get fired?
- If multiple employees recently quit, what is the reason? Does this indicate a risk in the way the department is operating or in its leadership?

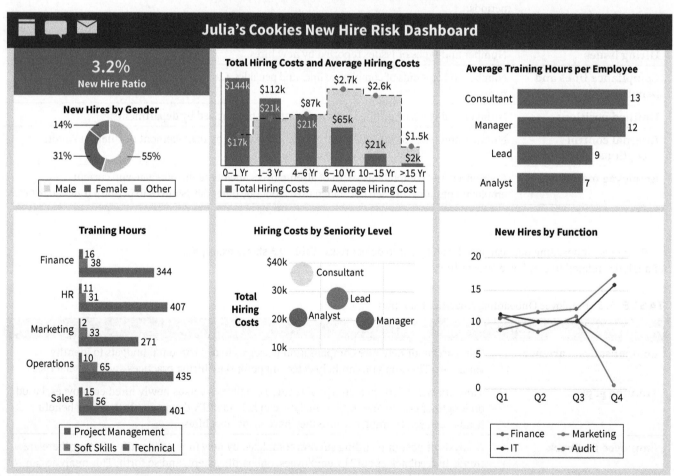

Illustration 9.12 Julia's Cookies' Internal Audit department maintains a new hire risk dashboard that includes various key risk indicators for new employees.

Employee Terminations

Employee terminations present a high risk to companies because onboarding new employees takes a lot of resources, and changing employees decreases productivity. The data created during the employee terminations output is limited, as indicated by the short list of reports in **Table 9.6**. However, this data is highly valuable to a company's review of its processes and risks. In particular, employee **turnover rate** is an essential metric for a business to monitor. This calculation provides a numeric assessment of the risks related to employee terminations because risk increases as the number of terminations rises.

TABLE 9.6 Employee Termination Reports

Report	Description
Completed terminations	Number of and reasons for employee terminations. Can be summarized by departments to examine trends for specific managers or in particular areas of the business.
Turnover rate	Terminated employees compared to available head count. Can be summarized by departments or time periods. Various turnover calculations are available.

Analysis of employee termination data focuses on improving other business processes, such as onboarding and departmental performance. **Table 9.7** shows examples of analytics related to employee terminations.

TABLE 9.7 Employee Termination Analytics Examples

Analytic	Example
Exit interviews	Trend analysis of reasons provided during exit interviews for voluntary terminations. This analytic can help identify ongoing corporate issues such as poor management and below-market pay rates.
Retention and onboarding	Analysis of length of employment compared to feedback from employee's onboarding activities. This analytic can help identify a relationship between onboarding experiences and retention risks.
Seasonal trends	Time series analysis of seasonal trends in voluntary terminations. This analytic can help identify whether employees are frequently leaving after annual promotions and bonuses are announced.

The Enterprise Risk Management department at Julia's Cookies has a dashboard that uses information captured during employee exit interviews to identify risks at an enterprise-wide level (**Illustration 9.13**). The exit dashboard shows company-wide termination activity, based on information from employee termination reports. The dashboard provides insights into the reasons employees leave the company. For example, if the ERM team sees a sudden increase in the exit reasons "culture" or "pay," the team considers questions like these:

- Is there a specific area of the business that is developing an unhealthy culture?
- Is someone recently promoted to a leadership position treating employees poorly?
- Is our pay competitive in the local market?

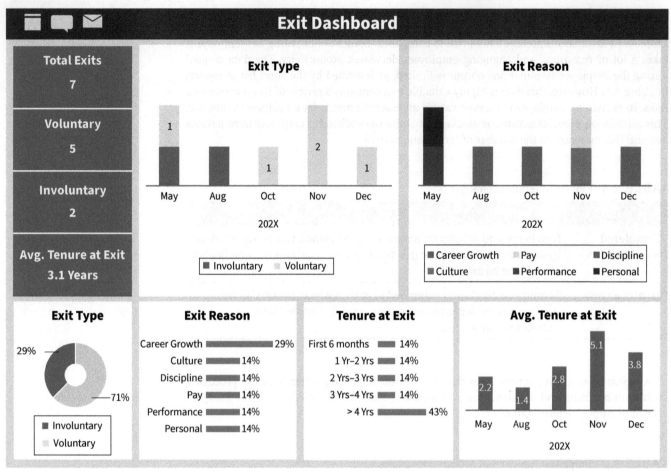

Illustration 9.13 Julia's Cookies' ERM department uses a dashboard populated with data gathered during employee exit interviews to identify enterprise-wide risks.

Payroll Processing

Payroll is a transaction-based and regulated process, so it is not surprising that payroll generates large quantities of data that can be useful to a company. Reports range from custom performance metrics to listings of tax documents for verification purposes. **Table 9.8** lists and describes a number of reports that can be used for payroll processing.

TABLE 9.8 Payroll Processing Reports

Report	Description
Payroll journal	A record of payroll accounting entries for a pay period. Includes employee hours worked, gross pay, net pay, deductions, and payroll rate.
Cumulative payroll journal	The year-to-date payroll journal.
Pay stubs	An individual employee's gross pay, deductions, and net pay for both the payment period and cumulative year-to-date totals.
Form W-2	Wage and tax statements sent to employees at the end of each year (due January 31).
Form W-3	Summary of all W-2 forms. This report is sent to the IRS at the end of each year (due February 28).
Accrued payroll	Hours to be accrued that were not paid at the end of the reporting period.

Because payroll is a high-fraud-risk area, payroll data can be analyzed to detect fraud. **Table 9.9** shows examples of analytics related to payroll processing.

TABLE 9.9 Payroll Processing Analytics

Analytic	Example
Ghost employees	Analysis of payroll processed for employees before their start dates or after their termination dates. This analytic provides a fraud test for ghost employees receiving inappropriate payroll.
Excessive payments	Comparison of wages earned to employee job classification to identify excessive wages.
Duplicate payroll	Identification of instances where employees received multiple payments in a single pay period.
Variances	Comparison of current payroll period wages with previous payroll periods' wages to identify adjustments in salaries. This analytic provides a fraud test for unauthorized payroll adjustments.
Timecard verification	Comparison of timecard data to payroll data to identify variances.
Trend analysis	Analysis of payroll, overtime, and special pay by departments and business leaders. This analytic can help identify high areas of expense for the business.
Wage equality	Analysis of payroll by gender and minority status to review for wage equality risk.

Payroll is an essential area for businesses to monitor, especially when it comes to wage equality. **Illustration 9.14** shows how basic payroll reports provide insights when summarized by age, gender, and department.

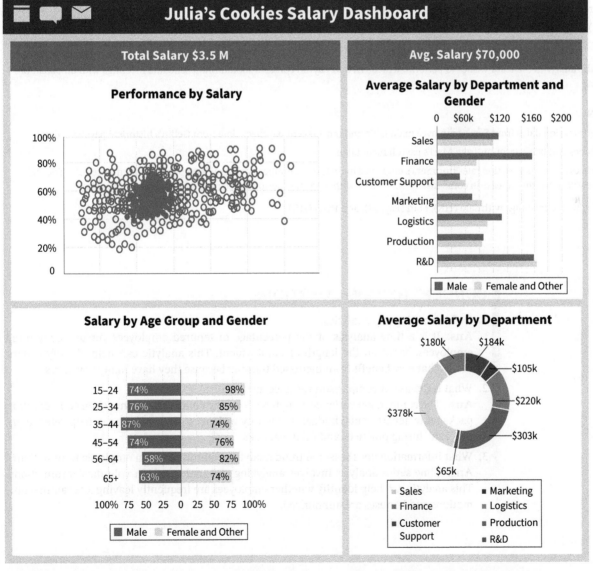

Illustration 9.14 A payroll fraud monitoring dashboard visualizes analytics investigating various fraud schemes.

As Julia's Cookies' Internal Audit team continues its audit of the Payroll department, who will Brant need to meet with to acquire the right data for the necessary analytics? Help him decide in Applied Learning 9.5.

Julia's Cookies	Applied Learning 9.5

Payroll Analytics: Identifying Data Requirements

As part of the ongoing payroll audit, the Internal Audit team is deciding which data it needs for the analytics to be performed. The audit team will perform the following analytics:

Analytic 1: Comparing the termination dates of inactive employees to the most recent date they received a paycheck.

Analytic 2: Identifying potential fictitious employees by comparing direct deposit bank accounts for duplications across multiple employees.

Analytic 3: Fraud test examining unexpected changes in salary rates (increases in compensation amount outside the normal promotion time period in February).

As a first-year auditor, Brant is tasked with scheduling meetings to begin discussions about data acquisition. His manager provides the following list of HR and Payroll contacts and the data they own:

Sara (HR): Employee main table (names, hire dates, termination dates, compensation rates)

Gellin (Payroll): Historical paycheck data (amounts, dates, withholdings)

Marl (Payroll): Payroll main table (names, benefits elections, bank accounts)

Ryan (HR): Employee performance data (performance ratings, bonuses, pay raises, manager comments)

Leslie (HR): Employee benefits (listing of which benefits each employee has elected to participate in)

Based on the analytics the team wishes to perform, which HR and Payroll contacts should Brant schedule meetings with on behalf of his audit team?

SOLUTION

Analytic 1: Termination dates from Sara's employee main table and most recent paycheck date from Gellin's historical paycheck data.

Analytic 2: Names and bank accounts from Marl's payroll main table.

Analytic 3: Names and compensation rates from Sara's employee main table combined with Ryan's employee performance data. The audit team can review whether an increase in compensation coincides with a positive performance review and bonus or pay raise.

Brant should schedule meetings with Sara (HR), Marl (Payroll), and Ryan (HR).

CONCEPT REVIEW QUESTIONS

1. Define training gap analytics.
   Ans. It is a time analysis of the percentage of tenured employees versus newly hired employees, based on the length of employment. This analytic can help identify departments that may benefit from increased training because they have many new hires.

2. What is the use of comparison variance analytics?
   Ans. The comparison variance analytics shows the comparison of new hire compensation packages to departmental budgets to identify variances. This analytic can help detect inappropriate hiring practices and financial risks.

3. What information does seasonal trend analytics communicate on employee termination?
   Ans. Time series analysis involves analyzing seasonal trends in voluntary terminations. This analytic can help identify whether employees are frequently leaving after annual promotions and bonuses are announced.

FEATURED PROFESSIONAL | Director of SOX Compliance

Photo courtesy of
Jonathan Cullen

Jonathan Cullen, CA,[2] CGMA,[3] Black Belt—Six Sigma

Jonathan is the director of SOX for an American health care company with more than 300,000 employees. He also has a career background in consulting and process improvement. As a Six Sigma black belt, Jonathan is experienced in redesigning organizational teams and controls, including developing reporting and analytics metrics to measure process performance. Jonathan enjoys creating buy-in and cooperation among stakeholders to achieve strategic objectives in his projects. He specializes in identifying ways to use available resources in the most effective manner. Jonathan holds degrees in both accounting and music.

What makes a business process successful?

A business is successful if the people doing the process support it and believe in it. This also includes sustainability of the process. If everyone feels that they have a responsibility for its success and are willing to participate in the process, you have the recipe for a great team and success.

What is a challenge you are facing in your day-to-day job, and how are you and your team managing it?

In this time of a global pandemic, our whole team is working remotely. Fortunately, my company embraces the use of technology, which allows us to deliver our work obligations even though we are not in the office. We use Microsoft Teams extensively and have regular video meetings and check-ins. This technology afforded us the ability to be more agile in getting people together for both formal and impromptu meetings. We have been forced to adapt to new ways of getting our work done, all with great success.

You have a music degree and graduated summa cum laude. How does that passion and experience make you a better accounting professional? Do you think your creativity helped you carve your career path?

My creative side has definitely helped me in my career path, which at present has me working in a SOX compliance role where I not only use all my accounting and auditing experience, but I also have the ability to implement process improvement ideas and concepts that reach beyond my immediate department.

What advice would you give regarding interaction with individuals in other parts of the organization?

Go out of your way to interact with people. Be genuinely interested in what they do and find out how your careers and jobs intersect, what you have in common, and what you could do together that would be mutually beneficial or would be an improvement for the organization.

What advice would you give accounting students who are looking for a career outside public accounting audit or tax departments?

Explore areas that may be of interest to you and don't be afraid to step out of your comfort zone. Opportunities often come from unexpected areas. Be adventurous and do what makes you happy. Rest assured that your background in accounting is a great foundation for any career you may choose.

Review and Practice

Key Terms Review

background check	Form W-2	pay stub
batch processing	Form W-3	payroll
cumulative payroll journal	HR processes	payroll batch
employee benefits	human resources (HR)	payroll journal
employee onboarding	labor-leisure trade-off	payroll processes
employee personal information	new hire package	payroll service administrator
employee termination	offer letter	severance
exit interview	outsourced HR model	timekeeping system
expense tracking system	overtime	turnover rate
fictitious employees test	paid time off (PTO)	

[2]Chartered Accountant—a globally recognized accounting certification similar to the CPA.
[3]Chartered Global Management Accountant—a globally recognized accounting certification for specialists in finance, operations, strategy, and management.

Learning Objectives Review

> ❶ Explain the relationship between human resources and payroll.

The human resources (HR) function in an organization is responsible for all employees and employee-related operations.

Major activities of an HR department include:

- Recruiting and hiring employees
- Training and developing employees
- Determining salaries and benefits
  - Compensation
  - Employee benefits (medical and life insurance, retirement, and more)
  - PTO and leaves
- Monitoring and evaluating employees
  - Performance evaluations
- Transitioning employees
  - Voluntary and involuntary termination
  - Retirement
- Updating and maintaining employee main table data

The payroll function in an organization calculates wages (hourly, salary, commission) and compensates employees with their entitled pay. Responsibilities for payroll should be separate from HR to ensure proper segregation of duties.

HR personnel are trained to handle sensitive, confidential, and legal HR issues. Finance professionals are trained to create journal entries in the payroll ledger.

Best practice is to divide payroll responsibilities between the two teams and promote an environment where they work together. In other words, HR owns the data used by the accounting department to process payroll.

> ❷ Evaluate the employee onboarding process.

Employee onboarding involves establishing new employees in the company's systems and helping them adapt to their new positions in the company.

A good onboarding process includes:

- Establishing the new employee in the company's system
- Socializing new employees with their teams
- Exposing new employees to the company culture
- Ensuring that new hires are comfortable and know what is expected of them

A good onboarding process increases the likelihood of employee retention, which mitigates risks related to employee turnover.

Control activities that address all the risks in employee onboarding are:

- Follow documented and authorized policies and procedures for hiring
- Complete a new hire checklist to ensure receipt of required documentation prior to employee record creation

> ❸ Evaluate the employee termination process.

Employee termination involves managing the removal of employees from active employment status. Terminations can be the result of:

- Voluntary resignation
- Retirement
- Involuntary layoff
- Involuntary firing
- Medical disability
- Death

Best practice requires the strategic involvement of HR in the termination process to manage legal risk and sensitive situations.

A good termination process involves HR in managing both the human element aspects and administrative activities such as collecting company assets, overseeing termination of employee access, and administering retirement or death benefits to appropriate beneficiaries.

Control activities that address all the risks in the termination process are:

- Follow documented and authorized policies and procedures for terminations
- Complete a termination checklist to ensure that all tasks related to the employee termination are performed

> ❹ Assess the payroll processing process.

Advantages of an integrated HR and payroll system include:

- Creating a single source for HR and payroll data
- Reducing data redundancies
- Improving data consistency, accuracy, and integrity
- Minimizing efforts for data collection (entering the data into only one system)
- Providing streamlined and quick access to data for business users

Payroll impacts the financial statements through Salaries and Wages Expense, which includes taxes, deductions, and benefits withholdings:

- Paying expenses reduces Retained Earnings on the Balance Sheet. This causes a reduction in Stockholders' Equity on both the Balance Sheet and the Statement of Stockholders' Equity.

- Paying liabilities reduces Cash on the Balance Sheet. This causes a reduction in Cash Flow from Operations on the Statement of Cash Flows.

Employee vacation and PTO are recorded as a liability and adjusted each month to reflect the liability outstanding at the end of that month. It is a debit to the liability account and a credit to the expense account, assuming that the balance in the liability account needs to decrease.

A good payroll process is separate from HR to provide adequate segregation of duties.

Important internal control activities related to payroll provide reasonable assurance that:

- Payroll is appropriately authorized.
- Payroll expenses and liabilities are calculated accurately.
- Payroll withholdings are remitted to appropriate agencies.
- Sensitive personal information is protected.

> **5** Connect the data in the underlying system and database to important reports and data analytics.

The Human Resources Management ERP module and Payroll feature should connect to streamline communication between the two related business processes.

Most tables in the human resources database relate to the employee main table.

Employee onboarding information supports decision making with a variety of reports:

- Number of new hires
- Number of hiring violations detected
- Number of hiring issues reported by new hires
- Number and amount of compliance fines and penalties
- Number of unfilled positions
- Internal control exception reports

Employee onboarding analytics include budget analysis of compensation, comparison of employment period of tenured employees to new hires, onboarding survey results, and fraud analytics looking for fictitious employees.

Employee termination reports include:

- Number of completed employee terminations
- Number of each type of completed employee termination (voluntary, involuntary, etc.)
- Turnover rate (with various types of calculations available)

Many companies use employee termination data to create dashboards that monitor the reasons for and locations of employee exits. These analytics help groups like ERM and Internal Audit identify risky areas in the business.

Payroll reports are used for decision making:

- Payroll journal (cumulative and noncumulative)
- Pay stubs
- Form W-2, wage and tax statement
- Form W-3
- Hours to be accrued at end of reporting period
- Payroll exceptions
- Other government agency reports

Analytics for payroll often focus on fraud risks and include identifying suspicious payroll activities and the potential for ghost employees to receive fictitious payroll.

CPA questions, as well as multiple choice, discussion, analysis and application, and Tableau questions and other resources, are available online.

Multiple Choice Questions

1. (LO 1) The human resources department activities are part of the

    a. acquisition and payment processes.

    b. conversion processes.

    c. marketing, sales, and collection processes.

    d. information processes.

2. (LO 1) The outsourced model helps HR perform the following kinds of value-driven tasks:

    a. Performing HR software development

    b. Promoting innovation, creativity, and flexibility in the work model

    c. Helping with HR and payroll audits

    d. Processing payroll

3. (LO 1) Why should payroll employees be separate from HR employees?

    a. Payroll personnel may work fewer hours.

    b. HR can better compensate employees.

    c. It ensures segregation of duties to prevent fraud.

    d. HR can focus on legal issues.

4. (LO 1) Mario works in the human resources (HR) department of Jimmy Sub Corporation. Mario's focus in HR involves employee hiring and transition. Which of the following employee activities will require Mario's involvement?

  a. April attends company orientation.

  b. May undergoes an annual performance review.

  c. June receives a promotion and a raise.

  d. July gets married and needs to update her W-4.

5. (LO 1) CPA Snickers Joke House hires illegal workers. Which of the core activities of the HR department should have identified and prevented this violation of law?

  a. Compliance with laws and regulations

  b. Training and development

  c. Salaries and benefits

  d. Recruiting and hiring of employees

6. (LO 2) Which of the following statements concerning employee onboarding is false?

  a. Employee onboarding is the process of establishing new employees in the company's systems and helping them quickly adapt to their positions and the company.

  b. Employee onboarding includes the administrative process of establishing the new employee in the payroll and benefits systems.

  c. Employee onboarding includes ensuring new hires are comfortable, facilitating socialization, and following up with the new hire.

  d. Employee onboarding starts on the employee's first day on the job and continues through the new-hire's first few weeks or months.

7. (LO 2) Which of the following activities should occur next after HR receives the offer acceptance from a candidate?

  a. Submit data to background check provider

  b. Send start date to IT department

  c. Process notice of offer withdrawal

  d. Review information for completeness

8. (LO 2) Which control activity would best mitigate the risk of violation of employment laws for hiring new employees?

  a. Review of payroll journal

  b. Credible background checks

  c. Extension of offer letters only by the HR department

  d. Hands-on approach to onboarding new employees

9. (LO 3) What key role does HR play during the employee termination process?

  a. Tracking hiring violations

  b. Minimizing potential damage

  c. Helping employees pack up their items

  d. Removing system access

10. (LO 3) Which of the following events constitutes an employee termination?

  a. Retirement

  b. Death

  c. Layoff

  d. All of the above

11. (LO 3) Which sample control activity is the best option for mitigating the risk of employee records remaining active in the payroll system?

  a. Executing a noncompete agreement

  b. Clearing all employee receivables

  c. Conducting independent reviews of the status of employee records

  d. Closing corporate card accounts

12. (LO 4) The primary purpose of a company is to

  a. create products.

  b. pay their employees.

  c. please shareholders.

  d. maximize profits.

13. (LO 4) The advantages of a higher level of maturity for payroll processing do *not* include

  a. having a single source of HR and payroll data.

  b. improving data accuracy.

  c. reducing data redundancies.

  d. having disparate or separate systems for HR and payroll.

14. (LO 4) Which sample control activity is best to mitigate the risk of incorrect employee data resulting in incorrect payments to the employee?

  a. Reviewing the payroll journal

  b. Reviewing the payroll calendar

  c. Reconciling the data in payroll records and HR main table

  d. Controller signing payroll checks

15. (LO 4) CPA Payroll accounting begins by recording _____ in the form of journal entries.

  a. business transactions involving an exchange of economic resources

  b. financial information

  c. corporate minutes

  d. business contracts

16. (LO 4) CPA Which of the following internal control activities would prevent an employee from being paid an inappropriate hourly wage?

  a. Having the supervisor of the data entry clerk verify that each employee's hours worked are correctly entered into the system

  b. Using real-time posting of payroll so there can be no after-the-fact data manipulation of the payroll register

  c. Giving payroll data entry clerks the ability to change any suspicious hourly pay rates to a reasonable rate

d. Limiting access to the employee main table to authorized employees in the HR department

17. (LO 5) What type of employee onboarding analytics may identify fictitious employees?

   a. Analysis of employee master data for nonmatching information

   b. Analysis of post-onboarding surveys completed by hiring managers

   c. Analysis of post-onboarding surveys completed by new hires

   d. Analysis of the percentage of tenured employees versus new hires in each department

18. (LO 5) What is the main use of employee termination analytics?

   a. Identify fraud in payroll

   b. Determine why employees tend to leave the organization

   c. Identify training opportunities

   d. Compare compensation packages

19. (LO 5) Which of the following data analytics tests identifies instances of payroll processed after an employee's termination date?

   a. Duplicate payroll

   b. Exit interviews

   c. Wage equality

   d. Ghost employees

Discussion and Research Questions

DQ1. (LO 1) What are the major activities of the HR business function?

DQ2. (LO 1) How has the focus of HR changed as companies moved to an outsourced model?

DQ3. (LO 1) Is it mandatory for HR to be segregated from payroll, and how does it benefit an organization if those areas are separate? Which functional area in the business should oversee payroll processing?

DQ4. (LO 1) Critical Thinking You are the lead HR consultant for BitbyBit Solutions. You are asked to speak to a group of new employees and explain the main activities of the HR department. In addition, you must explain how employees can interact with HR during their time at BitbyBit Solutions. What would you include in the discussion, and what examples would you use regarding the interaction between HR and employees?

DQ5. (LO 2) Why is it important to perform credible background checks before finalizing an offer of employment?

DQ6. (LO 2) How can the HR department help new hires feel connected to the company culture? What are the positive outcomes of those efforts?

DQ7. (LO 3) Discuss the process of employee termination and the part that HR plays in this process.

DQ8. (LO 3) Discuss two common risks in the employee termination process and identify one internal control activity for each.

DQ9. (LO 3) Critical Thinking You are a senior associate in the Business Process Management (BPM) division for a local accounting firm. One afternoon, a new HR consultant stops you in the hallway and mentions that the consulting team members have been looking at the employee termination process and believe there are too many people involved in what should be a simple process. They think that when someone leaves voluntarily or involuntarily, you should collect their company-owned items, and they should leave the building. How would you explain why this complex process is necessary and why multiple groups are involved in it?

DQ10. (LO 3) In Applied Learning 9.3, the CPA firm identified two control deficiencies. The first was that managers sometimes terminate employees without first providing notice to HR. The second was that the company conducts exit interviews inconsistently, and HR does not formally review the results. As part of its work, the CPA firm made two recommendations to help Julia's Cookies improve its process. What additional recommendations could be useful to Julia's Cookies?

DQ11. (LO 4) What are the advantages to an organization of achieving higher levels of maturity and integrating the information systems for the HR and payroll processes?

DQ12. (LO 4) Critical Thinking Many of AML Technical Services' employees are paid hourly, and they receive paychecks every Friday. Identify typical accounting transactions resulting from this process.

DQ13. (LO 5) Critical Thinking You are tasked with implementing new reports for the employee onboarding process that will provide HR managers with detailed information about the effectiveness of the process and help identify any issues. As you are gathering information, two of the HR managers tell you that you are wasting your time because they do not need reports to understand what is happening in their area. What would you say to the managers regarding the types of reports you are implementing and how they could be used to increase the effectiveness of their areas?

Application and Analysis Questions

A1. (LO 1) Each of the following HR activities belongs to one of three processes. In the following table, label each process with the appropriate activity or activities.

Activity options:

A. Administer insurance for employees

B. Track employee vacation days

C. Train employees

D. Administer health care benefits for employees

E. Administer flexible spending accounts for employees

F. Manage employee evaluations

G. Record time worked for hourly employees

Process	Activity or Activities
Employee administration	1. _____
Time management	2. _____
Benefit administration	3. _____

A2. (LO 2) **Early Career** You work for a local CPA firm hired by Touchstone Corporation to review its processes and procedures. The head of HR, Dilara Amin, has specifically asked that your team start by reviewing the employee onboarding process. Dilara feels that certain steps are not handled in the right areas and that the process could be more mature and efficient. Dilara has asked for feedback within a week, so they can present the preliminary findings at the next HR department meeting.

After completing your review, your team provides Dilara with the following control deficiencies in the onboarding process:

1. The company does not have a formal process for capacity planning or department budgeting in relation to employee decisions, as managers have full discretion over hiring and compensation.

2. In some instances, the hiring manager issues offer letters prior to notifying HR.

3. The company's background check provider does not have an independent internal control report in place.

4. The employee's job description is not communicated as part of the new hire package. In addition, the company has numerous positions with few differences in responsibilities.

5. The company has multiple stand-alone policies instead of a comprehensive employee handbook.

6. New hires must print and sign the new hire paperwork.

7. There is no formal process in place for internal/external job posting and recruitment.

8. The company has a networked hard drive that the HR department uses for document storage. The company stores its files there so that authorized employees can access them. There is no regular backup of this drive to keep the files safe.

Required: For each control deficiency, identify the risk and a control that can be used to mitigate that risk.

A3. (LO 2) **Early Career** **Critical Thinking** You are a first-year internal auditor for Investink, a global asset management firm. The Internal Audit department is undergoing a regulatory mandated quality assurance review (QAR) next year to review the effectiveness of the Internal Audit department's activities. During the QAR, your team's documentation, processes, policies, and audit activities will be assessed to provide an opinion on whether the department conforms to Internal Audit standards. One thing the QAR will look for is well-documented processes that are consistent and controlled.

In preparation for next year's QAR, you are asked to transform the following narrative for the Internal Audit department's onboarding and training processes into a process flowchart:

> When new hires for the Internal Audit department join the firm, they attend a company orientation for the first half of their first day. The HR department hosts this orientation and then escorts the new hires to their desk. A member of the IT department delivers the new hires' laptops after lunch and sits with them to ensure that their logins and passwords work.
>
> Before a new hire starts, their manager sends an email to their corporate email address with links and files to internal audit training materials. Then, on their first day, the new hire spends the afternoon reviewing these files, including an internal audit organization chart, an introduction to agile auditing slide deck, and a link to the company portal's 30-day onboarding task list. They are also given a Word document with a list of online training videos from the company intranet. (The list has not been updated in many years, and some names have changed.) New hires must find these videos on their own and view the trainings.
>
> New hires have the first week or so to complete their 30-day onboarding task list and trainings. They start on their first project as it becomes available.

1. Create a process flowchart for this narrative that includes at least five process icons and three swim lanes for responsible parties. Hint: For events that are facilitated by another party, you don't need to include the event in the new hire's swim lane. For example, if HR is responsible for something that the new hire attends, that event should go in the HR swim lane.

2. Provide at least two suggestions for how Internal Audit could improve its new hire onboarding and training to be a more consistent and controlled process.

A4. (LO 4) **Early Career** **Critical Thinking** At the Jim-Classy Clothing Factory, the normal workweek for full-time factory employees is 40 hours, measured from 12:01 a.m. Monday through midnight the following Sunday. Time worked in excess of 40 hours is paid at the overtime rate of time-and-a-half. The factory operates two eight-hour shifts a day, which run from 12:01 a.m. to 9 a.m. (the first shift) and 9 a.m. to 6 p.m. (the second shift) on weekdays. Employees are entitled to a one-hour unpaid meal break, beginning four hours after their shift starts.

The company's time-tracking and recordkeeping policy is as follows:

Departments are required to use the approved online timekeeping system for the final submission of time. Time records are the basic source of information for payroll purposes and must be accurate. Falsification of time or unauthorized submission is a serious offense and may result in termination. Supervisors or managers must approve time records for accuracy and completeness.

Supervisors and employees share the responsibility of ensuring an accurate record of time worked. Employees must accurately report time and make supervisors aware when problems arise. Supervisors are responsible for proper adherence to all policies, including but not limited to time tracking and recordkeeping.

In the recording system, employees should certify and approve their time prior to a supervisor or manager's approval. All hourly employees must punch in/out using the approved online timekeeping system. Employees are not permitted to work "off the clock" or voluntarily work without pay. Employees must record and be compensated for all time worked.

In order to be paid for a full shift, hourly employees must record time in and out within seven minutes of when a shift or lunch break begins and ends. This statement refers to the method of pay computation and does not imply permission to be up to seven minutes late or to leave seven minutes early.

The following withholding rates are in effect at the company:

Federal income taxes are 20% of gross pay minus employee retirement contributions.

State income taxes are 0 (some states have none).

Social Security (FICA) is 6.2% of gross pay.

Medicare is 1.45% of gross pay.

Employee retirement contribution is 5% of gross pay.

Elsa Kennedy is an hourly factory worker earning $21.25 an hour. She works the second shift. Her timesheet report generated by the information system for the week ending 07/10/2022 follows:

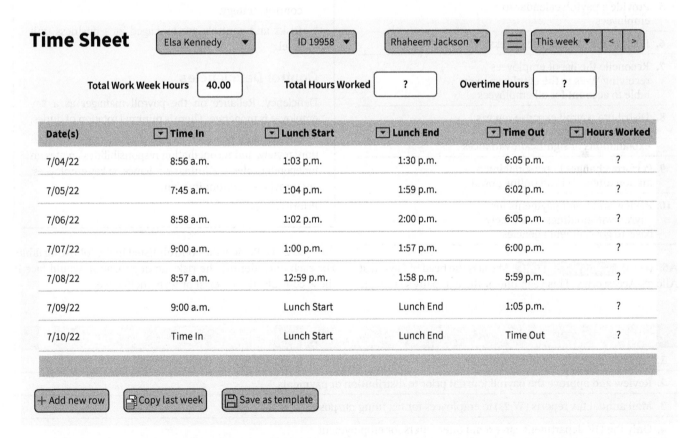

Time Sheet

| Elsa Kennedy ▼ | ID 19958 ▼ | Rhaheem Jackson ▼ | ≡ | This week ▼ | < | > |

| Total Work Week Hours | 40.00 | Total Hours Worked | ? | Overtime Hours | ? |

Date(s)	▼ Time In	▼ Lunch Start	▼ Lunch End	▼ Time Out	▼ Hours Worked
7/04/22	8:56 a.m.	1:03 p.m.	1:30 p.m.	6:05 p.m.	?
7/05/22	7:45 a.m.	1:04 p.m.	1:59 p.m.	6:02 p.m.	?
7/06/22	8:58 a.m.	1:02 p.m.	2:00 p.m.	6:05 p.m.	?
7/07/22	9:00 a.m.	1:00 p.m.	1:57 p.m.	6:00 p.m.	?
7/08/22	8:57 a.m.	12:59 p.m.	1:58 p.m.	5:59 p.m.	?
7/09/22	9:00 a.m.	Lunch Start	Lunch End	1:05 p.m.	?
7/10/22	Time In	Lunch Start	Lunch End	Time Out	?

[+ Add new row]   [📄 Copy last week]   [💾 Save as template]

1. Using Excel, prepare a payroll journal for the week for Elsa Kennedy. Use the following headings (where WH = withholding):

   Date, Employee ID, Pay Rate Regular, Hours Regular, Hours Overtime, Gross Pay, Federal Tax WH, FICA WH, Medicare WH, Retirement Contribution WH, Net Pay

2. To illustrate your understanding of the impact of this employee's weekly payroll on the financial statements, prepare a composite entry in general journal format to reflect an alternative to recording the weekly payroll entry for Elsa Kennedy in the payroll journal.

A5. (LO 4) You are the new payroll manager for the Build a Moose Toy Company. Build a Moose is a smaller manufacturer, and it is cost-effective for the company to process payroll in-house. As part of your initial work, you are reviewing the controls that are in place for payroll, and you want to ensure that the correct control owners are aligned with the controls. Using the table below, review the controls in place and identify the correct owner(s) for each control.

Control	Control Owner
1. Complete a payroll processing checklist	
2. Review and approve the payroll journal prior to distribution of payments	
3. Mail annual tax report (W-2) to each employee for tax filing purposes	
4. Conduct an independent review of employees receiving paychecks by comparing the list to other credible employee listings, such as an active company directory	
5. Provide a payroll calendar to employees	
6. Review and sign payroll checks	
7. Reconcile the list of employees receiving W-2s to the employee main table to account for all employees	
8. Distribute payroll expense reports to department managers for explanations of significant variances	
9. Perform changes to personal information directly via an online portal	
10. Review and remit payments for payroll withholdings on a timely basis to government agencies	

A6. (LO 4) `Critical Thinking` Maria is the head of Payroll at Alicia's Accessories. This year, one of the company's strategic goals is to increase performance optimization throughout all departments. Maria requests a business process maturity assessment of the payroll process from the Internal Audit department.

Internal Audit identifies one control deficiency and provides a summary of the strengths within the payroll process. Based on the following report from Internal Audit, what is the current phase of maturity for Alicia's Accessories' payroll process?

Key Observations

Based on a report provided by the external auditors, Alicia's Accessories has application controls embedded in its automated payroll system. The payroll manager and the controller review and approve payroll journals for each pay period, providing independent checks, and the payroll processing checklist is consistently implemented to prevent errors and omissions.

Most payroll controls are automated.

Processes are formally documented and consistently implemented.

There is no enterprise-wide risk management or control strategy.

Risks and controls are managed at a business unit level.

Control Deficiencies

Deficiency: Reliance on the payroll manager as a key employee is moderate. There is minimal rotation of duties.

Recommendation: Rotating payroll manager authorization, review, and reconciliation responsibilities creates an independent check, eliminates reliance on key employees, and provides a continuity plan.

Priority: High

A7. (LO 2–4) Review the controls listed in the following table. For each one, identify the risks an organization would face if those controls did not exist or were ineffective.

Control	Potential Risks
1. Provide notification of involuntary termination to the HR department the same day as notice is received	
2. Review and approve the payroll journal prior to distribution of payments	
3. Mail annual tax reports (W-2s) to employees for tax filing purposes	
4. Only the HR department can extend offer letters for employment	
5. The IT department removes systems access for terminated employees in a timely manner	
6. Collect corporate credit cards in possession of an exiting employee during the exit interview	
7. Reconcile the list of employees receiving W-2s to the employee main table to verify that the company accounts for all employees	

(*Continued*)

Control	Potential Risks
8. Maintain a comprehensive employee handbook	
9. Employees make changes to employee personal information directly via an online portal	
10. Review new hire documentation prior to employee record creation	

Employee Name	Exit Interview Date	HR Facilitator	Reason for Leaving	New Employer	How Would You Rank Company Culture?	Would You Recommend Alicia's Accessories as a Good Place to Work?
Jose Q.	9/2/202X	Miley N.	Better Offer	21 Improvements	Positive	Yes
Riley M.	9/12/202X	Eloise T.	Relocation	Unknown	Positive	Yes
Phillip P.	9/13/202X	Max R.	Unknown	Unknown		
Preston L.	9/18/202X	Max R.	Unknown	Unknown		
Levi M.	9/18/202X	Eloise T.	Dissatisfied	Vanguardium	Poor	No
Matthew B.	9/18/202X	Eloise T.	Dissatisfied	Vanguardium	Okay	Maybe
Dylan L.	9/20/202X	Max R.	Unknown	Unknown		

A8. (LO 5) `Fraud` `Early Career` `Data Analytics` The Internal Audit department at Alicia's Accessories is performing an audit of the HR department. As part of the engagement, the audit team plans to perform the following data analytics:

Analytic 1: Reperform turnover calculations that the HR department uses in a dashboard for decision making. If turnover calculations result in a number different from the one in the HR dashboard, it is possible that HR's dashboard is unreliable and should be reviewed further.

Analytic 2: Analyze exit interview data for missing fields. If data fields are missing, it is possible that HR is not asking all the exit interview questions or not inputting answers into the system correctly.

Analytic 3: Analyze the employee main table to determine the most recent date of a termination in the system. If the termination date is not in the last 30 days, it is possible that HR is not following its process of updating the employee data every week.

1. Which of the following data points will the Internal Audit team need in order to perform each of these three analytics? Match the data points selected with the analytic that needs it. (A data point may be needed by more than one analysis.)

   A. Employee main table (name, start date, end date, employment status)

   B. Employee compensation (salary, bonuses)

   C. Employee performance reviews (rating, raises, comments)

   D. Employee whistleblower hotline (complaints, fraud suspicions)

   E. Exit interview survey results (reason for leaving, new employer, rating of company culture)

2. The table above shows sample data for Analytic 2. Based on this sample, do you think Internal Audit should investigate the exit interview process further? Why or why not?

A9. (LO 1–5) `Critical Thinking` Kyle is the new director of HR at Manic Automotive. During his first month, Kyle asked the managers in the HR department for information about existing business processes and controls to familiarize himself with how the department currently operates.

Some of the managers provided formal documentation of processes and controls, including process flowcharts, narratives, and system diagrams. Other managers were only able to offer to meet with Kyle and tell him personally how things worked; there seemed to be no documentation for their teams' processes.

One manager had implemented a robust set of automated controls in his teams' processes, but the rest of the HR department managers said they rely on manual, and sometimes even ad hoc, controls.

Using the business process maturity model, what is the current maturity level of the HR department at Manic Automotive?

A10. (LO 3–5) `Fraud` `Early Career` `Critical Thinking` The Chester family owned and operated CEI, a manufacturer of electrical equipment. Mom and Dad Chester started the business. Their children grew up, became stockholders, and sat on the board of directors, which consisted entirely of family members.

The youngest son, Matthew, was in charge of human resources and payroll. He hired employees, authorized factory time sheets, calculated the net pay for each employee, and took custody of the payroll checks from the outside firm that generated the physical paychecks for employees. Many of the factory workers were low-income immigrants who did not trust direct deposits for their paychecks. Matthew distributed paychecks to these employees himself.

Matthew's sister, Maisie, was the CFO of the company and a member of the Board of Directors. By accident one day, she detected a payroll fraud perpetrated by her brother. When reviewing the fronts and backs of canceled payroll checks, she noticed endorsements to her brother on the backs of some payroll checks. Further checking revealed many more of instances of endorsements. As a CPA herself, she became frightened because she knew the implications of fraud. She hired a CPA firm to do an audit and to uncover the extent of the fraud.

A ghost, or fictitious, employee is someone who is on the payroll but who did not do work to earn the pay. When a ghost employee is paid, the money ends up in the hands of the fraudster. In this case, Matthew embezzled money from the family business by using ghost employees and stealing the checks—a form of asset misappropriation. He did not remove terminated employees from the main table. In this manner, he created 344 ghost employees over time.

He embezzled over $508,000 from the family business by creating more than 600 checks made out to ghost employees over a period of 8.5 years. He specifically targeted low-income immigrant workers who needed work and could not speak English well to be his ghost employees.

Maisie reported the fraud to the board of directors. Upon seeing the audit evidence, Matthew confessed to the fraud and apologized profusely. Matthew had violated the trust placed in him by his family. His motivation was greed. Even though he was a shareholder in the business and earned a good salary, it was not enough for him. He saw the opportunity to commit payroll fraud, and he took it.

All the family members on the board of directors, except for Maisie, accepted Matthew's apology, circled the family wagon, and tried to sweep the fraud under the rug. Maisie, however, was scared. She realized that, while family owned, the company was a separate legal entity and that the fraud resulted in significant risks for the company. There were criminal implications for all involved, such as identity theft. The employees used as "ghosts" could sue the company, the business insurance could be canceled if the fraud was not addressed, and the company's reputation in the community could suffer harm.

Employees suffered the consequences. The fictitious payroll payments of over $508,000 were included in the amounts reported to the state tax authorities and to the IRS. This created tax problems for the actual employees used as ghost employees. One employee, for example, was denied low-income housing because his "income" reported by the IRS to the housing authority was fraudulently overstated.

Following the advice of the auditors, Maisie reported the fraud to the police. Matthew received a sentence of 23 months in prison and was ordered to pay back $508,000 as restitution. As he had not included his ill-gotten gains in his taxable income, he was also charged with filing false tax returns. This is something that fraudsters often forget—they are required to declare and pay taxes on their ill-gotten gains!

The fraud caused a huge rift in the family. Maisie, the whistleblower, became the family outcast.

Required:

1. Identify the internal control weaknesses that provided the opportunity for this fraud that split apart a family

2. Suggest improvements in the process at CEI to reduce the risk of payments to fictitious employees

Tableau Case: Julia's Cookies' People Analytics

What You Need

Download Tableau to your computer. You can access www.tableau.com/academic/students to download your free Tableau license for the year, or you can download it from your university's software offerings.

Download the following file from the book's product page on www.wiley.com:

Chapter 9 Raw Data.xlsx

Case Background

Big Picture:

Analyze the current employee composition, including diversity.

Details:

Why is this data important, and what questions or problems need to be addressed?

- Human resources (HR) data gives the business valuable insights into the company corporate culture, as it can show the company current employee makeup and retention efforts.

- Analysis of this data helps in identifying areas of the company that are not diverse or inclusive, have a high turnover rate, or have employees who are nearing retirement age, which could mean a knowledge loss unless there is a succession plan in place.

Plan:

What data is needed, and how should it be analyzed?

- Data needed to answer the objective is pulled from Julia's Cookies' HR database. In most companies, the HR database contains not only data about employee demographics but payroll information. This data, however, is not available to everyone in the company, and the individuals who do have access to the HR data have different levels of access. For example, very few people in the company can view payroll data, as that is considered confidential, while all employees are able to view employees' full names, their supervisors' names, and their departments.

Now it's your turn to evaluate, analyze, and communicate the results!

Questions

1. How many employees are currently active? (Hint: Employment Status = "Active")

2. How many employees have been terminated at Julia's Cookies? (Hint: Employment Status = "Terminated")

3. What percentage of active employees are female?

4. Which department has the most active employees?

5. How many active employees are considered "Exempt" on the payroll? (Hint: Pay Group)

6. Of the active employees who received a performance review, how many employees were considered "Unsatisfactory"?

7. What is the average age of an active employee?

8. What is the average tenure of an active employee?

Take it to the next level!

9. During which month and year were the most employees terminated?

10. What is the most popular termination reason, and what percentage of employees left for that reason?

CHAPTER 10
Purchasing and Payments Processes

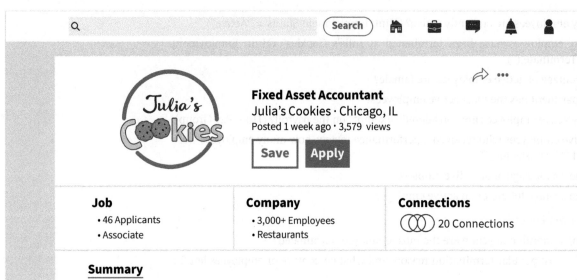

Fixed Asset Accountant
Julia's Cookies · Chicago, IL
Posted 1 week ago · 3,579 views

Save   **Apply**

Job	Company	Connections
• 46 Applicants	• 3,000+ Employees	20 Connections
• Associate	• Restaurants	

Summary
Julia's Cookies is seeking a recent college graduate to strengthen our General Ledger and accounting operations functions. The fixed asset accountant will manage day-to-day accounting activities in compliance with U.S. GAAP, internal policies, SOX controls, and external audits in relation to fixed assets and real estate leases.

Responsibilities
- Ownership of fixed assets module in information system
- Processing additions and disposals
- Reviewing invoices to ensure proper coding and capitalization under policy
- Preparing journal entries, account analyses, account reconciliations, and tie-outs to underlying detail
- Reporting for month-end and quarter-end closes
- Reviewing and tracking project costs into fixed assets accounts with proper accounting treatment
- Driving process improvement and automation efforts to streamline fixed asset and lease accounting and improve the quality of monthly, quarterly, and annual closes

Requirements
Preferred Education: Bachelor's degree or higher in accounting or finance
Preferred Certifications: CPA, CMA

Preferred Knowledge and Skills
The ideal candidate will demonstrate basic knowledge of U.S. GAAP, PCAOB standards, and SOX internal controls. Preference will be given to candidates who demonstrate:

- Ability to think independently, creatively, and opportunistically
- Sharp business acumen and process-oriented critical thinking
- Obsessed with data and unafraid to analyze to the lowest level of detail to discover the truth of a situation
- Advanced Excel skills

Salary: $55,000–75,000

CHAPTER PREVIEW   Companies can only perform business operations if they have resources. From manufacturing companies sourcing raw materials to public accounting firms buying laptops for their employees, the purchasing and payments processes are essential to all businesses' accounting operations.

You have learned that hiring employees is part of the acquisitions and payments processes in the basic business model. Now you will learn about business processes related to purchasing, paying for, and managing inventory, including:

- The relationship between purchasing and supply chain management
- How inventory is purchased
- How fixed assets are acquired
- How the accounts payable department handles payments
- How the AIS stores data generated in the purchasing and payments processes

In this chapter, we follow the purchasing and payments processes for inventory and fixed assets through the related information systems and examine the reports and analytics created by the generated data. And since every business process includes risks, we also explore the controls that mitigate risk in purchasing and payments.

There are many career opportunities involved in the purchasing and payments processes, including positions in accounts payable, business process improvements, SOX internal controls design, and fixed asset accounting positions like the one Julia's Cookies is hiring. While Julia's Cookies is a fictional company, this posting is based on a real job posting for a popular mobile app food delivery company with a comparable salary. ■

Chapter Roadmap

LEARNING OBJECTIVES	TOPICS	JULIA'S COOKIES APPLIED LEARNING
10.1 Describe the relationship between the inventory purchasing and payments processes, inventory management, and supply chain management.	• Inventory Purchasing and Payments Processes • Inventory Management • Supply Chain Management	Inventory Management: Working Capital
10.2 Summarize the purchasing process for inventory and other goods or services.	• Purchasing Process • Internal Control over Purchasing	Purchasing Controls: Process Improvements
10.3 Explain the fixed asset acquisitions process.	• Fixed Asset Acquisitions Process • Internal Control over Fixed Asset Acquisitions	Fixed Asset Acquisitions: Business Process Maturity Model
10.4 Evaluate the credit payments process.	• Credit Payments Process • Internal Control over Payments to Vendors	Accounts Payable: Continuous Fraud Monitoring
10.5 Use the key data in the underlying database for reporting and insights.	• Database Design • Reporting and Insights	Database Design: Three-Way Matching

CPA You will find the CPA tag throughout the chapter to call out any important topics you may see on the CPA exam.

10.1 What Is the Relationship Between Purchasing, Inventory Management, and Supply Chain Management?

Learning Objective ❶

Describe the relationship between the inventory purchasing and payments processes, inventory management, and supply chain management.

Purchasing processes, also known as procurement processes, are focused on acquiring the necessary resources for a business to operate, while **payments processes** are focused on paying for those resources. Both can significantly impact a company's success. From hiring vendors to paying for the raw materials needed to produce a product, the overall objectives of the purchasing processes are efficiency, or doing things right, and effectiveness, or doing the right things.

In the basic business model, purchasing and payments processes are part of the resource acquisitions and payments processes. We focus on inventory, goods, services, and fixed assets purchases and payments in this chapter. A company acquires, manages, and pays for inventory, goods, services, and fixed assets so it can do what it is in the business of doing—its operations. Acquired resources are used to generate sales, or cash. Whether it's raw materials that go directly into a product in the conversion processes or an office building used by sales and corporate administrative staff, all resources acquired in the purchasing and payments processes contribute to the company's goal of making a profit (**Illustration 10.1**).

Some business activities in the purchasing and payments processes result in the exchange of economic resources and recording of accounting transactions:

- Purchasing and receiving raw materials, merchandise inventory, other goods, fixed assets, and services (Dr. Asset or Expense, Cr. Accounts Payable)
- Paying for these purchases (Dr. Accounts Payable, Cr. Cash)
- Returning goods or negotiating allowances (Dr. Accounts Payable, Cr. Asset or Expense)

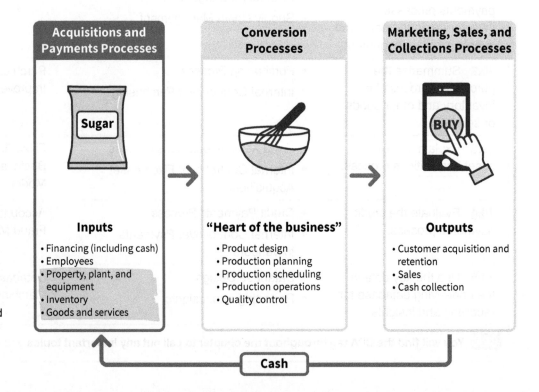

Acquisitions and Payments Processes	Conversion Processes	Marketing, Sales, and Collections Processes
Inputs	**"Heart of the business"**	**Outputs**
• Financing (including cash)	• Product design	• Customer acquisition and retention
• Employees	• Production planning	• Sales
• Property, plant, and equipment	• Production scheduling	• Cash collection
• Inventory	• Production operations	
• Goods and services	• Quality control	

Cash

Illustration 10.1 Purchasing and payments processes include PP&E (property, plant, and equipment), inventory, and goods and services, which are part of the acquisitions and payments processes in the basic business model.

Other activities in the process do not result in accounting transactions:

- Selecting vendors
- Negotiating contracts and payment terms with vendors
- Placing an order for resources such as raw materials, merchandise inventory, other goods, and fixed assets, which only results in an accounting transaction if there is a requirement for an upfront deposit or prepayment (Dr. Prepaid Asset, Cr. Cash)
- Entering contracts for services such as external auditing, cleaning, consulting, maintenance, recruiting, insurance, security, and utilities, which only results in an accounting transaction if there is a requirement for an upfront deposit or prepayment (Dr. Prepaid Asset, Cr. Cash)

While not every business activity in this process includes a transaction, purchasing involves connections with vendors, making it an essential part of supply chain management, which oversees business operations from the purchasing of resources to the sale of a product or service. Inventory management is an important consideration in purchasing as inventory availability drives purchases of raw materials. We give a more detailed review of how supply chain management, inventory management, and the business processes in the basic business model are all related in the Conversion Processes chapter.

Why Does It Matter to Your Career?

Thoughts from an Accounts Payable Associate, Manufacturing

Regardless of what kind of accounting you eventually practice, you will be exposed to purchasing and payments processes. You might work in the purchasing department or downstream from that department in a different finance function. Auditors perform audit engagements of these processes, and tax accountants need to know about them since they prepare tax documents that use data generated in the execution of those business processes.

Inventory Purchasing and Payments Processes

Inventory is a Balance Sheet line item that includes all items used in the creation of products. Inventory is classified as:

- **Raw materials:** Any components that are used in the creation of a product
- **Work in process:** Products that are in the process of being manufactured
- **Finished goods:** Products that are ready to ship to customers

Purchasing is the acquisition of resources, including raw materials, like cookie ingredients, cardboard packaging, and supplies. Other necessary items, such as shipping boxes, also go through the purchasing process, but they are classified as supplies on the Balance Sheet rather than as inventory. For the purposes of this section, we focus on the purchasing of raw materials.

While the process for purchasing raw materials seems simple, hidden dangers and risks can make it costly, inefficient, and ineffective for a business. From an internal control perspective, the raw materials purchasing process is summarized by the high-level business activities shown in **Illustration 10.2**, including relevant source documents. **Source documents** provide documentation of a transaction, such as a receipt, bill, or invoice, and may be electronic or paper documents, depending on the sophistication of the system.

Raw materials are purchased from a seller, called a supplier or vendor. While the terms "supplier" and "vendor" may sound interchangeable, there's a subtle difference between them. Both supply goods and/or services, but they are differentiated based on *who* they supply:

- **Vendors** engage in both business-to-consumer and business-to-business relationships.
- **Suppliers** engage in only business-to-business relationships.

Illustration 10.2 There are five high-level business activities in inventory purchasing.

Before we get into the details of the purchasing processes, let's look at the four departments in a company that are directly involved: inventory control, purchasing, receiving, and accounts payable. The following discussion assumes a digital system is used for these processes, including the creation of source documents. In a small business, these processes may be manually performed, and source documents may be hard copy documents.

Inventory Control

The inventory control department manages inventory and is responsible for ensuring that there is an optimal amount of inventory on hand. For example, at Julia's Cookies, the inventory control department must ensure there are adequate raw materials, such as baking ingredients and product packaging, at the company's regional factories and warehouses to meet customer demand. Customer demand is an important variable that is predicted using sales forecasts. Customer demand drives inventory management, which drives purchases of raw materials and supplies for production.

CPA When an inventory control department needs more raw material, it creates a **purchase requisition**, which is a request to obtain goods from an authorized source, and sends it to the purchasing department. Each purchase requisition must be approved and includes the same information:

- Name of the employee making the request
- Delivery location
- Date by which delivery is required
- Item numbers, descriptions, and quantities

In the Real World   Purchasing Gone Wrong[1]

An Oregon metals manufacturing company, Sapa Profiles Inc., admitted to falsifying thousands of certifications over 19 years for aluminum parts sold to NASA and hundreds of other customers.

The Fraud	Employees altered test results for the aluminum's reliability and strength when it was under pressure. They then provided certifications they knew to be false. NASA requested these tests and paid the supplier for them.
Motivation	The assistant attorney general of the criminal division of the U.S. Department of Justice (DOJ) described the company's motivation: "Corporate and personal greed perpetrated this fraud against the government and other private customers."

---

[1]Based on Stringer, David. May 1, 2019. NASA says metals fraud caused $700 million satellite failure. Boston Globe.

Implications for NASA	The faulty metal parts caused over $700 million in losses for NASA and two failed satellite launches. These parts were used to manufacture a rocket to deliver satellites that would study the Earth's climate. However, the rocket's payload fairing, which carries the satellite through the atmosphere, didn't open, and the launch was unsuccessful. NASA lost years of scientific work.
Consequences for the Perpetrator	The DOJ investigation resulted in criminal charges and alleged civil claims against Sapa Profiles. The company admitted that employees had faked test results and pleaded guilty to one count of mail fraud. Its parent company, Norsk Hydro ASA, paid $46 million to NASA, the U.S. government, and other customers. Sapa Profiles subsequently changed its name to Hydro Extrusion Portland Inc. and has been barred from U.S. federal government contracting.

How could this fraud have been prevented? Do you think it was NASA's responsibility to mitigate these fraud risks? If so, what type of risk mitigations could NASA have implemented?

Purchasing

At Julia's Cookies, the electronic purchase requisitions go to the Purchasing department, represented by a purchasing agent at a regional facility. The purchasing agents report to the purchasing manager at headquarters. Routing all purchases through the Purchasing department is an internal control that mitigates the risk of fraudulent or inappropriate purchasing.

CPA The purchase requisition evolves into a legally enforceable purchase order:

- The purchasing agent transforms the purchase requisition, which is an internal company document, to a **purchase order**, which is an external document used to request a supplier to sell and deliver the products in the quantities and for the prices specified in the purchase order.
- Once the supplier accepts the purchase order, it becomes a legal contract.

The purchasing agents at Julia's Cookies place the orders electronically with approved local suppliers identified by the system.

As part of the company's business strategy, Julia's Cookies' top management made an executive decision to purchase locally as much as possible. While there are benefits to purchasing locally, such as investing in local communities and reducing shipping costs, Julia's Cookies is sacrificing the benefits of volume discounts offered by purchasing centrally from larger distributors.

Receiving

A supplier delivers an order along with a supplier-generated **packing slip**, which shows quantities and descriptions of items delivered, to the receiving department at the specified warehouse location.

For internal control purposes, an employee in receiving opens a version of the purchase order that does not include the quantities. The employee then completes three steps:

1. Checks the condition of the shipment
2. Counts the quantities received
3. Inputs the data online

This data input generates an electronic **receiving report** that shows the descriptions and quantities of goods received from vendors, as well as a **discrepancy report** identifying variances between the receiving report and the purchase order. The employee in receiving attempts to resolve and correct any discrepancies. These steps are an internal control activity that ensures the employee in receiving performs an independent check of the goods received and reconciles it with what was ordered.

Next, the shipment is transferred to the warehouse, and a warehouse employee independently recounts the contents of the shipment, checks its condition, and inputs this data into the system as an additional independent check.

Accounts Payable

CPA In accounts payable, employees enter vendor invoices into the system upon receipt. A **vendor invoice** is a bill from a vendor that includes the related purchase order number, billing date, description and quantities of goods, amount due, and payment terms. The following internal controls should be in place, whether electronically or manually:

- A software application matches the data from the invoice to the purchase order and the receiving report in a three-way match.
- Vendors are paid on the due date, after the **payment voucher** is authorized by management. The payment voucher is an internal document that includes the vendor, amount due, and payment terms.
- The vendor receives a **remittance advice** along with the electronic payment. The remittance advice shows the invoices included in the payment to the vendor.

All these business events result in the accounting transactions covered in your financial accounting course. Using Julia's Cookies as an example, the following journal entries capture the initial purchase on credit and the subsequent payment, which includes a 2.5% discount because Julia's Cookies paid the invoice within the discount terms:

		Dr.	Cr.
May 2, 20XX	Inventory (or Purchases)[Note 1]	15,788.00	
	Accounts Payable		15,788.00
	Purchased inventory on credit from Flour Supplies		
May 31, 20XX	Accounts payable	15,788.00	
	Inventory (or Purchase Discounts)[Note 2]		394.70
	Cash		15,393.30
	Paid Flour Supplies for Invoice #224, less 2.5% discount		

Notes:

Note 1 Debit Inventory for a perpetual inventory system or Purchases for a periodic inventory system.

Note 2 Credit Inventory for a perpetual inventory system or Purchase Discounts for a periodic inventory system.

Inventory Management

If you don't know what you need, then how do you know what to buy? **Inventory management** is a process that coordinates the communication of inventory availability and needs across the purchasing, conversion, and sales processes. It's an essential source of information for the purchasing processes. At Julia's Cookies, inventory management is the responsibility of the Inventory Control department at the corporate office in San Francisco.

Efficient and effective inventory management is critical to success for Julia's Cookies and any other business. Poor inventory management may result in insufficient or excessive inventory.

Low inventory of raw materials and finished goods may result in a number of issues, including:

- Loss of revenue and cash flow, increased expenses for expedited shipping and increased cost of goods sold, and less profit for the company
- Finished goods (cookies, cookie dough) being unavailable to customers, leading to customer dissatisfaction
- Reduced competitive advantage
- Unplanned schedule changes or downtime in production, leading to excessive costs

On the other hand, having too much inventory can also lead to problems, including:

- Excessive expenses and reduced profits as a result of warehouse space, labor costs, insurance costs, and other expenses
- Potential spoilage or obsolescence and reduced profits, especially in the food industry
- Reduced cash flow since excess inventory has been paid for but receipt of revenue is delayed

Inventory records need to be correct. Inaccurate inventory records, or records that do not match the physical inventory on hand, have the same negative consequences as insufficient or excessive inventory. Inaccurate inventory records can be caused by inventory theft and damage, incorrect recording of inventory and inventory movements, or failure to record inventory or inventory movements, to name a few.

CPA Besides automating inventory purchasing and maintenance across a supply chain, good internal controls like segregation of duties, independent checks (such as regular physical inventory counts), training of employees, and adequate policies and procedures can significantly improve inventory management. Inventory management is a subprocess of supply chain management, which we discuss next.

Supply Chain Management

The **supply chain management (SCM)** process oversees the life cycle of a product from procuring raw materials through customer sales. It's a collaborative effort between a company and its suppliers, subcontractors, transportation providers, distributors, wholesalers, and retailers. The goal of supply chain management is to produce and distribute a product or service to customers efficiently and effectively by supplying goods and services at the lowest cost possible while providing the highest value to the customer and other stakeholders.

Supply chain business activities cover everything from sourcing raw materials to receiving goods and services from suppliers, managing inventory, producing the product, and distributing the product to retailers and/or customers.

There are two links between businesses that form the supply chain:

- **Physical flows:** The physical flows of inventory are the most visible part of the supply chain and involve storing, transforming, and moving inventory. **Illustration 10.3** shows the physical flow of the supply chain for Julia's Cookies and highlights the sections of the supply chain's physical flow that we cover in this chapter.

- **Information flows:** Information flows are just as important as physical flows. They require information technologies that allow supply chain participants to coordinate their activities and control the daily flow of goods and materials along the supply chain. A well-designed enterprise resource planning (ERP) system facilitates easy communication between the different areas of the supply chain through connected ERP system modules.

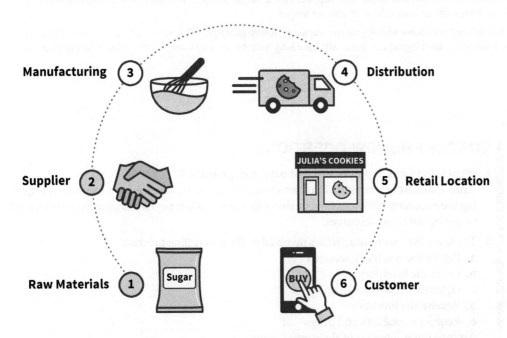

Illustration 10.3 The physical supply chain at Julia's Cookies begins with sourcing raw materials and ends with the customer purchasing a product.

In the next section, we explore key business processes supporting purchasing and payments using the example of Julia's Cookies. First, help Yalmaz and Darlene manage inventory in Applied Learning 10.1.

Julia's Cookies

Applied Learning 10.1

Inventory Management: Working Capital

Yalmaz is the chief operations officer (COO) at Julia's Cookies and oversees inventory control, purchasing, and the production of cookie dough at regional factories. Each factory has an inventory warehouse, a production line, and a packaging facility.

Currently, Julia's Cookies is facing supply chain issues caused by the increased demand for cookie deliveries due to the continuing global pandemic. It's Yalmaz's responsibility to ensure that sufficient raw materials are on hand to meet customer demand. He is currently working with Darlene, the chief financial officer (CFO), on addressing these supply chain issues. As CFO, Darlene optimizes the company's current assets and current liabilities to ensure that the right amount of working capital, or liquidity, is available for daily operations. Too little working capital implies an inability to pay short-term obligations, and too much is a waste of resources that could be put to more profitable use. Raw materials are a significant component of current assets.

Increased sales demands and the current struggle for suppliers to fulfill purchase orders during the pandemic highlights an unpredicted weakness in Julia's Cookies' supply chain. While the increase in sales is beneficial, the situation requires a renewed focus on working capital and inventory management:

- Production facilities must have sufficient raw materials to meet increased sales demand.
- Suppliers are being pressured by all their customers, not just Julia's Cookies. The current shortage in raw materials is affecting the entire industry.
- Increased pandemic sales have impacted working capital significantly:
  - Sales have increased by 15.3% over the past year.
  - Increased sales have increased accounts receivable.
  - Overall inventory levels have increased by 8% over the past year.
  - Increased raw materials purchases have increased accounts payable.

This week, Yalmaz and Darlene are attending a management meeting to explain the working capital and inventory issues Julia's Cookies currently faces and recommend ways to navigate the pandemic's impact on inventory management.

What recommendations should they make regarding supply chain issues and inventory management?

SOLUTION

Yalmaz and Darlene recommend the following:

1. Expand the supply chain by engaging with additional suppliers. This may take time but will have long-term benefits by reducing supply chain bottlenecks.
2. Negotiate with suppliers to increase accounts payable terms with suppliers for a longer payment period. This will increase working capital by keeping liquidity, or available cash, in Julia's Cookies' control longer.
3. Stockpile extra raw materials that are not perishable to mitigate the impact of future shortages. This may require an immediate cash outflow from Purchasing, which will lower working capital, but it will have long-term benefits by reducing the reliance on suppliers in the supply chain.

CONCEPT REVIEW QUESTIONS

1. What is the focus of purchasing and payments processes?

   Ans. Purchasing processes, also known as procurement processes, are focused on acquiring the necessary resources for a business to operate, while payments processes are focused on paying for those resources.

2. There are five business activities involved in the purchasing process:
   a. Pay for the inventory received
   b. Order the inventory
   c. Determine inventory to order
   d. Receive the inventory
   e. Request availability and prices
   Arrange these activities in the correct order.

   Ans. The correct order of activities is: c → e → b → d → a.

3. Which of the following activities do not result in accounting transactions?
   a. Purchasing and receiving raw materials, merchandise inventory, other goods, fixed assets, and services
   b. Negotiating contracts and payment terms with vendors
   c. Placing an order for resources such as raw materials, merchandise inventory, other goods, and fixed assets
   d. Placing an order for resources such as raw materials, merchandise inventory, other goods, and fixed assets and upfront deposit or prepayment
   e. Entering contracts for services such as external auditing, cleaning, consulting, and maintenance

   Ans. b, c, e

4. **CPA** What is a purchase requisition? When does a purchase requisition become a purchase order?

   Ans. Purchase requisition is a request to obtain goods from an authorized source, and sending it to the purchase department. When an inventory control department needs more raw material, it creates a purchase requisition. The purchase requisition evolves into a legally enforceable purchase order:
   - The purchasing agent transforms the purchase requisition, which is an internal company document, to a purchase order, which is an external document used to request a supplier to sell and deliver the products in the quantities and for the prices specified in the purchase order.
   - Once the supplier accepts the purchase order, it becomes a legal contract.

5. What are the two electronic reports generated after employees key in online data during internal control?

   Ans. The two electronic reports which are generated after employees key in online data during internal control are—an electronic receiving report which demonstrates the descriptions and quantities of goods received from vendors, and a discrepancy report identifying variances between the receiving report and the purchase order.

6. **CPA** List the internal checks that improve inventory management across supply chains.

   Ans. Besides automating inventory purchasing and maintenance across a supply chain, good internal controls like segregation of duties, independent checks (such as regular physical inventory counts), training of employees, and adequate policies and procedures can significantly improve inventory management.

7. What is supply chain management (SCM)?

   Ans. The SCM process oversees the life cycle of a product from procuring raw materials through customer sales. It's a collaborative effort between a company and its suppliers, subcontractors, transportation providers, distributors, wholesalers, and retailers.

10.2 How Are Inventory and Other Goods and Services Purchased?

Learning Objective ❷
Summarize the purchasing process for inventory and other goods or services.

So far, we have discussed the overall purchasing processes for inventory and how sales, purchases, inventory management, and supply chain management are related. Now we will examine the processes that companies use to make purchases of anything from raw materials to supplies, services, or software. The requests for these types of purchases may come from different functional areas of the business and are routed through the purchasing department.

Purchasing Process

To evaluate any process, we need to know what it looks like, how it works, and who does what. Julia's Cookies documents its current purchasing process for inventory and suppliers in a document flowchart (**Illustration 10.4**). Recall that document flowcharts map the movement of documents related to a business process through the underlying business events. The departments involved at Julia's Cookies are Inventory Control and other departments requesting goods, Purchasing, Receiving, Warehousing, and Accounts Payable. While the Inventory Control department has the primary responsibility for requesting inventory and supplies, other departments can also submit purchase requests.

Internal Control over Purchasing

CPA A company can mitigate risks related to purchases with effective control activities. Identifying the employee(s) typically responsible for each control activity is also necessary to ensure proper segregation of duties. The degree of control is a matter of judgment. A company's

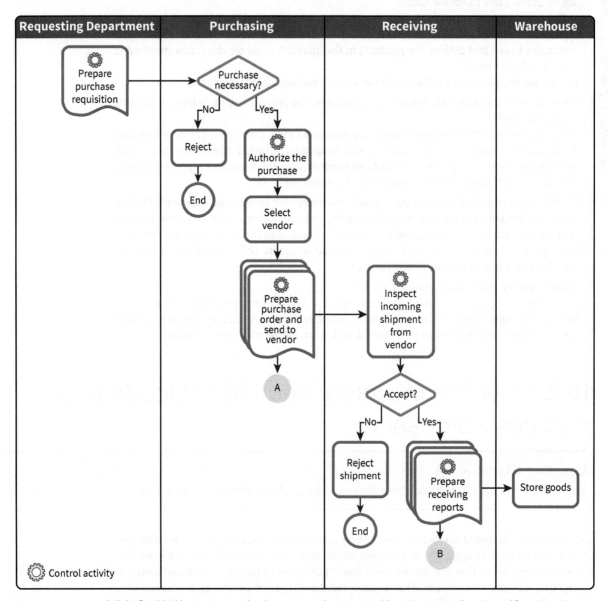

Illustration 10.4 Julia's Cookies' inventory purchasing process is presented in a document flowchart. (*Continued*)

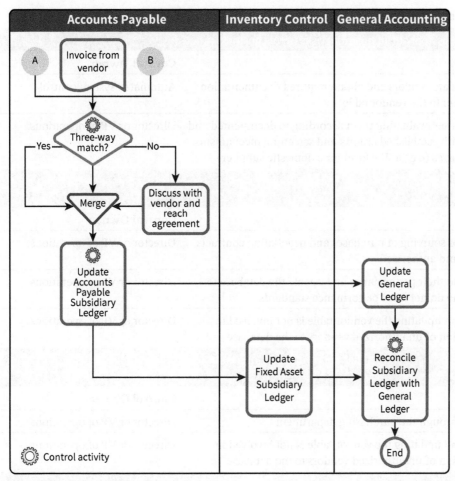

Illustration 10.4 (*Continued*)

management considers risk and costs versus benefit for each control activity. The cost of a control activity should not exceed the benefit.

Selecting and Managing Vendors

An organization can implement a number of internal controls related to vendor selection and management (**Table 10.1**). Formal processes should be in place to approve purchases from vendors who are not already in the system.

TABLE 10.1 Vendor Management Control Activities

Risk Statement: These control activities apply to all potential risks in this business process.	
Sample Control Activity	**Control Owner**
Use automated supplier portals to validate vendors and obtain required documentation before approving them and adding them to the vendor table	Automated system control
Add vendors to the vendor table only after evaluating them according to documented and authorized policies and procedures, with established criteria and screening mechanisms, and obtaining the proper vendor tax forms (e.g., a W-9 form for a domestic supplier)	Director or VP of operations
Risk Statement: Purchases from unapproved vendors may result in fraud, receipt of products that do not meet quality standards, or early or late deliveries.	
Sample Control Activity	**Control Owner**
Ensure that policies and procedures for sourcing of purchases and negotiating contracts or purchases are clearly documented and authorized	Director or VP of operations
Regularly review approved vendors and their performance and update the database to remove inactive vendors and those who do not meet performance standards	Director or VP of operations
Ensure that the person maintaining and updating the vendor table is not involved in supplier selection to prevent the addition of unauthorized vendors to the database	Director or VP of operations
Risk Statement: Purchases from unapproved vendors that are conflicts of interest or unauthorized related-party transactions may result in regulatory or reputational damage.	
Sample Control Activity	**Control Owner**
Ensure that all purchases are routed through the purchasing department	Director or VP of operations
Ensure that the person maintaining and updating the vendor table is not involved in supplier selection to prevent the addition of unauthorized vendors to the database	Director or VP of operations
Risk Statement: Unauthorized changes to the vendor table may result in fraudulent purchases or loss of financial assets.	
Sample Control Activity	**Control Owner**
Maintain segregation of duties by ensuring that the person maintaining and updating the vendor table is not involved in supplier selection	Purchasing manager
Risk Statement: Outdated information in the vendor table may result in financial losses due to inaccurate payments to vendors.	
Sample Control Activity	**Control Owner**
Regularly review approved vendors and their performance and update the table to remove inactive vendors and those who do not meet performance standards	Director or VP of operations
Risk Statement: Entering oral or written contracts prior to the completion of the vendor onboarding process may result in financial obligation to unapproved vendors.	
Sample Control Activity	**Control Owner**
Implement training for employees who communicate with vendors for purchasing	Purchasing manager/HR manager

For example, an organization may require that purchases be made only from vendors in the **main vendor table**, which is a list of all approved vendors the company does business with. A company should ensure that all vendors undergo screening and validation before being added to the main vendor table. Vendors should not be:

- Foreign officials
- Politically exposed
- On a government watch list
- In violation of the Foreign Corrupt Practices Act (FCPA)

The FCPA is a U.S. statute that prohibits businesses from paying bribes to foreign officials to benefit business deals. A company's failure to comply with the FCPA could result in fines, reputational harm, and potentially criminal charges. Ensuring only approved vendors are added to the main vendor table helps a company comply with the FCPA by prohibiting banned vendors in the system and fraudulent purchasing activities.

Placing Orders

It's essential that employees adhere to internal controls when placing orders, including properly filling out a purchase order. The responsibilities for placing orders should be defined, and it should ideally require all purchases to be routed through the purchasing department.

With an **e-procurement system**, purchase requisitions and orders can be created electronically and follow an electronic authorization sequence. In addition, such a system can perform three-way matches prior to vendor payment. The automation of an integrated system reduces the risk of error and fraud, speeds up processes, and leaves an electronic audit trail for accountability. E-procurement systems and other examples of internal controls for purchasing are described further in **Table 10.2**.

TABLE 10.2 Order Placement Control Activities

Risk Statement: These control activities apply to all potential risks in this business process.	
Sample Control Activity	**Control Owner**
Implement an e-procurement system, which can integrate with an ERP system, for automation of the purchasing process	Automated system control
Implement between suppliers and the company a paperless evaluated receipt settlement (ERS) system that ships goods based on system notices and confirms the corresponding purchase order upon receipt of the products	Automated system control
Prenumber and account for purchase requisitions and purchase orders	Automated system control
Risk Statement: Unauthorized purchase requisitions may result in unauthorized or fraudulent purchases.	
Sample Control Activity	**Control Owner**
Ensure that an authorized person from the department making a request approves a purchase requisition, within the dollar amount limits they are authorized to approve	Chief financial officer
Risk Statement: Unauthorized purchase orders submitted to an unauthorized vendor may result in unauthorized or fraudulent purchases.	
Sample Control Activity	**Control Owner**
Ensure that policies and procedures for processing and approving purchase orders are clearly documented and authorized	Director of operations
Separate the duties of ordering goods from receiving, payment, and accounting responsibilities	Director of operations
To enforce segregation of duties, allow only authorized employees to access purchase order input screens and/or purchase order documents	Director of operations
Risk Statement: Purchase requisitions being split into more than one purchase order to circumvent authorized limits may result in unauthorized or fraudulent purchases.	
Sample Control Activity	**Control Owner**
Ensure that documented and authorized policies and procedures for processing and approving purchase orders prohibit the practice of splitting requisitions into multiple purchase orders	Director of operations
Match purchase requisitions with purchase orders and generate an exception report investigation	Automated system control
Risk Statement: Blanket purchase orders may result in excessive purchases.	
Sample Control Activity	**Control Owner**
Ensure that each blanket purchase order specifies monetary limits and has a specified duration	Director or VP of operations

Placing orders is subject to unique fraud risks. In one type of fraud, employees may use **split purchase orders** to intentionally separate a single purchase into two or more purchase orders to stay within a single purchase authorization limit. For example, if the purchaser is only authorized to purchase up to $1,000, an $1,800 purchase may be split into two purchase orders—one for $1,000 and one for $800—to circumvent the purchase limit.

Let's look at an example at Julia's Cookies to see how this fraud is perpetrated. Recently, the Internal Audit department detected a purchase order anomaly by using data analytics to review purchase orders from the past six months. It investigated potential instances of split purchase orders, which were defined as multiple purchase orders that all:

- Were sent to the same supplier
- Were ordered by the same purchaser
- Were placed less than eight days apart

When confronted with the evidence, the purchaser admitted to receiving cash kickbacks from the vendor:

- She split 52 purchase orders into smaller value purchase orders of just under $5,000 each to bypass authorization limits and avoid additional approval checks.
- She knew that no one else needed to approve the purchases as only amounts higher than $5,000 required additional authorization.
- The intent was to circumvent Julia's Cookies' purchasing controls. The purchaser had significantly increased purchases from the vendor with whom she was colluding to increase kickbacks.

After this fraud was detected, the head of Internal Audit tasked an audit team with evaluating the internal control environment over the purchasing processes. Help the team evaluate the business process maturity level of the purchasing process in Applied Learning 10.2.

Julia's Cookies   Applied Learning 10.2

Purchasing Controls: Process Improvements

During the evaluation, the Internal Audit team identified three control deficiencies and ranked them as high, medium, or low in priority, depending on the team's assessment of each deficiency's related risk:

1. Because of its mission of buying local, Julia's Cookies does not have a formal process for consolidating purchase requests across the organization to obtain the best prices. Purchasers have significant discretion when choosing suppliers. The supplier that the employee was colluding with in this case also charged excessive prices—about 20% higher than the prices charged by other suppliers. [**High priority**]

2. Julia's Cookies does not have a formal and rigorous process for screening vendors. Individual purchasers select suppliers and request that they be added to the approved vendor table. [**High priority**]

3. The company is not effectively monitoring supplier performance for timely delivery of orders, quality of goods, and expiration dates of products upon delivery. [**Medium priority**]

KEY OBSERVATIONS

The Internal Audit team also noted that the remainder of the process and its controls are clearly defined, with formal documentation. While most controls are automated and integrated in the system, a number of manual controls exist that could be automated.

Julia's Cookies lacks a formal and rigorous process, applicable across the enterprise and for all facilities, for vetting and screening vendors. There is no formal enterprise-wide process to ensure that the company is getting the best prices from its local suppliers.

POTENTIAL IMPACTS

- Regulatory and compliance violations
- Conflicts of interest
- Unauthorized related-party transactions
- Inefficiencies and overpricing
- Purchasing fraud, such as the recently detected case

What improvements could Julia's Cookies make to address the control weaknesses identified by Internal Audit? Using the business process maturity model, how mature do you think Julia's Cookies' purchasing process is?

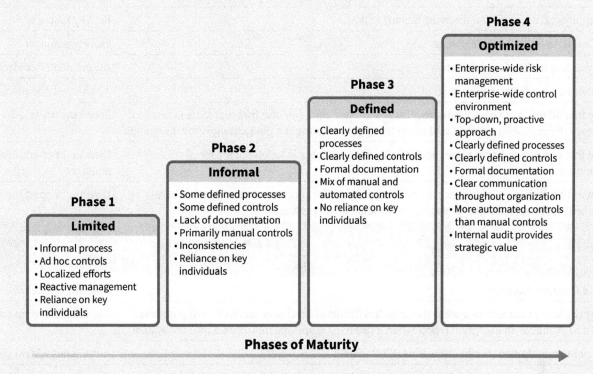

Phases of Maturity

SOLUTION

Julia's Cookies should implement the following improvements:

1. Use automated supplier portals to validate vendors and obtain required documentation before approving and adding them to the vendor table

2. Implement documented and authorized policies and procedures, with established criteria and screening mechanisms, to evaluate vendors before adding them to the vendor table

3. Retain the emphasis on support for local communities but implement centralized control from headquarters over purchasing

Julia's Cookies' purchasing process is in Phase 3—Defined of the business process maturity model.

Receiving Purchases

A company's receiving department is responsible for initially recording products received, and this record is the driver for paying for purchases. Physically separating the receiving area from production and shipping areas is a physical segregation of duties that protects against error and fraud. It also prevents purchases from being intermixed with shipments and production, whether accidentally or as an intentional theft.

Table 10.3 shows the main risks in the receiving process, how to mitigate each risk with one or more control activities, and a recommendation for who should be responsible for (own) the control activity.

TABLE 10.3 Receiving Control Activities

Risk Statement: These control activities apply to all potential risks in this business process.	
Sample Control Activity	**Control Owner**
To maintain segregation of duties, ensure that receiving employees do not initiate or authorize purchase transactions or have access to accounts payable and General Ledger records beyond the recording of goods received	Director of operations
Physically segregate receiving employees from warehouse storage areas, production, and shipping	Director of operations
Ensure that each physical facility has its own receiving location	Facility manager
Restrict physical access to the receiving department	Facility manager
Install cameras in the receiving areas	Facility manager
Control access to the receiving system	Automated IT control
Implement an e-procurement system	Automated system control
Ensure that all receiving exceptions are returned to the supplier or else investigated and resolved in a timely manner, with an audit trail of evidence documenting the physical movement of goods	Receiving supervisor
Ensure that policies and procedures and training for employees in receiving are clearly documented and authorized	Director of operations/HR manager
Implement an ongoing performance monitoring program for suppliers that is based on receiving department reports (shortages, overages, and product quality issues)	Director of operations
Risk Statement: Accepting goods that were not ordered, incorrect or excessive quantities, canceled orders, or goods that are damaged or of inferior quality may result in payment for unwanted items and excessive inventory or inventory shortfalls.	
Sample Control Activity	**Control Owner**
Implement an e-procurement system that matches details of inventory received with purchase orders and produces an exception report when a receiving employee inputs data into the system	Automated system control
Implement an evaluated receipt settlement (ERS) system	Automated system control
Conduct three-way matching of purchase order, receiving report, and vendor invoice prior to payment	Automated system control
Risk Statement: Accepting goods earlier or later than the scheduled delivery date may result in excessive or obsolete inventory.	
Sample Control Activity	**Control Owner**
Implement an e-procurement system that matches the scheduled delivery window period with the delivery date and produces an exception report when a receiving employee inputs data into the system	Automated system control
Risk Statement: Goods being received but not recorded, recorded at the wrong quantity, recorded to the wrong inventory account in the Subsidiary Ledger, or recorded in the wrong reporting period may result in misstatement of inventory and cost of goods sold, as well as incorrectly recorded liabilities.	
Sample Control Activity	**Control Owner**
Implement an e-procurement system	Automated IT control
Implement an ERS system	Automated IT control
Generate reports of all filled and open purchase orders for monthly review and follow-up by the requesting department	Automated IT control/ department manager
Match account numbers to each purchase requisition and purchase order	Automated IT control
Match goods received data to data on a purchase order	Automated IT control
Match the date goods are received with the accounting period in which the purchase is recorded	Automated IT control

CONCEPT REVIEW QUESTIONS

1. **CPA** How do internal controls help in risk mitigation related to purchases?
   Ans. A company can mitigate risks related to purchases with effective control activities. Identifying the employee(s) typically responsible for each control activity is necessary to ensure proper segregation of duties. The degree of control is a matter of judgment. A company's management considers risk and costs versus benefit for each control activity. The cost of a control activity should not exceed the benefit.

2. What is an e-procurement system?
   Ans. With an e-procurement system, purchase requisitions and orders can be created electronically and follow an electronic authorization sequence.

3. What do you understand by split purchase order?
   Ans. Placing orders is subject to unique fraud risks. In one type of fraud, employees may use split purchase orders to intentionally separate a single purchase into two or more purchase orders to stay within a single purchase authorization limit. For example, if the purchaser is only authorized to purchase up to $1,000, a $1,800 purchase may be split into two purchase orders—one for $1,000 and one for $800—to circumvent the purchase limit.

10.3 What Makes Fixed Assets Unique to Purchasing and Payments?

Learning Objective ❸
Explain the fixed asset acquisitions process.

Fixed assets include land, land improvements, buildings, equipment and machinery used in production, office equipment, computer equipment, furniture and fittings, warehouse shelving, and vehicles. In financial accounting, fixed assets are generally known as property, plant, and equipment (PP&E). The costs of acquiring fixed assets are referred to as **capital expenditures**, or **CAPEX**, in the business world.

Fixed assets differ from current assets in that they are revenue-producing assets used over the long term—that is, for more than one year. Unlike inventory, fixed assets are not held for resale. The purpose of these productive assets is to generate revenue for the company over the long term.

Illustration 10.5 shows the framework for the fixed asset acquisitions process, which consists of six stages.

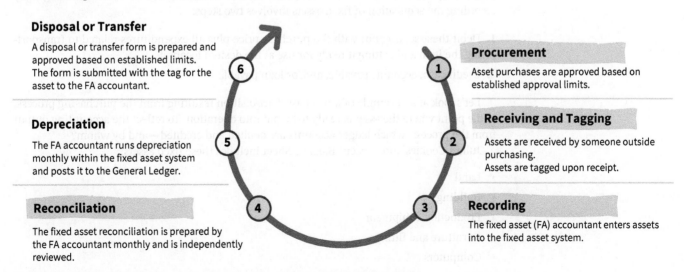

Disposal or Transfer

A disposal or transfer form is prepared and approved based on established limits. The form is submitted with the tag for the asset to the FA accountant.

6

Procurement

1

Asset purchases are approved based on established approval limits.

Depreciation

The FA accountant runs depreciation monthly within the fixed asset system and posts it to the General Ledger.

5

Receiving and Tagging

2

Assets are received by someone outside purchasing.
Assets are tagged upon receipt.

Reconciliation

The fixed asset reconciliation is prepared by the FA accountant monthly and is independently reviewed.

4

3

Recording

The fixed asset (FA) accountant enters assets into the fixed asset system.

Illustration 10.5 The fixed asset business processes framework includes six stages.

Fixed Asset Acquisitions Process

We will cover the first four stages of the fixed asset acquisitions process, which include the steps in the purchasing process, along with the fixed asset reconciliation, which is a necessary control. You may recall from introductory financial accounting classes that fixed assets are expensed as they are consumed over their revenue-generating service lives. The related expense is depreciation, which allocates the cost of a fixed asset to financial accounting reporting periods that benefit from them. This allocation results in matching the depreciation expenses with the revenue earned during a specific reporting period. Recording depreciation of fixed assets (Stage 5) and disposal or transfer of fixed assets (Stage 6) are beyond our scope here.

Stage 1: Fixed Asset Procurement

The department that uses a particular fixed asset generally initiates the purchasing process with a purchase requisition. Depending on the size of the business and how much the fixed asset costs, authorizations for fixed asset acquisitions can span several individuals or departments. For example, Julia's Cookies has certain authorization limits and authorizers:

- **Under $25,000:** Manager of requesting department (i.e., user department)
- **$25,000 to under $250,000:** Manager of requesting department and then the chief financial officer (CFO)
- **$250,000 to under $500,000:** Manager of requesting department, CFO, and then chief executive officer (CEO)
- **$500,000 and above:** Manager of requesting department, CFO, CEO, and then Board of Directors

Stage 2: Receiving and Tagging Fixed Assets

Routine purchases of fixed assets, such as equipment and furniture, follow a common pattern:

1. The fixed asset is inspected in receiving.
2. A receiving report is prepared.
3. The fixed asset is delivered to the requesting department for installation and/or use.
4. Fixed assets are tagged for future identification purposes.

Stage 3: Recording Fixed Assets

When a fixed asset is purchased, it is first procured (Stage 1) and received (Stage 2). The accounting for a fixed asset occurs when the asset is recorded (Stage 3). The accounting entry recording the acquisition of fixed assets involves two steps:

1. Debit the asset account with the purchase price plus all expenditures related to transporting the item and getting it ready for use at the desired location
2. Credit cash, accounts payable, and/or loan payable

Let's look at an example of a fixed asset acquisition resulting from the purchasing process, at the point where the asset is ready to be put into operation. To reflect the accounting output from the process, which ledger accounts are debited and credited—and by whom?

Julia's Cookies' most recent Balance Sheet includes these fixed assets:

- Land
- Buildings
- Production equipment
- Furniture and fittings
- Computers
- Vehicles

When Julia's Cookies acquired land and buildings for its most recent regional facility, it incurred the following costs for the purchase of the building and for preparing the building for use:

Purchase price building	$600,000
Title insurance	$3,500
Legal fees	$6,500
Commission to agent	$18,000
Remodel of building	$250,000
Total cost of building	**$878,000**

You may recall from financial accounting that the cost of the land is recorded separately in its own General Ledger account, as land generally has an unlimited life and is not depreciated. Buildings are subject to depreciation as they are "used up" in operations over time. For Julia's Cookies, the total cost of the land amounted to $410,000.

CPA Julia's Cookies took out a mortgage for $750,000 and paid the remainder in cash. The net journal entry is:

		Dr.	Cr.
August 17, 20XX	Land	$ 410,000	
	Building	878,000	
	Mortgage loan		$ 750,000
	Cash		538,000

Stage 4: Fixed Asset Reconciliation

In addition to the purchasing and payments journal entries, the fixed asset accountant ensures that the Fixed Asset Subsidiary Ledger is updated. The **Fixed Asset Subsidiary Ledger** shows details for each fixed asset:

- Date of purchase
- Historical cost
- Accumulated depreciation
- Net book value

It also provides details related to the disposal of a particular asset: the selling price and the profit or loss on disposal.

The Fixed Asset Subsidiary Ledger is reconciled to the Fixed Asset General Ledger accounts on a regular basis.

Why Does It Matter to Your Career?

Thoughts from a Senior Accountant, Professional Services

Knowing the fixed asset acquisitions process, risks, and controls is essential to your daily duties as an accountant since fixed assets can be the biggest line item for assets on the Balance Sheet.

Let's go back to Julia's Cookies. After reviewing the Internal Audit team's report for inventory purchases, Darlene, the CFO, considers the purchase of fixed assets:

- Fixed assets are more costly than inventory.
- Fixed assets are also constantly changing as the company adds or replaces assets that become outdated or worn out.
- The fixed asset acquisitions process is like the process for purchasing inventory.

Darlene asks the fixed asset accountant for a process flowchart of the existing process. Julia's Cookies uses a document flowchart for the acquisition of fixed assets (**Illustration 10.6**). Notice that this document flowchart is almost the same as the flowchart for the purchases of inventory and other goods, except for the replacement of inventory control with fixed asset accounting and the absence of a warehouse because the fixed asset is sent to the user or requesting department. These differences are highlighted in the document flowchart.

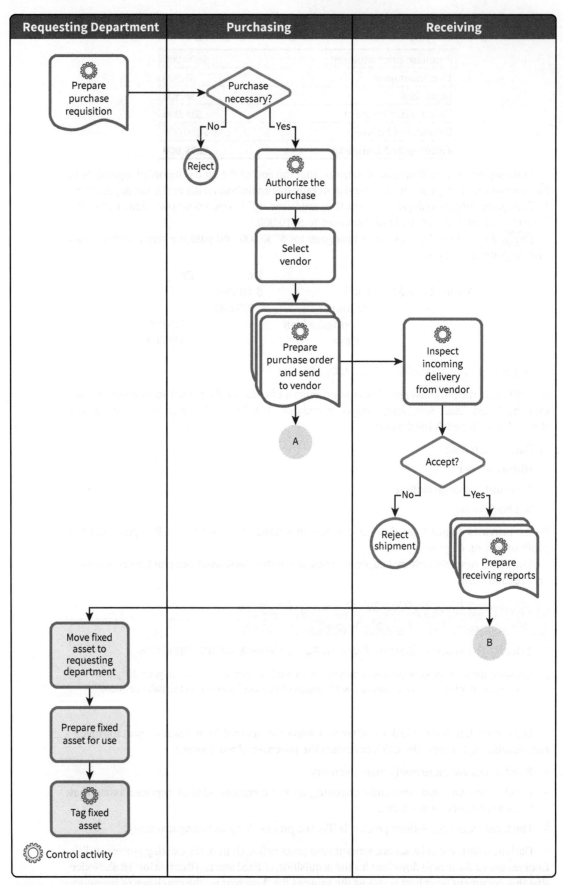

Illustration 10.6 The fixed asset acquisitions process at Julia's Cookies is similar to the inventory purchasing process but includes additional steps. (*Continued*)

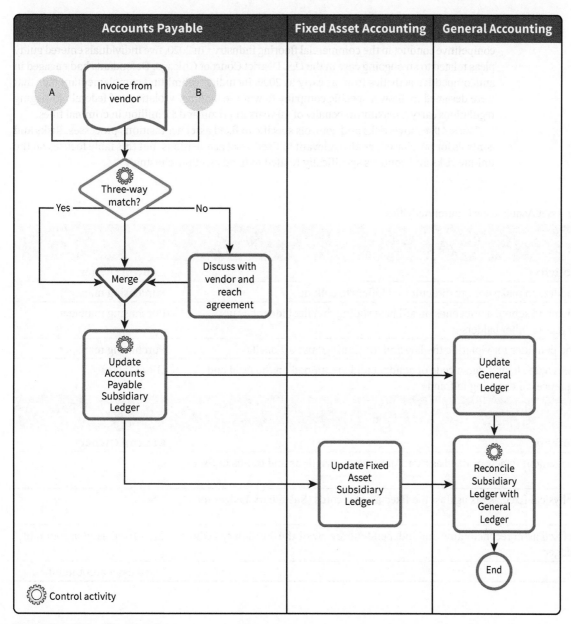

Illustration 10.6 *(Continued)*

Internal Control over Fixed Asset Acquisitions

Key accounting transactions associated with fixed assets are those that record the initial acquisition of these assets. Other than for material fixed assets such as land, buildings, and other significant acquisitions, fixed asset purchases are generally subject to the same risks and internal controls as purchases of other goods. Material fixed assets acquisitions should be subject to additional authorization to prevent unauthorized purchases.

Two additional risks for fixed asset acquisitions are bid rigging and the overstatement of fixed assets in the financial statements because of capitalizing expenses. We discuss the overstatement of assets and financial statement fraud in the Fraud chapter.

Bid rigging can happen in two ways:

- An employee colludes with a vendor to fraudulently obtain a contract meant to be subject to a competitive bidding process. Because of "insider information" illegally obtained from an employee, often in a kickback arrangement, the vendor wins the bidding process.
- Vendors collude with one another and reach advance agreement about which vendor will be the winning bidder for a particular contract. The winning bidder agrees to compensate the other vendors in some manner for intentionally losing the contract.

In recent years, the Antitrust Division's Chicago Office has been partnering with the FBI's Chicago Field Division to actively pursue cartels involved in bid rigging, price fixing, and anti-competitive conduct in the commercial flooring industry.[2] In 2020, five individuals entered guilty pleas related to an ongoing case in the U.S. District Court of Chicago. Defendants had engaged in anticompetitive activities from as early as 2009, including submitting complementary bids that were designed to allow a specific company to win the bidding. Violations of federal bid-rigging regulations carry a maximum penalty of 10 years in prison and $1 million in criminal fines.

Table 10.4 shows risks and controls specific to fixed asset acquisitions processes. Risks and controls for purchases are also relevant to fixed asset acquisitions, but this table focuses on the unique risks and controls specifically related to fixed asset purchasing.

TABLE 10.4 Fixed Asset Acquisitions Control Activities

Risk Statement: Bid rigging and kickbacks, especially for significant contracts, create unfair and uncompetitive bidding processes, which may result in financial losses due to paying higher prices in the absence of competition.	
Sample Control Activity	**Control Owner**
Expand the list of bidders to make it more difficult for bidders to collude	Purchasing manager
Require bidders to sign and submit a noncollusion affidavit stating that the bidder has not colluded with employees or other bidders	Purchasing manager
Inform bidders of the penalties for violating the law and for signing false affidavits	Purchasing manager
Ensure that employees agree to and sign a code of conduct and are trained on the legal and employment consequences of engaging in fraud	HR manager
Risk Statement: Capitalizing items that are not fixed assets may result in inflated net income and assets, financial statement misstatements, fines and penalties, or reputational damage.	
Sample Control Activity	**Control Owner**
Ensure regular management review of fixed asset accounting transactions and trends in fixed asset ratios	CFO
Periodically check physical fixed assets against the fixed asset records (Subsidiary Ledger for fixed assets)	CFO
Conduct a monthly fixed asset reconciliation and independent review of the Subsidiary Ledger with the General Ledger	CFO/fixed asset accountant
Tag all fixed assets	Fixed asset accountant

Now that you have reviewed the controls table, use the business process maturity model to evaluate Julia's Cookies' fixed asset acquisitions processes in Applied Learning 10.3.

Julia's Cookies   Applied Learning 10.3

Fixed Asset Acquisitions: Business Process Maturity Model

Darlene asks the Internal Audit team to conduct another review, this time over the acquisition of fixed assets. In addition to the control deficiencies reported in the purchases of inventory and goods, the Internal Audit team identified three control deficiencies:

1. There is no formal reconciliation of recorded fixed assets with physical assets. There should be periodic monitoring of fixed assets, including a review of new asset acquisitions. [**High priority**]

2. The fixed asset accountant maintains the fixed asset detail in an Excel spreadsheet and uploads it into a fixed asset system to calculate depreciation. This process should be automated to prevent errors and fraud. [**High priority**]

3. Currently, many of the assets include only a general description, such as "Mixer." Fixed assets should be more clearly labeled for identification and include additional details, such as model information and location. [**Medium-low priority**]

---

[2]www.justice.gov/opa/pr/commercial-flooring-contractor-agrees-plead-guilty-bid-rigging

ADDITIONAL KEY OBSERVATIONS

- A fixed asset on the books may not exist or the fixed asset records might be incorrect.
- Spreadsheets are prone to error and fraud due to a lack of internal controls.

POTENTIAL IMPACTS

- Stolen fixed assets
- Unauthorized removal of fixed assets
- Misstatements of the financial statements
- Erroneous calculations due to using poorly controlled spreadsheets

Darlene is surprised to learn that a spreadsheet is being used for fixed asset accounting—and she is concerned. What solution should she implement? How mature is Julia's Cookies' fixed asset acquisitions process?

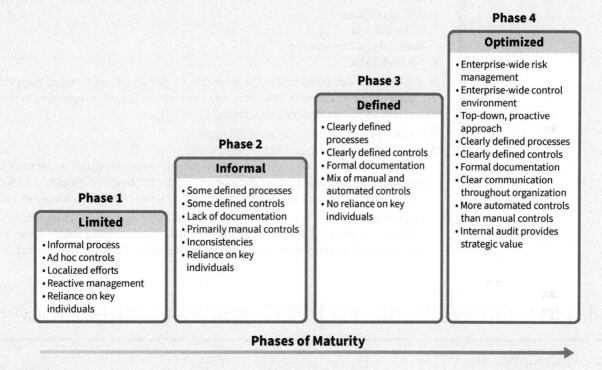

Phase 1

Limited

- Informal process
- Ad hoc controls
- Localized efforts
- Reactive management
- Reliance on key individuals

Phase 2

Informal

- Some defined processes
- Some defined controls
- Lack of documentation
- Primarily manual controls
- Inconsistencies
- Reliance on key individuals

Phase 3

Defined

- Clearly defined processes
- Clearly defined controls
- Formal documentation
- Mix of manual and automated controls
- No reliance on key individuals

Phase 4

Optimized

- Enterprise-wide risk management
- Enterprise-wide control environment
- Top-down, proactive approach
- Clearly defined processes
- Clearly defined controls
- Formal documentation
- Clear communication throughout organization
- More automated controls than manual controls
- Internal audit provides strategic value

Phases of Maturity

SOLUTION

There are a few solutions that Darlene, the CFO, could implement:

- Require recurring formal reconciliation of recorded fixed assets with physical fixed asset
- Implement a fixed asset system in place of the spreadsheet to improve the accuracy of the fixed asset acquisitions process
- Improve procedures for tagging fixed assets and updating the policies and procedures by requiring that tags be permanently adhered to assets or etched into assets to identify each asset's number and owner

Julia's Cookies' purchasing process for fixed assets is only in Phase 2—Informal of the business process maturity model, which is concerning for a company of its size.

CONCEPT REVIEW QUESTIONS

1. What are fixed assets?
   Ans. Fixed assets include land, land improvements, buildings, equipment and machinery used in production, office equipment, computer equipment, furniture and fittings, warehouse shelving, and vehicles. In financial accounting, fixed assets are generally known as property, plant, and equipment (PP&E).

2. What is meant by CAPEX?

Ans. The costs of acquiring fixed assets are referred to as capital expenditures, or CAPEX, in the business world.

3. What are the steps in receiving and tagging fixed assets?

Ans. Routine purchases of fixed assets, such as equipment and furniture, follow a common pattern:

1. The fixed asset is inspected in receiving.

2. A receiving report is prepared.

3. The fixed asset is delivered to the requesting department for installation and/or use.

4. Fixed assets are tagged for future identification purposes.

4. How is the fixed asset reconciliation done?

Ans. In addition to the purchasing and payments journal entries, the fixed asset accountant ensures that the Fixed Asset Subsidiary Ledger is updated. The Fixed Asset Subsidiary Ledger shows details for each fixed asset:

- Date of purchase
- Historical cost
- Accumulated depreciation
- Net book value

It also provides details related to the disposal of a particular asset: the selling price and the profit or loss on disposal. The Fixed Asset Subsidiary Ledger is reconciled to the Fixed Asset General Ledger accounts on a regular basis.

5. What are some common methods of bid rigging?

Ans. Bid rigging can happen in following ways:

- An employee colludes with a vendor to fraudulently obtain a contract meant to be subject to a competitive bidding process. Because of "insider information" illegally obtained from an employee, often in a kickback arrangement, the vendor wins the bidding process.

- Vendors collude with one another and reach advance agreement about which vendor will be the winning bidder for a particular contract. The winning bidder agrees to compensate the other vendors in some manner for intentionally losing the contract.

10.4 How Do We Evaluate the Credit Payments Process?

Learning Objective ❹
Evaluate the credit payments process.

The payments processes, also known as the cash disbursements processes, involve paying for acquisitions made in the purchasing processes. Payments processes impact the amount of the cash line item, the most liquid of current assets on the Balance Sheet, by decreasing the cash balance. Before we look at the business activities and internal controls for the payments processes, let's revisit some financial accounting concepts that are helpful for understanding payments.

Illustration 10.7 shows an example of a Cash ledger account for one month. The beginning balance (May 1) plus cash receipts (May 5) minus cash payments (May 31) equals the ending balance (June 1).

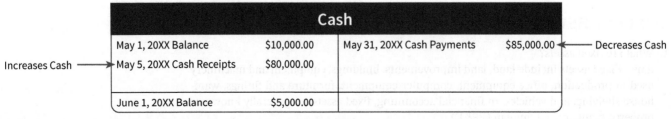

Cash			
May 1, 20XX Balance	$10,000.00	May 31, 20XX Cash Payments	$85,000.00
May 5, 20XX Cash Receipts	$80,000.00		
June 1, 20XX Balance	$5,000.00		

Increases Cash ⟶ (May 5)   Decreases Cash ⟵ (May 31)

Illustration 10.7 The Cash account is decreased during payments processes.

CPA The cash flow statement reports the impact of increases and decreases to cash over the reporting period, separating transactions into net cash inflow or outflow from operating activities, investing activities, and financing activities. Cash disbursements impact each of these activities on the financial statements:

- **Operating activity "Pay supplier invoice":** Reduce cash and accounts payable on the Balance Sheet. Reduce net cash flow from operating activities on the cash flow statement.
- **Investing activity "Purchase computer equipment for cash":** Reduce cash and increase computer equipment (a fixed asset) on the Balance Sheet. Reduce net cash flow from investing activities on the cash flow statement.
- **Financing activity "Repay long-term debt":** Reduce cash and long-term debt on the Balance Sheet and reduce net cash flow from financing activities on the cash flow statement. This would happen if the company previously borrowed money in the form of a long-term loan to purchase fixed assets.

Why Does It Matter to Your Career?

Thoughts from an Accounts Payable Clerk, Manufacturing

The accounts payable process is a high-risk area for fraud and financial loss due to duplicative payments and other process inefficiencies. Many businesses are adopting finance innovation opportunities to transform how this and other finance processes work. Understanding the payments process allows you to contribute to these cutting-edge initiatives and make recommendations for improvements at your job.

Credit Payments Process

There are two primary methods of paying for purchases: making cash payments and using credit. Payments made using credit are recorded in **accounts payable**, which is an account that records money the business owes to its suppliers and vendors. It is shown as a liability on the Balance Sheet. Here we focus on purchases bought on credit.

In the payments process, a company must approve payments and record them in the **cash disbursements journal**, in chronological order, to capture all transactions in debit/credit format.

Let's look at Julia's Cookies to see how the process works:

1. Management approves payment vouchers according to Julia's Cookies' authorization policies.
2. The computer system reports the amounts due to vendors daily. Businesses today often use the electronic funds transfer (EFT) from their bank accounts to make payments. While Julia's Cookies mainly uses EFT to pay its vendors, some vendors may require paper checks.
3. The Treasury department at Julia's Cookies, led by the treasurer, performs the cash management function. They monitor the company's cash position daily to ensure that funds are available so Accounts Payable can take advantage of vendor discounts by making payments on the due dates. Each day the information system extracts approved payment vouchers for Accounts Payable, and the vendors are paid. Payments are recorded in the cash disbursements journal, and the Accounts Payable Subsidiary Ledger and the General Ledger are updated.
4. For internal control purposes, an employee in Treasury performs a bank reconciliation each month by comparing the bank statement, which is an external record of receipts and payments from the bank, to the company's General Ledger to ensure that they are consistent.
5. Another internal control is the reconciliation of the monthly vendor statement with the Accounts Payable Subsidiary Ledger and the total from the Subsidiary Ledger with the Accounts Payable Control Account balance in the General Ledger.

From the initial three-way match of the purchase order, receiving report, and vendor invoice to the reconciliation, the payments process requires many business activities and participants (**Illustration 10.8**).

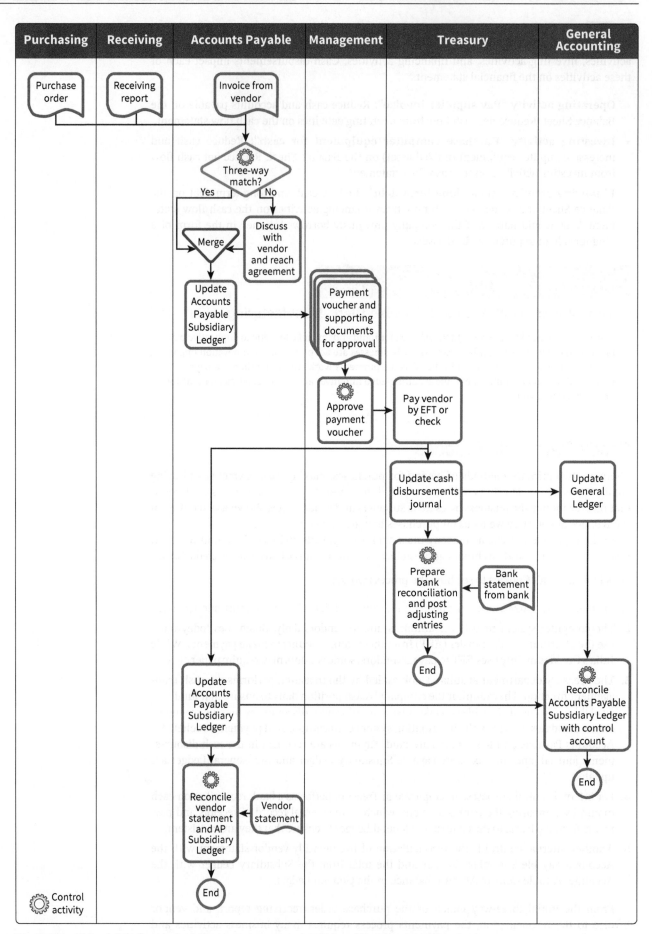

Illustration 10.8 Julia's Cookies' credit payments process is displayed in a document flowchart.

Internal Control over Payments to Vendors

Cash is highly susceptible to theft, and fraudulent disbursements schemes are common. One of the greatest fraud risks in the payments process is an employee creating a fictitious vendor and sending fraudulent payments to bank accounts the employee controls. The controls listed in **Table 10.5** can help a company maintain effective internal control over the payments processes.

TABLE 10.5 Payments Control Activities

Risk Statement: These control activities apply to all potential risks in this business process.	
Sample Control Activity	**Control Owner**
CPA Maintain segregation of duties among key responsibilities, such as receiving, purchasing, accounts payable, disbursements, bank reconciliation, and reconciliation of the Subsidiary Ledger with the Accounts Payable control account	CFO
Ensure independent bank reconciliation and review by management	Treasurer
CPA Ensure that every payment has a traceable audit trail and can be uniquely identified	Treasurer
CPA Do not allow checks to be made payable to "Cash" or "Bearer"	Treasurer
Check supplier invoices for accuracy by comparing them to purchase orders and checking quantities, price, calculations, extensions, taxes, etc.	Accounts payable manager
Use only original invoices (not duplicates) and authorized electronic invoices as the basis for payment	Accounts payable manager
Use vendor statements for reconciliation only and not for payment	Accounts payable manager
Risk Statement: Unrecorded payments may result in duplicate payments to vendors or misstatement of financial statements by overstating cash and accounts payable.	
Sample Control Activity	**Control Owner**
Report missing numbers in a sequence of prenumbered checks or EFTs for investigation and resolution	CFO/Automated system control
Compare the total of the authorized vouchers submitted for payment to the total in the cash disbursements journal for a specific period	CFO/Automated system control
Risk Statement: Payments recorded in the wrong vendor account may result in duplicate payments to vendors.	
Sample Control Activity	**Control Owner**
Compare the vendor ID in the cash payments journal with the vendor ID on supporting documentation and the payments voucher	CFO/Automated system control
Reconcile vendor statements with the Accounts Payable Subsidiary Ledger	Accounts payable manager
Risk Statement: Incorrect payment amounts may result in over- or underpayment of accounts payable.	
Sample Control Activity	**Control Owner**
Reconcile vendor statements with the Accounts Payable Subsidiary Ledger and investigate and resolve discrepancies	Accounts payable manager
Risk Statement: Payments made for unauthorized or nonexistent purchases may result in fraudulent misappropriation of cash.	
Sample Control Activity	**Control Owner**
Apply a limit test to large payments for additional review	CFO/Automated system control
CPA Apply a three-way match against the purchase report, the receiving report, and the vendor's invoice and ensure that payments are not processed until discrepancies are resolved	Authorizing manager of payment/ Automated system control
Compare payment information with purchase order and receiving report information	Authorizing manager of payment/ Automated system control

(Continued)

TABLE 10.5 (*Continued*)

Risk Statement: Paying invoices twice may result in overpayments to vendors.	
Sample Control Activity	**Control Owner**
Tag or cancel vendor invoice, payment voucher, and supporting documentation to prevent reuse	CFO/Automated system control

Risk Statement: Suboptimal use of cash may result in loss of assets and poor cash management.	
Sample Control Activity	**Control Owner**
Take advantage of all available supplier discounts that are favorable to the company	CFO/Treasurer

Many of these risks and controls are directly related to fraud, which is a large risk due to the financial nature of this business process. Unauthorized payments that are the result of fraud are referred to as "fraudulent disbursements." Help Julia's Cookies improve its internal controls to prevent fraud in Applied Learning 10.4.

Julia's Cookies   Applied Learning 10.4

Accounts Payable: Continuous Fraud Monitoring

Another fraud was uncovered at Julia's Cookies, this time via an anonymous tip on the corporate whistleblower hotline. The fraud involved duplicate payments to vendors, where the perpetrators circumvented the internal controls by colluding. An employee, a manager, and a vendor all worked together to perform the fraud. Fortunately, it was uncovered before significant losses occurred.

Darlene would like to implement a proactive fraud monitoring program that provides early detection prior to payment disbursement. The continuous fraud monitoring program will be a data analytics and automation solution that automatically emails the Internal Audit department whenever a fraud red flag is identified in the system data.

Darlene schedules a meeting with the corporate treasurer, the controller, and the VP of Internal Audit to discuss this fraud monitoring program. These stakeholders agree that the Internal Audit department has the technological capabilities to design and build this solution as part of its existing continuous analytics program.

What risks does this kind of continuous fraud monitoring analytics program mitigate? What risks could it create? Is this monitoring system part of the company's internal control environment?

SOLUTION

This tool addresses fraud risks related to duplicate and erroneous payments.

Examples of risks that could be created by this solution include:

- Improper design or erroneous implementation may result in inaccurate decisions being made by internal audit and other stakeholders.
- Sensitive information such as fraud red flags in a dashboard may result in unauthorized access and reputational damage of employees if not handled with the correct level of security and discretion.

Whether this system is part of the internal control environment depends on who is responsible for acting when a red flag is identified. If red flags are handled by the Compliance or Finance department, this is part of the internal control environment. However, since Julia's Cookies plans to have the continuous fraud monitoring program send alerts to the Internal Audit team, it's not part of the internal controls. Instead, it is part of the Internal Audit department's independent assurance practices.

CONCEPT REVIEW QUESTIONS

1. **CPA** What does the cashflow statement report?

   Ans. The cash flow statement reports the impact of increases and decreases to cash over the reporting period, separating transactions into net cash inflow or outflow from operating activities, investing activities, and financing activities.

2. How do cash disbursements impact each of the following activities: operating activity, investing activity, and financing activity?

Ans. The cash disbursements impact each of the following:

a. Operating activity "Pay supplier invoice": Reduce cash and accounts payable on the Balance Sheet. Reduce net cash flow from operating activities on the cash flow statement.

b. Investing activity "Purchase computer equipment for cash": Reduce cash and increase computer equipment (a fixed asset) on the Balance Sheet. Reduce net cash flow from investing activities on the cash flow statement.

c. Financing activity "Repay long-term debt": Reduce cash and long-term debt on the Balance Sheet and reduce net cash flow from financing activities on the cash flow statement. This would happen if the company previously borrowed money in the form of a long-term loan to purchase fixed assets.

3. **CPA** What is the three-way approach to avoid fraudulent misappropriation of cash for unauthorized payments?

Ans. Authorizing manager of payment/automated system control can apply a three-way match against the purchase report, the receiving report, and the vendor's invoice and ensure that payments are not processed until discrepancies are resolved.

10.5 How Does the AIS Capture Purchasing and Payments Data?

Learning Objective ❺
Use the key data in the underlying database for reporting and insights.

Beneath every good business process are an AIS and a database that capture and store the data that business events generate. When this system is an ERP system, reporting and analytics are supported across the organization with seamless connectivity. With decentralized, non-ERP systems, combining the data from the many business areas involved requires data modeling and aggregation.

There are five features, which are part of two modules, in the ERP system cloud map that support the specific purchasing and payments business processes you have learned about in this chapter: Inventory, Purchasing, Shipping/Receiving, Accounts Payable, and Fixed Assets (**Illustration 10.9**).

Database Design

The relational database that supports the ERP system modules and features used in the purchasing and payments processes is composed of many tables connected in multiple ways across modules. To keep things understandable, let's look at some of the key tables in the Accounts Payable, Purchasing, and Inventory features. The entity relationship diagram (ERD) is color coded to indicate to which ERP system modules the tables belong—Supply Chain Management or Financial (**Illustration 10.10**).

Recall that tables within a database are connected via different types of relationships. For example, the AP_Vendor table relates to both invoices and purchases:

- When the company initiates a purchase, it must submit the purchase order to the appropriate vendor.

- That same vendor then submits an invoice.

- **CPA** These two documents and the receiving report in the shipping and receiving tables, which would also include the vendor (which is not pictured in this ERD), constitute a three-way match.

- During the three-way match, the purchase order, invoice, and receiving report are reconciled to validate the details of a purchase before a payment is issued to the vendor.

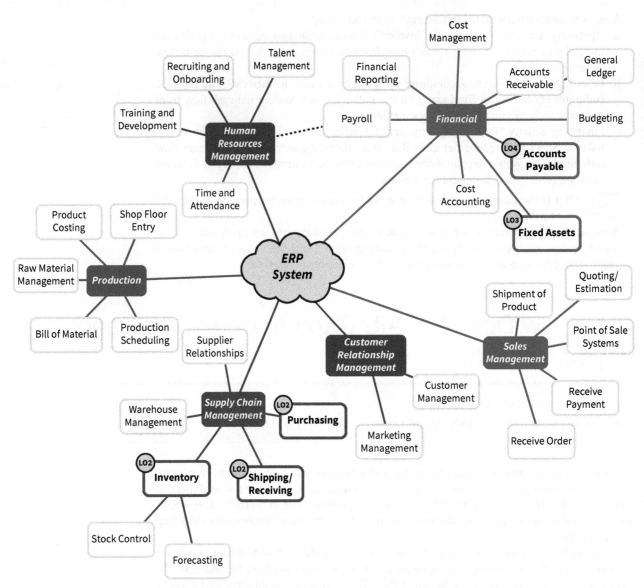

Illustration 10.9 Purchasing and payments business processes utilize five features in this ERP system.

In a non-ERP system, the three-way match is performed by manually querying each system for these three documents (purchasing, shipping and receiving, and financials) and manually reviewing the results of the queries against one another. In an ERP system, however, a three-way match can be performed automatically by reconciling data in these three interconnected tables using the primary and foreign keys, which are the identifier columns in a relational database. A three-way match is an essential internal control for purchasing and payments processes. Help Skylar in the Accounts Payable department of Julia's Cookies perform a three-way match in Applied Learning 10.5.

Julia's Cookies Applied Learning 10.5

Database Design: Three-Way Matching

Skylar, an Accounts Payable analyst, is performing a three-way match before issuing payments to a vendor. The receiving system is not yet integrated into an ERP system module, and Skylar must match the combined purchase order and invoice with a separate table that contains the receiving report data.

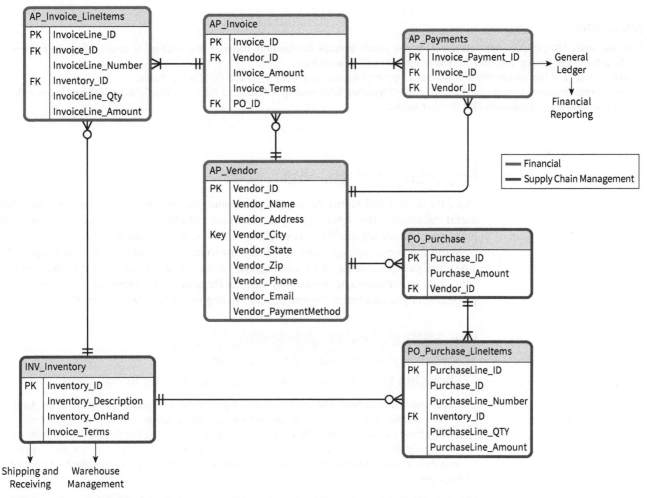

Illustration 10.10   The key tables in the purchasing and payments business processes are depicted in an ERD.

Do all of the following invoices pass the three-way match? What relationships between primary keys and foreign keys did you use to find the answer? Could these tables be joined as-is, or would data modeling be required?

Purchase and invoice data:

Vendor_ ID	Purchase_ ID	Purchase_ Date	Purchase_ Amount	Purchase_ Qty	Invoice_ ID	Invoice_ Date	Invoice_ Amount
A092923	100114	10/05/Y1	395.10	1.00	I-JC-3480	11/11/Y1	395.10
B248590	100116	10/05/Y1	448,950.20	8.00	INV 45229-1	11/15/Y1	449,900.20
B558403	100119	10/05/Y1	3,452.98	6.00	Nov-Y1-3942	11/15/Y1	3,450.09
A092923	100122	11/09/Y1	34,250.09	2.00	I-JC-3481	11/15/Y1	34,250.09

Receiving report data:

ID	PO Number	Quantity
1002560	100-114	1.00
1002578	100-116	10.00
1002601	100-119	6.00
1002620	100-122	2.00

SOLUTION

Purchase order 100-116 does not pass the three-way match because the quantity invoiced and received is greater than the amount purchased. The vendor sent and invoiced more than Julia's Cookies ordered.

The primary and foreign key relationships to join these tables are the Purchase_ID and PO Number fields.

To join these two data sets, the Purchase_ID and PO Number fields need to be formatted the same. The fields are different because the receiving system uses a hyphenated PO Number format.

Reporting and Insights

The data created and stored during the purchasing and payments processes is turned into useful information through reporting and analysis. Data from the purchasing and payments processes provides key insights into vendors, cash flow, and company assets.

Recall that reporting aggregates raw data to provide a historical view of what happened as a result of past purchasing activities. Analysis focuses on providing context to the historical data. It gives management meaningful insights for making decisions on how to improve a process. Analysis uses either the raw data or existing reports generated from that data.

Why Does It Matter to Your Career?

Thoughts from an External Audit Senior, Public Accounting

Procurement and payment data analytics is a hot topic for clients of public accounting firms. Auditors and internal audit consultants are finding ways to analyze data generated in these processes to identify fraud risks, trends, and efficiency opportunities. Accounting and finance departments are creating digital transformation teams to implement monitoring solutions. There are many opportunities in this space for you to add value, whether as an external auditor, consultant, or internal employee.

Raw Materials Purchasing

The data created and stored in a database during the purchasing of raw materials includes vendor ID, name, address, telephone number, email address, tax identification number (TIN), website, purchase requisition number, purchase order number, receiving report number, quantity, item number, item description, date, and item price. The collected data can be converted into typical purchasing reports such as vendor listings and backorder reports (**Table 10.6**).

TABLE 10.6 Raw Materials Purchasing Reports

Report	Description
Products received—by time	A summary of products received within a period of time.
Products received—by vendor	A summary of products received from particular vendors within a period of time. This report can show whether payments to a specific vendor have increased or decreased unexpectedly, which could indicate that a fictitious vendor is receiving payments.
Purchase requisitions filled and open	The total number of purchase requisitions that have been purchased or that remain outstanding within a period of time.
Purchase orders filled and open	The total number of purchase orders that have been completed by suppliers and vendors or that remain outstanding within a period of time.

TABLE 10.6 (Continued)

Report	Description
Purchase orders aging	The number of days purchase orders have been outstanding, classified in buckets. For example, all purchase orders that are between 30 and 60 days outstanding would be summarized into a total amount.
Backorder report	A list of items on backorder from suppliers and vendors.
Main vendor table	A list of all approved vendors from the main vendor table. This type of report is often used alongside other data sources to perform fraud analytics.

The output from the raw materials database can be analyzed to provide management with insight into how to improve processes. **Table 10.7** lists some examples of analytics that can be used to create insights from raw materials data.

TABLE 10.7 Raw Materials Purchasing Analytics

Analytics	Description	How It's Used
Vendor performance	Identifying how long it took to receive an order, the quality of goods received, and the condition of goods received	Indicates issues with vendors so purchasing can be optimized
Receiving reconciliation	Comparing the goods received against the approved purchase order	Identifies discrepancies between what has been received and what was ordered
Vendor prices	Analyzing vendor prices that have increased above a threshold amount over a period of time	Can detect collusive fraud by employee buyers and vendors where the buyers receive kickbacks or other rewards from the vendors
Vendor frequency	Analyzing the frequency of purchasing from a single vendor that has increased above a threshold over time	Can detect collusive fraud or fictitious vendors as such fraud results in increased spending with the fraudulent vendor
Duplicate vendor data	Analyzing vendors with the same telephone number, address, bank account, or email	Indicates whether a vendor is duplicated in the system due to fraud or error, potentially causing duplicate payments or payments sent to the wrong vendor
Vendor–employee comparison	Comparing vendor telephone numbers, addresses, emails, and bank accounts to the main employee table	Looks for red flags of fraud where an employee establishes a fictitious vendor to receive fraudulent payments
Vendor address	Identifying vendors with address issues in the main vendor table, such as no physical address or vendors with post office box number	Can indicate a fictitious vendors because a legitimate vendor is expected to have a physical mailing address
Discounts	Analyzing discount terms given, discounts used, and discounts forfeited	Identifies areas to improve management of cash
Financial ratios	Calculating purchasing ratios such as accounts payable turnover days, purchasing to sales, and purchases growth to sales growth	Compares these ratios to prior periods to identify unusual activity or to external benchmarks to measure performance

Management uses combinations of these reports and analytics for decision making, and dashboards like the one in **Illustration 10.11** provide at-a-glance information in real time.

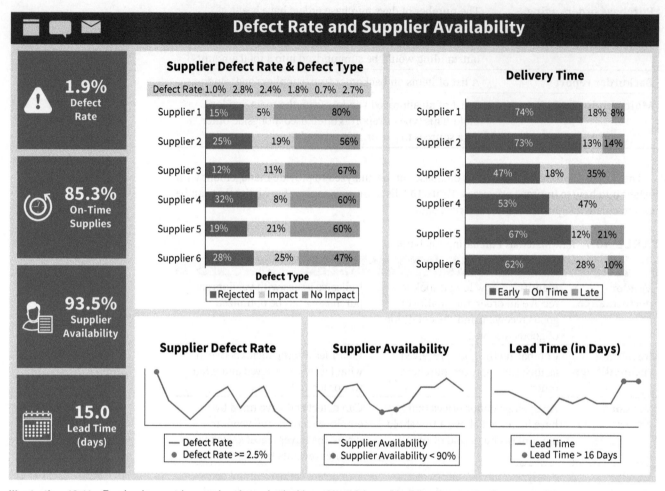

Illustration 10.11 Purchasing metrics can be shown in dashboards, which are visualized reports.

Fixed Assets Purchasing

The data created and stored in the database during the fixed asset purchasing process is similar to the data stored in the raw materials purchasing process. It includes vendor ID, name, address, telephone number, email address, tax identification number (TIN), purchase requisition number, purchase order number, receiving report number, fixed asset description, date received, ready-for-use date, cost price, tag number, and location. Processing this data creates output that can appear in reports that show changes in the company's assets and more (**Table 10.8**).

TABLE 10.8 Fixed Assets Purchasing Reports

Report	Description
Additions	A list of scheduled additions to the company's fixed assets.
Purchases by vendor	A list of fixed asset purchases, summarized by vendors within a period of time. This can show any unexpected expenditure with a particular vendor.
Purchase requisitions filled and open	The total number of purchase requisitions that have been filled or that remain outstanding within a period of time.
Purchase orders filled and open	The total number of purchase orders that have been completed by suppliers and vendors or that remain outstanding within a period of time.

TABLE 10.8 (*Continued*)

Report	Description
Purchase orders aging	The number of days purchase orders have been outstanding, classified in buckets. For example, all purchase orders that are between 30 and 60 days outstanding would be summarized into a total amount.
Backorder report	A list of items on backorder from suppliers and vendors.
Fixed asset listings	A list of fixed assets, their original costs, and their current book values.

A list of fixed assets by original cost and book value is a simple report, but it can be enhanced by presenting information in a data visualization, such as the pie charts in **Illustration 10.12**.

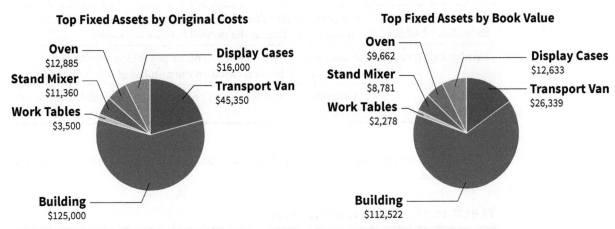

Illustration 10.12 Fixed asset data visualizations show the value of assets by original cost versus book value.

Analyzing the reported data from the fixed asset purchasing process can also provide valuable information. **Table 10.9** lists some examples of analytics that can be used to create insights from fixed assets purchasing data.

TABLE 10.9 Fixed Assets Purchasing Analytics

Analytic	Description	How It's Used
Fixed asset ratios	Calculating ratios such as the rate of return on assets and the fixed asset turnover ratio	Analyzing ratios by comparing them to prior periods for unusual activity or to external benchmarks to measure performance
Untagged assets	Analyzing a list of fixed assets with no tag numbers by location, buyer, and cost	Determining whether fraudulent activity is occurring
Fixed assets with no location	Analyzing a list of fixed assets with no location by buyer, cost, or usage	Determining whether fraudulent activity is occurring
Bidding patterns	Performing statistical analysis of bidding patterns	Detecting potential bid rigging. For example, all vendors in a group win an equal volume of business or an equal number of contracts over time

Accounts Payable

The payments process creates data such as vendor ID, check number, payment date, bank ID, amount, authorization date, and payee bank routing number and stores it in a database. This data can be used to create reports such as cash disbursement and vendor aging reports, among others (**Table 10.10**).

TABLE 10.10 Accounts Payable Reports

Report	Description
Cash disbursements journal	An accounting journal of cash disbursements that captures all payments recorded
Purchases by vendor	A summary of purchases by vendor over a specific period of time to look for unusual activity
Accounts payable	A list of outstanding accounts payable balances, which can be summarized by vendor
Accounts Payable Subsidiary Ledger	A report that identifies debit balances in the Accounts Payable Subsidiary Ledger, as the normal balance is a credit
Vendor aging report	A summary of outstanding accounts payable by vendor and separated into buckets based on the number of days outstanding
Invoices	A summary of invoices based on status (overdue, paid, and open) and aging

Table 10.11 lists a number of data analytics that can be used with accounts payable data to detect fraud.

TABLE 10.11 Accounts Payable Analytics

Analytic	Description	How It's Used
Financial ratios	Calculating ratios such as accounts payable turnover in days, accounts payable as a percentage of total assets, and cost of goods sold to average accounts payable	Analyzing these ratios by comparing them to prior periods, forecasts, budgets, and industry ratios
Approval of payments	Identifying excessive time periods between the approval for payments and initial recording in the cash disbursements journal	Identifying risk of fraud or violation of corporate policies that require approval within a specified period of time
Vendor–employee testing	Identifying vendors and employees with matches between any of the following tax ID number, address, email address, bank routing number, or phone number	Identifying potential fraudulent payments
Early payments	Identifying payments made before invoice due dates	Identifying payments to a fictitious vendor
Vendor invoice numbers	Analyzing payments made to the same vendor with little or no sequence between vendor invoice numbers	Identifying payment of fictitious invoices that are made to look like they are from legitimate vendors
Three-way match	Performing a three-way match and investigating results that do not pass	Identifying potential suspicious activity

Accounts payable is an area where ongoing transaction monitoring systems and dashboards can give management a real-time understanding of what is happening in the business processes. **Illustration 10.13** shows an example of a dashboard that provides information about accounts payable data at a glance.

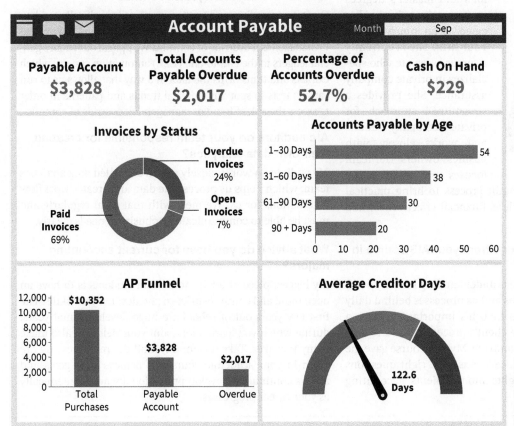

Illustration 10.13 Accounts payable data presented in a dashboard gives management quick insights into the KPIs of the business processes.

CONCEPT REVIEW QUESTIONS

1. What information does the purchase orders aging report give?

   Ans. Purchase orders aging report gives details on the number of days purchase orders have been outstanding, classified in buckets. For example, all purchase orders that are between 30 and 60 days outstanding would be summarized into a total amount.

2. What key insights can a vendor performance analytics provide?

   Ans. Vendor performance analytics identifies how long it took to receive an order, the quality of goods received, and the condition of goods received. This helps in identifying issues with vendors so purchasing can be optimized.

3. What is vendor prices analytics?

   Ans. Vendor prices analytics analyzes vendor prices that have increased above a threshold amount over a period of time. This can help detect collusive fraud by employee buyers and vendors where the buyers receive kickbacks or other rewards from the vendors.

4. What is the use of duplicate vendor data analytics?

   Ans. By analyzing vendors with the same telephone number, address, bank account, or email, the duplicate vendor data analytics helps in identifying whether a vendor is duplicated in the system due to fraud or error, potentially causing duplicate payments or payments sent to the wrong vendor.

FEATURED PROFESSIONAL | **External Auditor for Private Companies**

Photo courtesy of Holly Giang

Holly Giang, CPA

Holly, who holds bachelor's and master's degrees in accounting, began her career as an intern at a Big Four firm. She is currently a senior associate who specializes in private company assurance. She provides a streamlined approach for private company audits and works closely with business owners. Her team focuses on collaborating with clients through the audit process to bring practical insights around issues such as financial effectiveness and internal controls.

How do you use knowledge from your AIS course in your daily job?

An integral part of auditing is understanding how my audit client creates journal entries and its processes behind daily operations. In order to do that, it's important to have a good understanding of the client's processes and the type of systems in place at the company. My AIS course gave me the baseline knowledge I need to ask the right questions in order to gain better insights into my clients' accounting processes.

When auditing a client's purchasing or payments processes, what data analytics does your team use to look for fraudulent journal entries?

Our team uses firm audit software created specifically to identify journal entries that meet our fraud criteria and risk related to management override of controls. We upload our client's general ledgers to the end-to-end (E2E) automation system, which extracts and transforms the data in a way that allows us to run various tests to spot any unusual trends and patterns in order to assess the risk of fraud or management override of controls.

Are auditors on your team responsible for creating their own data analytics?

My audit team works closely with a dedicated data analytics team, which helps us process the data and creates workflow automations for us. We meet with that team regularly and must be able to communicate our business needs clearly.

What advice do you have for current accounting majors?

My biggest piece of advice to current students is to have an open mind and continue to learn and develop your skills. The first few years out of school are huge developmental years, during which you learn a lot about your field and also make many mistakes. Take advantage of all the resources you are given in your academic courses to achieve your goals and always continue to develop professionally and academically as your career progresses.

Review and Practice

Key Terms Review

accounts payable
bid rigging
capital expenditures (CAPEX)
cash disbursements journal
discrepancy report
e-procurement system
finished goods
fixed asset
Fixed Asset Subsidiary Ledger
inventory

inventory management
main vendor table
packing slip
payment voucher
payments processes
purchase order
purchase requisition
purchasing processes
raw materials
receiving report

remittance advice
source document
split purchase order
supplier
supply chain management (SCM)
vendor
vendor invoice
work in process

Learning Objectives Review

1. Describe the relationship between the inventory purchasing and payments processes, inventory management, and supply chain management.

Purchasing processes involve acquiring resources that businesses use in operations. Payments processes focus on paying for the acquired resources, either with cash at the time of purchase or on credit.

Inventory consists of:

- Raw materials: Purchased components that are used to create a product
- Work in process: Products that are in the process of being manufactured
- Finished goods: Products that are ready to be shipped to customers

Purchasing and payments processes source documents, which provide documentation of transactions, include:

- Purchase requisitions
- Purchase orders
- Receiving reports
- Checks or electronic money transfers

Vendors supply to both business-to-consumer and business-to-business sales relationships, while suppliers only enter business-to-business relationships.

The five high-level business activities of purchasing and payments processes are:

- Determine inventory that needs to be ordered (inventory control department)
- Request availability and prices (purchasing department)
- Order inventory (purchasing department)
- Receive the inventory (receiving department)
- Pay for the inventory received (accounts payable department)

Receiving employees must reconcile the received products to the purchase order and:

- Check the condition of the shipment
- Count quantities received
- Input data into the system

Accounts payable is responsible for paying vendors and suppliers when a vendor invoice is received. The initial purchase journal entry is a credit to Accounts Payable. When the invoice is paid, Accounts Payable is debited, and Cash is credited.

Inventory management oversees the flow of inventory through the life cycle of a product. Inventory management determines what raw materials need to be purchased based on customer demand forecasts from the sales processes.

The physical flow of the supply chain is linear, but the information flow of the supply chain involves a number of departments. Information travels upstream and downstream to create collaboration across departments.

❷ Summarize the purchasing process for inventory and other goods or services.

Purchase requests come from various parts of the business, based on what each department needs, and are routed to the purchasing department, where purchasing is consolidated and controlled.

Vendor selection and management involves maintaining the vendor table, ensuring that all purchases go to approved vendors, and keeping the vendor table current. Controls that address all the risks of vendor selection and management include:

- Using automated supplier portals to validate vendors and obtaining required documentation
- Maintaining documented authorized policies and procedures that establish criteria and screening for onboarding new vendors

Placing orders requires routing purchases through the purchasing department, approving purchases, and filling out and submitting purchase orders. Controls that address all the risks of purchasing orders include:

- Implementing an e-procurement system
- Implementing a paperless evaluated receipt settlement system
- Prenumbering and accounting for purchase requisitions and purchase orders

Receiving purchases consists of verifying quality and quantity, preventing physical theft, and informing the accounts payable department that payments can be issued. Controls that address all the risks of receiving purchases include:

- Segregating duties between receiving and initiating purchases
- Physically segregating the warehouse storage areas from production and shipping
- Dedicating an area to receiving in each facility
- Restricting physical access to the receiving area
- Installing cameras in the receiving area
- Controlling access to the receiving system
- Implementing an e-procurement system
- Returning receiving exceptions to the shipper with an audit trail documenting physical movement of product
- Maintaining documented and authorized policies and procedures for training receiving employees
- Implementing ongoing performance monitoring of suppliers

❸ Explain the fixed asset acquisitions process.

Fixed assets are a Balance Sheet line item called Property, Plant, and Equipment (PP&E), and costs of acquisition are capital expenditures.

The framework for fixed assets involves six stages:

1. Procurement
2. Receiving and tagging
3. Recording
4. Reconciliation
5. Depreciation
6. Disposal or transfer

Authorization limits determine which employee is allowed to authorize a purchase based on the size of the transaction.

Fixed assets are inspected and tagged upon receipt.

When a fixed asset is purchased, the accounting information system captures the journal entries that debit the asset account and credit cash, accounts payable, and/or loan payable.

The Fixed Asset Subsidiary Ledger shows the details for each fixed asset. It is reconciled to the fixed asset General Ledger accounts.

Bid rigging can occur when employees collude with a vendor or when external vendors collude with one another to ensure the winner of a contract bid.

Important controls for fixed assets include:

- Expanding the list of bidders to make it more difficult for bidders to collude in bid-rigging schemes
- Providing proactive code of conduct and fraud training for employees related to bid rigging and penalties
- Periodically checking physical fixed assets against the records
- Tagging all fixed assets with permanent tags or etching the fixed asset number into the surface of each asset

❹ Evaluate the credit payments process.

The payments process, which is also known as the cash disbursement process, involves paying for acquisitions made in the purchasing process. Accounts payable is an account that records money the business owes to its suppliers and vendors and is a liability on the Balance Sheet.

Cash disbursement journals record approvals for payments.

Bank reconciliations compare external records from the bank to the company's General Ledger to ensure consistency.

A three-way match between the purchase order, receiving report, and vendor invoice is a control performed before payments are issued to vendors.

Cash is highly susceptible to fraud. Controls that address risks related to payments include:

- Segregate responsibility for receiving goods, purchasing goods, overseeing accounts payable, disbursing payments, reconciling bank statements, and reconciling the Subsidiary Ledger to the control account
- Independently reconcile bank statements
- Maintain a traceable audit trail for all payments
- Do not allow checks to be made payable to "Cash" or "Bearer"
- Check supplier invoices for accuracy by comparing them to purchase orders
- Use only original invoices and authorized electronic invoices for payments—never duplicates
- Base payments only on purchase orders and not vendor invoices, which are used for reconciliation only

❺ Use the key data in the underlying database for reporting and insights.

Purchasing and payments processes leverage five features in the ERP system:

- Purchasing
- Shipping/Receiving
- Inventory
- Accounts Payable
- Fixed Assets

The first three of these features in the Supply Chain Management module, and the last two are Financial module features. The Purchasing and Accounts Payable features are joined by relationships between inventory and vendors in the ERD.

Raw materials purchasing reports, including these, show purchasing patterns and information:

- Products received—by time
- Products received—by vendor
- Purchase requisitions filled and open
- Purchase orders filled and open
- Purchase orders aging
- Backorder report
- Main vendor table

Raw materials analytics such as these can provide insight into improving business processes:

- Vendor performance
- Receiving reconciliation
- Vendor prices
- Vendor frequency
- Duplicate vendor data
- Vendor–employee comparison
- Vendor address
- Discounts
- Financial ratios

Fixed asset reports, including these, can show changes in a company's assets and purchases:

- Additions
- Purchases by vendor
- Purchase requisitions filled and open
- Purchase orders filled and open
- Purchase orders aging
- Backorder report
- Fixed asset listings

Fixed asset analytics, including the following, can measure performance and detect fraud:

- Fixed asset ratios
- Untagged assets
- Fixed assets with no location
- Bidding patterns

Accounts payable reports, including these, can identify outstanding accounts and suspicious activity:

- Cash disbursements journal
- Purchases by vendor
- Accounts payable

- Accounts Payable Subsidiary Ledger
- Vendor aging report
- Invoices

Accounts payable analytics, including the following, are especially useful for fraud detection:

- Financial ratios
- Approval of payments

- Vendor–employee testing
- Early payments
- Vendor invoice numbers
- Three-way match

CPA questions, as well as multiple choice, discussion, analysis and application, and Tableau questions and other resources, are available online.

Multiple Choice Questions

1. (LO 1) Which transaction would create an increase in accounts payable?

   a. Selecting vendors

   b. Entering contracts

   c. Ordering resources

   d. Receiving raw materials

2. (LO 1) In which financial statement is a line item for inventory found?

   a. Balance sheet

   b. Income statement

   c. Cash flow statement

   d. Statement of shareholder equity

3. (LO 1) Review the illustration below:

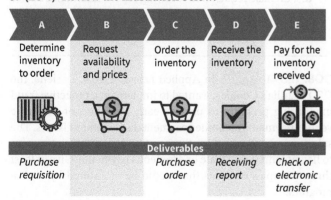

What business activity does B represent?

   a. Inventory control   **c.** Receiving

   b. Purchasing   **d.** Accounts payable

4. (LO 1) What is the main result of insufficient inventory and finished goods?

   a. Spoilage issues

   b. Inaccurate inventory records

   c. Loss of revenue and cash flow

   d. Decreased production

5. (LO 2) Which of these departments is responsible for updating the General Ledger for acquisitions and payments?

   a. General accounting

   b. Accounts payable

   c. Receiving

   d. Requesting department

6. (LO 2) What should management consider for each control activity?

   a. Time to implement

   b. Number of people to perform the activity

   c. Risk and cost versus benefit

   d. Profitability

7. (LO 2) CPA Which of the following is a violation of the segregation of duties control activity?

   a. An employee adds vendors and makes changes to a main vendor file.

   b. An employee enters purchase orders into the system and approves them.

   c. An employee matches invoices to purchase orders and receiving reports, and applies coding of account distributions.

   d. An employee receives goods from vendors and signs off on the deliveries.

8. (LO 2) CPA Reggie is the purchasing agent for a wholesale paint store, Ye Olde Paints. Reggie's cousin, Earl, owns a small paint store. Reggie arranged for paint to be delivered to Earl's stores from paint manufacturers COD, thereby allowing Earl to get the paint at a wholesale (cheaper) price, which violates a policy of Ye Olde Paints. Reggie was most likely able to violate this policy because of a failure in Ye Olde Paints' controls related to

   a. purchase orders.

   b. cash disbursements.

   c. bills of lading.

   d. inventory control.

9. **(LO 3)** How do fixed assets differ from current assets?

   a. They are held for resale.

   b. They are used for more than one year.

   c. They are nondepreciating.

   d. They include short-term holdings.

10. **(LO 3)** Numerous departments are involved in the fixed assets purchases and payments processes. Which of the following departments is involved in the fixed assets purchases and payments processes?

   a. Sales   c. Operations

   b. Receiving   d. Marketing

11. **(LO 3)** When a machine in the factory is tagged for future identification purposes, which record is updated?

   a. Accounts Payable Subsidiary Ledger

   b. Machinery Ledger

   c. Cash Ledger

   d. Fixed Asset Subsidiary Ledger

12. **(LO 4)** What is the most liquid asset on the Balance Sheet?

   a. Accounts Receivable

   b. Cash

   c. Inventory

   d. Goodwill

13. **(LO 4)** What does a cash flow statement provide to an organization?

   a. A detailed list of items purchased

   b. The impact of increases and decreases to cash

   c. The current value of all assets

   d. Net operating losses for the month

14. **(LO 4)** Which ledger accounts are impacted when payment is made to a vendor?

   a. Accounts receivable/cash

   b. Inventory/vendor payment

   c. Accounts payable/cash

   d. Current assets/vendor payment

15. **(LO 5)** The raw material purchasing reports can provide management with insight into how to improve processes. Additional raw materials purchasing analytics can be used for decision making and dashboards. Which raw material purchasing analytic calculates purchasing ratios, such as accounts payable turnover days, purchasing to sales, and purchases growth to sales growth?

   a. Vendor performance

   b. Receiving reconciliation

   c. Vendor prices

   d. Financial ratios

16. **(LO 5)** The data created and stored in the database during the _____ purchasing process includes vendor ID, name, address, telephone number, email address, tax identification number (TIN), purchase order number, receiving report number, asset description, date received, ready-for-use date, cost, tag number, and location.

   a. inventory

   b. raw materials

   c. fixed assets

   d. intangible assets

17. **(LO 5)** Prior to the payment of an invoice, the following documents are matched as a control activity:

   a. Remittance advice, invoice, receiving report

   b. Invoice, purchase requisition, receiving report

   c. Purchase order, receiving report, invoice

   d. Purchase requisition, receiving report, remittance advice

Discussion and Research Questions

DQ1. (LO 1) Explain why some of the business activities in the purchasing and payments processes do not result in accounting transactions.

DQ2. (LO 1) In the basic business model, acquisitions and payments processes outputs flow to the conversion processes. Why is acquisitions and payments a critical part of the success of conversion?

DQ3. (LO 1) Why must manufacturing companies closely monitor levels of inventory?

DQ4. (LO 2) What foundational controls should exist for purchasing, and why are they necessary?

DQ5. (LO 2) What data can be captured during the purchasing process, and how can management use it?

DQ6. (LO 3) Explain the importance of the fixed asset acquisition process. Cite examples of segregation of duties controls in this process.

DQ7. (LO 3) Fraud How can the use of bid rigging for fixed asset purchases introduce risk to an organization?

DQ8. (LO 4) Fraud In Applied Learning 10.4, Darlene, the CFO of Julia's Cookies, wanted to implement a proactive fraud monitoring program to provide early detection of duplicate vendor payments and other payment disbursement issues. The solution created was a continuous fraud monitoring program to flag potential duplicate or erroneous payments. Give at least three examples of items that would be monitored by such a program.

DQ9. (LO 4) How can an organization use the data gathered through the payments process to improve operations or mitigate error and fraud?

DQ10. (LO 4) Explain what a three-way match means in the payments processes and discuss its importance in risk mitigation. Is this control manual or automated?

DQ11. (LO 5) Identify key tables in database design for purchasing and payments processes for inventory and explain how they are related.

Application and Analysis Questions

A1. (LO 1) [Early Career] [Critical Thinking] You are an accounts payable clerk for a small manufacturer that creates designer flowerpots. You received three scenarios with specific dates. Answer the following two questions for each of the scenarios:

1. Would you enter accounting transactions?
2. If so, what accounting entries would you make?

Scenario 1:

- Copy of vendor invoice #201 for $10,000 received on February 15 showing terms of net 2/10
- Payment voucher with the vendor name, the amount due, and terms with management approval
- Copy of the remittance advice sent to the vendor showing #201 included in the payment to the vendor on February 24

Scenario 2:

- Copy of vendor invoice #4412 for $27,000 received on March 3 showing terms of net 30
- Payment voucher with the vendor name and amount due
- Copy of the remittance advice sent to the vendor showing #4412 included in the payment to the vendor made on March 28

Scenario 3:

- Copy of vendor invoice #332 for $70,000 received on April 11 showing terms of net 3/15
- Payment voucher with the vendor name, the amount due, and terms with management approval
- Copy of the remittance advice sent to the vendor showing #332 included in the payment to the vendor made on April 29

A2. (LO 1) [Fraud] For each of the following major business activities of the purchasing and payments processes, describe two controls that help mitigate the risk of error or fraud.

1. Managing inventory
2. Purchasing—vendor selection and management
3. Purchasing—placing orders
4. Receiving purchases
5. Paying for purchases

A3. (LO 2) [Critical Thinking] As an internal auditor for YoSee & Chan Company, which builds housing for low-income families, you are reviewing the controls in place to purchase inventory and supplies. Your objective is to ensure that the proper control owners are aligned to the controls. For each of the following controls, identify the correct owner(s).

1. Obtain vendor tax forms
2. Allow only authorized personnel to access ordering programs
3. Set limits on the amounts of purchases
4. Create receiving locations at physical facilities
5. Train purchasing employees
6. Prevent the owner of the vendor file from selecting vendors
7. Prevent Receiving employees from authorizing purchases
8. Install cameras in the Receiving areas
9. Train Receiving employees
10. Three-way match a purchase order, receiving report, and vendor invoice

A4. (LO 2) [Fraud] [Early Career] You are a fraud examiner performing an initial investigation involving potential fraud committed by Demitriv, the budget director at a local department store. You receive the following information during your investigation:

- Demitriv was a budget director in the men's department of the company.
- Demitriv's regular duties included overseeing the budget process for each department's cost centers and working with the company's budget officer to integrate the men's department budget within the store's overall budget.
- Demitriv often did not follow procedures, but management took no actions.
- Demitriv was delegated additional responsibilities by the head of the clothing department, including creating vendors and approving and processing vendor payments for other departments.
- The accounts payable clerks allowed departments to request that checks be returned to the requestors so the department could mail them.
- Demitriv requested that all checks from the men's department be returned to him for mailing.

Describe the opportunities for Demitriv to commit fraud and how the fraud could be covered up. What controls could the store implement to mitigate the risk of future occurrences of fraud?

A5. (LO 3) [Critical Thinking] As an accounting manager for a global organization, Rohler, you have been asked to attend new hire training and explain the fixed asset acquisition process to a group of newly hired college graduates who will be part of a rotational program. They will spend nine months in various parts of the organization, including the accounting department. Some of them will have their first rotation assignment in accounting. Choose from the key terms in the word bank to fill in the blanks in the speech you will give to the new hires.

Word Bank:	
historical cost	receiving department
theft	detail
vehicles	fixed asset sub-ledger
depreciated	IT personnel
capital expenditures	authorization limits

"Once the order is delivered, the **(1)** _____ inspects the items and accepts them into inventory, which helps mitigate the risk of **(2)** _____. Our fixed asset clerk updates the **(3)** _____, which shows the **(4)** _____ and **(5)** _____ for each fixed asset. To help mitigate the risk of fraud, we have put **(6)** _____ in place, which are set by the fixed asset cost. Fixed assets are also known as **(7)** _____ and include land, buildings, and **(8)** _____. As a fixed asset is consumed, the asset is **(9)** _____, which is allocated over the asset's life."

A6. (LO 3) `Early Career` `Critical Thinking` You are a new hire in the Accounting department of Gellin's Gelatins, a global manufacturer of snack foods. For your first assignment, you must review the risk and controls for fixed asset acquisitions to ensure that the correct alignment of risk and controls exists, and if it doesn't, you need to create an updated version of the alignment and submit it for approval. Review the table below and match each control with the risk it is intended to mitigate.

Control	Risk
Noncollusion affidavits	Fraudulent bidding
Periodically review physical assets	Fraudulent bidding or approval of nonbudgeted items
Have management review accounting transactions	Acquisitions not being conducted in adherence with policy
Perform fixed asset reconciliations	Fraudulent bidding or approval of nonbudgeted items

Initially approve fixed asset purchase	Inability to properly track the asset
Enter assets into the main fixed asset table	Fixed asset being expensed instead of being capitalized
Tag fixed assets	Fraudulent bidding
Have employees review and sign a code of conduct	Improper use of the asset
Have management review acquisition agreements	Fixed asset being expensed instead of being capitalized
Ensure policies limiting fixed assets expenditures are clearly documented and authorized	Inability to properly track the asset

A7. (LO 4–5) `Fraud` `Data Analytics` `Critical Thinking` You are a forensic accountant for a public accounting firm whose client hired your team to perform a fraud investigation of the accounts payable processes. As part of your fraud testing, you have acquired vendor data including bank accounts to which payments are sent and employee data including bank accounts for direct deposit of paychecks. You need to compare the main vendor table to the main employee table to search for potential fictitious vendors. Analyze the fields in the two tables on the next page, looking for identical or similar fields. Based on what you find, identify three red flags for accounts payable fraud. Provide the record numbers from the tables in your answer.

Main vendor table:

	A	B	C	D	E	F
1	Record	Vendor ID	Vendor Name	Address	City State	Bank Account
2	001	VICTFLO	Victor's Flowers	65875 Peach Road	Atlanta, GA	6500897531
3	002	REMMA	Remy's	1200 Sixth Street	Decatur, IL	100896213
4	003	REGIEX	Regina Extracts	48920 South Route 3	Boise, ID	152238546
5	004	JOHNDURA	J. Duram Landscaping	221 N. Ave	Chicago, IL	556321958221
6	005	BELL	Bella Telephones	4985 Oak Street	Philadelphia, PA	63258794
7	006	ACACC	Alicia's Accessories	1634 N. 98th Rd.	Orlando, FL	115668453
8	007	MCLEA	Mighty Cleaner Company	1114-A Plaza 19	Austin, TX	5221684446
9	008	JANIT	Janitorial Services R Us	869 Champion St.	Santa Fe, NM	112255348
10	009	ALPACA1	Alpaca Services	45901 Route 15	Boise, ID	5516848
11	010	REFUNI	Referee Universal	10091 Highland Drive	Birmingham, AL	5551556489
12	011	CHIKFAR	Idaho Chicken Farm	1679 N. 11th St.	Boise, ID	1008961555
13	012	BLUCLOWN	Blue Clown Events	1000 Pittsburgh Street	Philadelphia, PA	1358168515
14	013	MASSEFF	Mass Effect Visual Arts	78 East Atlanta Drive	Lafeyette, LA	188886
15	014	ATLASS	Atlass Software Services	11202 Routweiller Court	Chicago, IL	156484651
16	015	RENODEMO	Renovations and Demolition	46 Suite B Boston Avenue	Denver, CO	599135515
17	016	DELAUTH	Delaware Pest Authority	881 Ranchero Blvd	Savannah, GA	24406060600
18	017	JOEJOE	Joe's Joe Coffee Catering	1200 Coffee Court	Lexington, KY	20020672132
19	018	LUISAIR	Luis Air and Heating	908 Plant St.	Denver, CO	1000004666
20	019	PUTPUT	Computer Computer	5209 Long Ridge Circle	Denver, CO	6960005464
21	020	RELATIV	Relativity Media	0291 Ledge Cliff Dr.	Orlando, FL	321500054866
22	021	MILKNIF	Milly's Knife Polishing	39201-B Complexity Circle	Hartford, CT	4486483773
23	022	SERVCO	Serve Co. Disaster Cleaning	2 Meriam Way	Evansville, IL	45341345354
24	023	BRASSPOL	Brass Polishing - Commercial Services	29 Suite C Oxford Street	New Orleans, LA	453453543453
25	024	FLUSHIT	FLUSH-IT Toilet Installation	9087 Avenue C	Chicago, IL	1155283
26	025	MODE	Modem's Monitors and More	1 Tech Drive	Philadelphia, PA	3438786155

Main employee table:

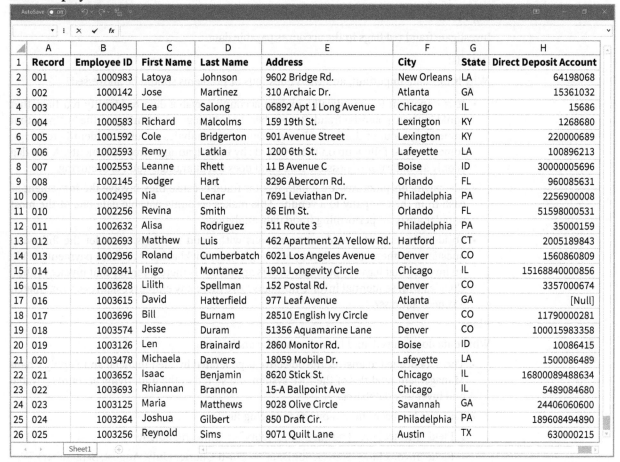

Record	Employee ID	First Name	Last Name	Address	City	State	Direct Deposit Account
001	1000983	Latoya	Johnson	9602 Bridge Rd.	New Orleans	LA	64198068
002	1000142	Jose	Martinez	310 Archaic Dr.	Atlanta	GA	15361032
003	1000495	Lea	Salong	06892 Apt 1 Long Avenue	Chicago	IL	15686
004	1000583	Richard	Malcolms	159 19th St.	Lexington	KY	1268680
005	1001592	Cole	Bridgerton	901 Avenue Street	Lexington	KY	220000689
006	1002593	Remy	Latkia	1200 6th St.	Lafeyette	LA	100896213
007	1002553	Leanne	Rhett	11 B Avenue C	Boise	ID	30000005696
008	1002145	Rodger	Hart	8296 Abercorn Rd.	Orlando	FL	960085631
009	1002495	Nia	Lenar	7691 Leviathan Dr.	Philadelphia	PA	2256900008
010	1002256	Revina	Smith	86 Elm St.	Orlando	FL	51598000531
011	1002632	Alisa	Rodriguez	511 Route 3	Philadelphia	PA	35000159
012	1002693	Matthew	Luis	462 Apartment 2A Yellow Rd.	Hartford	CT	2005189843
013	1002956	Roland	Cumberbatch	6021 Los Angeles Avenue	Denver	CO	1560860809
014	1002841	Inigo	Montanez	1901 Longevity Circle	Chicago	IL	15168840000856
015	1003628	Lilith	Spellman	152 Postal Rd.	Denver	CO	3357000674
016	1003615	David	Hatterfield	977 Leaf Avenue	Atlanta	GA	[Null]
017	1003696	Bill	Burnam	28510 English Ivy Circle	Denver	CO	11790000281
018	1003574	Jesse	Duram	51356 Aquamarine Lane	Denver	CO	100015983358
019	1003126	Len	Brainaird	2860 Monitor Rd.	Boise	ID	10086415
020	1003478	Michaela	Danvers	18059 Mobile Dr.	Lafeyette	LA	1500086489
021	1003652	Isaac	Benjamin	8620 Stick St.	Chicago	IL	16800089488634
022	1003693	Rhiannan	Brannon	15-A Ballpoint Ave	Chicago	IL	5489084680
023	1003125	Maria	Matthews	9028 Olive Circle	Savannah	GA	24406060600
024	1003264	Joshua	Gilbert	850 Draft Cir.	Philadelphia	PA	189608494890
025	1003256	Reynold	Sims	9071 Quilt Lane	Austin	TX	630000215

A8. (LO 1–5) [Fraud] Access and download the Association of Certified Fraud Examiners (ACFE) 2020 *Report to the Nations* from acfepublic.s3-us-west-2.amazonaws.com/2020-Report-to-the-Nations.pdf; if a more recent version is available, download it instead.

1. Identify a fraud case from a reputable news source such as the *Wall Street Journal*, the *New York Times*, your local news, or the ACFE website (www.acfe.org). Explain how the fraud case you chose relates to acquisitions and/or payments of inventory, supplies, fixed assets, or other resources that the business needs.

2. Describe the fraud and explain why it is workplace fraud. If the information is available, identify how it was detected. For the type of fraud you found, find information about that type of fraud in the ACFE report, such as the prevalence of that type. Record the page numbers of the report on which you found that information.

3. Explain how the risk of this type of fraud could have been mitigated by the victim organization.

Tableau Case: Accounts Payable Red Flags at Julia's Cookies

What You Need

Download Tableau to your computer. You can access www.tableau.com/academic/students to download your free Tableau license for the year, or you can download it from your university's software offerings.

Download the following file from the book's product page on www.wiley.com:

Chapter 10 Raw Data.xlsx

Case Overview

Big Picture:

Investigate fraud red flags in the accounts payable data.

Details:

Why is this data important, and what questions or problems should be addressed?

- It is important to periodically analyze accounts payable data to identify red flags that could indicate potential fraud. Remember that red flags are warnings to the business that something is out of the normal range. Once data analytics are used to identify red flags, someone must follow up on these records by investigating source documents. A red flag is only an indicator of possible fraud and does not guarantee fraud is occurring.

- The payments processes are a high risk for fraud because they involve the movement of cash from the company to a vendor. This makes accounts payable data one of the most popular areas for performing fraud data analytics.

- To identify accounts payable transactions with fraud red flags, consider the following questions: Is there an employee receiving vendor kickbacks? Are there payments made on invoices that have no purchase orders approved? Is there a vendor that invoices Julia's Cookies with sequential invoice numbers? Are there any employee addresses that match a vendor address?

Plan:

What data do you need, and how should it be analyzed?

- The data needed to answer the objective is generated by the Financial and Supply Chain Management modules of the ERP system and stored in the underlying accounts payable and inventory databases.

- The data has been filtered on the following fields:
  - Field "InvoiceLine_TransactionCategory" = "Raw Ingredients"
  - Field "InvoiceLine_TransactionDate" = Third Quarter (July, August, September)

Now it's your turn to evaluate, analyze, and communicate the results!

To answer the following questions, connect the tables using their ID fields (Hint: ApproverID = Employee_ID):

Questions

1. In July, payments were made the most number of times for which ingredient?
2. How many payments were made to Spice World in Q3?
3. A red flag that indicates possible fraudulent vendor kickbacks is a single employee approving all the payments to a particular vendor. Identify this vendor in the data set.
4. For the vendor you identified in question 3, identify the employee who approves all of this vendor's payments.
5. Another red flag for potential fraud is payments being approved for purchases that do not have associated purchase orders. Which employee approved payments that do not have associated purchase orders?
6. Which vendor(s) received the potentially fraudulent payments identified in question 5?

7. A vendor invoicing the company with invoices that have sequential numbers may indicate that the vendor has no other customers. This is a red flag for fraud, potentially signaling the existence of a shell company. Identify the vendor(s) that used sequential invoice numbers. (Hint: Split the field "Invoice ID" so that Split 2 indicates the vendor invoice sequence.)

8. A vendor submitting duplicate invoices for the same purchase order is another red flag indicating potential fraud. While submitting duplicate invoices may be done in error, vendors may do this intentionally to receive additional, unearned payments from Julia's Cookies. Which Julia's Cookies vendor submitted duplicate invoices?

Take it to the next level!

To solve these two problems, connect the HR_Employee to the AP_Vendor table on the "address" field:

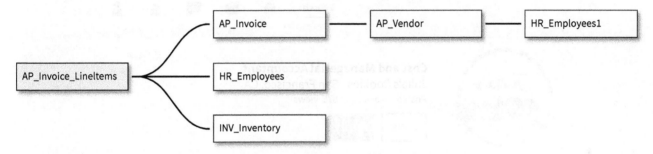

9. A vendor with the same address as an employee is a fraud red flag that indicates a possible shell company has been created by the employee. How many vendors have the same address as an employee? (Hint: Use the employee address from the HR_Employees 1 table.)

10. Which vendors have the same address as an employee? (Hint: Use the employee address from the HR_Employees 1 table.)

CHAPTER 11
Conversion Processes

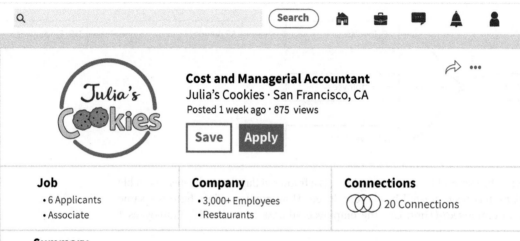

Summary

Julia's Cookies is seeking an accountant to join the managerial accounting team that oversees manufacturing processes, price calculations, and reporting. This position has a flexible salary point and is open to entry-level candidates ranging from recent college graduates to candidates with up to five years' experience.

Responsibilities

- Review cost variances for all products manufactured onsite
- Develop variable and fixed splits, price calculations, and activities revaluations
- Maintain existing Tableau dashboard of departmental KPIs and present insights to leadership
- Work closely with other areas of the business and corporate functions (HR, Corporate Accounting and Finance, Financial Planning and Analysis, Legal) to ensure that all expenses are properly accrued each month end and all issues are resolved in a timely manner
- Develop monthly forecast of standard operating costs for the remaining year
- Use data analytics tools and SAP reporting to analyze and provide meaningful commentary around variances to budget, forecast, and prior-year monthly costs
- Participate in internal/external audits at factory sites, explaining systems and processes and providing auditors with guidance regarding controls
- Maintain pertinent documentation of internal controls within factories

Requirements

Preferred Education: Bachelor's degree or higher in accounting, finance, or related field

Preferred Knowledge and Skills

The ideal candidate will demonstrate basic knowledge of cost accounting, month-end closing, and journal entries. Priority will be given to candidates who demonstrate:

- Exposure to or experience with SAP ERP systems
- Understanding of data analytics tools (Tableau experience a plus)
- Analytical and organization skills

Salary: $65,000–115,000

CHAPTER PREVIEW   Whether creating a product or offering a service, the process of combining resources and converting them into something that will appeal to customers or clients is the core of every business. It's easy to understand how this works with a manufactured product. Resources like raw materials and labor are combined and converted into a product that can be purchased and used. Not surprisingly, the process is more difficult to visualize for less tangible products like services. For example, external auditors don't need raw materials to provide a service to an organization, but resources like employees and computer technology are combined to provide the specific service of an external audit.

In earlier chapters, you learned how businesses acquire important resources like employees, inventory, and fixed assets. In this chapter, we explain how these resources are converted into a product or service. In particular, we look at:

- The relationship between production, inventory, and supply chain management
- The production business process
- The impact of digital manufacturing trends on systems
- How to turn data captured by the AIS into actionable insights

Conversion processes are crucial to how businesses achieve their strategic goals, so it's no surprise that career opportunities related to conversion are numerous and diverse. Accounting professionals can become managerial and cost accountants who specialize in recording, analyzing, and reporting costs associated with the conversion processes—like the cost and managerial accountant position at Julia's Cookies. Or they can become auditors and financial accountants who understand conversion processes as they relate to a company's use of resources and generation of revenue. In fact, every part of a company is connected to conversion processes, so familiarity with these processes is important regardless of your career path in professional accounting. ■

Chapter Roadmap

LEARNING OBJECTIVES	TOPICS	JULIA'S COOKIES APPLIED LEARNING
11.1 Describe the relationship between conversion processes, inventory, and supply chain management.	• Conversion Processes • Managing Inventory and Product Life Cycle	Production: Quality Management
11.2 Explain how the cost accounting system records conversion expenditures that impact the financial statements.	• Traditional Cost Accounting • Activity-Based Cost Accounting • Product Costing Internal Controls	Product Costs: ERP System Implementation
11.3 Identify opportunities and challenges in digital manufacturing.	• Digital Manufacturing Environment • Opportunities and Challenges • Digital Manufacturing Use Cases	Digital Manufacturing: Barriers to Automation
11.4 Explain how data generated by the AIS is converted to reporting and analytics.	• Database Design • Reporting and Insights	ERP System Modules: Production Authorization

CPA You will find the CPA tag throughout the chapter to call out any important topics you may see on the CPA exam.

11.1 What Is the Relationship Between Conversion Processes, Inventory, and Supply Chain Management?

Learning Objective ❶
Describe the relationship between conversion processes, inventory, and supply chain management.

In the basic business model, conversion processes form the heart of the business (**Illustration 11.1**). Inputs, which are resources, are pumped in; outputs, like products and services, are pumped out.

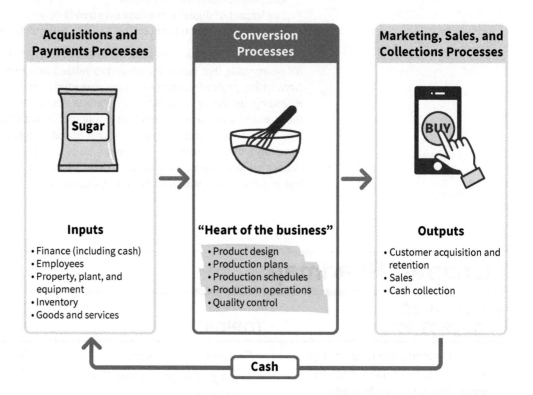

Acquisitions and Payments Processes	Conversion Processes	Marketing, Sales, and Collections Processes
Inputs	**"Heart of the business"**	**Outputs**
• Finance (including cash) • Employees • Property, plant, and equipment • Inventory • Goods and services	• Product design • Production plans • Production schedules • Production operations • Quality control	• Customer acquisition and retention • Sales • Cash collection

Cash

Illustration 11.1 Converting resources is at the center of the basic business model.

Conversion processes are operating business activities that combine resources (inputs) and convert them into products or services (outputs) that appeal to customers, whether they are clients, patients, or even students. The resources used differ depending on the type of business.

Some businesses—such as public accounting firms, law firms, and barber shops—convert their human resources into services for clients. In this course, we focus on production-based conversion, which involves converting physical raw materials into a tangible product that is sold to customers, such as Julia's Cookies' menu items.

Whether it's cookies or smart phones, producing products to sell is the primary objective of a manufacturing business. Doing this successfully depends on an efficient and effective manufacturing conversion process.

Manufacturing efficiency is a balance between three goals:

- Controlling the costs of resources
- The rate of production
- The quality of finished goods

CPA For example, manufacturing efficiency is increased when more output is produced from the same amount of resource inputs, like raw materials, labor, and overhead costs, without sacrificing product quality. The goal is to produce the same product at the lowest average total cost.

Overall equipment effectiveness (OEE) is a key performance indicator (KPI) that measures how well production resources are used by identifying the percentage of productive manufacturing time. An OEE of 100% means all products produced are acceptable (100% quality), produced at the fastest speeds (100% performance), and manufactured without interruptions in production (100% availability). Management uses OEE to identify process and performance improvement potential.

Conversion Processes

Conversion consists of five high-level business processes that connect to another key area of the business: inventory and supply chain management (**Illustration 11.2**). In the remainder of this section, we explore these five key conversion processes and their relationship to inventory and supply chain management.

Manufacturing Conversion Processes

Product Development	Production Planning	Production Scheduling	Manufacturing Operations	Quality Management
Transform product ideas into product specifications	Develop a long-term outlook of production activities	Schedule production	Manufacture the products	Test products for quality

Source Documents

Bill of materials, operations list	*Production plan*	*Production schedule, orders, material requisitions, move tickets*	*Production reports, job time tickets*	*Testing reports*

Inventory and Supply Chain Management
Source raw materials, oversee inventory, distribute to customers

Inventory and supply chain management has a two-way relationship with conversion processes. The production plan is an input that drives the raw materials the supply chain will procure, and the supply chain provides the raw materials needed in production.

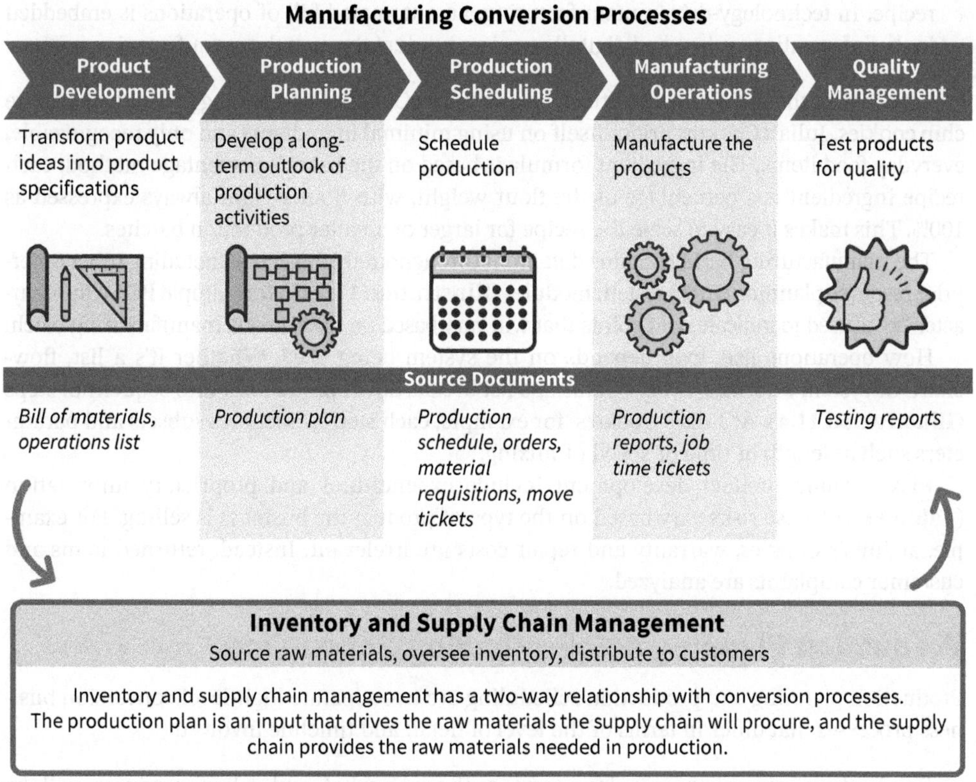

Illustration 11.2 The five business processes involved in conversion are both inputs and outputs of the inventory and supply chain management processes.

Product Development

Product development is the research and testing of new products or potential changes to existing products. At Julia's Cookies, the Product Development team creates new products, such as the seasonal menu item Exam-Time Cookie. Product Development conceptualizes and tests recipes for these new cookies.

Two source documents are essential to the control of product development:

- The **bill of materials (BOM)** is a document that specifies the components of a product, including descriptions and quantities of required raw materials and parts. The BOM at Julia's Cookies is the list of ingredients in a recipe. The **engineering BOM** is created at the time of product design, and a **manufacturing BOM** is created for every production run of the product.

- The **operations list**, also called the **bill of operations (BOO)**, provides a sequence of production events. This list, which the Engineering department prepares, includes the locations of raw ingredients (inputs), required production time, equipment needed, and destination of work-in-process and finished goods (outputs). At Julia's Cookies, the operations list is the recipe. In technology-driven manufacturing, an automated bill of operations is embedded in the information system and digitally tracks a product through the manufacturing process.

Let's look at the BOM and operations list for Julia's Cookies' best-selling product, chocolate chip cookies. Julia's Cookies prides itself on using minimal ingredients and only recognizable, everyday food items. The ingredient formula is based on the baker's percentage method: each recipe ingredient is a percentage of the flour weight, with flour weight always expressed as 100%. This makes it easy to scale the recipe for larger or smaller production batches.

The manufacturing BOM contains data from throughout the business, including other enterprise resource planning (ERP) system modules (**Illustration 11.3**). In this sample BOM, the character "x" is used to indicate data points that will vary based on the size of a manufacturing batch.

How operations lists look depends on the system being used. Whether it's a list, flowchart, or system interface, every operations list breaks down production into sequential steps (**Illustration 11.4**). At Julia's Cookies, for example, each step ID includes subsets and parameters such as length of time or speed of mixing.

Risks around product development include expenditures and proprietary information (**Table 11.1**). These risks vary based on the type of product the business is selling. For example, at Julia's Cookies, warranty and repair costs are irrelevant. Instead, returned items and customer complaints are analyzed.

Production Planning and Production Scheduling

Production planning and production scheduling are two separate high-level conversion business processes that differ in terms of the level of detail and timeline involved:

- **Production planning** is a long-term outline of what and when products will be manufactured.

- **Production scheduling** is the short-term allocation of plant machinery and resources to the manufacturing of products.

We discuss these two processes together because of their close relationship and similarities in their risks and controls. Once a product has been developed, the planning and scheduling business processes work together to move it from idea to reality.

Production planning balances product demand with resources over the long term. A production plan, which is a source document, can cover six months, one year, or longer. The one-year production plan at Julia's Cookies breaks each plan element into monthly requirements (**Table 11.2**).

After establishing the big picture with production planning, the next step is to create a detailed production schedule. Production scheduling bridges production planning and production execution and creates important source documents:

- In a **master production schedule (MPS)**, every production operation is scheduled at a specific calendar time, resources and workers are assigned, and steps are outlined to utilize

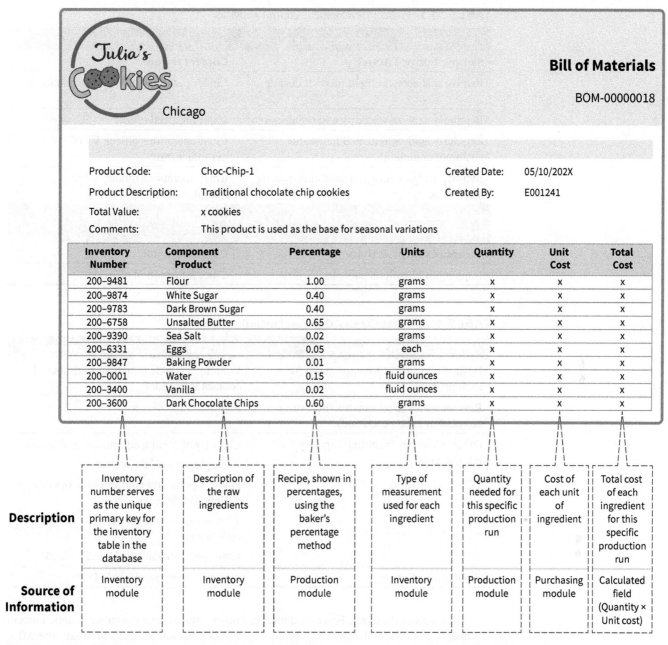

Julia's Cookies — Chicago

Bill of Materials

BOM-00000018

Product Code:	Choc-Chip-1	Created Date:	05/10/202X
Product Description:	Traditional chocolate chip cookies	Created By:	E001241
Total Value:	x cookies		
Comments:	This product is used as the base for seasonal variations		

Inventory Number	Component Product	Percentage	Units	Quantity	Unit Cost	Total Cost
200–9481	Flour	1.00	grams	x	x	x
200–9874	White Sugar	0.40	grams	x	x	x
200–9783	Dark Brown Sugar	0.40	grams	x	x	x
200–6758	Unsalted Butter	0.65	grams	x	x	x
200–9390	Sea Salt	0.02	grams	x	x	x
200–6331	Eggs	0.05	each	x	x	x
200–9847	Baking Powder	0.01	grams	x	x	x
200–0001	Water	0.15	fluid ounces	x	x	x
200–3400	Vanilla	0.02	fluid ounces	x	x	x
200–3600	Dark Chocolate Chips	0.60	grams	x	x	x

	Description	Source of Information
	Inventory number serves as the unique primary key for the inventory table in the database	Inventory module
	Description of the raw ingredients	Inventory module
	Recipe, shown in percentages, using the baker's percentage method	Production module
	Type of measurement used for each ingredient	Inventory module
	Quantity needed for this specific production run	Production module
	Cost of each unit of ingredient	Purchasing module
	Total cost of each ingredient for this specific production run	Calculated field (Quantity × Unit cost)

Illustration 11.3 The bill of materials for a specific product contains information from multiple ERP system modules.

⚙ ○ Help ✕

Step ID	Event Name	Description	Equipment
1010	Ingredients preparation	Prepare ingredients in correct premix proportions	Measuring
1020	Mixing A	Cream sugars, butter, salt, eggs, and baking powder	Mixing 1
1030	Mixing B	Mix water and vanilla	Mixing 2
1040	Mixing C	Combine Mixing A and Mixing B	Mixing 3
1050	Mixing D	Combine flour and chocolate chips	Mixing 4
1060	Mixing E	Combine Mixing C and Mixing D	Mixing 5
1070	Baking preparation	Transfer cookie dough for cutting and shaping	None
1080	Cutting and shaping	Cut and shape dough into formed cookies	Cutter 1
1090	Freezing	Freeze formed cookies	Freezer 1
1100	Packaging	Package for shipment to stores	Packer 1

Illustration 11.4 Although an operations list may look different in different systems, it is always a list of detailed steps and parameters for production.

TABLE 11.1 Product Development Control Activities

Risk Statement: Poorly designed products may result in excessive expenditures.	
Sample Control Activity	**Control Owner**
Involve cost accounting in product design	Chief operations officer, chief financial officer
Regularly analyze warranty and repair costs	Chief financial officer
Regularly analyze returned items and customer complaints	Chief operations officer, VP of manufacturing
Identify design issues and solutions as early as possible	Chief operations officer, VP of manufacturing
Risk Statement: Unauthorized access to proprietary information may result in loss of competitive advantage.	
Sample Control Activity	**Control Owner**
Implement IT general controls	Chief information officer

TABLE 11.2 Julia's Cookies' One-Year Production Plan

Production Plan Element	Julia's Cookies Example (Monthly)
Desired quantity of finished goods for each product	Volume of cookie dough and number of cookies to produce
Raw materials requirements (inventory on hand or to be purchased)	Required ingredients
Other resources, including capacity and related costs	Capacity of mixing equipment and ovens
	Packaging materials needed
	Space, layout, and equipment to operate without bottlenecks
	Workers and skills needed to operate equipment
	Employee shifts available and needed
Capital investments	Any new equipment needed

all resources effectively. Forecast demand, known outstanding customer orders, current inventory levels, and marketing promotion predictions are all used to create the MPS, which shows the quantity of each product to be produced on a weekly basis. At Julia's Cookies, forecasted demand is higher than usual the second week in February due to Valentine's Day promotions, resulting in increased production on the MPS for that week (**Illustration 11.5**). In turn, the MPS feeds into inventory and supply chain management by specifying which required materials must be procured and when. We explore this relationship further in the next section.

- The MPS determines what will be included in a **materials requisition request**, which is a document that authorizes the movement of raw materials from inventory into production.

- Some businesses also create **move tickets** (or routing tickets), such as a barcode tag, to authorize and track movements of a single manufacturing job from one location in production to another.

The control activities for these essential processes ensure that a company cost-effectively produces the right product at the right time (**Table 11.3**). Forecasting is an especially important control activity. The business must understand upcoming product requirements to properly facilitate manufacturing; otherwise, it may be unable to meet customer demand and could lose business to its competitors.

Product:	Variation:	202X								TOTAL
		February				March				
		Week								
		1	2	3	4	1	2	3	4	
In-Store Cookies	Chocolate Chip	200	300	100	200	200	200	200	200	1,600
	Peanut Butter	150	250	100	150	150	150	150	150	1,250
	Snickerdoodle	150	250	100	150	150	150	150	150	1,250
	Oatmeal Raisin	125	250	75	125	125	125	125	125	1,075
	M&M	100	200	75	100	100	100	100	100	875
	Sugar	125	250	100	125	125	125	125	125	1,100
Prepackaged Frozen Dough	Chocolate Chip	600	500	300	500	300	300	300	300	3,100
	Peanut Butter	360	360	150	360	150	150	150	150	1,830
	Snickerdoodle	360	360	150	360	150	150	150	150	1,830
	TOTAL	2,170	2,720	1,150	2,070	1,450	1,450	1,450	1,450	13,910

Illustration 11.5   Forecast demand, known orders, and current inventory levels combine to determine the necessary production volume of each product in a master production schedule (MPS).

TABLE 11.3 Production Planning and Scheduling Control Activities

Risk Statement: Failure to use resources efficiently and effectively may result in excessive costs or inability to meet customer product demands.	
Sample Control Activity	**Control Owner**
Document and authorize policies and procedures for production operations	Chief operations officer
Define roles and responsibilities for all functions	Chief operations officer
Use a formal review process to identify production improvement opportunities	Chief operations officer
Ensure that sales forecasting, product profitability analysis, and inventory management are integrated into management decision making about production	Chief executive officer/C-suite leadership
Risk Statement: Unauthorized production or underutilization of resources may result in a negative impact on the cost of goods produced and sold or inability to meet customer product demands.	
Sample Control Activity	**Control Owner**
Use formal sales and production planning processes, including approving sales and production forecasts	Chief executive officer/C-suite leadership
Manufacture products according to authorized BOM, BOO, and MPS documents	Chief operations officer
Use formal policies and procedures for reviewing, changing, and authorizing existing BOM, BOO, and MPS documents	Chief operations officer

Manufacturing Operations

The **manufacturing operations** process focuses on creating finished goods. Like the other conversion processes, these operations also require source documents:

- **Job time tickets** capture the cost of labor to manufacture the product.
- **Production reports** summarize the total manufacturing cost of a product, which is important in recording the cost of inventory and cost of goods sold in the general ledger.

TABLE 11.4 Manufacturing Operations Control Activities

Risk Statement: Theft or damage of fixed assets may result in disruptions in manufacturing operations, financial losses, or inability to meet customer demands.	
Sample Control Activity	**Control Owner**
Restrict physical access to fixed assets	Chief operations officer/plant manager
Maintain fixed asset records with sufficient detail	Controller
Conduct regularly scheduled physical inventory counts of fixed assets	Chief financial officer
Periodically reconcile the fixed assets subsidiary ledger to control accounts in the general ledger	Chief financial officer
Ensure that insurance coverage is adequate	Chief financial officer
Risk Statement: Inadequate maintenance of fixed assets may result in breakdowns and disruption of operations.	
Sample Control Activity	**Control Owner**
Implement a well-documented maintenance program	Plant manager
Risk Statement: Suboptimal performance by manufacturing employees may result in excessive costs or poor-quality products.	
Sample Control Activity	**Control Owner**
Automate manufacturing operations	Automated system controls
Regularly conduct performance evaluations	HR director/plant manager
Implement robust employee training and safety programs	HR director/plant manager
Risk Statement: A disruptive event may result in interruption of production operations and inability to meet customer demands.	
Sample Control Activity	**Control Owner**
Ensure that the disaster recovery plan includes considerations for production downtime	Disaster recovery manager
Implement physical safeguards such as fire alarms and sprinklers	Chief operations officer/plant manager
Ensure that insurance coverage is adequate	Chief financial officer

These source documents are sent back to production planning and scheduling and used to identify opportunities for improvement.

The manufacturing operations process varies across companies and industries. The particular process used in a company affects cost accounting information and the types of controls the company must implement (**Table 11.4**).

Companies also must consider disruptive events that may impact business operations. A disaster recovery plan, which specifies what the business will do if a disruptive event like a storm or fire occurs, should include plans for power backups, and physical controls in the plant must include detective safety devices such as fire alarms.

Quality Management

Throughout a product's manufacturing life cycle, businesses must make sure the product does what it's intended to do and meets internal and external requirements.

The **quality management** process involves testing products to ensure that they meet regulatory and corporate specifications. At Julia's Cookies, quality management is embedded in the manufacturing conversion processes to ensure food safety through continual chemical and microbiological testing of production line samples. Even visual pre-delivery cookie inspection is important since most people prefer cookies that look appealing!

Poor-quality products may result in bad reviews on social media or even safety hazards and lawsuits. In Applied Learning 11.1, help the director of operations at Julia's Cookies manage quality risks around the raw materials the company uses to make cookies.

Julia's Cookies   Applied Learning 11.1

Production: Quality Management

Yalmaz, the chief operations officer, is startled by a news headline he sees one morning while drinking coffee:

Nestlé is recalling some cookie dough products due to possible rubber contamination[1]

Julia's Cookies sells ready-to-bake cookie dough to grocery stores for consumers in addition to the cookie dough used in its stores to bake hot cookies for delivery. Since Yalmaz's responsibilities include product quality, this headline gets his attention.

Yalmaz learns that the Nestlé recall happened after consumers reported finding rubber bits in cookies. The recall was nationwide and included 26 different types of products that were distributed in the continental United States and Puerto Rico. The source of the rubber bits wasn't clear, but nobody who ate the products required medical attention.

Next, Yalmaz learns that a similar incident occurred a decade earlier, when the company recalled its dough products because of *E. coli* contamination. In that case, 72 people in 30 states got sick, and nearly half of them were hospitalized. The Food and Drug Administration found a contaminated sample at the company's plant in Virginia, and it was traced to flour used in the products.

Are Yalmaz's concerns about something similar happening at Julia's Cookies justified? Why? What can he do to reduce the risk of product contamination?

SOLUTION

Yalmaz's concerns are justified. If it can happen to Nestlé (twice), it can happen to Julia's Cookies!

There are many reasons to be concerned:

- Customers getting sick and requiring hospitalization is not a good scenario for any company, from a humanitarian perspective.
- The threat to a company's reputation and a decline in consumer trust would adversely affect sales and profits.
- Potential lawsuits can be costly.
- Yalmaz could lose his job and professional reputation.

Yalmaz should prioritize food safety and invest in quality assurance testing to meet internal quality requirements, as well as all regulatory requirements for manufacturing equipment and product and ingredient quality.

As you can tell, product safety is crucial—especially in the food industry, where contamination can be biological (bacteria like *Listeria* or *E. coli*), physical (rubber, glass, or metal), or chemical (equipment grease or cleaning products). Companies implement robust controls to ensure product safety (**Table 11.5**).

TABLE 11.5 Quality Management Control Activities

Risk Statement: Defective or contaminated products may result in reputational damage, financial losses, or lawsuits.	
Sample Control Activity	**Control Owner**
Ensure policies and procedures for product safety and quality are clearly documented, authorized, and enforced	Chief operations officer
Adhere to industry regulations and safety standards	Chief executive officer/ chief compliance officer
Define roles and responsibilities for inspectors and product handling	Chief operations officer
Embed a quality control program	Chief operations officer

Production Process Flowchart

The different conversion processes work together to ensure a business meets its goal: providing a quality product to its customers. Using a process flowchart is the best way to show how some of these manufacturing conversion processes are connected. **Illustration 11.6** shows

---

[1]www.cnn.com/2019/11/01/health/nestle-cookie-dough-recall-trnd/index.html

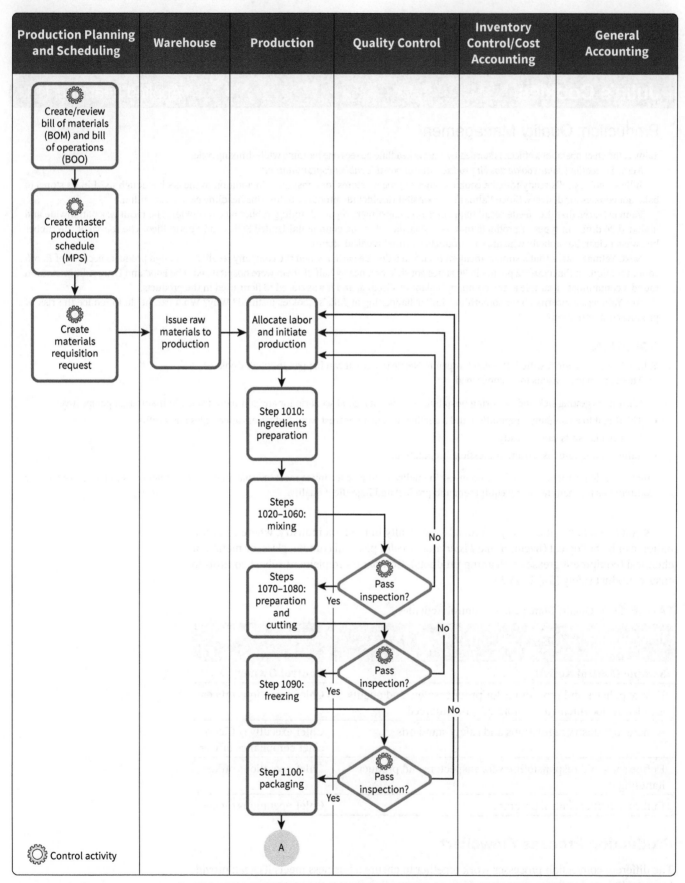

Illustration 11.6 The connections between manufacturing conversion business processes are easy to identify in a process flowchart. (*Continued*)

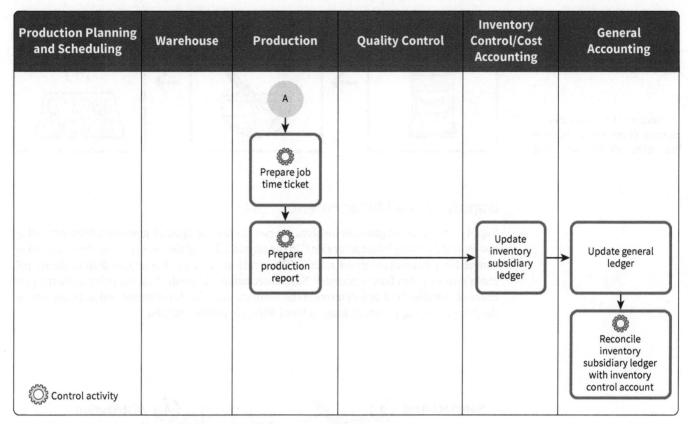

Illustration 11.6 (*Continued*)

a sample of some of the conversion processes we've discussed and how different business departments work together to achieve production goals.

Managing Inventory and Product Life Cycle

Here we discuss inventory management and supply chain management in relation to conversion processes, but these business processes also work with purchasing and sales processes. You have learned that purchasing processes focus on acquiring raw materials needed for conversion processes to create a finished good. The finished good is sold to customers, and forecasts of customer demand are used to create the production plan. The production plan tells the purchasing department what raw materials to purchase. Inventory management and supply chain management ensure that a business has the necessary materials, at the right time, to create products.

Inventory Management

Inventory management involves overseeing the processes of ordering, storing, and using a business's inventory. Inventory management is an essential business process because it coordinates communication between purchasing and acquisitions processes, conversion processes, and sales processes. Here we focus on inventory management from the production perspective, with the assumption that purchasing is adequately supporting production scheduling.

CPA You may recall from financial and cost accounting classes that manufacturing inventory is composed of raw materials (input) that flow through to production and become work-in-process and finally become finished goods (output) (**Illustration 11.7**).

Julia's Cookies' Inventory Control department ensures that enough raw materials (ingredients), packaging materials, and finished premixed dough are available at the company's 10 regional factories. The quantities must meet production demands and create sufficient finished goods to meet customer demand.

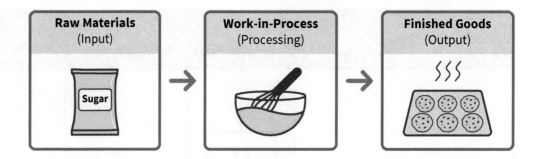

| Raw Materials (Input) | Work-in-Process (Processing) | Finished Goods (Output) |

Illustration 11.7 Inventory consists of raw materials, work-in-process, and finished goods.

Supply Chain Management

Supply chain management involves overseeing the life cycle of a product from procuring raw materials through customer sales. In the physical flow of the supply chain, manufacturing conversion processes are in the middle (**Illustration 11.8**), but the relationship to the supply chain's information flow is complex. Sales forecasting and production planning drive the purchase of raw materials and determine the products available for customer sales. In this sense, the parts of the supply chain management life cycle are interrelated.

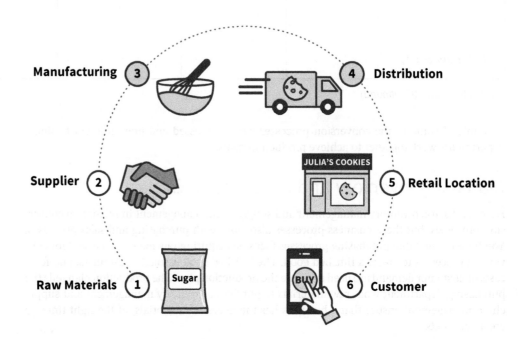

Illustration 11.8 Conversion processes include distribution and are in the middle of the supply chain.

Product Life Cycle Internal Controls

Controls for inventory management focus on providing manufacturing production processes with necessary raw materials to meet customer demand (**Table 11.6**). An **e-procurement system** is an electronic procurement system that integrates into an ERP system to automate the purchase of raw materials based on demand. It creates purchase requisitions and purchase orders using an electronic authorization process to meet predicted production needs. At Julia's Cookies, the e-procurement system automatically sends a purchase order to Flowers & Flours when flour inventory is below the predicted level needed for the next month's production schedule. Internal controls for this e-procurement system include purchase amount limitations, regular review of purchases made, and approvals for purchases above a dollar amount threshold.

Inventory should also be safeguarded from theft and damage. If the product is a perishable item, like Julia's Cookies' menu items, inventory control also considers risks such as power outages and other business disruptions.

TABLE 11.6 Inventory and Supply Chain Management Control Activities

Risk Statement: Insufficient on-hand raw materials may result in inability to meet production needs.	
Sample Control Activity	**Control Owner**
Implement an integrated e-procurement system	Automated system control
Risk Statement: Poor-quality raw materials, damage to finished goods, and improper storage or handling that creates inferior or contaminated products may result in customer dissatisfaction or regulatory violations.	
Sample Control Activity	**Control Owner**
Hold employee training focused on safeguarding quality, checking expiration dates, and preventing damage to inventory	Chief operations officer/HR director
Physically secure the warehouse to prohibit unauthorized access	Chief operations officer/ warehouse manager
Create a business continuity plan that includes a backup power system for critical storage equipment (refrigerators and freezers)	Chief operations officer/ enterprise risk management
Conduct product safety testing on raw materials	Chief operations officer
Risk Statement: Theft or destruction of inventory may result in inability to meet the production schedule and customer demand.	
Sample Control Activity	**Control Owner**
Maintain inventory records that provide accurate information on the inventory availability	Chief financial officer
Periodically reconcile inventory records to control accounts in the general ledger	Chief financial officer
Conduct regularly scheduled physical inventory counts	Chief financial officer
Ensure segregation of duties between manufacturing, inventory custody, and inventory accounting	Chief financial officer

CONCEPT REVIEW QUESTIONS

1. **What is a conversion process?**
   Ans. Conversion process is an operating business activity that combines resources (inputs) and converts them into products or services (outputs) that appeal to customers, whether they are clients, patients, or even students. The resources used differ depending on the type of business.

2. **CPA** **What is balancing in manufacturing efficiency?**
   Ans. Manufacturing efficiency is a balance between three goals:
   - Controlling the costs of resources
   - The rate of production
   - The quality of finished goods

   For example, manufacturing efficiency is increased when more output is produced from the same amount of resource inputs, like raw materials, labor, and overhead costs, without sacrificing product quality. The goal is to produce the same product at the lowest average total cost.

3. **What is a bill of materials (BOM)?**
   Ans. A bill of materials (BOM) is a document that specifies the components of a product, including descriptions of quantities of required raw materials and parts.

4. **Differentiate between production planning and production scheduling.**
   Ans. Production planning is a long-term outline of what and when products will be manufactured, whereas production scheduling is the short-term allocation of plant machinery and resources to the manufacturing of products.

5. **What is a job time ticket?**
   Ans. The manufacturing operations process focuses on creating finished goods. Like the other conversion processes, these operations also require source documents. One such document is the job time ticket that captures the cost of labor to manufacture the product.

11.2 Why Is Cost Accounting Important to the Accounting Information System?

Learning Objective ❷
Explain how the cost accounting system records conversion expenditures that impact the financial statements.

Accounting and reporting for production business activities span various accounting areas besides financial accounting. The accounting transactions generated flow directly through the AIS to the financial statements, making the risk of material financial misstatements an important consideration in conversion processes.

Managerial accounting is a subset of accounting that focuses on using accounting information to aid in decision making and management of control activities. Managerial accountants (also known as management accountants) perform analyses and create reports for use within the company. They might focus on different areas:

- Cost accounting
- Cost behavior and cost-volume-profit analyses
- Operational budgeting
- Capital budgeting to support production
- Variance analysis
- Analysis of the profitability of product lines, customers, and territories

Management uses these analyses and reports for decision making and for planning and controlling business operations.

A subset of managerial accounting, **cost accounting**, focuses on capturing and recording a company's total cost of production by identifying and recording the variable costs in each step of production, in addition to fixed costs such as factory rent or depreciation. It is part of managerial accounting, but it is specific to the conversion processes and has a narrower focus: quantitative product cost measured in monetary terms and entered into the accounting records. Product costs are required for external financial reporting, which must comply with generally accepted accounting principles (GAAP).

GAAP for financial reporting require that a manufacturer's inventory on the balance sheet and cost of goods sold on the income statement consist of:

- The cost of direct materials
- The cost of direct labor
- The cost of manufacturing overhead

Financial success or failure depends on how a business's resources are combined to add value to produce goods customers want to buy. The result of this process from an accounting perspective is financial statements that reflect the success of the company's conversion processes. These statements can tell us if the company is successfully producing a product or service that customers want.

There are two methods for assigning indirect costs to products. Both methods comply with GAAP, and cost accounting courses cover them extensively:

- Traditional cost accounting
- Activity-based cost accounting

Traditional Cost Accounting

Traditional cost accounting assigns production costs differently, depending on the product or service. Traditionally, costs are either assigned to a specific product or service or to the production process (**Table 11.7**):

TABLE 11.7 Job-Order Costing Versus Process Costing

Production Costing Method	Product or Service Type	How Costs Are Captured
Job-order costing	Product or service is unique for each customer.	Separately captures costs for each product or service, including materials, labor, and overhead.
Process costing	All customers receive a standard product that is continuously mass produced.	Captures the cost of the process for producing the product. Total cost is averaged over the number of units produced.

- **CPA** **Job-order costing** assigns costs to products or services that meet the specific needs of an individual customer. The costing system captures how much it costs to produce each product or service. Construction companies building custom homes, dentists treating patients, and a CPA firm auditing a client would use this method of costing.

- **CPA** On the other hand, if a company produces the same mass-produced product and sells it to everyone, then it uses **process costing** by determining the total cost of the production and averaging it over the units produced. The cost per unit equals the cost of all production inputs divided by expected output units. Julia's Cookies uses process costing.

CPA **Standard costing** is often used alongside both job-order and process costing to control production costs and promote production efficiency. Standard costs are projections of unit of production costs that we can measure against actual costs. In other words, actual costs are "what happened," and standard costs are "what should have happened." Significant variances between the two usually prompt investigation into the causes so management can take steps toward improvement. Cost accountants develop standard costs for all items that are or will be added to the master production schedule. On a regular basis—normally annually—the cost accountants prepare a standard cost update for all products.

Regardless of whether a company uses job-order or process costing, the data collected for costs of production from the resource acquisition processes covered next are the same. Only the way the data are allocated to manufacturing overheads differs. Let's look at allocating costs using these traditional approaches, then compare them to activity-based costing methods.

How costs are allocated depends on what resource is being assessed. Employees, raw materials, and fixed assets all involve different considerations for cost allocation (**Illustration 11.9**).

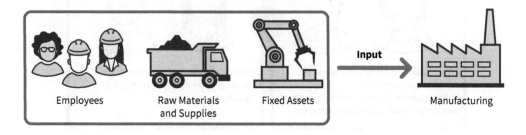

Illustration 11.9   The inputs to the manufacturing process are employees, raw materials and supplies, and fixed assets.

Human Resources and Payroll Processes

The success of a manufacturing company depends on its people—including the production innovators, those who work daily with the production processes, and the rest of the employees. Human resources and payroll processes enable us to hire, manage, and compensate these people depending on how their work is classified.

For accounting purposes, the salaries, wages, and benefits expenses of employees directly involved in the production process are classified as **direct labor**:

- This includes employees involved in hands-on production, like working on the assembly line or operating manufacturing machinery and equipment.

- **CPA** Direct labor is included in the cost of goods manufactured during a financial accounting reporting period. It is therefore part of **product costs,** which are costs incurred in manufacturing a product.
- The basis for charging product costs is the number of hours of labor worked on production during a period. The number of hours worked is then multiplied by an average hourly wage rate to calculate the dollar amount.

CPA Employees indirectly involved in manufacturing are allocated to **indirect factory labor:**

- These types of employees can be production supervisors, quality control inspectors, those managing and handling raw materials, factory cleaners, and factory maintenance.
- The indirect factory labor cost pool is allocated to the different units of product manufactured during the reporting period by using an allocation method that best reflects reality.
- In this manner, indirect factory labor is also included in the cost of goods manufactured during a reporting period and is part of product costs.

Can a manufacturer successfully produce its output without these employees? What about the CEO, the accounting staff, the internal auditors, and the janitorial staff for the administration premises? No. Every employee is hired to help the business succeed in its mission. The expenses incurred for these employees are not, however, allocated to the cost of goods manufactured but are expensed and appear as a line item on the income statement. **CPA** As such, these expenses do not become part of the cost of each finished product but are called **period costs.**

In the accounting system, direct labor and indirect factory labor are captured as part of the cost of the goods manufactured (product cost). The expenses for other employees of the business are captured as salaries and wages, employee benefits, and other line item expenses on the income statement. These period costs are not incurred in manufacturing a product and, therefore, cannot be assigned to product costs. **Illustration 11.10** summarizes how labor is categorized between product costs and period costs.

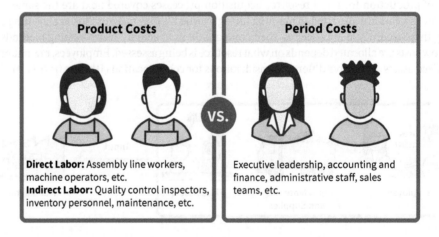

Illustration 11.10 Employee labor expenses are divided between product costs and period costs.

Product Costs	Period Costs
Direct Labor: Assembly line workers, machine operators, etc. **Indirect Labor:** Quality control inspectors, inventory personnel, maintenance, etc.	Executive leadership, accounting and finance, administrative staff, sales teams, etc.

Purchase of Raw Materials, Parts, and Production Supplies Process

The purchasing process provides another crucial type of input to the manufacturing process. Raw material, parts, and supplies consumed in manufacturing are also part of product costs:

- **CPA** **Direct material costs** are the costs of raw materials or parts that go directly into making products, like flour, butter, and sugar for making cookie dough or engine parts for an automobile manufacturer.

- **CPA** **Indirect material costs** are the costs of materials and supplies used in the manufacturing process that are not directly traceable to a product. For example, Julia's Cookies uses cooking spray and cleaning supplies in the conversion process as indirect materials.

In the accounting system, direct and indirect materials are captured as part of the cost of goods manufactured (product costs).

Why Does It Matter to Your Career?

Thoughts from a Cost Accountant, Manufacturing

- As a cost accountant in this industry, your responsibilities would include production cost analyses, standard costing, and variance analysis. This means that knowing about the production process and its risks and controls is essential to your daily duties.
- Since internal and external auditors work with cost accountants to review formulas, processes, and controls, they need to be familiar with this area, too. Cost accounting also generates journal entries, which auditors test.

Purchase of Fixed Assets for Production Processes

Production facilities require buildings, machinery, and equipment. These are called fixed assets, and businesses must allocate both the purchase and maintenance of these resources:

- Purchase of fixed assets is expensed as these assets are consumed over their revenue-generating service lives. The related expense is depreciation, which for nonproduction assets is charged to the income statement as an expense (a period cost).
- **CPA** The depreciation, repairs, maintenance, property taxes, and insurance for fixed assets used in production are classified as **manufacturing overhead**. Other types of production overhead, such as utilities, cleaning, and security, are classified the same way. All are allocated to product cost by using an overhead rate.

Traditional Cost Accounting Systems

Well-designed cost accounting systems mitigate the various risks related to the inaccurate allocation of production costs to units of production. These risks include:

- Financial statement misrepresentation
- Misleading managerial accounting reports
- Misleading cost accounting reports
- Erroneous decision making based on misleading reports
- Decreased profitability and financial performance

CPA In cost accounting, production costs are allocated to the units of product manufactured during the reporting period. Let's use Julia's Cookies to illustrate product costs:

- **Direct material:** The ingredients and packaging for the cookie dough directly used in production
- **Direct labor:** The cost of wages and benefits for the employees directly involved in production
- **Manufacturing overhead (indirect material):** The cost of cooking spray and other production supplies that can't be directly allocated to any batch of cookie dough
- **Manufacturing overhead (indirect labor):** The cost of wages and benefits for employees like production supervisors and cleaning staff in the production facility
- **Manufacturing overhead (other):** The costs of production utilities, depreciation on equipment, etc.

CPA The product costs generated by production processes during a reporting period end up in one of two places:

- Ending inventory (work-in-process and unsold finished goods), a current asset on the balance sheet
- Cost of goods sold (finished goods sold), an expense on the income statement

Illustration 11.11 reinforces this concept.

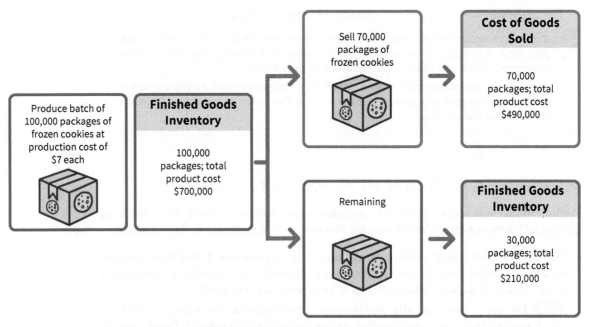

Illustration 11.11 Product costs end up as either ending inventory or cost of goods sold.

It's important to remember that expenses from outside the manufacturing facilities, like selling, general, and administrative (SG&A) expenses, are *not* product costs and are never included in the cost of inventory. They are expensed on the income statement in the accounting period in which they are incurred. In contrast, indirect labor is an indirect cost and is allocated to the cost of inventory produced.

Now that we have covered traditional cost accounting methods, let's look at the alternative.

Activity-Based Cost Accounting

When managerial accounting reports are inaccurate, management makes flawed decisions based on incorrect information. Consider the traditional assignment of indirect costs to products based on direct labor hours. Since we are increasingly relying on automation and technology in the workplace, direct labor hours may no longer be a good measure because this measure does not reflect business reality. **CPA** To avoid issues like this, businesses can use **activity-based costing (ABC)**, which involves assigning indirect overhead costs to business activity pools or processes based on direct consumption of resources rather than allocating them arbitrarily using traditional costing:

- In an ABC reporting process, management accountants identify specific business activity pools or fundamental business processes and then assign costs based on the resources directly consumed by that activity or process.
- Management can allocate more resources to profitable activities and processes and eliminate or reengineer those that are wasteful.
- Accurate cost drivers and overhead allocations result in improved, more streamlined business processes.

Let's go back to Julia's Cookies to illustrate how the company assigns indirect costs. Note that ingredients and labor to make the cookies are direct costs. The company initially had individual bakeries in various large-city locations and used activity-based costing to assign indirect overhead costs to each product. This was before the company started selling frozen dough, and there were only four types of cookies in the product lineup: chocolate chip, sugar, oatmeal raisin, and peanut butter. Each Julia's Cookies bakery had identified two activity cost pools and two cost drivers:

- **Activity cost pools:** Mixing and baking in their bakeries
- **Cost drivers:** Batch numbers and oven hours

This information should help management make good pricing and product decisions! Additionally, cost of goods sold on the income statement will better reflect business reality.

Illustration 11.12 shows the activity-based costing process for Julia's Cookies bakeries and the five steps in the process of assigning costs.

Activity-Based Costing Process

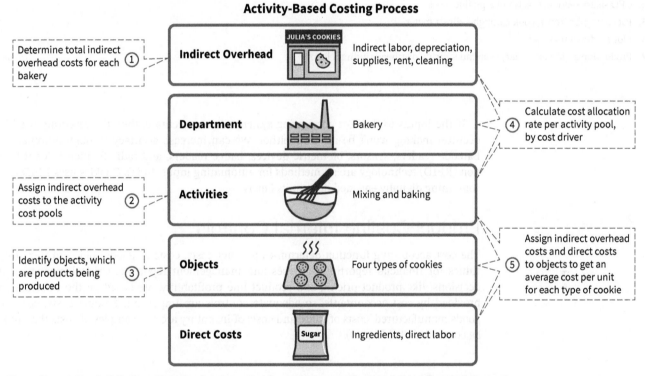

Illustration 11.12   Activity-based costing involves applying costs to specific objects based on activity pools.

ERP systems make activity-based costing easier to implement. Despite the benefits of ABC, the traditional method remains widely used. Julia's Cookies is implementing its new ERP system, SAP, using a phased approach that involves rolling out the ERP system modules to departments one at a time. Help the Cost Accounting team create business requirements for the SAP implementation in Applied Learning 11.2.

Julia's Cookies   Applied Learning 11.2

Product Costs: ERP System Implementation

As part of the implementation of the new SAP ERP system, the Cost Accounting team must identify cost categories for product costs. The Systems team will code this into the ERP system so items are automatically mapped to the proper cost categories when purchased.

The Systems team plans to use the categories direct material, direct labor, manufacturing overhead (indirect material), manufacturing overhead (indirect labor), and manufacturing overhead (other). Can you match each of the following costs to the appropriate product cost category?

1. Line manufacturing employee hourly wages
2. Cost of cooking spray
3. Depreciation on commercial ovens in the factory
4. CFO salary
5. Packaging for frozen cookie dough
6. Flour
7. Production supervisor salary

SOLUTION

These costs are categorized as:

1. Line manufacturing employee hourly wages—direct labor
2. Cost of cooking spray—manufacturing overhead (indirect material)
3. Depreciation on commercial ovens in the factory—manufacturing overhead (other)
4. CFO salary—none; this is not a product cost
5. Packaging for frozen cookie dough—direct material
6. Flour—direct material
7. Production supervisor salary—manufacturing overhead (indirect labor)

If the inputs to the cost accounting system are not accurate, then the reporting used in decision making won't be accurate either. We can increase accuracy through automation. Barcode readers, sensors, biometric devices, badge readers, and radio-frequency identification (RFID) technology are all methods for automating input. Julia's Cookies uses RFID tags containing digitally encoded data on its labels.

Product Costing Internal Controls

The cost accounting function determines product costs, costs of goods sold, and inventory values for financial reporting purposes and management reporting. Critical management decisions, like product pricing and product line profitability, are based on the information provided by cost accountants, so adequate controls are important. Product costs, costs of goods manufactured, costs of sales, and costs of inventory are all examples of costs that must be controlled (**Table 11.8**).

TABLE 11.8 Summary of Risks and Controls for Production Processes

Risk Statement: Misstatements in costs may result in material misstatement of financial reports.	
Sample Control Activity	**Control Owner**
Document and authorize product cost accounting procedures that describe costing methods	Chief financial officer
Risk Statement: Inadequate product cost recording may result in error, fraud, or financial losses.	
Sample Control Activity	**Control Owner**
Authorize a cost accounting system that accurately identifies and records costs	Chief financial officer
Create a cost accounting system that provides standard and actual manufacturing costs and variance analysis	Chief financial officer

TABLE 11.8 (*Continued*)

Develop standard costs for products and revise the list of costs on a regular basis	Chief financial officer
Use a BOM for every product in all steps of production	Chief operations officer
Control and account for raw materials issued to production	Chief financial officer
Allocate indirect labor and overhead to products on an approved and consistent basis	Cost accountant
Ensure that cost allocation complies with policies and procedures	Cost accountant
Allocate variances to cost of goods sold and goods in inventory equally	Chief financial officer
Investigate and resolve variances in a timely manner	Chief financial officer
Reconcile the general ledger control accounts to detailed records	Chief financial officer

Risk Statement: A poorly designed cost accounting system may result in misallocation of costs to products.

Sample Control Activity	Control Owner
Ensure that system development is reviewed by appropriate IT and accounting staff	Chief technology officer/ chief financial officer
Implement change management and supporting IT general controls	Chief technology officer

CONCEPT REVIEW QUESTIONS

1. What is managerial accounting?

   Ans. Managerial accounting is a subset of accounting that focuses on using accounting information to aid in decision making and management of control activities.

2. What do you mean by cost accounting?

   Ans. Cost accounting is a subset of managerial accounting which focuses on capturing and recording a company's total cost of production by identifying and recording the variable costs in each step of production, in addition to fixed costs such as factory rent or depreciation. It is part of managerial accounting, but it is specific to the conversion processes and has a narrower focus—quantitative product cost measured in monetary terms and entered into the accounting records.

3. **CPA** Differentiate between job-order and process costing.

   Ans. Job-order costing assigns costs to products or services that meet the specific needs of an individual customer. The costing system captures how much it costs to produce each product or service. On the other hand, if a company produces the same mass-produced product and sells it to everyone, then it uses process costing by determining the total cost of the production and averaging it over the units produced. The cost per unit equals the cost of all production inputs divided by the expected output units.

4. **CPA** Define standard costing.

   Ans. Standard costing is often used alongside both job-order and process costing to control production costs and promote production efficiency. Standard costs are projections of unit of production costs that we can measure against actual costs.

5. **CPA** What items are classified as manufacturing overhead?

   Ans. The depreciation, repairs, maintenance, property taxes, and insurance for fixed assets used in production are classified as manufacturing overhead. Other types of production overhead, such as utilities, cleaning, and security, are classified the same way. All are allocated to product cost by using an overhead rate.

6. What risks can be mitigated using a well-designed cost accounting system?

   Ans. The following risks can be mitigated by a well-designed cost accounting system:
   - Financial statement misrepresentation
   - Misleading managerial accounting reports
   - Misleading cost accounting reports
   - Erroneous decision making based on misleading reports
   - Decreased profitability and financial performance

7. **CPA** What is activity-based costing (ABC)?

   Ans. Activity-based costing (ABC) involves assigning indirect overhead costs to business activity pools or processes based on direct consumption of resources rather than allocating them arbitrarily using traditional costing.

11.3 What Is Digital Manufacturing?

Learning Objective ❸
Identify opportunities and challenges in digital manufacturing.

CPA **Digital manufacturing** involves automated, digital processes using Industrial Internet of Things (IIoT) technologies. Recall that the Internet of Things (IoT) is a network of intelligent devices connected to form digital systems that collect, exchange, monitor, and analyze data. A smart watch is a consumer-facing example. The IIoT consists of smart equipment, such as manufacturing machinery equipped with monitors and sensors. IIoT devices continually analyze data, in real time, to detect underutilization of resources, report inefficiencies, and expose errors. Because they are receiving this information immediately, employees are able to make real-time corrections.

Connectivity between information systems, factory assets like equipment and machinery, and employees allows businesses to leverage data-driven business insights. And the potential for insights increases over time as the information system collects more data. Production efficiency and productivity, as well as the company's profitability, also may benefit when artificial intelligence (AI) algorithms are applied to data. AI can detect real-time patterns and trends in performance and the condition of factory equipment.

Digital Manufacturing Environment

The physical factory, an individual machine, or even a single product can have a virtual **digital twin**, which is a digital duplicate or software model of the physical object:

- The software uses real-world data about the subject (inputs) to produce predictions or simulations on how the inputs impact the subject (outputs).
- Sensors on the subject gather data that is sent to the digital twin in real time, allowing the twin to simulate the counterpart to immediately provide insights into performance and potential faults.

Digital twins can also be prototypes for new products that simulate and test the products prior to production.

In the digital environment, an idea for a new or improved product or a new process or system can be digitized into a design, digitally visualized, and then optimized for manufacturing. In the physical factory environment, equipment and machinery are highly automated with disruptive technologies, such as IIoT and AI.

In the Real World Inside the Siemens Digital Factory[2]

Siemens, one of the largest industrial manufacturing companies in Europe, has spent the past decade digitizing its manufacturing plant. As a result, the company saw productivity improve by 1,400%.

Digital Twin	Siemens is using a digital twin of its factory, which calculates the daily manufacturing workload and produces identical products using different combinations of work cells. The optimization of production resources and daily production schedules determine which combination of work cells is most efficient. These work cells are logical, strategic organizations of manufacturing resources. Essentially, Siemens' production employees can now access the entire factory on their smart phones.
How It Works	A smart factory robot has more functionality than a traditional factory machine. Instead of just drilling holes, a smart factory robot may drill holes, solder, assemble, place components, and even perform tests. By performing multiple tasks, smart factory robots allow Siemens to produce identical products using efficient combinations of work cells. Previously, one work cell would have been dedicated solely to drilling holes. The digital twin allows the factory to optimize the entire production process rather than optimize production at an individual work cell.
Clearing a Bottleneck	While defects dropped from 150 to only 9 per million products manufactured, the manufacturing speed suffered. Every product was examined via x-ray to identify missing components or defects. The massive bottleneck created to ensure that Siemens wasn't sacrificing quality required an intelligent use of data analytics. Data sets from x-rays, machines used, operators, temperature monitors, and more were fed into a machine learning algorithm that predicted whether there would be quality issues. Siemens no longer needs to x-ray unless the algorithm alerts the production teams. The bottleneck is gone without sacrificing quality.
Outcomes	Siemens' plant grew from manufacturing 5 unique products to manufacturing more than 1,300 unique products, and the time from an order being received to being delivered is only 24 hours.

The vice president of Digital Enterprise at Siemens said, "Any product can go on any journey through the factory interacting with any combination of machines and people. The product can interact with one machine, 10 machines, 15 machines."

What companies could you work for that might use digital manufacturing? Do you think this technology is too advanced for most companies, or do you think it will be commonplace in the future? Could Julia's Cookies benefit from technology like production cells, robotic twins, or machine learning?

Opportunities and Challenges

What advantages do companies see by using digital manufacturing? A digital factory that is connected, networked, and fully integrated creates opportunities to minimize costs of downtime and underperformance in production and to enable the best output from factory assets and employees:

- Predicting and preempting machinery and equipment failure by performing functions like self-calibration and self-diagnosis
- Maintaining machinery and equipment using proactive real-time monitoring with a predictive maintenance model
- Connecting equipment and asset sensors to the cloud to improve equipment reliability and reduce unplanned outages
- Processing employee performance metrics through machine learning data models to identify at-risk factory employees and use the data to improve productivity and reduce attrition
- Using a digital twin for a product to improve measurement and manufacturing accuracy
- Eliminating manufacturing traffic jams
- Decreasing manufacturing cycle times, which is the time required to produce an order
- Improving production quality and output
- Providing more flexibility to meet customer demands

---

[2]www.themanufacturer.com/articles/what-is-digital-manufacturing/

Along with opportunities come challenges. Major challenges include:

- **CPA** **Cyber and privacy risks:** A manufacturer needs to secure every network, cloud, platform, operating system, and application across its supply chain and production network.
- **Data storage:** IIoT generates huge amounts of data.
- **Risk exposure:** Corporate risk appetites may not align with IIoT risks.
- **Process fragmentation:** Immature and fragmented business processes present a barrier to delivering intelligent automation. According to Deloitte, process fragmentation happens when there is not a unified workflow for critical business processes in terms of physical production and/or information flow.[3] Instead, a series of handoffs occur between departments, teams, and systems, introducing the risk of error and delay. The result is a barrier to delivering intelligent automation.
- **Resistance to change:** Employees might resist change if they fear losing their jobs. They might enjoy a comfort level and familiarity with existing processes and systems.
- **Limited existing technology support and capabilities:** Implementing advanced technologies like these can be challenging for many IT departments.
- **A clear vision and strategy with top management support:** Leadership support plays an essential role in the success of an initiative.

Why Does It Matter to Your Career?

Thoughts from a Senior Internal Auditor, Manufacturing

- Digital manufacturing is the future of business. Accounting professionals have the ability to combine their knowledge of systems, controls, processes, and accounting to play a major role in this space. Not many other majors of study have the well-rounded and diverse skills needed to make that kind of meaningful impact.
- Using emerging and disruptive technology creates new risks. If you pursue a career in audit, you need to be aware of the risks related to this area. It can be difficult to keep up with new technology, so proactively finding sources of information like online articles and whitepapers will be important throughout your entire career.

Digital Manufacturing Use Cases

There are many instances of successful and varied digital manufacturing cases. Here are a few examples[4]:

- The Bosch Automotive Diesel System factory in Wuxi, China, embedded sensors in the factory's machinery to collect data about the condition and efficiency level of its assets. Real-time alerts, created by advanced data analytics tools, warn workers about production operation bottlenecks. This initiative resulted in better maintenance of the machinery, a production output increase greater than 10%, improved customer delivery time, and increased customer satisfaction.
- Mobile robots at a Dutch DHL distribution center are picking and moving inventory. These robots automatically learn and share the most efficient routes. This has significantly decreased the order cycle time and significantly increased productivity in picking, moving, and placing inventory into production.

---

[3]www2.deloitte.com/us/en/insights/focus/technology-and-the-future-of-work/intelligent-automation-2020-survey-results.html

[4]amfg.ai/2019/03/28/industry-4-0-7-real-world-examples-of-digital-manufacturing-in-action/

- General Electric is testing augmented reality glasses at its jet engine manufacturing facility in Ohio. In the past, production employees had to frequently stop working to reference user manuals with detailed directions. Smart glasses provide those same instructions digitally and directly in employees' field of view. Workers can also use voice commands to bring up training videos and connect quickly with experts when they need help. GE has reported productivity gains of up to 11% from implementing these technologies.

You have learned that digital manufacturing uses emerging and disruptive technologies to create new approaches to manufacturing. Help Julia's Cookies improve its manufacturing by using these technologies in Applied Learning 11.3.[5]

Julia's Cookies	Applied Learning 11.3

Digital Manufacturing: Barriers to Automation

An article called "Digital Manufacturing and the CFO" in the CMA's *Strategic Finance* magazine catches the attention of Darlene, who is the chief financial officer. She knows automation in the production facilities is lacking and wants to discuss the article with Yalmaz, the chief operations officer. Her intention is to help Julia's Cookies mature its production processes.

When Darlene and Yalmaz meet, they agree that increased automation could mean significant improvement to the bottom line. Darlene is thrilled and wants to investigate this initiative. First, she wants to know if any barriers are preventing Julia's Cookies from advancing in this space. She asks Yalmaz to create a cross-functional task force to investigate and report on potential barriers.

What barriers do you think could prevent Julia's Cookies from pursuing digital automation?

SOLUTION

These are the top three barriers:

1. Lack of a clear vision for digital automation and its strategic fit for Julia's Cookies. Top management must lead the initiative and set the direction for change. This includes identifying the level of automation and the impact on business performance, profitability, and employees. Appetite for change will depend on the tone at the top.

2. Resistance to change. Employees are afraid a digital colleague or robot may replace them. Buy-in from workers is essential, and top management must immediately involve production employees by holding information sessions, training them on the new technologies, allowing them to help identify opportunities for automation, and offering training to update and build new skills so they can work with the technologies.

3. Limited IT capabilities. IT physical infrastructure may require substantial upgrades to support a digital factory.

CONCEPT REVIEW QUESTIONS

1. **CPA** What is meant by digital manufacturing?
   Ans. Digital manufacturing is the use of an integrated, computer-based system comprising of automated, digital processes using Industrial Internet of Things (IIoT) technologies to create new products and approaches to manufacturing.

2. What is a digital twin?
   Ans. A digital twin is a digital duplicate or software model of the physical object. The software uses real-world data about the subject (inputs) to produce predictions or simulations on how the inputs impact the subject (outputs). Digital twins can also be prototypes for new products that simulate and test the products prior to production.

---

[5]sfmagazine.com/post-entry/may-2019-digital-manufacturing-and-the-cfo/

11.4 How Is Data Collected and Used?

Learning Objective ❹

Explain how data generated by the AIS is converted to reporting and analytics.

The manufacturing conversion and supply chain management processes covered in this chapter involve 11 ERP features from the Financial, Production, and Supply Chain Management modules (**Illustration 11.13**). Remember that if a business is not using an integrated ERP system, there is still an information system in place; however, that information system is not connected directly to the information systems that support other parts of the process. For example, if a company has a stand-alone warehouse management system, it may not easily connect to the cost accounting financial system. Cost accountants may find it difficult to leverage warehouse data that requires extensive validation and modeling to join it with accounting data.

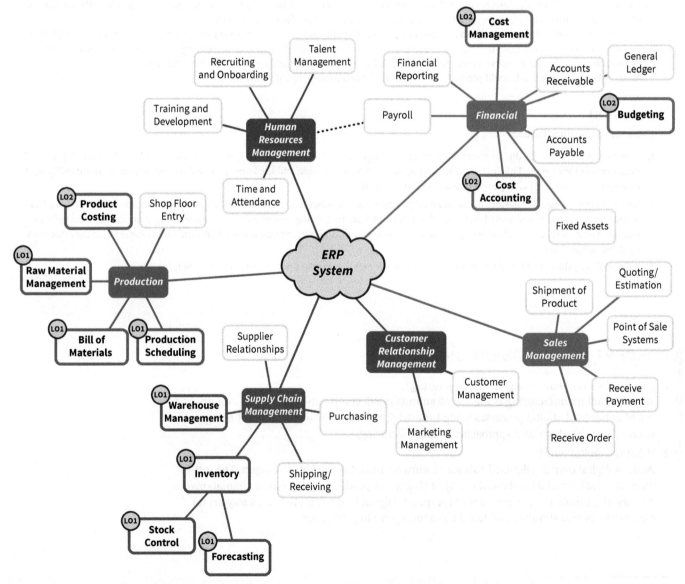

Illustration 11.13 Eleven modules from the ERP system are involved in the key production conversion processes.

Database Design

Illustration 11.14 shows a close-up view of some of the key tables that store data needed in the manufacturing conversion process. These tables connect to other parts of the ERP system, as depicted with arrows in the entity relationship diagram (ERD).

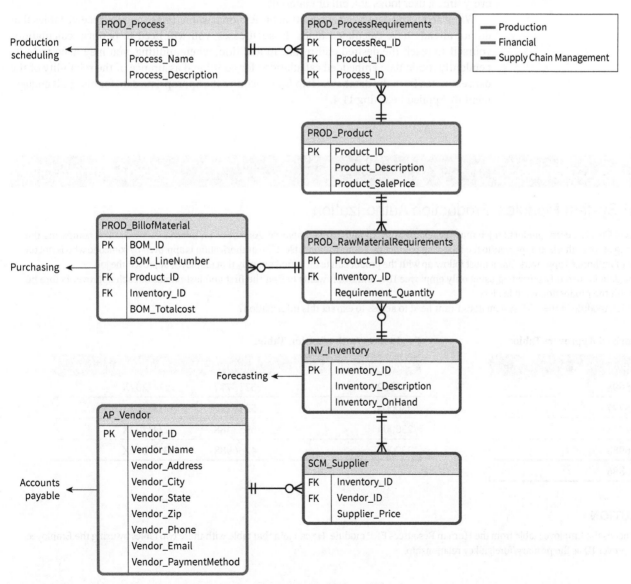

Illustration 11.14 A physical ERD highlights important tables related to the bill of materials, products, and production processes.

Table Relationships

Recall that the bill of materials (PROD_BillofMaterial) leverages data from the purchasing and inventory modules to drive its calculations. You will notice that data points such as Quantity are not included in the PROD_BillofMaterial table. This is because tables in a relational database reference other tables to pull necessary data without duplicating storage of a single data point. Since the attribute Requirement_Quantity is found in the raw material requirements table, it's not necessary to also store that number in the bill of materials table. The query that generates data for the final bill of materials report will join necessary tables together to make it possible to access data in real time.

Calculated Fields

Calculated fields, such as the bill of materials total cost (BOM_TotalCost), can be stored as a hardcoded number in the table, as it is in this example. Database designers may choose to store these calculated fields if they are accessed frequently to prevent unnecessary processing impacts on the database. If end users need to see the BOM_TotalCost every time a bill of materials is accessed, it makes sense to store it so that it is readily available instead of taxing the database with the additional processing requirements it would take to calculate that amount every time a user looks at a bill of materials.

When acquiring data as an accounting professional, sometimes you may receive tables that do not already have calculated fields. In such cases, you will need to perform calculations yourself to reach the desired end result. In addition, when auditing, you may need to independently recalculate embedded calculations for additional assurance of the reliability of the data extracted from the database. Help Brant acquire the appropriate data for his audit engagement in Applied Learning 11.4.

Julia's Cookies	Applied Learning 11.4

ERP System Modules: Production Authorization

At Julia's Cookies, every production job must be approved by an authorized employee. As part of an internal audit, Brant is comparing the following list of authorized approvers to the following production authorization table. If an authorization is approved by someone who is not on the list of authorized approvers, Brant must follow up with the production team to find out why that employee approved the job.

The data is currently presented using only employee IDs, and Brant wants to find the first and last names of each approver before he talks with the production team leaders.

Which module in the ERP system does Brant need to access to extract this information?

Authorized Approvers Table:

Employee ID
1005698
5215777
5252215
4256988
2648886

Production Authorization Table:

Production Run Number	Approver ID	Authorization Date
230002	5215777	1/4/202X
230003	5215777	2/3/202X
230004	6953488	2/4/202X
230005	4256988	3/1/202X

SOLUTION

Brant needs the Employee table from the Human Resources ERP module. He can join that table with these two tables by using the Employee ID/Approver ID as the primary/foreign key relationship.

Reporting and Insights

The data created and stored in a database during the production process includes BOM number, standard quantity, product number, product description, raw material ID number, material issue number, material issue date, material quantity issued, material cost, material quantity on hand, actual direct labor hours, material request number, material request date, and overhead rate. This data is processed, and the output may appear in typical production reports, or it may be analyzed using various types of data analysis.

Recall that reporting aggregates the raw data to provide a historical view of what happened because of past production activities. Analysis focuses on providing context to the historical data. It gives management meaningful insights for making decisions on how to improve a process. Analysis uses either the raw data or existing reports generated from that data. Examples of reports and analytics follow.

Production reports range from source documents to key metrics (**Table 11.9**).

TABLE 11.9 Production Reports

Report	Description
Production plan	A long-term plan depicting what will be produced and when based on the customer product demand and allocation of resources.
Bill of materials (BOM)	A list of raw materials, steps, and parts needed to manufacture a product.
Bill of operations (BOO)	A list of sequential steps followed to manufacture a product.
Master production schedule (MPS)	A build plan that compiles planned orders into a short-term schedule.
Production orders filled and open	The total number of orders that have been filled or remain outstanding within a period of time. This can indicate if production is ahead of or behind schedule.
Total manufacturing costs of products by period	Summary of costs by product within a period of time. This can indicate if a product is costing more than anticipated.
Actual versus standard or budget production costs	Comparison of the actual production costs to standard production costs. This can indicate deviations from expected costs that result from a production or supplier issue.
Top-selling products	Revenue from the sales processes showing top-selling products for production management decision making.
Production volume by machinery	Summary of volume produced by machinery type. This can indicate if a machine is underperforming compared to similar machines, possibly as a result of needed maintenance or other issues.
Downtime causes	Summary of machine downtime, including reasons for the downtime. This can indicate if there are ongoing downtime issues, such as excessive missing parts, which could be an issue in the maintenance inventory department.
Return items by reason	Summary of customer-returned items, including reasons for the returns. This can indicate if products are returned for similar reasons that are due to a larger issue, such as poor product design or faulty parts from a supplier.

These reports can be visualized and aggregated into a dashboard that is easy for management to understand (**Illustration 11.15**).

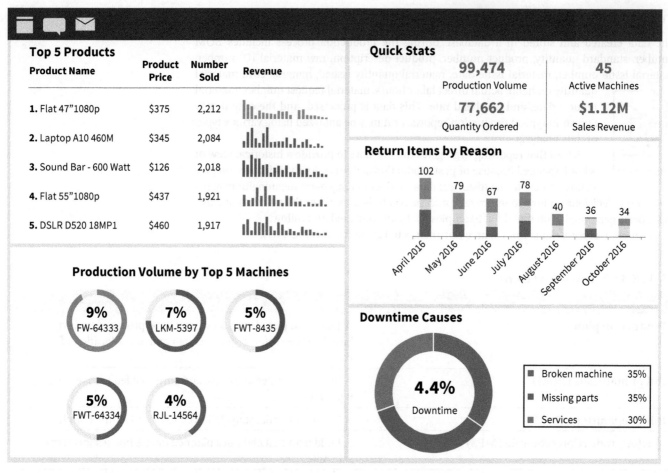

Illustration 11.15 Management uses dashboards to monitor KPIs related to the conversion processes.

Analytics can be used to monitor production efficiency and operating capacity compared to benchmarks (**Table 11.10**).

TABLE 11.10 CPA Production Analytics

Analytic	Description	How It's Used
Overall equipment effectiveness (OEE) comparison	Compares the overall equipment effectiveness to competitors and industry standards	Used to determine if equipment is underperforming or outperforming benchmarks.
Manufacturing yield	Indicates percentage of produced units that are nondefective	Indicates if production processes are operating effectively. If the percentage of defective products is high, management should investigate the processes to determine the root cause.
Capacity utilization rate	Measures production efficiency as a percentage of actual production output compared to the potential maximum output	Used to determine if production is underperforming or outperforming benchmarks.
CPA **Throughput**	Measures production efficiency by multiplying the productive capacity (total units produced/processing time), the productive processing time (processing time/total time), and the yield (nondefective units/total units produced)	Indicates whether customer demand can be met and whether production lines are performing effectively.

CONCEPT REVIEW QUESTIONS

1. What is a production orders filled and open report?

   Ans. The total number of orders that have been filled or remain outstanding within a period of time is reported in production order filled and open report. This can indicate if production is ahead of or behind the schedule.

2. What does a downtime report communicate?

   Ans. A downtime report communicates a cause summary of machine downtime, including reasons for the downtime. This can indicate if there are ongoing downtime issues, such as excessive missing parts, which could be an issue in the maintenance inventory department.

FEATURED PROFESSIONAL | **Program Manager, Electric Vehicle Manufacturer**

Photo courtesy of Yanek Michel

Yanek Michel, CPA, CFE

Yanek is a risk and compliance professional who specializes in enterprise risk. With over 12 years of experience in continuous improvements to internal control structures, Yanek combines his expertise as a CPA and CFE with his accounting education to perform analytical work over the business processes of his clients and employer. Yanek began his career in Big Four accounting as a fraud and forensics expert, and he approaches all his projects in internal audit with a fraud risk point of view. His experience in the conversion processes stems from five years as an internal audit manager at a global manufacturing firm. Currently, he is a program manager for a company that manufactures electric vehicles.

How important is it for accounting students to learn about accounting information systems?

Now that almost all successful companies rely on technology, the financial and operational data derived from the various enterprise systems is the most important commodity in a company. AIS allow companies and C-suite executives to accurately report information and make strategic decisions.

What can students do to pursue a career like yours?

Determine the specialties you are interested in and pursue certifications in those areas. The early part of your career should be spent developing a deep understanding of risk, how risks affect business strategy, and how to leverage technology to preemptively mitigate risks or detect deficiencies.

What major risks have you recently seen in conversion and production processes?

The largest risk in the conversion process is cybersecurity risk, such as ransomware events that limit a company's ability to access key data.

What is the conversion process like at a company that manufactures a digital product compared to at a company that has a physical product?

The conversion process is very different with digital (intellectual property driven) products than with physical goods. The largest difference relates to input and output. A physical manufacturer relies on planning, raw material inputs, fixed asset management, and, ideally, a repeatable process. A technology company relies primarily on human capital and has virtually no raw material costs. The development activities are generally unique. The cloud services model enables technology services companies to scale quickly and rely on a pay-as-you-go model rather than invest in their own physical servers. In accounting terms, technology costs of goods sold are overwhelmingly R&D labor and service maintenance costs (generally for cloud services).

How does fraud risk present itself in conversion and production processes?

The most obvious risk of fraud in the conversion process is existing fraudulent data, such as ghost employees or fraudulent vendor data that is transitioned to a new system. Although a robust process may exist for the new system, the rollover of existing data bypasses the setup process, where preventive controls generally exist.

Review and Practice

Key Terms Review

activity-based costing (ABC)
bill of materials (BOM)
bill of operations (BOO)
conversion processes
cost accounting
digital manufacturing
digital twin
direct labor
direct material costs
e-procurement system
engineering BOM
indirect factory labor

indirect material costs
inventory management
job-order costing
job time ticket
managerial accounting
manufacturing BOM
manufacturing efficiency
manufacturing operations
manufacturing overhead
master production schedule (MPS)
materials requisition request
move ticket

operations list
overall equipment effectiveness (OEE)
period costs
process costing
product costs
product development
production planning
production report
production scheduling
quality management
standard costing
supply chain management

Learning Objectives Review

❶ Describe the relationship between conversion processes, inventory, and supply chain management.

Conversion processes are operating business activities that combine resources (inputs) and convert them into products or services (outputs) that appeal to customers.

Manufacturing efficiency ensures a balance exists between:

- Controlling costs
- Production rate
- Quality

The five high-level conversion business processes are:

- Product development
- Production planning
- Production scheduling
- Manufacturing operations
- Quality management

Based on sales forecasts, these processes work with inventory and supply chain management to ensure that the right raw materials are available for production.

During product development, new products are researched and designed. Source documents include:

- Bill of materials (BOM) (either engineering or manufacturing)
- Operations list (also called the bill of operations)

Production planning involves a long-term outline of what and when products will be manufactured, while production scheduling involves the short-term allocation of plant machinery and resources to the manufacturing of products. Source documents include:

- Master production schedule (MPS)
- Materials requisition request
- Move tickets

Manufacturing operations involves the actual creation of the finished goods. Source documents include:

- Job time tickets
- Production reports

Quality management involves ensuring that products meet regulatory and corporate specifications. It is an essential part of manufacturing because poor-quality products may result in reputational damage or even safety hazards and lawsuits.

Inventory and supply chain management oversee communication between purchasing, conversion, and sales process to ensure that needed inventory is available and that the supply chain from supplier to customer is clearly integrated with lines of open communication.

❷ Explain how the cost accounting system records conversion expenditures that impact the financial statements.

Managerial accounting focuses on using accounting information to aid in decision making. Cost accounting is a subset of managerial accounting that captures and records the cost of production by allocating costs to the products being manufactured.

There are two types of traditional costing methods:

- Job-order costing: Each customer gets a unique product or service.
- Process costing: Every customer receives a standard product or service that is mass produced or distributed.

Standard costing measures units of production cost against actual costs. This is a comparison of what happened to what should have happened.

Labor costs are allocated as:

- Direct labor: Employees directly involved in hands-on production

- Indirect labor: Employees who are less involved, like production supervisors and factory janitorial staff
- Period costs: Administrative and salaried support staff like the CEO, auditor, or office janitorial staff

Materials are either:

- Direct material costs, which go directly into the product
- Indirect material cost, such as cleaning supplies

Manufacturing overhead includes production fixed assets, utilities, cleaning, and security costs.

Indirect costs can be assigned using an alternative method to traditional costing, activity-based costing (ABC):

- ABC is based on a product's usage of the activities.
- ABC uses activity cost pools and objects to group costs together to create accurate cost drivers.

❸ Identify opportunities and challenges in digital manufacturing.

The transition to digital manufacturing changes a manual plant to a plant that uses automated digital process.

A physical factory can have a digital twin, which uses real-world data about the subject to produce predictions or simulations about production activities.

Opportunities for digital manufacturing include:

- Predicting machinery failure
- Maintaining machinery in real time
- Using the cloud and equipment sensors
- Leveraging employee performance metrics
- Using digital twins for simulations
- Improving quality and output
- Enabling flexibility in meeting customer demands

Challenges to digital manufacturing include:

- Cybersecurity
- Resistance to change
- Limited existing technology and capabilities
- Lack of a clear vision

❹ Explain how data generated by the AIS is converted to reporting and analytics.

Conversion processes leverage the following features in an ERP system.

Production module features:

- Product Costing
- Raw Material Management
- Bill of Materials
- Production Scheduling

Supply Chain Management module features:

- Warehouse Management
- Inventory
- Stock Control
- Forecasting

Financial module features:

- Cost Accounting
- Budgeting
- Cost Management

The bill of materials data is stored in multiple tables that are related to the inventory, supplier, and vendor data in the ERD.

Production reports such as these aggregate raw data to provide a historical view of past production activities:

- Production plans
- Bill of materials (BOM)
- Bill of operations (BOO)
- Master production schedule (MPS)
- Production orders completed and outstanding
- Total manufacturing costs of products by period
- Actual versus standard or budget production costs
- Production performance by machinery
- Machine downtime
- Product returns and defects

Production analytics can monitor production efficiency and operating capacity compared to benchmarks:

- Overall equipment effectiveness (OEE) comparison
- Manufacturing yield
- Capacity utilization rate
- Throughput

CPA questions, as well as multiple choice, discussion, analysis and application, and Tableau questions and other resources, are available online.

Multiple Choice Questions

1. (LO 1) Which of the following shows the correct order of business processes in the manufacturing conversion process?

a. Product development, production planning, production scheduling, manufacturing operations, quality management

b. Production scheduling, product development, production planning, manufacturing operations, quality management

c. Product development, production planning, quality management, production scheduling, manufacturing operations

   d. Production planning, production scheduling, product development, manufacturing operations, quality management

2. (LO 1) What are the source document output(s) of the quality management process?

   a. Testing reports

   b. Production plan

   c. Production schedule, production orders, material requisitions, and move tickets

   d. Production reports and job time tickets

3. (LO 1) Which of the following is an overall equipment effectiveness (OEE) measure?

   a. Time spent on a job ticket

   b. Time spent developing a product

   c. Overall production run time

   d. Percentage of productive manufacturing time

4. (LO 1) CPA Hamish works in a factory that builds tractors in Des Moines, Iowa. He needs a B352 sprocket to build a X793 tractor. The document, form, or screen that would authorize this action is a

   a. bill of materials.

   b. move ticket.

   c. materials requisition.

   d. picking ticket.

5. (LO 1) CPA Hamish works in a factory that builds tractors in Des Moines, Iowa. He can't remember whether the B352 or the C917 sprocket is needed in building a X793 tractor. The document, form, or screen that would help him decide is a

   a. bill of materials.

   b. materials requisition.

   c. move ticket.

   d. picking ticket.

6. (LO 1) CPA A master production schedule is most likely to be useful in

   a. identifying erroneous journal entries.

   b. inventory shrinkage.

   c. pricing of goods for sale.

   d. reducing excess production of inventory.

7. (LO 2) Which of the following accounting subdisciplines applies only to conversion processes?

   a. Managerial accounting

   b. Financial accounting

   c. Cost accounting

   d. Data analytics

8. (LO 2) What is the objective of production planning and scheduling?

   a. Increase cost efficiency

   b. Decrease excessive costs

   c. Provide the right product at the right time

   d. Reduce the number of defective products manufactured

9. (LO 2) Traditional cost accounting assigns production costs differently, depending on the product or service. Which cost accounting method would likely be used for a mass-produced frozen cookie mix?

   a. Activity-based costing

   b. Machine setup costing

   c. Job-order costing

   d. Process costing

10. (LO 2) GAAP for financial reporting requires that a manufacturer's inventory on the balance sheet and cost of goods sold on the income statement consist of—the cost of direct materials, the cost of direct labor, and

   a. the cost of shipping.

   b. the cost of sales, general, and administration (SG&A).

   c. the cost of manufacturing overhead.

   d. the expense of IT.

11. (LO 2) Depreciation expenses on fixed assets used in production for a reporting period are classified as

   a. current assets.

   b. indirect materials.

   c. direct materials.

   d. manufacturing overhead.

12. (LO 2) CPA Book Co. uses the activity-based costing approach for cost allocation and product costing purposes. Printing, cutting, and binding functions make up the manufacturing process. Machinery and equipment are arranged in operating cells that produce a complete product starting with raw materials.

   Which of the following are characteristic of Book's activity-based costing approach?

   i. Cost drivers are used as a basis for cost allocation.

   ii. Costs are accumulated by department or function for the purposes of product costing.

   iii. Activities that do not add value to the product are identified and reduced to the extent possible.

   a. i only

   b. i and ii

   c. i and iii

   d. ii and iii

13. (LO 3) CPA Concerns about IoT include all of the following *except*

   a. reduced privacy.

   b. cycle times.

   c. data storage.

   d. risk exposure.

14. (LO 3) Which of the following provides the best definition of a digital twin?

   a. A digital twin involves using Industrial Internet of Things (IIoT) technologies to virtually manufacture a product.

b. A digital twin is a digital duplicate or software model of the physical object.

c. A digital twin is manufacturing a duplicate product in clay for testing purposes.

d. A digital twin is when an organization tests a product in the field.

15. (LO 3) What do we call a network of intelligent devices that collect and analyze data?

a. Intranet

b. Industrial Internet of Things

c. Data analytics

d. Data warehouse

16. (LO 3) A digital factory that is connected, networked, and fully integrated creates opportunities to minimize costs of downtime and underperformance in production and to enable the best output from factory assets and employees. What is a challenge that companies face when using digital manufacturing?

a. Employees resisting change out of fear of losing their jobs

b. Eliminating manufacturing traffic jams

c. Maintaining machinery and equipment using proactive real-time monitoring with a predictive maintenance model

d. Decreasing manufacturing cycle times, which is the time required to produce an order

17. (LO 3) Process fragmentation in production happens when

a. there are different production processes for different products.

b. there are efficient handoffs between departments, teams, and systems.

c. there is not a unified workflow for critical production processes.

d. different manufacturing teams handle different parts of the production process.

18. (LO 4) The manufacturing conversion and supply chain management processes involve 11 ERP features from the Financial, Production, and Supply Chain Management modules. Which of the following modules is part of the manufacturing conversion and supply chain management processes?

a. Production

b. Human resources management

c. Customer relationship management

d. Sales management

19. (LO 4) Which of these reports does *not* relate to production?

a. Bill of materials

b. Accounts payable aging analysis

c. Machine downtime

d. Bill of operations

20. (LO 4) Which of these dashboards is *not* used by management to monitor KPIs for production processes?

a. Machine downtime causes

b. Top five customers

c. Defective products by reason

d. Throughput

Discussion and Research Questions

DQ1. (LO 1) The basic business model shows the inputs and outputs for the conversion process. Which part of the model adds value to business resources, and why is this part of the business model so important?

DQ2. (LO 1) `Early Career` `Critical Thinking` You are a production manager for PlayItWell Inc, a mid-sized company that produces hockey equipment, primarily hockey sticks, pucks, and helmets. While reviewing data, you determine that inventory levels are too high and stop production of hockey sticks. Brunilda, a new intern in the production operations area, asks you to explain why you stopped producing products when you have the raw materials on hand. How do you explain the connection between inventory levels and production of a product?

DQ3. (LO 1) Consider the impact of the conversion process on a company's ability to make a profit. Explain why conversion processes must be both efficient and effective.

DQ4. (LO 1) What is an e-procurement system, and how does it benefit the production process?

DQ5. (LO 2) Describe the main differences between job-order and process costing.

DQ6. (LO 2) Why is the human resources process critical to the success of conversion processes?

DQ7. (LO 3) What is artificial intelligence (AI), and how can it improve other areas of digital manufacturing?

DQ8. (LO 3) `Early Career` `Critical Thinking` In Applied Learning 11.3, Darlene, the CFO of Julia's Cookies, asked Yalmaz to create a task force to report on barriers to the use of intelligent factory automation. As part of their work, the task force identified three top barriers: (1) lack of clear vision for digital automation, (2) resistance to change, and (3) limited IT capabilities. Yalmaz has asked you to research and report on the resistance to change barrier. Specifically, why does resistance to change exist, how do people resist change, how does management play a role in why resistance to change exists, and what can be done to mitigate it?

DQ9. (LO 3) How can a digital twin improve output from the production process?

DQ10. (LO 3) `Research` Conduct research using credible sources and explain how artificial intelligence (AI) can be used to enhance digital manufacturing. Provide an appropriate and interesting use case (real-world example). Cite your source(s).

Here is an example of a credible source that is a great read, but please find your own source: https://www.forbes.com/sites/forbestechcouncil/2020/06/12/artificial-intelligence-powers-flexibility-in-digital-manufacturing/?sh=7755502d32aa

DQ11. (LO 4) Discuss the disadvantages of not having an integrated ERP system between warehouse management and cost accounting.

DQ12. (LO 4) How does a bill of materials differ from a bill of operations in the production process?

DQ13. (LO 4) A database's bill of materials (BOM) table includes the attributes BOM_ID, Product_ID, Inventory_ID, and BOM_TotalCost. Which other tables in the database would the BOM table need to pull data from without duplicating storage of a single data point, and why? Which attribute has a calculated field, and why?

Application and Analysis Questions

A1. (LO 1) Critical Thinking At Quality Cabinets, six departments are involved with the conversion process involved in manufacturing kitchen cabinets. Consider the list of departments and answer the following questions:

Departments:

- Manufacturing
- Product Development
- Quality Management
- Production Scheduling
- Production Planning
- Inventory Management

1. When a new product is created, in what order should these departments be involved in the production process?

2. Why is it important for the departments to be involved in the correct order?

3. Describe two controls for each department.

Internal Control	Control Owner	Area
1. The system analyzes standard and actual manufacturing costs and variances.		
2. An annual review of employee performance is performed.		
3. Access to the warehouse is limited to authorized employees only.		
4. Inventory counts are completed on a monthly basis.		
5. The system creates purchase requisitions and orders electronically based on customer demand.		
6. Production decisions made by management must be based on sales forecasting, product profitability analysis, and inventory management.		
7. The inventory records must be periodically reconciled to the control accounts in the general ledger and to the physical inventory on hand.		
8. Documented policies and procedures for product safety and quality include roles and responsibilities of inspectors and the handling of exceptions.		
9. Product costs are standardized and reviewed and revised regularly, in accordance with documented policies and procedures.		
10. Policies and procedures related to the review, change, and authorization of existing bills of materials, operations lists, and production schedules are clearly documented.		

A2. (LO 1–2) As an internal auditor at HazelWood's Manufacturing, you have been tasked with preparing internal control testing plans for this year's business operations audit over the conversion processes. You have been given a list of controls from the prior year's workpapers. Unfortunately, last year's internal audit senior failed to include the control owners or the area of the conversion process for each, and the senior is no longer with HazelWood's Manufacturing. In preparation for this year's audit, complete the following two questions using the list of internal controls in the table above.

A. Identify the business stakeholders your team needs to meet with during the engagement by assigning an employee job title to the Control Owner column for each internal control.

B. To assist your team in planning the scope of the engagement, identify in which of the following areas of the conversion process the internal control is found:

   i. Product development

   ii. Production planning and scheduling

iii. Manufacturing operations

iv. Quality management

v. Inventory management

vi. Supply chain management

vii. Product cost management

Each area can be used more than once in the table above.

A3. (LO 2) `Early Career` You are a second-year external audit associate at a regional public accounting firm whose audit team focuses on manufacturing clients. You have been asked to be a peer coach to your team's newest first-year hire, which means you will need to provide mentoring, answer questions, and help them acclimate to the firm. In preparation for your mentee's first audit engagement with your team, you meet for a coffee coaching session and ask if they have any immediate questions. You find out that your mentee is concerned they won't understand terminology at the client and is feeling overwhelmed.

Help your mentee acclimate to the manufacturing-specific terms your audit team frequently encounters by providing a short explanation of each of the following production terms:

1. Job-order costing

2. Activity-based costing

3. Direct materials

4. Conventional cost accounting

5. Indirect materials

6. Period costs

7. Product costs

8. Process costing

9. Direct labor

10. Manufacturing overhead

A4. (LO 2) `Critical Thinking` CrownCorp is a manufacturer of beach equipment such as umbrellas, chairs, and tables. Currently, CrownCorp uses process-based costing. As a member of the Cost Accounting department, you have been tasked with compiling a single PowerPoint slide that compares and contrasts CrownCorp's current process-based costing methods with activity-based costing. Your manager plans to present this slide in an upcoming strategy meeting with executive stakeholders.

Complete the following table, which will be turned into an infographic centerpiece for your slide.

Activity-Based Costing	
Advantages	**Disadvantages**
1.	1.
2.	2.
3.	3.

A5. (LO 3) You are a senior consulting associate at a Big Four public accounting firm. One of your clients has asked for your team's help in determining if digital manufacturing could be an effective way for it to improve operations and create new opportunities for employees. The client's CEO is very interested in the Industrial Internet of Things (IIoT) and requests more information on the challenges the organization would face by adding a large number of smart devices. Compile a bulleted list of eight main challenges related to IIoT for the senior manager of your consulting team to review.

A6. (LO 4) `Data Fundamentals` The Production module of the ERP system stores important production-related data in an underlying relational database. Choose two related tables in the ERD below, which shows a sample of some of the tables housed in the production database, to complete the following prompts:

1. Select one of the tables to be your primary table, making sure it has a PK field. Then choose another one to be your secondary table.

2. Is the cardinality between these two tables one-to-one, one-to-many, or many-to-many? Provide one answer and

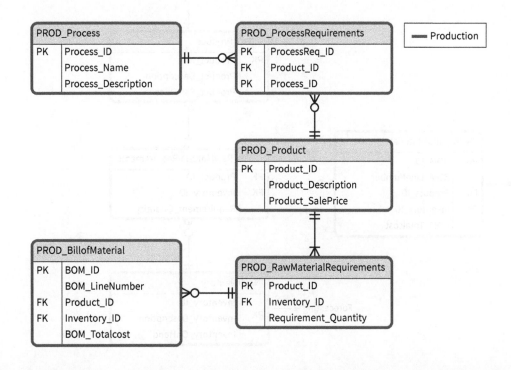

explanation using your primary table as the first table in your statement. For example, Table A (the primary table you chose) has a one-to-many relationship with Table B because one record in Table A may be related to many records in Table B (the secondary table you chose).

3. Is the optionality between these two tables mandatory or optional? Provide one answer using your primary table as the first table in your statement. For example, Table A has an optional relationship with Table B.

4. Identify the PK in your primary table.

5. Identify the PK/FK relationship that connects your primary table to your secondary table. There may be more than one.

6. Write a business rule that explains the relationship of your primary table to your secondary table.

A7. (LO 4) Leason Surgical operates surgery centers around the country. Its customers consist of surgeons from various medical fields who pay to perform their patient operations in the surgery center facilities. As part of the nonproduction conversion processes at Leason, surgical technicians assemble carts with the necessary medical instruments and medicine for a scheduled surgical procedure. A materials manager who oversees inventory and places orders to Leason's distribution centers when new supplies are required needs to see the quantity of available inventory at the center at a point in time.

The lead surgical technician at Leason's largest surgical center created a data visualization (given in the next column) that shows the current available inventory summarized by the surgery type to assist the materials manager in ordering supplies when needed. Review the visualization and answer the following questions:

1. Which table in the accompanying ERD is primarily used to populate this data visualization?

2. Do you think this is the most useful way to present the data? Suggest a change in the visualization that may be useful to the materials manager.

Data visualization:

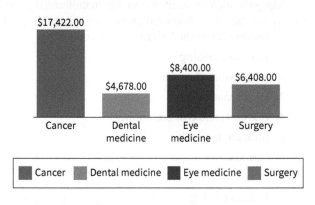

INV_Inventory is primarily used to populate the visualization.

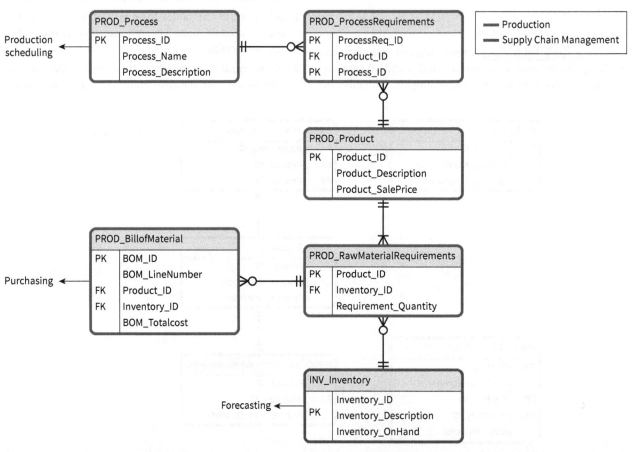

A8. (LO 4) `Early Career` `Data Analytics` `Critical Thinking`
As an internal auditor for Bliss & Shine Accessories, a manufacturer of jewelry and fashion accessories sold at popular chain stores throughout the United Kingdom, you are assigned to an advisory engagement for warehouse operations.

The warehouse schedules pickup and delivery times based on data points like order frequency, pickup locations, available employees, and the layout of the warehouse. To support these scheduling decisions, the information system captures data, including demand, stock, layout, and daily operations like hours worked and equipment uptime, which is the time a piece of equipment is operating each day.

Last year, the Internal Audit department partnered with the company's Process Improvement Six Sigma team to perform an advisory review and identify inefficiencies in warehouse operations. The review resulted in recommendations that the warehouse modify the layout by optimizing rack arrangements and redesigning where the conveyors are located. At the time, Internal Audit predicted that there would be a 35% reduction in distance finished goods traveled and a 70% reduction of workforce hours.

Now that the implementation of these recommendations is complete, the chief operations officer has asked Internal Audit to perform data analytics to assess the actual impact of the modifications. You are given the following sample of historical data and sample of post-implementation data. Identify the actual reduction in average distance traveled and workforce hours and compare your numbers to the predicted impact. Determine if the recommendations have had more or less of an impact on the efficiency of the warehouse or if they have had no effect. Perform this analysis based on individual product types.

Sample of historical data:

Product Type	Production Quantity	Travel Distance	Hours Labored
A	189261	620	205
A	189620	695	246
A	189722	645	252
B	189630	456	126
B	190201	485	152
B	190322	501	149
B	190410	492	160

Sample of post-implementation data:

Product Type	Production Quantity	Travel Distance	Hours Labored
A	189261	490	70
A	189620	540	55
A	189722	530	62
B	189630	225	32
B	190201	315	55
B	190322	266	43
B	190410	290	48

A9. (LO 1–4) `Early Career` `Critical Thinking` You are a member of an Internal Audit team at Moots Treats, a bakery, and are performing an evaluation of the company's manufacturing yield. The yield is calculated by dividing the number of nondefective items by the number of manufactured items. However, the maximum production yield for Moots Treats is unknown. Your team recommends building a predictive data analytics model that can predict the maximum production yield. This model could potentially pinpoint and identify yield losses in the production process and improve production yield. Internal Audit's calculations reveal that a 0.3% increase in yield can improve the bottom line by over $2 million at current production levels. This is a difficult but worthwhile data analytics project to tackle!

Your team completes its predictive model over a period of six weeks and is eager to try it out. The top six issues identified, and their potential impacts and causes, are:

1. Ingredients were added in incorrect proportions. Potential impacts are poor flavor and appearance of the cookies. Potential cause is poor employee training.

2. Storage was too warm for eggs, which require refrigeration. A potential impact is bacterial contamination. Potential cause is a poor warehouse storage program.

3. Ingredients were mixed for too long. Dough did not rise properly. Potential cause is poor employee training.

4. Incorrect equipment settings. Cookies were misshapen and incorrectly sized. Potential cause is poor employee training.

5. The metal detector malfunctions. Potential impact is that metal fragments remain in cookies and reach the consumer. Potential cause is poor equipment maintenance.

6. Freezer was too warm for frozen cookie storage. Cookies were too soft to pack for shipping and turned mushy. Potential cause is poor equipment maintenance.

Now that the issues and impact are clear, you have been asked to identify controls to mitigate the potential impacts. For each of the six issues, outline at least two controls that could be implemented. The same controls may be used in multiple areas.

Tableau Case: Julia's Cookies' Raw Ingredient Costs

What You Need

Download Tableau to your computer. You can access www.tableau.com/academic/students to download your free Tableau license for the year, or you can download it from your university's software offerings.

Download the following file from the book's product page on www.wiley.com:

Chapter 11 Raw Data.xlsx

Case Overview

Big Picture:

Calculate the costs of raw materials used to make cookies.

Details:

Why is this data important, and what questions or problems should be addressed?

- Julia's Cookies must determine the actual cost of raw materials to produce a certain type of cookie for an order of a particular size.
- Determining pricing for each type of cookie requires the analyst to break down the recipe into its core ingredients and analyze the raw material cost per cookie.
- To do this, consider the following questions: How much do the raw material ingredients cost? Which cookie is the most expensive to produce in terms of raw materials? How much of each raw material ingredient is required to fulfill specific orders?

Plan:

What data do you need, and how should you analyze it?

- Product cost data needed to answer these questions is pulled from the ERP system.
- The data for this exercise only focuses on the raw material costs. It does not include direct labor and manufacturing overhead.

Now it's your turn to evaluate, analyze, and communicate the results!

To answer the following questions, connect the tables by using their ID fields:

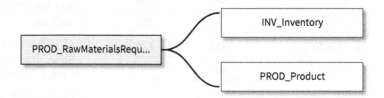

Questions

1. How many chocolate chip cookies does the chocolate chip cookie recipe make?

2. How much does one egg cost?

For questions 3 through 8, assume that Julia's Cookies is currently making six kinds of cookies and has received an order for 100,000 cookies of each type (600,000 total).

3. How many eggs does Julia's Cookies need to bake all the cookies for this order? (Hint: Create a calculated field.)

4. How much will it cost the company to purchase the eggs for this order? (Hint: Create a calculated field.)

5. How many total pounds of cinnamon are needed to fulfill this order? How much will cinnamon cost for this order? (Hint: Create a calculated field.)

6. How many pounds of light brown sugar are needed for this order? How much will light brown sugar cost for this order? (Hint: Create a calculated field.)

7. Which ingredient for this order will cost the most (total cost)? (Hint: Create a calculated field.)

8. Now that you have calculated the ingredients needed by pounds or count (for eggs), you're ready to submit the order to your vendors. What will be the total cost of raw materials for this order? (Hint: Create a calculated field.)

Take it to the next level!

9. Which type of cookie is the most expensive to produce?

10. How much does it cost to make one M&M cookie? (Hint: Create a calculated field.)

Marketing, Sales, and Collections Processes

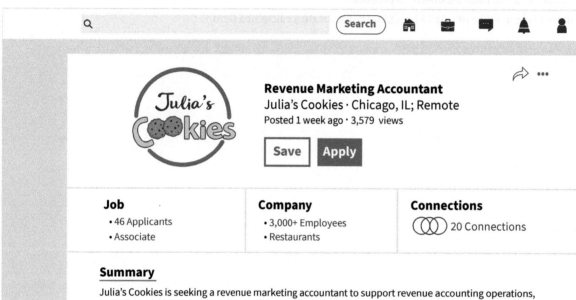

Revenue Marketing Accountant

Julia's Cookies · Chicago, IL; Remote

Posted 1 week ago · 3,579 views

Save | Apply

Job	Company	Connections
• 46 Applicants	• 3,000+ Employees	20 Connections
• Associate	• Restaurants	

Summary

Julia's Cookies is seeking a revenue marketing accountant to support revenue accounting operations, including establishing accounting policies and internal controls, developing technical accounting conclusions, and supporting our monthly close procedures.

Responsibilities

- Provide support in determining proper accounting for products and services, including new introductions
- Build expanding revenue reporting to bridge the gap from accounting to analytics
- Improve revenue accounting processes through simplification and automation
- Analyze interim financials for accuracy and consistency for transaction reporting
- Prepare monthly revenue-related reconciliations
- Improve and maintain process documentation
- Assist with annual external audit
- Ensure compliance with U.S. GAAP, SOX, and all relevant company policies and procedures

Requirements

Preferred Education: Bachelor's degree or higher in accounting
Preferred Certifications: CPA

Preferred Knowledge and Skills

The ideal candidate will demonstrate strong technical knowledge of accounting principles. Preference will be given to candidates who also demonstrate:

- Strong experience in Excel, including pivot tables and VLOOKUPs
- Experience with an ERP system (SAP is a plus!)
- Experience applying revenue accounting guidance (ASC 606)
- Experience with or desire to learn SQL
- Comfort learning new systems and ability to work with different applications

Salary: $65,000–85,000

CHAPTER PREVIEW   After a business has converted resources into products or services, it's time to generate revenue. This is done by marketing and selling products and services and collecting cash payments for those sales. In this chapter, you will learn about the core activities in these business processes:

- The importance of marketing, sales, and collections
- Differences between credit and cash sales
- Types of revenue recognition
- Methods of receiving payments, or collections
- How system-generated data is converted into reports and analytics

We will follow the sales and collections processes through the related information systems. You will learn about the controls that mitigate risk and the reports and analytics created with the data generated by these business processes.

Positions in marketing, sales, and collections for accounting professionals include specific subject matter expert roles like the revenue marketing accountant position at Julia's Cookies. This position, based on real job postings at two popular software service companies headquartered in Atlanta, Georgia, requires an accounting professional with strong knowledge of accounting principles and exposure to accounting information applications and databases. The AIS concepts in this chapter could be essential skills you will need on the job one day.

There are more accounting careers related directly to these processes, such as managing accounts receivable, business-process improvements, and SOX internal controls design. Auditors and forensic accountants must also achieve an understanding of this business area to perform their roles effectively. ∎

Chapter Roadmap

LEARNING OBJECTIVES	TOPICS	JULIA'S COOKIES APPLIED LEARNING
12.1 Describe the marketing, sales, and collections processes for business-to-consumer sales.	• Business-to-Consumer Sales • Managing Inventory and Product Flow	Supply Chain Management: Revenue Data Selection
12.2 Evaluate the credit sales process and its related risks and controls.	• Marketing • Pricing and Contracts • Sales Orders • Shipping • Billing and Collections • Credit Sales Process Flowchart	Marketing, Sales, and Collections: Opportunities and Challenges
12.3 Identify risks and controls related to revenue recognition in the sales process.	• Revenue Recognition Model • Controlling for Mistakes and Fraud	Revenue Recognition: Unusual Revenue Red Flags
12.4 Assess the risks and controls related to the cash collections and accounts receivable processes.	• Receiving Payments • Bank Deposits • Recording Cash Receipts • Collections Process Flowchart	Customer Invoicing: Business Process Maturity Assessment
12.5 Connect the ERP system and underlying database to potential reports and analytics.	• Database Design • Reporting and Insights	Customer Orders: Fuzzy Matching Fraud Test

CPA You will find the CPA tag throughout the chapter to call out any important topics you may see on the CPA exam.

12.1 How Do Marketing, Sales, and Collections Complete the Business Model?

Learning Objective ❶
Describe the marketing, sales, and collections processes for business-to-consumer sales.

Did you have a lemonade stand as a child or hold a bake sale to raise money for a good cause? If you did, you probably know that, while the process of creating a product can be rewarding, collecting your hard-earned cash is important. Once a company has manufactured its products or created its services, it must sell them.

Marketing, sales, and collections processes follow conversion processes in the basic business model. Just as a child running a lemonade stand converts lemons into lemonade, sets up a booth in a high-traffic area, waves down potential customers, and exchanges a glass of lemonade for a dollar or two, a company converts its resources into products and/or services and sells them to generate revenue that is collected as cash (**Illustration 12.1**).

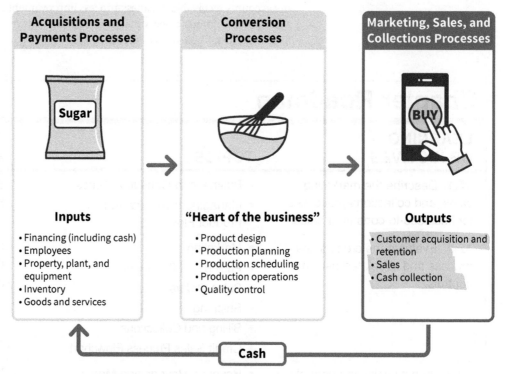

Illustration 12.1   Marketing, sales, and collections processes are the final steps in the basic business model.

At Julia's Cookies, the type of sale that occurs depends on the customer:

- **CPA** **Business-to-consumer (B2C) sales:** Julia's Cookies sells cookies via its mobile app to consumer customers who directly purchase the cookies.

- **CPA** **Business-to-business (B2B) sales:** Julia's Cookies also manufactures frozen cookie dough that is sold to other businesses, like grocery stores and other retailers, for resale.

Companies take various approaches to information systems for sales, from limited controls and processes through optimized, best-in-class operations. The sophistication and degree of integration of marketing, sales, and collections systems depend on many factors—including the cost of a fully integrated and sophisticated enterprise resource planning (ERP) system, the size of the business, management support, and user buy-in.

Using Julia's Cookies as our example, we will next examine the sales processes for B2C sales, and later we will explore the more complex processes involved in B2B sales, including risks and control activities.

Business-to-Consumer Sales

Remember that Julia's Cookies' B2C customers either use an app to connect to local stores where cookies are baked and delivered to the customer's location or order in person at a store counter. The high-level activities for marketing, selling, and delivering warm cookies are simpler than the B2B activities we'll discuss later. For B2C, sales and cash collections occur simultaneously via the mobile app (**Illustration 12.2**).

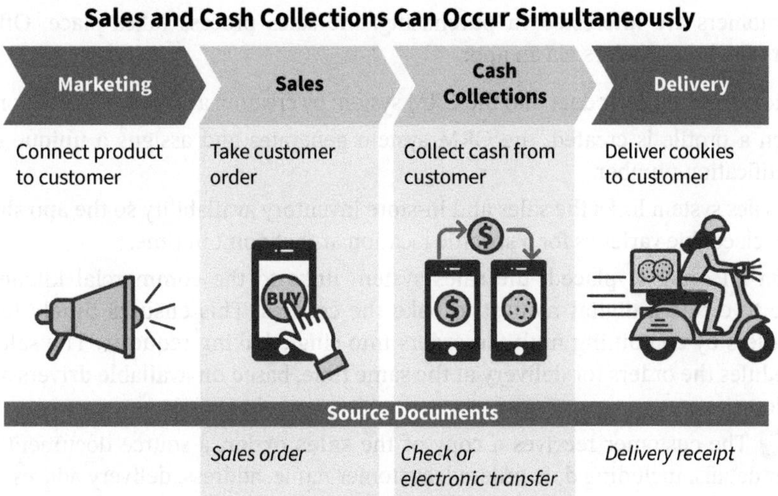

Sales and Cash Collections Can Occur Simultaneously

Marketing	Sales	Cash Collections	Delivery
Connect product to customer	Take customer order	Collect cash from customer	Deliver cookies to customer

Source Documents

Sales order	Check or electronic transfer	Delivery receipt

Illustration 12.2   Business-to-consumer (B2C) sales and cash collections occur simultaneously as customers purchase and pay via the mobile app.

Marketing

Marketing departments are generally responsible for marketing research, advertising, branding, promotional programs, and search engine optimization. Marketing processes bring together idea generation, research and development, and creative campaigns to reach potential clients and generate revenue for the company.

Many organizations purchase customer relationship management (CRM) software packages or ERP modules (as part of their ERP system) that manage interactions with existing, past, and potential customers. Marketing is different depending on the sales model, and B2C marketing at Julia's Cookies focuses on drawing people to the website, user experience of the website and mobile app, and social media branding.

Marketing activities may result in *accounting transactions for purchases* when a business *buys* marketing services and advertisements from vendors.

Control activities for marketing processes include those related to protecting how the business interacts with potential customers (**Table 12.1**). From ownership of social media accounts to logging passwords, policies must be in place to protect the business in the event that a key employee leaves the company. Additionally, adequate controls around who posts and what is posted on social media protect the business from legal and reputational risks.

TABLE 12.1 B2C Marketing Control Activities

Risk Statement: An unauthorized user posting inappropriate content to the corporate social media accounts may result in legal or reputational damage.	
Sample Control Activity	**Control Owner**
Maintain and enforce clearly documented policies and procedures for what content can be posted on social media sites	Marketing director
Make password logs available to authorized users only	Marketing director
Use standardized scripts for responding to recurring scenarios	Marketing director
Review and approve social media posts before allowing them to be posted	Marketing director

Sales

Once customers are interested in purchasing, the sales process takes place. Offsite B2C customers send their orders via an app:

1. Customers input their data into the CRM system by creating a customer profile on the app.
2. When a profile is created, the CRM system generates and assigns a unique customer identification number.
3. The sales system links the sales and in-store inventory availability so the app shows only in-stock cookie varieties for a specific location at that point in time.
4. When an order is placed, the sales system links to the commercial kitchen in the store to create a digital request to bake the cookies. This ensures timely fulfillment of orders by combining multiple orders into single baking requests. The sales system schedules the orders for delivery at the same time, based on available drivers and delivery locations.
5. **CPA** The customer receives a copy of the **sales order**, a source document with the order details, including date ordered, customer name, address, delivery address, description, individual price, quantity of goods ordered, and total selling price of the order.

The sales order is the customer's request for the purchase of goods. Even though it's a source document designed for documentation purposes, a sales order to a B2C customer can include company marketing. For example, at Julia's Cookies, the sales order includes links to social media and app downloads to engage customers to purchase again (**Illustration 12.3**).

Cash Collections

Whether cash is received at the checkout counter at a clothing retailer or digital payments are made on a mobile app for an e-commerce sales transaction, the cash collections process for B2C customers usually occurs at the time the sale is made. These payments can be made with cash, checks, mobile payment apps, or credit cards, but they are referred to as "cash" because the accounting transactions are all recorded in the Cash account in the General Ledger.

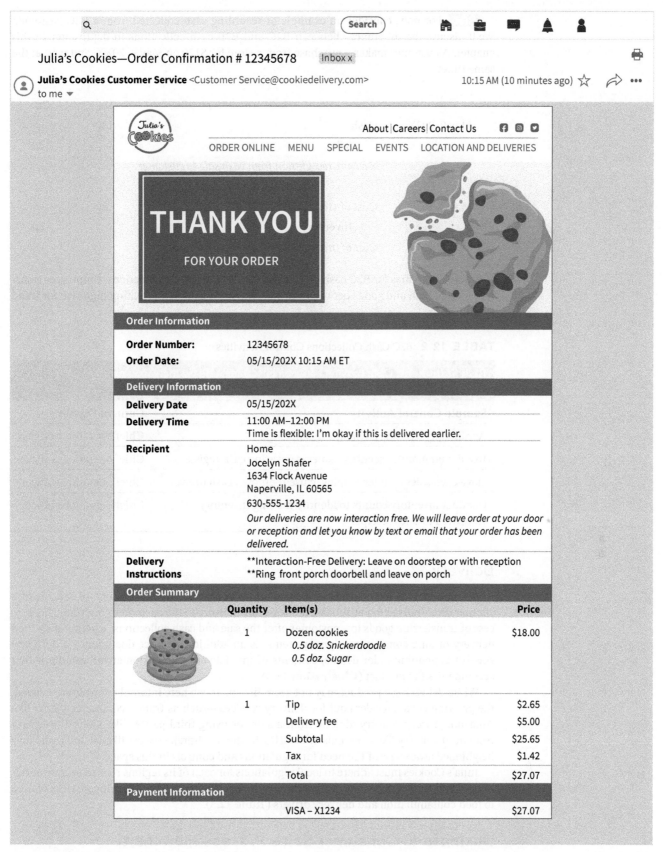

Illustration 12.3 The sales order is sent to the customer as an order confirmation and includes details of the products ordered and the selling price.

CPA For now, consider an example of recording cash collected from a B2C customer. We'll discuss the differences between B2C and B2B cash collections in depth later in this chapter. A customer makes a purchase from a store for $120 on May 9, 20XX, and pays at the same time:

		Dr.	Cr.
May 9, 202X	Cash	120	
	Sales		120
	Revenue recognition from cash sale to customer		
May 9, 202X	Cost of Goods Sold	80	
	Inventory		80
	Cost of inventory for cash sale to customer		

Control activities for B2C cash collections focus on in-store transactions. Employees transfer physical cash and goods between the business and customers, creating high risk for fraud (**Table 12.2**).

TABLE 12.2 B2C Cash Collections Control Activities

Risk Statement: Cash passing between customers and cashiers may result in cashiers pocketing cash.	
Sample Control Activity	**Control Owner**
Accept only cashless payments in stores	Chief operations officer
Install and monitor security cameras covering cash registers	Chief operations officer
Have each sales counter employee use their own cash drawer	Chief operations officer
Conduct inventory counts to identify missing inventory compared to sales receipts	Chief operations officer

Delivery

A B2C company delivers goods to a customer in-person at or near the time of sale, as in a counter sales transaction at Julia's Cookies, or by delivery to the customer's address. This process of transferring goods to a customer after the sale and cash collections, whether it's a food delivery or an e-commerce shipment, requires an additional source document—a **delivery receipt** containing order details, contents of the delivery, and customer information—that accompanies the product (**Illustration 12.4**).

While delivering a product may not seem like an area where internal controls are needed, the growing consumer demand for delivery services—such as from e-commerce giants like Amazon, grocery delivery directly from a store or using third parties like Shipt, third-party restaurant delivery like Uber Eats or DoorDash, and meal-prep services like Hello Fresh—has heightened awareness of the need for regulations and controls in this space.

Julia's Cookies must adhere to local regulations for each of its regions related to transportation and delivery of food, and it must have sufficient controls in place to mitigate risks related to food contamination and delivery drivers (**Table 12.3**).

Business-to-Consumer Sales Process Flowchart

To evaluate the controls of any process, we need to understand the process—what is done, who does it, and when it happens. The B2C process at Julia's Cookies varies depending on whether a sale is made in store or via the mobile app. In either case, a sales order is generated, and cash is collected at the time of the sale. The similarities are easy to note when the processes are presented in a process flowchart (**Illustration 12.5**).

Illustration 12.4 Delivery of products to e-commerce customers requires an additional source document, like a packing slip or an order confirmation.

TABLE 12.3 B2C Delivery Control Activities

Risk Statement: Failure to protect food during delivery may result in delivery of a subpar product to customers, food contamination, or theft of product.	
Sample Control Activity	**Control Owner**
Ensure adherence to local, state, and federal food handling and transportation regulations	COO
Use food tampering stickers or seals on delivery containers	COO
Risk Statement: Using unskilled delivery drivers may result in accidents, reputational damage, medical lawsuits, or legal fines.	
Sample Control Activity	**Control Owner**
Subject delivery drivers to background checks, driving record reviews, and robust onboarding	COO
Periodically deliver driver safety training	COO
Risk Statement: Customers filing fictitious claims that packages were not received may result in fraudulent refunds to customers.	
Sample Control Activity	**Control Owner**
Have delivery drivers take photos of packages in their delivery locations and send them to customers via email or text message	COO
Risk Statement: Customers filing fictitious claims that products were damaged upon receipt may result in fraudulent refunds to customers.	
Sample Control Activity	**Control Owner**
Require customers to submit a photo of the product condition in order to return the product and/or get a refund	COO

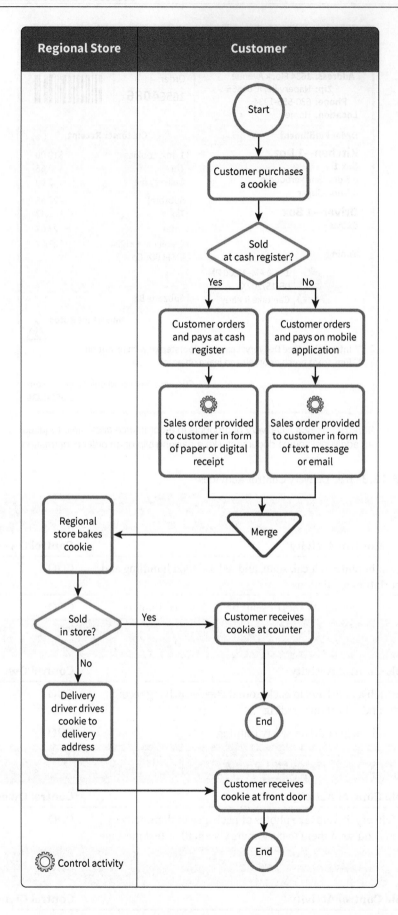

Illustration 12.5 The B2C sales process at Julia's Cookies varies depending on whether a sale is made in a store or via the mobile app.

Managing Inventory and Product Flow

While the B2C sales processes seem simple, there are risks that could make them costly and ineffective for a business. Effectively managing inventory and the supply chain is as important during the sales process as it is in the purchasing and conversion processes.

Inventory Management

Inventory management is the oversight of inventory from purchase to sales. After all, there can't be a sale without enough premixed cookie dough to make cookies when they are ordered. Inventory management is also important because sales orders and forecasts determine inventory requirements, which in turn drive purchases of raw materials and supplies and the production of finished goods (**Illustration 12.6**). Finally, keep in mind that baking the cookies, even when it happens in real time with a sale, is part of the production process and not the sales process. Production and sales must be in sync. Customers don't want a cold cookie.

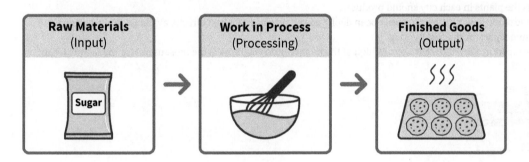

Illustration 12.6 Raw materials are turned into finished goods that are sold to customers in local stores.

Supply Chain Management

Supply chain management is the management of the life cycle of a product from procuring raw materials through customer sales (**Illustration 12.7**). The sales and collections processes are at the end of the physical life cycle of a product, but the information generated in these processes is used throughout the supply chain. For example, customer demand forecasts based on historical sales and marketing research are used to determine how much of a product must be manufactured and what supplies must be purchased for that production. An integrated

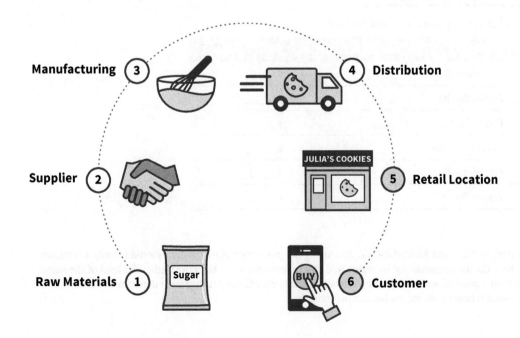

Illustration 12.7 The sales and collections processes are at the end of the physical flow of the supply chain.

accounting information system, such as an ERP system, makes the communication of this information throughout the supply chain efficient and clear.

While supply chain management may not seem like something an accounting professional is involved with, consider all the areas along the supply chain where accounting professionals manage processes and data. From purchasing to revenue and at many stops along the way, auditors, accounting analysts, and corporate accountants are involved in the supply chain, even if indirectly. Help Aniyah, a revenue accountant, fulfill a data request from the Supply Chain Management department in Applied Learning 12.1.

Julia's Cookies   Applied Learning 12.1

Supply Chain Management: Revenue Data Selection

The Supply Chain Management department at Julia's Cookies wants to create sales forecasts for the upcoming year that will be used to predict the quantity of products the plants in each city should produce.

Because the Financial module of the new ERP system hasn't been deployed yet, revenue data isn't directly available. Aniyah, a revenue accountant, must pull the revenue report for the past quarter.

Aniyah can pull the revenue report in a few different ways. Which of the following do you think is the most useful for the Supply Chain Management department's needs?

1. Revenue summarized by region:

Region	Total Revenue
Northeast	$_____
Southeast	$_____
Midwest	$_____

2. Number of sales and revenue summarized by product:

Product	Number of Sales	Total Revenue
Chocolate Chip	_____	$_____
Snickerdoodle	_____	$_____
Peanut Butter	_____	$_____

3. Number of sales and revenue summarized by region, city, and product:

Region	City	Product	Number of Sales	Total Revenue
Northeast	New York	Chocolate Chip	_____	$_____
Northeast	New York	Snickerdoodle	_____	$_____
Northeast	New York	Peanut Butter	_____	$_____
Northeast	Philadelphia	Chocolate Chip	_____	$_____
Northeast	Philadelphia	Snickerdoodle	_____	$_____
Northeast	Philadelphia	Peanut Butter	_____	$_____

SOLUTION

Because the data will be used for customer demand forecasting and developing the production plan, the data should include a summary by product. It's also important to have the data summarized by region and city so forecasting can be performed at the level of the plants that manufacture the products. Option 3 provides sufficient granular detail for the Supply Chain Management department's information needs that this department knows what it needs to do for production planning.

CONCEPT REVIEW QUESTIONS

1. **CPA** What is a sales order?

    Ans. A sales order is a source document with the order details, including date ordered, customer name, address, delivery address, description, individual price, quantity of goods ordered, and total selling price of the order.

2. A delivery receipt is a source document that is sent to the customer. What is some of the information that would be included on a delivery receipt?

    Ans. A delivery receipt would include order details, contents of the delivery, and customer information.

12.2 Why Are Business Credit Sales More Complex Than Consumer Cash Sales?

Learning Objective ❷
Evaluate the credit sales process and its related risks and controls.

Now that you have had an overview of the marketing, sales, and collections processes for B2C transactions, we can examine the process for B2B customers. Recall that B2C sales result in collection of "cash," which can be physical money, checks, credit cards, or mobile app payments. While these receipts are immediately recorded in the Cash account in the General Ledger, B2B sales often take a different form:

- Business credit sales are sales on account, meaning that the company offers a line of credit to its B2B customers.

- Instead of being recorded immediately as Cash receipts in the accounting records, these credit transactions are recorded to a different asset account, Accounts Receivable, because the customer has not yet paid.

We'll discuss the accounting implications of these transactions later in the chapter, but first, let's look at the B2B processes from a supply chain perspective.

In B2B sales, the company making the sale is the supplier. Consider how Julia's Cookies purchases flour from Flowers & Flours and then later sells frozen prepackaged cookie dough to Good Foods (**Illustration 12.8**).

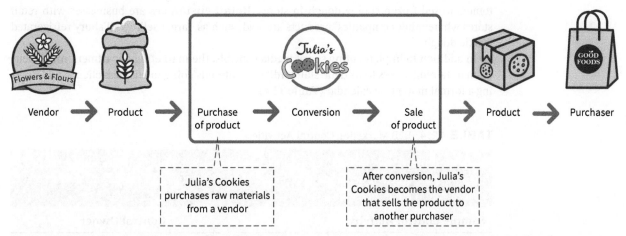

Illustration 12.8 A production company like Julia's Cookies starts as a purchaser and then becomes the vendor after converting raw materials to finished goods that are sold in B2B transactions.

Julia's Cookies goes from purchaser to vendor after converting raw materials to finished goods. As we continue exploring the B2B sales and collections processes, consider how the customer is performing purchasing and payments processes at the same time.

Why Does It Matter to Your Career?

Thoughts from a Senior External Audit Associate, Public Accounting

As an accounting professional, you could be associated with these business processes in different ways. You might work in the accounts receivable, financial reporting, or treasury department or work upstream from sales in a different finance function. You might audit these business processes or prepare tax documents that use data generated from them.

Illustration 12.9 summarizes a generic process with five high-level business activities for B2B sales. Note that pricing and contracts, shipping, and accounts receivable are highlighted in yellow. These are all new processes you have not learned about yet because they are specific to B2B sales.

Marketing	Pricing and Contracts	Sales	Shipping	Accounts Receivable
Connect product or service to customer	Negotiate price, payment terms, and/or sales contract terms	Take customer order	Provide goods to customer	Collect cash from customer

Source Documents

| | Signed sales contract | Sales order | Shipping notice | Invoice, check, or electronic transfer |

Illustration 12.9 Business-to-business (B2B) sales include marketing, pricing, sales, shipping, and accounts receivable.

Marketing

While the goal of B2C marketing is getting the product in front of potential consumers via web advertisements and marketing campaigns, B2B marketing focuses on finding retail customers to sell frozen cookie dough in stores. **Retail customers** are businesses with retail stores where other companies' products are sold, such as Target selling Pillsbury refrigerated cookie dough.

In addition to implementing social media controls, the marketing department must focus on maintaining access to its data, standardizing materials going to business clients, and keeping a formal marketing calendar (**Table 12.4**).

TABLE 12.4 B2B Marketing Control Activities

Risk Statement: An unauthorized user accessing the marketing database and gaining inappropriate access to sensitive data related to business customers and leads may result in legal and reputational damage.	
Sample Control Activity	**Control Owner**
Maintain and enforce clearly documented and authorized policies and procedures for user access	Information security manager/marketing director

TABLE 12.4 (*Continued*)

Risk Statement: Inconsistent marketing materials that provide unclear messaging may result in loss of customers and leads.	
Sample Control Activity	**Control Owner**
Use standardized scripts and templates for marketing materials	Marketing director
Risk Statement: Sending too much marketing material to customers and leads may result in loss of potential revenues from customers and leads.	
Sample Control Activity	**Control Owner**
Maintain and communicate a marketing schedule to employees	Marketing director

Pricing and Contracts

Marketing processes generate leads for new customers. From there, prices are negotiated, potential new customers are evaluated, and sales contracts are created.

Pricing

The selling prices of products and services are set in the **pricing process**, and pricing goes hand in hand with the marketing processes. Companies generate interest in their products with marketing, but setting a competitive price that customers are willing to pay is equally essential. Existing customers have negotiated prices and sales contracts already established with the company, as retailer Good Foods does with Julia's Cookies. Different customers get different pricing, which depends on factors such as the customer's buying power and sales volume. However, there are standard prices for retailers that do not have as much bargaining power as a buyer like Good Foods.

Pricing processes are subject to fraud risk. An employee at Julia's Cookies could give Good Foods an inappropriate discounted sales price as part of a collusion fraud. In that case, Good Foods would buy at a lower sales price and pay the employee a portion of the savings. Internal control activities over pricing should focus on oversight of price changes, communication of pricing updates, authorization policies, and customer discount procedures (**Table 12.5**).

TABLE 12.5 Pricing Control Activities

Risk Statement: Collusion between an employee and a buyer may result in fraud activity and financial losses.	
Sample Control Activity	**Control Owner**
Maintain a whistleblower hotline that takes anonymous tips from employees who suspect fraudulent activity	CFO
Conduct independent checks on pricing and sales team members' work	Controller/sales manager
Require every pricing and sales employee to periodically take vacation so other employees perform their job duties	Human resources manager
Risk Statement: Inappropriately given or unauthorized customer discounts may result in financial losses.	
Sample Control Activity	**Control Owner**
Maintain and enforce clearly documented policies and procedures for discount pricing	Sales manager
Define roles and responsibilities for pricing functions	Controller/sales manager
Implement system controls that prevent unauthorized users from making pricing adjustments, including discounts	Automated system control

(*Continued*)

TABLE 12.5 (*Continued*)

Risk Statement: Pricing pressures from customers that prompt employees to offer lower prices to maintain relationships may result in financial losses.	
Sample Control Activity	**Control Owner**
Maintain and enforce clearly documented policies and procedures for customer relationship management	Marketing and sales director
Define roles and responsibilities for customer relationship management	Marketing and sales director
Implement system controls that prevent unauthorized users from making pricing adjustments, including discounts	Automated system control

Evaluating Customers

Much as a car dealership or a credit card company checks an individual's credit score before extending that person a new line of credit, such as a car loan or a credit card, a company checks the creditworthiness of a new customer before extending a line of credit. Existing customers are also reviewed to ensure that their creditworthiness remains in good standing. **CPA** **Credit criteria** are the factors used to determine the financial strength of customers.

Credit terms are dependent on a customer's creditworthiness. A company needs to check the customer's credit and payment history and set a credit limit before accepting an order from a customer. The goal of this evaluation is to limit the bad debt expense and the allowance for doubtful accounts you may have learned about in financial accounting. Responsibilities for credit terms and checks should be independent of sales, the General Ledger, and accounts receivable (**Table 12.6**).

TABLE 12.6 Credit Customer Control Activities

Risk Statement: Inadequate or inconsistently applied creditworthiness checking may result in excessive bad debts and a wide variety of credit terms.	
Sample Control Activity	**Control Owner**
Maintain and enforce clearly documented credit policies and procedures for all customers	Controller
Risk Statement: Sales made to unreliable customers may result in unacceptable credit risks and excessive bad debts.	
Sample Control Activity	**Control Owner**
Maintain and enforce clearly documented credit policies and procedures for all customers, including a credit application and approval process for new customers	Controller
Establish a credit limit for each customer, based on the customer's ability to pay, and capture this limit in the information system as an attribute of customer main data	Controller
Review credit limits periodically and adjust them if required	Controller
Require management approval for credit in excess of credit limits	Controller
Conduct system checks for past due accounts receivable balances prior to approving a new sales order	Automated system control
CPA Establish segregation of duties between the person granting credit to customers and the sales, shipping, accounts receivable, and accounting functions	Controller

Sales Contracts

If the company's standard terms and conditions for credit sales do not apply to a particular order or customer, then the amended terms should be laid out in appropriate legally enforceable contracts, accepted by both parties and approved by management. These agreements should be accessible in the customer records. For example, if Julia's Cookies offers Good Foods a discounted price if Good Foods orders a specific quantity at a specified frequency, a sales contract is created.

It's important for legal counsel to review and approve sales contracts that deviate from standard sales terms and conditions (**Table 12.7**).

TABLE 12.7 Sales Contracts Control Activities

Risk Statement: Charging similar customers different prices for the same products may result in customer dissatisfaction, loss of reputation, or penalties.	
Sample Control Activity	**Control Owner**
Use standardized, authorized sales contracts that are legally enforceable	Director of legal and compliance
Risk Statement: Verbal agreements may result in legally binding agreements with unfavorable outcomes.	
Sample Control Activity	**Control Owner**
Notify customers that all agreements must be in writing to be legally binding	Director of legal and compliance/director of sales
Conduct employee training covering appropriate and inappropriate wording when speaking with customers	Director of legal and compliance/HR director

We've now examined marketing, pricing, and contracts. Next, we will consider how customers place, receive, and pay for orders. First, review Julia's Cookies' opportunities and challenges in sales and marketing flexibility in Applied Learning 12.2.

Julia's Cookies
Applied Learning 12.2

Marketing, Sales, and Collections: Opportunities and Challenges

Victoria is the vice president of marketing and sales at Julia's Cookies. Given economic uncertainties, government policies, a global pandemic, and increased competition, she realizes that the company's continued success requires flexibility when it comes to marketing and sales.

Of course, changes to business processes require cost-benefit analyses to ensure informed decision making. Flexibility is only one of the areas Victoria needs to consider. Review the following factors that may impact sales and marketing flexibility and help Victoria identify opportunities and challenges related to each of them.

1. The company uses its own salespeople to sell frozen product to retailers directly. Some competitors use third-party representatives rather than full-time employees.
2. Salespeople earn a combination of salaries and commissions, with higher salaries than the competition but lower commissions.
3. The company has both short-term and longer-term price agreements with different retail customers.
4. The company has several long-term advertising agreements with advertising vendors.
5. The company hires wage-earning drivers at its stores for cookie deliveries. They use company-owned vehicles for deliveries.

SOLUTION

Some of the opportunities and challenges Victoria faces are:

1. Independent representatives offer more flexibility in terms of cutting costs, but sales employees offer more flexibility by quickly changing selling points and sales strategies. Sales employees also have more loyalty to the company because they have long-term interests in the business.

2. In periods of strong sales, the company can afford higher commissions, and salespeople can make more money. In periods of weak sales, higher fixed salaries can be a drain on cash resources.

3. Shorter-term price agreements provide more flexibility to increase prices in periods of strong sales or inflation.

4. Longer-term advertising contracts likely offer quantity discounts, while shorter-term contracts offer more flexibility to change the message in line with current circumstances.

5. Hiring independent drivers who use their own vehicles offers more flexibility in terms of cutting costs when needed, but hiring employees offers more stability in terms of dependability, experience, and consistency related to customer interaction.

Sales Orders

Once pricing is negotiated, creditworthiness is approved, and a sales contract is established, the customer is onboarded:

1. Customers are included in the approved main customer table, with additional checks in place to approve credit sales to customers not already established in the database.

2. Once established in the sales system, customers can submit purchase orders to the seller, which are fulfilled under the existing pricing, credit terms, and contract terms and conditions.

3. A customer's purchase order becomes a numerically controlled sales order to the seller. This document includes all relevant information related to the order, so each order has an audit trail for accountability. At the time a sales order is received, no accounting transaction occurs, unless there is a requirement for advance payment. Upfront payments made before the conditions of the order are fulfilled result in deferred revenue, which is a liability:

		Dr.	Cr.
May 9, 202X	Cash	3,470	
	Deferred Revenue		3,470

Order #OD-20004938 on 04/20/202X

4. Sales orders are entered into the system, which is connected to the main customer table and inventory data for fulfillment.

IT general controls (ITGCs) for securing data, such as data integrity and access controls, as well as automated system controls, should be in place (**Table 12.8**).

TABLE 12.8 Sales Order Control Activities

Risk Statement: An unauthorized sales order may result in fraudulent or inappropriate sales.	
Sample Control Activity	**Control Owner**
Maintain and enforce clearly documented policies and procedures for processing and approving sales orders	Director of sales
CPA Separate the duties of authorizing sales from shipping, inventory control, and accounting responsibilities	CFO
To enforce segregation of duties, allow only authorized employees to access sales order input screens and/or sales order documents	IT manager/CFO
Have the ERP system match the customer on the sales order to the main customer data	Automated system control

TABLE 12.8 (*Continued*)

Risk Statement: A sales order without credit approval or above the credit limit may result in an uncollectible account.	
Sample Control Activity	**Control Owner**
Have the ERP system match the amount of the sales order with the credit limit in the main customer data	Automated system control
Risk Statement: Changes to the main customer data may results in sales orders being altered or deleted.	
Sample Control Activity	**Control Owner**
Require that all changes to the main customer data be authorized by management prior to other data entry	Director of sales/ controller/automated IT authorization sequence
Risk Statement: Inappropriate access to the main customer table may result in creation of a fictitious customer and revenue fraud.	
Sample Control Activity	**Control Owner**
Require that all changes to the main customer data be authorized by management prior to other data entry	Director of sales/ controller/automated IT authorization sequence
Periodically compare the main customer data to the main employee data to test for similarities and identify fraud red flags	Director of sales

Shipping

In B2C sales, delivery drivers deliver product to the customer's location, or the customer receives it at the counter of a store. In B2B sales, products are shipped to Julia's Cookies' B2B customers (**Illustration 12.10**).

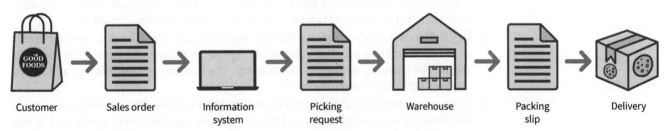

| Customer | Sales order | Information system | Picking request | Warehouse | Packing slip | Delivery |

Illustration 12.10 Shipping products to customers involves multiple departments and source documents.

The information system schedules the delivery:

1. The information from the sales order generates a request to the regional warehouse facility closest to the retail customer. **CPA** The **picking request** is an instruction to warehouse employees to prepare the correct quantity and product for shipping to the customer. This source document authorizes the transfer of finished goods from the warehouse.

2. **CPA** Warehouse employees prepare an order for delivery. As part of this process, they use the information in the picking request to create a **packing slip**, which is also a source document, showing the customer's name, the delivery destination, and the contents of the delivery (**Illustration 12.11**).

3. Once the delivery is packaged and ready, the information system selects a delivery vehicle and driver and schedules the most cost-effective route for the driver to take to the

Julia's Cookies

Packing Slip

Date: 05/05/202X

Julia's Cookies	**Receiving**	**Accounts Payable**
4128 Buford Highway	Good Foods	Good Foods
Duluth, GA 30096	1250 Shackleford Road	6548 Abernathy Road
470-555-1234	Duluth, GA 30096	Atlanta, GA 30328
470-555-5678	678-516-1234	770-448-1234
	Customer ID: V1-GF-0239	Customer ID: V1-GF-0200

Order Date	**Order Number**	**Job**
04/20/202X	OD-20004938	1285

Item Number	**Description**	**Quantity**
2156	Chocolate Chip Cookies (Box of 100)	30
2158	Sugar Cookies (Box of 100)	20
2198	Lemonade Cookies (Box of 100)	20

Please contact customer service at 770-555-1234 with any questions or comments.
Thank you for your business!

Illustration 12.11 Information from the sales order is transferred to the picking request and ultimately ends up on the packing slip that is returned to the customer with the product delivery.

customer. One driver may be responsible for many order deliveries in a single trip. While some companies use third-party carriers for shipping, Julia's Cookies has its own fleet of delivery vehicles for deliveries from stores and warehouses.

4. After an order is loaded into a delivery vehicle, the customer is notified that their purchase is on the way. The customer can track the delivery status via a tracking link.

5. **CPA** The delivery driver shows the customer a **shipping notice** that provides details of the shipment and proof of delivery. By signing on a handheld device, the customer accepts the shipping notice and the delivery. The business retains this digitally signed shipping notice as a source document.

6. Upon acceptance of the shipment on the handheld device, the information system reduces the inventory of finished goods and records the sale and the cost of goods sold in real time. The customer is billed immediately, and accounts receivable records are updated with an accounting transaction. For example, say that the Good Foods order to Julia's Cookies in Illustration 12.11 is for $3,470:

		Dr.	Cr.
May 5, 202X	Accounts Receivable	3,470	
	Sales		3,470

Order #OD-20004938 on 04/20/202X

Business events related to shipping that result in accounting transactions include delivering raw materials, merchandise inventory, other goods, and/or services to customers to generate revenue. Such events result in the important (and complex) concept of revenue recognition in financial accounting. Remember that the movement of inventory is recorded in the inventory records, from raw materials to work in process, to finished goods. Finished goods then move to cost of goods sold when the revenue from a sale is recognized, which for Julia's Cookies is upon delivery of the product to the customer. We dedicate the next learning objective to the complexities of revenue recognition.

Internal controls for shipping should include a focus on source documents. These shipping documents, although electronic, must be numerically controlled and allow for accountability for each shipment. The shipping function plays a vital role in revenue recognition, as ownership of the products passes to the customer upon acceptance of delivery of an order, at which stage the risks and rewards also pass on to the customer (**Table 12.9**).

TABLE 12.9 Shipping Control Activities

Risk Statement: Shipments made to incorrect customers or locations may result in customer dissatisfaction, complaints, and financial losses.	
Sample Control Activity	**Control Owner**
Maintain and enforce clearly documented policies and procedures for all shipments	COO
Require properly authorized shipping documents and an appropriate delivery address for every shipment	COO
Clearly communicate shipping policies for customers to warehouse delivery personnel	COO
Maintain and enforce clearly documented policies and procedures for investigating and resolving customer disputes and complaints	COO
Risk Statement: Lost or fraudulently diverted undelivered shipments may result in customer dissatisfaction, complaints, and financial losses.	
Sample Control Activity	**Control Owner**
Maintain and enforce clearly documented policies and procedures for all shipments	COO
Track shipments using tracking software	COO
Restrict access to the shipping area	CSO
Segregate the physical shipping location from the warehouse and the receiving location	COO
Maintain and enforce clearly documented policies and procedures for timely investigation and resolution of customer disputes and complaints	Controller
Risk Statement: Shipping incorrect products or quantities may result in customer dissatisfaction, complaints, sales returns, and financial losses.	
Sample Control Activity	**Control Owner**
Maintain and enforce clearly documented policies and procedures for all shipments	COO or VP of operations
Have the ERP system match goods and quantities taken from the warehouse to approved sales orders	Automated system control
Maintain and enforce clearly documented policies and procedures for timely investigation and resolution of customer disputes and complaints	Controller

(Continued)

TABLE 12.9 (*Continued*)

Risk Statement: Premature shipments or late shipments that don't meet customer requirements may result in customer dissatisfaction, complaints, sales returns, and financial losses.	
Sample Control Activity	**Control Owner**
Maintain and enforce clearly documented policies and procedures for all shipments	COO or VP of operations
Maintain and enforce clearly documented policies and procedures for timely investigation and resolution of customer disputes and complaints	Controller
Match sales orders to shipping documents and customer shipment receipts	Automated system control
Control the sequence of shipping documents and investigate anomalies	Automated system control
Have the ERP system identify unfilled sales orders in a timely manner for investigation and resolution	Automated system control
Risk Statement: Unauthorized orders may result in goods being released for shipping.	
Sample Control Activity	**Control Owner**
Have the ERP system match goods and quantities taken from the warehouse to approved sales orders	Automated system control
Risk Statement: Lack of shipping documentation may result in inaccurate shipments, fraudulent shipments, or missed shipments.	
Sample Control Activity	**Control Owner**
Have the ERP system generate shipping documentation when a sales order is processed	Automated system control

Billing and Collections

After it sells goods, a company must bill its customers:

- **CPA** The billing system generates an electronic **sales invoice** using data recorded from the sales order, picking slip, and packing slip and sends it to the customer. The sales invoice is a source document that shows data related to a specific order and delivery. **Illustration 12.12** is an example of a sales invoice for Julia's Cookies. Recall that Good Foods is a retail customer that orders Julia's Cookies frozen cookie dough to sell in stores.
- The data in this invoice repeats the sales order, and it also includes payment terms and due dates.
- Since accounts receivable is responsible for collecting payment from customers, this data is essential for the collections process.

At the end of each month, the billing system generates a monthly sales invoice for the customer, which is similar to the monthly bill you might receive from a credit card company. **CPA** The sales invoice is sent to the customer with another source document, called a remittance advice. When the B2B customer pays, it sends the **remittance advice** with its payment to show which invoices the payment applies to. For example, if Good Foods ordered Julia's Cookies frozen cookie dough more than once this month, Good Foods may choose to combine all its outstanding invoices into one payment to Julia's Cookies and include all the relevant remittance advices.

Tel 470-555-1234
Fax 470-555-5678
billing@juliascookies.com
www.juliascookies.com

Bill To	**Ship To**	**Invoice**
Good Foods	Good Foods	**# 2211**
6548 Abernathy Road	1250 Shackleford Road	Date: June 5,
Atlanta, GA 30328	Duluth, GA 30096	202X

Item Number	Description	Quantity	Unit Price	Total
2156	Chocolate Chip Cookies (box of 100)	30	$50.00	$1,150.00
2158	Sugar Cookies (box of 100)	20	$55.00	$1,110.00
2198	Lemonade Cookies (box of 100)	20	$55.00	$1,110.00

Terms
2/14 net 30

Subtotal	$3,370.00
Shipping and Handing	$100.00
Grand Total	$3,470.00
Total due by June 20, 202X (2% discount)	$3,400.60
Total due after June 20, 202X	$3,470.00

Thank you for your business!

Illustration 12.12   Julia's Cookies' sales invoice includes important data such as the amount due, the customer, and the terms of sale, including discounts available.

For B2B customers, all goods sold on credit result in accounts receivable. Accounting transactions for B2B collections of accounts receivable include:

- Collecting payment for credit sales, which reduces the Accounts Receivable balance and debits Cash:

		Dr.	Cr.
June 20, 202X	Cash	3,470.00	
	Accounts Receivable		3,470.00

- Collecting payment for credit sales that have discount terms applied, such as the 2% discount Good Foods receives if it pays within 14 days (that is, 2/14 net 30):

		Dr.	Cr.
June 20, 202X	Cash	3,400.60	
	Sales Discounts	69.40	
	Accounts Receivable		3,470.00

- Accepting returns from customers or negotiating allowances. This activity must recognize the returns, which includes recording the return of finished goods to inventory and removing the cost of goods sold:

		Dr.	Cr.
June 20, 202X	Sales Returns and Allowances	3,470.00	
	Accounts Receivable		3,470.00
June 20, 202X	Inventory	2,800.00	
	Cost of Goods Sold		2,800.00

Cash collections is a complex process. This overview focuses on accounts receivable for business credit customers, and we cover other aspects of cash collections later in this chapter.

Credit Sales Process Flowchart

Let's use a process flowchart to evaluate the complex credit sales process. **Illustration 12.13** shows the process flowchart for credit sales to retailers at Julia's Cookies. The Sales, Inventory Control, Warehouse, Delivery, Accounts Receivable, and Accounting departments are all involved, and the Production department may be involved as well if goods ordered are not in inventory but must be produced.

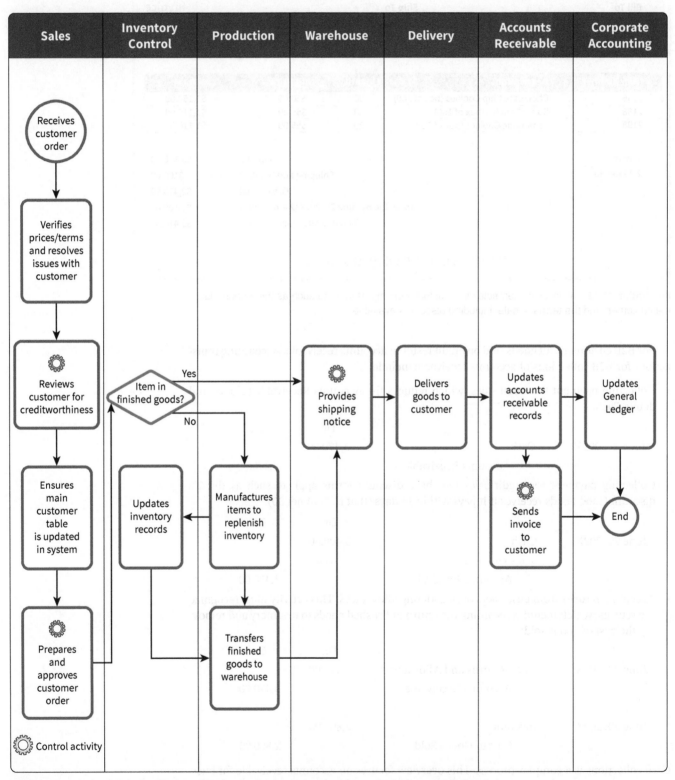

Illustration 12.13 Julia's Cookies' credit sales business process is documented in a process flowchart.

CONCEPT REVIEW QUESTIONS

1. **CPA** What is meant by credit criteria?
   Ans. Credit criteria are the factors used to determine the financial strength of customers. Credit terms are dependent on a customer's creditworthiness. A company needs to check the customer's credit and payment history and set a credit limit before accepting an order from a customer.

2. **CPA** Define electronic sales invoice or a sales invoice.
   Ans. The billing system generates an electronic sales invoice using data recorded from the sales order, picking slip, and packing slip and sends it to the customer. The sales invoice is a source document that shows data related to a specific order and delivery.

3. **CPA** Write a short note on remittance advice.
   Ans. The sales invoice is sent to the customer with another source document, called a remittance advice. When the B2B customer makes the payment, it sends the remittance advice with its payment to show which invoices the payment applies to.

4. When an independent retail outlet submits payment, what account is debited and what account is credited?
   Ans. When the independent retail outlet submits payment, Cash is debited and Accounts Receivable is credited.

5. Discuss some of the opportunities and challenges companies face by employing their own sales team versus using third-party sales representatives.
   Ans. Independent, third-party sales representatives offer more flexibility to cut costs, but full-time sales employees offer more flexibility by quickly changing selling points and sales strategies. Sales employees also have more loyalty to the company as the company and their long-term interests intersect.

12.3 How Do We Ensure That Revenue Is Correctly Recognized?

Learning Objective ❸
Identify risks and controls related to revenue recognition in the sales process.

Whether it is simple and verbal or recorded and complex, every sale is a contract between a seller and a buyer. Once the contract is made, the revenue from the sale must be recognized. **Revenue recognition** includes a set of determined conditions that must be met to justify a business's recognition of revenue as earned. This is a critical part of accrual accounting, and it is another complex process.

Revenue recognition for Julia's Cookies' B2C sales is straightforward: the revenue is recognized at the point the customer accepts the delivery. But businesses may have complex sales arrangements, perhaps involving the sale of goods plus service obligations. Some sales contracts include several complicated service obligations.

Why Does It Matter to Your Career?

Thoughts from a Senior External Auditor, Public Accounting

A few years ago, revenue recognition underwent a massive change in regulatory requirements that significantly impacted external auditors. Teams had to learn new reporting requirements to perform audit engagements, and advisory teams—including internal audit consultants at public accounting firms—were hired for engagements focused solely on implementing new revenue recognition principles for clients.

Revenue Recognition Model

To deal with the complexities of revenue recognition, U.S. GAAP (ASC 606) and IFRS (IFRS 15) include the same five steps for revenue recognition (**Illustration 12.14**). All public and private companies complying with GAAP are required to adopt ASC 606. Here we focus on step 5, the point at which the revenue is recognized, both from a systems perspective and with an emphasis on the related risks and controls. Knowing how revenue is recognized and how performance obligations are satisfied in the AIS will be valuable when you encounter revenue recognition in an advanced financial accounting class.

The Revenue Recognition Model

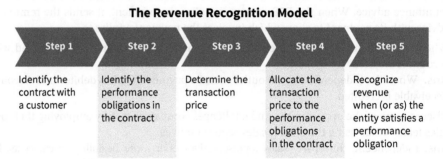

Step 1	Step 2	Step 3	Step 4	Step 5
Identify the contract with a customer	Identify the performance obligations in the contract	Determine the transaction price	Allocate the transaction price to the performance obligations in the contract	Recognize revenue when (or as) the entity satisfies a performance obligation

Illustration 12.14 There are five steps in revenue recognition according to ASC 606 and IFRS 15.

In step 5, revenue is recognized when a company satisfies its contractual obligations by transferring control of the promised goods or services to a customer. **Illustration 12.15** maps how revenue recognition can be satisfied at a single point in time or over many different points. In the case of Julia's Cookies, revenue recognition obligations are satisfied at a single point in time.

Revenue Recognition

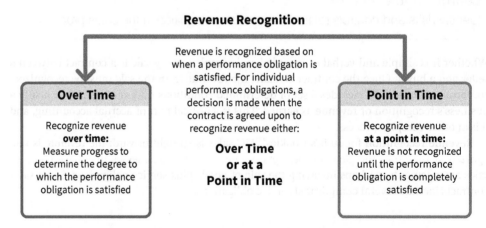

Revenue is recognized based on when a performance obligation is satisfied. For individual performance obligations, a decision is made when the contract is agreed upon to recognize revenue either:

Over Time or at a Point in Time

Over Time

Recognize revenue **over time:** Measure progress to determine the degree to which the performance obligation is satisfied

Point in Time

Recognize revenue **at a point in time:** Revenue is not recognized until the performance obligation is completely satisfied

Illustration 12.15 Revenue is recognized either over time or at the point in time when the performance obligation is satisfied.

In the Real World	Wirecard and the Missing $2 Billion of Revenue and Cash[1,2]

Wirecard was a high-performing online payment company that offered businesses software and systems to accept in-store or online credit cards and digital payments like Apple Pay or PayPal. Wirecard confirmed, processed, and settled transactions between buyers and sellers, and its revenue came from commissions ensuring that sellers received their money. Third-party partners processed payments on Wirecard's behalf in markets where Wirecard wasn't licensed to do business, like the Philippines.

The Fraud	In 2019, the *Financial Times* published evidence that Wirecard had inflated its sales and profits, and a special investigation into the allegations ensued. EY was Wirecard's external auditor, so a different auditor, KPMG, was brought in to perform this investigation.
	Once KPMG began the investigation, the case moved quickly. KPMG found that $2 billion—which Wirecard claimed was commission revenue from third-party processers in Asia and kept in a bank escrow account in the Philippines—was actually missing. In fact, Wirecard had not controlled that account for several years. EY had signed off on three years of Wirecard's financial statements without catching the missing cash. EY claimed that Wirecard had "duped" the audit team. The missing $2 billion comprised all the profits the company had reported over 10 years.
Motivation	It appears that the motivation for this financial statement fraud was to report fictitious revenue and inflate the company's stock price.
Consequences	After the fraud was revealed, Wirecard filed for insolvency. Shareholders lost most of their investments as the stock price dropped to almost nothing. The former CEO and three top managers were arrested, and Wirecard's former second-in-command went missing.

What kind of impact do you think this situation had on EY? Do you think EY lost any clients or suffered reputational damage? How would a better understanding of the client's information system have helped the audit team detect this fraud?

Controlling for Mistakes and Fraud

The most common financial statement fraud cases involve revenues and receivables and are perpetrated by management. Management is often incentivized and under pressure to overstate revenue to meet profit targets. Misstatements can also occur due to errors.

One of the most effective controls is an automated sales process (**Table 12.10**). An automated and integrated sales system reduces the risk of error and fraud, speeds up the process, and leaves an electronic audit trail for accountability. It is more efficient and effective than processes that have more manual controls than automated controls. Such a system updates inventory records upon revenue recognition, invoices customers at the point of recognizing revenue, and updates accounts receivable records.

TABLE 12.10 Revenue Recognition Control Activities

Risk Statement: These control activities apply to all potential risks in this business process.	
Sample Control Activity	**Control Owner**
Implement a sales module in an ERP system to automate the sales process	CFO and director of sales
Proactively conduct data analysis and monitoring	CFO
Implement anti-fraud policies and conduct training	HR director/director of legal and compliance

[1]wsj.com/articles/wirecard-scandal-puts-spotlight-on-auditor-ernst-young-12593286933
[2]ft.com/content/6a660a5f-4e8c-41d5-b129-ad5bf9782256

Revenue Misstatements

Even with an automated sales process, revenue recognition is a high risk for financial misstatements, whether caused by errors or the result of management financial statement fraud. **Table 12.11** shows the main risk exposures related to revenue recognition and sample control activities.

TABLE 12.11 Revenue Misstatement Control Activities

Risk Statement: Improper revenue recognition may result in incorrect recordings during a reporting period and misstatement of financial statements.	
Sample Control Activity	**Control Owner**
Strictly enforce the company's sales cutoff policy	Controller
Control the sequence of shipping documents and investigate anomalies	Automated system control
Match the sales invoice with the accounting period in which the goods were transferred to the customer and obligations were fulfilled	Automated system control
Risk Statement: Sales billed to customers that are not recorded as revenue in the General Ledger may result in misstatement of financial statements.	
Sample Control Activity	**Control Owner**
Reconcile totals for invoices to gross sales in the General Ledger to verify completeness and accuracy	Controller
Risk Statement: Sales to customers not resulting in billing or recognizing the revenue may result in loss of cash because customers may never pay, leading to misstatement of financial statements.	
Sample Control Activity	**Control Owner**
Generate invoices and recognize revenue when the customer electronically signs to accept a shipment	Automated system control
Segregate the billing function from the shipping and accounts receivable functions	Controller
Use numerically sequenced shipping documents and match them with customer billing	Automated system control
Generate a report listing all shipment documents that do not have sales invoice matches	Automated system control
Risk Statement: Improperly recorded sales returns and credits and adjustments for returns may result in misstatements in accounting records.	
Sample Control Activity	**Control Owner**
Review returns, credits, and adjustments to determine timing for revenue recognition	Controller
Risk Statement: Sales invoices with incorrect quantities and/or prices may result in misstatement of sales revenue and accounts receivable.	
Sample Control Activity	**Control Owner**
Match the sales invoice quantities to the shipping information and the prices to the sales contract or main price list	Automated system control

Fraud Risk

Another important consideration for revenue recognition is the risk of fraud (**Table 12.12**).

TABLE 12.12 Fraud Risk Control Activities

Risk Statement: Fictitious sales may result in overstatement of revenues (a credit) and receivables (a debit) or understatement of expenses (a debit).	
Sample Control Activity	**Control Owner**
Maintain a strong audit committee, board of directors, and control environment	Board of directors, CEO
Match each sales invoice with shipping information and customer acknowledgment of fulfillment of seller obligations	Automated system control
Provide a reporting hotline where whistleblowers remain anonymous	Director of legal and compliance
Periodically review accounts receivable, including write-offs and aging	Controller
Sample Control Activity	**Control Owner**
Maintain and enforce clearly documented anti-fraud policies and procedures that include consequences for committing fraud	Director of legal and compliance
Provide anti-fraud and corporate ethics training for executives and employees	HR director/director of legal and compliance
Risk Statement: Shipping more products to retailers or distributors than they are capable of selling near the end of a reporting period, such as a quarter or fiscal year end, may result in an inflated statement of revenue and channel stuffing fraud.	
Sample Control Activity	**Control Owner**
Avoid setting unrealistic bonus targets and instead use other forms of compensation and a good balance between revenue targets and incentivizing employees	CEO/CFO
Provide a reporting hotline where whistleblowers remain anonymous	Director of legal and compliance
Provide anti-fraud training for executives and employees that includes information on channel stuffing awareness	HR director/director of legal and compliance
Review reports and data analyses for unusual trends or unexpected results	CFO/controller
Match revenue transactions with approved customer orders	Automated system control
Examine customer returns that occur near the cutoff	Automated system control

One type of fraud, **channel stuffing**, occurs when revenue and profits are intentionally inflated by recognizing revenue from unnecessary sales in the current quarter or year:

- Channel stuffing may involve inflating revenues and profits for a particular reporting period to meet targets.
- This practice often has a detrimental impact on the company in the following period. Retailers or distributors may return the products, or the company may sell less the following period because retailers and distributors have excess inventory.

Besides having financial consequences, channel stuffing in a public company can result in charges of securities fraud. Guilty companies may be subject to shareholder actions, and the SEC can enact civil enforcements.

While fraud-specific analytics are an important piece of a company's fraud monitoring system, sometimes data analytics designed for a different purpose can reveal unexpected trends or activities. Discover how Julia's Cookies' monthly revenue report, which is not a fraud analytics, revealed sales fraud in Applied Learning 12.3.

| Julia's Cookies | Applied Learning 12.3 |

Revenue Recognition: Unusual Revenue Red Flags

CFO Darlene met with the company's controller to review the monthly revenue report and compare this month to the same month of the prior year. The report indicated a significant and unexpected increase in revenue at one of the regional facilities in December, which is the last month of the fiscal year.

Darlene and the controller drilled down into the underlying data and identified several unusually large shipments in the last three days of the month, which increased the monthly revenue significantly. This was suspicious because:

- The regional managers and employees get year-end bonuses based on meeting revenue targets for their facility.
- This facility was going to miss its target until these last shipments were recorded.

The Internal Audit team performed a management request engagement and uncovered a channel stuffing scheme:

- A new manager confessed that she feared that she would lose her job if she didn't meet performance targets.
- She persuaded some retail customers to order and buy more products than they needed by offering them big discounts, rebates, and extended payment terms.

The ease with which the facility manager did this may indicate that it was not her first time committing this kind of fraud. Her fear of losing her job became a reality, and she was fired on the spot for her dishonest and illegal actions. Legal counsel considered reporting the incident to law enforcement, and external auditors were notified.

Darlene is concerned. What controls should be implemented to prevent channel stuffing from happening again?

SOLUTION

This fraud was detected through an internal audit engagement shortly after it happened. However, prevention is better than detection.

For fraud prevention, management should eliminate or reduce opportunities to commit fraud. Reducing the motivation to commit fraud helps as well. Common fraud prevention controls that could have prevented this fraud include:

1. Enforce segregation of duties. The facility manager is not a salesperson, and she should not have been negotiating directly with customers.

2. Provide anti-fraud training for all employees. The sales employees were aware of the transactions. Although they were uncomfortable because the manager's behavior was not the norm, they did not know she was committing fraud.

3. Create an expectation of punishment for fraud or dishonesty.

4. Implement an anonymous reporting hotline and encourage employees to report anything that makes them uneasy. The experts can discern whether a reported incident is an issue or not.

5. Avoid setting unrealistic bonus targets to remove the incentive to manipulate revenues. Consider other forms of compensation and find the right balance between revenue targets and incentivizing employees. A focus on profitability instead of only sales quantities could make fraud a less attractive option.

6. Extensively onboard and validate new management hires by examining work history and background checks for red flags.

CONCEPT REVIEW QUESTIONS

1. Define revenue recognition concept.

    Ans. Revenue recognition includes a set of determined conditions that must be met to justify a business's recognition of revenue as earned. This is a critical part of accrual accounting, and it is another complex process.

2. Discuss what impact (beneficial or detrimental) channel stuffing may have in the company's following period and why.

    Ans. Channel stuffing often has a detrimental impact on the company in the following period. Retailers or distributors will return the products, or the company may sell less the following period because retailers and distributors have excess inventory.

12.4 How Are Customer Payments Collected?

Learning Objective ❹

Assess the risks and controls related to the cash collections and accounts receivable processes.

Once revenue is recognized, it's time to collect payment. Cash collection involves receiving cash from customers, depositing it, and recording the cash receipts. The collections process, also known as the cash receipts process, increases the amount of the Cash line item, the most liquid of current assets on the balance sheet.

You can refer to the Purchasing and Payments Processes chapter for an illustration of a Cash ledger account. As a reminder, in the Cash ledger account:

Beginning balance + Cash receipts − Payments +/− Bank adjustments = Ending balance

The Cash Flow Statement reports the impact of increases and decreases on the Cash account over the reporting period. It separates the impact into Net Cash Inflow or Outflow from operating, investing, and financing activities. Cash collections or receipts may impact each of these activity categories, depending on the nature of the business event (**Table 12.13**).

TABLE 12.13 Activities That Impact the Financial Statements

Activity	Business Event	Impact
Operating activity	Receive payment from customer for goods bought on credit	Increases Cash and reduces Accounts Receivable on the balance sheet (both current assets). Increases Net Cash Flow from operating activities on the Cash Flow Statement.
Investing activity	Sell used machinery and equipment for cash	Increases Cash and decreases Machinery and Equipment (a fixed asset) on the balance sheet. Increases Net Cash Flow from investing activities on the Cash Flow Statement.
Financing activity	Issue 10,000 new shares of common stock	Increases Cash and Common Stock (Equity) on the balance sheet. Increases Net Cash Flow from financing activities on the Cash Flow Statement.

Now that we have revisited the impact of the collections process on the financial statements, let's evaluate collections related to accounts receivable for credit sales to customers.

Receiving Payments

A critical part of the sales and collections processes for accounting professionals to understand is the collection of payments. The method of payment collection depends on how the customer purchases products (**Table 12.14**).

TABLE 12.14 Payment Methods and Examples

Payment Method	Payment Timing	Example
Cash sale (B2C)	At time of sale	A consumer customer walks into Starbucks, places an order at the counter, pays at the register, and receives coffee almost immediately.
Advance payment (B2C or B2B)	Before sale	A customer pays for Amazon purchases at the time of order, even though the items sold have not yet been packaged or shipped. In financial accounting, this is classified as deferred revenue in Amazon's records—a liability until ownership of the item transfers from Amazon to the customer.
Credit sale (B2B)	After sale	As a business customer, Amazon orders cardboard boxes from a corrugated box manufacturer WestRock. Amazon will use the boxes to ship its products to its consumer customers. Amazon orders regularly from WestRock on credit, which Amazon pays after the sale. WestRock begins fulfilling an order for boxes before Amazon pays for that individual order.

Collecting cash from credit customers, or those who are paying for good or services over an extended period of time, involves Accounts Receivable:

- Each customer's account in the Accounts Receivable Subsidiary Ledger shows how much the customer owes at the end of each month.
- The customer receives a monthly statement as a reminder to pay their outstanding bill to the company.

When there are strong controls over credit sales, sales adjusting entries, and cash collections, it follows that the controls over Accounts Receivable (the other side of the double-sided journal entry) will generally be strong (**Table 12.15**).

TABLE 12.15 Cash Receipt Control Activities

Risk Statement: These control activities apply to all potential risks in this business process.	
Sample Control Activity	**Control Owner**
CPA Segregate authorization responsibilities and duties for accounts receivable, cashier or cash receipts, accounting, sales, credit approval, bank reconciliation, and reconciliation of the Subsidiary Ledger with the Accounts Receivable control account	CFO
CPA Regularly conduct independent reconciliations of the Subsidiary Ledger with Accounts Receivable control account	Treasurer
CPA Ensure that every receipt has a traceable audit trail and is uniquely identifiable	Treasurer
CPA Physically count cash and compare actual cash on hand with accounting records	Treasurer
Risk Statement: Checks received in the mail that are lost or misappropriated after receipt may result in financial loss and customer dissatisfaction.	
Sample Control Activity	**Control Owner**
Implement electronic funds transfer directly to the company's bank account or a lockbox system	Treasurer/automated system control
Prepare a daily remittance list immediately upon opening mail and restrictively endorse checks	Treasurer
Deposit checks received in the mail daily	Treasurer
Risk Statement: Checks received in the mail failing to agree with the daily remittance list may result in misstatement of financial statements and incorrect Accounts Receivable records.	
Sample Control Activity	**Control Owner**
CPA Perform independent checks of remittance advices from customers against daily remittance list	Treasurer/controller
Risk Statement: Incorrect cash discounts to customers may result in loss of profit and future cash receipts.	
Sample Control Activity	**Control Owner**
CPA Automate the calculation of discounts	Controller

Bank Deposits

Most cash receipts from credit sales today don't involve physical collections, and company employees rarely physically handle checks from customers. However, for physical check payments that do occur, a company should implement a lockbox to manage bank deposits. CPA A **lockbox** is a post office box that can only be accessed by a company's bank. The bank collects the checks daily, deposits them into the company bank account, and sends three source documents to the company electronically:

- All remittance advices explaining the payments customers made
- CPA A **bank remittance report** for the day that lists the checks received from customers

- **CPA** A **deposit slip** as proof of the amount deposited into the company's bank account, with the amount of the deposit equal to the total on the bank remittance report

Another cash receipt method is an electronic funds transfer (EFT), which is a direct transfer from the customer's bank account into the company's bank account. In this case, the bank also sends the company a remittance report for each cash receipt, as well as a deposit slip.

The company uses the remittance advices from the customers, the bank remittance reports, and the bank deposit slips as source documents for recording cash receipts from credit customers in its books. This recording includes the update of the Accounts Receivable Subsidiary Ledger and the General Ledger control account.

With EFT and lockboxes, the receipt of cash and the deposit into the company's bank account merge into one business event or activity because the company does not physically handle any collections. Receipts from customers go directly into the company's bank account, reducing the risk of cash going missing before it is recorded (**Illustration 12.16**).

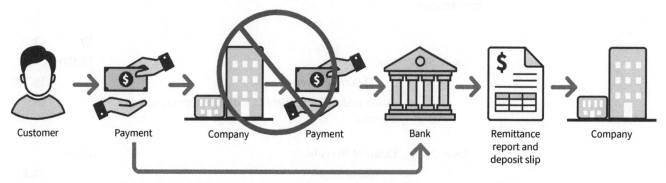

| Customer | Payment | Company | Payment | Bank | Remittance report and deposit slip | Company |

Illustration 12.16 EFT and lockboxes allow customers to submit payments directly to the bank, removing risk of error and fraud related to the extra step of the company processing payments and sending them to the bank on behalf of customers.

Customers still often mail checks to smaller businesses to settle their accounts. This creates an extra layer of risk for a business because there are more steps, each with more potential risks, before the check gets to the business's bank account. To ensure segregation of duties, an employee who is independent of accounts receivable, accounting, and bank reconciliation responsibilities should be responsible for receiving customer checks and creating a record of the receipts. **Table 12.16** summarizes the key control activities discussed in this section. A cashier, reporting to the treasurer, is a good example. **CPA** Upon opening the mail each day, the cashier would do four things:

1. Immediately endorse all checks for deposit
2. Detach the remittance advices from the customers for Accounts Receivable
3. List all the checks on a daily remittance list for Accounts Receivable (manually or by using a software application)
4. Deposit the checks

TABLE 12.16 Cash Deposit Control Activities

Risk Statement: Checks received in the mail that are not deposited intact may result in missing cash.	
Sample Control Activity	**Control Owner**
Implement electronic funds transfer directly to the company's bank account or a lockbox system	Treasurer/automated system control
Conduct regular independent bank reconciliations with management review	Treasurer

Recording Cash Receipts

The various payment methods create accounting transactions that are covered in financial accounting courses. The following examples use a perpetual inventory system to demonstrate the connection between the AIS business processes and financial accounting journal entries. You've already seen the journal entry for a B2C cash sale. Now let's examine how to record the two types of B2B payments: advance payments and credit sales.

Advance Payment (B2B)

A new Julia's Cookies customer, Wholesalers LLC, orders goods on May 2, 202X, for later delivery and pays cash in advance for the order. The selling price of the goods is $18,500, and the cost of the goods is $13,000. The goods are delivered on May 8, 202X, and revenue is recognized because ownership of the goods has transferred to Wholesalers LLC, and sales obligations were fulfilled by the seller. This sequence of events gives rise to three accounting transactions:

		Dr.	Cr.
May 2, 202X	Cash	18,500	
	Deferred Revenue		18,500
	Goods sold to Wholesalers LLC and payment received in advance		
May 8, 202X	Deferred Revenue	18,500	
	Sales		18,500
	Goods delivered to Wholesalers LLC and revenue recognized		
May 8, 202X	Cost of Goods Sold	13,000	
	Inventory		13,000
	Cost of inventory sold to Wholesalers LLC		

Credit Sale (B2B)

Good Foods, one of Julia's Cookies' top customers, submits a sales request on April 10, 202X. No journal entry is recorded at this time because no accounting event has occurred. The goods are shipped on April 28, 202X. Good Foods receives the delivery, and revenue is recognized on May 1, 202X, for $25,700.00. It pays the invoice on May 31, 202X. These events create several accounting transactions:

		Dr.	Cr.
May 1, 202X	Accounts Receivable	25,700	
	Sales		25,700
	Credit sale to Good Foods		
May 1, 202X	Cost of Goods Sold	19,000	
	Inventory		19,000
	Cost of inventory sold to Good Foods		
May 31, 202X	Cash	25,700	
	Accounts Receivable		25,700
	Receipt of electronic payment from Good Foods for goods purchased on credit		

Besides the monthly bank reconciliation already discussed in the Purchasing and Payments Processes chapter, another internal control performed is the reconciliation of the Accounts Receivable Subsidiary Ledger with the Accounts Receivable control account in the General Ledger. It's probably not surprising that cash is highly susceptible to theft, and cash fraud schemes are common. This makes strong controls around cash collections important (**Table 12.17**).

TABLE 12.17   Recording of Cash Receipts Control Activities

Risk Statement: Recording inflated receipts from customers may result in overstated revenue.	
Sample Control Activity	**Control Owner**
Perform monthly bank reconciliations with management review	Treasurer
Mail monthly statements to customers and investigate and fix discrepancies that customers report in a timely manner	Controller
Risk Statement: Posting receipts to the incorrect customer account may result in customer dissatisfaction.	
Sample Control Activity	**Control Owner**
Mail monthly statements to customers and investigate and fix discrepancies that customers report in a timely manner	Controller

Next we review a process flowchart to better understand how the cash collections process steps work together.

Collections Process Flowchart

Illustration 12.17 shows the process flowchart for collections for credit sales at Julia's Cookies. By agreement between Julia's Cookies and its retail customers, all payments to Julia's Cookies are made electronically:

- **CPA** **Financial electronic data interchange (FEDI)** is the electronic transfer of payments and payment-related information like invoices, in a standardized, machine-readable format.
- The customer formats the payment data and transmits it to their bank, which in turn reformats the data as necessary for transmission.
- Electronic payment data is transmitted through the **Automated Clearing House (ACH) Network**, which is an electronic system that serves financial institutions and facilitates financial transactions in the United States.
- The ACH Network delivers a payment and its associated data to Julia's Cookies' bank and transmits information to update Accounts Receivable, where Julia's Cookies' employees in Accounts Receivable can see receipts coming in as credits to customers' accounts.

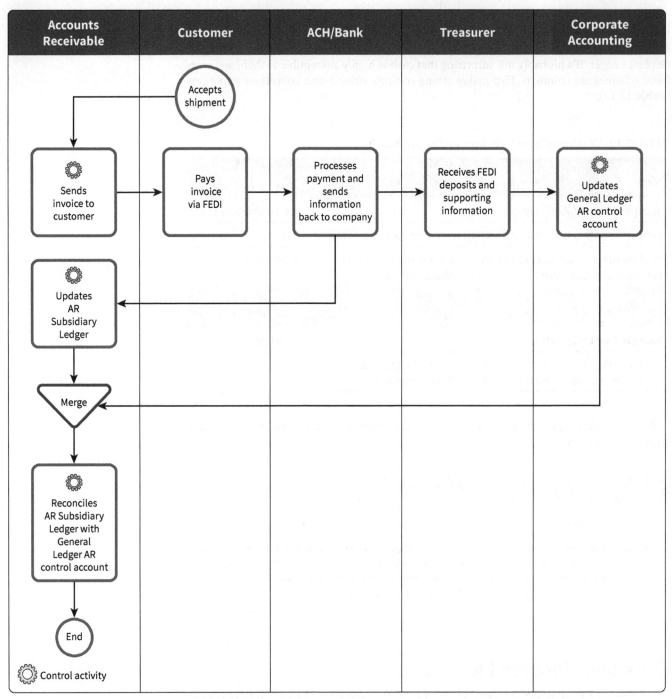

Illustration 12.17 Steps and control activities are depicted in a process flowchart of the collections process for credit sales at Julia's Cookies.

Using the credit sales flowchart in Illustration 12.17 and the risks and control activities in Table 12.17, help the Internal Audit department assess the maturity of the accounts receivable business processes in Applied Learning 12.4.

Julia's Cookies   Applied Learning 12.4

Customer Invoicing: Business Process Maturity Assessment

The VP of Internal Audit, Dylan, is responsible for managing the annual audit plan, which includes every audit his team will perform this year. The plan takes months to design, and an important consideration is making sure there's a budget for management requests, which occur when department leaders unexpectedly request audit assistance or identify a risk that Internal Audit should investigate. These requests must be prioritized since Dylan's team can audit only a limited number of requests each year.

Last month, Internal Audit received a management request to review the Accounts Receivable department. There is no suspicion of fraud, but management is concerned that errors or inefficiencies may be causing financial losses.

To assess the request, Dylan assigns Eduardo, a senior manager of Internal Audit, to discuss the existing business processes with the director of Accounts Receivable. Eduardo takes notes about the current state of the department's processes.

Using the business process maturity model and Eduardo's notes, how mature do you think the credit sales processes are currently? Do you think Dylan should prioritize this management request and assign an Internal Audit team to this project?

Eduardo's Notes

- Fifteen customers contacted the AR department in Q3 complaining that they were being invoiced for sales orders that had already been paid. This is a 20% increase from the same time period last year.

- In Q3, four customers complained that they received late notices after never having received an invoice. The KPI metric for this is a maximum of one per quarter.

- One customer complained about receiving invoices at an outdated mailing address they had updated with Julia's Cookies six months earlier.

- Policies and procedures are well documented.

- There is an annual rotation of duties and regularly scheduled training to ensure that employees are cross-trained for one another's roles.

- The department's risk assessment is performed by the enterprise-wide risk management team, which oversees the enterprise-wide control environment.

- There is a process improvement initiative to overhaul the AIS for accounts receivable to implement additional automated application controls.

- Accounts Receivable came to Internal Audit for advice because they know Internal Audit can provide strategic value through advisory projects.

Business Process Maturity Model

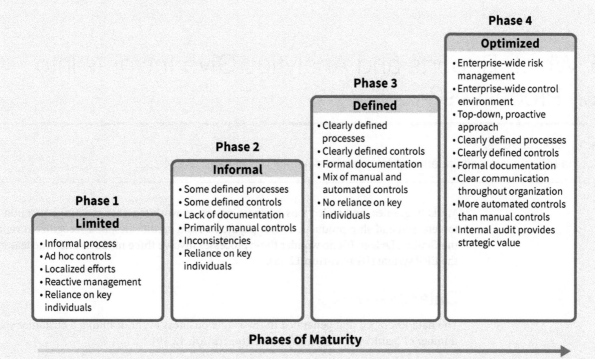

SOLUTION

According to the business process maturity model, the Accounts Receivable department is at Phase 4—Optimized. However, there are a number of customer complaints and issues that should be addressed. While the control environment is robust and well designed, as evidenced in the business process maturity model, somewhere controls are not being implemented correctly or there is a system issue creating problems with invoicing. Dylan should strongly consider dedicating a team to this area because customer relationships are essential to business operations.

CONCEPT REVIEW QUESTIONS

1. Label the following as investing, operating, or financing activity:
   a. Receive payment from the customer for goods bought on credit
   b. Issue 10,000 new shares of common stock
   c. Sell used machinery and equipment for cash
   Ans. a. Operating activity   **b.** Financing activity   **c.** Investing activity

2. **CPA** List any four cash receipts control activities.
   Ans. Following are the cash receipts control activities:
   • Segregating authorization responsibilities and duties for accounts receivable, cashier or cash receipts, accounting, sales, credit approval, bank reconciliation, and reconciling the Subsidiary Ledger with the Accounts Receivable control account
   • Regularly conducting independent reconciliations of the Subsidiary Ledger with Accounts Receivable control account
   • Ensuring that every receipt has a traceable audit trail and is uniquely identifiable
   • Physically counting cash and comparing the actual cash on hand with accounting records

3. **CPA** Differentiate between a bank remittance report and a deposit slip.
   Ans. A bank remittance report for the day lists the checks received from the customers, whereas a deposit slip is a proof of the amount deposited into the company's bank account, with the amount of the deposit equal to the total on the bank remittance report.

4. **CPA** What does financial electronic data interchange (FEDI) do?
   Ans. FEDI is the electronic transfer of payments and payment-related information like invoices, in a standardized, machine-readable format.

5. What is an automated clearing house (ACH)?
   Ans. Electronic payment data is transmitted through the ACH network, which is an electronic system that serves financial institutions and facilitates financial transactions in the United States.

12.5 Which Reports and Analytics Give Insights into These Processes?

Learning Objective ❺
Connect the ERP system and underlying database to potential reports and analytics.

Marketing, sales, and collections business processes work together to engage potential customers, sell and ship products, collect payments from credit sales, and recognize revenue in the General Ledger. It's no wonder these processes involve three modules and nine features in the ERP system (**Illustration 12.18**).

Database Design

The data leveraged and generated in the single business event of billing a customer spans a number of features of the ERP system (**Illustration 12.19**):

• Inventory
• Customer Management
• All Sales Management features
• Accounts Receivable

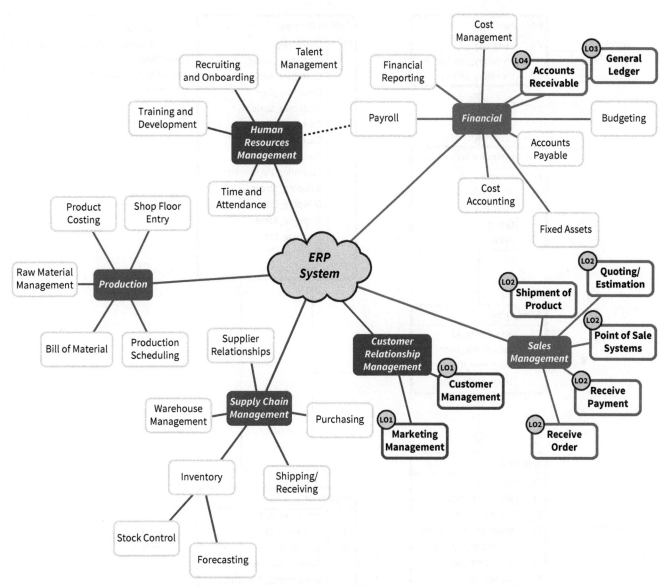

Illustration 12.18   The marketing, sales, and collections business processes involve features from the Customer Relationship Management, Sales Management, and Financial modules of the ERP system.

In a decentralized environment where each of these modules is a stand-alone system, redundant data is often stored. The sales, marketing, shipping, and accounts receivable departments must each maintain its own version of a customer table. This opens the company to the risk of data redundancy—that is, the same data kept in multiple locations—and to the possibility of data changing in one location but not another. For example, if accounts receivable sends an invoice and is notified that the customer's address has changed, the address may not be updated across the other departments, which creates data inconsistency.

Recall that business rules determine the types of relationships between tables in a relational database. The business rules for the relationships between the Sales_Order table and Shipment table and the Sales_Order table and AR_Invoice table are as follows:

- A sales order may be referenced in zero or one invoice.
- An invoice must belong to one and only one sales order.
- A sales order may result in zero or many shipments.
- A shipment must include products for one and only one sales order.

Relationships are defined by both cardinality, which is one or many, and optionality, which is mandatory or optional. The "zero" indicates an optionality of optional, meaning there

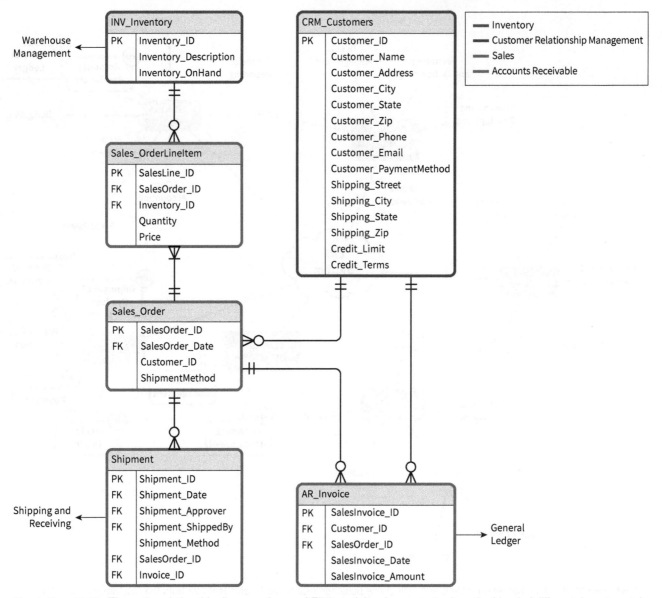

Illustration 12.19 The entity relationship diagram of several ERP modules demonstrates how the blend of different departmental data needed is easier to maintain and acquire in an integrated ERP system.

doesn't have to be a record in the related table and is represented as a circle on the ERD. There are a couple of reasons that a sales order may not result in a shipment or an invoice. For example, if Julia's Cookies has discontinued or is out of stock of a product, the sales order may not be fulfilled. Similarly, a shipment may be returned by the customer, resulting in the existence of a sales order and shipment but no invoice.

Reporting and Insights

The marketing, sales, and collections processes generate valuable data that is created and stored in databases. The AIS captures and processes this data, and the output may appear in sales reports or be analyzed through various data analytics.

Recall that reporting involves aggregating the raw data to provide a historical view of what happened because of past purchasing activities. Analysis focuses on providing context to the historical data and gives management meaningful insights for making decisions on how to improve a process. Either the raw data or existing reports generated from it can be analyzed.

Next, we examine reporting and analytic opportunities for sales, revenue recognition, and accounts receivable.

Sales

The sales process generates data such as customer information, sales contracts terms, credit-worthiness, pricing, and historical product sales. The processed data can appear in reports that can help a company improve processes and mitigate risks (**Table 12.18**).

TABLE 12.18 Sales Reports

Report	Description
Historic sales	A summary of inventory sold over a specific time period by customers.
Sales orders filled and open	The total number of orders that have been filled or that remain outstanding within a period of time. This can indicate if there are issues with production and availability of finished goods.
Sales orders aging	The number of days sales orders have been outstanding, classified in buckets. For example, all sales orders between 30 and 60 days outstanding would be combined into a total amount.
Back orders	A list of items on back order that customers have ordered.
Main customer table	A list of customers and their credit limits.
Order discrepancies	A list of orders delivered that do not match the approved sales order.
Noninvoiced shipments	A list of shipments to customers that did not include a recorded invoice for that customer.
Missing documentation	A list of invoices that do not have associated shipping documentation.

Analytics using sales data provide insights for decision makers and help detect fraud risk (**Table 12.19**).

TABLE 12.19 Sales Analytics

Analytic	Description	How It's Used
Sales forecasts	Compares actuals by product, region, facility, or salesperson.	Used to plan for future activities. For example, sales forecasts are used by the production department to determine what products to produce and when. This drives what raw materials purchasing needs to acquire.
Delivery timing	Compares delivery time to returns with customer complaints.	Used to explore opportunities for process improvement and efficiencies.
Price decreases	Shows customer price decreases greater than a specified percentage year over year.	Identifies collusion between salespersons and customers.
Increased orders	Combines decreasing prices with increasing order quantities for a single customer.	Identifies collusion between salespersons and customers.
Main customer table	Compares the main employee table to the main customer table to identify duplications of phone numbers, addresses, and other information.	Searches for fictitious customer accounts.

(Continued)

TABLE 12.19 (*Continued*)

Analytic	Description	How It's Used
Duplicate customers	Compares customer names and information for duplications. For example, record A may be "Walmart," while record B is "Wal-Mart."	Examines the reliability of the main customer table and addresses the risk of missing payments, invoices not matching payments or sales orders, and fraud.
Three-way match	Specifies exceptions to the three-way match of customer order, shipping documents, and sales invoice.	Used as an internal control to detect inappropriate sales.
Key performance indicators	Uses sales ratios such as purchasing to sales or purchase growth to sales growth.	Enable comparison over time to review company performance and comparison to external benchmarks.

Collusion between salespersons and customers, which results in the salesperson receiving kickbacks or other rewards for selling at a discounted price to the customer, is a significant fraud risk in this area. You have already learned about another unique risk in the sales process: channel stuffing. This fraud inflates sales for the company and can result in excessive returns from the distribution customer. In **Illustration 12.20**, salesperson Ian Malcolm's returns are significantly higher than those of his peers, and his sales transactions should be investigated to determine if the reason is channel stuffing.

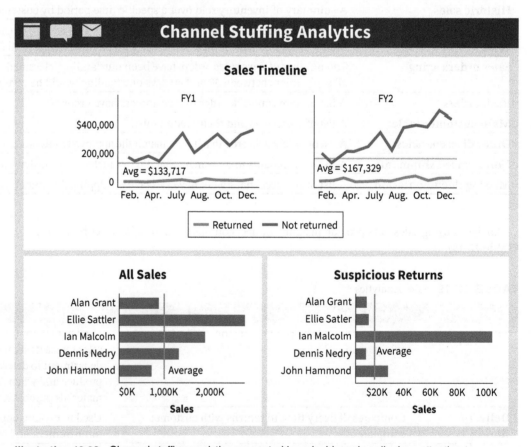

Illustration 12.20 Channel stuffing analytics presented in a dashboard easily draw attention to suspicious activity such as Ian Malcolm's returns.

While sales and customer data can be used for a variety of analytics, from performance measurement to predictive sales forecasting, some of the most important a company can implement are fraud analytics. Help identify sales fraud at Julia's Cookies in Applied Learning 12.5.

Julia's Cookies	Applied Learning 12.5

Customer Orders: Fuzzy Matching Fraud Test

As a licensed Certified Fraud Examiner (CFE), Oliana leads the Internal Audit department's fraud program. This year, she partnered with the Internal Audit department's dedicated data analyst, Joe, to design a fraud analytics program. They are piloting this program as part of an audit engagement, but the analytics designed for this audit will be programmed to run at regular intervals over real-time data so the Internal Audit team will have an ongoing fraud monitoring system.

Oliana designed a fraud test that compares the main customer table to the main employee table. The analytics specifically compares the name fields using fuzzy matching, which identifies similar text fields that may have slight differences. The match percentage indicates the similarity of the two fields.

Joe designed a first iteration of the analysis, and Oliana checks it for false positives. A false positive occurs when the analysis identifies an item that isn't a risk. Joe will use Oliana's feedback to edit his logic so that false positives are excluded in the final system.

Review the analysis output to help Oliana determine which records are false positives.

Customer Name	Employee Name	Match Percentage
Jill D. Inc.	Jill Donavon	80%
Good Foods	Rich Good	90%
Merry Markets	Meredith Roberts	75%
Josh Jackson Co.	Joshua Jackson	90%

SOLUTION

Oliana gives the following feedback to Joe:

Please mark the following as a false positive and exclude the customer name from analysis:

- Good Foods and Rich Good: Good Foods is a reputable, nationwide grocery chain that is not at risk of being a fake company.

Please pull the following information from the Customer table and Employee table so I can investigate further:

- Jill D. Inc. and Jill Donavon
- Merry Markets and Meredith Roberts
- Josh Jackson Co. and Joshua Jackson

Revenue Recognition

Like sales data, data from revenue recognition is processed by the AIS, and it can appear in a variety of reports, which can be analyzed using data analytics (**Table 12.20**). These reports can be run on a monthly or yearly basis, depending on management's needs for decision making.

TABLE 12.20 Revenue Recognition Reports

Report	Description
Customer revenue	Summary of historical revenue by customer.
Type of revenue	Summary of historical revenue by type—either product type or sales channel type. Julia's Cookies could summarize by individual products or summarize by B2C versus B2B revenue.
Revenue over time	Revenue by month or quarter.
Revenue changes	Increase or decrease in revenue between months, quarters, or years.
Recognized revenue	Summary of revenue by whether it's recognized.
Deferred revenue	Summary of revenue by whether it's deferred.

Illustration 12.21 shows how some of these basic reports can be aggregated into a management dashboard for easy decision making.

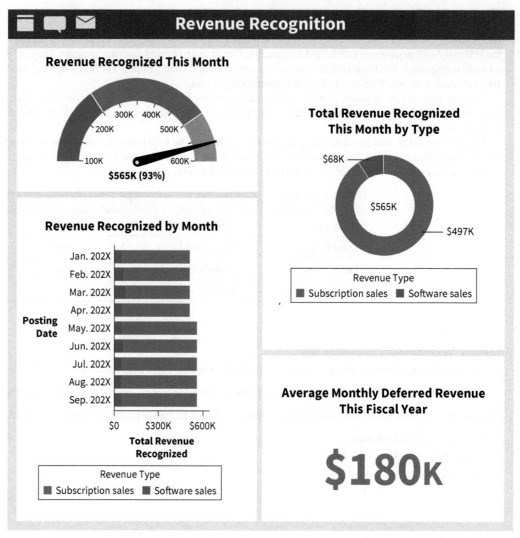

Illustration 12.21 Revenue recognition reports are easy to review in a dashboard presentation.

Additionally, analytics around revenue recognition, like those listed in **Table 12.21** are essential to successful monitoring.

TABLE 12.21 Revenue Recognition Analytics

Analytics	Description	How It's Used
Revenue growth root cause	Compares revenue growth to nonfinancial performance measures such as number of employees or square footage of operation facilities	Searches for revenue increasing at a faster rate than nonfinancial measures, which may be a red flag of financial statement fraud involving overstatement of revenue
Revenue cost	Compares revenue to costs	Identifies unusual relationships such as low costs and high revenue that may require investigation
Cutoff analysis	Analyzes the transactions around the General Ledger cutoff date for unusual activity immediately before or after close dates	Determines timeliness of revenue recognition and overlap of accounting periods

Cash Collections

As in other business processes like sales and revenue recognition, the AIS processes and stores cash collection data. The collected data, such as the current amounts past due, can be converted into reports that show information about past performance.

Reports for cash receipts and accounts receivable are used for identifying outstanding debt, estimating the allowance for doubtful accounts, and performing controls like reconciliations (**Table 12.22**).

TABLE 12.22 Cash Collections Reports

Report	Description
Cash receipts journal	All receipts over a period of time
Sales amounts	Summary of sales by customer over a period of time
Accounts receivable balances	Summary of the current outstanding balance in the Accounts Receivable Subsidiary Ledger for each customer at a specific point in time
Unusual account balances	Credit balances in the Accounts Receivable Subsidiary Ledger to identify abnormal accounts, as the normal account balance in Accounts Receivable should be a debit
Reconciliations	Bank reconciliation between bank statements and the Control account in the General Ledger

Analytics for these business processes are designed to answer questions, drive decision making, and detect fraud (**Table 12.23**).

TABLE 12.23 Cash Collections Analytics

Analytic	Description	How It's Used
Unusual activity	Identifies customers with no cash receipts during a period of time.	Searches for fraud or premature revenue recognition.
Ratios	Uses accounting ratios such as bad debt expense compared to net credit sales.	Reviews ratios over time for internal performance or compared to external benchmarks to analyze how the company is performing compared to its competition.
Bad debt expense comparison	Compares this year's bad debt expense as a percentage of accounts receivable to the prior year's.	Identifies anomalies to investigate. Often used by internal or external auditors.
Accounts receivable growth	Compares accounts receivable growth to sales growth.	Finds receivables growing faster than sales to identify potential collection issues.
Invoice comparison	Compares total sales invoices to paid invoices.	Provides an internal control reconciling sales invoices and paid invoices. Also identifies outstanding sales invoices, which can be compared to Accounts Receivable balances to verify accuracy.
Accounts Receivable Aging Schedule	Shows the customer's unpaid invoice balances based on the invoice date, bucketed into time periods. For example, all customers who have invoices that are 60 to 90 days outstanding could be included in one bucket.	Determines the age and collectibility of Accounts Receivable. Used to calculate allowance for doubtful accounts.

You probably learned about ratio analysis in your introductory financial accounting course. If you did, the ratios referenced in some of these analytics examples will be familiar to you.

Illustration 12.22 shows how some common reports and analytics for cash receipts and accounts receivable can be combined in a dashboard format. Note in the accounts receivable aging report that $140,000 is between 91 and 119 days overdue (<120 days), and $76,000 is 120 days or more overdue.

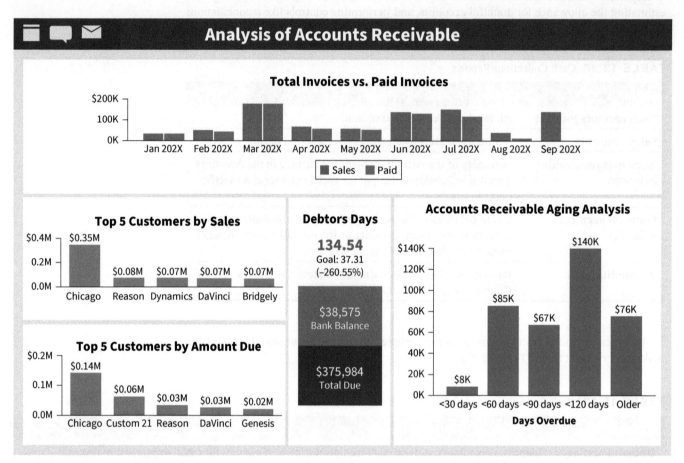

Illustration 12.22 Accounts receivable dashboards include metrics like an aging report and a comparison of total sales invoices to paid invoices.

While accounts receivable aging is a traditional report, presenting it as a simple bar chart visualization can effectively communicate the necessary information to decision makers.

CONCEPT REVIEW QUESTIONS

1. What does revenue growth root cause analytics communicate?

   Ans. The analytics compares revenue growth to nonfinancial performance measures such as the number of employees or square footage of operation facilities.

2. What is accounts receivable aging schedule?

   Ans. The accounts receivable aging report shows the customer's unpaid invoice balances based on the invoice date, bucketed into time periods. For example, all customers who have invoices that are 60 to 90 days outstanding could be included in one bucket.

FEATURED PROFESSIONAL | Finance Transformation Manager

Photo courtesy of Bharti Sukhani

Bharti Sukhani, CPA, CA

Bharti is a Chartered Accountant from India who has worked in three countries, including the United States, where she is a licensed CPA. Bharti has experience in compliance, management information systems, and internal audit and has worked in the software, banking, and manufacturing industries. Currently, Bharti lives in Canada, where she is a manager of finance transformation. Bharti specializes in internal controls for business processes and using technology to enhance the finance operations. She loves to hike, garden, and travel.

Finance transformation is a hot topic in the industry right now. Can you describe your daily role as a finance transformation manager?

As a finance transformation manager, I am a thought leader and project manager for multiple projects in the core finance processes across my company. These projects focus on improving, or transforming, areas to reach a higher level of business process maturity. We use process maturity models to assess the current state, identify gaps, and implement process improvements.

What skills are required to work in finance transformation?

Extensive exposure and an in-depth understanding of business processes is essential. Project management skills are also important. I gained these skills through years of internal controls work, including being an internal auditor and a business controls analyst.

How does technology, including the AIS, relate to your role in finance transformation?

In my current role, I work with business process owners to develop the optimum technological landscape. This includes systems integrations and designing dashboards and reports that work together to reach the optimum level of business process maturity. If an existing system is not meeting our standards, I develop a business case for procuring and implementing the desired system. I am also a member of our finance information management systems committee. This committee is dedicated to reviewing technology improvement ideas from employees in the Finance department.

Review and Practice

Key Terms Review

Automated Clearing House (ACH) Network
bank remittance report
business-to-business (B2B)
business-to-consumer (B2C)
channel stuffing
credit criteria
delivery receipt

deposit slip
financial electronic data interchange (FEDI)
inventory management
lockbox
packing slip
picking request
pricing process

remittance advice
retail customer
revenue recognition
sales invoice
sales order
shipping notice
supply chain management

Learning Objectives Review

1 Describe the marketing, sales, and collections processes for business-to-consumer sales.

Business-to-consumer (B2C) sales sell finished goods directly to customers, while business-to-business (B2B) sales sell finished goods to other businesses, like distributors and retail companies.

The four business activities for B2C sales are:

- Marketing
- Sales
- Cash collections
- Delivery

Marketing activities create purchasing accounting transactions when the company buys marketing services, materials, or advertisements from a supplier. Controls for marketing include:

- Maintain and enforce clearly documented policies and procedures for what content can be posted on social media sites
- Make password logs available to authorized users only

- Use standardized scripts for responding to recurring scenarios
- Review and approve social media posts before allowing them to be posted

Sales orders are source documents that contain order details and are sent as order confirmations to customers.

Cash collections for B2C sales result in an accounting journal entry that debits Cash and credits Sales to recognize revenue earned at the time of the sale. Control activities for cash collections focus on fraud risk:

- Accept only cashless payments in stores
- Install and monitor security cameras covering cash registers
- Have each sales counter employee use their own cash drawer
- Conduct inventory counts to identify missing inventory compared to sales receipts

Delivery to a B2C customer occurs in person at the time of sale or via shipments or driven deliveries if the sale is an e-commerce transaction. Delivery receipts contain order details and are included in delivery boxes, like packing slips. Delivery controls apply to boxed shipments and personal deliveries and include:

- Ensure adherence to local, state, and federal food handling and transportation regulations
- Use food tampering stickers or seals on delivery containers
- Subject delivery drivers to background checks, driving record reviews, and robust onboarding
- Periodically deliver driver safety training
- Have delivery drivers take photos of packages in their delivery locations and send them to customers via email or text message
- Require customers to submit a photo of the product condition in order to return the product and/or get a refund

Inventory management involves overseeing the life cycle of inventory from purchase to sales. Supply chain management involves overseeing the life cycle of a product, including managing customer and vendor relationships. Together they ensure open communication throughout operations.

❷ Evaluate the credit sales process and its related risks and controls.

In B2B sales, the company making the sale is the supplier. The five high-level business activities for B2B sales are:

- Marketing
- Pricing and contracts
- Sales
- Shipping
- Billing and collections

B2B marketing focuses on generating customer leads from other businesses, and controls focus on procedures and standardization:

- Maintain and enforce clearly documented policies and procedures for user access
- Create standardized scripts and templates for marketing materials
- Maintain and communicate with employees about a primary marketing schedule

Pricing processes focus on determining the sales price of products. B2B customers may receive standard pricing or custom pricing that requires individualized contracts. Pricing processes are subject to fraud risk, and controls focus on risks of collusion:

- Maintain a whistleblower hotline that allows anonymous tips from employees who suspect fraudulent activity
- Require independent checks on pricing and sales team members' work
- Require pricing and sales employees to periodically take vacations so other employees perform their job duties
- Maintain and enforce clearly documented policies and procedures for discount pricing
- Define roles and responsibilities for pricing functions
- Implement system controls that prevent unauthorized users from making pricing adjustments, including discounts
- Maintain and enforce clearly documented policies and procedures for customer relationship management
- Define roles and responsibilities for customer relationship management

Business customers must be evaluated for creditworthiness before they are extended business lines of credit. Controls ensure that credit terms and checks are independent of sales, General Ledger, and accounts receivable:

- Maintain and enforce clearly documented credit policies and procedures for all customers, including a credit application and approval process for new customers
- Establish credit limits for customers, based on each customer's ability to pay and capture these limits in the information system as attributes of main customer data
- Review credit limits periodically and adjust if required
- Require management approval for credit in excess of credit limits
- Perform system checks for past due accounts receivable balances prior to approving a new sales order
- Establish segregation of duties between the person granting credit to customers and the sales, shipping, accounts receivable, and accounting functions

Sales contracts are created if standard terms and conditions don't apply to a particular order or customer. Legal counsel must review and approve sales contracts that deviate from standard terms. Controls in this area include:

- Use standardized, authorized sales contracts that are legally enforceable

- Notify customers that all agreements must be in writing to be legally binding
- Provide employee training covering appropriate and inappropriate wording when speaking with customers

After pricing and sales contracts are negotiated and creditworthiness is checked, customers are onboarded and able to submit purchase orders, which become the seller's sales orders. No accounting transaction is recorded in the AIS at the time the sales order is received. Standard IT general controls (ITGCs) and automated system controls are essential for securing data in the sales process:

- Maintain and enforce clearly documented policies and procedures for processing and approving sales orders
- Separate the duties of authorizing sales from shipping, inventory control, and accounting responsibilities
- To enforce segregation of duties, allow only authorized employees to access input screens and/or sales order documents
- Have the ERP system match the customer on the sales order to the main customer data
- Have the ERP system match the amount of the sales order with the credit limit in the main customer data
- Require that all changes to the main customer data are authorized by management prior to other data entry

B2B sales orders are turned into picking requests. Information in the picking requests is used to create packing slips, which are included in deliveries to customers. Revenue is often recognized when the customer acknowledges receipt of delivery via a handheld device. Shipping controls focus on appropriate use of source documents:

- Maintain and enforce clearly documented policies and procedures for all shipments
- Ensure that all shipments have properly authorized shipping documents with appropriate delivery addresses
- Clearly communicate shipping policies of customers to warehouse delivery personnel
- Maintain and enforce clearly documented policies and procedures for investigating and resolving customer disputes and complaints
- Track shipments using tracking software
- Restrict access to the shipping area
- Segregate the physical shipping location from the warehouse and the receiving location
- Maintain and enforce clearly documented policies and procedures for timely investigation and resolution of customer disputes and complaints
- Have the ERP system match goods and quantities taken from the warehouse to approved sales orders

A sales invoice is a source document used to bill a B2B customer who purchases on a line of credit. Another source document, the remittance advice, is returned to the business along with a customer payment to identify which invoice the payment relates to.

③ Identify risks and controls related to revenue recognition in the sales process.

Revenue recognition is a set of determined conditions that must be met to justify a business recognizing revenue as earned. The five steps of the revenue recognition model are:

1. Identify the contract with a customer
2. Identify the performance obligations in the contract
3. Determine the transaction price
4. Allocate the transaction price to the performance obligations in the contract
5. Recognize revenue when (or as) the entity satisfies a performance obligation

Revenue is recognized over time by measuring progress toward satisfying performance obligations or at a point in time once the obligation is completely satisfied. Essential controls for revenue recognition include:

- Implement a sales module in an ERP system to automate the sales process
- Implement proactive data analysis and monitoring
- Implement anti-fraud policies and conduct training

There are also controls that specifically address the risk of revenue misstatements:

- Strictly enforce the company's sales cutoff policy
- Control the sequence of shipping documents and investigate anomalies
- Match the sales invoice with the accounting period in which the goods were transferred to the customer and obligations were fulfilled
- Reconcile totals for invoices to gross sales in the General Ledger to verify completeness and accuracy
- Automatically generate invoices and recognize revenue when the customer electronically signs to accept a shipment
- Segregate the billing function from the shipping and accounts receivable functions
- Use numerically sequenced shipping documents and match them with customer billing
- Generate a report listing all shipment documents that do not have sales invoice matches
- Review returns, credits, and adjustments to determine timing for revenue recognition
- Match the sales invoice quantities to the shipping information and the prices to the sales contract or main price list

The last set of revenue recognition controls mitigate the risk of fraud such as channel stuffing:

- Maintain a strong audit committee, board of directors, and control environment
- Match each sales invoice with shipping information and customer acknowledgment of fulfillment of seller obligations

- Provide a reporting hotline where whistleblowers remain anonymous
- Periodically review accounts receivable, including write-offs and aging
- Maintain and enforce clearly documented anti-fraud policies and procedures that include consequences for committing fraud
- Provide anti-fraud and corporate ethics training for executives and employees
- Avoid setting unrealistic bonus targets and instead use other forms of compensation and a good balance between revenue targets and incentivizing employees
- Provide a reporting hotline where whistleblowers remain anonymous
- Review reports and data analyses for unusual trends or unexpected results
- Match revenue transactions with approved customer orders
- Examine customer returns that occur near the cutoff

4 Assess the risks and controls related to the cash collections and accounts receivable processes.

The collections process is also known as the cash receipts process. The method for collecting payment depends on the type of sales transaction:

- Cash sale (B2C): Payment at the time of the sale
- Advance payment (B2B): Payment before the sale
- Credit sale (B2B): Payment after the sale

Collections consists of three steps:

1. Receiving payments
2. Depositing payments
3. Recording payments

Payments received for credit sales decrease the balance of Accounts Receivable, which shows the amount the customer owes at the end of each month. Controls for receiving cash must be strong:

- Segregate authorization responsibilities and duties for accounts receivable, cash receipts, accounting, sales, credit approval, bank reconciliation, and reconciliation of the Subsidiary Ledger with the Accounts Receivable control account
- Conduct regular independent reconciliations of the Subsidiary Ledger with the Accounts Receivable control account
- Ensure that every receipt has a traceable audit trail and is uniquely identifiable
- Physically count cash and compare actual cash on hand with accounting records
- Implement electronic funds transfer directly to the company's bank account or a lockbox system
- Prepare a daily remittance list immediately upon opening mail and restrictively endorse checks

- Deposit checks received in the mail daily
- Perform independent checks of remittance advices from customers against daily remittance list
- Automate calculation of discounts

Bank deposits are often put into lockboxes, accompanied by a remittance advices and deposit slips. Bank deposits can also be made via electronic funds transfers (EFT). Both of these methods mitigate the risk of a company receiving a check directly, which can result in errors and fraud. Controls that address this include:

- Implement electronic funds transfer directly to the company's bank account or a lockbox system
- Conduct regular independent bank reconciliations with management review

Journal entries to record cash receipts differ for cash sales (B2C), advance payments (B2B), and credit sales (B2B). Strong internal controls include bank reconciliations and identifying discrepancies:

- Perform monthly bank reconciliations with management review
- Mail monthly statements to customers and investigate and fix discrepancies reported in a timely manner

Electronic payments may be submitted by customers through an Automated Clearing House (ACH) Network.

5 Connect the ERP system and underlying database to potential reports and analytics.

Sales and collections processes leverage nine features in the ERP system.

Financial module features:

- Accounts Receivable
- General Ledger

Sales Management module features:

- Shipment of Product
- Quoting/Estimation
- Point of Sale Systems
- Receive Payment
- Receive Order

Customer Relationship Management module features:

- Customer Management
- Marketing Management

Sales orders may have a zero-to-many relationship with both shipments and invoices because an initiated sale may be canceled due to lack of product stock or customer returns.

Sales reports show sales patterns and information:

- Historic sales
- Sales orders filled and open
- Sales orders aging
- Back orders

- Main customer table
- Order discrepancies
- Noninvoiced shipments
- Missing documentation

Sales analytics can provide insight into customer demand, production needs, and fraud risk:

- Sales forecasts
- Delivery timing
- Price decreases
- Increased orders
- Main customer table
- Duplicate customers
- Three-way match
- Key performance indicators

Revenue recognition reports can show the historical and current state of the company's revenue:

- Customer revenue
- Type of revenue
- Revenue over time
- Revenue changes
- Recognized revenue
- Deferred revenue

Revenue recognition analytics can measure performance and detect fraud:

- Revenue growth root cause
- Revenue cost
- Shipping information
- Cutoff analysis

Cash collections reports can identify outstanding debts and perform reconciliations:

- Cash receipts journal
- Sales amounts
- Outstanding balances
- Accounts receivable balances
- Unusual account balances
- Accounts receivable aging
- Reconciliations

Cash collections analytics are especially useful for identifying errors and fraud detection:

- Unusual activity
- Ratios
- Bad debt expense comparison
- Accounts receivable growth
- Invoice comparison

CPA questions, as well as multiple choice, discussion, analysis and application, and Tableau questions and other resources, are available online.

Multiple Choice Questions

1. (LO 1) _____ is the oversight of the inventory life cycle from purchase to sales.

  a. Inventory management
  b. Supply chain management
  c. Customer relationship management
  d. Enterprise resource planning

2. (LO 1) What is the source document for data capture when a customer makes a request to buy goods?

  a. Pick request
  b. Inquiry program
  c. Sales order
  d. Intent to buy

3. (LO 1–3) For revenue recognition purposes, when does a sale officially occur?

  a. When a customer commits to buying a product
  b. When the business produces the product for sale
  c. When the shipping department prepares the product for delivery
  d. When ownership of goods is passed to the customer

4. (LO 2) Julia's Cookies has identified the following B2B marketing control activity risk: "Inconsistent marketing materials that provide unclear messaging, which may result in loss of customers and leads." Which of the following is an appropriate control activity for this risk statement?

  a. Standardized scripts and templates for marketing materials
  b. Master marketing schedule maintained and communicated to employees
  c. Independent checks on pricing and sales team member's work
  d. Defined roles and responsibilities for pricing functions

5. (LO 2) How does a numerically controlled purchase order help an organization?

  a. It creates an audit trail.
  b. It is used to run a credit check.
  c. It ensures products are in stock.
  d. It enters customers into the database.

6. (LO 2) _____ are dependent on the customers' creditworthiness.

    a. Credit terms

    b. Debit terms

    c. Sales orders

    d. Purchase orders

7. (LO 2) `CPA` Fictitious customers are an important risk to the

    a. general ledger cycle.

    b. revenue cycle.

    c. financing cycle.

    d. expenditure cycle.

8. (LO 2) `CPA` The most important document in the billing process is the

    a. picking ticket.

    b. sales invoice.

    c. packing slip.

    d. bill of lading.

9. (LO 2) `CPA` Juvehair works at Amazon in the warehouse. What does she most likely use to assemble the goods for customers' orders for shipping?

    a. Sales order

    b. Invoice

    c. Picking request

    d. Bill of lading

10. (LO 2) `CPA` Which of the following describes a company's credit criteria?

    a. The length of time a buyer is given to pay for their purchases

    b. The percentage of discount allowed for early payment

    c. The diligence to collect slow-paying accounts

    d. The required financial strength of acceptable customers

11. (LO 3) Who is responsible for ensuring that revenue recognition practices comply with generally accepted accounting principles?

    a. Chair of the board

    b. Sales manager

    c. CFO and controller

    d. Business unit president

12. (LO 3) Which of the following provides the best definition of revenue recognition?

    a. A set of determined conditions that must be met to justify a business recognizing the revenue as earned

    b. A set of determined conditions that must be met to justify a business recognizing the expenses as incurred

    c. The oversight of inventory from purchase to sales

    d. A system to oversee the life cycle of a product from procuring raw materials through customer sales

13. (LO 3) Julia's Cookies has identified the following revenue recognition fraud control activity risk: "Sales invoices with incorrect quantities and/or prices may result in misstatement of sales revenue and accounts receivable." Which of the following is an appropriate control activity for this risk statement?

    a. Review returns, credits, and adjustments to determine timing and revenue recognition

    b. Match the sales invoice quantities to the shipping information and the prices to the sales contract or main price list

    c. Segregate billing function from shipping and accounts receivable functions

    d. Review accounts receivable periodically including write-offs and again

14. (LO 3) Who is the most likely perpetrator of financial statement fraud?

    a. Accounts receivable employees

    b. Audit committee

    c. Management

    d. Employees who handle cash

15. (LO 3) The practice of shipping more goods to a distribution customer than the customer is likely to use to fraudulently inflate sales is called

    a. excessive sales.

    b. cutoff fraud.

    c. channel stuffing.

    d. revenue recognition.

16. (LO 4) Which of the following ERP modules is responsible for the accounts receivable function?

    a. Financial

    b. Sales Management

    c. Customer Relationship Management

    d. Supply Chain Management

17. (LO 4) A(n) _____ is a source document that the bank sends of the daily listings of each check received from the customers.

    a. lockbox

    b. bank remittance report

    c. deposit slip

    d. electronic funds transfer

18. (LO 4) Which common practice motivates customers to pay their bills sooner?

    a. Free products

    b. Discount incentives

    c. Lower interest rates

    d. Enhanced customer service

19. (LO 4) What is the electronic system that facilitates financial transactions?

   a. XBRL

   b. Metro 2

   c. ACH

   d. FDIC

20. (LO 4) `CPA` The procedures followed by the firm for ensuring payment of its accounts receivables are called its

   a. discount policy.

   b. credit policy.

   c. collections policy.

   d. payables policy.

21. (LO 5) Which of the following is an example of a typical report for a credit sales process?

   a. Noninvoiced shipments

   b. Cash payments journal

   c. Accounts payable aging report

   d. Analysis of sales patterns to detect potential bid rigging

22. (LO 5) `CPA` Maham reviews a report showing each customer and how long any amount owed has been outstanding. Which report is this?

   a. An aged balance list, to determine the age and collectibility of accounts receivable

   b. A customer order document, to determine if the correct items were shipping to a customer

   c. A customer invoice, to determine if a customer's bill is correct

   d. A bill of lading, to determine if the correct items were shipped to a customer

23. (LO 5) An optionality of "optional" means there does not have to be a related record in the joined table and is best represented by which of the following business rules:

   a. A sales order must contain one or more line items.

   b. A sales order may be referenced in zero or one invoice.

   c. An invoice must include one and only one customer.

   d. A shipment must belong to one and only one sales order.

24. (LO 5) The sales order table contains the Customer_ID, which comes from the customer table. In the sales order table, the Customer_ID field is the

   a. foreign key.

   b. primary key.

   c. composite key.

   d. relationship.

Discussion and Research Questions

DQ1. (LO 1) `Critical Thinking` Identify and explain the two types of sales, differentiated by type of customer. Choose a business and a product. Use that product to provide an example of the two types of sales.

DQ2. (LO 1) Describe the three ways a customer can pay for a sales order and identify one risk for each payment method.

DQ3. (LO 2) `Critical Thinking` The headline for an article from May 13, 2021 is "Yelp Ramps Up Spending on Ad Products to Boost Revenue." Yelp is selling advertising to restaurants and other businesses on its website and plans to spend more on marketing itself to potential advertisers. One of the Yelp representatives interviewed in the article was Yelp CFO David Schwarzbach, but the head of sales and marketing was not interviewed. Why are marketing expenditures of interest to a CFO? How does marketing relate to accounting?

DQ4. (LO 2) `Critical Thinking` Identify three internal controls for credit sales. Why are effective controls over credit sales important? What are some of the unique risks to credit sales compared to cash sales?

DQ5. (LO 2–3) `Fraud` `Critical Thinking` Halal Burtaz, the CFO at Totenheim Corp., authorized a credit sales transaction that resulted in increasing sales revenue and accounts receivable. While there was a legitimate purchase order from the customer, the customer was not yet ready to accept delivery of the product on the date of the sale recording. He arranged for the undelivered goods to be temporarily stored at a facility close to the customer to facilitate quick delivery once the customer was ready. Is this more likely to be an error or fraud? Discuss the implications of this scenario.

DQ6. (LO 3) Identify the steps in the revenue recognition model and outline specific actions required to satisfy each.

DQ7. (LO 3) What are the differences between over-time revenue recognition and point-in-time revenue recognition? Which steps in the revenue recognition process are impacted by choosing one over the other?

DQ8. (LO 3) `Research` `Fraud` `Critical Thinking` Access and download the recent article "Improper Revenue Recognition Tops SEC Fraud Cases" from www.cfodive.com/news/improper-revenue-recognition-sec-fraud-cases/583889/. Then follow the instructions below.

   a. Choose a revenue recognition fraud case from the examples the report provides

   b. Describe the fraud case and explain why it is revenue recognition fraud

   c. Do further research to uncover at least three other interesting facts about this case. Include references to your sources

   d. Explain how the risk of this type of fraud could have been mitigated by the victim organization

DQ9. (LO 4) `Early Career` `Data Analytics` `Critical Thinking`
You are an internal audit data analytics intern at a regional medical center's corporate headquarters. You are running a data analytics test to identify supplier names in the main vendor table that have similarities to employee names in the main employee table. Your analysis is searching for red flags for vendor fraud. You show the output of your test to your manager, who is surprised at the number of results you have generated. Your manager recommends that you review the testing parameters to eliminate any false positives they may have generated. When running data analytics, what is a false positive? What steps must be taken to address false positives? Use the internet to assist in finding an answer.

DQ10. (LO 4) `Fraud` `Early Career` `Critical Thinking`
You are a senior internal auditor at a global cell phone manufacturer. Your company sells finished smart phones that are ready for consumer use to retail chains and cell phone service providers for sale in their storefronts and e-commerce sites. One of your friends is a first-year internal auditor working on a revenue engagement. She's new to the company, and you regularly meet with her to answer questions she has. One day, during lunch, she asks you about channel stuffing. She's not familiar with it but was asked to compile a list of possible audit tests to assess channel stuffing fraud risk. How would you explain channel stuffing to your team member? Provide an example of how it would work at your company.

DQ11. (LO 4) Give three examples of how cash collections can impact the balance sheet.

DQ12. (LO 4) Describe a lockbox, how it is used by an organization, and what source documents are created when a lockbox is used.

DQ13. (LO 5) Identify the key database tables needed for selling finished goods on credit and explain how they are related using cardinality and optionality or business rules.

DQ14. (LO 5) Explain how sales forecasts are used by (1) the conversion processes and (2) the purchasing and payments processes.

Application and Analysis Questions

A1. (LO 1) `Critical Thinking` For each of the following scenarios, identify whether the sale that occurs is a business-to-consumer (B2C) or business-to-business (B2B) sale.

1. A college student purchases a cup of coffee at Starbucks.
2. Target purchases Starbucks coffee beans.
3. Starbucks purchases paper cups.
4. An honors society orders and receives 12 reusable coffee mugs on Starbucks' website.
5. The chair of a nonprofit purchases bags of coffee beans at Starbucks for a silent auction gift basket.
6. A college student purchases a cup of coffee at Starbucks inside of Target.
7. A Starbucks manager buys paper towels from Target because the café ran out.

8. A Starbucks manager orders and receives paper towels from a Bounty distributor.

A2. (LO 1) Accepting only cashless payment forms, such as credit cards or mobile app payments, is an internal control that mitigates the risk of cash being stolen by a cashier in charge of a cash register. Identify three other controls that could be used to address this risk in a physical store.

A3. (LO 2) Use the word bank to label the participants and source documents in the following illustration:

Word Bank:

delivery	warehouse
customer	packing slip
picking request	information system
sales order	

A4. (LO 3) `Critical Thinking` You are a financial systems analyst for Parker, LLC. You are reviewing existing controls to identify opportunities to migrate manual revenue controls, which are performed by individuals in the department, to automated system controls. Automated system controls will perform a control on behalf of individuals and either prohibit an action in the information system or provide an exception report indicating violations of the control's parameters. From the following list of controls, identify which are good candidates to be migrated to automated system controls by labeling each with "Yes" or "No."

1. Review reports and data analyses for unusual trends or unexpected results
2. Match revenue transactions with approved customer orders
3. Examine customer returns around the cutoff period
4. Maintain a strong audit committee, board of directors, and control environment (the tone at the top)
5. Match sales invoice with shipping information and customer acknowledgment of fulfillment of seller obligations

6. Provide a reporting hotline where whistleblowers remain anonymous

7. Automatically generate invoices and recognize revenue when the customer electronically signs to accept the shipment

8. Segregate billing function from shipping and accounts receivable functions

9. Sequence shipping documents and match them with customer billing

A5. (LO 4) `Critical Thinking` From Blizzard's perspective, identify the type of customer relationship, type of payment method, and General Ledger accounts involved in the journal entry made at the time of each of the following scenarios. Each scenario must be labeled with (1) one type of customer relationship, (2) one payment method, (3) one debit account, and (4) one credit account.

Customer relationships: B2C | B2B

Payment methods: Cash sale | Advance payment | Credit sale

Debit accounts: Cash | Accounts Receivable

Credit accounts: Sales Revenue | Deferred Revenue

Scenarios:

1. Joe purchases Blizzard's latest video game from Game Stop.

2. Game Stop orders a shipment of new video games from Blizzard to resell on its shelves. It will pay for them next month.

3. Blizzard orders a custom-designed graphic for its new video game and pays at the time of the order. The designer promises to deliver by a certain date.

4. Jose pays for his monthly subscription to Blizzard's latest online game.

A6. (LO 2–4) The following internal control activities mitigate risks in the marketing, sales, and collections processes. For each control listed, identify the risk the control activity mitigates.

Control activities:

A. Ensure that a policy for sales cutoff timing is documented and approved

B. Create programming that calculates sales discounts

C. Use standard sales contracts that are authorized by management

D. Do automated matching of sales invoice quantities to shipping information and to pricing in the sales contract

E. Automate the creation of monthly statements for customers

F. Implement a policy that states cash is not accepted and only cards can be used for payment

G. Ensure that a policy for credit checks is documented and approved

H. Check remittance advices against the daily remittance list

I. Control access to the warehouse

J. Automate the matching of the customer's name on the sales order to a main data list for customers

A7. (LO 5) Label each attribute listed below with the term from the word bank that best describes it.

Word Bank:		
data	report	analytics

Attributes:

1. Customer name

2. Customers with the same phone number

3. Average number of items sold per day

4. Customer type description

5. Product description

6. Sales order aging

7. Calculation of sales ratios

8. Service ID

9. Amount billed by date

10. Review of sales ratios

11. Items currently out of stock

12. Review of shipments without an invoice

A8. (LO 1–4) `Early Career` `Critical Thinking` You are an accounts receivable analyst for Amazing Nature, a manufacturer of camping and outdoor gear. The fiscal year ends on 12/31, and you received information about a number of scenarios, including dates. For each scenario, answer these questions:

A. What type of payment method is being used (e.g., credit, cash, advance payment)?

B. What type of customer is buying products (B2B or B2C)?

C. Which journal entries reflect the input into the AIS from these transactions during the second quarter?

Scenarios:

1. On April 3, ShopCo orders $18,500 worth of products. The cost of goods sold is $14,500. ShopCo is a new customer, and the terms of the sale are a 3% discount if paid with 10 days, otherwise full payment in 30 days. The product is shipped on April 12 and delivered on April 14. Payment for the product in the amount of $17,945 is received on April 16.

2. On April 5, Walmart orders $118,600 worth of products. The cost of goods sold is $84,450. Walmart pays the invoice when the products are ordered. The product is shipped on April 13 and delivered on April 14.

3. On April 12, Michelle O'Danre orders $125 worth of products in the retail store. The cost of goods sold is $75. Michelle receives and pays for the product in the store.

4. On April 18, Kroger orders $40,250 worth of products. The cost of goods sold is $29,125. The terms of the sale are net 30. The product is shipped on April 22 and delivered on April 24, and payment in the amount $40,250 is received on May 14.

5. On June 27, Target orders $94,200 worth of products. The cost of goods sold is $71,560. The terms of the sale are net 30. The product is shipped on July 1 and delivered on July 2, and payment for the product in the amount $94,200 is received on July 5.

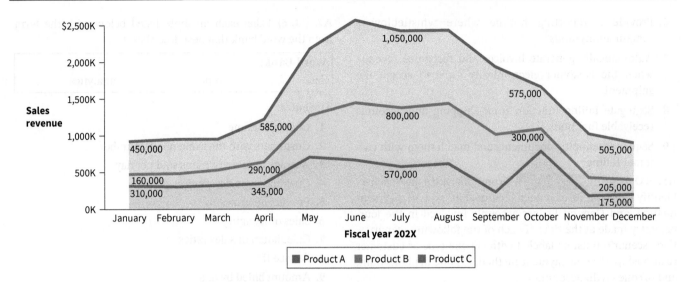

Fiscal year 202X

■ Product A ■ Product B ■ Product C

A9. (LO 1–5) `Fraud` `Data Analytics` `Critical Thinking`
You are an external auditor performing revenue testing on Lounging Luxury's sales data. Lounging Luxury is a provider of cabana rentals to tourists at premier beaches throughout the Caribbean. Sales peak in the summer months from May through August, then experience a drastic decrease through the fall and winter months.

You have received the visualization shown above from your team's audit data analyst. It shows the sales of products over time for fiscal year 202X in a stacked area chart. Each area of color shows the total for a particular product, and the top line indicates the total of all products. To help you use the stacked area chart, the audit data analyst included totals for each product on a quarterly basis. For example, in April 202X, Product A's sales were $85,000, Product B's sales were $290,000, and Product C's sales were $345,000.

Based on this visualization, which product do you think should be investigated for revenue fraud risk and at what point in time? Explain your answer.

A10. (LO 1–5) `Critical Thinking` You just started your third year at Nature's Naturals, a mid-sized company in the northwestern United States. Nature's Naturals has three local stores, and it also sells its products in grocery stores across the country.

You are an internal auditor working on a marketing and sales engagement. The company's marketing department has a strong connection to the Sales and Accounting departments. As part of the audit, you have been interviewing personnel throughout the Marketing, Sales, and Accounting departments. You need to document the notes you have taken in these interviews by writing a process narrative, which is a description of a process and its steps, written in paragraph form.

Using the word bank, fill in the missing portions of your process narrative. An item in the word bank may be used more than once. You may use a term more than once or not at all.

Word Bank:

business-to-consumer (B2C)	financial
business-to-business (B2B)	shipping notice
sales order	packing slip
sales invoice	picking request
remittance advice	controls
credit sale	cash
sales order	advance payment
credit	total sales
accounts receivable	lockbox

"When a customer wishes to buy a product, the company receives a(n) **(1)** _____. If the customer buys the product from the local company store, it is considered a(n) **(2)** _____ sale, but if the order comes from a reseller, it is a(n) **(3)** _____ sale. If the customer pays for the order before we give them the product, it is considered a(n) **(4)** _____. In our local company stores, we do not allow **(5)** _____ sales. When a customer pays via bank deposit in a **(6)** _____, they will send back a **(7)** _____ with the payment. For **(8)** _____ sales, the main warehouse will receive a(n) **(9)** _____ which instructs them on the items that have been purchased and need to be shipped to the customer. To help ensure the integrity of the processes, the organization implements **(10)** _____ to mitigate the risk of error or fraud. To ensure that a customer receives the correct amount due for any purchases, Nature's Naturals sends out a(n) **(11)** _____ to the customer. The amount the customer owes is stored in the **(12)** _____ table of the database, which stores data for one of the **(13)** _____ modules of the ERP system."

Tableau Case: Julia's Cookies' Accounts Receivable Analysis

What You Need

Download Tableau to your computer. You can access www.tableau.com/academic/students to download your free Tableau license for the year, or you can download it from your university's software offerings.

Download the following file from the book's product page on www.wiley.com:

Chapter 12 Raw Data.xlsx

Case Overview

Big Picture:

Identify outstanding balances and collections risks.

Details:

Why is this data important, and what questions or problems need to be addressed?

- Julia's Cookies analyzes its accounts receivable data to monitor how much it's invoiced customers, the amount of payments received, and the ratio of receipts from customers to outstanding accounts.
- An accounts receivable aging report breaks the outstanding accounts into buckets, based on the length of time the account has been outstanding. For example, an aging report may use buckets for 0–30 days, 31–60 days, 61–90 days, 91–120 days, and >120 days.
- An accounts receivable aging report is used to identify debts for collection and estimate bad debt expenses and the allowance for doubtful accounts.
- Consider the following questions during your analysis: What total amount is due from customers at a point in time? Which customer owes the largest amount at a point in time? How many days outstanding are the accounts receivable balances? Which customer consistently makes late payments?

Plan:

What data is needed, and how should it be analyzed?

- The data needed to answer these questions is extracted from the ERP database.
- The data consists of the accounts receivable data for retail customers who purchased frozen cookie dough on account in 2022.

Now it's your turn to evaluate, analyze, and communicate the results!

To answer the questions, connect the tables using their ID fields:

Questions

1. How much did Julia's Cookies invoice its customers in December 2022?
2. During which months did Julia's Cookies receive the largest total dollar amount of payments from its customers?
3. Which customer charged the largest total dollar amount for credit purchases in 2022?
4. Which state had the largest total dollar amount of credit sales in 2022?
5. What was the balance for Accounts Receivable on December 31, 2022? (Hint: "Null.")
6. Which customer had $19,094 in outstanding Accounts Receivable on December 31, 2022?

7. What was the total dollar amount of invoices sent to customers in March 2022 and paid by customers in July 2022?

8. What was the total dollar amount of invoices sent to customers in July 2022 and paid by customers in October 2022?

Take it to the next level!

9. What was the average number of days outstanding, rounded to the nearest whole number, for an invoice during 2022? (Hint: DATEDIFF.)

10. What was the total dollar amount of outstanding Accounts Receivable that were 61 to 90 days overdue as of December 31, 2022?

Financial Reporting Processes

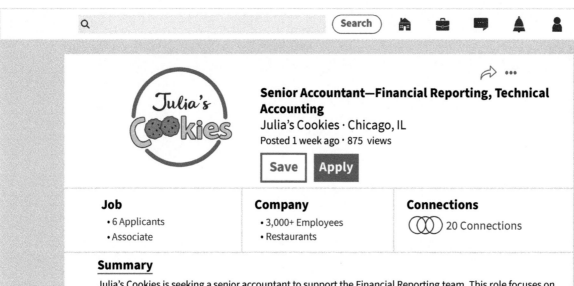

Senior Accountant—Financial Reporting, Technical Accounting

Julia's Cookies · Chicago, IL

Posted 1 week ago · 875 views

Save   **Apply**

Job	**Company**	**Connections**
• 6 Applicants	• 3,000+ Employees	20 Connections
• Associate	• Restaurants	

Summary

Julia's Cookies is seeking a senior accountant to support the Financial Reporting team. This role focuses on delivering value to the business through accurate and efficient preparation of external financial statements and internal reports. The senior accountant must be able to work at technical (accounting research) and tactical (analyzing data, applying accounting standards, and problem solving) levels.

Responsibilities

- Assisting in preparation, review, and analysis of required SEC external financial statements (10-Q, 8-K, 10-K, 11-K)
- Ensuring compliance with U.S. GAAP and SEC regulations
- Assisting with the completion and submission of XBRL filings
- Working directly with internal business partners, including various teams
- Assisting with research and implementation of new accounting standards
- Assisting with preparation and review of monthly internal reports for executive management
- Preparing the monthly cash flow statement

Requirements

Preferred Education: Bachelor's degree or higher in accounting

Preferred Certifications: CPA

Preferred Knowledge and Skills

The ideal candidate will demonstrate a solid foundation in accounting and advanced Excel, including formulas and pivot tables. Preference will be given to candidates who demonstrate the following experience:

- Two to four years in audit, corporate accounting, or financial reporting
- Data visualization (Tableau or PowerBI preferred)
- ERP systems (SAP, Oracle, etc.)
- Exposure to XBRL

Salary: $60,000–75,000

CHAPTER PREVIEW   During this course, you have learned that the AIS supports business decisions by turning accounting data into quality information. Many companies use reports and analytics to support quality decision-making information, but every company uses accounting data to generate financial statements.

In this chapter, you will learn:

- Why financial statements are an important output of the AIS
- How businesses use the AIS to produce financial statements
- Digital financial statement reporting requirements (XBRL)
- Some essential reporting for managerial accounting
- How to use system-generated reports and data analytics using financial reporting data

Remember that everything you are learning in this course, from management's role in internal control to using data analytics and visualization to turn accounting data into insights, is designed to result in accurate financial reporting.

Financial reporting is, unsurprisingly, a large area of career opportunity for accounting professionals. The senior accountant position at Julia's Cookies is based on a job at a global home improvement corporation. Notice that experience with SAP and digital financial statement reporting requirements (XBRL) are considered nice to have, but not necessary, qualifications. A candidate with familiarity with these concepts will have an advantage when interviewing for this kind of role. ■

Chapter Roadmap

LEARNING OBJECTIVES	TOPICS	JULIA'S COOKIES APPLIED LEARNING
13.1 Identify the role of the accounting information system in financial reporting.	• Meeting Financial Reporting Objectives • Consolidated Reporting Requirements	Financial Reporting: Useful Information
13.2 Document the generation of financial statements within the accounting information system.	• Chart of Accounts • The Financial Reporting Process • Financial Reporting Internal Controls	General Ledger: Journal Entry Testing
13.3 Explain how XBRL promotes reporting efficiency.	• Tagging Financial Data • Standardized Financial Reporting • XBRL in Action	XBRL: Creating a Business Case
13.4 Describe when to use key management accounting reports.	• Cost Accounting • Responsibility Accounting • Balanced Scorecard	Balanced Scorecard: Strategic Planning
13.5 Summarize the importance of data analytics and reporting for financial reporting decision making.	• Database Design • Financial Modeling for Decision Making • Reporting and Insights	Data Extraction: Trial Balance Rollforward

CPA   You will find the CPA tag throughout the chapter to call out any important topics you may see on the CPA exam.

13.1 How Is an AIS Involved in Financial Reporting?

Learning Objective ❶
Identify the role of the accounting information system in financial reporting.

Imagine friends approached you with a business idea and asked for investment money to help them start it. Would you give them thousands of dollars without question? Probably not. You would want to know details like what the business will do, why they think it will be successful, how it will make money, and how they plan to use your money. Investors generally won't invest in a company until they know the financial details of the business.

Financial reporting is a standardized practice that provides external stakeholders, like investors, with an accurate depiction of a company's financial situation. The result of a company's financial reporting processes is a set of formalized financial statements, which, in the order of their creation, are:

- Income statement
- Balance sheet
- Statement of stockholder's equity
- Statement of cash flows

Financial reporting uses accounting data generated from business processes, like purchasing, human resources, conversion, and sales, as the inputs to create the output of financial statements. These financial statements are used for decision making, which is one of the objectives of financial reporting.

Before our in-depth discussion of financial reporting, let's look at who the primary control owners are for these processes. Job titles may differ between companies, but the organizational structure of financial reporting processes is often similar. There are two key roles in an organization: the chief financial officer (CFO) and the controller.

The CFO oversees all financing-related activities:

- Participating in strategy development
- Overseeing functions like internal audit
- Being a key decision maker in the executive management team
- Being responsible for financial reporting, taxation, budget management, cost-benefit analysis, and financial forecasting

One of the CFO's direct reports—the controller—focuses specifically on accounting processes:

- Overseeing all accounting activities, including business process areas such as payroll and accounts receivable
- Overseeing managerial accounting functions and taxation
- Collaborating with management and other accounting functions to ensure a strong control environment

Together, the CFO and controller ensure that the financial reporting department is working with other areas of the business and using the data captured by the accounting information system (AIS) throughout the company to meet financial reporting objectives. Financial reporting objectives, which we discuss next, are based on the needs of the users of the information.

Meeting Financial Reporting Objectives

The financial reporting process produces financial statements that are useful to users external to the business. These financial statements must present, in all material aspects:

- The financial position of the business at specific points in time
- The results of its operations and cash flows over specific reporting time periods (i.e., annually, quarterly, and monthly)

In other words, they must fairly present the financial story of the business. Management also uses monthly, quarterly, and annual financial statements when managing business processes to achieve desired financial outcomes. The goal in both cases is to provide the most useful information in the most cost-effective manner.

Decision Usefulness

Financial accounting information only serves its purpose if it is useful for decision making. Recall from the Accounting as Information chapter that information quality is the suitability of information for a particular purpose in a specific task. **CPA** The FASB identifies the characteristics of quality information for financial information shown in **Illustration 13.1**. To meet the objective of decision usefulness, information must have these characteristics. Review these characteristics again and remember that there are always cost constraints that make it necessary to prioritize these characteristics.

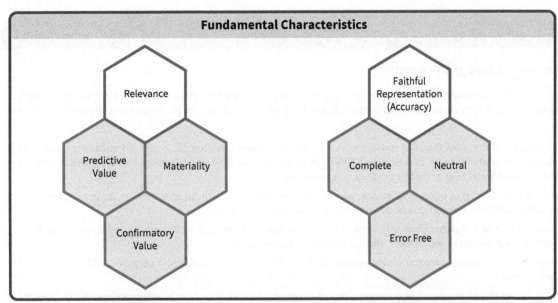

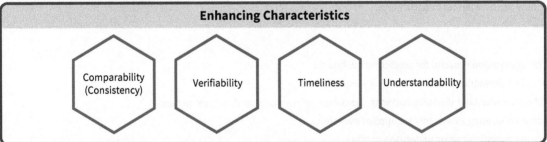

Illustration 13.1 Qualitative characteristics of accounting information create a hierarchy.

Cost-Effectiveness

The cost-effectiveness of accounting information is determined by weighing the costs of providing it against the value of the information. Examples of these costs include:

- Gathering the data
- Processing the data
- Storing the data
- Communicating the information

Determining cost-effectiveness requires professional judgment. If the cost of achieving a particular characteristic exceeds the perceived benefit of increased decision usefulness, then the cost is not justifiable. For example, expending more time and resources to process financial data from different subsidiaries' AIS will improve comparability, which is the enhancing characteristic that ensures data is consistent. If the process causes the company to miss its financial reporting deadlines, the characteristic may not be worth the cost.

Consider the decision usefulness and cost-effectiveness of financial reporting at Julia's Cookies in Applied Learning 13.1.

Julia's Cookies   Applied Learning 13.1

Financial Reporting: Useful Information

Financial reporting at Julia's Cookies serves a variety of purposes. The following situations rely on data within the AIS to create useful information via financial reports. Which characteristic of useful information is the highest priority for each of the following financial reporting use cases?

1. The treasurer provides a set of the latest financial statements to the bank to support a request for a material increase in its line of credit. The bank uses the financial statements to determine Julia's Cookies' ability to achieve a certain threshold for the financial ratios specified in the debt covenant, for as long as the line of credit is in existence.

2. Each quarter after the line of credit is in effect, the treasurer provides an updated set of financial statements to the bank so the bank can check whether Julia's Cookies achieved the debt covenant ratios in subsequent quarters.

3. Julia's Cookies calls a line item on its balance sheet "Allowance for Doubtful Accounts" instead of "Reserve for Bad Debts" to clarify to users that these amounts are estimates of loss of value and not reserves of cash or funds.

4. Julia's Cookies always discloses its significant accounting policies in Note 1 to its financial statements and provides full disclosure of any changes to those policies.

5. Julia's Cookies is planning to offer stock options to employees. Management understands it needs to provide employees with financial information before they decide whether to participate.

SOLUTION

1. Predictive value: The information is useful for predicting the future.
2. Confirmatory value: The information confirms the bank's expectations.
3. Understandability: Users understand the information in the context of the decision they have to make.
4. Consistency: The same accounting treatments are applied over time.
5. Timeliness: Information is available prior to decision making.

Consolidated Reporting Requirements

Financial reporting is important and complex. Companies consider many things when designing their financial reporting process, including which accounting system to use and how to prepare the financial statements. From mergers and acquisitions that bring legacy systems into the business to implementing advanced enterprise resource planning (ERP) systems, we have learned about many of the complexities businesses face. Now, let's examine a complexity that is unique to the financial reporting system.

CPA **Consolidated financial statements** are the financial statements of a company that has multiple divisions or subsidiaries. Normally covered in advanced financial accounting, consolidations have important financial reporting process considerations. From an AIS reporting perspective, consolidations add an additional layer of complexity, especially at fiscal year end, when timelines are tight.

A parent company has control over its subsidiary if it owns more than 50% of the subsidiary's voting stock. The companies remain separate legal entities and have individual financial statements, but the parent company is required to report consolidated financial statements to reflect its controlling interest in the subsidiary. This is based on the concept that when preparing financial statements, economic substance takes precedence over legal form.

The consolidated financial statements present the parent and all of its subsidiaries as one company by eliminating intercompany transactions and aggregating the different sets of financial statements into one set of consolidated financial statements. For example, Company A uses SAP as its AIS. Meanwhile, Company B uses Oracle, and Company C uses Sage. Company A gains a controlling interest in Company B and Company C through investing activities (**Illustration 13.2**). Now, Company A must combine Company B's financial data from Oracle, Company C's financial data from Sage, and its own financial data from SAP into a single set of consolidated financial statements.

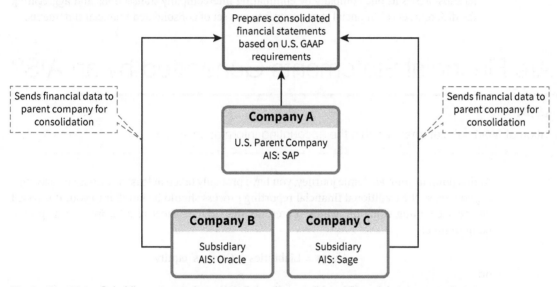

Illustration 13.2 Subsidiary companies report through consolidated financial statements that are prepared by the parent company.

In this example, all three companies are using different AIS. Field names, data formats, and even account numbers may differ greatly across the three companies, which makes aggregating the data into a unified format difficult.

Larger companies use dedicated consolidation software to automate the process, validate the data, and create a reliable audit trail. This approach can be too costly for smaller companies, which may resort to using spreadsheets, which come with all the related risks of using a mostly manual system. In addition to the difficulties of combining data from subsidiaries with different AIS software, companies also face difficulties with:

- Consolidating subsidiaries with different fiscal year ends
- Dealing with manual consolidation adjustments

Effective consolidation software includes the following functionalities:

- Maps multiple general ledgers to a single chart of accounts
- Determines hierarchies of control
- Manages and converts multiple currencies
- Performs eliminations of intercompany transactions
- Automatically generates consolidated financial statements
- Integrates XBRL, which you will learn about later in this chapter

A recent Gartner report identifies the leading consolidation vendors as Oracle Financial Consolidation, Workiva, Blackline, Tagetik, and OneStream.[1]

---

[1]Gartner, Inc. October 19, 2019. *Magic Quadrant for Cloud Financial Close Solutions.*

CONCEPT REVIEW QUESTIONS

1. What is meant by financial reporting?

   Ans. Financial reporting is a standardized practice that provides external stakeholders, like investors, with an accurate depiction of a company's financial situation.

2. **CPA** What according to the Financial Accounting Standards Board (FASB) are the fundamental characteristics that determine the quality of financial information?

   Ans. The FASB identifies the fundamental characteristics of quality information for financial information as relevancy and faithful representation of information. The enhancing characteristics are consistency, verifiability, timeliness, and understandability.

3. **CPA** What is a consolidated financial statement?

   Ans. Consolidated financial statement is a company's financial statement that has multiple divisions or subsidiaries. The consolidated financial statements present the parent and all of its subsidiaries as one company by eliminating intercompany transactions and aggregating the different sets of financial statements into one set of consolidated financial statements.

13.2 How Are Financial Statements Generated by an AIS?

Learning Objective ❷

Document the generation of financial statements within the accounting information system.

At this point in your academic journey, you have probably taken at least one financial accounting course, so the traditional financial reporting process should be familiar to you. It is based on the accounting equation, which represents the balance sheet of a business at a specific point in time:

$$\text{Assets} = \text{Liabilities} + \text{Owners' equity}$$

or:

$$A = L + OE$$

The accounting equation must always balance. This is an embedded control inherent to the traditional financial reporting process. We can expand the basic accounting equation reflecting the balance sheet to include the income statement and the statement of stockholders' equity and to conclude with the statement of cash flows. If you love math, see Appendix A, which provides detailed calculations for these financial reporting processes.

Financial reporting processes are different from the business processes discussed in other chapters. Instead of looking at who is performing physical actions, we will explore the steps of establishing a solid foundation for reporting in the AIS and look at the processes from the perspective of when each financial statement is created during the reporting process.

Chart of Accounts

CPA Before beginning the financial statement process, businesses must develop a **chart of accounts**, which is a classification scheme to organize financial data and summarize financial measurements of assets, liabilities, and owners' equity. The chart of accounts lists the reference numbers assigned to income statement and balance sheet accounts so accounting transactions are entered into the proper ledger accounts. By appropriately classifying and summarizing data, the chart of accounts makes it possible to prepare financial statements.

Recall the complexities of consolidated reporting when the subsidiaries use different AIS. A consistent chart of accounts across all entities allows a company to ensure there is a consistent method of aggregating financial data, regardless of which systems are being used.

A chart of accounts **coding system** logically records, classifies, stores, and extracts financial data using coding techniques made up of numbers and/or letters. A chart of accounts in a traditional system often uses **block coding**, with blocks of sequential numbers reserved for specific types of accounts. For example, current assets accounts could belong to the 100 block, with the individual current asset accounts, like Cash on Hand and Accounts Receivable, having account numbers that range from 100 to 199. Each assigned number is unique to a specific ledger account.

Illustration 13.3 shows an abbreviated chart of accounts using block coding for Julia's Cookies, which uses a stand-alone AIS for accounting and financial reporting.

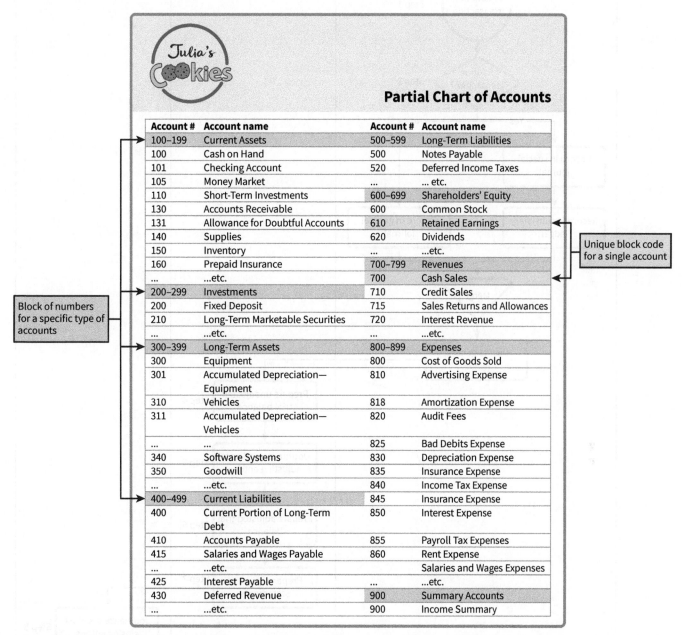

Partial Chart of Accounts

Account #	Account name	Account #	Account name
100–199	Current Assets	500–599	Long-Term Liabilities
100	Cash on Hand	500	Notes Payable
101	Checking Account	520	Deferred Income Taxes
105	Money Market	...	... etc.
110	Short-Term Investments	600–699	Shareholders' Equity
130	Accounts Receivable	600	Common Stock
131	Allowance for Doubtful Accounts	610	Retained Earnings
140	Supplies	620	Dividends
150	Inventory	...	...etc.
160	Prepaid Insurance	700–799	Revenues
...	...etc.	700	Cash Sales
200–299	Investments	710	Credit Sales
200	Fixed Deposit	715	Sales Returns and Allowances
210	Long-Term Marketable Securities	720	Interest Revenue
...	...etc.	...	...etc.
300–399	Long-Term Assets	800–899	Expenses
300	Equipment	800	Cost of Goods Sold
301	Accumulated Depreciation—Equipment	810	Advertising Expense
310	Vehicles	818	Amortization Expense
311	Accumulated Depreciation—Vehicles	820	Audit Fees
...	...	825	Bad Debits Expense
340	Software Systems	830	Depreciation Expense
350	Goodwill	835	Insurance Expense
...	...etc.	840	Income Tax Expense
400–499	Current Liabilities	845	Insurance Expense
400	Current Portion of Long-Term Debt	850	Interest Expense
410	Accounts Payable	855	Payroll Tax Expenses
415	Salaries and Wages Payable	860	Rent Expense
...	...etc.		Salaries and Wages Expenses
425	Interest Payable	...	...etc.
430	Deferred Revenue	900	Summary Accounts
...	...etc.	900	Income Summary

Block of numbers for a specific type of accounts

Unique block code for a single account

Illustration 13.3   Julia's Cookies' chart of accounts is coded using block coding that assigns each type of account to one block of account numbers.

The Financial Reporting Process

The chart of accounts categorizes the transactions that occur during the accounting process. This section provides a condensed refresher of the traditional accounting process (also known as the accounting cycle) covered in financial accounting courses. The steps are illustrated in Julia's Cookies' financial reporting process flowchart (**Illustration 13.4**). This process flowchart is horizontal, meaning the swim lanes move from left to right, while the process moves from top to bottom. The swim lanes in process flowcharts in other chapters have represented responsible parties, but here the swim lanes represent financial reporting activities during the reporting period, after the reporting period, and at the end of the fiscal year.

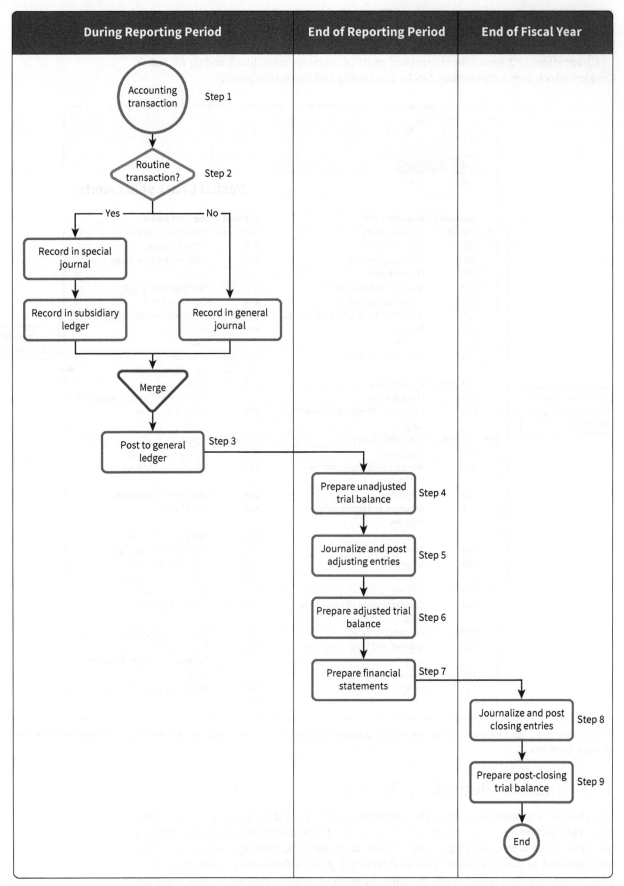

Illustration 13.4 This process flowchart uses swim lanes to indicate the timing of events during the reporting period.

During the Reporting Period

From when the business event occurs to when the accounting transaction is posted to the general ledger, there are three steps during the reporting period. These steps take place throughout the reporting period, as needed.

Step 1: Identify the accounting transactions
Recall that accountants filter the business data collected during business processes. Not every business event that occurs during a business process results in accounting data:

- We only classify an event as an accounting transaction if it impacts the accounting equation in monetary terms.
- Even if it is considered an accounting transaction, the accounting system does not necessarily capture all the data about that business event.

For example, a corporate customer places a large online order for frozen cookie dough from Julia's Cookies, to be paid within 30 days of delivery. This is a crucial business event. Without orders, there would be no sales and no revenues! While we can quantify the amount of the order, this business event does not yet result in an accounting transaction. Do we want to collect data about this order? Of course, but it does not impact the financial statements until the cookies are delivered to the customer and ownership has passed. At that point, the sale is made, and we will recognize the revenue for this order, whether as cash received or accounts receivable.

`CPA` When accounting transactions occur, **source documents** are generated. These documents provide evidence and an **audit trail**, which allows auditors to verify the accuracy and validity of accounting transactions. With a source document, transactions can be followed through the reporting process from origination to final output in the financial statements.

Step 2: Journalize the accounting transactions
A **journal**, also known as a book of prime entry, is where the economic impact of an accounting transaction is first recorded chronologically in the system. There are two types of journals:

- `CPA` A **special journal** (such as a sales journal, purchases journal, cash receipts journal, or cash payments journal) captures routine transactions that repeat often.
- `CPA` The **general journal** is for transactions that do not repeat often during a reporting period and for adjusting and closing entries.

It is unlikely you will encounter a manual journal these days. Journal entries are normally electronic entries into an accounting system. In an automated system, the entries are electronic, such as scanning a barcode. Journal entries show the most detail about an accounting transaction before it is further classified and summarized in ledgers. For example, when Julia's Cookies receives an order for 10,000 units of frozen cookie dough at $5 each from LowCost Wholesalers, the accounting team inputs a journal entry into the AIS:

- This journal entry shows the invoice number, date of the transaction, description of the transaction (a credit sale), and the name and/or account number of the individual customer for recording in the Accounts Receivable feature of an accounting system, so the business can keep track of which customer owes what amount.
- It also shows the amount of the debit and credit ($50,000) for posting to the general ledger.[2]

---

[2]You may recall from your financial accounting class that there will also be a debit to Cost of Goods Sold and a credit to Inventory to record the related expense and decrease in the Asset account.

Why Does It Matter to Your Career?

Thoughts from a First-Year External Auditor, Public Accounting

Journal entry testing is an essential part of an external audit, so you should understand where the journal entries came from. While journal entries are traditionally learned in a financial accounting class, your AIS course shows how the transactions that create journal entries occur and are captured by a company's systems.

Step 3: Post journal entries to ledgers   The AIS posts journal entries to the general ledger. It is the record-keeping system that captures all journal entries, validates them using the trial balance, and posts to subsidiary ledgers, if required. A company's chart of accounts provides the structure for its general ledger:

- Each general ledger account (often called a T-account because it was shaped like a T in manual systems) has a unique account number, as shown in the chart of accounts in Illustration 13.3.
- Every accounting transaction results in a journal entry of a debit amount that equals a credit amount in the general ledger.

For our Julia's Cookies example, this journal entry is a debit to Accounts Receivable and credit to Credit Sales. In T-accounts on paper, debits are on the left, and credits on the right.

CPA Subsidiary ledgers provide more detail about certain general ledger accounts. For example, the Accounts Receivable Subsidiary Ledger contains the ledger account and customer ID for each customer that owes money to the business. Recall that accounts receivable only applies to customers who purchase from the business on a line of credit.

Every time a customer makes a payment, the general ledger account is updated. Additionally, the associated customer's Accounts Receivable Subsidiary Ledger is also updated. For example, if Good Foods pays Julia's Cookies $200,000 on December 19 for a sales order purchased on credit, a journal entry is recorded in the general ledger, and the Good Foods' subsidiary ledger is also updated (**Illustration 13.5**).

Illustration 13.5   Julia's Cookies has an Accounts Receivable Subsidiary Ledger for each customer that records the amount a customer owes.

Julia's Cookies
Accounts Receivable Subsidiary Ledger
YE December 31, 202X

Account: Good Foods Inc.					Account Number: 100653-A
Date	**Details**	**Reference**	**Debit**	**Credit**	**Account Balance (Dr)**
Dec 1	Beginning Balance				$150,000
Dec 8	Sales Journal	87	$210,000		$360,000
Dec 19	Cash Receipts	44		$200,000	$160,000

In summary, every credit customer has an Accounts Receivable Subsidiary Ledger to record their individual transactions, while the general ledger records a summary of everyone's transactions. Reconciling these two ledgers is an important internal control. Other common general ledger accounts that also have subsidiary ledgers are Accounts Payable, Inventory, and Fixed Assets.

Journal entries are a large source of data stored in the AIS. External auditors use technology to aid their required fraud journal entry tests by applying data analytics in full population testing. Help the external auditors at Julia's Cookies decide which journal entry tests to perform this year in Applied Learning 13.2.

| Julia's Cookies | Applied Learning 13.2 |

General Ledger: Journal Entry Testing

The external audit team is planning its annual audit of Julia's Cookies. As part of Auditing Standard AU-C 240, which is a regulatory requirement for the external auditors to consider fraud in the financial statement audit, the team plans to use data analytics to analyze Julia's Cookies' journal entries for fraud risks. The external audit team has a list of journal entry tests that can be performed based on a client's unique risk profile. Help Arlo, the external auditor in charge of journal entry testing, select three of the following journal entry fraud tests. Then explain why they are useful at Julia's Cookies.

- Keyword testing: Searches for fraud-related wording in journal entry descriptions, such as "miscellaneous," "per CFO," "per manager," or "true up"
- Round dollar entries: Journal entries where the dollar amount ends in .00
- Revenue reversals: Reversed month-end entries related to revenue accounts
- GL close: Journal entries posted near the general ledger close date
- Dormant accounts: Journal entries posted to any inactive or dormant accounts
- Authorized users: Journal entries entered by system users who are not on the list of authorized users

SOLUTION

Arlo needs to use judgment, historical audit information, and the current year's fraud risk assessment to select the journal entry tests that will have the most impact. Here are some reasons each test could be useful to the external audit:

- Keyword testing: While searching for keywords like "fraud" wouldn't be helpful, finding unusual words or explanations for journal entries related to someone telling the accountant to enter them (like "per CFO" or "per manager") can uncover journal entries that may not follow normal procedures or that could be indicative of management override.
- Round dollar entries: It's unusual for a transaction to end in an even dollar amount. Reviewing round dollar journal entries can help identify fraudulent journal entries.
- Revenue reversals: Financial statement fraud can involve an increase in revenues just before the year end and a reversal of those fraudulent transactions post-close. Therefore, revenue journal entries that have been subsequently reversed can point to fraud.
- GL close: Because financial statement fraud relates to the year-end financial statements, fraudulent journal entries are sometimes posted near the close date to narrow the time frame in which fraud could be discovered.
- Authorized users: Unauthorized users should not be able to post journal entries, but the external audit team should check if it's happened. Such posting may indicate that the ITGCs (controls specifically related to the technology of the information system) are not functioning as designed, which creates an opportunity for fraud.

End of the Reporting Period

The next four steps can occur at the end of the reporting period, which is either a month, quarter, or fiscal year.

Step 4: Prepare an unadjusted trial balance CPA A trial balance is a listing of all the accounts in the general ledger, showing their ending balances at the end of the reporting period. By balancing the trial balance, you know that debits equal credits. We use the unadjusted trial balance as a starting point for creating adjusting journal entries. The Julia's Cookies unadjusted trial balance for the month of January 202X is shown in **Illustration 13.6**.

Step 5: Enter adjusting entries in the general journal and post them to the general ledger CPA Adjusting journal entries properly record accrued expenses, prepaid expenses, deferred revenues, depreciation, amortization, and allowance for doubtful accounts. They are the result of internal business events that impact the accounting equation. A business makes adjusting entries to update the general ledger account before preparing financial statements.

Step 6: Prepare an adjusted trial balance CPA The unadjusted trial balance is updated with the adjusting journal entries to create the adjusted trial balance. Again, a business should check that debits equal credits. The adjusted trial balance is used to prepare the financial statements.

Julia's Cookies		
Unadjusted Trial Balance		
January 31, 202X		
Account	**Debit ($)**	**Credit ($)**
Cash	6,500	
Accounts Receivable	3,000	
Inventory	4,800	
Accumulated Depreciation		5,000
Equipment	25,000	
Accounts Payable		6,000
Long-Term Liabilities		5,500
Common Stock		20,000
Retained Earnings		3,050
Dividends	500	
Sales Revenue		8,600
Cost of Goods Sold	4,200	
Rent Expense	750	
Supplies Expense	200	
Utilities Expense	500	
Wages Expense	2,500	
Interest Expense	200	
Total	48,150	48,150

Illustration 13.6 The unadjusted trial balance debits and credits must balance.

Step 7: Prepare financial statements CPA These statements are the primary output of the financial reporting system.

End of the Fiscal Year

The final two steps occur at the end of the fiscal year only.

Step 8: Prepare closing journal entries and post to the general ledger CPA Closing journal entries close the temporary income statement accounts (revenue and expense accounts) and the dividends account by transferring them to retained earnings. The balances on revenue, expense, and dividends ledger accounts revert to zero in preparation for the new fiscal year.

Step 9: Prepare a post-closing trial balance CPA This trial balance lists all the balances in the general ledger accounts after the closing entries have been posted and checks that debits equal credits.

Because the financial statement preparation process occurs on a regularly scheduled basis and the steps stay the same, financial reporting is an area where technology is often used to reduce the workload of employees and lower the risk of error. Most routine functions, like extracting trial balances and performing closing procedures at the end of a fiscal year, are now automated. Instead of being captured by a bookkeeper or accounts receivable clerk, data is often recorded in real time by scanning barcodes at a cash register or when a customer creates an online customer account. In fact, the popularity of online shopping means that transactions often occur between parties without any human interaction. The system captures digital versions of source document data instead of creating a physical paper trail. While modern accounting systems have adapted, the basic accounting equation is still the same!

Financial Reporting Internal Controls

Since modern accounting systems are so data centric, it follows that technology risks are just as important to address as traditional accounting risks. CPA To address both, management implements **internal controls over financial reporting (ICFRs)**, which are control activities specific to the financial reporting process.

The increasing complexity of accounting standards, like revenue recognition and the passage of the Sarbanes-Oxley (SOX) Act, and unusual business transactions means demands on ICFRs are higher than in the past. These demands can lead to potentially costly changes, and many companies try to reduce costs while still complying with regulations. The first steps in designing or evaluating ICFRs are to do a financial statement risk assessment and then identify controls to mitigate each risk to an acceptable level.

The first set of ICFRs we examine pertain to the corporate accounting policies and procedures (**Table 13.1**).

TABLE 13.1 Accounting Policies and Procedures Risks and Control Activities

Risk Statement: Failure to adhere to proper financial reporting regulations and standards, such as U.S. GAAP, may result in regulatory fines, fraud, and misstatements to the financial statements.	
Sample Control Activity	**Control Owner**
Ensure that accounting policies and procedures comply with GAAP and are authorized by the controller, documented, and implemented	Controller
Make the current version of policies and procedures available to users	Controller
Review, authorize, and document changes to policies and procedures	Controller
Implement changes to policies and procedures in a timely manner	Controller
Ensure that policies and procedures are followed at all times with no exceptions	Controller

Every company should have a good control environment that includes entity-level controls. Additional controls can vary based on the process levels they address, from a granular control over a single activity in a business process to broader department-wide controls. We focus on some broader internal controls in **Table 13.2**. These controls ensure that everything in financial reporting operates correctly and apply to a multitude of risks throughout these processes. For example, reconciliation of general ledgers and bank accounts or general ledgers and subsidiary ledgers ensures that the financial statements are an accurate representation of the company's performance by identifying errors, and this control also mitigates fraud risk. It's harder to commit fraud when there are two sets of ledgers that must be updated and that are maintained by separate parties through segregation of duties.

TABLE 13.2 Broad Financial Reporting Risks and Control Activities

Risk Statement: These control activities apply to a multitude of risks throughout the broad financial reporting processes.	
Sample Control Activity	**Control Owner**
Use a reporting schedule for monthly, quarterly, and annual reporting periods	Controller
Include in the reporting schedule cutoff dates that are consistently applied across the company	Controller
Verify journal entries posted to the general ledger for accuracy	Automated system control
Post journal entries to the general ledger only in the correct reporting period	Automated system control
Review and resolve error reports during the correct reporting period	Controller/automated system control

(Continued)

TABLE 13.2 (*Continued*)

Sample Control Activity	Control Owner
Ensure that irregular or manual journal entries undergo a higher level of review, approval, and documentation than standardized journal entries	Controller/automated system control
Review monthly accruals for all known liabilities and monthly prepayments	Controller
Identify contingent liabilities and make accruals per GAAP requirements	Controller
Ensure segregation of duties for incompatible responsibilities in corporate accounting and financial reporting	Controller
Reconcile general ledger accounts each month and automate where possible (such as bank reconciliations)	Controller
Review all reconciliations and document that this review was performed	Controller/treasurer
Resolve reconciliation discrepancies in a timely manner	Controller/treasurer

These broad control activities are only a sampling of the controls a business may implement. While companies direct their time and efforts toward the critical controls specific to their unique operations, some controls over financial reporting are used across a variety of industries and companies. **Table 13.3** presents some of these internal controls.

But it doesn't end there. Even the best-designed controls are subject to failure or circumvention. Top management may think the internal controls over financial reporting are healthy, but they should periodically evaluate these controls internally. A lapse can have serious consequences, including fines, loss of reputation, a decrease in stock price, shareholder litigation, issues with lenders, and a significant increase in external audit fees and other costs.

For example, the SEC fined insurance company MetLife $10 million in 2019. According to the SEC, over a period of 25 years, MetLife had assumed that customers had died or couldn't be found if they didn't respond to two mailings made five and a half years apart. This accounting policy resulted in MetLife inflating its profits by releasing reserves that had been set aside to cover claims. This issue was the result of material weaknesses in the company's internal control environment.

TABLE 13.3 Specific Financial Reporting Risks and Control Activities

Risk Statement: Financial statements that do not comply with GAAP, contain inconsistencies, or violate SEC requirements may result in regulatory fines, penalties, and litigation.	
Sample Control Activity	**Control Owner**
Ensure legal compliance with all statutory requirements, including tax law for reporting purposes	CEO/CFO
Perform periodic reviews of financial reporting standards	Head of legal and compliance
Risk Statement: Reporting complexities may result in financial statements and other reports being inaccurate, unreliable, or not issued in a timely manner.	
Sample Control Activity	**Control Owner**
Determine general ledger account responsibilities	Controller
Ensure accountability by assigning to general ledger accounts "owners" who are responsible for overseeing accuracy	Controller
Risk Statement: Loss of assets due to fraud, theft, negligence, or destruction may result in a lack of proper reflection in the financial statements.	
Sample Control Activity	**Control Owner**
Review asset accounts at regular intervals to check that balances do not exceed lower of cost or market and make authorized adjustments, if required	CFO/controller
Document evidence of the review being performed	CFO/controller

TABLE 13.3 (*Continued*)

Risk Statement: Incorrect, fictitious, omitted, duplicative, or incorrectly recorded journal entries may result in misstated financial statements.	
Sample Control Activity	**Control Owner**
Grant journal entry system permissions only to authorized individuals and require approvals and periodic independent checks	Controller/automated system controls/IT general controls
Risk Statement: Unauthorized access to documents and other accounting-related records may result in destruction, alteration, or loss of these documents or records.	
Sample Control Activity	**Control Owner**
Ensure that only authorized individuals have access to the AIS, databases, records, and documents and only authorized individuals discuss financial information with third parties	Controller/automated system controls/IT general controls
Risk Statement: Complex and nonroutine accounting transactions may result in incorrect recording.	
Sample Control Activity	**Control Owner**
Hire and retain knowledgeable accounting staff and provide continuing professional education opportunities to ensure accounting staff is up to date on reporting requirements	CFO/HR director
Risk Statement: Improper authorization of entries and transaction processing may result in errors or fraud.	
Sample Control Activity	**Control Owner**
Grant journal entry system permissions only to authorized individuals and require approvals and periodic independent checks	Controller/automated system controls/IT general controls
Risk Statement: Unauthorized access to proprietary and confidential information may result in reputational damage or loss of competitive advantage.	
Sample Control Activity	**Control Owner**
Ensure that only authorized individuals have access to the AIS, databases, records, and documents	CFO/controller
Ensure that only authorized individuals discuss financial information with third parties	CFO/controller
Risk Statement: Related party transactions may result in improper identification of the parties or incorrect recording of entries.	
Sample Control Activity	**Control Owner**
Identify related parties and report transactions, including intercompany transactions for consolidation purposes, in accordance with GAAP	CFO/controller

CONCEPT REVIEW QUESTION

1. Arrange the following steps in the financial reporting process in order from beginning to end:
   a. Accounting transaction occurs
   b. Prepare post-closing trial balance
   c. Prepare financial statements
   d. Post to general ledger
   e. Journalize and post adjusting entries
   f. Journalize and post closing entries
   g. Prepare adjusted trial balance
   h. Prepare unadjusted trial balance
   i. Record transaction in appropriate journal
   Ans.
   Step 1. Accounting transaction occurs
   Step 2. Record transaction in appropriate journal
   Step 3. Post to general ledger
   Step 4. Prepare unadjusted trial balance
   Step 5. Journalize and post adjusting entries
   Step 6. Prepare adjusted trial balance
   Step 7. Prepare financial statements
   Step 8. Journalize and post closing entries
   Step 9. Prepare post-closing trial balance

13.3 How Does XBRL Create Efficient Financial Reporting?

Learning Objective ❸
Explain how XBRL promotes reporting efficiency.

Mark Willis, a partner at PwC (PricewaterhouseCoopers) and the founding chair for XBRL International, wrote: "For accountants, business information is business. XBRL was developed by the accounting industry, and it is the language of our business. That's why every CPA needs to understand what it is and what it does for us and for clients."[3]

You have seen the challenges companies face when trying to consolidate financial reporting information from different systems to create their financial statements. Imagine the challenges the SEC faces on a global scale to collect, interpret, and present the financial statements from thousands of companies worldwide—each with their own interpretations of their relevant accounting standards. The need for standardized, reliable, and timely financial and other business data reporting that can be done electronically to a variety of regulatory bodies around the world resulted in the creation of a specific electronic language for business information.

CPA **XBRL (eXtensible Business Reporting Language)** is an open standard markup language for business information, specifically for electronic financial reporting. XBRL is an adaptation of the computer language **XML (eXtensible Markup Language)** that is suitable for reporting business and financial data in a standardized, computer-readable manner. In the United States, the SEC has mandated the use of XBRL for SEC filings.

The XBRL International Consortium, a nonprofit organization, creates XBRL standards anyone can use. Many accounting software products are XBRL enabled and have the ability to insert XBRL tags into files automatically, so you will not need to write the code. Even though your career path as an accounting professional may never require you to implement XBRL, it's an important concept for accounting professionals to understand.

Tagging Financial Data

When we buy groceries at a physical store, we bring our items to the cashier or self-checkout kiosk to scan their barcodes. These barcodes enable the store's system to retrieve item information and price from the store's system. They also help the store track the product and manage inventory levels by capturing how many items have been sold in a day.

Like barcodes on products, XBRL creates unique identifiers with a standardized labeling system for portions of financial reporting (**Illustration 13.7**):

- XML tags the data, or **financial information**, with standard identifying information, according to a **taxonomy**—which is a classification system, like the Dewey Decimal system used by libraries to classify books by division and subdivisions.

- **XBRL tags** associate the concepts in the taxonomy to pieces of data to make the electronic distribution, interpretation, extraction, and analysis of the data easier. In information systems, a *tag* is a standardized piece of a taxonomy assigned to a piece of data called an *element*, and a tag is enclosed in angle brackets that look like <> (like meta tags used to assign structured data descriptors to unstructured data).

- An **XBRL instance document** is an XBRL version of the financial statements prepared by a business. Similar to a barcode reader's programming, it includes the standardized "code" for the tags and the structure for the tagged data (e.g., number of decimal points, currency). These instance documents are structured to produce standardized financial statements. The document provides data plus structure for human readability and electronic recognition (e.g., for annual reports, earnings releases, reports to financial institutions).

---

[3]www.pwc.com/gx/en/xbrl/pdf/pwc_xbrl_willis.pdf

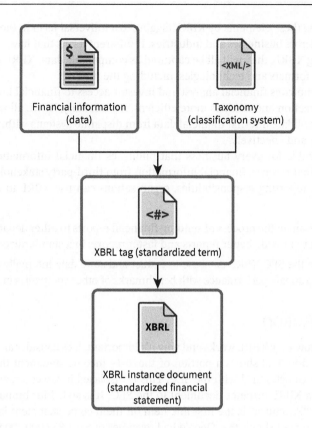

Illustration 13.7 XBRL is a markup language used for tagging financial statement concepts in a taxonomy.

SEC Release No. 33-10514, *Inline XBRL Filing of Tagged Data*, requires public companies to embed interactive data tags directly into their financial statements using a process called inline XBRL (iXBRL). Interactive iXBRL data tags allow users to drill down into the details of the financial statements. The intent of this SEC rule is to improve the timeliness, quality, and accessibility of XBRL financial information.

Why Does It Matter to Your Career?

Thoughts from a Senior Manager of Financial Reporting, Technology Manufacturing

XBRL is more than a regulatory requirement. It makes it easy to access and interpret financial statements of competitors, which can be used in benchmark comparisons.

Standardized Financial Reporting

XBRL provides standardization of financial reporting in a digital, reusable format. Accounting standards are not rigid and allow for flexibility, but this flexibility makes it difficult to compare financial performance and financial statement line items across companies, industries, and time:

- Different companies may use different terminologies for sales. One company might call sales "net sales," while another might use the term "sales revenue."

- Companies also use different date formats. For example, July 11, 2021, can also be shown as 11 July 2021, 07/11/2021, or 11/7/2021 (depending on the country).

Standardizing these elements by XBRL tagging to a universal term in the taxonomy allows comparability across businesses and industries. If different terms that have the same meaning are tagged using XBRL, they will all be captured as comparable data. XBRL is also compatible across software formats and technologies, including the internet.

XBRL also improves financial analyst and investor access to financial information since it makes data extraction and analysis more efficient. Additionally, XBRL allows the accounting function to consolidate internal financial data from disparate systems within an organization more efficiently and effectively.

XBRL is suitable for every business that publishes financial information internally and externally and that receives financial information from third-party stakeholders. Even if they don't have SEC reporting responsibilities, organizations can use XBRL to improve financial reports:

- They can automate the process of sending financial reports to other departments inside the organization to provide better reports and faster reports in a standardized manner.

- They can use the SEC XBRL database to extract and store data internally and then use it to analyze and compare performance with benchmarks of other companies in the same industry.

XBRL in Action

Now that we know how XBRL works and why it's important, let's consider an example of XBRL in use. **Illustration 13.8** shows a portion of the 2019 income statement that Alphabet (parent company of Google) filed with the SEC. This is displayed in a web browser after the company submits an XBRL instance document to the SEC. It is styled for human readability. The explanation for "Revenues" is the first line item on the income statement in Illustration 13.8. The income statement shows that Google had revenues of $161,857,000,000 for the year ended December 31, 2019.

Alphabet Inc.
CONSOLIDATED STATEMENTS OF INCOME
(In millions, except per share amounts)

	Year Ended December 31, (A)		
	2017	**2018**	**2019 (A)**
Revenues	$ 110,855	$ 36,819	$ 161,857 (C)
Costs and expenses:			
Cost of revenues	45,583	59,549	71,896
Research and development	16,625	21,419	26,018
Sales and marketing	12,893	16,333	18,464
General and administrative	6,840	6,923	9,551
European Commission fines	2,736	5,071	1,697
Total costs and expenses	84,677	109,295	127,626
Income from operations	26,178	27,524	34,231
Other income (expense), net	1,015	7,389	5,394
Income before income taxes	27,193	34,913	39,625
Provision for income taxes	14,531	4,177	5,282
Net income	$ 12,662	$ 30,736	$ 34,343
Basic net income per share of Class A and B common stock and Class C capital stock	$ 18.27	$ 44.22	$ 49.59
Diluted net income per share of Class A and B common stock and Class C capital stock	$ 18.00	$ 43.70	$ 49.16

Illustration 13.8 XBRL tags tie out to the consolidated income statement from Alphabet Inc.

Illustration 13.9 shows the XBRL code extracted from the XBRL instance document that produced the human-readable income statement in Illustration 13.8.

                    (A)   **(B)**

<us-gaap:RevenueFromContractWithCustomerExcludingAssessedTax contextRef="FD2019Q4YTD" decimals="–6" id="d16602969e858-wk-Fact-8DF1A010310F5901918847800D497951" unitRef="usd">161857000000</us-gaap:RevenueFromContractWithCustomerExcludingAssessedTax>

                     (C)

A) Reported as of Q4 2019 and includes year to date (YTD) activity for the fiscal year.
B) Delete six zeros to round to the nearest million for presentation in Income Statement.
C) $161,857,000,000 in Revenues as of Dec. 31, 2019.

Illustration 13.9   XBRL code contains references to the information displayed in the XBRL instance document.

The XBRL code tells us:

- The amount 161,857 shown in the income statement is based on U.S. GAAP (rather than an alternative like IFRS). We know this because the element for "revenues" opens with <us-gaap:RevenueFromContractWithCustomerExcludingAssessedTax...> and closes with </us-gaap:RevenueFromContractWithCustomerExcludingAssessedTax>. All companies complying with U.S. GAAP, no matter how they describe their revenue item from contracts with customers, will have the same tag for this element in their XBRL code.

- Next, we see contextRef="FD2019Q4YTD". This means the element covers a four-quarter time period ending December 31, 2019.

- decimals="-6" means the amount on the income statement is rounded to the nearest million. The -6 means delete the six zeros.

- unitRef="usd" means the value is in U.S. dollars.

Now that you've reviewed how XBRL works, decide if there's a business case for adopting XBRL at Julia's Cookies in Applied Learning 13.3.

Julia's Cookies   Applied Learning 13.3

XBRL: Creating a Business Case

Julia's Cookies is considering becoming a publicly traded company, so CFO Darlene is pushing company leadership to adopt XBRL. Since XBRL is a regulatory requirement for publicly traded companies, Julia's Cookies can prepare for the long-term goal of going public by adopting these practices now.

Darlene reasons that even if Julia's Cookies chooses not to go public, all companies benefit by internally sharing information in XBRL format. After all, the creators of XBRL wanted to improve the accountability and transparency of businesses, which can benefit even privately owned companies.

Darlene suggests hiring an accountant with XBRL experience to help the company fully integrate XBRL into its information systems. When Darlene meets with the Board of Directors to discuss this, she needs to have a business case that includes the benefits of hiring an XBRL accountant.

What are some of the benefits of XBRL reporting Darlene could present to the Board?

SOLUTION

Some examples of benefits Darlene could present to the Board of Directors include:

1. Data in XBRL format can be shared within the company, and the structure and the context of data will stay exactly the same. If you send someone an Excel spreadsheet, for example, and they move the data in a specific cell, the formulas and the context of the data don't move with the data.

2. XBRL can provide real-time data to decision makers across the business and also to external constituents, like financial institutions.

3. Sharing information between functional areas becomes more collaborative with XBRL. The information becomes more contextual and aids tracking and analysis.

4. XBRL data is software agnostic and can be read by any software with an XBRL processor. It is easily transferred between computers and software.

5. XBRL can integrate financial and nonfinancial data.

6. XBRL improves data analytics used for decision making.

> **CONCEPT REVIEW QUESTIONS**
>
> 1. **CPA** What is eXtensible Business Reporting Language (XBRL)?
>   **Ans.** XBRL is an open standard markup language for business information, specifically for electronic financial reporting. XBRL is an adaptation of the computer language eXtensible Markup Language (XML) that is suitable for reporting business and financial data in a standardized, computer-readable manner.
>
> 2. Support the argument for a private company to implement XBRL.
>   **Ans.** Public companies are required by the U.S. SEC to utilize XBRL for financial reporting. Though privately held companies are not required to utilize XBRL for financial reporting, there are several benefits to XBRL. XBRL formatting allows for ease of sharing of data across units, across various platforms, and to outside entities. Additionally, using XBRL allows for efficient data analysis and benchmark comparisons. Each of these benefits improves decision making and can improve business financial outcomes.

13.4 Are There Other Important Financial Accounting Reports?

Learning Objective ❹
Describe when to use key management accounting reports.

While the financial statements are the most widely known reports that come from the financial reporting process, the data captured by the AIS can also generate various management accounting reports for internal use. Companies are required to have a financial reporting system, but a management reporting system is optional. **Management accounting** provides managers with accounting information that helps them make decisions within the organization. These reports help managers perform their routine management and control functions.

As you may recall from your managerial and cost accounting studies, management accounting isn't as prescriptive or standardized as financial reporting. There is no GAAP for management accounting, and there are no pre-specified formats for presentation. Companies choose which report formats, data captures, and computational techniques best suit their decision-making needs. As you will see from the case in this chapter, management accounting options that are well regarded in theory may not have the same acceptance in practice, even for large manufacturing companies.

There are many kinds of management accounting reports, and your introductory management accounting, financial management, and cost accounting courses probably cover. Here we cover, from a systems perspective, some of the established types of managerial accounting reports, such as cost accounting reports and balanced scorecards.

Cost Accounting

CPA The **cost accounting** part of the AIS helps management with a very important responsibility—measuring and controlling costs associated with activities related to the purchasing, conversion, and sales processes. You've learned that businesses create value (profit) by combining and converting resources into goods or services that customers want. **CPA** To be successful, a company must have a **competitive advantage**, which is a position or strategy that places it in a superior position to its competitors.

There are two types of competitive advantage a company can choose (**Illustration 13.10**):

- **Low costs:** Companies with low-cost strategies can target a broad market, like Walmart's cost leadership strategy, or a niche market like Monster energy drinks' cost focus strategy,

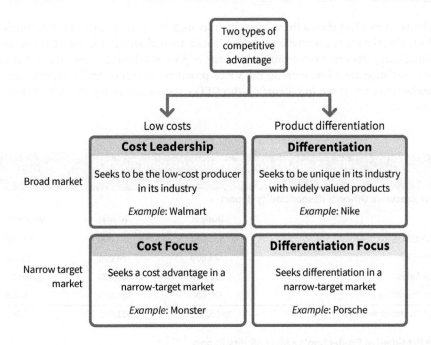

Illustration 13.10 Low costs are the primary focus of two of the four generic strategies of a business.

which offers a lower-cost alternative in a specialty beverage market. Since half of the corporate strategies in use today focus on low-cost approaches, measuring and controlling costs in a company is important.

- **Product differentiation:** Businesses like Nike or Porsche that focus on product differentiation by offering a unique, high-quality product are more successful than their competitors when their costs are controlled.

While areas of cost accounting techniques have been around for a long time, advances in integrated information systems have vastly improved the ability to track and report costs to management.

Why Does It Matter to Your Career?

Thoughts from an Internal Audit Advisory Manager, Public Accounting

Connecting management concepts like corporate strategy to accounting principles like cost accounting will set you up to understand the big picture of how your company operates and how your contributions help drive it toward strategic objectives and profitability.

Responsibility Accounting

Responsibility accounting is used to trace performance to the responsible department or manager to improve accountability. The type of managerial report needed depends on the business function:

- A production manager needs reports about material usage, number of units produced, labor hours, machine hours, defective products, and machine downtime.

- An accounts payable manager needs reports that show whether vendors are paid at the right time to take advantage of discounts and to avoid interest and other penalties.

A sophisticated AIS can provide information beyond the regular outputs for financial accounting purposes, including nonfinancial information.

Illustration 13.11 shows three layers of responsibility accounting reports at Julia's Cookies. Note that the lower responsibility budget totals are included in the report of the next level up. The Mixing department's controllable costs of $350,000 budget, $390,000 actual, and the $40,000 variance are a line item on the VP of production's responsibility report, and the VP of production's totals are line items on the CEO's responsibility report, as indicated by the arrows.

Illustration 13.11 The responsibility report shows the hierarchy of responsibility for controllable costs from individual teams up to the chief executive officer of Julia's Cookies.

Julia's Cookies Responsibility Account Reports
Reporting Period Ending January 31, 202X

Chief Executive Officer's Responsibility Report

	Budget	Actual	Variance
CEO's Office	$50,000	$53,000	$3,000
Controller	25,000	24,000	(1,000)
VP of Sales	610,000	600,000	(10,000)
VP of Production	920,000	954,000	34,000
Total Controllable Costs	1,605,000	1,631,000	26,000

Vice President of Production's Responsibility Report

	Budget	Actual	Variance
VP's Office	10,000	11,000	1,000
Mixing Department	350,000	390,000	40,000
Freezing Department	60,000	55,000	(5,000)
Packaging Department	500,000	498,000	(2,000)
Total Controllable Costs	920,000	954,000	34,000

Mixing Department's Responsibility Report

	Budget	Actual	Variance
Direct Material	150,000	175,000	25,000
Direct Labor	90,000	100,000	10,000
Variable Overhead	30,000	35,000	5,000
Fixed Overhead	80,000	80,000	0
Total Controllable Costs	350,000	390,000	40,000

Balanced Scorecard

CPA Another form of managerial reporting is the **balanced scorecard**, which is an internal assessment, improvement, and reporting tool that ties a measurement system to an organization's strategic plan. It provides key performance indicators for management to perform its function. The key to the scorecard's success is the link to the entity's strategic plan: it turns strategy into action.

CPA A balanced scorecard measures performance by combining financial measures with nonfinancial measures—for a *balanced* perspective. It has four traditional dimensions, as shown in **Illustration 13.12**:

- Financial
- Customer relationships
- Internal business processes
- Learning and growth (including innovation)

These four dimensions are traditional components of a balanced scorecard, but companies adapt the components to fit their strategic goals.

Balanced Scorecard

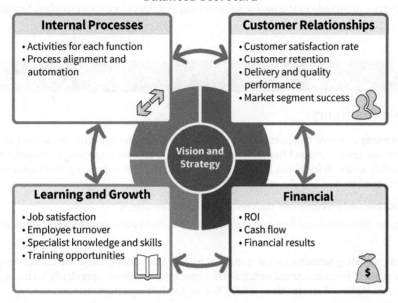

Illustration 13.12   The four parts of the balanced scorecard are financial, customer relationships, internal processes, and learning and growth.

Managers use balanced scorecards to monitor metrics, often by using a dashboard to provide easily understood graphical illustrations. The balanced scorecard has been around for decades, but technological advances have made it much easier to implement. The rich variety of data in a data warehouse provides great opportunities for developing sophisticated balanced scorecards that integrate data from the AIS, such as real-time updating dashboards (**Illustration 13.13**).

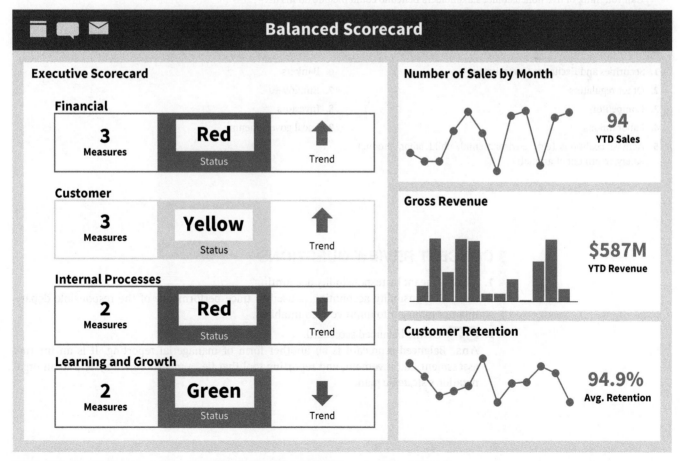

Illustration 13.13   A company can present its balanced scorecard in a dashboard format.

After you've reviewed the balanced scorecard in Illustration 13.13, help Benedito identify which metrics to include in the balanced scorecard at Julia's Cookies in Applied Learning 13.4.

Julia's Cookies Applied Learning 13.4

Balanced Scorecard: Strategic Planning

The CEO, Emilia, is developing and implementing a revised balanced scorecard for a new strategic plan being considered at Julia's Cookies. While she knows financial measures are easily extracted from the AIS, she wants to balance improving managerial performance for long-term organizational sustainability with a shorter-term focus on profits. She explains to her management team that this shift would require them, when developing metrics, to:

- Identify and improve internal business functions and processes and their resulting external outcomes
- Focus on indirect external stakeholders in addition to traditional stakeholders like customers, stockholders, creditors, and employees

Emilia invited three new accounting interns, including Benedito, to this meeting as part of their training. She asked all meeting participants (including the interns!) to come up with a list of indirect external stakeholders whose interests haven't specifically been considered or addressed in prior strategic plans and traditional balanced scorecards at Julia's Cookies. Emilia's argument:

Why stick to a traditional balanced scorecard format? We can change it to benefit our company and all its stakeholders, both traditional and nontraditional, internal and external. We are going to change the customer dimension to include all stakeholders. If our focus is on success in the longer term, then we should consider and preempt any regulatory and political actions these nontraditional stakeholders may bring. By including them, we will include performance considerations that otherwise would have been ignored.

Emilia gives everyone 15 minutes to write down their list of potential nontraditional stakeholders. Benedito very recently covered the traditional balanced scorecard in his management accounting class, so he's intrigued by Emilia's challenge and impressed she does not accept the status quo.

Can you think of five noncustomer stakeholders Benedito could include on his list?

SOLUTION

Benedito's list can include:

1. Securities and Exchange Commission
2. Other regulators
3. Competitors
4. Labor unions
5. Activist coalitions (e.g., environmental, child labor, product safety, treatment of animals)

6. Bankers
7. Employees
8. Investors
9. Local governments

CONCEPT REVIEW QUESTIONS

1. What is meant by responsibility accounting?

    Ans. Responsibility accounting is used to trace performance of the responsible department or manager to improve accountability.

2. **CPA** Define balanced scorecard.

    Ans. Balanced scorecard is an another form of managerial reporting. It is an internal assessment, improvement, and reporting tool that ties a measurement system to an organization's strategic plan.

13.5 How Is Financial Reporting Data Used for Insights and Decision Making?

Learning Objective ❺
Summarize the importance of data analytics and reporting for financial reporting decision making.

Think about everything you have learned about business processes and the AIS so far. Any business event that creates an accounting transaction is captured in the AIS and recorded in the General Ledger feature. For this reason, even though only two ERP features—General Ledger and Financial Reporting—are shown as being applicable to the financial reporting processes, we know that the majority of the modules and features in an ERP system contribute to these processes with the data they generate and record (**Illustration 13.14**).

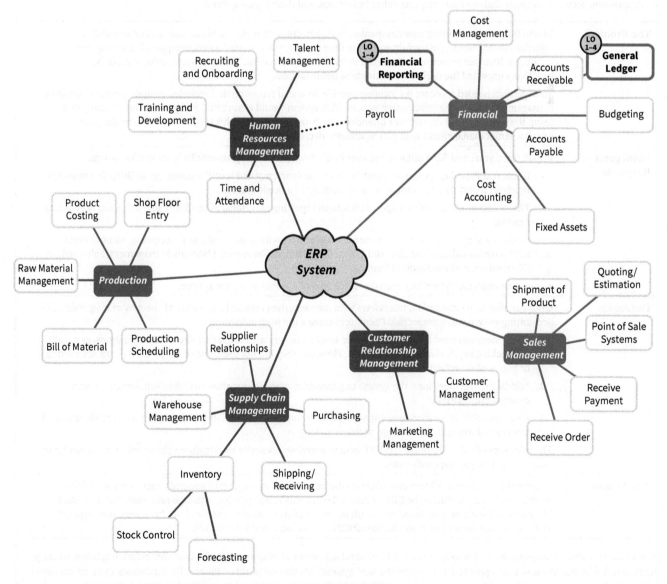

Illustration 13.14   Features in the ERP system contribute to financial reporting.

Recall that the general ledger system of a company is the record-keeping system that captures all journal entries and validates them using the trial balance. Every financial transaction that occurs is captured in the general ledger. This is why the ERP features throughout the company all feed to the general ledger. The general ledger summarizes detailed transactions that occur in sub-ledger accounts. The General Ledger feature of the AIS is complicated, especially when the business implementing the system performs mergers and acquisitions that involve legacy systems.

In the Real World — **A New Financial Reporting and Management Accounting System[4]**

Company A is a multinational, publicly traded manufacturer. It is an existing company, but its name isn't disclosed here due to confidentiality. Here is a quick summary of Company A:

- Top 10 performer in its market segment
- Physical presence in 27 countries
- Sells products in more than 100 countries
- Acquisition-focused company that regularly acquires other businesses, and their legacy systems

The Problem	Due to frequently acquiring new companies, management felt the financial and managerial accounting information was lacking in usefulness. Every time Company A acquired a new company, it also acquired a different financial reporting and management accounting system. These separate, incompatible systems negatively impacted the decision usefulness of financial data.
	Management needed a system for location-specific financial reporting that included a single, globally accessible management accounting information system. This system would ensure that everyone in the company was using the same, up-to-date, relevant financial data. Most importantly, this system needed to be designed to assist senior management with global strategic decision making.
Management Response	It took three years and $250 million, but eventually management implemented a leading ERP system:
	• It had real-time data processing with built-in multicurrency and multilanguage capabilities that provided financial reporting and management accounting in a single system.
	• The system enabled location-specific financial reporting and global accessibility to managerial accounting reports.
	• It integrated information on all resources, business activities, and business processes by using distinct ERP modules called Financials and Controlling, Human Resources, Materials Management, Sales and Distribution, and Production Planning.
	The system implementation met management's goal of a global, real-time system.
Outcomes	One year after implementation, interviews with top executives revealed that usage of the new management accounting system was unexpected. There were some surprising outcomes:
	1. The system was used frequently by lower-level managers who supported day-to-day operations, especially for tracking key performance indicators. However, they did not use some of the advanced cost accounting or balanced scorecard features.
	2. Middle management used the system to generate relevant information that they supplemented with external information.
	3. Unexpectedly, senior management barely used the system. Instead, they relied on financial statements and external information for strategic decision making.
	The relevance of this state-of-the-art ERP system decreased as senior management chose not to implement it in performing their job responsibilities.
The Lesson	Despite significant expenditure and effort on the new system, management decided to remove some of the functionality and customize the ERP system to be more like their previous management information system. They believed the new system did not result in improved information, and it did not have wide user support. The lesson: look before you leap and spend $250 million on a new ERP module!

Where do you think Company A went wrong? Could it have involved senior management in the decision before implementation to understand whether there was an appetite for adopting the new system? Do you think it is common for businesses to make decisions without fully understanding the reality of what will happen? What kinds of risks are related to making decisions in this way?

---

[4]Watts, D., P.W.S. Yapa, and S. Dellaportas. 2014. The Case of a Newly Implemented Modern Management Accounting System in a Multinational Manufacturing Company. *Australasian Accounting, Business and Finance Journal*, 8(2): 121–137.

Database Design

The general ledger system is complex, and you probably don't need to understand how the database supporting it is designed unless you pursue a career in accounting systems or IT audit. Therefore, we provide a high-level entity relationship diagram (ERD) that summarizes the key information from the General Ledger feature that you may interact with (**Illustration 13.15**).

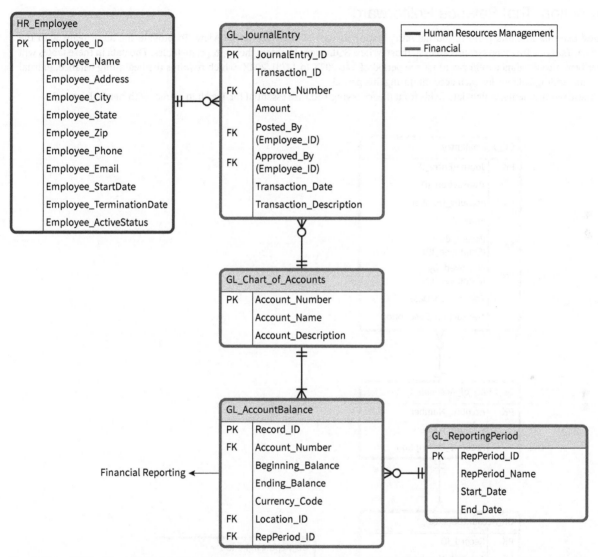

Illustration 13.15 The General Ledger feature uses a complex database design that is simplified here for demonstrative purposes.

In an actual system, the two tables used to show journal entries, GL_JournalEntry and GL_Transaction, consist of multiple tables and connect to the subledger account tables. We've simplified this for the purposes of this course.

Internal and external auditors commonly use two of the tables shown here for journal entry testing, which analyzes the general ledger for errors and fraud risk:

- The GL_JournalEntry table provide the transactions, or account activity.
- The GL_AccountBalance table provides the beginning and ending trial balance amounts for each account.

The first analytic an audit team performs for journal entry testing is a **trial balance rollforward**, which uses a calculation to verify the completeness of the journal entry data.

A rollforward recreates the ending balance by adding the net journal entry activity to the beginning balance and compares it to the actual ending trial balance. If there's a difference, the journal entry data may not be complete, and auditors must follow up on it before continuing their analytics. Help Tsz Ni extract data for a GL rollforward in Applied Learning 13.5.

Julia's Cookies   Applied Learning 13.5

Data Extraction: Trial Balance Rollforward

Julia's Cookies' external auditors perform journal entry testing as part of their year-end review. To provide the audit team with the appropriate data, Tsz Ni, a financial systems analyst, must write a SQL query to access the appropriate tables. The data in these tables will be used to perform a trial balance rollforward for the period of 1/1/202X to 12/31/202X, which requires the beginning balance, journal entry activity, and ending balance for each account during this period.

Based on these requirements, which data fields from the following ERD are essential for Tsz Ni to extract with her SQL query?

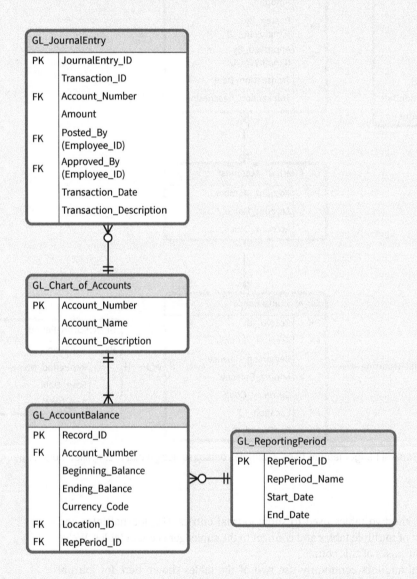

SOLUTION

Tsz Ni must extract the following fields for the auditors to perform a rollforward:

GL_JournalEntry Table

Account_Number: to join to the GL_AccountBalance table
Amount: for the calculation
Transaction_Date: to filter the data for journal entries in the correct time period

GL_AccountBalance Table

Account_Number: to join to the GL_JournalEntry table

Beginning_Balance: for the calculation

Ending_Balance: for the calculation

RepPeriod_ID: to join to the GL_ReportingPeriod table

GL_ReportingPeriod Table

RepPeriod_ID: to join to the GL_AccountBalance table

End_Date: to pull the account balances from the current beginning and ending trial balance dates (Tsz Ni will pull the beginning balance from the reporting period End_Date of 12/31 of the prior year and the ending balance from the reporting period End_Date of 12/31 of the current year being tested.)

GL_Chart_of_Accounts Table

Technically, none of the fields in this table are *required* for this analysis, but Tsz Ni will include them to give the external audit team insights into which accounts they are analyzing.

Financial Modeling for Decision Making

Financial modeling, as the name suggests, is the process of creating models for making business decisions involving finance. It is used to estimate the valuation, performance, or risk of a business, project, or investment. Financial modeling involves building a numerical representation of a financial situation by taking into account historical data, relevant factors, and assumptions. Financial models may vary in complexity and accuracy depending on the purpose and inputs.

Some examples of financial models are:

1. Discounted cash flow (DCF) model: It is a method of valuing an asset or a company by projecting its future cash flows and discounting them to the present value using an appropriate discount rate. The DCF model is based on the principle that the value of an asset is equal to the present value of its expected future cash flows.

2. Capital asset pricing model (CAPM) model: It is a model that describes the relationship between the expected return and the risk of an asset or a portfolio. The CAPM model states that the expected return of an asset or a portfolio is equal to the risk-free rate plus a risk premium that depends on the asset's or portfolio's beta (a measure of systematic risk) and the market risk premium.

3. Monte Carlo simulation model: It is a technique that uses random sampling and statistical analysis to estimate the probability distribution of possible outcomes of a complex system or process. The Monte Carlo simulation model can be used to analyze the uncertainty and variability of various factors that affect the performance or outcome of a project or investment.

There are many types of financial models with a wide range of uses. The output of a financial model is used for decision making and performing financial analysis, whether inside or outside of the company. Financial models are used to make decisions about:

- Raising capital (debt and/or equity)
- Making acquisitions (businesses and/or assets)
- Growing the business organically (e.g., opening new stores, entering new markets)
- Selling or divesting assets and business units
- Budgeting and forecasting (planning for the years ahead)
- Capital allocation (priority of which projects to invest in)
- Valuing a business
- Financial statement analysis/ratio analysis
- Management accounting

Majorly, modeling is used for determining reasonable forecasts, prices for markets or products, asset or enterprise valuation (discounted cash flow analysis, relative valuation, etc.), the share price of companies, synergies, effects of merger/acquisition on the companies, leveraged buy-out (LBO), corporate finance models, option pricing, etc.

There are many different types of professionals who build financial models. The most common types of career tracks are:

- Corporates—for internal management decisions based upon future business performance as predicted in financial models
- Investment banking firms—on behalf of both their clients and their investors for the company's valuation
- Equity research firms—for publishing reports on public sources to recommend buying or selling of any security
- Management consultancy and portfolio management firms—for advising their clients on various growth prospects
- Private equity funds, hedge funds, and venture capital funds—for the calculation of their investment exit return

Reporting and Insights

Whenever the AIS is involved with a business process, it collects and stores information that can eventually be converted into reports that provide management with crucial decision-making information. Financial statements are summary-level reports that gather important financial information to present it to the public (**Table 13.4**).

TABLE 13.4 Financial Statement Reports

Report	Description
Income statement	Results of operations and financial activities within a period of time, including revenue, expenses, gains, and losses
Balance sheet	Assets, liability, and owners' equity as of the report date
Statement of cash flows	Inflow and outflow of cash during the reporting period, including financing activities, operating activities, and investing activities
Statement of stockholders' equity	Changes in the company's equity from opening balance to the end of the reporting period, including earned profits, net losses, dividends, and inflow or outflow of equity investments
Notes to the financial statements	Explanations of various activities and details of accounts

These reports give us information that is useful in decision making. External stakeholders can use these reports to determine the overall financial health of a business, and management can use them to monitor the company's financial performance.

Why Does It Matter to Your Career?

Thoughts from a Senior Internal Auditor, Financial Services

It's easy to forget that the financial statements are reports generated by a system. Other reports are also helpful on the job, and you're more likely to be an end user of something like a managerial report. If you have access to your company's accounting information system, familiarize yourself with the existing prepackaged reports you can generate through the user interface.

We can use financial analytics to analyze the income statement and the balance sheet (**Table 13.5**).

TABLE 13.5 Financial Statement Analytics

Analytic	Description	How It's Used
Income statement vertical analysis	Ratios like cost of goods sold as a percentage of revenue or gross profit as a percentage of revenue	Identifies company performance and may indicate financial statement fraud risk.
Income statement horizontal analysis	Year-over-year time trend analysis comparing this period's ratios to prior-period ratios	Identifies changes in performance or unusual activity in income statement accounts that may indicate financial statement fraud risk.
Balance sheet ratios	Ratios of balance sheet accounts like quick ratio, current ratio, debt to equity, or inventory turnover	Analyzes company performance and can be compared to external benchmarks of competitors. May also indicate financial statement fraud risk.
General ledger monitoring	Monitoring of journal entry activity to perform real-time testing of journal entries for fraud risk tests	Identifies fraud red flags by testing journal entries against predetermined risky behaviors.

Vertical and horizontal financial statement analysis are the most common analytics in the financial reporting area. Dashboards like the one in **Illustration 13.16** give business leaders quick insights into overall company performance. This dashboard shows KPIs, such as the days payable outstanding, as of a specific point in time.

Illustration 13.16 Vertical and horizontal financial statement analysis ratios and time comparisons are presented in an easy-to-read dashboard for management and other decision makers.

The general ledger is an essential source of data for any business. Journal entries are generated throughout all business processes, from purchases to sales to investing, and we focus on journal entry testing analytics in **Table 13.6**. CPA These tests are used to address fraud risk after the general ledger rollforward validates the completeness of the journal entries.

TABLE 13.6 Journal Entry Testing Analytics

Analytic	Description	How It's Used
Round dollar entries	Transactions where the dollar amount ends in .00	Fraudulent journal entries that are manually input into the general ledger may have round dollar values.
Intercompany to non-intercompany accounts	Identifies debits to intercompany accounts with credits to non-intercompany accounts	Intercompany accounts may be used to hide fraudulent journal entries.
Revenue reversals	Reversed month-end entries related to revenue	Revenue inflation is financial statement fraud that involves posting to increase revenue inappropriately then reversing it after month-end close.
Fraud keyword testing	Fraud-related wording such as "miscellaneous," "per CEO," and "per manager"	Fraudulent journal entries that are manually input into the general ledger may contain vague journal entry descriptions.
Balancing keyword testing	Searches for words in journal entry descriptions such as "plug," "true up," "reconcile," and "balance account"	Journal entries with these descriptions may indicate errors in the general ledger that were addressed with inappropriate journal entries meant to balance the accounts.
Unusual dates	Transactions entered on unusual days, such as weekends and holidays	Fraudulent journal entries may be entered outside traditional working hours to avoid detection.
Management override	Posted by management authorized to override	Looks for risks of management fraud.
General ledger close	Journal entries posted near general ledger close date	Journal entries posted close to close date have a higher risk of fraud.
Daily revenue	Average revenue per day	Identifies unusual spikes in revenue journal entry activity that may indicate fraud.
Dormant accounts	Journal entries posted to any inactive or dormant accounts	Inactive or dormant accounts may be used to hide fraudulent journal entries.
Field analysis	Journal entries with missing items or invalid items in a field	Fraudulent journal entries that are manually input into the general ledger may be missing fields that are traditionally captured by the AIS.
Duplicate journal entries	Same account and amount with different dates	Identifies risks of erroneously double posted journal entries.
Benford analysis	Compares journal entry amounts to an expectation of anomalous numbers	Identifies unexpected numeric values in the journal entry population that may indicate fraud.
Summary of manual entries	Summarize manual journal entries by date, user, amount, account, etc.	Manual journal entries have a higher risk of fraud and should be reviewed carefully.
Unbalanced journal entries	Details of journal entries where debit amount does not equal credit amount	Unbalanced journal entries may indicate errors or fraud.
Unauthorized users	Compares journal entry approvers to list of authorized users	Identifies journal entries that were approved by an unauthorized user.

CONCEPT REVIEW QUESTIONS

1. What are the most common analytics in the financial reporting area?
   Ans. Vertical and horizontal financial statement analysis are the most common analytics in the financial reporting area.

2. What do you mean by financial modeling?
   Ans. Financial modeling is the process of building a numerical representation of a financial situation. It is used to estimate the valuation, performance, or risk of a business, project, or investment.

FEATURED PROFESSIONAL | Chief Financial Officer

Photo courtesy of
Hafiz Chandiwala

Hafiz Chandiwala, CPA

Hafiz's career started in public accounting in the audit practice. After seven years as an auditor in public accounting, Hafiz moved to corporate accounting. For the past 20 years, Hafiz has been with his current company, a household brand manufacturer. He has held positions as the corporate controller and treasurer, and is now the chief administrative officer and chief financial officer. Hafiz is a key leader involved with developing and executing the company's transactional strategy for franchise acquisitions. Hafiz is involved with numerous business and civic organizations, such as the National Multiple Sclerosis Society Board, and also serves on numerous collegiate boards, including the alumni society board at his alma mater.

What type of accounting information system does your company use?

Like most large corporate entities these days, we use an integrated ERP system for our accounting processes. Specifically, we use SAP.

How does your company use automation to support financial reporting?

We use Microsoft Power BI to provide a series of automated reports and a library of financial reports. Relevant reports are sent automatically to users at whatever frequency level they choose. For example, I can select to receive my reports in my email every morning. I can interact with them, select parameters, log in directly from the report screen, and even drill down into the data to align the report with my preferences for information.

What advice do you have for students about the importance of learning about financial reporting and accounting information systems?

It's not only about getting the data out of the system, it's how you present it and the information you present has to be in a user-friendly format that the user can understand. The big shift now is not about just providing reports but about giving insights. Things are moving toward not just static reporting but also providing actionable insights from data so that the user does not have to spend time deciphering information in the report. We use artificial intelligence to do this. For example, at my company, whatever happens at the output level—at each grocery store, at each venue, etc.—is crucial, and I want to know where the voids are so that we can call on that customer and sell them the product. Insights into these voids allow me to push the actionable items surrounding those voids into the inbox of a person who is responsible for that territory rather than have them go and search for those actionable items.

What's the biggest piece of advice you can give current accounting students?

Be a continual learner in your field. Take full advantage of internship opportunities. Have a strong work ethic. I can train people to understand a task, process, or system, but I can't train them to have a strong work ethic or to be curious. Focus on oral and written communication skills so that you have the ability to walk up to me, shake my hand, look me in the eye, and have a conversation and also write an articulate, well-thought-out memo to a client or to management rather than short-burst texts.

Review and Practice

Key Terms Review

audit trail	financial modeling	special journal
balanced scorecard	financial reporting	taxonomy
block coding	general journal	trial balance rollforward
chart of accounts	internal control over financial reporting	XBRL (eXtensible Business Reporting
coding system	(ICFR)	Language)
competitive advantage	journal	XBRL instance document
consolidated financial statements	management accounting	XBRL tag
cost accounting	responsibility accounting	XML (eXtensible Markup Language)
financial information	source document	

Learning Objectives Review

① Identify the role of the accounting information system in financial reporting.

Financial reporting is a standardized practice providing an accurate depiction of the company's financial situation to external stakeholders whose needs drive financial reporting objectives.

Five financial statements are:

- Trial balance and adjusted trial balance

- Income statement

- Balance sheet

- Statement of stockholder's equity

- Statement of cash flows

The chief financial officer (CFO) and the controller, who reports directly to the CFO, collaborate to ensure that financial reporting objectives are achieved.

The primary objective of financial reporting is to ensure that financial statements are useful to their users. Companies balance the usefulness of financial information with its cost-effectiveness. Costs of financial information include costs related to:

- Gathering the data

- Processing the data

- Storing the data

- Communicating the information

When a company owns more than 50% of a subsidiary's voting stock, it must file consolidated financial statements. Consolidated financial reporting is a complex process that is made more difficult when the subsidiaries use disparate general ledger systems. Companies can use consolidation software to:

- Map disparate general ledgers to a single chart of accounts

- Determine hierarchies

- Manage and convert multiple currencies

- Perform eliminations and intercompany transactions

- Generate consolidated financial statements

- Integrate XBRL

② Document the generation of financial statements within the accounting information system.

A company needs to create a chart of accounts that classifies accounts into an organized scheme. Coding systems logically record, classify, store, and extract financial data. Block coding is a traditional coding system that assigns account numbers based on the leading digit.

The steps of the financial reporting process are:

1. Identify accounting transactions
2. Journalize the accounting transactions
3. Post journal entries to ledgers
4. Prepare unadjusted trial balance
5. Enter adjusting entries in the general journal and post these to the general ledger
6. Prepare an adjusted trial balance
7. Prepare financial statements
8. Prepare closing journal entries and post to the general ledger
9. Prepare a post-closing trial balance

Policies and procedures are an important type of internal control for financial reporting. Some examples of policies and procedures controls are:

- Ensure that accounting policies and procedures comply with GAAP and are authorized by the controller, documented, and implemented

- Make the current version of policies and procedures available to users

- Review, authorize, and document changes to policies and procedures
- Implement changes to policies and procedures in a timely manner
- Ensure that policies and procedures are followed at all times with no exceptions

Internal controls for financial reporting can be broad or targeted. Examples of entity-level controls include:

- Use a reporting schedule for monthly, quarterly, and annual reporting periods
- Include in the reporting schedule cutoff dates that are consistently applied across the company
- Verify journal entries posted to the general ledger for accuracy
- Post journal entries to the general ledger only in the correct reporting period
- Review and resolve error reports during the correct reporting period
- Ensure that irregular or manual journal entries undergo a higher level of review, approval, and documentation than standardized journal entries
- Review monthly accruals for all known liabilities and monthly prepayments
- Identify contingent liabilities and make accruals per GAAP requirements
- Ensure segregation of duties for incompatible responsibilities in corporate accounting and financial reporting
- Reconcile general ledger accounts each month and automate where possible (such as bank reconciliations)
- Review all reconciliations and document that this review was performed
- Resolve reconciliation discrepancies in a timely manner

Companies must also have specific internal control that target unique, specific risks, such as:

- Ensure legal compliance with all statutory requirements, including tax law for reporting purposes
- Perform periodic reviews of financial reporting standards
- Determine general ledger account responsibilities
- Ensure accountability by assigning to general ledger accounts "owners" who are responsible for overseeing accuracy
- Review asset accounts at regular intervals to check that balances do not exceed lower of cost or market and make authorized adjustments, if required
- Document evidence of the review being performed
- Grant journal entry system permissions only to authorized individuals and require approvals and periodic independent checks
- Hire and retain knowledgeable accounting staff and provide continuing professional education opportunities to ensure accounting staff is up to date on reporting requirements

- Ensure that only authorized individuals have access to the AIS, databases, records, and documents
- Ensure that only authorized individuals discuss financial information with third parties
- Identify related parties and report transactions, including intercompany transactions for consolidation purposes, in accordance with GAAP

After designing a robust set of internal controls for financial reporting, a company must also periodically evaluate the controls to ensure that they are operating correctly.

③ Explain how XBRL promotes reporting efficiency.

eXtensible Business Reporting Language (XBRL) uses XML (eXtensible Markup Language) to standardized financial data. XBRL works by:

- Assigning financial data XBRL tags using a taxonomy
- Creating an XBRL instance document

XBRL addresses the complexities of using different systems, terminologies, charts of accounts, and financial statements. It allows for comparability across businesses and industries.

Companies use XBRL to improve financial reporting by:

- Automating the process of report sharing
- Using the SEC XBRL database to extract and store data
- Analyzing and comparing performance with benchmarks of other companies in the same industry

④ Describe when to use key management accounting reports.

Cost accounting helps management measure and control costs associated with activities related to the purchasing, conversion, and sales products.

Companies use cost accounting to help execute their business strategies, such as:

- Cost leadership: Seeking to be the low-cost producer in its industry
- Cost focus: Seeking a cost advantage in a narrow-target market

Responsibility accounting traces performance to the responsible department or manager to improve accountability in terms of costs related to business operations. In a responsibility account report, costs like direct labor for a production department can be traced upward, all the way to the CEO.

A balanced scorecard is used to internally assess performance and identify improvement opportunities. There are four traditional dimensions:

- Financial
- Customer relationships
- Internal processes
- Learning and growth

⑤ Summarize the importance of data analytics and reporting for financial reporting decision making.

Financial reporting processes consist of two features in the ERP system:

- Financial Reporting
- General Ledger

A trial balance rollforward recalculates the ending trial balance by adding the net journal entry activity to the beginning trial balance. If the calculated ending balance does not match the ending trial balance, journal entry activity may be missing or erroneous.

Financial modeling is the process of building a numerical representation of a financial situation. It is used to estimate the valuation, performance, or risk of a business, project, or investment.

Financial statement reports are the official financial statements businesses issue to stakeholders and include the following:

- Income statement
- Balance sheet
- Statement of cash flows
- Statement of stockholders' equity
- Notes to the financial statements

Financial statement analytics can provide insight into performance, changes over time, and fraud risk:

- Income statement vertical analysis
- Income statement horizontal analysis
- Balance sheet ratios
- General ledger monitoring

Special financial reporting analytics focus on testing journal entries for indicators of fraud activity. These fraud tests are an essential part of an external audit and internal audit monitoring activities:

- Round dollar entries
- Intercompany to nonintercompany accounts
- Revenue reversals
- Fraud keyword testing
- Balancing keyword testing
- Unusual dates
- Management override
- General ledger close
- Daily revenue
- Dormant accounts
- Field analysis
- Duplicate journal entries
- Benford analysis
- Summary of manual entries
- Unbalanced journal entries
- Unauthorized users

CPA questions, as well as multiple choice, discussion, analysis and application, and Tableau questions and other resources, are available online.

Multiple Choice Questions

1. (LO 1) Financial reports are prepared to provide an accurate depiction of a company's financial situation to _____.

   a. CFO

   b. CEO

   c. external stakeholders

   d. controller

2. (LO 1) **CPA** Within the context of the qualitative characteristics of accounting information, which of the following is a fundamental qualitative characteristic?

   a. Relevance

   b. Timeliness

   c. Comparability

   d. Confirmatory value

3. (LO 1) Financial reporting provides external stakeholders

   a. shares of the company.

   b. an accurate depiction of the company's financial situation.

   c. a clear determination on whether they should or should not invest in the company.

   d. a breakdown of key performance indicators.

4. (LO 1) **CPA** The objectives of financial reporting are based on which of the following sources?

   a. The need for conservatism

   b. The needs of the external users of the information

   c. Reporting on management's consistency

   d. Reporting on management's stewardship

5. (LO 1) The cost-effectiveness of accounting information is determined by evaluating the cost of providing the information versus the

    a. consistency of the information.

    b. timeliness of the information.

    c. value of the information.

    d. accuracy of the information.

6. (LO 1) When a parent company owns one or more subsidiaries, it prepares

    a. data visualization dashboards.

    b. an enhanced statement of cash flows.

    c. consolidated financial statements.

    d. a balanced scorecard.

7. (LO 1) CPA Consolidated financial statements are based on the concept that

    a. in the preparation of financial statements, legal form takes precedence over economic substance.

    b. in the preparation of financial statements, economic substance takes precedence over legal form.

    c. financial information should be presented separately for each legal entity.

    d. separate financial statements are more meaningful than consolidated financial statements.

8. (LO 2) The accounting equation is presented as A = L + OE, which stands for:

    a. Assets = Losses + Operational expenses.

    b. Assets = Liabilities + Operational equity.

    c. Assets = Losses + Owners' expenses.

    d. Assets = Liabilities + Owners' equity.

9. (LO 2) What must businesses do before starting the financial reporting process?

    a. Develop a chart of accounts

    b. Identify accounting transactions

    c. Determine cash on hand

    d. Run baseline financial reports

10. (LO 2) Which of the following is a series of sequential numbers that are reserved for accounts?

    a. Blockchain

    b. Chart of accounts

    c. Block coding

    d. Primary key

11. (LO 2) Which step of the financial reporting process occurs after the preparation of an unadjusted trial balance?

    a. Post journal entries to ledgers

    b. Enter adjusting entries

    c. Prepare financial statements

    d. Prepare an adjusted trial balance

12. (LO 2) With respect to internal controls over financial reporting, what accounting role should be the control owner for general ledger reconciliation?

    a. CFO   **c.** Controller

    b. AIS   **d.** Treasurer

13. (LO 3) Which of the following statements is true?

    a. XBRL is an adaptation of XML.

    b. XBRL use is mandated for SEC filings.

    c. XBRL standards are available for anyone to use.

    d. All of the above

14. (LO 3) Which of the following is the underlying language that eXtensible Business Reporting Language (XBRL) uses?

    a. XML

    b. Java

    c. HTML

    d. Python

15. (LO 3) A(n) _____ is a piece of data assigned a tag by XBRL.

    a. sheet

    b. element

    c. instance

    d. taxonomy

16. (LO 3) What is the term associated with XBRL standardized structure to produce financial statements?

    a. Tag

    b. Format

    c. Layout document

    d. Instance document

17. (LO 4) Which of the following best describes a balanced scorecard?

    a. Internal assessment tool

    b. Provides key performance indicators

    c. Turns strategy into action

    d. All of the above

18. (LO 4) Which of the following generic business strategies seeks to be the low-cost producer in its industry?

    a. Cost leadership

    b. Differentiation

    c. Cost focus

    d. Differentiation focus

19. (LO 4) CPA Which of the following is *not* one of the four traditional dimensions of a balanced scorecard?

    a. Customer relationships

    b. Learning and growth

    c. Internal processes

    d. Research and development

20. **(LO 4)** **CPA** Which of the following balanced scorecard perspectives examines a company's success in targeted market segments?

 a. Financial

 b. Customer relationships

 c. Internal processes

 d. Learning and growth

21. **(LO 4)** **CPA** What is the most important purpose of a balanced scorecard?

 a. Develop strategy

 b. Measure performance

 c. Develop cause-and-effect linkages

 d. Set priorities

22. **(LO 5)** Which of the following best explains a trial balance rollforward?

 a. It uses calculations to ensure that all of the journal entries in the general ledger are present.

 b. It uses calculations to create the ending trial balance.

 c. It recalculates the beginning trial balance to perform a completeness test.

 d. It reperforms the work of internal auditors to provide external auditors with sufficient assurance over the general ledger.

23. **(LO 5)** The notes to the financial statements is an important financial statement report that includes

 a. results of operations and financial activities within a period of time, including revenue, expenses, gains, and losses.

 b. inflow and outflow of cash during the reporting period, including financing activities, operating activities, and investing activities.

 c. explanations of various activities and details of accounts.

 d. assets, liabilities, and owners' equity as of the report date.

24. **(LO 5)** Which of the following keywords does *not* indicate inappropriate journal entries meant to balance the accounts?

 a. "reconcile"

 b. "plug"

 c. "allowance for doubtful accounts"

 d. "true up"

25. **(LO 5)** What is the record-keeping system that captures all journal entries and validates them using the trial balance?

 a. Financial reporting

 b. General ledger

 c. Budget

 d. Chart of accounts

26. **(LO 5)** You are an investment banker and offer wealth management services to customers. You are to advise a customer on the companies and their risks. In which financial model will you create a set of hypothetical outcomes that include the possible range of outcomes?

 a. DCF model analysis

 b. Buyout model analysis

 c. Three-statement models analysis

 d. Monte Carlo analysis

Discussion and Research Questions

DQ1. (LO 1) Explain the relationship between the chief financial officer (CFO) and the controller.

DQ2. (LO 1) Describe the four main financial statements and how they help fulfill the primary objective of the financial reporting process.

DQ3. (LO 1) Describe consolidated financial statements and explain when a company must use them.

DQ4. (LO 2) Explain the purpose of a chart of accounts and why it is critical to the traditional financial reporting process.

DQ5. (LO 2) Explain the first three steps in the financial reporting process and what would happen to the overall process if the steps failed.

DQ6. (LO 2) **Research** Use the internet to research internal controls over financial reporting (ICFRs). Explain why ICFRs are important to an organization. What is the relationship between ICFRs and COSO's internal controls?

DQ7. (LO 3) Explain XBRL and its components.

DQ8. (LO 3) List three benefits of using XBRL.

DQ9. (LO 4) What are the four traditional dimensions of the balanced scorecard? Provide an example of each.

DQ10. (LO 4) **Research** Use the internet to research a company of your choice that uses either the cost leadership or cost focus generic business strategies. Use the company to provide examples of how cost accounting, responsibility accounting, or balanced scorecards could be used to achieve this business strategy.

DQ11. (LO 4) **Critical Thinking** You are a cost accountant in the corporate office of the national coffee chain Sips and Drips. You have been assigned to a strategic project to design a new balanced scorecard. What elements will you include in the balance scorecard to ensure that Sips and Drips can effectively monitor its business?

DQ12. (LO 5) Describe a trial balance rollforward and its importance to an audit.

DQ13. (LO 5) [Research] Select one of the journal entry testing analytics from the following list and explain why it is useful in detecting journal entry fraud risk. Use the internet to find examples to support your answer.

- Round dollar entries
- Revenue reversals
- Unusual dates
- Management override
- General ledger close
- Dormant accounts

Application and Analysis Questions

A1. (LO 1) [Early Career] [Critical Thinking] You work at 13 Clues, a regional company that operates escape rooms in major cities. As part of the finance transformation team, a group that specializes in process improvements within the Accounting department, you are working on a strategic review of 13 Clues' current financial reporting processes to identify areas of improvement. You have been conducting interviews with finance data users throughout the organization. One of the opportunities your team has identified is leveraging the FASB characteristics of useful information to improve the usefulness of 13 Clues' financial data for end users.

The following are complaints from users of the financial data throughout 13 Clues' Accounting department that you have collected during your interviews. For each complaint, identify which characteristic of useful information could address the issue. An issue may be addressed using more than one characteristic.

a. "It takes a few weeks for the analysts to turn the data into reports we can use. I understand they are busy and have a long list of requests, but by the time we receive quarterly reports, we have already made major decisions for the next quarter. The reports aren't useful because we don't have them when we are making our decisions."

b. "The Finance department's system uses a different taxonomy for customer numbers than the Production department uses. When I need to perform reconciliations, I have to manually map customers using their names, and it isn't always easy to do."

c. "When I receive reports from Accounts Payable, the vendor information is presented using the Vendor ID field. I haven't memorized the Vendor IDs for all our suppliers and vendors, so I have to ask the Accounts Payable department to remind me of the difference between certain IDs. It would be easier to just receive the business names of the vendors instead."

A2. (LO 2) [Critical Thinking] You are a financial systems analyst at Forbidden Island, a parent company of multiple luxury resort companies. As part of implementing a new financial reporting system, your team is creating a new chart of accounts that will be used across your company's subsidiaries. Using the following block coding categorizations, assign an account number to each of the accounts.

- Current assets: 100–199
- Shareholders' equity: 300–350
- Revenues: 500–575
- Expenses: 900–950

Accounts:

1. Cash on hand
2. Sales returns and allowances
3. Bad debts expense
4. Inventory
5. Allowance for doubtful accounts
6. Cash sales
7. Cost of goods sold
8. Audit fees
9. Interest revenue

A3. (LO 2) You are a first-year financial accountant at Isabella's, a manufacturing company that specializes in cat condos and beds. The following table lists activities that occur in the normal course of business at Isabella's. For each activity, identify which step, using the step's name, it is in the financial reporting process. Also include the step's timing in relationship to the reporting period (during the reporting period, end of the reporting period, or end of the fiscal year).

Activity	Step Name	Timing
Receive an order for $5,000 of inventory		
Close income summary		
Run quarterly trial balance		
Run finalized general ledgers balances		
Record payment for advertising that will start in one month		
Run statement of cash flows		
Make agreement to purchase a new warehouse		
Post debit entry to accounts payable and credit entry to cash		
Finalize adjusting entries and run GL balances		
Run statement of owners' equity		
Close expense accounts		
Buy equipment with sales terms of 2/10 net 30		

A4. (LO 2) `Fraud` `Early Career` `Critical Thinking` As a senior internal auditor at Braxton's, a global clothing manufacturer, you are responsible for reviewing audit findings, including activities deemed inappropriate or high risk, from the prior year to create a summary of risks throughout the business. This list of risks will be used during this year's audit risk assessment, which helps internal audit leadership determine which audits to plan next year. For each of the following business activities, identify the risks it creates.

1. The entire IT support team has access to all GL accounts.
2. Sales between intercompany departments are not identified.
3. Some transactions are not recorded in U.S. dollars.
4. It is discovered that quarterly taxes have not been paid for two straight quarters.
5. General ledger accounts do not have clearly assigned account owners.
6. Because documents were not marked as paid, duplicate expenses were recorded for a period of three days.
7. Plans for a newly designed product are saved on a shared drive with no security.
8. The company benefits plan is canceled.
9. The monthly cost of vehicle insurance, which is paid in full as a yearly premium, was miscalculated.
10. Reviews of the inventory account are not occurring frequently.

A5. (LO 3) The illustration on the next page shows the consolidated income statement for Alphabet Inc. Use the statement to replace each XXXXXX in the following XBRL code with the correct information.

1. `<us-gaap:XXXXXX contextRef="FD2017Q4YTD" decimals ="-6" id="d16602969e974-wk-Fact-D431B4281DAE5E8BA E33013D08C16250"unitRef="usd">2736000000</us-gaap: XXXXXX>`

2. `<us-gaap:CostofRevenuescontextRef="XXXXXX"decimals ="-6" id="d16602969e974-wk-Fact-D431B4281DAE5E8BA E33013D08C16250"unitRef="usd">45853000000</us-gaap: CostofRevenues >`

3. `<us-gaap:XXXXXX contextRef="FD2019Q4YTD" decimals ="-6" id="d16602969e974-wk-Fact-D431B4281DAE5E8BA E33013D08C16250"unitRef="usd">127626000000</us-gaap: XXXXXX>`

4. `<us-gaap:Incomefromoperations contextRef="XXXXXX" decimals="-6" id="d16602969e974-wk-Fact-D431B4281DA E5E8BAE33013D08C16250" unitRef="usd">26178000000 </us-gaap: Incomefromoperations >`

5. `<us-gaap:Totalcostsandexpenses contextRef="FD2018Q4 YTD" decimals="-6" id="d16602969e974-wk-Fact-D431B4 281DAE5E8BAE33013D08C16250"unitRef="usd">XXXXXX </us-gaap: Totalcostsandexpenses>`

6. `<us-gaap:SalesandMarketing contextRef="FD2019Q4YTD" decimals="-6" id="d16602969e974-wk-Fact-D431B4281DA`

`E5E8BAE33013D08C16250"unitRef="usd">XXXXXX</us-gaap: SalesandMarketing >`

A6. (LO 3) `Early Career` `Critical Thinking` You are a senior consultant in the risk and advisory practice at your Big Four public accounting firm, working on a financial reporting engagement. Your client, Socrates, is a software as a service provider. You are presenting at an upcoming meeting of Socrates' department managers and senior leadership. Currently, Socrates' financial reporting is not as sophisticated as the reporting of competitors in the industry. Your consulting team thinks moving to XBRL is a way to close the reporting gap. You have been asked to give a brief talk on XBRL, including providing a general understanding of its functionality and benefits. This is what you say:

"Fundamentally, XBRL is a way to **(1)** _____ and **(2)** _____. XBRL was created by using a form of **(3)** _____, which is a well-known computer language. It uses a(n) **(4)** _____, which is an open standard that is managed by the **(5)** _____. Using an open standard for this type of reporting makes the use of XBRL **(6)** _____. It uses **(7)** _____ to associate parts of XBRL taxonomy to corresponding data, which is known as a(n) **(8)** _____. If we moved to XBRL instead of using our current process, which involves sending numerous copies to external parties, we would create a(n) **(9)** _____ that would be used to share financial information with all interested parties. One main benefit of moving to XBRL is that we would have a more effective way to **(10)** _____, which will increase the efficiency of the Accounting department."

Using the word bank below, fill in the blanks of your presentation at the leadership meeting.

Word Bank:	
XML	automate the process
tags	consolidate financial
element	information
XBRL instance document	taxonomy
improve access to financial	XBRL tags
information	XBRL International
suitable for any business	Consortium

A7. (LO 4) `Early Career` `Critical Thinking` You are responsible for preparing the annual responsibility accounting report as a cost accountant at Aero Inc., a manufacturer of luxury private aircraft. Use the information in the report given on the next page to complete the following tasks:

1. Complete the missing line items in the report using the existing information.
2. Which of the CEO's direct reports is responsible for the greatest variance?
3. Which area in the Assembly department would you recommend be analyzed for potential cost savings, and why?

Alphabet Inc.
CONSOLIDATED STATEMENTS OF INCOME
(In millions, except per share amounts) (B)

	Year Ended December 31, (A)		
	2017	2018	2019 (A)
Revenues	$ 110,855	$ 136,819	$ 161,857 (C)
Costs and expenses:			
Cost of revenues	45,583	59,549	71,896
Research and development	16,625	21,419	26,018
Sales and marketing	12,893	16,333	18,464
General and administrative	6,840	6,923	9,551
European Commission fines	2,736	5,071	1,697
Total costs and expenses	84,677	109,295	127,626
Income from operations	26,178	27,524	34,231
Other income (expense), net	1,015	7,389	5,394
Income before income taxes	27,193	34,913	39,625
Provision for income taxes	14,531	4,177	5,282
Net income	$ 12,662	$ 30,736	$ 34,343
Basic net income per share of Class A and B common stock and Class C capital stock	$ 18.27	$ 44.22	$ 49.59
Diluted net income per share of Class A and B common stock and Class C capital stock	$ 18.00	$ 43.70	$ 49.16

Aero Inc. Responsibility Accounting Reports
Reporting Period Ending January 31, 202X

Chief Executive Officer's Responsibility Report

	Budget	Actual	Variance
CEO's Office	$450,000	$ 720,000	$270,000
Controller	820,000	900,000	80,000
VP of Sales	1,260,000	1,600,000	340,000
VP of Production			
Total Controllable Costs			

Vice President of Production's Responsibility Report

	Budget	Actual	Variance
VP's Office	78,000	82,000	4,000
Quality Department	650,000	665,000	15,000
Assembly Department			
Research & Development Department	375,000	380,000	5,000
Total Controllable Costs			

Assembly Department's Responsibility Report

	Budget	Actual	Variance
Direct Material	670,000	662,000	(8,000)
Direct Labor	120,000	100,000	(20,000)
Variable Overhead	80,000	85,000	5,000
Fixed Overhead	205,000	205,000	0
Total Controllable Costs	1,075,000	1,052,000	(23,000)

A8. (LO 4–5) `Critical Thinking` You are a cost accountant, working on creating a balanced scorecard for your company. To create the scorecard, you must identify where the necessary data is generated and stored throughout the organization. Label the following data points from the AIS with (1) the ERP feature where it is generated, (2) the business process that generates it, and (3) the dimension of the balanced scorecard where it is used. Note that the process automation data point uses multiple ERP features, and the data comes from all business processes.

ERP features:

- Production
- Training and Development
- Financial Reporting
- Customer Management
- Talent Management

Business processes:

- Human resources and payroll
- Purchases and payments
- Conversion
- Marketing, sales, and collections
- Financial reporting

Balanced scorecard dimensions:

- Customer relationships
- Financial
- Internal processes
- Learning and growth

Data Points	ERP Feature	Business Process	Balanced Scorecard Dimension
1. Job satisfaction			
2. Customer retention			
3. Cash flow			
4. Product quality			
5. Employee turnover			
6. Process automation			
7. Return on investment			
8. Product reach			
9. Training opportunities			

A9. (LO 5) `Early Career` `Data Analytics` `Critical Thinking` You are a first-year external audit data analyst at a global public accounting firm. One of the audit teams you regularly work with just sent you the beginning trial balance, ending trial balance, and general ledger journal entry activity for its client, Lenya Lighting. Validate the completeness and accuracy of the general ledger journal entry activity file by performing a trial balance rollforward. Add the journal entry activity to each account's beginning balance and compare it to the ending balance. Identify any accounts that do not balance and the amount of the discrepancy.

Beginning account balances:

Lenya Lighting, LLC
Beginning Trial Balance
January 31, 202X

Account	Debit ($)	Credit ($)
Cash	1,562,000	
Accounts Receivable	568,000	
Inventory	639,000	

Ending account balances:

Lenya Lighting, LLC
Ending Trial Balance
December 31, 202X

Account	Debit ($)	Credit ($)
Cash	1,020,000	
Accounts Receivable	750,000	
Inventory	495,000	

Total debit and credit journal entry activity by account:

Account	Debit ($)	Credit ($)
Cash	5,675,215	6,217,215
Accounts Receivable	226,023	244,023
Inventory	865,726	1,009,726

A10. (LO 5) `Early Career` `Data Analytics` `Critical Thinking` You are a senior external auditor for a global public accounting firm. This morning, you received an email from a first-year associate in the firm's Audit Data Analytics group containing the output of the fraud analytics they ran for your current engagement. Unfortunately, this first-year forgot to label each journal entry they identified with the test that identified it. Before bothering this first-year during their first busy season, try to match up each of the following fraud analytics to the journal entry (shown in A–D) it identified as a red flag for fraud.

Fraud analytics:

1. Field analysis: Journal entries with missing items or invalid items in a data field
2. Unbalanced journal entries: Debit amount does not equal credit amount
3. Keyword testing: Searches for words in the journal entry description that indicate fraud
4. Round dollar entries: Transactions where the dollar amount ends in .00.

A.

JE Number	Date	Entered By	Approved By	Account	Account Name	Journal Entry Description	Debit Amount	Credit Amount
10023568	01/15/202X	BPIPER	DTENANT	100	Cash	True up month-end deferred revenue	6,235.02	
10023568	01/15/202X	BPIPER	DTENANT	430	Deferred revenue	True up month-end deferred revenue		6,235.02

B.

JE Number	Date	Entered By	Approved By	Account	Account Name	Journal Entry Description	Debit Amount	Credit Amount
10062354	06/22/202X	BPIPER		130	Accounts receivable	Sales order #1566-B	12,235.68	
10062354	06/22/202X	BPIPER		710	Credit sales	Sales order #1566-B		12,235.68

C.

JE Number	Date	Entered By	Approved By	Account	Account Name	Journal Entry Description	Debit Amount	Credit Amount
10098631	08/12/202X	BPIPER	DTENANT	100	Cash	Sales order #4052 2/10 discount terms	12,680.68	
10098631	08/12/202X	BPIPER	DTENANT	782	Sales discounts	Sales order #4052 2/10 discount terms	235	
10098631	08/12/202X	BPIPER	DTENANT	130	Accounts receivable	Sales order #4052 2/10 discount terms		12,235.68

D.

JE Number	Date	Entered By	Approved By	Account	Account Name	Journal Entry Description	Debit Amount	Credit Amount
10042615	12/23/202X	BPIPER	DTENANT	150	Inventory	Sales order #100000	250,000.00	
10042615	12/23/202X	BPIPER	DTENANT	800	Cost of goods sold	Sales order #100000		250,000.00

Tableau Case: Julia's Cookies' General Ledger Journal Entries

What You Need

Download Tableau to your computer. You can access www.tableau.com/academic/students to download your free Tableau license for the year, or you can download it from your university's software offerings.

Download the following file from the book's product page on www.wiley.com:

Chapter 13 Raw Data.xlsx

Case Overview

Big Picture:

Monitor general ledger journal entries.

Details:

Why is this data important, and what questions or problems need to be addressed?

- Julia's Cookies must monitor general ledger journal entries and transactions to check for unusual entries to the general ledger because incorrect or fraudulent entries could result in misrepresentation of the financial statements.

- One area to focus on is determining who approves and posts journal entries, as well as the times and days of the journal entry approvals and postings. Consider the following questions: Who posts the most journal entries? How many entries were posted outside of normal work hours? Does the same employee ever approve and post an entry?

Plan:

What data is needed, and how should it be analyzed?

- The data needed to answer these questions is extracted from the ERP database. It is data for the 2021 fiscal year general ledger for part of Q1 and the human resources database. In this data set, the journal entry header information is in one table, which includes all identifying information for each journal entry number, such as who posted the journal entry. The line items for each journal entry are in a second table. Remember, journal entries will always have at least two line items: one debit and one credit.

Now it's your turn to evaluate, analyze, and communicate the results!

To answer the questions, connect the tables using their ID fields:

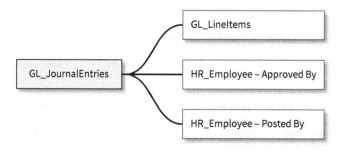

Hint: When connecting the HR_Employee table, connect the first instance on "Approved By" to "Employee Number" (primary key) and the second connection on "Posted By" to "Employee Number" (primary key).

Questions

1. Which employee posted the most journal entries? How many journal entries did this employee post? (Hint: Make sure you are only counting each journal entry number once.)
2. On which date were the most journal entries posted? How many journal entries were posted that day? (Hint: Make sure you are only counting each journal entry number once.)
3. On which date was the highest total dollar amount posted? How much was posted on this day? (Hint: Because journal entries net to zero, you should only consider the debit [positive] side of the journal entries.)
4. A common journal entry fraud test is to look for journal entries posted outside normal business days. Julia's Cookies' Accounting department has a normal business week of Monday through Friday. How many journal entries were posted outside normal business days? On which day of the week were they posted? (Hint: Make sure you are only counting each journal entry number once.)
5. For the day of the week you identified in question 4, what was the total amount posted on that day? (Hint: Because journal entries net to zero, you should only consider the debit [positive] side of the journal entries.)
6. A common journal entry fraud test is to look for journal entries posted outside normal business hours. Most of Julia's Cookies' accounting employees start work no earlier than 5 a.m. and log off before 8 p.m., Monday through Friday. How many transactions were posted on Monday through Friday outside these hours? (Hint: Make sure you are only counting each journal entry number once.)
7. For the journal entries you identified in question 6, what was the total dollar amount posted? (Hint: Because journal entries net to zero, you should only consider the debit [positive] side of the journal entries.)

8. A common journal entry fraud test is to identify journal entries posted or approved by unexpected employees. How many employees who do not work in the Accounting department posted journal entries? For each of these employees, identify their employee ID, name, employee type, and department, as well as the number of journal entries they posted. (Hint: Filter the HR data for an employee status of "Active" to get each employee's most recent department.)

Take it to the next level!

9. Because Julia's Cookies uses a double-sided accounting system, all journal entries are expected to net to zero. A common journal entry data validation test is to verify that all journal entries net to zero. How many unbalanced journal entries (that is, entries that do not net to zero) are there? Identify the journal entry number, poster ID, approver ID, and net dollar amount for each of these unbalanced journal entries.

10. A common journal entry fraud test is to identify journal entries that are both posted and approved by the same person, which violates segregation of duties internal controls. Analyze the "Posted By" and "Approved By" fields to identify any employees who are both posting and approving journal entries. Identify the employee ID(s), employee name(s), number of journal entries posted, and total dollar amount posted for each of the employees. (Hint: Because journal entries net to zero, you should only consider the debit [positive] side of the journal entries.)

Appendix A
Expanding the Accounting Equation:
From Balance Sheet to Statement of Cash Flows

Financial statements are one of the most important outputs of the AIS.

1. **Statements required by generally accepted accounting principles (GAAP):**

   Income statement: Revenues – Expenses = Net income (Net loss) = NI (–NL)

   Retained earnings: Beginning balance + NI (–NL) – Dividends +/– Adjustments = Ending balance

   Owners' equity: Owner contributions +/– Other adjustments + Retained earnings

   Balance sheet: Assets = Liabilities + Owners' equity

   Statement of cash flows: Cash = Δ Cash to/from operating activities + Δ Cash to/from investing activities + Δ Cash to/from financing activities (Δ = change, which can be positive or negative)

2. **Balance Sheet**

   Balance sheet: Assets = Liabilities + Owners' equity

   Expanding owners' equity to include the **income statement:**

   Assets = Liabilities + OE + (Revenue – Expenses)

   or equivalently:

   Assets + Expenses = Liabilities + OE + Revenue

   Assets + Expenses = Costs = Resources unused (assets) and used (expenses)

   Note: Costs are capitalized or expensed depending upon whether the expenditure benefits future periods.

   Resources need (=) Sources of funding = Liabilities + OE + Revenue

   Debits (assets and expenses) = Credits (liabilities, owners' equity, and revenue)

3. Statement of Cash Flows

Δ Cash = Δ Cash to/from operating activities + Δ Cash to/from investing activities + Δ Cash to/from financing activities (Δ = change)

Let us start with the balance sheet for a company (at a point in time indicated by t):

Assets (A_t) = Liabilities (L_t) + Stockholders' equity (SE_t)

$A_t = L_t + OE_t$

$A_{t-1} = L_{t-1} + SE_{t-1}$ and taking differences, we have:

$\Delta A = \Delta L + \Delta SE$, then splitting assets into Cash and Non-Cash Assets (NCA), we have:

Δ Cash + Δ NCA = Δ L + Δ SE, and recall what Δ SE is, we have, with Contributed Capital (CC):

Δ Cash = $- \Delta$ NCA + Δ L + NI ($-$NL) $-$ Div + Δ CC

Split Δ NCA and Δ L into current (c) and long-term (lt), and recalling what NI is, we rearrange terms and we get:

Δ Cash = Rev-Ex $- \Delta$ NCA$_c$ + Depreciation + Δ L$_c$	Operating activities
$- \Delta$ NCA$_{lt}$ (adjusted for depreciation)	Investing activities
$+ \Delta L_{lt} + \Delta$ CC $-$ Dividends	Financing activities

Note: Non-Cash changes to Current Assets, Current Liabilities, and Depreciation are called "accruals."

Note: "Disaccruing" NI to cash flow entails adjusting for accruals.

Information Systems and Controls

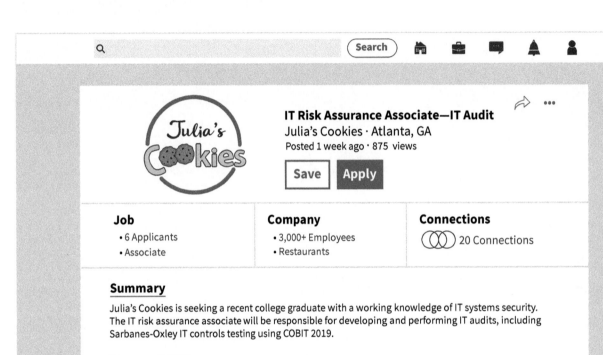

IT Risk Assurance Associate—IT Audit
Julia's Cookies · Atlanta, GA
Posted 1 week ago · 875 views

Save **Apply**

Job
- 6 Applicants
- Associate

Company
- 3,000+ Employees
- Restaurants

Connections
20 Connections

Summary
Julia's Cookies is seeking a recent college graduate with a working knowledge of IT systems security. The IT risk assurance associate will be responsible for developing and performing IT audits, including Sarbanes-Oxley IT controls testing using COBIT 2019.

Responsibilities
- Develop a thorough understanding of Julia's Cookies' operations and IT infrastructure
- Assist with risk assessments and with developing audit and audit testing plans
- Remain heavily involved in IT control testing and documentation of results
- Communicate issues with internal controls to management
- Maintain effective relationships with internal and external audit teams
- Evaluate the design, operational effectiveness, and efficiency of IT control processes and procedures
- Communicate IT concepts and risks to non-IT auditors and management

Requirements
Preferred Education: Bachelor's degree or higher in accounting, information systems, or related subjects
Preferred Certifications: CPA, CISA, CRISC, CITP, or CISM

Preferred Knowledge and Skills
The ideal candidate will demonstrate basic knowledge of internal controls, SOX regulatory compliance, business processes, and IT governance. Preference given to candidates with an understanding of or experience in the following areas:
- Relevant IT audit experience, including information security, IT general controls, IT application controls, and technology control frameworks (such as COBIT 2019)
- Role-based application access controls
- Segregation of duties
- Financial and business process controls
- IT policy and governance

Salary: $55,000–65,000

CHAPTER PREVIEW   Regardless of career path, all accounting professionals must have information technology (IT) skills. At Julia's Cookies, accounting professionals of all types need an understanding of IT risks and controls—including the IT Audit department, which is currently hiring a new IT risk assurance associate.

IT is a complex part of every business. Most business leaders spend a great deal of time thinking about IT, since it is an area that both addresses and creates risk. How do we know our IT systems are secure? Can we assure stakeholders that our technology is safe and efficient? How do we balance our IT needs with our allocated budgets? Companies face these kinds of questions daily.

This chapter explains how companies respond to these issues by describing one of the most important frameworks companies use in managing their IT risks: COBIT. COBIT sets out a potential roadmap that businesses can follow—and customize—to meet their organization's needs. The framework used in this chapter helps companies:

- Decide who can access their systems
- Physically protect systems
- Keep systems running
- Make changes to their systems

Frameworks manage IT risks through specific sets of policies and procedures that ensure the risks in these systems areas are being mitigated. Since IT systems are the foundation of the business processes and tools we cover throughout the course, accounting information systems students must understand the risks faced by these systems. ■

Chapter Roadmap

LEARNING OBJECTIVES	TOPICS	JULIA'S COOKIES APPLIED LEARNING
14.1 Describe the COBIT framework and its five domains.	• Introducing COBIT • The Five Domains of COBIT	Frameworks: Achieving Objectives
14.2 Evaluate logical user access controls.	• Assigning and Authenticating Users • Adding and Removing Users • Reviewing Existing Users • User Access Internal Controls	User Access: Assigning Roles
14.3 Explain how physical access controls protect equipment and systems.	• Data Center Components and Security • Physical Access Internal Controls	Physical Access: Company Tour
14.4 Compare backup and recovery efforts.	• Business Continuity Planning • Backup Sites • Backup Strategies • Backup Cycles • Data Storage Internal Controls	Business Continuity Planning: Global Pandemic
14.5 Summarize the change management process.	• The Change Management Process • Differentiating Between Normal and Emergency Changes • Change Management Internal Controls	Change Management: ServiceNow Ticket Review

CPA   You will find the CPA tag throughout the chapter to call out any important topics you may see on the CPA exam.

14.1 What Framework Can We Use to Mitigate Risk Around Our Systems?

Learning Objective ❶
Describe the COBIT framework and its five domains.

You have learned that there are many different ways to categorize controls. A control can be automated or manual, an application control or an IT general control (ITGC), and more. In this chapter, we focus on ITGCs that protect the business.

Recall that ITGCs protect the IT structure, components, and data stored in systems. ITGCs mitigate risks to systems, processes, and data by protecting them from external and internal risks. ITGCs cover all areas of the information technology infrastructure in a company, creating a great deal of complexity for leaders working to manage risk.

Information technology (IT) includes the technology and processes involved in developing, maintaining, and using computer systems, hardware, software, and networks for the processing and distribution of data. An IT department's goal is to keep the organization's technology up and running for business users and customers, which means this department creates and manages unique risks. The IT department is involved in supporting application controls for business processes that use information systems, which you'll recall are controls related to transaction processing. The IT department also focuses on ITGCs.

Companies must have a strategy to navigate these complexities. **IT governance** is the process that ensures effective and efficient use of IT so a company can achieve goals and provide value. The key point to remember is that IT governance is a *process*. It is not a department or a static state of existing; rather, it is an ongoing effort by different parts of an organization to monitor and make IT decisions that have an impact on business operations. While mitigating risk is part of IT governance, it is not the only focus. The methods of identifying and evaluating IT performance and bringing value to the company are also important parts.

To implement best IT governance practices, companies turn to frameworks. **IT governance frameworks** define the criteria a company can use to implement, manage, and monitor IT governance, including measurements for effectively leveraging IT resources. There are a number of widely accepted IT governance frameworks, and for the purposes of AIS, we focus on one that is specifically designed for security and risk management: COBIT.

Do you remember what a *framework* is? When you start a course, you receive a syllabus that lists all the learning objectives of the class, assignments, due dates, and more. The syllabus acts as your guide and instructions for the course. It is a framework for the class.

Introducing COBIT

CPA COBIT was developed by the Information Systems Audit and Control Association (ISACA), and its name originally stood for "Control Objective for Information and Related Technology." Recently, both ISACA and COBIT adopted their acronyms as their official names—a move that reflects how far they have evolved over the years.

Source: ISACA
COBIT is the most widely used international standard for IT governance. The most recent version, **COBIT 2019**, is designed to help companies meet regulatory compliance requirements, manage IT risks, and ensure that IT strategies are aligned with corporate goals.

COBIT has an online platform that allows users to provide feedback and recommend updates to enhance future versions. You could even have an impact on the framework someday! COBIT 2019 is an extensive document, but we focus on highlights you should know for your AIS course, including topics covered on the CPA exam.

CPA COBIT 2019 is one of many frameworks accounting professionals use. These two frameworks are also commonly used:

- The *COSO Internal Control—Integrated Framework* takes a control-based approach to assessing risk and providing assurance throughout an organization.
- Similarly, the *COSO Enterprise Risk Management—Integrating with Strategy and Performance Framework (ERM Framework)* takes a risk-based approach to addressing risk from a strategic perspective.

COBIT 2019 provides a way to achieve COSO objectives of assessing risks and providing assurance, but only for IT controls. **Table 14.1** shows the main differences between the two COSO frameworks and COBIT 2019. After examining this table, help the leadership of Julia's Cookies determine which framework to implement for its objectives in Applied Learning 14.1.

TABLE 14.1   COSO Versus COBIT 2019 Frameworks

Framework	Organizational Focus	Control Scope	Audience
COSO Internal Control—Integrated Framework and COSO ERM Framework	Corporate governance	All internal controls	Management Board of directors Internal and external audit
COBIT 2019	IT governance	Only IT-specific controls	IT managers IT professionals Internal and external audit

Julia's Cookies — Applied Learning 14.1

Frameworks: Achieving Objectives

Julia's Cookies' leadership recognizes that the company will benefit from implementing frameworks for both corporate and IT governance. There's a bit of confusion among the leadership team about which frameworks will address which areas. For each of the following areas of focus, would you suggest a COSO framework or a COBIT framework?

1. The IT managers want to make sure their systems are protected.
2. The board of directors wants to make sure the internal control environment is SOX compliant.
3. Internal Audit wants to make sure the IT department is meeting its control objectives.
4. Management wants to make sure that business processes and internal controls are meeting strategic objectives.

SOLUTION

1. The COBIT framework is used by IT managers for IT system controls.
2. COSO frameworks are used by the board of directors for all internal controls.
3. The COBIT framework is used by Internal Audit to assess IT control objectives.
4. COSO frameworks are used by management for all internal controls and strategic objectives.

The Five Domains of COBIT[1]

CPA COBIT 2019 provides more than 300 generic IT controls. These controls fall under 40 control objectives, which are categorized into five domains. (Note that COBIT 2019 calls control

---

[1]ISACA: *COBIT® 2019 Framework: Introduction and Methodology.*

objectives "practices"; we use the term "control objectives" because that is how accounting professionals refer to these practices.) We give an overview of the specific control objectives in each domain later, but for now it is important to understand that each of the domains contains many objectives.

The five domains of COBIT 2019 are divided into two categories, based on their objectives. First, an organization creates strategy through IT governance-related objectives.

IT Governance Objectives—Creating the Strategy:

1. **Evaluate, Direct, and Monitor (EDM)** is the *only* IT governance–focused domain in COBIT 2019. This domain states that the board of directors or governing body of an organization must evaluate stakeholder needs and IT strategic options, create direction by prioritizing and making decisions about these options, and monitor these IT strategies for performance, progress, and compliance. The control objectives in this domain include frameworks, resource optimization, and transparency with stakeholders.

Second, the organization turns the strategy into action by implanting a variety of domains whose objectives are focused on management.

Management IT Objectives—Turning the Strategy into Action:

2. **Align, Plan, and Organize (APO)** addresses the way IT is used to meet organizational objectives. APO includes some control objectives around risk, security, budgets, and innovation.

3. **Build, Acquire, and Implement (BAI)** is where management assesses IT requirements, acquires technology, and implements the technology. In this objective, IT is integrated with business processes. BAI control objectives cover topics like defining project requirements, addressing change management, and executing projects.

4. **Deliver, Service, and Support (DSS)** relates to the operational side of IT projects, including IT support. IT projects are delivered to end users. The DSS component includes service requests, business process controls, and IT security support among its control objectives.

5. **Monitor, Evaluate, and Assess (MEA)** focuses on existing IT projects and whether they are meeting the organization's objectives. IT projects are compared to internal performance targets, control objectives, and external regulatory requirements. Some of the MEA control objectives focus on the internal control system, regulatory compliance, and performance.

Why Does It Matter to Your Career?

Thoughts from a Lead IT Auditor, Insurance

- The CPA may be the most common certification you'll encounter during your accounting education, but it is not the only one. ISACA and many other organizations that provide frameworks also offer certifications that can enhance your skillset and help drive a successful career:

  - Certified Information Systems Auditor (CISA)
  - Certified in Risk and Information Systems Control (CRISC)
  - Certified Information Security Manager (CISM)
  - Certified in Governance of Enterprise IT (CGEIT)

- You do not have to memorize frameworks. They are accessible online, so you only need to know what they are and where to find them. You will find the COBIT framework on the ISACA website. Some companies use audit software that is integrated with COBIT. In those cases, all COBIT controls are included, and people can even export them as an Excel file for referencing outside the audit software.

Illustration 14.1 shows the five COBIT domains and their 40 control objectives. This seems like a lot, but don't worry: It's not necessary to know all of these ITGCs. For this course, you should understand how COBIT and internal controls are related. COBIT defines

① Governance:
Evaluate, Direct, and Monitor

- Ensure IT governance framework setting and maintenance
- Ensure IT benefits delivery
- Ensure risk realization
- Ensure resource optimization
- Ensure stakeholder transparency

② Management:
Align, Plan, and Organize

- Manage the IT management framework
- Manage strategy
- Manage enterprise architecture
- Manage innovation
- Manage portfolio
- Manage budget and costs
- Manage human relations
- Manage relationships
- Manage service agreements
- Manage suppliers
- Manage quality
- Manage risk
- Manage security
- Manage data

③ Management:
Build, Acquire, and Implement

- Manage programs and projects
- Manage requirements definition
- Manage solutions identification and build
- Manage availability and capacity
- Manage organizational change enablement
- Manage changes
- Manage change acceptance and transitioning
- Manage knowledge
- Manage assets
- Manage configuration
- Manage projects

④ Management:
Deliver, Service, and Support

- Manage operations
- Manage service requests and incidents
- Manage problems
- Manage continuity
- Manage security services
- Manage business process controls

⑤ Management:
Monitor, Evaluate, and Assess

- Manage performance and conformance monitoring
- Manage system of internal control
- Manage compliance with external requirements
- Manage assurance

Illustration 14.1 This chapter covers the highlighted controls from four domains of the COBIT 2019 framework.

specific controls—like the ones we will talk about next—and those specific controls are mapped to control objectives and domains. Essentially, internal controls help a company meet its control objectives. Throughout this chapter, you'll learn about controls that Julia's Cookies uses to do the following:

- Manage security services by limiting access to systems and physical equipment
- Manage operations by protecting facilities against intruders and environmental threats
- Manage continuity by having a plan for dealing with disasters
- Manage data by making sure it is saved in multiple ways
- Manage changes to systems by having a formal process in place for system updates
- Manage the system of internal control by monitoring these controls for effectiveness

Remember, a company's IT risks are vast and complex. This chapter focuses on a handful of the controls a business can implement—those highlighted in Illustration 14.1, which represent only a small piece of the COBIT framework.

CONCEPT REVIEW QUESTIONS

1. What is meant by IT governance, and how does IT governance framework work?
   Ans. IT governance is the process that ensures effective and efficient use of IT so that a company can achieve goals and provide value. To implement best IT governance practices, companies turn to frameworks. IT governance frameworks define the criteria a company can use to implement, manage, and monitor IT governance, including measurements for effectively leveraging IT resources.

2. **CPA** What is COBIT, and why is it important?
   Ans. COBIT is the most widely used international standard for IT governance. It was developed by the Information Systems Audit and Control Association (ISACA), and its name originally stood for "Control Objective for Information and Related Technology." Recently, COBIT adopted the acronym as its official name. The most recent version, COBIT 2019, is designed to help companies meet regulatory compliance requirements, manage IT risks, and ensure that IT strategies are aligned with corporate goals.

3. What are the other two commonly used internal control frameworks?
   Ans. The following frameworks are widely used:
   - The COSO Internal Control—Integrated Framework takes a control-based approach to assessing risk and providing assurance throughout an organization.
   - The COSO Enterprise Risk Management—Integrating with Strategy and Performance Framework (ERM Framework) takes a risk-based approach to addressing risk from a strategic perspective.

14.2 How Do We Decide Who Can Access Systems?

Learning Objective ❷
Evaluate logical user access controls.

Think about the laptop that you are using for your classes. When you purchased the laptop, did you create a logon password to keep intruders from accessing the computer? By doing so, you implemented a very simple ITGC that decreases the risk of your system's data being stolen. Maybe you have left the laptop in your car, locking it in the trunk so nobody can see it while you run an errand. At the local coffee shop, you may have left it at a table while placing an order at the counter, but you kept it in your line of sight to make sure nobody took it. By doing these things, you have implemented both logical and physical access controls:

- *Logical access controls* identify, authorize (grant permission), authenticate (ensure that users are who they say they are), and provide access to users of a computer information system. Much as a security badge is programmed to let you through a locked door, logical access controls are programmed into a system to let you into locked networks, files, databases, and more. Examples of logical access controls include usernames and passwords, biometric authentication, such as a fingerprint or a facial recognition scan, and specific permissions assigned to users in the system, based on user ID. As technologies improve, companies are implementing biometric access controls more often due to their strength of security.

- *Physical access controls* help a company keep track of who is coming and going to prevent unauthorized individuals from entering a facility. Physical access controls can include security badges or fingerprints for locked doors, a requirement for visitors to check in at the security desk, and even systems that store information on who entered a building and at what time, based on badge or fingerprint scans.

At one time, logical access controls were not widely available, and physical access control was the primary method of protecting information on systems. Computers housing systems were kept in locked rooms or had security guards restricting access. Once access was physically granted to a computer, users had unlimited ability to access any information it contained. While this was not a problem in all environments, for many companies, the information on a system needs to be secured on a need-to-know basis, and one individual may not require access to the entire system's information. For example, someone in the HR department may need to access the payroll system to input a newly hired employee's bank information and salary. That same employee may not need to see the salaries and bank accounts of every employee in the company—especially immediate colleagues or the company's executive team. In these environments, where not all information should be available to all users, logical access controls enhance the precision of the overall internal control environment.

To achieve an effective control environment, companies use an integrated approach that combines both logical and physical controls. The user access controls discussed next are logical. We'll explain physical access controls later in this chapter, when we discuss how systems are protected in data centers.

Assigning and Authenticating Users

The logical access controls we discuss first are related to assigning access in the system and confirming the identity of users logging into the system. These foundational user access controls are essential to an effective control environment. Let's start with assigning access.

User Access Roles

Have you ever shared a document with someone else on Google Drive or a similar cloud platform? If so, you were most likely presented with options similar to those shown in **Illustration 14.2**. This screenshot presents options for the level of access another person should receive. From viewing to editing, you have control over what others can do with your file.

By choosing one of these options, you are essentially assigning user access roles for your file. Similarly, to address the need of each user requiring a specific level of access, companies implement a type of authorization called **role-based access control (RBAC)**. RBAC restricts network access by assigning individuals specific roles that have predefined criteria for what they can and cannot access in the system:

- **User access roles** are groups with predefined permissions to which users are assigned, with each user assigned to only one role at a time.

- A **permission** is a listing of access rights, or privileges, a user has once assigned to a role. RBAC streamlines the logical access control process for IT personnel by eliminating the need to program access to every system for every employee. Instead, access is programmed for each employee only once, when that person is assigned a role.

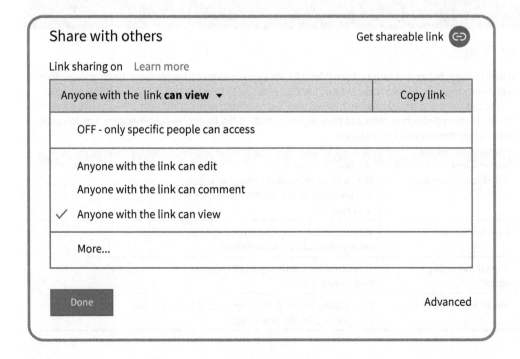

Illustration 14.2 File owners are asked which level of permissions to grant another user when sharing a file.

- The **administrator role** is the highest role in the hierarchy and has permissions for all objects. In other words, people in this role not only have unlimited access themselves, they are also the ones who assign access roles to the other users. This role is assigned to very few people. There may, for example, be only two people with this level of access: the primary administrator and the backup person who fills in if the primary administrator is not available. The administrator role is almost always a high priority when reviewing internal controls for user access because administrators can do anything in the system; they have all the privileges.

CPA Each user role has different levels of permissions. For example, a first-year tax associate may have a read-only role to access a team's shared drive. With this role, the associate can view files but cannot rename or delete files and folders on the drive. The associate's manager may have a creator role, which allows the manager to access the shared drive *and* make changes to folder names, delete files, and more. This role-based access control addresses the risk that a newly hired employee may delete essential team files from the shared drive.

Examine the permissions assigned to various user roles in **Illustration 14.3**. Then try to identify which roles users should have at Julia's Cookies in Applied Learning 14.2.

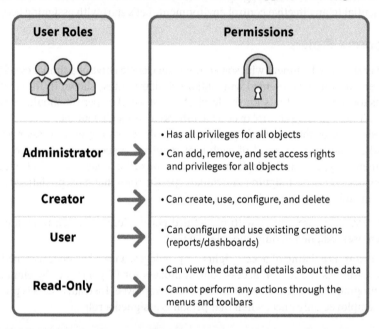

Illustration 14.3 User roles identify which level of permissions a user is granted.

Julia's Cookies   Applied Learning 14.2

User Access: Assigning Roles

Julia's Cookies started out as a local bakery, but it has grown into a national brand with a strong online sales presence. Its corporate office has adopted large-scale information systems to manage its operations. From Human Resources to Internal Audit, Julia's Cookies has many different employees who need specific access to its systems. Using a role-based user access control approach, Julia's Cookies assigns roles based on a user's job needs. Based on the hierarchy of access roles and permissions, which of the four roles (administrator, creator, user, and read-only) do you think each of these employees should be assigned?

System Name	User's Job Title	Why User Needs Access	Role Granted
Salesforce customer relationship management (CRM) system	VP of sales analytics	Newly hired employee in charge of setting and reviewing access rights in Salesforce for data analysts	
Payroll system	Internal auditor	Viewing senior executive payroll details to confirm the accuracy of a 10-K statement	
Company's website	Digital marketing intern	Downloading a daily report of website traffic statistics	
General ledger	Senior tax accountant	Configuring the tax percentages, per the new tax law, and deleting the old percentages	

SOLUTION

The VP of sales analytics needs the *administrator* role because only the administrator role grants permission to assign and change other users' permissions.

The internal auditor can perform the required actions with the *read-only* role.

The digital marketing intern requires the *user* role to be able to download reports. Read-only will only grant the ability to view the reports in the system. Downloading is a user role permission.

The senior tax accountant needs the *creator* role to make changes in the system. Configuring tax percentages to match the new law requires updating values in the system. Changing the system information is limited to creators and higher.

User Authentication

CPA Once a user has been granted a role in a system, how do we know this is the person using their account to log in? **User authentication** is the process of associating the username of each authorized user with a unique identifier. There are various kinds of identifiers, and they can be used individually or in combination for stronger control. **Multifactor authentication** occurs when a strong combination of identifiers is required when a user logs in. You may be familiar with two-factor authentication—a type of multifactor authentication—if you have ever tried to log into an account on a website and been prompted to have a verification code sent to your text messaging or email address. This verification code is an identifier.

An identifier could be something the user knows, has, or is (**Illustration 14.4**).

Knows	Has	Biometric
Something the user **KNOWS:**	Something the user **HAS:**	Something the user **IS:**
• Logon ID	• ID badge	• Fingerprint
• Password	• Smart card	• Voiceprint
• PIN	• Smart key	• Facial scan

Illustration 14.4 Authentication can be granted based on something a user knows, has, or is.

Adding and Removing Users

Now that we've reviewed the roles of users and how users are authenticated in a system, let's look at how users are added and removed. Because system access is a high-risk area, proper internal controls are essential when granting and removing permissions. Both processes must follow formalized steps and must be documented.

User Access Provisioning

User access provisioning is the formal process of granting access to a new user. This process can be different from one company to another, but it will have steps similar to those highlighted in **Illustration 14.5**.

To ensure that access is granted for legitimate business reasons:

- The service request ticket for new user access usually has a field where the employee explains why access to the system is needed to perform job duties. The ticket also includes the employee's job title, department, direct supervisor, and more.

Access Requested	Access Approved	Access Granted
An employee requests access to the system through a service request system—or a ticketing system—like ServiceNow. A ticket for the request is created.	The ticket is routed to the employee's manager and the system owner, who both review the request in the service request system and either approve or deny the ticket.	If access is approved by the required parties, the system administrator grants access to the system and closes the access request ticket.

Illustration 14.5 User access provisioning using a service request system follows proper approval request procedures.

- Managers and system owners must review this explanation and other job-related information to ensure that the access requested is appropriate.

For example, an internal auditor should not be granted administrative or creator access to the general ledger system, as this would circumvent the segregation-of-duties control activity. The process of reviewing and approving the user access request ticket is a manual control that is subject to the judgment and errors of approvers. This means the approval process is often considered a high-risk area surrounding user access provisioning.

User Access De-provisioning

User access de-provisioning is the formal process of changing a user's access. The steps for de-provisioning are generally similar to those in **Illustration 14.6**.

Table 14.2 summarizes the two types of user access status changes: termination and transfer.

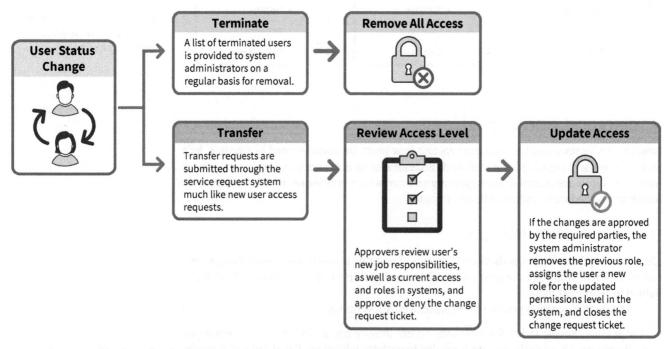

Illustration 14.6 The flow of actions for user access de-provisioning depends on whether the access is being terminated or transferred.

TABLE 14.2 Two Types of User Access Changes

Termination	Upon notification of a termination, all access for the user should be immediately revoked. It is rare to require further approvals, as removing someone's access does not create risk for the company.
Transfer	If an employee's status in the company changes—such as transferring to a different department or their current job changing its scope of responsibilities—it is important to perform an analysis of the employee's current access and to assess whether that access is still appropriate in the new role. This lowers the risk of a lack of segregation of duties.

For example, suppose you were in the accounting department and had creator-level access to the general ledger but decided to move to a new position in the internal audit department. Your general ledger access would go from creator to read-only to prevent a violation of segregation of duties—because internal auditors shouldn't have access that allows them to make changes in the general ledger system. |

Reviewing Existing Users

What about users who have not accessed the system for a long time? Do we leave users active even when they are not using the system? Great question! There is a specific internal control just for this situation.

Remove User?

Dormant access exists when a user has not accessed the system for a significant period of time but still has an active role that grants them access. Assume you were assigned to a project that uses the Salesforce system—a customer relationship management system that contains vital information for marketing, sales, and other areas of your company. The system administrator set you up with a creator role in that system so that you could download and update sales reports used in the project. Now that the project is done, you still have access to the system even though you are not using it anymore. This is where an important user access control comes into play: user access reviews.

User access reviews are periodic reviews of all current users and their system roles. This internal control protects the data and security of the system by lowering a variety of inappropriate use risks:

- Terminated employees gaining network or email access
- Violations of segregation of duties when employees change departments but retain previous access roles
- Dormant administrator accounts being misused if they are still active
- System being compromised through passwords that haven't expired

For the user access review control to be effective, it is important to identify certain users:

- Users with excessive privileges—those who have privileges that don't align with their job duties
- Users with dormant access privileges—those who haven't logged into the system for a significant time
- Users with outdated access—those whose access has not been updated to reflect job duty changes

When the system owners review the list, they consider the following questions:

- Who has the most access?
- Who doesn't need this access anymore?
- Do people have more access than they need, based on their role in the organization?
- Who hasn't logged into the system in a long time?
- Who has had a change in job title since our last user access review?

Why Does It Matter to Your Career?

Thoughts from an External Auditor, Public Accounting

- If you are thinking about a career in audit, as an internal, external, or IT auditor, you will test the roles of users as one of many user access tests. An external or internal auditor will test for segregation of duties, and an IT auditor will test to ensure appropriate level of access.

- If you are not planning to work in audit, you are still likely at some point to play one of the most important roles in user access controls: as a manager, you will be responsible for reviewing your employees' requests and approving them.

User access review is often a manual internal control that is tedious and time-consuming for system owners and auditors. It is an excellent opportunity for companies to implement automated controls using data analytics and robotic process automation to identify users who match the risk criteria and eliminate nonrisky users from the review. Taking it a step further, machine learning algorithms can be leveraged to make efficient decisions on whether access is appropriate with minimal human input.

User Access Internal Controls

There are many risks associated with unauthorized access to systems. The damage unauthorized users can cause varies based on which system or data source they've accessed. For example, an unauthorized user gaining access to the payroll system may result in payroll fraud. An unauthorized user gaining access to sensitive client data may result in the data being held for ransom, which happens when a cyber attacker—someone maliciously gaining unauthorized access to the company's systems—threatens to release sensitive information unless certain demands are met.

Unauthorized access to a company's systems or data may result in:

- Employee fraud
- Malicious attacks on systems and data
- Systems and data being held for ransom
- Data breaches

Logical controls for system access are essential to an effective internal control environment. **Table 14.3** summarizes the control activities discussed in this section and their control owners. Recall that a control owner is responsible for implementing a control. For example, it is the job of the system owner to ensure that users have only the information access rights they need to perform their job duties. It is not their responsibility to design or mandate this control; that is the responsibility of the company's management.

TABLE 14.3 Summary of Risks and Controls in Logical Security

Risk Statement: An unauthorized user gaining access to the company's systems or data may result in a variety of damaging consequences, such as fraud, malicious attacks, and data breaches.	
Sample Control Activity	**Control Owner**
Policies and procedures for user access are clearly documented and authorized.	Information security manager
Access to systems is granted to each user based on the user's business need.	System owner
User access to systems is periodically reviewed for appropriateness. Inappropriate access is immediately revoked.	System owner
Users are prohibited from saving information on flash drives or portable hard drives and cannot email sensitive information outside the company network.	Information security manager
Roles, responsibilities, and access privileges are designed to create proper segregation of duties needed to support business process objectives.	System owner
New access requests are reviewed and approved before being granted.	System owner/information security manager
Access for transferred or terminated employees is revoked in a timely manner.	System owner

CONCEPT REVIEW QUESTIONS

1. What are logical access controls?

   Ans. Logical access controls identify, authorize (grant permission), authenticate (ensure that users are who they say they are), and provide access to users of a computer information system. These controls are programmed into a system to let the authorized user into locked networks, files, databases, and more. Examples of logical access controls include usernames and passwords, and biometric authentication.

2. What are physical access controls?

   Ans. Physical access controls help a company keep track of who is coming and going to prevent unauthorized individuals from entering a facility. These controls can include security badges or fingerprints for locked doors, a requirement for visitors to check in at the security desk, and even systems that store information on who entered a building and at what time, based on badge or fingerprint scans.

3. What is a role-based access control (RBAC)?

   Ans. RBAC is a type of authorization which restricts network access by assigning individuals specific roles that have predefined criteria for what they can and cannot access in the system.

4. What do you mean by user access role?

   Ans. User access roles are groups with predefined permissions to which users are assigned, with each user assigned to only one role at a time.

5. Differentiate between the two types of user access changes—termination and transfer.

   Ans. The differences between the two types of user access changes are:

   Termination: Upon notification of a termination, all access for the user should be immediately revoked. It is rare to require further approvals, as removing someone's access does not create risk for the company.

   Transfer: If an employee's status in the company changes—such as transferring to a different department or their current job changing its scope of responsibilities—it is important to perform an analysis of the employee's current access and to assess whether that access is still appropriate in the new role. This lowers the risk of a lack of segregation of duties.

14.3 How Do We Physically Protect Our Systems?

Learning Objective ❸

Explain how physical access controls protect equipment and systems.

So far, we have focused on the risk to data within systems, but what about risks to the places where data is physically stored? Recall that physical access controls protect tangible assets such as equipment and facilities. These controls can include badges to access a building, locked doors to protect a room containing computer equipment, and mandatory visitor check-ins at the front security desk. In this section, you'll learn why and how companies keep computer equipment in a secure storage facility called a data center.

 A company uses a **data center** to protect the physical components on which systems and data are stored. Also known as a network operations center (NOC), a data center is an area in a building—or even an entire building—that is dedicated to the physical storage of computer and telecommunication systems. Data centers can be either onsite or offsite.

Onsite data centers have certain characteristics:

- They exist within the primary building where the business operates.
- Onsite data storage includes local hard drives, flash drives, or servers in a dedicated data center of the building.

Offsite data centers mitigate a specific risk:

- They store data in a different physical location than the center of business operations.
- Offsite storage prevents the risk that a company might lose the center of operations *and* all of its IT equipment and data at the same time.

Many companies implement a combination of onsite and offsite data centers.

Data Center Components and Security

Many components make up a successful data center. Let's follow along with one of Julia's Cookies' internal auditors to explore a data center in depth. Data centers are hard to audit remotely, so internal auditors commonly travel to the physical location of a data center and personally visit the building. Julia's Cookies uses an onsite data center that is in its corporate office building in San Francisco. Secondary storage is located at a facility in northern New Jersey—far away from the higher-risk locations in the United States where earthquakes, tornadoes, and hurricanes may be common. This secondary facility is available for use in the event that a disaster hits the San Francisco building, and we will talk about that later. For now, we will follow the internal auditor who is reviewing the onsite data center.

Why Does It Matter to Your Career?

Thoughts from an Internal Auditor, Financial Services

Even though doctors who are not cardiologists don't work on the heart on a regular basis, they still have to understand how it functions in order to perform medical duties on other parts of the body. In the same way, it is helpful for employees in all parts of a company to understand basic principles about a data center. You are using systems—you have email, a messenger program, and other software that runs on servers and is stored on drives in your company's data center. Maybe you won't be an auditor and will never see the inside of the data center, but you'll know it is there and that it is important.

Outside Environment

CPA The data center is the heart of a business—it keeps the business alive by providing connectivity across all business functions and maintaining operations. Just as your heart is located within your chest and protected by your rib cage, the location of the data center should also provide protection—from fire, flood, and changes in climate.

Illustration 14.7 shows that the data center should be near the bottom floors of its physical building, and an ideal building will be on higher ground to avoid flooding. Julia's Cookies follows the best practice of having no windows in the data center. The internal auditor notes that it is an interior room. This protects the data center from damage caused by users breaking in and entering through windows as well as from damage caused by windows being blown out by a large storm.

The data center is also built on raised, hollow floors. This decreases the risk of damage due to water covering the floors and improves air circulation around the equipment to minimize the risk of overheating.

Julia's Cookies has two access points to its data center: an entrance and an exit. Security protocols are followed at the entrance to allow employees to enter the data center. The exit is used only as a fire exit. To prevent anyone from entering the data center by using this door, it has no door handles on the outside. The internal auditor will review security protocols in the context of the physical security environment, as discussed later.

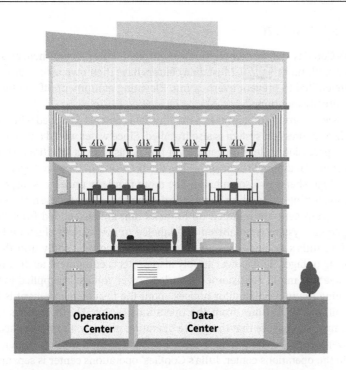

Illustration 14.7 Julia's Cookies' data center is located in the basement of one of its corporate office buildings.

In the Real World   Google and Amazon Data Centers

As the world's biggest companies use more and more computer power, they must expand their data centers. After all, even the cloud exists on equipment in physical locations.

Google, founded in 1998, specializes in search engines, cloud computing, software, and hardware. Amazon, founded in 1994, specializes in e-commerce, cloud computing, and digital streaming. Both multinational technology companies are headquartered in expensive zip codes, with Google in Mountain View, California ("Silicon Valley"), and Amazon in Seattle, Washington.

Due to their immense growth in those areas over the years, expanding data centers near their headquarters has not been financially feasible for either company. To address these financial issues, both companies thought outside the box (or, rather, their zip codes) and searched areas around the United States to purchase land for new data centers.

In 2020, Google purchased more than 165 acres in Ellis County, which is south of the Dallas–Fort Worth area in Texas. Amazon's existing Amazon Web Services (AWS) data center is located near Albany, Ohio, and the company bought 112 *additional* acres in this area for an expansion in 2020. Within 50 miles of the acreage in Albany, there are 15 other data centers.[2] This number includes a data center that Facebook opened in February 2020[3] and another for which Google broke ground in November 2019.[4]

The location of these data centers is strategic. It spreads the risk for Google and Amazon by placing the data centers in geographic areas with relatively mild climates and relatively low risk of hurricane or tornado damage.

Building a new data center is not the only way major companies are managing risk. Other internet giants, including Apple and Netflix, have transferred the risk of building their own data centers by renting space and computing power from Amazon.[5]

What are your thoughts on Amazon and Google choosing central Texas and Albany, Ohio, as locations for opening new data centers? What other outside environment considerations do you think were involved in selecting building locations? How do you think a new data center affects a community?

[2]www.datacenters.com/amazon-aws-new-albany
[3]www.thisweeknews.com/news/20200206/facebook-brings-data-center-online-announces-expansion-in-new-albany
[4]www.google.com/about/datacenters/locations/new-albany/
[5]www.nytimes.com/interactive/2020/05/27/magazine/amazon-coronavirus.html

Inside Environment

Inside, Julia's Cookies' data center is climate controlled. This prevents heat and humidity from damaging the equipment. **CPA** Most data centers have their own air-conditioning units, and the rooms are chilled to prevent overheating. Elevating equipment off the floor allows air to circulate, as already mentioned.

Julia's Cookies' internal auditor notices that the data center is equipped with smoke and water detectors. A fire suppression system is also installed. Since water would damage the equipment, the first fire suppression system triggered by a fire releases a gas to extinguish the fire using a chemical reaction. Traditional water sprinklers are present, but they are triggered only as a last resort. Fire extinguishers are also on hand. The room regularly undergoes inspection by the fire department, and the internal auditor checks the date and signature for the most recent inspection.

Cables for equipment are bundled up to racks that are suspended from the ceiling. This cable management system is organized and labeled to keep cables clean and visible for regular inspection. Julia's Cookies uses an uninterruptible power supply unit that keeps power available during outages. This power supply also protects equipment against power surges to prevent damage that might be sustained if varied power voltage is supplied to it.

The last thing the internal auditor notices about the inside environment is that conditions here are monitored at all times from the operations center. The operations center is where data center employees ensure that things are operating properly. Employees also maintain and update an inventory of the equipment, systems, and data within the data center, and this inventory is kept in the operations center. Julia's Cookies' operations center is separate from the rest of the data center to keep employees away from the equipment when possible. **Illustration 14.8** shows the operations center and other components of Julia's Cookies' inside environment.

Physical Security

CPA Not everyone can enter the data center. In fact, most employees will never see the inside of it. This is the center of the company's IT infrastructure, and unauthorized access

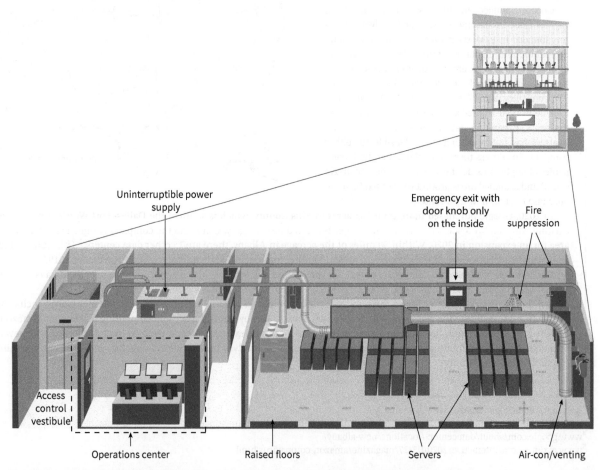

Illustration 14.8 Julia's Cookies' operations center is separate from the rest of the data center.

to this room is a high risk to the equipment that is powering the business. Only employees directly involved with operating the data center are authorized to enter.

To control access, Julia's Cookies uses a multifactor authentication security door. Employees first scan their badges at the door's badge reader. The badges are programmed to authorize entry based on a user's physical access role. To authenticate that the employee scanning a badge is the badge owner, the person enters a PIN on the neighboring keypad. Other authentication options include fingerprint scanning and use of a verbal passcode.

The door is also monitored by cameras that record anyone trying to enter the data center. The authorized personnel have been trained not to hold the doors for others to prevent a second person from entering without scanning through security themselves—a method of circumventing physical access controls often called **piggybacking** or **tailgating**.

For increased security, a second set of doors with security controls could be used. This setup, called an **access control vestibule** (or sometimes a mantrap), creates yet another level of security by allowing only one employee to be in the middle of the two sets of doors at a time.

Julia's Cookies' security doors lead directly to the operations center. From there, any employees who want to continue into the main data center must sign a log and record the times they enter and leave. This allows data center employees to track who enters the room and the duration of their access.

Guests should be granted access to the data center only for legitimate business purposes. Try to determine if Julia's Cookies' new VP of tax insights and analytics should be allowed into the data center in Applied Learning 14.3.

Julia's Cookies   Applied Learning 14.3

Physical Access: Company Tour

Sabree Allil is a staff-level employee who has volunteered to give building tours to new hires as an extra activity. He's done such a great job with tours in the past that today he's escorting a newly hired VP of tax insights and analytics—even though this new hire is levels above Sabree in the organization.

During the tour, Sabree takes the new employee to the doors to the data center and explains that this is where all the company's systems and equipment are secured. The VP asks if the tour could include the data center, and Sabree says no. The VP argues, "I'm the new VP of analytics. Shouldn't I be able to see where the systems my team uses are stored?"

How do you think Sabree should explain to this VP the reasons they are not able to go inside?

SOLUTION

There's no single right way for Sabree to explain the situation to the VP. As long as Sabree is professional and respectful, the VP should respect that Sabree is abiding by company policy. He could emphasize that only necessary personnel are allowed inside to protect the systems and that this rule applies to everyone—not just this VP. He could also point out that the analytics team's own systems are in the data center, so this rule also protects the VP and his team. If that doesn't work, Sabree could tactfully say he will check with his leadership about whether it can be arranged. Sabree's leaders can then take responsibility for ensuring that the VP understands the corporate policy. This takes the pressure off Sabree to say "no" to someone of a significantly higher level than he is, while allowing him to follow company policy and controls.

Physical Access Internal Controls

A robust IT governance process ensures all physical computer systems and data equipment are protected. Common risks to physical equipment and systems include:

- A natural disaster causing damage to systems and equipment may result in a disruption of business activities and financial losses.

- An unauthorized user gaining access to physical equipment may result in theft, malicious attacks, fraud, or data breaches.

- Failure to maintain facilities in accordance with laws and regulations may result in fines and reputational losses.

Managing these risks involves multiple control owners, including the information security manager, data center manager, and facilities manager.

Physically protecting computer systems and data is a critical function of IT governance. These activities can fall under multiple areas of an IT governance plan. **Table 14.4** summarizes internal controls for change management risks, according to the COBIT 2019 framework.

TABLE 14.4 Summary of Risks and Controls in Physical Security

Risk Statement: These control activities apply to all potential risks in this business process.	
Sample Control Activity	**Control Owner**
Policies and procedures for maintaining physical equipment are clearly documented and authorized.	IT security manager
Physical equipment is subject to clear accounting and inventory management policies.	IT security manager/ inventory manager
Risk Statement: A natural disaster causing damage to systems and equipment may result in a disruption of business activities and financial losses.	
Sample Control Activity	**Control Owner**
Specialized equipment and devices are installed to monitor and control the environment of the data center.	Data center manager
IT equipment is stored in a location that minimizes and mitigates susceptibility to environmental threats including air, fire, smoke, and water.	Data center manager
Eating and drinking are prohibited where IT equipment is stored.	Data center manager
Detection devices such as fire alarms are regularly monitored and maintained.	Facilities manager
Risk Statement: An unauthorized user gaining access to physical equipment may result in theft, malicious attacks, fraud, or data breaches.	
Sample Control Activity	**Control Owner**
Access to premises, buildings, and areas is justified, authorized, logged, and monitored.	Facilities manager
Physical access to IT equipment is granted to each user, based on business need.	IT security manager
Physical access to IT equipment, including access level and authorization of receiving access, is clearly documented.	IT security manager
Physical access to IT equipment is periodically reviewed for appropriateness. Inappropriate access is immediately revoked.	IT security manager
Users entering rooms where IT equipment is held are required to scan a badge or a fingerprint to gain access.	IT security manager/ facilities manager
Risk Statement: Failure to maintain facilities in accordance with laws and regulations may result in fines and reputational losses.	
Sample Control Activity	**Control Owner**
Facilities are managed in line with regulatory, health, and safety guidelines.	Data center manager

CONCEPT REVIEW QUESTIONS

1. What is a data center, and how does a data center interact with the outside environment?
   Ans. A company uses a data center to protect the physical components on which systems and data are stored. Also known as a network operations center (NOC), it is an area in a building—or even an entire building—that is dedicated to the physical storage of computer and telecommunication systems. Data centers can be either onsite or offsite. A data center is the heart of a business; it keeps the business alive by providing connectivity across all business functions and maintaining operations.

2. What is an access control vestibule?

   Ans. For increased security of data center, a second set of doors with security controls can be used. This setup, called an access control vestibule (or sometimes a mantrap), creates yet another level of security by allowing only one employee to be in the middle of the two sets of doors at a time.

3. Google and Amazon have invested in off-site data centers, but other companies, like Apple and Netflix, have not. What is another way for these companies to reduce risk?

   Ans. Another way for these companies to reduce risk is by renting off-site data center space and computer power.

14.4 How Do We Keep Our Systems Running?

Learning Objective ❹
Compare backup and recovery efforts.

While it is impossible to predict every situation that could cause a company's business operations to be disrupted or put its data at risk, businesses must consider multiple worst-case scenarios when designing their internal control environments. Data loss is a significant risk that can be addressed with IT governance planning. The prevention of data loss, including a plan for backing up data, is an important part of ensuring that a business continues operations regardless of disruptive events like disasters or system failures.

Business Continuity Planning

CPA **Business continuity planning (BCP)** is a set of procedures that a business undertakes to protect employees, other stakeholders, and assets in the event of a disruptive event. Disruptive events come in many forms: floods, tornadoes, cyberattacks, political disturbances, and even global pandemics. The need to prepare for and respond to these events is crucial. Events businesses have faced in recent years include Hurricane Harvey in Houston, Texas, and the unprecedented hurricane season in 2020; social unrest in Hong Kong; and the global COVID-19 pandemic.

BCP ensures that a business and all its processes continue running. BCP is an internal control that includes multiple plans:

- *Crisis reaction plans* indicating who leads the organization's response
- *Communication plans,* which could include global emergency messaging systems or call trees at smaller companies
- *Evacuation directions* for physical evacuation of a building or city
- *Essential equipment* for operations being protected or having alternative equipment available in a secondary location
- *Alternative operation sites* where employees can work should the primary building become unavailable
- *Return to normal procedures* that prescribe how the business will return to normal operations following a disruptive event

A BCP program is always evolving, and companies use lessons learned from previous events to improve their BCP programs.

BCP is an area where many accounting professionals have made interesting careers for themselves. Accounting majors are uniquely prepared for this area due to their studies of holistic business operations, financial and operating specifics, risk identification, and business processes.

Illustration 14.9 shows that **disaster recovery (DR)** is a subset of BCP. While disasters have been around forever, the 9/11 terrorist attacks in New York City in 2001 intensified companies' interest in DR planning. **CPA** DR plans focus on the restoration of a firm's IT infrastructure and operations after a crisis. DR is a key part of a business continuity plan; it covers all the procedures related to backups for servers, systems, and data.

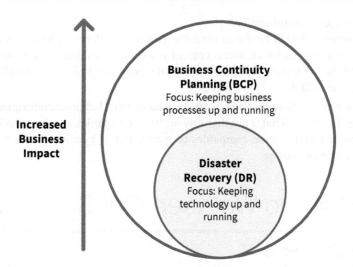

Illustration 14.9 Disaster recovery (DR) is a subset of business continuity planning (BCP).

Julia's Cookies uses a variety of BCP activities to ensure that its operations continue during a disruptive event. Like other companies, Julia's Cookies prepares these plans well in advance, as no one knows when a disaster might happen. Explore Julia's Cookies' response to a global pandemic in Applied Learning 14.4.

Julia's Cookies | Applied Learning 14.4

Business Continuity Planning: Global Pandemic

In response to a global pandemic, Julia's Cookies closes all its brick-and-mortar stores and directs its corporate employees to work from home to decrease the spread of a new virus. While frontline employees, such as cashiers and bakers, are unable to work remotely, Julia's Cookies provides additional paid time off and sick days to ensure these employees are protected during the lockdown closures.

Julia's Cookies requires all nonessential corporate employees to work remotely, including those in the Accounting, Internal Audit, and Human Resources departments. The company even provides financial support to employees who need to purchase equipment like monitors or desks to create a long-term work-from-home environment.

Julia's Cookies has activated its business continuity plan. Do you think moving corporate employees from working in-office to working from home falls under any of the following BCP areas?

Crisis reaction plans   Disaster recovery

Communication plans   Alternative operation sites

Return to normal procedures

SOLUTION

Having a plan in place for employees to work remotely is a large endeavor that is part of the business continuity plan for alternative operation sites. Julia's Cookies' BCP team must monitor the location of employees and ensure they are provided with adequate equipment and internet access to perform their work remotely.

During DR planning, companies categorize systems and data based on importance. Importance is determined by things like how the business would be impacted if it couldn't access the system or if it lost the data, as well as the acceptable amount of downtime a system can endure before it significantly interrupts business activities. For example, Julia's Cookies uses a three-category system for prioritizing the importance of its data (**Table 14.5**).

TABLE 14.5 Three-Category System of Prioritization

Category	Impact	Example of Business Process	Maximum Downtime
Critical (or "high")	Detrimental	**Customer Website/Application** Julia's Cookies' mobile ordering application is a critical part of the company's ability to earn revenue by making sales. If the app is down too long, customers may not trust Julia's Cookies in the future; they may decide to order from a competitor.	Up to 2 hours

TABLE 14.5 (*Continued*)

Category	Impact	Example of Business Process	Maximum Downtime
Moderate (or "medium")	Moderate	**Human Resources Hiring System** Julia's Cookies uses an HR system that captures data from new hires. If this system is down for up to three days, it doesn't stop Julia's Cookies from operating. It will be problematic if the system is down for long enough to interrupt payroll processing as employees need their biweekly paychecks.	Up to 72 hours
Low	Minimal	**Employee Benefits System** Julia's Cookies uses an internal website to grant employees access to their benefits: health insurance, 401(k) contributions, and even a legal support program. While this access is helpful for employees, they can also access their benefits directly from each provider's website. Having the Julia's Cookies' site down for multiple days will not impact employees' ability to work or access their benefits.	Over 72 hours

The importance of an organization's data determines the location, quantity, and frequency of backups. Not all systems and data need to be backed up at a fully operational facility or every day. Companies use the level of importance to determine three key considerations: the backup site (location), the backup strategy (quantity), and the backup cycle (frequency).

Backup Sites

 CPA A **backup site** is a physical location where company personnel will go to recover systems and data after a disaster. A backup site is a re-creation of a data center and provides the company with a place of operations if the data center is impacted during a disaster. Backup sites can be hot, warm, or cold. The names relate to the amount of effort it will take to make the backup site operational in the event of a disaster.

From hot to cold, the difficulty of restarting operations goes from easier to harder, and the costs of maintaining the backup site go from more expensive to cheaper.

CPA A hot backup site, which is immediately operational after a disaster, is the most expensive:

- A **hot backup site** runs and backs up continuously. Data is continuously backed up on a second-by-second or minute-by-minute basis, making the hot backup site a ready-to-go center of data operations.
- A unique risk for hot backup sites is that a virus entering the live systems is immediately backed up to the hot site.
- Most hot backup sites are offsite and contain an exact copy of the main server and live systems. This provides the best protection against natural disasters that might destroy the building where operations take place by separating the backup site geographically.
- It is not cheap to maintain two data centers at the same time. Companies need to consider the costs and benefits of a hot backup site versus more affordable options.

Many companies, like Julia's Cookies, choose a geographically safe location for offsite backups. Julia's Cookies' hot backup site is located in a rented facility in northern New Jersey. It contains servers, telecommunications devices, and all equipment found in the San Francisco data center. If Julia's Cookies' corporate office in San Francisco were damaged in a disaster such as an earthquake, the hot backup site could be up and running in no time.

CPA Another option is a warm backup site:

- A **warm backup site** is equipped with servers ready for systems to be installed and contains only some of the equipment needed to ramp up operations.

- It might take more than a couple of hours to switch over to a warm backup site, but the cost of maintaining it is significantly less than the cost of maintaining a hot backup site.
- When it comes to importing data backups, the data at a warm backup site may only be updated at the end of each day instead of in real time.

Companies that use warm backup sites face the possibility of losing one day or more of work, depending on how frequently data is backed up.

`CPA` A cold backup site is the final type of backup site:

- A **cold backup site** is an almost empty room with no servers or equipment ready. It has physical space, power, climate control, and physical security controls but is otherwise unequipped.
- It is offline—and it is empty! Data is not stored in a cold site because systems are not installed. Significant time must be spent installing equipment, systems, and data. Recovering to a cold backup site often takes days or weeks.
- A cold backup site is the cheapest option, but it is the type of site that takes the most time to begin using.

Table 14.6 provides an easy reference summarizing the three types of backups.

TABLE 14.6 Hot, Warm, and Cold Backups

Site Type	Cost	Backup Speed	Recovery Speed
Hot	Highest	Continuous	Fastest
Warm	Medium	Depends on data backup cycle	Medium
Cold	Lowest	Depends on data backup cycle	Slowest

Backup Strategies

A backup site is invaluable if an entire data center goes down, but problems can also arise with the day-to-day data being created in a business. The data center may be operational, but a specific system or database may be subject to a technical issue that results in the loss of data. For this reason, companies use more than just a backup site for their data center; they also make and store backups of their data.

When a disaster strikes, a business focuses on two metrics (**Illustration 14.10**):

- **Recovery time objective (RTO):** How much time a system can be down before it causes significant damage to the business
- **Recovery point objective (RPO):** How much data can be lost before it causes significant damage to the business

RTO also considers how long it takes the IT department to restore the system and reload the data from backups. Systems that have higher criticality are prioritized to be recovered first. Some systems can be down for only seconds. Imagine if the New York Stock Exchange system went down in the middle of a trading day. It could be disastrous to the market, as millions of trades are made throughout the day. In contrast, if a business is down in the middle of the night and the business is not performing major operations at that time, there won't be as much data loss.

Illustration 14.10 Recovery point objective (RPO) is the time since the last backup, while recovery time objective (RTO) is the time it takes to resume operations.

To mitigate the risk of losing data, it is important to perform data backups. A **data backup** involves copying computer data and storing the copy in a separate location so it can be used to restore data to a system if the original data is lost. Backups can take up a lot of storage space and time, so companies use the importance of a system to determine which backup strategy to implement.

A **backup strategy** determines *which* data is being stored during a data backup. There are three basic types of backup strategies: full, differential, and incremental.

Full Backups

CPA **Full backups** involve copying all existing data in its entirety every time. This is the slowest of the backup strategies and requires a lot of storage, as it means creating a full copy of your data every day.

To understand full backups, let's use the following assumptions:

1. You use your laptop for classwork and create multiple files every day for your various courses.
2. You use a cloud storage solution like Dropbox to save copies of your files as backups in case something happens to your laptop.
3. You do schoolwork Monday through Friday.
4. You save the copies of your files to Dropbox every night after you complete your schoolwork.
5. When you save the copies of your files to Dropbox, you create a new folder with that day's date.

Illustration 14.11 shows your process of creating full backups for a week:

- On Monday night, you copy everything you have ever done for your classes to a folder on Dropbox labeled "Monday." This includes work you did in previous weeks (A) and new work you completed on Monday (B).
- On Tuesday, you repeat this process, and the "Tuesday" folder contains preexisting data (A), Monday's data (B), and the new files you made on Tuesday (C).
- By Friday, you have six folders that contain data: one for the initial full backup and one for each subsequent day. That is, you have five copies of the data you generated on Monday (B) because you saved Monday's data on Monday, Tuesday, Wednesday, and so on; you have four copies of Tuesday's data (C), three copies of Wednesday's data (D), two copies of Thursday's (E), and one copy of Friday's (F).

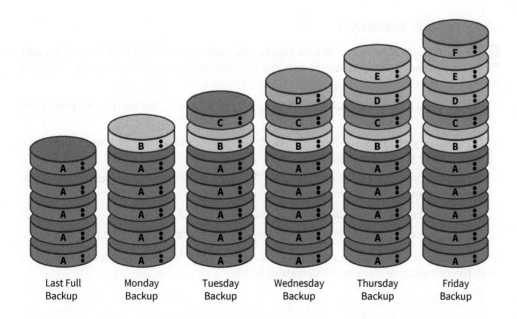

| Last Full Backup | Monday Backup | Tuesday Backup | Wednesday Backup | Thursday Backup | Friday Backup |

Illustration 14.11 Full backups build on one another every day throughout the week.

If you continue this method throughout your course term, you might run out of space on Dropbox very quickly, and your folders could take hours each day to transfer to Dropbox as they continue to get larger.

Differential Backups

CPA **Differential backups** involve copying all data created since the most recent full backup every time. Differential backups are the middle ground of backup strategies. They take a moderate amount of time and storage space.

We're going to add one more assumption to your Dropbox backups to explain a differential backup strategy:

- On Sundays, you perform a full backup of your preexisting data.
- Your most recent full backup was on Sunday (A).
- Your differential backup on Monday will only contain new data made on Monday (B), which is all the new data that has been created since your most recent full backup.
- On Tuesday, your backup will contain Monday's data (B) and Tuesday's data (C).
- The Wednesday backup has all the files you have created since the full backup on Sunday (B, C, and D).
- By Friday, you have one copy of your preexisting data—your most recent full backup (A), five copies of the files you made on Monday (B), four copies of the files you made on Tuesday (C), and so on.

As you can see in **Illustration 14.12**, a differential backup has some similarities to a full backup but takes up less storage space.

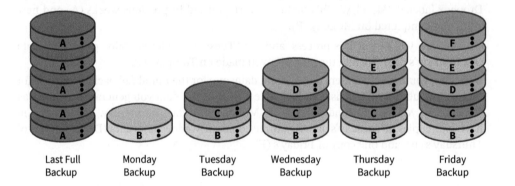

Illustration 14.12 Differential backups only save new files made since the last full backup, and these files build on one another throughout the week.

Incremental Backups

CPA **Incremental backups** involve copying only new or updated data with each backup. This is the cheapest strategy, and it uses the least amount of storage space. Here's how it works:

- Just as with a differential backup, on Sunday you perform a full backup of your preexisting data (A).
- On Monday, you only save Monday's new data (B), which is all the new data that has been created since your last full backup.
- On Tuesday, your backup will *only* contain Tuesday's new data (C). On Tuesday, your most recent backup was Monday night's incremental backup.
- On Wednesday's backup, only Wednesday's data (D) is saved.
- This continues throughout the week. By Friday, each day's data has been saved only one time.

Unlike differential backups, incremental backups save only the new data created since your most recent backup of *any type* (**Illustration 14.13**).

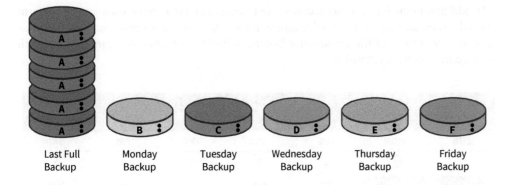

Illustration 14.13 Incremental backups only restore new files made since the last backup of any type, and these files do not build on one another.

To address the differing levels of importance of different systems and their data, businesses mix the different backup strategies. Don't be surprised if your company uses more than one backup strategy to achieve its data storage goals. While all three strategies are often used, incremental backups are the most cost-effective as they use the least space and take the least time. **Table 14.7** summarizes the three types of backup strategies.

TABLE 14.7 The Three Types of Backup Strategies

Strategy	Data Backed Up	Backup Time	Storage Space
Full backup	All data	Slowest	High
Differential backup	All data since last full backup	Moderate	Moderate
Incremental backup	New data since most recent backup of any type	Fast	Lowest

Backup Cycles

In our discussion of backup sites, you may have noticed that only a hot backup site has a continuous backup of data. At warm and cold backup sites, the availability of data depends on the backup cycle used because data backups must be brought to the backup site to get it up and running.

A **backup cycle** determines *when* data is being stored during a data backup. This is the frequency with which data is backed up. All three of the data backup strategies in the previous section can be implemented using various backup cycles. In our Dropbox example, you were backing up your school folders every day. In a hot backup site, data is backed up every second or minute. Backup cycles are important when planning for RPO. Recall that RPO determines how much data can be lost before it impacts the business. Critical systems with lower RPO values use more frequent backup cycles. Each company will have its own process of determining which backup cycle is needed.

CPA One of the most common backup cycles is known as the **grandfather-father-son redundant backup** scheme (**Illustration 14.14**). This scheme is based on three backup cycles (monthly, weekly, and daily):

- **Grandfather cycle:** Full backup, once a month
- **Father cycle:** Full backup, once a week
- **Son cycle:** Incremental or differential backup, every day

These three cycles implement an incremental or differential backup strategy. Grandfather and father are full backups, while son is incremental or differential. Recalling the Dropbox example, you can understand why. Making a full backup every day quickly monopolized Dropbox storage space, and by Friday, it took a significant amount of time for the folder to upload. When you did a differential or incremental backup daily but did a full backup only on Sunday, it took significantly less time and space. This is why the grandfather-father-son backup scheme only does incremental or differential backups on a daily basis.

In addition to the backup cycles that we've discussed so far, companies may also perform quarterly, semi-annual, and annual backups for safekeeping. Businesses may also keep as many as four or more of the grandfather-father-son backup schemes to ensure they have full coverage from previous months.

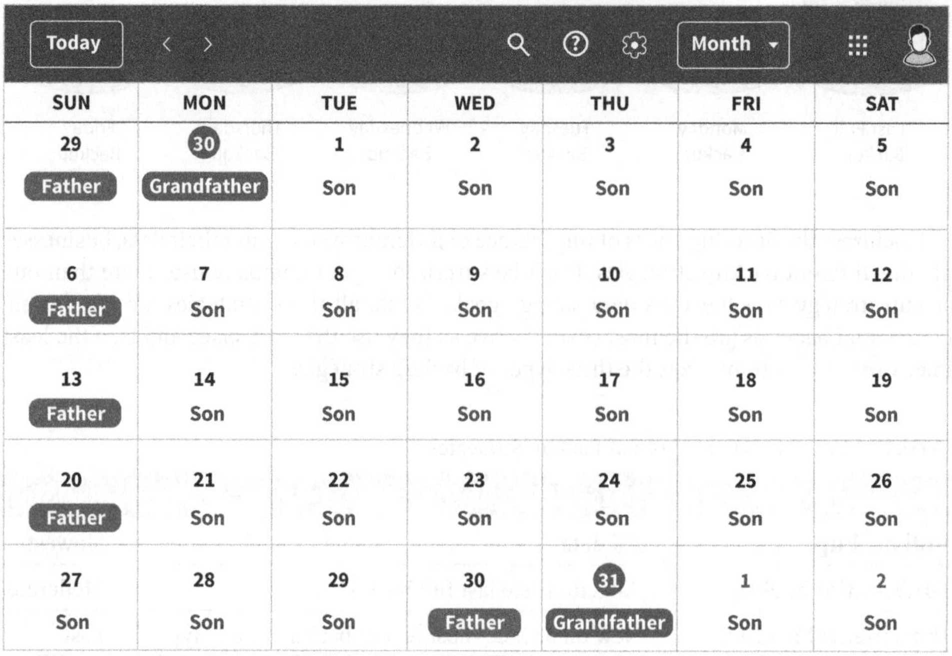

Today < >				🔍 ⑦ ⚙	Month ▾	⸬ 👤
SUN	**MON**	**TUE**	**WED**	**THU**	**FRI**	**SAT**
29 Father	③⓪ Grandfather	1 Son	2 Son	3 Son	4 Son	5 Son
6 Father	7 Son	8 Son	9 Son	10 Son	11 Son	12 Son
13 Father	14 Son	15 Son	16 Son	17 Son	18 Son	19 Son
20 Father	21 Son	22 Son	23 Son	24 Son	25 Son	26 Son
27 Son	28 Son	29 Son	30 Father	③① Grandfather	1 Son	2 Son

Illustration 14.14 The grandfather-father-son redundant backup scheme using monthly, weekly, and daily backups.

Why Does It Matter to Your Career?

Thoughts from an Accounting Analytics Manager, Investment Firm

- IT auditors often test a company's backup strategies and cycles to determine if the backups are successful and whether the selected strategies and cycles address the importance of the data being saved. It is part of annual SOX compliance testing, and many businesses use COBIT 2019 as their control testing framework.

- All of your work will reside on your company's systems. It would be devastating to find out that systems crashed, and years' worth of work was lost. So as an accounting professional, you may not be the one performing backups, but you can rest assured knowing your company has backup strategies and cycles in place.

Data Storage Internal Controls

Shutting down operations or losing data can lead to financial loss, inability to perform daily operations, violations of regulatory requirements such as financial reporting, or reputational damage related to being unprepared. Disruptive events may result in interruption of business operations, the primary data center becoming inoperable, or the loss of company data.

Recall that disruptive events can come in many forms. Whether caused by a natural disaster striking the data center or a malicious cyber attacker corrupting the company's systems, data loss has a critical impact on a company. Businesses plan for data loss and mitigate the risk by implementing internal controls such as business continuity planning, backup sites for the data center, and regularly scheduled backup cycles for data.

While frameworks like COBIT 2019 have dozens of controls to mitigate the risks of disruptive events, the ones you have learned about provide a glimpse into the steps that companies take to plan for the unexpected. **Table 14.8** summarizes and expands on sample control activities and control owners based on the discussion in this section.

TABLE 14.8 Summary of Risks and Controls in Business Continuity

Risk Statement: A disruptive event may result in the interruption of business operations and systems.

Sample Control Activity	Control Owner
A BCP is developed and maintained based on the strategy and objectives of the company.	BCP manager
All concerned internal and external parties are provided with regular training regarding BCP procedures and their roles and responsibilities in the event of disruption.	BCP manager
A separate disaster recovery plan is developed and maintained based on the strategy and objectives of the company.	IT manager/disaster recovery manager
The BCP is reviewed periodically to ensure it is up to date and reflects current business requirements.	BCP manager

Risk Statement: A disruptive event may result in the primary data center becoming inoperable.

Sample Control Activity	Control Owner
The disaster recovery plan includes considerations for alternative equipment sites (hot site, warm site, cold site) to ensure operational continuity.	Data center manager

Risk Statement: A disruptive event may result in loss of data stored on the primary servers.

Sample Control Activity	Control Owner
The availability of critical data is managed to ensure operational continuity.	IT manager
Data backup strategies and cycles are implemented to meet the needs of the business's objectives.	IT manager/disaster recovery manager

CONCEPT REVIEW QUESTIONS

1. **CPA** What do you understand by business continuity planning (BCP)?
   Ans. BCP is a set of procedures that a business undertakes to protect employees, other stakeholders, and assets in the event of a disruptive event. Disruptive events come in many forms: floods, tornadoes, cyberattacks, political disturbances, and even global pandemics.

2. List the multiple plans under BCP.
   Ans. BCP is an internal control that includes multiple plans:
   - Crisis reaction plans indicating who leads the organization's response
   - Communication plans including global emergency messaging systems or call trees at smaller companies
   - Evacuation directions for physical evacuation of a building or city
   - Essential equipment for operations being protected or having alternative equipment available in a secondary location
   - Return to normal procedures that prescribe how the business will return to normal operations following a disruptive event

3. **CPA** What does the term "backup site" mean?
   Ans. A backup site is a physical location where company personnel go to recover systems and data after a disaster. A backup site is a re-creation of a data center and provides the company with a place of operations if the data center is impacted during a disaster. Backup sites can be hot, warm, or cold. The names relate to the amount of effort it will take to make the backup site operational in the event of a disaster.

4. What are the two metrics that are focused during disaster strikes at the data center?
   Ans. The two metrics that are focused during disaster strikes at the data center are:
   - Recovery time objective (RTO): How much time a system can be down before it causes significant damage to the business?
   - Recovery point objective (RPO): How much data can be lost before it causes significant damage to the business?

5. **CPA** What are full, differential, and incremental backups?

   Ans. Full backups involve copying all existing data in its entirety every time. This is the slowest of the backup strategies and requires a lot of storage, as it means creating a full copy of the data every day. Differential backups involve copying all data created since the most recent full backup every time. Differential backups are the middle ground of backup strategies. They take a moderate amount of time and storage space. Incremental backups involve copying only new or updated data with each backup. This is the cheapest strategy, and it uses the least amount of storage space.

6. **CPA** If a company were to utilize the grandfather-father-son backup scheme, what backup cycles are implemented?

   Ans. One of the most common backup cycles is known as the grandfather-father-son redundant backup scheme. It is based on three backup cycles (monthly, weekly, and daily):

   - Grandfather cycle: full backup, once a month
   - Father cycle: full backup, once a week
   - Son cycle: incremental or differential backup, every day

14.5 How Do We Make Changes to Systems?

Learning Objective ❺
Summarize the change management process.

When Julia's Cookies decided to go public, it began planning its initial public offering (IPO) and became subject to new regulations—specifically, the Sarbanes-Oxley Act of 2002 (SOX), which has extensive internal control requirements and requires the use of a framework for creating the control environment. Julia's Cookies made a few preparations for these new regulatory requirements:

- A team devoted to enterprise risk management was assembled to assess the company's risks and control environment.
- The team performed an enterprise risk assessment and designed an adequate system of internal controls. Team members used COSO and COBIT as frameworks to guide them in the decision-making process.
- As the final step before its IPO, Julia's Cookies hired an external audit firm to perform a SOX audit.

The team was confident that it had in place an effective system for internal controls that would pass regulatory review. Things seemed to be going well until the IT audit team came to Julia's Cookies' leaders with a question: Why does the new financial reporting system produce mathematically inaccurate numbers?

The system in question was developed in house, which means that Julia's Cookies employees built it rather than buying software from a third party. The system takes numbers from a heavily used database, calculates some formulas, and inputs them into another system that generates the financial reports. While this seems simple enough, the enterprise risk management team members realized they'd never heard of this system, and it was not part of their internal control planning.

The team asked the financial accounting analysts, who seemed to be the only users of this system, for an update. It turned out that the financial accounting analytics manager had a brilliant idea: his team was manually calculating necessary formulas by copying and pasting data into an Excel sheet with the formulas, then uploading the results into a system by hand. He thought automating this process would be a value-add to his team and Julia's Cookies' accounting process. The manager didn't know how to request this, so he contacted a friend in the IT department who specialized in robotic process automation (RPA).

This friend built a simple automation process in Alteryx that directly connected to the source data, calculated the formulas, and automatically imported the results into the system. Unfortunately, the formula calculation was programmed incorrectly. The accounting manager didn't understand programming and was unable to review the code used. At the same time, the programmer didn't understand accounting formulas and was unable to validate the formula's accuracy. **Illustration 14.15** shows the change from the manual process to the automated RPA process when this system was implemented.

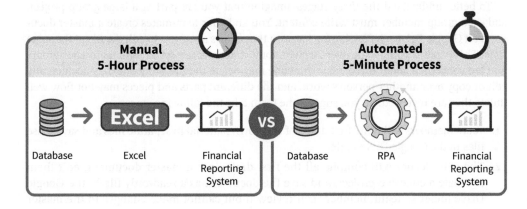

Illustration 14.15
A five-hour manual process is transformed into a five-minute automated process using robotic process automation (RPA).

Employees with programming skills are often presented with small requests like changing the way a system operates. Without formal procedures explaining how to request these updates, programmers don't know how to respond when direct requests come their way. As a result of the situation at Julia's Cookies, the external auditors advised the company to implement a formal change management process that provides specific steps to follow when a new system needs to be designed or an existing system needs to be updated.

The Change Management Process

In the 21st century, most organizational data resides in databases and is captured by systems. The data is often captured by the following automated business processes, among others:

- General ledger
- Human resources administration
- Finance trading
- Customer relationship management

These systems require updates as technology or business needs change. You have probably received an email from your school, warning you that a certain site or program will be unavailable for a brief period. During that time, the IT department might be implementing changes to the system.

Changes to a system are not always visible to users. For example, when the new tax rates are published each year, the tax department may work with the IT department to code new tax rates into the system. In this case, as a user of the program, you won't notice a change in the program, except for the tax rate that performs the internal calculations. Sometimes you will see such a change. For example, if the marketing department decides to change the color of the company website, it works with the IT department to code the change for a visible impact.

Change management is a standardized process that decreases risk by controlling the identification and implementation of required changes to a system. Updates to a system can have a significant impact on users. Changes must be made quickly and reliably, and they need to be reviewed appropriately before they are finalized. Poorly executed system changes can result in instability or lack of integrity.

A formal **change management process** consists of three stages that changes to a system's code must pass through. These stages occur in isolated environments that enforce segregation of duties for each of the three steps of the change management process:

1. Creating changes in the test environment
2. Evaluating accuracy of changes in the model environment
3. Implementing changes in the production environment

These three environments are isolated from one another to prevent a change from being accidentally implemented. An incorrect code change could be devastating to a company. Imagine that a developer accidentally codes an extra 0 on the end of everyone's paycheck and publishes it. Your employer could potentially pay millions of dollars in excess of regular employee salary before the mistake is fixed. Change management is important because it helps mitigate risk.

To better understand the three stages, imagine that you are part of a large group project, and each group member must write content. You and your teammates create a master document on Google Drive—a file-sharing location that allows all of you to edit the file at the same time. This paper is going to be over 20 pages long, and there are seven authors in your group. You are concerned about three risks: someone may delete the file, someone may accidentally edit or copy over another person's work, and the different parts and pieces may not flow well unless they are reviewed. So you suggest the team take the following steps:

1. Team members will write first drafts of their own material in separate files and save those files in the Google Drive folder.

2. The team leader will compile all the first drafts into a master document, edit them to create a cohesive project, and save the document as a read-only file in the Google Drive folder so team members can review it but cannot make changes to the master document.

3. After making all edits, the team leader will then save the final draft file and submit it to the professor on behalf of the group.

This is a change management process. **Illustration 14.16** relates the steps your group takes to the three stages of a formal change management process.

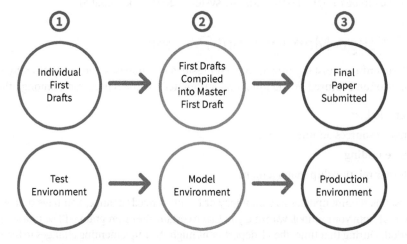

Illustration 14.16 The stages in the change management process can be compared to the steps involved in writing a group assignment.

By having team members write individual first drafts, your group is using a test environment. These individual document files won't give each team member an idea of the final results because they are separated from the rest of the paper. However, they are controlled and allow all of the members to write their own sections to the best of their abilities. Errors made here won't impact anyone's grade.

The master first draft file is similar to the model environment. This is where changes are put into a model of the final system. Your paper is now combined into a cohesive document that team members can review for issues. Again, errors here won't affect anyone's grade, but this environment gives everyone a better idea of whether the final product will work.

The final draft your team leader submits will affect your grade. Essentially, your paper has entered the production environment, where all the changes have an impact.

Now that we have looked at the basics of these environments, let's get into the details of how they work for systems.

Test Environment

The **test environment** is often called a "sandbox" because developers can "play" here without having any impact on the actual system. This is where developers design and test their code.

They receive a copy of the existing code and make changes in their own developer programs. The test environment is not connected to the system the code belongs to, so nothing developers do in it will impact the system. Using a sandbox also provides security protection for a business, as developers only have access to the test environment, and their code must be approved prior to publication. This ensures that developers don't make rogue changes that might disrupt the business.

While the test environment is in use, the system is still available for users to access. This limits the necessary downtime and allows the developers to take the time needed to code changes. **Illustration 14.17** shows the steps followed when using a test environment.

You might wonder why code changes should matter to you when you're studying accounting. We can use a tax example to illustrate. Assume you are a tax accountant at Julia's Cookies. Your team uses in-house-developed tax software, which is an information system, to calculate taxes. The IRS has issued new tax rates, but the system is currently programmed with the old rates, and the IT department needs to update it.

To update the system with the new tax rates, the Julia's Cookies tax team decides to follow these steps:

1. **User submits a request ticket.** As the user, you submit a request ticket in the IT ticketing system. You include in the ticket details of all the needed changes so the developer knows what needs to be done. After the ticket is submitted, it goes into the developer's work queue.

2. **Developer writes code.** The developer codes the new tax rates into a test environment. You are able to access your tax system while this is happening.

3. **Code is routed to the model environment.** Once the coding is finished, the developer attaches the code, along with testing documentation, to the request-for-change ticket in the IT ticketing system, and the ticket is routed to the next stage, which operates in the model environment.

User Submits
Request Ticket

Developer
Writes Code

Code Routed to
Model Environment

Illustration 14.17 In the test environment, users submit requests, developers write code, and code is sent to be modeled.

Model Environment

The **model environment** is a recent copy of the live system which is used to implement the code in an environment that looks almost like production. Due to the need for segregation of duties, the developer no longer has access to the model environment. The steps of the model environment continue from the test environment as follows (**Illustration 14.18**):

4. **Code creates a model system for testing.** The code that the developer designed is implemented, and Julia's Cookies' tax accountants must test it to see if it works.

5. **User approves changes.** As the user, you must sign off and approve the results of the coding change. This stage of the process is called **user acceptance testing**. In this tax example, you are given access to a copy of your tax software that contains fake data for you to test. You run the software as you normally do to ensure that the tax rates the developer coded are doing the correct calculation based on the IRS standards you provided when you submitted the request-for-change ticket. After you check for accuracy and accept the code, you sign off on the model stage of the request-for-change ticket in the IT ticketing system, and the ticket is routed to an IT analyst for approval.

6. **IT analyst approves and documents testing.** The IT analyst again tests the functionality of the code to see if the code works as it should—this time from a technical programming perspective. The analyst documents details and the results of the test but cannot make changes to the code. Only developers can change code, once again to maintain segregation of duties.

7. **Code routed to production environment.** When the IT reviewers approve the change in the IT ticketing system, the ticket is routed to the next stage, which operates in the production environment.

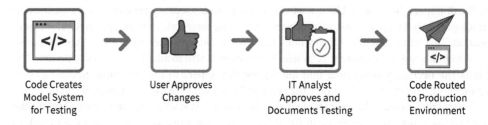

Illustration 14.18   In the model environment, the changes are tested before the code is sent to the production environment.

Code Creates Model System for Testing → User Approves Changes → IT Analyst Approves and Documents Testing → Code Routed to Production Environment

Production Environment

The final stage involves the **production environment**, during which the updated system goes live and is available for end users. This stage involves the following steps, which build on the steps from the previous stages (**Illustration 14.19**):

8. **Code is saved in production environment.** The production environment is separate from the other environments, and only Production Control employees have access to it.

9. **Production Control implements code.** Production Control cannot make changes to the authorized code. They are only responsible for implementing the code in the live system. During the code implementation, the system may go offline for some time. Such updates are often made over a weekend, when fewer users are working.

10. **Code is live in system.** Once the new code is published in the system's production environment, the system updates go live, and users accessing the system begin using the changes.

11. **Request ticket is closed.** The request-for-change ticket is closed, and the requestor (you) is notified that the requested change is now live.

Illustration 14.19   Code is implemented and systems go live in the production environment.

Code Is Saved in Production Environment → Production Control Implements Code → Code Is Live in System → Request Ticket Is Closed

Review the change management environments in **Table 14.9** and then help match Julia's Cookies' request tickets to its current change management environment in Applied Learning 14.5.

TABLE 14.9 The Three Change Management Environments

Environment	What Happens	Who Has Access	Output(s) of the Environment
Test	The developer writes the code that the user requested.	Developer	Code
Model	The user reviews the outcome of the code when it runs in the model environment. If the outcome is accurate, the user approves the change. The IT analysts test the functionality of the code and authorize it. They document their testing.	Business user (requestor) IT analyst	User approver IT approver Testing documentation
Production	The Production Control employee implements the code into production. This employee cannot change the code, to ensure that only the code that was tested and approved by IT and the user is implemented in the system.	Production Control employee	"Live" system with updates

---

Julia's Cookies   Applied Learning 14.5

Change Management: ServiceNow Ticket Review

Julia's Cookies uses IT service request software called ServiceNow. This software allows users to open request tickets for change management. The system routes request tickets through the three stages of the formal change management process.

As an auditor, Kae is testing the change management process. Part of her testing is to check the status of request tickets to ensure they are in the correct stages of the change management process. Which of the three stages (test, model, or production) of the change management process should each of the follow request tickets be in?

 Ticket A: Currently needs user acceptance testing.
 Ticket B: Developers are coding in the sandbox.
 Ticket C: An IT analyst is documenting all testing that has been completed.
 Ticket D: Production Control just finished implementing code.

SOLUTION

Ticket A: User acceptance testing is part of the *model environment*, where code goes into a copy of the real system. Users use the system as they normally would and note whether things are working as expected or whether bugs are encountered.

Ticket B: The sandbox is another term for the *testing environment*. This is where developers write and edit code to create the requested changes.

Ticket C: Testing documentation is done in the *model environment*. After user acceptance testing, the IT analyst performs technical testing. The results of both tests are documented before the code moves to the production environment.

Ticket D: Code is considered "live" once it is implemented. This is the last step that occurs in the *production environment*. After the code is implemented, the request ticket is closed.

Differentiating Between Normal and Emergency Changes

When you need medical attention, you assess your current situation and decide whether you should go immediately to an emergency room or whether you can wait to see your primary caregiver during a scheduled visit. Businesses use a similar philosophy when they decide how to categorize system changes.

The formal system change process involves several steps and approvers, which can impact how long it takes to go from the initial request to completion. For this reason, companies must prioritize change requests based on their users, impact on the business, and costs. Companies might have multiple priority ranges, but there are two categories of change requests that most businesses use:

- *Normal changes* follow the formal change management process to avoid the risk of mistakes. Normal changes are for organizational benefit (such as efficiency) or to update information (as in our tax rate update example). This is the most common type of change implemented in an organization.

- *Emergency changes* require immediate action to mitigate significant risks such as a system outage, compliance issue, or security risk. If you are an accountant for an organization and you find a system error that results in a significant misstatement for financial reporting, you'll file an emergency change request ticket. When Julia's Cookies fixed the calculation in its system that was identified during its SOX audit, it was making an emergency change because the error was creating miscalculations in financial reports.

The emergency change process differs from the normal change process because an emergency change must be completed as soon as possible. For emergency changes, the process is shortened by excluding the model stage. The code goes straight from the testing stage into production. After the code is live, the IT analyst and the business stakeholder both approve and the IT analyst documents the testing, normally within 24–48 hours. While eliminating the model stage is risky, it is less risky than leaving the system in a vulnerable state. **Illustration 14.20** shows the full life cycle of an emergency change request as it bypasses the model environment.

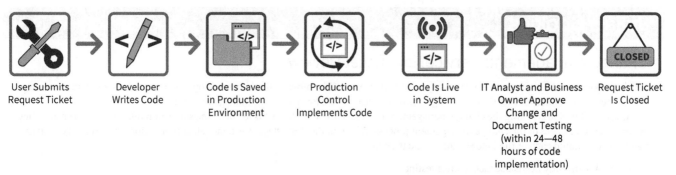

| User Submits Request Ticket | Developer Writes Code | Code Is Saved in Production Environment | Production Control Implements Code | Code Is Live in System | IT Analyst and Business Owner Approve Change and Document Testing (within 24—48 hours of code implementation) | Request Ticket Is Closed |

Illustration 14.20 Emergency change bypasses the model environment and moves directly to the production environment.

Change Management Internal Controls

Making any changes to existing systems is a high risk for many companies. Unauthorized or incorrectly executed changes to a system may result in:

- Incompatibility with existing infrastructure
- Disruptions in ongoing business processes due to system malfunctions or outages
- Data breaches or malicious code being programmed into the systems
- Internal fraud, which occurs when an employee steals from the business

Change management controls address such risks by providing a formal procedure for approving, executing, and reviewing changes to the company's systems. **Table 14.10** summarizes the internal control activities for change management found in COBIT 2019 that were discussed in this section.

TABLE 14.10 Summary of Risks and Controls in Change Management

Risk Statement: Unauthorized or incorrectly executed changes to a system may result in infrastructure issues, business disruptions, malicious attacks, or internal fraud.	
Sample Control Activity	**Control Owner**
Change requests are evaluated, prioritized, and authorized to determine the impact on business processes and IT services.	IT manager/system owner
Changes are logged, prioritized, categorized, authorized, and scheduled.	IT manager/system owner
A secure test environment is defined and established that mirrors the actual environment of the business.	IT manager/system owner
User acceptance testing independently verifies that changes meet the defined test plan before the changes migrate to the live environment.	IT manager/system owner

TABLE 14.10 (*Continued*)

Completed changes are formally documented to indicate the changes made and the procedures affected by the changes.	Production Control manager
A tracking and reporting system documents which changes are rejected, approved, in process, and completed.	Production Control manager
Emergency changes are managed and authorized using a formal procedure that minimizes further incidents.	System owner
A post-implementation review tests the outcome of the changes to ensure that the new or changed service meets the planned performance and outcomes.	IT analyst/system owner

CONCEPT REVIEW QUESTIONS

1. What is meant by change management?

   Ans. Change management is a standardized process that decreases risk by controlling the identification and implementation of required changes to a system. Changes must be made quickly and reliably, and they need to be reviewed appropriately before they are finalized as poorly executed system changes can result in instability or lack of integrity.

2. List the steps in change management process.

   Ans. The three steps of the change management process are:

   1. Creating changes in the test environment

   2. Evaluating accuracy of changes in the model environment

   3. Implementing changes in the production environment

3. How does a test environment reduce risk by ensuring that a developer does not make rogue changes to the production system?

   Ans. The test environment where developers write and test their code is not connected to the production system. Before their code can be implemented in the production system, it must be loaded to the model system for testing and user approval before being routed to production.

4. Differentiate between normal and emergency changes.

   Ans. Normal changes follow the formal change management process to avoid the risk of mistakes. These changes are for organizational benefit (such as efficiency) or to update information (tax rate update example). On the other hand, emergency changes require immediate action to mitigate significant risks such as a system outage, compliance issue, or security risk.

FEATURED PROFESSIONAL | IT Governance Thought Leader

Photo courtesy of Mark Thomas

Mark Thomas, CGEIT, CRISC, COBIT Assessor

As a former Army officer with over 28 years of professional experience, Mark has a wide array of industry experience, including government, health care, finance/ banking, manufacturing, and technology services. Mark has held roles ranging from CIO to IT consulting and is considered a thought leader in frameworks such as COBIT, NIST, ITIL, and multiple ISO standards. Mark routinely speaks at U.S. and international conferences and earned the ISACA John Kuyers award twice for Best Speaker/Conference Contributor of the year.

Key Certifications

- CGEIT, CRISC
- COBIT 4.1, 5, 2019
- NIST Cybersecurity Framework (CSF)
- ITIL v3 Expert Designation
- ITIL v4
- PRINCE2 Practitioner

Areas of Expertise

- Enterprise governance of information and technology
- Risk governance and management
- Cybersecurity strategy
- Information controls assurance and compliance
- IT strategy development and implementation

- Agile, Lean, and DevOps
- GRC frameworks (COBIT, NIST, COSO, ISO, ITIL)

What did you study in college, and why?

I have a management major with a minor in military history. My goal was to be a military officer, which I was for the first 10 years of my career.

Why should accounting students care about COBIT 2019?

Information and technology are pervasive throughout any organization. Regardless of what specific path accounting students take in their careers, they will undoubtedly see how information and technology enable the business. This is why I believe it is important to understand the principles of IT governance and how to tailor a system to meet specific enterprise needs.

What do you think makes COBIT 2019 a cutting-edge framework for IT risk planning?

I think COBIT got this right. Not only are there two primary objectives in the framework that encompass both risk governance and risk management, but COBIT links many of its processes and components to making informed decisions, which is what risk enables. Risk is not static, and having a tailorable governance system that uses risk scenarios to continuously modify a governance system based on these is key to business agility and resilience.

You are a well-known speaker and author on the COBIT topic. How did you find this niche?

I was once told by a mentor of mine not to "major in minors," and her advice was well received. She was basically telling me to pick something that I like and am good at and become the best at it. I love the idea of IT governance. I've been in many different roles in IT organizations, most notably a VP of IT operations as well as CIO. I decided to use my experience to offer very specific advice by linking the COBIT framework to common issues that organizations are experiencing. It is one thing to review bullet points, but it is a completely different experience when you can offer practical advice on how to put COBIT into practice.

As someone with an IT background, why do you believe IT internal controls are important for someone who doesn't work in IT?

I strongly believe in the three lines of defense. I see many organizations assume that controls are owned by the risk and audit functions. Not true. Controls are in place for a reason, and the first line of defense must understand that these controls are responses to identified risks; therefore, controls must be understood, owned, and maintained as a part of normal IT operations. The link to anyone who does not work in IT is this: these are business process controls and are designed to maintain information integrity and the security of information assets, which are all business assets. Therefore, understanding these is key to enabling and supporting the business.

If you had to eat one type of cuisine for lunch every day for a month, what would it be?

It is a bit embarrassing to say, but you have just revealed one of my vulnerabilities with this question. I have a hot dog addiction and could eat them every day!

Review and Practice

Key Terms Review

access control vestibule
administrator role
backup cycle
backup site
backup strategy
business continuity planning (BCP)
change management
change management process
COBIT 2019
cold backup site
data backup
data center
differential backup

disaster recovery (DR)
dormant access
full backup
grandfather-father-son redundant
 backup
hot backup site
incremental backup
information technology (IT)
IT governance
IT governance framework
model environment
multifactor authentication
permission

piggybacking
production environment
role-based access control (RBAC)
tailgating
test environment
user acceptance testing
user access de-provisioning
user access provisioning
user access review
user access role
user authentication
warm backup site

Learning Objectives Review

1 Describe the COBIT framework and its five domains.

Information technology (IT) is the technology that supports a company's operations. IT governance involves ensuring the effective use of IT resources to obtain company goals. The most widely used IT governance framework is COBIT 2019.

COBIT helps companies design an IT strategy that meets regulatory compliance requirements, manages IT risks, and aligns with corporate goals. COBIT 2019 provides more than 300 generic IT controls. Accounting professionals don't need to memorize them all, but they should understand how COBIT controls are used in a business to mitigate IT risks.

The five domains of COBIT are:

1. Evaluate, Direct, and Monitor (EDM)
2. Align, Plan, and Organize (APO)
3. Build, Acquire, and Implement (BAI)
4. Deliver, Service, and Support (DSS)
5. Monitor, Evaluate, and Assess (MEA)

2 Evaluate logical user access controls.

Logical access controls provide security for digital assets such as systems and networks.

User access roles group individuals with similar access needs according to specific roles. These roles determine what permissions a user has within a system.

The four commonly used roles are:

- Administrator
- User
- Creator
- Read-only

The highest role available is the administrator role, which has all privileges for the system and can add, remove, and change access rights for other users.

New users are granted access through a formal process called user access provisioning. Once users have access rights, they must prove to the system that they are the persons who are supposed to use the account when they log in. User authentication validates ownership of an account through controls like passwords, multifactor authentication (such as entering a code sent to your text messaging or email address), or biometrics (such as fingerprint scans).

User access de-provisioning changes a user's access when it needs to be terminated or transferred.

An essential control for user access is a periodic user access review that assesses everyone in the system and their roles to determine if access is appropriate. Data analytics can be used to analyze user access listing for trends and anomalies.

An unauthorized user gaining access to a company's systems or data may result in:

- Employee fraud
- Malicious attacks on systems and data
- Systems and data being held for ransom
- Data breaches

3 Explain how physical access controls protect equipment and systems.

Physical access controls protect physical assets such as equipment and facilities.

Physical components are protected in a data center, which is a specialized facility dedicated to storing the computer and telecommunication system.

Key controls in a data center include:

- Environment
- Power supplies
- Construction
- Heating and cooling
- Fire protection
- Cabling
- Security systems
- Physical access

Security doors can use multifactor authentication by combining two or more controls, such as badge scanning, password or PIN entry, and biometric fingerprint scans.

Piggybacking, also called tailgating, occurs when an unauthorized individual follows closely behind an authorized person when passing through a secure entry point. The authorized person scans a badge or uses another access method, and the unauthorized individual passes through the door before it closes.

Risks related to physical equipment and systems include:

- A natural disaster causing damage to systems and equipment may result in a disruption of business activities and financial losses.
- An unauthorized user gaining access to physical equipment may result in theft, malicious attacks, fraud, or data breaches.
- Failure to maintain facilities in accordance with laws and regulations may result in fines and reputational losses.

4 Compare backup and recovery efforts.

Companies plan for disruptive events by implementing an internal control called business continuity planning (BCP). A subpart of BCP that relates specifically to restoring IT operations is disaster recovery.

Companies mitigate the risk that their primary data centers will become inoperable by having a backup site ready. The three types of backup sites are:

- Hot: Fully operational and backing up data continuously
- Warm: A room with some equipment available and possibly data as well
- Cold: A room with an internal environment ready but no equipment or data, which means equipment must be installed before the site is operational

Backup strategies determine which data is being stored when data is backed up. The three basic types of backup strategies are:

- Full backups: Copy all existing data in its entirety every time
- Differential backups: Copy all data created since the most recent full backup in its entirety with each backup

- Incremental backups: Copy only new or updated data every time

Backup cycles schedule when a data backup occurs. A common backup cycle is the grandfather-father-son cycle.

Disruptive events present risks including the following:

- A disruptive event may result in interruption of business operations and systems.
- A disruptive event may result in the primary data center becoming inoperable.
- A disruptive event may result in the loss of data stored on the primary servers.

⑤ Summarize the change management process.

The standardized process that decreases risks around making changes to a company's system is called change management.

The three stages in a formal change management process operate in three environments:

- Test environment: Developers create the changes in a separate, secure environment designed to replicate the production environment.

- Model environment: Tests are performed in a recent copy of the production environment.
- Production environment: Code is implemented in the live business systems and released for use.

System changes are categorized as either:

- Normal changes that follow the formal change management process
- Emergency changes that require immediate action due to a significant risk such as a system outage or security breach

Changes to systems that do not follow the formalized change management process may result in:

- Incompatibility with existing infrastructure
- Disruptions in ongoing business processes due to system malfunctions or outages
- Data breaches or malicious code being programmed into the systems
- Internal fraud, which occurs when an employee steals from the business

---

CPA questions, as well as multiple choice, discussion, analysis and application, and Tableau questions and other resources, are available online.

Multiple Choice Questions

1. (LO 1) What is the most widely used international standard for IT governance?

  a. ISACA

  b. COSO ERM

  c. COBIT

  d. COSO Internal Control—Integrated Framework

2. (LO 1) Which of the following statements about COBIT 2019 is true?

  a. COBIT is an open-source model that has an online platform for feedback.

  b. COBIT is a part of the COSO Internal Controls.

  c. COBIT focuses on addressing risk from a strategic perspective.

  d. COBIT has a control scope that encompasses all internal controls.

3. (LO 1) Which item is *not* an objective of the IT Evaluate, Direct, and Monitor domain?

  a. Ensure IT governance framework setting and maintenance

  b. Ensure IT risk realization

  c. Ensure stakeholder transparency

  d. Manage an IT system of internal control

4. (LO 1) CPA One important purpose of COBIT is to

  a. guide managers, users, and auditors in adopting best practices related to the management of information technology.

  b. identify specific control plans that could be implemented to reduce the occurrence of fraud.

  c. specify the components of an information system that should be installed in an e-commerce environment.

  d. suggest the type of information that should be made available for management decision making.

5. (LO 2) New users to a system are granted access through what formal process?

  a. User access provisioning   **c.** User role assignment

  b. User authentication   **d.** User validation

6. (LO 2) Which of these access roles would you assign to the internal audit manager of a public company?

  a. Administration   **c.** Read-only

  b. Creator   **d.** Manager

7. (LO 2) Eleanor Rigby's Crematorium and Pet Custodian Services wants to choose the strongest control method for accessing its systems. Eleanor should choose

a. a sign-in log.

b. biometrics.

c. passwords.

d. a two-way mirror.

8. (LO 2) CPA When a client's accounts payable computer system was relocated, the administrator provided support through a dial-up connection to a server. Subsequently, the administrator left the company. No changes were made to the accounts payable system at that time. Which of the following situations represents the greatest security risk?

a. User passwords are not required to be in alphanumeric format.

b. Management procedures for user accounts are not documented.

c. User accounts are not removed upon termination of employees.

d. Security logs are not periodically reviewed for violations.

9. (LO 3) Why did Amazon and Google choose to *not* build their new data centers near their headquarters?

a. It wasn't financially feasible.

b. They already owned land elsewhere.

c. It was against regulations.

d. They plan to leave those areas and relocate their headquarters.

10. (LO 3) A security guard opens the door to allow an authenticated person into the data center. A second person enters behind the first person without properly scanning through security. This method of circumventing physical access controls is called

a. piggybacking, or tailgating.

b. the access control vestibule.

c. a backup plan.

d. unlawful access.

11. (LO 3) CPA Which of the following best characterizes the function of a physical access control?

a. Protects systems from Trojan horses

b. Provides authentication of users attempting to log into the system

c. Separates unauthorized individuals from computer resources

d. Minimizes the risk of a power or hardware failure

12. (LO 3) Which of the following roles have control ownership related to protecting the physical computer systems?

a. Information security manager

b. Data center manager

c. Facilities manager

d. All of the above

13. (LO 4) What statement about the functionality of a cold backup site is false?

a. A cold backup site may be an almost empty room.

b. A cold backup site is the least expensive type of backup site for a company to implement.

c. A cold backup site imports data at the end of each business day.

d. A cold backup site may take days or weeks to recover.

14. (LO 4) CPA A controller is developing a disaster recovery plan for a corporation's computer systems. In the event of a disaster that makes the company's facilities unusable, the controller has arranged for the use of an alternative location and the delivery of duplicate computer hardware to this alternative location. Which of the following recovery plans would best describe this arrangement?

a. Hot site   **c.** Backup site

b. Cold site   **d.** Hot spare site agreement

15. (LO 4) Which type of backup copies all data during every backup?

a. Hot backup

b. Full backup

c. Differential backup

d. Incremental backup

16. (LO 4) CPA Womping Wembley Corp. maintains three sets of backups, which are updated monthly, weekly, and daily. This approach illustrates a

a. checkpoint and restart approach.

b. RAID approach.

c. redundant backup approach.

d. storage area network (SAN) approach.

17. (LO 5) The three stages in a change management process, in consecutive order, are

a. production, test,   **c.** model, test,
model.   implement.

b. test, model, production.   **d.** produce, test, model.

18. (LO 5) Which of the following change management steps occurs in the model environment?

a. Developer writes code.

b. Code is implemented into production.

c. User reviews and approves code.

d. User requests change.

19. (LO 5) Only _____ have access to the test environment.

a. end users

b. company leaders

c. developers

d. data analysts

Discussion and Research Questions

DQ1. (LO 1) `Critical Thinking` Explain what IT governance is and why it is not a department or state of existing in a company.

DQ2. (LO 1) `Critical Thinking` You are an IT auditor who is also a CPA, and you work in the internal audit department of a large private company. Your manager is a CPA but not an IT auditor. She asks you to explain why the COBIT framework is important for IT governance and how it differs from the COSO Internal Control and COSO ERM frameworks, which she knows well. How do you respond?

DQ3. (LO 2) Use an internet search engine to identify and list specific physical and logical access controls that an organization could use.

DQ4. (LO 2) Explain the difference between authentication and authorization for logical access controls and provide an example of each.

DQ5. (LO 3) `Early Career` What controls should you check for if you are auditing physical data center security at a specific offsite location that is over 300 miles away from the organization's regular location?

DQ6. (LO 4) Discuss the types of data backup strategies for organizations. Include factors that influence the choice of a backup strategy.

DQ7. (LO 4) Data is critically important to any organization. You are an internal auditor tasked with preparing and presenting a plan to top management for disaster recovery planning. You decide to recommend using guidance provided by the COBIT 2019 framework. Explain which internal controls you think should be implemented as part of the DR planning.

DQ8. (LO 5) `Research` `Critical Thinking` Software failures have caused millions of dollars of losses for companies and their stockholders. Use an internet search engine to find and describe one example of a significant failure that a robust change management program could possibly have prevented.

DQ9. (LO 5) `Critical Thinking` Differentiate between normal and emergency coding changes and provide examples of each that differ from those provided in the book.

Application and Analysis Questions

A1. (LO 1–5) `Early Career` `Critical Thinking` Alicia's Accessories is a global manufacturer of jewelry and hair accessories. The company currently relies on the COSO Internal Control—Integrated Framework to manage its corporate governance and risk response plans. The new chief information security officer (CISO) has proposed that leadership adopt the COBIT 2019 framework to strengthen its IT governance process. The CISO wants to use COBIT 2019 to help identify key IT internal controls that can mitigate some of Alicia's Accessories' biggest technology problems, such as users accessing inappropriate data, inappropriate system changes resulting in failures, loss or damage of physical IT equipment where its stored, and the risk of the business losing access to its data in the event that a natural disaster destroys its equipment.

Some of Alicia's Accessories' leadership thinks this is a great idea, but others are skeptical. The CISO asks your team—a group that specializes in risk analysis—to put together a short slide deck that explains the key benefits of using COBIT 2019. Your specific task is to come up a handful of one-line explanations that will catch leadership's attention. For example, "When disaster strikes, COBIT 2019 keeps you up and running."

Write three one-liners your team can use in its PowerPoint presentation to leadership.

A2. (LO 2) `Critical Thinking` TLL Motors is an online motorcycle equipment store that sells motorcycle helmets, boots, jackets, and more. With no brick-and-mortar stores, it relies on many systems to provide an excellent customer buying experience.

You are the accounting director at TLL Motors and are overseeing the implementation of a new general ledger system called GL Solutions. As part of the final steps of implementing the system, you need to assign users to the appropriate user access roles within GL Solutions.

Users can be assigned to only one of four roles or can be denied access:

A. Administrator

B. Creator

C. User

D. Read-only

E. Denied access

The table on the next page shows a list of all employees who requested access to GL Solutions. Match each user with the appropriate system user access role, based on the business needs of the user's job summary. You can also deny access to users if you feel they don't require access to GL Solutions, based on their job summary. To indicate your choice, fill in the appropriate letter from the list above.

Employee Title	Job Summary	Appropriate Role
Chief operations officer	Responsible for overseeing and guiding the day-to-day operations of the company. Relies on prebuilt dashboards and reports for revenue and sales growth information, expense, cost and margin control, and monthly, quarterly, and annual financial goal management.	_____
Tax accountant	Responsible for financial tax statements. Researches the financials to ensure that the company is following tax laws. Creates different reports that help in preparing payments, identifying tax savings, and analyzing tax issues.	_____
Accounting director	Responsible for directing the accounting department. Monitors data access to accounting data.	_____
Regional sales manager	Responsible for overseeing the Sales department within TLL Motors. Sets regional sales quotas, manages sales support staff, and advises the company about sales performance. Relies on prebuilt reports for forecasting.	_____
Public relations manager	Responsible for directing publicity programs and campaigns to improve the public image of TLL Motors and to clarify the company's point of view on important issues.	_____
Internal auditor	Responsible for ensuring compliance with established internal control procedures by examining records, reports, operating practices, and documentation. Relies on prebuilt documentation.	_____
Compensation and benefits manager	Responsible for overseeing the compensation and benefits division of the company. Analyzes compensation data within the organization and evaluates job positions to determine classification and salary. Administers employee insurance, pension, and savings plans and works with insurance brokers and plan carriers.	_____
Marketing manager	Responsible for measuring, enhancing, and enriching the position and image of the company through various goals and objectives.	_____

A3. (LO 3) `Early Career` `Critical Thinking` As a staff auditor working for an international accounting firm, you are performing a data center walkthrough of Lookout Adventures. Lookout Adventures is an outdoor company that primarily sells mountain climbing and camping gear.

Upon arriving at the Lookout Adventures headquarters in Colorado, you are introduced to Lilly Walters. As the manager of Lookout Adventures' data center, she will be giving you a tour today. You have your clipboard so that you can take notes during the walkthrough—specifically, about things Lilly says.

Lilly: Hi! My name is Lilly Walters, and I'm the data center manager at Lookout Adventures.

You: Nice to meet you, Lilly. Thanks for taking the time out of your day to walk us through the data center as part of the annual SOX testing that we perform. To kick off our testing, could you tell us a little more about the location where we're standing?

Lilly: Sure. We are at our headquarters in Denver, Colorado. We are currently on the ground level of the building, where the data center is located. We are about to enter through the front doors of the data center. We have a backdoor as well.

You: Thank you for that. How do you secure the doors of the data center?

Lilly: We have an access control vestibule. We have the first doors, which we're currently standing outside of, and a second set of doors on the inside, which I will walk you through. Before we go in, I wanted to point out that we have cameras right outside of the first and second doors. This allows us to go back through video footage of who's entered and exited, if necessary.

You: Great, thank you. Who has access to the primary and secondary doors in the access control vestibule?

Lilly: We program all employee badges with physical access to different areas in the building. Access is on a need basis. Only data center employees have access to these doors, so their badges are programmed to allow them into the data center. Anyone else coming in will have to have an appointment, like you had, so they can be escorted into the data center. We review the listing of employees who have access to the data center on a quarterly basis. Are you ready to enter, or do you have other questions?

You: I'm ready, thanks.

Lilly: As we enter the access control vestibule, you can see that the second set of doors also has a badge scanner and a camera. As we continue through these doors, we enter the operations center. Here is where the data center employees sit and monitor the data center. You will need to sign in since you are a visitor. You also need to provide us with a reason for coming. You can just put "internal audit review."

You sign into the system.

You: Okay, I'm signed in.

Lilly: As you can see, we have multiple computer monitors here in the operations center. This data is updated continuously. We monitor the environment of the inside of the main room. One of the screens gives us the current temperature and humidity of the room and even provides a heatmap of where there is higher temperature. Heatmapping is a cool technology that we recently implemented. It tells us if there's a section in the room that is warmer than other parts and can alert the data center personnel to air circulation issues.

You: That is cool. How do you cool the temperature in the data center?

Lilly: We have a separate air conditioning unit in the room. The cool air enters through vents located in the ceiling. Let's move into the main data center room so you can see the vents for yourself.

You: That would be great. Now that we're here, I notice how many power cords are running along the ceiling. How do you handle any power outages?

Lilly: We use an uninterruptible power supply that helps with any power outages or surges.

You: What about the backup environments? Could you talk about where your data backups are located?

Lilly: Sure. We have a hot backup site in Miami, Florida. It is fully operational and ready for our data center personnel to work there if needed. Our critical data is continuously backed up at the hot site. This way, we won't lose any data if there's an emergency. We also perform full and incremental backups of less critical data on a regular basis. These backups are stored here at our headquarters.

You: You mentioned a second entrance to the data center—a backdoor. How do you secure that door?

Lilly: That door is secured through badge access only—same as the front doors.

You: Okay.

Lilly: Do you have any other questions for me now?

You: Not right now, thank you. I will take my notes and type them up into a workpaper and create a listing of observations. I will email you if I have any more questions. Thank you so much for taking time to meet with me and walk me through the data center.

Lilly: No problem, I'm always happy to help. Don't hesitate to email me if you think of any more questions.

Lilly escorts you back into the operations center so you can sign out. After that, she takes you through the access control vestibule and back to the hallway.

Once you are back at your desk, you review the notes you took during the walkthrough. You need to compile a list of audit observations (things that you are worried might be risky about the data center) for your manager. If Lilly did not specifically talk about something, it is safe to assume that the data center doesn't have it. List at least three things you think are concerns in the Lookout Adventures data center. Be as specific as possible.

A4. (LO 4) `Critical Thinking` You work for a major consulting firm, and you just completed a team training on data backup strategies. Your manager has prepared a post-training assignment to test your team's knowledge after the training session.

Label each of the following with the correct backup strategy:

A. Full backup

B. Differential backup

C. Incremental backup

1. The backup strategy that copies all existing data every time: _____

2. A backup strategy used in the son backup cycle: _____

3. The cheapest data backup strategy, which uses the least amount of storage space: _____

4. The middle ground of backup strategies: _____

5. The data strategy used in the father backup cycle: _____

6. The backup strategy illustrated below: _____

7. The backup strategy that copies all data created since the most recent full backup for each backup: _____

8. The backup strategy illustrated below: _____

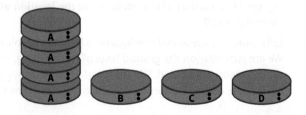

9. The slowest backup strategy: _____

10. The backup strategy illustrated below: _____

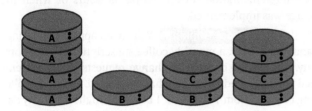

11. The backup strategy that copies only new or updated data for each backup: _____

12. The data strategy used in the grandfather backup cycle: _____

A5. (LO 4) [Critical Thinking] As a college student, you have a lot of files stored on your laptop: essays and assignments from classes, pictures from spring break trips, tax returns, and more. You have decided to clear some storage space on your computer, but you don't want to delete any of your files. Instead, you decide to use three storage options for your personal data, as described in the table below.

Assign one of these three storage options to the files you have, based on the priority of each file type:

1. Personal pictures and videos: _____

2. Annual tax documents: _____

3. Current class assignments: _____

4. Last semester's research project, which you plan to submit with graduate school application: _____

5. Meeting minutes, which you take for an honors society where you are an officer: _____

6. Personal finance documents, which include your student loan and FAFSA information: _____

Provide a written explanation of how you have prioritized the files.

Backup Type	Backup Space	Backup Cost	Pros	Cons
A. Cloud storage	100 GB	$1.99 per month	You can access your files anywhere at any time	You have to pay a monthly fee
B. Local storage on laptop	100 GB	Free—came with laptop	It is free	Your things are only stored on your laptop— if it crashes, they might be lost
C. External drive	100 GB	$19.99 one-time cost	One-time cost	It is a hassle to hook it up and save items on an external site

	A	B	C	D	E	F	G	H	I	J
1	Change #	Change Opened Date	Business Approver Date	IT Manager Approver Date	Implementation Date	Post-Implementation Review Date	Change Closed Date	Emergency Closed Date	Type	Effective or Ineffective?
2	1	12/29/2021	1/5/2021	1/10/2021	1/13/2021		1/14/2021		Regular	
3	2	12/22/2021	12/25/2021	12/30/2021	12/30/2021		12/30/2021		Regular	
4	3	12/21/2021	12/31/2021	1/3/2022	12/30/2021		1/4/2021		Regular	
5	4	12/20/2021	12/20/2021	12/25/2021	12/22/2021		12/31/2021		Regular	
6	5	12/20/2021	12/23/2021	12/28/2021	12/27/2021		12/28/2021		Regular	
7	6	12/20/2021	12/23/2021	12/24/2021	12/24/2021		12/24/2021		Regular	
8	7	12/19/2021	12/19/2021	12/19/2021	12/23/2021		12/23/2021		Regular	
9	8	12/18/2021	12/24/2021	12/29/2021	12/29/2021		12/30/2021		Regular	
10	9	12/18/2021	12/18/2021	12/29/2021	12/20/2021		12/21/2021		Regular	
11	10	12/31/2021			12/31/2021	1/1/2022		1/2/2022	Emergency	
12	11	12/18/2021	12/18/2021	12/23/2021	12/28/2021		12/29/2021		Regular	
13	12	12/25/2021			12/25/2021	12/28/2021		12/28/2021	Emergency	
14	13	12/17/2021	12/23/2021	12/25/2021	12/27/2021		12/27/2021		Regular	
15	14	12/31/2021			12/31/2021	1/4/2022		1/4/2022	Emergency	
16	15	12/16/2021	12/27/2021	12/24/2021	12/22/2021		12/28/2021		Regular	
17	16	12/16/2021	12/21/2021	12/23/2021	12/27/2021		12/28/2021		Regular	
18	17	12/15/2021	12/19/2021	12/19/2021	12/17/2021		12/21/2021		Regular	
19	18	1/1/2022			1/1/2022	1/5/2022		1/5/2022	Emergency	
20	19	12/15/2021	12/20/2021	12/23/2021	12/22/2021		12/28/2021		Regular	
21	20	12/15/2021	12/15/2021	12/16/2021	12/20/2021		12/20/2021		Regular	

A6. (LO 5) Early Career Data Analytics Critical Thinking
You are an internal auditor at an organic pet products company named Shaggy. Shaggy's main line of business focuses on the unique pet hair needs of its clients and providing customized products to individual pets.

As part of regular IT testing, you need to perform a change management analysis of Shaggy's customer management system. The changes shown in the table given on the previous page have occurred in the system. Determine whether a change is *effective*, in which case it received proper approval, or *ineffective*, in which case it did not receive proper approval prior to being implemented (put into production).

Watch out for emergency changes—changes that do not have to have approval prior to implementation but must have a postimplementation review within 48 hours of when the change was implemented.

A7. (LO 5) Critical Thinking You are an application change manager for Drip, a monthly coffee subscription service company. You have a backlog of change requests where systems need to be updated based on what users need. Order the following requests from 1 to 5, with 1 being the highest priority and 5 being the lowest priority. Then label each request with the type of change: regular or emergency. Hint: There are at least two emergency requests.

Priority	Request	Regular or Emergency?
_____	**General ledger:** Add $ to the front of each monetary amount. Currently, this is being manually added during reporting.	_____
_____	**HR administrative system:** Add *nonbinary* as a gender selection option. Currently, the only options are *male* and *female*.	_____
_____	**Customer relationship management system:** Add more memory. Currently, sales managers are unable to add more customers to the system.	_____
_____	**Virtual signature application:** Fix login issue. Currently, customers cannot log in to sign contracts.	_____
_____	**Backups/data protector:** Rerun backup. One of the incremental backups did not finish last night.	_____

A8. (LO 5) Following are defining statements for the three types of change management environments. Label each statement with the most appropriate change management environment. A statement may have more than one label.

Change management environments options:
A. Test environment
B. Model environment
C. Production environment

Statement	Environment
Also known as the "sandbox," this is where developers design and test their coding.	1. _____
Developer no longer has access to ensure segregation of duties.	2. _____
User acceptance takes place here.	3. _____
Outputs include testing documentation.	4. _____
Outputs include live code in the system.	5. _____
Outputs include initial code.	6. _____
The business user or IT analyst no longer has access to the code to ensure segregation of duties.	7. _____

Tableau Case: Change Management at Julia's Cookies

What You Need

Download Tableau to your computer. You can access www.tableau.com/academic/students to download your free Tableau license for the year, or you can download it from your university's software offerings.

Download the following file from the book's product page on www.wiley.com:

Chapter 14 Raw Data.xlsx

Case Background

Big Picture:
Analyze system change patterns.

Details:
Why is this data important, and what questions or problems need to be addressed?

- Companies follow a change management process to ensure that any changes made to a system are accurate before they are implemented. An incorrect change could have devastating effects on the business, as it opens the business to risks. Imagine that Julia's Cookies needed to increase the price of chocolate chip cookies from $1.45 to $1.50 and, instead, the developer accidentally coded $15.00 per cookie. A well-designed change management process, with a thorough chain of approval, would be able to prevent this kind of mistake before it could be published to the website, the app, and the financial system.

- To analyze the system change patterns at Julia's Cookies, consider these questions, among others: Which month had the most changes? Which application had the most *emergency* changes? How many changes did not receive timely post-implementation review?

Plan:
What data is needed, and how should it be analyzed?

- The data needed to answer the objective is pulled from the workflow management system.

- The data should be filtered to an appropriate time frame, usually an audit testing period, to help IT auditors identify which changes did not receive appropriate approvals prior to being implemented.

Now it's your turn to evaluate, analyze, and communicate the results!

Recall from the text:

- Regular changes require a business approver and an IT approver *before* they can be implemented.

- Emergency changes *do not* have to have business or IT manager approval; however, they *require* a post-implementation approval *after* they are implemented.

Questions

1. Which month had the highest count of changes opened?
2. How many emergency changes were opened in July 2021?
3. Which application had the highest count of regular changes submitted?
4. Which application had the highest count of emergency changes submitted?
5. How many *infrastructure* emergency changes were opened in September 2021?
6. How many *high-risk* changes did Julia's Cookies' firewall have opened overall?
7. How many days, on average, did it take for a change to be implemented after it received IT approval?
8. How many regular changes *did not* receive IT manager approval before being implemented?

Take it to the next level!

9. How many changes received post-implementation review within three days or more from the time the change was implemented? (Hint: Use a DATEDIFF calculation.)
10. Which application had 17 emergency changes during the testing period and received a post-implementation review three days *after* the changes were implemented?

CHAPTER 15

Fraud

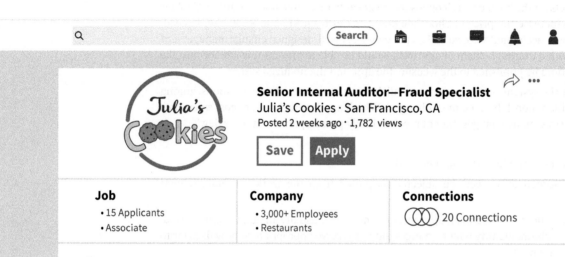

Summary

Julia's Cookies is seeking a senior internal auditor who specializes in fraud investigations. The senior auditor will perform audit work that impacts a variety of financial, operational, and compliance programs, in conformance with company policies and procedures, while supporting fraud investigations, as requested by Julia's Cookies' Compliance department.

Responsibilities

- Support fraud investigations by designing and conducting advanced data analytics to proactively identify fraud, waste, and abuse in business processes
- Investigate cases and work with Julia's Cookies' compliance and legal teams to support creation of case documentation for instances of expense fraud and other fraud cases
- Coordinate with Finance and Operations to create remediation plans for control weaknesses and enhance corporate policies to address risks related to fraud and abuse
- Investigate tips submitted to the employee whistleblower hotline and report findings to legal team
- Develop audit test programs and perform audit tests to evaluate the design and operating effectiveness of internal controls

Requirements

- Preferred Education: Bachelor's degree in accounting, law, or related field
- Preferred Certifications: CPA, CFE
- Minimum Experience: Two or more years in internal audit, external audit, forensics, law enforcement, or legal

Preferred Knowledge and Skills

The ideal candidate will possess critical-thinking skills and data analytics experience. Experience in fraud interviews and continuous monitoring data analytics is a plus.

Salary: $90,000–110,000

CHAPTER PREVIEW   Fraud is a global problem that negatively affects every type of organization—small businesses, multinational corporations, nonprofits, and governmental entities. No organization is immune, not even those with strong systems of internal control. Regardless of your specialization, as an accounting professional, it's crucial that you recognize the warning signs or red flags that signal possible fraud against your clients, employer, or even your own business. This chapter focuses on what you need to know about fraud, including:

- Types of fraud
- How accounting professionals manage the risk of fraud
- How to identify and prevent asset misappropriation schemes
- The impact of fraud on financial statements

There are many job opportunities for accounting professionals interested in pursuing a career in fraud examination. For example, the FBI employs accounting professionals as forensic accountants to investigate cases, public accounting firms have specialized teams that investigate fraud at their clients' companies, and larger companies hire internal auditors with a passion for fraud detection in roles like the internal auditor job posting at Julia's Cookies. ∎

Chapter Roadmap

LEARNING OBJECTIVES	TOPICS	JULIA'S COOKIES APPLIED LEARNING
15.1 Identify the main types of fraud.	• Fraud Is a Risk • External Fraud • Occupational Fraud • Behavioral Red Flags	Behavioral Red Flags: Anonymous Tips
15.2 Describe the role of an accounting professional in fraud management.	• The Fraud Triangle • Preventing Fraud • Detecting Fraud	Fraud Triangle: New Senior Manager
15.3 Explain how to identify, prevent, and detect asset misappropriation schemes.	• Skimming • Larceny • Fraudulent Disbursements	Expense Reimbursement Fraud: Travel Red Flags
15.4 Identify financial statement fraud and explain how to mitigate its risks.	• Overstating Financial Performance • Understating Financial Performance • Management's Involvement in Financial Statement Fraud	Financial Statement Fraud: Improper Revenue Recognition

CPA   You will find the CPA tag throughout the chapter to call out any important topics you may see on the CPA exam.

15.1 What Is Fraud?

Learning Objective ❶
Identify the main types of fraud.

Fraud is the "knowing misrepresentation of the truth or concealment of a material fact to induce another to act to his or her detriment."[1] This definition of fraud has four elements:

- **A false statement:** The perpetrator either lies directly or hides the truth.
- **Knowledge:** The perpetrator knows the statement is false at the time it's stated.
- **Reliance:** The victim relies on information when deciding or acting.
- **Damages:** The victim suffers damages as a result of relying on this false statement.

The first two elements—a false statement and knowledge—indicate that the perpetrator has intent. Intent is a key element to legally identify any crime, including fraud. For fraud to occur, the victim must trust—or have confidence—in the perpetrator. In fact, the terms "con man" and "con artist" originated from perpetrators gaining the *confidence* of their victims before swindling them. Victims of fraud can range from an individual person to an entire company:

- Individual fraud targets victims directly in schemes such as identity theft, elder fraud, Ponzi schemes,[2] mail fraud, tax refund fraud, and more.
- Employee fraud targets the employer, which results in the business suffering losses and becoming the victim.

For example, an employee at Julia's Cookies submits fake receipts to the company's expense reimbursement program. As a result of paying the employee for fictitious expenses, the company will increase expenses and lose cash. In this example, the company is the primary victim. For AIS, we focus on fraud against companies.

There are three components to fraud: the act, the concealment, and the conversion:

- The act of the Julia's Cookies employee submitting fake receipts for reimbursement is the fraud.
- Once the act is committed, perpetrators must cover up their tracks with concealment. When the Julia's Cookies employee creates false receipts to justify his fraudulent expense reports, he is concealing the fraud.
- Conversion happens when the perpetrator transforms the stolen item into usable cash. The Julia's Cookies employee uses cashing his reimbursement check for conversion. This type of asset misappropriation is a popular type of fraud because it is easy to convert.

Fraud Is a Risk

According to the 2020 Association of Certified Fraud Examiners (ACFE) *Report to the Nations*, organizations lose around 5% of their revenues to fraud.[3] But in practice, many risk management professionals underestimate or ignore fraud risk at a corporate level.

In this chapter, we look closely at statistics provided in the ACFE's *Report to the Nations: 2020 Global Study on Occupational Fraud and Abuse*. This report, issued every two years, is a valuable resource not only for fraud professionals but for students who are interested

---

[1]Bryan Garner, ed. 2004. *Black's Law Dictionary*. 8th ed.
[2]A Ponzi scheme lures investors to invest in a seemingly legitimate business, which then pays fictitious "profits" to earlier investors with funds from more recent investors. An example is the well-publicized fraud perpetrated by Bernie Madoff.
[3]www.acfe.com/report-to-the-nations/2020/

in pursuing fraud examination as a career. You can download a copy of the report from the ACFE's website. According to the report, "the amount of money lost to occupational fraud each year represents a staggering drain on the global economy. It directly impacts organizations' abilities to create jobs, produce goods and services, and provide public services."[4]

Companies can manage fraud proactively by:

- Performing fraud risk assessments
- Creating an anti-fraud culture
- Promoting fraud awareness through employee training
- Establishing and maintaining an effective system of internal control
- Instituting a formal fraud investigation process

A fraud risk assessment can be integrated into the enterprise risk assessment or performed as a stand-alone process. During a fraud risk assessment, fraud risks are usually categorized as financial, operational, or compliance risks. Like all other risks, fraud risks are addressed by creating a risk response and implementing internal controls to mitigate the risks.

Some regulations, including the Sarbanes-Oxley Act of 2002 (SOX), require companies to evaluate their system of internal controls specifically in relation to their ability to prevent and detect fraud. Public Company Accounting Oversight Board (PCAOB) regulations state that an external auditor should evaluate whether a company is sufficiently addressing fraud risks with its internal controls.

Even when not required by regulation, companies should address fraud risks since fraud can significantly impact profits and reputation, and it is not only the victim company that suffers. The labor union AFL-CIO estimated in 2005 that 28,500 employees had lost their jobs because of the Enron, WorldCom, and Arthur Andersen scandals. Thousands of people who did not even work for those companies were victims because their mutual funds, often for retirement savings, lost value. The AFL-CIO also estimated that those people lost $1.5 trillion from their retirement savings between 2002 and 2005.[5]

Given the COVID-19 pandemic and the accompanying financial difficulties for individuals and organizations, it is important to keep in mind that crises and economic difficulties can increase the frequency and severity of fraud. When economic survival is at stake, the line between acceptable and unacceptable behavior may become blurred. As people lose their jobs and those still employed feel threatened, the pressure to commit fraud increases if the opportunity exists.

During the COVID-19 pandemic, fraud in procuring masks, protective clothing, ventilators, and other medical equipment exploded, endangering the health of employees and patients who needed these resources. Two of many news reports provide examples of fraud attempts that highlight these recent life-threatening risks:

- A Georgia man attempted to sell 125 million nonexistent items of personal protective equipment (PPE) to the Department of Veterans Affairs for an advance payment.[6]
- An attempt to sell 39 million N95 masks through overseas brokers and suppliers for an advance payment would have cost victim organizations (including the state of California, Kaiser Permanente, Stanford Health Care, and Santa Clara County) a total of $78 million.[7]

Now that we have explored some of the many reasons considering fraud risk is important, let's examine two broad categories of fraud: external and occupational fraud.

---

[4]We mention the ACFE's *Report to the Nations: 2020 Global Study on Occupational Fraud and Abuse* a number of times in this chapter. To find more details or read the report, see www.acfe.com/report-to-the-nations/2020/.
[5]abcnews.go.com/Business/story?id=86817&page=1
[6]www.justice.gov/opa/pr/georgia-man-arrested-attempting-defraud-department-veterans-affairs-multimillion-dollar-covid
[7]abc7news.com/coronavirus-supplies-how-feds-uncovered-fraud-involving-39-million-n95-masks/6104173/

External Fraud

External fraud is fraud perpetrated by customers, vendors, or other outside parties against a company. Since they are external risks and less preventable, companies often devote significantly less time to them in risk assessments. A business may consider various types of external fraud during its fraud risk assessment:

- Dishonest customers may write bad checks for payment.
- Customers may shoplift items and then try to return them for refunds.
- Vendors may bill the company for services or goods that were never provided.
- Political figures in other countries may demand bribes to allow a product to pass local regulations.
- Vendors may work together to "rig a bid."

Let's talk about this last fraud. A company puts out a request for vendors to bid on a contract when it looks for new vendors. Vendors submit their proposals, including the cost of their services. A bid-rigging scheme is an illegal circumvention of the competitive bidding process. According to the Federal Trade Commission, vendors who are competitors may collude to take turns as the low bidder, exclude themselves from a bidding round, or subcontract part of the main contract to the losing bidders. They may even form a joint venture that submits a single bid. As a result, the organization pays an inflated price for the contract.

Let's take a look at an example of bid-rigging at Julia's Cookies. Julia's Cookies put out a request for vendors to bid on a setup for the company's new enterprise resource planning (ERP) system. Jacob works for the software contracting company Alpha. His old college roommate, Abhishek, works for a different software contracting company, Beta. Jacob and Abhishek have colluded to undermine the bidding process, and this time it's Jacob's turn to win the contract. Abhishek submits a high bid to Julia's Cookies. Jacob submits a slightly lower bid to Julia's Cookies. Julia's Cookies chooses Jacob's bid because it's lower than Abhishek's, not realizing the two coordinated their bids to be substantially above the current market price.

Besides bid-rigging, there are many other types of external fraud schemes. Hacking, data breaches, compromised business emails, and wire fraud are examples of fraud that uses technology to access a company from the outside. This technology-enabled external fraud is so important for companies to consider that we look at it separately in the Cybersecurity chapter.

Occupational Fraud

Occupational fraud, also called *internal fraud*, is committed by owners, executives, management, and employees who use their positions to enrich themselves at the expense of the company. The ACFE identifies almost 50 different types of occupational fraud schemes, and **Illustration 15.1** shows the three categories the ACFE uses to map them—asset misappropriation, financial statement fraud, and corruption—and their immediate subcategories.

Fraud schemes are further categorized into even more granular levels. Let's briefly talk about corruption schemes first. Then we will discuss the two most important occupational fraud categories—asset misappropriation and financial statement fraud—and the details of their specific schemes and important internal controls to prevent or detect them.

Corruption	Asset Misappropriation	Financial Statement Fraud
		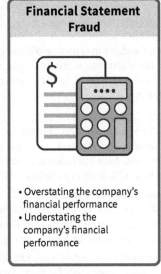
• Conflicts of interest • Illegal gratuities • Bribery • Economic extortion	• Fraud directly related to cash • Fraud related to inventory and all other assets (including information)	• Overstating the company's financial performance • Understating the company's financial performance

Illustration 15.1 The three categories of occupational fraud are corruption, asset misappropriation, and financial statement fraud.

Corruption is the inappropriate use of influence to obtain a benefit contrary to the perpetrator's responsibility or the rights of other people. According to the 2020 ACFE *Report to the Nations*, 43% of fraud committed falls into this category, with a median loss of $200,000 per case.

There are four types of corruption fraud schemes (**Table 15.1**). These examples of occupational fraud schemes only scratch the surface of the creative ways people inside a company perpetrate fraud. We'll cover asset misappropriation and financial statement fraud in their own sections.

TABLE 15.1 Types of Corruption Schemes

Type of Scheme	Description	Example
Conflicts of interest	Employees prioritize their personal interests over those of the organization. • This results in an adverse impact on the organization. • The relationship or the activity that the person engages in conflicts with the employer's interests.	A purchasing manager awards a contract worth $2 million to a firm owned by a family member rather than to the most qualified vendor. This relationship can result in unfair pricing, preferential treatment, an inability to deliver on the contract, and other problems.
Illegal gratuities	Executives, managers, or employees give or receive something of value as a reward for favorable business decisions.	A purchasing manager awards a contract worth $2 million to a vendor. Afterward, the vendor delivers an expensive vehicle to the purchasing manager, and she accepts it. While this exchange happens after the fact and is not prearranged, it may lead to bribery and future expectations of favorable treatment by that vendor.
Commercial bribery	Employees accept a covert offer of payment or something of value for favorably influencing a business decision. • The offer is made before the decision, without the employer's knowledge. • Merely making the offer is illegal.	A vendor offers to give the purchasing manager an expensive vehicle *if* she awards him a $2 million contract. The purchasing manager may select the vendor over others just to receive the vehicle.
Economic extortion	Employees threaten someone to pay up or else bear the consequences.	A purchasing manager *demands* that a vendor buy her an expensive vehicle in exchange for a $2 million contract for that vendor. If the vendor refuses, the purchasing manager threatens to award the contract to a competitor.

In the Real World   A Fraud with Deadly Consequences[8]

It's impossible to predict how far a fraudster may go to avoid the consequences if their criminal acts are detected. The story of Sallie Rohrbach provides insights into the worst way a criminal may react during a fraud investigation. This case is a valuable lesson for accounting professionals who encounter fraud in their careers. Watch out for the behavioral red flags that indicate dangerous situations! Your life may depend on it.

The Fraud	Sallie Rohrbach, who was an auditor for the North Carolina Department of Insurance, was performing an investigation of Michael Howell, the owner of Dilworth Insurance Agency in Charlotte, North Carolina. Sallie drove to Charlotte from her Raleigh, North Carolina, office in May 2008 to perform an onsite investigation of Howell's finances. Nobody expected that Sallie would never return from her trip.
	Sallie's investigation revealed that Howell was embezzling funds from customers. He stole over $150,000 between 2004 and 2008. Howell stole both insurance premiums that were documented (cash larceny) and undocumented (skimming). Because of Howell's misappropriation of insurance premiums, customers were driving around uninsured without knowing it.
	Fraudsters are often con artists. They are able to perpetrate fraud because people trust them, which contributes to the opportunity for fraud. One of Howell's former customers said that it was difficult to take her business elsewhere: "It was very hard, because I like him. He's such a nice guy." Howell was not a nice guy after all.[9]
The Red Flags	Sallie reported that she had reviewed months of bank statements from Howell and identified instances of him floating money by using multiple bank accounts to cover overdrafts. However, she never mentioned any concerns about Howell personally and did not notify her supervisor of behavioral red flags indicating Howell was potentially dangerous.
	The behavioral red flags that Sallie failed to recognize involved an escalation in Howell's emotional demeanor. According to Howell's wife's testimony, Howell became argumentative and verbally aggressive toward Sallie as she came closer to uncovering his fraud.
	When the conversation became increasingly intense, Sallie should have terminated it and sought assistance from her team in the investigation. Instead, Sallie continued the conversation, likely believing she was speaking with a reasonable person who would not resort to hurting her.
The Murder	Sallie never came home. She was reported missing, and her car was found near Howell's agency. Blood was found on the rug in his office and in the back of his vehicle. Prosecutors cut a deal with Howell: in exchange for information about the whereabouts of Sallie's body, they would pursue a lesser murder charge with a shorter prison sentence. Police subsequently found her body in a wooded area in South Carolina.
	While Howell never provided details, police believe she was killed during a conversation in which Howell became aggressive and agitated. Howell's wife stated in her testimony that Howell admitted to her that he became aggressive and eventually struck Sallie with a computer stand.
A Deadly Lesson	Sallie's final fraud investigation was like many such investigations she had performed in her career as an insurance auditor. A seasoned professional, Sallie followed the routine she had used many times during investigations. The lesson of Sallie's death is to be aware of your surroundings and use professional skepticism not only when looking at internal controls but also when looking at people—especially when investigating potential fraud. Recognizing behavioral red flags of not only a possible fraudster but of one who could turn violent might have saved Sallie's life.

What do you think is the most important takeaway of this case? Does it make you uncomfortable about the idea of investigating fraud yourself? What do you think Sallie could have done differently to be more aware of her own safety during her investigation?

Behavioral Red Flags

Normal, everyday people may compromise their integrity for a variety of reasons to engage in fraudulent behavior. An occupational fraudster is most likely a trusted employee or a member of the management team. According to the ACFE's 2020 *Report to the Nations*, 89% of

---

[8]Perri, Frank S., and Brody, Richard G. 2011. "The Sallie Rohrbach Story: Lessons for Auditors and Fraud Examiners." *Journal of Financial Crime* 18(1): 93–104.

[9]www.wbtv.com/story/8361472/sallie-rohrbach-murder-investigation/

occupational fraudsters did not have prior criminal convictions. **Behavioral red flags** are clues that indicate the *possibility* a person may be involved with a fraud. The presence of red flags does *not* mean a fraud is being committed. Instead, red flags are warning signs for potential fraud. There are six common behavioral red flags, as detailed in **Table 15.2**.

TABLE 15.2 Behavioral Red Flags at Julia's Cookies

Behavioral Red Flag	Julia's Cookies Employee
Financial difficulties	Shuo is an HR generalist who has been coming into work tired and underperforming. She says that she and her husband are experiencing financial difficulties that are keeping her up at night.
Living beyond one's means	Ricardo is an Accounts Payable clerk who recently bought a new sports car that cost twice as much as his annual salary.
Close association with vendor or customer	Lacy often goes out to lunch with the vendor representative for Flowers & Flours, but she never goes out with other vendors when they send representatives.
Recent divorce or family problems	Brady leaves the office regularly to meet with his lawyer and attend court hearings related to his divorce. His wife is demanding most of their assets, and Brady is worried about losing custody of his son. He's spending a lot of time and money on legal representation and is coming into work stressed and frustrated.
Control issues or unwillingness to share duties	Mariel works in Payroll and hasn't taken a vacation in two years, even though they have plenty of available paid time off. They say they love their job and that nobody else would "do it right" if they went out of office.
Unscrupulous "big shot" attitude	Nobody likes John. He's cut-throat and throws his teammates under the bus to get assigned to the best projects. He's been promoted at Julia's Cookies and acts like he can do whatever he wants.

Now that you know these common red flags, evaluate employees who raise red flags based on anonymous tips at Julia's Cookies in Applied Learning 15.1.

Julia's Cookies — Applied Learning 15.1

Behavioral Red Flags: Anonymous Tips

Hing is a fraud investigator at Julia's Cookies. He's been asked to review anonymous tips received by the Legal department and identify potential behavioral red flags. Which of these do you think are behavioral red flags? Do you think any of them is likely to be committing fraud?

- "Erik wouldn't stop bragging about his new car at our staff meeting. He went on and on about how much it cost. We have the same job title, and I couldn't afford that car. He must be stealing."
- "Mark wouldn't staff me on a project because I'm a woman. He always treats the men on our team better."
- "Sissett has been coming into the office late every day. She seems depressed and distracted. I asked her about it in our last one-on-one meeting, and she mentioned money problems. She was rather aggressive when she told me she's going through what sounds like a nasty divorce. She's working an extra job at nights to pay for her lawyer. I am her manager, and I am worried about her. She's acting differently."
- "When Lee got the promotion that I wanted, they rubbed my face in it and were rude. They used nasty language and acted inappropriately in front of our team."

SOLUTION

Erik and Sissett are both exhibiting behavioral red flags for fraud, which are warning signs that *may* indicate an increased fraud risk. Red flags do not provide evidence that fraud is occurring, but they warn you to be alert to fraud.

The second anonymous tip indicates that Mark might be sexist, but it doesn't mean he is committing fraud against the company. There are no financial indicators for fraud in this statement. Similarly, Lee has a bad attitude, and their rudeness might be impacting team morale, but this tip does not indicate fraud. Julia's Cookies can follow up on these tips to address the issues, but sexism and a bad attitude aren't fraud indicators.

Keep reading to find out what factors we look at to identify the possibility of someone committing fraud!

CONCEPT REVIEW QUESTIONS

1. What do you understand by external fraud?

   Ans. External fraud is the fraud perpetrated by customers, vendors, or other outside parties against a company; for example, a dishonest customer may write bad checks for payment. Since they are external risks and less preventable, companies often devote significantly less time to them in risk assessments.

2. What do you know about internal fraud?

   Ans. Internal fraud, also called occupational fraud, is committed by owners, executives, management, and employees who use their positions to enrich themselves at the expense of the company. The ACFE identifies almost 50 different types of occupational fraud schemes.

3. What is meant by conflict of interest?

   Ans. When employees prioritize their personal interests over those of the organization, it is termed as conflict of interest. This results in an adverse impact on the organization. The relationship or the activity that the person engages in conflicts with the employer's interests.

4. What do you understand by illegal gratuities?

   Ans. When executives, managers, or employees give or receive something of value as a reward for favorable business decisions, it is known as illegal gratuities.

5. What is commercial bribery?

   Ans. When employees accept a covert offer of payment or something of value for favorably influencing a business decision, this is known as commercial bribery. The offer is made before the decision, without the employer's knowledge.

6. Explain behavioral red flags. List any three behavioral red flags.

   Ans. Behavioral red flags are clues that indicate the possibility that a person may be involved with a fraud. The presence of red flags does not mean a fraud is being committed. Instead, red flags are warning signs for potential fraud. The three behavioral red flags are: financial difficulties, close association with vendor or customer, and control issues or unwillingness to share duties.

15.2 How Do We Manage Fraud Risk?

Learning Objective ❷
Describe the role of an accounting professional in fraud management.

As you learned in the Risk Management and Internal Controls chapter, companies have first, second, and third lines of defense against risk. Regardless of which line of defense they represent, accounting professionals are responsible for deterring, preventing, and detecting fraud:

- Accounting professionals are in the first line of defense when they use and comply with internal controls in their organizations.

- Compliance and financial accounting professionals are responsible for designing and monitoring internal controls as part of the second line of defense.
- Internal auditors, the third line of defense, evaluate accounting systems for internal control deficiencies that provide opportunities for fraud.
- External auditors may not be one of the three lines of defense, but they provide additional assurance and perform fraud risk assessments during audit planning.

Knowledge of fraud and the motivation of perpetrators can help you deter and prevent fraud. This knowledge combined with an understanding of how internal controls mitigate risk helps accounting professionals to both detect and prevent fraud. Accounting professionals can also play a key role in investigating potential fraud. At many companies, employees can report suspected fraud through calls to an anonymous hotline. These hotlines let reporting employees avoid potential retaliation and are often managed by legal or compliance departments that partner with internal audit to investigate allegations. Section 806 of the Sarbanes-Oxley Act makes employer retaliation illegal and provides protections for whistleblower employees who disclose corporate fraud.

The Fraud Triangle

CPA The **fraud triangle** is a commonly used framework that identifies three motivational elements generally associated with fraud (**Illustration 15.2**).

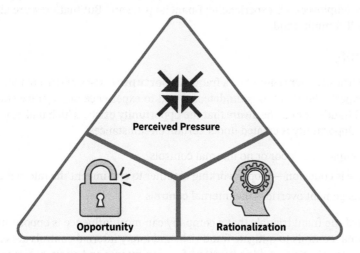

Illustration 15.2 The three elements of the fraud triangle are perceived pressure, rationalization, and opportunity.

The three elements that create the environment needed for committing fraud are perceived pressure (incentive or motive), opportunity, and rationalization (attitude). In auditing, these three elements of the fraud triangle are referred to as fraud risk factors. Where frauds have occurred, these fraud risk factors were evident after the fact. Let's look at the definition of each of these elements so we can later apply them to specific fraud schemes.

Perceived Pressure

First, there is perceived pressure. **Perceived pressure** is a motive or an incentive that pushes a person toward the decision to commit a fraud. A potential fraudster believes they have a need that is "nonshareable"; individuals feel they can't share this need with anyone else, which adds to their perceived pressure. Perceived pressure can come in many forms:

- The inability to pay debts
- The need to maintain a certain lifestyle
- Habits such as drugs and gambling
- Feeling underpaid or underappreciated at work
- A challenge to beat the system

The lower a person's integrity, the less pressure it takes for that person to commit fraud. If the opportunity arises, the chance that a person like this will commit fraud is higher than for someone with a more advanced moral compass. Recall our Julia's Cookies employees who exhibited behavioral red flags? Three of these employees demonstrated that they are under financial pressure (**Table 15.3**).

TABLE 15.3 Julia's Cookies Employees Exhibiting Financial Pressure

Perceived Pressure	Julia's Cookies Employee
Financial difficulties	Shuo is an HR generalist who has been coming into work tired and underperforming. *She says that she and her husband are experiencing financial difficulties that are keeping her up at night.*
Living beyond one's means	*Ricardo is a second-year Accounts Payable clerk who recently bought a new sports car that costs twice as much as his annual salary.*
Recent divorce or family problems	Brady leaves the office regularly to meet with his lawyer and attend court hearings related to his divorce. His wife is demanding most of their assets, and Brady is worried about losing custody of his son. *He's spending a lot of time and money on legal representation and is coming into work stressed and frustrated.*

Between financial difficulties at home and living beyond their means, it's apparent that all three of these employees are experiencing financial pressure. But that pressure alone doesn't mean they will commit fraud.

Opportunity

Without opportunity, there cannot be a fraud. **Opportunity** arises when a potential fraudster reasonably expects the fraud to go undetected and to experience no negative consequences. The potential fraudster must be *aware* that the opportunity exists, which makes it a perceived opportunity. Opportunity is created under certain circumstances:

- When a company has poor or no internal controls
- When there is collusion—people working together to circumvent the internal controls
- When management overrides the internal controls

The element of the fraud triangle that a company can most influence is opportunity. Companies use internal controls to mitigate fraud risk, and many internal controls are embedded in the AIS of an organization, making it critical for accountants and auditors to ensure that the system of internal controls is effective and efficient. An organization's control environment can create a culture of honesty and integrity to mitigate fraud opportunities. We explore internal controls that address the opportunity for specific fraud schemes throughout this chapter.

Rationalization

A fraudster who recognizes the opportunity for fraud typically must justify the act of committing it. **Rationalization** causes a potential fraudster to believe the crime is a justifiable act before they commit it. Some personality types, such as psychopaths, don't need to rationalize a crime. Specialized fraud examiners can help deter fraud by observing psychopathic tendencies in employees. Certified Fraud Examiners (CFEs) undergo training well beyond the scope of this course to ensure that they factor in this type of exception to the fraud triangle in their investigations.

Most people must rationalize committing fraud to overcome their consciences. Common rationalizations include:

- "I'll pay it back."
- "I'm not paid enough."
- "I deserve a promotion anyway."
- "The company is so large that it won't even notice."
- "I need this money for a good cause."

Explore an opportunity to commit fraud at Julia's Cookies in Applied Learning 15.2 to see if you can identify which part of the fraud triangle is missing and why that can make the difference between the potential for fraud and the fraud actually being committed.

Julia's Cookies | Applied Learning 15.2

Fraud Triangle: New Senior Manager

Savannah is the lead data analyst for the Internal Audit department at Julia's Cookies. Her manager quit four months ago, leaving her in charge. Only one year away from being eligible for promotion to manager, Savannah had been hired for "grooming" to one day take her manager's place.

- The vice president of Internal Audit tells Savannah he is accepting job applications for a new manager or senior manager of data analytics at the request of executive leadership and that she is under strong consideration for the promotion.
- Recently Savannah has worked long days, staying late and troubleshooting issues her previous manager left undone.
- Savannah has been reporting directly to the vice president of Internal Audit on a weekly basis, and together they have developed a five-year plan for the Internal Audit analytics fraud monitoring program. As part of this fraud monitoring program, Savannah has designed and implemented a system that alerts management when someone submits an unusual expense in the expense reimbursement system.

Yesterday the vice president of Internal Audit announced to the team—without telling Savannah first—that they had extended an offer for the senior manager of data analytics position, and the candidate had accepted the offer. The new senior manager has 10 more years of internal audit experience than Savannah, but he has none of Savannah's technical skills.

- When the new senior manager arrives, Savannah quickly realizes that her new boss doesn't understand coding or systems design.
- Savannah is the only person on the Internal Audit team who understands how her most recent project works. In fact, Savannah could easily change her fraud monitoring program to exempt her own name from ever raising an alert to management if she were to submit incorrect expenses for reimbursement.

Which parts of the fraud triangle are present for Savannah? Are any parts missing? Do you think Savannah will commit fraud?

SOLUTION

The opportunity to commit fraud is present because there are no internal controls over how Savannah makes changes to her system. With no oversight—nobody on her team understands the code she is writing—she could make inappropriate changes and ensure that nobody is notified if she submits inappropriate expenses.

The rationalization to commit fraud may be present because Savannah has been working overtime to earn a promotion. When passed up and not even informed about the new hire privately, she could easily rationalize that the "company owes her" for her hard work over the past year.

The missing piece is pressure. Savannah has no perceived financial need or pressure to commit fraud other than maybe wanting to get even with her employer. While she may be unhappy with her employer, it's less likely that she will commit fraud than if she had a stronger perceived need for the crime resulting from perceived financial pressure.

This story is based on a true story about one of the authors of this text. Rather than commit fraud, the author found a new position with a different employer.

Preventing Fraud

Preventing fraud before losses occur should always be the priority over detecting it after it happens. Since fraud investigations can be expensive and the company may never recover its loss, prevention is the most cost-effective approach to fighting fraud. In addition to assessing fraud risk, an effective fraud prevention approach includes a strong system of internal controls and creates a culture of ethical behavior in an organization.

Internal Controls

It's impossible to be certain that fraud will not occur. A perpetrator can get around even the strongest system of internal controls. For example, if Zi, a payroll clerk at Julia's Cookies, needs the electronic approval of the senior director of Accounting, Mary, to add new employees to the payroll, what will stop them from colluding to do so for a fictitious employee? Even with an effective internal control for approvals, two employees can work together to circumvent the control.

According to the ACFE's report, 51% of frauds in 2020 involved collusion. A larger number of colluders translated into larger losses due to fraud and greater difficulty detecting fraud. Collusion is used to circumvent two controls:

- Segregation of duties, where one person is not allowed to have conflicting responsibilities
- Independent checks, where one person reviews the work of another for accuracy and objectivity

While internal controls are essential for fraud prevention, a company's culture is equally important.

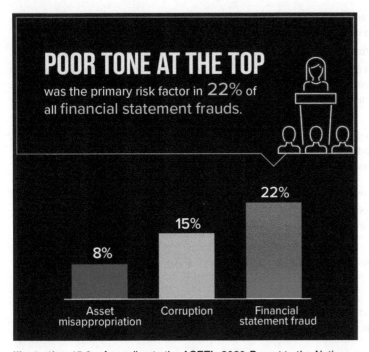

Illustration 15.3 According to the ACFE's 2020 *Report to the Nations*, poor tone at the top is a primary risk factor in financial statement frauds.

Source: 2020 *Report to the Nations.* Copyright 2020 by the Association of Certified Fraud Examiners, Inc.

Tone at the Top

An overarching part of a company's control environment is its culture surrounding fraud. The **tone at the top** is the culture of an organization that flows downstream from executive leadership to impact all functional areas. A culture of zero tolerance for fraud and unethical behavior is a strong deterrent to fraud. Corporate leadership must model behavior consistent with their policies. Company leadership should also communicate in writing and regularly reinforce the expectation of integrity and honesty. Codes of conduct for executives, employees, and external parties like vendors can communicate company expectations and consequences. Making it clear that criminal acts result in dismissal and prosecution will deter potential fraudsters.

Let's go back to Zi and Mary's collusion to commit payroll fraud at Julia's Cookies. If Zi and Mary are fired for collusion and Julia's Cookies reports them to the police, do you think others might be less willing to risk colluding? When Zi and Mary provide an example of what Julia's Cookies does with fraudsters, engaging in a fraudulent act *and not getting caught* becomes less certain in the minds of others. According to the ACFE report, a poor tone at the top was the primary risk factor in 22% of financial statement frauds, which are frauds that often require management complicity (**Illustration 15.3**).

Why Does It Matter to Your Career?

Thoughts from an Internal Audit Manager of Fraud Investigations, Manufacturing

- At many companies, whistleblower tips go to the compliance/legal team. Those that merit review are sent to internal audit, where a fraud investigations auditor will review the data. Often, fraud investigation auditors are pulling data for possible frauds—like expense fraud—and using data analytics to check for red flags.
- Many companies are moving from manual investigations to proactive fraud monitoring programs. Data analysts in your company may help design programs that alert their teams as soon as a transaction matches a fraud red flag. Business leaders in the second line of defense may ask internal auditors what they would look for during a fraud investigation and then have their data analysts and systems developers implement the audit fraud risk assessment logic in continuous monitoring systems. This proactive approach helps identify red flags for fraud before internal or external audit performs a review of the processes and the related transactions.

Detecting Fraud

Since we can't prevent fraud altogether, the next best alternative is early detection. How do we find out it has happened? Companies implement specific controls to detect fraud:

- Identifying **non-behavioral red flags** at a process or entity level, which are company-imposed goals or expectations that drive individuals to commit fraud. At the entity level, pressure to meet financial forecasts or benchmarks, deteriorating financial conditions, financial ratios that don't make sense, pressure from lenders, and a poor control environment—including a negative tone at the top—can all be indicators of possible fraud.

- Setting up anonymous **whistleblower** hotlines so employees can report observations of possible misconduct, concerns about external financial reporting, or other issues. A third party often administers the hotline, and tips received are managed by specified departments, most often legal, compliance, or internal audit.

- Using data analytics specifically designed to continuously monitor processes and systems for fraud trends or anomalies.

- Conducting independent checks of people's work.

- Reviewing adequate documentation that leaves an audit trail.

Two types of financial statement analysis are important to identify red flags that may indicate financial statement fraud:

- **Horizontal analysis:** This type of analysis involves investigating the changes in financial statement items by comparing two or more financial statements from different periods.

- **Vertical analysis:** This type of analysis involves calculating each line item in the same financial statement as a percentage of another line item in the same financial statement. Vertical analysis becomes more insightful when used in conjunction with horizontal analysis. The combination makes it possible to compare the vertical analysis of one reporting period with others.

The most common methods for detecting fraud based on the ACFE's 2020 *Report to the Nations* appear in **Illustration 15.4**.

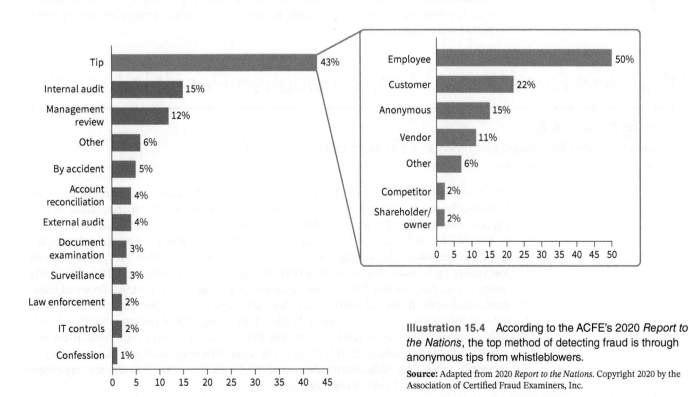

Illustration 15.4 According to the ACFE's 2020 *Report to the Nations*, the top method of detecting fraud is through anonymous tips from whistleblowers.

CONCEPT REVIEW QUESTIONS

1. **CPA** What is a fraud triangle?

   Ans. A fraud triangle is a commonly used framework that identifies three motivational elements generally associated with fraud. The three elements that create the environment needed for committing fraud are perceived pressure (incentive or motive), opportunity, and rationalization (attitude). In auditing, these three elements of the fraud triangle are referred to as fraud risk factors.

2. In the context of the culture of an organization, what does "tone at the top" mean?

   Ans. The tone at the top is the culture of an organization that flows downstream from executive leadership to impact all functional areas. A culture of zero tolerance for fraud and unethical behavior is a strong deterrent to fraud. Corporate leadership must model behavior consistent with their policies. Company leadership should also communicate in writing and regularly reinforce the expectation of integrity and honesty.

3. How can you detect frauds using non-behavioral red flags?

   Ans. Frauds can be detected by identifying non-behavioral red flags at the process level or entity level, which are company-imposed goals or expectations that drive individuals to commit fraud. At the entity level, pressure to meet financial forecasts or benchmarks, deteriorating financial conditions, financial ratios that don't make sense, pressure from lenders, and a poor control environment—including a negative tone at the top—can all be indicators of possible fraud.

4. How does maintaining a whistleblower hotline help to detect frauds?

   Ans. In the organizations with whistleblower hotline, employees can report observations of possible misconduct, concerns about external financial reporting, or other issues. A third party often administers the hotline, and tips received are managed by specified departments, most often legal, compliance, or internal audit.

5. What are the two types of financial analysis used to detect frauds?

   Ans. The two types of financial analysis used to detect frauds are:

   Horizontal analysis: This type of analysis involves investigating the changes in financial statement items by comparing two or more financial statements from different periods.

   Vertical analysis: This type of analysis involves calculating each line item in the same financial statement as a percentage of another line item in the same financial statement. Vertical analysis becomes more insightful when used in conjunction with horizontal analysis. The combination makes it possible to compare the vertical analysis of one reporting period with others.

15.3 How Does Asset Misappropriation Result in Fraud?

Learning Objective ❸

Explain how to identify, prevent, and detect asset misappropriation schemes.

You have already learned about corruption, which is one of the three main categories of fraud schemes. The second is **asset misappropriation**, which is the theft of corporate assets, including cash, inventory, fixed assets, and information such as customer lists and intellectual property.

The ACFE's 2020 *Report to the Nations* indicates that asset misappropriation schemes are the most common and least costly fraud schemes for businesses, based on the typical financial loss caused by an individual fraud case (**Illustration 15.5**). While these schemes frequently occur, the median amount lost in a single case is only $100,000. In contrast, financial statement fraud—which you will learn about in the next section—occurs less often, but an individual case is far more costly to a business. The most appealing type of asset to misappropriate is cash because it is the most liquid business asset. Remember that a perpetrator needs to convert a stolen asset into usable cash. A fraudster who steals inventory must sell that inventory to convert it to cash. This adds an extra element of risk for the fraudster. Cash schemes are attractive because they don't require conversion.

Illustration 15.5 According to the ACFE's 2020 *Report to the Nations*, asset misappropriation is the most common and least costly occupational fraud scheme.

Source: 2020 *Report to the Nations*. Copyright 2020 by the Association of Certified Fraud Examiners, Inc.

CPA Asset misappropriation can impact a company's financial statements—specifically when the perpetrator creates fraudulent journal entries to conceal the theft. For this reason, asset misappropriation is one of the two types of fraud that external auditors—and the CPA exam—focus on.

Why Does It Matter to Your Career?

Thoughts from an Accounts Payable Analyst, Manufacturing

Control deficiencies in business processes create the opportunity for fraud. From small to large companies, you are likely to encounter areas where controls can be improved. Even if it's not your specific job to design controls, don't be afraid to mention areas for improvement to your leadership. New hires can offer a fresh set of eyes to identify weaknesses that people who have been on the team for a long time might miss.

There are three major classes or subcategories of asset misappropriation: skimming, larceny, and fraudulent disbursements.

Skimming

The most difficult type of misstatement to detect is fraud based on the nonrecording of transactions. When a transaction is never recorded, investigators and auditors have no starting point as a reference. **Skimming** happens when an employee steals cash *before* the cash is recorded in the accounting records.

Cash Skimming

What happens if a Julia's Cookies cashier pockets the cash from a walk-in customer who buys three dozen cookies, and the cashier does not ring up the sale on the cash register (**Illustration 15.6**)?

- The sales transaction never shows up in Julia's Cookies' accounting records.
- The cash register will reconcile at the end of the night, but the inventory count will be off.
- The employee conceals this fraud by recording the three dozen cookies as expired dough that was disposed of.

Illustration 15.6 Skimming at the cash register happens when the cashier pockets the money without inputting the transaction into the sales system.

Controls can mitigate the risk of skimming. While it may not be feasible to eliminate cash transactions at Julia's Cookies' brick-and-mortar stores, controls such as daily bank deposits, reconciling the cash register to sales receipts every night, and inventory procedures can help mitigate the risk. The following are some controls that could help Julia's Cookies prevent the type of fraud described here:

- We know the cashier could write off the cookie dough as expired product. A preventive control is having the store manager approve every write-off to mitigate the risk of inappropriate write-offs. Besides, the cashier should not be recording accounting entries, as this is a control weakness in the form of a lack of segregation of duties.

- A regularly scheduled inventory count is a type of control. A store manager who performs an inventory count every week and notices that cookie dough is missing should investigate why the inventory is missing.

- But what if the cashier is the one who does inventory count? They could falsify the inventory report and say the cookies are in inventory. Separating responsibility for sales and reconciling inventory mitigates this risk.

Table 15.4 explores cash skimming concealment methods and methods of preventing and detecting this type of fraud.

TABLE 15.4 Cash Skimming Opportunities and Control Activities

Opportunity: Cashier pockets cash payment from face-to-face sale without ringing the transaction on the register		
Concealment Method	**Preventive Controls**	**Detective Controls**
Not ringing up transaction in sales system	• Not accepting cash at stores • Checking customer receipts when they exit the store (e.g., Costco)	Performing inventory counts; the inventory will be missing, and there will be no cash receipt to indicate that it was sold
Writing off missing inventory as expired	• Requiring manager approval for write-offs • Implementing segregation of duties so that employees executing sales do not perform inventory write-offs	• Data analytics comparing the expiration date in the company's database for all in-store products with the write-off list of products to identify conflicting dates of write-offs or items written off before their recorded expiration dates • Summarizing inventory write-offs by employee to determine if specific employees are performing excessive write-offs
Including product in inventory count when it isn't there	Implementing segregation of duties so that employees executing sales do not perform inventory counts	Audit teams performing independent inventory counts

Accounts Receivable Skimming

CPA Another example of skimming is an accounts receivable employee receiving a check from a customer that is meant to settle the customer's balance. If the employee pockets the check and later cashes it themselves, they could write off the accounts receivable balance as a bad debt. Without proper controls, the company wouldn't know the money was missing because no documentary evidence of the transaction exists.

Segregation of duties can mitigate risk of skimming for checks in this manner. The following responsibilities should be segregated:

- Receiving checks from customers
- Posting payments to the accounts receivable accounts
- Sending invoices to customers

Cross-training employees and rotating staff will ensure that no single person is always responsible for the same role. Custody of assets, authorization of transactions, and recording of transactions are duties that should be segregated. If an accounts receivable employee is responsible for all three of these duties, they can (1) pocket the check and deposit it into a personal account, (2) not record the receipt into the accounts receivable account, and (3) divert invoices and late notices so the customers do not receive notice that their payment wasn't received. There are many methods to prevent and detect accounts receivable skimming schemes (**Table 15.5**).

TABLE 15.5 Accounts Receivable Skimming Opportunities and Control Activities

Opportunity: Accounts receivable clerk receives a check from a customer and pockets the check		
Concealment Method	**Preventive Controls**	**Detective Controls**
Writing off accounts receivable balance as bad debt	• Implementing segregation of duties so that employees receiving payments do not also write off bad debt • Rotating employees across roles in the department on a regular basis	• Data analytics comparing accounts receivable write-offs over time for different customers to identify unusually high write-offs • Data analytics summarizing accounts receivable bad debt write-offs by employee to determine if specific employees are performing excessive bad debt write-offs
Diverting invoices and late notices so customers don't receive notice of payments not being recorded	• Implementing segregation of duties so that employees receiving payments do not also send invoices or late notices to customers • Rotating employees across roles in the department on a regular basis	Independent or supervisory checks

Larceny

Skimming is a type of misappropriation that happens before a transaction is recorded, while **larceny** is the theft of company assets *after* the company has recorded the assets in its books. Cash larceny is stealing cash. Non-cash larceny is defined based on the concealment method the perpetrator uses. Imagine that an employee at a store selling smart phones steals one. The employee could use either of these forms of concealment:

- **Unconcealed larceny:** The employee does not make an effort to conceal the theft.
- **Fictitious sales larceny:** The employee creates a fake sales receipt for the stolen phone.

Asset misappropriation can also refer to the theft of information, such as the selling of proprietary information to a competitor. This type of larceny is likely to be unconcealed larceny as there is no accounting transaction needed to cover for the theft.

Let's go back to the Julia's Cookies cashier. How can the cashier commit fraud *after* the cash receipt has been recorded in the books? Pocketing cash out of the register and stealing cash from the bank deposit bag at the end of the night are both examples of cash larceny. Additionally, the cashier could walk into the kitchen and steal equipment or cookies, which are both non-cash larceny frauds. These frauds could be concealed by faking sales receipts or writing off the inventory. **Table 15.6** summarizes opportunities for larceny and the related concealment, prevention, and detection methods.

TABLE 15.6 Larceny Opportunities and Control Activities

Opportunity: Cash larceny: Cashier pockets cash from register after recording sales transaction		
Concealment Method	**Preventive Controls**	**Detective Controls**
None	• Not accepting cash • Requiring employees to have separate cash drawers • Using cameras to record cashier actions • Using locked cash deposit bags and segregating duties between locking the bag and submitting the deposit to the bank	Reconciling the cash register to sales receipts whenever a cashier's shift ends or a new cashier starts
Opportunity: Non-cash larceny: Cashier walks into kitchen and steals cookies from inventory		
Concealment Method	**Preventive Controls**	**Detective Controls**
Writing off inventory as expired	• Requiring manager approval for write-offs • Implementing segregation of duties so that employees executing sales must not perform inventory write-offs	• Data analytics comparing the expiration date in the company's database for all products in-store with the write-off list of products to identify conflicting dates of write-offs or items written off before their expiration date on record • Summarizing inventory write-offs by employee to determine if any specific employees are performing excessive write-offs

Fraudulent Disbursements

Fraudulent disbursements occur when an employee causes the business to make a payment for an inappropriate purpose. Fraudulent disbursements occur on the books, as the company will have a record of the payment. These schemes are the most common type of asset misappropriation. The record of the payment creates an audit trail, and proper controls can assist in identifying fraudulent disbursements after the fact. Companies often use data analytics to monitor for red flags indicating possible fraudulent disbursements.

Let's look at three common fraudulent disbursement schemes that occurred at Julia's Cookies: expense reimbursement schemes, payroll schemes, and billing schemes.

Expense Reimbursement Schemes

In an **expense reimbursement scheme**, the business reimburses the perpetrator for expenses they never incurred. Jesse is a regional store manager at Julia's Cookies who regularly visits the stores he manages. Because he travels and submits expenses so frequently, he does not believe he will get caught if he submits fake expenses. He creates fictitious receipts in a document on his computer, prints them, and scans them back to his computer. He attaches these fake receipts to his expense reimbursement requests for meals he never ate.

Eventually Jesse takes his scheme a step further by submitting expenses that don't qualify for reimbursement. He begins submitting personal expenses for his dry cleaning and for coffee on the weekend. As these small-ticket items make it through the system and are reimbursed, he gets greedier and starts submitting large-ticket items like purchases from Best Buy and Amazon.

When he realizes that nobody is reviewing his expense submissions, Jesse starts double dipping. **Double dipping** involves submitting a valid credit card expense two times—once as a credit card transaction and once as a cash transaction. By double dipping his hotel and meal expenses, Jesse gets Julia's Cookies to pay for these transactions twice (**Illustration 15.7**). By the time Internal Audit at Julia's Cookies detects this fraud, Jesse has already stolen thousands of dollars.

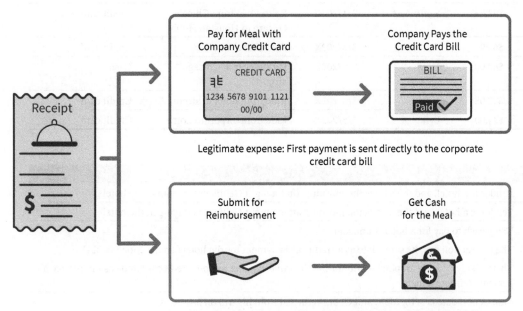

Illustration 15.7   Double dipping involves submitting a single credit card transaction two times: once as a legitimate credit card transaction and once as a cash transaction, which creates a fraudulent reimbursement to the employee.

One of the authors assists the legal department at her company with fraud investigations, and she uncovered a fraud similar to this one. The internal audit team performed an expense reimbursement review and provided the expense management team with recommendations on ways to implement better controls, including continuous monitoring data analytics. Explore expense reimbursement fraud further in Applied Learning 15.3.

Julia's Cookies   Applied Learning 15.3

Expense Reimbursement Fraud: Travel Red Flags

Gellin, who is a baking trainer at Julia's Cookies, lives in Chicago. He traveled from Chicago to Houston last week to host training on how to bake a new product:

- He flew to Houston on 3/6/202X.
- His return flight was the morning of 3/8/202X.

Gellin submitted this expense report using Julia's Cookies' expense reimbursement system.

Review the transactions to find common red flags for possible expense reimbursement schemes. Examine each transaction, state whether or not it raises a red flag, and explain why or why not.

Transaction	Category	Amount	Vendor	Date	Description	Transaction Type
000010	Hotels	$178.02	Marriott Houston	3/7/202X	Hotel room—one night	Credit card
000011	Hotels	$178.02	Marriott Houston	3/8/202X	Hotel room—one night	Credit card
000012	Hotels	$178.02	N/A	3/8/202X	Hotel room—one night	Cash
000013	Meals	$54.58	Uber Eats	3/10/202X	Dinner at hotel	Credit card
000014	Meals	$22.63	N/A	3/8/202X	Breakfast at airport	Cash
000015	Meals	$72.48	Amazon	3/7/202X	Dinner with team	Credit card
000016	Airline	$439.98	Southwest	3/1/202X	Round trip from Chicago O'Hare to Houston Hobby	Credit card
000017	Meals	$6.89	Starbucks	3/8/202X	Breakfast at airport	Credit card
000018	Travel	$60.00	N/A	3/8/202X	Parking car at Chicago airport	Cash
000019	Travel	$32.08	Lyft	3/8/202X	Ride from hotel to airport	Credit card
000020	Travel	$24.90	Lyft	3/8/202X	Ride from airport to home	Credit card

SOLUTION

Transaction	Red Flag?	Reason
000010	No	Vendor is a hotel, and the date is the morning after a night Gellin was staying at the hotel
000011	No	Vendor is a hotel, and the date is the morning after a night Gellin was staying at the hotel
000012	Yes	Using cash to pay for a hotel is unusual
		The transaction has the same date as a credit card payment for the hotel (Transaction 000011)
		This is likely "double dipping"—submitting the same expense as both credit card and cash to receive a personal reimbursement
000013	Yes	Transaction date is 3/10/202X, and Gellin returned from his trip on 3/8/202X
		Dinner at the hotel is unlikely to be from Uber Eats
000014	Yes	Cash transaction means you can't see who the vendor was
		This is breakfast on the same day as 000017
		Review the receipt to see if it matches the time and amount
000015	Yes	Vendor is Amazon, which is not a restaurant
000016	No	Transaction date is before the trip, which is okay because Gellin booked his flights in advance
000017	No	Vendor is a restaurant/coffee shop on the day Gellin was flying home in the morning
000018	Yes	Paying cash for parking isn't unusual, but Gellin also submits an expense for taking a Lyft home from the airport (transaction 000020), and he would not need to take a Lyft if his car were parked at the airport
000019	No	Vendor and date match Gellin's travel from his hotel to the airport
000020	No	Vendor and date match Gellin's travel from the airport to his home

When investigating possible expense reimbursement schemes, data analytics can be used to analyze expense reports and transactions. These are common red flags related to expense reimbursement schemes:

- Transactions with dates outside the dates of travel
- Transactions with expense categories that do not match vendor products or services
- Transactions for the same amount and date (double dipping)
- Transactions classified as cash for categories that are not usually paid in cash (hotels, airlines, etc.)
- Transactions for a car rental, taxi, or ride-share service while also submitting transactions to be reimbursed for mileage (driving a personal vehicle)

- Transactions for airline costs submitted twice—once before the trip and once in the trip report (**Illustration 15.8**)
- Transactions just under the threshold for requiring receipts (as most companies only require receipts if the transaction is over a set amount)

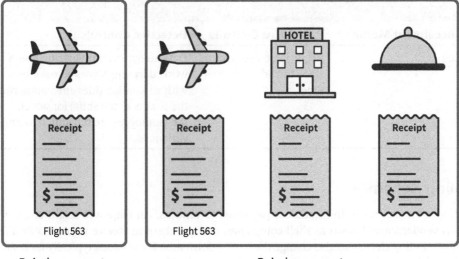

Reimbursement
March 4, 2022

Reimbursement
April 8, 2022

Illustration 15.8 An example of double dipping is submitting an airline cost twice: once when the ticket is purchased and again when submitting expenses after the trip.

A control implemented relatively recently by some companies mitigates the risk of fraudulent mileage expense reports by requiring traveling sales staff to use company-issued cell phones and to turn on the GPS tracking to capture data for mileage reimbursement. An employee who fails to record the GPS data in this manner receives no reimbursement for mileage.

Table 15.7 lists prevention and detection methods for expense reimbursement fraud.

TABLE 15.7 Expense Reimbursement Opportunities and Control Activities

Opportunity: An employee submits a credit card expense for an inappropriate personal purchase made at Amazon		
Concealment Method	**Preventive Controls**	**Detective Controls**
Categorizing the expense as a business meal and creating a fictitious receipt	• Requiring receipts to be submitted for all expenses over a certain dollar threshold • Manager approval and review of attached receipts for expense reimbursements	Data analytics comparing the "merchant code"—a categorical code attached to all credit card transactions—to reconcile the location where the credit card purchase was made to the expense category submitted; an online retailer has a different code than a restaurant

Payroll Schemes

In a **payroll scheme**, the business pays the perpetrator for time not worked. These schemes come in many forms—from a friend punching the timeclock for his buddy at a warehouse to payroll clerks creating ghost, or fictitious, employees in the payroll system. The perpetrator also must manage the bank accounts of the fictitious employee, who may be a real person not employed at the company and whose Social Security number may have been stolen.

At Julia's Cookies, cashiers are paid hourly wages and record their time in a computerized time system at the end of each shift. This creates an opportunity for cashiers to record **unauthorized hours** by padding their time sheets. One employee does this regularly by adding 15 minutes to their start and end time every day. This employee works 6 days a week, so the scheme results in over 12 hours of fraudulent pay every month.

Payroll schemes can also be detected using data analytics. **Table 15.8** explores payroll scheme opportunities and methods of preventing and detecting this type of fraud.

TABLE 15.8 Payroll Opportunities and Control Activities

Opportunity: A cashier pads their time sheet with unauthorized hours every shift		
Concealment Method	**Preventive Controls**	**Detective Controls**
None	Requiring employees to clock in and out in real time	Data analytics summarizing hours worked by employees across stores with similar job titles and comparing the results to the shifts for which the employees are scheduled to find variances

Billing Schemes

Billing schemes result in fraudulent payments to vendors. An employee might create fictitious vendors, also known as shell companies, and use them to receive payments for false invoices. Billing clerks can also change the bank information for vendors, typically for a short period of time, to divert payments to personally controlled bank accounts.

A Julia's Cookies billing clerk frequently engages in a **pay and return** fraud scheme by inputting inflated amounts in the payment system, thus arranging for Julia's Cookies to overpay an invoice. When the vendor returns the overpayment amount, the billing clerk intercepts the return check and deposits it in a personal account. **Table 15.9** explores billing scheme opportunities and methods of preventing and detecting this type of fraud.

TABLE 15.9 Billing Scheme Opportunities and Control Activities

Opportunity: An accounts payable clerk creates fictitious vendors and invoices, then directs payments to personal bank accounts		
Concealment Method	**Preventive Controls**	**Detective Controls**
Fictitious invoices	• Maintaining rigorous control over the vendor master file	• Data analytics looking for unusual or similar vendor names
	• Implementing segregation of duties so that employees responsible for vendor creation in the system are not responsible for issuing payments	• Data analytics comparing vendor names, bank accounts, phone numbers, and addresses to the employee directory's names, bank accounts, phone numbers, and addresses
	• Requiring manager approval for checks issued	• Data analytics looking for post office boxes or incomplete information in addresses

CONCEPT REVIEW QUESTIONS

1. **CPA** What is meant by asset misappropriation?

    Ans. Asset misappropriation is the theft of corporate assets, including cash, inventory, fixed assets, and information such as customer lists and intellectual property. Asset misappropriation can impact a company's financial statements—specifically when the perpetrator creates fraudulent journal entries to conceal the theft. For this reason, asset misappropriation is one of the two types of fraud that external auditors and Certified Public Accountants focus on.

2. What do you understand by cash skimming? List the concealment methods used in cash skimming.

   Ans. Cash skimming happens when an employee steals cash before the cash is recorded in the accounting records. Concealment methods used in cash skimming are:

   - Not ringing up transaction in the sales system
   - Writing off missing inventory as expired
   - Including product in inventory count when it isn't there

3. What is accounts receivable skimming?

   Ans. When an accounts receivable employee receiving a check from a customer that is meant to settle the customer's balance pockets the check and later cashes it themselves, they could write off the accounts receivable balance as a bad debt. This is an example of accounts receivable skimming. Without proper controls, the company wouldn't know the money was missing because no documentary evidence of the transaction exists.

4. What is the difference between skimming and larceny?

   Ans. Skimming is a type of misappropriation that happens before a transaction is recorded, whereas larceny is the theft of company assets after the company has recorded the assets in its books.

5. What are fraudulent disbursements?

   Ans. Fraudulent disbursements occur when an employee causes the business to make a payment for an inappropriate purpose. Fraudulent disbursements occur on the books, as the company will have a record of the payment. These schemes are the most common type of asset misappropriation.

6. What do you understand by the term "double-dipping"?

   Ans. Double-dipping involves submitting a valid credit card expense two times—once as a credit card transaction and once as a cash transaction.

15.4 What Are the Characteristics of Financial Statement Fraud?

Learning Objective ❹
Identify financial statement fraud and explain how to mitigate its risks.

CPA Management is responsible for producing the financial statements. Section 302 of SOX makes the CEO and CFO of a company subject to SOX regulations directly responsible for the accuracy, documentation, and submission of all financial reports, as well as a report on the adequacy of the system of internal control, to the SEC. Management producing inaccurate or fraudulent financial statements can face prison time and fines. Because management reviews and signs off on the accuracy of the financial statements—and can be legally liable for any inaccuracy—it is unlikely that significant financial statement fraud can be committed without the involvement or consent of management. **Financial statement fraud** involves materially misrepresenting the financial results and position of a company by manipulating amounts or inappropriately disclosing information in the financial statements to deceive investors, creditors, and other users of the financial statements. *Materiality* means that the misrepresentation is large enough that users who rely on this misrepresented financial information to make decisions may suffer financial damage. The ACFE's 2020 *Report to the Nations* indicates that financial statement fraud schemes are the least common and most costly of frauds (**Illustration 15.9**).

Internal victims of this type of fraud could be employees who hold stock of the company, including their retirement plans, and executives and managers who are innocent and may lose their jobs and reputations. Victims external to the organization include suppliers, investors, customers, and creditors—all of whom may suffer adverse consequences if a company misrepresents itself in its financial statements.

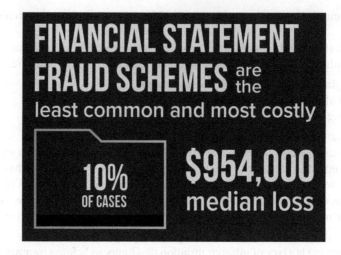

People commit financial reporting fraud for many reasons. Often, the end goal is to make a company seem like it is performing better than it really is. One reason is to sell their stock at an inflated price or exercise their stock options at a profit. Management may want to meet earnings forecasts or hide problems, such as meeting the terms of loan covenants. Management may also need to obtain financing that would not be possible if they fairly presented the financial statements. Management may also want to meet benchmarks for performance-based compensation.

The objective of financial statement fraud is to either overstate or understate the company's financial performance and position.

Overstating Financial Performance

Two kinds of financial statement frauds are commonly used to make a company's performance and financial position seem better than they really are. The first kind involves overstating assets, revenues, and profits. The second kind involves understating liabilities, expenses, and losses.

Overstating Assets, Revenues, and Profits

Let's look at how overstating assets, revenues, and profits impacts the financial statements to create an overstatement of the company's net worth. Recall the basic accounting equation:

$$\text{ASSETS} \quad = \quad \text{LIABILITIES} \quad + \quad \text{OWNERS' EQUITY}$$

If we *overstate* assets, revenues, or profits, we are increasing the assets side of the equation. One example would be to prematurely record revenue (earned in the subsequent fiscal year but recorded in the current fiscal year). The entry for a service organization would be:

		Dr.	Cr.
May 4, 20XX	Dr. Accounts Receivable	$10,000	
	Cr. Service Revenue		$10,000

By debiting accounts receivable (a balance sheet account), we are overstating assets. We are also overstating revenues for the reporting period by crediting service revenue (an income statement account). By overstating revenues, we are overstating net income because revenue increases net income (profits), which is credited to retained earnings in the closing process. Retained earnings, which is part of stockholders' equity, is now overstated. Retained earnings is a stockholders' equity account. Essentially, by overstating assets, revenues, and profits, we overstate the stockholders' equity and increase the book value of the company.

Let's use the following accounting equation as an example:

ASSETS	=	LIABILITIES	+	OWNERS' EQUITY
$50,000		$20,000		$30,000

If we overstate our assets by $10,000, we can balance the accounting equation by increasing our owners' equity by $10,000:

$$\text{ASSETS} = \text{LIABILITIES} + \text{OWNERS' EQUITY}$$
$$\$60,000 \qquad \$20,000 \qquad \$40,000$$
$$(\$50,000 + \$10,000) \qquad\qquad\qquad (\$30,000 + \$10,000)$$

To increase the net worth of the company on the balance sheet, assets, revenues, and profits can be overstated. The most common financial statement fraud schemes involve manipulating the revenue and accounts receivable balances. Recording fictitious sales in the income statement and overstating accounts receivable on the balance sheet increases the overall book value of the company, which may then meet or exceed analysts' forecasts and increase the stock price.

There are several ways to fraudulently overstate revenue. Let's look more closely at some common fictitious revenue fraud schemes and explore prevention and detection methods.

Sham sales fraud schemes occur when the perpetrator conceals fictitious revenue fraud with falsified documentation. Creating fake shipping documentation and sending the inventory to another location to physically hide it is a common method of concealment that ensures removal of the inventory from the inventory count.

For example, management at a bicycle manufacturer may rationalize that they need to meet their annual sales goals. To inflate revenue, finished bicycles are recorded as "sold" and shipped to a temporary rented storage location. The company's revenues have now increased, and forecasts are met. After the inventory count is completed, management brings back the bicycles. By physically moving the bicycles and hiding them at another location, the company will show an appropriate inventory count that reconciles to perpetual inventory records during an audit.

This type of fraud scheme is easiest to implement when a company has a large amount of finished goods in its warehouse. This is why we used a bicycle manufacturer instead of Julia's Cookies as our example. Julia's Cookies' business model involves perishable products that are made in a just-in-time environment to prevent spoilage, so finished goods do not stay in inventory for long. It would be difficult for a fraudster to use the sham sales scheme to conceal fictitious revenue fraud in this environment.

Table 15.10 gives examples of the various ways sham sales can be concealed, prevented, and detected.

TABLE 15.10 Sham Sales Opportunities and Control Activities

Opportunity: Management uses sham sales to inflate sales revenue		
Concealment Methods	**Preventive Controls**	**Detective Controls**
Shipping goods to another location	Requiring approvals for moving all finished inventories	• Performing simultaneous location inventory counts • Using data analytics to trace the life cycle of a product throughout the enterprise system • Implementing vertical or horizontal financial statement analysis
Creating a fake customer and falsifying sales documents and then hiding inventory from auditors	• Requiring approvals for creation of new customers in the system • Implementing systems controls that prevent the creation of customers with similar names so that fake customer accounts cannot be confused with legitimate customers	Using data analytics to review the master list of customers for red flags such as: • Sales only occurring near the end of an accounting period • Unusually high sales near the end of an accounting period • Long periods with no sales and then an abnormally large sale • Similarities in customer names to legitimate customer names but missing other data fields (e.g., Krogger, Walmarts, Amazin)

Unauthorized shipments enable a company to overstate revenues by creating sales and shipping goods that were never ordered by customers. This fraud scheme is most commonly executed at year end, so the return from the customer is processed in the subsequent accounting period.

Suppose that Julia's Cookies ships a large order of its frozen make-at-home cookie dough to one of its biggest customers, Kroger, on December 30, Year 1, even though Kroger did not order the product. The Year 1 financial statements include the revenue from this sale. When Kroger returns the order on January 1, Year 2, the return isn't reflected in the Year 1 financial statements. In a poor internal control environment, this could be done without concealment. Requiring a purchase order to be attached to every shipment in the system is a preventive control that requires the perpetrator to create a fictitious purchase order to conceal this fraud. To detect this fraud, Julia's Cookies could use data analytics to look at the sales and shipment systems and match every shipment with its sales documentation. It could also analyze sales and shipments close to the cutoff date to mitigate revenue fraud risks (**Table 15.11**).

TABLE 15.11 Unauthorized Shipments Opportunities and Control Activities

Opportunity: Management uses unauthorized shipments to inflate sales revenue		
Concealment Method	**Preventive Controls**	**Detective Controls**
Shipping to a customer product that was not ordered at the end of the accounting period	Implementing segregation of duties between processing of sales receipts and preparation of shipping requests	• Using data analytics to review sales made at year end for unusually large amounts close to the cutoff date • Implementing vertical or horizontal financial statement analysis

Channel stuffing is a fraud scheme where the seller encourages the sales of extra inventory to increase the current year's sales, when it is stated or implied that the customer can return the goods after the year end but not providing a reserve against these expected returns in the current year (**Table 15.12**). Because Julia's Cookies' products do not have a long shelf life, the company has a low risk of channel stuffing. Let's look at the real case of Monster Beverage Corp., where shareholders accused management of channel stuffing by selling too many drinks to Anheuser-Busch, with executives then taking advantage of the inflated share price. After an investigation and the release of accurate results, the share price fell by 25%.

TABLE 15.12 Channel Stuffing Opportunities and Control Activities

Opportunity: Management ships more products than were ordered into its distribution channel to inflate sales revenue and does not provide for returns that might come in the next reporting period		
Concealment Method	**Preventive Controls**	**Detective Controls**
Recording sales with the expectation that they will be returned but not providing for the returns in the current period	• Ensuring an ethical control environment • Creating a whistle-blower hotline	• Using data analytics to review sales made at year end for unusually large amounts close to the cutoff date and for unusually large amounts of returns after the cutoff date • Using vertical or horizontal financial statement analysis

Sales cutoff fraud schemes involve recording sales that occur after the balance sheet date in the current year's financial statements to inflate sales even though they belong in the subsequent accounting period.

Automated journal entries and appropriate journal entry approval controls in the general ledger system can help prevent this fraud scheme. General ledger systems that lock out back-dated journal entries after the cutoff date (the date of the month on which journal entries should no longer be applied to the prior accounting period) will prevent fictitious creation or manipulation of journal entries (**Table 15.13**).

TABLE 15.13 Sales Cutoff Opportunities and Control Activities

Opportunity: Management uses sales cutoff manipulation to inflate sales revenue		
Concealment Method	**Preventive Controls**	**Detective Controls**
Recording sales from the subsequent accounting period in the current period	• Implementing system controls that prevent recording or manipulating journal entries past the cutoff date • Implementing segregation of duties in the general ledger system • Requiring appropriate approvals in the general ledger system	• Using data analytics to review journal entry data from the general ledger system for post-cutoff entries • Using vertical or horizontal financial statement analysis

Data analytics can detect this fraud by performing cutoff date reviews of journal entries from the general ledger system. Data analytics can also look at revenue by month compared to previous years to see if there are times when revenue seems unusually high. If Julia's Cookies' sales in December seem disproportionately high compared to previous years, sales journal entries should be reviewed to ensure that dates were not changed to count sales from the subsequent period in December.

While revenue fraud involving physical inventory and shipments is only applicable to product businesses—that is, companies that produce tangible products to sell—sales cutoff fraud can occur at service businesses as well. For example, a software consulting firm that specializes in assisting companies in implementing enterprise resource planning systems may recognize revenue from contracts in the subsequent accounting period to inflate revenues.

CPA At Julia's Cookies, the fiscal year runs from January 1 through December 31. If Julia's Cookies records sales from January Year 2 in its Fiscal Year 1 data, it will inflate the revenues for Fiscal Year 1 (**Illustration 15.10**). Decide how you would handle a request to recognize revenue prematurely at Julia's Cookies in Applied Learning 15.4.

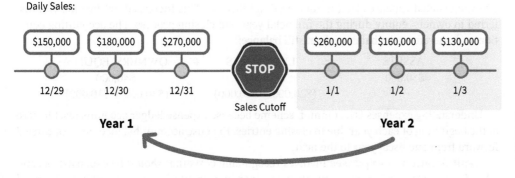

Daily Sales:

| $150,000 | $180,000 | $270,000 | STOP Sales Cutoff | $260,000 | $160,000 | $130,000 |

12/29   12/30   12/31   1/1   1/2   1/3

Year 1   **Year 2**

Illustration 15.10 Sales cutoff recognizes sales transactions from the beginning of Year 2 in Year 1's income statement.

Julia's Cookies   Applied Learning 15.4

Financial Statement Fraud: Improper Revenue Recognition

Julia's Cookies' year end is December 31. It's January Year 2, and the business is working on closing its books and preparing its year-end financial statements for Fiscal Year 1.

Chris is a financial accountant whose job is to enter journal entries into the accounting system.

- Chris has received the data from the Sales department for January Year 2 and is approached by one of the executives, who asks Chris to include all the sales from the first two weeks of January Year 2 in the December Year 1 sales data.
- This will increase the total revenue Julia's Cookies reports on its financial statements for Fiscal Year 1.
- Chris knows the executives in the Sales department receive large bonuses that are dependent on achieving specific revenue goals every fiscal year.
- Looking at the data, Chris sees that adding these two weeks from January Year 2 will change the year-end revenue to just above the target revenue amount.

What should Chris do?

SOLUTION

Manipulating the revenue balance is financial statement fraud. Sales should be recognized in the time period they occur, and including January sales in the prior year's revenues is not acceptable revenue recognition practice. Chris can tell the executive that they aren't comfortable completing the request, discuss the request with their direct manager and let them step in, or report the fraudulent request to the company's whistleblower hotline to anonymously provide information about the suspected fraud and inappropriate behaviors without fear of retaliation.

Understating Liabilities, Expenses, and Losses

Like overstating revenue, understating expenses increases a company's net income. Because net income is calculated by subtracting expenses from revenue, understating expenses increases net income. The lower the expenses, the higher the net income, given revenue as a constant.

Let's consider a fraudster CEO who decides to *understate* liabilities, expenses, and losses to show improved performance and a better financial position:

- The company is in danger of not meeting debt covenant liquidity requirements, which means the debt will have to be repaid immediately.
- To meet the liquidity ratio specified in the debt agreement, the CEO and CFO collaborate to omit liabilities (accrued liabilities for expenses) totaling $10,000 from the balance sheet and the related expenses of $10,000 from the income statement.

The impact would be to understate liabilities and expenses by $10,000 each because the journal entry to record the liability and related expenses payable, which was never processed, should have been:

		Dr.	Cr.
May 5, 20XX	Dr. Expenses	$10,000	
	Cr. Accrued Expenses Payable		$10,000

The understated expenses lead to increased net income. This increased net income is transferred to owners' equity during the financial year-end closing process. The accounting equation and, therefore, the balance sheet still balance:

ASSETS	=	LIABILITIES	+	OWNERS' EQUITY
$50,000		$10,000		$40,000
		($20,000 − $10,000)		($30,000 + $10,000)

Understating expenses is a common scheme because expense ledger accounts reset to zero at the beginning of each year due to closing entries. Expense account balances are not carried forward from one fiscal year to the next.

Capitalization of expenses involves recognizing costs that *should* be expensed as capitalized assets. Converting expenses into assets increases profits. You may recall from financial accounting that costs are recorded in one of two ways:

- Expensed in the current period's income statement
- Capitalized as an asset and expensed over more than one accounting period through depreciation or amortization

Capitalizing expenses is appropriate when a company can expect a *future value* from an expense that benefits the company over more than one accounting period. For example, if Julia's Cookies has routine maintenance performed on its delivery trucks, this expenditure is recorded as an expense. If the company installs hydraulic lifts on trucks to reach loading docks, this is considered an improvement that provides future long-term value to the company. Julia's Cookies capitalizes this cost by debiting it to the asset account and expensing it as depreciation over its useful life.

Capitalizing expenses as a fraud scheme involves recognizing inappropriate costs as assets and expensing them over time instead of in the current period. If Julia's Cookies reported its routine delivery truck maintenance as a capitalized cost, it would understate the expenses the company incurred this year and overstate the financial position of the company by overstating the asset.

In 2001, external auditors for HealthSouth, a Birmingham, Alabama, provider of post-acute health care services, received a letter from one of its previous bookkeepers. This whistleblower pointed the auditors toward multiple accounts where the bookkeeper believed HealthSouth had been capitalizing expenses. The eventual forensic investigation revealed that HealthSouth had overstated revenues by $3.8 to $4.6 billion through various fraud schemes, including fictitious sales. The fraud scandal badly damaged HealthSouth's reputation, and in 2017, the company rebranded itself as Encompass Health. **Table 15.14** lists prevention and detection methods for this type of fraud scheme.

TABLE 15.14 Capitalization of Expenses Opportunities and Control Activities

Opportunity: Management understates expenses to inflate profit		
Concealment Method	**Preventive Controls**	**Detective Controls**
Inappropriately capitalizing expenses to an asset account	• Implementing segregation of duties in the general ledger system • Requiring appropriate approvals in the general ledger system	• Using data analytics to identify significant capitalization during the year and reviewing for appropriateness • Using vertical or horizontal financial statement analysis

Expense cutoff fraud occurs when expenses are *not* recorded until the subsequent accounting period. The opposite of sales cutoff, expense cutoff pushes the transactions to the subsequent period to avoid recognizing the expense in the current period (**Illustration 15.11**). Detection methods for expense cutoff include data analytics tests similar to those used in sales cutoff tests—but on the opposite side of the date range. If Julia's Cookies has unusually high expenses occurring at the beginning of Year 2, auditors may want to check those expenses to confirm that they were not incurred during or related to revenues recorded in Year 1.

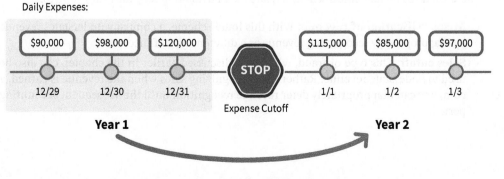

Daily Expenses:

$90,000 — 12/29
$98,000 — 12/30
$120,000 — 12/31
STOP — Expense Cutoff
$115,000 — 1/1
$85,000 — 1/2
$97,000 — 1/3

Year 1 → Year 2

Illustration 15.11 Expense cutoff recognizes expenses from the end of Year 1 at the beginning of Year 2.

Table 15.15 summarizes prevention and detection methods for expense cutoff fraud.

TABLE 15.15 Expense Cutoff Opportunities and Control Activities

Opportunity: Management understates expenses to inflate profit		
Concealment Method	**Preventive Controls**	**Detective Controls**
Postponing recognition of expenses until the subsequent accounting period	• Implementing system controls that prevent postdating of journal entries • Implementing policies regarding timeliness of recording journal entries	• Using data analytics to summarize expenses at the beginning of the subsequent accounting period • Using vertical or horizontal financial statement analysis

Understating Financial Performance

It is easy to understand why management might want to *overstate* the company's financial performance, and this is by far the most common type of financial statement fraud. However, there are also a few reasons management might want to *understate* the company's financial performance:

- To decrease taxes owed
- To reduce the amount of money distributed in dividends to shareholders
- To defer earnings to subsequent periods if current goals have been met
- To reduce investors' current expectations to create perception of growth in the future

The fraud schemes for understating company performance are the inverse of the fraud schemes used to overstate company performance (**Illustration 15.12**).

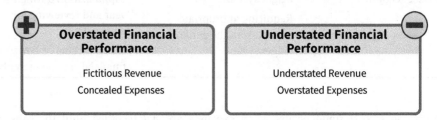

Illustration 15.12   Understating financial performance schemes are the inverse of overstating financial performance schemes.

Let's look at some examples of understating financial performance.

Understated Revenue

There are three notable fraud schemes related to understating revenue (**Table 15.16**):

- **Misclassification of revenue:** With this fraud scheme, a company understates revenue by inappropriately recognizing revenue as a different type of income.
- **Sales cutoff:** This type of fraud, which was discussed earlier in the chapter, can also be used to understate revenue. Rather than recognizing sales when the revenue is earned, a company can inappropriately defer revenue recognition until the subsequent accounting period.

TABLE 15.16 Understated Revenue Opportunities and Control Activities

Opportunity: Management misclassifies revenue to understate revenue		
Concealment Method	**Preventive Controls**	**Detective Controls**
Recording revenue as capital gain transactions	• Implementing segregation of duties in the general ledger system • Requiring appropriate approvals in the general ledger system	• Using data analytics to perform a time trend analysis of revenue from previous years to identify unusually low sales periods in the current year • Using vertical or horizontal financial statement analysis

Opportunity: Management uses sales cutoff to understate sales revenue		
Concealment Method	**Preventive Controls**	**Detective Controls**
Recording sales from the current accounting period in the subsequent accounting period	• Implementing system controls that prevent recording or manipulation of journal entries past the cutoff date • Implementing segregation of duties in the general ledger system • Requiring appropriate approvals in the general ledger system	• Using data analytics to review journal entry data from the general ledger system for entries that are postdated • Using vertical or horizontal financial statement analysis

Opportunity: Revenue is unrecorded and therefore understated		
Concealment Method	**Preventive Controls**	**Detective Controls**
Failing to record revenue transactions	• Electronic funds transfer directly to the bank • Use of cash registers or point-of-sales devices • Preparing a prelist of mail receipts and restrictively endorsing checks immediately to ensure independent agreement of prelist with bank deposits • Conducting bank reconciliations regularly	• Using data analytics to perform a time trend analysis of revenue from previous years to identify unusually low sales periods in the current year • Using vertical or horizontal financial statement analysis

• **Unrecorded revenue:** This fraud scheme, which is most easily perpetrated by smaller businesses, involves not documenting sales or destroying sales documentation and diverting funds, especially cash, elsewhere. A local restaurant or another small business often has cash transactions from daily sales. These situations lend themselves well to unrecorded revenue.

Overstated Expenses

There are a couple of ways a company might overstate its expenses:

• **Expensing capitalized costs:** With this fraud scheme, a company recognizes capital costs that should be recorded to an asset account as an expense, thus reducing net income. This is the opposite of the approach used to understate expenses.

- **Expense cutoff:** This type of fraud, which was discussed earlier in the chapter, can also be used for overstating expenses by prematurely recording them in the current accounting period rather than in the subsequent period. The impact is to increase expenses and reduce net income. The same data analytics used for expense cutoff fraud schemes that overstate the company's financial position can be used to test for this type of fraud.

If Julia's Cookies' internal auditors are using data analytics to review the expenses for Year 1, they will look at expenses recorded at the beginning of Year 2 to investigate for overstatement of expenses. In contrast, they will look at the end of Year 1 for expenses that belong in Year 2 to investigate for the understatement of expenses.

Explore these fraud schemes and their related concealment, prevention, and detection methods in **Table 15.17.**

TABLE 15.17 Overstated Expenses Opportunities and Control Activities

Opportunity: Management overstates expenses to understate profits		
Concealment Method	**Preventive Controls**	**Detective Controls**
Inappropriately expensing costs that should be capitalized to an asset account	• Implementing segregation of duties in the general ledger system • Requiring appropriate approvals in the general ledger system	• Using data analytics to review trends of expenses over time and identify unusually high expenses • Using vertical or horizontal financial statement analysis
Prematurely recording expenses from the subsequent accounting period in the current period	• Implementing system controls that prevent recording or manipulation of journal entries past the cutoff date • Implementing segregation of duties in the general ledger system • Requiring appropriate approvals in the general ledger system	• Using data analytics to summarize expenses at the end of the current accounting period • Using vertical or horizontal financial statement analysis

Management's Involvement in Financial Statement Fraud

As you have reviewed the summaries of preventive controls for financial statement fraud, have you noticed a trend? Often, they rely on a series of approvals or segregation of duties. **Management override** occurs when management decides to ignore controls that are in place. You can see throughout this chapter how management override could be used to circumvent these preventive measures. Management override is a big concern to a company's internal control environment, and it should be a consideration at the forefront of a fraud risk assessment.

Financial statement fraud, also known as "cooking the books," misleads investors and largely impacts the public. For this reason, the U.S. SEC releases cases to the public whenever it makes allegations against publicly traded companies. You can look at data from these actual fraud cases by reviewing the SEC's Accounting and Auditing Enforcement Releases (AAERs). A recent comprehensive study of AAERs shows that the SEC investigated 347 public company cases of alleged financial reporting fraud over a 10-year period.[10] Key findings from the cases in this study include:

---

[10]Research report commissioned by the Committee of Sponsoring Organizations (COSO): *Fraudulent Reporting: 1998–2007, An Analysis of U.S. Public Companies.*

- 89% of cases named the CEO and/or the CFO and indicated that fraud occurred as a result of control environment issues resulting from a compromised tone at the top.
- The average amount of fraud at these public companies was $400 million.
- 61% of cases involved inappropriate revenue recognition, mostly involving creation of fictitious revenue transactions or premature recognition of revenue.
- 51% of cases involved overstatement of assets.
- 31% of cases involved understatement of expenses and liabilities.
- The most common motivations for the frauds were attempts to meet earnings expectations, hide deteriorating financial conditions, inflate stock prices, improve financial performance for pending equity or debt financing, and increase performance-based compensation.

Why Does It Matter to Your Career?

Thoughts from an External Audit Data Analyst, Public Accounting

- Many online resources list various financial fraud data analytics tests you can use. Reviews that auditors used to perform manually on a sample are now performed on full populations using analytics. Cutoff analysis, backdated journal entries, reviews for segregation of duties, and trend analysis for key accounts such as revenue and expenses are some of the many tests you may encounter if you pursue a career in accounting data analytics.

- When you perform data analytics, it's important to obtain data from the source system. Rather than trust a report provided by management, go directly to the data in the system and request an extract. You can compare the source data to the financial statements to see if somewhere along the way management has manipulated the data. You can't always trust management, as they are most often responsible for—or at least involved in—financial statement fraud. Use your professional skepticism and critical-thinking skills to ask questions, dig deeper, and verify results through your own data analysis.

CONCEPT REVIEW QUESTIONS

1. What is meant by financial statement fraud?
   Ans. Financial statement fraud involves materially misrepresenting the financial results and position of a company by manipulating amounts or inappropriately disclosing information in the financial statements to deceive investors, creditors, and other users of the financial statements. Two commonly used financial statement frauds involve overstating assets, revenues, and profits, or understating liabilities, expenses, and losses.

2. What is channel stuffing?
   Ans. Channel stuffing is a fraud scheme where the seller encourages the sales of extra inventory to increase the current year's sales, when it is stated or implied that the customer can return the goods after the year end but not providing a reserve against these expected returns in the current year.

3. What are sales cutoff fraud schemes?
   Ans. Sales cutoff fraud schemes involve recording sales that occur after the balance sheet date in the current year's financial statements to inflate sales even though they belong in the subsequent accounting period.

4. What is expense cutoff fraud?
   Ans. Expense cutoff fraud occurs when expenses are not recorded until the subsequent accounting period. The opposite of sales cutoff, expense cutoff pushes the transactions to the subsequent period to avoid recognizing the expense in the current period.

FEATURED PROFESSIONAL | Fraud Analytics Specialist

Photo courtesy of John Aubrey Pickens

John Aubrey Pickens, CFE, CISA

John is a risk and compliance professional with over 13 years of experience identifying, managing, and mitigating risk through compliance and internal audit departments. He earned a bachelor's degree with a double major in accounting and management information systems and began his career as an IT and financial auditor for one of the Big Four firms. John soon realized that he wanted to make a lasting impact from within the companies he was auditing. Since then, he has led internal audits, helped build compliance and internal audit functions, and led the risk and control portions of major software implementations. He has also built fraud detection and anti-fraud programs at multiple Fortune 500 companies. He is now working as a senior manager in a compliance function and helping revamp compliance processes with his peers and team. He enjoys spending time with his wife and daughter, traveling abroad, and, when he can, sneaking away to fish or hike.

What types of fraud risks have you encountered throughout your career?

I have seen the most fraud risks and cases of fraud around business processes where employees have fast, easy access to money or something they can convert to money. Whether it's buying extra inventory and selling some of it, abusing corporate cards by expensing inappropriate expenses, or setting up fictitious vendors, these methods of stealing assets are common. In my experience, fraudsters tend to get as much as they can while under the radar so that they can act fast, before they are detected.

Is there a specific example of fraud you have uncovered that you can share with us?

I can't be very specific, but corporate cards, which are used to expense travel and for corporate purchasing, are often abused in interesting ways and are frequently involved in frauds, typically involving low dollar amounts. It is very easy for fraudsters to swipe a card with certain merchant providers and call it something that seems like a legitimate business expense. They can also use a corporate card to buy something that does not exist by creating shell companies. I once caught someone who put their own address as the business address when creating a shell company in the AIS. They ended up having a long conversation with me.

What data analytics tools do you find most useful for fraud testing?

I believe that to be good at data analytics or data science, you need to be tool agnostic. Not all data is the same, and not every company uses the same tools. I have used basic SQL queries and Excel to catch just as much fraud as I have caught using specialized software. If you don't enjoy coding, you can use a number of specialized software options that come with prebuilt scripts that enable you to start performing fraud data analytics quickly.

What recommendations do you have for an accounting major who is interested in pursuing a career path like yours?

Try to get as much exposure as you can to information systems through classes or real-life experiences. If possible, pursue an internship in this area and include specific experiences—even those as simple as shadowing someone—on your resume. It's important to give yourself the credit you deserve on your resume to set yourself apart when making career changes.

Review and Practice

Key Terms Review

asset misappropriation	financial statement fraud	payroll scheme
behavioral red flag	fraud	perceived pressure
billing scheme	fraud triangle	rationalization
capitalization of expenses	fraudulent disbursement	sales cutoff
channel stuffing	larceny	sham sale
corruption	management override	skimming
double dipping	misclassification of revenue	tone at the top
expense cutoff	non-behavioral red flag	unauthorized hours
expense reimbursement scheme	occupational fraud	unauthorized shipment
expensing capitalized cost	opportunity	unrecorded revenue
external fraud	pay and return	whistleblower

Learning Objectives Review

① Identify the main types of fraud.

Fraud is knowingly misrepresenting the truth or concealing a material fact to induce another to act to his or her detriment. This definition of fraud has four elements:

- A false statement: The perpetrator either lies directly or hides the truth.
- Knowledge: The perpetrator knows the statement is false at the time it's stated.
- Reliance: The victim relies on the information when deciding or acting.
- Damages: The victim suffers damages as a result of relying on this false statement.

Occupational fraud is committed by owners, executives, management, and employees who use their positions to enrich themselves at the expense of the company. The ACFE identifies three high-level categories to map all fraud schemes:

- Asset misappropriation
- Financial statement fraud
- Corruption

Corruption is the inappropriate use of influence to obtain a benefit contrary to the perpetrator's responsibility or the rights of other people. Perpetrators internal to the organization may engage in four possible types of corruption fraud schemes:

- Conflicts of interest
- Illegal gratuities
- Commercial bribery
- Economic extortion

External fraud is fraud perpetrated against an organization by customers, vendors, or other outside parties.

Behavioral red flags are clues that indicate the *possibility* a person may be involved in a fraud. The presence of red flags does *not* mean a fraud is being committed. There are six common behavioral red flags:

- Financial difficulties
- Living beyond one's means
- Close association with a vendor or customer
- Recent divorce or family problems
- Control issues or unwillingness to share duties
- Unscrupulous "big shot" attitude

② Describe the role of an accounting professional in fraud management.

The fraud triangle is a framework that identifies three motivational elements generally associated with fraud:

- Perceived pressure: The motive or incentive that pushes a person toward the decision to commit a fraud

- Opportunity: The element of the fraud triangle that a company can most influence, which is created when a company has poor or no internal controls, when there is collusion to circumvent internal controls, or when management overrides the internal controls
- Rationalization: The attitude of the fraudster that justifies the fraud act in the fraudster's mind

Auditors refer to these three elements of the fraud triangle as "fraud risk factors," and they are typically observed after fraud occurs.

Internal controls and an anti-fraud culture at a company can prevent fraud. Collusion circumvents two controls:

- Segregation of duties, where one person is not allowed to have conflicting responsibilities
- Independent checks, where one person reviews the work of another for accuracy and objectivity

The tone at the top is the culture of an organization that flows downstream from leadership to impact all functional areas. A culture of zero tolerance for fraud and unethical behavior is a strong deterrent to fraud.

Companies implement specific controls to detect fraud:

- Identifying non-behavioral red flags at a process or entity level
- Implementing anonymous whistleblower hotlines so employees can report observations or provide tips of possible misconduct, concerns about external financial reporting, or other issues
- Using data analytics specifically designed to continuously monitor processes and systems for fraud trends or anomalies
- Conducting independent checks of people's work
- Reviewing adequate documentation that leaves an audit trail

Two types of financial statement analysis can be used to identify red flags that may indicate financial statement fraud:

- Horizontal analysis involves investigating changes in financial statement items by comparing two or more financial statements from different periods.
- Vertical analysis involves calculating each line item in the same financial statement as a percentage of another line item in the same financial statement. Vertical analysis becomes more insightful when used in conjunction with horizontal analysis. The combination makes it possible to compare the vertical analysis of one reporting period with others.

Most frauds are detected based on tips from employees and external parties (e.g., vendors).

❸ Explain how to identify, prevent, and detect asset misappropriation schemes.

Asset misappropriation is the theft of corporate assets including cash, inventory, fixed assets, and information such as customer lists and intellectual property. Asset misappropriation can impact a company's financial statements—specifically when the perpetrator creates fraudulent journal entries to conceal the theft.

The three major classes or subcategories of asset misappropriation are:

- Skimming, which happens when an employee steals cash and does not enter the transaction in the accounting records, leaving no audit trail or documentary evidence of the transaction.
- Larceny, which is the theft of company cash and non-cash assets *after* the company has recorded the assets in its books. The common types are unconcealed larceny, where the fraudster does not attempt to conceal the fraud, and fictitious sales larceny, where the fraudster creates falsified documents or fraudulent journal entries.
- Fraudulent disbursements, which occur when an employee causes the business to make a payment for an inappropriate purpose. Fraudulent disbursements occur on the books, creating an audit trail.

Common fraudulent disbursement schemes include:

- Expense reimbursement schemes, where the business reimburses the perpetrators for expenses they never incurred
- Payroll schemes, where the business pays the perpetrator for time not worked
- Billing schemes, where the business makes fraudulent payments to vendors, including fictitious vendors

Companies mitigate all of these fraud risks by implementing in their processes and systems internal controls such as segregation of duties, authorization, and independent review.

❹ Identify financial statement fraud and explain how to mitigate its risks.

Financial statement fraud materially misrepresents the financial results and position of the company by manipulating amounts or inappropriately disclosing information in the financial statements to deceive investors, creditors, and other users of the financial statements. Financial statement fraud generally requires management complicity.

Section 302 of SOX makes the CEO and CFO directly responsible for the accuracy, documentation, and submission of all financial reports, as well as a report on the adequacy of the system of internal controls, to the SEC.

Financial statement fraud is designed to achieve one of two goals:

- Overstate the company's financial performance by overstating assets, revenues, and profits and/or understating liabilities, expenses, and losses. This can be done in the following ways:
  - Sham sales to overstate revenue
  - Unauthorized sales to overstate revenue
  - Channel stuffing to overstate revenue
  - Improper sales cutoffs to overstate revenue
  - Capitalizing expense by reporting them as assets to understate expenses
  - Improper expense cutoffs by deferring expense recognition to understate liabilities

- Understate the company's financial performance. Common schemes include:
  - Misclassification of sales revenue to something other than sales to understate sales revenue
  - Improper sales cutoff to defer revenue recognition and understate sales
  - Failure to record revenue
  - Expensing of costs that should be capitalized to overstate expenses
  - Improper expense cutoffs to overstate expenses
  - Recording of fictitious expenses to overstate expenses

Controls to prevent and detect financial statement fraud include vertical and horizontal analyses, segregation of duties, proper authorization procedures, independent reviews, data analytics, a good control environment, a whistleblower hotline, and systems controls.

CPA questions, as well as multiple choice, discussion, analysis and application, and Tableau questions and other resources, are available online.

Multiple Choice Questions

1. (LO 1) Which of the following scenarios is *not* an example of a behavioral fraud red flag?

   a. Your coworker complains he didn't get a large enough bonus this year and won't be able to afford his son's soccer registration fees.

   b. Your coworker dislikes your manager and regularly complains about her.

   c. Your coworker brags about buying a new house in one of the most expensive parts of town, where a lot of the company's executives live.

   d. Your coworker never takes vacation days or sick days because he says nobody else could do his job right.

2. (LO 1) Corruption fraud schemes include

   a. asset misappropriation, financial statement fraud, conflicts of interest, and illegal gratuities.

   b. economic extortion, illegal gratuities, asset misappropriation, and expense reimbursement fraud.

   c. asset misappropriation, bribery, stolen cash, and billing schemes.

   d. bribery, conflicts of interest, economic extortion, and illegal gratuities.

3. (LO 1) Which of the following could help a company manage fraud?

   a. Creating an antifraud culture

   b. Establishing and maintaining an effective system of internal controls

   c. Performing fraud risk assessments

   d. All of the above

4. (LO 2) **CPA** Which of the following is correct concerning a fraud risk factor?

   a. Its presence indicates that the risk of fraud is high.

   b. It has been observed in circumstances where frauds have occurred.

   c. It always requires modification of planned audit procedures.

   d. It is also a material weakness in internal control.

5. (LO 2) "The company is so large that it won't even notice it" is a type of

   a. opportunity.   b. concealment.

   c. perceived pressure.   d. rationalization.

6. (LO 2) Doorefishan and Gulfam approve each other's reimbursement requests. Their collusion on fictitious receipts allows their fraud to go undetected for some time. Which element of the fraud triangle is most closely associated with the collusion of Doorefishan and Gulfam?

   a. Perceived pressure

   b. Opportunity

   c. Rationalization

   d. All of the above

7. (LO 2) Which of the following statements is true?

   a. Fraud investigations are less expensive than fraud prevention.

   b. Preventing fraud is the most cost-effective approach to fighting fraud.

   c. To mitigate the risk that fraud will occur an organization implements internal controls.

   d. All of the above

8. (LO 2) If perceived pressure and opportunity to commit fraud are high and personal integrity is low, then the risk of fraud is

   a. low.

   b. medium.

   c. high.

   d. certain.

9. (LO 3) The most difficult asset misappropriation fraud scheme to detect, because it leaves no starting point or audit trail for auditors to investigate, is

   a. non-cash larceny.

   b. skimming.

   c. fraudulent disbursements.

   d. expense reimbursement fraud.

10. (LO 3) An example of an asset misappropriation scheme is

    a. larceny.

    b. economic extortion.

    c. illegal gratuities.

    d. fictitious revenues.

11. (LO 3) Which of the following controls could mitigate cash skimming efforts in a restaurant?

    a. Requiring receipts to be submitted

    b. Requiring manager approval for cash and check disbursement

    c. Implementing segregation of duties so that employees receiving payments do not also send invoices to customers

    d. Implementing segregation of duties so that employees executing sales do not also perform inventory counts and write-offs

12. (LO 3) The major classes of asset misappropriation are

    a. skimming, larceny, and fraudulent disbursements.

    b. skimming, double dipping, and payroll fraud.

    c. skimming, fraudulent disbursements, and vendor fraud.

    d. skimming, larceny, and corruption.

13. **(LO 4)** **CPA** Which of the following is an example of fraudulent financial reporting?

   a. Company management changes inventory count tags and overstates ending inventory while understating cost of goods sold.

   b. The treasurer diverts customer payments to his personal bank account, concealing his actions by debiting an expense account, thus overstating expenses.

   c. An employee steals inventory, and the "shrinkage" is recorded in cost of goods sold.

   d. An employee steals small tools from the company and neglects to return them; the cost is reported as a miscellaneous operating expense.

14. **(LO 4)** Which of the following is the best definition of materiality?

   a. Materiality means that the misrepresentation is large enough that users who rely on the information to make decisions may suffer financial damage.

   b. Materiality means that the misrepresentation is shared in such a way as to purposely dissuade potential investors from investing in the company.

   c. Materiality means that the financial statements are not misstated by enough to make a difference to those using the statements for decision making.

   d. Materiality means that any misrepresentations in the financial statements are negligible in amount and should not be considered wrong by malicious intent.

15. **(LO 4)** A fraud committed to lessen the amount of earnings that will be taxed this year is an example of

   a. misappropriation of assets.

   b. financial statement fraud that understates company performance.

   c. financial statement fraud that overstates company performance.

   d. skimming cash before it is recorded in the company's accounting books.

16. **(LO 4)** The fraud in which a company inflates its sales revenue by forcing more products through a distribution channel than the channel is capable of selling is called

   a. unauthorized sales.

   b. sham sales.

   c. cutoff fraud.

   d. channel stuffing.

Discussion and Research Questions

DQ1. (LO 1) **Critical Thinking** In the December 2020 edition of the *Fraud in the Wake of COVID-19: Benchmarking Report*, the ACFE reports the results of a survey of its members. Overall, 79% of the survey respondents observed an increase in fraud over the previous quarter, and 90% expected an increase in the next 12 months.[11] Discuss why the COVID-19 pandemic might result in an increase in occupational fraud.

DQ2. (LO 1–4) **Research** **Critical Thinking** Identify an occupational corporate fraud case from a reputable news source like *The Wall Street Journal*, *The New York Times*, your local news, or the ACFE website (www.acfe.org). Discuss the fraud and explain why it is occupational fraud. Identify the various victims of the fraud and explain how they have been victimized.

DQ3. (LO 1) **Fraud** **Early Career** **Critical Thinking** An anonymous tip received at your company's whistleblower hotline goes as follows: "The new Purchasing manager, Robin, started six months ago. I think she is slowly squeezing out some of our top vendors. She awards all the good contracts to a small vendor named Blisst. We have never worked with Blisst before this. Vendors we have used for years are disgruntled that they are no longer receiving work and are threatening not to bid on our projects again. I think Robin is engaged in some kind of illegal activity. Maybe she knows someone at Blisst?" Which of the three fraud categories do you think may be occurring in the Purchasing department? Is there a specific fraud scheme Robin may be involved in?

DQ4. (LO 2) Explain the difference between perceived pressure that could result in the misappropriation of assets and perceived pressure that could result in financial statement fraud. Give examples of both types of pressure.

DQ5. (LO 2) Which of the three elements of the fraud triangle can a company most easily influence and why?

DQ6. (LO 2) The illustration on the next page provides useful information on the most successful methods used recently for detecting occupational fraud, including the importance of tips from a whistleblower hotline. Do any of the results surprise you? Explain.

---

[11]www.acfe.com/uploadedFiles/ACFE_Website/Content/covid19/Covid-19%20Benchmarking%20Report%20December%20Edition.pdf

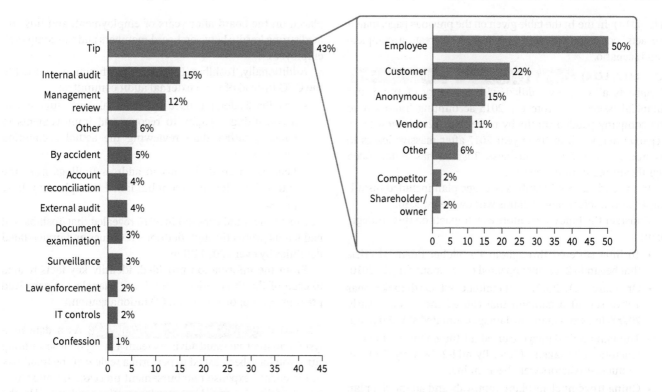

DQ7. (LO 3) `Fraud` `Critical Thinking` Talha, a trusted book-keeper at a medical practice, regularly forged the signature of an authorized signatory on the business bank account because he had access to blank checks. He wrote business checks to a shell company he maintained. He stole more than $500,000 over a five-year period before another employee accidentally detected and reported the fraud. Talha debited various expense accounts to conceal his criminal activities. Identify the main category and one subcategory for this fraud and explain your answer by discussing the impact on the financial statements.

DQ8. (LO 4) `Research` Perform an internet search for financial statement fraud and look for news articles posted in the past year. Find an example of a fraud, or suspected fraud, involving asset misappropriation. Summarize the case and include details about the fraud scheme used or suspected. Include a link to the original article in your submission.

DQ9. (LO 4) Distinguish financial statement fraud from other fraud types by explaining the role of management and who ultimately benefits from financial statement fraud compared to other types.

DQ10. (LO 4) Define capitalization and explain how it relates to fraud. Include the types of fraud schemes that use capitalization.

Application and Analysis Questions

Act	Concealment	Conversion
A. A salesperson steals an iPhone from the display case	**1.** Falsifying timesheet entries	**i.** Cashing company checks to a shell company's bank account and transferring the money to a personal bank account
B. A cashier pads their time sheet with unauthorized hours every shift	**2.** Creating fictitious receipts	**ii.** Selling it online or at a local pawn shop
C. An employee submits personal purchases as restaurant expenses	**3.** Billing to a shell vendor	**iii.** Inflating company revenue on financial statements
D. An accounts payable clerk creates fraudulent disbursements of company checks	**4.** Shipping at the end of the accounting period to cause returns to come back after the end of the accounting period	**iv.** Receiving a paycheck to a personal bank account
E. Management inflates sales revenue by shipping unauthorized sales to customer	**5.** Including it in the store inventory count when it's not there	**v.** Receiving reimbursement to a personal bank account

A1. (LO 1) In the In the table given on the previous page, match the acts, concealments, and conversions to create a complete fraud scenario.

A2. (LO 2, LO 4) `Fraud` `Early Career` `Critical Thinking`
Toshiba is a company riddled with a history of fraud and financial issues.[12,13] From the 2015 accounting fraud where the company padded profits by more than ¥200 billion to its negative net worth in fiscal year 2017 after massive losses to its nuclear power plant business, Toshiba has experienced significant reputational damage.

In the early 2000s, Toshiba's strategic plan included installing 45 new nuclear power plants worldwide by 2030.

Consider the following unforeseen impacts on this strategic plan:

- Toshiba suffered throughout the global financial crisis that began in 2008 but appeared to be rebounding in 2010.
- On March 11, 2011, a magnitude 9.1 earthquake near Tokyo set off a tsunami that caused the loss of nearly 20,000 lives and material damage estimated at ¥25 trillion.
- The tsunami's damage caused all the country's nuclear reactors to be taken offline. By mid-2018, only 9 of the 54 nuclear reactors were back online.
- China froze nuclear plant approvals and adopted a plan to decrease its usage of nuclear energy by 2020, and the United States canceled or postponed plans to build 12 power plants.
- The global reaction to the tsunami changed the demand for and acceptance of nuclear power.

During this time, the corporate culture at Toshiba was to push for success:

- The CEO in 2008 set income targets, known as "challenges," for each division. The income targets were so aggressive that they were often unattainable.
- The CEO insisted that the targets be achieved and even suggested that the company would sell off underperforming divisions, putting both division leaders and their employees at risk of losing their jobs.
- The pressure from the CEO filtered through the company, all the way through division leaders, managers, and employees.

Even though the CEO never directly demanded that his employees commit fraud, he relied on expected obedience—a significant part of the Japanese corporate culture—to cause his employees to do whatever was necessary to meet his demands.

Toshiba's corporate structure failed to rotate key accounting and finance personnel. Employees were assigned to the same division for their entire careers at Toshiba, which created a rapport among division employees that spanned decades. This culture created an environment in which it was difficult for an employee to speak out against inappropriate actions. Toshiba's board of directors consisted primarily of employees who were placed on the board after years of employment, and this created strong loyalty between board members and the company's employees.

Additionally, Toshiba's Internal Audit function reported to the CEO instead of to an external audit committee:

- Toshiba leadership used the Internal Audit function in a consulting capacity to recommend improvements to controls rather than reviewing the actual accounting methods.
- Leadership created plans to address findings from the Internal Audit department but failed to implement those plans.

The resulting fraud exposed in 2015 revealed that Toshiba had padded its profits through fictitious revenues and understated liabilities by over ¥200 billion.

From the information provided, identify key facts related to each of the three sides of the fraud triangle: (1) perceived pressure, (2) opportunity, and (3) rationalization.

A3. (LO 3) `Early Career` `Data Analytics` As a data analyst for an internal fraud advisory team at a regional accounting firm, you have been asked to perform a review of the fraud risk in the client's expense reimbursement process. You must analyze the following travel expense transactions, submitted by the company's vice president of sales. To assess the transactions for the presence of fraud flags, you will perform the following four data analytics tests. Read about each test and visually review the spreadsheet given on the next page. Identify which transactions numbers each test would identify.

Tests:

Double dipping: Transactions where the amounts are the same and the transaction dates are the same, but the types are different (one is credit card and one is cash).

Duplicate expenses: Transactions where all fields are the same except for the expense submission date.

Inappropriate cash: Transactions with transaction type "Cash" and category that is "out of policy" for cash payment. See "Out of policy cash categories" (below) for a list of categories to analyze.

Late expense submissions: Transactions with an expense submission date more than 30 days after the transaction date.

Out of policy cash categories:

Airline

Hotel

Rental Car

Meals (Over $35)

Rideshares (Uber, Lyft, etc.)

---

[12]www.investopedia.com/articles/investing/081315/toshibas-accounting-scandal-how-it-happened.asp

[13]Unmasking the Fraud at Toshiba, Caplan, D., S.K. Dutta, & D.J. Marcinko. *Issues in Accounting Education* 34(3), 2019.

	A	B	C	D	E	F	G	H
1	Transaction	Category	Amount	Vendor	Transaction Date	Description	Transaction Type	Expense Submission Date
2	1125	Airline	$827.34	Delta	1/28/202X	Roundtrip flight	Credit Card	2/15/202X
3	1126	Hotel	$983.09	Ritz Carlton	2/4/202X	Three-night stay	Credit Card	3/1/202X
4	1127	Meal	$33.28	N/A	2/2/202X	Dinner	Cash	3/1/202X
5	1128	Airline	$827.34	Delta	1/28/202X	Roundtrip flight	Credit Card	3/1/202X
6	1129	Taxi	$29.54	Uber	2/4/202X	Ride from airport to home	Cash	3/1/202X
7	1130	Meal	$14.05	Starbucks	2/1/202X	Breakfast	Cash	3/1/202X
8	1131	Meal	$19.54	Chipotle	2/1/202X	Lunch	Credit Card	3/1/202X
9	1132	Rental Car	$224.09	Enterprise	2/4/202X	Four-day rental	Credit Card	3/1/202X
10	1133	Taxi	$14.56	Lyft	2/1/202X	Ride from home to airport	Credit Card	3/1/202X
11	1134	Meal	$85.38	Jimmy's Steakhouse	2/3/202X	Dinner with client	Credit Card	3/1/202X
12	1135	Taxi	$29.54	Uber	2/4/202X	Ride from airport to home	Credit Card	3/27/202X

A4. (LO 3) Fraud Critical Thinking Ms. Conover recently purchased a local coffee shop in Burlington, Vermont, after its previous owners were unable to continue paying the lease. She hired a young couple to run the business and pays them each a monthly salary. The couple live rent-free in the apartment upstairs and are responsible for daily operations of the coffee shop. Ms. Conover asks them to hire and supervise four to five part-time employees. The couple are also responsible for keeping financial records, including expenses, payroll, and sales (both cash and credit card). They will keep cash received in a safe and make a weekly deposit at a local bank.

Ms. Conover lives almost four hours away, in Boston. She plans to drive up to Burlington to check on the coffee shop periodically.

Identify two areas of opportunity for the couple to commit fraud and identify a control that could be introduced to reduce the risk of fraud.

A5. (LO 3–4) Early Career Critical Thinking You are an external auditor performing an interview with a senior manager of financial accounting at your firm's new client. During the interview, you ask the senior manager to explain the overall operations and control environment of the department. Assess each of the statements the senior manager gives you and identify it as either (**i**) a fraud risk or (**ii**) not a fraud risk. If it is a fraud risk, explain whether it is most likely to indicate the possibility of (**A**) asset misappropriation, (**B**) financial statement fraud, or (**C**) either. Explain why.

1. Access to blank checks and signature plates is restricted to the cash disbursements bookkeeper, who personally reconciles the monthly bank statements.

2. There is a lack of independent checks in the accounts receivable process.

3. The accounting department has experienced high turnover among senior management.

4. There was a strained relationship between management and its previous external auditors.

5. Vendor invoices are matched with related purchase orders and receiving documents (a three-way match) by the accounts payable bookkeeper, who then approves the payments.

6. Management has been pushing for using aggressive accounting practices to maintain an increasing trend of earnings.

7. The company has been consistently reporting substantial earnings growth but struggles to generate cash flows from operations.

SEC Press Release Scenario

Read the following press release from the SEC and use it to answer A6 through A8:

Washington D.C., Sept. 4, 2018 —

The Securities and Exchange Commission today charged a telecommunications expense management company for its use of fraudulent accounting practices that artificially boosted company revenues between 2013 and 2015. Four former members of the company's senior management team were also charged for their roles in the alleged misconduct.

As alleged in the complaint, Tangoe Inc., formerly a public company headquartered in Connecticut, improperly recognized approximately $40 million of revenue out of the total of $566 million reported between 2013 and 2015. In some instances, Tangoe allegedly reported revenue prematurely for work that had not been performed, including service prepayments, and for transactions that did not produce any revenue at all. The SEC alleges that Donald J. Farias, a Tangoe executive, falsified business records, some of which were provided to Tangoe's external auditors to support revenue recognition decisions.

"Without accurate financial reporting our public markets cannot function fairly or efficiently," said Paul G. Levenson, Director of the Boston Regional Office. *"We are committed to protect the investing public against illegal accounting tactics that artificially boost company performance."*

The SEC's complaint, filed in federal court in Connecticut, charges Tangoe, its former CEO Albert R. Subbloie, former CFO Gary R. Martino, former vice president of finance Thomas H. Beach, and former senior vice president of expense management operations Donald J. Farias. Each is charged with violating provisions of the federal securities laws. Tangoe, Subbloie, Martino, and Beach have agreed to settle the SEC's charges without admitting or denying the allegations. They agreed to pay penalties in the amount of $1.5 million, $100,000, $50,000, and $20,000, respectively. The settlement is subject to court approval.[14]

A6. (LO 1) `Fraud` `Critical Thinking` According to Paul G. Levenson, director of the Boston Regional Office, who was a victim of this fraud?

A7. (LO 3–4) `Fraud` `Critical Thinking` Was Tangoe Inc. charged with fraud resulting from asset misappropriation or financial statement fraud? What type of fraud scheme was Tangoe Inc. using? What concealment method is mentioned in the press release?

A8. (LO 4) `Fraud` `Critical Thinking` Members of the senior management team at Tangoe Inc. were personally charged and fined by the SEC. What regulation specifies that management is responsible for the accuracy of financial statements and includes provisions that allow management to be personally charged and fined for fraud?

Tableau Case: Employee Reimbursement Expenses at Julia's Cookies

What You Need

Download Tableau to your computer. You can access www.tableau.com/academic/students to download your free Tableau license for the year, or you can download it from your university's software offerings.

Download the following file from the book's product page on www.wiley.com:

Chapter 15 Raw Data—Employee Expenses.xlsx

Case Background

Big Picture:

Analyze fraud red flags in expense reports.

Details:

Why is this data important, and what questions or problems need to be addressed?

- The employee expenses data reflects how employees are spending company money on expenses related to the office, travel, subscriptions, memberships, food, and more. Before you can start spending money and calling it a reimbursable business expense, you should review the company's policies and procedures. There may be a prohibited vendor list or cost limits to comply with.
- Analysis of this data helps identify potential fraud (the objective). While some employees may accidentally submit noncompliant expenses for reimbursement, there may be other employees who try to take advantage of internal control deficiencies and attempt to defraud the company. For example, fraudsters may attempt to:
  - Double dip for a single purchase and be reimbursed twice
  - Provide fraudulent mileage that might have been for personal travel instead of business travel (usually around the holiday months)
  - Ask the vendor to split a single invoice into multiple smaller ones in order to stay within the dollar amount limits that the business sets for a single purchase

---

[14]www.sec.gov/news/press-release/2018-175

Plan:

What data is needed, and how should it be analyzed?

- Data needed to answer the objective is pulled from Julia's Cookies' Employee Expenses database.

- Analyzing this data involves performing tests for four common employee reimbursement fraud schemes: employees approving their own reports, purchases at prohibited vendors, inappropriate mileage, and duplicate reimbursements.

Now it's your turn to evaluate, analyze, and communicate your results!

Questions

1. Which department had the largest count of unique expense claims submitted?

2. Which department had the highest *average* amount *per transaction*?

3. Which expense category had the highest total transaction amount?

4. Employees *should not* approve their own expense reports. Usually their manager is the approver; however, someone other than the employee should approve a claim for segregation of duties purposes. Test the data to see which employees approved their own expenses. (Hint: Create a true/false calculation.) What are their names?

5. How much, in total, did the employees from question 4 approve for themselves?

6. Julia's Cookies has a list of prohibited vendors that employees are not allowed to use while on business travel. One prohibited vendor is Airbnb. Julia's Cookies prohibits employees from staying at Airbnbs as they could be owned by the employee or a family member, creating a conflict of interest. How many employees broke the rules and used Airbnb as a vendor?

7. Employees at Julia's Cookies can use their personal vehicles to travel to customer sites. An employee who chooses to do so is reimbursed based on mileage. Sometimes employees abuse the system. A red flag exists when an employee reports more miles than their monthly average. Test the data between the transaction dates 7/1/2025 and 12/31/2025 for above-average mileage. (Hint: Use a line chart.) Identify the employee(s).

8. How many total miles did the employee(s) from question 7 report for the month for which they potentially committed this type of fraud?

Take it to the next level!

9. When booking a flight, an employee books and pays for the flight in advance, which means they can submit their air ticket reimbursement prior to their trip. After they come back from the trip, some employees may claim reimbursement again, along with their other expenses, accidentally or with the intent of defrauding the company. Test the data to see if there were any duplicated ticket numbers in the data set. How many air tickets were reimbursed twice?

10. Which employee had duplicate reimbursements of airline tickets?

Cybersecurity

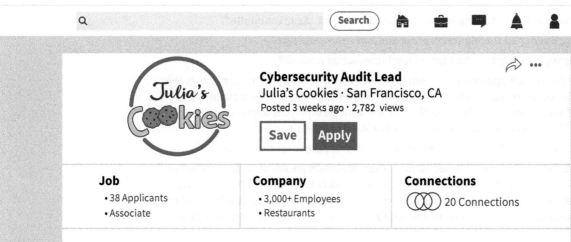

Summary

The cybersecurity audit lead will work closely with IT partners to identify and manage risks to our networks and applications. This role is a critical part of our line of defense for our technical environment.

Responsibilities

- Challenge established processes and controls to ensure that they are adequate to mitigate risk
- Facilitate delivery of high-quality internal workpapers and deliverables such as process/control narratives, flowcharts, testing documentation, conclusions, and recommendations
- Work closely with IT partners to identify and manage risks to our networks and applications
- Act as critical third line of defense for the technical environment
- Assess risks and effectiveness of controls by leveraging your technical knowledge and experience
- Focus on security information and event management, password vaults, vulnerability management, secure baseline configuration, email protection, and incident response

Requirements

Education: Bachelor's degree or higher in information systems, computer science, accounting, or another related field

Certifications: CISSP, CIA, CISA, CompTIA Security+, CISM, CCSP

Experience: Five to seven years of business experience, with at least two years in project management

Preferred Knowledge and Skills

The ideal candidate will possess hands-on security testing and assessment experience in areas such as network security, encryption, endpoint detection and response, and intrusion detection and prevention. Preference will be given to candidates who also demonstrate:

- Experience with risk and controls, such as operational audits, financial statement audits, internal audits, consulting, or compliance
- Strong IT security knowledge, such as application security architecture, cloud architecture and security, network security, IT infrastructure, data security administration, or database security
- Working experience with common security risk frameworks, such as ISO 27000, NIST, OWASP, COBIT, and CIS Critical Security Controls

Salary: $100,000–120,000

CHAPTER PREVIEW   As companies continue to rely on technology to improve processes, connect global operations, and drive strategies, the importance of cybersecurity in risk management is growing. You have learned that technology both provides opportunities to mitigate risk and creates risks of its own. While information technology general controls (ITGCs) address technological risks within a company, this chapter specifically addresses unique technology risks related to malicious attacks from external parties—cyber attackers.

Cyber threats are a top concern for companies and leaders because these attacks can cause long-lasting reputational damage. Once an emerging threat, cybersecurity is now ranked consistently as one of the top challenges facing companies.

In this chapter, we will explore several issues around cybersecurity:

- How the accounting profession approaches cybersecurity risks
- How attackers plan their attacks
- The methods used to gain unauthorized access
- How attackers shut down an entire system

While cybersecurity may not be the first thing you think of when planning your future as an accounting professional, companies are looking for professionals with a passion for understanding technology risk and controls. Career opportunities for accounting professionals range from an IT audit role, like the cybersecurity auditor job posting at Julia's Cookies, to dedicated data privacy and cybersecurity compliance teams. If you have an interest in technology and enjoy investigating, problem solving, or creative thinking, a career in cybersecurity may be the path for you. ■

Chapter Roadmap

LEARNING OBJECTIVES	TOPICS	JULIA'S COOKIES APPLIED LEARNING
16.1 Describe the relationship between cybersecurity risks and the accounting profession.	• Recent Cybersecurity Threats • Relevance to Accounting Professionals • Governance and Policies	Frameworks: Data Privacy Project
16.2 Describe the characteristics of reconnaissance attacks.	• Physical Reconnaissance Attacks • Logical Reconnaissance Attacks	Social Engineering: Reporting Suspicious Emails
16.3 Compare and contrast physical and logical access attacks.	• Physical Access Attacks • Logical Access Attacks	Physical Access: Mail Delivery
16.4 Explain how hackers perform disruptive attacks.	• Denial-of-Service Attacks • Malware Attacks	Disruptive Attacks: Cybersecurity Program Pitch

CPA   You will find the CPA tag throughout the chapter to call out any important topics you may see on the CPA exam.

16.1 How Is Cybersecurity Relevant to the Accounting Profession?

Learning Objective ❶
Describe the relationship between cybersecurity risks and the accounting profession.

You may be familiar with the media version of "hackers" as people logging into laptops with black screens and green fonts, swiftly accessing bank vault codes, programming doors to open, and even triggering explosive devices.

While mainstream media may imply that hackers are elite individuals with insurmountable technological knowledge, real-life cybersecurity threats are simply skilled programmers with unauthorized objectives. They use their technical knowledge to achieve a goal, which is often to gain unauthorized access to data. Cyber threats can come from individual hackers, criminal groups, or even corporate spies (**Illustration 16.1**). For the purposes of this discussion, we use the terms "hacker" and "attacker" to refer to any programmers with malicious intentions that pose a risk to a company.

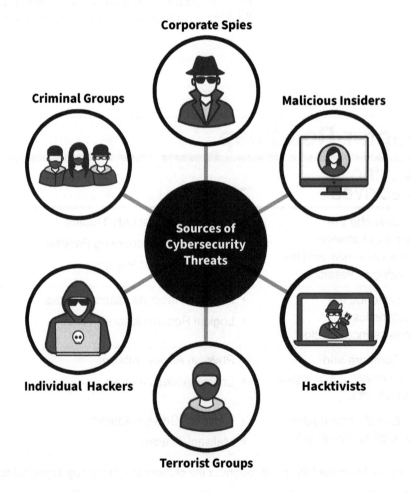

Illustration 16.1   Cyber threats come from many sources, including hackers and corporate spies.

Cybersecurity encompasses the measures a company takes to protect a computer or system—including those on the internet—against unauthorized access or attacks. Executive leaders in all industries are concerned about threats to their companies' information because information is a source of power and leverage to attackers. Cyberattacks, including data breaches, are regularly reported in the news. Managing these threats requires preventing cyberattacks and also addressing those that occur even though preventive and corrective controls are in place. It's the responsibility of management and executives to ensure that their company adopts a proactive cybersecurity plan.

Recent Cybersecurity Threats

Unfortunately, many companies take a reactive, rather than proactive, approach to cybersecurity threats. Let's look at what happened at Optus, as well as some other real-life stories, to understand the importance of a proactive cybersecurity program.

Optus Data Breach[1,2]

Optus, the Australian telecommunications giant, revealed in September 2022 that approximately 9.8 million customers, which is about 40% of Australia's population, had their personal data stolen. This data included sensitive information like names, birth dates, home addresses, phone and email contacts, as well as passport and driving license numbers. Optus, a subsidiary of Singapore Telecommunications Ltd., made the breach public about 24 hours after noticing suspicious activity on its network.

The breach was attributed to a cyberattack, and it's believed that cybercriminals gained access via an unauthorized API endpoint. This means that the attackers didn't need valid user credentials to access the data.

The Australian government recognized the severity of the breach, especially for the approximately 2.8 million individuals whose passport or license numbers were stolen. These individuals faced a heightened risk of identity theft and fraud, and the government characterized it as a "quite significant" risk.

Optus promptly reported the breach to the relevant authorities, including the police, financial institutions, and government regulators. Investigations into the breach were initiated, and the breach's origins appeared to be overseas. If it was confirmed to be a state-sponsored operation, this could indicate a significant and highly sophisticated cyber espionage or cyberattack campaign. Optus clarified that payment information and account passwords had not been compromised. This is a critical distinction because it means that financial losses for affected customers would have been minimal, although the risk of identity theft and fraud remained significant.

This incident underscores the importance of cybersecurity and the need for organizations to continually update and improve their security measures to protect customer data from data breach attempts.

National Health Service (NHS)

On May 12, 2017, the WannaCry ransomware caused the NHS to stop working for several days. This affected hospitals and GP offices in England and Scotland. Even though the NHS wasn't directly targeted, the global cyberattack revealed security flaws and caused thousands of appointments and surgeries to be canceled. It also forced emergency patients to be moved quickly from emergency centers that had been hit. After the attack broke key systems, staff had to go back to using pen and paper, as well as their own cell phones.

Most of the NHS devices that were attacked with ransomware were found to be running a supported but unpatched version of Microsoft Windows 7. The ransomware also spread through the internet, including the N3 network, which is a broadband network that connects all NHS sites in England. However, the ransomware did not spread through NHSmail, which is the email system for the NHS. NHS England said that at least 80 of the 236 trusts and 603 primary care and other NHS organizations, such as 595 GP practices, were impacted. No NHS organization paid the ransom, according to the Department, NHS England, and the National

[1]https://www.optus.com.au/about/media-centre/media-releases/2022/09/optus-notifies-customers-of-cyberattack#:~:text=Following%20a%20cyberattack%2C%20Optus%20is%20investigating%20the%20possible,Security%20Centre%20to%20mitigate%20any%20risks%20to%20customers
[2]https://www.theguardian.com/business/2022/sep/29/optus-data-breach-everything-we-know-so-far-about-what-happened

Crime Agency (NCA). The Department does not know how much the disruption of services cost the NHS, but figures add up to £92 million.

At the time of the attacks, the NHS was criticized for using old IT systems like Windows XP, which was then 17 years old and open to cyberattacks. In an unusual move, Microsoft put out a WannaCry patch for systems that it no longer supported, like Windows XP, which it stopped providing support for in 2014.

The NCA says that ransomware is still the most common type of cyber attack in the United Kingdom. Experts in security warn that cybercriminals see the health sector as a particularly attractive target because health records are worth up to 10 times as much as other kinds of data, like banking information.

Equifax

Credit reporting agencies have personal data on every American with a credit history. They offer products and services such as providing you and your future lenders with your credit score. These companies collect data to compile your credit history and create a snapshot of your credit health. A data breach occurred in 2017 at Equifax, one of the three largest consumer credit reporting agencies in the United States, affecting over 140 million Americans and their personal information:

- Names, Social Security numbers, birth dates, addresses, and even driver's license information were stolen.
- Equifax noticed suspicious activity at the end of July but didn't disclose the breach and its impact for two more months.
- Because of this delayed communication, Equifax experienced public backlash and suffered reputational damage, and Equifax's customers had their personal data exposed for months without knowing it.
- In February 2020, the U.S. Department of Justice indicted four hackers on nine charges related to the Equifax hack.
- Luckily for Equifax, the data breach stopped there. The hackers stole information but did not leave anything behind that could have damaged the systems.

A company targeted in a data breach should disclose information to its customers and to the public as soon as possible to mitigate reputational damage. The factors considered in deciding when to disclose a breach are part of a company's cybersecurity program.

Relevance to Accounting Professionals

Cybersecurity programs are subject to different resource constraints and business needs depending on the size of the company. At larger companies, the cybersecurity program is usually the responsibility of a dedicated executive leader, such as a chief information officer (CIO), chief information security officer (CISO), or chief technology officer (CTO). Other executive leaders, including the chief financial officer (CFO), also play pivotal roles in cybersecurity efforts:

- The CFO's responsibilities cover the enterprise resource planning (ERP) system, including the accounting information system (AIS), which gives the CFO an important view into information that could be targeted in a cyberattack.
- Cybersecurity planning requires balancing risks and aligning risk mitigation strategies with the company's risk appetite and strategic plan, which is an exercise that accounting professionals like the CFO are experienced in doing.
- Collaborative efforts between the CIO and CFO will increase the effectiveness of cybersecurity and support management in their individual efforts and control activities.

Accounting professionals understand the importance of safeguarding their companies' data in all areas of business. Employees with backgrounds in financial accounting, internal audit, external audit, and IT audit are uniquely positioned to work with teams that address cybersecurity risk, including data privacy and governance.

The positions and experience identified in LinkedIn job postings in the following tables demonstrate career paths accounting professionals may choose to pursue if they are passionate about technology and interested in cybersecurity. First, let's look at some options for people just starting their careers (**Table 16.1**).

TABLE 16.1 Early Career Job Postings for Cybersecurity Careers

	Baker Tilly, Public Accounting Firm	FBI	Google
Department:	Risk advisory consulting	Accounting/finance	Finance
Job title:	Summer technology process intern	Special agent	Treasury governance risk analyst
Education:	Studying: • Management information systems • Computer science • Accounting information systems	Bachelor's degree or higher in: • Accounting • Business administration • Finance • Forensic accounting	Bachelor's degree in related field with a preference for an MBA
Experience:	GPA of 3.0 or above preferred	College graduate	3 years in treasury or finance
Relevant certifications:	• Certified Information Systems Auditor (CISA) • Certified Information Systems Security Professional (CISSP) • Certified Information Security Manager (CISM) • Certified Public Accountant (CPA)	Eligibility for the FBI's Top Secret Sensitive Compartmented Information (SCI) clearance	None listed
Responsibilities and skills:	• Cybersecurity and privacy assessments • Vulnerability assessments • Business continuity and disaster recovery planning	• Tracing transactions to their source • Solving crime • Counterintelligence • Cybersecurity	• Cybersecurity • Data privacy • Relationship building

Next, let's see where your long-term career could take you by exploring real-world positions requiring five or more years of experience (**Table 16.2**). These job details also come directly from LinkedIn job postings.

TABLE 16.2 Experienced Job Postings for Cybersecurity Careers

	Coca-Cola	Tesla	JPMorgan Chase & Co.
Department:	Global cyber services	Internal audit	Finance
Job title:	Cyber policy and standards analyst	IT audit program manager	Vice president of cybersecurity and tech controls
Education:	Bachelor's degree or equivalent in appropriate business field	Bachelor's degree in: • Accounting • Finance • Computer science • Management information systems	Bachelor's degree in: • Accounting • Finance • Economics
Experience:	3–5 years in information technology or security operations 2+ years writing procedures, standards, and controls	6+ years in IT or audit	12+ years in core finance and business management

(Continued)

TABLE 16.2 (*Continued*)

	Coca-Cola	Tesla	JPMorgan Chase & Co.
Relevant certifications:	• Certified Information Systems Security Professional (CISSP) • Certified Forensic Computer Examiner (CFCE) • Certified Computer Examiner (CCE)	• Certified Information Systems Auditor (CISA) • Certified Information Systems Security Professional (CISSP) • Certified Public Accountant (CPA)	None listed
Responsibilities and skills:	• Designing cybersecurity policy and linking to relevant frameworks • Risk management	• ERP systems • Cybersecurity • Databases • Software as a service (SaaS) • Understanding of IT processes including change management, access security, and network operations	• Exceptional communication skills • Results oriented • Highly adaptable interpersonal skills

These jobs are just a sample of the specialized careers in the cybersecurity space. Whether the jobs involve hands-on technical work like implementing or auditing controls, governance and policy responsibilities, or solving cybercrimes, employers are looking for accounting professionals to help them fight the increasing threat of cyberattacks.

Governance and Policies

One of the jobs previously highlighted focuses on designing a cybersecurity policy and linking it to relevant frameworks. **CPA** You have learned about a variety of frameworks throughout this course, including COBIT, which is the most widely used international standard for IT governance. COBIT focuses on achieving control objectives specifically for IT risks, which include malicious activities. While the COBIT framework covers cybersecurity risk and controls, there is another framework designed for this niche area of risks.

CPA The **National Institute of Standards and Technology (NIST)** is a U.S. Department of Commerce agency that promotes innovation in science, standards, and technology to improve the quality of life in the United States. NIST's Cybersecurity Framework includes five functions a company should adopt to address cybersecurity risks (**Illustration 16.2**). It is considered the best practices framework for cybersecurity programs.

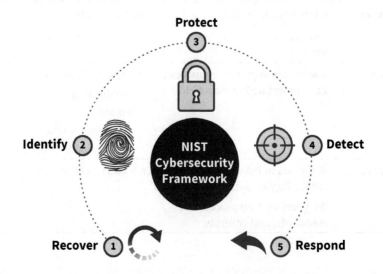

Illustration 16.2 The NIST Cybersecurity Framework includes five functions that work together to address cyber threats.

Do these functions seem familiar? We have seen similar approaches for risk assessments—including fraud, COBIT, and COSO—in this course. For accounting professionals, identifying, protecting, and detecting are especially important functions in the NIST Cybersecurity Framework since they are specifically related to risk identification and establishing effective control environments.

NIST has published *Security and Privacy Controls for Federal Information Systems and Organizations* (NIST 800-53), which is a catalog of security control baselines for businesses.[3] As the security world evolves, so do the standards. The NIST 800-53 standard is a living document that is revised periodically and has gone through five revisions. Important things to know about this standard include:

- While the publication is lengthy, NIST stresses that not all security controls apply to every business and that businesses should tailor the controls in NIST 800-53 to their needs.
- The standard is divided into 18 control families (**Table 16.3**).

TABLE 16.3 18 NIST Control Families

ID	Family	Number of Related Internal Controls	ID	Family	Number of Related Internal Controls
AC	Access Control	25	MP	Media Protection	8
AT	Awareness and Training	5	PE	Physical and Environmental Protection	20
AU	Audit and Accountability	16	PL	Planning	9
CA	Security Assessment and Authorization	9	PS	Personnel Security	8
CM	Configuration Management	11	RA	Risk Assessment	6
CP	Contingency Planning	13	SA	System and Services Acquisition	22
IA	Identification and Authentication	11	SC	System and Communications Protection	44
IR	Incident Response	10	SI	System and Information Integrity	17
MA	Maintenance	6	PM	Program Management	16

- Throughout the rest of this chapter, you will see a NIST reference in the internal controls tables that includes the letter of the control family and the control number. For example, PE-4 is a physical access control in the Physical and Environmental Protection family.
- NIST 800-53 categorizes each of the controls with a suggested priority label that helps businesses identify which controls they should implement first, where P1 indicates controls of the highest priority, P2 of medium priority, and P3 of low priority.

As you read through this chapter, you'll discover that the internal controls we discuss tie directly back to the NIST framework.

Many companies adopt NIST and COBIT frameworks together since both cover IT controls for cybersecurity threats. In fact, NIST and COBIT reference one another, which makes it easier to adopt both:

- **COBIT:** Provides an overarching information technology control structure
- **NIST:** Enhances the COBIT control structure by providing details regarding cybersecurity and privacy controls

Now that you understand the difference between NIST and COBIT, help the Internal Audit department at Julia's Cookies select the appropriate framework in Applied Learning 16.1.

---

[3]NIST 800-53 is available at https://csrc.nist.gov/publications/detail/sp/800-53/rev-5/final

Julia's Cookies   Applied Learning 16.1

Frameworks: Data Privacy Project

Dylan, the VP of Internal Audit, is working with the chief technology officer, Ahmad, to propose an enterprise-wide data strategy project to the Audit Committee.

Dylan suggests that the Internal Audit department perform an advisory review of the company's data management and privacy procedures. This review will involve interviewing various departments throughout Julia's Cookies to ask questions such as:

- What guidelines are in place for data privacy?
- How is data being shared?
- Are communications masked or encrypted securely?
- What are the differences between internal communications and communication with third parties?
- Where is data being stored?
- What procedures are in place for data retention?
- Is data disposed of through proper deletion methods in an appropriate time frame?
- Do these procedures meet regulatory standards?

Dylan and Ahmad must decide which framework(s) to use as guidance for proposing recommendations for this project to the audit committee. Do you think they should choose COBIT, NIST, or both?

SOLUTION

This project will benefit from both COBIT and NIST frameworks. COBIT contains guidelines for IT general controls, which are being reviewed. Additionally, NIST offers specific guidelines related to data privacy and security. Dylan and Ahmad should include both frameworks as guidance recommendations when proposing this project to the audit committee.

CONCEPT REVIEW QUESTIONS

1. **CPA** What control objectives do COBIT and NIST's Cybersecurity Framework help to achieve?

   Ans. COBIT focuses on achieving control objectives specifically for IT risks, which include malicious activities. While the COBIT framework covers cybersecurity risk and controls, NIST's Cybersecurity Framework is designed for this niche area of risks. It is considered the best practices framework for cybersecurity programs, and includes functions a company should adopt to address cybersecurity risks.

2. **CPA** Cybersecurity programs are subject to different resource constraints and business needs depending on the size of the company. Who might be responsible for leading the cybersecurity program in a larger organization?

   Ans. The chief information officer (CIO), chief information security officer (CISO), or chief technology officer (CTO) are likely to lead the cybersecurity team at larger companies.

16.2 How Do Cybercriminals Plan Attacks?

Learning Objective ❷
Describe the characteristics of reconnaissance attacks.

Cyber threats come in many forms, and the objective of an individual attack ranges from information gathering to destroying entire networks. The **cyber-kill chain** is the life cycle of a cyberattack from early stages of information gathering through final steps of damaging the network (**Illustration 16.3**). As we explore common types of threats, we look at the three steps in the cyber-kill chain:

1. Gathering information about the network
2. Accessing the network
3. Disrupting the network, including causing damage to the network or destroying it

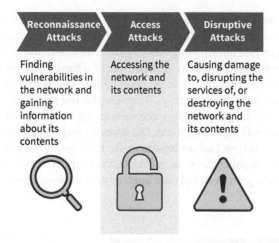

Illustration 16.3 Attackers use these three types of attacks to plan, enter, and damage the victim's network.

Attackers use combinations of attacks from these stages, and some attackers may never make it to the point of disruption.

The first stage is gathering information to plan an attack. **Reconnaissance attacks** are knowledge-gathering attacks that help attackers identify targets and plan their operations:

- These attacks may set the stage for later access and disrupt the network.
- Cybercriminals look for vulnerabilities in the network, through either a person who exposes valuable information or a technical weak point in the network.

While it's impossible for a company to completely avoid the risk of reconnaissance attacks, it is possible to mitigate the risk. Controls are designed to mitigate risk by making it difficult for attackers to get the information they need and hopefully deterring them from eventually accessing the network or causing damage. We cover reconnaissance attacks in this section and the other two stages of the cyber-kill chain in the following sections.

Whether a cyberattack is designed to gather information or cause disruption, it falls into one of two categories, based on the criminal's method:

- **Physical attacks:** Attackers threaten elements a network administrator has no control over, such as physical security, hardware, and people.
- **Logical attacks:** Attacks occur on a fully digital spectrum and require no human interaction other than the attacker instigating the attack.

 To remember the difference between physical and logical attacks, think of a bank robbery. There are two ways to rob a bank. Someone can enter the bank building and steal money from the vault, which is a physical attack. In contrast, in a logical attack, the bank robber steals from the bank from the comfort of their couch via an internet connection.

Physical Reconnaissance Attacks

A **physical reconnaissance attack** uses human interaction—on the part of the target, the attacker, or both—to generate information about the network.

Phishing

Social engineering involves persuading people to perform acts that would give the hackers access to confidential information, such as birth dates, passwords, and user IDs. Social engineering is one of the most robust categories of cyberattacks: it can be used for reconnaissance, access, and even to cause damage. As the weakest part of a network's security, humans can be easily tricked by hackers. Social engineering attacks are always physical in nature, as the target is always a person.

There are many ways in which people can fall into hackers' traps; however, phishing is the most common technique. **CPA** **Email phishing** is a deceptive request designed to trick victims into sharing private information. Phishing often involves a fraudulent email that appears to be from a reputable source, such as an employer or a bank. This email may ask victims to respond with sensitive information or may contain a link that takes victims to a fake website, where they input the sensitive information. Attackers also use mobile phishing (by sending text messages) and voice phishing (by leaving voicemails urging victims to call a number and provide information before something bad happens, like access to their bank account being suspended).

Do you think **Illustration 16.4** is a legitimate email? If you received the email and believed it was legitimate, you might click on the login link in order to resolve this issue. At that point, attackers could capture your personal data, such as your password. So, what makes this email suspicious?

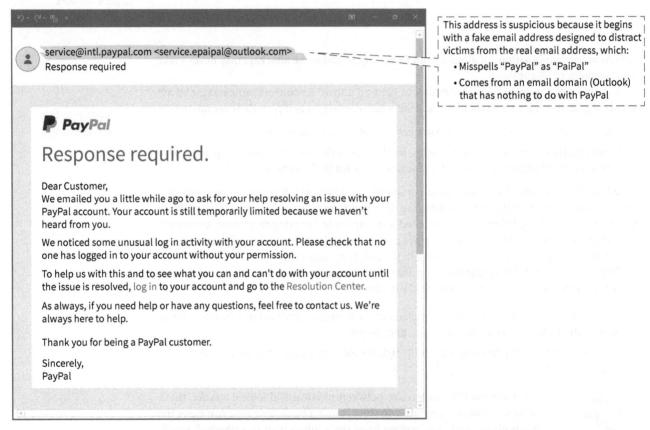

Illustration 16.4 Phishing emails are designed to look as if they came from a legitimate source, like PayPal.

Hackers intentionally send phishing emails when victims may be distracted:

- The increase in online shopping during winter holidays like Christmas, Thanksgiving, and Hanukkah provides opportunities for hackers to use emails that are disguised as coming from UPS, FedEx, or Amazon.

- During the COVID-19 pandemic, hackers sent fraudulent emails masked as U.S. government communications concerning the COVID-19 stimulus checks that many Americans received. The included link asked victims to enter their Social Security numbers and personal information into the website to check the status of their checks. Sadly, many Americans became victims of the attack.

A company's best defense against phishing attacks is to train employees to recognize and report red flags (**Table 16.4**). To understand red flags, users must know how it's possible to manipulate the information in emails. For example, the text that appears in an email link can be edited to display anything the sender wishes, and users must hover over that link to see the real link.

TABLE 16.4 Email Phishing Red Flags

Red Flag	Example
Incorrect sender address	Sending from obscure domains that are designed to look similar to legitimate domains, such as @arnazon.com instead of @amazon.com
Vague salutation	Addressing the email to a generic recipient, such as using "Dear employee" or "Dear colleague" instead of "Dear [*Individual's Name*]"
Poor grammar or spelling	Including grammar or spelling mistakes, such as "Your accounts information has need to be confirmed"
Urgency	Using words like "suspended," "security concerns," and "immediately"
Unusual links	Hovering over a link in the email shows the actual link is not the same as the displayed text; the link may take you to a fake website such as "paipal.com" instead of "PayPal.com"
Surveys	Asking for personal information in a survey instead of taking you to a company portal to input information directly in the corporate system

Darrell, a staff accountant in Julia's Cookies' Accounting department, received an email from the CEO that appeared unusual. Help them review their inbox for other unusual emails in Applied Learning 16.2.

Julia's Cookies   Applied Learning 16.2

Social Engineering: Reporting Suspicious Emails

An email from the CEO asked Darrell to wire money for a payment the CEO must make on behalf of Julia's Cookies. Darrell thought it was odd that the CEO was emailing a staff accountant instead of the chief accounting officer. They remembered that the company has a formal business process for wiring money and that even the CEO must follow it. Darrell contacted their manager and the Cybersecurity department. The Cybersecurity department asked Darrell to forward the suspicious email for further investigation and delete it immediately from their inbox. The Cybersecurity department reminded Darrell to always report suspicious emails and never forward them to anyone else, as others may also get caught in the con if the email is not handled properly.

After talking to the cybersecurity department, Darrell reviewed their inbox for other potential phishing emails. Are any of these emails suspicious?

Email	Phishing?
1. A reminder from Darrell's manager to fill out the weekly timesheet in the accounting system	
2. An email addressed to "Dear staff accountant at Julia's Cookies"	
3. A request from Julia's Cookies' vendor management analyst, Brooklyn, for a copy of the accounts payable codes for new vendors she added into the system	
4. A request from an employee for Darrell to escalate the approval of a requested payment reimbursement within the accounting system, as the employee submitted the request late and wants to avoid a late penalty	
5. A message from someone with an email address ending with @JuliasCoookies.com	
6. A request from the CFO for a rapid transfer of money from one bank account to another	
7. A request from Julia's Cookies' Internal Audit department, asking for General Ledger user access information for testing	

SOLUTION

Email 2 is suspicious because it's addressed to a nonpersonal recipient.
Email 5 is suspicious because the company name is misspelled with too many O's.
Email 6 is suspicious because Darrell's CFO is required to follow a specific formal business process for requesting money transfers.

Dumpster Diving

CPA It's exactly what you are thinking. **Dumpster diving** is looking through someone else's physical trash. In the corporate world, criminals look for discarded sensitive information like passwords or network diagrams (**Illustration 16.5**).

Network/application
diagrams

Organizational
charts

Credit card receipts

Expense reports

Passwords and
access codes

Printed emails

Employee names

Illustration 16.5 Dumpster divers look for sensitive information like passwords, network diagrams, and emails.

While more businesses are minimizing their use of printed documents, many companies still generate paper that must be discarded. An important internal control dictates how these papers are disposed of. Sensitive information should be shredded and discarded securely to keep it away from Dumpster divers.

Eavesdropping

CPA **Eavesdropping**, or sniffing, is the unauthorized interception of communication. It includes listening to phone calls, as well as intercepting emails, text messages, and other forms of communication.

CPA To mitigate the risk of attackers gaining information by intercepting communications, businesses encrypt data and use secure communication lines. **Encryption** is the process of using an algorithm to encode a plaintext message, like readable text, and converting it to something that is seemingly meaningless, called ciphertext. Encrypting the text helps ensure confidentiality. The recipient of the communication then decrypts the message back into its original, understandable format.

CPA To securely send files, companies use **File Transfer Protocol (FTP)**, which is a standard network protocol that allows users to transfer files between the company network and outside parties. For example, Julia's Cookies provides its employee data to its health insurance provider monthly. Because personal data is being sent to a third-party vendor outside the company network, an encrypted FTP channel is used to mitigate the risk of unauthorized interception.

Why Does It Matter to Your Career?

Thoughts from a Manager of Accounts Payable, Banking

- Employees of all types—especially accounting professionals—must know how to treat sensitive data. The information accounting professionals work with is sensitive in nature; therefore, it is important that all documentation is disposed of properly and secured even from the eyes of people in the workplace.

- Everyone receives phishing emails. While many cybersecurity teams implement prevention methods to filter potentially harmful emails, some emails can still get through the filter. As a recipient of any email, it is always wise to be skeptical and not click on any links or download any materials unless you know the email's origins and were expecting it.

Physical Reconnaissance Control Activities

As the first stage of a cybersecurity threat, reconnaissance attacks are an area where a company can mitigate the risk of external threats through proactive measures—like preventive controls. NIST states that "a well-trained workforce provides another organizational safeguard that can be employed as part of a strategy to protect organizations against malicious code coming into organizations via email or web applications."[4] NIST also recommends using

---

[4]https://nvlpubs.nist.gov/nistpubs/SpecialPublications/NIST.SP.800-172.pdf

physical access controls to help prevent eavesdropping or in-transit modification of unencrypted transmissions.

The NIST internal controls for phishing and eavesdropping are P1, which means they are at the highest priority level (**Table 16.5**).

TABLE 16.5 Physical Reconnaissance Internal Controls

Cybersecurity Threat	Control Activity	NIST Reference
Phishing	Train personnel to look for indications of potentially suspicious emails, such as unexpected emails or emails with strange or poor grammar	AT-3(4): Role-based Security Training
Dumpster diving/ eavesdropping	Control physical access to information system distribution and transmission lines with company facilities using security safeguards	PE-4: Access Control for Transmission Medium

Logical Reconnaissance Attacks

A **logical reconnaissance attack** uses digital attacks and does not require a human target. The target is a network vulnerability that could eventually allow the hacker to get into the system.

To execute the Equifax data breach in 2017, four hackers performed reconnaissance for weeks, scanning for vulnerable servers on Equifax's network. They discovered that Equifax used a specific software with a known weakness. The software provider disclosed the issue and provided a system update to its customers, but Equifax ignored the update. This allowed the hackers to exploit that weakness and eventually access Equifax's network.

To better understand how hackers get information, consider an example. If you are looking for information, you might type a few words into a search engine like Google, hoping the search will produce a web page with the information you need. Sometimes the first few searches aren't quite right, but changing the keywords results in a good match. Hackers do something similar. They search network traffic to see if they can operate within it, unseen.

Ping Sweeps

Before we describe specific logical attacks, there are some basics about computer networks that are essential to understanding the cybersecurity threats throughout this chapter:

- Communication over a computer network is based on sending **packets** between hosts. A **packet** is a small portion of the full message being sent over the network.
- Messages are broken into multiple packets when transferred through the network.
- Devices that connect to the network each have a unique **IP address**, which is composed of a string of characters.
- Devices use their IP addresses to communicate over the network.

The purpose of a **ping sweep**, also called an IP probe, is to identify which hosts are active in the network by sending a communication to each IP address to see if there is a response packet. The hacker pings, or calls, each network IP address, one at a time, and waits for the response packet. If an IP address does not send a response packet, the hacker assumes that IP address is not currently active and removes it from the list of prospective access points.

Port Scans

By performing ping sweeps, hackers can create a list of active IP addresses. The next step is for hackers to narrow their results using **port scans**, which indicate which ports are open and sending or receiving data on the network. A **network port** is a location in the network where communication packets are sent and received. A port scan is like a ping sweep because hackers attempt to connect to a series of ports and wait for response packets to indicate if the ports are active.

Attackers use port scans to identify the types of communication occurring on the network:

- For example, a specific port number can indicate if the information being sent is an FTP data transfer, an unencrypted text communication, or a website.
- Port scans also reveal whether firewalls exist between the sender and the port, which is valuable reconnaissance information for an attacker because firewalls are a defense mechanism against cyber attackers.

The downside of port scans for attackers is that they are easily detectable, provided the business has internal controls in place that monitor for this activity.

Logical Reconnaissance Control Activities

For all logical reconnaissance attacks, companies can be proactive by running sweeps and scans internally to identify weaknesses before a hacker does. The company can then address deficiencies before they are discovered by an external threat:

- **Vulnerability scans:** NIST recommends that companies perform vulnerability scans to detect and classify security loopholes in their infrastructure. A company should determine the level of vulnerability scanning required based on the security categorization of the system and should include all potential sources of vulnerabilities—even network-connected printers, scanners, and copiers.
- **CPA** **Penetration tests:** Companies commonly perform penetration testing—also called pen testing—by attempting to hack their own systems. Accounting professionals who are cybersecurity and technology risk specialists engage in pen testing as part of IT audits or technology consulting engagements. Even if you aren't performing pen testing, you may find yourself reviewing results of these tests to assess risks for a company.
- **Patches:** A company should ensure that systems are running up-to-date security by applying patches as soon as they are available. A patch is a software update, released by the software's providers, that may include upgrades, fixes, or improvements. For Equifax, the failure to patch its third-party-provided software opened the network to hackers. Equifax was aware that the patch was necessary to fix a security vulnerability in the software.

Table 16.6 lists the controls that NIST 800-53 recommends to mitigate a company's risk of logical reconnaissance attacks.

TABLE 16.6 Logical Reconnaissance Internal Controls

Cybersecurity Threat	Control Activity	NIST Reference
Various logical reconnaissance attacks	Scan for vulnerabilities in the information systems and hosted applications both randomly and when new vulnerabilities are identified or reported	RA-5: Vulnerability Scanning
	Conduct penetration testing on the information systems or individual system components to identify vulnerabilities that could be exploited by adversaries	CA-8: Penetration Testing
	Maintain the currency, accuracy, and availability of consistent baseline configurations for systems and use tools to track software installed or current patch levels	CM-2: Baseline Configuration

CONCEPT REVIEW QUESTIONS

1. What are reconnaissance attacks?

   Ans. Reconnaissance attacks are knowledge-gathering attacks that help attackers identify targets and plan their operations.

2. Differentiate between physical and logical attacks.

   Ans. Physical attacks occur when attackers threaten elements a network administrator has no control over, such as physical security, hardware, and people. On the other hand, logical attacks occur on a fully digital spectrum and require no human interaction other than the attacker instigating the attack.

3. What do you mean by social engineering?

   Ans. Social engineering involves persuading people to perform acts that would give the hackers access to confidential information, such as birth dates, passwords, and user IDs.

4. **CPA** What is email phishing?

   Ans. Email phishing is a deceptive request designed to trick victims into sharing private information. Phishing often involves a fraudulent email that appears to be from a reputable source, such as an employer or a bank.

5. **CPA** What is Dumpster diving?

   Ans. Dumpster diving is looking through someone else's physical trash. In the corporate world, criminals look for discarded sensitive information like passwords or network diagrams.

6. **CPA** Briefly explain encryption.

   Ans. Encryption is the process of using an algorithm to encode a plaintext message, like readable text, and converting it to something that is seemingly meaningless, called ciphertext. Encrypting the text helps ensure confidentiality. The recipient of the communication then decrypts the message back into its original, understandable format.

16.3 How Do Hackers Gain Unauthorized Access?

Learning Objective ❸
Compare and contrast physical and logical access attacks.

Once attackers acquire information about a network, it's time to gain access. During an **access attack**, hackers attempt to gain unauthorized access to the network and its information by exploiting vulnerabilities discovered during reconnaissance. Recall that not every attacker will follow the full cycle of reconnaissance, access, and disruption.

Attackers can use physical or logical attacks to access a network, so we explore common methods for both types of network access throughout this section.

Physical Access Attacks

CPA **Physical access attacks** result in access to either hardware or people. That access can be gained with the assistance of an unknowing victim or through force.

Tailgating

We have discussed some of the most common social engineering reconnaissance attacks, but social engineering can also be used to gain physical access. You have learned that humans are the biggest weakness in a company's internal control environment. Most humans want to avoid the appearance of rudeness, and social engineering takes advantage of this fundamental human characteristic.

Tailgating, also known as piggybacking, is the physical act of gaining unauthorized entry by closely following someone else through a physical security checkpoint and using that person's credentials to gain access. Basically, an authorized user allows an unauthorized user access due to proximity. This can happen in two ways:

- **Accidental tailgating:** Authorized users are unaware that there is a tailgater. If you get on an elevator that requires swiping a badge to reach your floor, someone else may jump on the elevator and follow you to that floor without you realizing that the person didn't swipe a badge. With dozens of people working on the same floor, it's natural to assume they all belong, but one of them may be tailgating you to get access.

- **Polite tailgating:** The authorized user is aware of the other person but may politely hold the door for the tailgater—which is something many people do out of courtesy!

Physical Access Control Activities

Many techniques, besides slamming a door in someone's face, can be used to prevent unauthorized entry. We explore some control activities from NIST's physical access controls list in **Table 16.7**, but this is not a comprehensive list. Companies can implement these controls based on their unique needs. For example, many companies install physical barriers using half-walls and turnstiles where employees must scan a badge or fingerprint to enter the office. The turnstile only allows one person to pass through at a time, preventing tailgating.

TABLE 16.7 Physical Access Internal Controls

Cybersecurity Threat	Control Activity	NIST Reference
Physical access attacks	Develop, approve, and maintain a list of individuals authorized to access the facility where the information resides	PE-2: Physical Access Authorizations
	Issue authorization credentials for facility access and review the access list on a routine basis to remove access when it is no longer required	PE-2: Physical Access Authorizations
	Require two forms of approved identification for visitor access to the facility where the system resides	PE-2: Physical Access Authorizations
	Escort visitors and control visitor activity	PE-3: Physical Access Authorizations
	Enforce physical access authorizations to the system in addition to the physical access controls for the facility	PE-3: Physical Access Control
	Employ guards to control access points to the facility where the system resides 24 hours per day, 7 days per week	PE-3: Physical Access Control
	Limit access using physical barriers including bollards, concrete slabs, Jersey walls, and hydraulic active vehicle barriers	PE-3: Physical Access Control
	Monitor physical access to the facility where the system resides using physical intrusion alarms and surveillance equipment	PE-6: Monitoring Physical Access

Even with proper physical access controls in place, companies are at risk. People can circumvent controls, whether intentionally or innocently. Help Sanglap handle an awkward situation at Julia's Cookies in Applied Learning 16.3.

Julia's Cookies   Applied Learning 16.3

Physical Access: Mail Delivery

As an employee of Julia's Cookies, Sanglap has an employee ID badge that allows access to the corporate headquarters. When Sanglap arrives at the office this morning, he uses a side door entry that unlocks with his badge. As he approaches, he sees a mail delivery person knocking on the door. She wants someone to let her inside.

She forgot her mail access badge and needs to deliver some packages. She is in a hurry and can't go back to her truck for the badge because she is already behind schedule. She assures Sanglap that she brings the mail every day and knows exactly where to take it.

Sanglap has never seen this person before, but he has only been working at Julia's Cookies for a few weeks. What do you think Sanglap should do?

SOLUTION

Sanglap should not let her in the door. He could do a few things:

- Offer to take the mail to the front desk for her
- Insist that she retrieve her badge from her truck

- Direct her to the visitor entrance to speak to a security guard

Even if Sanglap did recognize her from previous deliveries, she could be a risk to the company. She may have left her badge behind intentionally so she could enter the building without being tracked.

Logical Access Attacks

CPA **Logical access attacks** seek unauthorized access to a system or an application by either exploiting a network vulnerability unveiled during reconnaissance attacks or attempting to use force to get through network security.

Let's start with the most direct logical access method, the **brute-force attack**, in which attackers force access to the network by attempting many passwords or phrases until finding the correct one.

Brute-Force Attacks

Passwords protect networks like locks protect homes, and using weak passwords is like putting your house key under the doormat. Most criminals will look under the doormat for a house key, and most hackers know basic password formats and can easily bypass weak and infrequently updated passwords.

Have you ever forgotten a website password and tried as many different passwords as possible to see if they worked? That is a brute-force attack on yourself. In fact, as the workforce migrated primarily to a work-from-home environment in 2020 due to the COVID-19 pandemic, criminals increasingly used brute-force attacks to hack passwords. Even governments are not immune to these unsophisticated efforts. In early 2021, Australia's parliamentary network was the victim of 24 hours of password hacking attacks. While the parliament's network was not breached, the attack impacted network access for legitimate users for several days.

Hackers have many ways to figure out passwords. Many people recycle credentials by changing one or two characters and using the same password across locations. You probably have accounts that use the same username, like your email address. Do you also use the same password for these accounts? Once a hacker discovers one of your username and password combinations, it's easy to leverage that information across other accounts.

Hackers may try to guess passwords using social cues such as birth dates, hometowns, and middle names. This is the information that they may acquire during reconnaissance attacks, such as email phishing. They may also mount **dictionary attacks**, using lists of commonly used words and combinations of words and letters to guess passwords.

Alternatively, brute-force attacks can be highly sophisticated processes that use algorithms to run various combinations of passwords (**Illustration 16.6**). These programs are designed to run continuously, waiting even if the system locks out the user ID from logging in for a period of time.

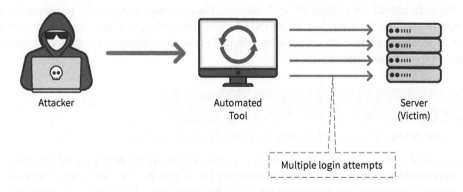

Attacker   Automated   Server
                   Tool   (Victim)

Multiple login attempts

Illustration 16.6 Attackers use automated programs that continually run login attempts to quickly carry out brute-force attacks.

To combat these automated systems, the strength of the password, which is based on its length and complexity, is essential. The use of strong passwords should be enforced by company policies. **CPA** NIST provides explicit guidelines that companies can require for password strength:

- **Length:** The recommended length is 8–64 characters.
- **Character types:** Use a mixture of letters, numbers, and special characters.
- **Construction:** Avoid dictionary words that would allow for dictionary attacks.
- **Reset:** Only reset your password if you know it has been compromised.
- **Historical:** Avoid using previously used passwords.
- **Multifactor:** Use multifactor authentication, where possible.
- **Log-in attempts:** Limit the number of allowed failed login attempts before locking the account.

The more complex the password, the longer it will take a program to identify the correct one, which means the company has more time to detect the brute-force attack.

On-Path Attacks

CPA While brute-force attacks are direct trial-and-error efforts, other attacks require planning and stealth. **On-path attacks,** which were once known as man-in-the-middle attacks, attempt to gain access to an ongoing communication between two endpoints by pretending to be each of the parties. This is similar to eavesdropping, discussed earlier, with the following difference:

- **Eavesdropping:** The hacker is only listening to or intercepting the communication.
- **On-path attack:** The hacker is actively injected into the connection.

Illustration 16.7 demonstrates how the original connection between a user and a server is intercepted by a hacker who establishes a new connection between the user and the server.

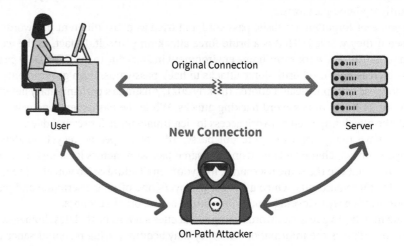

Illustration 16.7 An on-path attack creates a new connection that interrupts a legitimate communication.

This attack keeps the hacker hidden, so targets don't realize someone is gathering their information. Targets think they have connected to the server and enter their username and password, but now the hacker has these credentials and can log into the server without the company's or system administrators' awareness.

On-path attacks are technically sophisticated. Hackers must successfully impersonate the server to convince the user they are performing a legitimate login, which requires a combination of techniques and software to be successful. (Those techniques and software are beyond the scope of this discussion.)

Why Does It Matter to Your Career?

Thoughts From an IT Audit Associate, Consulting

Successful auditors often think like criminals. In the case of cybersecurity, think like a hacker! Understanding different attack methods and brainstorming how a cyber attacker could execute them will help identify controls to prevent or detect the attacks. Brainstorming like this can be fun if you are interested in technology or enjoy creative thinking. Your ideas could save your company millions of dollars.

IP Spoofing

Another access attack that involves impersonating a legitimate part of the network is IP spoofing. In **IP spoofing,** an attacker creates IP packets with modified source addresses to disguise their identity and impersonate a legitimate computer on the network (**Illustration 16.8**).

You have learned that sending and receiving IP packets is the primary way devices on the network communicate:

- **Normal packets:** In normal packets, the source address is the IP address of the packet sender.

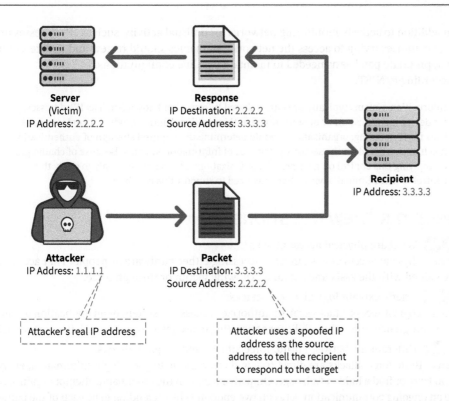

Illustration 16.8 IP spoofing disguises a hacker's real IP address by using the IP address of the target as the fake source address.

- **Spoofed packets:** When a packet has been spoofed, it has a forged source address. It's like sending a package in the mail with the wrong return address listed. The hacker sends the message to the system, and the system responds to a real user who is the target of the attack instead of to the real source, which is the attacker.

  Why would an attacker do this? Most commonly, it is to make the server send excessive data or requests to an IP address, overwhelm the host of that IP address, and take down that system. We'll explore this further when we discuss denial-of-service attacks in the next section.

Logical Access Control Activities

Attacks that attempt to access corporate systems are the core of cyber threats. If these attacks are not prevented, the hacker can access the company systems and wreak havoc, which we will discuss next. It is essential for a business to have controls in place to detect and avoid these attacks (**Table 16.8**).

TABLE 16.8 Logical Access Internal Controls

Cybersecurity Threat	Control Activity	NIST Reference
Brute-force attacks	Ensure that the information system does the following for password-based authentication: • Enforce minimum password complexity of specified case sensitivity, character numbers, and mix of uppercase and lowercase letters, including minimum requirements for each type • Enforce a specified number of changed characters when new passwords are created • Prohibit password reuse for a specified number of generations	IA-5: Authentication Management
On-path attacks	Review and update the baseline configuration of the information system: • Using a company-defined frequency • When required due to specified circumstances • As an integral part of information system component installations and upgrades	CM-2: Baseline Configuration
IP spoofing	Ensure that the information system uniquely identifies and authenticates devices before establishing a connection	IA-3: Device Identification and Authentication

In addition to actively monitoring networks for unusual activity, such as IP addresses from foreign countries trying to access the network, companies should review and update systems with appropriate patches as needed to maintain baseline configurations.

According to NIST:

> Information systems typically use either shared information known (such as IP addresses) for device identification or organizational authentication solutions. When it comes to controls for IP spoofing, organizations should determine the required strength of authentication mechanisms based on the security categories of information systems. Because of challenges of applying this control on a large scale, organizations are encouraged only to apply the control to those limited devices that truly need to support this capability.[5]

CONCEPT REVIEW QUESTIONS

1. **CPA** What are physical access attacks?

   Ans. Physical access attacks involve accessing either hardware or people. That access can be gained with the assistance of an unknowing victim or through force.

2. **CPA** Briefly explain logical access attacks.

   Ans. Logical access attacks seek unauthorized access to a system or an application by either exploiting a network vulnerability or attempting to use force to get through network security.

3. **CPA** Differentiate between brute-force attacks and on-path attacks.

   Ans. Brute-force attacks are direct trial-and-error efforts to guess login information, encryption keys, or find a hidden web page. On-path attacks, on the other hand, attempt to gain access to an ongoing communication between two endpoints by pretending to be each of the parties.

4. What is IP spoofing?

   Ans. IP spoofing involves an attacker impersonating a legitimate part of the network. An attacker creates IP packets with modified source addresses to disguise their identity and impersonate a legitimate computer on the network.

16.4 How Do Attackers Shut Down a System?

Learning Objective ❹
Explain how hackers perform disruptive attacks.

What do attackers do once they are in a network? It depends on their motives:

- Attackers can steal data.
- They can hold information hostage and demand a ransom.
- They can crash systems or even permanently damage the network.
- They can also perform physical attacks or terrorist actions.

Before we look at the different types of disruptive attacks, let's go back to the Equifax data breach. We know that four hackers gained access to Equifax's network through a vulnerability they found in Equifax's third-party software that was not patched in a timely manner. But what did the hackers do once they had access?

First, they created profiles for themselves using credentials of Equifax employees to mask suspicious network activity that might have been detected by Equifax's controls. With these profiles, the attackers could freely utilize the network. They remained disguised for so long by doing the following things:

- Hiding their location of origin by using at least 34 servers in more than 20 countries
- Purchasing remote computing services from other countries

---

[5]https://csrc.nist.gov/publications/detail/sp/800-53/rev-5/final

- Using encrypted communication channels within the Equifax network to blend into the normal network activity
- Compressing and dividing the data files
- Deleting the compressed files after downloading the sensitive data
- Wiping log files daily to eliminate any activity trail

While data breaches like the Equifax breach are common, and companies should address their risk when designing internal controls for cyberattacks, two other types of disruptive attacks should also cause businesses concern: denial-of-service attacks and malware.

Why Does It Matter to Your Career?

Thoughts from a Staff IT Auditor, Materials and Industrial Services

- Many accounting professionals have lucrative and rewarding careers in the cybersecurity or information security realms, whether as IT auditors or cybersecurity professionals. The unique capability of an accounting professional to identify risks makes them desirable candidates for these roles.
- Few words create more stress for leadership of an organization than "cybersecurity risk." Whether you are an auditor providing feedback from an engagement or a core business member observing a risk, you must understand when to notify the IT department about suspicious activity. It's even better if you can explain why it's suspect.

Denial-of-Service Attacks

CPA **Denial-of-service (DoS) attacks** prohibit users from using resources such as computers, websites, servers, or an entire network. DoS attacks deny users access to resources they have a legitimate need to use. To accomplish this, attackers continuously send fake requests to the business to consume the system's capacity, resulting in loss of availability for real users (**Illustration 16.9**). The resources become temporarily or even indefinitely unavailable.

Remember IP spoofing? Hackers can use IP spoofing to direct the recipient to overload the victim's network. For example, requesting excessive amounts of data from the recipient will cause the recipient to respond to the spoofed source address—the victim's IP address—with the request.

This disruption can be devastating to a company because it prohibits the company from completing business processes and transactions. It's a common tactic against internet-facing systems because attackers must access the system via the internet to perform these attacks. While anyone can be a target of a DoS attack, attackers often target businesses with high-traffic, high-profile websites such as banks and infrastructure providers.

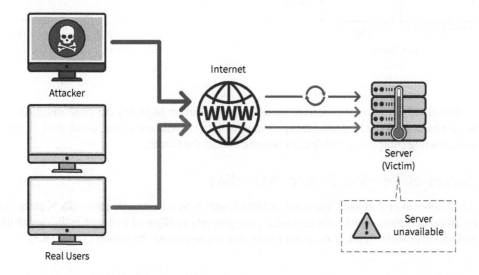

Illustration 16.9 The goal of a denial-of-service attack is to send excessive traffic to a server so that it is unavailable for real users.

Botnets

CPA While there are different DoS attack tools and techniques, the most common method is a brute-force attack. Attackers use computers infected with malware that function like robots. These computers, called **botnets**, are programmed to do whatever attackers want, such as flooding a specific host with repetitive requests to consume the target system's capacity.

At Julia's Cookies, orders are placed through the website or mobile app. A DoS attack on Julia's Cookies' website or mobile app floods the servers with fake requests. The requests are immediately noticeable because they don't follow the normal pattern of sales. Normal sales orders come in at a steady but spaced rate, while these attacks send orders at a rate of thousands per second. They overload the server for Julia's Cookies' transactional system and prevent legitimate customers from placing orders on the website or mobile app.

Distributed Denial-of-Service

A cyber attacker who wants to perform a large-scale DoS attack can carry out a **distributed denial-of-service (DDoS) attack** that uses multiple machines or IP addresses to force the target to shut down (**Illustration 16.10**). Since the hacker uses multiple originating points of attack, it's more difficult for a company to stop such attacks, as it must identify each source. This also makes it difficult for a company to differentiate between an attack and legitimate business traffic.

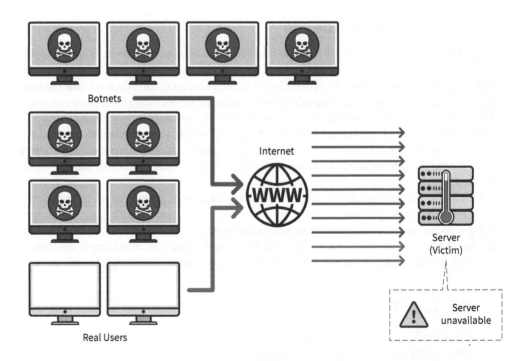

Illustration 16.10 A distributed denial-of-service attack uses multiple computers to increase pressure on the victim server until it's unavailable.

The distributed denial-of-service example in Illustration 16.10 is a complex attack. It uses email phishing to send a destructive program, which you will learn more about next, to many unsuspecting computers, which then become bots in the botnet.

Denial-of-Service Control Activities

A business can protect itself from DoS and DDoS attacks by ensuring that firewalls, routers, and intrusion detection systems are up-to-date, are properly configured to detect malicious traffic, and will automatically block the ports where fake requests enter the system (**Table 16.9**).

TABLE 16.9 Denial-of-Service Internal Controls

Cybersecurity Threat	Control Activity	NIST Reference
Denial-of-service attacks	Manage capacity, bandwidth, or other redundancy to limit the effects of denial-of-service attacks	SC-5: Denial-of-Service Protection
	Employ monitoring tools to detect indicators of denial-of-service attacks against, or launched from, the system	SC-5: Denial-of-Service Protection
	Monitor system resources to determine if sufficient resources exist to prevent effective denial-of-service attacks	SC-5: Denial-of-Service Protection

To help identify a DoS attack, a business should monitor incoming traffic, including the number of requests that come through a port at a given time. At Julia's Cookies, the Cybersecurity department continuously monitors incoming traffic and the number of requests that each system receives. If the requests cross a pre-established threshold, the port is closed to prevent requests from flooding the system and making it unavailable.

Malware Attacks

While DoS attacks use ongoing fake requests that crash a system, the requests themselves are harmless. In contrast, hackers can use destructive programs to take down a system with malware attacks. **CPA** **Malware**, short for "malicious software," is software specifically designed to damage, disrupt, or gain unauthorized access to systems:

- Malware contains **malicious code** that is written to cause harm and attack the target system.
- Malware can be a deliberate external cyberattack or can be created by a programmer who works for the company and intends to do harm from within.
- Malware packages malicious code in specific software that is often delivered via a link or file that requires users to interact with it to execute the malware. When malware is used to hold a system hostage in exchange for a demand, like monetary payment, it's called **ransomware**.

A company can minimize the risk of internally generated malicious code by mandating training for programmers on how to write secure code and implementing code testing procedures before new code is released into the business.

Viruses

CPA A **virus** is a type of malware that replicates itself in a system and spreads quickly, causing damage to core system functions. Like a biological virus, such as COVID-19, which spreads from person to person, malware viruses replicate in a system and cause widespread corruption to systems and data. Attackers create viruses that cause a variety of problems. For example, viruses can steal usernames and passwords, spam email inboxes, corrupt files, or lock users out of systems. Systems with viruses are considered infected, meaning these systems can actively cause damage to other systems if the viruses are not stopped.

Viruses can be extremely dangerous to businesses due to their high contagion levels. They move throughout an organization, seeking to infect as many systems as possible. However, viruses can only spread through ongoing human interaction. For example, a virus may be attached to an email that is then forwarded by an employee throughout an organization, but the email doesn't do any damage unless a user opens the file attachment, which is a human interaction (**Illustration 16.11**).

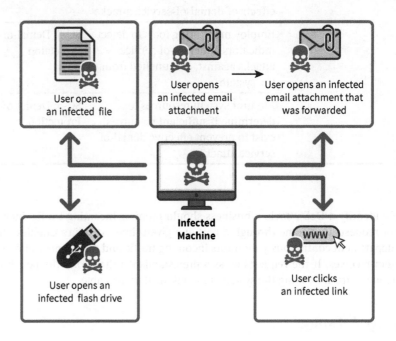

Illustration 16.11 Viruses replicate with the help of human interaction.

If your computer is infected with a virus, it may show signs like these:

- Emails sent from your email account that you didn't send
- Computer crashing consistently
- Pop-up windows displaying without explanation
- Slow computer processing
- Social media accounts sending messages or posting without your involvement
- Unfamiliar programs starting when you turn on your computer

To avoid spreading viruses, never open attachments, click links, or download files in emails if you are not sure of their source. Companies address the risk of viruses by employing protection mechanisms at a system's entry and exit points to detect and eradicate malicious code and perform periodic scans of systems when files are downloaded. Additionally, companies use email protection to identify suspected malware when it's received and redirect it from employees' inboxes to eliminate the risk of an employee clicking on an infected item.

Worms

CPA While viruses replicate through user interaction, **worms** replicate without the assistance of human interaction. They have the same destructive power as viruses and pose significant risks to the network security of a company:

- Worms arrive similarly to viruses, attached to emails in the form of links or files to download.
- Once a worm is installed on a machine, it infects every system it can reach, often without the initial user's awareness. A company with integrated systems such as an enterprise-wide ERP system would be infected very quickly, since the system connects to the entire organization's business processes. An unchecked worm could result in disaster.

- The replication of worms can drain a system by taking over hard drive space. This slows down the system and consumes its processing power.

 But this final characteristic of worms is also one way a company can detect their presence—by monitoring the system's performance and memory. A sudden spike in hard drive utilization or decrease in performance could indicate worm replication.

To address the risk of worms affecting security functions in systems, NIST recommends that businesses isolate security functions from nonsecurity functions. Companies should control the information that flows between security and nonsecurity functions and minimize the number of nonsecurity functions that are kept within the same system boundaries as the security functions. This limits the amount of code that must be trusted to ensure that security policies are enforced in the system, thus limiting exposure risk.

Logic Bombs

CPA A **logic bomb** is a piece of malicious code that is programmed into a system and remains dormant until certain conditions are met:

- Cyber attackers program logic bombs to be dormant until the time is right, and then the malicious code is released into the system. The principle is similar to setting a timer on a bomb or lighting a fuse.
- The conditions that trigger a logic bomb vary based on the creativity of the cyber attacker. In its simplest form, a logic bomb can be triggered by launching a specific program or logging into a website.
- These attacks are difficult to detect or prevent until they have been activated. Companies try their best to protect information by limiting user access to specified files or folders, but robust business continuity and disaster recovery plans are essential to ensure that systems and data are amply backed up to mitigate the damage in the event that a logic bomb is triggered.

 In the mid-2010s, Siemens, a multinational industrial manufacturing company headquartered in Europe, hired a contractor named David Tinley. Tinley intentionally programmed logic bombs within the software he wrote for Siemens and set the trigger for a future date. Since the software was a custom build, it had complex code that ensured Tinley would be hired to fix the software for a fee. Essentially, Tinley set his own software to self-destruct so he would be hired to come back and fix it. It was two years before Siemens' IT team received access to Tinley's code while the contractor was out of town and discovered the logic bombs hidden in the software's code. The lesson from Siemens for companies' IT departments is one learned the hard way: always ensure that you have processes in place to validate code independently—whether the code was written by a contractor or an internal employee. You never know who may have malicious intentions.

Trojan Horses

 In classical mythology, the Greeks used a gigantic hollow wooden horse to gain access to the city of Troy. They deposited the horse outside the city gates and appeared to sail away. When the Trojan soldiers pulled the horse into the city, the Greek soldiers hiding inside jumped out, opened the gates to the Greek army, and conquered the city.

Over the years, the term "Trojan horse" became a metaphor, a parable, and eventually a term to describe a specific type of malware. **CPA** A **Trojan horse** malware is disguised as benign software but carries malicious code that may be activated via a logic bomb. Unlike viruses and worms, Trojan horses are nonreplicating. While Trojan horses may differ in their purposes, they are commonly used to obtain back door access to a target system. The result is unauthorized access that allows attackers to destroy data, much like the Greeks destroyed the city of Troy.

In the Real World | Hostage Systems

The NHS attack in 2017 isn't the only recent hostage cyberattack to gain international attention. Ransomware and denial-of-service attacks occur more often than you may realize.

Denial-of-Service Attacks at Dyn, Inc. in 2016	Dyn, Inc. offered domain registration services, providing clients an internet name, such as the website name you enter into a web browser, mapped to a specific IP address: • In a single day, Dyn was the victim of two denial-of-service attacks. The first attack ran from 7:00 a.m. to 9:20 a.m., and the second lasted from 4:00 p.m. to 6:11 p.m. • During these attacks, hackers sent lookup requests from tens of millions of different IP addresses to overwhelm Dyn's servers. • Internet users experienced difficulties accessing websites, including services like Airbnb, Amazon.com, HBO, Etsy, Netflix, PayPal, the PlayStation Network, and Spotify. • Multiple hacker groups, including Anonymous, claimed responsibility for the attacks, but little evidence was available to validate those claims.
SamSam Ransomware, 2018	Two Iranian hackers executed the SamSam ransomware attack on the city of Atlanta using brute-force attacks that targeted weaknesses in the IT infrastructure of its victims: • This attack was one of the largest against a major American city to date. • It affected more than 6 million people, shut down systems for five days, and affected over a third of the city's systems. • Residents resorted to using paper bills and forms, legal documents and dashcam footage were deleted, and the city suffered substantial reputational damage for failing to maintain its systems' security ahead of the attack.
RobbinHood Ransomware, 2019	Another major U.S. city, Baltimore, suffered a similar ransomware attack the following year: • RobbinHood took down all the city's services, and the attackers demanded a ransom worth approximately $75,000 to restore access. • It took weeks to restore the city's systems. • Baltimore was the second victim of RobbinHood in 2019. The ransomware had also been used to attack Greenville, North Carolina, earlier that year.
Ransomware Attack at ISS World, 2020	ISS World is a Denmark-headquartered facilities management firm that suffered a ransomware attack that left thousands of employees without access to systems: • It took three days to identify the root cause of the attack and almost a month to regain control of most of the company's systems. • It's estimated that it cost ISS $45 to $75 million just to regain access to its systems after the attack. • The additional loss of IT assets potentially doubled the cost of the attack.
Ransomware Attack at Colonial Pipeline, 2021	In 2021, as fuel prices soared in the southeastern United States, Colonial Pipeline, which provides almost 50% of the fuel for the East Coast, was attacked with ransomware: • Shortly after discovering the attack, the CEO of Colonial Pipeline paid a $4.4 million ransom to the hackers who were holding the company's data hostage. • The hackers provided the company with the means to unlock its systems, but the damage took more to undo than simply typing in a password. • Colonial Pipeline subsequently shut down fuel lines because it feared the attack had infected its billing systems.. • In response, motorists rushed to local stations to fill containers and caused a shortage of gasoline at gas pumps across the region.

These attacks are a few examples of ransomware and denial-of-service attacks impacting businesses and the general public in the recent past. Have you heard of any recent attacks like these? How did the perpetrators perform those attacks?

To mitigate the risks of malware attacks, IT professionals recommend downloading software only if you are certain that the software is coming from a legitimate source. At your company, there may be IT policies that prevent downloading software to computers if that software is not sanctioned by the IT department. The goal of such policies is to prevent unintentionally bringing malware—like a Trojan horse—into the organization's network. Review the ways malware and DoS attacks can enter a company and test your identification skills by helping Mason prepare for a cybersecurity program pitch in Applied Learning 16.4.

| Julia's Cookies | Applied Learning 16.4 |

Disruptive Attacks: Cybersecurity Program Pitch

Mason is an IT auditor at Julia's Cookies, working on an advisory project for the Cybersecurity department. Currently, the department assigns attacks to team members for management based on the order in which they are received. All Cybersecurity department members must therefore be cross-trained on every type of attack.

Mason has recommended that the Cybersecurity department instead divide attacks into categories and train team members to become subject matter experts in specific types of attacks. While team members will still be cross-trained to act as support as necessary, this new approach will provide experts for every attack.

Mason needs buy-in from Cybersecurity department leadership and Julia's Cookies' chief information security officer (CISO) to get the project approved. As part of his pitch meeting, Mason is using descriptions of real cyberattacks that have occurred in the last two years to demonstrate how this approach can be implemented for the Cybersecurity department.

Mason has prioritized the following cyberattack categories:

- Denial-of-service attacks
- Viruses
- Worms
- Logic bombs
- Trojan horses

Help him match each category to one of the following attack descriptions:

1. On Monday, March 3, at exactly 3:00 p.m., a program stopped allowing users to log in.

2. Dozens of employees received an email from "@juliascookies_securrity.com," prompting them to download new time-tracking software. Employees who downloaded the software experienced no noticeable disruptions in their processing capabilities, and the attack did not appear to replicate itself.

3. Mobile app orders experienced an unprecedented increase at an unusual time of day that resulted in the order system being unavailable.

4. An employee was granted a large increase in memory on her laptop and then requested an additional increase one week later. Upon investigation, highly replicative malicious code was found on the computer.

5. Employees received an email with a funny meme that was forwarded throughout the company. The email contained a link that employees clicked on to view the meme. Users who interacted with the link in the email then experienced unexpected pop-ups on their computers.

SOLUTION

1. Logic bomb. This attack took place at a specific time and date without interaction. Logic bombs are often coded to detonate at a specified point in time.

2. Trojan horse. Because this attack did not replicate, it is a Trojan horse.

3. Denial-of-service attack. Unexpected traffic on a website or an application that bogs down the target system to the point that legitimate users are unable to access it is a denial-of-service attack.

4. Worm. Requiring an increase in memory is indicative of a self-replicating worm that eats away processing capabilities without requiring human interaction.

5. Virus. Unlike worms, viruses require human interaction to replicate across the network.

Malware Control Activities

Malware can cripple a company's systems and prevent it from completing essential business processes. Controls for these attacks should be both preventive and detective. For example, let's consider the two controls in **Table 16.10**. Control SI-3: Malicious Code Protection is a preventive control that stops malicious code from entering the company's systems.

According to NIST:

> Traditional malicious code protection mechanisms cannot always detect such malware code. In these situations, organizations rely instead on other safeguards including, for example, secure coding practices, configuration management and control, trusted procurement processes, and monitoring practices to help ensure that software does not perform functions other than the functions intended.[6]

If malicious code manages to bypass this control, then Control SI-4: Information System Monitoring should be designed to detect the presence of malicious code in the systems.

---

[6]https://csrc.nist.gov/publications/detail/sp/800-53/rev-5/final

TABLE 16.10 Malware Internal Controls

Cybersecurity Threat	Control Activity	NIST Reference
Malware	Employ malicious code protection mechanisms at information system entry and exit points to detect and eradicate malicious code	SI-3: Malicious Code Protection
	Configure malicious code detection to perform periodic scans of the information system, block malicious code, quarantine malicious code, and notify the administrator	SI-3: Malicious Code Protection
	Monitor the information system to detect attacks and indicators of potential attacks, including unauthorized local, network, and remote connections	SI-4: Information System Monitoring

CONCEPT REVIEW QUESTIONS

1. **CPA** How does a denial-of-service (DoS) attack work?
   Ans. DoS attacks prohibit users from using resources such as computers, websites, servers, or an entire network. DoS attacks deny users access to resources they have a legitimate need to use.

2. **CPA** What are botnets?
   Ans. Attackers use computers infected with malware that function like robots. These computers, called botnets, are programmed to do whatever attackers want, such as flooding a specific host with repetitive requests to consume the target system's capacity.

3. **CPA** What is malware?
   Ans. Malware, short for "malicious software," is software specifically designed to damage, disrupt, or gain unauthorized access to systems.

4. **CPA** What are viruses? How do they differ from worms?
   Ans. A virus is a type of malware that replicates itself in a system and spreads quickly, causing damage to core system functions. Like a biological virus, which spreads from person to person, malware viruses replicate in a system and cause widespread corruption to systems and data. While viruses replicate through user interaction, worms replicate without the assistance of human interaction.

5. **CPA** What are logic bombs?
   Ans. A logic bomb is a piece of malicious code that is programmed into a system and remains dormant until certain conditions are met.

6. **CPA** What is a Trojan horse?
   Ans. A Trojan horse malware is disguised as benign software but carries malicious code that may be activated via a logic bomb. Unlike viruses and worms, Trojan horses are nonreplicating.

FEATURED PROFESSIONAL | Public Accounting Cybersecurity Director

Photo courtesy of Rob Valdez

Rob Valdez, CPA, CISM, CISA

Rob is the director of cybersecurity and automation for a public accounting firm and performs advisory engagements including robotic process automation (RPA). Rob's work includes engagements for financial institutions and fintech companies, as well as health care and software developers. Helping clients manage cyber risk and defend against cyberattacks is a large part of Rob's work. With an undergraduate degree in finance and a master's degree in accounting, Rob started his career in corporate accounting for technology providers and software developers. Rob is an advocate for technology training and education, and he served as the president of the local ISACA chapter. (ISACA is an organization dedicated to technology-related governance, risk compliance, security, and IT audit.)

How is your accounting degree applicable to your role as a cybersecurity and automation director?

I ended up working in accounting roles before pursuing a degree in accounting because these operations were so critical to the businesses I worked for. That encouraged me to pursue a master's in accounting and sit for the CPA exam. Accounting is at the heart of decisions around risks and opportunities because both are measured financially. That is why becoming an accounting professional and obtaining a CPA license can open almost any door for someone who is motivated and enthusiastic. I combined my passion and propensity for technology with my accounting experience to become an information systems auditor. From there, I eventually started helping clients design, develop, and implement cybersecurity programs and automation solutions. Even when discussing technology, though, we are always measuring risk and opportunity in financial terms, and my background allows me to speak in terms that matter to clients, turning ideas into potential business value.

Why are frameworks like NIST's Cybersecurity Framework important for accounting professionals and businesses?

Frameworks establish time-tested, robust collections of knowledge. Using authoritative frameworks for guidance is like interviewing a thousand professionals before you start a project and turning their advice into checklists, explanations, and guides. They frequently help you include things that you would not have thought to include, and as a result they can save you time or reduce the likelihood of making certain types of mistakes.

How does your team utilize data analytics in its daily work?

At the firm where I work, we use data analytics constantly. Many of our clients are financial institutions, so they have lots of data relating to customer accounts and transactions. We develop solutions and products to help those institutions identify indicators of risk and fulfill their regulatory obligations to establish programs for preventing financial crime. As businesses become increasingly digital, and their information becomes more voluminous and complex, accountants will find more and more value in using data analytics for driving strategic decisions.

Review and Practice

Key Terms Review

access attack
botnet
brute-force attack
cyber-kill chain
cybersecurity
denial-of-service (DoS) attack
dictionary attack
distributed denial-of-service (DDoS) attack
Dumpster diving
eavesdropping
email phishing
encryption
File Transfer Protocol (FTP)
IP address

IP spoofing
logic bomb
logical access attack
logical attack
logical reconnaissance attack
malicious code
malware
National Institute of Standards and Technology (NIST)
network port
normal packet
on-path attack
packet
patch
penetration test

physical access attack
physical attack
physical reconnaissance attack
ping sweep
port scan
ransomware
reconnaissance attack
social engineering
spoofed packet
tailgating
Trojan horse
virus
vulnerability scan
worm

Learning Objectives Review

❶ Describe the relationship between cybersecurity risks and the accounting profession.

Sources of cybersecurity threats include:

- Corporate spies
- Criminal groups
- Malicious insiders
- Individual hackers

Companies use cybersecurity to protect computers and systems against unauthorized access and attacks. Management is responsible for ensuring that companies adopt proactive cybersecurity plans.

Recent cybersecurity threats include:

- Optus
- National Health Service
- Equifax

The CFO has a unique view into enterprise systems that can help with cybersecurity planning. Accounting professionals can pursue careers in the cybersecurity field such as the following recent job postings:

- Risk advisory technology process intern at Baker Tilly
- Special agent for accounting and finance at the FBI
- Treasury governance risk analyst at Google
- Cyber policy and standards analyst at Coca-Cola
- IT audit program manager at Tesla
- Vice president of cybersecurity and tech controls at JPMorgan Chase & Co.

Essential aspects of a cybersecurity program are governance and policies. Businesses use best practices frameworks like NIST 800-53 to identify, protect, detect, respond to, and recover from cybersecurity threats.

❷ Describe the characteristics of reconnaissance attacks.

A full-scale cyberattack consists of three stages:

- Reconnaissance
- Access
- Disruption

Cyberattacks are one of the following:

- Physical
- Logical

Reconnaissance attacks gather information that hackers use to subsequently access the network. Physical reconnaissance attacks use human interaction to generate information about the network:

- Phishing
- Dumpster diving
- Eavesdropping

The red flags for phishing emails are:

- Incorrect sender address
- Vague salutation
- Poor grammar or spelling
- Urgency
- Unusual links
- Surveys

Control activities for physical reconnaissance attacks include:

- Training
- Physical access controls

Logical reconnaissance attacks are digitally based and look for vulnerabilities in the network. They may use:

- Ping sweeps
- Port scans

Companies proactively control for logical reconnaissance attacks with:

- Vulnerability scans
- Penetration testing
- Patch updates

❸ Compare and contrast physical and logical access attacks.

Access attacks are designed to grant hackers unauthorized access to a network and its contents.

Physical access attacks, such as tailgating, often gain access through unknowing victims. Controls for physical access attacks include:

- Implement authorized lists of approved individuals
- Routinely review access lists
- Require two forms of visitor identification
- Escort visitors
- Control access to physical facilities and physical system hardware
- Hire security guards
- Establish physical barriers
- Install alarms and surveillance equipment

Logical access attacks exploit network vulnerabilities:

- Brute-force attacks
- On-path attacks
- IP spoofing

Essential controls to mitigate access attacks are password-based authentication and policies that require complex passwords. Complex passwords are more difficult for brute-force attacks to crack and buy the company time to detect attacks.

Other control activities include:

- Maintain baseline configurations and apply patches
- Identify and authenticate devices before allowing them to connect to a network

❹ Explain how hackers perform disruptive attacks.

The actions hackers take once they have accessed a network vary based on the hackers' motives:

- Data breaches
- Hostage and ransom
- System disruption
- Network damage
- Physical attacks
- Terrorist actions

Common disruptive attacks include:

- Denial-of-service (DoS) attacks
- Distributed denial-of-service (DDoS) attacks

Controls for these disruptive attacks include:

- Limit the effects by managing capacity, bandwidth, and other redundancies
- Monitor for indicators
- Monitor system resources to ensure that they effectively prevent attacks

Malware is malicious software designed to damage, disrupt, or gain access to systems. There are four types of malware:

- Viruses
- Worms
- Logic bombs
- Trojan horses

Control activities for malware range from preventive to detective:

- Implement protection mechanism to detect and eradicate malicious code
- Periodically scan systems to block and quarantine malicious code
- Monitor to detect attacks

CPA questions, as well as multiple choice, discussion, analysis and application, and Tableau questions and other resources, are available online.

Multiple Choice Questions

1. (LO 1) What is a type of malware used by hackers that replicates itself in a system and spreads quickly, causing damage to core system functions?

a. Virus

c. Logic bombs

b. Worms

d. Trojan horse

2. (LO 1) The National Institute of Standards and Technology (NIST) Cybersecurity Framework is displayed below.

What is function D?

a. Recover

c. Protect

b. Identify

d. Detect

3. (LO 1) CPA Cyberattacks are

a. preventable.

b. addressed in the original COSO pronouncements.

c. assumable.

d. inevitable.

4. (LO 1) CPA Managing cyber risks requires

a. blocking all cyber breaching by relying on preventive controls.

b. blocking all cyber breaching by relying on detective and corrective controls.

c. attempting to prevent cyber breaching but addressing those that occur through detective and corrective controls.

d. attempting to prevent cyber breaching but addressing those that occur through preventive controls.

5. (LO 1) Who plays a pivotal role in a company's cybersecurity program?

a. Chief information officer (CIO)

b. Chief financial officer (CFO)

c. Chief executive officer (CEO)

d. All of the above

6. (LO 2) CPA The IT department at Moonlight & Co. has recently learned of phishing attempts that rely on social engineering to break into its financial systems. Information about these attempts should be communicated to

a. internal auditors.

b. other personnel.

c. all personnel.

d. support functions.

7. (LO 2) Which of the following is *not* a method of attack used in the process of a full cyberattack?

a. Reconnaissance

c. Distancing

b. Disruption

d. Access

8. (LO 2) What step do reconnaissance attacks correspond to in the cyber-kill chain?

a. Steal passwords

b. Gather information about the network

c. Access the network

d. Disrupt the network

9. **(LO 2)** What is a company's best defense against phishing attacks?

   a. Only allowing email from certified businesses

   b. Shutting down email

   c. Monitoring employee's email

   d. Training employees to recognize and report red flags

10. **(LO 2)** _____ identifies active IP addresses, while _____ identifies the types of communication occurring on the network.

   a. Eavesdropping; phishing

   b. Phishing; port scanning

   c. Port scanning; ping sweeping

   d. Ping sweeping; port scanning

11. **(LO 3)** **CPA** An auditor was examining a client's network and discovered that the users did not have any password protection. Which of the following would be the best example of a strong network password?

   a. trjunpqs   c. tr34ju78

   b. 34787761   d. tR34ju78

12. **(LO 3)** In _____ tailgating, the authorized user holds the door open for the tailgater.

   a. accidental   c. polite

   b. spoofing   d. forced

13. **(LO 3)** The difference between eavesdropping and on-path attacks is that eavesdropping is _____ the communication, and an on-path attack is _____ the communication.

   a. writing over; injecting into

   b. listening to; writing over

   c. injecting into; listening to

   d. listening to; injecting into

14. **(LO 3)** What type of logical access attack disguises the source identity and impersonates a legitimate computer on the network?

   a. Brute-force attack

   c. IP spoofing

   b. On-path attack

   d. Tailgating

15. **(LO 4)** **CPA** A company's web server has been overwhelmed with a sudden surge of false requests that caused the server to crash. The company has most likely been the target of

   a. spoofing.

   c. an eavesdropping attack.

   b. piggybacking.

   d. a denial-of-service attack.

16. **(LO 4)** **CPA** Which of the following is true about denial-of-service attacks?

   (1) A denial-of-service attack takes advantage of a network communications protocol to tie up the server's communication ports so that legitimate users cannot gain access to the server.

   (2) If the denial-of-service attack is successful, the attacker can gain access to unprotected resources on the server.

   a. 1 only

   c. Both 1 and 2

   b. 2 only

   d. Neither 1 nor 2

17. **(LO 4)** **CPA** Which of the following is a computer program that appears to be legitimate but performs an illicit action when it is run?

   a. Redundant verification

   c. Web crawler

   b. Parallel count

   d. Trojan horse

18. **(LO 4)** Which of the following is *not* one of the ways that the Equifax hackers hid their suspicious network activity?

   a. Purchased subscriptions to Equifax's third-party software service

   b. Created profiles using Equifax employee credentials

   c. Purchased remote computing services from other countries

   d. Blended into normal activity with encrypted communication channels

19. **(LO 4)** What is a type of malware used by hackers that replicates without the assistance of human interaction?

   a. Virus

   c. Logic bombs

   b. Worms

   d. Trojan horses

20. **(LO 4)** What is the term for an attack that prohibits users from accessing resources, such as computers, websites, servers, or an entire network?

   a. Denial-of-service attack

   b. Malware attack

   c. Virus attack

   d. Logic bomb attack

Discussion and Research Questions

DQ1. (LO 1) **Early Career** **Research** Use LinkedIn or another online job board service to do one of the following: (1) Find a job posting for a cybersecurity role that you could be qualified to apply for upon graduation and summarize the educational requirements and job responsibilities of the posting. (2) Find a job posting for an accounting position that you will be eligible for upon graduation and explain how this position will give you the experience needed to be qualified for one of the following cybersecurity positions: special agent of accounting/finance at FBI, treasury governance risk analyst at Google, or IT audit program manager at Tesla.

DQ2. (LO 2) Explain the relationship between reconnaissance attacks, access attacks, and disruptive attacks.

DQ3. (LO 2) Compare and contrast ping sweeps and port scans. Focus on the difference between their targets in the network and outcomes for hackers' next steps.

DQ4. (LO 3) Give an example of why a hacker would perform IP spoofing. If necessary, include the names of other attacks that may be used in conjunction with IP spoofing and explain what the attacker is trying to accomplish in each case.

DQ5. (LO 3) `Critical Thinking` It's Monday morning at Fantom Productions, and Javier and Zarina arrive at the office's elevator at the same time as Moninder Fantom Productions' elevator requires all passengers to scan their corporate badges in order to press the button for their floor. Javier and Zarina are colleagues who regularly work together, so Javier knows which floor Zarina works on. He has never seen Moninder before. Javier stands near the keypad and scans his badge. He then presses the buttons for both his floor and Zarina's. Moninder looks at him expectantly, so he politely asks him "Which floor?" He then scans his badge and presses the button for Moninder's floor. Explain (1) the risk related to Javier's actions, (2) the internal control Javier circumvented, and (3) an alternative internal control that would have prevented this behavior.

DQ6. (LO 4) Explain how a logic bomb works and provide one control activity related to logic bombs. Are logic bombs easy to prevent and detect? Identify one control for logic bombs and explain whether it is preventive or detective.

Application and Analysis Questions

A1. (LO 1) `Critical Thinking` You are an IT auditor in the internal audit department of a financial services firm headquartered in the United States. The cybersecurity team has recently seen an increase in incident reports that has management concerned. Management asks your team to review the cybersecurity incidents to identify any trends that may indicate internal control weaknesses in the IT department. While reviewing the cybersecurity incident data, you notice that some of the incidents have been miscategorized as cybersecurity. Determine whether each of the following incident reports is a potential cybersecurity issue by labeling each "Yes" or "No."

1. A company website is down for two hours after a software update resulted in compatibility issues.
2. A staff accountant opened an email attachment that contained the CryptoLocker virus.
3. An employee lost an external hard drive while on a business trip. The hard drive contained corporate financial information.
4. The data center's backup power failed to turn on during a power outage.
5. Three servers cannot be backed up due to the backup size exceeding a system's storage capacity.
6. Employees have stated that they are receiving an increased number of pop-up ads on company computers.

A2. (LO 2) When you arrived at the office this morning, you found the following four emails in your inbox. Each of these emails is a type of phishing email that is soliciting a reaction from you to attempt to gain personal information or inappropriate access to company resources. For each email, identify what emotion in the word bank the cyber attacker is attempting to evoke. An emotion may be used more than one time.

Word Bank:	
fear	helpfulness
curiosity	urgency

Emails:

1. There is currently a motion being filed to suspend all bank accounts and tax returns bearing your name and Social Security number. To review immediate rights and details and avoid all further proceedings, please contact our firm by clicking the link provided.
2. Help a family in need this holiday season by providing them with a warm meal. A small donation of only $3 can provide a meal for a community member needing your help. Click the following link to make your donation on our easy-to-use web portal.
3. We have been reviewing your bank account information and it seems someone has made a large, unauthorized purchase. Please call us now at 1-800-123-4567 to discuss these charges and protect your accounts.
4. You and your attorney have a very brief window to address this matter with our office. It would serve your best interest to contact our offices before close of business today or immediately upon the receipt of this message, at 1-800-987-6543. This message serves as legal notification of a civil complaint filed against you. Thank you.

A3. (LO 2) `Early Career` `Critical Thinking` When you logged into your corporate laptop this morning, you noticed the following email. You have a bank account with Wells Fargo, so you briefly consider following the email's instructions before you notice something suspicious. What do you notice that makes you believe this email is a phishing scheme?

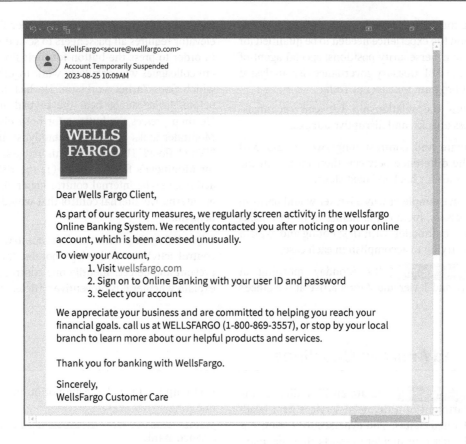

A4. (LO 3) Use one of the following websites to design a password that will take at least 100 years to crack:

howsecureismypassword.net

www.experte.com/password-check

A5. (LO 4) Data Analytics Critical Thinking You are a financial systems analyst in the finance and accounting department of a global financial institution. Currently, you are testing system access to determine whether there have been any unusual user activities this month. To do so, you transform the system login data set into the following data visualization:

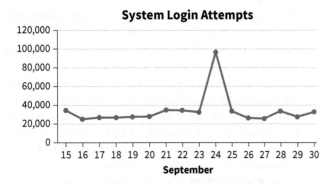

System Login Attempts

September

Based on this data visualization, you investigate the IT support tickets that employees submitted on September 24 and find that employees had issues logging into the system that day due to system errors.

On the basis of these facts, what type of attack did your financial system potentially experience on September 24?

A6. (LO 1–4) Critical Thinking Identify the cyberattack in each of the following recent real-world scenario:

1. The Metropolitan Police Department of the District of Columbia's system was compromised, and attackers demanded $50 million to unlock the system. During the attack, the attackers posted examples of the stolen data on the internet, including lists of arrests and the police chief's reports.

2. A German technology company whose clients include top financial institutions experienced a flood of data traffic on its network that paralyzed the network's operations. Within 24 hours, the network, including the company's clients' websites, shut down.

3. U.S. Army payroll systems started malfunctioning after a transfer between service providers occurred. Days after the transfer, a cyberattack activated in the system. The attack became progressively destructive and delayed paychecks to Army personnel for 17 days.

A7. (LO 1–4) Critical Thinking Nolls is an online retailer that specializes in connecting local artisans directly to consumers. You work for a public accounting firm as an IT audit consultant and have been staffed on the Nolls cybersecurity engagement. Nolls hired your firm to help implement the NIST Cybersecurity Framework. Your team is performing a gap analysis to identify areas where Nolls lacks internal controls, and you have been tasked with mapping Nolls' existing internal controls to specific NIST control families.

Use the word bank to identify the NIST family in which each of the following internal controls belongs:

Word Bank:

Physical and Environmental Protection	Configuration Management
Awareness and Training	Risk Assessment
Personnel Security	System and Communications Protection
Access Control	System and Information Integrity
Identification and Authentication	Security Assessment and Authorization

Internal controls:

1. The Human Resources and IT departments collaborate to provide annual training about phishing emails.

2. Nolls' IT department conducts penetration testing on an annual basis.

3. System resources are monitored to ensure that sufficient resources exist to support unexpected network traffic.

4. Nolls' corporate office requires two forms of identification for visitors to the data center.

5. System capacity, bandwidth, and redundancy are managed proactively.

6. Malicious code protection mechanisms are employed at access points of the information system.

7. Nolls' IT department scans for vulnerabilities randomly.

8. The corporate password requirements include a minimum of eight characters, along with at least one symbol, at least one number, and at least one capital letter.

A8. (LO 2–4) Every exchange of information can be the subject of a cybersecurity attack. The following scenarios are situations you may encounter in your daily life. Use the cyberattack types in the word bank to identify the type of attack that occurred in each scenario. Not every word in the word bank will be used.

Word Bank:

on-path attack	phishing
denial-of-service attack	virus
ping sweep	brute-force attack
eavesdropping	

Scenarios:

1. You didn't realize that instead of going to your bank's website (www.onebank.com), you were redirected to a fake website (www.onebank.net) that mimics the original one. Since you weren't aware that you were on the wrong website, you input your user and password information. The attacker then used it on the real website to access your banking information. You were a victim of a(n) _____.

2. Your passwords are very simple and incorporate not only your personal information but also dictionary words that are easy to guess (ILoveMyCat2002). You reuse the same password for many accounts because you would forget your passwords if you didn't. You could be a victim of a(n) _____.

3. Your friend told you he had seen a weird post on your social media account saying you were selling designer sunglasses at 80% off. Your account is infected with a(n) _____.

4. You are awaiting an Amazon package; however, you receive an email that the package might be running late. The email includes a "Check Status of Package" button that you decide to click because you want to know where your package is. You don't notice that the email is from CustomerService@Amaz0n.com. You are a victim of _____.

5. You were enjoying a cup of coffee at your local coffee shop. You were lucky to find a table as it was crowded that morning. You decided to do some administrative things from your to-do list, like pay your doctor's bill. You called the doctor's office to pay your bill. You gave the credit card number over the phone, along with the expiration date and the code on the back. You felt gratified by working on your to-do list. Later that week, you realized that the credit card had been used at many online retailers. You could have been a victim of _____.

Tableau Case: Network Logins at Julia's Cookies

What You Need

Download Tableau to your computer. You can access www.tableau.com/academic/students to download your free Tableau license for the year, or you can download it from your university's software offerings.

Download the following file from the book's product page on www.wiley.com:

Chapter 16 Raw Data.xlsx

Case Overview

Big Picture:

Identify suspicious network login activity.

Details:

Why is this data important, and what questions or problems need to be addressed?

- Analyzing the network logs ensures that only authorized employees are logging into the network.
- Access to the network by nonemployees or unauthorized employees creates significant risk for a company. These unauthorized users could steal financial information, cause a data breach, damage a system, or put the company in violation of data privacy regulations.
- To monitor the network, you should consider the following questions: Who is logging into the network outside of regular business hours? Do all IP addresses match the expected physical locations of the employees logging into the network?

Plan:

What data is needed, and how should you analyze it?

- The necessary data for this analysis is pulled from three sources: (1) network logs pulled from a login authentication application; (2) employee data pulled from the human resources database; and (3) IP address log pulled from an external website that includes cities, GPS coordinates, and IP addresses by physical location.

Now it's your turn to evaluate, analyze, and communicate the results!

Hint: Connect the data as follows:

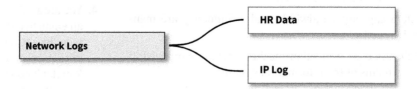

Questions

1. What hour of the day is the most popular for logging into Julia's Cookies' network?
2. Sometimes suspicious network activity can be related to employees logging into the network outside of normal business hours. Which employee logged into the network between 8:00 p.m. and 4:00 a.m. (considered "nonbusiness" hours)? How many times did this occur during the months of September and October?
3. Sometimes suspicious network activity can be linked to employees logging into the network over the weekend. Which employee logged into Julia's Cookies' network on a Saturday and Sunday during the months of September and October? How many times did this occur overall?
4. Julia's Cookies' employees only reside in the United States, meaning that all IP address traffic should be coming from within the United States. How many times was Julia's Cookies' network accessed by an IP address originating from outside of the United States?
5. During what hour of the day was Julia's Cookies' network accessed the most by a non-U.S. IP address?
6. It is possible for an employee's network ID to be spoofed and used to gain unauthorized access to the network. Which employees were associated with the non-U.S. IP network logins?
7. Which office location was targeted with logins from a non-U.S. IP network?
8. On what day did the most non-U.S. IP network logins occur?

Take it to the next level!

9. Sometimes suspicious activity can be linked to numerous logins in one day. The average number of logins per day is three. Which employee logged into the network the greatest number of times in one day? How many logins was it?

10. It is important to correlate the number of network logins per IP address to the number of employees who reside in the area for a particular IP address. Which city's IP address logged into Julia's Cookies' network the most times during the months of September and October? In what city do most of Julia's Cookies' employees reside?

CHAPTER 17
Data Analytics

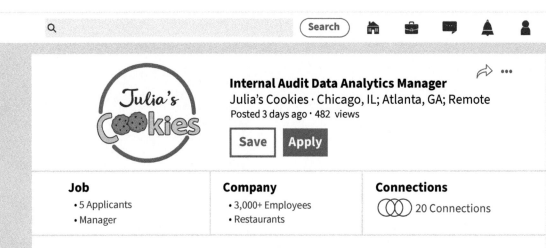

Summary

Julia's Cookies is looking for an internal audit data analytics manager to advance the Internal Audit department's use of analytics. This role will conduct complex data analysis and explore the use of existing and emerging technologies to support and enhance the audit plan and Internal Audit's operations.

This role can work remotely. Must be willing to travel 10–15% of the time to the Chicago or Atlanta corporate offices for in-person meetings and trainings.

Responsibilities

- Support the development and implementation of a long-term audit analytics strategy that leverages data and analytics to generate business insights
- Plan and execute data analysis, extraction, and visualization to support individual audits, investigations, or ad hoc projects
- Conceptualize and implement continuous auditing initiatives
- Be an internal champion of data analytics and technology by serving as a subject matter resource who can coach and advance the Internal Audit team's collective data analytics competencies
- Be able to think critically and actively solve problems by effectively identifying risks, connections, and patterns; investigating issues; analyzing root causes; and recommending solutions

Requirements

Preferred Education: Bachelor's degree or higher in accounting, finance, or related field

Preferred Certifications: CPA, CISA, CFE, CFA, CIA, CISSP, CAP

Preferred Knowledge and Skills

The ideal candidate will have four or more years' experience in audit, data analysis, or risk management roles. Candidates must have the ability to effectively design and execute data analytics and visualizations throughout all phases of an audit engagement. Preference will be given to candidates who demonstrate:

- Experience in data cleansing and manipulation tools such as Alteryx, R, or Python
- Familiarity with database management and querying such as SQL
- Proficiency in visualization software such as Tableau, Microsoft Power BI, QlikView, RStudio, or Excel
- Client service disposition that focuses on understanding stakeholder needs and providing sound advice and clear solutions

Salary: $115,000–145,000

CHAPTER PREVIEW   Data analytics is a growing field for accounting professionals. When companies first began adopting data analytics, accounting majors with those skills were rare and highly sought after. Today, performing fundamental data analytics is a requirement for accounting professionals. Whether you work in an accounts payable department at a small business or as a consultant at a Big Four public accounting firm, you will see that traditional reporting methods are evolving with technology, and stakeholders are increasingly expecting all organizations to adopt data analytics.

Accounting professionals are also expected to add value to their companies by influencing decision-making processes. You can do this by leveraging data analytics to present facts, trends, and future outcomes. If you are interested in technology, you might look for a job like the internal audit data analytics manager position at Julia's Cookies, which is based on a role one of the authors of this course held. This position combines accounting knowledge with technical skills to add value to the company's third line of defense against risk.

This chapter introduces:

- Career opportunities for accounting students in data analytics
- How to use data analytics to explore a new data set
- Analysis of data captured over time
- Advanced data analytics techniques that are impacting the accounting industry

The techniques in this chapter include a selection of the data analytics you will encounter throughout your accounting career—whether you are performing analytics or leveraging the results for decision making. ■

Chapter Roadmap

LEARNING OBJECTIVES	TOPICS	JULIA'S COOKIES APPLIED LEARNING
17.1 Identify career opportunities for accounting professionals working with data.	• Types of Analysts • Types of Analytics • Machine Learning (ML)	Types of Analysts: Finding the Best Role
17.2 Describe data analytics techniques that can explore data.	• Anomaly Detection • Data Summarization • Clustering and Classification	Exploratory Analytics: Journal Entry Testing
17.3 Evaluate data analytics techniques that explain changes over time.	• Linear Regression • Forecasting • Monte Carlo Simulation	Linear Regression: Journal Entry Testing
17.4 Summarize advanced data analytics techniques that transform data into insights.	• Process Mining • Network Analysis • Geospatial Analytics • Natural Language Processing (NLP)	Process Mining: Journal Entry Testing

CPA   You will find the CPA tag throughout the chapter to call out any important topics you may see on the CPA exam.

17.1 How Is Data Analytics Changing the Accounting Profession?

Learning Objective ❶
Identify career opportunities for accounting professionals working with data.

If you are unwell and have the means, you might visit a doctor's office or a clinic. There, a health care professional gathers data—recording vital signs like temperature and blood pressure and possibly drawing blood or performing a nasal or throat swab for testing.

Gathering data about symptoms allows health care professionals to understand an illness, why it happened, what will happen in the next days, and how to treat it. Businesses collect a variety of data using a similar process. Every time you pick up your phone and open an app, purchase a latte from your favorite coffee shop, or use a ride-hailing service like Uber, your data is collected by companies, analyzed, and then used in making business decisions.

Types of Analysts

A company that collects data needs people who can transform it into useful information. There are many career paths that involve working with data. Some require technical training, like statistics or computer science, and others rely on skills learned on the job as an accounting professional. Different accounting roles—including those in internal audit, external audit, and tax—have different purposes, and the same is true for data analytics roles. **Table 17.1** describes data analytics–related jobs and lists the expert understanding required for each role. You may not pursue a career path that focuses exclusively on data analytics, but you will certainly work alongside professionals who do.

TABLE 17.1 Data Analytics–Related Job Titles and Descriptions

Job Title	Description	Expert Understanding
Data engineer	• Builds the technological infrastructure and architecture for gathering, growing, and storing raw data. • Data analysts, data scientists, and statisticians depend on the work of data engineers to have access to data.	• Data modeling • Hardware • Networking • Database administration
Data scientist	• Works with large volumes of data. • Designs and programs algorithms to collect and analyze data and perform predictive analytics. • Possesses technical skills such as understanding of higher-level math and proficiency in coding.	• Data modeling • Statistics • Programming/coding
Statistician	• Provides a methodology for drawing conclusions from data. • The role is math oriented and focuses on collection and interpretation of quantitative data using defined scientific methods.	• Data • Statistics
Data analyst	• Collects, manipulates, and analyzes data across a business. • Understands the business processes and technical aspects of an organization. • Less scientifically focused than a data scientist or statistician but more coding oriented than a business analyst. • This role requires both technical and interpersonal skills.	• Data transformation • Programming/coding • Business processes

TABLE 17.1 *(Continued)*

Job Title	Description	Expert Understanding
Business analyst or business intelligence analyst	• Works with data to find trends and leverage insights. • Possesses a deep understanding of business processes and can evaluate them, analyze key metrics, and provide strategic recommendations. • Must assess requirements from a business perspective and understand data visualization. • Communication skills are important. People in this role must effectively present information and actionable insights to business leaders.	• Data transformation • Business processes • Visualization

Ideally, the different data-related activities in an organization are managed by separate employees, such as database administrators, data architects, data analysts or scientists, and business intelligence analysts or visualization specialists. However, only the largest companies generally have the resources to hire these many individual data specialists. Small to medium-sized companies often look for prospective employees who are multi-skilled, so the same individual may be responsible for data analytics and data visualization. You will likely be expected to manage multiple areas of your company's data journey should you pursue a career in this field.

In the Real World   Employment Opportunities in Accounting Data Analytics

Businesses are racing to harness data and draw insights from it. Data is growing exponentially, and when used correctly, it can provide a competitive advantage in the marketplace.

This growth of available data is also driving demand for data-based jobs. In recent years, colleges and universities have begun to offer undergraduate and graduate degrees in business analytics and data science. Additionally, companies like Big Four accounting firms are expanding their hiring scope to include information systems and computer science majors to support accounting professionals through data analysis.

All the Big Four accounting firms provide data analytics services to their clients. They also provide data analytics tools. Consider these examples:

- PwC's Risk Command suite includes a third-party tracker to monitor high-risk third parties and address regulatory requirements, a detection and monitoring hub that focuses on compliance and fraud analytics, and a risk atlas that centralizes a company's global privacy and security monitoring in an easy-to-use dashboard. PwC clients have successfully used Risk Command to create a singular, global view of corporate activities that eliminates the silos that decentralized data creates. Risk Command also uses artificial intelligence to reduce errors.[1]

- KPMG's Sofy Suite is a cloud-based analytics platform that provides clients with in-depth, real-time tax-related insights. It enables clients to perform tax, compliance, and transfer pricing analytics. Sofy Suite also helps clients with tax automation, root-cause analysis, and exception management.[2]

- E&Y's Helix is an audit analytics platform that gives clients an analytics-driven approach to auditing. Audit departments can use this tool on their general ledgers, inventory data, trade payables, revenue and trade receivables, mortgage portfolios, and more.[3]

- Deloitte's VisualChoice is a touchscreen decision analysis tool that allows clients to visualize their data in real time and apply what-if simulations on the data. The tool also gives clients drill-down capabilities, enabling them to pinpoint inefficiencies.[4]

These examples give you an idea of the importance of data analytics and data analytics tools in the accounting field today. If you are considering a career in accounting, especially with a Big Four firm, data analytics will be an important part of your career.

Did you already know that data analytics would be such a large part of your career if you work for a Big Four firm? Do you feel adequately prepared for a career using tools like these? If not, what can you do now as student to better prepare yourself?

---

[1]www.pwc.com/us/en/products/risk-command-suite.html
[2]www.kpmgsofy.com
[3]www.ey.com/en_us/audit/technology/helix
[4]www2.deloitte.com/us/en/pages/operations/solutions/visual-decision-xccelerator.html

With so many terms, tools, and skills included in job listings, identifying the positions you are qualified for can be difficult. The internal audit data analytics manager position for Julia's Cookies is an example: it requires extensive accounting and audit experience and also some advanced analytics skills like SQL and Python. Identify the appropriate role at Julia's Cookies for a recent accounting graduate in Applied Learning 17.1.

Julia's Cookies   Applied Learning 17.1

Types of Analysts: Finding the Best Role

Gabbi recently completed an accounting program and graduated with a master of accountancy degree. They double-majored in accounting and information systems in their undergraduate program. They have completed three of the four sections of the CPA exam and plan to sit for the fourth next month.

Gabbi wrote SQL queries during an internship as an internal audit data analyst and is passionate about turning data into useful information that impacts business operations. They want to know that their work will result in change for their future employer.

Julia's Cookies currently has several job openings posted on LinkedIn:

- Data scientist
- Data analyst

- Business analyst
- Data engineer

These positions are specific to the Finance and Accounting departments. Which jobs do you think Gabbi should apply for?

SOLUTION

Gabbi is qualified to apply for a position as a data analyst or a business analyst. They may need to gain some experience in a data analyst role to further their skills in coding before they can move into a data scientist position. While they may be qualified for a data engineer role based on their double major, they are passionate about data transformation and impacting business decisions, which they couldn't do as a data engineer. Gabbi should apply for the data analyst or business analyst position.

Types of Analytics

Do you recall the four most widely used categories of data analysis from the Data Storage and Analysis chapter? **CPA** They are descriptive, diagnostic, predictive, and prescriptive (**Illustration 17.1**). The first two categories, descriptive and diagnostic, look at the past and use historical data to learn more about what occurred and why it occurred. These two types of analysis are less complex than predictive and prescriptive analytics, which analyze historical data and also predict future events, providing recommendations on what the business should do.

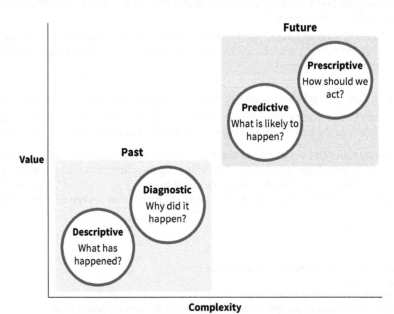

Illustration 17.1 The four categories of data analysis can be divided into two that look at the past and two that look at the future.

Table 17.2 describes the four types of analytics and lists their key characteristics and the questions they answer. In the following sections, we explore these categories, along with various popular analytics.

TABLE 17.2 The Four Categories of Analytics

Analytic	Description	Key Characteristics	Questions Answered
Descriptive analytics	• Tells us *what has happened* • Looks at historical data and condenses it into smaller, more meaningful bits of information • Is the most common form of analysis	• Easy to access • Easy to visualize • Based on historical data	• What is happening? • How many times did this happen? • When did it happen?
Diagnostic analytics	• Provides insight into *why something happened* • Drills down to a granular level • Often looks at data in a variety of ways to identify trends or investigate causes	• Used to troubleshoot and investigate issues • Drills down to root cause • Based on historical data	• Why did it happen? • Where did this come from? • How can we avoid this problem in future?
Predictive analytics	• Uses statistical modeling and algorithms to predict *what is likely to happen* • Provides powerful tools that assist in decision making and inform future actions • Requires assumptions and identifies possible outcomes based on these assumptions	• Uses statistical modeling and predictive algorithms • Yields better results for larger data sets • Based on historical and live data	• What is likely to happen? • What is the logical outcome?
Prescriptive analytics	• Identifies *what we should do* • Requires advanced programming • Consists of advanced, cutting-edge technology and design • Uses a decision-making protocol and historical data to train a program on what to do in a real-time situation	• Requires advanced technology and algorithms • Uses the three previous analytics types for insights • Based on live, historical, and external data • Costly to implement	• How should we act? • Should we make this decision?

Machine Learning (ML)

Compared to analytics that focus on the past, future-looking predictive and prescriptive analytics yield greater insights for businesses and provide greater value. However, due to the complexity of predictive and prescriptive analytics, they do not always easily generate value for a business. Companies must dedicate resources like time and talent to achieving the ideal state of advanced data analytics.

CPA Recall from the Emerging and Disruptive Technologies chapter that artificial intelligence (AI) uses complex algorithms, programmed to mimic human cognitive functions, to learn and solve problems independently. Advanced technologies like AI were traditionally used to perform predictive and prescriptive data analytics. However, as advanced technologies become more accessible, they are now also executing descriptive and diagnostic analytics. We will examine how AI works before moving on to explore specific data analytics techniques.

Machine learning (ML) uses algorithms and statistical models to train an AI system through patterns and trends in data sets. ML programs systems to perform tasks without explicit instruction and is a popular application of AI in data analytics. **Table 17.3** summarizes three primary approaches to ML algorithms and provides examples of their applications in data analytics.

TABLE 17.3 Machine Learning Approaches

Machine Learning Approach	Description	Examples
Supervised learning	• Uses labeled data sets to train the algorithm to classify data or predict outcomes from a data set. • Before it can begin, human intervention is necessary to establish the labels within the data set.	• Classification • Regression
Unsupervised learning	• Uses algorithms to analyze unlabeled data sets for hidden patterns. • It does not require human intervention.	• Clustering • Association • Dimensionality reduction
Reinforcement learning	• Focuses on decision making by rewarding desired behaviors and/or punishing undesired behaviors. • Decisions are made sequentially by the AI, and each decision is rewarded or punished to train the AI. • This hybrid approach may require human intervention.	• Task learning • Skills acquisition • Robot navigation • Real-time decisions • Monte Carlo simulation

Note that the primary difference between supervised and unsupervised learning is the use of human intervention to create labeled data sets. **Labeled data** contains predefined tags or descriptors that an ML algorithm uses to understand the data set or learn from it. Labeling data is a human act of intervention, which occurs only when using supervised ML analytics.

Four of the data analytics techniques listed in the table—classification, regression, clustering, and Monte Carlo simulation—are discussed in this chapter. You will learn more about each of them later. Additionally, you will explore a data analytics technique that is not usually a candidate for ML: data summarization. You will also learn about these machine learning analytics techniques that can involve either supervised or unsupervised learning, depending on how the data set is formatted and the ML is programmed:

- Forecasting
- Process mining
- Network analysis
- Geospatial analytics
- Natural language processing (NLP)

We'll explore the differences between supervised and unsupervised learning and discuss how classification and clustering techniques help you understand a data set. You will see hands-on applications of both types of ML as you learn about them. First, you need to understand how a new data set is explored.

Why Does It Matter to Your Career?

Thoughts from an Accounting Manager, Banking

- Organizations are adopting the four categories of analytics with more frequency. Understanding them will help you engage in and contribute to professional conversations.
- As expectations increase for all job functions to successfully use descriptive and diagnostic analytics, job opportunities for accounting professionals who understand analytics will continue to increase as well. Higher expectations for accounting professionals to be experts in multiple fields are creating pressure to diversify skillsets beyond traditional accounting knowledge.

CONCEPT REVIEW QUESTIONS

1. Differentiate between a data engineer and a data scientist.

   Ans. A data engineer builds the technological infrastructure and architecture for gathering, growing, and storing raw data. Data analysts, data scientists, and statisticians depend on the work of data engineers to have access to data. A data scientist designs and programs algorithms to collect and analyze data and perform predictive analytics. They possess technical skills such as an understanding of higher-level math and proficiency in coding.

2. What is the role of a business analyst in an organization? How does it differ from that of a data analyst?

   Ans. Business analysts work with data to find trends and leverage insights. They possess a deep understanding of business processes and can evaluate them, analyze key metrics, and provide strategic recommendations. Data analysts collect, manipulate, and analyze data across a business. They understand the business processes and technical aspects of an organization, and are more coding oriented than business analysts.

3. **CPA** What are the different types of analytics?

   Ans. The different types of analytics are descriptive, diagnostic, predictive, and prescriptive. The first two categories, descriptive and diagnostic, look at the past and use historical data to learn more about what occurred and why it occurred. These two types of analysis are less complex than predictive and prescriptive analytics, which analyze historical data and also predict future events, providing recommendations on what the business should do.

4. What is machine learning (ML)?

   Ans. ML uses algorithms and statistical models to train an AI system through patterns and trends in data sets. ML programs systems to perform tasks without explicit instruction and is a popular application of AI in data analytics.

17.2 How Do We Explore a Data Set?

Learning Objective ❷
Describe data analytics techniques that can explore data.

The first step in analyzing a data set is learning about its data. **Exploratory data analytics** techniques reveal the key characteristics of a data set. Whether this type of analytics is performed using ML algorithms or another technique, the purpose is the same. Exploratory data analytics techniques help us identify three key factors of a data set: categorical values, quantitative values, and patterns (or trends).

Data composition refers to the first two key factors:

- **Categorical values** are the descriptive components within a data set. For example, the gender identity of an employee is a categorical value in the main employee table of a human resources database. Categorical values are qualitative in nature.

- **Quantitative values** are the numeric data points that can be summed, counted, or otherwise analyzed using mathematical operations. Dates and dollar amounts are two examples of quantitative data values.

The third key factor that data exploration reveals is **patterns** of recurring or similar values, either categorical or quantitative. Patterns that occur over time are called *trends*, and you will learn more about them later. Besides discovering patterns, exploration can find unexpected data points, called *anomalies* or *outliers*, that fall outside the data set's norm.

Let's examine a data set you are familiar with to see how these three key factors are presented. Assume you have exam grades for a semester as follows: 94, 90, 94, 88, 70, 92, 92, and 94. These numeric grades are the quantitative values that make up part of the data composition of your exam data set. The other part of the data composition is that the data can be described using the categorical description "you have six As, one B, and one C." A pattern in your grades is an average exam score of 89, and the grade of 70 is an outlier significantly below the average score of 89. This is a simplified explanation of the three key factors that define the contents of a data set.

Anomaly Detection

Anomaly detection, also known as outlier analysis, reveals observations or events that are outside a data set's normal behavior. Anomaly detection is an important data analytics objective that can be the purpose of many of the data analytics techniques we will explore throughout this chapter. Anomaly detection is applicable to every part of a business. For example:

- **Banking:** If a bank customer regularly purchases in the same geographic area, near their hometown, and then suddenly starts incurring charges in a different state or country, these new charges are considered anomalies. These transactions will alert the bank's fraud program. The bank may decline the outlier charges and contact the customer to verify the authenticity of the unusual purchases.

- **Cybersecurity:** A company's cybersecurity department may monitor employee network activity. If an employee regularly logs on from an IP address in a known geographic area and then suddenly logs on from a different country, the cybersecurity team will be alerted of this outlier login. The team will investigate the suspicious login for fraudulent activity, and the network session may be terminated.

- **Marketing:** A marketing department may monitor website traffic and social media engagement as part of its marketing data analytics program. Suppose there is an unusual uptick in social media posts that mention the business when there are no special marketing campaigns currently happening. In this case, the marketing department may investigate those social media posts to ensure that they are not likely to damage the company's reputation.

As you work through the rest of this chapter, keep in mind that anomaly detection is an *objective* of data analytics that can be accomplished using a variety of different data analytics *techniques*.

Data Summarization

Exploring a new data set and understanding its composition commonly involve the data analytics technique **data summarization**, which involves simplifying data to quickly identify the composition of categorical and quantitative values. We compress the data into smaller, easier-to-understand outputs, called data summaries. To do this, we typically group a data set by a specific field, or column.

Let's consider an Excel file containing the data for a large customer order at Julia's Cookies (**Illustration 17.2**). A corporate office ordered snacks delivered for a team training session. The data set has one categorical value, which is the product name, and one quantitative value, which is the price.

Summarizing this data involves two steps:

1. Group according to categorical value (product name)
2. Perform mathematical functions on the quantitative value (price)

For example, the price can be summed to identify the customer's total dollar amount spent on each product type. Data summarization can also be used to count the number of records for each product name to determine the total quantity that the customer ordered. To take it a step further, we can find the grand total for both the number of products sold and the total sales price. **Illustration 17.3** depicts these calculations in a summarized data table.

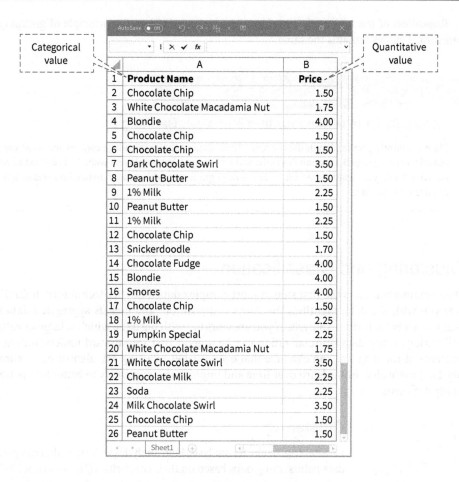

Categorical value

Quantitative value

	A	B
1	**Product Name**	**Price**
2	Chocolate Chip	1.50
3	White Chocolate Macadamia Nut	1.75
4	Blondie	4.00
5	Chocolate Chip	1.50
6	Chocolate Chip	1.50
7	Dark Chocolate Swirl	3.50
8	Peanut Butter	1.50
9	1% Milk	2.25
10	Peanut Butter	1.50
11	1% Milk	2.25
12	Chocolate Chip	1.50
13	Snickerdoodle	1.70
14	Chocolate Fudge	4.00
15	Blondie	4.00
16	Smores	4.00
17	Chocolate Chip	1.50
18	1% Milk	2.25
19	Pumpkin Special	2.25
20	White Chocolate Macadamia Nut	1.75
21	White Chocolate Swirl	3.50
22	Chocolate Milk	2.25
23	Soda	2.25
24	Milk Chocolate Swirl	3.50
25	Chocolate Chip	1.50
26	Peanut Butter	1.50

Illustration 17.2   This data set contains one categorical value and one quantitative value.

	A	B	C
1	**Product Name**	**Count of Product Name**	**Sum of Price**
2	1% Milk	3	6.75
3	Blondie	2	8.00
4	Chocolate Chip	6	9.00
5	Chocolate Fudge	1	4.00
6	Chocolate Milk	1	2.25
7	Peanut Butter	3	4.50
8	Pumpkin Special	1	2.25
9	Snickerdoodle	1	1.70
10	White Chocolate Macadamia Nut	2	3.50
11	Dark Chocolate Swirl	1	3.50
12	Smores	1	4.00
13	White Chocolate Swirl	1	3.50
14	Soda	1	2.25
15	Milk Chocolate Swirl	1	3.50
16	**Grand Total**	**25**	**58.7**

Illustration 17.3   A customer order is summarized by product name to calculate the quantity and total cost of each product ordered as well as a grand total.

Illustration 17.3 was created using a **pivot table** in Excel, which is a popular method of summarizing smaller data sets. Summarization can be performed on larger data sets with other tools, including:

- Writing GROUP BY queries in SQL or Python
- Using the Summarize tool in Alteryx
- Dragging field names to the appropriate locations in Tableau or Power BI

Regardless of the tool used to perform data summarization, the principle of grouping by categorical values remains the same.

Clustering and Classification

Data summarization is the first step in most complex data analytics techniques. It familiarizes you with the data, identifies the data's composition, and creates aggregated data sets that are ready for further analysis. If you are working with big data, which is large in volume and variety, using data summarization can be a great first step toward understanding the contents of the data set. You can take that even further by using ML algorithms to explore big data; these algorithms learn over time and improve their accuracy to better find patterns in big data sets.

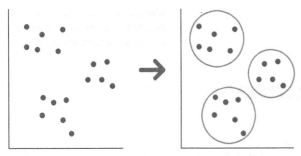

Illustration 17.4 Clustering identifies groupings of occurrences.

Clustering

Clustering, or cluster analysis, is an analytics technique that categorizes data points into groups based on their similarities (**Illustration 17.4**):

- The groups, called **clusters**, are determined by the distance between individual items, which indicates how closely related the data points are.
- Clustering is an unsupervised ML technique in which the data input contains unlabeled data.

In cluster analysis, the ML algorithm finds similarities between the data points to group them together without human intervention.

There are many business uses for clustering. For example:

- **Music streaming:** Services such as Spotify and Apple Music employ algorithms that use cluster analysis to categorize similar songs based on features such as length, popularity, danceability, acoustic levels, and energy. This categorization is then used to identify other songs with the same features that users may not have heard before. The services can then create stations where similar, recommended songs are played based on the first song a user selects.

- **Public health:** Scientists can cluster people based on geographic areas in terms of low or high tendencies toward certain illnesses. This information can suggest appropriate locations for specialty clinics or direct health education for various groups, or it may prompt investigation of local factors that might be influencing occurrences of illnesses.

- **Accounting:** An accountant in the insurance industry might cluster customers based on average claim costs or premium payments. At a bank, customers could be clustered by their credit card payment behavior to help target perpetually tardy customers and trigger reminders to pay their bills.

If we perform cluster analysis on the large corporate customer order data at Julia's Cookies, we might get the results shown in **Illustration 17.5**. In this example, the ML algorithm is grouping the order items by shape and chocolate content.

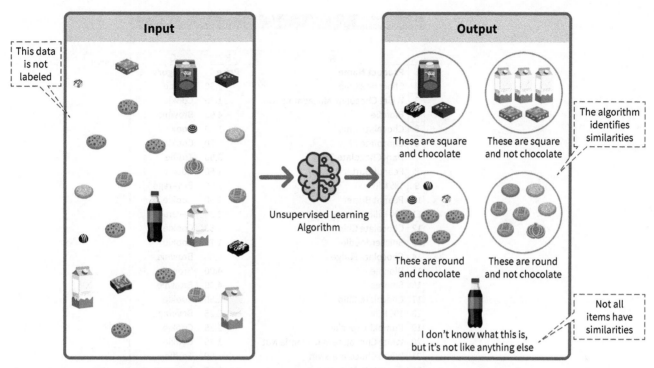

Illustration 17.5   Unsupervised learning algorithms cluster unlabeled data into groups based on similarities.

A potential drawback to this technique is that the output of unsupervised ML algorithms may not be reliable:

- If two products are square, they are not necessarily similar.
- If we want to group products by type, we might expect the soda to be close to the chocolate milk and 1% milk. The unsupervised learning algorithm doesn't know this, though, so it is clustering items together based on the similarities it is able to recognize.

Cluster analysis is more valuable with big data sets containing many categorical and quantitative values that the ML algorithm can analyze and learn from. Additionally, external data sources can help the ML algorithm become smarter. For the purposes of our customer order example, a more streamlined and controlled analytic should be used, and we can create it by using supervised learning.

Classification

Classification analysis is the categorization of data into groups based on similarities found in a data label that was previously defined. Classification analysis might sound closely related to clustering—and the two types of analysis do have similarities. While they are both methods of categorization, they differ in the type of ML they use:

- Clustering uses unsupervised ML to analyze unlabeled data inputs.
- Classification uses supervised ML to analyze labeled data inputs.

The first step in classification is ensuring that a data set has appropriate data labels. To prepare the large corporate customer order data at Julia's Cookies for classification, let's add labels for the categories of products (**Illustration 17.6**).

After we do this, our ML algorithm knows that we want it to organize data based on the category labels. In classification analysis, we program the supervised ML algorithm to identify whether items should have data labels applied. To demonstrate, let's use classification to identify the cookies and the noncookie items (**Illustration 17.7**).

	A	B	C
1	**Product Name**	**Price**	**Category**
2	Chocolate Chip	1.50	Cookie
3	White Chocolate Macadamia Nut	1.75	Cookie
4	Blondie	4.00	Brownie
5	Chocolate Chip	1.50	Cookie
6	Chocolate Chip	1.50	Cookie
7	Dark Chocolate Swirl	3.50	Truffle
8	Peanut Butter	1.50	Cookie
9	1% Milk	2.25	Beverage
10	Peanut Butter	1.50	Cookie
11	1% Milk	2.25	Beverage
12	Chocolate Chip	1.50	Cookie
13	Snickerdoodle	1.70	Cookie
14	Chocolate Fudge	4.00	Brownie
15	Blondie	4.00	Brownie
16	Smores	4.00	Brownie
17	Chocolate Chip	1.50	Cookie
18	1% Milk	2.25	Beverage
19	Pumpkin Special	2.25	Cookie
20	White Chocolate Macadamia Nut	1.75	Cookie
21	White Chocolate Swirl	3.50	Truffle
22	Chocolate Milk	2.25	Beverage
23	Soda	2.25	Beverage
24	Milk Chocolate Swirl	3.50	Truffle
25	Chocolate Chip	1.50	Cookie
26	Peanut Butter	1.50	Cookie

Label

Illustration 17.6 Human intervention is required to create labeled data for supervised machine learning.

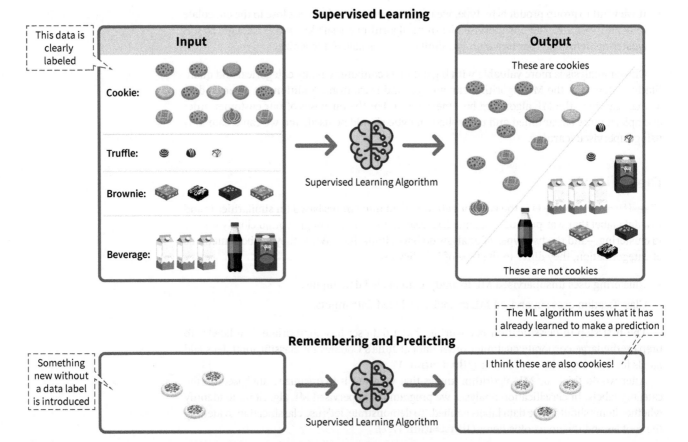

Supervised Learning

This data is clearly labeled

Input

Cookie:

Truffle:

Brownie:

Beverage:

Supervised Learning Algorithm

Output

These are cookies

These are not cookies

Remembering and Predicting

The ML algorithm uses what it has already learned to make a prediction

Something new without a data label is introduced

Supervised Learning Algorithm

I think these are also cookies!

Illustration 17.7 Classification identifies cookies and noncookie items in the customer order data set.

During supervised learning, the ML algorithm uses the clearly labeled data to learn the characteristics of what is and is not a cookie. The classification algorithm uses what it learns over time from the labeled data set to identify the categories for future records. When something new and unlabeled is introduced, like the sprinkled sugar cookies in Illustration 17.7, the ML algorithm predicts whether it is a cookie by comparing its characteristics with those of the products it knows.

A great example of classification analysis for accounting professionals is its application in fraud detection. Classification can detect anomalies in transactional data, which could be indicators of fraud:

- First, each business expense is labeled with a category, such as fixed cost, semi-variable cost, or variable cost.
- Based on the pre-programmed rules in the labeled data set, the ML algorithm can classify newly created business expenses as belonging to one of those categories.
- Over time, the ML algorithm will learn from itself and become more accurate in its identification.
- The outputs of the ML algorithm are then analyzed to identify fraud red flags, such as increasing fixed costs that may result from a vendor adding miscellaneous fees that weren't part of the company's contract with the vendor.

Based on what you have learned about classification and cluster analysis, help Kae determine which data analytics technique to use for her internal audit at Julia's Cookies in Applied Learning 17.2.

Julia's Cookies   Applied Learning 17.2

Exploratory Analytics: Journal Entry Testing

Kae is performing journal entry testing to identify any fraud red flags that require further investigation. She wants to group the journal entries based on whether they are manual or automated.

Kae plots the journal entry data on the following visualization, where the horizontal axis is the dollar amount of the journal entry, and the vertical axis is the time of day the journal entry was posted. She uses a field in the data set to determine which journal entries are manual (blue dots) and which are automated (orange dots).

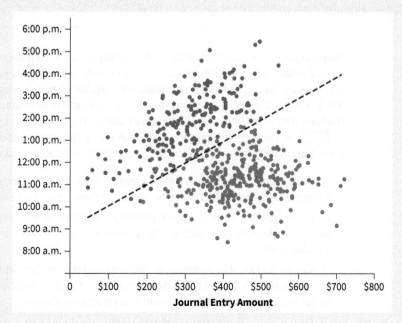

What type of data analytics technique is Kae performing?

SOLUTION

Kae is performing classification. This data is labeled with a field that identifies whether a journal entry is manually or automatically posted.

This section introduced exploratory data analytics techniques. Once a data set has been explored, additional data analytics techniques are used to investigate specific occurrences within the data set, which we review next.

CONCEPT REVIEW QUESTIONS

1. What are the three key factors identified by exploratory data analytics?
   Ans. Exploratory data analytics techniques help us to identify three key factors of a data set: categorical values, quantitative values, and patterns (or trends).

2. What do you mean by anomaly detection? Describe how anomaly detection could be used in the marketing department.
   Ans. Anomaly detection, also known as outlier analysis, reveals observations or events that are outside a data set's normal behavior. Suppose there is an unusual uptick in social media posts that mention the business when there are no special marketing campaigns currently happening. In this case, the marketing department may investigate those social media posts to ensure that they are not likely to damage the company's reputation.

3. What is classification, and how is it different from clustering?
   Ans. Classification analysis is the categorization of data into groups based on similarities found in a data label that was previously defined. Clustering, or cluster analysis, is an analytics technique that categorizes data points into groups based on their similarities. The difference between classification and clustering is:

   - Clustering uses unsupervised ML to analyze unlabeled data inputs.
   - Classification uses supervised ML to analyze labeled data inputs.

17.3 How Do We Investigate Interesting Occurrences in a Data Set?

Learning Objective ❸
Evaluate data analytics techniques that explain changes over time.

Runners can track their time and distance daily to see if their times are improving. If you are an influencer, you might track daily engagement, such as likes and views, with your social media posts. An avid reader could track the number of new books read each month to determine how reading habits ebb and flow during a year. These examples illustrate the benefit of tracking data over time, which businesses also do regularly.

CPA A **time series** captures data that occurs in chronological order across a period of time. Important considerations when investigating time series data include:

- A **time trend** is a consistent movement in the time series data that does not repeat. One example is an increase in revenue through a fiscal year due to a new product launch.

- **Seasonality** is a consistent movement in the time series data that repeats on a regular basis. An example is an increase in revenue every November and December due to winter holiday sales.

- **Noise** is additional movements in the time series data that cannot be explained as a trend or seasonality. A drastic spike in revenue at the end of February due to a large customer order for a one-time corporate event is an example of noise.

At Julia's Cookies, cookie sales have spiked consistently in October for the past two years. When analysts drill into sales data by cookie flavor, they realize there is a pumpkin spice cookie that is popular only during the fall season. An uptick in pumpkin spice cookie sales is causing these spikes, shown highlighted in orange in **Illustration 17.8**. This is an example of seasonality in Julia's Cookies' cookie sales time series data.

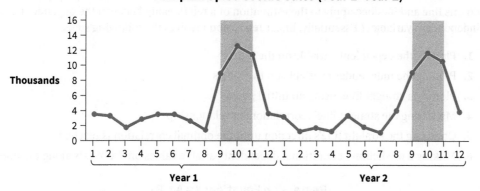

Illustration 17.8 A time trend analysis displayed in a line graph shows the sales of pumpkin spice cookies over two years.

Time series data is useful for a variety of purposes. For example:

- Time series data can be analyzed for outliers. For example, stock market data of a single company, like the stock price, changes daily. But when the company announces something exciting, the stock market price goes up for that day or week. When Apple announces an exciting new product, its price goes up, which would be an outlier to the rest of its usual stock market activity.

- Businesses use time series data to track their growth over time. A human resources department, for example, can track the number of new hires and employee terminations on a monthly basis. This would allow the company to see if its employee count is growing or decreasing over time.

Linear Regression

CPA One of the most popular techniques for analyzing time series data comes from statistics. You might have heard a professor say that the more hours you study, the better you will perform on a test. If you want to know if that is true, you need to collect data about the number of hours you spend studying and the grades you receive for each exam. Linear regression can help you determine whether there is a relationship between the hours you spend studying and your test scores. **Linear regression** is a statistical technique we use to estimate the relationships between a dependent variable and one or more independent variables:

- **CPA** **Dependent variable:** This is the value to be understood. It is often called the outcome.
- **CPA** **Independent variable:** This is the factor that may be influencing the dependent variable. There can be one or more independent variables, depending on the type of regression performed.

In the studying and exam grades example, your exam scores are the dependent variable, or outcome, of the number of hours you spend studying, which is the independent variable. Regression can determine the strength of the relationship between the hours spent studying and the test scores you receive.

You may recall from your statistics courses that regression *does not* establish a cause-and-effect relationship between the variables. It only *estimates* the existence of a relationship between them.

Linear regression is either simple or multiple.

- **Simple regression:** One dependent variable and only one independent variable
- **Multiple regression:** One dependent variable and multiple independent variables

In this course, we will only look at the simple linear regression equation:

$$Y = A + Bx$$

where:

Y = Dependent variable
x = Independent variable
A = Y-intercept (value of Y when x = 0)
B = Slope of line

Illustration 17.9 shows the simple regression equation plotted on a line graph. But how do this line and its slope apply to the estimation of a relationship between the dependent and independent variables? Essentially, linear regression involves the following steps:

1. Plotting the dependent variable on the Y-axis
2. Plotting the independent variable on the X-axis
3. Plotting a straight line, using an initial guess
4. Measuring the straight line's correlation, or relationship
5. Changing the straight line's direction until the optimal correlation is reached
6. Making a prediction of additional dependent variable values on the Y-axis along the line

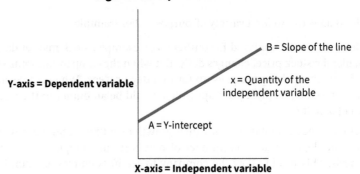

Regression Equation: Y = A + Bx

B = Slope of the line

Y-axis = Dependent variable

x = Quantity of the independent variable

A = Y-intercept

X-axis = Independent variable

Illustration 17.9 The equation for regression analysis is plotted on a line graph.

Does step 6 sound like a predictive analytic? That is because it is. If regression analysis stops at step 5, it's a diagnostic technique that estimates how various factors may have influenced an outcome, as we have discussed so far. Note that linear regression is not limited to time series data. It can be used for other data analytics applications. We discussed it here because you can expand upon linear regression to predict future values by following the trend of the straight line's slope to identify future outcomes. We'll look at that next. First, help Kae identify the variables she needs to perform linear regression in Applied Learning 17.3.

Julia's Cookies   Applied Learning 17.3

Linear Regression: Journal Entry Testing

Kae wants to perform linear regression to identify red flags for fraud in the journal entry data. Journal entries are posted to specific account types, which are identified by categories. Some categories of accounts are subject to increased fraud risks.

Kae's hypothesis is that if journal entries posted to high-fraud-risk categories increase at year end, when the fraud risk is highest, it is a red flag for fraud that should be investigated. She will use linear regression to determine if the number of journal entries posted to a high-fraud-risk account is related to the time of year it is posted.

In Kae's analysis, what is the dependent variable, and what is the independent variable?

SOLUTION

The two variables Kae is analyzing are:

- Number of journal entries posted to the high-fraud-risk accounts
- Time of year the journal entries are posted

The number of journal entries posted is the dependent variable. Kae wants to determine whether that is influenced by the independent variable, which is the time of year.

Forecasting

CPA **Forecasting** is the process of estimating future events based on the combination of past and present time series data. This predictive analytics method is a staple in accounting data analytics.

Several statistical methods, including linear regression, can create a forecast. Forecasting is not limited to linear regression, however, and other statistical models are also used (though they are beyond the scope of this discussion). Data professionals must decide which algorithms to use based on the business case and data in question.

One of the most common uses of forecasting is in sales. Historical sales data for each store is used to create a forecast of future sales. Sales forecasts are an essential part of planning for businesses. The anticipated sales drive decisions on what raw materials to purchase, which products to manufacture, what marketing campaigns to launch, and more. Recall the pumpkin spice cookie sales numbers from our time series analysis. Let's expand on that analysis to help with forecasting of future pumpkin spice cookie sales in **Illustration 17.10**.

Pumpkin Spice Cookie Sales (Year 1–Year 2) with Year 3 and Year 4 Forecast

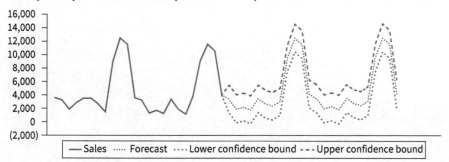

Illustration 17.10 Forecasting sales of pumpkin spice cookies for Y3 and Y4 builds on the existing sales data from Y1 and Y2.

Illustration 17.10 shows multiple lines representing the future possibilities:

- The "lower confidence bound" and "upper confidence bound" are part of a **confidence interval**, which is an estimate derived from observed data that shows a range of possible values.
- Businesses like to use a 95% confidence interval when they perform forecasting. This interval gives 95% certainty that the true mean of the population falls within those bounds.
- The upper and lower bounds are important elements of forecasting, as the forecast line is just an estimated mean.

Now that we have discussed both linear regression and forecasting, let's consider some business opportunities to use both techniques together to generate insights. In managerial accounting, accountants use forecasting for robust planning. For example:

- Forecasting is used to determine the amount of variable costs associated with expanding a product line or business segment.
- The known fixed costs are compared to the estimated variable costs to predict the point of loss, break-even point, and profitability. This analysis, called a **break-even analysis**, is covered in managerial accounting courses.

Monte Carlo Simulation

Forecasting can predict what will happen next, but it is limited because it predicts outcomes based solely on the historical time series data and confidence intervals. If sales have steadily increased over the past two years, a forecast will predict further increases next year. In reality, though, many future scenarios and external factors can impact sales. For example, we have seen what can happen to sales during a global pandemic when stores and offices are shut down.

CPA A **simulation** uses complex calculations to predict the outcomes and probabilities associated with a decision that influences a data set:

- It can study the causes and effects of various actions. For example, a sales simulation can use market research data to predict the outcome of sales in a region if a new product line is added.
- Simulations are adjusted to test different actions, and the predictions are reviewed each time the simulation is run to evaluate how the actions affect the model.

Many college students perform simulations on their GPAs by calculating a final class grade based on various scores for exams. They want to predict how the final class grade will react to different exam grades. A 70% on one exam may still yield an A in the class overall if the rest of the course grades are high enough. This is an example of a rather simple simulation involving limited data sources.

CPA A popular simulation is **Monte Carlo simulation**, which predicts the probability of different outcomes in the presence of many random variables. To use it, we generate models of potential outcomes and conduct a risk analysis for each one. Monte Carlo can use reinforcement learning to learn directly from its experiences to evolve the model. **Illustration 17.11** shows the visual output of a Monte Carlo simulation created in R, a statistical analytics software package, where every line is a possible outcome.

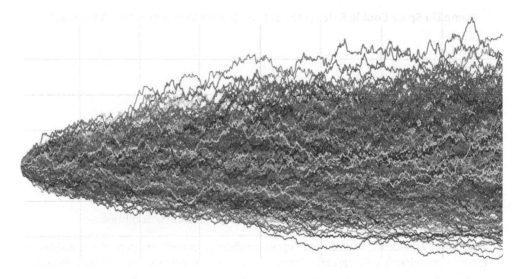

Illustration 17.11 Visualizing a Monte Carlo simulation in R creates hundreds of lines showing possible outcomes.

Source: Adapted from Ojasvin Sood, Monte Carlo Simulation in R with Focus on Option Pricing, Jun 25, 2019. https://towardsdatascience.com/monte-carlo-simulation-in-r-with-focus-on-financial-data-ad43e2a4aedf

Monte Carlo is an important simulation in the business world and can be used in many contexts, including:

- **Investment firms:** It can predict the value of a portfolio based on various investment options while considering the uncertainty of the financial market and other external factors.
- **Personal finances:** Monte Carlo can simulate investment options in a retirement account to predict outcomes and determine the amount of savings necessary to achieve a target income at retirement age. It considers financial market performance, investment selections, and other factors as the random variables.
- **Corporate risk management:** It is used to predict volatility and risks of various business decisions for executive leadership, such as selecting loans, investing corporate finances, and onboarding a new ERP system.
- **Project management:** Managers can predict project costs, schedules, and more using random values such as resource availability and project funding.
- **Cost accounting:** Cost accountants can simulate cash flows, costs, variances, and more to understand and plan budgets.

Why Does It Matter to Your Career?

Thoughts from a Senior Consultant, Public Accounting

- Technology is a two-way street for recruiting. Companies want talented individuals with technology awareness, and students are seeking companies at the forefront of data management and analysis. If companies want to attract top talent, they must stay relevant in the tools and processes they use to manage and analyze data.
- You don't have to be a data scientist to understand the capabilities of data analytics. Just knowing the different analysis techniques and appropriate times to utilize them will make you a competitive candidate as the accounting industry increasingly utilizes data analytics.

CONCEPT REVIEW QUESTIONS

1. **CPA** Define linear regression.

   Ans. Linear regression is a statistical technique used to estimate the relationships between a dependent variable and one or more independent variables. For example, linear regression can help us determine whether there is a relationship between the hours we spend studying and our test scores.

2. **CPA** What do you mean by forecasting? What confidence interval is used by businesses when they perform forecasting?

   Ans. Forecasting is the process of estimating future events based on the combination of past and present time series data. Business analysts often use a 95% confidence interval when they perform forecasting.

3. What is Monte Carlo simulation? Give an example of how Monte Carlo simulation could be used in cost accounting.

   Ans. A popular simulation, Monte Carlo simulation can predict the probability of different outcomes in the presence of many random variables. To use it, we generate models of potential outcomes and conduct a risk analysis for each one.

   Cost accountants can use Monte Carlo simulation to simulate cash flows, costs, variances, and more to understand and plan production budgets and actual compared to budgeted results.

17.4 Which Analytics Techniques Are Gaining Popularity in the Accounting Profession?

Learning Objective ❹
Summarize advanced data analytics techniques that transform data into insights.

So far, we have examined data analytics techniques that build on or relate to one another. For exploratory analysis, we progressed from summarizing a raw data set to using machine learning algorithms to analyze big data. We considered time series analysis, where we use time series data to predict what might happen in the future based on what has already happened.

Here we explore four data analytics techniques that are more standalone in nature. Each technique uses advanced data analytics processes to create insights from a company's data. Let's start with one that uses a special type of time series data to explore deviations between the expected and actual steps in a business process.

Process Mining

You have learned that time series data is a specific type of data captured over a period that is useful for regression, forecasting, and even simulations. Now let's examine a subtype of time series data that is specifically related to events and a unique data analytics technique that is used with it:

- **Event log data** is data about activities in a system and includes the timestamp of when the activities occur. For example, when a person interacts with a system's user interface to input new data, the system captures a record and timestamp for that update. This record and timestamp are part of the system's event log data.

- **Process mining** uses event log data to show what individuals, systems, and machines are doing in a visual format.

Any business process that captures system data with timestamps—such as accounts payable, supply chain processes, and even journal entries—can be analyzed with process mining. In addition to identifying segregation of duties violations, process mining can detect inefficiencies in business processes and circumvention of internal controls. The output of a process mining analytic is an easy-to-understand map that draws attention to unexpected events. Think of it this way:

- A business-process flowchart visually depicts what *should* happen in a business process.
- Process mining analytics reveal what *did* happen in a system-based business process.

Consider how the system captures each event in the process for purchasing:

- Purchase requisition creation
- Requisition approvals from managers
- Vendor verification to ensure that vendors requested are pre-approved
- Purchase order creation
- Purchase order approval from managers
- Orders placed with vendors

Ideally, these events would happen in this specific order. In reality, a purchasing process may happen out of order or might even omit particular steps, which could be a circumvention of an internal control. **Illustration 17.12** shows the process path of four new purchase requisitions. Each event these purchase requisitions goes through is shown inside a rectangle. As indicated with the numbers inside circles on the path, three of them go through appropriate manager approval in the system, and one skips straight to the vendor verification review. This purchase order may not have been reviewed, or it may have been inappropriately reviewed outside the system.

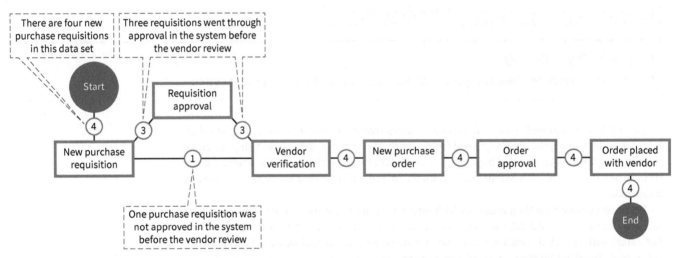

Illustration 17.12 Process mining visualizes event data and makes it easier to identify deviations in an expected process path.

Any part of the business that captures event data is a candidate for process mining. Here are some more examples:

- **Investment firms:** Process mining can be used to identify unusual activities of traders and portfolio managers, such as a trade being executed unexpectedly before it's been approved.
- **Journal entries:** Process mining can be used to show the chain of command of journal entries, including originator, poster, and approver, in order to identify segregation of duties.
- **Information technology (IT):** Events for IT requests can be analyzed for processes like change management, addition of new users to a system, and system error reports. This analysis can show whether processes are followed appropriately and whether the IT support team effectively addresses user issues.

Now that we have reviewed the insights that can be gained by using process mining, we'll discuss how we can explore relationships within a process. First, see if you can help Kae finish her journal entry testing in Applied Learning 17.4.

Julia's Cookies — Applied Learning 17.4

Process Mining: Journal Entry Testing

To finish her journal entry testing, Kae wants to use process mining to identify any deviations in the journal entry posting process for the purchasing of goods. For the data she is analyzing, Kae expects the process path to follow these steps:

1. Post received goods
2. Post received invoice
3. Clear postings
4. Payment
5. Post with clearing

Kae develops the following process mining visualization, which shows the process path for four journal entries.

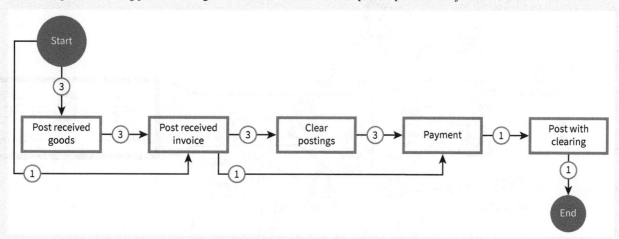

What anomalies can Kae detect using her process mining analytics?

SOLUTION

One journal entry bypasses the "Post received goods" step and goes straight to "Post received invoice." One journal entry bypasses the "Clear postings" step and goes straight to "Payment." Kae needs to tell the audit team to investigate these deviations to determine whether they are appropriate within the process of purchasing goods.

Network Analysis

During the COVID-19 pandemic, researchers began using contact tracing to track the infected people and everyone they have been near during a certain time. The goal is to isolate infected and exposed individuals to slow the spread of the disease. Contact tracing is an example of network analysis.

CPA **Network analysis** is an analytics technique that visualizes relationships among participants in a data set to learn about the social structure those relationships create. It can be used to study relations among people, who are displayed as **nodes** in a network analysis. The links between the nodes are the relationships, or interactions, that connect the participants. Let's look at examples of network analysis in practice.

Banking

Banks can analyze credit card transactions to investigate relationships between people, accounts, transactions, and events. Consider one example:

- Baron is one node of many in the network analysis visualization his bank uses.
- He made purchases at the Apple Store and on Amazon but reported that someone fraudulently used his information to make unauthorized purchases at the Apple Store.

- The network diagram updates to show a red line between Baron and the fraudulent purchase made with his account at the Apple Store.

- Financial analysts at the bank will identify other fraud risks by investigating other transactions related to this one.

In **Illustration 17.13**, fraudulent transactions to the Apple Store have also been reported by other customers. These are indicated with red lines. The bank will freeze these customers' credit cards to prevent further spread and mark further risky activity as purple in the network diagram, which includes all other transactions for the affected customers. These transactions will be monitored to ensure that they were authorized. Note that purple is used for the potentially risky transactions to ensure that end users can easily see the difference between those lines and the red lines of transactions at the Apple Store.

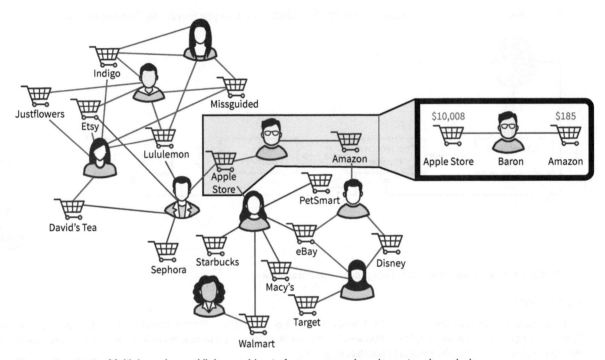

Illustration 17.13   Multiple nodes and links combine to form a comprehensive network analysis.

Social Networks

Social network analysis is a type of network analysis that investigates social structures on social media. On many social media platforms, you can see relationships among your friends by analyzing your "mutual friends" list. Some social media platforms even suggest "people you may know" based on your current connections. If a customer follows Julia's Cookies' competitors on a social media platform, then the Julia's Cookies account will be listed as "accounts you might want to follow." If customers follow those competitors, they may also enjoy following another cookie account. These are both examples of social network analysis.

Social network analysis is not the only useful data analytics technique for social media accounts. Let's look next at another popular method of analyzing the data created in these accounts.

Geospatial Analytics

Have you ever tagged a location in a social media post, tracked your run on a smart watch, or requested a ride service to drive you from point A to point B? All these actions generate location data that is collected and used for analytics.

Geospatial analytics is a technique that gathers, transforms, and visualizes geographic data and imagery, including satellite photographs, Global Positioning System (GPS) coordinates, and more. Geospatial analytics has grown in popularity as location data has become increasingly available. In the past, companies relied on customers to provide their zip code locations, which could be translated into longitude and latitude points and plotted on a map. Today, companies often track their customers through their mobile apps.

Has an app ever asked permission to track your location? Customers choose whether to share their location with the Julia's Cookies purchasing app. Julia's Cookies can then send a customer who has shared their location a push notification with a coupon, for example, if they are near a Julia's Cookies store. **Illustration 17.14** shows customer GPS data visualized on a city map.

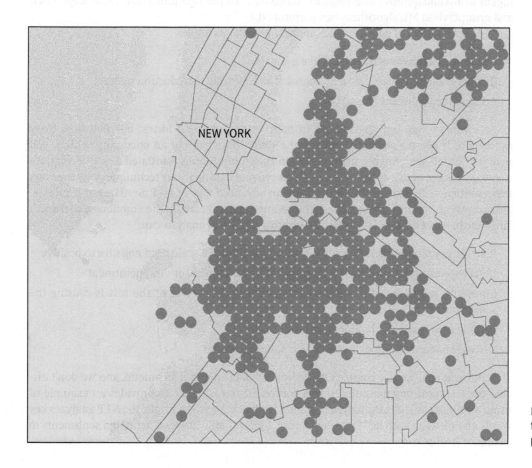

Illustration 17.14 GPS data from mobile app users is presented in a data visualization.

There are many other use cases for geospatial data. For example:

- **Delivery:** Amazon delivery trucks use GPS so customers can track the locations of their deliveries in real time. Geospatial data also allows Amazon to carefully craft routes for delivery trucks based on the current traffic in their delivery areas.

- **Banking:** The banking industry uses geospatial data to track credit card transactions. If you live in Salt Lake City, Utah, and your credit card is used in person in Portland, Maine, the bank will flag that transaction and (most likely) immediately call or text you to see if you made that purchase. If you did not, the bank will freeze your account to prevent further fraudulent transactions from occurring. This is an example of using geospatial analytics to perform anomaly detection.

For our last data analytics technique, let's explore analysis of something people use every day: language.

Natural Language Processing (NLP)

CPA To understand how we analyze language, let's start with **textual analysis,** a category of data analytics techniques used to interpret objects that include words. Textual analysis can interpret text transcriptions of conversations, emails, process narratives and flowcharts, and more to analyze a business process. It can be as simple as keyword searching and scraping text-based documents, but there are also more complex applications.

In this course we focus on textual analysis that analyzes communication. At its most basic level, communication is the exchange of information, and communication methods can be as unique as the individuals using them. But there is a common denominator to many forms of communication—language.

Natural language processing (NLP) is a form of textual analysis that gathers, processes, and interprets meaning from human language. NLP uses ML algorithms to learn the meanings of words and improve interpretation based on what the algorithms learn. Both supervised and unsupervised ML algorithms can perform NLP.

NLP has a variety of data analytics applications. For example:

- Create AI that answers questions, like a chat bot
- Classify documents based on content, such as reviewing legal documentation
- Analyze the sentiment of a text

Let's explore this last application. In both written and oral forms, our messages carry expression. If you see someone crossing the street in the path of an oncoming vehicle, you may yell "Stop!" with intense urgency. When communication is translated to text format, it's easy to lose some of this expression, and other types of data analytics techniques may overlook these subtleties. To address this, we can use an advanced type of NLP. **Sentiment analysis,** also known as opinion mining, uses NLP to interpret and classify the emotions underneath language in a text format. Using ML algorithms, sentiment analysis can:

- Rate the emotions underlying a text communication on a scale from negative to positive
- Detect specific emotions, such as happiness, anger, sadness, or disappointment
- Connect a sentiment to a cause by determining what aspect of the text is causing the sentiment
- Sort big data based on emotional context
- Discover patterns in big data based on emotional context

Sentiment analysis is a complex and advanced data analytics technique, and we don't discuss the technical programming in this course. **Illustration 17.15** provides an example of using sentiment analysis to analyze customer feedback. In this example, the NLP analyzes key words and phrases, such as "fantastic," "okay, I guess," and "useless," to assign sentiments to customer feedback.

My experience so far has been fantastic!

Positive

The product is okay, I guess

Neutral

Your support team is useless

Negative

Illustration 17.15 Sentiment analysis uses NLP to analyze keywords and phrases to assign emotion to textual data.

Now, let's review examples of how textual analysis—and specifically sentiment analysis— can create useful insights for businesses:

- **Social media posts:** Large businesses may be the subject of thousands of tweets on X (formerly Twitter) every day. Sentiment analysis quickly categorizes tweets into customer mood categories based on whether each tweet includes verbiage that is positive, negative, or neutral. In fact, Big Four accounting firms perform consulting engagements with clients to create dashboards that visualize the results of brand sentiment analysis over the client's social media data.

- **Board meeting minutes:** NLP and sentiment analysis can extract metadata by associating verbiage contained in board meeting minutes and categorizing it into metadata tags. The goal is to create an indexed and searchable categorization of unstructured data.

- **Employee satisfaction surveys:** Analyzing open text fields of employee satisfaction surveys can quickly quantify a company's culture and make fast work of reviewing hundreds, or even thousands, of comments.

- **Auditing documents:** NLP has gained popularity in the auditing field. It is being implemented, for example, to "read" through documents, such as contracts and leases, to identify the key terms, trends, and outliers, which would take a human many hours. Humans are still an important part of the equation as they must interpret the machine's output.

- **Journal entry analysis:** An NLP algorithm can search for questionable terminology in journal entries. While this function could be performed with keyword searching, the size of general ledger data sets often creates a valuable use case for leveraging NLP instead. ML algorithms can analyze multiple years of data in minutes to produce a report with outliers and high-risk items that the end user can investigate.

CONCEPT REVIEW QUESTIONS

1. Any part of the business that captures event data is a candidate for process mining. Give an example of how process mining could be used in investment firms.
   Ans. Process mining can be used to identify unusual activities of traders and portfolio managers, such as a trade being executed unexpectedly before being approved.

2. **CPA** Write a brief note on network analysis.
   Ans. Network analysis is an analytics technique that visualizes relationships among participants in a data set to learn about the social structure those relationships create. It can be used to study relations among people, who are displayed as nodes in a network analysis. The links between the nodes are the relationships, or interactions, that connect the participants.

3. What do you understand by geospatial analytics?
   Ans. Geospatial analytics is a technique that gathers, transforms, and visualizes geographic data and imagery, including satellite photographs, GPS coordinates, and more. Geospatial analytics has grown in popularity as location data has become increasingly available. In the past, companies relied on customers to provide their zip code locations, which could be translated into longitude and latitude points and plotted on a map. Today, companies often track their customers through their mobile apps.

4. What is natural language processing (NLP)? Give an example of how NLP could be used for auditing documents.
   Ans. NLP is a form of textual analysis that gathers, processes, and interprets meaning from human language. NLP uses ML algorithms to learn the meanings of words and improve interpretation based on what the algorithms learn. Both supervised and unsupervised ML algorithms can perform NLP.

   NLP has gained popularity in the auditing field. It is being implemented, for example, to "read" through documents, such as contracts and leases, to identify the key terms, trends, and outliers, which would take a human many hours to read.

FEATURED PROFESSIONAL | Audit Data Analytics Manager

Photo courtesy of Joshua Giles

Joshua Giles, CPA

Josh enjoys public speaking and is a people-oriented problem solver who is also drawn to the logic of streamlined machines and technology. With a dual major in accounting and information technology management, Josh specializes in the areas of IT and data science. His career began in Big Four public accounting as a data analyst. Data acquisition, analysis, and visualization are still part of Josh's daily work, and he is the only dedicated advisory and assurance data analyst on his team. In addition to his CPA, Josh is also a certified Alteryx Core Designer and Lean Six Sigma Yellow Belt.

Did you have experience in data analytics before your first full-time accounting role?

Before my first analytics role as a Big Four intern, I had taken a few introductory courses on database design, Java, and SQL, but there was definitely a gap in terms of what I had learned in the classroom from a syntax perspective and what was necessary to deliver projects in the real world. Looking back, the theory of how data is organized and presented was the biggest asset from my academic work. There are so many different tools, buzzwords, and languages available to analysts today, but a solid understanding of data concepts has been infinitely more valuable.

What suggestions do you have for accounting students who want to pursue a career in data analytics?

Take a basic database class. Understanding SQL and databases at the highest level is a great way to see if you enjoy the more mundane aspects of analytics. Many resources available online for little or no cost do a phenomenal job of presenting introductory concepts. After a little bit of exploration, try building something that solves a problem using Excel, Python, or something else. It really doesn't matter what tool you try. When all is said and done, can you use data to solve problems, and do you enjoy doing it?

Which data analysis techniques are the most important for accounting students to understand?

Summarizing data is critical for the consumption of the increasingly large volumes of records within financial applications. Similarly, the ability to parse through those large sets of data to detect anomalies allows accounting professionals to focus on interesting, fraudulent, or process-breaking areas. Finally, forecasting has high utility across an enterprise. Accountants benefit from the ability to estimate future risks, resourcing requirements, and propensity to commit fraud. At the end of the day, you will need to effectively combine multiple analytical procedures to guarantee success.

Review and Practice

Key Terms Review

anomaly detection
break-even analysis
categorical value
classification analysis
cluster
clustering
confidence interval
data composition
data summarization
dependent variable
event log data
exploratory data analytics
forecasting

geospatial analytics
independent variable
labeled data
linear regression
machine learning (ML)
Monte Carlo simulation
multiple regression
natural language processing (NLP)
network analysis
node
noise
pattern
pivot table

process mining
quantitative value
reinforcement learning
seasonality
sentiment analysis
simple regression
simulation
social network analysis
supervised learning
textual analysis
time series
time trend
unsupervised learning

Learning Objectives Review

❶ Identify career opportunities for accounting professionals working with data.

All accounting professionals work with data! In addition, certain career paths focus heavily on data analytics and require an expert understanding of data. For example:

- Data engineers: Build the IT infrastructure and architecture for the growth of data. Support data analysts and data scientists by providing them with tools and access to data. Build scalable infrastructure for collecting and managing raw data. Data analysts, data scientists, and statisticians depend on the work of data engineers to have access to data. They are experts in information technology.
- Data scientists: Work with large volumes of data. Design algorithms to collect and analyze data and conduct predictive analytics. Require expert technical skills in statistics and coding.
- Data analysts: Collect, manipulate, and analyze data from across a business. Understand business operations, including business processes, as well as technical aspects of a business. Less scientifically focused than a data scientist or statistician but more code oriented than a business analyst.
- Business or business intelligence analysts: Work with data to find trends and leverage that information to improve operations. Evaluate business processes, analyze key metrics, and provide strategic recommendations. Skilled at assessing requirements from a business perspective and in data visualization. Know how to present data and provide actionable items for business leaders. Require a deep understanding of business processes.
- Statisticians: Provide a methodology for drawing conclusions from data. Math oriented, with a focus on collection and interpretation of quantitative data using defined scientific methods.

Categories of data analytics are:

- Descriptive analytics: Tells us what has happened. Looks at historical data and condenses it into smaller, more meaningful bits of information. It is the most common form of analysis.
- Diagnostic analytics: Uses data mining to provide insights into why something happened. Drills down to a granular level. Looks at data in a variety of ways to identify trends or investigate causes.
- Predictive analytics: Uses statistical modeling and algorithms to predict what is likely to happen. Provides powerful tools to assist in decision making and inform future actions. Requires assumptions and identifies possible outcomes based on these assumptions.
- Prescriptive analytics: Uses the three previous analytics types to gain insights. Identifies what we should do.

Consists of advanced, cutting-edge technology and design. Uses a decision-making protocol and historical data to train a program on what to do in a real-time situation. Requires advanced programming skills.

Artificial intelligence (AI) uses complex algorithms programmed to mimic human intelligence. It is often used in predictive and prescriptive analytics to train the system to make decisions based on historical data.

With machine learning (ML), a system learns from data to create rules and categories that will enable it to make predictions about future data. It mimics human cognitive functions to learn and solve problems without human involvement. For example, ML can be used in auditing to review journal entries by searching for questionable terminology, entries from unauthorized employees and systems, and a high number of journal entries right under the authorized limit.

The three types of machine learning are:

- Supervised learning: Uses labeled data sets to train the algorithm
- Unsupervised learning: Uses algorithms to analyze unlabeled data sets for hidden patterns
- Reinforcement learning: Focuses on decision making by rewarding desired behaviors and/or punishing undesired behaviors

❷ Describe data analytics techniques that can explore data.

Exploratory data analytics reveals key characteristics of a data set. Data composition refers to the various characteristics of a data set, including:

- Categorical values, which are descriptive components
- Quantitative values, which are numeric data points that can be summed, counted, or otherwise analyzed using mathematical operations

Anomaly detection reveals observations or events that are outside of a data set's normal behavior.

Exploratory analytics techniques include:

- Data summarization: Simplifies data to quickly identify trends by compressing the data into smaller, easier-to-understand outputs such as charts or tables. For example, an Excel pivot table can be used to summarize sales order data based on location, type of product, and date of sale.
- Clustering: Uses unsupervised machine learning to categorize unlabeled data into groups based on similarities.
- Classification analysis: Uses supervised machine learning to categorize labeled data into groups based on predefined labels.

③ Evaluate data analytics techniques that explain changes over time.

Time series data occurs in chronological order across a period of time. Important considerations include:

- Time trend: A consistent movement that does not repeat
- Seasonality: A consistent movement that repeats on a regular basis
- Noise: Additional movement that cannot be explained as a trend or seasonality

Explanatory data analytics techniques include:

- Linear regression: Statistical techniques that predict the relationships between one dependent variable and one or more independent variables. It *does not* establish a cause-and-effect relationship between the variables. It only estimates the existence of a relationship between them. Example: Used in cost accounting to look for relationships between fixed costs, variable costs, and total costs.
- Forecasting: The process of estimating future events based on a combination of past and present data. This predictive analytics method uses statistics and is a staple in accounting data analytics. Example: Common in sales forecasting, where historical sales data is used to create a forecast of future sales.
- Monte Carlo simulation: Measures the sensitivity of changes in a simulation based on the existence of random variables. Example: Can help project cash flow, which is impacted by uncertainty of the markets.

④ Summarize advanced data analytics techniques that transform data into insights.

Advanced data analytics techniques include:

- Process mining: Uses event log data to show what individuals, systems, and machines are doing in a visual format. Example: A purchasing agent creates purchase orders and also approves them. This puts the business at high risk for purchasing fraud.
- Network analysis: Visualizes relationships among participants in a data set to learn about the social structure based on those relationships. Mostly used to study relationships among people, who are displayed as nodes in a network analysis. The links between the nodes are the relationships, or interactions, that connect the participants. Example: Used by banks to identify fraud risks by investigating transactions related to reported fraudulent transactions.
- Geospatial analysis: Gathers, transforms, and visualizes geographic data and imagery, including satellite photographs and GPS coordinates. Example: Banks use geospatial data to track credit card transactions and flag suspicious transactions.
- Natural language processing (NLP): An advanced type of textual analysis that uses artificial intelligence to read, understand, and derive meaning from human language. Example: A chat bot that helps with virtual communication with customers. Sentiment analysis (or opinion mining) is textual analysis that uses NLP to interpret and classify the emotions that lie behind text and speech. Example: Deloitte consultants analyze social media to improve branding of products by identifying key motivators for customers.

CPA questions, as well as multiple choice, discussion, analysis and application, and Tableau questions and other resources, are available online.

Multiple Choice Questions

1. (LO 1) What is the key role of a business analyst?

a. Designs and builds algorithms to collect and analyze data; proficient in coding

b. Provides actionable items for business leaders

c. Performs the same job as a data analyst

d. Helps produce information for database administrators

2. (LO 1) There are four widely used categories of data analysis. Which two look at the past and use historical data to learn more about what had occurred and why it occurred?

a. Descriptive and Diagnostic

b. Predictive and Prescriptive

c. Descriptive and Prescriptive

d. Diagnostic and Predictive

3. (LO 1) Five data analytics–related job titles were discussed in the text. Which of the following job titles would need an expert understanding of data modeling?

a. Business analyst   b. Data scientist

c. Statistician   d. Data analyst

4. (LO 1) **CPA** A manager of an insurance company asks a data analyst to investigate why collision losses on newer cars were so high, the highest in history, in New Jersey in 2017. The data analyst should perform which type of analytics?

a. Descriptive analytics

b. Diagnostic analytics

c. Predictive analytics

d. Prescriptive analytics

5. (LO 2) _____ identifies events outside the normal behavior of a data set.

    a. Data summarization   **b.** Anomaly detection

    c. Cluster analysis   **d.** Process mining

6. (LO 2) To identify fraudulent transactions by looking for unusual activities, you use

    a. unsupervised learning.

    b. classification.

    c. clustering.

    d. anomaly detection.

7. (LO 2) The primary difference between classification and clustering is that classification uses _____ machine learning, and clustering uses _____ machine learning.

    a. reinforcement; supervised

    b. supervised; unsupervised

    c. unsupervised; supervised

    d. unsupervised; reinforcement

8. (LO 2) You are presented with a data set of 10 test scores: 99, 85, 84, 83, 83, 81, 80, 80, 79, and 66. Which grade(s) is(are) an outlier?

    a. 82   **b.** 99 and 66

    c. 95   **d.** 79

9. (LO 3) The primary difference between simple regression and multiple regression is

    a. the number of independent variables.

    b. the number of dependent variables.

    c. the use of a mediator.

    d. the use of multiple data sets.

10. (LO 3) _____ is a consistent movement in the time series data that does not repeat. One example is an increase in revenue through a fiscal year due to a new product launch.

    a. A dependent variable   **b.** A time trend

    c. Seasonality   **d.** Noise

11. (LO 3) Joboy wants to know if the high summer temperatures in Sydney have influenced the increase in ice cream sales at his dessert shop. In his linear regression equation, the temperature would be the

    a. dependent variable.

    b. independent variable.

    c. simple regression.

    d. multiple regression.

12. (LO 3) Which of the following best describes a confidence interval?

    a. It is the range of certainty that the true mean of the population is within the forecasted bounds.

    b. It is the estimate of the mean of the population.

    c. It is the length of time during which the forecast is reliable.

    d. It is a method of performing a break-even forecasting analysis.

13. (LO 4) _____ uses _____ to present chronological activities in a visual flow format.

    a. Event data; network analysis

    b. Event data; process mining

    c. Process mining; event data

    d. Network analysis; event data

14. (LO 4) When natural language processing (NLP) is used to classify emotions within communications, it is called

    a. sentiment analysis.   **b.** building algorithms.

    c. process mining.   **d.** network analysis.

15. (LO 4) Which of the following statements best describes network analysis?

    a. Network analysis is data about activities in a system and includes the timestamp of when the activities occur.

    b. Network analysis uses data to show what individuals, systems, and machines are doing in a visual format.

    c. Network analysis is an analytics technique that visualizes relationships among participants in a data set to learn about the social structure those relationships create.

    d. Network analysis is a type of network analysis that investigates social structures on social media.

16. (LO 3–4) Which of the following is _not_ recommended for analyzing time series data?

    a. Natural language processing

    b. Process mining

    c. Forecasting

    d. Linear regression

Discussion and Research Questions

DQ1. (LO 1) **Early Career** You are a senior manager at one of the Big Four CPA firms. You have accepted an invitation to participate in a student mentorship program at your alma mater. You will mentor Yoshida, an accounting major, for one academic year. You will conduct monthly meetings with Yoshida and have them shadow you at work for one day each semester. At one of your monthly meetings, Yoshida expresses a strong interest in specializing in data analytics. Tell Yoshida about the various types of analysts, as well as their related job descriptions. How are they similar, and what are some of their main differences?

DQ2. (LO 1) What are some of the data analytics platforms offered by Big Four firms, and how are they used to help support the firms and their clients?

DQ3. (LO 1) `Research` Research and discuss how Turbo-Tax software uses prescriptive analytics and machine learning when you use it to prepare your tax returns.

DQ4. (LO 2) `Research` Explain what anomaly detection is and why it is an important tool for accounting professionals. Conduct research and provide an example of the use of anomaly detection by auditing professionals in the real world that differs from examples in the chapter. Cite your source.

DQ5. (LO 2) `Research` Explain the analytics technique used to consolidate a data set into smaller, easier-to-understand groups that present general properties of the data. Provide one example of this technique that is not an example from the chapter and explain why this technique is critical to the creation of useful information for accounting professionals. Cite your source if you use one.

DQ6. (LO 3) Explain the relationship between linear regression and forecasting.

DQ7. (LO 3) `Research` Research examples of analytics not included in the chapter that analyze *time series data*. You may use the internet to research use cases in business.

DQ8. (LO 3) `Research` What is the best way to determine if there is a relationship between items, events, or observations? Explain how this technique works. Provide an accounting example not used in the chapter. You may use the internet to research real-world use cases.

DQ9. (LO 4) `Research` Research and explain how auditors could use network analysis to detect fraud.

DQ10. (LO 1, 4) Explain process mining and provide a use case. Identify the analytics used in the case as descriptive, diagnostic, predictive, or prescriptive and explain your answer.

DQ11. (LO 1–4) `Research` There are four widely used data analytics categories (descriptive, diagnostic, predictive, and prescriptive), each using certain data analytics techniques (e.g., data summarization, clustering, process mining). Choose one technique discussed in the chapter and provide an example of its use that is not in the chapter. Then identify that use as descriptive, diagnostic, predictive, or prescriptive. You can use the internet to search for use case examples in the business world.

Application and Analysis Questions

A1. (LO 1) `Early Career` `Critical Thinking` As a recent new hire at a large international CPA firm, you are part of a team visiting colleges and universities across the country to both encourage specialization in data analytics and recruit for your firm. You are tasked with creating a presentation to show students the different types of data analytics jobs at your firm. Label each job description with a job title from the word bank.

Word Bank:	
Business intelligence analyst	Statistician
Data analyst	Data scientist
Data engineer	

Job descriptions:

1. Provides a methodology for drawing conclusions from data. Is math oriented and focuses on collection and interpretation of quantitative data using defined scientific methods.

2. Works with large volumes of data. Designs algorithms to collect and analyze data and conduct predictive analytics. Requires technical skills such as high-level statistics ability and proficiency in coding.

3. Builds scalable, high-performing infrastructure for collecting and managing raw data.

4. Works with data to find trends and leverage that information to improve business operations. Evaluates business processes, analyzes key metrics, and provides strategic recommendations. Knows how to present data and provide actionable items for business leaders.

5. Collects, manipulates, and analyzes data from across a business. Understands both business and technical aspects of an organization. Expert in coding.

A2. (LO 1) For the following data analytics techniques, identify which type of machine learning each can use by labeling it with a machine learning type from the word bank.

Word Bank:
Supervised learning
Unsupervised learning
Reinforcement learning
Either supervised or unsupervised learning
None

Data analytics techniques:

1. Monte Carlo simulation
2. Clustering
3. Forecasting
4. Process mining
5. Regression
6. Network analysis
7. Classification
8. Data summarization
9. Natural language processing (NLP)
10. Geospatial analytics

A3. (LO 2) `Data Analytics` `Critical Thinking` You are a staff auditor who is performing data analytics for a corporate culture audit for your client. For this analytic, your client provides you with the main employee data from the human resources department. The following data sample shows the data for 2022 in the accounting department.

	Results	Messages		
1	Manager	Department	Year	Turnover Rate
2	S. Holden	Accounting	2022	18%
3	M. Reynolds	Accounting	2022	14%
4	J. Pickens	Accounting	2022	15%
5	R. Stile	Accounting	2022	17%

You use data analytics techniques to prepare this data and create the following data visualization:

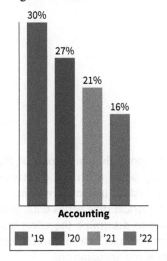

1. What data analytics technique did you use to prepare the data for this visualization? Include all relevant fields in your description.

2. What mathematical function did you perform while using this technique? Include all relevant fields in your description.

A4. (LO 2) `Early Career` `Data Analytics` `Critical Thinking`
You are an accounts receivable analyst at a regional manufacturing firm that specializes in automotive parts for vintage and antique cars. At the end of every month, you reconcile the sales invoice data with the accounts receivable subledger to ensure that all sales invoices were correctly recorded. Your first step is to identify the total invoice amount. To do this, you transform the raw data set to analytics output. Review the following raw data set and analytics output and then answer the following questions:

1. What type of analysis technique was used to turn the raw data set into the analytics output?

2. Identify one record in the analytics output that an anomaly detection might identify as an outlier. Explain why you believe it could be an outlier.

Raw data set:

	Results	Messages		
1	**SalesInvoice_ID**	**Customer_ID**	**SalesOrder_ID**	**SalesInvoice_Date**	**SalesInvoice_Amount**
2	SI_008476	C_0017	SO_0001-17-54880	1/3/202X	$ 1,859.00
3	SI_008477	C_0007	SO_0002-7-54731	1/4/202X	$ 3,369.00
4	SI_008478	C_0007	SO_0003-7-54732	1/4/202X	$ 7,918.00
5	SI_008479	C_0001	SO_0004-1-54625	1/5/202X	$ 3,402.00
6	SI_008480	C_0019	SO_0005-19-54908	1/5/202X	$ 9,500.00
7	SI_008481	C_0021	SO_0006-21-54941	1/5/202X	$ 1,329.00
8	SI_008482	C_0019	SO_0007-19-54909	1/6/202X	$ 2,019.00
9	SI_008483	C_0002	SO_0008-2-54640	1/6/202X	$ 9,778.00
10	SI_008484	C_0006	SO_0009-6-54700	1/7/202X	$ 9,703.00
11	SI_008485	C_0020	SO_0010-20-54928	1/8/202X	$ 36,000.00
12	SI_008486	C_0013	SO_0011-13-54811	1/12/202X	$ 9,315.00
13	SI_008487	C_0022	SO_0012-22-54954	1/13/202X	$ 3,269.00
14	SI_008488	C_0002	SO_0013-2-54641	1/16/202X	$ 2,410.00
15	SI_008489	C_0021	SO_0014-21-54942	1/18/202X	$ 3,109.00
16	SI_008490	C_0012	SO_0015-12-54801	1/19/202X	$ 2,348.00
17	SI_008491	C_0001	SO_0016-1-54626	1/19/202X	$ 1,656.00
18	SI_008492	C_0006	SO_0017-6-54701	1/20/202X	$ 7,164.00
19	SI_008493	C_0017	SO_0018-17-54881	1/23/202X	$ 9,448.00
20	SI_008494	C_0017	SO_0019-17-54882	1/23/202X	$ 7,071.00
21	SI_008495	C_0010	SO_0020-10-54772	1/23/202X	$ 6,474.00
22	SI_008496	C_0013	SO_0021-13-54812	1/24/202X	$ 82,168.00
23	SI_008497	C_0009	SO_0022-9-54758	1/24/202X	$ 2,046.00
24	SI_008498	C_0005	SO_0023-5-54691	1/24/202X	$ 3,141.00
25	SI_008499	C_0021	SO_0024-21-54943	1/24/202X	$ 1,995.00

Analytics output:

	Customer_ID	Total_Amount
1	Customer_ID	Total_Amount
2	C_0001	$ 5,058.00
3	C_0002	$ 12,188.00
4	C_0006	$ 16,867.00
5	C_0007	$ 11,287.00
6	C_0012	$ 2,348.00
7	C_0013	$ 91,483.00
8	C_0017	$ 18,378.00
9	C_0019	$ 11,519.00
10	C_0020	$ 36,000.00
11	C_0021	$ 6,433.00
12	C_0022	$ 3,269.00
13	C_0010	$ 6,474.00
14	C_0009	$ 2,046.00
15	C_0005	$ 3,141.00

A5. (LO 2) `Fraud` `Data Analytics` `Critical Thinking` You are an external audit associate at a public accounting firm, performing an audit engagement for a global manufacturing client. As part of your team's audit testing, you are analyzing your client's journal entries for fraud risk. To assist with the fraud testing, you have transformed your client's journal entry data into the following visualization. In this visualization, journal entries are grouped based on similarities that the machine learning algorithm identified. In this case, the similarities are the journal entry size (horizontal axis) and journal entry time of day (vertical axis). Using this visualization, answer the following questions:

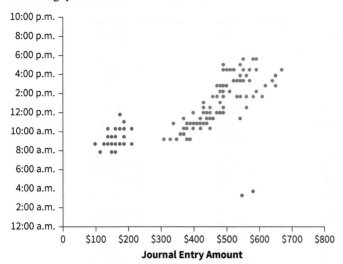

1. What type of data analytics technique did you use?
2. Does the technique use supervised or unsupervised machine learning?
3. Did this data analytics technique detect any anomalies? If so, explain.
4. If there are anomalies, do they indicate a risk of fraud? If so, explain.

A6. (LO 3) `Data Analytics` `Critical Thinking` You are a cost accountant at a paper manufacturing company that has

plants and mills along the Gulf Coast of the United States. You are currently working with the disaster recovery team on an impact analysis of inclement weather in the Gulf Coast region. Using historical time series data, you are performing linear regression to determine the effect a hurricane in the Gulf Coast region would have on overall company revenue. The two variables you are using are:

- Hurricane activity
- Corporate revenue

In your linear regression equation, which of these is the dependent variable, and which is the independent variable?

A7. (LO 4) `Fraud` `Data Analytics` `Critical Thinking` You are an internal auditor who specializes in data analytics at an investment firm. The audit engagement you are currently working on focuses on risks around trading activities. You know that the proper process for executing a trade in the company's trading system is as follows:

1. New order ID creation: This step creates a new order in the system, including all of its details.
2. Pre-trade compliance: The new order details are sent to the compliance team for a pre-trade compliance check to ensure that the new trade request is within regulatory requirements.
3. Order placed: The order is put in the market, ready to be filled.
4. Order filled: The trade is executed, which means the trade is completed.
5. Post-trade compliance: The trade details are reviewed to ensure that the trade still passes regulatory standards.
6. Accounting: Details of the completed order are sent to the accounting department for processing and posting.

By running the trading event log data through a process mining analysis, you generate the process mining map shown below. Based on this map, identify two issues with the trades occurring in the event log data. Why are these issues a fraud risk for the investment firm?

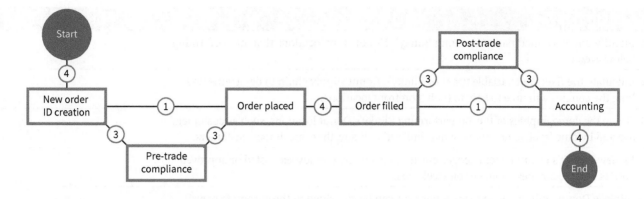

A8. (LO 2–4) `Data Analytics` `Critical Thinking` You are an accounting professional who specializes in data analytics. You recently transferred from the corporate accounting department to a new finance transformation team that is dedicated to using financial and employee data to generate meaningful insights for management and executives. You are tasked with performing data analytics using data from employee satisfaction surveys for the past five years. The data includes the following fields:

- Employee name
- Department
- Date hired, which is used to calculate the length of employment
- Salary
- Overall employee satisfaction rating (scale of 1–5)
- Work-life balance rating (scale of 1–5)
- Training and development rating (scale of 1–5)
- Corporate culture rating (scale of 1–5)
- Feedback, which is an open text field where employees enter commentary to communicate with executive leadership

You have developed the following analytics use cases. For each of them, identify the best data analytics technique you could use to perform that analysis.

1. You want to determine if variable factors are influencing an employee's overall employee satisfaction rating. For example, does an employee's department, length of employment, or salary relate to the overall employee satisfaction rating?

2. You want to use the results of your analysis of the case above to predict whether the company's overall employee satisfaction rating will increase or decrease next year.

3. You want to analyze the employee feedback to identify whether the overall commentary is positive or negative.

4. You want to analyze the relationships between employees in different departments by visualizing the connections between departmental employees, department managers, and executive leadership.

5. You want to identify any patterns or trends in the data without specifying a specific field to analyze.

6. You want to see all possible outcomes of future overall employee satisfaction ratings related to a number of different changes in relevant factors by modeling scenarios and results.

A9. (LO 2–4) Match each of the following business use cases with the appropriate data analytics technique:

1. Project management — Managers can predict project costs, schedules dules, and more using random values such as resource availability, project funding, and more.

2. Managerial accounting — Managerial accountants can perform a break-even analysis to predict the point of loss, break-even point, and profitability of costs.

3. Cost accounting — Cost accountants can simulate cash flows, costs, variances, and more to understand and plan budgets.

4. Accounting — An accountant in the insurance industry might group unlabeled customer data based on average claim costs or premium payments.

5. Banking — Banks analyze credit card transactions to investigate relationships between people, accounts, transactions, and events.

6. Journal entries — Auditors can analyze the chain of command in journal entries, including originator, poster, and approver, in order to identify segregation of duties.

A10. (LO 2–4) `Data Analytics` `Critical Thinking` As a manager of a local favorite, Blinky's Donut, you are trying to implement data analytics techniques that you have learned in your AIS course this semester to help the store gain important insights for business decisions. You have written out the scenarios that you would like to analyze, but now you want to ensure that you are using the appropriate data analytics technique. Match the following techniques to the scenarios listed below:

Data analytics techniques:

A. Anomaly detection

B. Sentiment analysis

C. Classification

D. Clustering

E. Regression

Scenario	Data Analytics Technique
1 Identify undetermined patterns among Blinky's Donut store locations that are performing below average.	
2 Calculate the fixed and variable times of Blinky's Donut supply chain to determine how long the cookies will take to ship to their storefront locations.	
3 Group the demographics of the top-performing Blinky's Donut locations, such as customers' age and income level, to determine what similarities, if any, there are among customers.	
4 Review Blinky's Donut general ledger entries to see if any employees posted or approved entries outside business hours or on weekends.	
5 Blinky's Donut auditors want to see what risks can be identified in the corporate board meeting minutes by analyzing the transcripts of the meetings for emotional content.	

Tableau Case: Julia's Cookies' Call Center Performance

What You Need

Download Tableau to your computer. You can access www.tableau.com/academic/students to download your free Tableau license for the year, or you can download it from your university's software offerings.

Download the following file from the book's product page on www.wiley.com:

Chapter 17 Raw Data.xlsx

Case Background

Big Picture:

Examine business-process performance for Julia's Cookies' call centers.

Details:

Why is this data important, and what questions or problems need to be addressed?

- Many companies have call centers that employ customer service representatives to address customers' questions or concerns.
- Call center data contains the volume of calls received and the reasons customers are calling. This data is useful for identifying trends in and risk related to customer concerns. For example, if customers from the same state have similar problems or complaints, then there might be an underlying issue at those regional stores that needs to be addressed.

Call center data can reveal if the business is fulfilling its service level agreement (SLA), which is a goal that the business has set as a standard of performance that it would like to achieve.

Plan:

What data is needed, and how should it be analyzed?

- The necessary data is extracted from the call center management system. This data set includes calls received during the month of October.
- The data can be used to determine schedules for hourly employees at the call center. Managers will use this historical data to create forecasts of the expected call volume during upcoming shifts and schedule an appropriate number of employees to cover the anticipated call volume.
- The data is also used to identify trends and potential issues based on customer call patterns. To analyze customer call patterns at Julia's Cookies, we should consider the

following questions: What contact method do customers prefer? What days of the week have the highest volume of calls? At what time of day does the center receive the highest volume of calls? How long must customers wait before connecting with a representative?

Now it's your turn to evaluate, analyze, and communicate the results!

Questions

1. What contact method is most commonly used by Julia's Cookies' customers?

2. Which two days of the week have the largest call volume?

3. In which state do customers most often use the chat bot method to contact Julia's Cookies?

4. What is the most common reason customers living in Utah contact Julia's Cookies?

5. What percentage of calls were rated as "Positive"? (Round your answer to a whole number.)

6. What is the average call wait time, in minutes, for calls with a response time "within SLA"? (Round your answer to a whole number.)

7. What hour of the day were the most calls received in the month of October?

8. On what date did Texas experience a service outage?

Take it to the next level!

9. What was the average number of calls per day received by the Georgia call center in the month of October? (Round your answer to a whole number.)

10. At what time of day did the California call center receive the lowest average customer score?

Data Visualization

Financial Data Analyst—Accounting

Julia's Cookies · Chicago, IL; Atlanta, GA; Remote

Posted 2 weeks ago · 3,822 views

Save | **Apply**

Job	**Company**	**Connections**
• 28 Applicants	• 3,000+ Employees	20 Connections
• Associate	• Restaurants	

Summary

The Julia's Cookies finance transformation team is hiring a data analyst to assist the Finance and Accounting departments in performing data analytics and visualization and implementing technology to enhance their business processes.

This role can work remotely. Must be willing to travel 10–15% of the time for in-person meetings and trainings.

Responsibilities

- Develop clear information and valuable insights from complex data
- Handle large amounts of financial data to support all areas of the Finance and Accounting departments
- Collaborate with stakeholders to gather user requirements for data analytics and visualizations
- Translate user requirements into technical specifications
- Implement a consistent design strategy across all reports and dashboards
- Partner with database administrators and other data owners throughout the business

Requirements

Preferred Education: Bachelor's degree in information systems, accounting, finance, or related field
Minimum Experience: One year in an accounting or finance-related role

Preferred Knowledge and Skills

The ideal candidate will possess experience using Tableau, Power BI, or similar software for ad hoc analysis and dashboards. Preference will be given to candidates who:

- Possess a deep understanding of finance and accounting business processes, risks, and internal controls
- Have experience using design principles and color theory to create aesthetically pleasing dashboards
- Prioritize performance, scalability, security, and users in all visualization designs

Salary: $80,000–95,000

CHAPTER PREVIEW   Throughout this course, we have established an essential fact: data is everywhere, and you will be working with it regardless of your career path in the accounting profession. You know data can be turned into valuable information through data analytics. But then what? How do we present data analytics outcomes to stakeholders meaningfully and with impact? Numbers convey information, but when we use data analytics to communicate a story, we exponentially increase the value of that communication. Human perception is attuned to visual information, and properly visualizing data analytics is an important skill for accounting professionals.

When data is transformed into a story, it tells us what happened, why, and what we should do with the information. If you can analyze large volumes of data and turn the insights gained in that analysis into a visual storyboard, you will be an asset to your company.

This chapter focuses on data visualization and its importance to your career, including:

- The relationship between storytelling and data visualization
- How to apply design fundamentals
- Exploring data sets using visualizations
- Using data visualizations to present insights to decision makers

Chapter Roadmap

LEARNING OBJECTIVES	TOPICS	JULIA'S COOKIES APPLIED LEARNING
18.1 Summarize the importance of user-centric design and storytelling in data visualization.	• Turning Data into a Story • Designing for a User • Setting the Tone	Setting the Tone: Internal Audit Analytics
18.2 Apply fundamental design principles to data visualizations.	• Color • White Space • Typography and Iconography	Design Fundamentals: Selecting Icons
18.3 Evaluate visualization techniques for exploratory analysis.	• Composition and Comparison • Distribution • Relationships • Geospatial Maps	Exploratory Analysis: Choosing Visualization Techniques
18.4 Describe visualization techniques that are used to create explanatory stories.	• Infographics • Dashboards • Storyboards	Storyboards: Corporate Culture Audit

CPA   You will find the CPA tag throughout the chapter to call out any important topics you may see on the CPA exam.

18.1 How Does Visualization Tell a Story with Data?

Learning Objective ❶
Summarize the importance of user-centric design and storytelling in data visualization.

There are a lot of people in the world:

- Asia: 4.6 billion
- South America: 430 million
- Europe: 747 million
- Australia/Oceania: 42 million
- Africa: 1.3 billion
- North America: 592 million
- Antarctica: 0

Compare this list to the visualization of the same data in **Illustration 18.1**. Which is easier to comprehend?

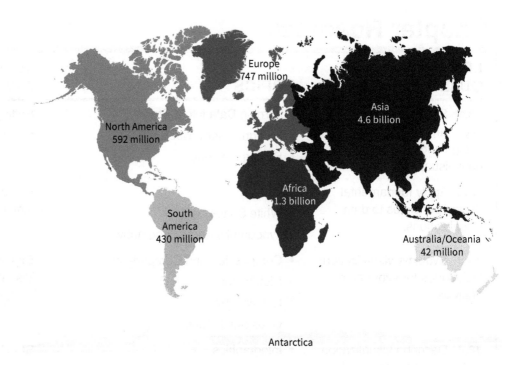

Illustration 18.1 A visualization of the world's population on a map is easier to understand than a bulleted list of numeric data.

This example gives you an idea of the power of data visualization: it quickly delivers information in a way that is easy to comprehend. In Illustration 18.1, continents are labeled with their population totals, and color indicates a continent's population density. This visualization tells a better story than the list of numeric data.

CPA **Data visualization** is a data analytics technique that presents data in a graphical format, such as a chart or graph, for analysis and communication. Creating a high-quality visualization requires certain things of the designer (that's you!):

- Understanding the audience and their requirements (as discussed in LO 1)
- Using fundamental design principles to create user-friendly visualizations (LO 2)
- Understanding the data and selecting the appropriate visualization technique (LO 3)
- Putting it all together to develop the visualization (LO 4)

In the Real World	Charles Schwab's Tableau Center of Excellence[1]

Charles Schwab is a financial services company headquartered in San Francisco. It is the 14th largest banking institution in the United States and the third largest asset management company in the world.[2] As a financial institution, Charles Schwab generates vast volumes of financial data. To tap into the potential of this data, the company adopted an enterprise-wide data visualization strategy:

- First, Charles Schwab equipped more than 6,000 employees with Tableau licenses. Within 18 months, the Tableau license count doubled to 12,000. The most recent report states that there are more than 16,000 Tableau licenses and users driving a data-driven culture at Charles Schwab.

- To support these users, Charles Schwab established a Tableau Center of Excellence (COE) that supports Tableau users and visualization end users throughout the business. The Tableau COE treats visualization projects like systems development endeavors. Visualization experts in the COE approach each new visualization development with a consistent project plan that ensures success and value for the final dashboard.

  One of the Tableau COE's success cases is a client monitoring dashboard. Retail branch managers use the dashboard to identify clients they should contact. This increased insight into customer data allows branch managers to have more impactful discussions when consulting with clients, which results in a better client experience.

  Charles Schwab reports these results from implementing Tableau across the company:

- An increase in team collaboration
- More transparency between departments
- Decreased wait times for data analytics results

  All accounting professionals are likely to interact with companies implementing data visualization tools like Tableau. Careful project planning, motivating leadership, and executive management support are required for companies to be as successful as Charles Schwab in enterprise-wide adoption.

  Do you think accounting professionals have a role in a Tableau COE like the one at Charles Schwab? How does aggregating the corporate data visualization strategy under a dedicated COE reduce enterprise risk?

Turning Data into a Story

There are many ways to create data visualizations:

- Many information systems, including enterprise resource planning (ERP) systems, have built-in reporting modules that can generate some of the basic visualizations we talk about in this chapter.
- Alternatively, data visualization software, like Tableau or Power BI, can visualize data captured by a system. These tools function by either connecting to data after its been extracted from the system to a stand-alone file, such as an Excel or .csv text file, or connecting directly to the system's underlying database and querying the data in real time.

The tools and data acquisition methods you use will be determined by your company. For example, a robotics firm's internal audit team extracts data from corporate systems and then inputs it into a database maintained by internal audit. Tableau dashboards then connect directly to the internal audit database. When hiring new talent, the team looks for experience in data visualization of any kind because data visualization skills translate across tools.

The good news is that you don't have to be a trained graphic designer or an advanced programmer to effectively tell a story with data. With tools like Tableau or Power BI, accounting professionals can easily create meaningful data visualizations. Let's start with the basics.

Do you remember learning about trends, noise, and seasonality in the Data Analytics chapter? Businesses value data visualizations because they can show movement within a data set, like trends and seasonality, that may be difficult to infer from numbers in a table. Let's explore an example. **Illustration 18.2** is the raw data for Julia's Cookies' sales figures in Year 1 (Y1).

---

[1]www.tableau.com/solutions/customer/charles-schwab-equips-more-12000-employees-tableau-advance-data-driven-culture

[2]https://content.schwab.com/web/retail/public/about-schwab/Charles_Schwab_2020_Proxy.pdf

	A	B	C	D	E	F	G	H	I	J	K	L
1	Jan ▾	Feb ▾	Mar ▾	Apr ▾	May ▾	Jun ▾	Jul ▾	Aug ▾	Sep ▾	Oct ▾	Nov ▾	Dec ▾
2	$1,983,000	$2,343,000	$2,593,000	$2,283,000	$2,574,000	$2,838,000	$2,382,000	$2,634,000	$2,938,000	$2,739,000	$2,983,000	$3,493,000

Illustration 18.2   Julia's Cookies' sales figures for Year 1 are shown in a table format.

Compare this to **Illustration 18.3**, which shows the same information in a data visualization. The blue line indicates the actual sales figures, while the orange line indicates the data pattern, or movement trend.

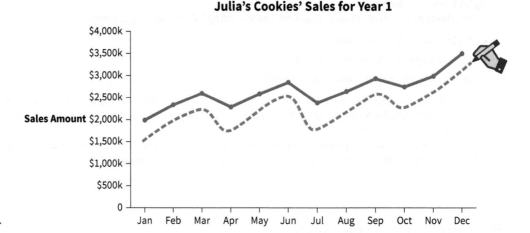

Illustration 18.3   Julia's Cookies' sales figures for Year 1 provide more insights when presented in a data visualization.

What information does the data visualization convey that we may have missed in the raw data?

- Sales trended upward overall throughout the year.
- Sales exhibited a cyclical up-and-down pattern that repeated throughout the year.
- Peak sales occurred during March, June, September, and December.

But raw data is not useless. In fact, the underlying data must be complete, accurate, and reliable for a visualization to be useful. Recall the characteristics of quality information, which are prioritized based on a cost-benefit analysis. If the systems capturing data or the databases storing it are not reliable, the data visualization isn't useful. In this course, you have learned that internal controls ensure that the data captured by an accounting information system (AIS) results in reliable and accurate financial reporting. This also applies to data analytics and visualizations used for decision making.

Why Does It Matter to Your Career?

Thoughts from a Manager of Internal Audit Data Analytics, Financial Services

Data visualization techniques have evolved dramatically in the past 20 years. Entering the workforce with an appreciation for well-designed data visualizations will make you a valuable addition to your company. Converting antiquated reports to user-friendly visualizations will demonstrate your passion for innovation and discovering new insights.

Designing for a User

While you don't have to be a graphic designer to create useful data visualizations, there's an art to creating dashboards that are beautiful, intuitive, and—most importantly—user-friendly.

The first step of any data visualization project is knowing your **visualization audience**, which includes all the end users of your data visualization, and understanding their requests. **Table 18.1** summarizes the questions you can consider to determine your audience and their needs.

TABLE 18.1 Determining a Visualization's Audience

Question	Example
Who is the end user?	The chief executive officer (CEO) needs a different approach than the internal audit department.
How will the visualization be used?	Design considerations are different when a visualization is going to be used as part of a PowerPoint presentation than when it is used to drill down into data to investigate fraud.
What are the technical user requirements?	End users may need certain filters to analyze a visualization, may have preferences as to the layout of a dashboard, and may even prefer specific colors, depending on the purpose of the visualization. You will learn more about colors in the next section.

Overlooking the audience when creating a data visualization is a mistake. There are many horror stories in businesses of developer-run data analytics teams creating dashboards without consulting the end users. These talented data scientists, data analysts, or data engineers may know advanced data analytics techniques, but they may not understand certain principles, such as:

- What a business presentation needs in order to be effective
- How a business stakeholder may interpret a visualization
- The appropriate level of detail for the business need
- The value of white space

That is where you come in. A deep understanding of business needs, the relationship skills to put the needs of end users first, and the ability to talk to business-minded users in a manner they understand can make you an asset in the data visualization space. Data visualizations that tell stories do more than present facts in a chart. They convey messages—even perhaps subliminal ones.

Setting the Tone

Subliminal messages in data visualizations influence end users by conveying emotions:

- A well-crafted visualization sets a tone the audience members will remember, even if they forget the exact numbers.
- An accounts payable manager may not remember that internal audit presented a visualization that included $1.2 million of duplicated vendor payments. But a visual cue like the one in **Illustration 18.4** will leave a lasting impression that is easy to understand: the number of duplicated vendor payments is *bad*.

$1.2 Million

Duplicate Vendor Payments

Illustration 18.4   Visual cues help create a lasting impression.

Setting the tone of a data visualization allows end users to feel the data as well as read it. A great data visualization strikes a balance between providing facts and communicating the desired emotional response from those facts. Keep the tone of your visualization in mind as you select colors, icons, fonts, and visualization techniques, as all these criteria help set the tone.

Sometimes data visualizations are used to convey bad news. Consider the accounts payable manager with $1.2 million of duplicated vendor payments, which is not good news:

- The business data used to create visualizations is generated by business processes, which employees are responsible for performing or overseeing. In other words, someone in the company is always responsible for the actions that create data.
- It's important for a designer to remember where the data originated and who the audience is. This is especially true if you are working in an internal audit department, which is often the bearer of bad news to business leaders.

Never forget the human aspect of data. An author of this textbook is a data analyst at a life insurance company. Data visualizations that use life insurance claims data are created with caution and intention to ensure that the visualizations present information in a respectful way. Before sharing your next visualization, consider the tone and see if the visualization triggers the appropriate emotions.

Consider whether Julia's Cookies' internal audit data analyst has set the right tone in Applied Learning 18.1.

Julia's Cookies — Applied Learning 18.1

Setting the Tone: Internal Audit Analytics

Kae, an internal audit data analyst, is designing an interactive Tableau dashboard that visualizes Internal Audit's quarterly risk assessment. Using data from across the business, this dashboard summarizes risk data by state, calculates risk scores, and displays the risk ratings on a map.

This quarter, the results of the risk assessment were positive. The worst possible risk score is a 3, and most of the risk scores were a 1 or 2.

Kae created this visualization with the following legend:

Low Risk Score (1): Peach   Medium Risk Score (2): Red   High Risk Score (3): Light Blue

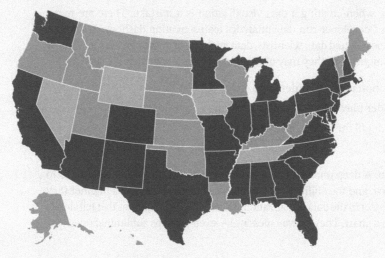

Do Kae's design choices set the appropriate tone for the message this visualization is trying to portray?

SOLUTION

Probably not. The color red can have negative associations, such as indicating something is wrong or failing. This visual implies that the risk assessment had an overall negative outcome. Kae could have used better choices in colors to portray the message that the results of the risk assessment were positive. You will learn more about color theory in the next section.

CONCEPT REVIEW QUESTIONS

1. **CPA** What is data visualization?
   Ans. Data visualization is a data analytics technique that presents data in a graphical format, such as a chart or a graph, for analysis and communication.

2. Why is setting the tone in data visualization important?
   Ans. Setting the tone helps audience members to remember the visualization and the message, even when/if they forget the numbers. Setting the tone also allows the end users to feel the data—whether it is good, bad, or neutral news.

3. What questions should be asked while determining visualization audience?
   Ans. The questions to be asked are:
   - Who is the end user?
   - How will the visualization be used?
   - What are the technical user requirements?

18.2 What Are the Fundamentals of Design?

Learning Objective ❷
Apply fundamental design principles to data visualizations.

Does your favorite company have a memorable logo? Business logos have meaning. From the colors to the icons or fonts, a logo represents something about a company. Consider the Olympic Games logo, which consists of five interlocked rings, each a different color. Did you know that each of the five rings represents a continent that competes, and the six colors (five colored rings and a white background) represent the flag colors of competing nations? This logo has been in use for over 100 years and is still recognized globally. That is the power of a visual cue!

Data visualizations, like all other visual cues and graphics, are based on design concepts. A **design concept** is the central idea, or theme, that drives a design's meaning and tone. In business, professionals who work with visual cues, including data visualizations, pay careful attention to details to ensure that the different elements of the design work together to tell the appropriate story.

Color

One of the most important decisions in a design concept is choosing colors. Colors draw attention, incite emotional reactions, and determine tone. **CPA** There are two families of colors (**Illustration 18.5**):

- **Warm colors:** Red, orange, and yellow are often associated with joy, energy, and playfulness. Note that red has special considerations, which we discuss later.
- **Cool colors:** Green, blue, and purple often evoke feelings of relaxation, calm, and stability.

Color Pairings

A color wheel, which is a useful tool for design, shows relationships among colors. The color wheels in **Illustration 18.6** represent different combinations a designer can choose. Designers often also use gradients, or shades, of a single color to create minimalist designs.

Best practice is to limit the number of colors used in a single visualization to no more than four. Using too many colors can create visual chaos and make it difficult for the audience to understand the message the visualization is trying to convey.

WARM COLOR FAMILY
versus
COOL COLOR FAMILY

Illustration 18.5   Colors are divided into two families: warm (reds, oranges, and yellows) and cool (greens, blues, and purples).

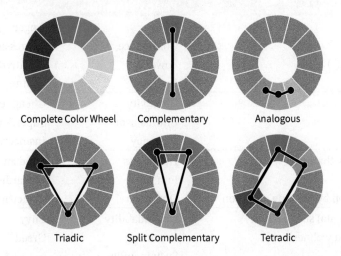

Complete Color Wheel   Complementary   Analogous

Triadic   Split Complementary   Tetradic

Illustration 18.6   Color wheels assist designers in choosing pleasing color combinations.

Does **Illustration 18.7** feel busy to you? The visualizations in this dashboard are simple, but its many colors—especially background colors—make it distracting. End users may miss the dashboard's central message: sales are increasing, especially in Russia and Mexico.

Illustration 18.7 Poor color choices, unclear labels, and busy visualizations distract from the message of a dashboard.

Color Psychology

Different colors convey different emotions. **Color psychology** is the study of human behavior related to colors. Every color is associated with positive and negative traits, and colors can influence human perception by evoking emotions. **Table 18.2** shows common associations and emotional responses to popular colors based on North American color psychology.

TABLE 18.2 North American Color Psychology

Color	Associations	Positive Qualities	Negative Qualities
Red	• Noticeable and bright • Negative business connotations • Associated with debt ("in the red")	Love Confidence Power Energy	Anger Aggression Negativity Failure
Orange	• Suggests adventure and fun • Used in products for children	Creativity Enthusiasm Vibrancy	Cheapness Superficiality Insincerity
Yellow	• Draws attention, but more subtly than red • Used in children's products • Highlights important information by drawing attention	Happiness Fun Optimism	Egotism Cowardice Criticism
Green	• Used in promotion of environmental sustainability • Associated with health, food, and wellness • Opposite effects from red • Indicates wealth and money • Used by financial companies and grocery stores	Dependability Nurturing Sustainability Improvement Good performance	Envy Greed

TABLE 18.2 (*Continued*)

Color	Associations	Positive Qualities	Negative Qualities
Blue	• Most used color in design	Loyalty	Coldness
	• Used by conservative businesses where trust and security are core values	Integrity	Conservativism
		Calmness	Rigidity
Purple	• Often appears in products targeting women or children	Mystery	Impracticality
	• Associated with femininity	Pride	Corruption
		Wisdom	Immaturity

Recall the dashboard in Applied Learning 18.1. The red in that image would be likely to emotionally influence end users to believe something bad is happening, even though the actual message is one of positivity and improvement. Kae could have instead used green, which is associated with improvement.

Why Does It Matter to Your Career?

Thoughts from a Staff Accountant, Logistics Consulting

Graphic designers create visual cues for external use, but you are most likely to create data visualizations for internal use. Senior management prefers to receive reporting in a graphical format, so even staff accountants should know simple design techniques.

Color Accessibility

The final color decision we consider, accessibility, is one of the most important. Not all sighted people experience color the same way. For example:

- Approximately 1 in 12 men (8%) and 1 in 200 women (0.5%) have *color vision deficiency (CVD)*. CVD is most commonly referred to as *color blindness*.
- In rare cases, color blindness is the complete inability to see color, but for most people, it means seeing colors differently than they appear to the rest of the population.
- Different types of CVD affect the appearance of different colors.
- The most common type of CVD is red-green color blindness, where the individual has difficulty seeing shades of red, green, and yellow.

In **Illustration 18.8**, the image on the left shows the intended colors, and the image on the right shows what a person with red-green CVD sees.

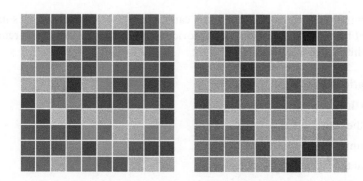

Illustration 18.8 This color blindness simulation shows the intended colors on the left and the colors a person with red-green CVD would see on the right.

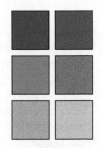

Illustration 18.9 A popular Tableau CVD-friendly palette includes shades of blue, orange, and gray.

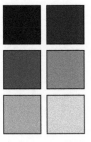

Illustration 18.10 People with CVD can typically distinguish shades of a single color.

Since accounting data is numeric and often financial, it's natural to want to use green to indicate positive numbers or increases and red to indicate negative numbers or decreases, but that message will be lost on someone with CVD. So how do we design accessible data visualizations for persons with CVD? Here are some tips:

- Use CVD-friendly color combinations. Tableau has built-in color blindness palettes (**Illustration 18.9**). A common combination of CVD-friendly colors includes shades of gray along with blue and orange or blue and red. You can use blue instead of green for accounting data visualizations to convey the same message.

- Select different tints of the same color. Using light and dark shades of one color allows an end user with CVD to associate the darker tints and lighter tints with differences in the visualization (**Illustration 18.10**).

- Explore alternative methods to distinguish data in visualizations. Add text, icons, arrows, annotations, different line widths, or different line styles (such as solid line versus dashed line) to clarify the message in a data visualization.

Remembering these color principles when designing data visualizations and dashboards will put you on the right path to creating an accessible, user-centric design concept that clearly sets the tone and delivers the message of your data visualizations.

White Space

While color is important, so is its absence. A cluttered data visualization distracts the end user from its intended message. **White space** is negative space that creates a visual pause (**Illustration 18.11**). White space allows end users to process a visualization's message and reduces cognitive load by eliminating unnecessary elements and distractions. Its use is also considered modern and visually appealing.

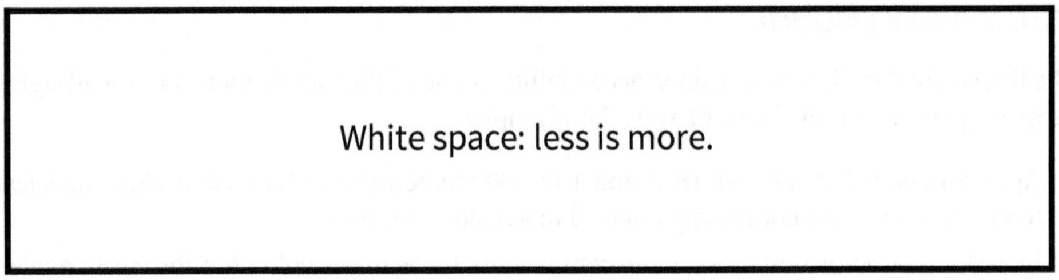

Illustration 18.11 White space's motto is "less is more"—in other words, visual simplicity is often more effective than visual complexity.

> White space: less is more.

White space is important when creating visualizations for many reasons, including:

- **Comprehension:** Eliminates distracting visual elements, which improves understanding

- **Simplicity:** Avoids overwhelming the reader

- **Focus:** Highlights key information by isolating it

Keep in mind that overusing white space can indicate a lack of content. It's important to find the right balance. **Illustration 18.12** provides some examples of ways to remove clutter and using white space well in an Excel chart:

- Remove grid lines

- Clean up the axis

- Remove the chart border

- Remove unnecessary chart markers

- Transform the legend to notations

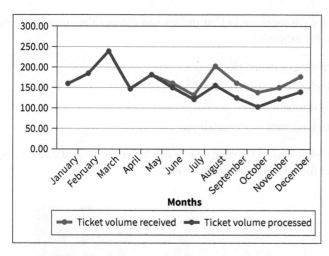
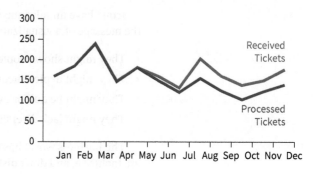

Illustration 18.12 Removing clutter and using white space well can make a chart easier to understand.

Source: Knaflic, C. N. (2015). *Storytelling with Data: A Data Visualization Guide for Business Professionals*. Hoboken, NJ: John Wiley & Sons, Inc. Reproduced with permission from John Wiley & Sons.

Typography and Iconography

Color is not the only element to consider when designing a data visualization. Typography and iconography are also fundamental design elements for data visualizations.

Typography

Typography describes the style and appearance of printed matter. One aspect of typography concerns the font choice for a visualization. Fonts influence the tone of a story, and using a professional font increases the credibility of a visualization with the audience. Fonts should be readable, even at small sizes. Popular font choices include:

- Benton Sans
- Fira Sans
- Gotham
- Noto Sans
- Source Sans Pro
- Merriweather

Not all fonts are free to use, and availability depends on company resources. Another typography choice besides font choice is sizing. There are different approaches for implementing typography:

- **One font and one size:** Using the same font and font size throughout a visualization creates a consistently subtle and modern visual impact.

- **One font and a big header:** Using a single font with larger headers highlights the headers (or titles) of a visualization for the audience.

- **Two fonts and with different emphases:** Using two complementary fonts with the header bolded draws attention to different parts of a visualization.

Iconography

Icons are another design tool in a data visualization designer's toolbox. **Iconography** is the use of visual images and symbols to represent ideas. In data visualization, **icons** are symbols that provide visual cues along with data, text, or charts and graphs.

An icon directly communicates information without distraction. The book icon in **Illustration 18.13** doesn't indicate which book it represents because it doesn't matter in this case. When the book title is irrelevant, showing the title creates a distraction.

Illustration 18.13 Business presentations use iconography to provide simplistic visual cues to an audience.

Icons have an advantage over photographs in that photos can distract the audience from the message of a visualization. For example:

- They might show people wearing outdated clothing.
- They might depict unconvincing behaviors (**Illustration 18.14**).
- They might be dull or overly dramatic.
- They might lack diversity and accurate representation.

The business world has therefore shifted to using icons, which provide helpful visual cues, are inclusive, and don't distract the reader from the message.

Illustration 18.14 Stock photos are often unconvincing and unrealistic.

Monkey Business Images / Shutterstock

Icons are an important part of polished business presentations. Help Brant prepare for an internal audit meeting with business stakeholders in Applied Learning 18.2.

Julia's Cookies   Applied Learning 18.2

Design Fundamentals: Selecting Icons

Brant is preparing a presentation for a quarterly meeting of Julia's Cookies' Internal Audit department with business stakeholders. He has included the information in a PowerPoint slide deck and wants to make his presentation more visually appealing by adding icons. Here are the topics of the slides:

  Slide 1: Success

  Slide 2: Process

  Slide 3: Negotiation

What icons could Brant use for each slide? You can use the internet for ideas.

SOLUTION

The following are examples of some of the many icons Brant could use for each slide.

Slide 1: Success

Slide 2: Process

Slide 3: Negotiation

CONCEPT REVIEW QUESTIONS

1. What is a design concept?

   Ans. A design concept is the central idea, or theme, that drives a design's meaning and tone. In business, professionals who work with visual cues pay careful attention to details to ensure that the different elements of the design work together to tell the appropriate story.

2. **CPA** What are the two families of colors?

   Ans. The two families of colors are:
   - Warm colors: Red, orange, and yellow are often associated with joy, energy, and playfulness.
   - Cool colors: Green, blue, and purple often evoke feelings of relaxation, calm, and stability.

3. What is a color wheel, and how can we use it in data visualization?

   Ans. A color wheel, which is a useful tool for design, shows relationships among colors. The color wheels represent different combinations a designer can choose. Designers often also use gradients, or shades, of a single color to create minimalist designs.

   Best practice is to limit the number of colors used in a single visualization to no more than four. Using too many colors can create visual chaos and make it difficult for the audience to understand the message the visualization is trying to convey.

4. Why is effective use of white space important when creating visualizations?

   Ans. White space is important since it increases comprehension by eliminating distracting visual elements, avoids overwhelming the reader, and focuses the audience's attention by highlighting key information.

18.3 How Do Visualizations Help Us Explore Data?

Learning Objective ❸
Evaluate visualization techniques for exploratory analysis.

Now that you have learned the importance of storytelling and the fundamentals of design, let's apply these concepts to data visualization techniques. There are as many options for visually presenting data as there are techniques for analyzing it, which we discuss in the Data Analytics chapter. In fact, some visualization techniques are specifically suited to certain data analytics techniques.

Data analytics can be performed in all types of software, including visualization software. This means data analysis and visualization are not always separate processes. Visualization tools like Tableau can perform descriptive, diagnostic, and even predictive analysis with the click of a mouse. We'll look at some descriptive and diagnostic use cases first:

- Descriptive analytics tell us *what has happened.*
- Diagnostic analytics tell us *why it happened.*

By turning raw data into a visual, we can easily perform flexible and insightful descriptive and diagnostic analytics. In visualization, we call this process of investigating unknown data **exploratory analysis.**

Let's illustrate exploratory analysis with a Julia's Cookies example. In **Illustration 18.15,** raw customer satisfaction survey data is summarized by location. Then the results for the San Francisco store are compared to the results for the rest of Julia's Cookies' locations to see how this store is performing. This exploratory analysis shows that the San Francisco location is outperforming in many areas but tends to run out of cookie flavors more than other stores. While there are other areas where the San Francisco location is underperforming, this area is most substantially below Julia's Cookies' other locations.

It's easier to select the most appropriate data visualization techniques once the data is understood. Let's take a closer look at the data visualization techniques we can use for exploratory analysis to answer a number of questions:

- **Composition of data:** What variables are included in the data set?
- **Comparison of data points:** How is one variable performing compared to other variables in the data set?
- **Distribution of data:** How often does a variable occur in the data set?
- **Relationships between data points:** How do the different variables in the data set relate to one another?
- **Geospatial location of data points:** Where are variables geographically located in the data set?

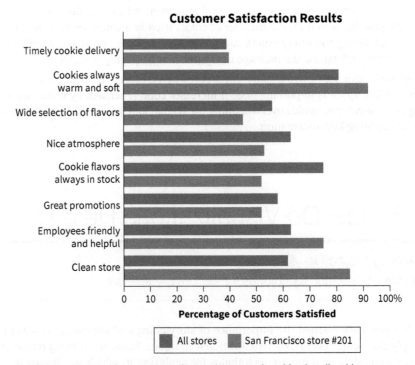

Illustration 18.15 It's easy to explore a data set when it's visualized in a simple chart or graph.

Composition and Comparison

The first step in exploring a data set is understanding its composition—what variables it contains. Understanding data composition includes answering questions like:

- What are the **categorical values**, or descriptive components, that we can use to summarize the data for analysis?

- Are there **quantitative values** that describe the categorical values with numbers we can analyze?

For example, in a journal entry data set, the journal entry ID, description, and approver name are all *categorical values* that summarize the data. The debit amounts, credit amounts, and posted data are all *quantitative values* that can be analyzed mathematically.

Let's consider some of the most popular visualization techniques for composition and comparison exploration.

Pie Charts

CPA One of the most basic composition visualizations is the **pie chart**, which divides data into groups proportional to their size within the data set. While pie charts are common visualizations, they don't always paint the clearest picture of data. The human brain is not trained to compare angles around a circle. For this reason, it can be difficult to correctly gauge the comparison between slices of a pie chart. However, there are some techniques we can use to make pie charts more valuable:

- Add numeric labels for the quantitative values. Labels provide visual cues to accompany the sizes of the slices. For pie charts, the percentage of the whole is the preferred numeric value to use.

- Sort the groups by largest to smallest in a clockwise direction.

- Reserve pie chart usage for small data sets with only five to six groups to avoid clutter.

In **Illustration 18.16**, it's difficult to differentiate between the marketing and accounting employee counts. The quantitative values, the largest-to-smallest order, and the minimal number of groups presented help provide clarity, but the visualization is still difficult to interpret. It's best to use a pie chart only if there is no other choice. There are many modern visualization techniques that better accomplish the same goals.

Tree Maps

One popular substitute for a pie chart is a **tree map**, which is a mosaic chart that presents groups and subgroups as rectangular portions of the larger whole. A key difference between a tree map and a pie chart is that a tree map can handle multiple groupings of categorical values, such as hierarchies. A visualization of hierarchies in pie charts would require multiple pie charts, side by side, with each chart belonging to one grouping.

Employee Distribution by Department

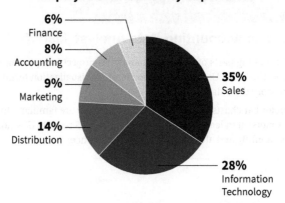

Illustration 18.16 This pie chart has six slices, or categories, of data.

A tree map is a useful, quick visual reference to a data set. Due to the rectangular shapes, a tree map makes it easy to interpret proportional sizes. In **Illustration 18.17**, users can quickly determine that the most common customer complaints relate to food quality, and Store 200 has the most complaints of this type.

Bar Charts

Pie charts and tree maps show the breakdown of categories within a data set as part of the whole, making them ideal for both composition and comparison. **CPA** In contrast, traditional **bar charts** present categorical data as rectangular bars with heights or lengths proportional

Julia's Cookies Customer Complaints by Type of Complaint

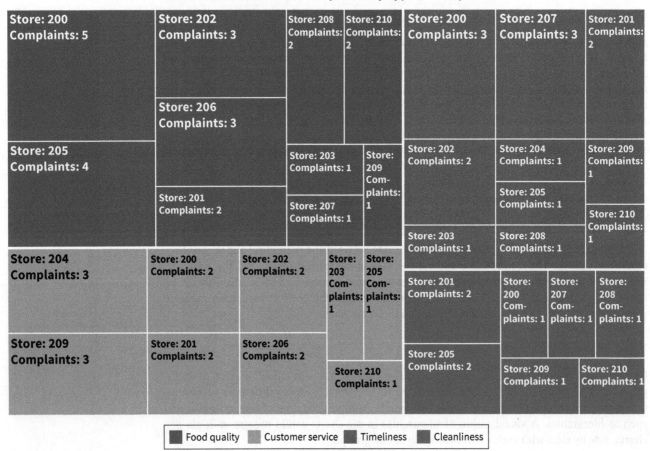

Illustration 18.17 A tree map visualizes hierarchies of categorical data.

to the quantitative values they represent. Because bar charts display the categories within a data set side by side, they're best used for comparison and aren't ideal for showing composition. That said, you can learn a lot about what is in a data set by creating various bar charts for different categorical and quantitative values.

Bar charts are popular visualizations because they are easy to understand (**Illustration 18.18**). Because they were some of the first data visualizations to be adopted by businesses, many professionals are comfortable creating and using them. You may find that your employer prefers bar charts because they are familiar.

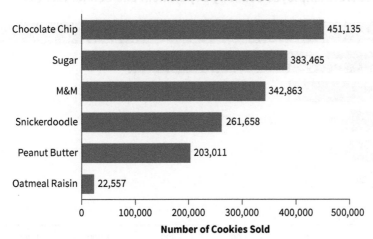

Illustration 18.18 A horizontal bar chart shows sales for the month of March, summarized by product type.

Here are some tips for creating meaningful bar charts:

- The Y-axis (vertical axis) should always start at zero to ensure consistency between categorical values.
- Sorting categories from highest to lowest quantity emphasizes which categorical values have the most quantitative impact on the data set. For example, in Illustration 18.18, the bars are arranged from largest to smallest sales count.
- If the categories are numeric values, such as date or number ranges, bars should be placed in numeric order. In **Illustration 18.19**, bars are arranged in order of age groups, from youngest to oldest.

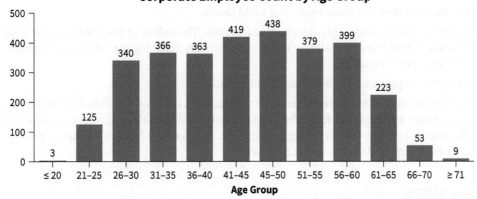

Illustration 18.19 A vertical bar chart summarizes employees by age groups.

Stacked Bar Charts

While traditional vertical and horizontal bar charts don't intuitively display composition, there is another type of bar chart that does. **CPA** **Stacked bar charts** illustrate parts of a whole within the rectangular bars of a traditional bar chart. They are useful when illustrating major and minor categories within one visualization.

Illustration 18.20 shows a stacked bar chart:

- It divides Julia's Cookies' employees into their respective departments, which is the first categorical value.
- The second categorical value is the gender identity of each employee, which is indicated with the colored stacks within the bars.
- The quantitative value is the total number of employees for each of the categorical value pairings.

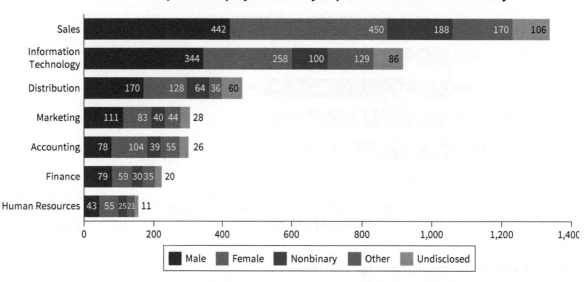

Corporate Employee Count by Department and Gender Identity

Illustration 18.20 A stacked bar chart adds another layer of categorical values to a traditional bar chart by showing gender identities of employees in colored stacks.

Although there are a similar number of female employees in the Finance and Human Resources departments, this is hard to visually identify because the colored stacks have different starting points on their respective bars. Therefore, numeric labels have been added to clarify the gender composition of each department.

Stacked bar charts can become complicated and cluttered very quickly. Tips for creating meaningful bar charts apply to stacked bar charts, but there are also some things to be aware of that are specific to stacked bar charts:

- Use no more than five subcategories to avoid clutter.
- Carefully select colors using design fundamentals. The colors in Illustration 18.20 were selected to meet color accessibility standards while also matching the colors used throughout this course's materials.
- Maximize impact with strategic use of white space.
- Include labels of quantitative values over the stacked bars when possible. If a stacked bar doesn't have enough space for a label, set the label just outside the color stack, as shown in Illustration 18.20 for the Marketing, Accounting, Finance, and Human Resources employees whose gender identities are undisclosed.

Heat Maps

The final composition and comparison visualization technique we cover here is one you have seen before in this course. **CPA** In the Risks and Risk Assessments chapter, you learned about *heat maps*, which are maps or diagrams that use different colors to represent the values of the data set they visualize. So far, you have only seen heat maps used for plotting risk scores, but this visualization technique is useful for any type of data where quantitative values can be separated into different ranges, or groups. In a heat map:

- Colors are applied from darker to lighter shades, based on quantitative values.
- A single color and its shades can be used.
- Gradients across multiple colors can be used, such as shades of green, yellow, and red that indicate lower to higher values (**Illustration 18.21**).

Julia's Cookies Call Center Volume of Calls

	Monday	Tuesday	Wednesday	Thursday	Friday	Saturday	Sunday
January	564	637	1,052	684	137	68	62
February	213	241	397	258	52	26	23
March	468	529	873	567	113	57	51
April	131	148	244	159	32	16	14
May	498	563	929	604	121	60	54
June	621	702	1,158	753	151	75	68
July	963	1,088	1,796	1,167	233	117	105
August	645	729	1,203	782	156	78	70
September	321	363	599	389	78	39	35
October	546	617	1,018	662	132	66	60
November	987	1,115	1,840	1,196	239	120	108
December	1,059	1,197	1,975	1,283	257	128	116

Illustration 18.21   Heat maps use shades of various colors to draw attention to anomalies and trends.

Note that a heat map uses red and green, even though this color combination can be difficult for color-impaired individuals. We use these colors in Illustration 18.21 because you are likely to encounter this color scheme in a business. However, we encourage you to be conscientious about accessibility in your color selections throughout your career.

A heat map compares values of data based on two categorical values, which are on the X-axis and Y-axis of the visualization. Illustration 18.21 shows the number of calls received at the customer service call center for each month of the year and each day of the week. A visualization like this is useful for anomaly detection. In this illustration, you can easily see that there is an unusually high call volume on Wednesdays in July, November, and December.

Now that we have reviewed some of the most popular composition and comparison visualization techniques, let's explore some techniques we use to examine the distribution of variables in a data set.

Distribution

Distribution techniques are used to determine how often a variable occurs in a data set. This is different from comparison in a bar chart or heat map because distribution is a statistical analysis. A summary of data in a bar chart or heat map doesn't consider the relationship of the data points. In contrast, distribution uses statistical functions to determine the relationships between categorical values and quantitative values. We can even use distribution analytics to calculate probability, as a predictive analytic.

For the sake of simplicity, let's examine two common visualizations that display statistical distributions: histograms and box plots.

Histograms

CPA A **histogram** is a visual representation of numeric distributions based on user-defined ranges:

- It graphs the frequency of values occurring in a data set.
- The defined ranges, called **bins**, are plotted as bars where each bar's height is equal to the total occurrences of that bin in the data set.
- The width of a bar is equal to the range of the bin, and all the ranges are the same size.

To understand how histograms are applied to business data visualizations, let's consider an inventory count example for Julia's Cookies:

- Julia's Cookies' warehouse contains spare parts for the kitchen appliances at each of its store locations.
- The warehouse manager wants to know the dollar value of the parts in the warehouse, including the number of on-hand inventory items for each dollar value range.
- The inventory data is divided into $30 range increments, starting with inventory worth $30 or less.
- Displaying the data in a histogram helps the warehouse manager quickly see that there are very few inventory items worth $200 or more (**Illustration 18.22**).

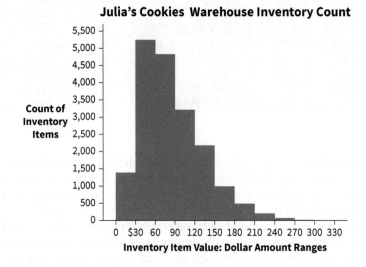

Illustration 18.22 A histogram shows data values grouped into same-sized ranges.

Box Plots

CPA Another distribution visualization, the **box plot**, illustrates the distribution of quantitative values for a categorical value. Within a box plot visualization, every category has its own box plot diagram, which identifies:

- **Minimum:** Smallest value in the category
- **Maximum:** Largest value in the category
- **Median:** Middle value in the category
- **Quartiles:** Division of the category values into four sections

Box plots are useful for showing details within a distribution, as well as anomaly detection. Assume that 12 students take an exam and receive the exam scores in **Illustration 18.23**, which are shown in order from lowest to highest. The minimum (65), median (79), and

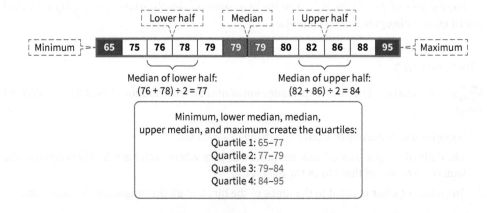

Illustration 18.23 Calculating the data points for a box plot requires identifying the four quartiles of the data set.

maximum (95) are easily determined. To create four quartiles, the median of the lower half (77) and upper half (84) are also calculated.

Software like Tableau will do these calculations automatically. Now we put this data into a box plot (**Illustration 18.24**). In the box plot, the minimum (65) and maximum (95) are represented as horizontal bars at the bottom and top of the diagram, respectively. The divider between Quartile 1 and Quartile 2 (77) is the bottom of the box, the divider between Quartile 2 and Quartile 3 (which is the median, 79) is inside the box, and the divider between Quartile 3 and Quartile 4 (84) is the top of the box.

The assumption of a box plot is that most of the quantitative values of the category fall inside the box:

- Values closer to the box are more expected.
- The further away the minimum or maximum bars are from the box, the more unexpected those values are.

In this example, the exam scores 65 and 95 are both considered outliers. Most students scored between 77 and 84 on the exam.

Let's apply a box plot to an example at Julia's Cookies. As part of a corporate culture audit, the Internal Audit department is reviewing salaries and wages for employees throughout the company to ensure that there are no major discrepancies within departments. Internal Audit established benchmarks for each department to support this review. For the Receiving department:

- There should be a gap of less than 15% between the highest- and lowest-paid employees with similar tenure.
- The minimum hourly wage should be $16 per hour to meet the current job market rates.

Using the pay rates for hourly employees, Internal Audit reviews the data for receiving clerks who have been working at Julia's Cookies for one to three years in the Receiving department (**Illustration 18.25**):

- The highest hourly wage is $19.25.
- The lowest hourly wage is $15.75.
- The median hourly wage is $18.25.
- The majority of employees are paid between $17.25 and $18.75 per hour.

Internal Audit notes that the lowest hourly wage is below the $16 per hour target threshold. Additionally, there is a 22% gap between the lowest- and highest-paid receiving clerks in this group.

The box plot visualization technique supports the compensation review for Julia's Cookies. While they are more complex, distribution techniques can generate insights beyond those of composition and comparison techniques. Let's explore two more exploratory visualization techniques that show relationships.

Relationships

Discovering relationships between categorical values in a data set is a common goal of descriptive, diagnostic, and predictive analytics. From *regression analysis*, to identify the impact of a value on the outcome of another, to *forecasting*, to predict what comes next, the visualization techniques described next identify essential cause-and-effect relationships that provide insights for decision makers.

Line Charts

One of the most popular types of relationships that visualizations can explore is changes over time. A **time series** captures data that occurs in chronological order across a period of time. **CPA** **Line charts** visualize *time series analysis*, which identifies trends or anomalies in time series data.

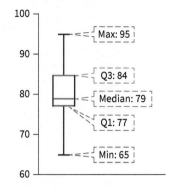

Illustration 18.24 A box plot of grades shows the expected range and outliers.

Warehouse Receiving Clerks

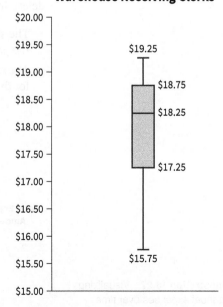

Illustration 18.25 Payroll data at Julia's Cookies is visualized as a box plot to provide insights for internal auditors.

Line charts are popular because they are simple to understand and can be used for trend analysis, forecasting, and even anomaly detection. When creating a line chart, keep in mind:

• Unlike in a bar chart, the Y-axis (vertical axis) in a line chart does not have to start at zero. Instead, it starts at a relevant value, such as a few values below the lowest value in the data set.

• Points should be spaced out evenly along the X-axis (horizontal axis).

• The progression should be defined logically. For example, in a time series line chart, the X-axis is ordered chronologically from oldest to newest.

• Dots along the line chart are connected with a line of the same color for clarity.

Illustration 18.26 shows employee expense data summarized by type of expense and year. Presenting this data in a line chart makes it easy to see the movement of each expense type between years. The sudden decrease in employee expenses in 2020 is due to the work-from-home movement prompted by the COVID-19 pandemic.

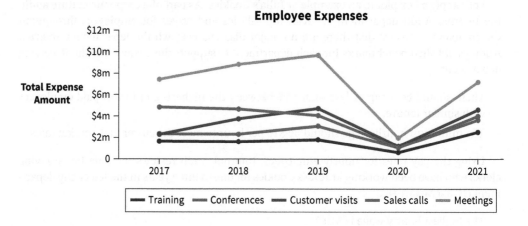

Illustration 18.26 Visualizing annual expenses over time with a line chart draws attention to the movements, or relationship, between the years.

This data could be presented in a traditional bar chart or stacked bar chart. However, bar charts would draw attention to the *comparison* of expenses over the years, while line charts naturally draw attention to the movement, or *relationship*, between years. It's important to consider nuances like this when choosing a visualization technique. The decision should be determined by the story the visualization is telling:

• The story in Illustration 18.26 is that employee expenses decreased suddenly in 2020 due the pandemic and were on the rise in 2021.

• The story in **Illustration 18.27** is that in 2020, employee expenses were at the lowest level for the five years shown.

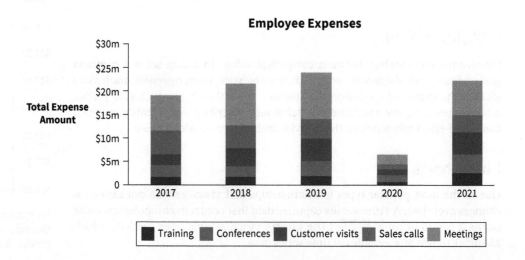

Illustration 18.27 Visualizing annual expenses over time in a stacked bar chart draws attention to the comparison and composition of expenses.

Scatter Plots

Important data analytics techniques that depict relationships also include *clustering* and *classification*, which group similar categorical values based on similarities in the data set. **CPA** The best visualization for depicting these types of relationships is a **scatter plot**, which shows the relationship between two variables. For the purposes of visualization techniques, scatter plots use shapes, such as dots or circles, mapped along the X-axis and Y-axis, which show the two variables being measured for relationships.

To understand scatter plots, let's consider an employee expense fraud test. The company in this example has a number of rules related to reimbursing employees for meals purchased during work trips:

- Employees use their corporate credit cards to pay for company-approved meals.
- Employees must record the number of guests that attend a meal in their expense reports, which are submitted in the employee reimbursement system.
- Company policy states that employees cannot spend more than $250 per person per day on meals when traveling.

The employee expense report data can be visualized in a scatter plot (**Illustration 18.28**):

- Each dot is a single meal expense.
- The number of guests attending each meal is plotted on the Y-axis.
- The dollar amount spent for each meal is plotted on the X-axis.
- Each meal is color-coded based on the amount spent per person, and the orange, and red circles indicate meals above the company policy limits. This presentation is CVD-friendly because it uses blue, orange, and red.
- The dot size indicates how far the meal expense is above the policy limits. This is calculated by dividing the total amount by the number of attendees.

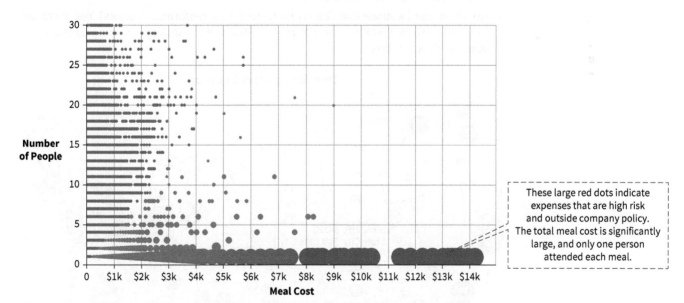

Illustration 18.28 Scatter plots are useful for visualizing analytics like fraud tests examining employee expenses.

It's easy to identify outliers, like the large red dots ranging from $8,000 to $14,000 with fewer than five attendees, in this scatter plot. Nobody can eat that much food in one meal! This type of visualization technique is useful for accounts payable analysts, expense reimbursement program analysts, and auditors.

Geospatial Maps

CPA The last type of exploratory visualization we cover is the **geospatial map**, which refers to analytics and visualizations that utilize geographic data such as map coordinates, GPS data, and more. Some key things to remember include:

- Visualization software like Tableau can automatically turn geographic coordinates into map plots.
- Not everyone will be familiar with every part of the world, so it's important to always include labels.
- White space and minimalist design choices can make a map more insightful and user-friendly.
- Legends and reference points can be used to avoid packing too much information on a map.
- Maps can be enhanced through the use of styles that are modern, clean, and visually appealing.

Business uses for mapping geospatial data include:

- Showing corporate activity, such as sales and expenses, across geographic regions
- Providing insights into distribution of employees, office locations, and customers around the globe
- Adding an easy-to-understand, real-world context to corporate data, such as presenting a map that relates corporate risk to physical locations

Illustration 18.29 shows sales data summarized by geographic location and visualized in a geospatial map. Additional context is provided through use of a **tooltip**, which is a pop-up in Tableau that appears when a user hovers over a data point and shows more information. In Illustration 18.29, the tooltip is showing the zip code, store city, and total revenue for the Salt Lake City location. Legends indicate that the circle size and color depict the amount of sales revenue. Management can use this map and visualizations like it to support decision making such as:

- Is it worth opening more stores in San Francisco? The existing stores there are doing well, so this option may be worth exploring.
- Are there any locations that should be reviewed for performance issues? Yes, there are stores in western Texas and New York state that may be underperforming compared to others in those regions.

Revenue by Store Location

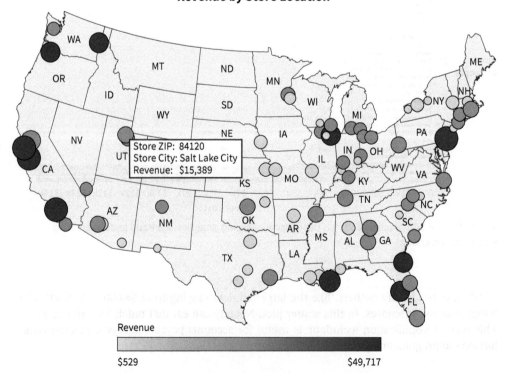

Illustration 18.29 Geospatial maps immediately draw attention to the relationship between data and the real world.

Now that we have reviewed many of the visualization techniques available for exploratory analysis, see if you can help a financial analyst at Julia's Cookies choose which visualization techniques to use in Applied Learning 18.3.

| **Julia's Cookies** | Applied Learning 18.3 |

Exploratory Analysis: Choosing Visualization Techniques

Claire is preparing visualizations for a presentation to senior management that will highlight recent work the financial analysts have been doing with corporate data using Alteryx and Tableau. Six data sets must be visualized.

Which visualization technique do you think Claire should use for each of the following data sources?

1. Network log: Log of individuals accessing the corporate network that includes all login attempts over a period of time
2. IT requests: IT requests system users submitted to the IT department last week, summarized by system
3. Employee composition: The number of employees, and their gender identities, for each department
4. Hours worked: Total hours worked by each employee in the warehouse for the past month
5. Quarterly earnings: Global revenue and expenses for last fiscal quarter, summarized by week
6. Sales: Regional sales, summarized by store location

SOLUTION

Since all of these data sets could be visualized using more than one of the visualization techniques you have learned about so far, there are no wrong answers. Claire decides to create the following:

1. Network log: A *line chart* visualizes network access by the minute and draws attention to the periods of time when network traffic is the highest.
2. IT requests: A *bar chart* easily identifies which systems have the most issues.
3. Employee composition: A *tree map* or a *stacked bar chart* shows employees by department and gender identity.
4. Hours worked: A *heat map* draws attention to the days employees are working longer hours, which will help with scheduling and managing risk of burnout.
5. Quarterly earnings: A *line chart* compares revenue to expenses over time.
6. Sales: A *geospatial map* displays revenue by location.

CONCEPT REVIEW QUESTIONS

1. What rules should you follow when creating a pie chart?
   Ans. The rules we can follow are: adding numeric labels for quantitative values (percentages preferred); sorting the pie slices from largest to smallest in a clockwise direction; and only using the pie chart if we are showing up to five or six groups within the pie chart.

2. **CPA** What do you know about stacked bar charts?
   Ans. Stacked bar charts illustrate parts of a whole within the rectangular bars of a traditional bar chart. They are useful when illustrating major and minor categories within one visualization.

3. What is a heat map?
   Ans. Heat map is a map or diagram that uses different colors to represent the values of the data set they visualize. In a heat map colors are applied from darker to lighter shades, based on quantitative values. A single color and its shades can be used. Gradients across multiple colors can be used, such as shades of green, yellow, and red that indicate lower to higher values.

4. **CPA** What is a box plot?
   Ans. A box plot is a distribution visualization which illustrates the distribution of quantitative values for a categorical value. Every category within a box plot visualization has its own box plot diagram, which identifies:
   - Minimum: Smallest value in the category
   - Maximum: Largest value in the category
   - Median: Middle value in the category
   - Quartiles: Division of the category values into four sections

5. **CPA** What are geospatial maps?

Ans. Geospatial maps utilize geographic data, such as map coordinates, GPS data, and more, to draw attention to the relationship between data and the real world. For example, an interactive dashboard can chart customer locations via a bank mobile app that tracks the customer location and the locations where the customer credit card payment is being made.

18.4 When Should Explanatory Visualizations Be Used for Storytelling?

Learning Objective ❹
Describe visualization techniques that are used to create explanatory stories.

During exploratory analysis, information that is gathered may not be pertinent to the audience or purpose of a data visualization. A bar chart of purchasing data may, for example, reveal that the cost of raw materials is significantly higher in San Francisco than in Los Angeles. But if the purpose of the data visualization is to identify regions where the cost of raw materials has increased by more than 15% in the past two years, it doesn't matter that San Francisco is more costly than Los Angeles.

Information gathered during exploratory analysis should only include relevant insights. **Explanatory analysis** occurs once the story, or purpose, of a visualization is known and the data is ready to be presented to the audience. During explanatory analysis, visualizations are crafted, the presentation is fine-tuned, and key points are highlighted. When crafting explanatory data visualizations, remember to consider these questions:

- Who is the audience?
- What is the key takeaway of this story?
- How does the data support the key takeaway?
- Which visualization techniques best portray the story?

Explanatory data visualization occurs at the sweet spot where data, visuals, and the story intersect (**Illustration 18.30**).

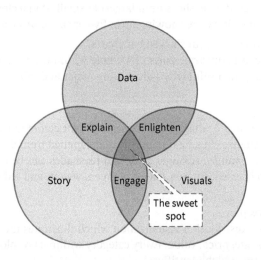

Illustration 18.30 Explanatory analysis occurs at the sweet spot where data, visuals, and the story intersect.

Recall the bar chart that visualizes customer satisfaction survey results for Julia's Cookies in the last section (Illustration 18.15). While this visualization portrays information—that San Francisco is outperforming other stores in delivering tasty cookies, hiring friendly employees, and keeping the store clean—there is more to the story.

Using the same data, we can create a more insightful explanatory visualization by calculating the difference in performance scores between the San Francisco store and other stores (**Illustration 18.31**).

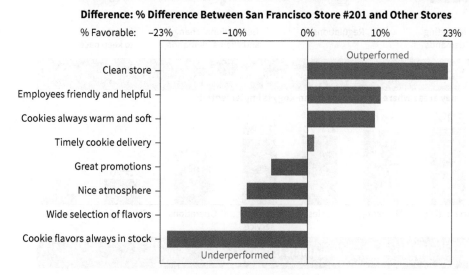

Illustration 18.31   An explanatory analysis is designed to deliver key takeaways of the story being told to the audience.

This explanatory analysis presentation is more effective than the bar chart for a few reasons:

- The bar chart doesn't immediately portray how San Francisco ranked against other stores.
- The explanatory analysis highlights categories management should focus on.
- The explanatory analysis includes notes about actionable items for management.

Next, we explore three important explanatory visualizations: infographics, dashboards, and storyboards.

Infographics

Sometimes data doesn't have to be formatted in charts and graphs. Visually appealing presentations of information come in many forms, including a popular graphic design style called an infographic. An **infographic** is a stand-alone visual that tells a story through graphic design and rarely needs to be accompanied by verbal communication. Effective infographics quickly engage the audience's attention using carefully crafted charts, statistics, quotes, and summarized information that highlight key takeaways.

The complexity of infographics ranges from simple, single illustrations to complex larger spreads, like the one in **Illustration 18.32**. In this infographic, there are three key takeaways:

- There have been cultural shifts in accounting.
- Opportunities for accounting automation are increasing.
- Accounting professionals need certain skills in order to be successful in today's technology-driven world.

These three takeaways tell a story: technology is the future of the accounting profession. The infographic tells that story in a succinct, visually pleasing manner.

You don't have to be a brilliant graphic designer to create appealing infographics. Power-Point skills can achieve similar results, and websites like infograpia.com make infographic creation accessible for even the least creative individuals.

Dashboards

This chapter has presented visualizations that can be created using software like Tableau or Power BI. Alone, each of these visualizations is its own chart or graph, but they can be combined

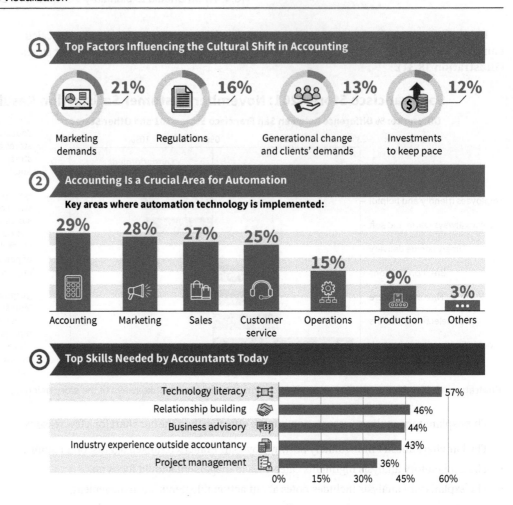

Illustration 18.32 This infographic succinctly delivers three key takeaways that support the story that technology is changing the accounting profession.

to create dashboards. **CPA** A **dashboard** is a collection of individual visualizations that allows the audience to view multiple pieces of data at once.

Dashboard Use Cases

A company should perform a cost-benefit analysis when planning a large dashboard project to ensure that the value of the insights the dashboard provides is worth the investment of time, talent, and other resources.

For accounting professionals, whose work often focuses on financial data captured by an AIS, dashboards are commonly used, and highly desired, for reporting. Examples of dashboard use cases include analyzing financial *key performance indicators (KPIs)* and more:

- Tracking of revenue, expenses, gross profit, and net income
- Data monitoring for suspicious transactions or fraud risk
- Visualization of the balance sheet and accompanying financial ratios
- Variance analysis of budgets to actual expenses
- Predictive forecasting of sales, costs, and more
- Accounts payable vendor management
- Analysis of taxes geographically or over time

This list is only a sampling of the types of accounting data analytics that can be visualized in a dashboard for easy comprehension.

Dashboard Characteristics

By compiling different visualizations, a dashboard presents multiple key takeaways supporting the overall story of the dashboard. It's important to make sure the visualizations included in a dashboard have certain characteristics:

- They relate to one another.
- Each visualization supports the overall story.
- Each visualization has unique and important takeaways.
- They are necessary.
- They do not distract from the message.

Dashboards can be static or interactive:

- A **static dashboard** is a still image with no interactivity, such as a JPEG of a Tableau dashboard exported into a PowerPoint presentation.
- An **interactive dashboard** is presented within the software used to create it or on a website in such a way that the audience can interact with it. Interactions include drilling down into the underlying data, exporting images and underlying data, viewing tooltips, changing filters, and more.

An interactive dashboard has a **landing page**, which is the first dashboard view when the dashboard is opened. **Dashboard views** allow users to save specific settings, like filters, for ease of use. For example, a compliance analyst in North America may create a dashboard view that only shows data for North American businesses, as that is the scope of the analyst's work. Dashboard views prevent the audience from having to reapply filters every time they open the dashboard.

Let's consider a sales dashboard for Julia's Cookies. This interactive dashboard uses two visualizations:

- A geospatial map of revenue by store location
- A vertical bar chart that shows total number of cookies sold for each cookie type

This dashboard is interactive: when a store location is selected on the geospatial map, the bar chart updates to show revenue by cookie type for that specific location. In both visualizations, darker colors indicate higher revenue.

Illustration 18.33 shows the landing page for the dashboard, which provides a national view of Julia's Cookies' U.S. sales. In this view, we can see that:

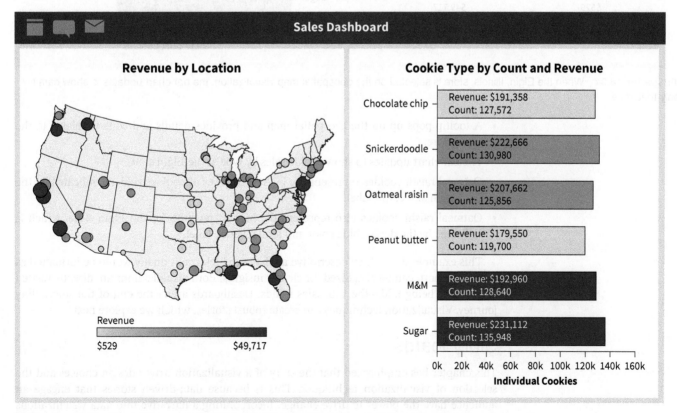

Illustration 18.33   The landing page for this sales dashboard includes all of the United States.

- Los Angeles, Chicago, and New York have the most revenue, as indicated by the large, dark blue circles on the geospatial map.
- Fewer oatmeal raisin cookies were sold than M&M cookies, as indicated by the bar length along the horizontal axis and the count labels in the bars.
- Oatmeal raisin cookies generated more revenue than M&M cookies, as indicated by the darker blue color and the total revenue label.

Illustration 18.34 shows the interactive view that appears when the Elgin, Illinois, location is selected:

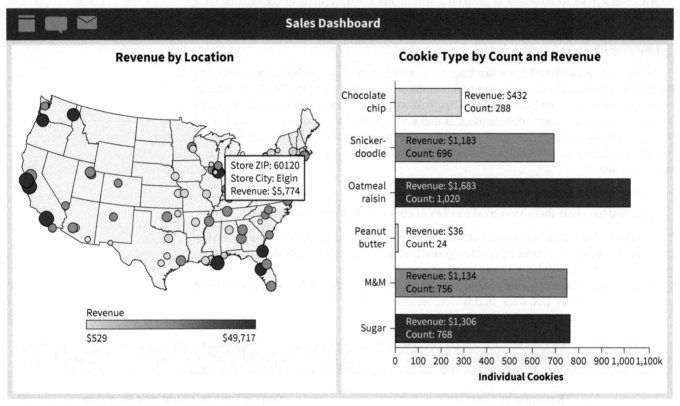

Illustration 18.34 When the Elgin, Illinois, store is selected on the geospatial map visualization, the bar chart updates to show data for only that store.

- A tooltip pops up on the geospatial map and provides details and context related to the Elgin store.
- The bar chart updates to show cookie sales by type at the Elgin store.
- Oatmeal raisin cookies represent the highest number of cookies sold, as indicated by the bar length and count label.
- Oatmeal raisin cookies also represent the highest revenue for the Elgin store, which is indicated by the darker blue color and total revenue label.

This example shows how descriptive analytics, which traditionally would be formatted as a simple report, can be visualized for clearer insights. Both visualizations are directly related to the story being told—the U.S. sales trends. Dashboards aren't the end of the storytelling journey. Visualization techniques can create robust stories, which we explore next.

Storyboards

This chapter has emphasized that the story of a visualization drives design choices and the selection of visualization techniques. This is because data-driven stories that engage an audience have the power to drive change. Incorporating a narrative into data visualizations illustrates the key takeaways of the data set more memorably than would simply stating facts.

Designing data visualizations to tell a story is like being an author of a film script or novel. Data visualization stories follow a story arc (**Illustration 18.35**).

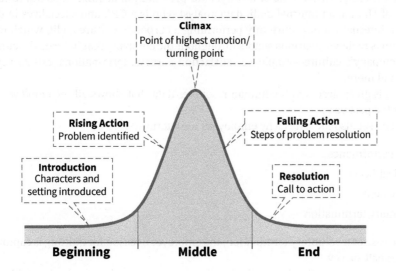

Illustration 18.35 A story arc has five important parts: the introduction, rising action, the climax, falling action, and the resolution.

Presenting a Story

A **storyboard** is a collection of dashboards, stand-alone visualizations, infographics, and other presentation materials that turn the data analytics and visualization into a business presentation. When we use a storyboard to present data analytics and visualizations, the storyboard follows the story arc, which has five parts:

- **Introduction:** Characters and settings are introduced. This involves describing the presentation, including the subject matter and why it is being presented. It's important to convince the audience that they should pay attention because this presentation may affect them.
- **Rising action:** This includes articulating the problem being addressed or the question being answered. It presents the overall story that all the data visualization work supports.
- **Climax:** The climax shows the results of the analytics that have been performed. Whether it's the success of a high-performing department or the discovery of risky behaviors or transactions, this is where the audience is most interested. If the *rising action* set the stage properly, the audience will be invested in seeing the visualizations during the climax. Avoid overwhelming the audience with too much information.
- **Falling action:** If the presentation has identified something negative, like a problem or risk, the falling action may include suggestions for improvements. Alternatively, a data visualization can be used to show predictive analytics—what *may happen* if the audience takes certain actions.
- **Resolution:** At the end of the presentation, the audience is presented with a powerful call to action. Whether the presentation has identified areas for improvement or areas to continue doing things well, the audience should leave the presentation with a clear understanding of what to do next.

Why Does It Matter to Your Career?

Thoughts from a Senior Risk Consultant, Public Accounting

- In public accounting, dashboards are used to analyze a team's work. They track the amount of work remaining on a project and the number of projects coming up next this quarter. They also provide insights into the availability of employees in the client firm, which can be used to schedule future engagements.
- Clients also love seeing their data presented in dashboards. Storyboarding with dashboards is a way to add value to client engagements with data analytics.

Internal Audit Example

Let's walk through an example of a storyboard presentation at Julia's Cookies from the perspective of Hanna, an internal audit data analyst who is a CPA and specializes in data visualization. Internal Audit is currently performing a corporate culture audit, which means the audit team is reviewing various factors throughout the company that indicate the current state of the company's culture—employee satisfaction surveys, terminations, exit surveys, salary ranges, and more.

Hanna is given access to the human resources data that shows all the employee terminations for the past year.

The data set also indicates why employees were terminated:

- Poor performance
- Medical Leave
- Retirement
- Voluntary termination

In the case of a voluntary termination, the employee's reason for quitting is captured in the employee exit survey.

Hanna summarizes the data set by termination reason and uses a horizontal bar chart to compare the reasons (**Illustration 18.36**):

- The terminated employees are the characters of this story.
- Data exploration reveals that most employees voluntarily quit because they found another company with a more flexible work environment or they were not happy with the lack of training opportunities at Julia's Cookies.

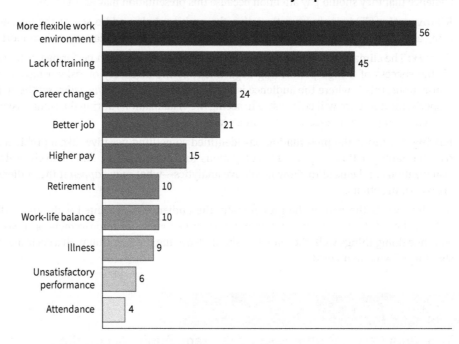

Total Number of Terminations by Top Termination Reasons

Illustration 18.36 A horizontal bar chart easily compares the categorical values, which are the reasons employees left the company.

Hanna meets with a human resources generalist to discuss how Julia's Cookies could address the two primary reasons employees are quitting. They rank each termination on a scale of 1 to 5, according to the likelihood that Julia's Cookies could affect the termination reason. Using this information, Hanna creates another visualization that plots termination reasons based on the number of terminations (horizontal axis) and the ability of Julia's Cookies to influence the terminations (vertical axis) (**Illustration 18.37**).

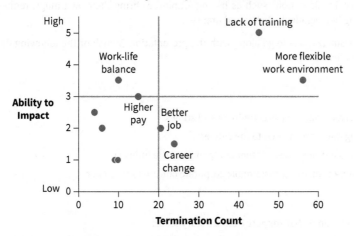

Ability to Impact Termination

Illustration 18.37 This visualization depicts the climax and falling action, which assist management in identifying next steps to take in addressing the corporate culture issues at Julia's Cookies.

In the middle of her storyboard presentation, Hanna presents the climax and falling action. Julia's Cookies can minimize employees quitting due to work-life balance concerns, an offer with higher pay at a different company, the lack of training opportunities, and issues with the company's flexible work policy. Because lack of training and the flexible work policy are the top two reasons employees voluntarily quit, management should focus on these two areas first.

To conclude her story, Hanna provides recommendations, or a call to action, to management:

- Lack of training:
  - Management should review training opportunities throughout the company to identify departments and positions where training is lacking.
  - Exit interview data should be summarized by department to see if there are specific departments where employees are quitting for these two reasons.
  - Department managers should work with Human Resources to design and implement increased training opportunities.
- Flexible work policy:
  - Management should review positions throughout the company to identify opportunities for flexible schedules and implement a hybrid return-to-office plan.

Now that you have seen how Hanna presented a storyboard of her data analytics and visualizations to management, see if you can identify the data Internal Audit needs to review another area of corporate culture in Applied Learning 18.4.

Julia's Cookies   Applied Learning 18.4

Storyboards: Corporate Culture Audit

As part of the corporate culture audit, Hanna is helping the Internal Audit team analyze whether the onsite benefits at Julia's Cookies' corporate headquarters, like the gym and discounted cafeteria, are creating value for corporate employees.

Through data analytics, Hanna has discovered that there's been a recent decline in the number of employees purchasing discounted meals in the corporate cafeteria. She outlines a proposed storyboard to present these findings to the rest of her Internal Audit team:

- **Introduction:** The corporate cafeteria opened when the company moved its headquarters to the current office building.
- **Rising action:** The cafeteria has been consistently popular with employees until this year.
- **Climax:** The decline in employee use of their corporate discount at the cafeteria may reflect a decrease in corporate culture. Employees believe that Julia's Cookies uses too many disposable dishes and utensils in the cafeteria, and some people are opting for sustainable lunch choices.
- **Falling action:** Implementing a sustainability program in the cafeteria may improve how employees view their corporate meal discounts as well as employee morale. This may increase employee retention and satisfaction, which will improve overall corporate culture.

- **Resolution:** Management should consider sustainable options such as having employees bring their own mugs, removing plastic straws from the cafeteria, and switching to using biodegradable dishes and utensils.

Hanna's audit manager asks her to create the visualizations to go along with the presentation. Which of the following data sets will Hanna need to create the visualizations for this storyboard?

1. Cafeteria sales: Menu items purchased per day
2. Cafeteria menu: Sales price of each menu item
3. Cafeteria inventory: List of supplies used in the cafeteria, such as containers and straws
4. Employee satisfaction: Survey results containing questions related to the cafeteria
5. External benchmarks: Sustainability metrics showing successes of other companies in the industry
6. External statistics: Survey results showing the importance of a sustainable corporate culture to customers

SOLUTION

All these data sets are useful for creating data visualizations that support Hanna's storyboard:

(1) Cafeteria sales, (2) menu items, and (3) inventory can be used to show the current state of cafeteria operations.

(4) Employee survey results can show the rising action and climax of the current issues.

(5) External benchmarks and (6) statistics can create a case that supports the falling action and resolution, where Hanna presents her call to action to Julia's Cookies' management team.

CONCEPT REVIEW QUESTIONS

1. What is an infographic, and how can it help achieve your communication objectives?
   Ans. An infographic is a stand-alone visual that tells a story through graphic design and rarely needs to be accompanied by verbal communication. Effective infographics quickly engage the audience's attention using carefully crafted charts, statistics, quotes, and summarized information that highlight key takeaways.

2. Differentiate between static and interactive dashboards.
   Ans. A static dashboard is a still image with no interactivity, such as a JPEG of a Tableau dashboard exported into a PowerPoint presentation. On the other hand, interactive dashboard is presented within the software used to create it or on a website in such a way that the audience can interact with it. Interactions include drilling down into the underlying data, exporting images and underlying data, viewing tooltips, changing filters, and more.

3. What is a storyboard?
   Ans. A storyboard is a collection of dashboards, stand-alone visualizations, infographics, and other presentation materials that turn the data analytics and visualization into a business presentation.

FEATURED PROFESSIONAL | Health Insurance Business Analyst

Photo courtesy of Alana Baumann

Alana Baumann

Alana obtained a bachelor's degree in accounting with a concentration in forensics and is now pursuing a master of business administration (MBA). As an undergraduate, Alana worked at various internships that provided opportunities to network, explore career interests, and map a long-term career path. Alana is currently a business analyst in the health insurance field and uses tools like Tableau to create insights for company decision makers. Alana enjoys traveling with friends and family and bingeing good series on various streaming services.

Why do you believe it is important for accounting professionals to understand data visualization?

Because data visualizations interpret information in a visual format, they can transform information that may be complex into an understandable format for all types of audiences. In today's workforce, data visualizations are crucial because the world around us is constantly evolving. Information is captured and turned into fresh, relevant presentations with data visualizations.

How do you use data visualizations in your daily work?

In my current role, I use tools such as Tableau to create various data visualizations. With Tableau, I can import data and produce dashboards that are utilized by multiple departments throughout my company. These visualizations are mainly used by upper management to measure productivity. They represent what is going well in our business and draw attention to where things can be improved.

Using dashboards in presentations influences a department to set new goals, adapt to future productivity needs, and improve processes. The information in dashboards I create is the basis for departmental changes that increase productivity and efficiency throughout the company.

What recommendations do you have for accounting majors who wish to pursue a career path that includes data visualization?

My biggest advice is to trust the process. This is not something that can be learned, or taught, overnight and it takes time to refine your skills. Your growth heavily depends on your willingness to learn. It's crucial to know how to interpret these visualizations yourself so you can feel confident in presenting your findings. Don't be discouraged if you are not exceling as quickly as you would like. Just be sure to note all the new tips and tricks that you learn along the way and use that for your future growth. In addition, utilize the advice and guidance of your colleagues around you.

Review and Practice

Key Terms Review

bar chart	exploratory analysis	resolution
bin	falling action	rising action
box plot	geospatial location	scatter plot
categorical value	geospatial map	stacked bar chart
climax	histogram	static dashboard
color psychology	icon	storyboard
comparison	iconography	time series
composition	infographic	tooltip
cool colors	interactive dashboard	tree map
dashboard	introduction	typography
dashboard view	landing page	visualization audience
data visualization	line chart	warm colors
design concept	pie chart	white space
distribution	quantitative value	
explanatory analysis	relationship	

Learning Objectives Review

❶ Summarize the importance of user-centric design and storytelling in data visualization.

Data visualization is the presentation of data in a graphical format, such as charts and graphs, that is used for analysis and communication. It turns complete, reliable, and accurate data into a story. Creating a high-quality visualization requires determining how the visualization will be used:

- Understand the visualization audience and their requirements.
  - Who is the user? For example, is it the CEO or the internal audit team?
  - How will the audience use the visualization? Will they view a PowerPoint presentation or drill down into the data?

- What are the audience's technical requirements, such as filters, dashboard layout, or colors?
- Understand the data
- Select the proper visualization technique
- Develop the visualization

To create an effective visualization, a designer should be aware of these things:

- What an effective business presentation should look like
- How a business stakeholder may interpret a visualization
- The appropriate level of detail for the business need
- The value of white space

❷ Apply fundamental design principles to data visualizations.

Data visualizations are based on design concepts. A design concept is the central idea, or theme, of a visualization that drives the design's meaning and tone. Design concepts include color, white space, typography, and iconography.

Color draws attention, incites emotional reactions, and sets the tone:

- There are two families of color. Warm colors are vivid colors like red, orange, and yellow, which are associated with joy, energy, and playfulness. Cool colors like green, blue, and purple evoke feelings of relaxation, calm, and stability.
- Color wheels show the relationships among colors and represent different combinations of colors that go together. It's best to limit the number of colors in a single visualization to no more than four.
- Color psychology is the study of human behavior related to colors. Every color has positive and negative associations, and they can influence human perceptions.
- Color accessibility is important because some people have color vision deficiency (CVD), or color blindness, and they experience colors differently. A solution is to use CVD-friendly color combinations, different tints of the same color, and alternative methods to distinguish data, like text, icons, arrows, annotations, different line widths, or different line styles.

White space is negative space that creates a visual pause in a visualization. It provides many benefits, including:

- Improves comprehension by avoiding distracting visual elements
- Reduces cognitive load by avoiding clutter and distractions
- Focuses attention on the message by isolating it
- Draws attention to interactive opportunities like filters and drilldowns
- Balances important visual elements in an organized manner
- Communicates more clearly by separating unrelated elements into sections

Typography is the choice of a font and its size for use in a visualization. There are some best practices for typography:

- Using the same font and font size throughout an entire visualization creates consistency.
- Using the same font with larger headers makes the headers, or titles, of visualizations stand out.
- Using two fonts that complement one another with the header bolded draws attention to different parts of a visualization.

Iconography involves the choice of which icons to use in a visualization. Icons are symbols of common concepts that provide visual cues along with data, text, or charts and graphs.

❸ Evaluate visualization techniques for exploratory analysis.

Exploratory analysis is the first phase of using visualizations to understand and analyze unknown data:

- It determines what story a visualization can tell.
- Converting raw data into a visual format makes it easier to perform descriptive and diagnostic analyses.

Once we understand the data, we can select the appropriate data visualization techniques to answer these questions:

- Composition of data: What variables are included in the data set?
- Comparison of data points: How is one variable performing compared to other variables in the data set?
- Distribution of data: How often does a variable occur in the data set?
- Relationships between data points: How do the different variables in the data set relate to one another?
- Geospatial location of data points: Where are variables geographically located in the data set?

There are several popular composition and comparison visualizations:

- A pie chart divides a data set into groups proportional to their sizes within the data set.
- A tree map presents groups and subgroups as rectangular portions of the larger whole.
- A bar chart presents categorical data as rectangular bars with heights or lengths proportional to the quantitative values they represent.
- A stacked bar chart illustrates parts of a whole within the rectangular bars of a traditional bar chart.
- A heat map uses different colors to represent values of the data set it visualizes.

Distribution uses statistical functions to determine the relationships between categorical values and quantitative values. There are two common distribution visualizations:

- A histogram provides a visual representation of a numeric distribution based on a user-defined range. It graphs the frequency of values occurring in a data set.
- A box plot illustrates the distribution of quantitative values for a categorical value. Every category has its own box plot diagram, which identifies minimum, maximum, median, and quartile values.

Some visualization techniques identify essential cause-and-effect relationships that provide insights for decision makers:

- A line chart visualizes a time series analysis, which identifies trends or anomalies in data that occurs in chronological order across a time period.
- A scatter plot shows the relationship between two variables by using shapes, such as dots or circles, mapped along the X-axis and Y-axis, which are the two variables being measured for relationships.

Geospatial maps utilize geographic data such as map coordinates, GPS data, and so forth.

4 Describe visualization techniques that are used to create explanatory stories.

Explanatory analysis occurs once the story, or purpose, of a visualization is known and the data is ready to be presented to the audience. During explanatory analysis, visualizations are crafted, the presentation is fine-tuned, and key points are highlighted.

An infographic is a stand-alone visual that tells a story through graphic design and is not likely to require verbal communication for explanation.

A dashboard, which can be static or interactive, is a collection of individual visualizations that allow the audience to view multiple pieces of data at one time.

A storyboard is a collection of dashboards, stand-alone visualizations, infographics, and other presentation materials that turn the data analytics and visualizations into a business presentation. The storyboard follows the story arc, which has five parts:

- Introduction: Introduces characters and settings and describes the presentation, including the subject matter and why it is being presented
- Rising action: Articulates the problem being addressed or question being answered and is the overall story of the presentation that all the data visualization work supports
- Climax: Shows the results of the analytics
- Falling action: Often includes suggestions for improvements or may predict what may happen if the audience takes certain actions
- Resolution: Presents the audience with a powerful call to action

CPA questions, as well as multiple choice, discussion, analysis and application, and Tableau questions and other resources, are available online.

Multiple Choice Questions

1. (LO 1) **CPA** Which statement best describes data visualization?

    a. It creates complex displays using data.

    b. It is the presentation of data in graphical format.

    c. It reduces the demands on human working memory.

    d. It uses technology to create data extractions.

2. (LO 1) Which of the following is *not* one of the steps for creating a high-quality, user-centric data visualization?

    a. Understand the audience

    b. Gather user requirements

    c. Understand the data

    d. Ask which visualization technique to use

3. (LO 1) Charles Schwab wanted to tap into the potential of its data, so it adopted an enterprise-wide data visualization strategy using which software?

    a. Excel

    b. Canva

    c. SAS

    d. Tableau

4. (LO 1) Naureen is creating visualizations that will present big ideas about the core functions of the business, such as accounting, finance, marketing, and sales. Who is most likely her visualization audience?

    a. CEO

    b. Staff accountant

    c. Mid-level manager

    d. Intern

5. (LO 2) Which of the following colors represents loyalty, calmness, and coldness?

    a. Purple

    b. Green

    c. Blue

    d. Yellow

6. (LO 2) Which of the following is *not* one of the reasons white space is important?

    a. It reduces clutter.

    b. It creates balance.

    c. It combines thoughts.

    d. It focuses attention.

7. (LO 2) When using icons, you should *never*

    a. assume that what you see clearly means the same thing for every other person.

    b. ask at least one person to interpret the icon before you use it.

    c. add text labels to the icon.

    d. consider accessibility of the icon.

8. (LO 2) CPA Typography is the choice of _____ in a visual display, while iconography is the choice of _____ in a visual display.

    a. color; icons

    b. fonts; colors

    c. fonts; icons

    d. icons; fonts

9. (LO 3) CPA The following visualization is an example of what type of visualization technique?

    a. Word cloud

    b. Bar chart

    c. Scatter plot

    d. Line chart

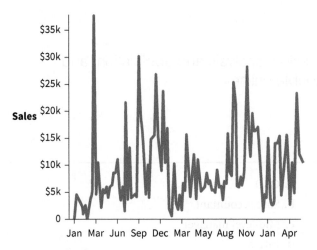

10. (LO 3) CPA The type of visualization shown below, which shows changes in Apple's stock price, is useful in displaying

    a. a distribution of multiple data points.

    b. changes in data over time.

    c. part-to-whole relationships.

    d. simple changes to data across multiple categories.

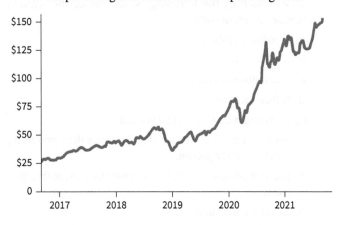

11. (LO 3) CPA The following visualization is an example of a

    a. line chart.   **b.** graph line.

    c. scatterplot.   **d.** bar chart.

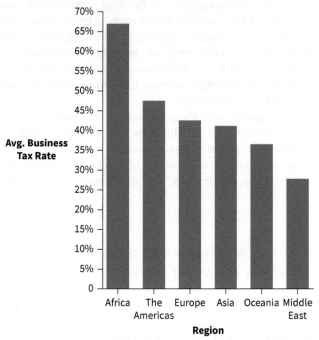

12. (LO 3) CPA A problem with the following visualization is that

    a. this information would be better displayed in a pie chart.

    b. the categories should be sorted alphabetically instead of by "hours worked."

    c. the vertical axis of a bar chart should always start at zero.

    d. bar charts should always include numbers on the bars.

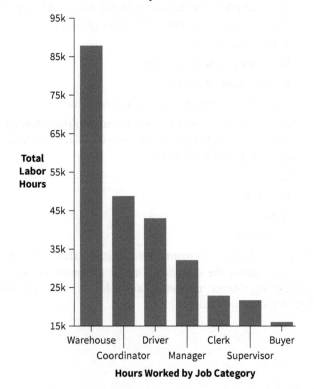

13. (LO 4) A(n) _____ is a visualization that stands alone and tells a story through graphic design.

   a. static dashboard

   b. storyboard

   c. infographic

   d. interactive dashboard

14. (LO 4) Which of the following is a collection of individual visualizations that allows the audience to view multiple pieces of data at once?

   a. Excel workbook

   b. Database

   c. Infographic

   d. Dashboard

15. (LO 4) Which part of the story arc presents suggestions for improvement or predictions of what may happen if the audience takes certain actions?

   a. Rising action

   b. Climax

   c. Falling action

   d. Resolution

Discussion and Research Questions

DQ1. (LO 1) Describe the purpose of data visualization and why it is important in business.

DQ2. (LO 1) `Critical Thinking` You are a lead internal auditor for a medium-sized health care company. You are creating a data visualization to include in a report to the audit committee, which is the governing body that the internal audit department reports to quarterly. The topic of your data visualization is corporate diversity, equity, and inclusion (DEI). What level of information does the audit committee need to see? Describe at least two types of data points your data visualization requires. For example, you may include the number of DEI-related workshops the human resources department hosted last year.

DQ3. (LO 2) `Critical Thinking` A company logo is a visualization created by a graphic designer who carefully selects colors, typography, and iconography that reflect the company's values, mission, and culture. Based on what you have learned about these fundamental design principles, discuss the messaging the Julia's Cookies' logo portrays. Specifically discuss the color selection, typography, and iconography messaging.

DQ4. (LO 2) `Research` Explain the importance of color psychology. Choose two colors and provide examples of how each of them impacts the emotions of a visualization's audience. Use the internet to identify one example of a business logo or visualization that exemplifies this emotional impact for each color.

DQ5. (LO 2) Explain how white space helps an audience understand a visualization.

DQ6. (LO 3) `Research` Choose two of the following public companies and use the internet to locate the latest quarterly (Q1, Q2, Q3, or Q4) financial results presented to shareholders for these companies. Identify, discuss, and compare the visualization techniques used by the two companies in their financial statements. Which type of visualization technique is used most often?

Companies: Walmart, Amazon, Unilever, Samsung, Berkshire Hathaway, Toyota, Alphabet, Exxon Mobil, Tesla

DQ7. (LO 3) Explain two ways in which a data visualization may mislead its audience based on design, structure, or incorrect technique.

DQ8. (LO 3) `Research` `Fraud` Download the most recent charts and graphs from the Association of Certified Fraud Examiners (ACFE) *Report to the Nations.* You can find the charts and graphs in .pdf or .jpg format by navigating to www.acfe.com/rttn-archive.aspx and selecting "Charts and Graphs Only (PDF)" for the most recently archived report, which will be at the top of the web page.

Choose three data visualizations from the report, each illustrating a different type of data visualization technique. Provide the figure number for each visualization you choose (e.g., Fig. 32), identify the visualization technique used for each one, and explain how effective each illustration is at exploratory analysis.

DQ9. (LO 4) `Critical Thinking` You are a senior tax associate at a Big Four public accounting firm. The human resources department is working on new campus recruiting initiatives for accounting majors. They ask you to help brainstorm a one-page infographic to attract college student candidates to join the company. Suggest five data points that should be included in this infographic to grab the attention of accounting majors considering a career with your firm. For example, you may choose to include the fact that your company pays for training materials for candidates who choose to take the CPA exam.

DQ10. (LO 4) `Early Career` `Critical Thinking` You are a senior financial analyst in the accounting department of your company. As part of implementing a new AIS, you are training employees in the accounting and finance departments on enhanced features the new AIS will offer. At the beginning of the training sessions, you surveyed attendees to identify how everyone felt about the new AIS adoption. You then sent a post-training survey to attendees, including the same question. Using the before and after survey data, you have created the vertical bar chart shown on the next page. Describe how you will use this data visualization to tell your managers about the impact of the training sessions you facilitated.

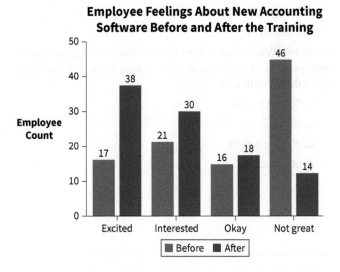

Employee Feelings About New Accounting Software Before and After the Training

DQ11. (LO 1–4) Research Use the internet to find an example of a bad data visualization. Use the fundamentals of design, principles of user-centric design, and tips for the visualization technique to critique the visualization and identify what makes it a bad data visualization.

Application and Analysis Questions

A1. (LO 1–2) Critical Thinking You are a staff accountant preparing data visualizations related to financial reporting that are distributed to department managers throughout the company. Your visualizations compare the budgeted spending to the actual spending of each department over time. Each department will receive the same visualization but populated with that department's specific data.

Visualizations A and B depict two ways of designing your visualization. Identify the emotions each visualization evokes in its audience and select which visualization is the most appropriate version to distribute to department managers.

Visualization A:

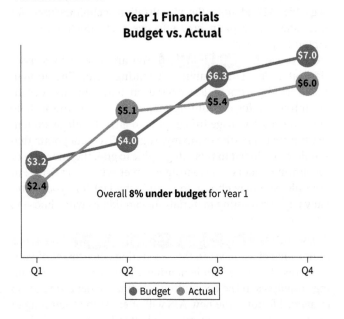

Visualization B:

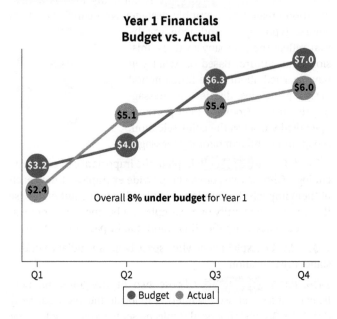

A2. (LO 1–2) Identify an issue in the following dashboard that is caused by not following the fundamental principles of design. Suggest how this dashboard could be improved to address this issue.

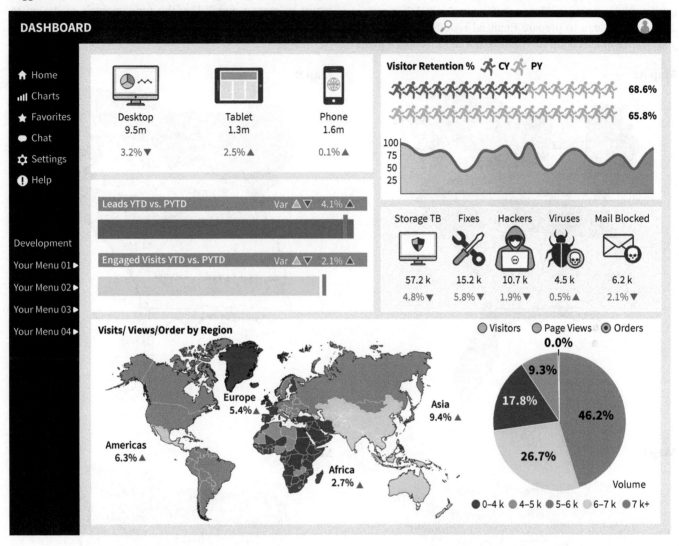

A3. (LO 1–3) [Critical Thinking] You are a financial analyst for Bolt, a fitness gym offering small-group, focused workout classes with a strong market in the eastern United States. You are using Tableau to prepare financial reporting metrics for your management team to visualize the net income of gyms by state location. The following geospatial map visualizations depict the same data. Which of these maps should you use to report to management? Use the fundamentals of design to explain why this map is the best choice.

Map A:

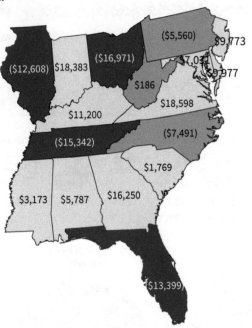

Map B:

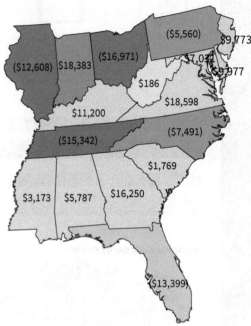

Map C:

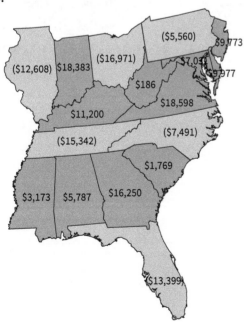

Map D:

A4. (LO 3) [Early Career] [Critical Thinking] As a recent college graduate, you have accepted a position as a cost accountant supporting the supply chain management team at a regional ice cream chain, ScoopsAhoy. As one of your first projects, you are asked to analyze historical data for the number of ice cream cones sold each month for the past year (see the spreadsheet). This analysis will be used to create forecasts of product demand to help the Purchasing department acquire the appropriate raw materials for the Production department.

Visualizations A through E are examples of how you could present this data to your manager. For each visualization example, identify the visualization technique it uses. Then select which visualization is the most appropriate option for visualizing this time series sales data.

	A	B
1	Month	Ice Cream Sales (Number of Cones Sold)
2	January	1,650
3	February	2,005
4	March	2,456
5	April	3,081
6	May	7,900
7	June	14,137
8	July	22,469
9	August	26,146
10	September	18,783
11	October	8,573
12	November	4,243
13	December	1,891

Visualization A:

Visualization B:

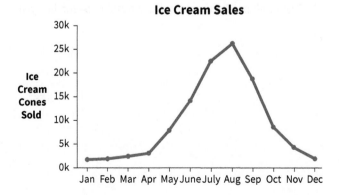

Visualization C:

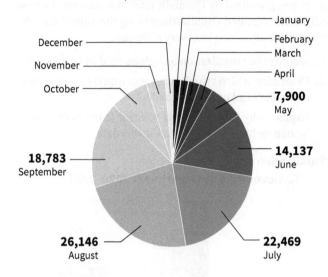

Visualization D:

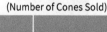

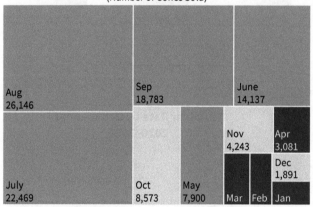

Visualization E:

Month	Ice Cream Sales (Number of Cones Sold)
January	1,650
February	2,005
March	2,456
April	3,081
May	7,900
June	14,137
July	22,469
August	26,146
September	18,783
October	8,573
November	4,243
December	1,891

A5. (LO 3) [Data Analytics] [Critical Thinking] As an audit manager, you have assigned two of your staff auditors to create a visualization depicting the turnover rate for three departments being audited by the audit team this quarter. The two staff auditors created visualizations using the same data; however, the visualizations look very different.

1. Identify the visualization technique used in each option.

2. Determine which visualization you would choose to present to the head of internal audit.

3. Explain why the option you selected is the better visualization technique for presenting this data.

Visualization A:

Turnover Rate by Department 2020–2022

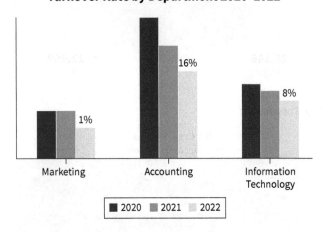

Visualization B:

Turnover Rate by Department 2020–2022

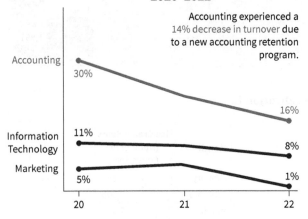

A6. (LO 4) [Critical Thinking] You are a senior data analyst in the compliance department of a global investment firm. You are creating a visualization to inform compliance executive leadership about key metrics related to compliance violations throughout the organization. You have decided to create a one-page infographic to potentially present the following data points:

A. Number of compliance issues opened and closed each month

B. Total vacation time (paid time off) taken by compliance employees each month

C. Compliance employee gender composition, as a percentage of total compliance employees

D. Source of identification of compliance issues each month, such as employee reports, email, and whistleblower hotline

E. Comparison of actual and budgeted employee spending each month

F. Average time of a compliance investigation, from identification to resolution

G. Total number of employee code of conduct violations each month

To ensure that your infographic follows the principles of design by telling a story, using minimalist aesthetics, and avoiding distractors, you decide to include only four of these data points. Which four data points will you include in your one-page infographic? Explain the story these data points tell.

A7. (LO 1–4) The following scenarios describe data analytics that will be visualized for a national pizza chain. For each scenario, identify whether it is best categorized as an exploratory analysis or an explanatory analysis.

Scenarios:

1. Top 10 reasons budgets were increased this year

2. Total number of new customers who joined the rewards program last month

3. Top three reasons customers are reporting dissatisfaction with pizza orders last year

4. This year's annual budget, by regional location

5. Reasons behind different types of customer feedback last year

6. Top 10 store locations with highest sales last month

7. Best-selling pizza topping types in the state of Virginia last year

8. List of all products sold in store number 54265 last year

A8. (LO 1–4) `Data Analytics` `Critical Thinking` You and a college classmate, Ebitzel, have recently been hired by an electric scooter manufacturer, Volt. You are both working on the finance transformation team. Your team's focus is to identify opportunities to improve business processes, use analytics to drive insights, and implement robotic process automation (RPA) to create efficiencies for the finance and accounting teams.

You and Ebitzel are working together on an analytics project to redesign financial reports used by senior management, department managers, and staff accountants. Currently, these three audiences receive the same report, but each group complains that the report does not meet their specific needs.

For the past month, you have been gathering user requirements and assisting in acquiring data. Then you and Ebitzel shared the project information with a data analyst on your team, Greg, who is responsible for developing the dashboards.

This morning, you met with Greg, and he presented Dashboards A through C. Match each of the three dashboards with the audience group and user requirements from the list. Each dashboard belongs to only one audience group.

Audience groups:

1. Senior managers, including the chief executive officer, who need a strategic overview
2. Middle managers, such as managers of individual departments, who need actionable insights
3. Staff accountants, who need detailed information

Dashboard A:

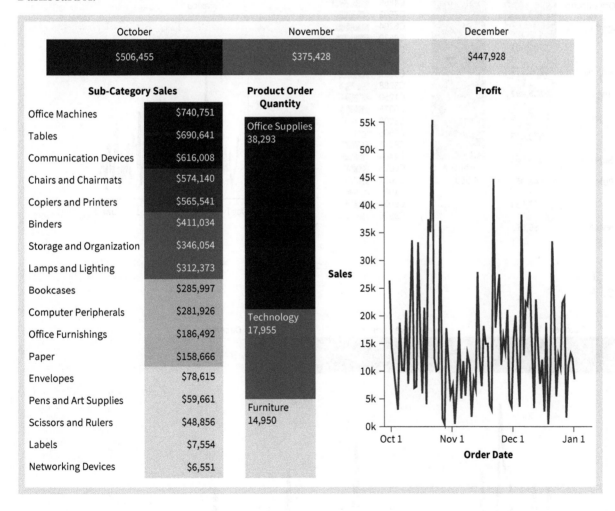

Dashboard B:

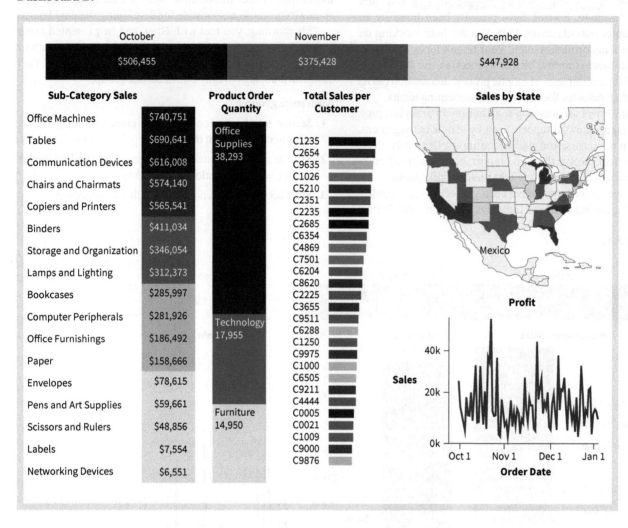

Dashboard C:

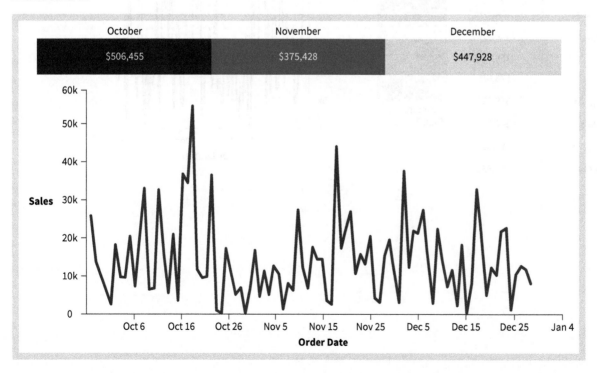

A9. (LO 1–4) `Early Career` `Fraud` `Critical Thinking` You are an external audit associate at a public accounting firm, performing an audit engagement for a global manufacturing client. As part of your team's audit testing, you are analyzing your client's journal entries for fraud risk. To assist with the fraud testing, you have transformed your client's journal entry transaction data into Visualizations A through C. For each of these data visualizations, match the visualization to the fraud journal entry test it's performing and identify the visualization technique used.

Fraud journal entry tests:

1. Testing for unusual dollar activities by reviewing the average journal entry amounts each month for the past year. This test revealed that there was an unusually high average dollar amount for journal entries posted in one month.

2. Testing for unusual user activities by reviewing the number of journal entries posted by each user. This test revealed that there is one user who posted an unusual number of journal entries.

3. Testing for unusual cutoff activities by reviewing the number of journal entries posted every day for the reporting period and the subsequent three days. This test revealed that there was an unusual increase in the number of journal entries posted on the final day of the reporting period followed by a steep decrease in the number of journal entries posted on the first day after cutoff.

Visualization A:

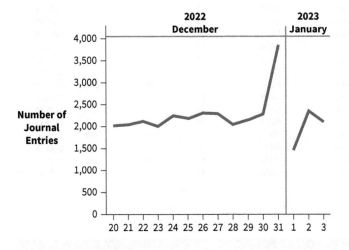

Visualization B:

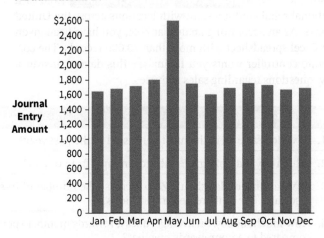

Visualization C:

User ID	Q1	Q2	Q3	Q4
L00001	602	680	625	637
L00002	710	752	740	732
L00003	650	621	663	684
L00004	675	730	704	728
L00005	620	694	702	708
L00006	702	763	1,235	1,320
L00007	646	721	734	698
L00008	691	736	766	757

A10. (LO 3–4) [Early Career] [Critical Thinking] Zolo is a national retail clothing store with locations across the United States. As an accounting analyst at Zolo, you have been given an Excel spreadsheet with more than 70,000 records. The corporate controller wants you to analyze this data to answer a few questions regarding sales activities.

For each of the following scenarios, identify the spreadsheet data field names that you need to answer the scenario's question and the visualization technique that best fits. Use the sample of the first 30 records in the Excel spreadsheet to identify the data field names you need.

Scenario	Data Fields Needed	Visualization Technique
1. In which state were the most items sold in the past year?		
2. Which day did Zolo make the most money from orders?		
3. At what time of day should Zolo increase the number of in-store associates due to increased transactions?		
4. How much money, on average, does a rewards member spend compared to a nonrewards member?		
5. What are the highest, lowest, and median order amounts in this data set?		

Sample spreadsheet data:

	A	B	C	D	E	F	G	H	I	J
1	transaction_ID	transaction_date	transaction_hour	location_state	location_city	rewards_member	num_of_items	coupon_flag	discount_amt	order_amt
2	TID_00012546	10/1/2021	5:46 PM	Georgia	Albany	TRUE	9			$183.93
3	TID_00012547	10/1/2021	2:25 PM	Florida	Pompano Beach	TRUE	22			$119.07
4	TID_00012548	10/1/2021	4:55 PM	Florida	Fort Lauderdale	TRUE	12			$ 82.88
5	TID_00012549	10/1/2021	4:31 PM	Florida	Tampa	TRUE	6			$282.55
6	TID_00012550	10/1/2021	6:04 PM	Florida	Jacksonville	TRUE	45			$269.31
7	TID_00012551	10/1/2021	12:53 PM	Alabama	Montgomery	FALSE	31			$162.01
8	TID_00012552	10/1/2021	2:09 PM	Florida	Daytona Beach	TRUE	5			$ 96.18
9	TID_00012553	10/1/2021	7:13 PM	Florida	Miami	FALSE	19			$281.38
10	TID_00012554	10/1/2021	1:29 PM	Mississippi	Jackson	FALSE	41			$213.08
11	TID_00012555	10/1/2021	5:55 PM	Florida	Orlando	TRUE	25			$139.18
12	TID_00012556	10/1/2021	6:27 PM	Georgia	Lawrenceville	FALSE	47			$ 90.63
13	TID_00012557	10/1/2021	8:29 PM	Florida	Naples	FALSE	28	Yes	16%	$113.58
14	TID_00012558	10/1/2021	7:02 PM	Florida	North Port	TRUE	27			$109.77
15	TID_00012559	10/1/2021	8:52 PM	Florida	Miami	FALSE	22			$172.49
16	TID_00012560	10/1/2021	5:34 PM	Alabama	Birmingham	FALSE	50			$219.45
17	TID_00012561	10/1/2021	4:16 PM	Florida	Orlando	TRUE	9	Yes	31%	$199.06
18	TID_00012562	10/1/2021	11:22 AM	Georgia	Savannah	FALSE	6			$ 43.19
19	TID_00012563	10/1/2021	6:07 PM	Georgia	Atlanta	FALSE	53	Yes	16%	$216.81
20	TID_00012564	10/1/2021	3:09 PM	Alabama	Huntsville	FALSE	51			$ 32.37

Tableau Case: Julia's Cookies' Sales Dashboard

What You Need

Download Tableau to your computer. You can access www.tableau.com/academic/students to download your free Tableau license for the year, or you can download it from your university's software offerings.

Download the following file from the book's product page on www.wiley.com:

Chapter 18 Raw Data.xlsx

Case Background

Big Picture:

Design an interactive dashboard that tells the story of corporate sales.

Details:

Why is this data important, and what questions or problems need to be addressed?

- Analyzing daily sales data can create insights into customers' buying behavior.
- Armed with insights into customers' buying behavior, management can make decisions about marketing campaigns, sales revenue forecasting, inventory purchasing requirements, and product scheduling needs.
- In this analysis, we consider three questions: Which state sells the most products? At what time of day do Julia's Cookies' locations receive the most orders? Which product type generates the highest revenue?

Plan:

What data is needed, and how should it be analyzed?

- The data needed to answer these questions is captured by the Sales and Production modules of the ERP system and stored in the Orders, Products, and Stores tables in the underlying database.
- The extracted data has been filtered to include only one day of product sales in the United States.

Now it's your turn to evaluate, analyze, and communicate the results!

To answer the questions, connect the tables using their ID fields:

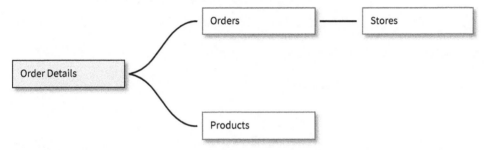

Questions

1. How many different types of products does Julia's Cookies offer?
2. Which two products have the highest sales price? (Hint: Consider the unit price.)
3. Which state had the largest number of orders? (Hint: Consider OrderID.)
4. What is the total number of products sold in Texas?
5. Which product was sold the most in Alabama? (Hint: Consider individual cookie counts.)
6. In which city were the fewest M&M cookies sold?
7. In which city was the total number of products sold the highest?
8. At what time did the highest total number of products sold throughout the United States occur?

Take it to the next level!

9. Which product generated the highest dollar amount of gross sales in the United States?
10. Which city generated the highest dollar amount of gross sales from the sale of sugar cookies?

Glossary

A

access attack An attack in which hackers attempt to gain unauthorized access to a network and its information by exploiting vulnerabilities discovered during reconnaissance.

access control vestibule A pair of doors in which only one of the doors can be open at any one time. It increases security by allowing only one person to be in the middle of the two sets of doors at a time. Also called a *mantrap*.

accounting information system (AIS) An information system that performs data collection, transformation, and reporting that is specific to financial data. It captures accounting data created by business events (or activities) that involves an exchange of economic resources.

accounts payable An account that records money which business owes to its suppliers and vendors. It is shown as a liability on the balance sheet.

acquisition One company's purchase of all or the majority of another company's shares to gain control over that company.

acquisition-based growth Growth in a company that occurs when it purchases and integrates other companies into its infrastructure.

activity-based costing (ABC) A method of assigning costs to products and services that involves assigning indirect overhead costs to business activity pools or processes based on direct consumption of resources rather than allocating them arbitrarily using traditional costing.

actual residual risk The risk that actually remains after a risk is addressed.

administrator role The highest role in the role-based access control hierarchy, which has permissions for all objects. In other words, people in this role have unlimited access themselves and are also the ones who assign access roles to the other users. This role is assigned to very few people. There may, for example, be only two people with this level of access: the primary administrator and the backup person.

Agile auditing A type of auditing that is performed in short time spans called sprints—such as two or four weeks for all the fieldwork for one engagement—by auditors who are fully dedicated to a single engagement until it's completed.

Agile methodology A group of systems development life cycle (SDLC) methodologies that focus on iterative development, collaboration, and self-organized, cross-functional teams. Characterized by multiple short cycles of work that simultaneously include multiple SDLC stages, Agile involves end users in real-time decision making as the project progresses.

aligned assurance An Institute of Internal Auditors–supported initiative that promotes the cohesive and collaborative efforts of the second and third lines of defense to provide appropriate coverage over a company's risks. Without aligned assurance, the second and third lines of defense work independently.

analysis stage The second stage of the systems development life cycle, in which systems analysts meet with end users to understand business requirements of a project. This is a critical step in a systems development project. The information captured here provides a roadmap for programmers.

anomaly detection A data analytic objective that reveals observations or events that are outside of a data set's expected or normalized behavior. Also called *outlier analysis*.

application control A control that only applies to a specific application, including all the business processes and accounts that are linked to it.

application software A type of software that allows end users to perform specific functions. Application software may be designed for general use or a specific function. It may also be custom developed for a specific function. Also called an *application* or an *app*.

artificial intelligence (AI) A type of automation that involves computer systems trained to perform tasks that typically require human intelligence. It uses complex algorithms to learn and solve problems without human intervention.

asset misappropriation Theft of corporate assets, including cash, inventory, fixed assets, and information such as customer lists and intellectual property.

audit canvas An Agile version of a planning memo that includes audit information that stakeholders need to know.

audit committee A committee of a company's board of directors that includes outside committee members with special qualifications in finance or accounting. The audit committee provides objective oversight of a company's financial reporting, internal controls, and regulatory compliance, and the company's internal audit department should have a direct line of communication to this committee.

audit deliverable A formal communication of information, such as results or plans, that internal audit provides to an auditee, management, or leaders in the internal audit department.

audit fieldwork The assessment of the adequacy of internal controls, compliance, and business processes. It involves testing transactions, data, and other procedures necessary to accomplish the audit objectives. Fieldwork consists of information gathering, tests of controls, and substantive audit procedures.

audit findings The results of an audit, such as written explanations of errors, improper activities, control weaknesses or deficiencies, and discovered fraud.

audit kickoff meeting A meeting during which an internal audit team presents its plans—including the audit planning memo—to the auditee and captures any immediate feedback or concerns before the audit begins.

audit opinion The section of an audit report that presents the auditors' conclusions.

audit plan A complete list of all audit engagements an audit team will perform in the upcoming period. This plan requires an audit risk assessment, during which internal audit leadership and managers use data points collected from the business and professional judgment to identify risky areas in the company's operations.

audit planning memo A document that includes key audit planning information, such as the reason for the audit, audit team members, timelines, and scope details.

audit recommendations Information auditors provide to an auditee that includes the cause of an issue, details about the root cause, and suggested actions management can take to address the finding.

audit report The results of an audit engagement, which must be filed according to applicable regulatory requirements.

audit trail Documentation that allows auditors to verify the accuracy and validity of accounting transactions. For example, source documents from the purchase of raw materials, conversion to finished goods, and sale of a product are combined to show the audit trail of an inventory item's life cycle.

audit workpapers Formal documentation capturing the control testing performed by auditors. During wrap-up, auditors ensure that workpapers are complete, organized, and properly reviewed by audit managers. These workpapers are then referenced in the audit report.

auditee A business function that is being audited.

auditing The systematic and independent review of data, information, records, and operations of a business to provide assurance of the design and effectiveness of internal controls and the efficiency of processes.

Automated Clearing House (ACH) Network An electronic system that serves financial institutions and facilitates financial transactions in the United States.

automated control A control that uses technology to implement control activities and requires no human intervention. Automated controls are often more reliable and consistent than manual controls because they are not susceptible to human error, judgment, or override. Automated controls include embedded IT controls and controls that use other automation technologies, such as robotics, to perform what have traditionally been manual tasks.

autonomous things (AuT) Physical devices controlled by computers using complex algorithms. Human interaction is required to establish the programming, but from there, these devices are self-regulating. The devices come in the form of drones and robots.

B

background check Verification from a third-party company of a prospective hire's historical residential addresses, prior employment, and criminal history.

backup cycle A schedule that determines when data backup occurs—that is, the frequency with which data is backed up. A common backup cycle is the grandfather-father-son cycle.

backup site A physical location where company personnel will go to recover systems and data after a disaster. A backup site is a re-creation of a data center and provides the company with a place of operations in the event that the data center is impacted during a disaster.

backup strategy A plan that determines which data is being stored during a data backup. There are three basic types of backup strategies: full, differential, and incremental.

balanced scorecard An internal assessment, improvement, and reporting tool that ties a measurement system to an organization's strategic plan. It provides key performance indicators for management to perform its function and turn strategy into action.

bank remittance report A source document that lists the checks received from customers throughout a day.

bar chart A visualization that presents categorical data as rectangular bars with heights or lengths proportional to the quantitative values they represent.

basic business model A fundamental model that consists of three primary types of business processes: acquisitions and payments processes; conversion processes; and marketing, sales, and collections processes.

batch processing In a transaction processing system, a type of processing in which data is collected as it is generated and then is processed later, at a scheduled time. Because transactions are processed together in a batch—whether at the end of a day, week, or month—batch processing is most suitable for transactions that are not time sensitive.

behavioral red flag A clue that indicates the possibility a person may be involved with a fraud. The presence of red flags does not mean a fraud is being committed. Instead, red flags are warning signs indicating potential fraud.

bid rigging A risk for acquisition of assets or services that involves collusion between competitors or between a vendor and an employee. In one form of bid rigging, an employee colludes with a vendor to obtain by fraudulent means a contract meant to be subject to a competitive bidding process. Because of "insider information" illegally obtained from an employee, often in a kickback arrangement, the vendor wins the bidding process. In another form of bid rigging, vendors collude with one another and reach advance agreement about the winning bidder for a particular contract. The winning bidder agrees to compensate the other vendors in some manner.

big data Extremely large and complex data sets that can be analyzed to reveal patterns and associations. Big data often is so large, generated so fast, and so unstructured that it surpasses the limitations of traditional systems and databases.

bill of materials (BOM) A source document that specifies the components of a product, including descriptions and quantities of required raw materials and parts.

bill of operations (BOO) A source document that specifies the sequence of production events. In technology-driven manufacturing, an automated bill of operations is embedded in the information system and digitally tracks a product through the manufacturing process. Also called an *operations list*.

billing scheme A fraudulent disbursement scheme in which an employee fraudulently submits or alters an invoice for personal gain, and the employer pays the invoice.

bin A defined range in a histogram that is plotted as a bar where the height is equal to the total occurrences of that range in the data set.

binary code A two-symbol system in a digital computer environment that uses the digits 1 and 0 to assign a pattern that represents a letter, a digit, or another character. Computer systems operate in binary code, storing data and performing calculations using only binary digits.

bitcoin The first cryptocurrency, which has been the most successful use case of blockchain technology because of the decentralized and transparent validation of bitcoin transactions.

block coding A type of coding used in a chart of accounts in which blocks of sequential numbers are reserved for specific types of accounts.

blockchain A system that enables the recording of digital transactions packaged in blocks that form a sequence, like a chain, in a peer-to-peer network. These blocks are distributed and visible to all participants in the network in a way that makes changing, cheating, or hacking the system almost impossible. Blockchain is a sequence of blocks containing unchangeable ledgers of transactions, and each block in the chain has a logical relationship with the preceding block.

botnet A number of computers infected with malware that function like robots. The botnets are programmed to do whatever attackers want, such as flooding a specific host with repetitive requests to consume the target system's capacity.

box plot A visualization that illustrates the distribution of quantitative values for a categorical value. Every category has its own box plot diagram, which identifies minimum, maximum, median, and quartile values.

break-even analysis The process of comparing known fixed costs to estimated variable costs to predict the point of loss, break-even point, and profitability.

brute-force attack An attack in which attackers force access to a network by attempting many passwords or phrases until they find the correct one.

business activity *See* business event.

business continuity planning (BCP) A set of procedures that a business undertakes to protect employees, other stakeholders, and assets in the event of a disruptive event (for example, flood, tornado, cyberattack, political disturbance, or pandemic). BCP ensures that a business and all its processes continue running.

business event A single business activity in a business process that takes place during the normal operation of a business. Examples of business events include "sell goods to customer" and "purchase equipment from vendor." Business events give rise to accounting transactions if they involve an exchange of economic resources that impacts the accounting equation. Also called a *business activity*.

business function A high-level business area or department that performs business processes to achieve company goals. More than one business function may be necessary to complete a single business process.

business model A company's plan for operations. It identifies the customer base, products, operation plans, and sources of revenue and financing.

business process A group of related business events designed to accomplish the strategic objectives of a business.

business process automation The process of managing information, data, costs, resources, and investments by increasing productivity through automating key business processes with computing technology.

Business Process Model and Notation (BPMN) A documentation method that depicts the steps of a business process from start to finish. BPMN is a standardized methodology managed by the Object Management Group, which is an organization that offers certifications for process improvement specialists to become credentialed BPMN analysts. BPMN creates a visualization that can be easier to understand than a narrative description.

business rule A written statement that precisely captures a business event occurring during a process as it relates to the entities in a database. When written correctly, business rules define the entities, relationships, cardinalities, and constraints of a database.

business-to-business (B2B) Describes a company that sells finished goods to other businesses, like distributors and retail companies.

business-to-consumer (B2C) Describes a company that sells finished goods directly to customers. It delivers goods to a customer in person at or near the time of sale or by delivery to the customer's address.

C

capital expenditures (CAPEX) The business world term for the costs of acquiring fixed assets.

capitalization of expenses A fraud scheme that understates expenses and overstates net income by recognizing inappropriate costs as assets and expensing them over time instead of in the current reporting period.

cardinality In relational databases, a numeric relationship between two tables that consists of two constraints: plurality and optionality.

cash disbursements journal An accounting journal that contains a record of a company's payments, in chronological order.

categorical value A descriptive component of a data set that can be used to summarize data for analysis. Categorical values are qualitative in nature.

center of excellence (COE) A specialized team in a company that is dedicated to providing unique support, usually technological, to the entire business.

centralized ledger A ledger system in which participants have access to a central ledger. For example, the general ledger is a centralized ledger that businesses use as the backbone for financial accounting; it contains all the ledger accounts for recording transactions related to a company's assets, liabilities, owners' equity, revenue, and expenses.

centralized system An information system that connects all users to one central location that is built around a server or cluster of servers that all authorized users can access. All the network's main business processing occurs at, and business information is stored in, that one place.

change management A standardized process that decreases risk by controlling the identification and implementation of required changes to a system.

change management process A process that consists of three stages that changes to a system's code must pass through. These stages occur in isolated environments that enforce segregation of duties for each of the three steps of the process: (1) creating changes in the test environment, (2) evaluating accuracy of changes in the model environment, and (3) implementing changes in the production environment.

channel stuffing A type of fraud that occurs when revenue and profits are intentionally inflated by recognizing revenue from unnecessary sales in the current quarter or year.

chart of accounts A classification scheme used to organize financial data and summarize financial measurements of assets, liabilities, and owners' equity. It provides a list of all the accounts in the general ledger, organized in subcategories.

checklist A questionnaire that may consist of questions, items to review, or steps to perform during an audit engagement.

class In the context of object-oriented databases, an entity that connects similar objects together.

classification analysis The categorization of data into groups based on similarities found in a data label that was previously defined. Classification uses supervised machine learning (ML) to analyze labeled data inputs.

climax The point of highest emotion or turning point in a story. It shows the results of the analytics that have been performed. Whether it's the success of a high-performing department or the discovery of risky behaviors or transactions, the climax is where the audience is most interested.

cloud computing A type of computing that provides access to shared resources over the internet, such as computer processing, software applications, data storage, and other services. In the business context, cloud computing allows companies to minimize computer resources kept on hand, which can be expensive to both purchase and securely store. The costs are absorbed by the cloud provider, which maintains the physical equipment at its facility and provides access to customers via the cloud network.

cluster A group of data points.

clustering An analytics technique that categorizes data points into groups based on their similarities. Also known as *cluster analysis*.

COBIT 2019 The most widely used international standard for IT governance, which is designed to help companies meet regulatory compliance requirements, manage IT risks, and ensure that IT strategies are aligned with corporate goals.

coding system A chart of accounts system that logically records, classifies, stores, and extracts financial data using coding techniques made up of numbers and/or letters.

cold backup site A backup site that is an almost empty room with no servers or equipment ready. It has physical space, power, climate control, and physical security controls but is otherwise unequipped. A cold backup site is the cheapest option, but it is the type of site that takes the most time to begin using.

collusion A secretive agreement to deceive others when two or more people work together to circumvent controls. For example, if a control requires one employee to input invoices into the accounts payable system and a different employee to approve payments for the invoices, these two employees could work together (that is, collude) to commit fraud by inputting a fictitious invoice and authorizing the payment to go to a bank account they control.

color psychology The study of human behavior related to colors. Every color has positive and negative associations that can influence human perceptions.

commands A programming language instruction. In particular, a SQL command is an instruction sent to a database to perform tasks like creating items and querying existing data.

Committee of Sponsoring Organizations of the Treadway Commission (COSO) An organization that is committed to fighting corporate fraud. It is composed of five private organizations that focus on providing guidance to executives and government entities on fraud prevention and response. COSO helps publicly traded companies comply with SOX and the SEC requirement of using an internal control framework.

comparison How one variable is performing compared to other variables in a data set.

compensating control A control that can be used to reduce risk when more expensive or more complex controls are not available.

competitive advantage A position or strategy that places a company in a superior position to its competitors.

compliance risk Risk that occurs when a company fails to follow regulation and legislation and is subjected to legal penalties, including fines.

composition The variables that are included in a data set.

conceptual design A document created by the lead system analyst that summarizes a system's purpose and resource requirements, as well as the planned flow of data through the system.

conditional statement A statement used in a variety of programming situations to pre-program "rules," or decisions, into the software. A conditional statement may take the form "IF THIS THEN THAT." Conditional statements are used in a variety of programming situations, including robotic process automation, data analytics, systems and software development, and website development. You can even program a conditional statement in an Excel field.

confidence interval An estimate derived from observed data that shows a range of possible values.

configurable ERP system An enterprise resource planning (ERP) system that has some add-ins and features that can be customized for customers' needs.

confirmation bias The tendency to make decisions based on what we already believe. When we ask advice only from people who share our own worldview, we risk hearing only what we want to hear. By using inherently biased data for an analytics task, we risk decision making that omits relevant facts about the big picture.

connector In a process flowchart, a shape that is used when a flowchart is large enough to span multiple pages. Connectors are always filled with a letter, starting with "A." The connector on the first page appears at the end of the flowchart on that page, and the connector on the next page appears at the beginning. The letter inside the two related connectors is the same. Essentially, you end at "A" on one page and begin again at "A" on the next page.

consolidated financial statements Financial statements of a company that has one or more subsidiaries. The separate financial statements of the companies are combined into a single set of financial statements, as if all the companies were a single entity. From an AIS reporting perspective, consolidations add an additional layer of complexity, especially at fiscal year end, when timelines are tight.

consortium blockchain A consortium of companies that collaborate and leverage information to improve workflows, accountability, and transparency. An example is a manufacturer working with logistics companies to form a blockchain supply chain. This type of blockchain allows for transaction privacy, with a selected group of participating members controlling the network and setting the rules. Its permissions structure is more complex than for a private blockchain, as individual companies still want to keep certain transactions private.

continuous monitoring Data analytics technology that internal auditors use to create detective controls that use rules-based programming to monitor a business's data for red flags of risks. Continuous monitoring is often programmed to keep tabs on key performance indicators (KPIs) or to look for red flags indicating possible fraud.

control A mechanism that is part of the internal control process—such as a rule, policy, or procedure—and that is put in place to mitigate risks by providing reasonable assurance that risk is at an acceptable level. Also known as a *control activity*.

control component One of the five key steps of the COSO Internal Control Framework involved in implementing an effective system of internal control. The control components flow from the top to the bottom of a business, starting with the control environment and ending with monitoring. Control components and their related principles help framework users understand what an effective control is and how to judge whether a control is effectively designed and implemented.

control environment The first of the COSO Internal Control Framework control components. It is the foundation for other components and includes the attitude of management concerning integrity and ethical behavior. It is the most important component because it sets the overall tone for integrity and ethics for the organization.

control objective One of the three areas on which the COSO Internal Control Framework focuses to achieve results: operations objectives, reporting objectives, and compliance objectives.

conversion processes Operating business activities that combine resources (inputs) and convert them into products or services (outputs) that appeal to customers, whether they are clients, patients, or students. The resources used differ depending on the type of business.

cool colors Colors like green, blue, and purple that evoke feelings of relaxation, calm, and stability.

corrective control A control that changes undesirable outcomes and occurs after the potential outcome of a risk has become a reality. Corrective controls are used when it is not cost-effective to implement preventive or detective controls to mitigate a specific risk. They are also used as a backup plan in the event of a failure of preventive or detective controls.

corruption The inappropriate use of influence to obtain a benefit contrary to the perpetrator's responsibility or the rights of other people.

cost accounting A subset of managerial accounting that focuses on capturing and recording a company's total cost of production by identifying and recording the variable costs in each step of production, in addition to fixed costs such as factory rent or depreciation. It is part of managerial accounting, but it is specific to the conversion processes and has a narrower focus: quantitative product cost measured in monetary terms and entered into the accounting records.

credit criteria The factors used to determine the financial strength of customers.

crow's foot notation In an entity relationship diagram, shapes at the end of each line between entities that indicate relationships. Each side of a relationship line has two symbols: one for the plurality constraint and one for the optionality constraint.

cumulative payroll journal The year-to-date payroll journal.

Customer Relationship Management (CRM) module An enterprise resource planning (ERP) system module that captures and stores all customer information. It captures communication with customers like emails and phone calls and can generate leads of prospective customers for sales team members to contact.

customizable ERP system An enterprise resource planning (ERP) system in which the features are customized for an individual customer's needs.

cyber risk A unique type of technology risk that occurs when an external party accesses a company's technology assets and performs unauthorized actions that are malicious. For example, cyberattacks can cause data breaches or lock down a company's systems and hold them for ransom. Attackers may simply mean to prove that they have the skill needed to perform attacks successfully.

cyber-kill chain The life cycle of a cyber-attack from early stages of information gathering through final steps of damaging the network. The cyber-kill chain has three steps: (1) gathering information about the network, (2) accessing the network, and (3) disrupting the network.

cybersecurity The measures a company takes to protect a computer or system—including those on the internet—against unauthorized access or attacks.

D

dashboard A static or interactive collection of individual visualizations that allow the audience to view multiple pieces of data at one time.

dashboard view A dashboard function that allows users to save specified filters within a dashboard for easy access during future dashboard usage.

data Facts or statistics collected together for reference or analysis, including numbers, words, measurements, observations, or even just descriptions. For example, your personal data includes your first and last names, birthdate, address, and more. This information doesn't have to be stored on a computer to be considered data.

data analytics The process of using technology to transform raw data, or facts, into useful information. Data analytics answers strategic questions beyond historical reporting by transforming data into insights. It can use either raw data from an information system or reports generated by an information system.

data backup   A copy of computer data that is stored in a separate location so it can be used to restore data to a system if the original data is lost.

data center   An area in a building—or even an entire building—that is dedicated to the physical storage of computer and telecommunication systems. Data centers can be either onsite or offsite. Also known as a *network operations center (NOC).*

data composition   The various characteristics of a data set.

data control language (DCL)   A subset of SQL that grants access to or removes access from a database user.

data definition language (DDL)   A subset of SQL that changes the structure of a database by adding or changing tables and relationships.

data dictionary   A detailed description of the fields in a table and their data type (text, numeric, date, etc.). A data dictionary provides descriptions that end users can reference when they need data from the database.

data flow diagram (DFD)   A graphical representation of the flow of data in an information system. A DFD describes the processes used in a system to manage the life cycle of the data, from generation (input) to storage (databases) to reporting (output).

data flow line   In a Gane-Sarson data flow diagram, an arrow that indicates movement of data between external entities, processes, and data stores. The data flow line is labeled with the type of data being transmitted, such as "Purchase order" or "Order data." Data flow lines can have arrows at both ends to depict a two-way flow of information.

data integrity   The completeness, accuracy, reliability, and consistency of data throughout its life cycle in an information system.

data lake   A vast pool of data in its raw format—before it's cleaned, aggregated, or filtered—that is designed to contain all of a company's data. A data lake acts as a central repository for data that is stored even though its purpose may not yet be known.

data manipulation language (DML)   A subset of SQL that modifies the data within a database.

data mart   A subset of a data warehouse that is designed for a specific business function. A department uses a data mart for its individual reporting needs. Companies often have multiple data marts throughout their various business areas.

data modeling   The process of documenting data that will be stored in a database and identifying its specifications. These specifications include the fields that will be stored, the associations between fields and tables, and the rules that govern the associations.

data privacy principles   Organizations must follow the data privacy principles that tell people how to gather, use, and share personal information.

Data Query Language (DQL)   A subset of SQL that retrieves data from a database based on user requests.

data redundancy   Repetition of the same piece of data stored in multiple places.

data store shape   A Gane-Sarson data flow diagram shape that represents a data repository such as a database or data warehouse. The data store retains data for later use. A data store can also be the beginning or ending of a data flow diagram. A "D" and numeric, such as the "D1" label, identifies the data store for quick reference.

data subject   A data subject is a person. In order to give individuals control over their personal data, laws have specified data subject rights, which may be generic or applied under specific circumstances.

data summarization   The process of simplifying data to quickly identify trends. It involves compressing the data into smaller, easier-to-understand outputs such as charts or tables.

data type   A data attribute that indicates to a system how the user will use the data. The system stores the data in the specific data type format. Examples of data types include text, number, and date.

data visualization   The presentation of data in a graphical format, such as a chart or graph, for analysis and communication.

data warehouse   An enterprise-wide data repository that is designed specifically for reporting and data analysis and contains relevant data that has already been transformed for reporting use. Data warehouses are relational databases; they store historical data that's structured into related tables. Since a data warehouse is designed to be used for reporting, it has a predefined schema, and data ingested into the warehouse must fit that format.

database   A set of logically related tables (files) containing an organized collection of data that is accessible for fast searching and retrieval.

DCF model   It is a method of valuing an asset or a company by projecting its future cash flows and discounting them to the present value using an appropriate discount rate. The DCF model is based on the principle that the value of an asset is equal to the present value of its expected future cash flows.

decentralization   A characteristic of blockchain that eliminates the need for an intermediary or a central authority to process, validate, or authenticate transactions. Decentralization of power leads to transparency, which in turn leads to immutability.

decentralized ledger   A ledger system in which groups of users have access to hubs that have copies of the same ledgers.

decentralized system   An information system that, rather than having a single location, utilizes multiple locations that each maintain a copy of the data needed for connected systems. In a decentralized network, there are multiple access points for users, but not all users are connected to all access points. Decentralized systems may be used when there are regional offices that process data, then summarize it and communicate the data back to headquarters.

decision context   The preferences, constraints, and other factors that affect how a decision is made. The decision context helps understand the intended use of information: Who are the users, and why do they need the information?

decision shape   A process flowchart shape that represents a yes/no or true/false question that must be answered for the process to continue on the correct flowline. When the flowchart reaches a decision, it splits into two branches—one for the answer "Yes" and one for the answer "No." A decision shape must have a single flowline entering it and two flowlines exiting it.

decision support system (DSS)   An information system that assists in nonroutine problem solving and unstructured decision making.

decryption   The process of converting an encrypted message back to its original form by decoding it so that the recipient can read it. To break the secret code, an authorized user needs a secret key.

delivery receipt   A source document that contains order details, contents of the delivery, and customer information and that accompanies a product.

denial-of-service (DoS) attack   An attack that prohibits users from using resources such as computers, websites, servers, or an entire network. DoS attacks deny users access to resources they have a legitimate need to use. To accomplish this, attackers continuously send fake requests to the business to consume the system's capacity, resulting in loss of availability for real users. The resources become temporarily or even indefinitely unavailable.

dependent variable   In linear regression, the value to be understood. It is often called the *outcome.*

deposit slip   A source document that provides proof of the amount deposited into a company's bank account, with the amount of the deposit equal to the total on the bank remittance report.

descriptive analytics   A category of data analytics that uses historical data to examine what has happened. Descriptive analytics provides decision makers with information about historical activities and performance to assist them in making decisions. It is the first phase of data analytics in the Gardner model.

design concept The central idea, or theme, of a visualization that drives the design's meaning and tone.

design effectiveness A test that determines whether a control, if operated as prescribed, meets a company's control objectives and effectively prevents or detects errors or fraud.

design stage The third stage of a systems development life cycle project, which involves translating the requirements definition into technical specifications.

detective control A control that alerts management to an issue once it has occurred. Detective controls monitor business processes to identify problems like fraud, quality control, or legal compliance issues.

development stage The fourth stage of a systems development life cycle project, during which programmers create a system based on technical specifications identified in the design stage.

diagnostic analytics A category of data analytics that uses historical data to examine why something happened. Diagnostic analytics provides decision makers with insights into descriptive analytics by identifying the influencing factors in the data. It is the second phase of data analytics in the Gardner model.

dictionary attack An attack in which attackers use lists of commonly used words and combinations of words and letters to guess passwords.

differential backup A backup that involves copying only the new data created since the most recent full backup. Differential backups are the middle ground of backup strategies. They take a moderate amount of time and storage space.

digital manufacturing Manufacturing that involves automated, digital processes using Industrial Internet of Things (IIoT) technologies. IIoT devices continually analyze data, in real time, to detect underutilization of resources, report inefficiencies, and expose errors. Because employees are receiving this information immediately, they are able to make real-time corrections.

digital twin A digital duplicate or software model of a physical object that uses real-world data about the subject (inputs) to produce predictions or simulations of how the inputs impact the subject (outputs). Sensors on the subject gather data that is sent to the digital twin in real time, allowing the twin to simulate the counterpart to immediately provide insights into performance and potential faults.

direct labor For accounting purposes, the salaries, wages, and benefits expenses of employees directly involved in the production process.

direct material costs Costs of raw materials or parts that go directly into making products, like flour, butter, and sugar for making cookie dough or engine parts for an automobile manufacturer.

direct-to-consumers business model A business model that involves selling directly to customers.

Directive 2014/56/EU The European Union (EU) equivalent of the Sarbanes-Oxley Act (SOX) for internal controls is the EU Audit Regulation and Directive (Directive 2014/56/EU) which was adopted in 2014. This directive was an amendment to Directive 2006/43/EC.

disaster recovery (DR) A subset of business continuity planning (BCP) that focuses on the restoration of a firm's IT infrastructure and operations after a crisis. DR is a key part of a business continuity plan; it covers all the procedures related to backups for servers, systems, and data.

discrepancy report From a receiving perspective for purchases, a document that identifies variances between the receiving report and the purchase order.

disruptive technology An innovation that changes the way that companies function. Disruptive technologies force companies to adapt their operations to stay competitive.

distributed denial-of-service (DDoS) attack A large-scale DoS attack that uses multiple machines or IP addresses to force a target to shut down. Since the hacker uses multiple originating points of attack, it's more difficult for a company to stop such attacks, as it must identify each source. This also makes it difficult for a company to differentiate between an attack and legitimate business traffic.

distributed ledger A ledger system in which all participants receive an electronic copy of the ledger. Instead of only one copy, as in a centralized system, multiple copies showing identical records of transactions are distributed to all participants in a network. If a transaction is added to the ledger, all participants in the network can see it.

distributed system An information system in which all the users and systems are directly connected to one another across the network. In a distributed system, the processing and databases are distributed among several business locations. All users have access to all data, depending on their user access privileges, and all users are connected throughout the business.

distribution How often a variable occurs in a data set.

document flowchart A flowchart that shows the flow of documents, such as physical or digital purchase orders, through a process.

document request A formal list of all documentation needed for an audit, such as flowcharts, organizational charts, PowerPoint presentations, and raw data.

documentation A formal record that describes a system or process. Documentation can serve as a future reference, such as a user guide for training, or as an official record, such as an audit trail.

dormant access A situation that exists when a user has not accessed a system for a significant period of time but still has an active role that grants them access.

double dipping A type of fraud that involves submitting a valid expense twice: once as a credit card transaction and once as a cash transaction.

Dumpster diving An attack that involves looking through someone else's physical trash. In the corporate world, criminals look for discarded sensitive information like passwords or network diagrams.

dynamic data Data that may change after it is recorded and must be updated. Dynamic data is like a website: users can update the content at any point in time, causing the data to change when they do so.

E

eavesdropping The unauthorized interception of communications. It includes listening to phone calls and intercepting emails, text messages, and other forms of communication. Also known as *sniffing*.

email phishing A deceptive request designed to trick victims into sharing private information. Phishing often involves a fraudulent email that appears to be from a reputable source, such as an employer or a company. This email may ask victims to respond with sensitive information or may contain a link that takes victims to a fake website, where they input the sensitive information.

emerging technology A new technology that has entered the market but is not yet regularly used by companies.

emerging technology COE A specialized team in a company that evaluates emerging and disruptive technologies to see how they may fit into current operations.

employee benefits Nonmonetary employee compensation, which includes medical and life insurance, retirement pay, and more.

employee onboarding The process of establishing new employees in a company's systems and helping them quickly adapt to their positions and the company. Onboarding starts when a job offer is made and continues through an employee's first day, weeks, or even months.

employee personal information Information an employee provides before starting employment, including emergency contacts, tax ID number, tax withholding details, and mailing address.

employee termination A business process that involves managing the removal of an employee from active employment status. A termination may be voluntary (resignation, retirement), involuntary (layoffs, firing), or medical (disability, death).

encryption The process of using an algorithm to encode a plaintext message, like readable text, and to convert the plaintext to something that is seemingly meaningless, called ciphertext. Encryption helps ensure confidentiality.

engineering BOM A bill of materials that is created at the time of product design.

enhancing characteristics Additional characteristics beyond the fundamental characteristics of relevance and faithful representation that enhance the usefulness of information. There are four of these characteristics: verifiability, timeliness, understandability, and comparability.

enterprise resource planning (ERP) A solution that offers a single system with aggregated parts that meet the needs of each business function. An ERP system integrates multiple systems into a single, cohesive communication system.

enterprise risk management (ERM) The comprehensive process of identifying, categorizing, prioritizing, and responding to a company's risks. It involves creating a formal risk assessment and plans for addressing the risks.

entity integrity The database design principle that a primary key cannot be null, or empty.

entity relationship diagram (ERD) A graphical illustration of all the tables in a database and their relationships. ERDs are designed for business end users who don't have the technical skills to read a database schema. ERDs help users understand the layout and data within a relational database. There are three types of ERD: conceptual ERD, logical ERD, and physical ERD.

e-procurement system An electronic procurement system that integrates into an enterprise resource planning (ERP) system to automate the purchase of raw materials based on demand. It creates purchase requisitions and purchase orders using an electronic authorization process to meet predicted production needs.

ERM Framework Enterprise Risk Management—Integrating with Strategy and Performance, a set of five interrelated components that highlight the importance of risk in creating strategies and driving a company's performance. The ERM Framework aims to improve the risk management process by addressing more than just internal control.

ERP feature A specific capability for a business process within an enterprise resource planning (ERP) system module. Each feature is specifically designed to support the unique requirements of its business processes. Accounts Receivable is an example of a feature within the Financial module of an ERP system.

ERP module A function within an enterprise resource planning (ERP) system. ERP modules can be purchased as a full, all-inclusive package or individually to create custom combinations that meet a business's needs.

event log data Data about activities in a system plus the timestamp showing when the activities occur.

executive support system (ESS) An information system that supports strategic decision making. An ESS is a subset of a decision support system.

exit interview A meeting that occurs on the last day of employment, when an employee meets with HR to discuss why they are leaving, provides forwarding contact information, and learns about benefits post-termination. This is also when the employee turns in their badge, equipment, and corporate credit card. HR may then escort the employee from the building.

exit meeting A meeting between auditors and management of the business area being audited to discuss findings and get management's response.

expense cutoff A type of fraud that occurs when expenses are not recorded until the subsequent accounting period. Expense cutoff fraud pushes the transactions to the subsequent period to avoid recognizing the expense in the current period.

expense reimbursement scheme A fraudulent disbursement in which a business reimburses a perpetrator for expenses they never incurred.

expense tracking system A system, maintained by the accounting department, that allows employees to input their reimbursable business expenses with appropriate documentation (such as receipts). Such a system is often purchased from a third-party software company (such as SAP) but directly administered by the company's accounting department.

expensing capitalized cost A fraud scheme in which a company recognizes capital costs that should be recorded to an asset account as an expense, thus reducing net income.

explanatory analysis A type of analysis that occurs once the story, or purpose, of a visualization is known and the data is ready to be presented to the audience. During explanatory analysis, visualizations are crafted, the presentation is fine-tuned, and key points are highlighted.

exploratory analysis The process of investigating unknown data.

exploratory data analytics Techniques that reveal the key characteristics of a data set. This type of analytics can be performed using machine learning (ML) algorithms or other techniques.

extended reality (XR) An environment that is a combination of real and virtual experience and involves human–machine interactions generated by computer technology and wearables. XR technology takes three forms, which progress from completely real to completely virtual: augmented reality (AR), mixed reality (MR), and virtual reality (VR).

external auditor Someone who evaluates whether the financial statements of an audited company ("the client") are free from material misstatements and are presented in accordance with accounting standards such as generally accepted accounting principles (GAAP). An external auditor is employed by an outside organization, such as an accounting firm.

external entity shape A Gane-Sarson data flow diagram (DFD) shape that represents an input or output of the DFD. These entities are called "external" because they are either entering the system from an external place or exported out of the system to an external place. External entities only provide or receive data; they do not process data.

external fraud Fraud perpetrated by customers, vendors, or other outside parties against a company. Since they are external risks and less preventable, companies often devote significantly less time to them in risk assessments.

external risk A risk that is not related to business operations and comes from outside a company. External risks are not related to business operations. While external risks are often unpredictable, companies still prepare for them to the best of their abilities.

F

falling action The part of a story that describes the steps of problem resolution.

feasibility study An analysis of the technical, economic, and operational factors that will impact a project. Some critical decisions are made at this point, such as whether to build or buy the system and whether it should be a cloud-based solution. The project plan is used to perform the feasibility study, and the results of the feasibility study will update the project plan.

fictitious employees test Analysis of employee data to identify employees with matching information, such as different names but the same bank accounts. This analytic provides a fraud test for fictitious employees.

File Transfer Protocol (FTP) A standard network protocol that allows users to transfer files between a company network and outside parties.

financial electronic data interchange (FEDI) The electronic transfer of payments and payment-related information like invoices in a standardized and machine-readable format.

financial information In XBRL, data related to the monetary transactions of a business that is included in the financial statements.

Financial module The enterprise resource planning (ERP) system module that captures accounting data and generates financial documents, including financial statements, tax forms, and receipts. Accounting data from all other modules flows to the Financial module for reporting.

financial reporting A standardized practice that provides external stakeholders, like investors, with an accurate depiction of a company's financial situation. Financial reporting uses accounting data generated from business processes, like purchasing, human resources, sales, and conversion, as the inputs to create the output in the form of financial statements. These financial statements are used for decision making, which is one of the objectives of financial reporting.

financial risk A risk specifically related to money going into and out of a company and the potential loss of a substantial sum. This type of risk is associated with various types of financial transactions, including investments, sales, purchases, and loans.

financial statement fraud Fraud that involves materially misrepresenting the financial results and position of a company by manipulating amounts or inappropriately disclosing information in the financial statements to deceive investors, creditors, and other users of the financial statements. The objective of financial statement fraud is to either overstate or understate the company's financial performance and position. Also known as "cooking the books."

financing event A business event that helps a company operate by acquiring incoming cash flows to fund operating events.

finished goods Products that are ready to be provided to customers.

first line of defense The business operations portion of the Institute of Internal Auditors' three lines of defense model. In this line of defense, management has the ownership and the responsibility of enforcing mitigating measures to prevent identified risk from occurring. This line of defense reports only to executive management.

fixed asset Long-lived assets that generate revenue such as land, land improvements, buildings, equipment and machinery used in production, office equipment, computer equipment, furniture and fittings, warehouse shelving, and vehicles. In financial accounting, fixed assets are generally known as property, plant, and equipment (PP&E).

Fixed Asset Subsidiary Ledger A ledger that shows details for each fixed asset—date of purchase, historical cost, accumulated depreciation, and net book value. It also provides details related to the disposal of a particular asset—the selling price and the profit or loss on disposal. The Fixed Asset Subsidiary Ledger is reconciled to the Fixed Asset General Ledger accounts on a regular basis.

flowchart A documentation method that depicts the actions or movements of individuals or items in a system or process as a diagram. Flowcharts present visuals of the management, operations, controls, outside vendors, and systems involved in a business process. A flowchart may be able to fit on a single page, or it may span multiple pages.

flowline In a process flowchart, an arrow that connects shapes together. Each shape in a flowchart must have at least one incoming flowline and one outgoing flowline, unless it's a terminator. The arrow of the line points in the direction of the flowchart flow. A flowline cannot have arrows on both sides.

forecasting The process of estimating future results based on the combination of past and present data. This predictive analytic method uses statistics and is a staple in accounting data analytics.

foreign key (FK) In relational databases, a key in one table that references the primary key of another table, such as the Customer_ID field in the Orders table.

Form A form is a user interface that allows users to enter data into the database.

Form W-2 A wage and tax statement sent to an employee by January 31 each year.

Form W-3 A summary of all W-2 forms. This report is sent to the IRS by February 28 each year.

framework A published set of specifications and criteria that defines a strategy to achieve certain objectives. Accounting frameworks are specific to the information appearing in a company's financial statements, and risk management frameworks focus on how a company defines its strategy for eliminating or minimizing the impact of risks.

franchise business model A business model in which individuals purchase and run a franchise, such as a franchise of a popular fast food chain (for example, McDonald's).

fraud Intentional misrepresentation of the truth or concealment of a material fact. Fraud has four elements: a false statement (the perpetrator either lies directly or hides the truth), knowledge (the perpetrator knows the statement is false at the time it's stated), reliance (the victim relies on information when deciding or acting), and damages (the victim suffers damages as a result of relying on this false statement).

fraud triangle A commonly used framework that identifies three motivational elements generally associated with fraud: perceived pressure (incentive or motive), opportunity, and rationalization (attitude).

fraudulent disbursement A payment that a company makes for an inappropriate purpose. Fraudulent disbursements occur on the books, as the company will have a record of the payment. These schemes are the most common type of asset misappropriation.

freemium business model A business model that involves offering free services but charging a fee to access upgraded features (for example, Dropbox).

full backup A backup that involves copying all existing data in its entirety every time. This is the slowest of the backup strategies and requires a lot of storage, as it means creating a full copy of your data.

fundamental characteristics The two characteristics that are required to make information useful for decision making, according to the Financial Accounting Standards Board (FASB): relevance and faithful representation.

G

gamification A merger of video game principles and real-world simulations in which users earn badges and points while they learn new skills they might need on the job. Gamification can be a low-key badge-earning system, as when a public accounting firm awards employees badges and points for engaging in health and wellness activities. Gamification can also be complex, as when gamification principles are combined with virtual reality and head-mounted displays to create job simulations.

general journal A journal used for transactions that do not repeat often during a reporting period and for adjusting and closing entries.

geospatial analytics An advanced data analytics technique that involves gathering, transforming, and visualizing geographic data and imagery, including satellite photographs, and GPS coordinates.

geospatial location The geographic location of a variable in a data set.

geospatial map An analytic or visualization that utilizes geographic data such as map coordinates, GPS data, and more.

geotag A digitally assigned geographic location associated with a piece of data like a photo and other locational data. Geotags allow management accountants to provide analyses that are more extensive and substantive.

grandfather-father-son redundant backup A common backup scheme that is based on three backup cycles: (1) grandfather cycle, which is a full backup, once a month; (2) father cycle, which is a full backup, once a week; and (3) son cycle, which is an incremental or differential backup, every day.

graphical documentation Refers to the use of visual elements, such as diagrams, charts, graphs, illustrations, and other graphical representations, to convey information, concepts, or instructions.

graphical user interface (GUI) A screen that allows users to interact with a system.

H

hash string With blockchain, a string that is created using an algorithm as part of the encryption process to ensure that third parties are unable to access the information. The hash string is embedded in the blockchain, and auditors search for the hash string within the blockchain. If the search is successful, the auditors know the record has remained unmodified.

heat map A type of risk matrix that uses different colors to represent values of data in a map or diagram format. The different colors in the risk matrix heat map typically represent the priority of a risk based on the risk score; for example, green may indicate a lower priority and red a higher priority.

histogram A visualization that represents a numeric distribution based on user-defined ranges. It graphs the frequency of values occurring in a data set.

hot backup site A backup site that runs and backs up continuously. Data is continuously backed up on a second-by-second or minute-by-minute basis, making the hot backup site a ready-to-go center of data operations. A hot backup site is typically offsite and contains an exact copy of the main server and live systems. Separating the backup site geographically provides the best protection against natural disasters that might destroy the building where operations take place.

HR processes Acquisition and payment processes that involve acquiring and managing employees.

human resources (HR) A business function that is responsible for all employees and employee-related operations. An HR department is responsible for a number of major activities, including recruiting and hiring employees, training and developing employees, and determining salaries and benefits.

Human Resources Management (HRM) module An enterprise resource planning (ERP) system module that manages detailed employee records, training and development, and even time tracking. The HRM module must communicate with the Financial module because employee data and timekeeping are in the HRM module, while payroll processing is in the Financial module.

I

icon A type of symbol that provides visual cues along with data, text, or charts and graphs.

iconography The use of visual images and symbols to represent ideas.

immutability A characteristic of blockchain that gives users assurance that their assets and information are secure and cannot be changed.

impact The estimation of damage that could be caused if a risk occurs. It is equivalent to the outcome in a risk statement.

implementation stage The sixth stage of a systems development life cycle project, when a system is moved into production and goes live for use in the company. This stage is the culmination of the work put into the systems development project.

in-house development A method of developing software in which the software is programmed by a company's own software developers, from scratch.

incremental backup A backup that involves copying only new or updated data with each backup. This is the cheapest backup strategy, and it uses the least amount of storage space.

independence A condition in which an auditor is removed from a business process and has no stake in or influence over the outcome of the business processes that they are auditing. It is important for an auditor to remain independent in order to audit the business objectively.

independent variable In linear regression, the factor that may be influencing the dependent variable. There can be one or more independent variables, depending on the type of regression being performed.

indirect factory labor Employees indirectly involved in manufacturing (for example, production supervisors, quality control inspectors, those managing and handling raw materials, factory cleaners, and factory maintenance).

indirect material costs The costs of materials and supplies used in the manufacturing process that are not directly traceable to a product. For example, a cookie company uses cooking spray and cleaning supplies in the conversion process as indirect materials.

infographic A stand-alone visual that tells a story through graphic design and rarely requires verbal communication to accompany it.

information event A business event that involves an exchange of information and never involves an exchange of economic resources.

information gathering The part of fieldwork during which the audit team reviews existing audit documentation (such as process narratives, flowcharts, and prior-year audit workpapers) and conducts a process walkthrough by interviewing employees and letting them explain their daily job functions.

information quality The suitability of information for a particular purpose in a specific task.

information system A system that consists of interrelated components including physical hardware like monitors and laptops, the software that users interact with, databases used for storage, networks that send data and information throughout the system, and the people who use and maintain it.

information technology (IT) The technology and processes involved in developing, maintaining, and using computer systems, hardware, software, and networks for the processing and distribution of data.

inherent risk The natural level of risk in a business process or activity if there are no risk responses in place. It is the risk before implementing a risk response. Inherent risk consists of two parts: likelihood and impact.

input In an information system, raw and unorganized data captured by the system.

interactive dashboard A dashboard presented within the software used to create it or on a website. The audience can interact with this type of dashboard by drilling down into the underlying data, exporting images and underlying data, changing filters, and more.

internal audit An independent function in a company that tests internal controls to provide assurance of their effectiveness to executive management and the board of directors. Internal audit adds value to a business by providing assurance, insight, and objectivity to the company.

internal auditor Someone who is employed by a company and provides independent assurance that the company's risk management, governance, and internal control processes are operating effectively. An internal auditor has a professional duty to provide an unbiased and objective view of the organization that employs them. An internal auditor looks beyond financial risks and financial statements to consider wider issues related to the company, including its reputation, growth, environmental impact, and employee satisfaction; this differentiates an internal auditor from an external auditor.

internal control A process that specifically mitigates risks to the company's financial information. Internal control, as it relates to accounting information, focuses on providing quality information to internal decision makers and external stakeholders.

internal control over financial reporting (ICFR) Controls that are specific to the financial reporting process.

Internal Control—Integrated Framework A controls-based approach to risk management that is widely accepted as the authoritative guidance on internal controls and SOX compliance. It defines internal control and gives the criteria for developing, implementing, and monitoring an effective internal control system.

internal risk A risk that occurs throughout a company's operations and arises during normal operations. Most internal risks are preventable through careful risk identification and management. Note that an internal risk may relate to an external party, such as the company's reputation with customers.

Internet of Things (IoT) A collection of electronic devices (the "things") connected to the internet through sensors, software, and other technologies. The IoT is designed to monitor and control devices while extracting the data each device generates. For example, smart light bulbs connect to the internet and are controllable via smartphone app. These light bulbs can be programmed with automated decision statements that create a smart home environment.

introduction The part of a story where characters and settings are introduced.

inventory A current asset balance sheet line item that includes all goods awaiting sale (finished goods or purchased for resale), goods in the course of production (work in process), and goods that will be used in production (raw materials).

inventory management A process that involves coordinating the communication of inventory availability and needs across the purchasing, conversion, and sales processes. It's an essential source of information for all three of these processes because sales orders and forecasts determine inventory requirements, which in turn drive purchases of raw materials and supplies and the production of finished goods.

investing event A business event that provides long-term value to a company by purchasing long-term assets that will deliver value in the future.

IP address A string of characters that a device uses to communicate over a network.

IP spoofing An attack in which an attacker creates IP packets with modified source addresses to disguise their identify and impersonate a legitimate computer on the network.

IT general control (ITGC) A control that applies to the entire operation of a system and its environment. All corporate applications, like email, web browsers, time-keeping software, benefits management systems, and more, are subject to ITGCs.

IT governance The process that ensures effective and efficient use of IT so a company can achieve goals and provide value. IT governance is a process, not a department or a static state of existing; it is an ongoing effort by different parts of an organization to monitor and make IT decisions that have an impact on business operations.

IT governance framework A framework that defines the criteria a company can use to implement, manage, and monitor IT governance, including measurements for effectively leveraging IT resources. COBIT is an example of an IT governance framework.

J

job time ticket A source document that captures the cost of labor to manufacture a product.

job-order costing A method of assigning costs to products and services based on how much it costs to produce each product or service. Construction companies building custom homes, dentists treating patients, and a CPA firm auditing a client would use this method of costing.

JOIN operator In SQL, an operator that retrieves interconnected data from related tables by declaring a primary key and foreign key relationship as the join column. For example, when joining the Customers and Orders tables, the Customer_ID column is the join column: it's the primary key in the Customers table and a foreign key in the Orders table.

journal A chronological record of all the financial accounting transactions of a business. Also known as a *book of prime entry*.

K

key The unique ID that identifies a record in a database.

key performance indicator (KPI) A quantifiable metric used to measure and evaluate the success of a company based on its objectives.

L

labeled data Data that contains predefined tags or descriptors that a machine learning (ML) algorithm uses to understand the data set or learn from it. Labeling data is a human act of intervention, which occurs only when using supervised ML analytics.

labor-leisure trade-off The balance between the amount of time you spend earning your salary and the satisfaction you receive during your leisure, or unpaid, time. A primary determinant of this balance is the amount of salary you are earning.

landing page The first dashboard view when a dashboard is opened.

larceny Theft of company assets after the company has recorded the assets in its books. Larceny can be either cash or non-cash larceny.

Level 0 diagram A data flow diagram that gives a high-level overview of data flows. It must fit on one page, and it provides a snapshot of the data flow that is designed to be understood by all business audiences—from stakeholders to developers. It illustrates the exchange of information between external entities and the system. Also referred to as a *context diagram*.

Level 1 diagram A data flow diagram (DFD) that highlights the main functions carried out by the system and drills down further into the DFD process by "decomposing" the system. It breaks down each process into further subprocesses.

Level 2 diagram The most detailed data flow diagram, which allows the end user to understand the system and process in depth. This type of diagram assists in identifying control weaknesses or inefficiencies. Process numbers include decimal places to indicate subprocesses of a Level 1 process.

lift and shift An acquisition in which the acquiring company moves the acquired systems, physically placing the systems' servers in the data center and maintaining the existing systems as they are. Users have access to all the systems simultaneously. Lift and shift is one of the easiest and lowest-cost ways to integrate systems.

likelihood The estimated probability of risk occurrence. Companies use different methods to calculate likelihood, but likelihood is always ranked on a spectrum. In different industries, likelihood is described as "frequency" or "probability"; these terms are synonymous.

line chart A visualization that shows time series analysis and can be used to identify trends or anomalies in time series data.

linear regression Statistical techniques that predict the relationships between one dependent variable and one or more independent variables. It does not establish a cause-and-effect relationship between the variables. It only estimates the existence of a relationship between them.

lockbox A post office box that can only be accessed by a company's bank.

logic bomb A piece of malicious code that is programmed into a system and remains dormant until certain conditions are met. Cyber attackers program logic bombs to be dormant until the time is right, and then the malicious code is released into the system. The conditions that trigger a logic bomb vary based on the creativity of the cyber attacker. These attacks are difficult to detect or prevent until they have been activated.

logical access attack An attack in which the attackers seek unauthorized access to a system or application by either exploiting a network vulnerability unveiled during reconnaissance attacks or attempting to use force to get through network security.

logical attack An attack that occurs on a fully digital spectrum and requires no human interaction other than the attacker instigating the attack.

logical reconnaissance attack A digital attack on a network vulnerability that could eventually allow the hacker to get into the system. This type of attack does not require a human target.

M

machine learning (ML) A form of artificial intelligence (AI) that uses algorithms and statistical models to train the AI system through patterns and trends in data sets.

main vendor table A list of all approved vendors (and their attributes) a company does business with.

maintenance stage The final stage of a systems development life cycle project, which occurs after the system goes live and continues throughout the system's life. During this stage, the system is monitored, updated, and changed. Changes to the system go through the company's formal change management process.

malicious code Code that is written to cause harm and attack a target system.

malware Software specifically designed to damage, disrupt, or gain unauthorized access to systems. Short for "malicious software."

management accounting A type of accounting that provides managers with information that helps them make decisions within the organization. Management accounting reports help managers perform their routine management and control functions.

management information system (MIS) An information system that provides managers with useful information for effective and timely decision making. An accounting information system is part of the overall management information system.

management override A control weakness that occurs when internal control activities are ineffective because management is not following policy or procedure—as when managers tell employees who report directly to them to ignore specific controls. The American Institute of Certified Public Accountants (AICPA) describes management override as the Achilles heel of fraud prevention.

management's response A plan for remediation that management of the business area being audited provides to the audit team.

managerial accounting A subset of accounting that focuses on using accounting information to aid in decision making and management of control activities. Managerial accountants (also known as management accountants) perform analyses and create reports for use within the company.

manual control A control that is executed by people or physical interaction. Manual controls are used when human judgment or physical interaction is required. Manual controls are subject to human error or intentional manipulation and override, which means there is an increased risk that a manual control might fail. For this reason, auditors—both internal and external—frequently focus on manual controls during their assessments.

manufacturing BOM A bill of materials that is created for every production run of a product.

manufacturing efficiency A balance between three goals: controlling (1) the costs of resources, (2) the rate of production, and (3) the quality of finished goods.

manufacturing operations A process that focuses on creating finished goods.

manufacturing overhead The depreciation, repairs, maintenance, property taxes, and insurance for fixed assets used in production.

master production schedule (MPS) A source document that shows the specific calendar time when every production operation is scheduled to occur, the resources and workers assigned, and the steps required to utilize all resources effectively. The MPS shows the quantity of each product to be produced on a weekly basis. It feeds into inventory and supply chain management by specifying which required materials must be procured and when.

materials requisition request A source document that authorizes the movement of raw materials from inventory into production.

maturity model A model that shows how far along a company is on its journey to reach the ideal state by comparing the current state to a predetermined set of best practices. Companies use maturity models to judge their current performance and create a roadmap, or plan, for continuous improvement.

merge shape A process flowchart shape that connects two or more paths of a flowchart into a single flowline. There is no limit on the number of paths that can merge through this shape. A merge should always have multiple flowlines entering it and a single flowline exiting it.

merger The combination of two separate companies into a new legal entity. In a merger, one of the companies generally maintains its leadership and operating environment.

meta tag A keyword that helps describe content. For example, a human can categorize the image of a green turtle swimming with meta tags such as "turtle," "green," "swimming," "animal," and "happy." These meta tags convert the image into data that is searchable.

miner In the context of blockchain, someone who creates ledgers of transactions in chained blocks by using computing power (nodes in the network) to solve the mathematical encryption puzzles that secure the transactions.

misclassification of revenue A fraud scheme in which a company understates revenue by inappropriately recognizing revenue as a different type of income.

model environment A recent copy of a live system or application which is used to implement the code in an environment that mirrors the production environment of the system or application.

Monte Carlo simulation A popular simulation method that predicts the probability of different outcomes in the presence of many random variables. It generates models of potential outcomes and conducts a risk analysis over each one. Monte Carlo can use reinforcement learning to learn directly from its experiences to evolve the model.

move ticket A source document in the form of a ticket, such as a barcode tag, that authorizes and tracks movements of a single manufacturing job from one location in production to another. Also known as a *routing ticket*.

multifactor authentication A type of user authentication in which a strong combination of identifiers is required when a user logs in. For example, two-factor authentication might require a username and password as well as a verification code sent in a text message or email.

multiple regression A type of linear regression with one dependent variable and multiple independent variables.

N

narrative A written description of a system or process that describes responsibilities in detail, as well as the processes and controls that are in place. A narrative is often accompanied by a visual depiction, such as a flowchart.

National Institute of Standards and Technology (NIST) A U.S. Department of Commerce agency that promotes innovation in science, standards, and technology to improve the quality of life in the United States.

natural language processing (NLP) An advanced type of textual analysis that uses artificial intelligence to read, understand, and derive meaning from human language.

network analysis An advanced data analytics technique that visualizes relationships among participants in a data set to learn about their social structure based on those relationships. It is mostly used to study relationships among people, who are displayed as nodes in a network analysis. The links between the nodes are the relationships, or interactions, that connect the participants.

network port A location in a network where communication packets are sent and received.

new hire package Documentation that contains a newly hired employee's start date, summary of benefits offered, where to report on the first day, and a link to an online portal the employee will use to provide information before starting employment.

node (1) In network analysis, a representation of a participant. The links between the nodes are the relationships, or interactions, that connect the participants. (2) In the context of blockchain, a computer, laptop, or server of a participant in the network who chooses to be a miner.

noise In time series analysis, additional movement that cannot be explained as a trend or seasonality.

non-behavioral red flag A company-imposed goal or expectation that drives individuals to commit fraud. For example, pressure to meet financial forecasts or benchmarks may drive employees to commit fraud to meet financial goals and achieve bonus targets.

normal packet A packet in which the source address is the IP address of the packet sender.

NoSQL database A database that stores each item individually, rather than in rows and columns, and retrieves them by using key values. There is no structured schema, resulting in a flexible storage solution for unstructured data. NoSQL databases were introduced to respond to the increasing velocity of big data and the need for faster processing of unstructured data.

null Empty.

O

object In the context of object-oriented databases, an item contained within a class. It is like a record in a relational database.

object-oriented database A hybrid database that has a relational database framework with the data presented and stored in a form other than tables. It can store both structured numbers and text and complex unstructured data.

occupational fraud Fraud committed by owners, executives, management, and employees who use their positions to enrich themselves at the expense of the company. The Association of Certified Fraud Examiners (ACFE) identifies almost 50 different types of occupational fraud schemes and uses three categories to map them—asset misappropriation, financial statement fraud, and corruption. Also called *internal fraud.*

offer letter The initial offer to a job candidate, which contains the position details and salary for the prospective employee and states that the employment offer is contingent on a background check.

on-path attack An attack in which the attacker attempts to gain access between two endpoints during an ongoing communication and can impersonate either of the parties. In an on-path attack, the hacker can intercept or modify the communication. Also known as a *man-in-the-middle attack.*

online analytical processing (OLAP) An information system that focuses on leveraging data for information.

online transaction processing (OLTP) An information system that supports core business functions by handling sales, accounting, purchasing, and more.

operating effectiveness A test that determines whether a control operates as designed by a person with appropriate authority and training to perform the control.

operating event A business event that occurs during the normal operations of a company and directly relates to the company's creation and provision of a good or service to its customers.

operating system (OS) Systems software that supports a computer's basic functions, such as task management, executing applications, and starting up and shutting down. Two widely used operating systems are Microsoft Windows and Apple macOS.

operational risk The most important type of risk for an AIS, which occurs during day-to-day business operations and causes breakdowns in business activities. These risks are a priority for an AIS because they result from inadequate or failed procedures within the company.

operations list *See* bill of operations (BOO).

operator documentation Documentation that provides information necessary to execute a program and make it work. Often referred to as the "run manual."

opportunity A situation that arises when a potential fraudster reasonably expects a fraud to go undetected and to experience no negative consequences. The potential fraudster must be aware that the opportunity exists, which makes it a perceived opportunity.

organic growth Growth in a company that occurs when the company uses its own resources and business processes to increase sales, customers, and market share.

organizational chart A documentation method that shows the employees in a company and their reporting relationships with one another as a diagram. The chief executive officer (CEO) or the company president is usually at the top of the chart, with everyone else cascading down from there. Often called an "org chart."

out-of-the-box ERP system An enterprise resource planning (ERP) system that is preconfigured to work one way when implemented. Customers are expected to adapt their business processes to match the system's existing configuration.

output In information systems, information that comes from a system in a format that is useful to users.

outsourced HR model An HR model in which a third-party company is responsible for certain administrative tasks. Examples include companies that specialize in administration of benefits such as health insurance and search firms that find the best candidates for a key position. This outsourced model frees up the company's dedicated HR team to perform more value-driven tasks.

overall equipment effectiveness (OEE) A key performance indicator that measures how well production resources are used by identifying the percentage of productive manufacturing time. An OEE of 100% means all products produced are acceptable (100% quality), produced at the fastest speeds (100% performance), and manufactured without interruptions in production (100% availability).

overtime Extra pay for hourly employees who work more than a standard work week. Overtime typically requires prior approval from the employee's manager.

P

packet A small portion of a full message sent over a network.

packing slip A supplier-generated source document that shows quantities and descriptions of items delivered as part of an order. It is provided to a customer with a delivered product, often inside the shipment package or digitally at the time of delivery.

paid time off (PTO) Company-paid vacation, personal, or sick time. PTO requires approval from the employee's manager.

patch A software update, released by the software's providers, that may include upgrades, fixes, or improvements. Failure to patch software can open a network to hackers.

pattern Recurring or similar values, which can be categorical or quantitative.

pay and return A fraud scheme that involves inputting inflated amounts in the payment system, thus arranging for a company to overpay an invoice. When the vendor returns the overpayment amount, the billing clerk intercepts the return check and deposits it in a personal account.

pay stub A record of an individual employee's gross pay, deductions, and net pay for both the payment period and cumulative year-to-date totals.

payment voucher An internal document that includes the vendor, amount due, and payment terms.

payments processes Processes focused on paying for the resources necessary for a business to operate.

payroll The process involved in calculating wages (hourly, salary, commission) and compensating employees with their entitled pay.

payroll batch The accumulated payroll transactions for batch processing.

payroll journal A record of payroll accounting entries for a pay period. It includes employee hours worked, gross pay, net pay, deductions, and payroll rate.

payroll processes Payment processes that involve paying employees for their work.

payroll scheme A fraudulent disbursement in which a business pays the perpetrator for time not worked. These schemes come in many forms—from a friend punching the timeclock for their friend at a warehouse to payroll clerks creating ghost, or fictitious, employees in the payroll system. The perpetrator also must manage the bank accounts of the fictitious employee, who may be a real person not employed at the company and whose Social Security number may have been stolen.

payroll service administrator A third party that handles payroll processing for other companies. Automatic Data Processing, Inc. (ADP) is an example.

peer-to-peer business model A business model that connects individuals with one another (for example, Airbnb).

penetration test A test that a company performs on its own network (or that a third party performs on the company's network) to identify network vulnerabilities. Penetration testing is often performed as part of IT audits or technology consulting engagements. Also called a *pen test.*

perceived pressure A motive or an incentive that pushes a person toward the decision to commit fraud. The potential fraudsters believe they have a need that is "non-shareable"; they feel they can't share this need with anyone else, which adds to their perceived pressure.

period costs All costs that are not included in product costs but that are required to help a business succeed in its mission. A period cost is listed as an expense in the accounting period in which it occurred.

permission A listing of access rights, or privileges, a user has once assigned to a role.

physical access attack An attack that results in access to either hardware or people. That access can be gained with the assistance of an unknowing victim or through force.

physical attack An attack in which the attacker threatens elements a network administrator has no control over, such as physical security, hardware, and people.

physical reconnaissance attack An attack that uses human interaction—on the part of the target, the attacker, or both—to generate information about a network.

physical risk A threat such as adverse weather, crime, or physical damage. Physical risk is the easiest type of risk to understand, and it is one of the most important types of risk to identify because the impact is usually high. The losses from physical risks range from financial loss to legal actions and reputational loss due to mismanagement of assets.

picking request An instruction to warehouse employees to prepare the correct quantity and product for shipping to the customer. This document authorizes the transfer of finished goods from the warehouse.

pie chart A visualization that divides a data set into groups proportional to their sizes within the data set.

piggybacking *See* tailgating.

ping sweep An attack that involves identifying which hosts are active in a network by sending a communication to each IP address to see if there is a response packet. The hacker pings, or calls, each network IP address, one at a time, and waits for the response packet. By performing a ping sweep, a hacker can create a list of active IP addresses. Also called an *IP probe*.

pivot table An Excel feature that can be used to summarize relatively small data sets.

planning stage The first stage of a systems development life cycle project, which includes defining the scope of the project, identifying necessary resources, and determining if the project will likely be successful.

port scan A method hackers use to narrow their results by finding which ports are open and sending or receiving data on a network. Attackers use port scans to identify the types of communication occurring on a network.

portfolio view A view of risk that examines risk at the entity level.

predictive analytics A category of data analytics that uses historical and external data to examine what is likely to happen. Predictive analytics provides decision makers with predictions of what may happen based on the data analyzed. It is the third phase of data analytics in the Gardner model.

prescriptive analytics A category of data analytics that uses historical and external data to examine what should happen or how to act. Prescriptive analytics provides decision makers

with insights by providing recommendations on what to do next. It is the fourth phase of data analytics in the Gardner model.

preventive control A control that prevents problems from happening. Examples of preventive controls include firewalls to prevent unauthorized access to an organization's computer network and policy and procedure documentation that specifies how employees should execute procedures and clarifies company policies to reduce the organization's risk of error and misconduct.

pricing process The process of setting selling prices of products and services.

primary key (PK) In a relational database, a key that is the unique ID of a table, such as the Customer_ID field in the Customers table.

private blockchain A blockchain network that includes an intermediary. A single entity (the business) governs the network.

process costing A process that involves determining the total cost of the production and averaging it over the units produced for companies that mass produce identical products. The cost per unit equals the cost of all production inputs divided by expected output units.

process flowchart A flowchart that shows the flow of activity through the company, including the key parties and actions that they perform. Also known as a *business-process diagram*.

process mining The process of using event log data to show, in a visual format, what individuals, systems, and machines are doing.

process shape (1) A process flowchart shape that represents an event, or step, within the flow. A process shape always has a single line entering it and can have multiple lines exiting it. This is because flowcharts can split into two paths if a process event results in two subsequent events, such as sending an email to two different departments. (2) A Gane-Sarson data flow diagram (DFD) shape that represents an activity that transforms, or changes, the data. A decimal number, such as the "1.0" label, identifies the process for quick reference. A process shape must be connected to at least one external entity.

process walkthrough An interview during which auditees explain their daily job functions to an auditor.

process-based information system An information system that captures all the data of interest generated in a business process, including informational events.

product backlog In scrum, a list of all the desired features for a system being developed. Each feature is its own item on the backlog. As the team works through the project, it builds all the features through to completion, in order of priority. Features on the product backlog are broken into smaller parts and worked on simultaneously by the core team.

product costs Costs incurred in manufacturing a product.

product development The process of researching and testing new products or potential changes to existing products.

product increment In scrum, the current version of a system that is presented to business stakeholders for feedback at the end of a sprint. Feedback is returned to the core team, which prioritizes the feedback, adjusts the product backlog accordingly, and creates a sprint backlog for the next sprint.

production environment In systems development, an environment that is separate from the other environments and accessible only to production control employees. In the production environment, code is implemented in the live business systems and released for use.

Production module An enterprise resource planning (ERP) system module that manages production activities, including machine operations and scheduling. The Production module should communicate seamlessly with the Supply Chain Management module.

production planning A long-term outline of what and when products will be manufactured.

production report A source document that summarizes the total manufacturing cost of a product, which is important in recording the cost of inventory and cost of goods sold in the accounting records.

production scheduling The short-term allocation of plant machinery and other resources to the manufacturing of products.

profile view A view of risk that considers risk at the granular level of a business function, process, or event.

program documentation Documentation that describes the details of a program and its logic. This documentation is helpful if programmers who are unfamiliar with a system must troubleshoot it during an emergency. Also referred to as *software documentation* or *technical documentation*.

program flowchart A flowchart that shows the sequence of coded instructions in a computer program that enable it to perform specified logical and mathematical operations.

programming language A written set of coded instructions that a computer system understands. These instructions can be as simple as opening a file or as complex as performing calculations for a rocket to land on the moon. Structured Query Language (SQL) is an example of a programming language that an accounting professional might use.

project plan A plan that identifies the system scope and project goals. A project plan covers three elements: (1) critical factors that must be met for the project to be successful, (2) a defined project scope, including an overview of goals and limitations, and (3) milestones and responsibilities that break down project goals into timelines and identify individuals responsible for each goal.

proof of work A proven consensus protocol that replaces third-party intermediaries or a central authority in a blockchain network. With bitcoin, no third-party intermediaries are necessary to approve and enter transactions in the system. This eliminates reliance on a central bank or other third-party entities.

public blockchain A blockchain network that is open to all, with no restrictions on accessing or leaving the network.

purchase order A document used to request a supplier to sell and deliver the products in the quantities and for the prices specified in the purchase order.

purchase requisition A request to obtain goods from an authorized source that is sent to the purchasing department by an inventory control department that needs more raw material.

purchasing processes Processes focused on acquiring the necessary resources for a business to operate. From hiring vendors to paying for the raw materials needed to produce a product, the overall objectives of the purchasing processes are efficiency, or doing things right, and effectiveness, or doing the right things. Also known as *procurement processes*.

purpose of a business The goal of making a profit and generating enough cash flow to continue operating. Without the profit motive, a business would not be a business (at least not for very long).

Q

quality management A process that involves testing products to ensure that they meet regulatory and corporate specifications.

quantitative value A numeric data point that can be summed, counted, or otherwise analyzed using mathematical operations. Dates and dollar amounts are two examples of quantitative data values.

questionnaire A documentation method that includes a list of questions to ask the business team in charge of a process in order to gather information about specific procedures and internal controls. Questionnaires are often used by people outside a business, like auditors, who need to understand what is happening in the business. *See also* checklist.

R

ransomware Malware that is used to hold a system hostage in exchange for a demand, like monetary payment.

rationalization Justification of the act of committing fraud. Rationalization causes a potential fraudster to believe a crime is a justifiable act before they commit it.

raw materials Any components that are used in the production of a product.

real-time processing In a transaction processing system, a type of processing in which a transaction is processed as it occurs. This requires the company to have high processing capabilities readily available.

receiving report A document that shows descriptions and quantities of goods received from vendors.

reconnaissance attack A knowledge-gathering attack that helps an attacker identify targets and plan operations. In this type of attack, cybercriminals look for vulnerabilities in the network, through either a person who exposes valuable information or a technical weak point in the network.

referential integrity A property of database design which states that a foreign key cannot be entered into a table unless it exists as a primary key in the base table. For example, you cannot enter the customer ID into the Orders table if the customer ID does not exist in the Customers table.

reinforcement learning A type of machine learning that focuses on decision making by rewarding desired behaviors and/or punishing undesired behaviors.

relational database A database that organizes structured data in interrelated tables connected by similarities between tables. Data within relational databases is stored in tables that share commonalities—relationships—with one another. Most accounting information systems use relational databases.

relationship The way that different variables in a data set relate to one another.

remittance advice A source document that is returned to a business along with a customer payment to identify which invoice the payment relates to.

reperformance A test of operating effectiveness in which auditors independently re-create a control situation, often using data analytics.

report A report is a formatted presentation of data from the database.

reporting The process of aggregating data into information on the activities and performance in a company. Reporting provides a strictly descriptive view of what happened and does not seek insights into the context or reasons.

reputational risk Risk that occurs when the reputation—or good name—of a company is damaged. With reputational risk comes financial loss through a loss of customers and revenue. Reputational risk can be both internal and external in nature. The exact financial loss tied to a reputational risk is hard to quantify, but reputation is so important to a company that in accounting it is considered an intangible asset.

requirements definition Formal documentation of the final goal of a project, which identifies the steps needed to achieve the goal and outlines the overall system plan.

residual risk The remaining risk posed by a process or an activity once a plan to respond to the risk is in place. It is the risk after implementing a risk response.

resolution The wrap-up of a story that occurs at the end and includes the call to action.

responsibility accounting A type of accounting that is used to trace performance to the responsible department or manager to improve accountability.

retail customer A business with retail stores where other companies' products are sold, such as Target.

retailer business model A business model in which a manufacturer sells goods to a retailer to sell to consumers on its behalf.

revenue recognition A set of determined conditions that must be met to justify a business recognizing revenue as earned. These conditions determine when a revenue account will be credited.

rising action The part of a story that articulates the problem being addressed or the question being answered.

risk The likelihood of an unfavorable event occurring. Risks differ by business type, size, industry, and location.

risk acceptance A risk response in which an inherent risk is present but the organization chooses not to act. The company chooses to live with the risk.

risk appetite The amount of risk a company is willing to take on at a particular time.

risk assessment An assessment that identifies, categorizes, and prioritizes individual risks in a company. After assessing risk, management decides how to manage it.

risk avoidance A risk response that involves eliminating the risk by completely avoiding the events causing the risk. Rather than accept or reduce risk, companies avoid risk when it is both significant and highly likely to occur.

risk inventory A listing of all a business's known risks. A risk inventory is an essential part of approaching risk at the entity level and creating a portfolio view.

risk matrix A diagram that helps paint a clearer picture of risk by helping users visualize variations in risk scores. Using a risk matrix allows management to plot risk and move prioritization around; it is especially helpful for risks that are scored the same numerically.

risk mitigation The most commonly used risk response. It involves reducing risk based on careful consideration and calculation. Risk mitigation enables a company to take on risks in order to create a competitive advantage.

risk severity The likelihood of risks occurring and their potential impact on a company.

risk statement A statement that summarizes a potential problem that needs to be addressed. It contains two parts: the issue and the possible outcome. The outcome of a risk varies greatly, from delaying the launch of an information system to preventing the success of an entire company.

risk transfer A risk response that involves shifting a risk to a third party. In other words, a third party assumes the liabilities for the risk. Most often, this is done through a contract, such as an insurance policy.

robotic process automation (RPA) A type of automation that involves software that can be programmed and managed easily, using a drag-and-drop interface that does not require coding knowledge. With RPA, you basically create a software robot that can launch and operate other software.

Rogers Adoption Curve A model that shows the percentage of businesses that fall in each technology adoption category.

role-based access control (RBAC) A type of authorization companies implement to address the need of each user requiring a specific level of access. RBAC restricts network access by assigning individuals specific roles that have predefined criteria for what they can and cannot access in the system. RBAC streamlines the logical access control process for IT personnel by eliminating the need to program access to every system for every employee. Instead, access is programmed for each employee only once, when that person is assigned a role.

rolling audit plan A plan that includes a prioritized list of audit engagements.

S

sales cutoff A fraud scheme that involves recording sales that occur after the balance sheet date in the current year's financial statements to inflate sales even though they belong in the subsequent accounting period.

sales invoice A source document that is used to bill a B2B customer who purchases on a line of credit. It shows data related to a specific order and delivery.

Sales Management module An enterprise resource planning (ERP) system module that tracks orders from the time they are received from customers through shipment of products. It is important for the Sales Management module to communicate with the Supply Chain Management and Production modules because sales requirements drive what production will prioritize and when.

sales order A source document that contains the order details, including date ordered, customer name, address, delivery address, description, price, quantity of goods ordered, and total selling price of the order.

Sarbanes-Oxley Act of 2002 (SOX) A U.S. federal law that protects investors from fraud and other risks by improving the reliability and accuracy of financial statements. SOX primarily focuses on the internal control structure of a company. It changed the way companies operate by mandating audit trails and shifting the responsibility for financial reporting misstatements. Responsibility for control failures moved directly to management, and violation of internal control requirements now comes with serious criminal penalties—with fines up to $5 million and/or imprisonment for up to 20 years.

scatter plot A visualization that shows the relationship between two variables. Scatter plots use shapes, such as dots or circles, mapped along the X-axis and Y-axis, which are the two variables being measured for relationships.

scope creep A problem that occurs when a project evolves during development beyond its original specifications and becomes too large to meet its deadlines. It is often the result of end users asking "Can it also do this?" and adding more features. Scrum addresses this risk by ordering the suggestions of the end users by priority.

scoping document A document that describes the areas of a process that are subject to audit. It lists all identified risks and relevant controls to be tested and the likelihood and impact of risks. This document helps prioritize the controls to include in the scope of work.

scraped Describes textual data that has been pulled and cleaned from an unstructured format and placed into a structured table.

scrum A set of project management practices focused on daily communication and flexible planning. This flexible planning allows mid-project changes that do not impact budgets or timelines. Scrum breaks a systems development project into short cycles of work. After each cycle, the team reflects on successes and failures, and appropriate adjustments are made before continuing to the next cycle.

seasonality In time series analysis, a consistent movement that repeats on a regular basis.

second line of defense The risk management and compliance portion of the Institute of Internal Auditors' three lines of defense model. In this line of defense, the ERM team identifies and assesses organizational risks. This line of defense aids the first line of defense in ensuring that controls are designed to adequately address risk and monitors the controls to ensure that the first line of defense is complying with internal control requirements. This line of defense reports only to executive management.

segregation of duties A type of preventive control that reduces the risk of error and fraud by ensuring that different employees are responsible for the separate parts of a business activity: authorizing, recording, and custody. The work of one employee acts as a check on the work of another employee. Also called *separation of duties*.

SELECT command A DQL command that retrieves data from a database and that has the basic form SELECT [field name] FROM [table name].

sensitive information requires explicit consent from the individuals unless it is required for legal or regulatory purposes.

sentiment analysis Textual analysis that uses natural language processing to interpret and classify the emotions that lie behind text and speech. Also known as *opinion mining*.

severance A pay package given to an employee who is involuntarily terminated, such as in a layoff, not as a result of poor employee performance.

sham sale A fraud scheme that occurs when the perpetrator conceals fictitious revenue fraud with falsified documentation. Creating fake shipping documentation and sending the inventory to another location to physically hide it is a common method of concealment that ensures removal of the inventory from the inventory count.

shipping notice Details of a shipment and proof of delivery. By signing on a handheld device, a customer accepts a shipping notice and delivery.

simple regression A type of linear regression with one dependent variable and only one independent variable.

simulation The process of using complex calculations to predict the outcomes and probabilities of a decision that influences a data set.

skimming Asset misappropriation that happens when an employee steals cash before the cash is recorded in the accounting records.

smart contract A computer program that acts as an intermediary to create, execute, and settle contracts automatically under certain conditions. An accounting example is the automatic payment of an invoice after the program checks that goods have been received, that they match the purchase order, and that sufficient funds are available in the buyer's bank account to pay the invoice.

social engineering A physical reconnaissance attack in which an attacker persuades another human to perform an act that would allow the hacker access to confidential information. Social engineering can be used for reconnaissance, access, and to cause damage.

social network analysis A type of network analysis that investigates social structures on social media.

software The interface between hardware components and users that governs how the other components work with one another and provides users with the means of interacting with the system. Software includes mobile apps and internet browsers.

source document Documentation of a transaction, such as a receipt, bill, or invoice. Source documents may be electronic or paper documents, depending on the sophistication of the system.

special journal A journal that captures routine transactions that repeat often. Examples include a sales journal, purchases journal, cash receipts journal, and cash payments journal.

split purchase order A type of fraud in which employees intentionally separate a single purchase into two or more purchase orders to stay within a single purchase authorization limit. For example, if the purchaser is only authorized to purchase up to $1,000, an $1,800 purchase may be split into two purchase orders—one for $1,000 and one for $800—to circumvent the purchase limit.

spoofed packet A packet that has a forged source address. A hacker sends a spoofed packet to a system, and the system responds to a real user who is the target of the attack.

sprint In scrum, a single iteration of a systems project that includes multiple systems development life cycle stages. Sprints are often biweekly increments, after which the core team regroups to discuss what went well and how to improve work during the next sprint.

sprint backlog In scrum, a list of what the core team will develop during the current sprint.

SQL statement Written syntax for communicating SQL commands to a database.

stacked bar chart A visualization that illustrates parts of a whole within the rectangular bars of a traditional bar chart.

standard costing A process that measures units of production cost against actual costs. This is a comparison of what happened to what should have happened.

static dashboard A still image with no interactivity, such as a report imported into a PowerPoint presentation.

static data Data that doesn't change after it's created. Think of static data as a book—once it's printed, its pages do not change.

storyboard A collection of dashboards, stand-alone visualizations, infographics, and other presentation materials that turn data analytics and visualization into a business presentation.

strategic risk The inevitable risk that results when a strategy becomes less effective. Companies constantly update their strategies—and change their risks—to stay ahead of the competition. Adopting new technology, overhauling a product design, and changing vendors to avoid high costs of materials are all examples of companies taking proactive measures to avoid strategic risk.

structured data Data that is stored in a fixed field of a file. Whether it's stored in a spreadsheet or a database, data in a table is considered structured data.

subscription business model A business model that involves charging a monthly subscription fee for unlimited access to a service or product (for example, Netflix).

substantive procedures Steps used to determine if material misstatements (from error or fraud) exist in the underlying data that is used to create the financial statements. While substantive procedures are primarily used in external audits, internal auditors often use data analytics to perform substantive procedures over full populations of data from the AIS.

supervised learning A type of machine learning that uses labeled data sets to train the algorithm.

supplier A provider of goods and services that engages in only business-to-business relationships.

supply chain management (SCM) A process that involves overseeing the life cycle of a product from procuring raw materials through customer sales. The goal of supply chain management is to produce and distribute products or services to customers efficiently and effectively by supplying goods and services at the lowest cost possible while providing the highest value to the customer and other stakeholders. The physical flow of inventory moves sequentially through and is the most visible part of the supply chain. The information flow moves in all directions throughout the supply chain and allows supply chain participants to coordinate activities.

Supply Chain Management (SCM) module An enterprise resource planning (ERP) system module that coordinates the entire supply chain, from purchasing of raw materials and supplies to inventory management and warehousing. It also has the ability to manage supplier relationships.

swim lane An area within a flowchart that delineates the responsibility for activities involved in a business process. Swim lanes provide clarity and accountability by placing activities within the swim lanes of particular individuals, groups, or departments. A flowchart with swim lanes also shows the handoff points between different contributors and can help identify inefficiencies, redundancies, or waste in the process.

system go-live The point after a system is developed and tested when it is officially available to users. This critical event in the systems development life cycle is followed by ongoing maintenance of the live system.

systems development life cycle (SDLC) A project management framework with clearly defined stages for creating and deploying new systems. The SDLC includes seven stages: planning, analysis, design, development, testing, implementation, and maintenance.

systems documentation Documentation that provides an overview of a computer system. Systems developers need a clear understanding of the system's purpose and design and use systems documentation to help create new systems, maintain existing systems, and troubleshoot problems.

systems flowchart A flowchart that illustrates the flow of information through a system, including how information is accessed and where data is stored.

systems integration The process of joining different systems or subsystems into one larger system and ensuring that they function as one system.

systems model A model created by the lead systems analyst that includes graphical models such as flowcharts and data flow diagrams (DFDs) to describe in technical detail how a system will interact with users, other technologies, and systems processes and components.

systems software Specialized software that runs a computer's hardware and other software. Systems software is a platform for other software that coordinates all the activities throughout the system.

T

tailgating A method of circumventing physical access controls by closely following an authorized person through a secure entry point. The authorized person scans a badge or uses another access method, and the unauthorized individual passes through the door before it closes. Also known as *piggybacking*.

target residual risk The goal level of residual risk after implementing a risk response.

tax data hub A specialized database designed to provide a centralized store for tax-related data. It automatically extracts data from source systems and loads it in a standard format optimized for the tax department. In addition to increasing efficiency, tax data hubs reduce errors and enable data analytics.

taxonomy A classification system. An example is the Dewey Decimal System, which libraries use to classify books by division and subdivisions.

technical architecture specifications A document created by the lead systems analyst that identifies software, hardware, and network technologies a system will need.

technology risk A specific subset of operational risk that exists when technology failures have the potential to disrupt business. Technology failures include threats, vulnerabilities, and exposures of information.

terminator shape A process flowchart shape that marks the start or end of a process. It can be filled with either the word "Start" or "End" or a description of the beginning of a process. Every flowchart must start and end with a terminator.

test environment An environment where developers can design and test their code without having any impact on the actual system. The test environment is not connected to the system the code belongs to, so nothing developers do in it will impact the system. Also called a *sandbox*.

testing stage The fifth stage of a systems development life cycle project, when a system is evaluated against the design specifications and requirements definition to ensure that it meets expectations.

textual analysis A category of data analytics techniques used to interpret objects that include words. Textual analysis can interpret text transcriptions of conversations, emails, process narratives and flowcharts, and more to analyze a business process. It can be as simple as keyword searching and scraping of text-based documents, but there are also more complex applications.

third line of defense The internal audit portion of the Institute of Internal Auditors' three lines of defense model. The primary objective of internal audit is to test internal controls to provide assurance of their effectiveness to executive management and the board of directors. Internal audit is an independent function of the company that reports both to executive management and to the board of directors.

time series Data that occurs in chronological order across a period of time.

time trend In time series analysis, a consistent movement that does not repeat.

time-based model of controls A model that measures the residual risk for technology attacks by comparing the relationship of preventive (P), detective (D), and corrective (C) control functions. If P > (D + C), then the controls are effective. Otherwise, the security measures are inadequate to protect the company's systems from intruders.

timeboxing In scrum, a practice that involves allocating a fixed length of time to each activity to both define the activity and limit the amount of time dedicated to it.

timekeeping system A system for keeping track of time worked by hourly employees.

tone at the top The culture of an organization that flows downstream from executive leadership to impact all functional areas.

tooltip A pop-up in Tableau that appears when a user hovers over a data point and shows more information.

Transaction Control Language (TCL) A subset of SQL that interacts with data manipulation language (DML) commands when transactions are processed in a database.

transaction processing system (TPS) An information system that processes day-to-day business activities, provides a foundation for other systems, and captures data that is fed through the higher-level systems.

transaction-based AIS A traditional information system that captures only accounting business events and ignores nonfinancial data and the relationships between business events and business processes.

transparency A characteristic of blockchain that ensures, by consensus, maintenance of the most accurate and recent record of transactions

(or ledgers) arranged in transaction blocks. The transactions are recorded in the ledger only after the network participants reach consensus.

tree map A visualization that presents groups and subgroups as rectangular portions of the larger whole.

trial balance rollforward An analytic that an audit team performs for journal entry testing. Trial balance rollforward uses a calculation to verify the completeness of journal entry data. A rollforward re-creates the ending balance by adding the net journal entry activity to the beginning balance and compares it to the actual ending trial balance.

Trojan horse Malware that is disguised as benign software but carries malicious code that may be activated via a logic bomb. Trojan horses are commonly used to obtain back-door access to a target system. The result is unauthorized access that allows attackers to destroy data.

turnover rate From a human resources perspective, a metric that provides a numeric assessment of the risks related to employee terminations by calculating the percentage of employees who have left the company during a given period of time. This is an important metric because risk increases as the number of terminations rises.

typography Font choice for a visualization.

U

unauthorized hours Extra time on an employee's time sheet. An employee may pad their time sheet, for example, by adding 15 minutes to their start and end time every day. If this employee works six days a week, the scheme results in over 12 hours of fraudulent pay every month.

unauthorized shipment A type of fraud that enables a company to overstate revenues by creating sales and shipping to customers goods that were never ordered. This fraud scheme is most commonly executed at year end, with the return from the customer processed in the subsequent accounting period.

unrecorded revenue A fraud scheme that involves not documenting sales or destroying sales documentation and diverting funds, especially cash, elsewhere. This type of fraud is most easily perpetrated by smaller businesses, such as local restaurants that often have cash transactions from daily sales.

unstructured data Any data that is not stored in a fixed field of a record or a file. Examples of unstructured data include photographs, emails, PDFs, and text. This type of data cannot be easily stored in a table.

unsupervised learning A type of machine learning that uses algorithms to analyze unlabeled data sets for hidden patterns.

user acceptance testing (UAT) A type of system testing in which a select group of end users get access to the system so they can use the system and verify that it meets their expectations. They are often provided scenarios to

execute and then record their observations and any errors encountered.

user access de-provisioning The formal process of changing a user's access.

user access provisioning The formal process of granting new users access to a system.

user access review A review of all current users and their system roles. A user access review is an internal control that protects the data and security of a system by lowering a variety of inappropriate use risks.

user access role A group with predefined permissions to which users are assigned, with each user assigned to only one role at a time.

user authentication The process of associating the username of each authorized user with a unique identifier, such as something the user knows, has, or is. There are various kinds of identifiers, and they can be used individually or in combination for stronger control.

user documentation Content provided to system users to ensure that they are successful at using the system.

V

value The big data characteristic related to the usefulness of data. Value is arguably the most important of the 5Vs of big data because data isn't useful to a business unless it can be converted into valuable information. Given the significant resources allocated to collecting, storing, and analyzing data, it is essential to identify data value.

variable In the context of object-oriented databases, a name assigned to similar characteristics of objects in a class, much like fields in a relational database.

variety The big data characteristic related to the diversity of data created or collected. Data variety can refer to the difference between unstructured and structured big data or the different types of unstructured data. Variety is one of the 5Vs of big data.

velocity The big data characteristic related to the speed at which data is generated. Velocity is one of the 5Vs of big data.

vendor A supplier of goods and services that engages in both business-to-consumer and business-to-business relationships.

vendor invoice A bill from a vendor that includes the related purchase order number, billing date, description and quantities of goods, amount due, and payment terms.

veracity The big data characteristic related to the accuracy and truthfulness of data—that is, the extent to which the data can be trusted for insights. Data must be accurate, objective, and relevant to be useful and have value. Veracity is one of the 5Vs of big data.

virus A type of malware that replicates itself in a system and spreads quickly, causing corruption to systems and data. Attackers create viruses that cause a variety of problems. For example, viruses can steal usernames and passwords, spam email inboxes, corrupt files, or lock users out of systems.

visualization A graphical representation of information and data.

visualization audience The end users of a data visualization.

volume The big data characteristic related to quantity and scale of data generated every second. Volume is one of the 5Vs of big data.

vulnerability scan A control activity whose goal is to detect and classify security loopholes in the infrastructure.

W

wallet application An application that allows blockchain participants to broadcast and receive transactions.

warm backup site A backup site that is equipped with servers ready for systems to be installed and that contains only some of the equipment needed to ramp up operations. The data at a warm backup site may only be updated at the end of each day instead of in real time. A warm backup site provides less protection than a hot backup site, but it also costs significantly less to maintain.

warm colors Vivid colors like red, orange, and yellow that are associated with joy, energy, and playfulness.

Waterfall methodology A systems development methodology that breaks the systems development life cycle (SDLC) into formal stages, which must be executed in a linear fashion. Waterfall usually uses the seven stages of the SDLC framework, but companies can customize this approach by adding, removing, or renaming stages.

Web 2.0 The second stage of development of the World Wide Web, specifically associated with user-generated content and user participation on the internet. Web 2.0 is rich in interactive applications and socialization. It is a "read and write" environment, as opposed to the "read-only" environment of the original internet.

WHERE clause In SQL, a clause added to a SELECT statement to filter which records the query returns by adding values such as mathematical comparisons (=, <, <=, >, >=, <>) or special operators (BETWEEN, LIKE, IN, etc.).

whistleblower Someone who reports observations of possible misconduct, concerns about external financial reporting, or other issues.

white space Negative space that creates a visual pause and allows end users to process a visualization's message by eliminating unnecessary elements and distractions.

work in process Products that are in the process of being manufactured.

worm Malware that replicates without the assistance of human interaction. Worms arrive attached to email in the form of links or a file to download. Once a worm is installed on a machine, it infects every system it can reach.

X

XBRL (eXtensible Business Reporting Language) An open-standard markup language for business information, specifically for electronic financial reporting. XBRL is an adaptation of the computer language XML (eXtensible Markup Language) and is suitable for reporting business and financial data in a standardized, computer-readable manner. In the United States, the SEC has mandated the use of XBRL for SEC filings.

XBRL instance document An XBRL document prepared by a business. An XBRL instance document is structured to produce standardized financial statements. The document provides data plus structure for human readability and electronic recognition (e.g., for annual reports, earnings releases, and reports to financial institutions).

XBRL tag A standardized piece of XBRL that associates a concept in the taxonomy to a piece of data to make the electronic distribution, interpretation, extraction, and analysis of the data easier.

XML (eXtensible Markup Language) A computer meta language that allows users to define their own customized markup languages. It is commonly used to display documents on the internet.

Company Index

13 Clues, 13-39
21st Century Fox, 4-17

A

ADP (Automatic Data Processing, Inc.), 9-8, 9-10, 9-17, 9-21, 9-23, 9-25
Aero, Inc., 13-40
Airbnb, 1-9, 15-43, 16-26
Airbus, 7-23
Alibaba/Alibaba Group Holding, 2-2, 7-43
Alicia's Accessories, 1-35, 9-44–9-45, 10-44, 14-40
Alpaca Services, 10-44
Alphabet, Inc., 13-18, 13-40, 13-41, 18-39
Alteryx, 6-39, 6-43–6-44, 8-28
Amazing Nature, 12-53
Amazon, 2-2, 2-29, 4-8, 6-4, 6-20, 6-50, 7-3, 7-11, 7-12, 12-6, 12-29, 12-50, 14-15, 14-19, 14-39, 15-19, 15-20, 15-21, 16-10, 16-11, 16-26, 16-35, 17-21, 17-22, 17-23, 18-39
American Express (Amex), 6-31–6-32
AML Technical Services, 9-41
Anheuser-Busch, 15-26
Ant Financial Group, 7-43
Apple, 2-2, 2-29, 4-6, 7-8, 12-25, 14-15, 14-19, 17-10, 17-15, 17-21, 18-38
Archer Solutions, 6-51
Arthur Andersen, 3-35, 15-3
Atlass Software Services, 10-44
Automatic Data Processing, Inc. (ADP), 9-8, 9-10, 9-17, 9-21, 9-23, 9-25

B

Baker Tilly, 16-5, 16-30
Bamboozled Doggos, 2-33
Beeman Sports, 8-32
Bella Telephones, 10-44
Berkshire Hathaway, 18-39
Best Buy, 8-33, 15-19
Blackline, 13-5
Blisst, 15-38
Blizzard, 12-53
Blockbuster, 2-12, 2-27, 7-3
Blue Clown Events, 10-44
Boeing, 2-29
Bolt, 18-42
Book Co., 11-34
Bosch, 11-24
Bounty, 12-52
Brandsgård, Thyrsted, 6-13
Brass Polishing - Commercial Services, 10-44
Braxton's, 13-40
Buffet, Warren, 2-11
Build a Moose Toy Company, 9-44
Burger King, 8-2

C

Cantey, Willis, 3-10
Cape Renovations, 3-35–3-36
Cash App, 7-28
CEI, 9-45
Charles Schwab, 18-3, 18-37

Chipotle, 8-34, 15-41
Christiansen, Ole Kirk, 6-13
Chrystelle, 6-48
Clever Cabinets, 1-36
Clover, 4-11
Cobblestone, 8-35
Coca-Cola, 4-12, 16-5–16-6, 16-30
Codecademy, 6-44
Colonial Pipeline, 16-26
Computer Computer, 10-44
Cookie Crunch, 4-17–4-18, 8-36
Cosco Shipping Holdings, 7-43
Covington Financial, 3-34
CrownCorp, 11-37
Crunchie Cookies, 4-34

D

David's Tea, 17-22
Delaware Pest Authority, 10-44
Dell, 4-11
Deloitte, 7-32, 7-41, 11-24, 17-3, 17-28
Delta, 15-41
DHL, 11-24
Dilworth Insurance Agency, 15-6
Disney, 1-35, 4-17, 17-22
Domino's, 1-35
DoorDash, 1-7, 1-9, 5-3, 6-2, 12-6
Drip, 14-44
Dropbox, 1-9, 4-7, 14-23, 14-24, 14-25
Dyn, Inc., 16-26

E

eBay, 17-22
Eleanor Rigby's Crematorium and Pet Custodian Services, 14-38
Encompass Health, 15-29
Enron, 3-23, 3-35, 3-37, 15-3
Enterprise, 15-41
Equifax, 16-4, 16-13, 16-14, 16-20, 16-21, 16-29, 16-32
Etsy, 2-31, 16-26, 17-22
Exxon Mobil, 18-39
EY (Ernst & Young Global Limited), 5-20, 7-41, 12-25, 17-3

F

Facebook, 2-2, 2-29, 5-5, 5-29, 6-20, 14-15
FBI, 10-22, 15-1, 16-5, 16-30, 16-33
FedEx, 16-10
Financial Times, 12-25
Fitbit, 7-8
Flowers & Flours, 1-15–1-16, 11-12, 12-11, 15-7
FLUSH-IT Toilet Installation, 10-44
Forbes, 2-8, 7-41
Forbidden Island, 13-39

G

Game Stop, 12-53
Gartner, 13-5
Gellin's Gelatins, 6-48, 10-44
General Electric, 11-25
GL Solutions, 14-40

Good Foods, 12-13–12-15, 12-18, 12-20–12-21, 12-32, 12-41, 13-10
Google, 2-29, 3-3, 4-7–4-8, 4-11–4-13, 5-4, 5-6, 7-3, 7-36–7-37, 13-18, 14-7, 14-15, 14-19, 14-30, 14-39, 16-5, 16-13, 16-30, 16-33
Grubhub, 1-7

H

HBO, 16-26
Health Foods Corporation, 8-35
HealthSouth, 15-29
Hello Fresh, 12-6
The Hill House, 8-33
Hilton, 8-33
Home Depot, 1-7
Honda, 4-26–4-27
Hydro Extrusion Portland Inc., 10-5

I

Idaho Chicken Farm, 10-44
Indigo, 17-22
Innovation Depot, 1-33
Insomnia Cookies, 1-7
Instagram, 5-4, 5-5
Insyte CPAs, 8-18
Investink, 9-42
Ion, 2-29
Isabella's, 13-39
ISS World, 16-26

J

J. Duram Landscaping, 10-44
Janitorial Services R Us, 10-44
Jellyfish, 4-31
Jimmy's Steakhouse, 15-41
Joe's Joe Coffee Catering, 10-44
JPMorgan Chase & Co., 16-5–16-6, 16-30
Julia's Cookies, 1-0–1-1, 1-4, 1-6–1-9, 1-11, 1-15–1-16, 1-20–1-22, 1-24–1-25, 1-27, 1-38–1-39, 2-1–2-4, 2-6–2-11, 2-13–2-18, 2-23, 2-26, 2-34, 3-0–3-1, 3-3, 3-5–3-7, 3-9, 3-11–3-12, 3-14–3-16, 3-19–3-21, 3-27–3-29, 3-40, 4-0–4-2, 4-9–4-21, 4-25, 4-35, 5-0–5-1, 5-3, 5-7, 5-10, 5-11–5-12, 5-16, 5-17, 5-22, 5-23–5-24, 5-33, 6-0–6-2, 6-4–6-8, 6-12, 6-15–6-18, 6-21–6-26, 6-28, 6-31–6-32, 6-36–6-37, 6-39–6-40, 6-53, 7-0–7-1, 7-5–7-6, 7-12, 7-21, 7-31, 7-35–7-36, 7-43–7-44, 8-0–8-1, 8-5, 8-9, 8-12, 8-15–8-25, 8-35–8-37, 9-0–9-1, 9-3, 9-5–9-9, 9-15, 9-19–9-23, 9-28, 9-32–9-36, 9-41, 9-46–9-47, 10-0–10-1, 10-4–10-10, 10-14–10-15, 10-18–10-24, 10-25–10-26, 10-28, 10-30–10-32, 10-42, 10-45–10-47, 11-0–11-2, 11-4–11-7, 11-8–11-9, 11-11–11-12, 11-15, 11-17–11-20, 11-23, 11-25, 11-28, 11-35, 11-40–11-41, 12-0–12-6, 12-8–12-13, 12-15, 12-17, 12-18–12-19, 12-20–12-24, 12-27–12-28, 12-32–12-35, 12-38, 12-40–12-41, 12-55–12-56, 13-0–13-1, 13-4, 13-7–13-12, 13-19, 13-22, 13-24, 13-28–13-29, 13-43–13-44, 14-0–14-1,

Julia's Cookies (*Continued*)
14-3, 14-5, 14-8, 14-14–14-17, 14-20–14-21, 14-28–14-29, 14-31–14-34, 14-44–14-45, 15-0–15-2, 15-4, 15-7–15-8, 15-10–15-12, 15-15–15-16, , 15-18–15-22, 15-25–15-29, 15-32, 15-42–15-43, 16-0–16-1, 16-7–16-8, 16-11–16-12, 16-16, 16-22–16-23, 16-27, 16-35–16-37, 17-0–17-1, 17-4, 17-8, 17-10–17-1117-13–17-14, 17-16, 17-21–17-23, 17-34–17-35, 18-0–18-1, 18-3–18-4, 18-6, 18-13–18-14, 18-16–18-21, 18-25–18-26, 18-29, 18-32–18-34, 18-39, 18-48–18-49
Justflowers, 17-22

K
Kaiser Permanente, 15-3
KiCo, 4-33
Kim's Auto Dealership, 5-30
Knack, 4-13
Kniberg, Henrik, 6-13
KPMG, 7-41, 12-25, 17-3
Kroger, 12-53, 15-26

L
Leason Surgical, 11-38
LEGO, 6-13
Lenya Lighting, LLC, 13-42
Lillianna's Crafts, 4-34
LinkedIn, 1-1, 1-34, 7-7, 7-11, 16-5, 16-32
Lookout Adventures, 14-41–14-42
Lounging Luxury, 12-54
LowCost Wholesalers, 13-9
Lucasfilm, 4-17
Luis Air and Heating, 10-44
Lululemon, 17-22
Lyft, 4-16–4-17, 15-20, 15-40

M
Macy's, 17-22
Maggianos, 8-34
Manic Automotive, 9-45
Marriott, 15-20
Marvel, 4-17
Mass Effect Visual Arts, 10-44
McDonald's, 1-9, 1-12, 1-17, 1-32, 8-2
Mega-Construction, 7-41
MetLife, 13-14
Microsoft, 4-6, 4-8, 4-11–4-13, 4-26, 4-30, 4-32, 4-34, 5-9, 6-31, 7-37, 8-14, 9-37, 13-33, 16-4
Mighty Cleaner Company, 10-44
MillerCoors, 4-27–4-28
Mirabel Enterprises, 5-31
Missguided, 17-22
Modem's Monitors and More, 10-44
MongoDB, 6-50
Monster Beverage Corp., 13-20, 13-21, 15-26
Moonlight & Co., 16-31
Moore, Emily, 9-26
Mr. Shankley's Medical Services Corp., 6-46

N
NASA, 10-4–10-5
Nature's Naturals, 12-54
Nestlé, 11-9
Netflix, 1-9, 1-12, 2-12, 3-9, 4-12, 4-20, 7-3, 7-7, 14-15, 14-19, 16-26
NetSuite, 4-14
New York Stock Exchange, 14-22

New York Times, 10-45
Nike, 13-21
Nolls, 16-34–16-35
Norsk Hydro ASA, 10-5
North Green Farms, 3-11–3-13

O
OneBank, 16-35
OneStream, 13-5
On-the-Spot, Inc., 8-31
Oracle, 4-6, 4-26, 4-34, 5-9, 6-31, 6-50, 13-5

P
Pacific Gas & Electric (PG&E), 2-29
Parker, LLC, 12-52
Parkwood Entertainment, 1-35
PayPal, 2-29, 6-31–6-32, 12-25, 16-10–16-11, 16-26
PeopleSoft, 4-22, 4-34
PetSmart, 17-22
Philips, 4-13, 7-7
Pillsbury, 12-12
Pizza Palace, 5-31
Pluto-Cola, 7-42
Porsche, 13-21
Portia's Ports, 3-37
Pride College, 2-27
Protiviti, 7-42
PwC (PricewaterhouseCoopers), 7-11, 7-41, 13-16, 17-3

Q
Quality Cabinets, 11-36

R
Referee Universal, 10-44
Refratechnik Group, 4-25
Regina Extracts, 10-44
Relativity Media, 10-44
Reliant, Inc., 6-49
Remy's, 10-44
Renovations and Demolition, 10-44
Ritz Carlton, 15-41
Rohler, 10-43
The Royal Cooks, 5-31–5-32

S
Sage, 1-6, 4-14, 4-26, 4-34, 8-26, 13-5
Salesforce, 4-8, 4-34, 14-8, 14-11
SAP, 4-17, 4-26–4-28, 4-34, 9-8, 13-1, 13-5
Sapa Profiles Inc., 10-4–10-5
SAS, 4-34
ScoopsAhoy, 18-43
Seagate, 4-27
Sephora, 17-22
Serenity Acres, 2-33
Serve Co. Disaster Cleaning, 10-44
ServiceNow, 14-33
Shaggy's, 14-44
Shipt, 12-6
ShopCo, 12-53
Siemens, 11-23, 16-25
Silverman, Mark, 9-26
Sips and Drips, 13-38
Slack, 4-8
Smith, John, 9-26
Snapchat, 7-10
Snickers Joke House, 9-40

Socrates, 13-40
Southeastern Paper, 3-36
Southwest, 15-20
SpaceX, 2-2
Spotify, 16-26, 17-10
Square, 4-11–4-12, 4-30, 7-29
Stanford Health Care, 15-3
Starbucks, 8-33, 8-34, 12-29, 12-52, 15-20, 15-41, 17-22
Subaru, 4-26
SumUp, 4-11

T
Tagetik, 13-5
Tallie, 4-17
Tangoe Inc., 15-41–15-42
Target, 12-12, 12-52–12-53
Teradata, 6-31
Tesla, 4-11, 16-5–16-6, 16-30, 16-33, 18-39
Tiff's Treats, 1-7
TikTok, 1-7, 5-4–5-5
Toshiba, 15-40
Touchstone Corporation, 9-42
Twitter, 17-25
Tyco, 3-23, 3-37

U
Uber, 1-7, 1-24, 4-20, 5-16, 5-27–5-28, 15-40–15-41, 17-2
Uber Eats, 5-3, 6-2, 8-20, 12-6, 15-20
UiPath Academy, 6-44
UPS, 16-10

V
Venmo, 4-5, 6-18, 6-31–6-32, 6-34, 7-28
Verizon, 8-33–8-34
Victor's Flowers, 10-44
Visa, 6-31–6-32, 7-28
Volkswagen, 2-10, 2-11, 2-27
Volt, 18-45

W
Wall Street Journal, 10-45, 15-38
Walmart, 7-36, 12-40, 12-53, 13-20–13-21, 17-22, 18-39
WanderLust, LLC, 6-47
Wells Fargo, 1-39, 16-33–16-34
WestRock, 12-29
Wholesalers LLC, 12-32
Wirecard, 12-25
Womping Wembley Corp., 14-39
Workday, 4-26
Workiva, 13-5
WorldCom, 3-23, 3-37, 15-3

X
XBRL International Consortium, 13-16
Xero, 4-14

Y
Ye Olde Paints, 10-41
Yelp, 12-51
YouTube, 5-5, 6-20, 6-44

Z
Zelle, 4-5, 7-28
Zoho, 4-13
Zolo, 18-48

Subject Index

A

AAA (American Accounting Association), 3-25
ABC (activity-based cost accounting), 11-18–11-21
Access (Microsoft), 4-6, 4-13, 5-9, 5-14, 5-18
Access, user. *See* User access
Access attacks
  cybersecurity for, 16-15–16-20
  defined, 16-15
  logical, 16-17–16-20
  physical, 16-15–16-16
Access control vestibule, 14-15
Accidental tailgating, 16-15
Accountants. *See* Accounting professionals
Accounting
  clustering in, 17-10
  cost, 11-14–11-21, 13-20–13-21, 17-18
  data analytics and, 1-25–1-27, 5-18–5-26
  decision making based on, 1-2–1-3
  financial, 1-4, 5-21–5-22, 7-34
  information importance in, 1-2–1-4
  managerial, 5-22–5-24, 11-14, 13-20–13-24, 13-26, 17-17. *See also* Cost accounting
  overview of, 1-1
  responsibility, 13-21–13-22
  software for startups, 4-14–4-15
  stereotypes and misconceptions about, 1-2
  subdisciplines in, 1-4
  tax, 5-24, 7-34, 14-26, 14-29
Accounting equation, 13-6, 13-45–13-46
Accounting information systems (AIS)
  complexity of, 1-3
  cost accounting in, 11-14–11-21
  data, 1-4–1-5
  defined, 1-3, 1-12, 1-19, 4-2
  established Procedures, 1-5
  evolution of, 1-13–1-18
  internal controls, 1-5
  IT infrastructure, 1-5
  financial reporting role of, 13-2–13-5
  financial statement generation in, 13-6–13-15
  internal controls. *See* Internal controls
  management and business process iterative relationship with, 1-20–1-22
  process-based, 1-13–1-18, 4-4
  risk management importance to, 3-1. *See also* Risk management
  software, 1-5–1-6
  terminology, 1-3
  as transaction processing system, 4-3
  transaction-based, 1-13–1-18, 4-4
  users, 1-6
Accounting professionals
  accounting support services, 1-29
  audit data analyst, 17-26
  auditors as. *See* Auditors
  Big Four external auditor, 8-28
  blockchain relevance to, 7-30–7-35
  career skills. *See* Career skills
  chief financial officer, 13-33–13-34

conversion process roles, 11-1, 11-31
critical thinking skills, 1-3, 7-21
cybersecurity roles, 16-1, 16-4–16-6, 16-28–16-29
data analytics roles, 17-1–17-4, 17-26
data use and management, 5-1, 5-18–5-26
data visualization roles, 18-1, 18-2, 18-34–18-35
director of innovation, public accounting firm, 7-37
director of SOX compliance, 9-37
disruptive technology interfaces, 7-8, 7-32–7-37
documentation roles, 8-1, 8-28
finance digital transformation analyst, 6-43
finance transformation manager, 12-45
financial reporting roles, 13-1–13-2, 13-33–13-34
fraud analytics specialist, 15-34
fraud management roles, 15-1, 15-8–15-13, 15-34
health insurance business analyst, 18-34–18-35
human resources and payroll roles, 9-1, 9-7
IT system roles, 14-33
job postings for. *See* Job postings
marketing, sales, and collections roles, 12-1, 12-45
MBA business analytics and management information systems, 5-26
nontraditional CPA firm, 2-24–2-25
program manager, electric vehicle manufacturer, 11-31
public accounting cybersecurity director, 16-28–16-29
purchasing and payments processes roles, 10-1
risk management firm managing partner, 3-30–3-31
risk management roles, 2-1–2-2, 2-19, 2-24–2-25, 3-1, 3-30–3-31. *See also* risk-related entries
robotic process automation benefiting, 7-13–7-23
senior accountant at local startup, 4-29
senior associate, internal audit analytics, 10-38
software and information systems roles, 4-1
systems and database interactions, 6-1, 6-43–6-44
Accounts payable
  billing schemes, 15-22
  blockchain effects, 7-34
  continuous fraud monitoring, 10-28
  credit payments processes and, 10-25–10-26
  defined, 10-25
  overview of, 10-6
  reporting and analytics, 10-36–10-37
  robotic process automation, 7-18–7-19, 7-20
Accounts receivable

business-to-business sales, 12-11–12-12, 12-18, 12-20–12-21, 12-29–12-30, 12-32–12-33
  maturity model, 12-34–12-35
  reporting and analytics, 12-44
  risks and controls, 12-29–12-35
  skimming, 15-17–15-18
  subsidiary ledgers, 13-10
Accrued payroll, 9-35
ACFE. *See* Association of Fraud Examiners (ACFE), *Report to the Nations*
ACH (Automated Clearing House) Network, 12-33
Acquisitions, 1-19. *See also* Acquisitions and payments processes; Purchasing processes
  acquisition-based growth, 4-16–4-17, 4-21
  defined, 4-16
  mergers vs., 4-16
  systems integration with, 4-17–4-18
Acquisitions and payments processes
  in accounting information systems, 1-13–1-18
  in basic business model, 1-10, 1-14, 2-3, 9-2
  business events in, 1-12
  human resources and payroll as, 9-2, 9-26
  purchasing and payments processes as, 10-2
  risks in, 2-4
Actual residual risk, 2-21, 2-24, 3-2
Adjusted trial balance, 13-11
Administrator role, 14-8
Advance payments, 12-29, 12-32
AFL-CIO, 15-3
Agile methodology
  defined, 6-10, 6-15
  real-world example, 6-13
  scrum, 6-11–6-13
  selection of, 6-13–6-14
  for systems development, 6-10–6-15
AI. *See* Artificial intelligence (AI)
AIS. *See* Accounting information systems
American Accounting Association (AAA), 3-25
American Institute of Certified Public Accountants (AICPA), 3-3, 3-6, 3-25, 7-32
Analysis stage, of SDLC, 6-3, 6-4
Analytics. *See* Data analytics
Anomaly detection, 17-8, 17-14, 18-22
Antivirus software, 4-6
Application software, 4-6
Applications
  defined, 3-10
  IT application controls, 3-8–3-10, 3-16
  wallet, 7-25–7-26
AR (augmented reality), 7-9–7-10, 11-25
Artifacts, scrum, 6-12–6-13
Artificial intelligence (AI). *See also* Robotics
  automated controls, 3-12–3-13
  data analytics with, 1-28, 17-5–17-6
  defined, 7-13

Artificial intelligence (*Continued*)
machine learning, 14-12, 17-5–17-6, 17-10–17-14, 17-24
robotic process automation vs., 7-14
Asset misappropriation
defined, 15-14, 15-22
fraud and, 15-5, 15-14–15-22
fraudulent disbursements as, 15-18–15-23
larceny as, 15-17–15-18
skimming as, 15-15–15-17
Assets
fixed. *See* Fixed assets
misappropriation of, 15-5, 15-14–15-22
overstatement of, 10-21, 15-24–15-27
Association of Fraud Examiners (ACFE),
Report to the Nations, 15-2–15-5, 15-6, 15-11–15-14, 15-23
Audit committees, 3-21, 3-22
Audit trail, 13-9
Auditors
blockchain use, 7-33–7-34
external, role of, 3-18
independence of, 3-21
misperceptions about, 1-2
skills required, 1-7–1-8
Audits
blockchain applications, 7-33–7-34
data analytics for, 5-19–5-21
documentation for, 8-7–8-8, 8-12, 8-28
external. *See* External audits
for fraud, 13-11, 15-6, 15-8, 15-13
internal. *See* Internal audits
natural language processing for, 17-25
Authorization, 3-4
Automated Clearing House (ACH) Network, 12-33, 12-36
Automated controls
automated sales process, 12-26
change to, management of, 14-28
defined, 3-12, 3-16
examples, 3-11, 3-12
manual combined with, 3-13
manual vs., 3-11
overview of, 3-12–3-13
user access review as, 14-10
Automation
artificial intelligence as, 7-14. *See also* Artificial intelligence
barriers to, 11-25
brute-force attacks using, 16-17–16-18
business process, 7-14, 7-22
ERP system, 4-23, 4-27–4-28
real-world example, 7-23
robotic process, 7-13–7-24, 14-12, 14-28
types of, 7-14
Autonomous Things (AuT), 7-11–7-12, 7-13

B

B2B sales. *See* Business-to-business (B2B) sales
B2C sales. *See* Business-to-consumer (B2C) sales
Background checks, 9-8
Backups
backup cycles, 14-25–14-26
backup sites, 14-19–14-20
data backup, defined, 14-23
differential, 14-24
full, 14-23–14-24
grandfather-father-son redundant, 14-25

incremental, 14-24–14-25
software for, 4-6
strategies for, 14-22–14-25
Balance sheets
accounting equation for, 13-45–13-46
defined, 13-30
ratios of accounts, 13-31
Balanced scorecard, 13-22–13-24
Ballesteros, Catalina, 8-28
Bank deposits, 12-30–12-31
Bank remittance reports, 12-30–12-31
Banking, data analytics for, 17-7, 17-21–17-23
Bar charts, 18-16–18-18, 18-27, 18-30, 18-32
stacked, 18-17–18-18, 18-22
Batch processing, 4-4, 4-10, 9-23
Baumann, Alana, 18-34–18-35
BCP. *See* Business continuity planning
"Being data-minded," 1-29
Behavioral red flags, 15-6–15-8
Benchmarks, 1-20, 3-19
Benefits. *See* Employee benefits
Bezos, Jeff, 2-2
Bid-rigging schemes, 10-21–10-22, 15-4
Big data
characteristics of, 5-13–5-17
data summarization of, 17-9–17-10
defined, 5-13, 5-17
geotags for, 5-22
Internet of Things creating, 7-7–7-9
mobile technologies and, 5-17
real-world example, 5-16
value of, 5-14, 5-16, 7-9
variety of, 5-15, 7-9
velocity of, 5-14–5-15, 7-9
veracity of, 5-13, 5-15, 7-9
volume of, 5-14, 7-9
Bill of materials (BOM), 11-4, 11-13
Bill of operations (BOO), 11-4–11-6
Billing, 12-20–12-21
Billing schemes, 15-22
Binary code, 5-2, 5-8
Bins, 18-19
Biometric access controls, 14-4, 14-7
Bitcoin, 7-24–7-29, 7-32
Bits, data, 5-2–5-3, 5-14
Block coding, 13-6–13-7
Blockchain
accounting profession relevance, 7-32–7-36
for audits, 7-33
basics of, 7-25–7-26
bitcoin, 7-24–7-29, 7-32
career opportunities with, 7-33–7-35
consensus or proof of work, 7-26, 7-29–7-30
consortium, 7-31
cryptology in, 7-26
data quality with, 7-33, 7-35
decentralization with, 7-30
defined, 7-24
as disruptive technology, 7-24–7-36
double-entry general ledgers vs., 7-33–7-34
fundamental principles, 7-29–7-30
hash strings, 7-33
immutability of, 7-29, 7-30
ledgers, 7-26–7-29
miners, 7-25–7-26, 7-29
nodes, 7-25–7-26, 7-29
private, 7-30–7-31
public, 7-30
small business use of, 7-35

smart contracts, 7-25, 7-35
transaction process, 7-24, 7-27
transparency of, 7-30
wallet applications, 7-25–7-26
Blockchain mining, 7-31
Blockchain system, 7-31
Board of directors
internal control accountability, 3-17–3-18
IT system strategies, 14-2–14-3
risk response responsibilities, 2-19–21-20
Bolus, Miriam, 1-29
Botnets, 16-22
Box plots, 18-20–18-21, 18-25
BPMN (business process model and notation), 8-9–8-10
Break-even analysis, 17-17
Bribery, commercial, 15-5
Brute-force attacks, 16-17–16-19, 16-22
Bureau of Labor and Statistics, U.S., 2-19
Business activities, 1-11, 1-13. *See also* Business events
Business analysts, 17-3
Business continuity planning (BCP)
as corrective control, 3-10
defined, 14-19, 14-27
disaster recovery, 11-8, 14-19–14-20. *See also* Backups
for IT systems, 14-17–14-19, 14-24
plans included in, 14-17
risks and controls, 14-26
Business disruptions
planning for. *See* Business continuity planning
software access and, 4-7
as technology risk, 7-4
Business events
in acquisitions and payments processes, 1-14
data from, 1-21, 1-27
defined, 1-3, 1-9, 1-13
financing events, 1-11, 10-25, 12-29
information events, 1-11, 1-14
investing events, 1-11, 10-25, 12-29
operating events, 1-11, 10-25, 12-29
terminology and language for, 1-10
Business functions, 2-3–2-4, 2-7
Business intelligence analysts, 17-3
Business models
basic, 1-9–1-10, 1-13, 2-3, 9-2, 10-2, 11-2, 12-2
business processes in, 1-9–1-10, 1-13, 2-3, 9-2, 10-2, 11-2, 12-2
defined, 1-8, 1-12
direct-to-consumers, 1-9
franchise, 1-9
freemium, 1-9
peer-to-peer, 1-9
retailer, 1-9
social responsibility in, 1-8–1-9
subscription, 1-9
Business operations. *See also specific topics below*
business events, 1-11–1-12
business models, 1-8–1-9
business processes, 1-9–1-10
extended reality technologies for, 7-10
internal controls for, 3-17–3-20, 3-26
Internet of Things products for, 7-7–7-8
purpose of business, 1-8
risk with, 2-8–2-9

Business process automation, 7-14, 7-22, 7-24.
    See also Robotic process automation (RPA)
Business process model and notation (BPMN),
    8-9–8-10, 8-13
Business processes
  acquisitions and payments processes, 1-10,
    1-13–1-17, 2-3–2-4, 9-2, 9-25, 10-2. *See also*
    Acquisitions; Payments processes;
    Purchasing processes
  automation of, 7-13, 7-22. *See also* Robotic
    process automation (RPA)
  in basic business model, 1-9–1-10, 1-13, 2-3,
    9-2, 10-2, 11-2, 12-2
  business events combined for, 1-12
  business functions implementing, 2-3–2-4
  changing and improving, 1-20
  conversion processes, 1-10, 1-14, 1-16–1-17,
    2-3–2-4, 11-1–11-31. *See also*
    Conversion processes
  defined, 1-9, 1-12, 2-3, 9-2
  documentation of, 8-8–8-25. *See also*
    Documentation
  flowcharts of. *See* Flowcharts
  human resources. *See* Human resources
  improvements to, 8-6, 8-18
  management and information system
    iterative relationship with, 1-20, 1-21
  management responsibilities for, 1-20–1-21
  marketing, sales, and collections processes,
    1-10, 1-14, 1-17–1-18, 2-3–2-4, 12-1–12-45,
    17-8. *See also* Marketing, sales, and
    collections processes
  maturity model, 3-18–3-20, 3-22
  payroll. *See* Payroll
  risks in, 2-3–2-4
Business rules, 6-26, 6-29
Business-to-business (B2B) sales
  accounts receivable, 12-11–12-12, 12-18,
    12-20–12-21, 12-29–12-30, 12-32–12-33
  customer evaluation, 12-14
  defined, 12-2
  inventory management, 12-18
  marketing, 12-12–12-13
  opportunities and challenges, 12-15
  pricing and contracts, 12-13–12-15
  process flowchart for, 12-22
  revenue recognition, 12-19
  risks and controls, 12-12–12-15, 12-16–12-17,
    12-19–12-20
  sales, 12-12, 12-17
  shipping, 12-12, 12-17–12-20
Business-to-consumer (B2C) sales
  cash collections, 12-3, 12-4, 12-29
  defined, 12-2
  delivery, 12-3, 12-4–12-7
  inventory management, 12-9
  marketing, 12-3–12-4
  process flowchart, 12-6–12-8
  risks and controls, 12-4, 12-4–12-7
  sales, 12-3–12-5
  supply chain management, 12-9–12-10
Bytes, data, 5-2–5-3, 5-13–5-14

C
C#, 4-5, 6-20
C++, 4-5
Calculated fields, database, 11-28
Cantey Technology, 3-10
Capacity utilization rate, 11-30

Capital expenditures (CAPEX), 10-17, 10-24
Capitalization of expenses, 15-29
Capitalized costs, expensing, 15-31–15-32
Cardinality, 6-26
Career skills. *See also* Skills
  accounting and information systems, 1-13,
    1-18, 1-24, 1-26
  conversion processes, 11-1, 11-4, 11-17,
    11-24, 11-27, 11-31
  cybersecurity, 16-5–16-6, 16-12, 16-18, 16-21
  data analytics, 17-2–17-4, 17-6, 17-10, 17-18,
    17-23
  data knowledge and analysis, 5-6, 5-11, 5-15,
    5-19–5-20
  data visualization, 18-5, 18-8–18-9, 18-15, 18-32
  documentation, 8-2, 8-11, 8-15
  emerging and disruptive technologies, 7-5,
    7-11, 7-16, 7-30, 7-33
  financial reporting, 13-4, 13-10, 13-17, 13-21,
    13-30
  fraud prevention, 15-4, 15-12, 15-15, 15-34
  human resources and payroll, 9-4, 9-7, 9-15,
    9-21, 9-30
  internal controls for risk management, 3-3,
    3-13, 3-18, 3-25
  IT systems, 14-2, 14-9, 14-12, 14-24, 14-27
  marketing, sales, and collections processes,
    12-11, 12-23, 12-32, 12-37
  purchasing and payments processes, 10-3,
    10-11, 10-19, 10-25, 10-32
  risk identification and assessment, 2-4–2-5,
    2-18, 2-20
  software and information systems, 4-3,
    4-14–4-15, 4-17, 4-26
  systems and database use, 6-6, 6-11,
    6-21–6-22, 6-33, 6-39–6-40
Case studies. *See* Tableau case studies
Cash
  larceny, 15-17
  skimming, 15-15–15-16
Cash collections
  bank deposits of, 12-30–12-31
  business-to-consumer sales, 12-3, 12-6, 12-29
  receipt of payments, 12-29–12-30
  recording, 12-32–12-33
  reporting and analytics, 12-43–12-44
  risks and controls, 12-6, 12-29–12-36
Cash disbursements journals, 10-25
Cash disbursements processes. *See* Payments
    processes
Cash flow statements, 10-24–10-25, 10-28,
    12-29, 13-30, 13-45
Categorical values of data, 17-7, 18-15–18-19
Centers of excellence (COEs)
  defined, 7-6, 7-7
  emerging technology, 7-4, 7-6
  robotic process automation, 7-14
  Tableau, 18-3
Centralized ledgers, 7-26
Centralized systems, 4-19–4-20, 4-22
Certified Fraud Examiners (CFEs), 15-10
Certified Information Systems Auditor
    (CISA), 16-5–16-6
CFO (chief financial officer), 13-2
Chandiwala, Hafiz, 13-33
Change management
  defined, 14-27, 14-35
  emergency changes, 14-32–14-33
  for IT systems, 14-25–14-33

management responsibility for, 1-19
  in model environment, 14-26–14-30
  normal changes, 14-32–14-33
  process, 14-28–14-32
  in production environment, 14-27–14-28, 14-30
  risks and controls, 14-33
  in test environment, 14-27–14-30
  user acceptance testing, 14-29
Channel stuffing, 12-27, 12-40, 15-26–15-27, 15-33
Chart of accounts, 13-6–13-7
Checklists, 8-7–8-8
Chief executives. *See* Management
Chief financial officer (CFO), 13-2
CISA (Cybersecurity and Infrastructure
    Security Agency), 16-5–16-6
Classes, in databases, 6-19–6-20
Classification, 17-14
  in data analytics, 17-6, 17-11–17-13, 18-23
  of internal controls, 3-8–3-15
  misclassification of revenue, 15-30–15-31
Cloud computing
  defined, 4-8, 4-11
  deployment models, 4-8
  hybrid clouds, 4-8
  Internet of Things and, 4-13
  overview of, 4-7–4-9
  private clouds, 4-8
  public clouds, 4-8
  risks of, 4-9–4-10
  service models, 4-8–4-11
Clustering, 17-6, 17-10–17-11, 18-23
Clusters, defined, 17-10
COBIT framework
  Align, Plan, and Organize (APO) objective, 14-4
  Build, Acquire, and Implement (BAI)
    objective, 14-4
  COBIT 2019 version, 14-3
  COSO frameworks compared, 14-3
  cybersecurity controls, 16-6–16-8
  Deliver, Service, and Support (DSS) objective,
    14-4
  domains of control objectives, 14-4
  Evaluate, Direct, and Monitor (EDM)
    objective, 14-4
  for IT systems, 14-2–14-6
  Monitor, Evaluate, and Assess (MEA)
    objective, 14-4
  name of, 14-2
Codes of conduct, 15-12
Coding system, 13-6–13-7
COEs. *See* Centers of excellence
Cold backup sites, 14-21–14-22
Collections. *See also* Accounts receivable;
    Cash collections; Marketing, sales, and
    collections processes
  bank deposits, 12-30–12-31
  business-to-business sales, 12-20–12-21,
    12-29–12-30, 12-32–12-33
  business-to-consumer sales, 12-3, 12-6, 12-29
  process flowcharts, 12-33–12-34
  receipt of payments, 12-29–12-30
  recording cash receipts, 12-32–12-33
  reporting and analytics, 12-43–12-44
  risks and controls, 12-6, 12-29–12-36
Collusion
  bid rigging and, 10-21–10-22, 10-24, 15-4
  blockchain risk of, 7-30
  defined, 3-6, 3-8
  fraud and, 12-13, 12-40, 15-11–15-12

Color
  accessibility of, 18-9–18-10
  cool, 18-7
  in data visualization, 18-7–18-10, 18-18–18-19
  pairings of, 18-7–18-8
  psychology and emotional response to, 18-8–18-9
  warm, 18-7
Color vision deficiency (CVD)/color blindness, 18-9–18-10, 18-18
Columns, database, 6-17–6-18
Commands
  JOIN operators, 6-35–6-40
  Select, 6-30–6-33, 6-37–6-40
  SQL, 6-30–6-40
  Where clause, 6-33–6-35, 6-37–6-40
Commercial bribery, 15-5, 15-8
Committee of Sponsoring Organizations of the Treadway Commission (COSO)
  Enterprise Risk Management Framework, 3-28–3-30, 14-3
  Internal Control–Integrated Framework, 3-25–3-28, 3-30, 14-3
    control components, 3-26–3-27, 3-30
    control objectives, 3-26
    cube illustration, 3-26–3-28
    members of, 3-25
    role of, 3-25
Communication
  COSO ERM Framework on, 3-27
  COSO Internal Control Framework on, 3-27
  data communication software, 4-6
  plans, for business continuity, 14-17
Comparability of information, 1-23, 13-3
Comparison of data, 18-14–18-19
Compensating controls, 4-13
Compensation. See Payroll
Competitive advantage, 13-20
Compliance
  data analytics for, 5-19–5-20
  internal control objectives for, 3-26
  risk management through, 3-1
  risks of noncompliance, 2-9, 2-9, 3-1
Compliance risks, 2-9, 2-9, 3-1
Composition of data, 17-7, 18-14–18-19
Conceptual designs, 6-5
Conceptual entity relationship diagrams, 6-22–6-23, 8-11
Conditional statements, 7-14–7-22
Confidence intervals, 17-16
Configurable ERP systems, 4-27
Confirmation bias, 5-15
Conflicts of interest, 15-5
Connector shapes, 8-14
Consolidated financial statements, 13-4–13-6
Consortium blockchain, 7-30
Continuous monitoring controls, 3-14–3-15, 3-16, 10-28
Contracts
  sales, 12-14
  smart, 7-25, 7-34
Controller, 13-2
Controls
  automated, 3-11–3-13, 12-26, 14-10, 14-25
  classification of, 3-8–3-15
  compensating, 4-13
  continuous monitoring, 3-14–3-15, 10-28
  control activities, 3-2, 3-27
  corrective, 3-5–3-7, 3-9

defined, 3-2
  detective. See Detective controls
  implementing, 3-11–3-13
  internal. See Internal controls
  IT application, 3-8–3-10
  IT general, 3-8–3-9, 14-2–14-36
  manual, 3-11, 3-13, 14-10, 14-25
  overview of, 3-15
  physical, 3-8, 3-11
  preventive. See Preventive controls
  time-based model of, 3-6–3-8
  user access, 4-14, 14-14–14-16, 16-15, 16-19
  weaknesses of, 3-5–3-6
Conversion processes
  in accounting information systems, 1-13, 1-16–1-17
  in basic business model, 1-10, 1-13, 2-3, 11-2
  cost accounting of, 11-14–11-20
  dashboards, 11-30
  data analytics, 11-30
  data collection and use, 11-26–11-31
  databases, 11-27–11-28
  defined, 1-19, 11-2, 11-13
  digital manufacturing in, 11-22–11-25
  in ERP system, 11-26–11-31
  inventory management and, 11-3, 11-11–11-13
  manufacturing operations in, 11-3, 11-7–11-8
  overview of, 11-1, 11-3–11-11
  product development in, 11-3–11-4
  production planning in, 11-3, 11-5–11-7
  production process flowchart of, 11-9–11-11
  production scheduling in, 11-3, 11-5–11-7
  quality management in, 11-3, 11-8–11-9
  real-world example, 1-16
  reporting and insights on, 11-29–11-30
  risks in, 2-4, 11-6, 11-7–11-8
  supply chain management and, 11-3, 11-12
"Cooking the books." See Financial statement fraud
Cool colors, 18-7
Copyrights, software, 4-7
Corrective controls, 3-5–3-7, 3-8, 3-9
Corruption schemes, 15-5
COSO. See Committee of Sponsoring Organizations of the Treadway Commission
Cost accounting
  activity-based, 11-14, 11-15, 11-18
  of conversion processes, 11-14–11-20
  defined, 11-14, 11-21, 13-20
  financial reporting for, 13-20–13-21
  job-order costing, 11-15
  labor costs, 11-15–11-16
  Monte Carlo simulations in, 17-18, 17-19
  process costing, 11-15
  purchasing process costs, 11-17
  risks and controls, 11-20
  standard costing, 11-15
  traditional, 11-14–11-18
Cost of goods sold, 11-18
Cost-benefit analysis, 1-25
  of dashboards, 18-27
  data processing and storage, 5-13
  emerging and disruptive technology risks, 7-5
  ERP system, 4-23
  information usefulness, 1-24, 13-4
  risk response based on, 2-22
Cost-effectiveness of financial reporting, 13-4

COVID-19 pandemic
  Agile methodology during, 6-13
  business continuity in, 3-9, 14-17–14-18
  contact tracing as network analysis in, 17-21
  corrective controls in, 3-9
  cyberattacks during, 16-10, 16-17
  fraud during, 15-3
  payroll impacts, 9-26
  remote work during, 3-10, 6-13, 9-7, 14-18, 18-22
  risk mitigation in, 3-10
Credit criteria, 12-13, 12-23
Credit payments processes, 10-25–10-26. See also Accounts payable
Credit sales. See Business-to-business (B2B) sales
Creditworthiness, customer, 12-14
Crisis reaction plans, 14-17
CRM (customer relationship management) software, 12-3–12-4
Crow's foot notation, 6-27–6-28
Cryptocurrencies, 7-24–7-26, 7-28–7-29, 7-34
Cryptology, 7-26
Cullen, Jonathan, 9-37
Culture. See Organizational culture
Cumulative payroll journal, 9-34
Custody, segregation of duties, 3-4
Customer evaluation, 12-14
Customer profile data, 6-18
Customer Relationship Management module (ERP system), 4-23–4-24, 12-36–12-37
Customer relationship management (CRM) software, 12-3–12-4
Customizable ERP systems, 4-27
CVD (color vision deficiency), 18-9–18-10, 18-18
Cyberattacks
  access, 16-15–16-20
  botnets for, 16-22
  brute-force, 16-17–16-19, 16-22
  cyber-kill chain of, 16-9
  denial-of-service, 16-21–16-23, 16-26
  dictionary, 16-17
  disruptive, 16-21–16-28
  distributed denial-of-service, 16-22
  Dumpster diving for, 16-11–16-12
  eavesdropping, 16-12, 16-18
  internal controls to avoid, 16-7, 16-13–16-15, 16-19–16-20, 16-23, 16-28
  IP spoofing, 16-18–16-19, 16-21
  logic bombs, 16-25
  logical access, 16-17–16-20
  logical reconnaissance, 16-9, 16-13–16-14
  malware, 16-3, 16-23–16-28
  on-path, 16-18–16-19
  phishing, 16-9–16-13
  physical access, 16-15–16-16
  physical reconnaissance, 16-9–16-13
  ping sweeps, 16-13
  planning methods for, 16-8–16-15
  port scans, 16-13–16-14
  ransomware, 16-3, 16-23, 16-26
  real-world examples, 16-3–16-4, 16-13, 16-15, 16-21, 16-25
  reconnaissance, 16-8–16-15
  red flags for, 16-10–16-11
  sources of, 16-2
  Trojan horses, 16-26–16-27
  user access and, 14-11

viruses, 16-23–16-24
worms, 16-24–16-25
Cyber risk, 2-9, 2-13, 11-24
Cyber-kill chain, 16-8–16-9
Cybersecurity. *See also* Data security
    for access attacks, 16-15–16-20
    accounting professional roles in, 16-1,
        16-4–16-6, 16-28–16-29
    anomaly detection in, 17-7
    COBIT framework for, 16-6–16-8
    defined, 16-2
    for disruptive attacks, 16-20–16-28
    Equifax, 16-4
    governance and policies for, 16-6–16-7, 16-27
    internal controls for, 16-7, 16-13–16-14,
        16-19–16-20, 16-22–16-23, 16-28
    job postings for careers in, 16-0, 16-5–16-6
    national health service, 16-3–16-4
    NIST framework for, 16-6–16-8
    optus data breach, 16-3
    overview of, 16-1
    real-world threats to, 16-3–16-4, 16-13, 16-15,
        16-21, 16-25
    for reconnaissance attacks, 16-8–16-15
    sources of threats to, 16-2

D
Dashboard views, 18-27–18-29
Dashboards
    accounts payable, 10-37
    accounts receivable, 12-44
    balanced scorecard, 13-23, 13-24
    channel stuffing, 12-40
    characteristics of, 18-28–18-30
    colors in, 18-8
    continuous monitoring controls, 3-14
    conversion processes, 11-30
    data analytics using, 5-18, 9-32–9-35, 11-30,
        12-40, 12-42, 12-44, 13-31, 18-27–18-30
    defined, 5-18, 5-25, 18-28
    exit interview, 9-33–9-34
    explanatory analysis with, 18-27–18-30
    financial statement, 13-30
    interactive, 18-28–18-30
    landing page of, 18-28–18-29
    new hire, 9-32
    purchasing metrics, 10-34
    revenue recognition, 12-42
    salary, 9-35
    static, 18-28
    use cases, 18-29
    viewing preferences, 18-28–18-29
Data
    accounting professional use of, 5-1,
        5-18–5-26
    analysis of. *See* Data analytics
    backups of, 14-19–14-24
    big. *See* Big data
    binary code, 5-2, 5-8
    bits of, 5-2–5-3, 5-14
    bytes of, 5-2–5-3, 5-14
    career opportunities with, 5-1
    categorical values of, 17-7–17-8,
        18-15–18-19
    comparison of, 18-14–18-19
    composition of, 17-7, 18-14–18-19
    conversion process, 11-26–11-30
    customer profile, 6-18
    databases of. *See* Databases

decision making driven by, 1-21–1-25
defined, 1-3, 5-2
distribution of, 18-14, 18-19–18-21
documentation of, 8-10–8-13, 8-20–8-25
dynamic, 5-6–5-7
elements of, 5-2–5-3
event log, 17-19
fields of, 5-2–5-3, 6-17–6-18
    calculated, 11-28
files of, 5-2–5-3, 6-17
financial accounting, 1-4
geospatial location of, 18-14. *See also*
    Geospatial analytics
geotags for, 5-22
input, 1-3
integrity of, 1-22–1-23, 4-4, 6-24, 7-33, 7-35
labeled, 17-6, 17-11–17-13
latency of, 5-16
meta tags for, 5-4
output, 1-3–1-4
patterns of, 17-7
prioritizing importance of, 14-19–14-20
purchasing and payments processes,
    10-29–10-38
quantitative values of, 17-7–17-8, 18-15–18-19
queries to interact with, 6-30–6-39
records of, 5-2–5-3, 6-16–6-17
redundancy of, 6-24
relationship between points of, 18-14,
    18-21–18-23
relevant, selecting, 1-24
retention of, 7-35
scraped, 5-4
security of. *See* Data security
static, 5-6
storage of. *See* Data storage
structured, 5-4–5-5
summarization of, 17-6, 17-8–17-10
time series, 17-14–17-16, 17-19, 18-21–18-22
transforming into information, 1-3–1-4, 1-21,
    5-2, 9-4–9-5
transparency of, 4-23, 7-35
types of, 5-2–5-6
unstructured, 5-4–5-7, 6-19–6-21
validity of, 7-35
variety of, 6-16
visualization of. *See* Data visualization
volume of, 6-16
Web 2.0 effects on, 5-5–5-6
Data analysts, 17-2
Data analytics
    accounting and, 1-25–1-29, 5-18–5-26
    accounting professional roles, 17-2–17-4, 17-26
    anomaly detection in, 17-8, 17-14, 18-19, 18-22
    for audits and compliance, 5-20
    channel stuffing, 12-40
    classification in, 17-6, 17-11–17-13, 18-23
    clustering in, 17-6, 17-10–17-11, 18-23
    collections and accounts receivable,
        12-43–12-44
    conversion processes, 11-30
    dashboards in, 5-18, 9-32–9-35, 11-30, 12-40,
        12-42, 12-44, 13-31, 18-27–18-30
    data summarization in, 17-6, 17-8–17-9
    database queries for, 6-39
    defined, 1-26, 1-29, 5-18
    descriptive, 5-18, 5-20–5-22, 17-4–17-5, 18-14
    diagnostic, 5-18, 5-21–5-23, 5-25, 17-4–17-5,
        17-16, 18-14

employee onboarding, 9-31–9-32
employee termination, 9-33–9-34
explanatory, 18-26–18-35
exploratory, 17-7–17-13, 18-13–18-25
for financial accounting, 5-21–5-22
financial statement, 13-31
for forecasting, 17-6, 17-16–17-17, 18-21
for fraud detection, 15-13, 15-21, 15-27,
    15-29, 15-31, 15-39, 17-13
geospatial, 17-6, 17-23–17-24, 18-14,
    18-24-18-25, 18-29–18-30
human resources and payroll data,
    9-29–9-36
internal controls, 3-15
linear regression in, 17-15–17-16, 18-21
machine learning and, 17-5–17-6, 17-10–17-14,
    17-27
for managerial accounting, 5-22–5-24, 17-17
Monte Carlo simulations in, 17-6, 17-17–17-18
natural language processing in, 17-6,
    17-24–17-25
network analysis in, 17-6, 17-21–17-22
outlier analysis in, 17-8, 17-14
overview of, 17-1
popular techniques in, 17-19–17-26
predictive, 5-18, 5-21–5-23, 5-25, 17-4–17-5,
    17-16–17-17
prescriptive, 5-18, 5-21–5-23, 5-25, 17-4–17-5
process mining in, 17-6, 17-19–17-21
production, 11-30
purchasing and payments processes,
    10-32–10-38
real-world examples, 17-3
regression in, 17-6, 17-15–17-16, 18-21
reporting vs., 1-26–1-27
revenue recognition, 12-42
sales, 12-39–12-40, 17-17
skills for, 1-28, 5-18–5-20
social responsibility, 1-38–1-39
software, 4-12–4-13
for tax accounting, 5-24–5-25
time series, 17-14–17-16, 17-19, 18-21–18-22
types or categories of, 17-4–17-5
veracity of data for, 5-15
visualization of. *See* Data visualization
Data centers
    backup sites, 14-21–14-22
    defined, 14-13
    inside environment, 14-16
    onsite vs. offsite, 14-13–14-14
    outside environment, 14-14–14-15
    physical access controls, 14-13–14-18
    physical security, 14-16–14-17
    real-world example, 14-15
Data communication software, 4-6
Data composition, 17-7, 18-14–18-19
Data control language (DCL), 6-30
Data definition language (DDL), 6-30
Data dictionaries, 6-24, 6-29
Data-driven risk analysis, 2-19
Data engineers, 17-2
Data flow diagrams (DFDs)
    defined, 8-11, 8-13, 8-25
    for documentation, 8-10, 8-21–8-25
    examples, 8-21–8-24
    Level 0, 8-21–8-22
    Level 1, 8-22–8-23
    Level 2, 8-23–8-24
    shapes in, 8-20–8-21

Data flow lines, 8-21
Data integrity
  blockchain, 7-33, 7-35
  defined, 1-22, 1-25, 6-24
  FASB standards, 1-22–1-23
  in relational databases, 6-24
  transaction processing ensuring, 4-4
Data lakes, 5-10–5-12
Data manipulation language (DML), 6-30
Data mart, 5-11
Data modeling, 6-21, 6–29
Data Query Language (DQL)
  database queries, 6-30–6-39
  defined, 6-29
  JOIN operators, 6-35–6-39
  SELECT command, 6-30–6-33, 6-38–6-39
  Where clause, 6-34–6-35, 6-38–6-39
Data redundancy, 6-24
Data retention, 7-35
Data scientists, 17-2
Data security. *See also* Cybersecurity
  blockchain, 7-35
  cloud risks, 4-9
  internal controls and, 3-24
  logical access controls, 14-6–14-12
  physical access controls, 14-6, 14-13–14-18
  regulatory requirements, 3-24
  software vendors', 4-7
Data storage
  backups as, 14-21–14-24
  cloud-based, 4-7–4-10
  data centers for, 14-13–14-15, 14-19–14-21
  data lakes for, 5-10–5-12
  data warehouses for, 5-11–5-12
  databases for, 5-1, 5-9–5-10. *See also*
    Databases
  for digital manufacturing, 11-24
  onsite vs. offsite, 14-13–14-14
  risks and controls, 14-26
  software, 4-13
  tax data hubs for, 5-25
  terminology, 6-17
Data store shape, 8-20
Data summarization, 17-6, 17-8–17-9
Data transparency, 4-23, 7-35
Data validity, 7-35
Data variety, 5–17
Data visualization. *See also* Visualizations
  accounting professional roles in, 18-1, 18-3,
    18-34
  audience for, 18-5
  bar charts as, 18-16–18-18, 18-22, 18-26–18-27,
    18-29–18-30, 18-32
  box plots as, 18-20–18-21, 18-25
  of business value, 18-4
  color in, 18-7–18-10, 18-18–18-19
  comparison in, 18-14–18-19
  composition of data in, 18-14–18-19
  dashboards as. *See* Dashboards
  for data analytics, 5-18, 5-23–5-24, 9-32–9-35,
    11-30, 12-40, 12-42, 12-44, 13-31,
    17-18–17-20, 17-23, 18-1–18-35
  data flow diagrams as, 8-11, 8-20–8-25
  defined, 18-2, 18-6
  design concepts for, 18-5, 18-7–18-13
  distribution of data in, 18-14, 18-19–18-21
  explanatory, 18-26–18-34
  for exploratory analysis, 18-13–18-25
  of fixed asset data, 10-35

for geospatial analytics, 17-23–17-24, 18-14,
    18-24–18-25, 18-29–18-30
  geospatial maps as, 18-24–18-25, 18-30
  heat maps as, 18-18–18-19
  histograms as, 18-19–18-20
  iconography in, 18-11–18-12
  infographics as, 18-27
  line charts as, 18-21–18-22
  of Monte Carlo simulations, 17-17–17-18
  overview of, 18-1
  pie charts as, 18-15
  of population, 18-2
  power of, 18-2
  real-world example, 18-3
  relationships between data points in, 18-14,
    18-21–18-23
  scatter plots as, 18-23
  selection of techniques, 18-25
  setting tone with, 18-5–18-6
  stacked bar charts as, 18-17–18-18, 18-22
  storyboards as, 18-30–18-34
  storytelling with, 18-3–18-4, 18-26–18-33
  tree maps as, 18-16
  typography in, 18-11
  user-focused design for, 18-5
  white space in, 18-10–18-11
Data warehouses, 5-11–5-12
Database management systems (DBMS), 4-6,
    4-9, 4-11, 5-9, 5-12
Databases
  accounting professional use of, 6-1
  classes in, 6-19–6-20
  cloud-based, 4-9
  columns in, 6-17–6-18
  conversion processes, 11-27–11-28
  creating form, 6-40–6-42
  as data element, 5-2–5-3
  data interaction in, 6-30–6-39
  data storage in, 5-1, 5-9–5-10
  database management systems, 4-6, 4-9,
    4-11, 5-9
  database shapes, 8-15
  defined, 5-2, 5-9, 6-17
  entity relationship diagrams of, 6-21–6-29,
    8-11–8-12, 9-30, 10-29–10-31, 11-27,
    12-36, 13-27
  field names in, 6-17–6-18
  human resources, 6-17–6-18, 9-30
  marketing, sales, and collections processes,
    12-36–12-38
  NoSQL, 6-20–6-21
  object-oriented, 6-19–6-20
  objects in, 6-19–6-20
  overview of, 5-9–5-10, 6-1
  production, 5-10
  purchasing and payments processes,
    10-29–10-32
  purpose of, 6-16
  queries in, 5-9, 6-30–6-39
  querying languages for, 5-9, 6-30–6-39
  relational, 5-9, 6-16–6-19, 6-21–6-39, 8-11–8-
    12, 11-27–11-28, 12-36–12-38, 13-27
  reports, 6-42–6-43
  scalability of, 5-10, 6-16, 6-20–6-21
  schema for, 5-9, 8-11
  selection of, 6-16–6-18
  tax data hubs as, 5-24
  types of, 6-16–6-21
  variables in, 6-19–6-20

Data-driven decision making, 1-21–1-24
DBMS (database management systems), 4-6,
    4-9, 4-11, 5-9
DCL (data control language), 6-30
DDL (data definition language), 6-30
DDoS (distributed denial-of-service) attacks,
    16-22
Debt-to-equity ratio, 1-22
Decentralization, with blockchain, 7-28
Decentralized ledgers, 7-27–7-28
Decentralized systems, 4-19–4-20, 4-22
Decision context, 1-24, 1-25
Decision making
  context for, 1-24
  data-driven, 1-21–1-24
  decision support systems, 4-3
  financial reporting for, 13-2–13-3,
    13-25–13-32
  information for, 1-2–1-3, 1-19–1-24, 13-3
Decision shapes, 8-14
Decision support systems (DSS), 4-3
Decryption, 7-26
Delivery
  business-to-business sales, 12-12, 12-17–12-20
  business-to-consumer sales, 12-3, 12-4–12-6
  delivery receipts, 12-6–12-7
  geospatial analytics for, 17-23–17-24
  risks and controls, 12-8–12-9
Denial-of-service (DoS) attacks, 16-21–16-23,
    16-26
Dependent variables, 17-15–17-16
Deposit slips, 12-31
Depreciation of fixed assets, 10-18
Descriptive analytics
  for audits and compliance, 5-21
  data visualization of, 18-14
  defined, 5-18, 17-4–17-5, 18-14
  for financial accounting, 5-21–5-22
  for managerial accounting, 5-22–5-23
  for tax accounting, 5-24–5-25
Design concepts
  color in, 18-7–18-10
  defined, 18-7, 18-13
  fundamental, 18-7–18-13
  iconography in, 18-11–18-12
  typography in, 18-11
  user-focused, 18-5
  white space in, 18-10–18-11
Design stage, of SDLC, 6-2, 6-5
Detective controls
  for asset misappropriation, 15-17, 15-21
  continuous monitoring controls as, 3-14–3-15,
    10-28
  defined, 3-5, 3-8
  examples, 3-6–3-7
  for financial statement fraud, 15-26,
    15-29–15-32
  overview of, 3-5
  in time-based model, 3-7
Development stage, of SDLC, 6-2, 6-6
DFDs. *See* Data flow diagrams (DFDs)
Diagnostic analytics
  for audits and compliance, 5-20–5-21
  data visualization of, 18-14
  defined, 5-18, 17-4–17-5, 18-14
  for financial accounting, 5-21–5-22
  linear regression as, 17-15
  for managerial accounting, 5-23
  for tax accounting, 5-25

Dictionary attacks, 16-17
Differential backups, 14-24
Digital manufacturing, 11-22–11-25
Digital twins, 11-22–11-23, 11-25
Direct cutover implementation, 6-8
Direct labor, 11-15–11-16
Direct material costs, 11-16
Direct-to-consumers business models, 1-9
Directive 2014/56/EU, 3-25, 3-30
Disaster recovery (DR), 11-8, 14-17–14-18.
　　See also Backups
Discrepancy reports, 10-5
Disruptive attacks
　cybersecurity for, 16-20–16-28
　denial-of-service, 16-21–16-23, 16-26
　malware, 16-3, 16-23–16-28
　real-world examples, 16-21, 16-25
Disruptive technologies
　Autonomous Things as, 7-11–7-12, 7-13
　blockchain as, 7-24–7-36
　defined, 7-3
　emerging technologies distinguished, 7-3
　extended reality as, 7-9–7-10, 7-12
　gamification as, 7-10–7-11
　Internet of Things as, 7-7–7-9, 7-12
　opportunities with, 7-7–7-12, 7-22–7-23
　overview of, 7-1
　risk assessment and mitigation, 7-3–7-6
　robotic process automation as, 7-13–7-23
Distributed denial-of-service (DDoS) attacks,
　　16-22
Distributed ledgers, 7-28. See also Blockchain
Distributed systems, 4-20
Disruptive technology, 7-7
Distribution
　conversion processes including, 11-12
　of data, 18-14, 18-19–18-21
Distributed system, 4-22
DML (data manipulation language), 6-30
Document flowcharts
　defined, 8-10
　for fixed asset purchasing processes,
　　10-19–10-21
　for inventory purchasing processes,
　　10-9–10-11
　for payments processes, 10-26
Document shapes, 8-15
Documentation. See also Recording;
　　Reporting
　accounting professional role, 8-1, 8-28
　for audit effectiveness, 8-7, 8-12, 8-28
　business process model and notation for,
　　8-9–8-10, 8-13
　checklists for, 8-7–8-8
　of data, 8-10–8-12, 8-20–8-25
　data flow diagrams for, 8-11, 8-20–8-25
　defined, 8-2, 8-6
　for efficient knowledge transfer, 8-6
　entity relationship diagrams for, 8-11–8-12
　flowcharts for, 8-9, 8-13–8-19
　goals of, 8-2–8-5
　of internal controls, 8-2, 8-18
　narratives for, 8-9
　operator, 8-3–8-4
　of organizational charts, 8-7
　of overall business, 8-7–8-8
　overview of, 8-1
　for process improvements, 8-6, 8-18
　of processes and systems, 8-8–8-19

program, 8-3–8-4
　questionnaires for, 8-7–8-8
　source documents as, 10-3–10-4, 13-9
　for standardization, 8-6
　systems, 8-2–8-3, 8-8–8-25
　user, 8-3–8-5
Dormant access, 14-11
DoS (denial-of-service) attacks, 16-21–16-23,
　16-26
Double dipping, 15-19, 15-20, 15-23
DQL. See Data Query Language
DR (disaster recovery), 11-8, 14-21–14-22.
　　See also Backups
Drones, 3-12–3-13, 7-11
DSS (decision support systems), 4-3
Dumpster diving, 16-11–16-12, 16-15
Dynamic data, 5-6–5-7

E
Eavesdropping, 16-12, 16-13, 16-18
Economic extortion, 15-5
Economic feasibility, 6-4
Electronic funds transfers (EFTs), 12-31
Email
　data communication software, 4-6
　phishing, 16-9–16-13, 16-15
Emerging technologies
　center of excellence evaluating, 7-4, 7-6
　defined, 7-3, 7-6
　disruptive technologies distinguished, 7-3
　overview of, 7-1
　risk assessment and mitigation, 7-3–7-7
　systems development incompatibility
　　with, 6-2
Employee benefits, 9-3, 9-5, 9-22–9-23
Employee hiring
　background checks, 9-8
　employee personal information collection,
　　9-8
　human resources management of, 9-2,
　　9-5–9-13
　job postings for. See Job postings
　new hire packages, 9-8
　offer letters, 9-8
　onboarding process, 9-7–9-13, 9-31–9-32
Employee onboarding
　best practices, 9-7–9-8
　defined, 9-7, 9-13
　maturity model for, 9-12–9-13
　process flowchart of, 9-7–9-8
　reporting and analytics, 9-31–9-32
　risks and control activities, 9-8, 9-11–9-12
Employee reimbursement
　double dipping, 15-19, 15-20
　expense reports for, 7-21–7-22, 15-2,
　　15-18–15-21
　expense tracking system, 9-8
　fraud in, 15-2, 15-18–15-21, 15-42–15-43,
　　18-23
　human resources management of, 9-5, 9-8
Employee termination
　data visualization of, 18-32–18-35
　defined, 9-14
　exit interviews, 9-14, 9-33–9-34
　human resources management of, 9-2, 9-5,
　　9-14–9-20
　maturity model for, 9-19–9-20
　process flowchart of, 9-15
　reporting and analytics, 9-33–9-34

risks and control activities, 9-15–9-20
　severance pay, 9-15
　turnover rates, 9-33
　user access changes, 14-10
Employees
　codes of conduct for, 15-12
　compensation of. See Payroll
　direct labor, 11-15–11-16
　efficient knowledge transfer between, 8-6
　employment life cycle of, 9-3
　fictitious, 9-32
　fraud awareness training, 15-3
　fraud by, 15-2, 15-4–15-5, 15-7–15-8,
　　15-18–15-21, 15-42, 18-23
　fraud disclosure, 15-9, 15-13
　fraud effects on, 15-3, 15-23
　ghost, 9-35
　hiring of new. See Employee hiring
　human resources management. See Human
　　resources
　indirect factory labor, 11-15–11-16
　labor-leisure trade-off, 9-20
　in organizational charts, 8-7
　payroll for. See Payroll
　remote work by, 6-13, 9-7, 14-20, 18-22
　termination of. See Employee termination
　as transaction processing system users, 4-3
　transfers of, 14-11
　turnover rates, 9-33
　turnover risks, 9-7
　whistleblowers among, 15-9, 15-13
Encryption, 7-25–7-26, 7-31, 16-12
End users, 1-25
Engineering bill of materials, 11-4
Enterprise resource planning (ERP) systems
　activity-based cost accounting for, 11-19
　benefits of, 4-23
　bill of materials data from, 11-4, 11-13
　configurable, 4-27
　conversion processes in, 11-26–11-31
　costs of, 4-28
　customizable, 4-27
　data visualization tools in, 18-2
　defined, 4-22, 4-28
　financial reporting in, 13-25–13-33
　as ideal state, 4-23
　implementation of, 4-25–4-29
　marketing, sales, and collections processes
　　in, 12-36–12-45
　modules and features, 4-23–4-26. See also
　　specific modules
　need for, 4-22–4-23
　out-of-the-box, 4-26
　purchasing and payments processes in,
　　10-29–10-38
　real-world example, 4-27, 13-26
　for systems integration, 4-22–4-25
Enterprise risk management (ERM)
　COSO ERM Framework, 3-28–3-31, 14-3
　database selection and, 6-16
　defined, 2-5, 2-7
　of emerging and disruptive technology risks,
　　7-3–7-7
　human resources and payroll analytics for,
　　9-29–9-37
　internal controls for, 3-16
　overview of, 2-5
　risk assessments for, 2-5–2-19
　risk response for, 2-5, 2-19–2-25

Entity integrity, 6-25
Entity relationship diagrams (ERDs)
    conceptual, 6-22–6-23, 8-11
    of conversion processes database, 11-27
    defined, 6-22, 6-29, 8-11
    for documentation, 8-10–8-11
    of general ledger database, 13-27
    of human resources database, 9-30
    logical, 6-23–6-24, 8-11
    of marketing, sales, and collections processes
        database, 12-37
    physical, 6-24–6-30, 8-11, 11-27
    of purchasing and payments processes
        database, 10-29–10-30
    of relational databases, 6-21–6-30, 8-10–8-11,
        11-28, 12-37, 13-27
E-procurement systems, 10-13, 10-17, 11-12
ERDs. See Entity relationship diagrams
    (ERDs)
ERM. See Enterprise risk management (ERM)
ERP systems. See Enterprise resource planning
    (ERP) systems
Errors
    change management to minimize,
        14-25–14-33
    internal controls to avoid, 3-3, 3-5
    manual controls subject to, 3-11–3-12
    revenue recognition, 12-26–12-28
ESS (executive support systems), 4-2
Event log data, 17-19
Exabytes, data, 5-14
Excel (Microsoft)
    conditional statements in, 7-15
    data analytics in, 1-26, 4-12–4-13, 5-18,
        17-27
    data in, 5-1, 5-3, 5-14, 18-3
    data visualization in, 18-11
    flowcharts, 8-14
    formulas and functions, 4-12
    pivot tables in, 17-9
    software, 4-6, 4-12–4-13
Executive support systems (ESS), 4-2
Executives. See Management
Exit interviews, 9-14, 9-20, 9-33–9-34
Expense cutoff fraud, 15-33
Expense reports
    fraudulent, 15-2, 15-18–15-21
    robotic process automation examination of,
        7-22–7-23
Expense tracking system, 9-8
Expenses
    capitalization of, 15-28–15-29
    capitalized costs shown as, 15-31–15-32
    data visualization of, 18-23
    expense cutoff schemes, 15-28–15-32
    overstatement of, 15-31–15-32
    understatement of, 15-28–15-30
Explanatory analysis
    dashboards for, 18-27–18-30
    data visualization of, 18-26–18-35
    defined, 18-26
    infographics for, 18-27
    storyboards for, 18-30–18-35
    sweet spot for, 18-26
Exploratory data analytics
    anomaly detection in, 17-8
    classification in, 17-11–17-13
    clustering in, 17-10–17-11
    data summarization in, 17-8–17-10

data visualization of, 18-13–18-25
    defined, 17-7, 18-14
Extended reality (XR), 7-9–7-10, 7-13
eXtensible Business Reporting Language
    (XBRL), 5-22, 13-16–13-20
eXtensible Markup Language (XML), 13-16
External audits, 3-30
    blockchain applications, 7-33
    data analytics for, 5-19
    documentation for, 8-6, 8-7, 8-11
    for fraud, 15-8
    of internal controls, 3-17, 3-24
    regulatory requirements, 3-24
    risk mitigation, 3-17
External entity shape, 8-20
External fraud, 15-4, 15-8
External risks
    compliance, 2-9, 2-10
    defined, 2-8, 2-13
    financial, 2-9
    physical, 2-9, 2-12
    strategic, 2-9, 2-11–2-12

F

Faithful representation, information as, 1-22,
    13-3
FASB (Financial Accounting Standards Board),
    1-22, 13-6
FCPA (Foreign Corrupt Practices Act),
    10-12–10-13
FDA (Food and Drug Administration), 2-11,
    11-9
Feasibility
    economic, 6-4
    operational, 6-4
    risk response based on, 2-22
    robotic process automation analysis of, 7-18,
        7-20–7-22
    studies, 6-4
    technical, 6-4
Featured professionals. See Accounting
    professionals
Federal Trade Commission, 15-4
FEDI (financial electronic data interchange),
    12-33, 12–36
FEI (Financial Executives Institute), 3-25
Fictitious employees tests, 9-32
Fictitious invoices, 15-22
Fictitious sales larceny, 15-17
Field names, database, 6-17–6-19
Fields, data, 5-2–5-3, 6-17–6-18
    calculated, 11-28
File Transfer Protocol (FTP), 4-6, 16-12
Files, data, 5-2–5-3, 6-17
Financial accounting, 1-4, 5-21–5-22, 7-34
Financial Accounting Standards Board (FASB),
    1-22, 13-6
Financial electronic data interchange (FEDI),
    12-33, 12–36
Financial Executives Institute (FEI), 3-25
Financial information, tagging, 13-17–13-19
Financial losses
    as technology risk, 7-4
    understatement of, 15-28–15-30
Financial modeling, 13-29–13-30, 13-33
Financial module (ERP system)
    conversion processes in, 11-26
    defined, 4-23
    features of, 4-24, 4-26

financial reporting in, 13-25–13-26
    marketing, sales, and collections processes
        in, 12-36–12-37
    purchasing and payments processes in,
        10-29–10-30
Financial reporting. See also Financial
    statements
    accounting information system role in,
        13-2–13-6
    accounting professional roles in, 13-1–13-2,
        13-33–13-4
    accounting transaction identification for,
        13-9
    accounting transaction journalization for,
        13-9
    adjusted trial balance for, 13-11
    for balanced scorecard, 13-22–13-24
    chart of accounts for, 13-6–13-7
    consolidated reporting requirements,
        13-4–13-6
    for cost accounting, 13-20–13-21
    cost-effectiveness of, 13-4
    decision making with, 13-3, 13-25–13-33
    defined, 13-2, 13-6
    during reporting period, 13-8–13-11
    end of fiscal year, 13-12
    end of reporting period, 13-8, 13-11–13-12
    in ERP system, 13-25–13-33
    financial statement generation for,
        13-6–13-15
    financial statement preparation for,
        13-12
    internal controls over, 13-13–13-15
    journal entries adjusted and posted to
        ledgers for, 13-11
    journal entries closed and posted to ledgers
        for, 13-12
    journal entries posted to ledgers for,
        13-10–13-11
    journal entry testing for accurate, 13-11,
        13-27–13-29, 13-32
    for managerial accounting, 13-20–13-24,
        13-26
    objectives of, meeting, 13-3
    overview of, 13-1
    post-closing trial balance for, 13-12
    process flowchart for, 13-7–13-8
    process of, 13-7–13-12
    real-world example, 13-26
    reporting and insights on, 13-30–13-33
    for responsibility accounting, 13-21–13-22
    standardized, 13-17–13-18
    trial balance roll-forward for, 13-27–13-29
    unadjusted trial balance for, 13-11–13-12
    XBRL for, 13-16–13-19
Financial risks, 2-8–2-9, 2-13
Financial statement fraud
    asset misappropriation vs., 15-14
    assets, revenues, and profits overstatement
        as, 10-21, 12-26, 15-24–15-28
    characteristics of, 15-23–15-33
    defined, 15-23, 15-33
    financial performance overstatement as,
        15-24–15-30
    financial performance understatement as,
        15-30–15-32
    frequency and cost of, 15-23–15-24
    horizontal analysis for, 15-13
    journal entry testing for, 13-11, 13-32

liabilities, expenses, and losses understated for, 15-28–15-30
management involvement in, 15-32–15-33
overview of, 15-5
revenue recognition, 12-24–12-27
tone at the top affecting, 15-12
vertical analysis for, 15-13
Financial statements. *See also* Financial reporting
accounting information system generation of, 13-6–13-15
activities impacting, 12-29
balance sheet as, 13-30–13-31, 13-45
consolidated, 13-4–13-6
dashboards of data from, 13-31
fraud. *See* Financial statement fraud
horizontal analysis of, 13-31, 15-13
income statement as, 13-30–13-31, 13-45
notes to, 13-30
payroll effects on, 9-21–9-23
regulatory requirements for, 3-23–3-24, 15-23
retained earnings statement as, 13-45
risk management with accurate, 3-1
robotic process automation of, 7-22
statement of cash flows as, 10-24–10-25, 12-29, 13-30, 13-45
statement of stockholders' equity as, 13-30, 13-46
vertical analysis of, 13-31, 15-13
Financing events, 1-11, 1-13, 10-24–10-25, 12-29
Finished goods, 10-3
Fixed Asset Subsidiary Ledger, 10-19
Fixed assets
business processes framework for, 10-17
capital expenditures on, 10-17
cost accounting for, 11-17
defined, 10-17, 10-23
depreciation of, 10-18
disposal or transfer of, 10-17
document flowcharts for, 10-19–10-21
internal controls for acquiring, 10-21–10-24
PP&E as, 10-2, 10-17
procurement of, 10-18
purchasing and payments processes for, 10-1–10-2, 10-17–10-24, 10-34–10-35, 11-17
receiving and tagging of, 10-18
reconciliation of, 10-19
recording of, 10-18–10-19
reporting and analytics, 10-34–10-35
Flowchart shapes
connector, 8-14
database, 8-15
decision, 8-14
document, 8-15
flowline, 8-14
horizontal, 8-15
input/output, 8-15
manual input, 8-15
manual operation, 8-15
merge, 8-14
process, 8-14
terminator, 8-14
vertical, 8-15
Flowcharts. *See also* Data flow diagrams
for bank reconciliation, 8-16–8-17
for business-to-business sales, 12-22
for business-to-consumer sales, 12-6, 12-8

for collections, 12-33–12-34
defined, 8-9
document, 8-10, 10-10, 10-19–10-21, 10-26
for documentation, 8-10, 8-13–8-20
examples, 8-13, 8-16, 8-19
process. *See* Process flowcharts
for production process, 11-9–11-11
program, 8-10
real-world applications, 8-18
shapes in, 8-14–8-17
swim lanes, 8-18–8-19, 13-7–13-8
systems, 8-10, 8-13–8-20
Flowchart swim lanes, 8-1, 8-18, 8-20
Flowlines, 8-14
Fonts, 18-11
Food and Drug Administration (FDA), 2-11
Forecasting, 17-6, 17-16–17-17, 17-19, 18-21. *See also* Predictive analytics
Foreign Corrupt Practices Act (FCPA), 10-12–10-13
Foreign keys, 6-25, 6-29
Form W-2, 9-34
Form W-3, 9-34
Frameworks
COBIT, 14-2–14-6, 16-6–16-8
COSO Enterprise Risk Management Framework, 3-28–3-30, 14-3
COSO Internal Control–Integrated Framework, 3-25–3-28, 3-30, 14-3
defined, 3-23
fraud triangle, 15-8–15-11, 15-14
internal control, 3-23–3-31
IT governance, 14-2
NIST Cybersecurity Framework, 16-6–16-8
Franchise business models, 1-9, 1-12
Fraud
accounting professional defense against, 15-1, 15-8–15-14, 15-34
anti-fraud culture as deterrent, 15-3, 15-12
asset misappropriation and, 15-5, 15-14–15-23
audits to uncover. *See* Audits
behavioral red flags indicating, 15-6–15-8
change management to avoid, 14-33
continuous fraud monitoring, 10-28
corruption schemes, 15-5
data analytics to detect, 15-13, 15-20–15-21, 15-25–15-27, 15-31, 15-34, 15-42, 17-13, 17-16
data visualization to detect, 18-23
defined, 15-2
encryption to prevent, 7-28
external, 15-4
financial statement. *See* Financial statement fraud
fraud triangle, 15-8–15-11, 15-14
internal controls to avoid, 3-3, 3-5, 3-14, 12-27, 15-3, 15-8, 15-11, 15-15–15-17, 15-21–15-22
management override allowing for, 3-6, 15-32
non-behavioral red flags indicating, 15-13, 15-19–15-21
occupational or internal, 15-4–15-5
opportunity as motivation, 15-10
overview of, 15-1
in payments processes, 10-27–10-28. *See also* Fraudulent disbursements
payroll, 9-4, 9-26, 9-35, 15-12, 15-21–15-22
perceived pressure as motivation, 15-9–15-10
prevention techniques, 15-11–15-12

pricing process, 12-13–12-14
in purchasing processes, 10-5, 10-14, 10-21–10-22
rationalization as motivation, 15-10–15-11
real-world example, 12-25, 15-6
reputational risks with, 2-11
revenue recognition, 12-24–12-28
as risk, 12-27, 15-2–15-3
risk assessments, 15-3, 15-9
risk management, 15-8–15-14
robotic process automation to uncover, 7-22
sales, 12-40–12-41, 15-17. *See also* Channel stuffing
software development and, 4-7
user access leading to, 14-10, 14-11, 14-16
whistleblowers on, 15-7, 15-13
Fraudulent disbursements
as asset misappropriation, 15-18–15-23
billing schemes as, 15-22
defined, 15-18
expense reimbursement schemes, 15-2, 15-18–15-21, 15-42, 18-23
to fictitious vendors, 10-27, 15-22
in payments processes, 10-27–10-28
payroll schemes, 15-21–15-22
Freemium business models, 1-9
FTP (File Transfer Protocol), 4-6, 16-12
Full backups, 14-21–14-22

G
GAAP (generally accepted accounting principles), 1-2, 11-14, 12-24–12-25, 13-13–13-14, 13-45
Gamification, 7-10, 7-13
General journals, 13-9
General ledgers
adjusted trial balance of, 13-11
database design for, 13-27–13-28
defined, 13-26
double-entry, vs. blockchain, 7-33–7-35
in ERP system, 13-25–13-26
journal entry testing for, 13-11, 13-27–13-29, 13-32
monitoring of, 13-31
post-closing trial balance of, 13-12
posting adjusted journal entries to, 13-11
posting closing journal entries to, 13-12
posting journal entries to, 13-10–13-11
trial balance roll-forward of, 13-27–13-29
unadjusted trial balance of, 13-11–13-12
Generally accepted accounting principles (GAAP), 1-2, 11-14, 12-24–12-25, 13-13–13-14, 13-45
Geospatial analytics, 17-6, 17-23–17-24, 17-25
data visualization of, 17-23, 18-14, 18-24–18-25, 18-29–18-30
Geospatial maps, 18-24–18-25, 18-26, 18-29–18-30
Geotags, 5-23
Ghost employees, 9-35
Giang, Holly, 10-38
Gigabytes, data, 5-14
Giles, Joshua, 17-26
Go, 4-5
Governance
COSO ERM Framework on, 3-27
cybersecurity, 16-6–16-7
IT, 14-2–14-6

Grandfather-father-son redundant backup, 14-25
Graphical documentation, 8-26–8-27
Gratuities, illegal, 15-5
Gross profit margin, 1-21
Growing businesses
information systems for, 4-16–4-22
systems configurations, 4-19–4-22
systems integration, 4-18–4-19
Growth
acquisition-based, 4-16–4-17
organic, 4-16–4-17
GUI (graphical user interface), 6-5

H
Hackers, 16-2. *See also* Cyberattacks
Hash strings, 7-34
Heat maps
data visualization with, 18-18–18-19
defined, 2-18, 2-19, 18-18, 18-25
of inherent risk, 2-20
of residual risk, 2-21
as risk matrix, 2-18–2-20
Hiring. *See* Employee hiring
Histograms, 18-19–18-20
Horizontal financial statement analysis, 13-31, 15-13
Horizontal flowchart shapes, 8-15
Horizontal organizational charts, 8-7
Horizontal scalability, 5-16
Hot backup sites, 14-21–14-22
HTML, 4-5
Human resources
as acquisition and payment process, 9-2, 9-26
categorization of responsibilities, 9-5
cost accounting for, 11-15–11-16
data analytics, 9-29–9-36
databases, 6-17–6-18, 9-30
defined, 9-3
employee operations, 9-2–9-4. *See also* Employee benefits; Employee hiring; Employee termination
outsourced model of, 9-3
overview of, 9-1
payroll relationship to, 9-2–9-6, 9-21
reporting and insights on, 9-31–9-35
segregation of duties, 9-6
virtual environment challenges for, 9-7
Human resources (HR) business function, 9-6
Human Resources Management module (ERP system), 9-29, 9-30
Hybrid cloud, 4-8, 4-30

I
IaaS (infrastructure as a service), 4-8
ICFR (internal controls over financial reporting), 13-13–13-15
Iconography, 18-11–18-13
IIA (Institute of Internal Auditors), 3-17–3-19, 3-25
IIoT (Industrial Internet of Things), 11-22, 11-24
Illegal gratuities, 15-5
IMA (Institute of Management Accountants), 3-25
Immutability of blockchain, 7-30, 7-33
Impact of risk, 2-15–2-21
Implementation

business functions for, 2-3–2-4
data lake, 5-11
data warehouse, 5-11
direct cutover, 6-7
ERP system, 4-25–4-28
internal controls, 3-11–3-13
management responsibility for, 1-20
parallel, 6-7
phased, 6-7
pilot, 6-7
systems development, 6-3, 6-6–6-7
Implementation stage, 6-9
Income statements, 13-30–13-31, 13-45
Incremental backups, 14-23
Independence of auditors, 3-21
Independent variables, 17-15–17-16
Indirect factory labor, 11-16
Indirect material costs, 11-17
Industrial Internet of Things (IIoT), 11-22, 11-24
Infographics, 18-27
Information. *See also* Accounting information systems; Data
comparability of, 1-23, 13-3
COSO ERM Framework on, 3-27
COSO Internal Control Framework on, 3-27
cost-benefit analysis of, 1-22–1-23, 13-4
data flow diagrams of, 8-11, 8-20–8-27
data transformed into, 1-3–1-4, 1-21, 5-2, 9-4
decision context for, 1-24
decision making with, 1-2–1-3, 1-20, 1-21–1-25, 13-3
defined, 1-3
enhancing characteristics of, 1-23, 13-3
as faithful representation, 1-22, 13-3
financial, tagging in XBRL, 13-16–13-18
flow of, in supply chain, 10-7
fundamental characteristics of, 1-22, 13-3
importance of, 1-2–1-13
larceny as theft of, 15-17–15-18
management use of, 1-19–1-25
overview of accounting and, 1-1
quality of, 1-21–1-23, 3-1, 4-23, 13-3
relevance of, 1-22, 1-24, 13-3
supply and demand, 1-2–1-3
timeliness of, 1-23, 13-3
understandability of, 1-23, 13-3
verifiability of, 1-23, 13-3
Information events, 1-11, 1-13, 1-14, 1-19
Information quality
for decision making, 1-21–1-23, 13-3
defined, 1-21, 1-25
in ERP systems, 4-23
internal controls for. *See* Internal controls
for risk management, 3-1
Information systems. *See also* Accounting information systems; IT systems; *Systems entries*
accounting professional use of, 6-1
basic business model comparison, 1-10
cloud computing, 4-7–4-11. *See also* Cloud computing
decision support systems, 4-3
defined, 1-3, 1-12
executive support systems, 4-2
for growing businesses, 4-16–4-22
management information systems, 4-3
online analytical processing, 4-2
online transaction processing, 4-2

software, 4-5–4-7. *See also* Software
transaction processing systems, 4-2–4-5, 6-2, 9-23
users of, 4-3
Information Systems Audit and Control Association (ISACA), 14-2, 16-27
Information technology. *See IT entries*
Infrastructure as a service (IaaS), 4-8
Inherent risks, 2-20, 2–23
In-house development of software, 4-6–4-7
Inline XBRL (iXBRL), 13-17
Innovation, risk driving, 2-2. *See also* Technology innovations
Input
business process, 1-9–1-10, 1-13–1-14, 9-2, 11-2
data, 1-3–1-4
defined, 1-3
input/manual input shapes, 8-15
Institute of Internal Auditors (IIA), 3-17–3-19, 3-25
Institute of Management Accountants (IMA), 3-25
Integrated process-based information system, 1-19
Interactive dashboards, 18-26–18-30
Internal audits
auditors performing, 3-21
blockchain applications, 7-33
data analytics for, 5-20–5-21
data visualization for, 18-32–18-34
documentation for, 8-6–8-7
of emerging and disruptive technology risks, 7-4–7-5
for fraud, 15-7, 15-13
of internal controls, 3-17–3-18, 3-21–3-22
of payroll, 9-36
of purchasing and payments processes, 10-37–10-38
risk assessments, 2-34
robotic process automation for, 7-19–7-22
skills required, 1-7–1-8
of user access, 7-19–7-21
Internal controls
assessment of, 3-17–3-22, 3-27
automated, 3-11–3-13, 12-26, 14-10, 14-12, 14-25
for business continuity, 14-24
for business-to-business sales, 12-12–12-14, 12-16, 12-18–12-19
for business-to-consumer sales, 12-3, 12-6–12-7
for change management, 14-33
classification of, 3-8–3-15
for collections, 12-4, 12-29–12-36
collusion to circumvent, 3-6
continuous monitoring, 3-14–3-15, 10-28
controls/control activities, 3-2, 3-27
corrective, 3-5–3-7, 3-11
COSO Internal Control–Integrated Framework, 3-25–3-28, 3-30, 14-3
for cost accounting, 11-20
for cybersecurity, 16-7, 16-12–16-15, 16-19, 16-22, 16-28
data analytics, 3-15
data security and, 3-24
defined, 3-2
for denial-of-service attacks, 16-22
detective. *See* Detective controls

documentation of, 8-2, 8-18
for employee onboarding, 9-8–9-11
for employee termination, 9-15–9-20
environment for, 3-27
external audits of, 3-19, 3-24
over financial reporting, 13-13–13-15
frameworks for, 3-23–3-31
for fraud detection and prevention, 3-3, 3-5,
    3-14, 12-27, 15-3, 15-7, 15-11, 15-15–15-17,
    15-21–15-22
functions of, 3-2–3-8
implementing, 3-11–3-14
internal audits of, 3-17–3-18, 3-21–3-22
for inventory, 3-5, 3-11–3-12, 11-12–11-13
IT application, 3-8–3-10
IT general, 3-8–3-9, 14-2–14-33
lines of defense for, 3-17–3-22
logical access, 4-14, 14-3–14-11, 16-19
for logical reconnaissance attacks, 16-14
for malware attacks, 16-27–16-28
management override of, 3-5–3-6, 15-32
management responsibilities, 3-17–3-22,
    3-24, 15-23
manual, 3-11, 3-14, 14-10, 14-25
for manufacturing operations, 11-8
maturity models and, 3-18–3-20, 9-12–9-13,
    9-18–9-19, 10-15, 10-22–10-24, 12-34–12-36
monitoring of, 3-27
number of, 3-3
for order placement, 10-13–10-14
overview of, 3-15–3-16
for payments processes, 10-27–10-28
for payroll, 9-24–9-28
penalties for violation of, 3-23
physical, 3-8, 3-11
physical access, 4-14, 14-4, 14-11–14-17, 16-16
for physical reconnaissance attacks, 16-12
policies and procedures as, 3-15–3-16, 3-27,
    13-13
preventive. See Preventive controls
for product development, 11-6
for production planning and scheduling, 11-7
over purchasing processes, 10-11–10-16,
    10-21–10-24
for quality management, 11-9
for receiving purchases, 10-15–10-16
regulatory requirements, 3-2, 3-23–3-24, 3-27,
    13-13, 14-25, 15-3, 15-23
reports on, 3-24, 3-26, 3-30
for revenue recognition, 12-26–12-28
risk assessments for, 3-27
for risk management, 3-1–3-37, 4-14–4-15,
    9-8–9-11, 9-15–9-20, 9-24–9-28,
    10-11–10-16, 10-22, 10-27, 11-6,
    11-7–11-8, 11-12–11-13, 11-20, 12-4,
    12-6–12-7, 12-12–12-14, 12-15,
    12-18–12-19, 12-25–12-36, 13-13–13-15,
    14-10, 14-16, 14-24, 14-33
segregation of duties, 3-3–3-4, 3-12, 4-14
for startups and small businesses, 4-14–4-15
for supply chain management, 11-12
time-based model of, 3-6–3-8
user access, 4-14, 14-14–14-16, 16-17, 16-19
for vendor selection and management,
    10-12–10-13
weaknesses of, 3-5–3-6
Internal controls over financial reporting
    (ICFR), 13-13–13-15
Internal fraud, 15-4–15-5

Internal Revenue Service (IRS), 1-2
Internal risks
    defined, 2-8, 2-13
    financial, 2-9
    operational, 2-8–2-9
    reputational, 2-10
Internet of Things (IoT), 4-13, 7-7–7-9, 7-12,
    7-13, 11-22, 11-24
Inventory
    asset misappropriation, 15-14–15-15
    control of, 10-4
    conversion processes and supply chain
        management relationship to, 11-2–11-13
    data visualization of, 18-20
    defined, 10-3
    document flowcharts for, 10-10–10-11
    documentation of processes, 8-8
    financial statement fraud and, 15-23–15-25
    finished goods as, 10-3
    internal controls, 3-5, 3-11–3-13, 11-12–11-13
    internal controls for purchasing, 10-10–10-17
    management of, 10-3, 10-6–10-7, 11-3,
        11-11–11-12, 12-9, 12-18
    physical count of, 3-5, 3-11, 8-8
    physical flow of, 10-7–10-8
    product costs and, 11-18
    purchasing and payments processes for,
        10-1–10-16, 10-32–10-34
    raw materials as, 10-3–10-6, 10-32–10-34,
        11-6, 11-16–11-17
    work in process as, 10-3
Inventory control, 10-4
Inventory management
    business-to-business sales, 12-11–12-12, 12-17
    business-to-consumer sales, 12-3–12-8
    conversion processes and, 11-3, 11-12–11-13
    defined, 10-6, 11-12, 12-10
    overview of, 10-6–10-7
    purchasing and payments processes and,
        10-3, 10-6–10-9
    working capital and, 10-8
Investing events, 1-11, 1-13
IoT (Internet of Things), 4-13, 7-7–7-9, 7-12,
    11-22, 11-24
IP addresses, 16-13
IP spoofing, 16-18–16-21
IRS (Internal Revenue Service), 1-2
ISACA (Information Systems Audit and
    Control Association), 14-2, 16-28
IT application controls, 3-8–3-10, 3-16
IT general controls (ITGCs)
    backups as, 14-21–14-26
    for business continuity, 14-19–14-21, 14-25
    for change management, 14-28–14-35
    COBIT framework, 14-2–14-5
    defined, 3-9, 3-16
    examples, 3-10
    for IT system risk mitigation, 14-2–14-35
    logical access controls, 14-6–14-13
    overview of, 3-9
    physical access controls, 14-6, 14-13–14-19
    user access, 14-6–14-18
IT governance, 14-2–14-5
    frameworks, 14-2.
        See also COBIT framework
IT systems. See also Information systems
    backups of, 14-21–14-25
    business continuity planning, 14-19–14-21,
        14-26

change management, 14-27–14-35
COBIT framework for, 14-1–14-5
data categorization and prioritization,
    14-20–14-21
governance of, 14-2–14-5
information technology, defined, 14-2
operational continuity, 14-19–14-27
overview of, 14-1
physical protection of, 14-6, 14-13–14-18
process mining, 17-19–17-20
user access controls, 14-6–14-13.
    See also User access
iXBRL (inline XBRL), 13-17

J
Java, 4-5, 6-20
JavaScript, 4-5, 8-27
Java Golf Club, 9-26
Job postings
    accounting intern, 1-0
    cost and managerial accountant, 11-0
    cybersecurity audit lead, 16-0
    cybersecurity careers, 16-5–16-6
    data governance specialist, 5-0
    enterprise risk associate—operational risk,
        3-0
    financial data analyst—accounting, 18-0
    financial systems analyst, 4-0
    fixed asset accountant, 10-0
    internal audit data analytics manager, 17-0
    internal controls manager, 8-0
    IT risk assurance associate—IT audit, 14-0
    manager—payroll tax and accounting, 9-0
    revenue marketing accountant, 12-0
    risk management intern, 2-0
    senior accountant—financial reporting,
        technical accounting, 13-1
    senior financial analyst—financial reporting,
        6-0
    senior internal auditor—fraud specialist, 15-0
Job time tickets, 11-7, 11-13
Job-order costing, 11-15
Jobs, Steve, 2-2
JOIN operators, 6-36, 6-37, 6-38, 6-40, 6-46
    database queries, 6-30–6-35
    full outer join, 6-37–6-38
    inner join, 6-35
    left outer join, 6-36–6-37
    right outer join, 6-36
Journals/journal entries
    cash disbursements, 10-25
    defined, 13-10
    general, 13-10
    natural language processing analysis of,
        17-24
    payroll, 4-4, 9-21–9-23, 9-34
    posting adjusted entries to ledgers, 13-11
    posting closing entries to ledgers, 13-12
    posting entries to ledgers, 13-10–13-11
    process mining entries, 17-19–17-21
    special, 13-9
    testing of entries, 13-11, 13-27–13-29, 13-31,
        17-13, 17-16, 17-21
Judgment-based risk analysis, 2–19

K
Key performance indicators (KPIs)
    for balanced scorecard, 13-22–13-24
    dashboards of, 18-28. See also Dashboards

Key performance indicators (*Continued*)
data analytics of, 1-25, 5-20, 5-22, 13-22
defined, 1-20, 1-25
information quality from, 1-22
maturity model, 3-19
monitoring and evaluation of, 1-19,
3-14–3-15
Keys, database, 6-25
Kilobyte, data, 5-14

L

Labeled data, 17-6, 17-11–17-13
Labor. *See* Employees; Human resources
Labor-leisure trade-off, 9-20
Landing page, 18-29
Larceny, 15-17–15-18
Laws and legislation. *See* Regulation and
legislation; *specific laws*
Leadership. *See* Board of directors;
Management
Ledgers
blockchain, 7-24–7-29
centralized, 7-26–7-27
decentralized, 7-28–7-29
distributed, 7-28
general. *See* General ledgers
subsidiary, 10-19, 13-10
LEGO Group, 6-13
Level 0 diagrams, 8-21–8-22
Level 1 diagrams, 8-22–8-23
Level 2 diagrams, 8-23–8-24
Liabilities, understatement of, 15-28–15-30.
See also Expenses
Lift and shift, 4-17
Likelihood of risk, 2-14–2-19
Line charts, 18-21–18-22
Linear regression, 17-6, 17-15–17-16, 17-19,
18-21
Lockboxes, 12-30–12-31
Logic bombs, 16-25
Logical access attacks
brute-force, 16-17–16-18, 16-20
cybersecurity for, 16-17–16-20
defined, 16-17
internal controls for, 16-19–16-20
IP spoofing, 16-18–16-19
on-path, 16-18
Logical access controls, 4-14, 4-15, 14-6–14-12,
14-13, 16-19–16-20
Logical entity relationship diagrams, 6-21–6-23,
8-11–8-12
Logical reconnaissance attacks
cybersecurity for, 16-9, 16-13–16-15
defined, 16-9, 16-13
internal controls for, 16-14–16-15
ping sweeps for, 16-13
port scans for, 16-13–16-14
Logos, 18-7
Losses. *See* Financial losses
Low-cost strategies, 13-20–13-21
Lucidchart, 8-14

M

Ma, Jack, 2-2
Machine learning, 14-12, 17-5–17-6, 17-7,
17-9–17-13, 17-19
macOS (Apple), 4-6
Main vendor tables, 10-12–10-13
Maintenance stage, of SDLC, 6-7, 6-9

Malicious code, 16-24
Malware attacks
cybersecurity for, 16-23–16-28
defined, 16-23, 16-28
internal controls for, 16-27–16-28
logic bombs, 16-25
ransomware, 16-3, 16-23, 16-26
Trojan horses, 16-25–16-26
viruses, 16-23–16-24
worms, 16-24–16-25
Management
business process responsibilities, 1-18
codes of conduct for, 15-12
cybersecurity responsibilities, 16-4
data-driven decision making, 1-21–1-24
financial reporting responsibilities, 13-2
fraud by, 15-4–15-5, 15-21, 15-30. *See also*
Financial statement fraud
information system and business process
iterative relationship with, 1-20–1-21
as information systems users, 4-3
information use by, 1-19–1-24
internal control environment shaped by, 3-26
internal control override by, 3-5–3-6, 15-32
internal control responsibilities, 3-17–3-22,
15-23
IT system objectives, 14-4–14-5
in organizational charts, 8-7
risk response responsibilities, 2-19
tone at the top, 3-27, 15-12. *See also*
Organizational culture
Management accounting, 13-20.
See also Managerial accounting
Management in business, 1–25
Management information systems (MIS), 4-3
Management override, 3-5–3-6, 15-32
Managerial accounting
break-even analysis in, 17-17
cost accounting as. *See* Cost accounting
data analytics for, 5-19–5-22, 17-16
defined, 11-14–11-15, 11-21
financial reporting for, 13-20–13-24, 13-26
forecasting in, 17-17
Manual controls
automated combined with, 3-13
automated vs., 3-11
change to automated, 14-28
defined, 3-11, 3-16
examples, 3-12
overview of, 3-10–3-11
physical vs., 3-9
user access review as, 14-11
Manual input shapes, 8-15
Manual operation shapes, 8-15
Manufacturing bill of materials, 11-4
Manufacturing efficiency, 11-2–11-3
Manufacturing operations, 11-3, 11-7–11-8
digital, 11-22–11-25
indirect factory labor for, 11-16–11-17
Manufacturing overhead, 11-17
Manufacturing yield, 11-30
Marketing, sales, and collections processes.
See also Sales
in accounting information systems, 1-12,
1-17–1-18
anomaly detection in, 17-7
in basic business model, 1-9, 1-13, 2-3, 12-2
business-to-business, 12-2, 12-11–12-23,
12-29–12-30, 12-32–12-33

business-to-consumer, 12-3–12-11, 12-29
cash collections and accounts receivable,
12-2, 12-6, 12-12–12-13, 12-19,
12-21–12-22, 12-29–12-35, 12-43–12-44,
13-10, 15-16–15-17
data analytics, 12-38–12-40, 12-42–12-44,
17-16
databases, 12-36–12-38
defined, 1-19
in ERP systems, 12-36–12-44
overview of, 12-1–12-3
reporting and insights, 12-38–12-44
revenue recognition, 12-19, 12-24–12-28,
12-41–12-42
risks and controls, 2-4, 12-4, 12-6, 12-8,
12-13–12-15, 12-17, 12-19–12-20,
12-29–12-35
Master production schedule (MPS), 11-7
Materiality, defined, 15-23
Materials requisition requests, 11-6
Maturity models
for accounts receivable, 12-33
for business processes, 3-18
defined, 3-17, 3-22
for employee onboarding, 9-12–9-13
for employee termination, 9-18–9-20
phases of maturity, 3-19
for purchasing processes, 10-10, 10-20
Megabytes, data, 5-14
Melancon, Barry, 7-32
Merge shapes, 8-14
Mergers, 4-16
Messaging, 4-6
Meta tags, 5-4
Michel, Yanek, 11-31
Miners, blockchain, 7-24–7-25, 7-28
MIS (management information systems), 4-3
Misclassification of revenue, 15-30
Mixed reality (MR), 7-9
Mobile technologies
big data and, 5-16
geospatial analytics from, 17-24
payment processing via, 4-11
phishing, 16-9–16-10
real-time processing, 4-5
Model environment, change management in,
14-29–14-31
Monitoring and evaluation
continuous monitoring controls, 3-14–3-15,
10-28
general ledger, 13-31
human resources roles, 9-3
information quality for, 1-22
internal controls, 3-25
key performance indicators, 1-19, 3-14–3-15
management responsibility for, 1-20–1-21
Monte Carlo simulation, 17-6, 17-17–17-18,
17-19
Move tickets, 11-6
MPS (master production schedule), 11-7
MR (mixed reality), 7-9
Multifactor authentication, 14-9
Multiple regression, 17-15
Musk, Elon, 2-2

N

Narratives, 8-9. *See also* Storytelling
National Institute of Standards and
Technology (NIST)

control activities, 16-12–16-16, 16-20, 16-23,
16-28
control families, 16-7
Cybersecurity Framework, 16-6–16-8
*Security and Privacy Controls for Federal
Information Systems and Organizations*
(NIST 800-53), 16-7
Natural language processing (NLP), 17-6,
17-24–17-25
Network analysis, 17-6, 17-21–17-22
Network operations centers (NOCs), 14-13
Network ports, 16-13
New employee hiring. *See* Employee hiring
New hire packages, 9-8
New technologies. *See* Emerging technologies;
Technology innovations
Nodes
blockchain, 7-24–7-25, 7-28
in network analysis, 17-21
Noise, 17-14
Normal packets, 16-18
NoSQL databases, 6-20, 6-21
Null, keys not, 6-25

O

Object Management Group, 8-9
Object-oriented databases, 6-19–6-20, 6-21
Objects, in databases, 6-18–6-19
Occupational fraud, 15-4–15-5
OEE (overall equipment effectiveness), 11-3,
11-30
Offer letters, 9-8
Onboarding
customer, 12-16
employee, 9-6–9-13, 9-30–9-31
vendors, 7-21
Online analytical processing (OLAP) systems,
4-2, 4-10
Online transaction processing (OLTP) systems,
4-2, 4-10
On-path attacks, 16-18–16-20
Operating events, 1-11, 1-13, 10-24, 12-29
Operating system (OS), 4-6
Operational feasibility, 6-4
Operational risks, 2-8–2-9, 2-13
Operations list, 11-4
Operations objectives, for internal controls,
3-26
Operator documentation, 8-4
Opinion mining, 17-24
Opportunity, as fraud motivation, 15-10
Optionality constraints, 6-26–6-27
Order placement
internal controls for, 10-13–10-14
purchase orders, 10-5, 12-17
split, 10-14
relational databases of, 6-17, 6-20–6-38
sales orders, 12-4–12-5, 12-17
Organic growth, 4-15–4-16, 4-21
Organizational charts, 8-6–8-7, 8-12
Organizational culture
anti-fraud, 15-3, 15-34
audit of, visualization tools for, 18-33–18-34
COSO ERM Framework on, 3-28
new employee exposure to, 9-7
risk appetite in, 2-20
risk-aware, 2-3, 3-25
tone at the top, 3-27, 15-12
OS (operating system), 4-6

Outlier analysis, 17-8, 17-14
Outlook (Microsoft), 4-6
Out-of-the-box ERP systems, 4-26
Output
business process, 1-8, 1-10, 1-12, 1-16, 9-2,
11-2
data, 1-3–1-4
defined, 1-3
output shapes, 8-14
Outsourced human resources model, 9-3
Outsourcing of payroll, 9-7, 9-20, 9-25
Overall equipment effectiveness (OEE), 11-3,
11-30
Overtime, 9-24

P

PaaS (platform as a service), 4-8
Packets, 16-13
normal, 16-18
spoofed, 16-19
Packing slips, 10-5, 12-18
Paid time off, 9-23
Parallel implementation, 6-7
Passwords, 14-6, 14-9, 16-17
Patches, 16-14, 16-20
Pathways Vision Model, 1-3, 7-22
Patterns of data, 17-7
Pay and return fraud scheme, 15-22
Pay stubs, 9-34
Payment processing software, 4-11
Payment vouchers, 10-6
Payments, receiving, 12-29–12-30
Payments processes
acquisitions and. *See* Acquisitions and
payments processes
cash flow effects, 10-25
credit, 10-25–10-26. *See also* Accounts
payable
data from, 10-29–10-37
database design for, 10-29–10-31
defined, 10-2, 10-24
document flowcharts for, 10-26
in ERP system, 10-29–10-37
fixed asset, 10-1–10-2, 10-17–10-23,
10-34–10-35
fraud in, 10-27–10-28. *See also* Fraudulent
disbursements
internal controls for, 10-27–10-28
inventory, 10-2–10-6, 10-32–10-34
overview of, 10-1
reporting and analytics, 10-32–10-37
three-way matches in, 10-6, 10-13, 10-25,
10-30–10-32
Payroll
accrued, 9-34
as acquisition and payment process, 9-2, 9-25
batch processing, 4-4, 4-10, 9-23
categorization of responsibilities, 9-4
cost accounting for, 11-16–11-17
data visualization of, 18-21
defined, 9-4
employee compensation via, 9-4–9-5,
9-19–9-27
employee onboarding role, 9-7–9-8, 9-9
employee termination role, 9-14, 9-15
fraud, 9-4, 9-26, 9-34, 15-12, 15-21
human resources relationship to, 9-2–9-6,
9-20
internal audits of, 9-35

journal/journal entries, 4-4, 9-21–9-23, 9-34
outsourcing of, 9-7, 9-20, 9-25
overtime, 9-24
overview of, 9-1
pay stubs, 9-34
payroll batch, 9-23
process flowchart of, 9-23–9-24
processing of, 9-5
real-world example of risks, 9-24
reporting and analytics, 9-31–9-36
risks and control activities, 9-24–9-27
segregation of duties, 9-6
severance pay, 9-15
timekeeping system, 9-23
vacation and paid time off, 9-22–9-23
Payroll journal, 9-34
Payroll service administrators, 9-8
PCAOB (Public Company Accounting
Oversight Board), 15-3
Peer-to-peer business models, 1-9
Peer-to-peer networks, 7-24
Penetration tests, 16-14
Perceived pressure, as fraud motivation,
15-9–15-10
Performance evaluation, 3-27, 9-3
Period costs, 11-16–11-17
Permission, user access, 14-7
Petabytes, data, 5-14
Phased implementation, 6-7
Phishing, 16-9–16-13
Photographs, icons vs., 18-12
Physical access attacks, 16-15–16-16
Physical access controls, 4-14, 14-6,
14-13–14-19, 16-16
Physical controls, 3-8, 3-11, 3-16
Physical entity relationship diagrams, 6-21,
6-22–6-28, 8-11, 11-27
Physical flow of inventory, 10-7
Physical reconnaissance attacks
cybersecurity for, 16-9–16-14
defined, 16-8
Dumpster diving as, 16-11–16-12
eavesdropping as, 16-12, 16-18
internal controls for, 16-13
phishing as, 16-9–16-13
Physical risks, 2-9, 2-12
Pickens, John Aubrey, 15-34
Picking requests, 12-17, 12-18
Pie charts, 18-15
Piggybacking, 14-17, 16-15
Pilot implementation, 6-7
Ping sweeps, 16-13
Pivot tables, 17-9
Planning
business continuity, 3-10, 11-9, 14-19–14-21,
14-26
cyberattacks, 16-8–16-15
cybersecurity, 16-3
management responsibility for, 1-20–1-21
production, 11-3, 11-6–11-8
strategic, 1-19–1-20, 2-3, 3-28, 13-22
as systems development life cycle stage,
6-2–6-4
Platform as a service (PaaS), 4-8
Plurality constraints, 6-26, 6-27
Policies and procedures
cybersecurity, 16-6–16-7, 16-27
as internal controls, 3-15, 3-25, 13-13
Polite tailgating, 16-15

Ponzi schemes, 15-2
Port scans, 16-13–16-14
Portfolio view of risk, 2-4, 2-7
Post-closing trial balance, 13-12
Power BI (Microsoft), 17-9, 18-3, 18-27
PowerPoint (Microsoft), 4-6, 5-3, 8-14, 18-29
PP&E (property, plant, and equipment), 10-2,
    10-17. *See also* Fixed assets
Predictive analytics
    for audits and compliance, 5-18
    defined, 5-18, 17-4–17-5
    for financial accounting, 5-18
    for forecasting, 17-7, 17-16
    linear regression as, 17-15
    for managerial accounting, 5-23
    for tax accounting, 5-25
Prescriptive analytics
    for audits and compliance, 5-18
    defined, 5-16, 17-4–17-5
    for financial accounting, 5-18
    for managerial accounting, 5-23
    for tax accounting, 5-25
Preventive controls
    for asset misappropriation, 15-16–15-18,
        15-21–15-22
    defined, 3-3, 3-8
    examples, 3-6–3-7
    for financial statement fraud, 15-24–15-25,
        15-27, 15-29, 15-30
    overview of, 3-3–3-4
    segregation of duties as, 3-3–3-4
    in time-based model, 3-6
Pricing processes, 12-13
Primary keys, 6-25–6-26
Privacy issues, 4-9, 7-8, 11-24, 16-8
Private blockchain, 7-30
Private clouds, 4-8
Process costing, 11-15
Process flowcharts
    for business-to-business sales, 12-22
    for business-to-consumer sales, 12-6–12-8
    for collections, 12-33–12-34
    defined, 8-9
    for documentation, 8-9, 8-10–8-19
    for employee onboarding, 9-7–9-12
    for employee termination, 9-14–9-19
    for financial reporting, 13-7–13-8
    for payroll process, 9-20–9-28
    for production, 11-6–11-9
Process fragmentation, 11-24
Process mining, 17-6, 17-19–17-21
Process shapes, 8-14–8-16, 8-20
Process-based information systems, 1-13–1-19,
    4-2
Procurement processes. *See* Purchasing processes
Product backlog, 6-12
Product costs, 11-16–11-21
Product development, 11-4–11-6
Product differentiation, 13-21
Product increment, 6-13
Product safety, 11-9
Production analytics, 11-30
Production databases, 5-10
Production environment, change management
    in, 14-29–14-30, 14-32–14-33
Production module (ERP system), 4-24, 11-26
Production planning, 11-4–11-7
Production process flowchart, 11-9–11-11
Production reports, 11-7, 11-29

Production scheduling, 11-3, 11-4–11-7
Professionals. *See* Accounting professionals
Profile view of risk, 2-4, 2-7
Profits
    gross profit margin, 1-21–1-22
    overstatement of, 15-24–15-27
    as purpose of business, 1-8
Program documentation, 8-3–8-4
Program flowcharts, 8-10
Programming languages, 4-5. *See also specific
    languages*
Project plans, 6-3
Proof of work, blockchain, 7-29
Property, plant, and equipment (PP&E),
    10-2, 10-17. *See also* Fixed assets
Public blockchain, 7-30
Public clouds, 4-8
Public Company Accounting Oversight Board
    (PCAOB), 15-3
Purchase orders, 10-5, 12-16
    split, 10-14
Purchase requisitions, 10-5, 10-13, 10-17,
    10-32, 10-34
Purchasing accounting transactions, 12-45
Purchasing processes. *See also* Acquisitions
    business activities in, 10-3
    cost accounting for, 11-17
    data from, 10-29–10-37
    database design for, 10-29–10-31
    defined, 10-2–10-3
    document flowcharts for, 10-10–10-11,
        10-19–10-21
    e-procurement systems in, 10-13, 11-13
    in ERP system, 10-29–10-37
    fixed asset, 10-2, 10-17–10-23, 10-34–10-35,
        11-17
    fraud in, 10-5, 10-14, 10-21–10-22
    internal controls over, 10-10–10-14,
        10-21–10-23
    inventory, 10-2–10-17, 10-29–10-31
    maturity models for, 10-15, 10-22
    order placement in, 10-13. *See also*
        Order placement
    overview of, 10-2, 10-8–10-14
    process mining, 17-19–17-21
    purchasing department role in, 10-5
    receiving in, 10-5, 10-15–10-16, 10-18
    reporting and analytics, 10-32–10-38
    three-way matches in, 10-6, 10-13, 10-25,
        10-29–10-32
    vendor selection and management in, 10-12
Python, 4-5, 5-18, 6-20, 6-39, 17-4, 17-9, 17-26

Q

Quality management, 11-1, 11-3, 11-8–11-9,
    11-32, 11-33, 11-34, 11-36, 11-37
Quantitative values of data, 17-7–17-8, 18-15,
    18-17, 18-18
Queries, 5-9, 6-30–6-40
Querying languages, 5-4, 5-9. *See also*
    Structured Query Language (SQL)
Questionnaires, 8-7–8-8
QuickBooks, 1-5, 4-13–4-14, 4-15, 4-30, 4-32,
    4-34, 5-2, 8-26

R

R (software), 17-18
Ransomware, 11-31, 16-3, 16-4, 16-23, 16-26,
    16-29

Rationalization, for fraud, 15-9
Raw materials
    conversion of. *See* Conversion processes
    defined, 10-3
    direct vs. indirect material costs, 11-16–11-17
    materials requisition requests, 11-6
    purchasing and payments processes for,
        10-3–10-6, 10-32–10-34, 11-17
    reporting and analytics, 10-32–10-37
RBAC (role-based access controls), 14-7
Real-time processing, 4-5, 4-10
Reasonable assurance, 3-7
Receiving
    of fixed assets, 10-18
    internal controls for, 10-14
    payments, 12-29–12-30
    in purchasing processes, 10-5, 10-15–10-16,
        10-18
Receiving reports, 10-5
Reconciliation
    fixed assets, 10-19
    human resources and payroll functions, 9-4
Reconnaissance attacks
    cybersecurity for, 16-8–16-15
    defined, 16-9, 16-14
    logical, 16-9, 16-13–16-15
    physical, 16-9–16-13
Recording. *See also* Documentation
    cash receipts, 12-32–12-33
    data records, 5-2–5-3, 6-16–6-17
    fixed assets, 10-18–10-19
    segregation of duties, 3-4
Recovery point objective (RPO), 14-22, 14-27
Recovery time objective (RTO), 14-22
Red flags
    behavioral, for fraud, 15-7–15-8
    for cyberattacks, 16-10–16-11
    non-behavioral, for fraud, 15-13, 15-19–15-20
Referential integrity, 6-25, 6-29
Regression, 17-6, 17-15–17-17, 18-21
Regulation and legislation. *See also specific laws*
    compliance risks, 2-10–2-11, 3-1
    compliance with. *See* Compliance
    on data security, 3-24
    on delivery and handling, 12-7–12-8
    on external audits, 3-24
    on financial statements, 3-24, 15-23
    on internal controls, 3-2, 3-23–3-24, 3-26,
        13-13, 14-26–14-27, 15-3, 15-23
    technology risks and, 7-4
Reinforcement learning, 17-6, 17-18, 17-27, 17-30
Relational databases
    business rules for, 6-26–6-27
    cardinality in, 6-26
    conversion processes, 11-27–11-28
    crow's foot notation for, 6-27–6-28
    data integrity in, 6-24
    defined, 5-9
    design of, 6-21–6-30
    entity relationship diagrams of, 6-21–6-30,
        8-10–8-12, 11-27, 12-38, 13-27–13-28
    general ledger, 13-27
    marketing, sales, and collections processes,
        12-38–12-39
    primary and foreign keys in, 6-25
    queries, 6-30–6-40
    selection of, 6-16–6-20
    table relationships in, 11-28
    terminology, 6-17

Relationships between data points, 18-14, 18-21–18-23

Relevance
of blockchain to accounting professionals, 7-32–7-36
of information, 1-22, 1-23, 13-3

Remittance advice, 10-6, 12-20, 12-30–12-31

Reporting
bank remittance reports, 12-30–12-31
collections and accounts receivable, 12-43–12-44
conversion processes, 11-29–11-30
COSO ERM Framework on, 3-28
data analytics vs., 1-26
defined, 1-26, 1-29
of employee expenses. *See* Expense reports
financial statement. *See* Financial reporting; Financial statements
human resources and payroll, 9-31–9-36
internal control, 3-23, 3-24
marketing, sales, and collections processes, 12-38–12-44
production reports, 11-8, 11-29–11-30
purchasing and payments processes, 10-32–10-38
receiving reports, 10-5
revenue recognition reports, 12-41–12-42
sales reports, 12-39–12-40

Reputational risks, 2-10, 2-14, 12-4
Requirements definition, 6-4
Residual risk, 2-21, 3-2
Responsibility accounting, 13-21–13-22, 13-24
Retail customers, 12-12
Retailer business models, 1-9
Retained earnings, 1-8, 13-45, 15-24
Returns, product, 12-21

Revenue recognition
business-to-business sales, 12-19
defined, 12-24, 12-28
fraud and mistakes in, 12-25–12-28
model for, 12-24–12-25
at point in time, 12-24
real-world example, 12-25
reporting and analytics, 12-41–12-42
risks and controls, 12-26–12-28
over time, 12-24

Revenues
data visualization of, 18-24
misclassification of, 15-30–15-31
overstatement of, 12-27, 15-24
recognition of, 12-19, 12-24–12-28, 12-41–12-42
sales forecasts based on, 12-11
understatement of, 12-27, 15-28–15-29
unrecorded, 15-31

Risk
acceptance of, 2-21–2-22, 2-23, 2-24
appetite for, 2-20, 3-2
applying to a business, 2-3–2-4
assessment of. *See* Risk assessments
avoidance of, 2-22, 2-23–2-24
categorization of, 2-5, 2-8–2-13
cloud, 4-9–4-10
compliance, 2-9–2-11, 3-17
cyber, 2-9, 11-24
defined, 2-2
digital manufacturing, 11-24
employee onboarding, 9-10–9-11
employee termination, 9-18–9-19
employee turnover, 9-7

external, 2-8, 2-10–2-12, 3-27
financial, 2-9
formulas for prioritizing, 2-16–2-17
fraud as, 12-27, 15-2–15-3
identification of, 2-3, 2-5, 2-7, 9-29–9-36
impact of, 2-14–2-19
importance of, 2-2–2-3, 2-7
inherent, 2-20–2-21
internal, 2-8–2-10
inventory of, 2-12–2-13
likelihood of, 2-14–2-19
management of. *See* Risk management
matrix illustrating, 2-18
mitigation of. *See* Risk mitigation
nature of, 2-2–2-7
operational, 2-8–2-9
optimal level of, 2-2–2-3
payroll, 9-22–9-27
physical, 2-10, 2-12
portfolio view of, 2-4, 2-7
prioritization of, 2-5, 2-14–2-19
profile view of, 2-4, 2-7
reputational, 2-8–2-10
residual, 2-21, 3-2
response to, 2-5, 2-19–2-23
risk-aware culture, 2-2, 3-27
severity, evaluating, 2-14–2-15
statements of. *See* Risk statements
strategic, 2-9–2-12
systems development, 6-2, 6-10, 6-13
technology. *See* Technology risks
transfer of, 2-20, 2-22–2-23

Risk acceptance, 2-21–2-22, 2-23, 2-24
Risk appetite, 2-20, 2-23, 3-2

Risk assessments
defined, 2-2
for enterprise risk management, 2-5, 2-7
fraud, 15-3, 15-8–15-13
internal audits, 2-34
for internal controls, 3-26
regulatory requirements for, 3-2
risk categorization in, 2-5, 2-8–2-13
risk identification in, 2-5, 2-7
risk prioritization in, 2-5, 2-14–2-19
risk response based on, 2-19–2-23

Risk avoidance, 2-22, 2-23–2-24
Risk formulas, 2-16–2-17
Risk inventory, 2-12–2-13, 2-14

Risk management
accounting professional roles in, 2-1–2-2, 2-19, 2-23, 3-1, 3-28
careers in, 2-19
cybersecurity in. *See* Cybersecurity
enterprise. *See* Enterprise risk management
fraud, 15-8–15-13
internal controls for, 3-1–3-40, 4-14, 9-11, 9-15, 9-19, 9-24–9-27, 10-10–10-14, 10-21–10-22, 10-27, 11-8–11-9, 11-12–11-13, 11-20–11-21, 12-4, 12-6–12-7, 12-12–12-17, 12-19–12-20, 12-26–12-35, 13-13–13-15, 14-12, 14-17–14-18, 14-26, 14-34–14-35
Monte Carlo simulations in, 17-18
startup and small business, 4-13–4-14

Risk matrix, 2-18–2-19

Risk mitigation
change management for, 14-28–14-35
defined, 2-22, 2-24
for emerging and disruptive technologies, 7-3–7-6

employee onboarding for, 9-7
internal controls for, 3-2–3-7
for IT systems, 14-2–14-35
as risk response, 2-19, 2-22

Risk response
acceptance as, 2-21–2-22, 2-23, 2-24
avoidance as, 2-22, 2-23–2-24
for enterprise risk management, 2-5, 2-19–2-23
example, 2-23
mitigation as, 2-19, 2-22. *See also* Risk mitigation
risk assessment informing, 2-20–2-21
transfer as, 2-20, 2-22–2-23

Risk scores, 2-19
Risk severity, 2-14–2-15, 2-19

Risk statements
on business continuity, 14-27
on business-to-business sales, 12-12–12-17, 12-19–12-20
on business-to-consumer sales, 12-4, 12-6, 12-7
on change management, 14-34–14-35
on collections, 12-6, 12-30, 12-33
on cost accounting, 11-20–11-21
defined, 2-6, 2-7
on employee onboarding, 9-11–9-12
on employee termination, 9-18–9-19
examples, 2-6
on fixed asset acquisitions, 10-22
internal controls targeting, 3-9, 9-11, 9-18–9-19, 9-26–9-17, 10-12–10-13, 10-16, 10-22, 10-27–10-28, 11-6, 11-8–11-9, 11-13, 11-20–11-21, 12-4, 12-6, 12-7, 12-12–12-15, 12-16–12-17, 12-19–12-20, 12-26–12-27, 12-30–12-31, 12-33, 13-13–13-15, 14-12, 14-18, 14-27, 14-34–14-35
on inventory, 11-13
on logical security, 14-12
on manufacturing operations, 11-9
on order placement, 10-13
on payments, 10-27–10-28
on payroll processing, 9-27–9-28
on physical security, 14-18
on product development, 11-6
on production planning and scheduling, 11-8
on quality management, 11-9
on receiving, 10-16
on revenue recognition, 12-26–12-27
risk formulas based on, 2-16–2-17
risk severity in, 2-14–2-15
source of risk identified in, 2-9
on supply chain management, 11-13
on vendor management, 10-12

Risk transfer, 2-20, 2-22–2-23, 2-24
RobbinHood ransomware attack, 16-26

Robotic process automation (RPA)
accounting professional benefits, 7-13–7-22
accounting use cases, 7-17–7-21
for accounts payable functions, 7-18–7-19
artificial intelligence vs., 7-14
change to, management of, 14-28
conditional statements in, 7-14–7-21
defined, 7-14, 7-24
efficiencies and opportunities with, 7-22–7-23
for financial reporting, 7-22
for fraud alerts, 7-22
for internal audit functions, 7-18–7-21
logic behind, 7-14–7-17
real-world example, 7-23
for user access review, 14-12

Robotics. *See also* Artificial intelligence
automated controls, 3-12
as Autonomous Things, 7-11–7-12, 7-13
in digital manufacturing, 11-23
robotic process automation, 7-13–7-14, 14-12, 14-28
Rogers Adoption Curve, 7-2
Role-based access controls (RBAC), 14-7, 14-13
RPA. *See* Robotic process automation (RPA)
RPO (recovery point objective), 14-22, 14-25
RTO (recovery time objective), 14-22

S
SaaS (software as a service), 4-1, 4-8–4-15, 4-30, 4-35, 16-6
Sales
analytics on, 12-39–12-40, 17-16
automated sales process, 12-25
business-to-business, 12-2, 12-11–12-22, 12-29–12-30, 12-32–12-33
business-to-consumer, 12-2, 12-3–12-10, 12-29
contracts, 12-15
fictitious sales larceny, 15-17
fraudulent, 12-40–12-41, 15-18. *See also* Channel stuffing
marketing, sales, and collections processes, 1-10, 1-14, 1-17–1-18, 2-3–2-4, 12-1–12-45, 15-16, 17-8, 17-17
reporting, 12-38–12-40
sales cutoff schemes, 15-26–15-27, 15-30
sham, 15-25
Sales invoices, 12-20
Sales Management module (ERP system), 4-24, 12-37
Sales orders, 12-4, 12-11, 12-16–12-17. *See also* Order placement
Sales reports, 12-39–12-40
SamSam ransomware attack, 16-26
Sandbox. *See* Test environment
Sarbanes-Oxley Act of 2002 (SOX), 3-22, 3-23, 3-30, 3-31
documentation requirements, 8-12
financial statement requirements, 3-23, 15-23
internal controls requirements, 3-23–3-24, 3-26, 13-13, 14-28, 15-3, 15-23
overview of, 3-23–3-24
risk assessment requirements, 3-1
user access testing requirements, 7-19–7-20
whistleblower protections, 15-9
Scala, 4-5
Scalability
database, 5-10, 6-16, 6-20
horizontal, 5-10
vertical, 5-10
Scatter plots, 18-23
Schema, database, 5-9, 5-12, 8-11
Scope creep, 6-12
Scraped data, 5-4
Scrum, 6-11–6-13, 6-15
SDLC. *See* Systems development life cycle (SDLC)
Seasonality, 17-14
Securities and Exchange Commission, U.S. (SEC)
Accounting and Auditing Enforcement Releases, 15-32
civil enforcements, 12-27
fraud investigations, 15-32
internal controls requirements, 3-24, 13-13–13-15

XBRL requirements, 13-16–13-18
Security. *See also* Cybersecurity; Data security
cloud-supported cameras, 4-13
internal controls for. *See* Internal controls
technology risks, 7-4
Segregation of duties, 3-3–3-4, 3-8, 3-12, 4-14, 9-6, 15-12, 15-16
SELECT command, 6-40
database queries, 6-30–6-33, 6-38–6-39
Select all, 6-32
Select multiple columns, 6-33
Select one column, 6-32
Sentiment analysis, 17-24
Severance pay, 9-15, 9-20
Sham sales, 15-25
Sheu, Eliza, 5-26
Shimamoto, Donny, 2-24–2-25
Shipping, 12-12, 12-17–12-20, 15-25. *See also* Delivery
Shipping notices, 12-18
Simple regression, 17-15
Simulations
defined, 17-17
Monte Carlo, 17-6, 17-17–17-18
Skills. *See also* Career skills
critical thinking, 1-2, 7-22
data analytics, 1-28–1-29, 5-18
internal audit, 1-7–1-8
Skimming, 15-15–15-17
Small businesses. *See also* Startups
blockchain applications, 7-35
risk management, 4-14–4-15
Smart contracts, 7-25, 7-31, 7-35
Smart glasses, 11-25
Smart lightbulbs, 4-13
Smart locks, 4-13
Social engineering, 16-1, 16-9–16-11, 16-15, 16-29, 16-31
Social media, 2-10, 17-22, 17-25
Social network analysis, 17-22
Social responsibility, 1-8–1-9, 1-17, 1-38–1-39
Software
accounting, 4-13–4-15
application software, 4-6
consolidation, 13-4–13-5
customer relationship management, 12-3–12-4
for data analytics, 4-12–4-13
data communication software, 4-6
for data storage, 4-13
defined, 4-5, 4-10
in-house development of, 4-6–4-7
malware, 16-23–16-28
overview of, 4-5–4-7
patches, 16-14, 16-20
for payment processing, 4-11
programming languages, 4-5. *See also specific languages*
sourcing of, 4-6–4-7
for startups, 4-11–4-14, 4-29
systems software, 4-6
utility programs, 4-6
Software as a service (SaaS), 4-8–4-14
Source documents, 10-3–10-4, 13-9
SOX. *See* Sarbanes-Oxley Act of 2002 (SOX)
Special journals, 13-9
Split purchase orders, 10-14, 10-17
Spoofed packets, 16-19
Sprint backlog, 6-12

Sprints, 6-12
SQL. *See* Structured Query Language (SQL)
Square, 4-11
Stacked bar charts, 18-17–18-18, 18-22, 18-25
Standard costing, 11-15, 11-21
Standardization
documentation for, 8-6
of financial reporting, 13-17–13-18
Startups
risk management, 4-14–4-15
software and technology for, 4-11–4-15, 4-29
Statement of cash flows, 10-25, 12-29, 13-30, 13-45
Statement of stockholders' equity, 13-30, 13-45
Static dashboards, 18-29
Static data, 5-6
Statisticians, 17-2
Stockholders' equity statements, 13-30, 13-45
Story arcs, 18-31
Storyboards, 18-30–18-34
Storytelling, 18-2–18-4, 18-26–18-35. *See also* Narratives
Strategic planning, 1-20, 2-3, 3-29, 13-22, 14-2
Strategic risks, 2-9, 2-11–2-12, 2-14
Structured data, 5-4, 5-8
Structured Query Language (SQL)
commands, 6-30–6-39
data analytics, 5-18, 17-4, 17-10, 17-24
data control language, 6-30
data definition language, 6-30
data manipulation language, 6-30
Data Query Language, 6-30–6-39
database queries, 5-9, 6-30–6-39
JOIN operators, 6-35–6-38
languages, 6-30
as programming language, 4-5
SELECT command, 6-31–6-33, 6-38–6-39
SQL statements, 6-31
Transaction Control Language, 6-30
Where clause, 6-34–6-35, 6-38–6-39
Subscription business models, 1-9, 1-12
Subsidiaries, consolidated financial statements for, 13-4–13-5
Subsidiary ledgers, 10-19, 13-10
Sukhani, Bharti, 12-44–12-45
Supervised learning, 17-6, 17-11–17-13, 17-24
Suppliers, 10-3. *See also* Vendors
Supply chain management (SCM)
for business-to-consumer sales, 12-9–12-10
conversion processes and, 11-3, 11-12–11-13
defined, 10-7, 10-9, 11-12, 12-9
information flow in, 10-7
overview of, 10-7–10-8
physical flow in, 10-7
purchasing and payments processes and, 10-3, 10-7–10-8
revenue data selection, 12-10
risks and controls, 11-12–11-13
Supply Chain Management module (ERP system), 4-22–4-23, 10-29–10-30, 11-26
Sustainability, 1-17
Swim lanes, flowchart, 8-18–8-19, 13-7–13-8
Sylvester, Dominic, 6-38–6-39
System go-live, 6-6–6-8
Systems configurations
centralized systems, 4-18–4-19
decentralized systems, 4-19–4-20
distributed systems, 4-20
for growing businesses, 4-18–4-21

Systems development
  buy-build decisions, 6-2
  life cycle, stages of, 6-2–6-9
  methodologies for, 6-9–6-15
    Agile, 6-10–6-15
    selection of, 6-13–6-15
    Waterfall, 6-9–6-10, 6-13–6-15
  overview of, 6-2
  real-world example, 6-13
  risks in, 6-2, 6-10, 6-13
Systems development life cycle (SDLC)
  Agile methodology for executing, 6-10–6-15
  analysis stage, 6-3, 6-4–6-5
  defined, 6-2, 6-8
  design stage, 6-3, 6-5
  development stage, 6-3, 6-6
  implementation stage, 6-3, 6-6–6-7
  maintenance stage, 6-3, 6-7
  planning stage, 6-3–6-4
  roles and responsibilities during, 6-3–6-4
  stages of, 6-2–6-9
  testing stage, 6-3, 6-6
  Waterfall methodology for executing, 6-9–6-10, 6-13–6-15
Systems documentation
  business process model and notation for, 8-9
  data flow diagrams for, 8-11, 8-20–8-24
  defined, 8-2–8-3
  entity relationship diagrams for, 8-11–8-12
  flowcharts for, 8-9, 8-13–8-19
  in hierarchy, 8-3
  narratives for, 8-9
  overview of, 8-2–8-3
Systems flowcharts, 8-9, 8-13–8-19
Systems integration
  defined, 4-17, 4-21
  ERP systems for, 4-22–4-25
  for growing businesses, 4-17–4-18
  immediate, 4-18
  lift and shift, 4-17
Systems models, 6-5
Systems security controls, 3-16
Systems software, 4-6, 4-10

T
Tableau
  case studies. See Tableau case studies
  data summarization in, 17-9
  data visualization with, 18-3, 18-6, 18-10, 18-14, 18-21, 18-24–18-25, 18-29, 18-35
Tableau case studies
  Accounts Payable Red Flags, 10-45–10-47
  Accounts Receivable Analysis, 12-55
  Call Center Performance, 17-34–17-35
  Change Management, 14-44–14-45
  Control Mapping, 3-40–3-41
  Cookies Cares Charitable Foundation, 1-38–1-39
  Employee Reimbursement Expenses, 15-42–15-43
  General Ledger Journal Entries, 13-43–13-45
  IT Help Desk, 5-33
  IT Help Desk Employee Insights, 6-53
  Network Logins, 16-35–16-37
  People Analytics, 9-46–9-47
  Raw Ingredient Costs, 11-40–11-41
  Risk Profile, 2-34
  Sales Dashboard, 18-48–18-49

Smart Freezers, 7-43–7-44
System Conversion, 4-35
System Migration, 8-35–8-37
Tagging
  of financial information in XBRL, 13-16–13-17
  of fixed assets, 10-18
Tailgating, 14-17, 16-15
Target residual risk, 2-21, 2-24, 3-2
Tax accounting, 5-24, 7-34, 14-26, 14-31
Tax data hubs, 5-25
Taxonomy, XRBL, 13-16, 13-18
TCL (Transaction Control Language), 3-16, 6-30, 6-44, 6-45
Technical architecture specifications, 6-5
Technical feasibility, 6-4
Technology for startups, 4-11–4-14
Technology innovations
  artificial intelligence as. See Artificial intelligence (AI)
  disruptive. See Disruptive technologies
  emerging. See Emerging technologies
  mobile. See Mobile technologies
  opportunities with, 7-7–7-12
  overview of, 7-1
  risk assessment and mitigation, 7-3–7-6. See also Technology risks
  robotics as. See Robotics
  Rogers Adoption Curve, 7-2
Technology risks
  business disruptions as, 7-4
  center of excellence evaluating, 7-6
  cyber risk as, 2-9, 11-24
  defined, 2-9, 2-13
  with emerging and disruptive technologies, 7-3–7-6
  enterprise risk management of, 7-5
  financial losses as, 7-4
  internal audits for, 7-4–7-5
  internal controls to manage, 3-2
  IT application controls for, 3-10
  IT general controls for, 3-9–3-10. See also IT general controls
  regulatory risks as, 7-4
  security-related, 7-4
Terabytes, data, 5-14
Termination. See Employee termination
Terminator shapes, 8-14
Test environment
  change management in, 14-28–14-33
  systems development in, 6-2, 6-6
Textual analysis, 17-24
Thomas, Mark, 14-35
Throughput, 11-30
Time management, 9-5
Time series data, 17-14–17-16, 17-19, 18-21–18-22
Time trends, 17-14
Time-based model of controls, 3-6–3-7, 3-8
Timeboxing, 6-12
Timekeeping system
  job time tickets, 11-7
  payroll process and, 9-23
  unauthorized hours recorded, 15-21
Timeliness of information, 1-23, 13-3
Tinley, David, 16-25
Tone, data visualization setting, 18-5–18-6
Tone at the top, 3-27, 15-12. See also Organizational culture
Tooltips, 18-24

TPS (transaction processing systems), 4-3–4-5, 6-2, 9-23
Traditional cost accounting
  of conversion processes, 11-14–11-18
  job-order costing, 11-15
  labor costs, 11-15–11-16
  process costing, 11-15
  purchasing process costs, 11-16
  sample system, 11-17–11-18
  standard costing, 11-15
Training gap analytics, 9-36
Transaction Control Language (TCL), 6-30
Transaction processing systems (TPS), 4-3–4-5, 6-2, 9-23
Transaction-based accounting information systems, 1-13–1-18, 1-19, 4-3–4-4
Transparency
  blockchain, 7-29
  data, 4-23, 7-35
Tree maps, 18-15–18-16
Trends, data, 17-7, 17-14, 18-22
Trial balance
  adjusted, 13-11
  post-closing, 13-12
  roll-forward, 13-27–13-29
  unadjusted, 13-11–13-12
Trojan horses, 16-26, 16-28
Turnover rates, 9-33
Typography, 18-11

U
Unadjusted trial balance, 13-8, 13-11–13-12, 13-15, 13-34, 13-37
Unauthorized hours, 15-21
Unauthorized shipments, 15-26
Understandability of information, 1-23, 13-3
Unrecorded revenue, 15-29
Unstructured data, 5-4–5-5, 5-8, 6-19–6-20
Unsupervised learning, 17-6, 17-10–17-11, 17-24
Updates, software, 4-7
User acceptance testing (UAT), 6-6, 6-9, 14-32
User access
  adding and removing users, 14-9–14-11
  administrator role, 14-8
  assigning access, 14-7–14-8
  de-provisioning, 14-10
  dormant, 14-11
  internal audits of, 7-19–7-21
  IT system controls, 14-3–14-19
  logical access controls, 4-14, 14-6–14-12, 16-19–16-20
  multifactor authentication, 14-9
  permission, 14-7
  physical access controls, 4-14, 14-6, 14-17–14-18, 16-16
  provisioning, 14-9–14-10
  reviews of, 14-11–14-12
  risks and controls, 14-12, 14-18
  role-based access controls, 14-7–14-8
  user authentication and, 14-11
User documentation, 8-4–8-5
Usernames, 14-6
Utility programs, 4-6

V
Vacation and paid time off, 9-23
Valdez, Rob, 16-28–16-29
Value of big data, 5-13, 5-16, 7-9

Variables
   in databases, 6-20
   dependent and independent, 17-15–17-16
Variety
   of big data, 5-15, 7-8
   of data in databases, 6-16
   defined, 5-15
Velocity of big data, 6-20
Vendor invoices, 10-6, 15-22
Vendor prices analytics, 10–37
Vendors. *See also* Suppliers
   bid-rigging schemes, 10-21–10-22, 15-4
   codes of conduct for, 15-12
   defined, 10-3
   of ERP systems, 4-26
   fraud by, 15-4
   fraudulent disbursements to, 10-27, 15-21
   invoices from, 10-6, 15-21
   main vendor table of approved, 10-12–10-13
   payments owed. *See* Accounts payable;
      Payments processes
   robotic process automation for onboarding,
      7-21
   selection and management of, 10-11–10-13
   software, 4-6–4-7
Veracity of big data, 5-13, 5-15, 5–18, 7-9
Verifiability, information, 1-23, 1-31, 1-32, 1-38,
   13-3, 13-6
Vertical financial statement analysis, 13-31, 15-13
Vertical flowchart shapes, 8-15

Vertical organizational charts, 8-8
Vertical scaling, 5-10
Virtual reality (VR), 7-9–7-10, 7-12
Viruses, 4-6, 16-23–16-24, 16-28
Visio (Microsoft), 8-14
Visualization audience, 18-5
Visualizations. *See also* Data visualization
   business process model and notation as,
      8-9–8-10, 8-13
   on dashboards, 5-18. *See also* Dashboards
   defined, 5-18
   diagrams as. *See* Data flow diagrams; Entity
      relationship diagrams
   flowcharts as. *See* Flowcharts
Voice assistants, 4-13
Voice phishing, 16-9–16-10
Volkswagen Emissions Scandal, 2-11
Volume
   of big data, 5-14, 7-9
   of data in databases, 6-16
   defined, 5-14
VR (virtual reality), 7-9–7-10, 7-12
Vulnerability scans, 16-14, 16-30

W
W-2 form, 9-34, 9-37
W-3 form, 9-34, 9-37
Wall Street Blockchain Alliance, 7-32
Wallet applications, 7-25–7-27, 7-38
Wang, Kevin, 7-37

WannaCry ransomware attack, 16-3
Warm backup sites, 14-21–14-22
Warm colors, 18-7
Waterfall methodology, 6-9–6-10, 6-13–6-15
Web 2.0, 5-5–5-6
Where clause, 6-34–6-35, 6-38–6-39, 6-40
Whistleblowers, 15-9, 15-13
White space, 18-10–18-11, 18-13
Williams, Laniesha, 4-29
Willis, Mark, 13-16
Windows (Microsoft), 4-6
Word (Microsoft), 4-6, 5-2, 8-14
Work in process, 10-3
Working capital, 10-8
Worms, 16-24–16-25, 16-27, 16-28, 16-31, 16-32
Wyatt, Cindy, 3-30–3-31

X
XBRL instance document, 13-16
XBRL tags, 13-16, 13-18
XML (eXtensible Markup Language), 13-16
XR (extended reality), 7-1, 7-9–7-10, 7-13, 7-37,
   7-38, 13-35, 13-40

Y
Yottabytes, data, 5-14

Z
Zettabytes, data, 5-14
Zuckerberg, Mark, 2-2